Fodor's 07

W9-BTQ-458

CARIBBEAN

Where to Stay and Eat
for All Budgets

Must-See Sights
and Local Secrets

Ratings You Can Trust

Fodor's Travel Publications   New York, Toronto, London, Sydney, Auckland
www.fodors.com

FODOR'S CARIBBEAN 2007

Editors: Douglas Stallings, Mark Sullivan

Editorial Production: Linda Schmidt

Editorial Contributors: Carol M. Bareuther, John Bigley, Cathy Church, Katherine Dykstra, Lynda Lohr, Elise Meyer, Jackie Mulligan, Vernon O'Reilly-Ramesar, Paris Permenter, Elise Rosen, Eileen Robinson Smith, Roberta Sotonoff, Jordan Simon, Mark Sullivan, Jane E. Zarem

Maps: David Lindroth, *cartographer;* Bob Blake and Rebecca Baer, *map editors*

Design: Fabrizio La Rocca, *creative director;* Guido Caroti, *art director;* Melanie Marin, *senior picture editor*

Production/Manufacturing: Robert Shields

Cover Photo (windsurfers, Aruba): Darrell Jones/Stone/Getty Images

ISBN-10: 1-4000-1675-4

ISBN-13: 978-1-4000-1675-4

ISSN: 1524-9174

SPECIAL SALES

This book is available for special discounts for bulk purchases for sales promotions or premiums. Special editions, including personalized covers, excerpts of existing books, and corporate imprints, can be created in large quantities for special needs. For more information, write to Special Markets/Premium Sales, 1745 Broadway, MD 6-2, New York, New York 10019, or e-mail specialmarkets@randomhouse.com.

AN IMPORTANT TIP & AN INVITATION

Although all prices, opening times, and other details in this book are based on information supplied to us at press time, changes occur all the time in the travel world, and Fodor's cannot accept responsibility for facts that become outdated or for inadvertent errors or omissions. So **always confirm information when it matters,** especially if you're making a detour to visit a specific place. Your experiences—positive and negative—matter to us. If we have missed or misstated something, **please write to us.** We follow up on all suggestions. Contact the Caribbean editor at editors@fodors.com or c/o Fodor's at 1745 Broadway, New York, New York 10019.

PRINTED IN THE UNITED STATES OF AMERICA

10 9 8 7 6 5 4 3 2 1

Be a Correspondent for Fodor's Caribbean

Your opinion matters. It matters to us. It matters to your fellow Fodor's travelers, too. And we'd like to hear it. In fact, we *need* to hear it.

When you share your experiences and opinions, you become an active member of the Fodor's community. That means we'll not only use your feedback to make our books better, but we'll publish your names and comments whenever possible. Throughout our guides, look for "Word of Mouth," excerpts of your unvarnished feedback.

Here's how you can help improve Fodor's for all of us.

Tell us when we're right. We rely on local writers to give you an insider's perspective. But our writers and staff editors—who are the best in the business—depend on you. Your positive feedback is a vote to renew our recommendations for the next edition.

Tell us when we're wrong. We're proud that we update most of our guides every year. But we're not perfect. Things change. Hotels cut services. Museums change hours. Charming cafés lose charm. If our writer didn't quite capture the essence of a place, tell us how you'd do it differently. If any of our descriptions are inaccurate or inadequate, we'll incorporate your changes in the next edition and will correct factual errors at fodors.com *immediately.*

Tell us what to include. You probably have had fantastic travel experiences that aren't yet in Fodor's. Why not share them with a community of like-minded travelers? Maybe you chanced upon a beach or bistro or B&B that you don't want to keep to yourself. Tell us why we should include it. And share your discoveries and experiences with everyone directly at fodors.com. Your input may lead us to add a new listing or highlight a place we cover with a "Highly Recommended" star or with our highest rating, "Fodor's Choice."

Give us your opinion instantly at our feedback center at www.fodors.com/feedback. You may also e-mail editors@fodors.com with the subject line "Caribbean Editor." Or send your nominations, comments, and complaints by mail to Caribbean Editor, Fodor's, 1745 Broadway, New York, NY 10019.

You and travelers like you are the heart of the Fodor's community. Make our community richer by sharing your experiences. Be a Fodor's correspondent.

Happy traveling!

Tim Jarrell, Publisher

CONTENTS

CLOSEUPS

MAPS

CONTENTS

HOW TO USE THIS BOOK

Our Ratings

Sometimes you find terrific travel experiences and sometimes they just find you. But usually the burden is on you to select the right combination of experiences. That's where our ratings come in.

As travelers we've all discovered a place so wonderful that its worthiness is obvious. And sometimes that place is so experiential that superlatives don't do it justice: you just have to be there to know. These sights, properties, and experiences get our highest rating, **Fodor's Choice,** indicated by orange stars throughout this book.

Black stars highlight sights and properties we deem **Highly Recommended,** places that our writers, editors, and readers praise again and again for consistency and excellence.

By default, there's another category: any place we include in this book is by definition worth your time, unless we say otherwise. And we will.

Disagree with any of our choices? Care to nominate a place or suggest that we rate one more highly? Visit our feedback center at www.fodors.com/feedback.

Budget Well

Hotel and restaurant price categories from ¢ to $$$$ are defined in the opening pages of each chapter. For attractions, we always give standard adult admission fees; reductions are usually available for children, students, and senior citizens. Want to pay with plastic? **AE, D, DC, MC, V** following restaurant and hotel listings indicate if American Express, Discover, Diners Club, MasterCard, and Visa are accepted.

Restaurants

Unless we state otherwise, restaurants are open for lunch and dinner daily. We mention dress only when there's a specific requirement and reservations only when they're essential or not accepted—it's always best to book ahead.

Hotels

Hotels have private bath, phone, TV, and air-conditioning and operate on the European Plan (a.k.a. EP, meaning without meals), unless we specify that they use the Continental Plan (CP, with a Continental breakfast), Breakfast Plan (BP, with a full breakfast), or Modified American Plan (MAP, with breakfast and dinner) or are all-inclusive (AI, including all meals and most activities). We always list facilities but not whether you'll be charged an extra fee to use them, so when pricing accommodations, find out what's included.

Many Listings
- ★ Fodor's Choice
- ★ Highly recommended
- ✉ Physical address
- ✛ Directions
- ⌂ Mailing address
- ☎ Telephone
- 🖷 Fax
- ⊕ On the Web
- ✉ E-mail
- 🎫 Admission fee
- ☉ Open/closed times
- ⚑ Start of walk/itinerary
- Ⓜ Metro stations
- ▭ Credit cards

Hotels & Restaurants
- ⌆ Hotel
- ↴ Number of rooms
- ⚲ Facilities
- ¶⊙¶ Meal plans
- ✕ Restaurant
- ✍ Reservations
- 🕭 Dress code
- ↘ Smoking
- 🕮 BYOB
- ✕⌆ Hotel with restaurant that warrants a visit

Outdoors
- 🏌 Golf
- ⛺ Camping

Other
- ☺ Family-friendly
- 🛈 Contact information
- ⇨ See also
- ✉ Branch address
- ☞ Take note

UNITED
STATES

Miami

Key West

Nassau

The Bahamas

Havana

Cuba

Turks and
Caicos Islands

George
Town

Little
Cayman

Cayman
Brac

Grand
Cayman

Puerto Plata

Haiti Hispaniola

Montego Bay

Ocho Rios

Port-au-Prince

Jamaica

Kingston

Santo
Domingo

GREATER

Greater Antilles

Caribbean   Sea

0   200 mi

0   200 km

Cartagena

COLOMBIA

Maracaibo

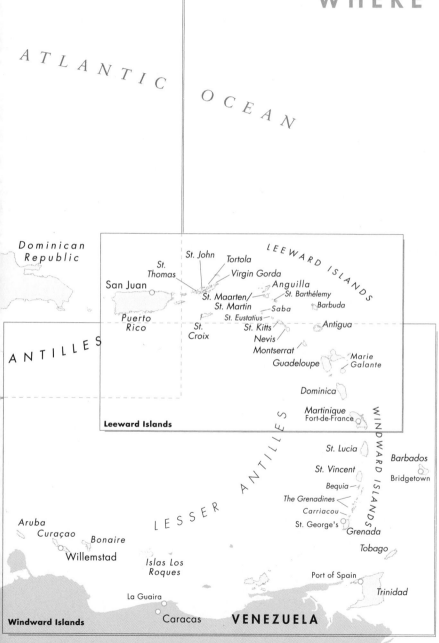

ATLANTIC OCEAN

Dominican Republic

LEEWARD ISLANDS

St. John
St. Thomas
Tortola
Virgin Gorda
San Juan
Anguilla
St. Maarten/ St. Barthélemy
St. Martin
Saba
Barbuda
Puerto Rico
St. Eustatius
St. Croix
St. Kitts
Antigua
Nevis
Montserrat
Marie Galante
Guadeloupe

ANTILLES

Dominica

Martinique
Fort-de-France

Leeward Islands

WINDWARD ISLANDS

St. Lucia

St. Vincent
Barbados
Bridgetown

Bequia

The Grenadines
Carriacou
St. George's
Grenada

Aruba
Curaçao
Bonaire
Willemstad

Tobago

LESSER ANTILLES

Islas Los Roques

Port of Spain
Trinidad

La Guaira
Caracas
VENEZUELA

Windward Islands

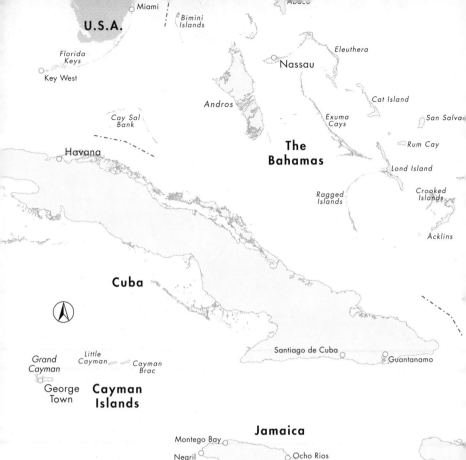

U.S.A.

Miami

Bimini Islands

Abaco

Florida Keys

Key West

Eleuthera

Nassau

Andros

Cat Island

San Salva

Cay Sal Bank

The Bahamas

Exuma Cays

Rum Cay

Havana

Lond Island

Ragged Islands

Crooked Islands

Acklins

Cuba

Santiago de Cuba

Guantanamo

Little Cayman

Cayman Brac

Grand Cayman

George Town

Cayman Islands

Jamaica

Montego Bay

Negril

Ocho Rios

Black River

Kingston

G R E A T E R

Caribbean

Cayman Islands, ⇨ Ch. 7
Vacationers appreciate the mellow civility of the islands, and Grand Cayman's exceptional Seven Mile Beach has its share of fans. Divers come to explore the pristine reefs or perhaps to swim with friendly stingrays. Go if you want a safe, family-friendly vacation spot. Don't go if you're trying to save money because there are few real bargains here.

Jamaica, ⇨ Ch. 13
Easy to reach and with resorts in every price range, Jamaica is also an easy choice for many travelers. Go to enjoy the music, food, beaches, and sense of hospitality that's made it one of the Caribbean's most popular destinations. Don't go if you can't deal with the idea that a Caribbean paradise still has problems of its own to solve.

The Greater Antilles

The islands closest to the United States mainland—composed of Cuba, Jamaica, Haiti, the Dominican Republic, and Puerto Rico—are also the largest in the chain that stretches in an arc from the southern coast of Florida down to Venezuela. Haiti and Cuba aren't covered in this book. The Cayman Islands, just south of Cuba, are usually included in this group.

WHAT'S WHERE

Turks & Caicos Islands, ⇨ Ch. 25
Miles of white sand beaches surround this tiny island chain, only eight of which are inhabited. The smaller islands seem to come from some long-forgotten era of Caribbean life. Go for deserted beaches and excellent diving on one of the world's largest coral reefs. Don't go for nightlife and a fast pace. And don't forget your wallet. This isn't a budget destination.

Dominican Republic, ⇨ Ch. 10
Dominicans have beautiful smiles and warm hearts and are proud of their island, which is blessed with pearl-white beaches and a vibrant, Latin culture. Go for the best-priced resorts in the Caribbean and a wide range of activities that will keep you moving day and night. Don't go if you can't go with the flow. Things don't always work here, and not everyone speaks English.

Puerto Rico, ⇨ Ch. 16
San Juan is hopping day and night; beyond the city, you'll find a sunny escape and slower pace. So party in San Juan, relax on the beach, hike the rain forest, or play some of the Caribbean's best golf courses. You have the best of both worlds here, with natural and urban thrills alike. So go for both. Just don't expect to do it in utter seclusion.

WHAT'S WHERE

Lesser Antilles: The Eastern Caribbean

The Lesser Antilles are larger in number but smaller in size than the Greater Antilles, and they make up the bulk of the Caribbean arc. Beginning with the Virgin Islands but going all the way to Grenada, the islands of the Eastern Caribbean form a barrier between the Atlantic Ocean and the Caribbean Sea. The best beaches are usually on the Caribbean side.

U.S. Virgin Islands, ⇨ Ch. 26

A perfect combination of the familiar and the exotic, the U.S. Virgin Islands are a little bit of America set in an azure sea. Go to St. Croix if you like history and interesting restaurants. Go to St. John if you crave a back-to-nature experience. Go to St. Thomas if you want a shop-till-you-drop experience and a big selection of resorts, activities, and nightlife.

British Virgin Islands, ⇨ Ch. 6

The lure of the British Virgins is exclusivity and personal attention, not lavish luxury. Even the most expensive resorts are selling a state of mind rather than state-of-the-art. So go with an open mind, and your stress may very well melt away. Don't go if you expect glitz or stateside efficiency. These islands are about getting away, not getting it all.

Montserrat, ⇨ Ch. 15

Montserrat has staged one of the best comebacks of the new century, returning to the tourism scene after a disastrous volcanic eruption in 1995. Go for exciting volcano eco-tourism and great diving or just to taste what the Caribbean used to be like. Don't go for splashy resorts or nightlife. You'll be happier here if you can appreciate simpler pleasures.

Anguilla, ⇨ Ch. 1

With miles of brilliant beaches and a range of luxurious resorts (even a few that mere mortals can afford), Anguilla is where the rich, powerful, and famous go to chill out. Go for the fine cuisine in elegant surroundings, great snorkeling, and funky late-night music scene. Don't go for shopping and sightseeing. This island is all about relaxing and reviving.

St. Martin, ⇨ Ch. 22

Two nations (Dutch and French), many nationalities, one small island, a lot of development. But there are also more white, sandy beaches than days in a month. Go for the awesome restaurants, excellent shopping, and wide range of activities. Don't go if you're not willing to get out and search for the really good stuff.

St. Barthélemy, ⇨ Ch. 18

If you come to St. Barths for a taste of European village life, not for a conventional full-service resort experience, you will be richly rewarded. Go for excellent dining and wine, great boutiques with the latest hip fashions, and an active, on-the-go vacation. Don't go for big resorts, and make sure your credit card is platinum-plated.

ATLANTIC OCEAN

Anguilla
Thr Valley
Marigot
t. Maarten
St. Martin Philipsburg
Gustavia
St. Barthélemy
Barbuda

Saba

Oranjestad
St. Eustatius   **St. Kitts**
Basseterre   St Johns   **Antigua**
Nevis
Charlestown   English Harbour

Montserrat

LEEWARD ISLANDS

Grande-Terre
Guadeloupe   Le Désirade
Abymes
Petite Terre
Pointe-à-Pitre
Basse-Terre
Marie
Galante
Basse-Terre
Les Saintes   Grande-
Bourg

Portsmouth   Dominica

Roseau

Martinique

St Pierre
Fort-de-France

Antigua, ⇨ Ch. 2
Beaches, bone-white and beckoning—one for every day of the year—can be secluded or hopping with activity. History buffs and nautical nuts will appreciate English Harbour, which sheltered Britain's Caribbean fleet in the 18th and 19th centuries. Go for those beaches but also for sailing. Don't go for local culture because all-inclusives predominate. Lovely as it is, the island is more for tourists than travelers.

St. Eustatius, ⇨ Ch. 19
St. Eustatius (Statia) is the quintessential low-key island, where the most exciting thing is finding an elusive blue iguana while hiking the Quill. The real thrills are below the surface. Go to dive the wrecks, to hike the island's extinct volcano, and to be among the Caribbean's friendliest people. Don't go if you want to do much else.

Saba, ⇨ Ch. 17
With few modern conveniences (no resorts, no fast food, no movie theaters), you can reacquaint yourself with Mother Nature or simply catch your breath. Go to dive in the clear water, to hike to the top of Mount Scenery, and to enjoy the peace. Don't go if you want to lounge on the beach. There is no beach.

St. Kitts & Nevis, ⇨ Ch. 20
Things are unhurried on lush, hilly St. Kitts and Nevis. And the locals seem more cordial and courteous—eager to share their paradise with you—than on more touristy Caribbean islands. Go to discover Caribbean history, to stay in a small plantation inn, or just to relax. Don't go for nightlife or shopping. These islands are about laid-back "liming" and maybe buying some local crafts.

Guadeloupe, ⇨ Ch. 12
An exotic, tropical paradise, Guadeloupe is covered by a lush rain forest and blessed with a rich, Creole culture that influences everything from its dances to its food. Go if you want to experience another culture—and still have your creature comforts and access to fine beaches. Don't go if you want five-star luxury because it's rare here.

The Windward and Southern Islands

The Windward islands—Dominica, Martinique, St. Lucia, St. Vincent, and Grenada— complete the main Caribbean arc. These dramatically scenic southern islands face the tradewinds head on. The Grenadines—a string of small islands between Grenada and St. Vincent—is heaven for sailors. The Southern Caribbean islands—Trinidad, Tobago, Aruba, Bonaire, and Curaçao—are rarely bothered by hurricanes.

Aruba, ⇨ Ch. 3

Some Caribbean travelers seek an undiscovered paradise, some seek the familiar and safe: Aruba is for the latter. On the smallest of the ABC islands, the waters are peacock blue, and the white beaches beautiful and powdery soft. For Americans, Aruba offers all the comforts of home: English is spoken universally, and the U.S. dollar is accepted everywhere.

Bonaire, ⇨ Ch. 5

With only 12,000 year-round citizens and huge numbers of visiting divers, Bonaire still seems largely untouched by tourism. Divers come for the clear water, profusion of marine life, and great dive shops. With a surreal, arid landscape, immense flamingo population, and gorgeous turquoise vistas, you can also have a wonderful land-based holiday.

Curaçao, ⇨ Ch. 8

Rich in heritage and history, Curaçao offers a blend of island life and city savvy, wonderful weather, spectacular diving, and charming beaches. Dutch and Caribbean influences are everywhere, but there's also an infusion of touches from around the world, particularly noteworthy in the great food. Willemstad, the picturesque capital, is a treat for pedestrians, with shopping clustered in areas around the waterfront.

Dominica, ⇨ Ch. 9

Dominica is the island to find your bliss exploring nature's bounty, not in the sun and surf. Go to be active, either diving under the sea or hiking on land. Don't go for great beaches or a big-resort experience. This is one island that's delightfully behind the times.

Martinique, ⇨ Ch. 14

Excellent cuisine, fine service, highly-touted rum, and lilting Franco-Caribbean music are the main draws in Martinique. Go if you're a Francophile drawn to fine food, wine, and sophisticated style. Don't go if you are looking for a bargain and don't have patience. Getting here is a chore, but there are definitely rewards for the persistent.

Caribbean

Aruba
Oranjestad

Bonaire
Kralendijk

Curaçao
Willemstad

Sea

Islas Los Roques

La Guaira

Isla La Tortuga

Caracas

0		100 mi
0	100 km	

VENEZUELA

St. Kitts

L E E W A R D

Nevis

Antigua

Montserrat

Grande-Terre

Guadeloupe

Abymes ⟋ Le Désirade

Basse-Terre ⟋ Pointe-à-Pitre

I S L A N D S

Basse-Terre ⟋ Marie Galante

Les Saintes ⟋ Grande-Bourg

Portsmouth

Dominica

Roseau

St Pierre ⟋ La Trinité

Fort-de-France

Martinique

W I N D W A R D

Castries

St. Lucia

Barbados

Bridgetown

St. Vincent

Kingstown

Bequia

The Grenadines

I S L A N D S

Carriacou

Grenada

St. George's

Tobago

Scarborough

Trinidad

Port of Spain

San Fernando

St. Lucia, ⇨ Ch. 21

One of the most green and beautiful islands in the Caribbean is, arguably, the most romantic. The scenic south and central regions are mountainous and lush, with dense rainforest, endless banana plantations, and fascinating historic sites. Along the west coast, some of the region's most picturesque and interesting resorts are interspersed with dozens of delightful inns, appealing to families as well as lovers and adventurers.

St. Vincent & The Grenadines, ⇨ Ch. 23

Thirty-two perfectly endowed islands and cays have no mass tourism but a lot of old-style Caribbean charm; several have not a small sense of luxury. Tourism isn't even the biggest business in lush, mountainous St. Vincent. Throughout the chain, wildlife trusts protect rare species of flora and fauna, and villa walls ensure privacy for the islands' rich and famous human visitors.

Grenada, ⇨ Ch. 11

The spice business is going strong, but tourism is just as important. On the laid-back island, the only sounds are the occasional abrupt call of a cuckoo in the lush rain forest, the crash of surf in the secluded coves, and the slow beat of a big drum dance. Resorts are mostly small and charming. St. George's, the island's capital, is often called the most beautiful city in the Caribbean.

Trinidad & Tobago, ⇨ Ch. 24

Trinidad and Tobago, the most southerly Caribbean islands, are two different places. Trinidad is an effervescent mix of cultures—mostly descendants of African slaves and East Indian indentured workers—who like to party but also appreciate the island's incredibly diverse ecosystem. Little sister Tobago is laid-back and rustic, with beaches that can match any in the Caribbean.

Barbados, ⇨ Ch. 4

Broad vistas, sweeping seascapes, craggy cliffs, and acre upon acre of sugarcane make up the island's varied landscape. A long, successful history of tourism has been forged from the warm, Bajan hospitality, welcoming hotels and resorts, sophisticated dining, lively nightspots, and, of course, magnificent sunny beaches.

ISLAND FINDER

To help you decide which island is best for you, we've rated each island in several areas that might influence your decision on choosing the perfect Caribbean vacation spot. Each major island covered in this book has been rated in terms of cost from $ (very inexpensive) to $$$$$ (very expensive), and since prices often vary a great deal by season, we've given you a rating for the high season (December through mid-April) and low season (mid-April through November). We've also compared each island's relative strength in several other categories that might influence your decision.

If an island has no marks in a particular column (under "Golf" for example), it means that the activity is not available on the island.

	Cost High Season	Cost Low Season
Anguilla	$$$$	$$$
Antigua	$$$	$$
Aruba	$$$	$$
Barbados	$$$$	$$$$
Bonaire	$$	$$
BVI: Tortola	$$$	$$
BVI: Virgin Gorda	$$$$$	$$$$
BVI: Anegada	$$$$	$$$
BVI: Jost Van Dyke	$$$$	$$$
Cayman Islands: Grand Cayman	$$$$	$$$
Cayman Islands: Little Cayman	$$$	$$$
Cayman Islands: Cayman Brac	$$	$$
Curaçao	$$$$	$$$
Dominica	$$	$
Dominican Republic	$$	$
Grenada	$$$	$$$
Grenada: Carriacou	$$	$
Guadeloupe	$$	$$
Jamaica	$$$	$$
Martinique	$$$	$$
Montserrat	$	$
Puerto Rico	$$$	$$
Saba	$$	$
St. Barthélemy	$$$$$	$$$$
St. Eustatius	$$	$
St. Kitts & Nevis: St. Kitts	$$$	$$
St. Kitts & Nevis: Nevis	$$$$	$$$
St. Lucia	$$$$	$$$
St. Maarten/St. Martin	$$$	$$$
SVG: St. Vincent	$$	$$
SVG: The Grenadines	$$$$	$$$
T&T: Trinidad	$$$	$$
T&T: Tobago	$$$	$$
Turks & Caicos Islands	$$$$*	$$$*
USVI: St. Thomas	$$$$	$$$
USVI: St. Croix	$$	$
USVI: St. John	$$$	$$

*   *Cost for Provo (Parrot Cay $$$$$, other islands $$)*

**   *Provo Only*

Beautiful Beaches	Fine Dining	Shopping	Casinos	Night-life	Diving	Golf	Eco-tourism	Good for Families

IF YOU LIKE

Great Beaches

Great beaches aren't all the same. You might dream of sifting your toes in soft white sand with just a hint of warmth. You may love to walk along a virgin beach that is lined with nothing but a 20-foot palm tree. You may be charmed by that cute little crescent that's reachable by a precipitous climb down an almost-sheer rock cliff. You may want to be surrounded by a hundred pairs of beautiful limbs, all smelling slightly of coconut oil. The Caribbean can give you all these. Our favorite beaches aren't always the most famous ones, but part of the fun of taking a tropical vacation is discovering your own favorites, which are sometimes the ones you'd least suspect. Here are a few of the beaches we like:

- **Baie Orientale, St. Maarten/St. Martin.** There's a good reason why everyone goes here.
- **The Baths, Virgin Gorda, British Virgin Islands.** Giant boulders form grottos filled with seawater that you can explore.
- **Eagle Beach, Aruba.** Once undeveloped, this beach on Aruba's southwestern coast is now hopping and happening.
- **Half Moon Beach, Providenciales, Turks & Caicos Islands.** A natural ribbon of ivory sand joins two tiny, uninhabited cays.
- **Macaroni Beach, Mustique, St. Vincent & the Grenadines.** The most famous beach on the most famous Grenadine.
- **Negril Beach, Jamaica.** Seven miles of sand lined by beach bars, casual restaurants, and hotels in westernmost Jamaica.
- **Seven Mile Beach, Grand Cayman, Cayman Islands.** After Hurricane Ivan, better than it's been in years.
- **Shoal Bay, Anguilla.** Sand or talcum powder? You decide.

Diving & Snorkeling

Many people would rather spend their days under the sea rather than on the beach. Generally, the best conditions for diving—clear water and lots of marine life—are also good for snorkelers, though you won't see as much from the surface looking down. If you haven't been certified yet, take a resort course. After learning the basics in a pool, you can often do a short dive from shore. Here are some of the Caribbean's best dive destinations:

- **Anegada, British Virgin Islands.** The reefs surrounding this flat coral and limestone atoll are a sailor's nightmare but a scuba diver's dream.
- **Bonaire.** The current is mild, the reefs often begin just offshore, visibility is generally 60 feet to 100 feet, and the marine life is magnificent.
- **Little Cayman, Cayman Islands.** The drop-off at Bloody Bay Wall goes from 18 feet to more than 1,000 feet—diving doesn't get much better than this.
- **Dominica.** Serious divers know that the pristine, bubbly waters around Dominica's submerged volcanic crater are among the best in the world.
- **Saba.** Beside one of the lively Caribbean reefs, the diving on Saba is some of the best in the world.
- **St. Eustatius.** The waters here are tops for wreck diving.
- **Tobago Cays, St. Vincent & the Grenadines.** A group of five uninhabited islands surrounds a beautiful lagoon studded with sponges, coral formations, and countless colorful fish.
- **Turks & Caicos Islands.** The world's third-largest coral reef is visible from the air and packed with exotic marine life, dramatic wall drop-offs, colorful fans, and pristine coral formations.

Boating & Sailing

Whether you charter a crewed boat or captain the vessel yourself, the waters of the Caribbean are excellent for boating and sailing, and the many secluded bays and inlets provide ideal spots to drop anchor and picnic or explore. Once deemed an outward-bound adventure or exclusive domain of the rich and famous, chartering a boat is now considered—and actually is—an affordable and attractive vacation alternative. If you're already a sailor, you may have always wanted to explore beyond your own lake, river, or bay. Well, you can always hire a certified skipper to come along and help you out. If you've never sailed before, you've probably not experienced the delight at dropping anchor at a different beautiful beach every day. There are many great yacht harbors, including these:

- **Antigua.** Yachtspeople favor the waters here and put in regularly in Nelson's Dockyard, which hosts a colorful annual regatta in late April or early May.
- **St. Martin.** Marigot's yacht harbor is a jumping-off spot for trips to the nearby islands of Anguilla and St. Barths.
- **St. Vincent & the Grenadines.** So many islands so close together give you more possibilities than you can possibly enjoy in one vacation.
- **St. Thomas, U.S. Virgin Islands.** It's easy to charter a yacht in the Virgin Islands, which offer some of the best sailing opportunities in the world.
- **Tortola, British Virgin Islands.** The marinas here have some of the Caribbean's best charter possibilities.

Golf

What's better than playing the back nine shaded by swaying palm trees with a view of the crashing surf? Golfers are drawn to excellent Caribbean courses and stunning views, often attached to comfortable and luxurious resorts, where the rest of the family can lounge by the pool while you head off for a morning round before the sun gets too hot. Mild weather year-round means you can be playing golf in the Dominican Republic or Barbados while everyone else is freezing. Here are a few of the best:

- **Four Seasons Golf Course, Nevis.** The combination of majestic scenery, unbelievably lush landscaping, and Robert Trent Jones, Jr.'s wicked layout incorporating ravines and sugar mills, makes this experience well above par even among classic golf resorts.
- **Hyatt Dorado Courses, Puerto Rico.** Dorado Beach has four world-class, Robert Trent Jones–designed courses that are renowned classics and among Chi Chi Rodríguez's favorites.
- **The Teeth of the Dog, Dominican Republic.** Casa de Campo's most well known course is considered among the best in the Caribbean. The resort's other courses—also designed by Pete Dye—are becoming their own legends.
- **Tobago Plantations Golf & Country Club, Trinidad & Tobago.** The oceanside course—the newest on the island—has amazing views, not to mention challenging greens and fairways.
- **Trump International Golf Club, Canouan.** This course, the only one in the Grenadines, was designed by Jim Fazio and has astounding views.

IF YOU LIKE

Caribbean History

From the 16th century until the early 19th century, the Dutch, Danes, Swedes, English, French, and Spanish fought bitterly for control of the Caribbean. Some islands have almost as many battle sites as sand flies. Having gained control of the islands and annihilated the Caribs, the Europeans established vast sugar plantations and brought Africans to work the fields. Today the Caribbean population is a rich gumbo of nationalities, and a good deal of the region's history has been preserved. Here are some of the more interesting historical sights:

- **Christiansted, U.S. Virgin Islands.** Fort Christiansvaern and other historic sights, which are spread out all over town, let you step back into St. Croix's colonial past.
- **Kurá Hulanda Museum, Curaçao.** This museum and cultural center is at the heart of a rebirth for Curaçao, and its collection documenting African history around the world is worth a special trip.
- **Nelson's Dockyard, Antigua.** An impeccable restoration of Lord Horatio Nelson's 18th-century headquarters has delightful hotels, restaurants, and crafts shops.
- **Rose Hall & the Appleton Estate, Jamaica.** Jamaica is home to many former plantation greathouses but none with as rich a history as Rose Hall, which comes complete with haunting legends.
- **Santo Domingo's Zona Colonial, Dominican Republic.** As you wander the narrow cobbled streets, it's easy to imagine what the city was like in the days of Columbus, Cortés, and Ponce de León, especially now that the zone is well lighted by antique lanterns.

Nightlife

Steel drums, limbo dancers, and jump-ups are ubiquitous in the Caribbean. Jump-ups? Simple. You hear the music, jump up, and dance. Or just indulge the art of "liming" (we call it "hanging out"), which can mean anything from playing pool or dominoes to engaging in heated political debate to dancing.

- **Aruba.** While it's not everyone's cup of tea, Aruba has a vibrant nighttime scene. You definitely do not have to wait until spring to break free here.
- **Jamaica.** Reggae Sumfest is the big summer music festival. Both Montego Bay's so-called Hip Strip and Negril's Norman Manley Boulevard are lined with bars and clubs that keep things hopping until late (or early, as the case may be).
- **Puerto Rico.** With a full range of bars, nightclubs, and every form of entertainment, San Juan is a big, small city that never sleeps. The year-round Le Lai Lo Festival is perhaps the most successful attempt to introduce visitors to local music and dance.
- **Trinidad.** Port-of-Spain is loaded with lively night spots, and spontaneity is prized, so you have to keep your ears open for the new parties. The one party you can't miss is Carnival, the Caribbean's biggest and most popular celebration, which draws thousands to the island for days of parades and street parties. Other good Carnival celebrations are on Curaçao and Guadeloupe.

Shopping

Almost as many people go to the Caribbean to shop as to lie on the beach. Whether it's jewelry in St. Maarten, fragrant spices in Grenada, high-end designer fashions in St. Barths, or island crafts almost anywhere, you're likely to come home with a bag full of treasures.

- **Grenada.** Visit a historic spice plantation, tour a nutmeg-processing plant, and replenish your spice rack with nutmeg, cinnamon sticks, cocoa, and cloves at an outdoor market.
- **Puerto Rico.** From the boutiques of Old San Juan to ateliers of the young designers elsewhere in metro San Juan to galleries scattered all over the island, there's plenty to see and buy. You may also consider picking up some of the santos created in San Germán.
- **St. Barthélemy.** Without a doubt, the shopping here for luxury goods and fashion is the best in the Caribbean. The variety and quality are astounding. The unfavorable exchange rates mean fewer bargains for Americans, but the prices here—all duty-free—are still less than what you'd pay in Paris or Saint Tropez.
- **St. Maarten/St. Martin.** Hundreds of duty-free shops in Phillipsburg make the island the best in the Caribbean for bargain hunters, especially for quality jewelry and perfumes. Marigot has its share of nice boutiques, but unfavorable exchange rates make for fewer good buys on the French side.
- **St. Thomas, U.S. Virgin Islands.** Main Street in Charlotte Amalie is well known for numerous duty-free shops, selling everything from rum to designer fashions and gems. The Caribbean's biggest cruise port also has several malls.

Staying Active

There's much more to do in the Caribbean than simply lying on the beach, sipping rum punches, or playing a round of golf. Try hiking through rain forests, kayaking through mangroves, or sailing on a board through a windswept bay.

- **Bird-watching, Trinidad & Tobago.** So the watching part isn't so active, but hiking through the rain forests and savannahs on these sister islands will give you the opportunity to see more bird species than any other place in the Caribbean.
- **Hiking the Quill, St. Eustatius.** The crater of Statia's extinct volcano is filled with a primeval rain forest and is a top hiking destination.
- **Horseback Riding at Chukka Cove, Jamaica.** Headquartered at the Ocho Rios polo fields, this company is now Jamaica's top soft-adventure outfitter, having added canopy tours, river rafting, and more to its excellent horseback-riding program.
- **Kayaking through Bahía Mosquito, Puerto Rico.** Vieques's bioluminiscent bay is best experienced on a kayak tour on a moonless night, when every stroke makes the water light up.
- **Trekking to Boiling Lake, Dominica.** This bubbly, brackish cauldron is actually a flooded fumarole. A trek here is an unforgettable trip into an otherworldly place.
- **Windsurfing in Sosúa Bay, Dominican Republic.** Ideal wind conditions have helped to create one of the Caribbean's major windsurfing centers on this north-coast beach.

IF YOU WANT

To Take It Easy on Your Wallet

The Caribbean isn't all about five-star resorts. Often, you may want to save a bit of your vacation cash to eat in elegant restaurants or to shop for the perfect gift. Saving money in the Caribbean doesn't have to mean sacrificing comfort. Sometimes it just means going to a cheaper island, such as the Dominican Republic, Saba, or Dominica. But there are some unique inns and resorts in the Caribbean, where you can sleep for much less and still have a great time.

- **Carringtons Inn, St. Croix, U.S. Virgin Islands.** A stay at this spacious bed-and-breakfast harks back to a gentler time, when people spent the winter, rather than a week, in the Caribbean.
- **Habitation Chabert, Dominica.** The poshest resort on Dominica—created with fine creole style—is still a relative bargain.
- **Horny Toad, St. Maarten/St. Martin.** A marvelous little oceanfront guest house with a funky name offers the island's best value for those who want to keep costs down.
- **Peach & Quiet, Barbados.** This small seaside inn on the southeast coast is the sweetest deal on Barbados.
- **Rockhouse, Jamaica.** Perched on the cliffs of Negril's West End, unique bungalows blend comfort and rustic style. Regular rooms keep costs down, but if you want to spend a bit more, the dramatic villas are worth every penny.
- **Turtle Nest Inn, Grand Cayman, Cayman Islands.** On otherwise expensive Grand Cayman, this Spanish-style seaside inn has roomy one-bedroom apartments on a small beach.

To Splurge

The Caribbean's most luxurious resorts are worlds unto themselves. You'll live a privileged existence, if only for the week, and you may be joined by the masters of Wall Street or Hollywood, the jet set or old money. Everyone deserves to splurge at least once, and if that's what you want to do, these are the best places to do it.

- **Anse Chastanet Hotel, St. Lucia.** Rooms were designed to meld with the mountainside; louvered wooden walls open to stunning Piton and Caribbean vistas or to the deep-green forest.
- **Cap Juluca, Anguilla.** This spectacular 179-acre resort wraps around the edge of Maunday's Bay and almost 2 mi (3 km) of sugary white-sand beach.
- **Coral Reef Club, Barbados.** Elegant and stylish without being stuffy, suites are individually designed, beautifully decorated, and wonderfully private.
- **Eden Rock, St. Barthélemy.** St. Barths' original hotel has been expanded and brought into the top tier of the island's offerings.
- **Meridien Club, Pine Cay, Turks & Caicos Islands.** This is luxury of a decidedly simple sort—based on relaxing and pampering, and there's nary a celebrity in sight.
- **Ottley's Plantation Inn, St. Kitts.** This greathouse inn with ravishing gardens epitomizes low-key, worldly sophistication and down-home Caribbean hospitality.
- **Sofitel Auberge de la Vieille Tour, Guadeloupe.** Guests love the split-level suites and luxurious amenities at this jewel, which has gotten better over the years. It also has one of the finest restaurants on Guadeloupe.

To Have the Perfect Honeymoon

Swaying palms, moonlight strolls on the beach, candlelit dinners: No wonder the Caribbean is a favorite honeymoon destination. Whatever you are looking for in a honeymoon—seclusion, privacy, or more active fun—you can certainly find it, and it will usually be on a perfect beach. You can be pampered or just left alone, stay up late or get up with the sun, get out and stay active or simply rest and relax. Our favorites run the gamut, so if you need a place with easy access, or if you want to really get away from it all, we have the perfect spot.

- **Horned Dorset Primavera, Puerto Rico.** Whisk your beloved to this sunset-kissed hotel and just disappear. You may never leave your elegant ocean-front room. When you do, the restaurant is one of the best in Puerto Rico.
- **Palm Island, Grenadines.** Enjoy five dazzling beaches for water sports, nature trails for quiet walks, a pool with waterfall, sophisticated dining, impeccable service, exquisite accommodations—and privacy.
- **Sandals Grande St. Lucian Spa & Beach Resort, St. Lucia.** Big, busy, and all-inclusive, this resort is a favorite of young honeymooners—particularly for its complimentary weddings.
- **Spice Island Beach Resort, Grenada.** After more than a year of rebuilding, Grenada's best is back; with impeccable service, it's one of the Caribbean's finest small resorts.
- **Windmills Plantation, Turks & Caicos Islands.** This eight-room resort has an eclectic blend of plantation-inspired, romantic hideaways on the powdery sand of the north shore of Salt Cay. If you want to get far off the beaten path, this is definitely the place to consider.

To Eat Well

Caribbean food is a complex blend of indigenous, African, and colonial influences. Native tubers such as yuca and taro, leafy vegetables like callaloo, and herbs such as cilantro recur in most island cuisines. Africans brought plantains, yams, pigeon peas, and assorted peppers. The Spanish introduced rice, and the British brought breadfruit from the South Pacific. Here are some of our favorite Caribbean restaurants:

- **Blue by Eric Ripert, Cayman Islands.** Grand Cayman's best restaurant is brought to you by one of New York's finest chefs.
- **Brandywine Bay, Tortola.** A romantic, candlelit atmosphere coupled with stellar food makes this Tortola's best restaurant.
- **Chez Pascal, Antigua.** Perched on a cliff overlooking the ocean, this restaurant is an authentic piece of sunny, southern France transplanted to the Caribbean. Melt-in-your-mouth seafood specialties particularly shine, as do the silken sauces.
- **Koal Keel, Anguilla.** One of the island's best new restaurants mixes French and West Indian styles to excellent effects.
- **Marandi, Aruba.** Directly on the water, Aruba's best restaurant has an eclectic menu, including everything from a delicious grouper fillet to wonderful pork tenderloin.
- **La Belle Epoque, Martinique.** The excellent, classic French cuisine brings this elegant restaurant to the forefront of formal dining experiences in Martinique.

WHEN TO GO

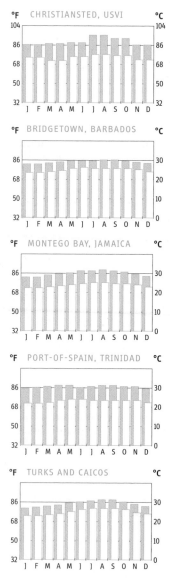

°F CHRISTIANSTED, USVI °C

°F BRIDGETOWN, BARBADOS °C

°F MONTEGO BAY, JAMAICA °C

°F PORT-OF-SPAIN, TRINIDAD °C

°F TURKS AND CAICOS °C

The Caribbean high season is traditionally winter—from December 15 to April 14—when northern weather is at its worst. During this season you're guaranteed the most entertainment at resorts and the most people with whom to enjoy it. It's also the most fashionable, the most expensive, and the most popular time to visit—and most hotels are heavily booked. You must make reservations at least two or three months in advance for the very best places (sometimes a year in advance for the most exclusive spots). Hotel prices drop 20% to 50% after April 15; airfares and cruise prices also fall. Saving money isn't the only reason to visit the Caribbean during the off-season. Temperatures are only a few degrees warmer than at other times of the year, and many islands now schedule their carnivals, music festivals, and other events during the off-season. Late August, September, October, and early November are the least crowded.

Climate

The Caribbean climate is fairly constant. The average year-round temperatures for the region are 78°F to 88°F. The temperature extremes are 65°F low, 95°F high; but, as everyone knows, it's the humidity, not the heat, that makes you suffer, especially when the two go hand in hand.

As part of the late-fall rainy season, hurricanes occasionally sweep through the Caribbean. Check the news daily and keep abreast of brewing tropical storms. The southernmost Caribbean islands (from St. Vincent to Trinidad, along with Aruba, Bonaire, and Curaçao) are generally spared the threat of hurricanes. The rainy season consists mostly of brief showers interspersed with sunshine. You can watch the clouds thicken, feel the rain, then have brilliant sunshine dry you off, all while remaining on your lounge chair. A spell of overcast days or heavy rainfall is unusual, as everyone will tell you.

🔳 **Weather Channel Connection** ☎ 900/932-8437 95¢ per minute from a Touch-Tone phone ⊕ www.weather.com.

The Caribbean's top seasonal events are listed below, and any one of them could provide the stuff of lasting memories. Contact local tourism authorities for exact dates and for further information.

ONGOING Jan.–Apr.	**Carnival** lasts longer on Curaçao than on many other islands: the revelries begin at New Year's and continue until midnight the day before Ash Wednesday. The highlight is the Tumba Festival (dates vary), a four-day musical event featuring fierce competition among local musicians for the honor of having their piece selected as the official road march during parades. Easter Monday's Seú Folklore Parade is made up of groups celebrating the harvest in traditional costumes.
WINTER Dec.	The week before Christmas, the Carriacou **Parang Festival** is a musical and cultural celebration. "Parang" is Spanish for ad-libbing. Costumed singers travel from village to village, creating spontaneous songs based on local gossip and accompanied by guitar, violin, and drums.
	In odd-numbered years, in early December, Martinique hosts its jazz festival, **Jazz à la Martinique**; in addition to showcasing the best musical talent of the islands, it has attracted such top American performers as Branford Marsalis.
	So Sabans don't forget what fun is, they hold a **Saba Day** the first weekend in December—three days of band contests, food tastings, and other events.
	Bicycle racing, arts and crafts exhibitions, caroling, and street parties with music and dancing mark **Nine Mornings,** a pre-Christmas tradition in St. Vincent that occurs during the nine days immediately before Christmas.
Dec. & Jan.	St. Croix celebrates Carnival with its **Crucian Christmas Festival,** which starts in late December. After weeks of beauty pageants, food fairs, and concerts, the festival wraps up with a parade in early January.
Jan.	In mid-January, the **Barbados Jazz Festival** is a weeklong event jammed with performances by international artists, jazz legends, and local talent.
	The **Air Jamaica Jazz & Blues Festival** takes place in Montego Bay, Jamaica, in late January, drawing both music fans and a wide range of talent.
Jan. & Feb.	The **Grenada Sailing Festival,** held at the end of January and early February, includes six days of races and regattas and a daylong crafts market and street festival—all organized by the Grenada Yacht Club.

ON THE CALENDAR

Feb.	Although the pre-Lenten **Carnival** is celebrated all over the Caribbean, the region's biggest and most elaborate celebration is undoubtedly in Trinidad, where it's become a way of life and the most widely anticipated event of the entire year.
	The biggest event of the year is the four-day **Carriacou Carnival**, held in mid-February. Revelers participate in parades, calypso contests, music and dancing, and general frivolity.
SPRING Mar.	Locals and yachties gather at Foxy's bar on Jost Van Dyke in the British Virgin Islands for the annual **St. Patrick's Day** celebration.
	Beginning around March 17 and lasting a week, the **St. Patrick's Day Fiesta** is celebrated in Sauteurs (St. Patrick's Parish), in the north of Grenada, with arts and crafts, agricultural exhibits, food and drink, and a cultural extravaganza with music and dancing.
	On the Dutch side of St. Maarten, early March has the **Heineken Regatta,** with as many as 300 sailboats competing from around the world. (For the experience of a lifetime, some visitors can purchase a working berth aboard a regatta vessel.)
Mar. & Apr.	The **National Music Festival** is held at Kingstown, St. Vincent's Memorial Hall during March and April. The best in Vincentian music and song is presented—folk songs, gospel, calypso, solos and duets, choirs, and group ensembles.
	The Bequia **Easter Regatta** is held during the four-day Easter weekend. Revelers gather to watch boat races and celebrate Bequia's seafaring traditions with food, music, dancing, and competitive games.
	On Union in the Grenadines, the **Easterval Regatta** occurs during the Easter weekend. Festivities include boat races, sports and games, a calypso competition, a beauty pageant, and a cultural show featuring the Big Drum Dance (derived from French and African traditions). Union is one of the few islands (along with Grenada's Carriacou) that perpetuate this festive dance.
	During Easter weekend, St. Thomas Yacht Club hosts the **Rolex Cup Regatta,** which is part of the three-race Caribbean Ocean Racing Triangle (CORT), which pulls in yachties and their pals from all over.
Late Apr.– early May	**Antigua Sailing Week** draws more than 300 yachts for a series of races in several boat classes. It's like a nautical Kentucky Derby, and the salt air crackles with excitement.

	May	Every May, hordes of people head to Tortola for the three-day BVI Music Festival to listen to reggae, gospel, blues, and salsa music by musicians from around the Caribbean and the U.S. mainland.
		In early May the weeklong St. Lucia Jazz Festival, one of the premier events of its kind in the Caribbean, sees international jazz greats entertain at outdoor venues on Pigeon Island and at various hotels, restaurants, and nightspots throughout the island; free concerts are also held at Derek Walcott Square in downtown Castries.
		On Canouan in the Grenadines, the Canouan Regatta is held in mid-May. Besides competitive boat races and sailing events, there are fishing contests, calypso competitions, donkey and crab races, and a beauty pageant.
		The St. Croix Half Ironman Triathlon attracts international-class athletes as well as amateurs every May for a 1-mi (2-km) swim, a 7-mi (12-km) run, and a 34-mi (55-km) bike ride; it includes a climb up the Beast on Route 69.
SUMMER June		The weeklong Bonaire Dive Festival is filled with educational and fun activities to raise people's awareness of the importance of the world's coral reefs.
		During Million Dollar Month, you'll find fishing tournaments on all three of the Cayman Islands (five tournaments in all), each with its own rules, records, and entrance fees; huge cash prizes are awarded, including one for a quarter of a million dollars that's given to the angler who breaks the existing blue marlin record (at this writing 584 pounds).
		The Creole Blues Festival is held on Marie-Galante annually, and it's gaining in fame.
		The St. Kitts Music Festival, held the last week of June, celebrates everything from R&B to reggae. Among the top international acts to perform have been Chaka Khan, Earl Klugh, Kool and the Gang, and Peabo Bryson.
	July	Dating from the 19th century, the Barbados Crop Over Festival, a monthlong event ending on Kadooment Day (a national holiday), marks the end of the sugarcane harvest.
		The St. Thomas Gamefishing Club hosts its July Open Tournament over the Fourth of July weekend. There are categories for serious marlin anglers, just-for-fun fishermen, and even kids who want to try their luck from docks and rocks.

ON THE CALENDAR

	St. John dishes up its own version of Carnival with the July 4 celebration. Weeks of festivities—including beauty pageants and a food fair—culminate in a parade through the streets of Cruz Bay on Independence Day.
Late July–early Aug.	Antigua's Summer Carnival is one of the Caribbean's more elaborate, with eye-catching costumes, fiercely competitive bands, and the only Caribbean queen show (a.k.a. the Miss Antigua Contest).
	The renowned Festival del Merengue is held in late July and early August in Santo Domingo in the Dominican Republic, showcasing name entertainers, bands, and orchestras.
	Music lovers also fill the island for the July and August Reggae Sumfest, which is getting hotter every year, because the best, brightest, and newest of the reggae stars gather to perform in open-air concerts in MoBay, Jamaica.
	Nevis's version of carnival—Culturama—is a summer event, held the end of July and beginning of August, and includes music competitions, queen shows, art exhibits, and cultural events. It culminates in the daylong last-day jump-up, a colorful parade around the island.
Aug.	Try your hand at sportfishing as anglers compete to land the largest catch at the BVI Sportfishing Tournament.
	A month of calypso road shows culminates in the Grenada Carnival the second week of August. It's the biggest celebration of the year, with a beauty pageant, a soca monarch competition, continuous steel-pan and calypso music, and a huge Parade of the Bands on the last Tuesday.
	On a Sunday in early August, Point-à-Pitre on Grande-Terre holds the Fête des Cuisinières, which celebrates the masters of creole cuisine with a five-hour banquet that's open to the public. The festival was started in 1916 by a guild of female cooks (they still represent a large contingent) who wanted to honor the patron saint of cooks, St. Laurent.
	The Caribbean Quest Musical Awards, a festival of regional music from around the islands, is held in early August on the French side of St. Martin.

FALL	
Late Sept.– early Oct.	The St. Lucia Billfishing Tournament, held in late September or early October, attracts anglers from all over the Caribbean, with prizes awarded for the biggest fish and the largest catch; the blue marlin is the most sought-after fish, and everyone hopes to find one that beats the 1,000-pound mark.
Oct.	Grand Cayman sees the carnival-like atmosphere of Pirates Week (which really lasts 10 days and includes a mock invasion of Hog Sty Bay by a mock Blackbeard and company). Visitors and locals dress up like pirates and wenches; music, fireworks, and competitions take place island-wide.
	Dominica's Annual World Creole Music Festival is held the last weekend in October or first weekend of November. This three-day music and cultural festival draws performers and creole music enthusiasts from around the globe.
	The Dominican Republic Jazz Festival is an impressive lineup of international (like Chuck Mangione) and Latino jazz stars (Bobby Sanabria and Carlos Estrada) that runs for three days during the first week of October, with venues in Cabarete, Sosúa, and Puerto Plata. Sea Horse Ranch is a hotbed of activity during the festival, and there's music, dance, and art.
Oct. & Nov.	Divali, held in October or November in Trinidad and Tobago and known as the Festival of Lights, is the climax of long spiritual preparation in the Hindu community. Small lamps beautifully illuminate the night, and there are events involving music, dancing, gift exchange, and much hospitality.
Nov.	BET (Black Entertainment Television) sponsors Anguilla's Tranquility Jazz Festival, which attracts major musicians such as Hilton Ruiz, James Moody, Bobby Watson, and Vanessa Rubin.

1

Anguilla

The beach at Little Bay

WORD OF MOUTH

"Anguilla's water looks like you are in a swimming pool, and the sand is so white it hurts your eyes!"

—mustang8

"All [the] beaches are beautiful—long with white sand & crystal clear water—although Shoal Bay East is busier & has day trip-pers from St. Martin ('busy' in Anguilla is a relative term—the beaches are never really crowded)."

—MaryD

WELCOME TO ANGUILLA

TRANQUIL AND UPSCALE

The island is only 16 mi (26 km) long and 3 mi (5 km) wide at its widest point. A low-lying limestone island, its highest spot is 213 feet above sea level. Since there neither streams nor rivers—only saline ponds used for salt production—water is provided by cisterns that collect rainwater or desalinization plants.

> In 1744, Anguillians (as well as privateers from St. Kitts) captured nearby French St-Martin and held it for 4 years; the French retaliated by attacking at Crocus Bay but were repelled.

In tiny Anguilla, where fishermen have been heading out to sea for centuries in handmade boats, the beaches are some of the Caribbean's best and least crowded. Heavy development has not spoiled the island's atmospheric corners, and independent restaurants still thrive. Resorts run the gamut from over-the-top places to quaint inns.

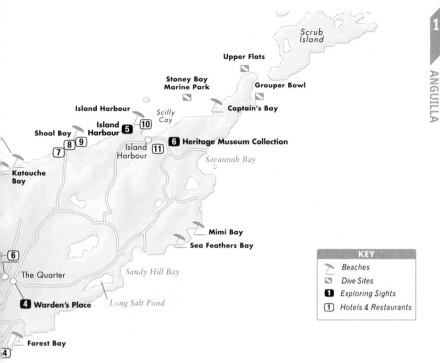

TOP 4 REASONS TO VISIT ANGUILLA

1 Miles of brilliant beach ensure you have a quality spot to lounge.

2 The dining scene offers fine cuisine in elegant surroundings as well as delicious local food in casual restaurants.

3 A funky late-night local music scene for reggae and string band fans means you don't have to go to bed early.

4 Excellent luxury resorts coddle you in a level of comfort to which you may or may not be accustomed.

ANGUILLA PLANNER

Getting to Anguilla

There are no nonstop flights to Anguilla (AXA) from the U.S., so you will almost always have to fly through San Juan, St. Maarten, or some other Caribbean island. Most of the airlines flying to Anguilla are Caribbean-based, including Caribbean Star, Winair, and LIAT, so you'll usually be making that short hop in a small plane, but American Eagle makes the trip from San Juan.

The other option is a ferry from Marigot in St. Martin or directly from the St. Maarten airport. Many people take this option because it's only a 20-minute trip and relatively inexpensive (about $15 each way).

Hassle Factor: Medium

On the Ground

It's possible to base yourself in Sandy Ground, Rendezvous Bay, Meads Bay, or Upper Shoal Bay and do without a car, but restaurants and resorts are quite spread out, so for the sake of convenience you may wish to rent a car for a few days or for your entire stay. If you do, prepare to drive on the left. Otherwise, the taxi ride from the airport to your hotel will be less than $25 even to the West End (and considerably less if you are going to Sandy Ground). Taxis are fairly expensive on Anguilla, another reason to consider renting a car.

Hotel & Restaurant Costs

Assume that hotels operate on the European Plan (**EP**—with no meals) unless we specify that they use either the Continental Plan (**CP**—with a Continental breakfast), Breakfast Plan (**BP**—with full breakfast), or the Modified American Plan (**MAP**—with breakfast and dinner). Other hotels may offer the Full American Plan (**FAP**—including all meals but no drinks) or may be All-Inclusive (**AI**—with all meals, drinks, and most activities).

WHAT IT COSTS in Dollars					
	$$$$	**$$$**	**$$**	**$**	**¢**
Restaurants	over $30	$20–$30	$12–$20	$8–$12	under $8
Hotels*	over $350	$250–$350	$150–$250	$80–$150	under $80
Hotels**	over $450	$350–$450	$250–$350	$125–$250	under $125

*EP, BP, CP   **AI, FAP, MAP
Restaurant prices are for a main course at dinner, excluding the customary 15% service charge. Hotel prices are per night for a double room in high season, excluding 10%–15% tax, service charges, and meal plans (except for all-inclusives).

Activities

Beach-going and **fine dining** are the two most popular activities on Anguilla. However, if you want to be active, it's not a problem. The **diving** is good, though not excellent. You'll have many options for **day sails** and **snorkeling** trips. And there's even **horseback riding**. For shopping, St. Martin is a short ferry ride away. At this writing, Anguilla's first **golf course**, the Temenos Golf Course, was set to open in late 2006.

Updated by
Elise Meyer

1:00 PM: "WHAT DO YOU MEAN, YOU CHANGED THE MENU? But my snapper," moaned the glamorous mother of three impeccably dressed children, her diamond earrings glittering in the midday sun. The maître d' listened attentively and nodded. "Don't worry, madam, I'm sure the chef will be happy to make it the way you like." "That's all right, Pierre. We'll do that tomorrow. What else would I like?" They consulted the menu together. When lunch materialized, lovely mom took one bite and realized that although she had insisted on eating the same lunch for a dozen years, she might actually like the new dish a teensy bit more.

1:00 AM: Under the full moon's glow, the beat of the rollicking calypso-tinged reggae had the whole room dancing. First-time visitors mingled with the regulars and the locals, brought together by the magic of the music, the sea air, the rum punch. At last call, they were all the best of friends and agreed to meet again the next night on the other side of the island, where a steel band might or might not appear.

Which is the "real" Anguilla? They both are. And if you want to have an incredibly special Caribbean holiday, make sure that you experience them both.

Peace, pampering, great food, and a wonderful local music scene are among the star attractions on Anguilla (pronounced ang-*gwill*-a). If you're a beach lover, you may become giddy when you first spot the island from the air; its blindingly white sand and lustrous blue-and-aquamarine waters are intoxicating. And, if you like sophisticated cuisine served in casually elegant open-air settings, this may be your culinary Shangri-La. Despite its small size, Anguilla has nearly 70 restaurants ranging from stylish temples of haute cuisine to classic, barefoot beachfront grills.

This dry limestone isle is the most northerly of the Leeward Islands, lying between the Caribbean Sea and the Atlantic Ocean. It stretches, from northeast to southwest, about 16 mi (26 km) and is only 3 mi (5 km) across at its widest point. The highest spot is 213 feet above sea level, and there are neither streams nor rivers, only saline ponds once used for salt production. The island's name, a reflection of its shape, is most likely a derivative of *anguille*, which is French for "eel." (French explorer Pierre Laudonnaire is credited with having given the island this name when he sailed past it in 1556.)

In 1631 the Dutch built a fort here, but so far no one has been able to locate its site. English settlers from St. Kitts colonized the island in 1650, with plans to cultivate tobacco and, later, cotton and then sugar. But the thin soil and scarce water doomed these enterprises to fail. Except for a brief period of independence, when it broke from its association with St. Kitts and Nevis in the 1960s, Anguilla has remained a British colony ever since.

From the early 1800s various island federations were formed and disbanded, with Anguilla all the while simmering over its subordinate status and enforced union with St. Kitts. Anguillians twice petitioned for direct rule from Britain and twice were ignored. In 1967, when St. Kitts, Nevis, and Anguilla became an associated state, the mouse roared; citizens kicked out St. Kitts's policemen, held a self-rule referendum, and for two years conducted their own affairs. To what *Time* magazine called "a cascade of laughter around the world," a British "peacekeeping force" of 100 paratroopers from the Elite Red Devil unit parachuted onto the island, squelching Anguilla's designs for autonomy but helping a team of royal engineers stationed there to improve the port and build roads and schools. Today Anguilla elects a House of Assembly and its own leader to handle internal affairs, while a British governor is responsible for public service, the police, the judiciary, and external affairs.

The territory of Anguilla includes a few islets (or cays, pronounced "keys"), such as Scrub Island, Dog Island, Prickly Pear Cay, Sandy Island, and Sombrero Island. The 10,000 or so residents are predominantly of African descent, but there are also many of Irish background, whose ancestors came over from St. Kitts in the 1600s. Historically, because the limestone land was unfit for agriculture, attempts at enslavement never lasted long; consequently, Anguilla doesn't bear the scars of slavery found on so many other Caribbean islands. Instead, Anguillians became experts at making a living from the sea and are known for their boatbuilding and fishing skills. Tourism is the stable economy's growth industry, but the government carefully regulates expansion to protect the island's natural resources and beauty. New hotels are small, select, and definitely casino-free; Anguilla emphasizes its high-quality service, serene surroundings, and friendly people.

Where to Stay

Tourism on Anguilla is a fairly recent phenomenon—most development didn't begin until the early 1980s, so most hotels and resorts are of relatively recent vintage. The lack of native topography and, indeed, vegetation, and the blindingly white expanses of beach have inspired building designs of some interest; architecture buffs might have fun trying to name some of the most surprising examples. Inspiration largely comes from the Mediterranean: the Greek Islands, Morocco, and Spain, with some Miami-style art deco thrown into the mixture.

Anguilla accommodations basically fall into two categories: grand, sumptuous resorts and luxury resort-villas, or low-key, simple, locally owned inns and small beachfront complexes. The former can be surprisingly expensive, the latter surprisingly reasonable. In the middle are some condo-type options, with full kitchen facilities and multiple bedrooms, which are great for families or for longer stays. Private villa rentals are becoming more common and are increasing in number and quality every season as development on the island accelerates. A good phone chat with the management of any property is in order, as some lodgings don't have TV, a few have no air-conditioning, and units within the same complex can vary greatly in layout, accessibility, distance to the beach, and view. When calling to reserve a room, inquire about special discount packages, especially in the spring and summer. Most hotels include Continental breakfast in the price, and many have meal-plan options. But keep in mind that Anguilla is home to dozens of excellent restaurants before you lock yourself into an expensive meal plan that you may not be able to change; consider the more flexible voucher offerings. All hotels charge a 10% tax, and most charge an additional 10% service charge, so be sure to factor this into your budget.

Hotels

⚙ $$$$ 🖼 **Cap Juluca.** Once you have stayed at Cap Juluca, you might think
Fodor'sChoice again before uttering the phrase: "Nothing is perfect." Chic, sybaritic, and
★ serene, this 179-acre resort wraps around breathtaking Maundays Bay, the glittering sand rivaled only by the dramatic domed, white, Moorish-style villas, superlative cuisine, and celebrity clientele. Enormous and private, guest rooms are furbished with Moroccan textiles and Brazilian hardwood furniture and have huge marble bathrooms, a few with tubs big enough for two. Private patios, balconies, or sun roofs render sea, sky, and sand part of the decor. The romantic atmosphere makes this resort popular for honeymoons and destination weddings. Facilities include a new fitness center and expanded spa in 2007, an aqua-golf driving range, and an extensive water-sports pavilion. There are three room categories, but even the standard ("luxury") accommodations are well laid out, spacious, and comfortable. Flexible multibedroom private villas are beautifully furnished and include a 24-hour-a-day butler. A high point: each morning at the exact moment you specify, Continental breakfast appears on your private veranda, with a basket of fresh-baked pastries, a platter of delicious fresh fruit, and piping-hot coffee. Room TVs are available by request only. ⌂ *Box 240, Maundays Bay* ☎ *888/858–5822 in U.S., 264/ 497–6779* 🖷 *264/497–6617* ⊕ *www.capjuluca.com* ↯ *72 rooms, 7 patio suites, 6 pool villas* ⚖ *3 restaurants, room service, fans, minibars, in-room broadband, driving range, putting green, 3 tennis courts, pool, health club, spa, beach, snorkeling, windsurfing, boating, croquet, bar, library, shops, babysitting, children's programs (ages 3–14), laundry service; no room TVs* ▭ *AE, D, MC, V* ☾ *Closed Sept. and Oct.* ▯◯▮ *CP.*

★ ⚙ $$$$ 🖼 **CuisinArt Resort & Spa.** This family-friendly beachfront resort's design—gleaming white-stucco buildings, blue domes and trim, glass block walls—blends art deco with a Greek Isle feel. Huge rooms are somewhat haphazardly appointed with an odd mixture of pine, wicker, and heavy Spanish wood furniture, and garish yellow-and-blue upholstery; but the upscale crowd doesn't seem to mind. Guests return in droves to enjoy the casual atmosphere, full-service spa, sports facilities, and the fulfill-every-wish concierge crew, who provide everything from vacation-long nannies to local cell phones to dinner reservations. An ambitious new manager, hired in 2006, is overseeing an upgrade of the facility, including a spacious new health club and expanded spa with thalassotherapy tubs. High-season children's programs give parents a chance to enjoy the holiday, too. A hydroponic farm provides ultrafresh organic produce for the two restaurants, and tours of the greenhouse, as well as the lush tropical gardens and orchards, are fun and interesting. Cooking classes and demonstrations are conducted in the "kitchen stadium," a cooking facility with audience seating. ⌂ *Box 2000, Rendezvous Bay* ☎ *264/ 498–2000 or 800/943–3210* 🖷 *264/498–2010* ⊕ *www.cuisinartresort. com* ↯ *93 rooms, 2 penthouses* ⚖ *3 restaurants, fans, in-room safes, refrigerators, cable TV, in-room broadband, 3 tennis courts, pool, health* *club, hot tub, spa, beach, snorkeling, windsurfing, boating, billiards, croquet, 2 bars, shops, babysitting, laundry service* ▭ *AE, D, MC, V* ⊘ *Closed Sept. and Oct.* ⦿| *EP.*

$$$$ ⊡ **Frangipani Beach Club.** This flamingo-pink Mediterranean-style complex on the beautiful champagne sands of Meads Bay is a great value for a luxury resort. Perfect for independent travelers, the feel here is more condo than resort. Accommodations range from simple rooms to a three-bedroom apartment, all with pleasant, if unremarkable, decor—typical Caribbean rattan furniture and softly colored textiles. Larger units have full kitchens and laundry facilities and are well suited for families and for longer stays. Try to get a room with an ocean view; Nos. 1 to 8 have the best vistas. A condo building was going up next door as this book went to press, so ask about the progress of construction when you reserve. Plumeria, gaudily dressed in frangipani yellows and reds, overlooks the ocean and has a well-executed French-influenced menu. ⌂ *Box 1566, Meads Bay* ☎ *264/497–6442 or 800/892–4564* 🖷 *264/497–6440* ⊕ *www.frangipaniresort.com* ⟳ *17 rooms, 8 suites* ⚴ *Restaurant, fans, some kitchens, cable TV, some in-room VCRs, in-room broadband, tennis court, pool, beach, snorkeling, windsurfing, bar, laundry facilities* ▭ *AE, MC, V* ⦿| *EP* ⊘ *Closed Sept. and Oct.*

★ ☝ $$$$ ⊡ **Malliouhana.** This superluxe enclave is European refinement in a tranquil beach setting, with impeccable service, world-class dining, and a plethora of activities that keep the mostly mogul clientele returning year after year. An elegant air surrounds the resort's white arches and soaring columns, accented by tile stairways that wrap dramatically around a rocky bluff. With high ceilings, large balconies, marble baths, and sumptuous, if somewhat dated, decor, rooms are so comfortable you might never want to leave. Some suites even have private hot tubs; one has a private swimming pool. Don't miss the divine cuisine in the main restaurant, Michael Rostang at Malliouhana, quite possibly the very best in all the Caribbean. Extensive facilities allow you to be as active—or not—as you wish: spend your days snorkeling, waterskiing, or fishing, or just relax at the spa or take a leisurely stroll along mile-long Meads Bay. Those with young ones need not be deterred by the opulence here—Malliouhana is also family-friendly, with special facilities and services catered to kids. ⌂ *Box 173, Meads Bay* ☎ *264/497–6111 or 800/835–0796* 🖷 *264/497–6011* ⊕ *www.malliouhana.com* ⟳ *34 double rooms, 9 junior suites, 8 1-bedroom suites, 2 2-bedroom suites* ⚴ *2 restaurants, room service, fans, in-room safes, minibars, in-room broadband, 4 tennis courts, 3 pools, health club, hair salon, hot tub, spa, 2 beaches, snorkeling, windsurfing, boating, waterskiing, basketball, bar, library, babysitting, playground, laundry service, Internet room, business services, meeting room; no room TVs* ▭ *AE, D, MC, V* ⊘ *Closed Sept. and Oct.* ⦿| *EP.*

$$$ ⊡ **Anguilla Great House Beach Resort.** These West Indian–style bungalows strung along one of Anguilla's longest beaches seductively evoke an old-time Caribbean feel with their cotton-candy colors. Gingerbread trim frames views of the ocean from charming verandas. Rooms are decked with local artwork, mahogany and wicker furnishings, tropical-print fabrics, and ceiling fans; some have hand-painted floral borders. Those numbered 111 to 127 offer beach proximity and the best views; newer units aren't as well sited and lack views but have television and Internet access. Not all rooms have air-conditioning. The restaurant serves a mix of West Indian, Italian, and Continental cuisines; the bartenders proudly ask you to sample their special concoctions, exemplifying the friendly service. The hotel can arrange in-room massage and other spa treats. ⊠ *Rendezvous Bay* 🏠 *Box 157, The Valley* ☎ *264/497–6061 or 800/ 583–9247* 🖷 *264/497–6019* ⊕ *www.anguillagreathouse.com* 🛏 *27 rooms* ⟋ *Restaurant, fans, refrigerators, some in-room data ports, pool, gym, beach, snorkeling, windsurfing, boating, shop, business services; no a/c in some rooms* ⊟ *AE, DC, MC, V* ⟐ *EP.*

$$$ ⊞ **La Sirena.** The friendly Swiss owners of this low-key resort overlooking Meads Bay have created an atmosphere of casual, lively hospitality that attracts many repeat customers. Standard rooms are small, with tiny bathrooms and decor ranging from dormitory stark to Euro-eclectic. The garden suites and larger villas—some of the best values on the island— all have fully equipped kitchens, and four have large hot tubs. Your room won't come with a TV, but you can rent one (along with VCR or DVD player). The restaurant, Top of the Palms, is a gathering spot for guests, many of whom choose a meal plan that includes breakfast and dinner or, for more flexibility, purchase meal vouchers for a part of their stay. Though the five-minute walk to the beach is not the prettiest, you'll find thatched umbrellas and chaises when you get there. The PADI dive shop on-site is another draw. 🏠 *Box 200, Meads Bay* ☎ *264/497–6827* 🖷 *264/497–6829* ⊕ *www.la-sirena.com* 🛏 *20 rooms, 6 suites, 6 villas* ⟋ *Restaurant, fans, in-room safes, some kitchenettes, 2 pools, massage, dive shop, bicycles, bar, Internet room, car rental; no room TVs* ⊟ *AE, D, MC, V* ⟐ *CP.*

★ ☾ **$–$$$** ⊞ **Rendezvous Bay Hotel & Villas.** Spread over 50 acres of coconut, date, and papaya trees and overlooking a sparkling 1½-mi-long beach on Rendezvous Bay, the location here is prime—no surprise, as this was Anguilla's first resort. Opened in 1962, the property has been continuously and ably run by the Gumbs family, the Anguillian equivalent of the Kennedys, since the very beginning. Feel like a true part of the Anguillian scene when you chat with matriarch Una Gumbs and her three political brothers. Accommodations vary from older "garden rooms" to modern oceanfront villas, which can be configured to accommodate up to 12. The Cedar Grove Cafe here is superlative, much like the other Gumbs family establishments on the island. There's a fine island art gallery, a small boutique, and a fun playroom with pool, big-screen television, and movies. Note that the resort was slated to close for extensive renovations in early 2007, so be sure to call ahead. ⊠ *Rendezvous Bay* 🏠 *Box 31, The Valley* ☎ *264/497–6549, 732/442–1968, 800/274–4893* 🖷 *264/497–6026* ⊕ *www.rendezvousbay.com* 🛏 *27 villa rooms, 19 garden rooms, 8 3-4 bedroom villas* ⟋ *2 restaurants, fans, some kitchens, refrigerators, in-room data ports, 2 tennis courts, windsurfing, bar, lounge, recreation room, shops, laundry service, Internet room, meeting room, car rental; no a/c in some rooms, no room TVs* ⊟ *AE, D, MC, V* ☾ *Closed Sept. and Oct.* ⟐ *EP.*

$$ ⊞ **Arawak Beach Inn.** An excellent choice for a low-key, funky Anguillian respite is this intimate gem. These breezy, hexagonal two-story villas sing with island warmth and color. The pricier units on the top floors are more spacious and a bit quieter and enjoy spectacular views of the rocky shores of boat-dotted Island Harbor and beyond to Scilly Key. Some rooms have large four-poster rattan beds, and some have kitchenettes. Most aren't air-conditioned, and those that are cost more, but the harbor breezes are usually sufficient. The inn's manager, Maria Hawkins, will make you feel like one of the family by the time you leave. Mix your own drinks at the bar—or, if co-owner Maurice Bonham-Carter is around, have him mix you the island's best Bloody Mary. The Arawak Cafe, splashed in psychedelic colors, serves special pizzas and lip-smacking Caribbean comfort food. A small private cove with a sandy beach is just a five-minute walk. The common areas have wireless Internet connections. ⊡ *Box 1403, Island Harbour* 🕾 *264/497–4888, 877/427–2925 reservations only* 🖷 *264/497–4889* ⊕ *www.arawakbeach.com* ⇘ *13 rooms, 4 suites* ♨ *Restaurant, fans, in-room safes, some kitchens, Wi-Fi, pool, beach, snorkeling, windsurfing, boating, bar, shop, Internet room; no a/c in some rooms, no TV in some rooms* ⊟ *AE, D, MC, V* ⫶◎⫶ *EP.*

Villas & Condominiums

The tourist office has a complete listing of the plentiful vacation apartment rentals. You can contact the **Anguilla Connection** (⊡ Box 1369, Island Harbour 🕾 264/497–9852 or 800/916–3336 🖷 264/497–9853 ⊕ www.luxuryvillas.com) for condo and villa listings.

$$$$ ▦ **Altamer.** Architect Myron Goldfinger's geometric symphony of floor-to-ceiling windows, cantilevered walls, and curvaceous floating staircases is fit for any king (or CEO)—as is the price tag that goes along with it. Each of the three villas here has a distinct decorative theme and must be rented in its entirety; choose from Russian Amethyst, Brazilian Emerald, or African Sapphire. Striking interiors are filled with custom-made and antique pieces—Murano fixtures, Florentine linens, Turkish kilims, Fabergé ornaments, Tsarist silver candelabras—but still manage to feel airy rather than cluttered. They are also outfitted with the latest gadgetry, from touch-pad stereo systems to wireless Internet. A private staff, including three butlers and a chef, anticipates your every whim. Full conference facilities make this an ideal location for corporate or family retreats of up to 40 people. ⊠ *Shoal Bay West* ⊡ *Box 3001, The Valley* 🕾 *264/498–4000* 🖷 *264/498–4010* ⊕ *www.altamer.com* ⇘ *3 5-bedroom villas* ♨ *Restaurant, fans, in-room hot tubs, kitchen, cable TV, in-room VCRs, Wi-Fi, tennis court, pool, gym, hot tub, beach, snorkeling, windsurfing, boating, recreation room, laundry service, Internet room, business services, meeting room* ⊟ *AE, D, DC, MC, V* ⚷ *1-week minimum* ⫶◎⫶ *AI.*

$$$$ ▦ **Covecastles Villa Resort.** Though this secluded Myron Goldfinger–designed enclave resembles a series of giant concrete prams from the outside, the sensuous curves and angles of the skylit interiors bespeak elegance and comfort. Decor in the soaring one- to six-bedroom villas is luxurious without being stuffy: custom-made wicker furniture, raw-silk cushions, and hand-embroidered linens in muted, soothing colors. Louvered Brazilian walnut doors and windows perfectly frame tranquil views of St. Martin, creating living canvases. Units are filled with such high-tech amenities as DVD and CD players. The restaurant exemplifies French savoir faire, the beach beckons, and an unobtrusive staff allows tranquility to reign. *Box 248, Shoal Bay West ☎ 264/497–6801 or 800/223–1108 ☒ 264/497–6051 ⊕ www.covecastles.com ↴ 15 apartments △ Restaurant, room service, fans, cable TV, in-room VCRs, in-room broadband, 2 tennis courts, beach, snorkeling, boating, bicycles, library, shops ═ AE, D, MC, V ◯ EP.*

★ **$$$$** ▦ **St. Regis Temenos Villas.** "Temenos" is Greek for "sanctuary," and the name is certainly justified. These incomparably glamorous villas were inspired by the pure, spare architecture of Mykonos and Santorini: sparkling white buildings contrast with the serene blues and greens of the ocean. The three villas—named Sea, Sky, and Sand—each have a different shimmering color scheme that evokes its name. All have cathedral ceilings, louvered French doors, infinity pools, and enormous marble bathrooms with indoor-outdoor showers. Textural elements are mixed beautifully; marble, granite, wrought iron, mosaic tiles, and woven rugs offset state-of-the-art kitchen and entertainment equipment. The private staff is friendly yet unobtrusive. Of course, sanctuary comes with a high price, but celebrities like Janet Jackson know that you will get what you pay for. Expansion plans include a Greg Norman–designed golf course slated to open in late 2006 and more villas planned for 2008. *Box 1656, Long Bay ☎ 264/498–9000 ☒ 264/498–9050 ⊕ www.starwoodhotels.com ↴ 1 5-bedroom villa, 2 4-bedroom villas △ Fans, kitchens, cable TV, in-room VCRs, in-room broadband, 3 tennis courts, 3 pools, gym, 3 hot tubs, beach, snorkeling, boating, laundry service, Internet room, business services ═ AE, D, MC, V ☞ 1-week minimum ◯ CP.*

★ **$$$–$$$$** ⊙ ▦ **Kú.** This all-suites hotel on beautiful Shoal Bay East opened to well-deserved raves in 2005. Modeled on the barefoot chic of South Beach, the airy white apartments have lime and turquoise decorative accents, glass and chrome furniture, and balconies overlooking the beach or the pool. Managed by the experienced folks at Cap Juluca, it is a great choice for young people because of its hip styling, great facilities, and gentle room rates. The location on Shoal Bay Beach, with its string of lively beach grills and dive shops, is a winner. The open-air restaurant with a 70-foot-long bar hops at breakfast, lunch, and dinner. *⊠ Box 51, Shoal Bay East ☎ 264/497–2011 or 800/869–5827 ☒ 264/497–3355 ⊕ www. ku-anguilla.com ↴ 27 suites △ Restaurants, fans, kitchens, cable TV, in-room broadband, pool, gym, spa, beach, snorkeling, bar, shop ═ AE, MC, V ◯ EP.*

$$$–$$$$ ▦ **Carimar Beach Club.** This horseshoe of bougainvillea-draped Mediterranean-style buildings on beautiful Meads Bay has the look of an upscale Sun Belt condo. Although only two units—No. 1 and No. 6—stand at the water's edge, all have balconies or patios with ocean views. Bright, white one- and two-bedroom apartments are individually owned and thus reflect their owners' tastes, but most are tastefully appointed, fully equipped, and carefully maintained. The cordial staff, supreme beachfront location, and several fine restaurants within walking distance make this a winner. Look for aggressive promotions on the Web site, including last-minute online auctions. Portable air-conditioning units are available for a fee. ⌂ *Box 327, Meads Bay* ☎ *264/497–6881 or 800/ 235–8667* 🖷 *264/497–6071* ⊕ *www.carimar.com* ⇆ *24 apartments* ⌂ *Fans, kitchens, 2 tennis courts, beach, snorkeling, Internet room; no a/c, no room TVs* ▭ *AE, D, MC, V* ⍥ *EP* ⊗ *Closed Sept.–mid-Oct.*

★ **$$–$$$$** ⊙ ▦ **Paradise Cove.** This pretty complex of luxury one- and two-bedroom apartments compensates for its location away from the beach with two whirlpools, a large pool, and tranquil tropical gardens where you can pluck fresh guavas for breakfast. The beautiful Cove and Rendezvous bays are just a few minutes' stroll away. Spotless units are attractively appointed with white rattan and natural wicker furniture, gleaming white-tile floors, large kitchens, and soft floral or pastel fabrics from mint to mango. Second-floor units have high beamed ceilings. Maid service and private cooks are available. Families will appreciate such thoughtful touches as cookies-and-cream pool parties and weekend pizza-making lessons. ⌂ *Box 135, The Cove* ☎ *264/497–6959 or 264/497–6603* 🖷 *264/497–6927* ⊕ *www.paradise.ai* ⇆ *12 studio suites, 17 1- and 2-bedroom apartments* ⌂ *Restaurant, fans, some kitchens, some kitchenettes, cable TV, in-room data ports, 2 pools, gym, 2 wading pools, outdoor hot tub, bar, shops, playground, laundry facilities, laundry service, Internet room, meeting room* ▭ *AE, D, MC, V* ⍥ *EP.*

$$$ ▦ **Caribella.** These spacious Mediterranean-style villas on the broad sands of Barnes Bay are a terrific bargain, especially at the discounted weekly rate. The two-bedroom, two-bathroom villas have full kitchens and daily maid service. The decor is not much to speak of, but the beach is beautiful. ⌂ *Box 780, Barnes Bay, West End* ☎ *264/497–6045* 🖷 *264/497–8929* ⇆ *6 villas* ⌂ *Fans, kitchens, cable TV* ▭ *MC, V* ⍥ *EP.*

$$ ▦ **Easy Corner Villas.** The price is right at these modest villas on a bluff overlooking Road Bay. They're a five-minute walk (up a steep hill) from the beach and have spectacular views of Salt Pond and the ocean beyond. Two- and three-bedroom units are cheerfully furnished and well equipped, belying the mousy facade; they also can be broken down into one-bedroom units or studios to accommodate couples or solo travelers. Packages, especially those with rental car, can offer even better value. ⌂ *Box 65, South Hill* ☎ *264/497–6433, 264/497–6541, 800/ 633–7411 reservations only* 🖷 *264/497–6410* ⇆ *12 villas* ⌂ *Fans, kitchens, kitchenettes, cable TV, car rental* ▭ *AE, D, MC, V* ⍥ *EP.*

⊙ **$–$$** ▦ **Allamanda Beach Club.** Youthful, active couples from around the globe happily fill this casual, three-story, white-stucco building hidden in a palm grove just off the beach. Units are neat and simply furnished, with tile floors and pastel matelassé bedspreads; ocean views are best from the top floor. On the ground floor are four large "deluxe" apartment suites that are great for families. People return year after year, thanks to the management's dedicated hospitality. The creative restaurant, Zara's, is a popular draw, as is the less expensive Gwen's Reggae Grill, a boisterous and colorful beachside joint with an upscale, frat-party atmosphere. Look into special summer packages. ⌂ *Box 662, Upper Shoal Bay Beach* ☎ *264/497–5217* 🖷 *264/497–5216* ⊕ *www.allamanda.ai* ⇆ *16 units* ⌂ *2 restaurants, fans, kitchens, cable TV, pool, gym, snorkeling, boating, Internet room* ▭ *AE, D, MC, V* ⍥ *EP.*

Where to Eat

Anguilla has an extraordinary number of excellent restaurants, ranging from elegant establishments to down-home seaside shacks. Many have breeze-swept terraces, where you can dine under the stars. Call ahead—in winter to make a reservation and in late summer and fall to confirm if the place you've chosen is open. Anguillian restaurant meals are leisurely events, and service is often at a relaxed pace, so settle in and enjoy. Most restaurant owners are actively and conspicuously present, especially at dinner. It's a special treat to take the time to get to know them a bit when they stop by your table to make sure that you are enjoying your meal.

What to Wear

During the day, casual clothes are widely accepted: shorts will be fine, but don't wear bathing suits and cover-ups unless you're at a beach bar. In the evening, shorts are okay at the extremely casual eateries. Elsewhere, women should wear sundresses or nice casual slacks; men will be fine in short-sleeved shirts and casual pants. Some hotel restaurants are more formal and may have a jacket requirement in high season; ask when you make your reservation.

BARBECUE
$-$$$

✕ **Smokey's.** There's no sign, so you'll have to ask the way to Cove Bay to find this quintessential Anguillian beach barbecue, part of the Gumbs family mini-empire of authentic and delicious eateries. African-style hot wings, honey-coated ribs, saltfish cakes, curried chicken roti, and grilled lobsters are paired with local staple side dishes such as spiced-mayonnaise coleslaw, hand-cut sweet-potato strings, and crunchy onion rings. If your idea of the perfect summer lunch is a roadside lobster roll, be sure to try the version here, served on a home-baked roll with a hearty kick of hot sauce. The dinner menu includes crayfish tails and chicken in orange sauce. On Saturday afternoons a popular local band, the Musical Brothers, enlivens the casual, laid-back atmosphere. ⊠ *Cove Rd., Cove Bay* ☎ *264/497–6582* ⊟ *AE, MC, V* ☺ *Closed Mon., except in winter.*

CARIBBEAN
$$$-$$$$

✕ **Overlook.** Perched on a cliff high above the bustling harbor of Sandy Ground, chef Deon Thomas's popular and friendly eatery showcases flavorful dishes that combine local and Continental cuisine with a sure hand and a distinct flair. The veranda is pretty, and the orange-and-blue dining room is decorated in island art. The soups stand out: try the carrot-and-apple or pumpkin to start, or perhaps a refreshingly brash gazpacho topped with a basil-Worcestershire granité. At dinner, main courses like roasted grouper curry with coconut-mango chutney as well as braised goat with fragrant rice and peas reflect local flavors, while international touches yield such dishes as oven-crisp duck with Chambord sauce or roasted rack of lamb with rosemary and eggplant tomato ragout. It's closed in summer, when Thomas cooks for lucky fans on Martha's Vineyard. Reservations are recommended. ⊠ *Back St., South Hill* ☎ *264/497–4488* ⊟ *AE, MC, V* ☺ *Closed May–Oct.*

★ $$-$$$

✕ **Tasty's.** Once your eyes adjust to the quirky kiwi, lilac, and coral color scheme, you'll find that breakfast, lunch, or dinner at Tasty's is, well, very tasty. Chef-owner Dale Carty trained at Malliouhana, and his careful, confident preparation bears the mark of French culinary training, but the menu is classic Caribbean. It's worth leaving the beach at lunch for the lobster salad here. A velvety pumpkin soup garnished with roasted coconut shards is superb, as are the seared jerked tuna and the garlic-infused marinated conch salad. Yummy desserts end meals on a high note. This is one of the few restaurants that do not allow smoking, so take your Cubans elsewhere for an after-dinner puff. ⊠ *On main road in South Hill* ☎ *264/497–2723* △ *Reservations essential* ☰ *AE, MC, V* ☉ *Closed Thurs.*

$–$$ ✕ **English Rose.** Lunch finds this neighborhood hangout packed with locals: cops flirting with sassy waitresses, entrepreneurs brokering deals with politicos, schoolgirls in lime-green outfits doing their homework. The decor is not much to speak of, but this is a great place to eavesdrop or people-watch while enjoying island-tinged specialties like beer-battered shrimp, jerk chicken Caesar salad, snapper creole, and baked chicken. ⊠ *Main St., The Valley* ☎ *264/497–5353* ☰ *MC, V* ☉ *Closed Sun.*

CONTEMPORARY ✕ **Blanchard's.** This absolutely delightful restaurant, a mecca for food-
$$$$ ies, is considered one of the best in the Caribbean, if not the world. Pro-
Fodor'sChoice prietors Bob and Melinda Blanchard moved to Anguilla from Vermont
★ in 1994 to fulfill their culinary dreams. A festive atmosphere pervades the handsome, airy white room, which is accented with floor-to-ceiling teal-blue shutters to let in the breezes and colorful artworks by the Blanchards' son Jesse on the walls. A masterful combination of creative cuisine, an upscale atmosphere, attentive service, and an excellent wine cellar (including a selection of aged spirits) pleases the star-studded crowd. The nuanced contemporary menu is ever-changing but always delightful; house classics like corn chowder, lobster cakes, and a Caribbean fish sampler are crowd pleasers. For dessert, concoctions like the key lime "pie-in-a-glass" or the justly famous "cracked coconut" will be remembered long after your suntan has faded. ⊠ *Meads Bay* ☎ *264/497–6100* △ *Reservations essential* ☰ *AE, MC, V* ☉ *Closed Sun. and No lunch.*

$$$$ ✕ **Covecastles.** Elegant, intimate dinners are served here in a garden overlooking beautiful Shoal Bay. Each season, Dominique Thevenet devises a new menu, innovatively mating French culinary traditions with Caribbean ingredients. Savory examples might include phyllo stuffed with warm goat cheese, truffle honey, and roasted hazelnuts; tuna tartare with citrus sauce; or pan-seared lobster in bordelaise sauce. Villa guests receive priority for the seven tables, so call ahead for reservations. ⊠ *Shoal Bay West* ☎ *264/497–6801* △ *Reservations essential* ☰ *AE, D* ☉ *Closed Sept.–Nov. No lunch.*

★ **$$$–$$$$** ✕ **Cedar Grove Cafe.** Along with the Blanchards, the Gumbs jump-started Anguilla's reputation as a gastronomic destination, and this breeze-swept, colonnaded terrace eatery at the Rendezvous Bay Hotel exemplifies the family's recipe for success. Everything, including the bread, is prepared on-site daily. Chef Smoke (who also oversees the wondrously refined Koal Keel) seduces diners with creative Caribbean–meets–Pacific Rim fare. Perfectly prepared, exquisitely presented standouts include teriyaki-ginger marinated tuna with Chinese vegetables and a sesame soy infusion, and tempura lobster tails with leeks and zucchini in chardonnay-butter sauce. The extensive wine list is miraculously priced. ⊠ *Rendezvous Bay* ☎ *264/497–6549* ⚒ *Reservations essential* ▭ *AE, MC, V* ☾ *Closed Sept.–Nov.*

★ $$$–$$$$ ✕ **Hibernia.** Some of the island's most creative dishes are served in this wood-beam cottage restaurant overlooking the water. Unorthodox yet delectable culinary pairings—inspired by chef Raoul Rodriguez's continuing travels from France to the Far East—include foie gras prepared two ways: one a Thai-style jasmine mousse, the other scented with gewürztraminer wine. Asian mushroom soup topped with cream of cauliflower is a great starter. Among the creative entrées are flambé duck breast with a grape sauce, a crayfish casserole with steamed rice noodles in basil and coconut milk, and roasted lobster tail served with a garnish of aromatic rice layered with papaya in a lime and cashew sauce. The painterly presentations echo Raoul's and wife Mary Pat O'Hanlon's passion for art; the adjacent gallery displays some of their acquisitions. ⊠ *Island Harbour* ☎ *264/497–4290* ▭ *MC, V* ☾ *Closed Mon. and Aug. and Sept. No lunch Sun., Dec.–Apr. Also closed Tues. and no lunch Thurs.–Tues., May–July and Oct.–Nov.*

★ $$$–$$$$ ✕ **Mango's.** One meal at Mango's and you'll understand why it's a perennial favorite of repeat visitors to Anguilla. Sparkling-fresh fish specialties have starring roles on the menu here. Light and healthy choices like a spicy grilled whole snapper are deliciously perfect. Save room for dessert—the warm apple tart and the coconut cheesecake are worth the splurge. There's an extensive wine list, and the Cuban cigar humidor is a luxurious touch. The proprietor, a former New Jerseyian known islandside as Mango Dave, keeps a watchful eye over his chic domain and over his stylish clientele, a veritable *People* magazine spread in high season. Excellent local live music several nights a week adds to the cheerful party atmosphere. ⊠ *Barnes Bay* ☎ *264/497–6479* ⚒ *Reservations essential* ▭ *AE, MC, V* ☾ *Closed Tues. No lunch.*

$$$–$$$$ ✕ **Pimms.** Local chef George Reid weaves culinary magic in an enchanted setting at Cap Juluca. The most coveted tables are so close to the water that you can actually see fish darting about as you dine. Reid's innovative fare is globally inspired haute Caribbean, and the menu includes such creations as pan-seared foie gras with English pea risotto, *tagine* of pompano with preserved lemon, and smoked sesame-crusted salmon with vanilla bean sauce. A sterling wine list complements the menu (look for regular winemaker dinners). Your perfect meal could end with chocolate mousse, an aged rum, and a pre-Castro *cubano* from G. M. Eustace "Guish" Guishard's personal selection. ⊠ *Cap Juluca, Maundays Bay* ☎ *264/497–6666* ⚒ *Reservations essential* ▭ *AE, MC, V* ☾ *Closed Sept. and Oct. No lunch.*

★ $$$–$$$$ ✕ **Straw Hat.** Seven picture windows frame seascapes, from floodlighted coral reefs to fishing flotillas, from this covered dock built on pilings directly over the water. By night, the lights of St. Martin and St. Barth twinkle in the distance. Sophisticated and original food is a feisty symphony of local, Asian, and Mediterranean elements. Start with tangy redsnapper ceviche tinged with local chilies or portabello mushroom "fries" with truffle sauce; then move on to the Thai curry snapper or the papaya-braised short ribs. Weird but wonderful habanero chile and lime cheesecake is on the dessert menu. ⊠ *Forest Bay* ☎ *264/497–8300* ⊟ *AE, D, MC, V* ⊘ *Closed Sun. No lunch.*

★ **$$–$$$$**   ✕ **Altamer.** High style characterizes this formal oceanfront restaurant—stark white geometric architecture patterned after sails, frosted-glass tables lit from below, stunning luminescent cast-glass tableware, and weighty custom-made silver with finials cast from a shell found on the adjacent beach. The fantastical decor and pampering service provide a lovely backdrop for chef Maurice Leduc's sumptuous inventions. His take on a traditional gumbo is superlative, with chunks of lobster and shrimp bathed in the rich saffron tomato broth and the heat of island hot sauce replacing the rouille. A Cuban-style garlic chicken with pineapple salsa and black bean cake is delicious. Those overwhelmed by the array of delectable choices can sample several of the fish specialties. For special occasions, a chef's table next to the open kitchen or multicourse sampler menus are memorable splurges. Altamer is also open for breakfast. ⊠ *Shoal Bay West* ☎ *264/498–4040* ⌑ *Reservations essential* ⊟ *AE, MC, V* ⊘ *Closed Sun. No lunch Wed.*

ECLECTIC   ✕ **Zara's.** Chef Shamash Brooks presides at this cozy restaurant with
$$–$$$$ beamed ceilings, terra-cotta floors, colorful artwork, and poolside seating. His kitchen turns out tasty fare that combines Caribbean and Italian flavors with panache. Standouts include a velvety pumpkin soup with coconut milk, crunchy calamari, lemon pasta scented with garlic, herbed rack of lamb served with a roasted apple sauce, and spicy fish fillet steamed in banana leaf. ⊠ *Allamanda Beach Club, Upper Shoal Bay* ☎ *264/497–3229* ⊟ *AE, D, MC, V* ⊘ *No lunch.*

★ **$$**   ✕ **Kemia.** Cap Juluca's seaside "hors d'oeuverie" looks like a posh pasha's oasis transported to the Caribbean. Arches, tables, and lamps are embedded with jewel-like mosaic and colored glass; cushy throw pillows and billowing tent ceilings complete the fantasy. Chef Vernon Hughes prepares a truly global selection of small tapaslike plates that are perfect for sharing in this romantic retreat at the edge of the cerulean waves. Spanish-style shrimp in garlic butter, tiny pots of curries, rare Thai beef salad—it's all delicious. ⊠ *Cap Juluca, Maundays Bay* ☎ *888/858–5822 in U.S., 264/497–6666* ⌑ *Reservations essential* ⊟ *AE, MC, V* ⊘ *Closed Sun., Mon., Sept., and Oct. No lunch May–Nov.*

FRENCH   ✕ **KoalKeel.** Originally part of a sugar and cotton plantation, KoalKeel
$$$–$$$$ is owned by descendants of the slaves once housed on this very site. A
Fodor's Choice   tour is a high point of any meal here, as the buildings are rich in his-
★   tory. A 200-year-old rock oven is used by the on-site bakery upstairs. With a day's notice, you can enjoy a whole chicken that has been slow-roasted from the inside. The menu features a combination of classic French and West Indian specialties. Start with goat cheese baked in puff pastry in a pool of honey vinaigrette; then continue with rack of lamb served with pumpkin gratin or veal chop in a rosemary sauce with caramelized shallots and truffled mashed potato. Be sure to save room for the incredible desserts made by pastry wizard Geraud Lavest, inventor of wonders like ginger streusel, a sweet cake with caramel and spiced roasted apricots, or warm milk-chocolate tart served on a sugar-almond crust. Wine lovers take note of the exceptional 15,000-bottle wine cellar, in

an underground cistern under the able stewardship of expert Manny Nieves. ⊠ *Coronation Ave., The Valley* ☎ *264/497–2930* ⚑ *Reservations essential* ☰ *AE, MC, V.*

$$$–$$$$
Fodor'sChoice
★
✕ **Michael Rostang at Malliouhana.** Sparkling crystal and fine china, exquisite service, a wonderful 25,000-bottle wine cellar, and a spectacularly romantic candlelit, open-air room complement exceptional haute cuisine rivaling any in the French West Indies—or anywhere else in the world. Consulting chef Michael Rostang, renowned for his exceptional Paris bistros, and chef Alain Laurent revamp the menu seasonally, brilliantly incorporating local ingredients in both classic and contemporary preparations. The ultimate in hedonism is sipping champagne as the setting sun triggers a laser show over the bay, before repairing to your table. ⊠ *Meads Bay* ☎ *264/497–6111* ⚑ *Reservations essential* ☰ *AE, D, MC, V* ☺ *Closed Sept. and Oct.*

$–$$
✕ **Madeariman Reef Bar & Restaurant.** Fans of St. Barth will feel right at home at this casual, feet-in-the sand bistro right on busy, beautiful Shoal Bay. It's open for breakfast, lunch, and dinner; the soups, salads, and simple grills here are served with a bit of French flair. Come for lunch and stay to lounge on the beach chaises, or bar-hop between here and Uncle Ernie's barbecue next door. ⊠ *Shoal Bay East* ☎ *264/497–5750* ☰ *AE, MC, V.*

ITALIAN
$$$–$$$$
✕ **Trattoria Tramonto & Oasis Beach Bar.** The island's only Italian restaurant features a dual (or dueling) serenade of Andrea Bocelli on the sound system and gently lapping waves a few feet away. Chef Valter Belli artfully adapts recipes from his home in Emilia-Romagna. Try the delicate lobster ravioli in truffle-cream sauce; for dessert, don't miss the authentic tiramisu. Though you might wander in here for lunch after a swim, when casual dress is accepted, you'll still be treated to the same impressive menu. You can also choose from a luscious selection of champagne fruit drinks, a small but fairly priced Italian wine list, and homemade grappas. Denzel Washington celebrated his 50th birthday here with such close friends as Robert De Niro and Sean "P. Diddy" Combs. ⊠ *Shoal Bay West* ☎ *264/497–8819* ⚑ *Reservations essential* ☰ *MC, V* ☺ *Closed Mon., Sept., and Oct.*

SOUTHWESTERN
☾ **$–$$$**
✕ **Picante.** This casual, bright-red roadside Caribbean *taqueria,* opened by a young California couple, is a refreshing addition to the Anguilla restaurant scene. Huge, tasty burritos with a choice of fillings, fresh warm tortilla chips with first-rate guacamole, and tequila-lime chicken grilled under a brick are all sure bets. Mexican chocolate pudding makes a great choice for dessert. Seating is at picnic tables; the friendly proprietors cheerfully supply pillows on request. Reservations are recommended. ⊠ *West End Rd., West End* ☎ *264/498–1616* ☰ *AE, MC, V* ☺ *Closed Tues. No lunch.*

Beaches

Renowned for their beauty, Anguilla's 30-plus dazzling white-sand beaches are the best reason to visit. You can find long, deserted stretches ideal for walking and beaches lined with bars and restaurants—all accompanied by surf that ranges from wild to glassy-smooth. As anywhere, exercise caution in remote locations, and never swim alone. Swimming is not recommended at Captain's Bay and Katouche Bay, due to strong westerly currents and potentially dangerous undertows.

Captain's Bay. Located on the north coast just before the eastern tip of the island, this quarter-mile stretch of perfect white sand is bounded on the left by a rocky shoreline where Atlantic waves crash. If you make the grueling four-wheel-drive-only trip along the inhospitable dirt road that leads to the northeastern end of the island toward Junk's Hole, you'll be rewarded with peaceful isolation. The surf here slaps the sands with a vengeance, and the undertow is strong—so wading is the safest water sport.

Island Harbour. These mostly calm waters are surrounded by a slender beach. For centuries Anguillians have ventured from these sands in colorful handmade fishing boats. There are several bars and restaurants (Arawak Cafe and Smitty's are best for casual lunches), and this is the departure point for the three-minute boat ride to Scilly Cay, where a thatched beach bar serves seafood. Just hail the restaurant's free boat and plan to spend most of the day (the all-inclusive lunch starts at $40 and is worth the price), Wednesday, Friday, and Sunday only.

Barnes Bay. Between Meads Bay and West End Bay, this beach is a superb spot for windsurfing and snorkeling, though in high season it can get a bit crowded with day-trippers from St. Martin. The only public access is on the road to Mango's restaurant and Caribella resort.

Little Bay. Little Bay is on the north coast between Crocus Bay and Shoal Bay, not far from the Valley. Sheer cliffs embroidered with agave and creeping vines rise behind a small gray-sand beach, usually accessible only by water (it's a favored spot for snorkeling and night dives). The easiest way to get there is a five-minute boat ride from Crocus Bay (about $10 round trip). The hale and hearty can also clamber down the cliffs by rope to explore the caves and surrounding reef; this is the only way to access the beach from the road and is not recommended to the inexperienced climber.

Road Bay. The clear blue waters here are usually dotted with yachts and cargo boats. Several restaurants, including evergreen classic Johnno's, a water-sports center, and lots of windsurfing and waterskiing activity make this area—often called Sandy Ground—a commercial one. The snorkeling isn't very good here, but the sunset vistas are glorious.

Sandy Island. A popular side excursion for Anguilla visitors, Sandy Island is a tiny islet with a lagoon, nestled in coral reefs about 2 mi (3 km) from Road Bay. From a distance, it seems no more than a tiny speck of sand and a few spindly palm trees. Still, Sandy Island has the modern-day comforts of a beach boutique, a bar, and a restaurant. Use of snorkeling gear and underwater cameras is free. A ferry heads here every hour during the day from Sandy Ground.

Sandy Hill. Not far from Sea Feathers Bay, this base for anglers sits between the Valley and Junks Hole at East End. Here you can buy fish and lobster right off the boats and snorkel in the warm waters. Don't plan to sunbathe—the beach is too narrow. But there's very good snorkeling here, and you'll also find great views of St. Martin and St. Barth.

Fodor's Choice
★
Shoal Bay. Anchored by sea-grape and coconut trees and covered in the most exquisite powdery-white coral sand, Shoal Bay—not to be confused with Shoal Bay West at the other end of the island—is one of the Caribbean's prettiest beaches. Restaurants like Gwen's Reggae Grill, Kú, and Madeariman Beach Club offer seafood and tropical drinks; shops sell T-shirts and sunscreen; and the water-sports center arranges diving, sailing, and fishing trips. You can even enjoy a beachside massage. The quieter east end has excellent snorkeling and the Fountain, an archaeological dig with a cave filled with millennia-old petroglyphs and tribal artifacts that the Anguilla National Trust is hoping to develop as a historic attraction.

SOUTHWEST COAST
Cove Bay. Lined with coconut palms, this is a quiet spot between Rendezvous Bay and Maundays Bay. You can walk here from Cap Juluca for a change of pace or a beach lunch at Smokey's. There's a fishing boat pier, a dive shop, and a place where you can rent floats, umbrellas, and mats.

Maundays Bay. The dazzling, 1-mi-long (1½-km-long) beach is known for good swimming and snorkeling. You can also rent water-sports gear.

Rendezvous Bay. Here you'll find 1½ mi (2½ km) of pearl-white sand lapped by calm water and with a view of St. Martin. The rockier stretch provides marvelous snorkeling. The expansive crescent houses three resorts, with plenty of open space to go around; stop in for a drink or a meal at one of the hotels. For public access to Rendezvous Bay Beach, take the turn off from the main road for Anguilla Great House (between South Hill Plaza and CuisinArt) and follow this road straight to the water.

Shoal Bay West. This glittering bay is a lovely place to spend the day. This mile-long sweep of sand, home to some major restaurants and resorts, is rimmed with mangroves, and there are coral reefs not too far from shore. Punctuate your day with a meal at beachside Trattoria Tramonto. You can reach Shoal Bay West by taking the main road to the West End and turning left at the end of the pavement on a gravel road around the pond. Note that similarly named Shoal Bay is a separate beach in a different part of the island.

Sports & the Outdoors

As this writing, Temenos Estate was slated to open in November 2006. The island's first golf course, designed by Greg Norman to accentuate the natural terrain and maximize ocean views, will be in Rendezvous Bay West. The Anguilla Tennis Academy, designed by noted architect Myron Goldfinger, was expected to open in 2007 in the Blowing Point area. The stadium, equipped with pro shop and seven lighted courts, was created to attract major international matches and to provide a first-class playing option to tourists and locals.

BOATING & SAILING
Anguilla is the perfect place to try all kinds of water sports. The major resorts offer complimentary Windsurfers, paddleboats, and water skis to their guests. If your hotel lacks facilities, you can get in gear at **Sandy Island Enterprises** (✉ Sandy Ground ☎ 264/772–0542), which rents Sunfish and Windsurfers and arranges fishing charters. **Island Yacht Charters** (✉ Sandy Ground ☎ 264/497–3743 or 264/235–6555) rents

A Day at the Boat Races

IF YOU WANT A DIFFERENT KIND of trip to Anguilla, try for a visit during Carnival, which starts on the first Monday in August and continues for about 10 days. Colorful parades, beauty pageants, music, delicious food, arts and crafts shows, fireworks, and nonstop partying are just the beginning. The music starts at sunrise jam sessions—as early as 4 AM—and continues well into the night. The high point? The boat races. They are the national passion and the official national sport of Anguilla.

Anguillians from around the world return home to race old-fashioned, made-on-the island wooden boats that have been in use on the island since the early 1800s. Similar to some of today's fastest sailboats, these are 15 to 28 feet in length and sport only a mainsail and jib on a single 25-foot mast. The sailboats have no deck, so heavy bags of sand, boulders, and sometimes even people are used as ballast. As the boats reach the finish line, the ballast—including some of the sailors—gets thrown into the water in a furious effort to win the race. Spectators line the beaches and follow the boats on foot, by car, and by even more boats. You'll have almost as much fun watching the fans as the races.

the 35-foot, teak *Pirate* powerboat and the 30-foot Beneteau *Eros* sailboat and organizes snorkeling, sightseeing, and fishing expeditions.

DIVING   Sunken wrecks; a long barrier reef; terrain encompassing walls, canyons, and hulking boulders; varied marine life, including greenback turtles and nurse sharks; and exceptionally clear water—all of these make for excellent diving. Prickly Pear Cay is a favorite spot. **Stoney Bay Marine Park,** off the northeast end of Anguilla, showcases the late-18th-century *El Buen Consejo*, a 960-ton Spanish galleon that sank here in 1772. Other good dive sites include **Grouper Bowl,** with exceptional hard-coral formations; **Ram's Head,** with caves, chutes, and tunnels; and **Upper Flats,** where you are sure to see stingrays. **Anguillian Divers** (⊠ Meads Bay ☏ 264/ 497–4750 ⊕ anguilliandivers.com) is a full-service dive operator with a PADI five-star training center. At Shoal Bay, contact **Shoal Bay Scuba & Watersports** (☏ 264/497–4371 ⊕ www.shoalbayscuba.ai). Single-tank dives start at $50, two-tank dives, $80.

FISHING   Albacore, wahoo, marlin, barracuda, and kingfish are among the fish angled after off Anguilla's shores. You can strike up a conversation with almost any fisherman you see on the beach, and chances are, you'll be a welcome addition on his next excursion. If you'd rather make more formal arrangements, **Johnno's Beach Stop** (☏ 264/497–2728) in Sandy Ground has a boat and can help you plan a trip.

HORSEBACK RIDING   The scenic Gibbons nature trails, along with any of the island's miles of beaches, are perfect places to ride, even for the novice. Ride English- or western-style at **El Rancho Del Blues** (☏ 264/497–6164). Prices start at $25 to $35 per hour ($50 for two-hour rides).

SEA EXCURSIONS   *Chocolat* (✉ Sandy Ground ☎ 264/497–3394) is a 35-foot catamaran available for private charter or scheduled excursions to nearby cays. Captain Rollins is a knowledgeable, affable guide. Rates for day sails with lunch are about $80 per person. For an underwater peek without getting wet, catch a ride ($20 per person) on **Junior's Glass Bottom Boat** (✉ Sandy Ground ☎ 264/497–4456 ⊕ www.junior.ai). Snorkel trips and instruction are available, too. Picnic, swimming, and diving excursions to Prickly Pear Cay, Sandy Island, and Scilly Cay are available through **Sandy Island Enterprises** (☎ 264/772–0542).

Shopping

Anguilla is by no means a shopping destination. In fact, if your suitcase is lost, you will be hard-pressed to secure even the basics on-island. If you're a hard-core shopping enthusiast, a day trip to nearby St. Martin will satisfy. Well-heeled visitors sometimes organize boat or plane charters through their hotel concierge for daylong shopping excursions to St. Barth. The island's tourist publication, *What We Do in Anguilla*, has shopping tips and is available free at the airport and in shops. Pyrat rums—golden elixirs blending up to nine aged and flavored spirits—are a local specialty available at the Anguilla Rums distillery and several local shops. For upscale designer sportswear, check out the small boutiques in hotels (some are branches of larger stores in Marigot on St. Martin). Outstanding local artists sell their work in galleries, which often arrange studio tours (you can also check with the Antigua Tourist Office).

CLOTHING   **Capri Boutique** (✉ CuisinArt Resort & Spa, Rendezvous Bay ☎ 264/498–
★   2000) carries custom designs by the renowned jewelers Alberto & Lina, as well as Helen Kaminski accessories and more brand-name merchandise. **Boutique at Malliouhana** (✉ Malliouhana, Meads Bay ☎ 264/497–6111) specializes in such upscale designer specialties as jewelry by Oro De Sol, luxurious swim fashion by Manuel Canovas and LaPerla, and Robert LaRoche sunglasses. **Caribbean Fancy** (✉ George Hill ☎ 264/497–3133) sells Ta-Tee's line of crinkle-cotton resort wear, plus books, spices, perfumes, wines, and gift items. **Caribbean Silkscreen** (✉ South Hill ☎ 264/497–2272) creates designs and prints them on golf shirts, hats, sweatshirts, and jackets. **Irie Lite** (✉ South Hill ☎ 264/497–6526) sells vividly hued beach and resort wear, Reef flip-flops, and French bikinis that appeal to the younger set who also jive to the java and the wireless Internet connection. **Sunshine Shop** (✉ South Hill ☎ 264/497–6964) stocks cotton pareus (saronglike beach cover-ups), silkscreen items, cotton resort wear, and hand-painted Haitian wood items. **Whispers** (✉ Cap Juluca, Maundays Bay ☎ 264/497–6666) sells Asian handicrafts and designer resort wear for men and women.

HANDICRAFTS   **Anguilla Arts & Crafts Center** (✉ The Valley ☎ 264/497–2200) carries island crafts, including textiles and ceramics. Of particular interest are unique ceramics by Otavia Fleming, lovely spotted glaze items with adorable lizards climbing on them. Look for special exhibits and performances—ranging from puppetry to folk dance—sponsored by the Anguilla National Creative Arts Alliance. **Cheddie's Carving Studios** (✉ West

End Rd., The Cove ☎ 264/497–6027) showcases Cheddie Richardson's fanciful wood carvings and coral and stone sculptures. **Devonish Art Gallery** (✉ West End Rd., George Hill ☎ 264/497–2949) purveys the wood, stone, and clay creations of Courtney Devonish, an internationally known potter and sculptor, plus creations by his wife, Carolle, a bead artist. Also available are works by other Caribbean artists and regional

★ antique maps. **Hibernia Restaurant & Gallery** (✉ Island Harbour ☎ 264/497–4290) has striking pieces culled from the owners' travels, from contemporary Eastern European artworks to traditional Indo-Chinese crafts. In the historic Rose Cottage, **Loblolly Gallery** (✉ Coronation St., Lower Valley ☎ 264/497–6006) showcases the work of three expats (Marge Morani, Paula Warden, Georgia Young) working in various media and also mounts exhibits from Anguilla's artistic grande dame, Iris

★ Lewis. **Savannah Gallery** (✉ Coronation St., Lower Valley ☎ 264/497–2263) specializes in works by local Anguillian artists as well as other Caribbean and Central American art, including watercolors, oil paintings from the renowned Haitian St. Soleil group, Guatemalan textiles, Mexican pottery, and brightly painted metal work. The peripatetic pro-

★ prietors of **World Arts Gallery** (✉ Cove Rd., West End ☎ 264/497–5950 or 264/497–2767), Nik and Christy Douglas, display a veritable United Nations of antiquities: exquisite Indonesian *ikat* hangings to Thai teak furnishings, Aboriginal didgeridoos to Dogon tribal masks, Yuan Dynasty jade pottery to Uzbeki rugs. There is also handcrafted jewelry and handbags.

Nightlife & the Arts

In late February or early March, reggae star and impresario Bankie Banx stages Moonsplash, a three-day music festival that showcases local and imported talent around the nights of the full moon. At the end of July is the International Arts Festival, which hosts artists from around the world. BET (Black Entertainment Television) sponsors Tranquility Jazz Festival in November, attracting major musicians such as Hilton Ruiz, James Moody, Bobby Watson, and Vanessa Rubin.

Nightlife

Most hotels and many restaurants offer live entertainment in high season and on weekends, ranging from pianists and jazz combos to traditional steel and calypso bands. Check the local tourist magazines and newspaper for listings. Friday and Saturday, Sandy Ground is the hot spot; Wednesday and Sunday the action shifts to Shoal Bay East.

The nightlife scene here runs late into the night—the action doesn't really start until after 11 PM. If you do not rent a car, be aware that taxis are not readily available at night. If you plan to take a taxi back to your hotel or villa at the end of the night, be sure to make arrangements in advance with the driver who brings you or with your hotel concierge.

★ The funky **Dune Preserve** (✉ Rendezvous Bay ☎ 264/497–2660) is the driftwood-fabricated home of Bankie Banx, Anguilla's famous reggae star. He performs here weekends and during the full moon. Kevin Bacon also plays here when he is on the island. Other nights, a DJ named Elvis spins and mixes an awesome rum punch. A dance floor and a beach bar are recent additions, and sometimes you can find a sunset beach barbecue in progress. Things are lively at **Johnno's Beach Stop** (✉ Sandy Ground ☎ 264/497–2728), with live music and alfresco dancing every night and on Sunday afternoon, when just about everybody drops by. This is *the* classic Caribbean beach bar, attracting a funky eclectic mix, from locals to movie stars. At the **Pumphouse** (✉ Sandy Ground ☎ 264/497–5154), in the old rock-salt factory, you can find live music most nights—plus surprisingly good pub grub, celebrities like Bruce Willis and Charlie Sheen, and a minimuseum of artifacts and equipment from 19th-century salt factories. It's open from noon until 3 AM daily except Sunday. **Uncle Ernie's** (✉ Shoal Bay ☎ 264/497–3907) often has live music, and a spirited crowd heads here almost every night, as much for the fabulous ribs and jerk chicken as the boisterous atmosphere.

Exploring Anguilla

Exploring on Anguilla is mostly about checking out the spectacular beaches and resorts. The island has only a few roads; some are in bad condition, but the lack of adequate signage is being addressed. Locals are happy to provide directions, but having a good map—and using it—is the best strategy. Get one at the airport, the ferry dock, your hotel, or the tourist office in the Valley.

Numbers in the margin correspond to points of interest on the Anguilla map.

WHAT TO SEE

❻ Heritage Museum Collection. Don't miss this remarkable opportunity to learn about Anguilla. Old photographs and local records and artifacts trace the island's history over 4 millennia, from the days of the Arawaks. The museum is painstakingly curated by Colville Petty. High points include the historical documents of the Anguilla Revolution and the albums of photographs chronicling island life, from devastating hurricanes to a visit from Queen Elizabeth in 1964. You can see examples of ancient pottery shards and stone tools along with fascinating photographs of the island in the early 20th century—many depicting the heaping and exporting of salt and the christening of schooners—and a complete set of beautiful postage stamps issued by Anguilla since 1967. ✉ *East End at Pond Ground* ☎ *264/497–4092* 🗃 *$5* ⏱ *Mon.–Sat. 10–5.*

★ ❺ Island Harbour. Anguillians have been fishing for centuries in the brightly painted, simple handcrafted fishing boats that line the shore of the harbor. It's hard to believe, but skillful pilots take these little boats out to sea as far as 50 or 60 mi (80 or 100 km). Late afternoon is the best time to see the day's catch. Hail the boat to Gorgeous Scilly Cay, a classic little restaurant offering sublime lobster and Eudoxie Wallace's knockout rum punches on Wednesday, Friday, and Sunday. The government is also excavating Arawak cave dwellings on the edge of town, which were tentatively slated to open for public visiting in 2006.

❸ Old Prison. The ruins of this historic jail on Anguilla's highest point—213 feet above sea level—offer outstanding views. ✉ *Valley Rd. at Crocus Hill.*

❶ Sandy Ground. Almost everyone who comes to Anguilla stops by its most developed beach. Little open-air bars and restaurants line the shore, and there are several boutiques, a dive shop, and a small commercial pier. This is where you catch the ferry for tiny Sandy Island, just 2 mi (3 km) offshore.

❷ Wallblake House. The only surviving plantation house in Anguilla, Wallblake House was built in 1787 by Will Blake (Wallblake is probably a corruption of his name) and has recently been thoroughly and thoughtfully restored. The place is associated with many a tale involving murder, high living, and the French invasion in 1796. On the grounds are an ancient vaulted stone cistern and an outbuilding called the Bakery (which wasn't used for making bread at all but for baking turkeys and hams). Tours are usually at 10 AM and 2 PM. ⊠ *Wallblake Rd., The Valley* ☎ *264/497–6613* ⊕ *www.wallblake.ai* ☑ *Free* ⊙ *Mon., Wed., and Fri.*

❹ Warden's Place. This former sugar-plantation greathouse was built in the 1790s and is a fine example of island stonework. It now houses Koal-Keel restaurant and a sumptuous bakery upstairs. But for many years it served as the residence of the island's chief administrator, who also doubled as the only medical practitioner. Across the street you can see the oldest dwelling on the island, originally built as slave housing. ⊠ *The Valley.*

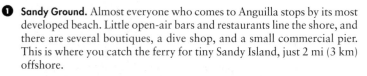

ANGUILLA ESSENTIALS

To research prices, get advice from other travelers, and book travel arrangements, visit www.fodors.com.

Transportation

BY AIR
There are no nonstop flights to Anguilla. American Eagle flies several times a day from San Juan, with connecting flights from other destinations through Continental and Delta. Caribbean Star/TransAnguilla offers daily flights from Antigua, St. Thomas, and St. Kitts and provides air-taxi service on request from neighboring islands. Windward Islands Airways (Winair) wings in daily from St. Thomas and several times a day from St. Maarten. LIAT comes in from Antigua, Nevis, St. Kitts, St. Maarten, St. Thomas, and Tortola. Note that LIAT requires all passengers to reconfirm 72 hours in advance, to avoid cancellation of their reservations.

Wallblake Airport is the hub on Anguilla. A taxi ride to the Sandy Ground area runs $7 to $10; to West End resorts it's $16 to $22.

The departure tax is $20, payable in cash at the airport.

🛪 Airline Contacts **American Eagle** ☎ 264/497–3500. **Caribbean Star/TransAnguilla** ☎ 264/497–8690. **LIAT** ☎ 264/497–5002. **Windward Islands Airways** ☎ 264/497–2748.

🛪 Airport Contacts **Wallblake Airport** ☎ 264/497–2719.

BY BOAT & FERRY
Ferries run frequently between Anguilla and St. Martin. Boats leave from Blowing Point on Anguilla approximately every half hour from 7:30 AM to 6:15 PM and from Marigot on St. Martin every half hour from 8 AM to 7 PM. Check for evening ferries, whose schedules are more erratic. You pay a $3 departure tax before boarding, in

addition to the $12 one-way fare ($15 in the evening). Don't buy a round-trip ticket, as it restricts you to the boat for which it is purchased. On very windy days the 20-minute trip can be bouncy, so bring medication if you suffer from motion sickness. An information booth outside the customs shed in Blowing Point is usually open daily from 8:30 AM to 5 PM, but sometimes the attendant wanders off. For schedule information, and info on special boat charters, contact Link Ferries.

🚢 **Link Ferries** ☎ 264/497-2231 ⊕ www.link.ai.

BY CAR

Although most of the rental cars on-island have the driver's side on the left as in North America, Anguillian roads are like those in the United Kingdom—driving is on the left side of the road. It's easy to get the hang of, but the roads can be rough, so be cautious, and observe the 30 mph speed limit. Roundabouts are probably the biggest driving obstacle for most. As you approach, give way to the vehicle on your right; once you are in the rotary you have the right of way.

A temporary Anguilla driver's license is required—you can get into real trouble if you're caught driving without one. You get it for $20 (good for three months) at any of the car-rental agencies; you'll also need your valid driver's license from home. Rental rates are about $45 to $55 per day, plus insurance.

🚗 **Apex/Avis** ✉ Airport Rd. ☎ 264/497-2642. **Connors/National** ✉ Blowing Point ☎ 264/497-6433. **Triple K Car Rental** ✉ Airport Rd. ☎ 264/497-5934.

BY TAXI

Taxis are fairly expensive, so if you plan to explore the island's many beaches and restaurants, it may be more cost-effective to rent a car. Taxi rates are regulated by the government, and there are fixed fares from point to point, which are listed in brochures the drivers should have handy and are also published in the local guide,

What We Do in Anguilla. Posted rates are for one or two people; each additional passenger adds $4 to the total. You'll always find taxis at the Blowing Point ferry landing and at the airport. You will need to call them to pick you up from hotels and restaurants, and arrange ahead with the driver who took you if you will require a taxi late at night from one of the night-clubs or bars.

🚕 **Airport Taxi Stand** ☎ 264/497-5054. **Blowing Point Ferry Taxi Stand** ☎ 264/497-6089.

Contacts & Resources

BANKS & CURRENCY EXCHANGE

Prices quoted throughout this chapter are in U.S. dollars unless otherwise indicated. ATMs dispense American and Eastern Caribbean dollars. Credit cards are not always accepted; some resorts will settle only in cash, but a few accept personal checks. Some restaurants add a charge if you pay with a credit card.

Though the legal tender here is the Eastern Caribbean (EC) dollar, U.S. dollars are widely accepted. (You'll often get change in EC dollars, though.) The exchange rate between U.S. and EC dollars is set at EC$2.68 to the U.S. dollar. Be sure to carry lots of small bills; change for a $20 is often difficult to obtain.

🏦 **Scotiabank** ☎ 264/497-3333 ⊕ www.scotiabank.ca.

BUSINESS HOURS

Banks are open Monday through Thursday from 8 to 3 and Friday 8 to 5. Most shops are open from 10 to 5 on weekdays only. Most commercial establishments are closed Saturday and Sunday, although some small groceries open for a few hours on Sunday afternoon, but call first, or adopt the island way of doing things: if it's not open when you stop by, try again.

ELECTRICITY

The current is 110 volts, the same as in North America; U.S.-standard two-prong plugs will work just fine.

EMERGENCIES

As in the U.S., Dial 911 in any emergency.
🔢 Ambulance & Fire **Ambulance** ☎ 264/497–2551. **Fire** ☎ 911.

🔢 Hospitals **Princess Alexandra Hospital** ✉ Sandy Ground ☎ 264/497-2551. Emergency room and ambulance operate 24 hours a day. **Hotel de Health** ✉ Palm Court at Sea Feathers Bay ☎ 264/497-4166 is a well-regarded private medical facility.

🔢 Pharmacies **Government Pharmacy** ✉ Princess Alexandria Hospital, The Valley ☎ 264/497-2551 ⊙ Daily 8:30-4. **Paramount Pharmacy** ✉ Water Swamp ☎ 264/497-2366 ⊙ Mon.-Sat. 8:30-7.

🔢 Police **Police emergencies** ☎ 911. **Police non-emergencies** ☎ 264/497-2333.

ETIQUETTE & BEHAVIOR

Anguillians are polite and very sociable people. They will always greet you with warmth and will expect to exchange polite comments about the day or the weather before getting down to business. It's considered quite rude not to do so—so smile and join in the pleasantries; you might even make a friend. Personal appearances are important, and it's considered unseemly not to dress neatly—this is not a gym-shorts and tank-top island. European visitors should note that topless bathing, by law, is not permitted anywhere on the island.

HOLIDAYS

Public holidays are New Year's Day, Easter (varies; Mar. or Apr.), Easter Monday (the day after Easter), Labour Day (1st Thurs. in May), Anguilla Day (last Fri. in May), Whitmonday (7th Mon. after Easter), Queen's Birthday (June 11), August Monday (1st Mon. in Aug.), Constitution Day (Aug. 8), Separation Day (Dec. 19), Christmas Day, Boxing Day (Dec. 26).

INTERNET, MAIL & SHIPPING

Airmail postcards and letters cost EC$1.50 (for the first ½ ounce) to the United States, Canada, and the United Kingdom and EC$2.50 to Australia and New Zealand. The only post office is in the Valley; it's

open weekdays 8 to 4:45. When writing to the island, you don't need a postal code; just include the name of the establishment, address (location or post-office box), and "Anguilla, British West Indies."

The post office, located in the Valley, is open weekdays 8 to 4:45. There is a FedEx office near the airport. It's open weekdays 8 to 5 and Saturday 9 to 1.

🔢 **Anguilla Post Office** ✉ Wallblake Rd., The Valley ☎ 264/497-2528. **FedEx** ✉ Hallmark Bldg., 227 Old Airport Rd., The Valley ☎ 264/497-3575.

MEDIA

Look for the local newspaper, the *Anguillian,* for information about local life and the monthly magazine *What We Do in Anguilla* for tourist news.

PASSPORTS & VISAS

U.S. citizens must carry a valid passport starting January 1, 2006. Canadian citizens need proof of identity, either a passport or a government-issue photo ID, such as a driver's license, *along with* a birth certificate (with raised seal) or naturalization papers. Everyone else must have passports. Everyone must also have a return or ongoing ticket. Visitor passes are valid for stays of up to three months. We strongly urge all travelers going to the Caribbean to carry a valid passport, whether or not it's an absolute requirement.

SAFETY

Anguilla is a quiet, relatively safe island, but there's no sense in tempting fate by leaving your valuables unattended in your hotel room, on the beach, or in your car. Avoid remote beaches, and lock your car, hotel room, and villa. Most hotel rooms are equipped with a safe to stash your valuables.

TAXES

The departure tax is $20, payable in cash at the airport, $3 payable in cash at Blowing Point Ferry Terminal. A 10% accommodations tax is added to hotel bills.

TELEPHONES

To make a local call, dial the seven-digit number. Most hotels will arrange with a local provider for a cell phone to use during your stay. Try to get a prepaid, local one for the best rates. Some GSM international cell phones will work, some not; check with your service before you leave. Hotels usually add a hefty surcharge to all calls.

Cable & Wireless is open weekdays 8–6, Saturday 9–1, and Sunday 10–2. Here, you can purchase Caribbean phone cards for use in specially marked phone booths. Inside the departure lounge at the Blowing Point ferry dock and at the airport there's an AT&T USADirect access phone for collect or credit-card calls to the United States.

To call Anguilla from the United States, dial 1 plus the area code 264, then the local seven-digit number. From the United Kingdom dial 001 and then the area code and the number. From Australia and New Zealand dial 0011, then 1, then the area code and the number.

To call internationally, dial 1, the area code, and the seven-digit number to reach the United States and Canada; dial 011, 44, and the local number for the U.K.; dial 011, 61, and the local number for Australia; and dial 011, 64, and the local number for New Zealand.

🗐 **Cable & Wireless** ⊠ Wallblake Rd. ☎ 264/497-3100.

TIPPING

A 10% to 15% service charge is added to all hotel bills, though it doesn't always go to staff.

It's usually expected that you will tip more—$5 per person per day for the housekeeping staff, $20 for a helpful concierge, and $10 per day for the group to beach attendants. It is not uncommon to tip more generously, particularly at higher-end resorts.

Many restaurants include a service charge of 10% to 15% on the bill; it is your choice to tip more if you feel the service is deserving. If there is no surcharge, tip about 15%. If you have taken most meals at your hotel's dining room, approximately $100 per week can be handed to the restaurant manager in an envelope to be divided among the staff.

Taxi drivers should receive 10% of the fare.

TOUR OPTIONS

A round-the-island tour by taxi takes about 2½ hours and costs $40 for one or two people, $5 for each additional passenger. Bennie's Tours is one of the island's more reliable tour operators. Malliouhana Travel & Tours will create personalized package tours of the island. The Old Valley Tour, created by longtime resident Frank Costin, ambles the road up Crocus Hill, a treasure trove of Anguilla's best-preserved historic edifices, including Ebenezer's Methodist Church (the island's oldest), the Warden's Place, and typical turn-of-the-20th-century cottages (most housing galleries). The tour is by appointment only and offers a fascinating insight into Anguillian architecture, past and present.

Contact the Anguilla Tourist Board to arrange the tour by Sir Emile Gumbs, the island's former chief minister, of the Sandy Ground area. This tour, which highlights historic and ecological sites, is on Tuesday at 10 AM. The $10 fee benefits the Anguilla Archaeological Historical Society. Gumbs also organizes bird-watching expeditions that show you everything from frigate birds to turtle doves.

🗐 **Anguilla Tourist Office** ⊠ Old Factory Plaza, The Valley ☎ 264/497-2759 ⊕ www.anguilla-vacation.com. **Bennie's Tours** ⊠ Blowing Point ☎ 264/497-2788. **Malliouhana Travel & Tours** ⊠ The Valley ☎ 264/497-2431. **Old Valley Tour** ☎ 264/497-2263.

VISITOR INFORMATION

The Anguilla Tourist Office can provide up-to-the-minute information about attractions, events, and tours.

🗐 **In Anguilla Anguilla Tourist Office** ⊠ Coronation Ave., The Valley ⊕ www.anguilla-vacation.com

com ☎ 264/497-2759, 800/553-4939 from U.S.
📠 264/497-2710.

WEDDINGS

Anguilla's beaches and sybaritic resorts, such as Cap Juluca and Malliouhana, provide ideal settings for destination weddings and honeymoons. Several resorts will help plan everything in advance. Some people are discouraged by a fairly lengthy residency period to get an inexpensive marriage license: if one partner lives on Anguilla at least 15 days before the wedding date, the license costs $40; otherwise, you must pay a fee of $284. Allow two working days to process applications, which can be obtained weekdays from 8:30 to 4 at the Judicial Department. Both parties must present proof of identity (valid passport, birth certificate, or driver's license with photo), as well as an original decree of divorce where applicable and death certificate if widowed. Blood tests are not required. There are additional requirements if you wish to marry in the Catholic Church.

Antigua & Barbuda

Heritage Quay, St. John's

WORD OF MOUTH

"Go for sailing week . . . and see why millionaires worldwide flock to Antigua with their multi-million dollar sailboats; English Harbour turns into a non-stop party."

—antigualover

"Our guide took us through the rain forest and we picked fruit right off the trees. You have to try a piece of black pineapple!"

—Roy_Boy

WELCOME TO ANTIGUA

KEY

➤ Beaches
⚓ Cruise Ship Terminal
◹ Dive Sites
1 Exploring Sights
① Hotels & Restaurants

0 — 2 mi
0 — 2 km

BARBUDA
12 **37**

Boon Pt.
Hodges Bay
26 **27**
Cedar Grove
Prickly Pear Island

28 - **31**

Dickenson Bay
Runaway Beach
32

Deepwater Harbour

Andes
35 **33**
Five Islands

36
34
Hawksbill's Beaches

Fullerton Pt.
Five Islands Harbour

Pearns Pt.

Beggar's Pt.
25
23 Lo Isla

24

V.C. Bird International Airport

1 St. John's
Potters
Parham Rd.
11 Parham

1 - **3**

Pare
Betty Hop

Jennings

4
5

Jolly Harbour
Bolans

Megaliths of Greencastle Hill **2**

Boggy Peak

All Saints

6
Darkwood Beach
7

Johnson's Point
Urlings
Fig Tree Drive
3
Fig Tree Drive
4 Ft. George

Johnson's Point

Falmouth **5**
11
Nelson Dockya

◹ Cades Reef
8 **10**
Old Road
9
Carlisle Bay
Pigeon Point
Rendezvous Bay
Falmouth Bay
6

12 - **15**
16
17
7
Shirle Height

Excellent beaches—365 of them—might make you think that this island has never busied itself with anything more pressing than the pursuit of pleasure. But for much of the 18th and 19th centuries, English Harbour sheltered Britain's Caribbean fleet. These days, pleasure yachts bob where galleons once anchored.

A BEACH FOR EVERY DAY

At 108 square mi (280 square km), Antigua is the largest of the British Leeward Islands. Its much smaller sister island, Barbuda, is 26 mi (42 km) to the north. Together, they are an independent nation and part of the British Commonwealth. The island was under British control from 1667 until it achieved independence in 1981.

The first large sugar plantation on Antigua, Betty's Hope, was established by Christopher Codrington in the 17th century; today, it's an open-air museum.

Though established in 1704, English Harbour was given much more prominence as a naval station when Horatio Nelson was assigned there in 1784; he expanded the port, which thrived for over 100 years.

TOP 4 REASONS TO VISIT ANTIGUA

① So many paradisaical beaches of every size provide a tremendous selection for an island its size.

② Some islands may offer more attractions, but Nelson's Dockyard alone is one of the Caribbean's best examples of historic preservation.

③ With several natural anchorages and tiny islets to explore, Antigua is a major sailing center.

④ Activities galore: land and water sports, sights to see, and nightlife.

ANTIGUA PLANNER

Getting to Antigua

A fair number of nonstop flights make getting to Antigua (ANU) reasonably easy from either North America or the U.K. You can also come on a charter flight from the U.K. Some flights connect through San Juan. Antigua itself is something of a Caribbean hub, as it's the home base of Caribbean Star. You can continue on a small Carib Aviation plane to Barbuda, or there is ferry service five days a week, though it's geared for day-trippers. Package deals can be a good deal for resorts here.

Hassle Factor: Low for Antigua, Medium for Barbuda.

Activities

Because it caters to large numbers of package tourists, Antigua has a fairly large number of sports and activity outfitters offering a variety of adventure and sightseeing tours that include **hiking**, **kayaking**, and **snorkeling** trips. The island even has its own "Stingray City" reminiscent of the original in Grand Cayman. Because of a strong **boating** culture on the island, day sails are also good, and you can rent a sailboat for a long or short time. The island is somewhat unsung as a **diving** destination. **Golfers** may not be overly impressed by the quality of Antigua's two courses, but they will be pleased with the greens fees compared to those on other islands. A trip to Barbuda and its exquisite **beach** is always welcome. The more adventurous may prefer a day-trip over to Montserrat to see its occasionally spewing, sputtering, active volcano.

On the Ground

Antigua's V.C. Bird International Airport, on the northeast coast, is a major hub for traffic between Caribbean islands and for international flights. Montserrat has a small airport with a few daily flights.

Taxis meet every flight to Antigua, and drivers will offer to guide you around the island. The taxis are unmetered, but rates are posted at the airport, and drivers must carry a rate card with them. The fixed rate from the airport to St. John's is $10 (although drivers have been known to quote in EC dollars), to Dickenson Bay $13, and to English Harbour $26.

Renting a Car

If you are staying at an isolated resort or wish to sample the island's many fine restaurants, then a car is a necessity, less so if you are staying at an all-inclusive and plan to limit your on-island excursions to a sightseeing tour or two. It's certainly possible to get by without a car, particularly if you are staying near St. John's or English Harbour, but taxi rates mount up quickly (it can cost $40 for the round-trip between St. John's and English Harbour, including a half-hour for you to do a bit of exploring). A temporary driving permit is required on the island ($20), and you drive on the left.

Where to Stay

The good thing about Antigua is that it is lined with excellent beaches, so you're almost certain to have a good beach regardless of where you stay. Dickenson Bay and Five Islands Peninsula suit beachcombers who want proximity to St. John's, while Jolly Harbour offers affordable options and activities galore. English Harbour and the southwest coast have the best inns and several excellent restaurants—although many close from August well into October; it's also the yachting crowd's hangout. Resorts elsewhere on island are ideal for those seeking seclusion; some are so remote that all-inclusive packages or rental cars are mandatory. Barbuda has three posh resorts.

TYPES OF LODGING

Luxury Resorts: A fair number of luxury resorts cater to the well-heeled in varying degrees of formality on both Antigua and Barbuda.	**All-Inclusive Resorts:** Most of the all-inclusives aim for a very mainstream, package-tour kind of crowd—to varying degrees of success—though Sandals Antigua offerings are more upscale.	**Small Inns:** A few restored small inns can be found around Antigua, but a large concentration is in or near English Habour. Montserrat has only a few guesthouses.

Hotel & Restaurant Costs

Assume that hotels operate on the European Plan (**EP**—with no meals) unless we specify that they use either the Continental Plan (**CP**—with a Continental breakfast), Breakfast Plan (**BP**—with full breakfast), or the Modified American Plan (**MAP**—with breakfast and dinner). Other hotels may offer the Full American Plan (**FAP**—including all meals but no drinks) or may be All-Inclusive (**AI**—with all meals, drinks, and most activities).

WHAT IT COSTS in Dollars					
	$$$$	**$$$**	**$$**	**$**	**¢**
Restaurants	over $30	$20–$30	$12–$20	$8–$12	under $8
Hotels*	over $350	$250–$350	$150–$250	$80–$150	under $80
Hotels**	over $450	$350–$450	$250–$350	$125–$250	under $125

*EP, BP, CP   **AI, FAP, MAP
Restaurant prices are for a main course at dinner and do not include 7% tax or customary 10% service charge. Hotel prices are per night for a double room in high season, excluding 8.5% tax, customary 10% service charge, and meal plans (except at all-inclusives).

When to Go

The high season runs from mid-December through April; after that time, you can find real bargains, for as much as 40% off the regular rates, particularly if you book an air/hotel package. A fair number of smaller properties close for at least part of the time between August and October.

The year's big event is **Antigua Sailing Week**, which draws some 300 yachts for a series of races in late April and early May. Mid-April sees the **Antigua Classic Yacht Regatta**, a five-day event that includes a Tall Ships race.

Antigua Tennis Week, usually the second week of May, has exhibition games by former greats plus a pro-am tournament.

Summer Carnival runs 10 days from the end of July to early August and is one of the Caribbean's more elaborate, with eye-catching costumes and fierce music competitions.

2

By Jordan
Simon

THE SKIFF SKIMS WATERS rippling from azure to aquamarine, colors so intense they seem almost artificial. An archipelago of islets unfolds before me. We moor off the aptly named Great Bird Island, where brown pelicans dive-bomb for tiny, sun-silvered flying fish inches from my feet as I stroll a stretch of powdered ivory sand. Later I clamber up the rocks, and my bird's-eye view takes in a flotilla of fishing boats as brightly colored as a child's finger painting. A halo of frigate birds circles overhead, unfurling their wings to a full 8-foot span, resembling a flag proudly flapping in the breeze.

The miracle of Antigua, and especially its astonishingly undeveloped sister island, Barbuda, is that you can still play Robinson Crusoe here. Travel brochures trumpet the 365 sensuous beaches, "one for every day of the year," as locals love saying, though when the island was first developed for tourism, the unofficial count was 52 ("one for every weekend"). Either way, even longtime residents haven't combed every stretch of sand.

The island's extensive archipelago of cays and islets is what attracted the original Amerindian settlers—the Ciboney—at least 4,000 years ago. The natural environment, which is rich in marine life, flora, and fauna, has been likened to a "natural supermarket." Antigua's superior anchorages and strategic location naturally caught the attention of the colonial powers. The Dutch, French, and English waged numerous bloody battles throughout the 17th century (eradicating the remaining Arawaks and Caribs in the process), with England finally prevailing in 1667. Antigua remained under English control until achieving full independence on November 1, 1981, along with Barbuda, 26 mi (42 km) to the north.

Boats and beaches go hand in hand with hotel development, of course, and Antigua's tourist infrastructure has mushroomed since the 1950s. Though many of its grande dames such as Curtain Bluff remain anchors, today all types of resorts line the sand, and the island offers something for everyone, from gamboling on the sand to gambling in casinos. Though many locals regrettably litter the islandscape, environmental activists have become increasingly vocal about preservation and the limiting of development, and not just because green travel rakes in the green. Antigua's allure is precisely that precarious balance and subliminal tension between its unspoiled natural beauty and its something-for-everyone, sun-sand-surf megadevelopment. And, of course, the British heritage persists, from teatime (and tee times) to fiercely contested cricket matches.

Where to Stay

Scattered along Antigua's beaches and hillsides are exclusive, elegant hideaways; romantic restored inns; and all-inclusive hot spots for couples. One trend: top restaurants, including Harmony Hall and Chez Pascal, are adding charming, affordable cottages. Check individual lodgings for restrictions (many have minimum stays during certain high-season periods). Look also for specials on the Web or from tour packagers, since hotels' quoted rack rates are often negotiable. At this writing, the deluxe Hermitage Bay was slated to open in late 2006 on a beach between Five

Islands Peninsula and Jolly Harbour; the 30 beachfront and hillside cottages will have private plunge pools and garden showers.

★ $$$$ ⊞ **The Beach House.** A dictionary could easily list this serene, secluded retreat under definitions for sanctuary. Cushy white sofas and rows of dazzling white columns offset hardwood coffee tables, purple heartwood decking, and a palate of Greek island–worthy blue accent pieces in the open-air Club House. Spacious, split-level, white-on-white digs are similarly sleek but not slick: black-and-white photos of local scenes line pristine walls, billowing curtains cordon huge private decks, and canopied four-poster beds face glass doors framing an ever-changing canvas of man-made lagoon, sand, and surf. If "civilization" must intrude, use of TVs with DVD players, personal direct-dial international cell phones, and Wi-Fi-ready laptops are complimentary. Each guest is assigned a multitasking Personal Service Ambassador who will give a free welcome massage, press clothes, run bubble baths brimming with bougainvillea blossoms, and patrol the beach with Evian spray and fruit kebabs. Italian-born Andrea Coppola's food is exceptional, from meltingly tender red snapper *en papillote* to velvety lobster tortellini. Presentation is as simple, elegant, and creative (broccoli gelato!) as the resort itself. ⊠ *Palmetto Point, Barbuda* ☎ *268/725–4042, 631/537–1352, 888/776–0333 reservations only* 📠 *516/767–6529* ⊕ *www.thebeachhousebarbuda. com* ⬐ *20 rooms, 1 1-bedroom cottage* ⌂ *Restaurant, room service, fans, in-room safes, minibars, Wi-Fi, pool, gym, massage, beach, snorkeling, bicycles, billiards, bar; no room TVs* ⊟ *AE, MC, V* ⦿ *BP.*

★ $$$$ ⊞ **Blue Waters Hotel.** A well-heeled Brit crowd goes barefoot at this swank yet understated retreat. The lobby strikes an immediate note of class, with cast-iron columns, mosaic lamps, towering earthenware urns, fountains, and a central mini-jungle. The twin beaches are minuscule, but sundecks and gazebos strategically dot the lush hillside for optimum privacy. Rooms are continually refurbished, with such trendy additions as flat-screen TVs and "rainwater" showerheads complementing appealingly old-fashioned vellum prints, intricately carved furnishings, and classic Italian tilework with a soothing blue or sparkling white motif. Rooms 104 to 116 lack direct beachfront access, but their sizable balconies practically jut over the water. Low-numbered units in the 200 through 600 blocks feature similarly splendid views. The two Rock Cottages define exclusive seclusion. Afternoon tea and nonmotorized water sports are complimentary. The Palm offers an unmatched setting and fine Caribbean fare and buffets; Vyvien's counters with a sophisticated fusion menu and comely neo-Colonial setting. ⊠ *Boon Point, Soldiers Bay* ⬆ *Box 256, St. John's* ☎ *268/462–0290, 800/557–6536 reservations only* 📠 *268/462–0293* ⊕ *www.bluewaters.net* ⬐ *73 rooms, 4 villas, 2 cottages* ⌂ *2 restaurants, room service, fans, in-room safes, minibars, cable TV, in-room broadband, tennis court, 3 pools, hot tub, gym, hair salon, spa, 2 beaches, snorkeling, windsurfing, boating, billiards, 2 bars, shops, children's programs (ages 5–13), Internet room, car rental* ⊟ *AE, D, DC, MC, V* ⊗ *Closed Sept.* ⦿ *AI.*

★ $$$$ ⊞ **Carlisle Bay.** This cosmopolitan, boutique sister property of London's trendy One Aldwych hotel daringly eschews everything faux colonial and creole. The monochromatic, magazine-worthy result combines cool, classy minimalism with un-snobbish warmth. Vast, split-level accommodations emulate the Japanese decorative ideal of perfection through simplicity with white walls, black-and-white snapshots of island plants and local life, mahogany-and-teak furnishings, and chrome-and-glass accents. The bougainvillea garlanding the enormous balcony adds just the right amount of color. Deluxe gadgetry runs the gamut from plasma TV/DVDs to fiber-optic bed lights to a movie-screening room and library with futuristic Internet stations. The two trendy restaurants (under executive chef Barnaby Jones's innovative direction), complimentary non-motorized water sports, and a soothing spa enhance the luxe ambience. There are kinks—uneven service, the murky sand-roiled bay, an inadequate separation of families and romantically inclined couples—but the buff bodies toting cell phones make this a hip, hopping, happening see-and-be-scene. ⊠ *Carlisle Bay, Old Road, St. Mary's* ⬧ *Box 2288, St. John's* ☎ *268/484–0000, 800/745–8883, 800/628–8929 reservations only* 🖷 *268/484–0003* ⊕ *www.carlisle-bay.com* ⚲ *88 suites ⚐ 2 restaurants, fans, some kitchens, minibars, cable TV, in-room VCRs, in-room DVDs, Wi-Fi, 9 tennis courts, pool, gym, hair salon, spa, beach, dive shop, snorkeling, kayaking, boating, 3 bars, library, children's programs (ages 3–12), Internet room, meeting rooms* ⊟ *AE, DC, MC, V* ⍲ *BP.*

$$$$ 🖭 **Curtain Bluff.** An incomparable beachfront setting, impeccable serv-
★   ice, diligent upgrading by attentive management, superb extras (free scuba diving and deep-sea fishing), effortless elegance: Curtain Bluff is that rare retreat that remains ahead of the times while exuding a magical timelessness. Owner Howard Hulford still patrols the property with cutting shears and wine glass in hand: the lavish gardens and legendary 25,000-bottle wine cellar bespeak his passions, which the loyal multigenerational clientele (yes, families are coddled) shares. Some might find Curtain Bluff stuffy and country-clubby, but guests merely respect one another's privacy. Regardless, the ravishing beaches and drop-dead rooms invite seclusion. Gorgeous junior suites—the majority of the rooms—have marble bathrooms, grass mats, Mexican earthenware, deco-funky lamps, and coffered raw-wood ceilings. Stunning duplex suites, in soothing whites and blues, scale the bluff; their hammock-slung terraces alone outclass many hotel rooms. Everyone eventually emerges for exceptional Continental dining and dancing to live bands in the lovely alfresco restaurant. ⊠ *Morris Bay* ⬧ *Box 288, St. John's* ☎ *268/462–8400, 888/289–9898 outside NY for reservations* 🖷 *268/462–8409* ⊕ *www.curtainbluff. com* ⚲ *18 rooms, 50 suites ⚐ 2 restaurants, fans, in-room safes, putting green, 4 tennis courts, pool, gym, hair salon, massage, 2 beaches, dive shop, snorkeling, windsurfing, boating, fishing, croquet, squash, bar, library, shops, children's programs (ages 4–12), playground, Internet room, meeting rooms; no room TVs* ⊟ *AE, D* ⊗ *Closed late July–mid-Oct.* ⍲ *AI.*

★ **$$$$**   🖭 **Galley Bay.** This posh all-inclusive channels the fictional Bali H'ai (with Yankee colonial architectural flourishes): man-made lagoon and grotto pool; bird sanctuary laced with nature trails; magnificent boardwalk-lined ecru beach; gardens as manicured as the discriminating clientele;

thatched-roof public spaces; custom-made bamboo furnishings; art naïf paintings; and African carvings. The soothing surf serenades the creole-style beachfront buildings and romantic Gauguin restaurant (with clever, thatched private-dining alcoves). The handsomely appointed beach-front units (numbers 47–48 are centrally located; avoid 77–80, which abut potential mosquito breeding grounds) represent the best value, though towering palms slightly obstruct even the second-floor views. The wattle-and-daub, stucco Gauguin Cottages are a charming conceit, especially with the addition of plunge pools. Alas, they're slightly claustrophobic and the walkways separating bedroom from bathroom insufficiently covered. The best rooms, such as 67–68, at least overlook the lagoon. But these are minor quibbles for honeymooning couples and corporate big-wigs escaping the rat race. ⊠ *Five Islands* ⏧ *Box 305, St. John's* ☎ *268/462–0302, 800/858-4618 or 800/345–0356 reservations only* 📠 *268/462–4551* ⊕ *www.eliteislandresorts.com* ⇆ *70 rooms* ⏴ *2 restaurants, fans, in-room safes, refrigerators, cable TV, tennis court, 2 pools, gym, hair salon, spa, beach, snorkeling, windsurfing, kayaking, boating, bicycles, croquet, horseshoes, bar, shops, Internet room; no kids under 16* ⊟ *AE, D, DC, MC, V* ⊘ *Closed mid-Aug.–early Sept.* ❍| *AI.*

$$$$ ⌂ **Jumby Bay.** This refined resort proffers all the makings of a classic Caribbean hideaway, yet the whole remains less than the sum of its considerable parts. The main beach is simply sublime—except when jets whoosh by. The air-conditioning is often insufficient, ironically because of the majestically high ceilings. Standard rooms and junior suites have hand-carved mahogany four-poster beds—yet the lighting is poor. Still, the details impress, from the rondavel suites' luxuriant indoor-outdoor bathrooms to the luxe villas' hand-painted tilework. The best value for the money are the refurbished Pond Bay Villa ocean-view suites. The cuisine, befitting a Rosewood-managed property, is usually unimpeachable. Birdsong and sea breeze fill the casual Verandah restaurant. Villa owners, including Robin Leach and Ken Follett, frequent the 18th-century stone-and-mahogany Estate House dining room and its fanciful, pineapple-theme lounge. And prized privacy is certainly paramount: you can bike along nature trails to the island's many secluded beaches (one lures nesting turtles in season). ⊠ *Long Island* ⏧ *Box 243, St. John's* ☎ *268/462–6000, 800/767–3966 reservations only* 📠 *268/462–6020* ⊕ *www.jumbybayresort.com* ⇆ *40 suites, 11 villas* ⏴ *2 restaurants, fans, in-room safes, minibars, putting green, 3 tennis courts, pool, gym, spa, 3 beaches, snorkeling, windsurfing, waterskiing, bicycles, croquet, 2 bars, shops, Internet room, business services; no room TVs* ⊟ *AE, D, MC, V* ❍| *AI.*

$$$$ ⌂ **Occidental Grand Pineapple Beach.** This bustling all-inclusive is not quite "grand," yet it still lures honeymooners, families, and mature couples to its remote location. It doesn't lack for facilities, from disco to slot machines, while neocolonial public spaces and facilities are quite handsome, from the polished piano bar to waterfall pool spanned by bridges. The restaurants—Tex-Mex, creole, and Italian—are just adequate. Odd-numbered (101–125) beachfront units sit steps from the sand, though even-numbered "garden-view" rooms in the 200 and 300 blocks feature sweeping views and beach proximity for far less money. The largest, freshest-looking rooms cling to the hillside, enjoying good breezes and better views (opt for those numbered in the 820s–830s and 920s–930s) but are a trek if you're not spry. The lush but overgrown grounds epitomize management's inattentiveness (or lack of funds), as do the tired chaises (rise early if you want a beach chair) and chronic fresh towel shortage. Still, the resort should please less-demanding travelers who finagle special rates. ☒ *Long Bay* ☐ *Box 2000, St. John's* ☏ *268/463–2006 or 800/858-4618, 800/345–0356 for reservations only* 🖶 *268/463–2452* ⊕ *www.eliteislandresorts.com* ⤴ *180 rooms* ☖ *3 restaurants, fans, in-room safes, cable TV, 4 tennis courts, 2 pools, gym, massage, beach, snorkeling, windsurfing, boating, waterskiing, fishing, croquet, horseshoes, volleyball, 5 bars, nightclub, shops, children's programs (ages 4–12), Internet room* ▭ *AE, D, DC, MC, V* ⫧ *AI.*

$$$$ ▦ **St. James's Club.** Forget any prestige the name connotes; this hotel has undergone many incarnations (including one as a Holiday Inn) as the discolored concrete terraces, chipped paint, and gimcrack plastic accents attest. That said, there's much to recommend it, starting with the peerless location straddling 100 acres on Mamora Bay. Recently refurbished rooms are commodious and vibrantly decorated (the larger, more distinctive Oceanfront units are worth the extra cost). Activities galore satisfy the most jaded travelers; in inclement weather you can enjoy movies, trivia contests, and dance classes in the opulent Jacaranda Bar. Though nonmotorized water sports and afternoon tea are complimentary for all guests, most opt for the pricey all-inclusive package, as the remote location discourages dining out. The self-catering two-bedroom villas cascading down the hillside can represent value for large families. Though the restaurants are spectacularly situated over the water, especially Coco's and Piccolo Mondo, food is mostly indifferent. The sometimes unhelpful (or honestly harried) staff and occasional invasion of younger, rowdy Brits on package deals further diminish deluxe pretensions, but this hotel is still a favorite with many travelers who return year after year. ☒ *Mamora Bay* ☐ *Box 63, St. John's* ☏ *268/460–5000 or 800/858–4618* 🖶 *268/460–3015* ⊕ *www.eliteislandresorts.com* ⤴ *187 rooms, 72 villas* ☖ *4 restaurants, room service, fans, cable TV, golf privileges, 7 tennis courts, 4 pools, gym, hair salon, hot tub, spa, 2 beaches, dive shop, dock, snorkeling, windsurfing, boating, croquet, 4 bars, casino, nightclub, children's programs (ages 2–12), Internet room, car rental* ▭ *AE, D, DC, MC, V* ⫧ *AI.*

$$$$ ▦ **Sandals Antigua Caribbean Village & Spa.** The opulent public spaces, lovely beach, glorious gardens, and plethora of facilities almost mask this once-sterling resort's worn lodgings and apathetic service. Recent renovations are merely cosmetic, including repainting of the buildings in appetizing colors of mango, lime, and saffron and adding plunge pools to garden-view rondavels. Alas, the few units claiming water vistas (numbers 301–305 are best, while 401–404 lack views but open onto the beach) are cramped, poorly ventilated, and directly in the busiest foot-traffic path. Pluses include a lively atmosphere (discounting disputes over reserving the scant, shabby beach chairs), activities from cardio training to karaoke, and such extras as complimentary tennis lessons and scuba diving (only spa treatments and weddings incur surcharges). The

$70 million Mediterranean Village expansion should debut by December 2006, adding 180 lavish units (starting at 500 square feet and mating marble, mosaic, and mahogany with such contemporary touches as flat-screen TVs); a swim-up bar (reputedly the Eastern Caribbean's largest); private check-in; two upscale restaurants; and posh retailers. ⊠ *Dickenson Bay* � *Box 147, St. John's* ☎ *268/462–0267, 888/726–3257 reservations only* 🖷 *268/462–4135* ⊕ *www.sandals.com* 🛏 *100 rooms, 257 suites, 16 rondavels* ⚐ *7 restaurants, room service, fans, in-room safes, refrigerators, cable TV, Wi-Fi, 2 tennis courts, 6 pools, gym, hair salon, 6 hot tubs, spa, beach, dive shop, snorkeling, windsurfing, boating, waterskiing, 5 bars, nightclub, shops, Internet room, meeting rooms* ⊟ *AE, D, DC, MC, V* ☞ *3-night minimum* ⍾ *AI.*

$$$–$$$$ ▦ **Hawksbill by Rex Resorts.** "Location, location, location" is the hospitality industry mantra, and four secluded beaches (including one clothing-optional strand) compose this resort's main attraction. A backdrop of jade mountains, verdant grounds with landscaped walkways, restored sugar mill, and plantation-style cottages trimmed with gingerbread fretwork and radiant purple or orange bougainvillea maximize Hawksbill's old-time Caribbean feel. Garden-view rooms enjoy restricted water views, making them the best buy; the original air-conditioned Club units (especially 138–142) are isolated from the action, but hand-painted tilework, beamed vaulted ceilings, and superlative vistas make them the choice accommodations—other than the restored, three-bedroom greathouse. Though a full slate of entertainment is on tap, the mix of honeymooners and mature couples is generally sedate, thanks to the restful surroundings. ⊠ *Five Islands* ⌂ *Box 108, St. John's* ☎ *268/462–0301* 🖷 *268/462–1515* ⊕ *www.hawksbill.com* 🛏 *111 rooms, 1 3-bedroom villa* ⚐ *2 restaurants, fans, refrigerators, tennis court, pool, spa, 4 beaches, snorkeling, windsurfing, boating, 2 bars, shops, Internet room, meeting rooms; no a/c in some rooms, no room TVs* ⊟ *AE, D, DC, MC, V* ⍾ *AI.*

$$–$$$$ ▦ **Inn at English Harbour.** This genteel resort, long a favorite with Brits and the boating set, is ideal for those seeking beachfront accommodations near English Harbour's attractions, yet it suffers from a split personality. The original hilltop buildings hold six well-worn guest rooms and flagstone bar and dining room with scintillating harbor panoramas. Four cramped beachfront rooms are serviceable (beware windless days and biting insects), though there's a funky-elegant beach bar and easy access to the complimentary water sports and launch into English Harbour. Three newer whitewashed, gray-shingle buildings bizarrely sit in a breezeless area behind the horizon pool far from the beach. Enormous rooms are plushly appointed with teak four-poster beds, hand-painted armoires, candelabra sconces, and porphyry bathrooms—however, water pressure is weak and they're dimly lighted and often stifling. Top-floor units at least offer cathedral ceilings and better views. Even the food and service range from spot-on to spoiler. ⊠ *Freeman's Bay, English Harbour* ⌂ *Box 187, St. John's* ☎ *268/460–1014, 800/970–2123 reservations only* 🖷 *268/460–1603* ⊕ *www.theinn.ag* 🛏 *34 units* ⚐ *2 restaurants, room service, fans, in-room safes, refrigerators, 2 tennis courts, pool, gym, beach, snorkeling, windsurfing, boating, waterskiing, 2 bars,*

Internet room; no a/c, no TV in some rooms ▤ *AE, D, DC, MC, V* ⊘ *Closed mid-Aug.–Oct.* ⦿ *EP.*

$$–$$$ ⊡ **CocoBay.** This healing hillside hideaway aims to "eliminate all potential worries," by emphasizing simple natural beauty and West Indian warmth. Pastel-hue creole-style cottages with gingerbread trim and distinctive wattle-and-daub terrace dividers have pine floors, sisal rugs, mosquito netting, and bleached wood louvers. Fresh flowers plucked from the exquisite gardens add splashes of color. The sparkling bay vistas from every room are restorative in themselves, though a wellness center offers massages, facials, and scrubs, many utilizing indigenous ingredients. Yoga classes and nature hikes further promote destressing, though worriers can request complimentary cell phones (you pay for calls). Only middling food—except at Sheer, which has a surcharge—and pokey beaches somewhat mitigate the relaxing vibe. ⊠ *Valley Church* ⬧ *Box 431, St. John's* ☏ *268/562–2400 or 800/816–7587* 🖷 *268/562–2424* ⊕ *www.cocobayresort.com* ⤳ *41 rooms, 4 2-bedroom houses* ♿ *2 restaurants, fans, in-room safes, refrigerators, pool, gym, spa, 2 beaches, snorkeling, bar, shops, Internet room; no a/c, no room TVs* ▤ *AE, D, MC, V* ⦿ *AI.*

★ **$$–$$$** ⊡ **Dickenson Bay Cottages.** If you don't mind a five-minute hike down to the beach, this small hillside complex offers excellent value for families. Lush landscaping snakes around the two-story buildings and pool. The handsomely appointed duplex accommodations feature most of the comforts of home, though the decor is hardly original and the ventilation poor. Larger units have verandas with ocean views but aren't worth the higher tariff. Guests enjoy privileges at Rex Halcyon Cove's bustling beach; use of its tennis and water-sports facilities is always discounted. Other dining and recreational options abound along Dickenson Bay. This agreeable enclave is often inexplicably empty, so ask about last-minute reductions and check its Web site for specials. ⊠ *Marble Hill* ⬧ *Box 1379, St. John's* ☏ *268/462–4940* 🖷 *268/462–4941* ⊕ *www.dickensonbaycottages.com* ⤳ *11 units* ♿ *BBQ, fans, some kitchens, some kitchenettes, cable TV, some in-room VCRs, pool* ▤ *AE, DC, MC, V* ⦿ *EP.*

$$–$$$$ ⊡ **Jolly Beach Resort.** If you're looking for basic sun-sand-surf fun, this active resort—Antigua's largest—fits the bill for few bills, luring a gregarious blend of honeymooners, families, and singles on the make. Management diligently gussies up the public areas: faux sugar mill, freeform fantasy pool, creole-style vendors' village, attractive gardens, and a riot of tropic-cocktail colors. Palapas and hammocks dot the long if crowded beach. The four main restaurants, Italian to Indian, are surprisingly competent, especially the waterfront seafood eatery, Lydia's. The range of activities and facilities surpasses that of many tonier all-inclusives. Alas, service is too often cursory if not curt, and the dilapidated cinderblock structures have peeling paint, chipped doors, and rusting railings. Most units are cramped and musty with ugly, bizarre built-in concrete furnishings; "supersaver" rooms, though the size of jail cells, represent the top value, especially for singles (only $10 supplement). Every room has at least a partial sea view. ⊠ *Jolly Harbour* ⬧ *Box 2009, St. John's* ☏ *268/462–0061 or 866/905–6559* 🖷 *268/562–2117* ⊕ *www.*

jollybeachresort.com ↵ *462 units* ⌂ *5 restaurants, in-room safes, some refrigerators, cable TV, 4 tennis courts, 2 pools, fitness classes, gym, hot tub, beach, dive shop, snorkeling, windsurfing, boating, waterskiing, 7 bars, nightclub, recreation room, shops, children's programs (ages 2–12), Internet room, meeting rooms* ⊟ *AE, D, MC, V* ⦿ *AI.*

$$–$$$ **Rex Blue Heron.** If it weren't for the sublime ecru beach (replete with superior snorkeling), this intimate but average all-inclusive wouldn't merit consideration. Still, all rooms (save for a few rip-off "standard" units lacking air-conditioning and TV) gaze or open onto that spectacular sweep of sand. German, Italian, and British tour operators book it heavily for huge discounts, though service, food, decor, and facilities are mediocre. The clientele runs from young and worldly types to flight crews to spillover from Rex Halcyon Cove that ups the average closer to retirement age, but all are chummy. Come here if you can get a good rate and simply want to relax on a secluded strand. ⊠ *Johnson's Point* ⌀ *Box 1715, St. John's* ☎ *268/462–8564 or 800/255–5859* 🖷 *268/462–8005* ⊕ *www.rexresorts.com* ↵ *64 rooms* ⌂ *Restaurant, fans, pool, beach, snorkeling, windsurfing, boating, 2 bars, shops; no a/c in some rooms, no TV in some rooms* ⊟ *AE, D, MC, V* ⦿ *AI.*

★ **$$–$$$** **Siboney Beach Club.** This affordable beachfront oasis nestled in a tranquil corner of Dickenson Bay delights with intimacy and warmth, and knowledgeable, affable Aussie owner Tony Johnson gladly acts as a de facto tourist board. Cleverly designed suites have a small bedroom, Pullman-style kitchen, living area, and patio or balcony. Atmospheric touches include island CDs, painted gourds, and driftwood wall hangings. A TV can be provided on request, though guests savor the soothing surf counterpointed by crickets, bananaquits, and tree frogs in Tony's extravagant, enchanted garden. Rooms 9 and 10 overlook the sea, and ground-floor units—number 3 virtually extends into that lushly landscaped pool area—represent fine buys for families. Their advantage can also be a drawback: the sofa beds are welcome, but patios lack screens, forcing a choice between sweltering and swatting pests on rare still days. ⊠ *Dickenson Bay* ⌀ *Box 222, St. John's* ☎ *268/462–0806 or 800/533–0234* 🖷 *268/462–3356* ⊕ *www.siboneybeachclub.com* ↵ *12 suites* ⌂ *Restaurant, fans, in-room safes, kitchenettes, pool, beach, bar, Internet room; no room TVs* ⊟ *AE, D, MC, V* ⦿ *EP.*

$$ **Jolly Harbour Villas.** These duplex, two-bedroom villas ring the marina of a sprawling, self-contained 500-acre compound offering every conceivable facility from restaurants to shops, casino to golf course. The Mediterranean Revival central activity area could put the florid in Florida, with its red-tile roofs, faux stucco, and mustard arcades. The sizable, fully equipped, pastel-hued villas themselves resemble a posh, cookie-cutter retirement village. Opt for those on the south finger, which is closer to the beach, eateries, and most activities, since the free shuttle is erratic and slow. You must pay separately for everything but pool and kids' club, and the extra $20 per night for air-conditioning is a wise investment: on still days, flies and mosquitoes come out in brute force and formation. Villas represent jolly good value for self-catering families and golfers (unlimited greens fees are $105 per week). ⊠ *Jolly Harbour* ⌀ *Box 1793, St. John's* ☎ *268/462–7771* 🖷 *268/462–7772*

⊕ *www.jollyharbourantigua.com* ⇥ *150 villas △ 7 restaurants, fans, in-room safes, kitchens, 18-hole golf course, miniature golf, 4 tennis courts, 3 pools, hair salon, 2 beaches, dive shop, snorkeling, windsurfing, boating, marina, waterskiing, squash, 6 bars, casino, nightclub, shops, children's programs (ages 3–11), playground, car rental, helipad; no a/c in some rooms, no TV in some rooms* ⊟ *AE, D, DC, MC, V* ⏇ *EP.*

★ **$–$$** ⊞ **Admiral's Inn.** This 18th-century brick edifice, originally the shipwright's offices in what is now Nelson's Dockyard, has withstood acts of God since the early 18th century. The sturdy walls, occasionally creaking floorboards, even the ancient bar exude history. The finest rooms at "The Ads," as yachties call it, feature the original timbered ceilings—replete with iron braces, whitewashed brick walls, polished hardwood floors, and four-poster beds swaddled in mosquito netting. Those upstairs (numbers 1–3) spy on the yachts in the harbor through Australian pines and stone pillars. Gulls and egrets seem poised to dart into the timbered living room of the two-bedroom Loft (once the dockyard's joinery). Commandeer the complimentary boat and shuttle to nearby beaches when crowds descend on the compound and the inn's captivating terrace restaurant for lunch. ⊠ *English Harbour* ⌂ *Box 713, St. John's* ☎ *268/460–1027 or 800/223–5695* 🖷 *268/460–1534* ⊕ *www.admiralsantigua.com* ⇥ *14 rooms, 1 2-bedroom apartment* △ *Restaurant, fans, boating, bar; no a/c in some rooms, no TV in some rooms* ⊟ *AE, D, MC, V* ⏇ *EP.*

☾ **$–$$** ⊞ **Sunsail Club Colonna.** Those who want to learn to sail or improve their skippering skills should cruise to this instructional facility justly celebrated worldwide for its affordable sailing and windsurfing schools and family-friendly approach. Sunsail has state-of-the-art equipment, a fine kids' club, and excellent group instruction (all complimentary), but nearly every other aspect of the resort is inferior. The expansive free-form pool (though often noisily overrun by kids), handsome public spaces and Mediterranean architecture, sizable rooms (recently brightened with stylish Italian fabrics), and such incentives as discounted greens fees compensate somewhat for the smallish, man-made beaches. The spa could be cleaner, and food veers from inventive to inedible. Fortunately, management is gradually upgrading every facet of the resort in an effort to make Colonna truly ship-shape. Weekly stays are preferred and often discounted. ⊠ *Hodges Bay* ⌂ *Box 591, St. John's* ☎ *268/462–6263, 800/327–2276, or 888/350–3568* 🖷 *268/462–6430* ⊕ *www. sunsail.com* ⇥ *102 rooms, 12 villas △ 2 restaurants, in-room safes, minibars, cable TV, tennis court, pool, gym, hair salon, spa, 2 beaches, dive shop, snorkeling, windsurfing, boating, 2 bars, shops, children's programs (ages 4 months–17), Internet room* ⊟ *AE, D, MC, V* ⏇ *FAP.*

★ **$** ⊞ **Catamaran Hotel.** The main building at the congenial, sand-fronted "Cat Club" evokes a plantation greathouse with verandas, white columns, and hand-carved doors. The efficiency apartments are ideal for families (the staff dotes on kids), while second-floor deluxe rooms have romantic canopy four-poster beds and scintillating views. Nonmotorized water sports are free at the minuscule, palm- and almond-lined beach, which gazes upon megayachts anchored in the marina. Owner-manager Feona Bailey rings improvements yearly and personally ensures

Other Hotels to Consider on Antigua

OBVIOUSLY, WE CAN'T INCLUDE every property deserving mention without creating an encyclopedia. Our favorites receive full reviews, but you might consider the following accommodations, many of which are popular with tour operators.

Coconut Beach Club (✉ Yepton Beach ☎ 268/462-3239 or 800/361-4621 ⊕ www.coconutbeachclub.com) was taken over by CocoBay Resort, which refurbished the neglected rooms in 2004. The beach overlooking the ruins of Fort James is lovely, the food in the restaurants creative; all units feature smashing sea views, and the price is right—for now.

Dian Bay Resort & Spa (✉ Dian Bay ☎ 268/460-6646 or 800/345-0356 ⊕ www.eliteislandresorts.com) occupies a remote if picturesque spit of land. This "spa-concept resort" provides everything from ayurvedic to aromatherapy treatments, manicures to mud wraps to meditation. The three-tier pool and panoramic restaurant (innovative lower-fat fare)

delight, but the beach is minuscule, and only half the rooms have (slightly impeded) water views: request upper-floor units.

Galleon Beach (✉ Freeman's Bay, English Harbour ☎ 268/460-1024 ⊕ www.galleonbeach.com) offers commodious if slightly worn self-catering one- to four-bedroom cottages. The lack of air-conditioning is rarely a problem. The views of yachts bobbing in Freeman's Bay, complimentary nonmotorized water sports at the smallish but attractive cove, tropical vegetation, infinity pool, and worthy restaurant are pluses.

Rex Halcyon Cove Beach Resort (✉ Dickenson Bay ☎ 268/462-9256 or 800/255-5859 ⊕ www.rexresorts.com) is a large, impersonal but admirably outfitted resort (from dive shop to car rental) on one of Antigua's top beaches. It reopened in late 2005 after renovations, though little has been done about the institutional buildings or stampeding tour groups.

smooth sailing for travelers seeking true Antiguan flavor. ✉ *Falmouth Harbour* 🖃 *Box 958, St. John's* ☎ *268/460-1036 or 800/223-6510* 🖷 *268/460-1339* ⊕ *www.catamaran-antigua.com* 🛏 *12 rooms, 2 1-bedroom suites* 🖒 *Restaurant, BBQ, fans, in-room safes, kitchenettes, cable TV, pool, beach, windsurfing, boating, marina, bar, shops, Internet room* ➡ *D, MC, V* ¶Ⓞ¶ *EP.*

$ 🖃 **Ocean Inn.** Smashing views of English Harbour, affable management, and affordability distinguish this homey inn. The main house has six snug guest rooms (two share a bathroom), but the four hillside cottages are recommended (especially numbers 8 and 9). The main drawback is a rickety wooden staircase careening as drunkenly as yachties celebrating a regatta victory. The owners can provide light dinners with advance notice, though restaurants are a short hike away. There are several beaches within 10 minutes' drive. In season, the small, mural-adorned pool hosts impromptu parties that lure local characters, sea dogs, and eccentric expats for cheap drinks and amusing tall tales. ✉ *English Har-*

bour ⊡ *Box 838, St. John's* ☎ *268/463–7950 or 888/686–8913* 🖷 *268/ 460–1263* ⊕ *www.theoceaninn.com* ☞ *6 rooms, 4 with bath, 4 cottages* ⚬ *BBQ, fans, some refrigerators, cable TV, pool, bar, Internet room; no a/c in some rooms* ▭ *AE, D, MC, V* ❙❂❙ *CP.*

Where to Eat

Antigua's restaurants are almost a dying breed since the advent of all-inclusives. But several worthwhile hotel dining rooms and nightspots remain, especially in the English Harbour and Dickenson Bay areas, in addition to many stalwarts. Virtually every chef incorporates local ingredients and elements of West Indian cuisine.

Most menus list prices in both EC and U.S. dollars; if not, ask which currency the menu is using. Always double-check if credit cards are accepted and if service is included. Dinner reservations are needed during high season.

What to Wear

Perhaps because of the island's British heritage, Antiguans tend to dress more formally for dinner than dwellers on many other Caribbean islands. Wraps and shorts (no beach attire) are de rigueur for lunch, except at local hangouts.

CARIBBEAN ✕ **george.** Owner Philip George-John's eatery is a loving evocation of
$$–$$$$ the original Georgian family home. The contemporary colonial design is stunning: beamed ceilings, teal-and-aqua walls, high-back hardwood chairs, and jalousie shutters that close off to form a second-floor gallery overlooking the busy street scene. The menu updates West Indian classics, from jerk burgers to slow-roasted spare ribs with a caramelized passion fruit–pineapple glaze to pepper-seared tuna marinated in sesame-ginger oil. If you avoid the priciest items (rack of lamb, lobster) you can dine affordably; indulge in the bartenders' extensive "Naughty List" of cocktails. ⊠ *Market and Redcliffe Sts., St. John's* ☎ *268/562– 4866* ▭ *AE, D, MC, V.*

$$–$$$ ✕ **Papa Zouk.** Who would have thought that two jovial globetrotting German gents could create a classic Caribbean hangout? But the madras tablecloths, fishnets festooned with Christmas lights, painted bottles of homemade hot sauce, colorful island clientele, and lilting rhythms on the sound system justify the name (which describes the sultry, musical stew of soul and calypso). Seafood is king, from Guyanese butterfish to Bajan flying fish, usually served either deep-fried or steamed with choice of such sauces as guava-pepper teriyaki or tomato-basil-coriander. Tangy Caribbean bouillabaisse and house-smoked tuna are specialties, as are the knockout rum punches. Dine family-style in front or more intimately in back. ⊠ *Hilda Davis Dr., Gambles Terrace, St. John's* ☎ *268/ 464–7576* ▭ *No credit cards* ❂ *Closed May–Oct. No lunch Sun.–Tues.*

$$–$$$ ✕ **Sticky Wicket.** With a dining room framed by flagstone columns and a trendily open kitchen, this is one of the classiest sports bars imaginable. Cricket is the overriding theme, but whether you're sitting in the posh lounge surrounded by cricket memorabilia or outside on the patio overlooking the equally handsome Stanford Cricket Ground, you can

2

enjoy everything from snacks, such as the definitive conch fritters, to standout that include ribs and beef brisket. The potent house cocktails and daily specials—sterling mahimahi with a passion-fruit, mango, and lime salsa—not to mention the ambience—remain pure Antillean. This is a splendid respite while waiting for your flight at the airport across the road. Avoid its pretentious, overpriced Pavilion sister restaurant (despite its hand-painted ceilings and extensive wine cellar). ⊠ *Airport Blvd., Coolidge* ☎ *268/481–7000* ⊟ *AE, D, MC, V.*

CONTEMPORARY
★ $$–$$$$

✕ **Coconut Grove.** Coconut palms grow through the roof of this open-air thatched restaurant, flickering candlelight illuminates colorful local murals, waves lap the white sand, and the warm waitstaff provides just the right level of service. Jean-François Bellanger's superbly presented dishes fuse French culinary preparations with island ingredients. Top choices include pan-seared snapper medallions served with roasted sweet potato in a saffron white-wine curry, and chicken stuffed with creole vegetables in mango-kiwi sauce. The kitchen can be uneven, the wine list is merely serviceable, and the buzzing happy-hour bar traffic lingering well into dinnertime can detract from the otherwise romantic atmosphere. Nonetheless, Coconut Grove straddles the line between casual beachfront boîte and elegant eatery with aplomb. ⊠ *Siboney Beach Club, Dickenson Bay* ☎ *268/462–1538* ⊟ *AE, D, MC, V.*

$$–$$$$
Fodor'sChoice
★

✕ **Julian's Alfresco.** Sea breezes and jazz waft through this open-air eatery that perfectly frames picture-postcard Runaway Bay, but the real artistry is that of chef-owner Julian Waterer. His merry mélange of influences spans the globe, but the food's beautifully counterpointed textures and flavors take the confusion out of fusion cuisine. Signature stunners include fish-and-crab cakes touched with Thai red-and-green curry with sweet chili sauce and green onions and such sublimely seasoned specials as jerk-spiced chicken breast and lobster medallions accompanied by pineapple cilantro salsa and guava peppercorn coulis. Meat-and-potato types will appreciate the simpler grilled offerings, including several prime cuts of steak, vegetarians the creative gâteaux exploding with flavor. Finish with an impeccable chocolate mousse or crème brûlée and beg for an extra ginger cookie to go. ⊠ *Barrymore Beach Hotel, Runaway Bay* ☎ *268/562–1545* ⊟ *AE, D, MC, V* ⊘ *Closed Mon. No lunch.*

ECLECTIC
$$$

✕ **Sheer.** This stylish, sensuous eatery carved into a sheer cliffside showcases one of the Caribbean's most ambitious menus. Start with a creative martini such as the white-chocolate saffron as you admire the setting sun's pyrotechnics from the staggered, thatched dining nooks, many separated by billowing white gauze curtains. Chef Nigel Martin revels in daringly unorthodox—even odd—combinations that trigger all sets of taste buds: foie gras and nori-seaweed-filled tortellini with sun-dried tomatoes, mung beans, and morels; coffee-glaze pork tenderloin with rhubarb-cinnamon tamales, lima beans, and poblano salsa; and a dessert of orange-blossom-braised endive (!) with white-chocolate-pistachio *kulfi* (Indian-style ice cream). Sheer closes twice weekly on a rotating schedule, so call ahead. ⊠ *CocoBay, Valley Church* ☎ *268/562–2400* ◿ *Reservations essential* ⊟ *AE, D, MC, V* ⊘ *Closed 2 nights per wk. No lunch.*

FRENCH
$$$–$$$$
Fodor'sChoice
★

✕ **Chez Pascal.** Pascal and Florence Milliat built this hilltop charmer with their own hands, and it begs comparison with any bistro in the French West Indies. The flagstone terrace overlooks a tinkling fountain and lighted pool; the tasteful, elevated dining room is furnished in dark rattan, with ceramics, local paintings, cast-iron gas lamps, and copper pots. Pascal's classic Lyonnaise cuisine exhibits his remarkably deft hand with subtle, silken sauces. Try the gossamer chicken-liver mousse in thyme sauce, practically translucent and transcendent scallops with leeks, or the sublime steamed grouper in beurre blanc. Finish with a heavenly flourless chocolate cake with strawberry coulis or a definitive tarte tatin and you've just defined joie de vivre. Four guest rooms ($225, including breakfast and a 10% discount on other meals) with whirlpool baths have splendid sea views. ⊠ *Galley Bay Hill, Five Islands* ☎ *268/462–3232* ⌕ *Reservations essential* ⊟ *AE, D, MC, V* ⊘ *Closed Aug.*

$$$–$$$$

✕ **Le Bistro.** This Antiguan institution's peach-and-pistachio accents subtly match the tile work, jade chairs, mint china, and painted lighting fixtures. Trellises cannily divide the large space into intimate sections. Chef Patrick Gaducheau delights in blending regional fare with indigenous ingredients, but the kitchen is surprisingly inconsistent, and the service can be stuffy. Opt for daily specials, such as fresh snapper with spinach and grapefruit in thyme-perfumed lime-butter sauce, lobster medallions in basil-accented old-rum sauce with roasted red peppers, and almost anything swaddled in puff pastry. Co-owner Phillippa Esposito doubles as hostess and pastry chef; her passion-fruit mousse and chocolate confections are sublime. ⊠ *Hodges Bay* ☎ *268/462–3881* ⌕ *Reservations essential* ⊟ *AE, MC, V* ⊘ *Closed Mon. No lunch.*

★ $$–$$$

✕ **Catherine's Café.** This little deck café overlooking English Harbour marina brims with Gallic verve thanks to ebullient hostess Catherine Ricard, whose definition of table-hopping sometimes includes strangers' laps. The food is simple: zucchini-Roquefort quiche, a proper salade niçoise, and lovely brochettes. Evening delights might include *moules marinières* (marinated mussels), or *gratin de cèpes* (wild mushrooms in a cheese sauce). Catherine's pert comments highlight the fairly priced, extensive wine list. This delightful place always percolates with life and good strong espresso. ⊠ *English Harbour* ☎ *268/460–5050* ⊟ *MC, V* ⊘ *Closed Tues. and Sept. No dinner Mon.*

$$–$$$

✕ **Le Cap Horn.** As Piaf and Aznavour compete with croaking tree frogs in a trellised room lined with a virtual jungle, it's easy to imagine yourself in a tropic St. Tropez. From the small but select menu begin with lobster bisque or escargots in a lovely tomato, onion, and pepper sauce (sop it up with the marvelous home-baked bread); then segue into tandoori tiger shrimp flambéed with rum or Dijon-crusted rack of lamb. Gustavo Belaunde (he's Peruvian of Catalan extraction) elicits fresh, delicate, almost ethereal flavors from his ingredients; his versatility is displayed in the restaurant's other half, a pizzeria replete with wood-burning oven. ⊠ *English Harbour* ☎ *268/460–1194* ⊟ *AE, D, MC, V* ⊘ *Closed Aug. and Sept.*

ITALIAN
★ $$–$$$

✕ **Alberto's.** Vivacious owner Alberto taught his culinary secrets to his English wife, Vanessa; she now bests her mentor with her Italian, Asian, and French inspirations. Try leek and Parmesan soufflé; great sushi; veal medallions in mushroom crust; or yummy gnocchi with sweet red-pepper sauce. The homemade, lusciously textured sorbets are a must for dessert: tangy passion fruit, creamy coconut, lip-smacking lemon. Tables line a trellised balcony open to the breezes and hung with bougainvillea, and whimsically painted china graces the walls of this justly popular trattoria. ⊠ *Willoughby Bay* ☎ *268/460–3007* ♙ *Reservations essential* ▭ *AE, D, MC, V* ⊘ *Closed Mon. and May–Oct. No lunch.*

★ **$$–$$$** ✕ **Harmony Hall.** Its remote location is a headache, but Harmony Hall's seamless blend of historic ambience, panoramic ocean views, stellar food, and sterling service provides a feast for all the senses. Consummate hosts Riccardo and Marilisa Parisi's near-obsessive attention to detail extends from the specially commissioned ceramic ware to the savvy, fairly priced wine list. The ultrafresh Italian fare sings with sun-drenched Mediterranean colors and flavors, from tender salmon in a crunchy sesame-poppy-seed crust to wahoo-herb ravioloni with cherry tomatoes. The amazing multitier antipasto is a meal in itself. You can also spend the night in one of the stylish, spacious cottages (just $185, including breakfast). ⊠ *Brown's Bay Mill, Brown's Bay* ☎ *268/460–4120* ▭ *AE, D, MC, V* ⊘ *Closed May–Oct. No dinner Sun.–Thurs.*

$–$$ ✕ **Big Banana–Pizzas in Paradise.** This tiny, often crowded spot is tucked into one side of a restored 18th-century rum warehouse with broad plank floors, wood-beam ceiling, and stone archways. Cool Benetton-style photos of locals and jamming musicians adorn the brick walls. It serves some of the island's best pizza—try the lobster or the seafood variety—as well as such tasty specials as conch salad, fresh fruit crushes, and sub sandwiches bursting at the seams. There's live entertainment Thursday night, and sports nuts congregate at the bar's huge satellite TV. ⊠ *Redcliffe Quay, St. John's* ☎ *268/480–6985* ▭ *AE, MC, V* ⊘ *Closed Sun.*

PAN-ASIAN   ✕ **East.** Imposing Indonesian carved doors usher you into this bold and
★ **$$–$$$** sexy Asian fusion spot. Flames flicker in the outdoor lily pond while candles illuminate lacquered dark-wood tables with blood-red napery and oversize fuchsia-color chairs; strategically spaced seating ensures you can't eavesdrop on the affairs, romantic or professional, likely being transacted. Exquisite pan-Pacific fare courts perfection through simplicity and precision: prawn spring rolls with hoisin-sweet chili sauce, superlative sashimi, Thai lobster with asparagus, and green tea crème brûlée. The comprehensive wine list is pricey, while the small main courses mandate tapas-style dining. ⊠ *Carlisle Bay, Old Road, St. Mary's* ☎ *268/484–0000* ♙ *Reservations essential* ▭ *AE, D, DC, MC, V.*

Beaches

Antigua's beaches are public, and many are dotted with resorts that have water-sports outfitters and beach bars. The government does a fairly good job of islandwide maintenance, cleaning up seaweed and garbage, though locals don't always adopt the same prideful attitude. Most restaurant and bars on developed beaches won't charge for beach-chair rentals if you buy lunch or even drinks; otherwise the going rate is usually $3 to $5. Access to some of the finest stretches of sand, such as those at the Five Islands Peninsula resorts (including Galley Bay, Hawksbill Beach Hotel, and Coconut Beach Club), is somewhat restricted by security gates. Sunbathing topless or in the buff is strictly illegal except on one small beach at Hawksbill Beach Hotel. Beware that when cruise ships dock in St. John's, buses drop off loads of passengers on most of the west-coast beaches. Choose such a time to tour the island by car, visit one of the more remote east-end beaches, or take a day trip to Barbuda.

ANTIGUA **Darkwood Beach.** This (1-km) beige ribbon on the southwest coast has stunning views of Montserrat. Although popular with locals on weekends, it's virtually deserted during the week. Waters are generally calm, but there's scant shade, no development other than a basic beach bar, and little to do other than bask in solitude. Its neighbor across the headland (a seven-minute walk along the road), Ffryes Bay, is another fine pristine stretch. ⌧ *2 mi (3 km) south of Jolly Harbour and roughly ½ mi ([3//4] km) southwest of Valley Church off the main coast rd.*

Dickenson Bay. Along a lengthy stretch of powder-soft white sand and exceptionally calm water you can find small and large hotels, water sports, concessions, and beachfront restaurants. Be forewarned that many operators such as Sea Sports (arguably the island's best venue for motorized water sports) and Big John's Dive can be rather chaotic. Vendors pass by but generally don't hassle sun worshippers. There's decent snorkeling at either point. ⌧ *2 mi (3 km) northeast of St. John's, along the main coast rd.*

★ **Half Moon Bay.** This ¾-mi (1-km) ivory crescent is a prime snorkeling and windsurfing area. On the Atlantic side of the island, the water can be quite rough at times, attracting a few intrepid hardcore surfers and wakeboarders. The northeastern end, where a protective reef offers spectacular snorkeling, is much calmer. A tiny bar has restrooms, snacks, and beach chairs. Vendors wander by intermittently; signs of life are few. Half Moon is a real trek (you might end up asking locals directions several times) but one of Antigua's showcase beaches. Follow signs for the villages of St. Philips or Freetown, and pray: all roads are unmarked, and the island's hinterland has no landmarks to guide us. ⌧ *On the southeast coast, 1½ mi (2½ km) from Freetown.*

★ **Johnson's Point/Crab Hill.** This series of connected, deliciously deserted beaches of bleached white sand on the southwest coast overlooks Montserrat, Guadeloupe, St. Kitts, and Nevis. You can explore a ruined fort at one end; notable beach bar-restaurants include OJ's (try the snapper) and Turner's. Just across the road, the amiable owners of 3 Martini (a restaurant-apartment complex) serve excellent, inexpensive Italian food and cocktails. All are superb places to applaud the spectacular sunsets. The water is generally placid, though snorkelers will be disappointed. ⌧ *3 mi (5 km) south of the Jolly Harbour complex on the main west-coast Rd.*

Pigeon Point. Near Falmouth Harbour are these two fine white-sand beaches; the leeward side is calmer, while the windward side is rockier, with sensational views and snorkeling around the point. Several restaurants and bars are nearby, though Billy's satisfies most on-site needs. There are two turnoffs from the main south-coast road; the easiest to identify is just past the turn for the Antigua Yacht Club. ⌧ *Off the main south-coast road, southwest of Falmouth.*

2

Runaway Beach. An often unoccupied stretch of bone-white sand, this beach is still rebuilding after years of hurricane erosion, with just enough palms left for shelter. Both the water and the scene are relatively calm, and beach restaurants such as the raucous Bikini's offer cool shade and cold beer. Hug the lagoon past the entrance to Siboney Beach Club to get here. ⊠ *Approx. 2 mi (3 km) northwest of St. John's, down the main north-coast road from Dickenson Bay.*

BARBUDA

Fodor'sChoice

★

Pink Beach. This practically deserted 8-mi (13-km) stretch reaches from Spanish Point to Palmetto Point: you can sometimes walk miles without encountering another footprint. This classic strand is champagne-hued and with sand soft as silk; crushed coral often imparts a rosy glint in the sun, hence its (unofficial) name. The only signs of life are Barbuda's three posh resorts, of which only the Beach House really offers meals (Barbudan lobster is a must), drinks, and chairs. The water can be rough with a strongish undertow in spots, though protected by the reefs that make the island a diving mecca. If you're coming for the day, hire a taxi to take you here, since none of the roads are well marked. ⊠ *1 mi (1½ km) from the ferry and airstrip along unmarked roads.*

Sports & the Outdoors

Several all-inclusives offer day passes that permit use of all sporting facilities from tennis courts to water-sports concessions, as well as free drinks and meals. The cost begins at $40 for singles (but can be as much as $180 for couples at Sandals), and hours generally run from 8 AM to 6 PM, with extensions available until 2 AM. Antigua has long been famed for its cricketers (such as Viv Richards and Richie Richardson); aficionados will find one of the Caribbean's finest cricket grounds right by the airport, with major test matches running January through June.

ADVENTURE

TOURS

★

Antigua is developing its ecotourist opportunities, and several memorable offshore experiences involve more than just snorkeling. The archipelago of islets coupled with a full mangrove swamp off the northeast coast is unique in the Caribbean. **Adventure Antigua** (☎ 268/727–3261 ⊕ www.adventureantigua.com) is run by enthusiastic Eli Fuller, who is knowledgeable not only about the ecosystem and geography of Antigua but also about its history and politics (his grandfather was the American consul). His thorough seven-hour excursion (Eli dubs it "re-creating my childhood explorations") includes stops at Guiana Island for lunch and guided snorkeling (turtles, barracuda, and stingrays are common sightings), Pelican Island (more snorkeling), Bird Island (hiking to vantage points to admire the soaring ospreys and frigate and red-billed tropic birds), and "Hell's Gate" (a striking limestone rock formation where the more intrepid may hike and swim through sunken caves and tide pools painted with pink and maroon algae). The company also offers a fun, wild, shorter "amusement park ride" variation on a racing boat catering to adrenaline junkies who "feel the need for speed." **"Paddles" Kayak Eco Adventure** (⊠ Seaton's Village ☎ 268/463–1944 or 268/560–3782 ⊕ www.antiguapaddles.com) takes you on a 3½-hour tour of serene mangroves and inlets with informative narrative about the fragile ecosystem of the swamp and reefs and the rich diversity of flora and fauna. The tour ends with a hike to sunken caves and snorkeling in the North Sound Marine Park. Experienced guides double as kayaking and snorkeling instructors, making this an excellent opportunity for novices.

Stingray City Antigua (⊠ Seaton's Village ☎ 268/562–7297 or 268/463–1944) is a carefully reproduced "natural" environment nicknamed by staffers the "retirement home," though the 30-plus stingrays, ranging from infants to seniors, are frisky. You can stroke, feed, even hold the striking gliders, as well as snorkel in deeper, protected waters. The tour guides do a marvelous job of explaining the animals' habits, from feeding to breeding, and their predators (including man).

BICYCLING Bicycling isn't terribly arduous on Antigua, except in the southernmost region, where the roads soar, dip, and corkscrew. **Bike Plus** (⊠ Independence Dr., St. John's ☎ 268/462–2453) offers rentals, which run about $15 a day. Everything from racing models to mountain bikes is available.

BOATING Antigua's circular geographic configuration makes boating easy, while its many lovely harbors and coves provide splendid anchorages. Experienced boaters will particularly enjoy Antigua's east coast, which is far more rugged and has several islets; be sure to get a good nautical map, as there are numerous minireefs that can be treacherous. If you're just looking for a couple of hours of wave hopping, stick to the Dickenson Bay or Jolly Harbour area. **Nicholson Yacht Charters** (☎ 268/460–1530 or 800/662–6066 ⊕ www.nicholson-charters.com) are real professionals, true pioneers in Caribbean sailing, with three generations of experience. A long-established island family, they can offer you anything from a 20-foot ketch to a giant schooner. **Sunsail Club Colonna** (☎ 268/462–6263 or 800/327–2276 ⊕ www.sunsail.com) has an extensive modern fleet of dinghies and 32-foot day sailers available (call ahead, as resort guests have priority) for $25 per half-day, $50 for a full day. They also arrange bareboat yachting, often in conjunction with hotel stays.

DIVING Antigua is an unsung diving destination, with plentiful undersea sights to explore, from coral canyons to sea caves. Barbuda alone features roughly 200 wrecks on its treacherous reefs. The most accessible wreck is the 1890s bark *Andes,* not far out in Deep Bay, off Five Islands Peninsula. Among the favorite sites are **Green Island, Cades Reef,** and **Bird Island** (a national park). Memorable sightings include turtles, stingrays, and barracuda darting amid basalt walls, hulking boulders, and stray 17th-century anchors and cannon. One advantage is accessibility in many spots for shore divers and snorkelers. Double-tank dives run about $90.

Big John's Dive Antigua (⊠ Rex Halcyon Cove Beach Resort, Dickenson Bay ☎ 268/462–3483 ⊕ www.diveantigua.com) offers certification courses and day and night dives. Advantages include the central location, knowledgeable crew, satellite technology sounding the day's best dive sites, free drinks after dives, and exceptionally priced packages. Drawbacks include generally noisy groups and inconsistent maintenance (less safety than hygiene concerns) now that John doesn't personally supervise trips. **Dockyard Divers** (⊠ Nelson's Dockyard, English Harbour ☎ 268/460–1178), owned by British ex-merchant seaman Capt. A. G.

"Tony" Fincham, is one of the island's most established outfits and offers diving and snorkeling trips, PADI courses, and dive packages with accommodations. They're geared to seasoned divers, but staff work patiently with novices.

FISHING
Antigua's waters teem with such game fish as marlin, wahoo, and tuna. Most boat trips include equipment, lunch, and drinks. Figure at least $400 for a half-day, $600 for a full day, for up to six people. The 45-foot Hatteras Sportfisherman *Obsession* (☎ 268/462–2824) has top-of-the-line equipment, including an international-standard fighting chair, outriggers, and handcrafted rods. *Overdraft* (☎ 268/464–4954 or 268/462–3112 ⊕ www.antiguafishing.com) is a sleek, spacious fiberglass 40-footer outfitted with the latest techno-gadgetry and operated by Frank Hart, a professional fisherman who knows the waters intimately and regales clients with stories of his trade.

GOLF
Though Antigua hardly qualifies as a duffer's delight, its two 18-hole courses offer varied layouts. **Cedar Valley Golf Club** (✉ Friar's Hill ☎ 268/462–0161), northeast of St. John's, has a par-70, 6,157-yard, 18-hole course. The bland, not terribly well-maintained terrain offers some challenge with tight hilly fairways and numerous doglegs. The 5th hole has exceptional vistas from the top of the tee, while the 9th offers the trickiest design. Greens fees are $45, $35 off-season; carts are $30, $15 off-season. **Jolly Harbour Golf Course** (✉ Jolly Harbour ☎ 268/462–3085 or 268/462–7771 ⊕ www.jollyharbourantigua.com) is a par-71, 6,001-yard, 18-hole course designed by Karl Litten. The layout is hilly and lushly tropical, with seven lakes adding to the challenge. Unfortunately, drainage is poor, upkeep spotty, and the pro shop and "19th hole" barely adequate. At least it's reasonable: greens fees are $50 ($85 including cart).

HORSEBACK RIDING
Comparatively dry Antigua is best for beach rides, though you won't find anything wildly romantic and deserted à la *The Black Stallion*. **Spring Hill Riding Club** (✉ Falmouth ☎ 268/460–7787 or 268/460–1333 ⊕ www.springhillridingclub.com) really specializes in equestrian lessons in show jumping and dressage but also offers $40 to $60 trail rides on the beach or through the bush past ruined forts; half-hour private lessons from a British Horse Society instructor are $25.

SAILING & SNORKELING
Not a sailor yourself? Consider signing up for one of the following boat tours. Each tour provides a great opportunity to enjoy the seafaring life while someone else captains the ship.

Miguel's Holiday Adventures (☎ 268/460–9978 or 268/723–7418 ⊕ www.pricklypearisland.com) leaves every Tuesday, Thursday, and Saturday morning at 10 AM from the Hodges Bay jetty for snorkeling, rum punches, and lunch at Prickly Pear Island, which offers both shallow- and deepwater snorkeling. In this comfortable family operation, Miguel's wife, Josephine, prepares an authentic, lavish West Indian buffet including lobster, while Miguel and his son Terrence are caring instructors. **Tropical Adventures** (☎ 268/462–2064 or 268/480–1225 ⊕ www.tropicalad.com) operates Barbuda day trips on the catamaran *Excellence* that overflow with rum and high spirits, as do circumnavigations of Antigua. The company also operates slightly more sedate, intimate catamaran cruises on the *Tiami*. **Wadadli Cats** (☎ 268/462–4792 ⊕ www.wadadlicats.com) offers several cruises, including a circumnavigation of the island and snorkeling at Bird Island or Cades Reef, on its three sleek catamarans, including the handsome, fully outfitted *Spirit of Antigua*. Prices are fair, and advance bookers get a free T-shirt.

TENNIS & SQUASH Most larger resorts have their own tennis courts, but guests have top priority. **BBR Sportive Complex** (⊠ Jolly Harbour ☎ 268/462–6260) offers two clay and two Astroturf courts, instruction, and a squash court. Its lively Steely Bar offers happy hours, theme buffet dinners, and occasional live entertainment or karaoke. **Carlisle Bay** (⊠ Old Road St., St. Mary's ☎ 268/484–0000) has nine lighted courts and an impressive pro shop and roster of instructors; nonguests can occasionally book court time. The **Temo Sports Complex** (⊠ Falmouth Bay ☎ 268/463–6376 or 268/460–1781) has four floodlighted, synthetic-grass tennis courts and two glass-backed squash courts.

WINDSURFING & KITEBOARDING Most major hotels offer windsurfing equipment. The best areas are Nonsuch Bay and the east coast (notably Half Moon and Willoughby bays), which is slightly less protected and has a challenging juxtaposition of sudden calms and gusts. **H2O** (⊠ Dutchman's Bay ☎ 268/562–3933 or 268/462–3094 for Lord Nelson Hotel ⊕ www.h2oantigua.com) offers state-of-the-art equipment and instruction; however, the entire outfit was for sale at this writing. The bay, replete with a man-made reef, is safe yet permits some challenge for the more experienced, who can also board at adjacent Jabberwock Beach, where winds are onshore rather than cross-on. Many people spend the day hanging out at the adjacent Lord Nelson Hotel beach bar, an excellent source for additional information. **KiteAntigua** (⊠ Jabberwock Beach ☎ 268/460–3414 or 268/727–3983 ⊕ www.kiteantigua.com) offers lessons in the Caribbean's hot new sport, kite boarding, where a futuristic surfboard with harness is propelled only by an inflated kite, and has kite-board rentals (for the certified). The varied lesson packages are expensive but thorough. KiteAntigua closes from September through November, when winds aren't optimal. The center is on a stretch near the airport, but road trips to secret spots are arranged for experienced kite surfers seeking that sometimes harrowing "high."

Shopping

Antigua's duty-free shops are at Heritage Quay, one reason so many cruise ships call here. Bargains can be found on perfumes, liqueurs, and liquor (including, of course, Antiguan rum), jewelry, china, and crystal. As for other local items, look for straw hats, baskets, batik, pottery, and hand-printed cotton clothing.

Areas

Redcliffe Quay, on the waterfront at the south edge of St. John's, is by far the most appealing shopping area. Several restaurants and more than 30 boutiques, many with one-of-a-kind wares, are set around landscaped courtyards shaded by colorful trees. **Heritage Quay,** in St. John's, has 35 shops—including many that are duty-free—that cater to the cruise-ship crowd, which docks almost at its doorstep. Outlets here include Benetton, the Body Shop, Sunglass Hut, Dolce and Gabbana, and Oshkosh B'Gosh. There are also shops along **St. John's, St. Mary's, High,** and **Long streets.** The tangerine-and-lilac-hue four-story **Vendor's Mall** at the intersection of Redcliffe and Thames streets gathers the pushy, pesky vendors that once clogged the narrow streets. It's jammed with stalls; air-conditioned indoor shops sell some higher-price, if not higher-quality, merchandise. On the west coast the Mediterranean-style, arcaded **Jolly Harbour Villa Resort & Marina** holds some interesting galleries and shops.

Specialty Items

ALCOHOL & TOBACCO
Manuel Dias Liquor Store (✉ Long and Market Sts., St. John's ☎ 268/462–0490) has a wide selection of Caribbean rums and liqueurs. **Quin Farara** (✉ Long St. and Corn Alley, St. John's ☎ 268/462–0463 ✉ Heritage Quay, St. John's ☎ 268/462–1737 ✉ Jolly Harbour ☎ 268/462–6245) has terrific deals on both hard liquor and wines as well as cigars.

ART
Fine Art Framing (✉ Redcliffe Quay, St. John's ☎ 268/562–1019) carries Jennifer Meranto's incomparable hand-colored black-and-white photos of Caribbean scenes; Heather Doram's exquisite, intricately
★ woven "collage" wall hangings; and ever-changing exhibits. **Harmony Hall** (✉ Brown's Mill Bay, Brown's Mill ☎ 268/460–4120) remains Antigua's top exhibition space. **Island Arts Galleries** (✉ Aiton Pl. at Sandy La., Hodges Bay ☎ 268/461–6324 ✉ Heritage Quay, St. John's ☎ 268/462–2787), run by artist-filmmaker Nick Maley, showcases artists from throughout the Caribbean, including such local notables as Gilly Gobinet and Jan Farara. The art naïf pieces and genre paintings of local life often have a raw, elemental power. Call first to ensure that Nick is around; he tells fascinating anecdotes about his helping to create Yoda from *Star Wars.*

BOOKS & MAGAZINES
The **Best of Books** (✉ Benjie's Mall, Redcliffe St., St. John's ☎ 268/562–3198) is an excellent source for everything from local cookbooks and nature guides to international newspapers. **Map Shop** (✉ St. Mary's St., St. John's ☎ 268/462–3993) has a "must" buy for those interested in Antiguan life: the paperback *To Shoot Hard Labour: The Life and Times of Samuel Smith, an Antiguan Workingman.* Also check out any of the books of Jamaica Kincaid, whose writing about her native Antigua has won international acclaim. The shop also offers a fine assortment of books on Caribbean cuisine, flora, fauna, and history.

CLOTHING
Exotic Antigua (✉ Redcliffe Quay, St. John's ☎ 268/562–1288) sells everything from antique Indonesian *ikat* throws to crêpe de chine caf-
★ tans to Tommy Bahama resort wear. At **Galley Boutique** (✉ Nelson's Dockyard, English Harbour ☎ 268/460–1525), Janey Easton personally seeks out exclusive creations from both international (Calvin Klein, Adrienne Vittadini) and local Caribbean designers, ranging from swimwear to evening garb. She also sells handicrafts and lovely hammocks. **Jacaranda** (✉ Redcliffe Quay, St. John's ☎ 268/462–1888) sells batik, sarongs, and swimwear as well as Caribbean food, perfumes, soaps, and artwork. **Jingjok**

(✉ Coolidge ☎ 268/462–2372), near the airport, sells gorgeously hued, handmade batik linen and cotton resort wear. **New Gates** (✉ Redcliffe Quay, St. John's ☎ 268/562–1627) is a duty-free authorized dealer for such name brands as Ralph Lauren, Calvin Klein, and Tommy Hilfiger. **Noreen Phillips** (✉ Redcliffe Quay, St. John's ☎ 268/462–3127) creates glitzy appliquéd and beaded evening wear—inspired by the colors of the sea and sunset—in sensuous fabrics ranging from chiffon and silk to Italian lace and Indian brocade. **Sunseakers** (✉ Heritage Quay, St. John's ☎ 268/462–3618) racks up every conceivable bathing suit and cover-up—from bikini thongs to sarongs—by top designers.

DUTY-FREE GOODS **Abbott's** (✉ Heritage Quay, St. John's ☎ 268/462–3108) sells luxury items from Breitling watches to Belleek china to Kosta Boda art glass in a luxurious, air-conditioned showroom. **Lipstick** (✉ Heritage Quay, St. John's ☎ 268/562–1133) imports high-priced scents and cosmetics, from Clarins to Clinique and Givenchy to Guerlain.

HANDICRAFTS **Cedars Pottery** (✉ St. Claire Estate, Buckleys ☎ 268/460–5293) is the
★ airy studio of Michael and Imogen Hunt. Michael produces a vivid line of domestic ware and Zen-simple teapots, vases, and water fountains featuring rich earth hues and sensuous lines. Imogen fashions ethereal paper-clay fish sculptures, and mask-shape, intricately laced light fixtures and candelabras. **Eureka** (✉ Thames St., St. John's ☎ 268/560–3654) spans the globe, from Azerbaijani handblown glass to Zambian weavings and carvings. **Isis** (✉ Redcliffe Quay, St. John's ☎ 268/462–4602) sells island and international bric-a-brac, such as antique jewelry, hand-carved walking sticks, and glazed pottery. The **Pottery Shop** (✉ Redcliffe Quay, St. John's ☎ 268/562–1264 or 268/462–9503) sells the work of gifted potter Sarah Fuller, whose hand-painted tiles,
★ wind chimes, and plates and cobalt-blue glazes are striking. **Rhythm of Blue Gallery** (✉ Dockyard Drive, English Harbour ☎ 268/460–1614 or 268/562–2230) is co-owned by Nancy Nicholson, who's renowned for her exquisite glazed and matte-finish ceramics, featuring Caribbean-pure shades, as well as her black-and-white yachting photos. Partner Michael "Scrim" Strzalkowski is noted for his intricate, delicate scrimshaw and original silver jewelry.

JEWELRY **Colombian Emeralds** (✉ Heritage Quay, St. John's ☎ 268/462–3462) is the largest retailer of Colombian emeralds in the world and also carries a wide variety of other gems. **Diamonds International** (✉ Heritage Quay, St. John's ☎ 268/481–1880) has a huge selection of loose diamonds as well as a variety of rings, brooches, bracelets, and pendants.
★ Several resorts have branches. The **Goldsmitty** (✉ Redcliffe Quay, St. John's ☎ 268/462–4601) is Hans Smit, an expert goldsmith who turns gold, black coral, and precious and semiprecious stones into one-of-a-kind works of art.

Nightlife & the Arts

Most of Antigua's evening entertainment takes place at the resorts, which occasionally present calypso singers, steel bands, limbo dancers, and folkloric groups. Check with the tourist office for up-to-date information.

Nightlife

BARS It's always a party at busy bright trattoria **Abracadabra** (✉ Nelson's Dockyard, English Harbour ☎ 268/460–2701). Late nights often turn into a disco with live music or DJs spinning reggae and 1980s dance music,
★ while special events run from masquerades to fashion shows. **beach** (✉ Dickenson Bay ☎ 268/480–6940) is a sophisticated-funky combination of casual beach bar, lounge, and bistro (with Asian-Euro fusion cuisine), all daubed in sexy reds and hung with striking photographs of local scenes. **Bikini's** (✉ Runaway Bay ☎ 268/562–5566) is a funky place that attracts world-renowned cricketers as well as a jovial crowd for liberal happy hours; late-night, dirt-cheap burgers and pizza; live bands weekends; and dirty dancing on the sand. **Castaways** (✉ Jolly Harbour ☎ 268/562–4445) is a boisterous beach bar-bistro with a thatched roof and colorful local murals that serves an inexpensive menu of tapas and pub grub along with occasional entertainment. The French fare is incidental at **HQ₂** (✉ Nelson's Dockyard, English Harbour ☎ 268/562–2563), whose plush lounge outfitted with cushy sofas and crystal chandeliers
★ hosts slinky jazz combos and pianists. **Indigo on the Beach** (✉ Carlisle Bay, Old Road ☎ 268/480–0000) is a soigné yet relaxed spot any time of day for creative tapas, salads, grills, and burgers, but the beautiful people turn out in force come evening to pose at the fiber-optically lit bar or on white lounges scattered with apricot and ecru throw pillows. The **Inn at English Harbour Bar** (✉ English Harbour ☎ 268/460–1014), with its green leather, wood beams, fieldstone walls, 19th-century maps, and maritime prints, is uncommonly refined. The **Mainbrace Pub** (✉ Copper & Lumber Store Hotel, English Harbour ☎ 268/460–1058) has a historic ambience, though it's really more of a beer, darts, and fish-and-chips kind of hangout for the boating set. The **Mad Mongoose** (✉ Falmouth Harbour ☎ 268/463–7900) is a wildly popular yachty (and singles) joint, splashed in vivid Rasta colors, with tapas and martini menus,
★ live music Tuesdays and Fridays, a game room, and satellite TV. **Shirley Heights Lookout** (✉ Shirley Heights ☎ 268/460–1785) hosts Sunday-afternoon barbecues that continue into the night with reggae, soca, and steel-band music and dancing that sizzle like the ribs on the grill. Residents and visitors gather for boisterous fun, the latest gossip, and great sunsets. Most tourist groups vanish by 7 PM, when the real partying be-
★ gins. **Trappa's** (✉ Main Rd., English Harbour ☎ 268/562–3534) is a hipster hangout set in a bamboo-walled courtyard amid a virtual jungle of greenery. It serves delectable, sizable tapas (tuna sashimi, deep-fried Brie with black-currant jelly, Thai mango chicken curry, seafood pizzetta) for reasonable prices (EC$20–EC$35) into the wee hours. Live music is often on the menu.

CASINOS There are three full casinos on Antigua, as well as several holes-in-the-wall that have mostly one-arm bandits. Hours depend on the season,
★ so it's best to inquire upon your arrival. **Grand Princess Casino** (✉ Jolly Harbour ☎ 268/562–9900) occupies slick, three-story digs combining English colonial and Mediterranean revival elements. You can find abundant slots and gaming tables at the somewhat dilapidated, unintentionally retro (icicle chandeliers, Naugahyde seats, and 1970s soul crooners on the sound system), smoky **King's Casino** (✉ Heritage Quay,

St. John's ☎ 268/462–1727). The best time to go is Friday nights, which jump with energetic karaoke competitions, live bands, and dancing. The **St. James's Club** (✉ Mamora Bay ☎ 268/463–1113) has a small but opulent casino, while the adjacent Jacaranda Bar features a handsome men's-clubby ambience: English plantocracy meets Bond.

DANCE CLUBS **18 Karat** (✉ Lower Church St., St. John's ☎ 268/562–1858) attracts a casually swanky over-21 crowd for rollicking island sounds and the latest in techno and house; the courtyard restaurant is a favored meeting place for Antigua's young elite. A wildly mixed crowd frequents **Liquid** (✉ Grand Princess Casino, Jolly Harbour ☎ 268/562–9900) for its equally sizzling sound system and singles scene and for its cool decor done up in blood red and black, with hallucinogenic sky murals. **Rush** (✉ Runaway Bay ☎ 268/562–7874) lures mostly young, lively locals in cool club gear or snazzy attire for disco, Latin, and reggae-soca mixes, sea views from the romantic terrace, and the Conors Billiards Lounge (which opens earlier, with happy hours and pub grub).

Exploring Antigua

Hotels provide free island maps, but you should get your bearings before heading out on the road. Street names aren't listed (except in St. John's), though *some* easy-to-spot signs lead the way to major restaurants and resorts. Locals generally give directions in terms of landmarks (turn left at the yellow house, or right at the big tree). Wear a swimsuit under your clothes—one of the sights to strike your fancy might be a secluded beach.

Numbers in the margin correspond to points of interest on the Antigua & Barbuda map.

WHAT TO SEE **Barbuda.** This flat, 62-square-mi (161-square-km) coral atoll—with 17
★ ⑫ mi (27 km) of gleaming white-sand beaches (sand is the island's main export)—is 26 mi (42 km) north of Antigua. Most of the island's 1,200 people live in Codrington. Nesting terns, turtles, and frigate birds outnumber residents at least 10 to 1. Goats, guinea fowl, deer, and wild boar roam the roads, all fair game for local kitchens. A few very basic efficiencies exist, but most visitors stay overnight at one of the three deluxe resorts: the Beach House, Coco Point Lodge, or K Club. Pink Beach lures beachcombers, a bird sanctuary attracts ornithologists, caves and sinkholes filled with rain forest or underground pools (containing rare, even unique crustacean species) attract spelunkers, while reefs and roughly 200 offshore wrecks draw divers and snorkelers. Barbuda's sole historic ruin is the 18th-century, cylindrical, 56-foot-tall **Martello Tower,** which was probably a lighthouse built by the Spaniards prior to English occupation. The **Frigate Bird Sanctuary,** a wide mangrove-filled lagoon, is home to an estimated 400 species of birds, including frigate birds with 8-foot wingspans. Your hotel can make arrangements.

You can fly to Barbuda from Antigua on Carib Aviation, a 15-minute flight, or go by boat on *Barbuda Express,* although despite the catamaran's innovative wave-cutting design and its friendly experienced crew,

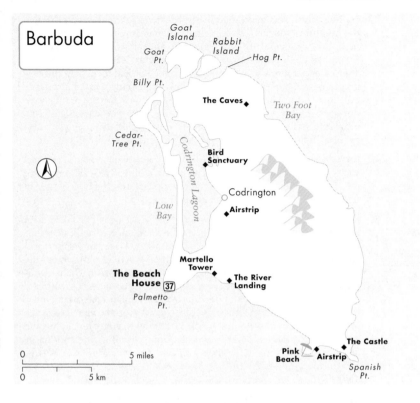

the 95-minute ride is extremely bumpy ("a chiropractor's nightmare—or fantasy," quipped one passenger). Day-trips by air are arranged by D&J Tours (see ⇨ Tour Options *in* Antigua Essentials).

❾ Betty's Hope. Just outside the village of Pares, a marked dirt road leads to Antigua's first sugar plantation, founded in 1650. You can tour the twin windmills, various ruins, still-functional crushing machinery, and the visitor center's exhibits on the island's sugar era. The private trust overseeing the restoration has yet to realize its ambitious, environmentally aware plans to replant indigenous crops destroyed by the extensive sugarcane plantings. ⊠ *Pares* ☎ *268/462–1469* ⊕ *www. antiguamuseums.org* ✉ *$2* ⊘ *Tues.–Sat.10–4.*

❿ Devil's Bridge. This limestone arch formation, sculpted by the crashing breakers of the Atlantic at Indian Town, is a national park. Blowholes have been carved by the hissing, spitting surf. The park also encompasses some archaeological excavations of Carib artifacts.

❺ Falmouth. This town sits on a lovely bay backed by former sugar plantations and sugar mills. The most important historic site here is St. Paul's Church, which was rebuilt on the site of a church once used by troops during the Nelson period.

❸ **Fig Tree Drive.** This often muddy, rutted, steep road takes you through the rain forest, which is rich in mangoes, pineapples, and banana trees (*fig* is the Antiguan word for "banana"). The rain-forest area is the hilliest part of the island—Boggy Peak, to the west, is the highest point, at 1,319 feet. At its crest, Elaine Francis sells seasonal local fruit juices—ginger, guava, sorrel, passion fruit—and homemade jams at a stall she dubs the Culture Shop. A few houses down (look for the orange windows) is the atelier of noted island artist Sallie Harker (shimmering seascapes and vividly hued fish incorporating gold leaf). You can also pass through several tranquil villages with charming churches.

❹ **Fort George.** East of Liberta—one of the first settlements founded by freed slaves—on Monk's Hill, this fort was built from 1689 to 1720. Among the ruins are the sites for 32 cannons, water cisterns, the base of the old flagstaff, and some of the original buildings.

❽ **Harmony Hall.** Northeast of Freetown (follow the signs), this delightful
Fodor'sChoice art gallery–cum–restaurant is built on the foundation of a 17th-century
★ sugar-plantation greathouse. Artists Graham Davis and Peter and Annabella Proudlock co-founded the original Jamaican outpost, but the Antigua operation is co-owned and run by an enterprising Italian couple who added a superb restaurant and charming cottages to an already enchanting spot. A large exhibit space is used for one-person shows; other rooms display works in various media, from Aussie aboriginal carvings to Antillean pottery. Allot the whole afternoon to enjoy lunch, browse through the exhibits, comb the beach, and perhaps even snorkel at nearby Green Island. ⊠ *Brown's Mill Bay, Brown's Mill* ☎ *268/463–8657 or 268/460–4120* ⊕ *www.harmonyhall.com* ⊗ *Mid-Nov.–June, daily 10–6.*

❷ **Megaliths of Greencastle Hill.** It's an arduous climb to these eerie rock slabs in the south-central part of the island. Some say the megaliths were set up by early inhabitants for their worship of the sun and moon or as devices for measuring time astronomically; others believe they're nothing more than unusual geological formations.

❻ **Nelson's Dockyard.** Antigua's most famous attraction is the world's only
Fodor'sChoice Georgian-era dockyard still in use, a treasure trove for history buffs and
★ nautical nuts alike. In 1671 the governor of the Leeward Islands wrote to the Council for Foreign Plantations in London, pointing out the advantages of this landlocked harbor. By 1704 English Harbour was in regular use as a garrisoned station.

In 1784 26-year-old Horatio Nelson sailed in on the HMS *Boreas* to serve as captain and second-in-command of the Leeward Island Station. Under him was the captain of the HMS *Pegasus,* Prince William Henry, duke of Clarence, who was later crowned King William IV. The prince acted as best man when Nelson married Fannie Nisbet on Nevis in 1787.

When the Royal Navy abandoned the station at English Harbour in 1889, it fell into a state of decay, though adventuresome yachties still lived there in near-primitive conditions. The Society of the Friends of English Harbour began restoring it in 1951; it reopened with great fanfare as Nelson's Dockyard, November 14, 1961. Within the compound are crafts shops, restaurants, and two splendidly restored 18th-century hotels, the Admiral's Inn and the Copper & Lumber Store Hotel, worth peeking into. (The latter, occupying a supply store for Nelson's Caribbean fleet, is a particularly fine example of Georgian architecture and has an interior courtyard evoking Old England.) The Dockyard is a hub for ocean-going yachts and serves as headquarters for the annual Sailing Week Regatta. Water taxis will ferry you between points for EC$5. The Dockyard National Park also includes serene nature trails accessing beaches, rock pools, and crumbling plantation ruins and hilltop forts.

The **Dockyard Museum,** in the original Naval Officer's House, presents ship models, mock-ups of English Harbour, displays on the people who worked there and typical ships that docked, silver regatta trophies, maps, prints, antique navigational instruments, and Nelson's very own telescope and tea caddy. ⊠ *English Harbour* ☎ *268/481–5022 or 268/ 463–1060, 268/481–5028 for the National Parks Department* ⊕ *www. antiguamuseums.org* ✉ *$2 suggested donation* ☉ *Daily 8–5.*

NEED A BREAK?

The restaurant at the **Admiral's Inn** (⊠ Nelson's Dockyard, English Harbour ☎ 268/460–1027) is a must for Anglophiles and mariners. Soak up the centuries at the inside bar, where 18th-century sailors reputedly carved their ships' names on the dark timbers. Most diners sit on the flagstone terrace under shady Australian gums to enjoy the views of the harbor complex; yachts seem close enough to eavesdrop. Specialties include pumpkin soup and fresh snapper with equally fresh limes.

⓫ Parham. This sleepy village is a splendid example of a traditional colonial settlement. St. Peter's Church, built in 1840 by English architect Thomas Weekes, is an octagonal Italianate building with unusual ribbed wooden ceiling, whose facade is richly decorated with stucco and keystone work, though it suffered considerable damage during an 1843 earthquake.

➊ St. John's. Antigua's capital, with some 45,000 inhabitants (approximately half the island's population), lies at sea level at the inland end of a sheltered northwestern bay. Although it has seen better days, a couple of notable historic sights and some good waterfront shopping areas make it worth a visit. Signs at the **Museum of Antigua & Barbuda** say PLEASE TOUCH, encouraging you to explore Antigua's past. Try your hand at the educational video games or squeeze a cassava through a *matapi* (grass sieve). Exhibits interpret the nation's history, from its geological birth to its political independence in 1981. There are fossil and coral remains from some 34 million years ago; models of a sugar plantation and a wattle-and-daub house; an Arawak canoe; and a wildly eclectic assortment of objects from cannonballs to 1920s telephone exchanges. The museum occupies the former courthouse, which dates from 1750. The superlative museum gift shop carries such unusual items as calabash purses, seed earrings, and lignum vitae pipes, as well as historic maps and local books (including engrossing, detailed monographs on varied subjects by longtime resident, Desmond Nicholson). ⊠ *Church and Market Sts.*

☎ 268/462–1469 ⊕ *www.antiguamuseums.org* 🖃 *$2 suggested donation* ⊙ *Sun.–Thurs. 8:30–4, Fri. 8:30–3, Sat. 10–2.*

At the south gate of the **Anglican Cathedral of St. John the Divine** are figures of St. John the Baptist and St. John the Divine said to have been taken from one of Napoléon's ships and brought to Antigua. The original church was built in 1681, replaced by a stone building in 1745, and destroyed by an earthquake in 1843. The present neo-Baroque building dates from 1845; the parishioners had the interior completely encased in pitch pine, hoping to forestall future earthquake damage. The church attained cathedral status in 1848. Tombstones bear eerily eloquent testament to the colonial days. ⊠ *Between Long and Newgate Sts.* ☎ *268/461–0082.*

Shopaholics head directly for **Heritage Quay,** an ugly multimillion-dollar complex. The two-story buildings contain stores that sell duty-free goods, sportswear, T-shirts, down-island imports (paintings, T-shirts, straw baskets), and local crafts. There are also restaurants, a bandstand, and a casino. Cruise-ship passengers disembark here from the 500-foot-long pier. Expect heavy shilling. ⊠ *High and Thames Sts.*

Redcliffe Quay, at the water's edge just south of Heritage Quay, is the most appealing part of St. John's. Attractively restored (and superbly re-created) buildings in a riot of cotton-candy colors house shops, restaurants, and boutiques and are linked by courtyards and landscaped walkways. At the far south end of town, where Market Street forks into Valley and All Saints roads, haggling goes on every Friday and Saturday, when locals jam the **Public Market** to buy and sell fruits, vegetables, fish, and spices. Ask before you aim a camera; your subject may expect a tip. This is old-time Caribbean shopping, a jambalaya of sights, sounds, and smells.

❼ **Shirley Heights.** This bluff affords a spectacular view of English Harbour. The heights are named for Sir Thomas Shirley, the governor who fortified the harbor in 1787. At the top is Shirley Heights Lookout, a restaurant built into the remnants of the 18th-century fortifications. Most notable for its boisterous Sunday barbecues that continue into the night with live music and dancing, it serves dependable burgers, pumpkin soup, grilled meats, and rum punches. Not far from Shirley Heights is the **Dows Hill Interpretation Centre,** where observation platforms provide still more sensational vistas of the English Harbour area. A multimedia sound-and-light presentation on island history and culture, spotlighting lifelike figures and colorful tableaux accompanied by running commentary and music, results in a cheery, if bland, portrait of Antiguan life from Amerindian times to the present. ☎ *268/460–2777 for National Parks Authority* 🖃 *EC$15* ⊙ *Daily 9–5.*

ANTIGUA ESSENTIALS

To research prices, get advice from other travelers, and book travel arrangements, visit www.fodors.com.

Transportation

BY AIR

American Airlines has daily direct service from New York and Miami. American Eagle has several daily flights from San Juan. Continental Airlines offers nonstop service from Newark and Miami. Delta Airlines schedules twice-weekly flights from Atlanta in high season. USAirways offers direct service from Baltimore and Philadelphia. Air Canada has nonstop service from Toronto. British Airways has daily nonstop service from London, as does Virgin Atlantic. BWIA has nonstop service from New York, Miami, and Toronto. Carib Aviation flies daily to Barbuda, as well as to neighboring islands. LIAT has daily flights to and from many other Caribbean islands. Antigua-based Caribbean Star promises a "whole new altitude" with daily flights to and from several islands, as well as Miami and San Juan.

Charter flights to Barbuda from Antigua on Carib Aviation cost $60 per person. However, daily seven-seater charter flights are often booked well in advance or canceled without sufficient bookings.

🚩 Airline Information **American Airlines/ American Eagle** ☎ 268/462-0950. **Air Canada** ☎ 268/462-1147. **British Airways** ☎ 268/462-0876. **BWIA** ☎ 268/480-2925 or 268/462-3101. **Carib Aviation** ☎ 268/462-3147 or 268/481-2900 ⊕ www.candoo.com/carib. **Caribbean Star** ☎ 268/480-2591 ⊕ www.flycaribbeanstar.com. **Continental Airlines** ☎ 268/462-5355. **Delta Airlines** ☎ 800/532-4777. **LIAT** ☎ 268/480-5600. **US Airways** ☎ 268/480-5700 **Virgin Atlantic** ☎ 268/560-2079.

🚩 Airport Information **V. C. Bird International Airport** ☎ 268/462-4672 or 268/462-0358.

BY BOAT & FERRY

Barbuda Express runs five days a week (call for the changing schedule), leaving Antigua's Heritage Quay Ferry Dock. The fare is EC$80 one-way, EC$140 round-trip (a day tour costs US$120).

🚩 **Barbuda Express** ☎ 268/560-7989, 268/460-0059, or 268/724-7027 ⊕ www.antiguaferries.com.

BY CAR

If you are staying on Dickenson Bay, in and around English Harbour, or at an all-inclusive resort, you may not want to rent a car. But if you plan to dine out, then one may be a necessity, since taxi rates can mount up quickly. To rent a car, you need a valid driver's license and a temporary permit ($20), available through the rental agent. Costs start about $50 per day in season, with unlimited mileage, though you may get a better rate if you rent for several days. Most agencies offer automatic, stick-shift, and right- and left-hand drive. Four-wheel-drive vehicles ($55 per day) will get you more places and are refreshingly open; they are also useful because so many roads are full of potholes.

Gasoline in Antigua tends to be more expensive than in the continental United States. The main roads, by and large, are in good condition, although there are bronco-busting dirt stretches leading to some more remote locations and a few hilly areas that flood easily and become impassable for a day or two. Driving is on the left, although many locals drive in the middle—or think nothing of stopping at the roadside to chat. Don't be flustered by honking: it's the Caribbean version of hello.

🚩 **Avis** ☎ 268/462-2840. **Budget** ☎ 268/462-3009. **Dollar** ☎ 268/462-0362. **Hertz** ☎ 268/481-4440. **Thrifty** ☎ 268/462-9532.

BY TAXI

Taxis are unmetered, and although fares mount up quickly, rates are fixed (your driver should have a rate card). Some cabbies may take you from St. John's to English Harbour and wait for a "reasonable" amount of time (about a half hour) while you look around, for about $50. You can always call a cab from the St. John's taxi stand.

🚩 St. John's taxi stand ☎ 268/462-5190, 268/460-5353 for 24-hour service.

Contacts & Resources

BANKS & EXCHANGE SERVICES

American dollars are readily accepted, although you can usually receive change in EC dollars, so it's really your call as to whether or not you exchange any currency. It's certainly not necessary if you are staying in an all-inclusive resort. The local currency is the Eastern Caribbean dollar (EC$), which is tied to the U.S. dollar and fluctuates only slightly. US$1 is worth approximately EC$2.70; you get a slightly better rate if you exchange money at a bank than at your hotel. Several island banks have ATMs.

Most hotels, restaurants, and duty-free shops take major credit cards; all accept traveler's checks. ATMs (dispensing EC$) are available at the island's banks and at the airport.

Prices quoted throughout this chapter are in U.S. dollars unless otherwise indicated.

🚩 **Bank of Antigua** ⊠ High and Thames Sts. ☎ 268/480-5300. **First Caribbean International Bank** ⊠ High St. ☎ 268/480-5000.

BUSINESS HOURS

Banks have varying hours but are generally open Monday through Thursday from 8 to 1 and 3 to 5, Friday 8 to noon and 3 to 5. Although some stores still follow the tradition of closing for lunch, most are open Monday through Saturday from 9 to 5, especially in season; if a cruise ship is in port, shops in Heritage and Redcliffe Quays are likely to open Sunday.

ELECTRICITY

Antigua runs on 110 volts, allowing use of most small North American appliances.

Outlets are both two- and three-pronged, so bring an adapter.

EMBASSIES & CONSULATES

🚩 United Kingdom **British High Commission** ⊠ 11 Old Parham Rd., St. John's ☎ 268/462-0008 or 268/562-2124 ⊕ www.fco.gov.uk. 🚩 United States **United States Consulate** ⊠ Hospital Hill, Pigeon Point, English Harbour ☎ 268/463-6531 🖷 268/460-1569 ⊕ usembassy.state.gov.

EMERGENCIES

🚩 Ambulance & Fire **Ambulance** ☎ 268/462-0251. **Fire** ☎ 268/462-0044.
🚩 Hospitals **Holberton Hospital** ⊠ Hospital Rd., St. John's ☎ 268/462-0251.
🚩 Pharmacies **City Pharmacy** ⊠ St. Mary's St., St. John's ☎ 268/480-3314. **Woods Pharmacy** ⊠ Woods Centre, Friar's Hill Rd., St. John's ☎ 268/462-9287.
🚩 Police **Police assistance** ☎ 268/462-0125.

HOLIDAYS

Public holidays are New Year's Day, Good Friday (usually late Mar.–Apr.), Easter Sunday and Monday (usually late Mar.–Apr.), Labour Day (1st Mon. in May), Whitmonday (usually late May or early June), Independence Day (Nov. 1), Christmas Day, and Boxing Day (Dec. 26).

INTERNET, MAIL & SHIPPING

Most hotels offer some kind of Internet service; if yours doesn't, the front desk should be able to direct you to one of the small Internet cafés In St. John's, Jolly Harbour, or English Harbour (the operations move around quite a bit).

Airmail letters to North America cost EC$1.50; postcards, EC75¢. Letters to the United Kingdom cost EC$1.50; postcards EC75¢. Letters to Australia and New Zealand are EC$1.80, postcards EC90¢. The main post office is at the foot of High Street in St. John's. Note that there are no postal codes; when addressing letters to the island, you need only indicate the address and "Antigua, West Indies."

2

PASSPORT REQUIREMENTS

U.S. citizens must carry a valid passport starting on January 1, 2007. Canadian citizens need proof of identity. A birth certificate is acceptable, provided it has a raised seal and has been issued by a county or state (not a hospital) and provided that you also have some type of photo identification, such as a driver's license. All others need passports. All visitors must present a return or ongoing ticket.

SAFETY

Throughout the Caribbean, incidents of petty theft are increasing. Leave your valuables in the hotel safe-deposit box; don't leave them unattended in your room, on a beach, or in a rental car. Also, the streets of St. John's are fairly deserted at night, so it's not a good idea to wander about alone.

TAXES & SERVICE CHARGES

The departure tax is $20, payable in cash only—either U.S. or EC currency. Hotels collect an 8½% government room tax; some restaurants will add a 7% tax. Hotels and restaurants also usually add a 10% service charge to your bill.

TELEPHONES

GSM tri-band mobile phones from the U.S. and U.K. usually work on Antigua; you can also rent one from Cable & Wireless and APUA (Antigua Public Utilities Authority), though service is occasionally spotty and tariffs can mount up. Basic rental costs range between EC$25 and EC$50 per day (you can buy a SIM card and top it up with regular phone cards), with a EC$300 refundable deposit; typical calls to the U.S. range between $1.25 and $2 per minute, but you'll certainly save on local calls.

Most hotels have direct-dial phones; other hotels can easily make connections through the switchboard. You can use the Cable & Wireless Phone Card (available in $5, $10, and $20 denominations in most hotels and post offices) for local and long-distance calls. Phone-card phones work much better than the regular coin-operated phones. To place a local call, simply dial the local seven-digit number. To call Antigua from the United States, dial 1 + 268 + the local seven-digit number.

To call the United States and Canada, dial 1 + the area code + the seven-digit number, or use the phone card or one of the "CALL USA" phones, which are available at several locations, including the airport departure lounge, the cruise terminal at St. John's, and the English Harbour Marina. These take credit cards and, supposedly, calling cards (though Cable & Wireless tacks on a fee).

🚩 **Cable & Wireless** ✉ Woods Centre, St. John's ☎ 268/480-2628 or 269/480-2636 ✉ Long St., St. John's ☎ 268/480-4236 ⊕ www.cwmobile.com or www.cwantigua.com. **APUA** ✉ St. John's ☎ 268/727-2782 ✉ English Harbour ☎ 268/562-3147 ⊕ www.apua.ag

TIPPING

In restaurants it's customary to leave 5% beyond the regular service charge added to your bill if you're pleased with the service. Taxi drivers expect a 10% tip, porters and bellmen about $1 per bag. Maids are rarely tipped, but if you think the service exemplary, figure $2 to $3 per night. Staff at all-inclusives aren't supposed to be tipped unless they've truly gone out of their way.

TOUR OPTIONS

Almost all taxi drivers double as guides, and you can arrange an island tour with one for about $25 an hour. Every major hotel has a cabbie on call and may be able to negotiate a discount, particularly off-season. Several operators specialize in off-road 4x4 adventures that provide a taste of island history and topography. Jolly Harbour–based Caribbean Helicopters offers bird's-eye views both of the island and of Montserrat's ruins and still simmering volcano. Trips last anywhere from 15 to 45 minutes; prices run $80 to $200. D&J Tours offers day-trippers the chance to experience Barbuda on a round-trip flight with a beach picnic and full tour for $120. Estate Safari Jeep Tours explores the interior, where there are few marked trails and roads are rough. The cost (about $90 per person) includes a visit to Betty's Hope, a hike to the summit of Monk's Hill (affording sensational near-360-degree panoramas of Montserrat, Guadeloupe, and English Harbor and Falmouth Harbor), a botanical walk through the rain forest, and lunch and snorkeling at a secluded beach. Four-wheel off-road adventures by Island Safaris enable you to fully appreciate the island's natural beauty, history, folklore, and cultural heritage as they zoom about the southwest part of Antigua. Hiking is involved, though it's not strenuous. Lunch and snorkeling are also included. Active adventurers will particularly enjoy the combo Land Rover/kayak outback ecotour. Prices start at $85 per person. Suntours, by far the most professional outfit on Antigua, gives half- and full-day island tours that focus on such highlights as Shirley Heights and English Harbour. Suntours is also the island's American Express representative.

🛈 **Caribbean Helicopters** ☎ 268/460-5900 ⊕ www.caribbeanhelicopters.com **D&J Tours** ☎ 268/773-9766 **Estate Safari Jeep Tours** ☎ 268/463-4713 Four-wheel off-road adventures by Island Safaris ☎ 268/480-1225 ⊕ www.tropicalad.com **Suntours** ✉ Long and Thames sts., St. John's ☎ 268/462-4788.

VISITOR INFORMATION

🛈 Before You Leave **Antigua & Barbuda Tourist Offices** ⊕ www.antigua-barbuda.org or www.barbudaful.net ✉ 610 5th Ave., Suite 311, New York, NY 10020 ☎ 212/541-4117 or 888/268-4227 ✉ 25 S.E. 2nd Ave., Suite 300, Miami, FL 33131

☎ 305/381-6762 ✉ 60 St. Clair Ave. E, Suite 304, Toronto, Ontario, Canada, M4T 1N5 ☎ 416/961-3085 ✉ Antigua House, 15 Thayer St., London, U.K., W1U 3JT ☎ 0207/486-7073.

🛈 In Antigua **Antigua & Barbuda Department of Tourism** ✉ Nevis St. and Friendly Alley, St. John's ☎ 268/463-0125 or 268/462-0480 📠 268/462-2483. **Antigua Hotels & Tourist Association** ✉ Newgate St., St. John's ☎ 268/462-0374.

WEDDINGS

Wedding planning is relatively simple in Antigua; most hotels can help with the arrangements, and many offer complete wedding packages (from flowers to catering to videography). No minimum residency or blood test is required for adults 18 and over. Visit the Ministry of Legal Affairs on the outskirts of St. John's any weekday to pay the license application fee of $150. Bring valid passports as proof of citizenship and, in the case of previous marriages, the original divorce or annulment decree; widows or widowers should present the original marriage and death certificates. Then visit the Registrar General's office in downtown St. John's and get a marriage certificate for $10. If you plan a civil ceremony at the courthouse, there's an additional registration fee of $40; if you marry anywhere else, you must pay the Marriage Officer $50. If you prefer a church ceremony, you must receive permission from the clerical authorities. Wherever the marriage occurs, you'll need two or more witnesses to sign the marriage certificate.

🛈 **Ministry of Legal Affairs** ✉ Queen Elizabeth Hwy., St. John's ☎ 268/462-0017. **Registrar General** ✉ High St., at Lower Thames St., St. John's ☎ 268/462-0609.

Aruba

Windsurfing

WORD OF MOUTH

"If you want a guarantee of sun, Aruba is it . . . though the "gentle breezes" they advertise are really better described as constant wind. If you have a high maintenance hair-do this is not the place for you!"
—Ann

"Aruba is dry . . . but the beaches, the water, the weather, are all beautiful . . . Too hot? Just get some shade as the . . . trade winds will keep you comfortable. Don't worry about your "doo," just have fun."
—Lee

WELCOME TO ARUBA

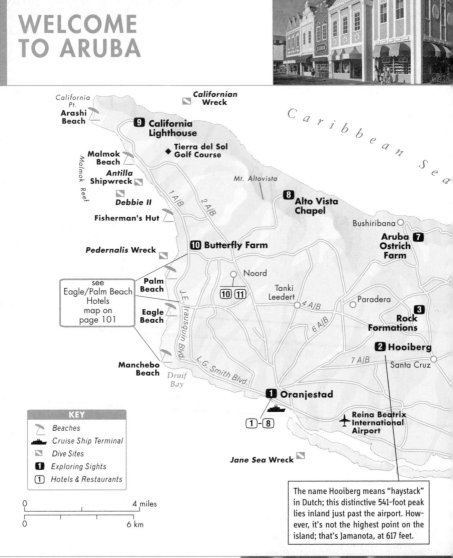

California Pt.
California Wreck

Arashi Beach

9 **California Lighthouse**

◆ **Tierra del Sol Golf Course**

Malmok Beach

Antilla Shipwreck

Malmok Reef

Mt. Altovista

8 **Alto Vista Chapel**

Bushiribana

Aruba Ostrich Farm 7

Debbie II

1 A/B

2 A/B

Fisherman's Hut

Pedernalis Wreck

10 **Butterfly Farm**

Noord

see Eagle/Palm Beach Hotels map on page 101

Palm Beach

10 11

Tanki Leedert

4 A/B

Paradera

6 A/B

Rock Formations 3

Eagle Beach

J.E. Irausquin Blvd.

2 **Hooiberg**

7 A/B

Santa Cruz

Manchebo Beach

Druif Bay

L.G. Smith Blvd.

1 **Oranjestad**

1 - 8

✈ **Reina Beatrix International Airport**

Caribbean Sea

KEY
- ⬎ Beaches
- 🚢 Cruise Ship Terminal
- ◪ Dive Sites
- 1 Exploring Sights
- 1 Hotels & Restaurants

```
0                    4 miles
0                    6 km
```

Jane Sea Wreck

The name Hooiberg means "haystack" in Dutch; this distinctive 541-foot peak lies inland just past the airport. However, it's not the highest point on the island; that's Jamanota, at 617 feet.

The pastel-colored houses of Dutch settlers still grace the waterfront in the capital city of Oranjestad. Winds are fierce, even savage, on the north coast, where you'll find a landscape of cacti, rocky desert, and wind-bent divi-divi trees. On the west coast the steady breezes attract windsurfers to the shallow, richly colored waters.

THE A IN THE ABC ISLANDS

The A in the ABC Islands (the other two being Bonaire and Curaçao), Aruba is small—only 19½ mi (31½ km) long and 6 mi (9½ km) across at its widest point. It became an independent entity within the Netherlands in 1986. The official language is Dutch, but almost every native speaks English and Spanish as well. The island's population is 72,000.

3

ARUBA

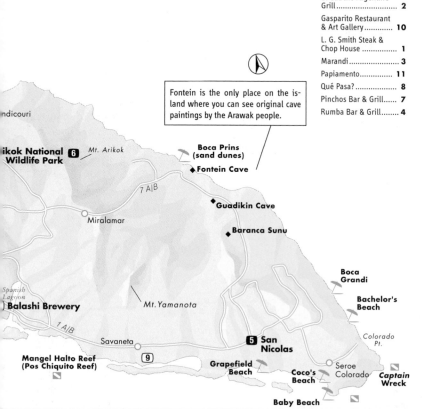

Fontein is the only place on the island where you can see original cave paintings by the Arawak people.

TOP 4 REASONS TO VISIT ARUBA

① Nightlife is among the best in the Caribbean. The colorful Kukoo Kunuku party bus picks you up and pours you out at your hotel.

② Powder-soft beaches and turquoise waters are legendary.

③ Great restaurants offer a wide range of cuisine as good as any in the Caribbean.

④ Aruba's casinos aren't as glitzy as their Las Vegas rivals, but they will please both casual and serious gamblers.

ARUBA PLANNER

Getting to Aruba

Many airlines fly nonstop to Aruba from North America, and if you need to make connections, it will usually be at a U.S. airport. You can also fly nonstop from Amsterdam if you are coming from Europe. Smaller airlines connect the Dutch islands in the Caribbean, often using Aruba as a hub.

The island's state-of-the-art Reina Beatrix International Airport (AUA) is equipped with thorough security, many flight displays, and state-of-the-art baggage handling systems. Travelers to the United States clear U.S. Customs and Immigration before leaving Aruba, so you should allow a little extra time going home.

Hassle Factor: Low

On the Ground

A taxi from the airport to most hotels takes about 20 minutes. It will cost about $17 to get to the hotels along Eagle Beach, $19 to the high-rise hotels on Palm Beach, and $10 to the hotels downtown. Few hotels offer a shuttle, but if you've booked an air/hotel package, your transfer is often included in your package price.

Renting a Car

If you want to explore the countryside at your leisure and try different beaches, then you should rent a car, but for just getting to and around town taxis are preferable, and you can use tour companies to arrange your activities. If you rent, try to make reservations before arriving, and rent a four-wheel-drive vehicle if you plan to explore the island's natural sights.

Activities

Soft, sandy **beaches** and turquoise waters are the biggest draw in Aruba. They are often crowded, particularly the best stretches of Eagle Beach, which is the island's—and perhaps one of the Caribbean's—finest. Baby Beach, on the east end of the island, is also good. But the island also comes alive by night and has

become a true **party hotspot**; casinos—though not as elaborate as those in Las Vegas—are among the best of any Caribbean island. **Restaurants** are very good, though sometimes expensive. **Diving** is good in Aruba, if not as spectacular as in nearby Bonaire. The island has two **golf courses**, but neither is

particularly wonderful, and the constantly blowing wind can be a problem for golfers. What's not good for golfers, though, is a boon for **windsurfers**, who have discovered that the combination of consistent breezes and tranquil, protected waters on the southwestern coast are ideal conditions for the sport. Aruba isn't

a good destination if you want to escape from it all as it is well-developed. But it still has a largely undeveloped region in **Arikok National Park**, the destination of choice for those wishing to hike and explore some wild terrain.

Where to Stay

Almost all of the resorts are along the island's southwest coast, along L.G. Smith and J.E. Irausquin boulevards, with the larger high-rise properties being farther away from Oranjestad. A few budget places are in Oranjestad itself. Since virtually all the hotels are right along the same lovely stretches of Palm and Eagle beaches, think carefully about whether your chosen resort has the atmosphere you are looking for. It's the resort, rather than its location, that's going to be a bigger factor in how you enjoy your vacation.

TYPES OF LODGINGS

Large resorts: These all-encompassing vacation destinations offer myriad dining options, casinos, shops, water-sports centers, health clubs, and car-rental desks. Few of these resorts include anything (even breakfast) in their rates. The island has only a handful of all-inclusives.	**Time-shares:** Large time-share properties are cropping up in greater numbers, luring visitors who prefer to prepare some of their own meals and have a bit more living space than you might find in the typical resort hotel room.	**Boutique Resorts:** You'll find a few small resorts that offer more personal service. Though they don't always offer the same level of luxury as the larger places—and certainly don't offer the wide range of amenities—smaller resorts are better suited to the natural sense of Aruban hospitality you'll find all over the island.

When to Go

Aruba's popularity means that hotels are usually booked solid during the high season from late November through May, so early booking is essential. During other times of the year, rate reductions can be dramatic. Aruba doesn't really have a rainy season and rarely sees a hurricane, so you take fewer chances by coming here during the late summer and fall.

February or March witnesses a spectacular **Carnival**, a riot of color whirling to the tunes of steel bands and culminating in the Grand Parade, where some of the floats rival the extravagance of those in the Big Easy's Mardi Gras.

Hotel & Restaurant Costs

Assume that hotels operate on the European Plan (**EP**—with no meals) unless we specify that they use either the Continental Plan (**CP**—with a Continental breakfast), Breakfast Plan (**BP**—with full breakfast), or the Modified American Plan (**MAP**—with breakfast and dinner). Other hotels may offer the Full American Plan (**FAP**—including all meals but no drinks) or may be All-Inclusive (**AI**—with all meals, drinks, and most activities).

WHAT IT COSTS in Dollars				
	$$$$	**$$$**	**$$**	**$**	**¢**
Restaurants	over $30	$20–$30	$12–$20	$8–$12	under $8
Hotels*	over $350	$250–$350	$150–$250	$80–$150	under $80
Hotels**	over $450	$350–$450	$250–$350	$125–$250	under $125

*EP, BP, CP   **AI, FAP, MAP
Restaurant prices are for a main course excluding the customary 10%–15% service charge. Hotel prices are for two people in a double room in high season excluding 8% tax, typical 11% service charge, and meal plans (except all-inclusive resorts).

By Vernon
O'Reilly-
Ramesar

EVERY EVENING THEY COME TO SIT BY THE SHORE to await the sunset: a family of six visiting from some distant land. During the day the parents may have been dining in style or perhaps laughing a couple of hours away as they gambled a few dollars in the glitzy casinos downtown. The kids may have been snorkeling or diving, or perhaps were driving an ATV across the arid, moonlike surface of the northern coast. The evening, though, is the time when they all come together as a family to see the sun dip down below water. In the tangerine light of another Aruba sunset, they hug and laugh, six happy silhouettes against the Caribbean sky.

Cruise ships gleam in Oranjestad Harbour. Thousands of eager tourists scavenge through souvenir stalls looking for the perfect memento. The mile-long stretch of L. G. Smith Boulevard is lined with cafés, designer stores, and signs for the latest Vegas-style show. The countryside is dotted with colorful *cunucu*-style houses and small neighborhood shops. Suddenly, the rocky desert landscape is startlingly austere.

Aruba offers an amazingly diverse experience in a small package. Tourists flock here for the sunny climate, perfect waters, and excellent beaches, so much so that the area around beautiful Eagle Beach is an almost unbroken line of hotels, restaurants, and bars. Here on the south coast, the action is nonstop both day and night. However, the fiercely rugged north coast is a desolate and rocky landscape that has resisted development.

Aruba is the smallest of the ABC islands—only 193 square km (120 square mi) in area—with Curaçao and Bonaire rounding out the trio. In 1986, after much lobbying, Aruba separated from the rest of the Netherlands Antilles to become a separate part of the Kingdom of the Netherlands. Perhaps the separation came so easily because there is so little Dutch presence on the island. The small population of 72,000 is of mainly mixed extraction, and many people show distinct traces of some Amerindian ancestry.

As with Bonaire and Curaçao, the island was originally populated by the Caquetio, an Amerindian people related to the Arawak. After the Spanish conquered the island in 1499, Aruba was basically left alone, since it held little agricultural or mineral appeal. The Dutch took charge of the island in 1636, and things remained relatively quiet until gold was discovered in the 1800s. Mining dominated the economy until the early part of the 20th century, when the mines became unsustainable. Shortly thereafter, Aruba became home to a major oil-refining operation, which was the economic mainstay until the early 1990s, when its contribution to the local economy was eclipsed by tourism.

Like the trademark *watapana* (divi-divi) trees that have been forced into bonsailike angles by the constant trade winds, Aruba has always adjusted to changes in the economic climate. Realizing that tourism was a valuable opportunity, Aruba has worked on developing the sector to the point where it has now overtaken oil as the island's primary source of income. Having been resolutely dedicated to tourism for so many years, the Aruban national culture and tourism industry are now inextricably intertwined.

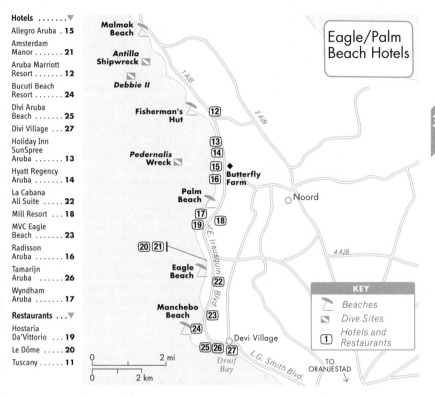

Eagle/Palm Beach Hotels

KEY
- Beaches
- Dive Sites
- Hotels and Restaurants

With more than half a million visitors a year, Aruba is not a destination that will appeal to those trying to avoid the beaten path. Instead, you should visit Aruba if you're looking for a nice climate, excellent facilities, lots of nightlife, and no surprises. The U.S. dollar is accepted everywhere, and English is spoken universally—this makes Aruba a popular spot for Americans who want an overseas trip to a place that doesn't feel foreign. In fact, Americans go through U.S. customs right at the airport in Aruba, so there are no formalities on landing in the United States.

Where to Stay

Hotels on the island are categorized as low-rise or high-rise and are grouped in two distinct areas along L. G. Smith and J. E. Irausquin boulevards north of Oranjestad. The low-rise properties are closer to the capital, the high-rises in a swath a little farther north. Hotel rates, with the exception of those at a few all-inclusives, do not generally include meals or even breakfast. The larger resorts feel like destinations unto themselves and come complete with shopping, entertainment, and casinos. Several hotels now offer Wi-Fi service, so if you need to stay in touch, consider these hotels and bring your laptop.

★ **$$$$** ⊡ **Aruba Marriott Resort & Stellaris Casino.** The gentle sound of the surf and splashing waterfalls compete for your attention in this sprawling compound, where everything seems to run smoothly, right down to the details. A spacious lobby leads either to gardens or to a chic shopping arcade and casino. Rooms are spacious (the largest on the island) with massive balconies; most have ocean views, and all have walk-in closets. Suites are even more expansive and have hot tubs. Some of the best dinner shows on the island are held at Wave's Beach Bar & Grill, which is also the perfect place to enjoy the sunset. ⊠ *L. G. Smith Blvd. 101, Palm Beach* ☎ *297/586–9000 or 800/223–6388* ⊟ *297/586–0649* ⊕ *www. marriott.com* ⇌ *375 rooms, 35 suites* ⅋ *5 restaurants, café, in-room safes, minibars, cable TV with movies, in-room VCRs, in-room broadband, in-room data ports, Wi-Fi, 2 tennis courts, pool, health club, hair salon, massage, saunas, spa, beach, dive shop, windsurfing, boating, jet skiing, volleyball, 4 bars, lobby lounge, casino, shops, concierge, meeting rooms, car rental* ⊟ *AE, D, DC, MC, V* ⊶ *EP.*

★ **$$$$** ⊡ **Hyatt Regency Aruba Beach Resort & Casino.** This 12-acre resort offers everything from a casino for adults to waterslides for kids, so it's popular with both honeymooners and families and is big enough that there are still some quietly romantic corners. The sand-color high-rise building is topped by a distinctive hacienda-style roof, and interconnected pools flow through the compound and end in an ornamental lagoon. Rooms are well equipped, but the balconies are rather small. There's no lack of activities for adults, as the resort offers horseback riding, water sports, tennis, and a highly regarded spa. Kids' programs are extensive as well. The restaurants are very good, most notably Ruinas del Mar, which serves fresh seafood with a Continental flair. ⊠ *J. E. Irausquin Blvd. 85, Palm Beach* ☎ *297/586–1234 or 800/554–9288* ⊟ *297/586– 5478* ⊕ *www.aruba.hyatt.com* ⇌ *342 rooms, 18 suites* ⅋ *5 restaurants, snack bar, room service, fans, in-room safes, minibars, cable TV with movies, 2 tennis courts, pool, health club, hair salon, 2 outdoor hot tubs, massage, sauna, spa, steam room, beach, dive shop, dock, snorkeling, windsurfing, boating, jet skiing, waterskiing, basketball, horseback riding, volleyball, 5 bars, casino, shops, babysitting, children's programs (ages 3–12), playground, concierge, Internet room, business services, car rental, travel services* ⊟ *AE, D, DC, MC, V* ⊶ *EP.*

$$$$ ⊡ **Allegro Aruba Resort & Casino.** Allegro resorts tend to be party centers, and this is no exception. Buoyed by the limitless benefits of all-inclusive drinks and activities, guests here are an animated bunch. Some sort of contest is always going on near the pool. Rooms are colorful and offer all the basic comforts needed for relaxing after a hard day of carousing. Kids are kept well occupied during the day by the children's program, allowing the adults to seek other diversions, including a range of water sports. The hotel underwent a major renovation in late 2004, so all rooms are in excellent shape. ⊠ *J. E. Irausquin Blvd. 83, Palm Beach* ☎ *297/586–4500 or 800/858–2258* ⊟ *297/586–3191* ⊕ *www. occidentalhotels.com* ⇌ *403 rooms, 14 suites* ⅋ *3 restaurants, in-room safes, cable TV with movies, 2 tennis courts, pool, gym, 2 outdoor hot* *tubs, beach, snorkeling, boating, waterskiing, Ping-Pong, volleyball, 3 bars, casino, dance club, shops, children's programs (ages 4–12), Internet room, meeting rooms* ▤ *AE, D, DC, MC, V* ⑩ *AI.*

★ **$$$$** ▦ **Radisson Aruba Resort & Casino.** Luxury is the key word at this 14-acre resort. Rooms are lavishly equipped and furnished with colonial West Indian–style furniture, including four-poster beds. Large balconies look out onto either ocean views or the tropical gardens. The pools are top notch, and even though there's a comprehensive children's program—not to mention a large family contingent—peace and quiet are not hard to find in this resort. The fitness center is dazzling, and the spa is the perfect place to unwind from the stresses of everyday life. ⊠ *J. E. Irausquin Blvd. 81, Palm Beach* ☎ *297/586–6555* 📠 *297/586–3260* ⊕ *www.radisson.com* 🛏 *358 rooms, 32 suites* ⚐ *4 restaurants, room service, in-room safes, minibars, cable TV with movies, Wi-Fi, golf privileges, 2 tennis courts, 2 pools, health club, spa, beach, dive shop, snorkeling, boating, jet skiing, 3 bars, video game rooms, babysitting, children's programs (ages 5–12), dry cleaning, laundry service, Internet room, business services, convention center, meeting rooms* ▤ *AE, D, DC, MC, V* ⑩ *BP.*

$$$–$$$$ ▦ **Divi Village Golf & Beach Resort.** The newest of the midsize Divi resorts focuses on golf, and although it's just across the road from its sister properties, the atmosphere at this all-suite version is much quieter and more refined. Another difference is the pricing structure; base rates are not all-inclusive, though AI plans that allow you to dine at the Divi Aruba and Tamarijn are available for an additional cost. Suites are massive and include kitchens; the beach is across the road. Those seeking the ultimate in luxury can book one of the golf villas that overlook the golf course and have private rooftop Jacuzzis. Happily, the hotel grounds are as lush and as well maintained as the 9-hole golf course, and regardless of the meal plan, you get to use the facilities of all Divi resorts on Aruba. ⊠ *J. E. Irausquin Blvd. 93, Oranjestad* ☎ *297/583–5000* 📠 *297/582–0501* ⊕ *www.divivillage.com* 🛏 *250 suites* ⚐ *3 restaurants, room service, kitchens, cable TV, in-room data ports, Web TV, 9-hole golf course, 3 tennis courts, pro shop, 3 pools, boating, jet skiing, 2 bars, car rental* ▤ *AE, D, DC, MC, V* ⚲ *3-night minimum* ⑩ *EP.*

★ **$$$–$$$$** ▦ **Renaissance Aruba Resort & Casino.** This downtown hotel consists of two distinct parts: the Renaissance Marina Hotel and the Renaissance Ocean Suites. Standard rooms are in the marina section, which is on Oranjestad's main drag and overlooks the harbor. The Ocean Suite rooms are larger and have separate living areas and kitchenettes. The main hotel pool actually juts out 25 feet above L. G. Smith Boulevard. Rooms here are spacious and well appointed, but some overlook the six-floor atrium filled with restaurants and stores. A 40-acre island just offshore has the only private beaches in Aruba and is reserved for hotel guests (the boat to the island leaves from the hotel lobby). Most restaurants in the attached Seaport Mall allow diners to sign for their meals. ⊠ *L. G. Smith Blvd. 82, Oranjestad* ☎ *297/583–6000 or 800/421–8188* 📠 *297/582–5317* ⊕ *www.renaissancearuba.com* 🛏 *291 rooms, 268* *suites ⅃ 5 restaurants, room service, some kitchenettes, minibars, cable TV with movies, tennis court, 3 pools, 2 gyms, spa, beach, dive shop, snorkeling, marina, fishing, volleyball, 5 bars, 2 casinos, nightclub, video game room, shops, children's programs (ages 5–12), playground, laundry facilities, concierge, Internet room, convention center, meeting rooms, no-smoking rooms ⊟ AE, D, DC, MC, V ⫸ EP.*

♻ **$$$** 🖾 **La Cabana All Suite Beach Resort & Casino.** Despite the name, this is not a charming little collection of huts but rather a massive complex of self-contained units across from Eagle Beach. Rooms have every imaginable home comfort, including hot tubs. A third of the suites have ocean views. Unfortunately, the resort has the feel of a large urban apartment block, and most common facilities, including the pools, are permanently crowded and usually noisy. An excellent children's program called Club Cabana Nana makes this a popular choice for families, but those not fond of masses of children should avoid this hotel completely ⊠ *J. E. Irausquin Blvd. 250, Eagle Beach* ☎ *297/587–9000 or 800/835–7193* 🖨 *297/587–0844* ⊕ *www.lacabana.com* ⇰ *811 suites* ⅃ *4 restaurants, café, grocery, ice cream parlor, pizzeria, in-room safes, kitchenettes, microwaves, cable TV, 5 tennis courts, 3 pools, health club, 3 outdoor hot tubs, spa, dive shop, basketball, racquetball, shuffleboard, squash, volleyball, 4 bars, video game room, shops, children's programs (ages 5–12), playground, Internet room, meeting rooms* ⊟ *AE, D, DC, MC, V* ⫸ *EP.*

★ **$$$** 🖾 **Wyndham Aruba Beach Resort & Casino.** Come to the Wyndham for pampering and impeccable service, both of which are in plentiful supply. The attention to detail even extends poolside, where attendants offer guests Evian spritzes and CD players. Rooms are not as large as those at some other resorts but are beautifully furnished with plentiful wood accents. The grand public spaces are always decorated with floral displays. Diversions are readily available in the casino and at the spa. The Scirocco Lounge is a fine place to end an evening over glamorous cocktails. The hotel's cabaret show, "One Night in Havana," is well worth seeing even if you aren't staying here. Although it isn't cheap, the hotel offers good value for a luxury hotel by Aruba standards. ⊠ *J. E. Irausquin Blvd. 77, Palm Beach* ☎ *297/586–4466 or 800/996–3426* 🖨 *297/586–8217* ⊕ *www.wyndham.com* ⇰ *481 rooms, 81 suites* ⅃ *8 restaurants, in-room safes, minibars, cable TV, Wi-Fi, tennis court, pool, wading pool, hair salon, 3 outdoor hot tubs, spa, beach, dive shop, snorkeling, windsurfing, boating, jet skiing, parasailing, waterskiing, 4 bars, casino, video game room, shops, concierge, Internet room, convention center* ⊟ *AE, D, DC, MC, V* ⫸ *EP.*

$$–$$$ 🖾 **Bucuti Beach Resort.** An extraordinary beach setting, impeccably understated service, and attention to detail help this elegant resort easily outclass anything else on the island. Hacienda-style buildings are surrounded by ecologically sensitive landscaping that suits the island's desertlike environment. Rooms are done in cool creams and feature cherrywood furnishings; there's a distinctly modern and European feel to the entire place. Wireless broadband is available throughout the resort. This hotel is very popular with return visitors, so book early, as it is frequently sold out in high season. ⊠ *L. G. Smith Blvd. 55B, Eagle*

FodorśChoice
★

Beach ☎ 297/583–1100 🖷 297/582–5272 ⊕ *www.bucuti.com* 🖙 *97 rooms, 39 suites, 12 huts* △ *Restaurant, grocery, fans, in-room safes, minibars, microwaves, refrigerators, cable TV, pool, beach, bicycles, 2 bars, shop, laundry facilities, Internet room, business services, travel services* ⊟ *AE, D, DC, MC, V* 🍴 *CP.*

☪ **$$–$$$** 🖼 **Divi Aruba Beach Resort Mega All Inclusive.** The main advantage to this small resort is that it offers a variety of room types along with the privilege of using the facilities of the adjoining Tamarijn Resort. The beachfront lanais offer the best combination of privacy and views. Because the crowd here can get quite animated—especially with free margaritas so readily available—rooms overlooking the main pool are best avoided. The "Mega" concept allows guests to dine and use the facilities at sister properties. Better yet, children under 18 stay free when accompanied by two adults, and the kids' camp even offers Papiamento lessons. The beach here is gorgeous, but if you can drag yourself off the lounge chairs, it's nice to know that nonmotorized water sports are all included in the price. ⊠ *L. G. Smith Blvd. 93, Manchebo Beach* ☎ *297/582–3300 or 800/554–2008* 🖷 *297/583–1940* ⊕ *www.diviaruba.com* 🖙 *203 rooms* △ *3 restaurants, fans, refrigerators, cable TV, golf privileges, children's programs (ages 5–12), tennis court, 2 pools, gym, hair salon, outdoor hot tub, beach, dive shop, snorkeling, windsurfing, boating, waterskiing, bicycles, shuffleboard, volleyball, 2 bars, shops, babysitting, laundry service, Internet room* ⊟ *AE, D, DC, MC, V* 🍴 *AI.*

$$–$$$ 🖼 **Tamarijn Aruba All Inclusive Beach Resort.** An upscale alternative to its sister property, the Divi Aruba next door, this resort is pleasantly laid back for an all-inclusive. Guests seeking additional excitement can take a short walk along the beach to the more rambunctious sister property. Rooms feature blond-wood furnishings and ample balconies. The rate covers food, beverages, entertainment, an array of activities, and even tickets to the weekly Bon Bini Festival. A free shuttle runs to the Alhambra Casino until 3 AM. ⊠ *J. E. Irausquin Blvd. 41, Punta Brabo* ☎ *297/525–5200 or 800/554–2008* 🖷 *297/525–5203* ⊕ *www.tamarijnaruba.com* 🖙 *236 rooms* △ *3 restaurants, snack bar, fans, cable TV, golf privileges, 2 tennis courts, 2 pools, health club, beach, snorkeling, windsurfing, boating, waterskiing, fishing, bicycles, Ping-Pong, shuffleboard, volleyball, 2 bars, shops, Internet room, meeting rooms, car rental* ⊟ *AE, D, DC, MC, V* 🍴 *AI.*

$$ 🖼 **Amsterdam Manor Beach Resort.** An intimate, family-run hotel with a
FodorśChoice genuinely friendly staff and an authentic Dutch-Caribbean atmosphere,
★ this little place offers an excellent value for the money. The gabled mustard-yellow hotel is built around a central courtyard with a waterfall pool and wading pool. Eagle Beach is right across the road (guests can have lunch served on the beach). The pool bar is buzzing late into the night, and Filo the bartender keeps everyone fully entertained. Tilefloor rooms range from small, simple studios (some with ocean-view balconies) to two-bedroom suites with peaked ceilings and whirlpool tubs; all have kitchenettes. The restaurant serves good, reasonably priced meals. A bank of computers near reception is free for Web junkies. ⊠ *J. E. Irausquin Blvd. 252, Eagle Beach* ☎ *297/527–1100 or 800/932–6509* 🖷 *297/527–1112* ⊕ *www.amsterdammanor.com* 🖙 *37 studios, 35*

suites ☼ *Restaurant, fans, in-room safes, kitchenettes, cable TV with movies, in-room data ports, Wi-Fi, pool, wading pool, snorkeling, 2 bars, playground, grocery, laundry facilities, Internet room, car rental, some pets allowed* ⊟ *AE, D, MC, V* �○l *EP.*

★ ☾ **$$** ⊡ **Mill Resort & Suites.** This lovely low-rise resort is deservedly popular with travelers in the know. Staff are genuinely friendly and are devoted to the needs of guests. Buildings are laid out around a busy pool and bar area. The open-air Mediterranean-style lobby has free coffee available day and night. The resort's all-inclusive plan, which can be added onto the basic room cost, allows guests the freedom to dine off-property if they wish, although the on-site restaurant is good. Wednesday night draws a crowd from across the island for the all-you-can-eat barbecue accompanied by live entertainment. The property is not on the beach, but guests get free access to the beach club at the Wyndham across the street. ✉ *J. E. Irausquin Blvd. 330, Palm Beach* ☎ *297/586–7700* 🖷 *297/586–7271* ⊕ *www.millresort.com* ♐ *64 studios, 128 suites* ☼ *Restaurant, grocery, in-room safes, some kitchens, some kitchenettes, cable TV, Wi-Fi, 2 tennis courts, 2 pools, wading pool, gym, sauna, spa, steam room, bar, babysitting, laundry facilities, Internet room, car rental, travel services* ⊟ *AE, D, DC, MC, V* ♠○l *EP.*

☾ **¢–$$** ⊡ **Holiday Inn SunSpree Aruba Beach Resort & Casino.** This popular, family-oriented package-tour hotel has three seven-story buildings filled with spacious rooms lining a sugary, palm-dotted shore. However, the pool's cascades and sundeck draw as large a crowd as the beach, where you can enjoy the Wednesday-evening cocktail party. The lobby is usually overflowing with suitcases as the throngs check in and out, so don't expect too much in the way of personalized service from the front desk or the concierge at these busy times. The SeaBreeze Grille is on the beach but has little to recommend it other than the location. The resort's free program for kids, however, is a boon for families. ✉ *J. E. Irausquin Blvd. 230, Palm Beach* ☎ *297/586–3600 or 800/465–4329* 🖷 *297/586–5165* ⊕ *www.ichotelsgroup.com* ♐ *600 rooms, 7 suites* ☼ *4 restaurants, refrigerators, cable TV with movies, Wi-Fi, 6 tennis courts, 2 pools, gym, hair salon, massage, beach, dive shop, dock, snorkeling, windsurfing, boating, waterskiing, basketball, Ping-Pong, volleyball, 3 bars, casino, video game room, shops, children's programs (ages 5–12), concierge, Internet room, meeting rooms* ⊟ *AE, DC, MC, V* ♠○l *EP.*

★ ☾ **¢–$** ⊡ **MVC Eagle Beach.** For the price and the excellent location across from Eagle Beach, this former vacation facility for the visiting families of Dutch marines is a great bargain. Most guests are still budget-minded Dutch tourists, who can live with impeccably clean but basic and simply furnished rooms. Don't come expecting the facilities of a Hilton; however, there's a tennis court, a good restaurant serving hearty fare, and a lively bar. The hotel is also well suited to the needs of families with smaller children, as there are ample play areas and a children's pool. ✉ *J. E. Irausquin Blvd. 240, Eagle Beach* ☎ *297/587–0110* 🖷 *297/587–*

3

0117 ⊕ www.mvceaglebeach.com ➷ 16 rooms, 3 suites ⅋ Restaurant, tennis court, pool, wading pool, beach, Ping-Pong, bar, playground, laundry facilities; no room TVs ▭ MC, V ⚊ EP.

Where to Eat

Aruba has many fine restaurants, so you can expect outstanding meals and international cuisine. Arubans tend to eat their main meal at lunchtime, so feel free to follow suit and save money by trying the lunch menus at the better restaurants. Be sure to try such Aruban specialties as *pan bati* (a mildly sweet bread that resembles a pancake) and *keshi yena* (a baked concoction of Gouda cheese, spices, and meat or seafood in a rich brown sauce). On Sunday you may have a hard time finding a restaurant outside a hotel that's open for lunch, and many restaurants are closed for dinner on Sunday or Monday. Reservations are essential for dinner in high season.

The **Aruba Gastronomic Association** (AGA; ⊕ www.arubadining.com) offers Dine-Around packages that allow visitors to have a three-course dinner at a number of affiliated restaurants. Restaurants listed as "VIP Members" of the AGA program are usually higher-priced establishments, and for these the plan allows for a $36 discount on dinner. A number of packages range from three dinners ($109) to seven dinners ($245) and can be ordered online.

What to Wear

Even the finest restaurants require at most a jacket for men and a sundress for women. If you plan to eat in the open air, remember to bring along insect repellent—the mosquitoes sometimes get unruly.

CARIBBEAN
$$–$$$$
✕ **Brisas del Mar.** Eating at this friendly place overlooking the sea is like dining in a private home. Old family recipes use such indigenous ingredients as the aromatic *yerbiholé* leaf (with a minty basil flavor). Try the steamy fish soup, *keri keri* (shredded fish kissed with annatto, also known as achiote), or some of the island's best pan bati. The catch of the day cooked Aruban-style (panfried and covered with creole sauce, or in garlic butter on request) has drawn a crowd for more than 20 years. Reserve early for sunset gazing on the breezy terrace. The restaurant is bus-accessible from hotels. ⊠ *Savaneta 222A, Savaneta* ☎ *297/584–7718* ▭ *AE, MC, V* ⊗ *Closed Mon.*

★ $$–$$$
✕ **Gasparito Restaurant & Art Gallery.** You can find this enchanting hideaway in a cunucu (country house) in Noord, not far from the hotels. Dine indoors, where works by local artists are showcased on softly lighted walls, or on the outdoor patio. Either way, the service is excellent. The Aruban specialties—pan bati, keshi yena—are feasts for the eye as well as the palate. The standout dish is the Gasparito chicken; the sauce recipe was passed down from the owner's ancestors and features seven special ingredients, including brandy, white wine, and pineapple juice. (The rest, they say, are secret.) AGA Dine-Around member. ⊠ *Gasparito 3, Noord* ☎ *297/586–7044* ▭ *D, MC, V* ⊗ *Closed Sun. No lunch.*

CLOSE UP

Cunucu Houses

PASTEL HOUSES surrounded by cacti fences adorn Aruba's flat, rugged *cunucu* ("country" in Papiamento). The features of these traditional houses were developed in response to the environment. Early settlers discovered that slanting roofs allowed the heat to rise and that small windows helped to keep in the cool air. Among the earliest building materials was *caliche*, a durable calcium carbonate substance found in the island's southeastern hills. Many houses were also built using interlocking coral rocks that didn't require mortar (this technique is no longer used, thanks to cement and concrete). Contemporary design combines some of the basic principles of the earlier homes with touches of modernization: windows, though still narrow, have been elongated; roofs are constructed of bright tiles; pretty patios have been added; and doorways and balconies present an ornamental face to the world beyond.

CONTEMPORARY

$–$$$

✕ **Rumba Bar & Grill.** In the heart of Oranjestad, this lively bistro has an open kitchen, where you can watch the chef prepare tasty international fare over a charcoal grill (mostly grilled seafood and beef). The presentations are fanciful, with entrées forming towering shapes over beds of colorful vegetables and sauces. You can dine on the terrace and soak up the local color, or inside, where the crowd is always worth watching. It's an AGA Dine-Around member. ✉ *Havenstraat 4, Oranjestad* ☎ *297/588–7900* ▭ *AE, D, MC, V* ☉ *Closed Sun.*

CONTINENTAL

★ **$$$$**

✕ **Chez Mathilde.** If you are looking for a cheap and cheerful meal, keep looking. Those seeking superb and imaginative French food with decor straight out of La Belle Epoque and excellent service will find their bliss here. This upscale restaurant is in one of the oldest buildings in Oranjestad and sets the standard for fine dining on the island. The obsession with authenticity here includes mango and champagne sherbet between courses to clear the palate. The wild boar and ostrich, a complex blending of flavors and textures, is a good example of the unusual flavor combinations on offer. Save room for dessert, as the chocolate soufflé is sure to cause rapture. If you are looking for more relaxed surroundings, the garden room in the back with potted palm trees and high ceilings offers an airy and bright alternative to the more traditional dining room, though the menu is usually the same. ✉ *Havenstraat 23, Oranjestad* ☎ *297/583–9200* ⬥ *Reservations essential* ▭ *AE, D, MC, V.*

★ **$$–$$$$**

✕ **Le Dôme.** Eleven thousand bricks were imported from Antwerp to add European flair to this fine dining spot. Although the ownership has changed, the fine cuisine and exquisite service have, if anything, improved. Four dining rooms are done in different themes, with the Old World and La Galerie rooms being the most atmospheric. The menu changes frequently, but scampi Le Dôme is always listed and worth ordering. The wine list includes more than 250 labels. Savor champagne with the prix-fixe Sunday brunch. AGA VIP member. ✉ *J. E. Irausquin Blvd. 224,*

Eagle Beach ☎ *297/587–1517* ⏃ *Reservations essential* ▭ *AE, D, MC, V* ⊗ *No lunch Sat.*

CUBAN
★ $–$$$

✕ **Cuba's Cookin'.** This funky little establishment is tucked away in an innocuous street downtown. Entertainment, great Cuban food, and a lively crowd are the draws here. The food is authentically Cuban. The empanadas are excellent, as is the chicken stuffed with plantains. Don't leave without trying the roast pork, which is pretty close to perfection. The signature dish is the *ropa vieja*, a sautéed flank steak served with a rich sauce. The name literally translates as "old clothes." There's always a crowd, as loyal fans and other fun-seekers usually crowd the bar area. ⊠ *Wilhelminastraat 27, Oranjestad* ☎ *297/588–0627* ▭ *AE, MC, V* ⊗ *Closed Sun.*

ECLECTIC
$$–$$$$
Fodor$Choice
★

✕ **Marandi.** With a name that means "on the water" in Malaysian, this seaside restaurant is at once cozy and chic. Everything is seductive, from the tables tucked under a giant thatched roof by the water's edge to the dining room, which is unencumbered by a ceiling. There are even couches set in a sandbox where you can enjoy a cocktail before your meal. The beef cooked in local beer with foie gras, apples, and cabbage is an unusual but tasty option. Reserve ahead, and you can dine at the chef's table, which is right in the kitchen. ⊠ *L. G. Smith Blvd. 1, Oranjestad* ☎ *297/582–0157* ▭ *MC, V* ⊗ *Closed Mon. No lunch.*

★ $$$

✕ **Papiamento.** Longtime restaurateurs Lenie and Eduardo Ellis converted their 175-year-old manor into a bistro with an atmosphere that is elegant, intimate, and always romantic. You can feast in the dining room filled with antiques or outdoors on a terrace surrounding a pool (sitting on plastic patio chairs covered in fabric). The chefs mix Continental and Caribbean cuisines to produce sumptuous seafood and meat dishes. Items cooked "on the stone" are popular as much for the drama of the sizzling stone as for the incredible aromas that envelop you when they are presented. ⊠ *Washington 61, Noord* ☎ *297/586–4544* ⏃ *Reservations essential* ▭ *AE, D, MC, V* ⊗ *Closed Sun. No lunch.*

$$–$$$

✕ **Pinchos Bar & Grill.** Built on a pier, this casual spot has the most romantic setting on the island. At night the restaurant glimmers from a distance as hundreds of lights reflect off the water. With only 11 tables, this is always an intimate dining experience. Chef Robby Peterson manages to prepare delectable meals on the grill as you watch him work his tiny kitchen. His wife and co-owner, Anabela, keeps diners comfortable and happy. The bar area is great for enjoying ocean breezes over an evening cocktail. There is live entertainment every weekend. ⊠ *L. G. Smith Blvd. 7, Oranjestad* ☎ *287/583–2666* ▭ *D, MC, V* ⊗ *Closed Mon. No lunch.*

$$–$$$

✕ **Qué Pasa?** This funky lemon-yellow eatery serves as something of an art gallery. Despite the name, there isn't a Mexican dish on the menu, which includes everything from sashimi to ribs, but everything is done with Aruban flair and is served by a helpful and friendly staff. The fish dishes are especially good. The bar area is lively and friendly. ⊠ *Wilhelminastraat 2, Oranjestad* ☎ *297/583–4888* ▭ *MC, V.*

ITALIAN
$$$–$$$$

✕ **Hostaria Da' Vittorio.** Part of the fun at this family-oriented spot is watching chef Vittorio Muscariello prepare authentic Italian regional specialties in the open kitchen. The staff helps you choose wines from the extensive list and recommends portions of hot and cold antipasti, risottos, and pastas. As you leave, pick up some *limoncello* (lemon liqueur) or olive oil at the gourmet shop. Be aware that the decibel level of the crowd is high and that this is one of the few restaurants in Aruba with a stringent dress code, so avoid jeans. A 15% gratuity is automatically added to your bill. AGA VIP member. ⊠ *L. G. Smith Blvd. 380, Palm Beach* ☎ *297/586–3838* ▤ *AE, D, MC, V.*

$$–$$$$ ✕ **Tuscany.** The personalized service, excellent wine list, carefully prepared food, and soft piano music make for a special evening at this casually elegant restaurant. The *spannochie prima donna con capellini d'angelo* (sautéed shrimp with prosciutto, shallots, wild mushrooms, and artichokes in a light grappa cream sauce on angel hair pasta) is among the many delights. Don't despair if the extensive menu doesn't feature your particular fancy—the kitchen may be up for a challenge. ⊠ *Aruba Marriott Resort & Stellaris Casino, L. G. Smith Blvd. 101, Palm Beach* ☎ *297/586–9000* ⩘ *Reservations essential* ▤ *AE, DC, MC, V* ◯ *No lunch.*

STEAK ✕ **El Gaucho Argentine Grill.** Faux-leather-bound books, tulip-top lamps,
☺ **$$–$$$$** wooden chairs, and tile floors decorate this Argentina-style steak house, which has been in business since 1977. The key here is meat served in mammoth portions (think 16-ounce steaks). A welcome new feature is a children's playroom, which allows adults to dine while the kids are entertained with videos and games. ⊠ *Wilhelminastraat 80, Oranjestad* ☎ *297/582–3677* ▤ *MC, V* ◯ *Closed Sun.*

★ **$$–$$$$** ✕ **L. G. Smith's Steak & Chop House.** A study in teak, cream, and black, this fine steak house offers some of the best beef on the island. Subdued lighting and cascading water create a pleasing atmosphere. The menu features quality cuts of meat, all superbly prepared. The view over L. G. Smith Boulevard to the harbor makes for an exceptional dining experience. The casino is steps away if you fancy a few slots after dinner. AGA VIP member. ⊠ *Renaissance Aruba Beach Resort & Casino, L. G. Smith Blvd. 82, Oranjestad* ☎ *297/523–6115* ⩘ *Reservations essential* ▤ *AE, D, DC, MC, V* ◯ *No lunch.*

Beaches

The beaches on Aruba are legendary: white sand, turquoise waters, and virtually no litter—everyone takes the NO TIRA SUSHI (no littering) signs very seriously, especially considering the island's $280 fine. The major public beaches, which back up to the hotels along the southwestern strip, are usually crowded. You can make the hour-long hike from the Holiday Inn to the Tamarijn without ever leaving sand. Make sure you're well protected from the sun—it scorches fast despite the cooling trade winds. Luckily, there's at least one covered bar (and often an ice cream stand) at virtually every hotel. On the island's northeastern side, stronger winds make the waters too choppy for swimming, but the vistas are great and the terrain is wonderful for exploring.

Arashi Beach. Just after Malmok Beach, this is a 1-km (½-mi) stretch of gleaming white sand. Although it was once rocky, nature, with a little help from humans, has turned it into an excellent place for sunbathing and swimming. Despite calm waters, the reputation for rockiness has kept most people away, making it relatively uncrowded. ⊠ *West of Malmok Beach, on the west end.*

★ ☾ **Baby Beach.** On the island's eastern tip (near the refinery), this semicircular beach borders a bay that's as placid and just about as shallow as a wading pool—perfect for tots, shore divers, and terrible swimmers. Thatched shaded areas are good for cooling off. Down the road is the island's rather unusual pet cemetery. Stop by the nearby snack truck for burgers, hot dogs, beer, and soda. The road to this beach (and several others) is through San Nicolas and along the road toward Seroe Colorado. Just before reaching the beach, keep an eye out for a strange 300-foot natural sea wall made of coral and rock that was thrown up overnight when Hurricane Ivan swept by the island in 2004. ⊠ *Near Seroe Colorado, on the east end.*

Boca Grandi. This is a great spot for windsurfers, but swimming is not advisable. It's near Seagrape Grove and the Aruba Golf Club toward the island's eastern tip. ⊠ *Near Seagrape Grove, on the east end.*

Boca Prins. You need a four-wheel-drive vehicle to make the trek here. Near the Fontein Cave and Blue Lagoon, this beach is about as large as a Brazilian bikini, but with two rocky cliffs and tumultuously crashing waves, it's as romantic as you get in Aruba. Boca Prins is famous for its backdrop of enormous vanilla sand dunes. This isn't a swimming beach, however. Bring a picnic, a beach blanket, and sturdy sneakers, and descend the rocks that form steps to the water's edge. ⊠ *Off 7 A/B, near the Fontein Cave.*

Fodor'sChoice **Eagle Beach.** On the southwestern coast, across the highway from what
★ is quickly becoming known as Time-Share Lane, is one of the Caribbean's—if not the world's—best beaches. Not long ago it was a nearly deserted stretch of pristine sand dotted with the occasional thatched picnic hut. Now that the resorts are completed, this mile-plus-long beach is always hopping. When other Caribbean beaches eroded after Hurricane Ivan in 2004, Eagle Beach actually became several feet wider. ⊠ *J. E. Irausquin Blvd., north of Manchebo Beach.*

Fisherman's Huts. Next to the Holiday Inn is a windsurfer's haven. Swimming conditions are good, too. Take a picnic lunch (tables are available) and watch the elegant purple, aqua, and orange sails struggle in the wind. ⊠ *1 A/B, at the Holiday Inn SunSpree Aruba.*

Grapefield Beach. To the southeast of San Nicolas, a sweep of blinding-white sand in the shadow of cliffs and boulders is marked by a memorial shaped like an anchor dedicated to all seamen. Pick sea grapes in high season (January to June). Swim at your own risk; the waves here can be rough. ⊠ *Southwest of San Nicolas, on the east end.*

Malmok Beach. On the northwestern shore, this small, nondescript beach (where some of Aruba's wealthiest families have built tony residences) borders shallow waters that stretch 300 yards from shore. It's the perfect place to learn to windsurf. Right off the coast here is a favorite haunt for divers and snorkelers—the wreck of the German ship *Antilla*, scuttled in 1940. Take J. E. Irausquin Boulevard to the very end of the road. ⊠ *At the end of J. E. Irausquin Blvd., Malmokweg.*

Manchebo Beach (Punta Brabo). Impressively wide, the shoreline in front of the Manchebo Beach Resort is where officials turn a blind eye to the occasional topless sunbather. This beach merges with Druif Beach, and most locals use the name Manchebo to refer to both. ⊠ *J. E. Irausquin Blvd., at the Manchebo Beach Resort.*

Palm Beach. This stretch runs from the Wyndham Aruba Beach Resort & Casino to the Marriott Aruba Ocean Club. It's the center of Aruban tourism, offering good opportunities for swimming, sailing, and other water sports. In some spots you might find a variety of shells that are great to collect but not as much fun to step on barefoot—bring sandals just in case. ⊠ *J. E. Irausquin Blvd., between the Wyndham Aruba Beach Resort and the Marriott Aruba Ocean Club.*

☺ **Rodger's Beach.** Near Baby Beach on the island's eastern tip, this is a beautiful curving stretch of sand only slightly marred by its proximity to the oil refinery at the bay's far side. Swimming conditions are excellent here, as demonstrated by the local kids diving off the piers. The snack bar at the water's edge has beach-equipment rentals and a shop. Local bands play Sunday nights from Easter through summer. Drive around the refinery perimeter to get here. ⊠ *Next to Baby Beach, on the east end.*

Sports & the Outdoors

On Aruba you can participate in every conceivable water sport, as well as play tennis and golf or go on a fine hike through Arikok National Wildlife Park.

BIKING   Pedal pushing is a great way to get around the island; the climate is perfect, and the trade winds help to keep you cool. **Melchor Cycle Rental** (⊠ Bubali 106B, Noord ☎ 297/587–1787) rents ATVs and bikes. **Rancho Notorious** (⊠ Boroncana, Noord ☎ 297/586–0508 ⊕ www.ranchonotorious.com) organizes mountain-biking tours.

DAY SAILS   If you try a cruise around the island, know that the choppy waters are stirred up by trade winds and that catamarans are much smoother than single-hull boats. Sucking on a peppermint or lemon candy may help a queasy stomach; avoid boating with an empty or overly full stomach. Moonlight cruises cost about $25 per person. There are also a variety of snorkeling, dinner and dancing, and sunset party cruises to choose from, priced from $25 to $60 per person. Many of the smaller operators work out of their homes; they often offer to pick you up (and drop you off) at your hotel or meet you at a particular hotel pier.

★ **Octopus Sailing Cruises** (⊠ Sali-a Cerca 1G, Oranjestad ☎ 297/583–3081) operates a trimaran that holds about 20 people at a time. The drinks flow freely during the three-hour afternoon sail, which costs $25. Having a captain named Jethro is almost worth the price of admission by itself. **Red Sail Sports** (⊠ J. E. Irausquin Blvd. 83, Oranjestad ☎ 297/586–1603, 877/733–7245 in U.S. ⊕ www.aruba-redsail.com) offers a number of sail packages aboard its four catamarans, including the 70-foot *Rumba*. The popular sunset sail includes drinks and a lively atmosphere for $35 per person. The dinner cruise package includes a three-course meal and open bar for $85. There are also locations at the Hyatt and Allegro. **Tranquilo Charters Aruba** (✉ Sibelius St. 25, Oranjestad ☎ 297/586–1418 ⊕ www.visitaruba.com/tranquilo), operated by Captain Hagedoorn, offers entertaining cruises, including a six-hour cruise to the south side of the island with lunch for $65. As strange as it sounds, the special "mom's Dutch pea soup" served with lunch is actually very good. Snorkeling equipment and free lessons are included in the package. **Wave Dancer Cruises** (✉ Ponton 90, Oranjestad ☎ 297/582–5520 ⊕ www.arubawavedancer.com), in business since the mid-1970s, offers excellent value for the money. Sunset sails are $25, including drinks and snacks, and half-day sails are $50, including snacks, lunch, and drinks. Snorkeling packages are also available.

DIVING &
SNORKELING

With visibility of up to 90 feet, the waters around Aruba are excellent for snorkeling and diving. Both advanced and novice divers will find plenty to occupy their time, as many of the most popular sites, including some interesting shipwrecks, are found in shallow waters ranging from 30 feet to 60 feet. Coral reefs covered with sensuously waving sea fans and eerie giant sponge tubes attract a colorful menagerie of sea life, including gliding manta rays, curious sea turtles, shy octopuses, and fish from grunts to groupers. Marine preservation is a priority on Aruba, and regulations by the Conference on International Trade in Endangered Species make it unlawful to remove coral, conch, and other marine life from the water.

Expect snorkel gear to rent for about $15 per day and trips to cost around $40. Scuba rates are around $50 for a one-tank reef or wreck dive, $65 for a two-tank dive, and $45 for a night dive. Resort courses, which offer an introduction to scuba diving, average $65 to $70. If you want to go all the way, complete open-water certification costs around $350.

The more seasoned diving crowd might check with **Aruba Pro Dive** (✉ Ponton 88, Noord ☎ 297/582–5520 ⊕ www.arubaprodive.com) for special deals. **Dax Divers** (✉ Kibaima 7, Santa Cruz ☎ 297/585–1270) has an instructor-training course. Some dives are less expensive, at $40 for 40 minutes with one tank and weights. **De Palm Watersports** (✉ L. G. Smith Blvd. 142, Oranjestad ☎ 297/582–4400 or 800/766–6016 ⊕ www.depalm.com) is one of the best choices for your undersea experience, and the options go beyond basic diving. You can don a helmet and walk along the ocean floor near De Palm Island, home of huge blue parrot fish. You can even do snuba—which is like scuba diving but without the heavy air tanks—either from a boat or from an island; it costs $55. **Dive Aruba** (✉ Williamstraat 8, Oranjestad ☎ 297/582–7337 ⊕ www.divearuba.com) offers resort courses, certification courses, and trips to interesting shipwrecks. **Mermaid Sport Divers** (✉ Manchebo Beach Resort, J. E. Irausquin Blvd. 55A, Eagle Beach ☎ 297/587–4103 ⊕ www.scubadivers-aruba.com) has dive packages with PADI-certified instructors. **Native Divers Aruba** (✉ Koyari 1, Noord ☎ 297/586–4763 ⊕ www.nativedivers.com) offers all types of dives. Underwater naturalist courses are taught by PADI-certified instructors. **Pelican Tours & Watersports** (✉ Pelican Pier, near the Holiday Inn and Playa Linda hotels, Palm Beach ☎ 297/587–2302 ⊕ www.pelican-aruba.com) has options for divers of all levels. Novices start with midmorning classes and then move to the pool to practice what they've learned; by afternoon they put their new skills to use at a shipwreck off the coast. **Red Sail Sports** (✉ J. E. Irausquin Blvd. 83, Oranjestad ☎ 297/586–1603, 877/733–7245 in U.S. ⊕ www.redsail.com) has courses for children and others new to scuba diving. An introductory class costs about $80.

FISHING   Deep-sea catches here include barracuda, kingfish, wahoo, bonito, and black-and-yellow tuna. November to April is the catch-and-release season for sailfish and marlin. Many skippered charter boats are available for half- or full-day sails. Packages include tackle, bait, and refreshments. Prices range from $250 to $450 for a half-day charter and from $400 to $600 for a full day.

Pelican Tours & Watersports (✉ Pelican Pier, near the Holiday Inn and Playa Linda hotels, Palm Beach ☎ 297/586–3271 ⊕ www.pelican-aruba.com) is not just for the surf-and-snorkel crowd; the company will help you catch trophy-size fish. **Red Sail Sports** (✉ J. E. Irausquin Blvd. 83, Oranjestad ☎ 297/586–1603, 877/733–7245 in U.S. ⊕ www.redsail.com) can arrange everything for your fishing trip. Captain Kenny of **Teaser Charters** (✉ St. Vincentweg 5, Oranjestad ☎ 297/582–5088 ⊕ www.teasercharters.com) runs a thrilling expedition. The expertise of the crew is matched by a commitment to sensible fishing practices, making this an excellent as well as enjoyable choice. The company's two boats are fully equipped, and the crew seem to have an uncanny ability to locate the best fishing spots.

GOLF   The **Aruba Golf Club** (✉ Golfweg 82, San Nicolas ☎ 297/584–2006) has a 9-hole course with 20 sand traps and five water traps, roaming goats, and lots of cacti. There are also 11 greens covered with artificial turf, making 18-hole tournaments a possibility. The clubhouse has a bar and locker rooms. Greens fees are $10 for 9 holes, $15 for 18 holes. Golf carts are available. Aruba-bound golfers can rejoice, because the **Links at Divi Aruba** (✉ J. E. Irausquin Blvd. 93, Oranjestad ☎ 297/581–4653), a 9-hole course designed by Karl Litten and Lorie Viola, opened in 2004. The par-36 course on paspalum grass (best for seaside courses) takes you past beautiful lagoons. Amenities include a golf school with professional instruction, a swing analysis station, a driving range, and a two-story golf clubhouse with a pro shop. Two restaurants are available: Windows on Aruba for fine dining and Mulligan's for a casual and quick lunch. Greens fees are $75 for 9 holes, $110 for 18 (high season); guests of the Divi Village Golf & Beach Resort pay a reduced rate. **Tierra del Sol** (✉ Malmokweg ☎ 297/586–0978), a stunning course, is on the northwest coast near the California Lighthouse. Designed by Robert Trent Jones Jr., this 18-hole championship course combines Aruba's native beauty—cacti and rock formations—with the lush greens of the world's best courses. The $133 greens fee ($70 in summer) includes a golf cart equipped with a communications system that allows you to order drinks for your return to the clubhouse. Half-day golf clinics (Monday, Tuesday, and Thursday), a bargain at $45, include lunch in the clubhouse. The pro shop is one of the Caribbean's most elegant, with an extremely attentive staff.

HIKING Despite the arid landscape, hiking the rugged countryside will give you the best opportunities to see Aruba's wildlife and flora. Arikok National Wildlife Park is an excellent place to glimpse the real Aruba free of the trappings of tourism. The heat can be oppressive, so be sure to take it easy, wear a hat, and have a bottle of water handy.

★ ♻ **Aruba Nature Sensitive Hikers** (✉ Pos Chiquito 13E, Savoneta ☎ 297/ 587–5017 ⊕ www.sensitivehikers.com) is run by Eddy Croes, a former park ranger, whose passion for the area is seemingly unbounded. Groups are never larger than eight people, so you'll see as much detail as you can handle. Expect frequent stops, when Eddy will ask for silence so that you can hear the sounds of the park. The hikes are done at an easy pace and are suitable for basically anyone.

HORSEBACK RIDING Ranches offer short jaunts along the beach or longer rides along trails passing through countryside flanked by cacti, divi-divi trees, and aloe vera plants. Ask if you can stop off at Cura di Tortuga, a natural pool that's reputed to have restorative powers. Rides are also possible in Arikok National Wildlife Park. Rates run from $25 for an hour-long trip to $65 for a three-hour tour. Private rides cost slightly more.

♻ **Rancho Daimari** (✉ Tanki Leendert 249, San Nicolas ☎ 297/587–5674 ⊕ www.visitaruba.com/ranchodaimari) will lead your horse to water— either at Natural Bridge or Natural Pool—in the morning or afternoon for $60 per person. The "Junior Dudes" program is tailored to young riders. There are even ATV trips. **Rancho Notorious** (✉ Boroncana, Noord ☎ 297/586–0508 ⊕ www.ranchonotorious.com) will take you on a tour of the countryside for $60, to the beach to snorkel for $55, or on a three-hour ride up to the California Lighthouse for $65. The company also organizes ATV and mountain-biking trips.

KAYAKING Kayaking is a popular sport on Aruba, especially along the south coast, where the waters are calm. It's a great way to explore a stretch of coastline. **Aruba Kayak Adventure** (✉ Ponton 90, Oranjestad ☎ 297/587–7722 ⊕ www.arubawavedancer.com/arubakayak) has excellent half-day kayak trips, which start with a quick lesson before you begin paddling through caves and mangroves and along the scenic coastline. The tour makes a lunch stop at De Palm Island, where snorkeling is included as part of the $77 package.

SUBMARINE EXCURSIONS Explore an underwater reef teeming with marine life without getting wet. **Atlantis Submarines** (✉ Renaissance Marina, L. G. Smith Blvd. 82, Oranjestad ☎ 297/583–6090 ⊕ www.atlantisadventures.net) operates a 65-foot air-conditioned sub, *Atlantis VI,* which takes 48 passengers 95 to 150 feet below the surface along Barcadera Reef for $84 per person. The company also owns the *Seaworld Explorer,* a semisubmersible that allows you to sit and view Aruba's marine habitat from 5 feet below the surface. Make reservations a day in advance.

WINDSURFING The southwestern coast's tranquil waters make windsurfing conditions ★ ideal for both beginners and intermediates, as the winds are steady but sudden gusts rare. Experts will find the Atlantic coast, especially around Grapefield and Boca Grandi beaches, more challenging; winds are fierce and often shift course without warning. Most operators also offer complete windsurfing vacation packages. The up-and-coming sport of kite surfing (sometimes called kite boarding) is also popular on Aruba.

Aruba Boardsailing Productions (✉ L. G. Smith Blvd. 486, near Fisherman's Huts, Palm Beach ☎ 297/586–3940 🖷 297/993–1111 ⊕ www.visitaruba.com/arubaboardsailing) is a major windsurfing center on the island. **Pelican Adventures Tours & Watersports** (✉ Pelican Pier, near Holiday Inn and Playa Linda hotels, Palm Beach ☎ 297/586–3600 ⊕ www.pelican-aruba.com) usually has boards and sails on hand. **Sailboard Vacations** (✉ L. G. Smith Blvd. 462, Malmok Beach ☎ 297/586–2527 ⊕ www.sailboardvacations.com) offers complete windsurf packages, including accommodation. Equipment can be rented for $60 a day. Trade jokes and snap photos with your fellow windsurfers at **Vela Aruba** (✉ L. G. Smith Blvd. 101, Palm Beach ☎ 297/586–9000 Ext. 6430 ⊕ www.velawindsurf.com). This is *the* place to make friends. It's a major kite-surfing center as well.

Shopping

"Duty-free" *is* a magical term in the Caribbean but not always accurate. The duty-free shopping zone in Aruba closed several years ago, so now the only true duty-free shopping is in the departure area of the airport. Passengers bound for the United States should be sure to shop before proceeding through U.S. customs in Aruba. Downtown stores often advertise "duty-free prices," and prices are sometimes discounted by as much as 25%. Comparison shopping is still advisable. Major credit cards are welcome virtually everywhere; U.S. dollars are accepted almost as readily as local currency; and traveler's checks can be cashed with proof of identity.

Aruba's souvenir and crafts stores are full of Dutch porcelains and figurines, as befits the island's heritage. Dutch cheese is a good buy (you're allowed to bring up to 10 pounds of hard cheese through U.S. customs), as are hand-embroidered linens and any products made from the native aloe vera plant—sunburn cream, face masks, or skin refreshers. Local arts and crafts run toward wood carvings and earthenware emblazoned with ARUBA: ONE HAPPY ISLAND and the like. Since there's no sales tax, the price you see on the tag is what you pay. (Note that although large stores in town and at hotels include the value-added tax of 6.5%, tiny shops and studios may add it separately.) Don't try to bargain. Arubans consider it rude to haggle, despite what you may hear to the contrary.

Areas & Malls

Oranjestad's **Caya G. F. Betico Croes** is Aruba's chief shopping street, lined with several duty-free boutiques and jewelry stores noted for the aggressiveness of their vendors on cruise-ship days.

For late-night shopping, head to the **Alhambra Casino Shopping Arcade** (✉ L. G. Smith Blvd. 47, Manchebo Beach), which is open until midnight. Souvenir shops, boutiques, and fast-food outlets fill the arcade, which is attached to the popular casino. Although small, the **Aquarius Mall** (✉ Elleboogstraat 1, Oranjestad) has some upscale shops. The **Hol-**

land **Aruba Mall** (⊠ Havenstraat 6, Oranjestad) houses a collection of smart shops and eateries. Stores at the **Port of Call Marketplace** (⊠ L. G. Smith Blvd. 17, Oranjestad) sell fine jewelry, perfumes, duty-free liquor, batiks, crystal, leather goods, and fashionable clothing. Five minutes from the cruise-ship terminal, the **Renaissance Mall** (⊠ L. G. Smith Blvd. 82, Oranjestad), also known as Seaport Mall, is where you can find the Crystal Casino. More than 120 stores sell merchandise to meet every taste and budget. The **Royal Plaza Mall** (⊠ L. G. Smith Blvd. 94, Oranjestad), across from the cruise-ship terminal, has cafés, a post office (open weekdays 8 to 3:30), and such stores as Nautica, Benetton, Tommy Hilfiger, and Gandelman Jewelers. This is where you can find the Cyber Café, where you can send e-mail and get your caffeine fix all in one stop.

Specialty Items

CLOTHING   If you're in the mood to splurge, **Agatha Boutique** (⊠ Renaissance Mall,
★   L. G. Smith Blvd. 82, Oranjestad ☎ 297/583–7965) has some high-style outfits (some up to size 18), shoes, and bags by Aruba-based New York fashion designer Agatha Brown. Sample at least one of her five signature fragrances, derived from floral and citrus scents. Agatha herself is usually on hand to help choose the perfect outfit. **Confetti** (⊠ Renaissance Mall, L. G. Smith Blvd. 82, Oranjestad ☎ 297/583–8614) has the hottest European and American swimsuits, cover-ups, and other beach
★   essentials. **Wulfsen & Wulfsen** (⊠ Caya G. F. Betico Croes 52, Oranjestad ☎ 297/582–3823) has been one of the most highly regarded clothing stores in Aruba and the Netherlands Antilles for 30 years. It carries elegant suits for men and linen cocktail dresses for women, and it's also a great place to buy Bermuda shorts.

PERFUMES   For perfumes, cosmetics, men's and women's clothing, and leather goods (including Bally shoes), stop in at **Aruba Trading Company** (⊠ Caya G. F. Betico Croes 12, Oranjestad ☎ 297/582–2602), which has been in business since the 1930s. A venerated name in Aruba, **J. L. Penha & Sons** (⊠ Caya G. F. Betico Croes 11/13, Oranjestad ☎ 297/582–4160 or 297/582–4161) sells high-end perfumes and cosmetics. It stocks such
★   brands as Boucheron, Cartier, Dior, and Givenchy. **Little Switzerland** (⊠ Caya G. F. Betico Croes 14, Oranjestad ☎ 297/582–1192 ⊠ Royal Plaza Mall, L. G. Smith Blvd. 94, Oranjestad ☎ 297/583–4057), the Caribbean retail giant, is the place to go for brand-name men's and women's fragrances as well as china, crystal, and fine tableware. At **Weitnauer** (⊠ Caya G. F. Betico Croes 29, Oranjestad ☎ 297/582–2790) you can find specialty Lenox items as well as a wide range of fragrances.

HANDICRAFTS   **Art & Tradition Handicrafts** (⊠ Caya G. F. Betico Croes 30, Oranjestad
★   ☎ 297/583–6534 ⊠ Royal Plaza Mall, L. G. Smith Blvd. 94, Oranjestad ☎ 297/582–7862) sells intriguing souvenirs. Buds from the *mopa mopa* tree are boiled to form a resin colored by vegetable dyes. Artists then stretch the resin by hand and mouth. Tiny pieces are cut and layered to form intricate designs—truly unusual gifts. The **Artistic Boutique** (⊠ L. G. Smith Blvd. 90–92, Oranjestad ☎ 297/588–2468 ⊠ Holiday Inn SunSpree Aruba Beach Resort & Casino, J. E. Irausquin Blvd. 230 ☎ 297/583–3383) is known for its Giuseppe Armani figurines from Italy,

usually sold at a 20% discount; Aruban hand-embroidered linens; gold and silver jewelry; and porcelain and pottery from Spain.

JEWELRY Filling 6,000 square feet of space, **Boolchand's** (✉ Renaissance Mall, L. G. Smith Blvd. 82, Oranjestad ☎ 297/583–0147) sells jewelry and watches. It also stocks leather goods, cameras, and electronics. If green fire is your passion, **Colombian Emeralds** (✉ Renaissance Mall, L. G. Smith Blvd. 82, Oranjestad ☎ 297/583–6238) has a dazzling array. There are also fine European watches. **Kenro Jewelers** (✉ Renaissance Mall, L. G. Smith Blvd. 82, Oranjestad ☎ 297/583–4847 or 297/583–3171) has two stores in the same mall, attesting to the popularity of its stock of bracelets and necklaces from Ramon Leopard; jewelry by Arando, Micheletto, and Blumei; and various brands of watches. There are also six other locations, including some in the major hotels.

Nightlife & the Arts

Nightlife

Unlike that of many islands, Aruba's nightlife isn't confined to the touristic folkloric shows at hotels. Arubans like to party, and the more the merrier. They usually start celebrating late; the action doesn't pick up until around midnight. One uniquely Aruban institution is a psychedelically painted '57 Chevy bus called the **Kukoo Kunuku** (☎ 297/586–2010 ⊕ www.kukookunuku.com). Weeknights you can find as many as 40 passengers traveling among three bars from sundown to around midnight. The $55 fee per passenger includes a so-so dinner, some drinks, and pickup at your hotel. The same company operates the infamous Tatoo party boat, which has a buffet, $1 drinks, live entertainment, and a lot of rowdy behavior for $49. The boat leaves at 7:15 PM from the De Palm pier near the Radisson.

BARS **Bambu** (✉ Babijn 53, Paradera ☎ No phone) is a local joint that offers typical Aruban food, cheap drinks, and a lively crowd on the terrace on weekends. Many visitors, including those on party buses, find their
★ way to **Carlos & Charlie's** (✉ Weststraat 3A, Oranjestad ☎297/582–0355), which may be why most locals shy away from it. You can find mixed drinks by the yard, Mexican fare, and American music from the 1960s, '70s, and '80s. **Charlie's Bar** (✉ Zeppenfeldstraat 56, San Nicolas ☎297/584–5086) has been an institution since 1941. Though it is a bit far from most hotels, it is certainly worth the trip. Expect a raucous (and, most likely, highly inebriated) crowd. The food here is quite good as well, so there is amble opportunity to pad your stomach before the margaritas.
★ You can watch the crowds from the terrace at **Choose a Name** (✉ Havenstraat 36, Oranjestad ☎ 297/588–6200) or climb up on the bar for your karaoke debut. Bands perform several nights a week. For specialty drinks, try **Iguana Joe's** (✉ Royal Plaza Mall, L. G. Smith Blvd. 94, Oranjestad ☎ 297/583–9373). The creative reptilian-theme decor is as colorful as the cocktails. With painted parrots flocking on the ceiling,
★ **Mambo Jambo** (✉ Royal Plaza Mall, L. G. Smith Blvd. 94, Oranjestad ☎ 297/583–3632) is daubed in sunset colors. Sip one of several concoctions sold nowhere else on the island; then browse for memorabilia

at a shop next door. With front-row seats to view the green flash—that ray of light that supposedly flicks through the sky as the sun sinks into the ocean—the **Palms Bar** (✉ Hyatt Regency Aruba Beach Resort & Casino, J. E. Irausquin Blvd. 85, Palm Beach ☎ 297/586–1234) is the perfect spot to enjoy the sunset, green flash or no.

CASINOS Aruban casinos offer something for both high and low rollers, as well as live, nightly entertainment in their lounges. Diehard gamblers might look for the largest or the most active casinos, but many simply visit the casino closest to their hotel.

★ In the casual **Alhambra Casino** (✉ L. G. Smith Blvd. 47, Oranjestad ☎ 297/583–5000), a "Moorish slave" named Roger gives every gambler a hearty handshake upon entering. The **Allegro Casino** (✉ Allegro Aruba Resort & Casino, J. E. Irausquin Blvd. 83, Palm Beach ☎ 297/586–9039) has 245 slot machines and nightly bingo. The **Carnaval Casino** (✉ Aruba Grand Beach Resort, J. E. Irausquin Blvd. 79, Palm Beach ☎ 297/586–3900 Ext. 149) is decorated with musical instruments. It opens at 10 AM for slots, 6 PM for all games. The smart money is on the **Casablanca Casino** (✉ Wyndham Aruba Beach Resort & Casino, J. E. Irausquin Blvd. 77, Palm Beach ☎ 297/586–4466). It's quietly elegant and has a Bogart theme. Overhead at the **Casino at the Radisson Aruba Resort** (✉ Radisson Aruba Resort, J. E. Irausquin Blvd. 81, Palm Beach ☎ 297/586–4045), thousands of lights simulate shooting stars that seem destined to carry out your wishes for riches. The slots here open at 10 AM, and table action begins at 4 PM. The ultramodern **Copacabana Casino** (✉ Hyatt Regency Aruba Beach Resort & Casino, J. E. Irausquin Blvd. 85, Palm Beach ☎ 297/586–1234) is an enormous complex with a Carnival in Rio theme and live entertainment. The **Crystal Casino** (✉ Renaissance Aruba Resort, L. G. Smith Blvd. 82, Oranjestad ☎ 297/583–6000) is open 24 hours a day. The **Excelsior Casino** (✉ Holiday Inn SunSpree Aruba Beach Resort & Casino, J. E. Irausquin Blvd. 230, Palm Beach ☎ 297/586–3600) has sports betting in addition to the usual slots and table games. **Royal Palm Casino** (✉ Occidental Grand Aruba, J. E. Irausquin Blvd. 250, Eagle Beach ☎ 297/587–4665) is the largest in the Caribbean. It has an expansive, sleek interior; 400 slot machines; no-smoking gaming tables and a slot room; and the Tropicana nightclub. Low-key gambling can be found at the waterside **Seaport Casino** (✉ L. G. Smith Blvd. 9, Oranjestad ☎ 297/583–6000). The **Stellaris Casino** (✉ Aruba Marriott Resort, L. G. Smith Blvd. 101, Palm Beach ☎ 297/586–9000) is one of the island's most popular.

DANCE & MUSIC CLUBS Popular with locals and tourists, **Café Bahia** (✉ Weststraat 7, Oranjestad ☎ 297/588–9982) draws a chic crowd every Friday for happy hour.
★ If you come for dinner, you can stick around for drinking and dancing as the music heats up. Tuesday nights a band from one of the cruise ships plays local favorites. The party starts late at **Euphoria** (✉ Royal Plaza Mall, L. G. Smith Blvd. 93, Oranjestad), and the beautiful crowd is usually dressed to the hilt. For jazz and other types of music, try the cozy
★ **Garufa Cigar & Cocktail Lounge** (✉ Wilhelminastraat 63, Oranjestad ☎ 297/582–7205), which serves as a lounge for customers awaiting a

table at the nearby El Gaucho Argentine Grill (you're issued a beeper so you know when your table is ready). While you wait, have a drink, enjoy some appetizers, and take in the leopard-print carpet and funky bar stools. The ambience may very well draw you back for an after-dinner cognac. There's live entertainment most nights, and the powerful smoke extractor system helps make life bearable for nonsmokers. The beautiful people head for **La Fiesta** (⊠ Aventura Mall, Oranjestad ☎ 297/583–5896), where popular music plays and a younger crowd parties the night away. Stop by the cozy **Sirocco Lounge** (⊠ Wyndham Aruba Beach Resort & Casino, L. G. Smith Blvd. 77, Palm Beach ☎ 297/586–4466) for jazz every night except Sunday.

The Arts

ART GALLERIES **Access** (⊠ Caya G. F. Betico Croes 16–18, Oranjestad ☎ 297/588–
★ 7837) showcases new and established artists and is a major venue for Caribbean art. In the downtown shopping district, the gallery is home to a thriving cultural scene that includes poetry readings, chamber music concerts, and screenings of feature films and documentaries. The owner, artist Landa Henriquez, is also a bolero singer. At **Galeria Eterno** (⊠ Emanstraat 92, Oranjestad ☎ 297/583–9607) you can find local and international artists at work. Be sure to stop by for concerts by classical guitarists, dance performances, visual-arts shows, and plays. **Galeria Harmonia** (⊠ Zeppenfeldstraat 10, San Nicolas ☎ 297/584–2969), the island's largest exhibition space, has a permanent collection of works by local and international artists. **Gasparito Restaurant & Art Gallery** (⊠ Gasparito 3, Noord ☎ 297/586–7044) features a permanent exhibition by Aruban artists.

ISLAND CULTURE The **Bon Bini Festival,** a year-round folkloric event (the name means "welcome" in Papiamento), is held every Tuesday from 6:30 PM to 8:30 PM at Fort Zoutman in Oranjestad. In the inner courtyard you can check out the Antillean dancers in resplendent costumes, feel the rhythms of the steel drums, browse among the stands displaying local artwork, and partake of local food and drink. Admission is $3.

Exploring Aruba

Aruba's wildly sculpted landscape is replete with rocky deserts, cactus clusters, secluded coves, blue vistas, and the trademark divi-divi tree. To see the island's wild, untamed beauty, you can rent a car, take a sightseeing tour, or hire a cab for $30 an hour (for up to four people). The main highways are well paved, but on the windward side (the north- and east-facing side) some roads are still a mixture of compacted dirt and stones. Although a car is fine, a four-wheel-drive vehicle will allow you to explore the unpaved interior.

Traffic is sparse, but signs leading to sights are often small and hand-lettered (this is slowly changing as the government puts up official road signs), so watch closely. Route 1A travels southbound along the western coast, and 1B is simply northbound along the same road. If you lose your way, just follow the divi-divi trees.

Numbers in the margin correspond to points of interest on the Aruba map.

WHAT TO SEE **Alto Vista Chapel.** Alone near the island's northwest corner sits the scenic little Alto Vista Chapel. The wind whistles through the simple mustard-colored walls, eerie boulders, and looming cacti. Along the side of the road back to civilization are miniature crosses with depictions of the stations of the cross and hand-lettered signs exhorting PRAY FOR US, SINNERS and the like—a simple yet powerful evocation of faith. To get here, follow the rough, winding dirt road that loops around the island's northern tip, or, from the hotel strip, take Palm Beach Road through three intersections and watch for the asphalt road to the left just past the Alto Vista Rum Shop.

Arikok National Wildlife Park. Nearly 20% of Aruba has been designated part of this national park, which sprawls across the eastern interior and the northeast coast. The park is the keystone of the government's long-term ecotourism plan to preserve resources and showcases the island's flora and fauna as well as ancient Arawak petroglyphs, the ruins of a gold-mining operation at Miralmar, and the remnants of Dutch peasant settlements at Masiduri. At the park's main entrance, Arikok Center houses offices, restrooms, and food facilities. All visitors must stop here upon entering so that officials can manage the traffic flow and hand out information on park rules and features. Within the confines of the park are Mount Arikok and the 620-foot Mount Yamanota, Aruba's highest peak.

Anyone looking for geological exotica should head for the park's caves, found on the northeastern coast. Baranca Sunu, the so-called Tunnel of Love, has a heart-shape entrance and naturally sculpted rocks farther inside that look like the Madonna, Abe Lincoln, and even a jaguar. Fontein Cave is marked with ancient drawings (rangers are on hand to offer explanations), as it was used by indigenous people centuries ago. Bats are known to make appearances—don't worry, they won't bother you. Although you don't need a flashlight because the paths are well lighted, it's best to wear sneakers.

★ **Aruba Ostrich Farm.** Everything you ever wanted to know about the world's largest living birds can be found at this farm. A large palapa houses a gift shop and restaurant (popular with large bus tours), and tours of the farm are available every half-hour. This is virtually identical to the facility in Curaçao and is owned by the same company. ⊠ *Makividiri Rd.* ☎ *297/585–9630* ⚞ *$10 adults* ☉ *Daily 9–5.*

Balashi Brewery. Beer drinkers may often wonder how their favorite brew is made. The factory that manufactures the excellent local beer, Balashi, offers daily tours to the public that will take you through every stage of the brewing process. It makes for a fascinating hour, and the price of the tour includes a free drink at the end. Those more interested in beer drinking than beer making might want to visit the factory any evening from 7 to 10 for happy hour (there is live music on Friday). ⊠ *Balashi 75, Balashi* ☎ *297/592–2544.*

Butterfly Farm. Hundreds of butterflies from around the world flutter about this spectacular garden. Guided 20- to 30-minute tours (included in the price of admission) provide an entertaining look into how these insects complete their life cycle, from egg to caterpillar to chrysalis to butterfly. There's a special deal offered here: after your initial visit, you can return as often as you like for free. ⊠ *J. E. Irausquin Blvd., Palm Beach* ☎ *297/586–3656* ⊕ *www.thebutterflyfarm.com* 🖃 *$12* ⊙ *Daily 9–4:30; last tour at 4.*

❾ **California Lighthouse.** The lighthouse, built by a French architect in 1910, stands at the island's far northern end. Although you can't go inside, you can ascend the hill to its base for some great views. In this stark landscape you can feel as though you've just landed on the moon. The lighthouse is surrounded by huge boulders that look like extraterrestrial monsters and sand dunes embroidered with scrub that resemble undulating sea serpents.

❷ **Hooiberg.** Named for its shape (*hooiberg* means "haystack" in Dutch), this 541-foot peak lies inland just past the airport. If you have the energy, climb the 562 steps to the top for an impressive view of the city.

❶ **Oranjestad.** Aruba's charming capital is best explored on foot. The palm-lined thoroughfare in the center of town runs between pastel-painted buildings, old and new, of typical Dutch design. There are many malls with boutiques and shops.

At the **Archaeological Museum of Aruba** you can find two rooms chock-full of fascinating artifacts from the indigenous Arawak people, including farm and domestic utensils dating back hundreds of years. ⊠ *J. E. Irausquin Blvd. 2A, Oranjestad* ☎ *297/582–8979* 🖃 *Free* ⊙ *Weekdays 8–noon and 1–4.*

★ Learn all about aloe—its cultivation, processing, and production—at **Aruba Aloe,** Aruba's own aloe farm and factory. Guided tours lasting about a half hour will show you how the gel—revered for its skin-soothing properties—is extracted from the aloe vera plant and used in a variety of products, including after-sun creams, soaps, and shampoos. You can purchase the finished goods in the gift shop. ⊠ *Pitastraat 115, Oranjestad* ☎ *297/588–3222* 🖃 *$6* ⊙ *Weekdays 8:30–4:30, Sat. 9–2.*

🕘 The **Experience Aruba Panorama** brings the island's history and culture to life in a 22-minute cinematic extravaganza that fills five massive screens measuring 13 feet high and 66 feet wide. The breathtaking shows begin in the Crystal Theater at the Renaissance Aruba Beach Resort every hour from 11 to 5. ⊠ *L. G. Smith Blvd. 82, Oranjestad* ☎ *297/ 583–6000* 🖃 *$10* ⊙ *Mon.–Sat. 11–5.*

One of the island's oldest edifices, **Fort Zoutman** was built in 1796 and played an important role in skirmishes between British and Curaçao troops in 1803. The Willem III Tower, named for the Dutch monarch of that time, was added in 1868 to serve as a lighthouse. Over time, the fort has been put to use as a government office building, a police station, and a prison. Now its historical museum displays Aruban artifacts in an 18th-century house. ⊠ *Zoutmanstraat* ☎ *297/582–6099* 🖃 *Free* ⊙ *Weekdays 8–noon and 1–4.*

★ The **Numismatic Museum** displays more than 40,000 historic coins and paper money from around the world. A few pieces were salvaged from shipwrecks in the region. Some of the coins circulated during the Roman Empire, the Byzantine Empire, and the ancient Chinese dynasties; the oldest dates to the 3rd century BC. The museum—which moved in 2003 to a new, larger location next to the central bus station—had its start as the private collection of one Aruban who dug up some old coins in his garden. It's now run by his granddaughter. ⊠ *Westraat* ☎*297/ 582–8831* ☜ *$5* ☼ *Mon.–Thurs. 9–4, Fri. 9–1, Sat. 9–noon.*

❸ **Rock Formations.** The massive boulders at Ayo and Casibari are a mystery, as they don't match the island's geological makeup. You can climb to the top for fine views of the arid countryside. On the way you'll doubtless pass Aruba whip-tail lizards—the males are cobalt blue, the females blue with dots. The main path to Casibari has steps and handrails (except on one side), and you must move through tunnels and along narrow steps and ledges to reach the top. At Ayo you can find ancient pictographs in a small cave (the entrance has iron bars to protect the drawings from vandalism). You may also encounter a boulder climber, one of many who are increasingly drawn to Ayo's smooth surfaces. Access to Casibari is via Tanki Highway 4A to Ayo via Route 6A; watch carefully for the turnoff signs near the center of the island on the way to the windward side.

❺ **San Nicolas.** During the heyday of the oil refineries, Aruba's oldest village was a bustling port; now its primary purpose is tourism. *The* institution in town is Charlie's Restaurant & Bar. Stop in for a drink and advice on what to see and do in this little town. Aruba's main red light district is located here and will be fairly apparent to even the most casual observer.

ARUBA ESSENTIALS

To research prices, get advice from other travelers, and book travel arrangements, visit www.fodors.com.

Transportation

BY AIR

Aruba is 2½ hours from Miami and 4½ hours from New York. There are nonstop flights from Atlanta, Charlotte, Chicago, Houston, Miami, Newark, New York–JFK, Philadelphia, and Washington, DC–Dulles, though not all flights are daily. You can also fly nonstop from Amsterdam. Smaller airlines provide connecting flights to and from other Dutch Caribbean islands, making day trips possible, though expensive.
🛈 **Dutch Antilles Express** ☎ 297/588-1900 ⊕ www.flydae.com. **American Airlines/American Eagle** ☎ 297/582-2700. **Continental** ☎ 297/ 588-0044. **Delta** ☎ 297/588-6119. **KLM** ☎ 297/

583-4406. **United Airlines** ☎ 297/588-6544. **US Airways** ☎ 297/588-4162.
🛈 Airport Information **Reina Beatrix International Airport** AUA ☎ 297/582-4800 ⊕ www. airportaruba.com.

BY BUS

Buses run hourly trips between the beach hotels and Oranjestad. The one-way fare is $1.25 ($2 round-trip), and exact change is preferred (so be sure to keep some U.S. change handy if you plan to pay in U.S. currency). Buses also run down the coast from Oranjestad to San Nicolas for the same fare.

BY CAR

Aruba has a well-organized public transit system, and taxis and tour companies are readily available, so a rental car is not really necessary for most visitors to the island. Many people come here for the nightlife, so using a taxi will prevent any temptation to drink and drive. To rent a car you need a driver's license, and you must meet the minimum age requirements of the company (Budget, for example requires drivers to be over 25; Avis, between 23 and 70; and Hertz, over 21). A deposit of $500 (or a signed credit-card slip) is required. Rates are between $35 and $65 a day (local agencies generally have lower rates).

Most of Aruba's major attractions are fairly easy to find; others you'll happen upon only by sheer luck. Aside from the major highways, the island's winding roads are poorly marked. International traffic signs and Dutch-style traffic signals (with an extra light for a turning lane) can be misleading if you're not used to them; use extreme caution, especially at intersections, until you grasp the rules of the road. Speed limits are rarely posted but are usually 80 kph (50 mph) in the countryside. Gas prices average about $1.05 a liter (roughly ⅓ gallon), which is reasonable by Caribbean standards.

🚗 **Avis** ✉ Kolibristraat 14, Oranjestad ☎ 297/582-8787 ✉ Airport ☎ 297/582-5496. **Budget** ✉ Kolibristraat 1, Oranjestad ☎ 297/582-8600 or 800/472-3325. **Dollar** ✉ Grendeaweg 15, Oranjestad ☎ 297/582-2783 ✉ Airport ☎ 297/582-5651 ✉ Manchebo Beach Resort, J. E. Irausquin Blvd. 55 ☎ 297/582-6696. **Economy** ✉ Kolibristraat 5 ☎ 297/582-5176 ⊕ www.economyaruba.com. **Hedwina Car Rental** ✉ Bubali 93A, Noord ☎ 297/587-6442 ✉ Airport ☎ 297/583-0880. **Hertz** ✉ Sabana Blanco 35, near the airport ☎ 297/582-1845 ✉ Airport ☎ 297/582-9112. **National** ✉ Tanki Leendert 170, Noord ☎ 297/587-1967 ✉ Airport ☎ 297/582-5451. **Thrifty** ✉ Balashi 65, Santa Cruz ☎ 297/585-5300 ✉ Airport ☎ 297/583-5335.

TAXIS

There's a dispatch office at the airport; you can also flag down taxis on the street (look for license plates with a "TX" tag). Rates are fixed (i.e., there are no meters; the rates are set by the government and

displayed on a chart), though you and the driver should agree on the fare before your ride begins. Add $1 to the fare after midnight and $1 to $3 on Sunday and holidays. An hour-long island tour costs about $40, with up to four people. Rides into town from Eagle Beach run about $5; from Palm Beach, about $8.

🚕 Taxi Information **Airport Taxi Dispatch** ☎ 297/582-2116.

Contacts & Resources

BANKS & EXCHANGE SERVICES

Arubans happily accept U.S. dollars virtually everywhere, so there's no real need to exchange money, except for necessary pocket change (for soda machines or pay phones). The official currency is the Aruban florin (Afl), also called the guilder, which is made up of 100 cents. If you need fast cash, you can find ATMs that accept international cards at banks in Oranjestad, at the major malls, and along the roads leading to the hotel strip.

🏦 Banks **RBTT Bank** ✉ Caya G. F. Betico Croes 89, Oranjestad ☎ 297/523-3100. **Caribbean Mercantile Bank** ✉ Caya G. F. Betico Croes 5, Oranjestad ☎ 297/582-3118.

BUSINESS HOURS

Bank hours are weekdays from 8 to 4:30; the Caribbean Mercantile Bank at the airport is open all day Saturday and Sunday morning. The central post office in Oranjestad is across from the San Francisco Church and is open weekdays from 7:30 to noon and 1 to 4:30. Stores are open Monday through Saturday from 8:30 or 9 to 6. Some stores stay open through the lunch hour (noon to 2), and many open when cruise ships are in port on Sunday and holidays. Most of the larger supermarkets are open on Sunday from 8 to noon.

ELECTRICITY

Aruba runs on a 110-volt cycle, the same as the United States; outlets are usually the two-prong variety. Total blackouts are rare, and most large hotels have backup generators.

3

EMERGENCIES

🚑 Ambulance, Fire & Police **General Emergencies** ☎ 911.

🏥 Hospitals **Dr. Horacio Oduber Hospital** ✉ L. G. Smith Blvd., across from Costa Linda Beach Resort and Alhambra Bazaar and Casino ☎ 297/587-4300.

💊 Pharmacies **Botica Eagle** ✉ L. G. Smith Blvd., Oranjestad ☎ 297/587-6103.

HOLIDAYS

Public holidays are New Year's Day, Betico Croes's Birthday (a politician who aided Aruba's transition to semi-independence; Jan. 25), Carnival Monday (Mon. before Ash Wednesday, usually in Feb.), National Anthem and Flag Day (Mar. 18), Good Friday (varies), Easter Monday (varies), Queen's Birthday (Apr. 30), Labor Day (May 1), Ascension Day (May 9), Christmas Day, Boxing Day (Dec. 26).

LANGUAGE

Everyone on the island speaks English, but the official languages are Dutch and Papiamento. Most locals speak Papiamento—a fascinating, rapid-fire mix of Spanish, Dutch, English, French, and Portuguese—in normal conversation. Here are a few helpful phrases: *bon dia* (good day), *bon nochi* (good night), *masha danki* (thank you very much).

INTERNET, MAIL & SHIPPING

Aruba is well wired by Caribbean standards. Almost every hotel offers some form of Internet access ranging from lobby Internet kiosks to high-speed wireless access. SETAR, a local Wi-Fi company, offers wireless access in most of the main hotel areas (and even on the beach if you want to risk your laptop). Prepaid cards must be purchased at SETAR's offices (there is an office right next to Brickell Bay Hotel in the high-rise hotel area). At a cost of only $10 for an entire 24 hours of usage, it is usually cheaper than paying for the service offered by the hotels.

From Aruba to the United States or Canada, a letter costs Afl 2.05 (about $1.15) and a postcard costs Afl 1 (56¢). Expect it to take one to two weeks. A letter to Europe is Afl 2.15 ($1.20) and a postcard is Afl 1 (56¢). It takes two to four weeks, so you'll probably make it home before your letter does. Prices to Australia and New Zealand (three to four weeks) may be slightly higher. When addressing letters to Aruba, don't worry about the lack of formal addresses or postal codes; the island's postal service knows where to go.

💻 Internet Cafés **Café Internet** ✉ 8 Royal Plaza Mall, Oranjestad ☎ 297/582-4500.

PASSPORT REQUIREMENTS

All arriving passengers require a valid passport; a few countries' citizens require a visa. The standard allowable stay is 90 days.

SAFETY

Arubans are friendly, so you needn't be afraid to stop and ask anyone for directions. It's a relatively safe island, but commonsense rules still apply. Lock your rental car and leave valuables in your hotel safe. Don't leave bags unattended in the airport, on the beach, or on tour transports. Tap water is okay to drink.

TAXES

The airport departure tax is a hefty $36.75 for departures to the United States and $33.50 to other international destinations (including Bonaire and Curaçao), but the fee is usually included in your ticket price. Hotels collect 8% in government taxes on top of a typical 11% service charge, for a total of 19%. A 6.5% A.B.B. tax (value-added tax) is included in the price charged in almost all shops that are not duty-free.

TELEPHONES

You can dial international calls directly or call from the SETAR office in the post office building in Oranjestad. Simply dial the seven-digit number in Aruba. AT&T customers can dial 800–8000 from special phones at the cruise dock and in the airport's arrival and departure halls. From other phones dial 121 to contact the

SETAR International Operator to place a collect or calling card call.

Local calls from pay phones, which accept both local currency and phone cards, cost 25¢.

Because hotel phone charges on Aruba can verge on obscene, renting a mobile for your stay can save you a ton of money. Chapeau Aruba Business Services offers one-week rental packages for about $75 that include 40 minutes of talk time to the United States; each additional day's rental is only $5. Aruba Office Center in the Port of Call Marketplace offers similar rates and will also deliver or pick up the phone for $15.

To call Aruba direct from the United States, dial 011–297, followed by the seven-digit number in Aruba.

🔝 **Aruba Office Center** ✉ Port of Call MarketPl. ☎ 297/583-8700. **Chapeau Aruba Business Services** ☎ 297/586-4250.

TIPPING

Restaurants generally include a 10% to 15% service charge on the bill; when in doubt, ask. If service isn't included, a 10% tip is standard; if it is included, it's still customary to add something extra, usually small change, at your discretion. Taxi drivers expect a 10% to 15% tip, but it isn't mandatory. Porters and bellhops should receive about $2 per bag; chambermaids, about $2 a day.

TOUR OPTIONS

You can see the main sights in one day, but set aside two days to meander. Romantic horse-drawn carriage rides through the city streets of Oranjestad run $30 for a 30-minute tour; hours of operation are from 7 PM to 11 PM, and carriages depart from the clock tower at the Royal Plaza Mall. Guided tours are your best option if you have only a short time. Aruba's Transfer Tour & Taxi will take you to the main sights on personalized tours that cost $40 per hour. De Palm Tours has a near monopoly on Aruban sightseeing; you can

make reservations through its general office or at hotel tour-desk branches. The basic 3½-hour tour hits such highlights as the Santa Anna Church, the Casibari Rock Formation, and the Gold Smelter Ruins. Wear tennis or hiking shoes, and bring a lightweight jacket or wrap, as the air-conditioned bus gets cold.

🔝 **Aruba's Transfer Tour & Taxi** ✉ Pos Abao 41, Oranjestad ☎ 297/582-2116. **De Palm Tours** ✉ L. G. Smith Blvd. 142, Oranjestad ☎ 297/582-4400 or 800/766-6016 ⊕ www.depalm.com.

VISITOR INFORMATION

🔝 **Aruba Tourism Authority** ☎ 800/862-7822 ⊕ www.aruba.com ✉ L. G. Smith Blvd. 172, Eagle Beach, Aruba ☎ 297/582-3777 ✉ 1 Financial Plaza, Suite 136, Fort Lauderdale, FL 33394 ☎ 954/767-6477 ✉ 1000 Harbor Blvd., Ground Level, Weehawken, NJ 07087 ☎ 201/330-0800.

WEDDINGS

Aruba is a popular destination for Caribbean weddings. You must be over the age of 18 and submit the appropriate documents one month in advance. Couples are required to submit birth certificates with raised seals, through the mail or in person, to Aruba's Office of the Civil Registry. They also need an apostille—a document proving they are free to marry—from their country of residence. Most major hotels have wedding coordinators, or there are independent wedding planners on the island as well.

With so many beautiful spots to choose from, weddings on Aruba are guaranteed to be romantic. The island's endless beaches are a natural, but other choices include the tropical gardens at Arikok National Wildlife Park, the top of Natural Bridge, or a sunset cruise. And be sure to register for the island's "One Cool Honeymoon" program for special discounts from local businesses.

🔝 Wedding Planners **Aruba Fairy Tales** 📠 Box 4151, Noord ☎ 297/993-0045 🖨 297/583-1511 ⊕ www.arubafairytales.com. **Aruba Weddings for You** ✉ Nune 92, Paradera ☎ 297/583-7638 🖨 297/588-6073 ⊕ www.arubaweddingsforyou.com.

Barbados

Carlisle Bay

WORD OF MOUTH

". . . [D]efinitely do Oistins fish fry on Friday nights—it doesn't really get busy until later in the night, so prepare yourself to stay out until at least 1 or 2 . . ."

—kspoerl

"Just returned from my 17th trip to Barbados, and I'm still finding new and different things to do!"

—Cathy

WELCOME TO BARBADOS

Broad vistas, sweeping seascapes, craggy cliffs, and acre upon acre of sugarcane... that's Barbados. Beyond that, what draws visitors to the island is the warm Bajan hospitality, the welcoming hotels and resorts, the sophisticated dining, the never-ending things to see and do, the exciting nightspots, and, of course, the sunny beaches.

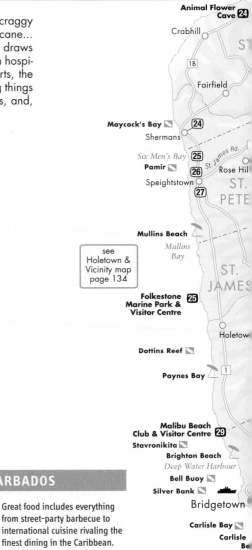

North Pt.

Animal Flower Cave 24

Crabhill

1B

Fairfield

Maycock's Bay 24

Shermans

Six Men's Bay 25

Pamir 26

Speightstown 27

Rose Hill

ST. PETE

Mullins Beach

Mullins Bay

see Holetown & Vicinity map page 134

Folkestone Marine Park & Visitor Centre 25

Holetown

Dottins Reef

Paynes Bay 1

ST. JAMES

Malibu Beach Club & Visitor Centre 29

Stavronikita

Brighton Beach
Deep Water Harbour

Bell Buoy

Silver Bank

Bridgetown

Carlisle Bay

Carlisle Be

3

4 - 7

TOP 4 REASONS TO VISIT BARBADOS

1. Great resorts run the gamut—from unpretentious to knock-your-socks-off—in terms of size, intimacy, amenities, and price.

2. Golfers can choose from some of the best championship courses in the Caribbean.

3. Great food includes everything from street-party barbecue to international cuisine rivaling the finest dining in the Caribbean.

4. With a wide assortment of land and water sports, sightseeing options, and nightlife, there's always plenty to do.

CHARM AND SOPHISTICATION

Barbados stands apart both geographically and geologically from its Caribbean neighbors; it's a full 100 mi (161 km) east of the Lesser Antilles chain. The top of a single submerged mountain of coral and limestone, the island is 21 mi (34 km) long, 14 mi (22½ km) wide, and relatively flat. The population is about 276,000, and the capital is Bridgetown.

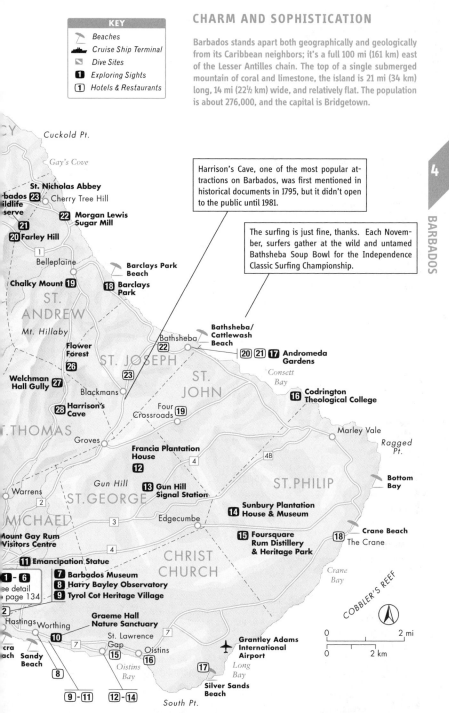

KEY
- Beaches
- Cruise Ship Terminal
- Dive Sites
- **1** Exploring Sights
- ① Hotels & Restaurants

4

BARBADOS

Harrison's Cave, one of the most popular attractions on Barbados, was first mentioned in historical documents in 1795, but it didn't open to the public until 1981.

The surfing is just fine, thanks. Each November, surfers gather at the wild and untamed Bathsheba Soup Bowl for the Independence Classic Surfing Championship.

Cuckold Pt.

Gay's Cove

St. Nicholas Abbey **23**
...bados **23** Cherry Tree Hill
...ildlife
...serve
21
20 Farley Hill

22 Morgan Lewis
Sugar Mill

1
Belleplaine

Barclays Park
Beach
Chalky Mount **19**
18 Barclays
Park

ST.
ANDREW
Mt. Hillaby

Flower
Forest
26

Welchman
Hall Gully **27**
Blackmans

23

Harrison's
28 Cave
Four
Crossroads **19**

ST. JOSEPH

Bathsheba **22**

Bathsheba/
Cattlewash
Beach

20 **21** **17** Andromeda
Gardens

Consett
Bay

ST.
JOHN

16 Codrington
Theological College

Marley Vale

Ragged
Pt.

T. THOMAS
Groves

Francia Plantation
House
12

Gun Hill
Warrens
ST. GEORGE

13 Gun Hill
Signal Station

4

4B

ST. PHILIP

Bottom
Bay

Sunbury Plantation
14 House & Museum

Edgecumbe

3

MICHAEL

Mount Gay Rum
Visitors Centre

4

11 Emancipation Statue

7 Barbados Museum
8 Harry Bayley Observatory
9 Tyrol Cot Heritage Village

① - ⑥
ee detail
page 134

②
Hastings Worthing
10

cra
ach
Sandy
Beach

⑧

Graeme Hall
Nature Sanctuary

St. Lawrence
Gap
⑮
Oistins
⑯

⑨-⑪

⑫-⑭

Oistins
Bay

South Pt.

CHRIST
CHURCH

⑮ Foursquare
Rum Distillery
& Heritage Park

⑱ Crane Beach
The Crane

Crane
Bay

COBBLER'S REEF

⑦

Grantley Adams
International
Airport

⑰

Silver Sands
Beach

Long
Bay

0   2 mi

0   2 km

BARBADOS PLANNER

Getting to Barbados

Many airlines fly nonstop to Barbados from North America, but you may have to make a connection in San Juan or Montego Bay. You can also fly nonstop from London. Barbados is a regional hub, so sometimes you'll actually make a stopover there en route to somewhere else.

Grantley Adams International Airport (BGI) is in Christ Church Parish, on the south coast. It's a large, modern facility. The airport is about 15 minutes from hotels situated along the south coast, 45 minutes from the west coast, and about 30 minutes from Bridgetown.

Hassle Factor: Low to Medium.

On the Ground

Ground transportation is available immediately outside the customs area. Airport taxis aren't metered, but fares are regulated (about $28 to Speightstown, $20 to $22 to west coast hotels, $10 to $13 to south coast ones). Be sure, however, to establish the fare before getting into the cab and confirm whether the price quoted is in U.S. or Barbadian dollars.

Renting a Car

If you're staying in a remote location, such as the southeast or east coasts, you may want to rent a car for the duration of your stay. In more populated areas, where taxis and public transportation are available at the door, you might rent a car or minimoke (a tiny, open-sided convertible, similar to a beach buggy, that's popular among tourists in Barbados) for a day or two of exploring on your own. Rates are about $55 per day during the high season.

Activities

There's always something to do in Barbados, and that's the way most visitors like it. The soft, white **beaches** are good whether you choose to stay in the millionaire's row of resorts on the west coast or the more affordable south coast. Exceptional **golf** courses bring a lot of players to the island, but the best courses—at Sandy Lane—aren't for the light of wallet. The island's **restaurant scene** is excellent; you can choose from street-party barbecue to international cuisine that rivals the finest dining on the planet. Getting out on the water is the favored activity, whether that's on a **snorkeling** day sail, in a **minisub**, on a deep-sea **fishing** boat, or from a **dive** boat to explore the island's reefs and wrecks. In season—from December through April—the conditions around the southern tip of Barbados are ideal for **windsurfing**. All year long, the pounding surf of the east coast draws **surfers** to the Bathsheba Soup Bowl, but the Independence Classic is the highlight every November.

Where to Stay

Most people stay either in self-contained enclaves on the fashionable west coast—north of Bridgetown—or on the action-packed south coast, within easier reach of small, independent restaurants, bars, and nightclubs. A few inns on the remote east coast offer ocean views and tranquility but don't offer easy access to good swimming beaches.

Prices in Barbados are sometimes twice as high in-season as during the quieter months. Most hotels include no meals in their rates, but some offer breakfast or a meal plan; others require you to purchase the meal plan in the high season, and a few offer all-inclusive packages.

TYPES OF LODGINGS

Resorts: Great resorts run the gamut—from unpretentious to knock-your-socks-off—in terms of size, intimacy, amenities, and price. Many are well suited for families

Villas & Condos: Families and longer-term visitors can choose from a wide variety of condos (everything from frenetic time-share resorts to more sedate holiday condo complexes). Villas can be luxurious or simple and everything in between.

Small Inns: A few small, cozy inns can be found in the east and southeast regions of the island.

Hotel & Restaurant Costs

Assume that hotels operate on the European Plan (**EP**—with no meals) unless we specify that they use either the Continental Plan (**CP**—with a Continental breakfast), Breakfast Plan (**BP**—with full breakfast), or the Modified American Plan (**MAP**—with breakfast and dinner). Other hotels may offer the Full American Plan (**FAP**—including all meals but no drinks) or may be All-Inclusive (**AI**—with all meals, drinks, and most activities).

WHAT IT COSTS in Dollars

	$$$$	$$$	$$	$	¢
Restaurants	over $30	$20–$30	$12–$20	$8–$12	under $8
Hotels*	over $350	$250–$350	$150–$250	$80–$150	under $80
Hotels**	over $450	$350–$450	$250–$350	$125–$250	under $125

*EP, BP, CP **AI, FAP, MAP

Restaurant prices are for a main course excluding the customary 10% service charge. Hotel prices are for two people in a double room in high season, excluding 7½% tax, customary 10% service charge, and meal plans (except at all-inclusive resorts).

When to Go

Barbados is busiest from December 15 through April 15. Rates in the off-season can be half what they are during this busy period. If you go to Barbados during the high season, be aware that some hotels require you to buy some kind of meal plan, which is usually not required in the low season.

In mid-January, the **Barbados Jazz Festival** is a week-long event jammed with performances by international artists, jazz legends, and local talent.

In February the week-long **Holetown Festival** is held at the fairgrounds to commemorate the date in 1627 when the first European settlers arrived in Barbados.

Gospelfest occurs in May and hosts performances by gospel headliners from around the world.

Dating from the 19th century, the **Crop Over Festival**, a month-long carnival beginning in July and ending on **Kadooment Day** (a national holiday), marks the end of the sugarcane harvest.

By Jane E.
Zarem

THE NUMBER OF TIMES I'VE ARRIVED at Barbados's Grantley Adams International Airport reaches well into the double digits. Recently, something new caught my eye—besides the huge reconstruction of the airport itself. On the east side of the terminal, a small hangar houses a Concorde—one of seven supersonic airliners retired from British Airway's fleet. That's certainly fitting. After all, a retirement home in Barbados, a British outpost and holiday destination for nearly four centuries, is the dream—and, in fact, the reality—for many Brits. Moreover, Barbados was Concorde's only Caribbean destination during the iconic jetliner's lofty heyday, delivering the well-heeled to their nifty tropical holidays at Mach 2 speed.

Without question, Barbados is the "most British" island in the Caribbean. In contrast to the turbulent colonial past experienced by neighboring islands, which included repeated conflicts between France and Britain for dominance and control, British rule in Barbados carried on uninterrupted for 340 years—from the first established British settlement in 1627 until independence was granted in 1966. That's not to say, of course, that there weren't significant struggles in Barbados, as elsewhere in the Caribbean, between the British landowners and their African-born slaves and other indentured servants.

With that unfortunate period of slavery relegated to the history books, the British influence on Barbados remains strong today in local manners, attitudes, customs, and politics—tempered, of course, by the characteristically warm nature of the Bajan people. ("Bajan," pronounced *bay*-jun, derives phonetically from the British pronunciation of "Barbadian.") In keeping with British-born traditions, many Bajans worship at the Anglican church, afternoon tea is a ritual, cricket is the national pastime (a passion, some admit), dressing for dinner is a firmly entrenched tradition, and patrons at some bars are as likely to order a Pimm's Cup as a rum and Coke. And yet, Barbados is hardly stuffy—this is still the Caribbean, after all.

The long-standing British involvement is only one of the unique attributes that distinguish Barbados from its island neighbors. Geographically, Barbados is a break in the Lesser Antilles archipelago, the chain of islands that stretches in a graceful arc from the Virgin Islands to Trinidad. Barbados is isolated in the Atlantic Ocean, 100 mi due east of St. Lucia, its nearest neighbor. And geologically, most of the Lesser Antilles are the peaks of a volcanic mountain range, while Barbados is the top of a single, relatively flat protuberance of coral and limestone—the source of building blocks for many a plantation manor. Many of those historic greathouses, in fact, have been carefully restored and are open to visitors.

Bridgetown, both capital city and commercial center, is on the southwest coast of pear-shaped Barbados. Most of the 280,000 Bajans live and work in and around Bridgetown, in St. Michael Parish, or along the idyllic west coast or busy south coast. Others live in tiny villages that dot the interior landscape. Broad sandy beaches, craggy cliffs, and picturesque coves make up the coastline, while the interior is consumed by forested hills and gullies and acre upon acre of sugarcane.

Tourist facilities are concentrated on the west coast in St. James and St. Peter parishes (appropriately dubbed the Platinum Coast) and on the south coast in Christ Church Parish. Traveling along the west coast to historic Holetown, the site of the first British settlement, and continuing to the northern city of Speightstown, you can find posh beachfront resorts, luxurious private villas, and fine restaurants enveloped by lush gardens and tropical foliage. The trendier, more commercial south coast offers more competitively priced hotels and beach resorts, and its St. Lawrence Gap area is jam-packed with shops, restaurants, and nightlife. The relatively wide-open spaces along the southeast coast appear ripe for development, and some wonderful inns and hotels already take advantage of the intoxicatingly beautiful ocean vistas. For their own holidays, though, Bajans escape to the rugged east coast, where the Atlantic surf pounds the dramatic shoreline with unrelenting force.

All in all, Barbados is a sophisticated tropical island with a rich history, lodgings to suit every taste and pocketbook, and plenty to pique your interest both day and night—whether you're British or not!

Where to Stay

Most people choose to stay on either the fashionable west coast, north of Bridgetown, or on the action-packed south coast. The west-coast beachfront resorts in the parishes of St. Peter and St. James are mostly self-contained enclaves. Highway 1, a two-lane road with considerable traffic, runs past these resorts, which makes casual strolling to a nearby bar or restaurant difficult. Along the south coast, in Christ Church Parish, many hotels are clustered near the busy strip known as the St. Lawrence Gap, convenient to dozens of small restaurants, bars, and nightclubs. On the much more remote east coast, a few small inns offer oceanfront views, cool breezes, and get-away-from-it-all tranquility. The hotels below all have air-conditioning, telephones, and TVs in guest rooms unless otherwise noted.

Villas, Apartments & Condominiums

Villas, private homes, and condos are available south of Bridgetown, in the Hastings-Worthing area, and along the west coast in St. James and in St. Peter. Most include maid service, and the owner or manager can arrange for a cook.

A number of time-share resorts have cropped up along the south and west coasts. Nonowner vacationers can rent the units by the week from the property managers. Two- and three-bedroom condos run $800 to $3,800 per week in summer—double that in winter. This can be an economical option for family groups or couples vacationing together.

The **Barbados Tourism Authority** (☎ 246/427–2623 ⊕ www.barbados.org) on Harbour Road in Bridgetown has a listing of apartments in prime resort areas on both the south and west coasts, complete with facilities offered and rates from $30 to $300 per night. Some apartment complexes are small, with only 3 or 4 units; others have 30 to 40 units—or even more.

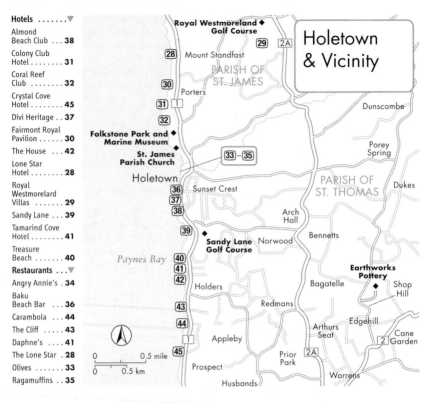

On the south coast, the seaside villas at **Bougainvillea Beach Resort** (⊠ Maxwell Coast Rd., Maxwell, Christ Church ☎ 246/418–0990 ⊕ www.bougainvillearesort.com) are appropriate for families, couples, or honeymooners.On the southeast coast the upscale private residences at the **Crane** (⊠ Crane Beach, St. Philip ☎ 246/423–6220 ⊕ www.thecrane.com) overlook Crane Beach's rolling waves and pink sand and are perfect for anyone seeking peace, tranquillity, and natural beauty.

On the west coast, just beyond Speightstown, the luxurious town homes at **Port St. Charles** (⊠ Hwy. 1B, Heywoods, St. Peter ☎ 246/419–1000 ⊕ www.portstcharles.com) are the perfect choice for boating enthusiasts, whether you arrive on your own yacht or plan to charter one during your stay; each villa has its own berth on the property's picturesque lagoon. **Royal Westmoreland Villas** (⊠ Hwy. 2A, Westmoreland, St. James ☎ 246/422–4653 ⊕ www.royal-westmoreland.com) overlook the Royal Westmoreland Golf Club's championship course and are, therefore, an ideal base for golfers.

Bajan Services (⊠ Seascape Cottage, Gibbs, St. Peter ☎ 246/422–2618 ⊕ www.bajanservices.com) is a real estate service that manages and rents luxury villas on the west coast of Barbados. All villas are fully furnished and equipped, including appropriate staff depending on the villa's size—which can range from one to eight bedrooms. Rates include utilities and government taxes; the only additional cost is for groceries and staff gratuities.

Hotels

SOUTH COAST 🏨 **Hilton Barbados.** Brand-new in 2005 and beautifully situated on the
☾ **$$$$** sandy peninsula of Needham's Point, the luxurious Hilton Barbados is just minutes from Bridgetown. All 350 rooms and suites in this high-rise have private balconies overlooking the ocean or Carlisle Bay; 77 rooms are on an executive floor, with a private lounge and concierge services. Meetings are big business here, as the property has the largest hotel meeting space in Barbados. The two broad white-sand beaches, the sprawling pool complex, and a host of activities on land and sea make this a hit with vacationing families, as well. Children under 18 stay free in a room with adults, children ages 5 to 12 get a break on meals, and children under 5 eat for free—and parents get one free night of babysitting with a three-night stay! ⊠ *Needham's Point, Aquatic Gap, St. Michael* ☎ *246/426–0200* 🖷 *246/228–7730* ⊕ *www.hiltoncaribbean. com* ⇨ *317 rooms, 33 suites* ⚬ *3 restaurants, room service, in-room safes, minibars, cable TV, in-room broadband, in-room data ports, Wi-Fi, pool, 3 tennis courts, health club, 2 bars, 2 beaches, children's programs (ages 3–12), concierge floor, business services, meeting rooms* ☰ *AE, D, DC, MC, V* ⧖ *EP.*

☾ **$$$$** 🏨 **Turtle Beach Resort.** Families flock to Turtle Beach because it offers large, bright suites and enough activities for everyone to enjoy—all the time, and all included. The Tommy Turtle Kids Club keeps children busy with treasure hunts, supervised swims, games, and other activities from 9 AM to 9 PM each day. That gives parents a chance to play tennis, learn to windsurf or sail, relax at the beach, or enjoy an elegant dinner for two at Asagio's Restaurant on the ground level of the lobby atrium, which opens to a clear view of the sea. Families also have good times together—cooling off in the three pools, riding the waves on Boogie boards, searching for baby turtles hatching on the beach, or having a casual meal at the beachfront restaurant. ⊠ *St. Lawrence Gap, Dover, Christ Church* ☎ *246/428–7131* 🖷 *246/428–6089* ⊕ *www.turtlebeachresortbarbados. com* ⇨ *161 suites* ⚬ *3 restaurants, snack bar, room service, fans, in-room safes, refrigerators, cable TV, golf privileges, 2 tennis courts, 3 pools, fitness classes, gym, hair salon, hot tub, beach, snorkeling, windsurfing, boating, waterskiing, 2 bars, sports bar, shops, babysitting, children's programs (ages 3–11), playground, dry cleaning, laundry service, Internet room, business services* ☰ *AE, D, DC, MC, V* ⧖ *AI.*

★ **$$–$$$$** 🏨 **The Crane.** Built in 1887 high on this seaside cliff on Barbados's southeast coast to catch the cooling Atlantic breezes, the Crane was the island's first resort. Today, the original hotel building (with much of the original furniture) is the centerpiece of a luxurious villa complex that combines the character and ambience of the 19th century with the comforts and amenities expected today. Step back in time and stay in an 1887 Resort Apartment, decorated with original antiques; corner suites have walls of windows and wraparound patios or balconies with panoramic ocean views. Alternatively, the Private Residences—in modern but architecturally compatible four-story buildings—are spacious timeshare villas with hardwood floors, hand-carved four-poster beds, multiple bathrooms with spa showers, fully equipped kitchens, entertainment centers, objets d'art, and private plunge pools. Expansion plans, under way at this writing and continuing in coming years, will triple the number of villas. The hotel's signature infinity pool is a frequent backdrop for photo shoots, while reef-protected, pink-sand Crane Beach is 200 steps down the cliff. You need a rental car to get around if you plan to leave the resort grounds. ⊠ *Crane Bay, St. Philip* ☎ *246/423–6220* 🖷 *246/423–5343* ⊕ *www.thecrane.com* ⟿ *4 rooms, 14 suites, 128 villas* ⚮ *2 restaurants, fans, in-room safes, kitchenettes, minibars, microwaves, refrigerators, in-room data ports, 4 tennis courts, 4 pools, beach, bar, laundry facilities, meeting room; no a/c in some rooms, no TV in some rooms* ⊟ *AE, D, DC, MC, V* ⦿| *EP.*

★ **$$$** 🏨 **Little Arches Hotel.** Off the beaten track just east of the picturesque fishing village of Oistins, this classy boutique hotel has a perfect vantage point overlooking the sea and is just 100 yards from pretty, palm-lined Miami Beach. This small hotel has a distinctly Mediterranean ambience; beautifully appointed rooms are decorated with Italian fabrics, local pottery, and terrazzo flooring. Bathrooms have showers only but feature locally made earthenware sinks and fluffy robes. The pool is on the roof, alongside the open-air Café Luna restaurant. Each unit has a unique layout and is named for a different Grenadine island. The Union Island and Palm Island suites each have a kitchen and a large, oceanfront patio with a private hot tub. Guests who book a 10-day stay are entitled to a choice of a complimentary round of golf at the Barbados Golf Club, an in-room champagne breakfast and massage, or a fully catered day sail aboard the hotel's 42-foot monohull yacht, *Soul Venture,* or 44-foot catamaran, *Silver Moon.* We recommend you leave the kids home if you're staying here, as Little Arches offers nothing less than pure romance. ⊠ *Enterprise Beach Rd., Enterprise, Christ Church* ☎ *246/420–4689* ⊕ *www.littlearches.com* ⟿ *8 rooms, 2 suites* ⚮ *Restaurant, fans, in-room safes, some kitchens, cable TV, in-room data ports, pool, boating, mountain bikes, bar, complimentary weddings, laundry service, Internet room* ⊟ *MC, V* ⦿| *EP.*

$$$ 🏨 **The Savannah.** Convenient, comfortable, and particularly appealing to independent travelers who don't expect or want organized entertainment and group activities, the Savannah is a hotel rather than a resort. Nevertheless, it's perfectly situated for walks to the Garrison historic area, the Barbados Museum, the race track, and the Graeme Hall Nature Centre—and minutes from Bridgetown by car or taxi. Two modern additions spill down to the beach from the main building, once the historic Sea View Hotel. Definitely opt for a room in one of the modern wings, which overlook a lagoon-style pool that flows between them in graduated steps, from a waterfall at the higher end to a more traditional pool by the beach; the oceanfront duplex suites at each end are the cat's meow. A favorite of local businesspeople, the Boucan Restaurant is a buzz of activity at lunchtime. ⊠ *Garrison Main Rd., Hastings, Christ Church* ☎ *246/435–9473* 🖷 *246/435–8822* ⊕ *www. gemsbarbados.com* ⟿ *90 rooms, 8 suites* ⚮ *2 restaurants, fans, in-room* *safes, refrigerators, cable TV, in-room VCRs, in-room data ports, golf privileges, 2 pools, gym, hair salon, spa, beach, 2 bars, wine bar, shop, babysitting, laundry service, Internet room, business services, meeting room, airport shuttle, car rental; no smoking ☰ AE, D, DC, MC, V ⦿⦿ CP.*

$$–$$$ ⊞ **Divi Southwinds Beach Resort.** The all-suite Divi Southwinds is uniquely situated on 20 acres of lawn and gardens that are bisected by action-packed St. Lawrence Gap. The bulk of the suites are north of the Gap in a large, unspectacular three-story building offering garden and pool views. The property south of the Gap wraps around a stunning half-mile of Dover Beach, where 16 beach villas provide an intimate setting steps from the sand. Whichever location you choose, all suites have separate bedrooms, sofa beds in the sitting room, and full kitchens. The large, rambling resort has many amenities and is within walking distance of lots of shops, restaurants, and nightspots, so it appeals equally to families with kids and fun-loving couples or singles. Kids under 15 stay free in their parents' suite. ✉ *St. Lawrence Main Rd., Dover, Christ Church* ☎ *246/428–7181* 🖷 *246/420–2673* ⊕ *www.diviresorts.com* ⇆ *121 1-bedroom suites, 12 2-bedroom suites △ 2 restaurants, grocery, kitchens, cable TV, golf privileges, putting green, 2 tennis courts, 3 pools, gym, hair salon, beach, basketball, volleyball, 2 bars, shops, babysitting, laundry facilities, Internet room* ☰ *AE, D, DC, MC, V* ⦿⦿ *EP.*

$$ ⊞ **Accra Beach Hotel & Resort.** One of the best choices for vacationers preferring a full-service resort in the middle of the busy south coast, Accra is large, it's modern, it faces a great beach, and it's competitively priced. Six duplex penthouse suites—the priciest accommodations—face the sea. Most rooms overlook the large cloverleaf pool or the beach—and some of the oceanfront suites have hot tubs on the balconies. The budget-minded can opt for the less expensive ("island view") rooms, which face the street. It's not unusual to witness a local couple being married here, and the hotel is a popular meeting venue for local businesspeople. That shouldn't interrupt your day lazing on the beach, mingling at the poolside swim-up bar, or dining sumptuously at Wytukai (pronounced Y2K)—the island's only (so far) Polynesian restaurant. ✉ *Hwy. 7, Box 73W, Rockley, Christ Church* ☎ *246/435–8920* 🖷 *246/435–6794* ⊕ *www.accrabeachhotel.com* ⇆ *109 rooms, 34 suites, 3 2-bedroom suites △ 3 restaurants, room service, fans, in-room safes, some in-room hot tubs, some refrigerators, cable TV, some in-room broadband, in-room data ports, pool, gym, hair salon, beach, snorkeling, squash, volleyball, 2 bars, shops, babysitting, laundry service, concierge, Internet room, business services, meeting rooms, no-smoking rooms* ☰ *AE, D, MC, V* ⦿⦿ *EP.*

$$ ⊞ **Grand Barbados Beach Resort.** Particularly geared to business travelers, this high-rise hotel is close to Bridgetown and offers executive rooms, abundant business services, and extensive meeting facilities. Leisure travelers also appreciate the comfortable rooms and attentive service—but especially enjoy the hotel's location on beautiful Carlisle Bay. Broad beaches on either side of the building are great for swimming and sunbathing, with powdery white sand and calm water. From guest-room balconies—especially those in the corner rooms—the panoramic view is spectacular. At the far end of a 260-foot-long Victorian pier, five unique suites with over-water patios offer a tempting choice for a romantic getaway; the pier is also a perfect spot to watch the sunset. Children under 12 stay free with their parents. ⌂ *Box 639, Aquatic Gap, St. Michael* ☎ *246/426–4000* 🖷 *246/429–2400* ⊕ *www. grandbarbados.com* ⇆ *128 rooms, 5 suites* ⚴ *2 restaurants, in-room safes, cable TV, in-room data ports, Wi-Fi, pool, gym, hair salon, hot tub, massage, sauna, beach, dive shop, snorkeling, 2 bars, shops, laundry service, concierge, concierge floor, Internet room, business services, convention center* ☰ *AE, DC, MC, V* ⍋ *EP.*

$ ⊡ **Peach & Quiet.** Perhaps Barbados's best-kept secret, this small sea-
Fodor'sChoice side inn on the southeast coast is the sweetest deal we've found on the
★   entire island. Forego the flashy accoutrements of a resort and, instead, claim one of these stylish suites as your own. With no in-room noise-makers and no children around, the only sounds you will hear are the gentle surf and your own conversations. Hands-on British owners Adrian and Margaret Loveridge purchased Peach, the first hotel designed by noted architect Ian Morrison, in 1988. In 2004, they renovated and refurbished the entire property. Decor in the spacious suites, arranged in whitewashed Mykonos-inspired buildings, is elegantly spare. Each has a large terrace or balcony and a stocked bookshelf; bathrooms have showers only. Besides lazing in the pool and windsurfing at nearby beaches (a five-minute walk), guests enjoy swimming and snorkeling among 120 noted varieties of tropical fish in a "rock pool" naturally created by the sea, joining 5-mi early-morning or late-afternoon walks, and stargazing at night. You're advised to rent a car. ⌧ *Inch Marlow Main Rd., Inch Marlow, Christ Church* ☎ *246/428–5682* 🖷 *246/428–2467* ⊕ *www.peachandquiet.com* ⇆ *22 suites* ⚴ *Restaurant, fans, in-room safes, refrigerators, pool, saltwater pool, snorkeling, hiking, bar, lounge; no a/c, no room phones, no room TVs, no kids under 16* ☰ *MC, V* ⊙ *Closed May–Oct.* ⍋ *EP.*

WEST COAST   ⊡ **Almond Beach Club & Spa.** Among several similar beachfront resorts
$$$$ south of Holetown, Almond Beach Club distinguishes itself with all-inclusive rates (only spa and salon services are extra), an adults-only environment, and reciprocal guest privileges (including shuttle service) at its sister resort, Almond Beach Village. A horseshoe of rooms and suites, decorated in a British-colonial theme, faces the sea, although most units overlook the pools and gardens. Lavish breakfast buffets, four-course lunches, afternoon teas, and intimate dinners are served in the main dining room—or dine on seafood at Water's Edge or West Indian cuisine at Enid's, the colorful Bajan restaurant that also offers free cooking classes. The soundproof piano bar remains open until the last guest leaves. ⌧ *Hwy. 1, Vauxhall, St. James* ☎ *246/432–7840* 🖷 *246/432–2115* ⊕ *www.almondresorts.com* ⇆ *133 rooms, 28 suites* ⚴ *3 restaurants, room service, fans, in-room safes, minibars, cable TV, tennis court, 4 pools, fitness classes, health club, hair salon, hot tub, sauna, spa, beach, snorkeling, windsurfing, boating, waterskiing, 4 bars, nightclub, shop, laundry service, Internet room, airport shuttle; no kids under 16* ☰ *AE, D, MC, V* ⍋ *AI.*

☾ **$$$$**   ⊡ **Almond Beach Village.** Barbados's premier family resort is both massive enough to be a popular conference venue and romantic enough to host intimate weddings. Situated on an 18th-century sugar plantation north of Speightstown, the Village's 32 acres front a mile-long, powdery beach. Rooms and pools at the north end of the property, near a historic sugar mill, are reserved for adults; at the south end, junior and one-bedroom suites targeted to families with children are near special facilities for kids and teens. A full-service spa and 150 additional rooms were part of a $10 million resortwide renovation in 2005. A plethora of activities—golf, sailing, waterskiing, shopping excursions to Bridgetown, an off-site Bajan picnic, and more—are all included. Not enough? Hop the shuttle to Almond Beach Club and enjoy the (adults-only) facilities there. ⊠ *Hwy. 1B, Heywoods, St. Peter* ☎ *246/422–4900* 🖷 *246/422–0617* ⊕ *www.almondresorts.com* ⤺ *355 rooms, 41 suites* ♨ *5 restaurants, room service, fans, in-room safes, cable TV, 9-hole golf course, 4 tennis courts, 10 pools, wading pool, fitness classes, health club, hot tubs, spa, beach, snorkeling, windsurfing, boating, waterskiing, fishing, billiards, Ping-Pong, squash, 5 bars, dance club, shops, children's programs (ages infant–17), playground, Internet room, business services, convention center, airport shuttle* ▭ *AE, D, MC, V* ¶⊙¶ *AI.*

★ **$$$$**   🖼 **Cobblers Cove Hotel.** "English Country" best describes the style of this pretty-in-pink resort, which is favored by wealthy British sophisticates who return year after year. The resort is flanked by tropical gardens on one side and the sea on the other. Each elegant suite has an air-conditioned bedroom and a comfy sitting room with a wet bar and a wall of louvered shutters that open onto a patio. From the four oceanfront suites, the view of the gently splashing surf or the starry evening sky is mesmerizing. The sublime Colleton and Camelot penthouse suites each have richly decorated sitting rooms, king-size four-poster beds, enormous dressing rooms, whirlpool baths, private sundecks, and plunge pools for all-out luxury. Water sports are available at the beach, while socializing occurs in the library (which doubles as a TV lounge) and at the alfresco restaurant, which receives well-deserved raves for superb dining. ⊠ *Road View, Speightstown, St. Peter* ☎ *246/422–2291* 🖷 *246/422–1460* ⊕ *www.cobblerscove.com* ⤺ *40 suites* ♨ *Restaurant, snack bar, room service, fans, in-room safes, minibars, in-room data ports, golf privileges, tennis court, pool, gym, beach, snorkeling, windsurfing, boating, waterskiing, bar, library, shop, babysitting, children's programs (ages 2–12), meeting room; no room TVs, no kids under 12 Jan.–Mar.* ▭ *AE, D, MC, V* ¶⊙¶ *BP.*

★ **$$$$**   🖼 **Colony Club Hotel.** As the signature hotel of six Elegant Hotel properties on Barbados, the Colony Club is certainly elegant—but with a quiet, friendly, understated style. The main building and grounds were once a private gentlemen's club. Today a similar sense of belonging transcends to hotel guests, who are made to feel very much at home. A lagoon pool meanders through the central gardens, and 20 rooms have private access to the lagoon directly from their patios. Relax on the beach, soak in one of four pools, and enjoy an exquisite meal in the air-conditioned Orchids restaurant or a more informal repast at the open-air Laguna Restaurant. Nonmotorized water sports, an in-pool scuba-diving lesson, and tennis are all included. A free water taxi provides transportation to three sister hotels located along the west coast. ⊠ *Hwy. 1, Porters, St. James* ☎ *246/422–2335* 🖷 *246/422–0667* ⊕ *www.colonyclubhotel.*

com 🏊 *64 rooms, 32 junior suites* ♿ *2 restaurants, room service, fans, in-room safes, minibars, cable TV, 2 tennis courts, 4 pools, gym, hair salon, hot tub, spa, beach, snorkeling, windsurfing, boating, waterskiing, 2 bars, library, shops, babysitting, dry cleaning, laundry service, Internet room, meeting room* ▤ *AE, DC, MC, V* ❀ *EP.*

$$$$

Fodor'sChoice

★

🏨 **Coral Reef Club.** Owned and operated by the O'Hara family since the 1950s, the upscale Coral Reef Club offers the elegance and style of Sandy Lane without the formality. Spend your days relaxing on the white-sand beach or around a pool, taking time out for afternoon tea. Individually designed and beautifully decorated suites are in pristine coral-stone manses and cottages scattered over 12½ acres of flower-filled gardens; the public areas ramble along the beach. Garden rooms suit one or two guests and have a small patio or balcony, while junior suites with sitting areas and larger patios or balconies are perfect for families. Luxury cottage suites have plunge pools and separate bedrooms. The five pricey Plantation suites and two villas have spacious living rooms, private sun decks and plunge pools, and stereos—and are the only accommodations here that come with TVs (other guests can watch TV in the lounge or request one in-room for an added charge). Catch a breeze while mingling at the bar before or after dining in Coral Reef's excellent restaurant. ✉ *Hwy. 1, Holetown, St. James* ☎ *246/422–2372* 🖨 *246/ 422–1776* ⊕ *www.coralreefbarbados.com* 🏊 *29 rooms, 57 suites, 2 villas* ♿ *Restaurant, room service, fans, some in-room faxes, in-room safes, refrigerators, in-room data ports, golf privileges, 2 tennis courts, 2 pools, gym, hair salon, massage, beach, dive shop, snorkeling, windsurfing, boating, waterskiing, billiards, shuffleboard, bar, shops, babysitting, children's programs (ages 2–12), playground, Internet room, business services; no TV in some rooms, no kids under 12 in Feb.* ▤ *AE, MC, V* ❀ *EP.*

★ **$$$$** 🏨 **The Fairmont Royal Pavilion.** Unique among west-coast hotels of the same upscale caliber, every suite in this adults-oriented resort has a view of the sea from its broad balcony or patio. From ground-floor patios, in fact, you can step directly onto the sand. In the style of a Barbadian plantation house, all rooms have rich mahogany furniture and sisal rugs on ceramic floor tiles; to meet current expectations, rooms are also equipped with 27-inch flat-screen TVs and DVD/CD players. The resort's traditional, personalized service continues on the beach, where "Beach Butlers" cater to your every seaside whim—a fresh towel, sunscreen, mineral water, or perhaps an icy treat delivered to your beach chair. Breakfast and lunch are served alfresco near the beach; afternoon tea and dinner, in the exquisite Palm Terrace. ✉ *Hwy. 1, Porters, St. James* ☎ *246/422–5555* 🖨 *246/422–3940* ⊕ *www.fairmont.com* 🏊 *72 rooms, 1 3-bedroom villa* ♿ *2 restaurants, room service, fans, in-room safes, minibars, cable TV, in-room data ports, golf privileges, 2 tennis courts, pool, health club, hair salon, outdoor hot tub, beach, dive shop, snorkeling, windsurfing, boating, waterskiing, billiards, croquet, Ping-Pong, volleyball, 2 bars, shops, babysitting, laundry service, concierge, Internet room, business services, meeting room, no-smoking rooms; no kids under 12 Nov.–Apr.* ▤ *AE, D, DC, MC, V* ❀ *EP.*

4

$$$$ 🖺 **Sandy Lane Hotel & Golf Club.** Few places on earth can compare to
Fodor'sChoice Sandy Lane's luxurious facilities and ultra-pampering service—or to its
★ astronomical prices. Taking "upscale" to an entirely new level, Sandy
Lane is by far the priciest and most exclusive resort in Barbados and is
among the most expensive in the world, but for the few who can afford
to stay here—royals, celebrities, and business moguls among them—it's
an unparalleled experience. The main building of this exquisite resort
is a coral-stone, Palladian-style mansion facing a sweeping stretch of beach
shaded by mature trees. Guest accommodations, sumptuous in every detail, include three plasma TVs and DVD, full in-room wet bar, a personal butler, and remote-controlled everything—even the draperies!
The world-class spa, housed in a magnificent Romanesque building, is
a vacation in itself. Add elegant dining, the Caribbean's best golf courses,
a tennis center, a full complement of water sports, a special lounge for
teenagers, incomparable style . . . you get the picture. Sandy Lane is extraordinary. ☒ *Hwy. 1, Paynes Bay, St. James* ☎ *246/444–2000* 🖶 *246/
444–2222* ⊕ *www.sandylane.com* ➥ *102 rooms, 10 suites, 1 5-bedroom
villa* ⇘ *3 restaurants, room service, fans, in-room faxes, in-room safes,
minibars, cable TV, in-room data ports, 1 9-hole golf course, 2 18-hole
golf courses, 9 tennis courts, pool, hair salon, spa, steam room, beach,
snorkeling, windsurfing, boating, 4 bars, shops, children's programs (ages
3–12), dry cleaning, laundry service, concierge, Internet room, business
services, convention center* ⊟ *AE, D, DC, MC, V* ⦅◎⦆ *BP.*

$$$$ 🖺 **Tamarind Cove Hotel.** This Mediterranean-style resort sprawls along
750 feet of prime west-coast beachfront and is large enough to cater to
sophisticated couples and active families while at the same time offering cozy privacy to honeymooners. Most rooms provide a panoramic
view of the sea, which is gorgeous by day and spectacular at sunset. Four-
poster beds in 10 luxury oceanfront suites add a touch of romance. Junior suites are great for couples or families with one or two small
children; families with older kids might prefer the space and privacy of
a one-bedroom suite. Tamarind offers an array of water sports, as well
as golf privileges at the Royal Westmoreland Golf Club. Among its three
restaurants, Daphne's Barbados is a fashionable oasis for grand wining
and dining. A free water taxi shuttles to two sister hotels. ☒ *Hwy. 1,
Paynes Bay, St. James* ☎ *246/432–1332* 🖶 *246/432–6317* ⊕ *www.
tamarindcovehotel.com* ➥ *58 rooms, 47 suites* ⇘ *3 restaurants, room
service, in-room safes, refrigerators, cable TV, golf privileges, 2 tennis
courts, 3 pools, gym, hair salon, beach, snorkeling, windsurfing, boating, waterskiing, 2 bars, cabaret, shops, babysitting, dry cleaning, laundry service, concierge, Internet room, business services, meeting room*
⊟ *AE, D, DC, MC, V* ⦅◎⦆ *EP.*

$$$$ 🖺 **Treasure Beach.** Quiet, upscale, and friendly, this boutique all-suites
hotel has an almost residential quality. Many guests—mostly British—
are regulars, returning for two- or three-week stays every year. But the
rates are relatively expensive when compared, say, to the posh and
much larger (in terms of facilities and amenities) Coral Reef Club. Nevertheless, the hotel's high number of repeat guests suggests that the ambience here is well worth the price. Two floors of one-bedroom suites
form a horseshoe around a small garden and pool. Most have sea views,

but all are just steps from the sandy beach. The superdeluxe Hemmingway Suite blends antiques with modern luxury, an enormous terrace, and whirlpool tub. All suites have comfortable sitting rooms with ceiling fans, plasma TVs, shelves of books, and open-air fourth walls that can be shuttered at night for privacy. Only the bedrooms are air-conditioned. Suites easily accommodate three adults or two adults and two children. The resort's restaurant enjoys a well-deserved reputation among guests and locals alike for its fine cuisine and pleasant atmosphere. ⊠ *Hwy. 1, Paynes Bay, St. James* ☎ *246/432–1346* 🖷 *246/432–1094* ⊕ *www.treasurebeachhotel.com* 🛏 *29 suites* 🍴 *Restaurant, room service, fans, in-room safes, refrigerators, cable TV, in-room data ports, pool, gym, beach, snorkeling, bar, library, dry cleaning, laundry service, Internet room; no kids under 2 Nov.–May 15, except Christmas and Easter* 🖃 *AE, MC, V* 🍽 *EP* ⊘ *Closed Sept.*

$$ 🏨 **Divi Heritage Beach Resort.** Perhaps the best value we've found in the heart of the "Platinum Coast," Divi Heritage is a small oceanfront enclave—a home away from home—for adults only. Intentionally quiet, on-site activities are limited to tennis, snorkeling, and the beach, although day passes are available to guests who wish to use the pools, gym, water sports, spa, and restaurants at Almond Beach Club right next door. All suites, whether studio-size or one-bedroom, are airy and spacious, with fully equipped kitchens, king-size beds, sleeper sofas in the sitting area, clay-tile floors, and arched doorways opening onto a patio or balcony. Oceanfront studios each have a private hot tub on the patio. Sunset Crest shopping mall (with a supermarket) is directly across the street, and it's a short walk to the restaurants, shops, and sights in the center of Holetown. ⊠ *Hwy. 1, Sunset Crest, St. James* ☎ *246/432–2968* 🖷 *246/432–1527* ⊕ *www.diviresorts.com* 🛏 *22 suites* 🍴 *Some in-room hot tubs, kitchens, cable TV, tennis court, beach, snorkeling; no kids under 16* 🖃 *AE, D, DC, MC, V* 🍽 *EP.*

EAST COAST 🏨 **Villa Nova.** For a truly luxurious Barbadian escape, Villa Nova is
★ **$$$$** uniquely situated in the middle of nowhere—well, actually it's located amid beautiful gardens in the hilly woodlands of St. John. Owner Lynne Pemberton, a romance novelist, had this tranquil, all-suite country retreat reconstructed on the remnants of a historic (1834) greathouse, once the home of Sir Anthony Eden. The pampering begins with a complimentary unpacking service and a free steaming of the outfit you plan to wear on the first evening and extends to the plush facilities and accommodations. Exquisitely decorated with antiques and works of art, suites have king-size beds, comfortable sitting areas, and bathrooms with claw-foot tubs; a butler will serve breakfast on your wraparound terrace. Relax in the lounge, on the veranda, or by the pool with a book from the extensive library, or explore the neighborhood on horseback (stables are nearby) before enjoying a superb meal in the Plantation Room. For a change of scenery, head to one of the hotel's two beach clubs (transportation is provided)—the west-coast club is ideal for swimming; the east-coast club at Cattlewash is a great picnic location. ⊠ *Villa Nova, St. John* ☎ *246/433–1505, 246/433–1524 reservations* 🖷 *246/433–6363* ⊕ *www.villanovabarbados.com* 🛏 *17 rooms, 11 suites* 🍴 *2 restaurants, room service, fans, in-room safes, cable TV, in-room data ports, golf priv-*

CLOSE UP

More Barbados Resorts, Hotels & Inns

BECAUSE WE WOULD LIKE to recommend more places to stay than we have room, here are some additional suggestions:

ON THE SOUTH COAST

$-$$ Coconut Court Beach Resort (✉ Main Rd., Hastings Bay, Christ Church ☎ 246/427-1655 ⊕ www. coconut-court.com). This resort is popular among families, who love the Coco Kids Club and children's pools. The 126 apartments and efficiencies have kitchenettes; request one with air-conditioning and, if you wish, satellite TV.

$ Hotel PomMarine (✉ Barbados Community College, Hastings, Christ Church ☎ 246/228-0900 ⊕ www. pommarinebarbados.com). Staffed by Hospitality Institute students at Barbados Community College, the 20 rooms and one self-catering suite here are simple yet comfortable. Enjoy the pool, tennis court, fine dining at Muscovado Restaurant—and perhaps observe students working in a demo kitchen. Hastings Beach is across the street.

$ Sandy Beach Island Resort (✉ Main Rd., Worthing, Christ Church ☎ 246/435-8000 ⊕ www. sandybeachbarbados.com). Broad Sandy Beach is the main attraction at this 127-room resort, which also offers a waterfall pool, water sports, and a full-time activities director.

ON THE WEST COAST

$$$$ Crystal Cove Hotel (✉ Hwy. 1, Appleby, St. James ☎ 246/432-2683 ⊕ www.crystalcovehotelbarbados. com). This 88-room resort spills down a hillside to the beach where you can swim, sail, snorkel, water-ski, windsurf, or kayak to your heart's

content—or play tennis, dip in the pool, or take advantage of the golf privileges.

$$$$ The House (✉ Hwy. 1, Paynes Bay, St. James ☎ 246/432-5525 ⊕ www.thehousebarbados.com). Privacy, luxury, and service are hallmarks of this 31-suite adult sanctuary next door to sister resort Tamarind Cove. A 24-hour "ambassador" service caters to your every whim.

$$$-$$$$ Little Good Harbour (✉ Hwy. 1B, Shermans, St. Peter ☎ 246/439-3000 ⊕ www. littlegoodharbourbarbados.com). A cluster of classy, spacious one-, two-, and three-bedroom, self-catering cottages overlooks a narrow strip of beach in the far north of Barbados— just beyond the picturesque fishing village of Six Men's Bay.

$$$$ Lone Star Hotel (✉ Hwy. 1, Holetown, St. James ☎ 246/419-0599 ⊕ www.thelonestar.com). A 1940s service station transformed into a chic four-suite hotel—now there's an idea! Two architecturally fascinating suites at beach level and two upstairs are furnished with Bajan mahogany and chic Italian-designed furniture. The restaurant is also extraordinary.

ON THE EAST COAST

$-$$ New Edgewater (✉ Bathsheba Beach, Bathsheba, St. Joseph ☎ 246/433-9900 ⊕ www.newedgewater. com). In 2004, new owners refurbished and significantly upgraded the rooms at this cliffside hideaway, while retaining its rustic beach-house atmosphere, handmade furniture, parquet ceilings, and leaded-glass windows.

4

ileges, 2 tennis courts, pool, gym, spa, billiards, hiking, 3 bars, library, piano, shop, laundry service, concierge, Internet room, meeting room, airport shuttle; no kids under 12 ⊟ *AE, D, MC, V* ⱳ *BP.*

Where to Eat

First-class restaurants and hotel dining rooms serve quite sophisticated cuisine—prepared by chefs with international experience—which rivals that served in the world's best restaurants. Most menus include seafood: dorado (also known as dolphin—a fish, not the mammal—or mahimahi), kingfish, snapper, and flying fish prepared every way imaginable. Flying fish is so popular that it has officially become a national symbol. Shellfish also abounds, as do steak, pork, and local black-belly lamb.

Local specialty dishes include *buljol* (a cold salad of pickled codfish, tomatoes, onions, sweet peppers, and celery) and *conkies* (cornmeal, coconut, pumpkin, raisins, sweet potatoes, and spices, mixed together, wrapped in a banana leaf, and steamed). *Cou-cou,* often served with steamed flying fish, is a mixture of cornmeal and okra, usually topped with a spicy creole sauce made from tomatoes, onions, and sweet peppers. Bajan-style pepper pot is a hearty stew of oxtail, beef chunks, and "any other meat" in a rich, spicy gravy and simmered overnight.

For lunch, restaurants often offer a traditional Bajan buffet of fried fish, baked chicken, salads, and a selection of local roots and vegetables. Be cautious with the West Indian condiments—like the sun, they're hotter than you think. Typical Bajan drinks, besides Banks beer and Mount Gay rum, are *falernum* (a liqueur concocted of rum, sugar, lime juice, and almond essence) and *mauby* (a nonalcoholic drink made by boiling bitter bark and spices, straining the mixture, and sweetening it). You're sure to enjoy the fresh fruit or rum punch.

What to Wear

The dress code in Barbados is conservative and, on occasion, formal—a jacket and tie for gentlemen and a cocktail dress for ladies in the fanciest restaurants and hotel dining rooms, particularly during the winter holiday season. Other places are more casual, although jeans and shorts are always frowned upon at dinner. Beach attire is appropriate only at the beach.

Bridgetown

CARIBBEAN/
SEAFOOD
$$

✕ **Waterfront Cafe.** This friendly bistro alongside the Careenage is the perfect place to enjoy a drink, snack, or meal—and to people-watch. Locals and tourists alike gather for all-day alfresco dining on sandwiches, salads, fish, pasta, pepper pot stew, and tasty Bajan snacks such as buljol, fish cakes, or plantation pork (plantains stuffed with spicy minced pork). The panfried flying fish sandwich is especially popular. In the evening you can gaze through the arched windows while savoring nouvelle Caribbean cuisine, enjoying cool trade winds, and listening to live jazz. There's a special Caribbean buffet and steel-pan music on Tuesday night from 7 to 9. ✉ *The Careenage, Bridgetown, St. Michael* ☎ *246/427–0093* ⊟ *AE, D, DC, MC, V* ✸ *Closed Sun.*

South Coast

CARIBBEAN
$$$–$$$$

✕ **David's Place.** Come here for sophisticated Bajan cuisine in a prime waterfront location on St. Lawrence Bay. Waves gently lap against the pilings of the open-air deck—a rhythmic accompaniment to the soft classical background music. Among the starters, the pumpkin soup is divine. Specialties such as grilled flying fish, pepper pot stew, curried shrimp, and vegetarian dishes come with homemade cheddar-cheese bread. Dessert might be bread pudding, carrot cake with rum sauce, or coconut cream pie. David's has an extensive wine list. ⊠ *St. Lawrence Main Rd., Worthing, Christ Church* ☎ *246/435–9755* ⚖ *Reservations essential* ▭ *AE, D, MC, V* ☯ *Closed Mon. No lunch.*

ITALIAN
$$–$$$

✕ **Bellini's Trattoria.** Classic northern Italian cuisine is the specialty at Bellini's, on the main floor of the Little Bay Hotel. The atmosphere here is smart-casual—as appropriate for a family meal as for a romantic dinner for two. Toast the evening with a Bellini cocktail (ice-cold sparkling wine with a splash of fruit nectar) and start your meal with bruschetta, an individual gourmet pizza, or perhaps a homemade pasta dish with fresh herbs and a rich sauce. If not already stuffed, move on to the signature garlic shrimp entrée or the popular chicken parmigiana—then top it all off with excellent tiramisu. We recommend making your reservations early; request a table on the Mediterranean-style verandah to enjoy one of the most appealing dining settings on the south coast. ⊠ *Little Bay Hotel, St. Lawrence Gap, Dover, Christ Church* ☎ *246/435–7246* ⚖ *Reservations essential* ▭ *AE, MC, V* ☯ *No lunch.*

SEAFOOD
$$$–$$$$

✕ **Josef's Restaurant.** The signature restaurant of Austrian restaurateur Josef Schwaiger, in a cliffside Bajan dwelling surrounded by gardens, is one of the most upscale seaside dining spots on the south coast. Josef's cuisine fuses Asian culinary techniques and Caribbean flavors with fresh seafood. Fruits of the sea—seared yellowfin tuna with mango-cilantro sauce or catch of the day with tomato fondue and creamed potatoes—are prominent, and the wine list is extensive. Try shredded duck with herbed hoisin pancakes as an innovative starter, or let the free-range chicken teriyaki with stir-fry noodles tingle your taste buds. Pasta dishes assuage the vegetarian palate. ⊠ *Waverly House, St. Lawrence Gap, Dover, Christ Church* ☎ *246/435–8245* ⚖ *Reservations essential* ▭ *AE, D, MC, V* ☯ *No lunch.*

★ $$$–$$$$

✕ **Pisces.** For seafood lovers, this is nirvana. Prepared here in every way—from charbroiled to gently sautéed—seafood specialties include conch strips in tempura, rich fish chowder, panfried fillets of flying fish with a toasted almond crust and a light mango-citrus sauce, and seared prawns in a fragrant curry sauce. Landlubbers in your party can select from a few chicken, beef, and pasta dishes on the menu. Whatever you choose, the herbs that flavor it and the accompanying vegetables will have come from the chef's own garden. Save room for the bread pudding, yogurt-lime cheesecake, or homemade rum-raisin ice cream. Twinkling white lights reflect on the water as you dine. ⊠ *St. Lawrence Gap, Dover, Christ Church* ☎ *246/435–6564* ⚖ *Reservations essential* ▭ *AE, D, DC, MC, V* ☯ *No lunch.*

$$-$$$ ✕ **L'Azure at the Crane.** Perched on an oceanfront cliff, L'Azure is an informal luncheon spot by day that becomes elegant after dark. Enjoy seafood chowder—prepared with lobster, shrimp, dorado, local vegetables, and a dash of sherry—or a light salad or sandwich while absorbing the breathtaking view. At dinner, candlelight and a soft guitar enhance a fabulous Caribbean lobster seasoned with herbs, lime juice, and garlic butter and served in its shell; if you're not in the mood for seafood, try the perfectly grilled filet mignon. Sunday is really special, with a Gospel Brunch at 10 AM and a Bajan Buffet at 12:30 PM. ✉ *The Crane, Crane Bay, St. Philip* ☏ *246/423–6220* ⚱ *Reservations essential* ▭ *AE, D, DC, MC, V.*

West Coast

CONTEMPORARY ✕ **The Cliff.** Chef Paul Owens' mastery is the foundation of one of the
$$$$ finest dining experiences in the Caribbean, with prices to match. Steep
Fodor'sChoice steps hug the cliff on which the restaurant sits to accommodate those
★ arriving by yacht, and every candlelight table has a sea view. Starters include smoked salmon ravioli with garlic sauce or grilled portobello mushroom on greens with truffle vinaigrette; for the main course, try Caribbean shrimp with a Thai green-curry coconut sauce, veal chop with a mustard and tarragon sauce, or red snapper fillet on a baked potato cake. Dessert falls in the sinful category, and service is impeccable. A $75 prix-fixe menu is a good deal. Reserve days or even weeks in advance to snag a table at the front of the terrace for the best view. ✉ *Hwy. 1, Derricks, St. James* ☏ *246/432–1922* ⚱ *Reservations essential* ▭ *AE, DC, MC, V* ☉ *Closed Sun. Apr. 15–Dec. 15. No lunch.*

$$$-$$$$ ✕ **Carambola.** Dramatic lighting, alfresco dining, and a cliffside location make this one of the island's most romantic restaurants. The menu is a mix of classic French and Caribbean cuisines—with Asian touches for good measure. Start with the tuna carpaccio with ginger and sesame seeds or a vegetable tartlet with pesto and apple. For an entrée, try wine-poached mahimahi with coriander and vegetables, or oven-roasted duck breast with anise and bitter orange marmalade. The *citron gâteau* (lime mousse on a pool of lemon coulis) is a wonderfully light finish to your meal. ✉ *Hwy. 1, Derricks, St. James* ☏ *246/432–0832* ⚱ *Reservations essential* ▭ *AE, D, MC, V* ☉ *Closed Sun. No lunch.*

★ **$$$-$$$$** ✕ **La Mer.** Master chef Hans Schweitzer, who earned a reputation in Barbados for elegant cuisine as executive chef of the original Sandy Lane Hotel, works his magic here in a more relaxed—but still stylish—way. His restaurant hugs the pretty, man-made lagoon at Port St. Charles, the tony villa community that particularly appeals to boating enthusiasts. Fresh fish from Six Men's Bay, just up the road, and tender cuts of meat are seared on either of two grills, wood or lava-rock, while vegetarian dishes might be stirred up at the wok station. This is a perfect place for a light meal at the bar, just steps from the dock, or a romantic dinner, with moonlight reflecting on the lagoon. ✉ *Port St. Charles, Speightstown, St. Peter* ☏ *246/419–2000* ⚱ *Reservations essential* ▭ *AE, DC, MC, V* ☉ *Closed Mon.*

ECLECTIC ✕ **The Lone Star.** In the 1940s this was the only garage on the west coast;
$$$-$$$$ today it's the snazzy restaurant in the tiny but chic Lone Star Hotel, where

top chefs in the open-plan kitchen turn the finest local ingredients into gastronomic delights. The menu is extensive but pricey, even for lunch. During the day, such tasty dishes as fish soup with rouille, Caesar or Thai chicken salad, tuna tartare, rotisserie chicken, and linguini with tomato-basil sauce and feta cheese are served in the oceanfront beach bar. At sunset, the casual daytime atmosphere turns trendy. You might start with an Oriental tasting plate or a half-dozen oysters, followed by crispy roast duckling, grilled fish of the day, or lamb cutlets—or choose from one of dozens of other tasty land, sea, and vegetarian dishes. ✉ *Lone Star Hotel, Hwy. 1, Mount Standfast, St. James* ☎ *246/419–0599* ▭ *AE, D, MC, V.*

★ **$$–$$$** ✕ **Angry Annie's.** You can't miss this place. Outside and inside, everything's painted in cheerful Caribbean pinks, blues, greens, and yellows—and it's just steps from the main road. The food is just as lively: great barbecued "jump-up" ribs and chicken, grilled fresh fish or juicy steaks, "Rasta pasta" for vegetarians, and several spicy curries. Eat inside on gaily colored furniture or outside under the stars, or take it away with you. Fun for people of all ages, Angry Annie's has a vibrant atmosphere and serves satisfying meals. ✉ *1st St., Holetown, St. James* ☎ *246/432–2119* ▭ *AE, DC, MC, V* ☾ *No lunch.*

$$–$$$ ✕ **Olives Bar & Bistro.** Chef Scott Ames presides over this intimate restaurant, a quaint Bajan residence in the center of Holetown but now a favorite west-coast dining spot. Mediterranean and Caribbean flavors enliven inventive pizzas and tasty salads at lunch; the dinner menu often includes fresh seafood, such as seared yellowfin tuna with ratatouille or pan-seared sea scallops with basmati rice and steamed greens. Vegetarian selections are always available. Dine inside, accompanied by the hint of soothing light jazz music, or in the courtyard; the upstairs bar is a popular spot to mingle over coffee, refreshing drinks, or snacks (pizza, pastas, salads). ✉ *2nd St., Holetown, St. James* ☎ *246/432–2112* ▭ *AE, D, MC, V.*

☾ **$$–$$$** ✕ **Ragamuffins.** The only restaurant on Barbados in an authentic chattel house, Ragamuffins is tiny, funky, lively, and informal. The menu offers seafood, perfectly broiled T-bone steaks, West Indian curries, and vegetarian dishes such as Bajan stir-fried vegetables with noodles. Dine inside or out. The kitchen is within sight of the bar—which is a popular meeting spot most evenings for vacationers and locals alike. ✉ *1st St., Holetown, St. James* ☎ *246/432–1295* ⌁ *Reservations essential* ▭ *AE, D, MC, V* ☾ *No lunch.*

☾ **$–$$** ✕ **Baku Beach Bar.** Whether you're going to the beach, coming from the beach, or just wanting to be near the beach, this is a great place for lunch or an informal dinner. Tables spill into the courtyard, through tropical gardens, and onto a boardwalk by the sea. Try a Caesar salad, a burger, spareribs, or grilled fish served with the salsa of your choice: fruit, pesto, herb lemon, or ginger soy. On the side, have garlic bread, sautéed onions, rice pilaf, or spicy potato wedges. Got room for crème brûlée, lemon tart, or a brownie with ice cream? Maybe dawdling over cappuccino is enough. ✉ *Hwy. 1, Holetown, St. James* ☎ *246/432–2258* ▭ *AE, D, MC, V.*

ITALIAN
★ $$$$ ✕ **Daphne's.** The chic and glamorous Caribbean outpost of the famed London eatery is wedged between the Tamarind Cove Hotel and its sister hotel, the House. British chef Kelly Jackson whips up contemporary versions of classic Italian dishes. Grilled mahimahi, for example, becomes "modern Italian" when combined with marsala wine, peperonata, and zucchini. Perfectly prepared pappardelle with braised duck, red wine, and oregano is a sublime pasta choice. Light meals, salads, and half-portions of pasta are available at lunch. The extensive wine list features both regional Italian and fine French selections. ⊠ *Paynes Bay, St. James* ☎ *234/432–2731* ⌕ *Reservations essential* ⊟ *AE, D, MC, V.*

SEAFOOD
★ $$$–$$$$ ✕ **The Fish Pot.** Just north of the little fishing village of Six Men's Bay, toward the far northern west coast of Barbados, this attractive seaside restaurant serves excellent Mediterranean cuisine and the freshest fish. Gaze seaward through windows framed with pale green louvered shutters while lunching on a seafood crêpe or perhaps pasta with seafood or puttanesca sauce; in the evening, the menu includes panfried red snapper with caper-and-thyme mashed potatoes, seared herb-crusted tuna on garlic and spinach polenta, sun-dried tomato risotto tossed with vegetables, and lamb shank braised in red wine. Bright and cheery by day and relaxed and cozy by night, the Fish Pot offers a tasty dining experience in a setting that's more classy than its name might suggest. ⊠ *Little Good Harbour, Shermans, St. Peter* ☎ *246/439–3000* ⌕ *Reservations essential* ⊟ *MC, V.*

East Coast

CARIBBEAN
$$–$$$ ✕ **Atlantis Hotel Restaurant.** People have been stopping by for lunch with a view here since 1945, when Mrs. Enid Maxwell bought this property, a quaint seaside hotel since the turn of the 19th century. Although it was sold in 2002, the new owners have kept up Mrs. Maxwell's tradition—all Bajan cuisine that complements the natural environment. Each Wednesday and Sunday the enormous Bajan buffet includes pumpkin fritters, rice and peas, breadfruit casserole, steamed fish creole, oven-barbecued chicken, pepper pot, macaroni pie, ratatouille, and more. Homemade coconut pie tops the dessert list. The Atlantis is a lunch stop for several organized day tours, so it sometimes get crowded. ⊠ *Atlantis Hotel, Tent Bay, Bathsheba, St. Joseph* ☎ *246/433–9445* ⊟ *AE, D, MC, V.*

★ $$–$$$ ✕ **Naniki Restaurant.** Rich wooden beams and stone tiles, clay pottery, straw mats, colorful dinnerware, and fresh flowers from the on-site anthurium farm set the style here. Huge picture windows and outdoor porch seating allow you to enjoy the exhilarating views of surrounding hills or a refreshing breeze along with your meal of exquisitely prepared Caribbean standards. For lunch, seared flying fish, grilled dorado, stewed lambi (conch), curried chicken, and jerk chicken or pork are accompanied by cou-cou, peas and rice, or salad. At dinner, grilled snapper, local black-belly lamb, seared shrimp, and pork loin are specialties. On Sunday, lunch is a Caribbean buffet. Vegetarian dishes are always available. ⊠ *Suriname, St. Joseph* ☎ *246/433–1300* ⊟ *AE, DC, MC, V* ☺ *Closed Mon.*

☾ $ ✕ **Bonito Beach Bar & Restaurant.** The Bonito's wholesome West Indian home cooking has soothed the hunger pangs of many folks who find themselves on the east coast at lunchtime. The view of the Atlantic from the second-floor dining room is striking, and the Bajan buffet lunch includes fried fish and baked chicken accompanied by salads and vegetables fresh from the garden. Beer, rum punch, fresh fruit punch, and lime squash are the refreshing choices to accompany your meal. ☒ *Coast Rd., Bathsheba, St. Joseph* ☎ *246/433–9034* ☰ *AE, D, DC, MC, V* ☉ *Closed Sun.*

Beaches

Bajan beaches have fine white sand, and all are open to the public. Most have access from the road, so nonguest bathers don't have to pass through hotel properties.

EAST COAST   With long stretches of open beach, crashing ocean surf, rocky cliffs, and verdant hills, the Atlantic (windward) side of Barbados is where Barbadians spend their holidays. But be cautioned: swimming at east-coast beaches is treacherous, even for strong swimmers, and is *not* recommended. Waves are high, the bottom tends to be rocky, the currents are unpredictable, and the undertow is dangerously strong.

Barclays Park. Serious swimming is unwise at this beach, which follows the coastline in St. Andrew, but there are tide pools where you can take a dip, wade, and play—and a lovely shaded area with picnic tables directly across the road. ☒ *Ermy Bourne Hwy., north of Bathsheba, St. Andrews.*

★ **Bathsheba/Cattlewash.** Although it's not safe for swimming, the miles of untouched, windswept sand along the East Coast Road in St. Joseph Parish are great for beachcombing and wading. As you approach Bathsheba Soup Bowl, the southernmost stretch just below Tent Bay, the enormous mushroomlike boulders and rolling surf are uniquely spectacular. This is also where expert surfers from around the world converge each November for the Independence Classic Surfing Championship. ☒ *East Coast Rd., Bathsheba, St. Joseph.*

SOUTH COAST   A young, energetic crowd favors the south-coast beaches, which are broad, blessed with powdery white sand, and dotted with tall palms. The reef-protected areas with crystal-clear water are safe for swimming and snorkeling. The surf is medium to high, and the waves get bigger and the winds stronger (windsurfers take note) the farther southeast you go.

Accra Beach. This popular beach next to the Accra Hotel has gentle surf and a lifeguard. There are plenty of nearby restaurants for refreshments and beach stalls for renting chairs and equipment for snorkeling and other water sports. There's also a convenient parking lot and a children's playground. ☒ *Hwy. 7, Rockley, Christ Church.*

Carlisle Bay. Adjacent to the Hilton Barbados and Grand Barbados hotels just south of Bridgetown, this broad half-circle of white sand is one of the island's best beaches—but it can become crowded on weekends and holidays. Park at Harbour Lights or the Boatyard, both on Bay Street, where you can also rent umbrellas and beach chairs and buy refreshments. ☒ *Needham's Point, Aquatic Gap, St. Michael.*

★ **Crane Beach.** An exquisite crescent of pink sand on the southeast coast, Crane Beach is protected by steep cliffs. As attractive as this location is now, it was named not for the elegant long-legged wading birds but for the crane used for hauling and loading cargo when this area was a busy port. Protected by a reef, the beach has lightly rolling surf that is great for bodysurfing. A lifeguard is on duty. Changing rooms are available at The Crane resort for a small fee (which you can apply toward drinks or a meal at the restaurant). Beach access is through the hotel and down about 200 steps. ⊠ *Crane Bay, St. Philip.*

Miami Beach. Also called Enterprise Beach, this isolated spot on Enterprise Coast Road, just east of Oistins, is a picturesque slice of pure white sand with cliffs on either side and crystal-clear water. You can find a palm-shaded parking area, snack carts, and chair rentals. Bring a picnic or have lunch across the road at Café Luna in Little Arches Hotel. ⊠ *Enterprise Beach Rd., Enterprise, Christ Church.*

Sandy Beach. Next to the Sandy Beach Island Resort, this fabulous beach has shallow, calm waters and a picturesque lagoon, making it an ideal location for families with small kids. Park right on the main road. You can rent beach chairs and umbrellas, and plenty of places nearby sell food and drink. ⊠ *Hwy. 7, Worthing, Christ Church.*

Silver Sands–Silver Rock Beach. Nestled between South Point, the southernmost tip of the island, and Inch Marlowe Point, Silver Sands–Silver Rock is a beautiful strand of white sand that always has a stiff breeze. That makes this beach the best in Barbados for intermediate and advanced windsurfers and, more recently, kite surfers. ⊠ *Off Hwy. 7, Christ Church.*

WEST COAST Gentle Caribbean waves lap the west coast, and the stunning coves and sandy beaches are shaded by leafy mahogany trees. The water is perfect for swimming and water sports. An almost unbroken chain of beaches runs between Bridgetown and Speightstown. Elegant homes and luxury hotels face much of the beachfront property in this area, Barbados's Platinum Coast.

West-coast beaches are mostly smaller and narrower than those on the south coast. Also, prolonged stormy weather in October or November may cause sand erosion, temporarily making the beach even narrower. Even so, west-coast beaches are seldom crowded. Vendors stroll by, selling handmade baskets, hats, dolls, jewelry—even original watercolors; owners of private boats offer waterskiing, parasailing, and snorkeling excursions. There are no concession stands, but hotels and beachside restaurants welcome nonguests for terrace lunches (wear a cover-up), and you can buy picnic items at supermarkets in Holetown.

Brighton Beach. Calm as a lake, this is where you can find locals taking a quick dip on hot days. Just north of Bridgetown, Brighton Beach is also the home to the Malibu Beach Club. ⊠ *Spring Garden Hwy., Brighton, St. Michael.*

★ **Mullins Beach.** This lovely beach just south of Speightstown is a perfect place to spend the day. The water is safe for swimming and snorkeling, there's easy parking on the main road, and Suga Suga Restaurant serves snacks, meals, and drinks—and rents chairs and umbrellas. ⊠ *Hwy. 1, Mullins Bay, St. Peter.*

Paynes Bay. The stretch of beach just south of Sandy Lane is lined with luxury hotels. It's a very pretty area, with plenty of beach to go around and good snorkeling. Parking areas and public access are available near the Coach House. Grab a bite to eat and liquid refreshments at Bomba's Beach Bar. ⊠ *Hwy. 1, Paynes Bay, St. James.*

Sports & the Outdoors

Cricket, football (soccer), polo, and rugby are extremely popular sports in Barbados among participants and spectators alike, with local, regional, and international matches held throughout the year. Contact the Barbados Tourism Authority or check local newspapers for information about schedules and tickets.

DIVING & SNORKELING
More than two dozen dive sites lie along the west coast between Maycocks Bay and Bridgetown and off the south coast as far as the St. Lawrence Gap. Certified divers can explore flat coral reefs and see sea fans, huge barrel sponges, and more than 50 varieties of fish. Nine sunken wrecks are dived regularly, and at least 10 more are accessible to experts. Underwater visibility is generally 80 to 90 feet. The calm waters along the west coast are also ideal for snorkeling. The marine reserve, a stretch of protected reef between Sandy Lane and the Colony Club, contains beautiful coral formations accessible from the beach.

On the west coast, **Bell Buoy** is a large, dome-shaped reef where huge brown coral tree forests and schools of fish delight all categories of divers at depths ranging from 20 to 60 feet. At **Dottins Reef,** off Holetown, you can see schooling fish, barracudas, and turtles at depths of 40 to 60 feet. **Maycocks Bay,** on the northwest coast, is a particularly enticing site; large coral reefs are separated by corridors of white sand, and visibility is often 100 feet or more. The 165-foot freighter *Pamir* lies in 60 feet of water off Six Men's Bay; it's still intact, and you can peer through its portholes and view dozens of varieties of tropical fish. **Silver Bank** is a healthy coral reef with beautiful fish and sea fans; you may get a glimpse of the *Atlantis* submarine at 60 to 80 feet. Not to be missed is the *Stavronikita*, a scuttled Greek freighter at about 135 feet; hundreds of butterfly fish hang out around its mast, and the thin rays of sunlight filtering down through the water make fully exploring the huge ship a wonderfully eerie experience.

Farther south, **Carlisle Bay** is a natural harbor and marine park just below Bridgetown. Here you can retrieve empty bottles thrown overboard by generations of sailors and see cannons and cannonballs, anchors, and seven unique shipwrecks (*Berwyn, Fox, CTrek, Eilon,* the barge *Cornwallis,* and *Bajan Queen*) lying in 25 to 60 feet of water, all close enough to visit on the same dive. The *Bajan Queen*, a cruise vessel that sank in 2002, is the island's newest wreck.

Dive shops provide a two-hour beginner's "resort" course ($70 to $75) followed by a shallow dive, or a weeklong certification course (about $350). Once you're certified, a one-tank dive runs about $50 to $55; a two-tank dive is $70 to $80. All equipment is supplied, and you can purchase multidive packages. Gear for snorkeling is available (free or for a small rental fee) from most hotels. Snorkelers can usually accompany dive trips for $20 for a one- or two-hour trip.

On the south coast, the **Dive Shop, Ltd.** (⊠ Bay St., Aquatic Gap, St. Michael ☎ 246/426–9947, 888/898–3483 in U.S., 888/575–3483 in Canada ⊕ www.divebds.com), the island's oldest dive shop, offers daily reef and wreck dives, plus beginner classes, certification courses, and underwater photography instruction. Underwater cameras are available for rent. On the west coast, **Dive Barbados** (⊠ Mount Standfast, St. James ☎ 246/422–3133 ⊕ www.divebarbados.net), on the beach next to the Lone Star Hotel, offers all levels of PADI instruction, two-or three-reef and wreck dives daily for up to six divers each time, snorkeling with Hawksbill turtles just offshore, as well as underwater camera rental and free transportation. **Hightide Watersports** (⊠ Coral Reef Club, Holetown, St. James ☎ 246/432–0931 or 800/513–5761 ⊕ www.divehightide.com) offers three dive trips—one- and two-tank dives and night reef/wreck/drift dives—daily for up to eight divers, along with PADI instruction, equipment rental, and free transportation.

FISHING   Fishing is a year-round activity in Barbados, but its prime time is January through April, when game fish are in season. Whether you're a serious deep-sea fisher looking for marlin, sailfish, tuna, and other billfish or you prefer angling in calm coastal waters where wahoo, barracuda, and other small fish reside, you can choose from a variety of half- or full-day charter trips departing from the Careenage in Bridgetown. Expect to pay $100 per person for a shared charter; for a private charter, expect to pay $400 per boat for a four-hour half-day or $750 for an eight-hour full-day charter.

Billfisher II (☎ 246/431–0741), a 40-foot Pacemaker, accommodates up to six passengers with three fishing chairs and five rods. Capt. Winston ("The Colonel") White has been fishing these waters since 1975. His full-day charters include a full lunch and guaranteed fish (or a 25% refund); all trips include drinks and transportation to and from the boat. *Blue Jay* (☎ 246/429–2326 ⊕ www.bluemarlinbarbados.com) is a spacious, fully equipped, 45-foot Sport Fisherman with a crew that knows the denizens of blue marlin, sailfish, barracuda, and kingfish. Four to six people can be accommodated—it's the only charter boat on the island with four chairs. Most fishing is done by trolling. Drinks, snacks, bait, tackle, and transfers are provided. *Cannon II* (☎ 246/424–6107), a 42-foot Hatteras Sport Fisherman, has three chairs and five rods and accommodates six passengers; drinks and snacks are complimentary, and lunch is served on full-day charters.

GOLF   Barbadians love golf, and golfers love Barbados. In addition to the courses listed below, Almond Beach Village has a 9-hole, par-3 executive course open to guests only. Learn to play or improve your game at the **Barbados Academy of Golf & Public Driving Range** (⊠ ABC Hwy., Balls Complex, Balls, Christ Church ☎ 246/420–7405). It has a chipping and putting green, with sand bunkers and 48 hitting bays. The adjacent 18-hole miniature golf course is fun for the whole family. Both are open daily 8 AM to 11 PM, and snacks are available. **Barbados Golf Club** (⊠ Hwy. 7, Durants, Christ Church ☎ 246/428–8463 ⊕ www. barbadosgolfclub.com), the first public golf course on Barbados, is an 18-hole championship course (6,805 yards, par 72) redesigned in 2000 by golf course architect Ron Kirby. Greens fees are $119 for 18 holes, plus a $13 per-person cart fee. Unlimited three-day and seven-day golf passes are available. Several hotels offer preferential tee-time reservations and reduced rates. Club and shoe rentals are available. At the prestigious **Country Club at Sandy Lane** (⊠ Hwy. 1, Paynes Bay, St. James ☎ 246/432–2829 ⊕ www.sandylane.com/golf), golfers can play on the Old Nine or on either of two 18-hole championship courses: the Tom Fazio–designed Country Club Course or the spectacular Green Monkey Course, which opened in October 2004 and is reserved for hotel guests and club members only. Greens fees in high season are $85 for 9 holes ($75 for hotel guests) or $200 for 18 holes ($150 for hotel guests). Golf carts are equipped with GPS, which alerts you to upcoming traps and hazards, provides tips on how to play the hole, and allows you to order refreshments! **Rockley Golf & Country Club** (⊠ Golf Club Rd., Worthing, Christ Church ☎ 246/435–7873), on the southeast coast, has a challenging 9-hole course (2,800 yards, par 35) that can be played as 18 from varying tee positions. Club and cart rentals are available. Greens fees on weekdays are $40 for 18 holes and $30 for 9 holes; on weekends, $56 for 18 holes and $38 for 9 holes. The **Royal Westmoreland Golf Club** (⊠ Westmoreland, St. James ☎ 246/422–4653) has a world-class Robert Trent Jones, Jr., 18-hole championship course (6,870 yards, par 72) that meanders through the former 500-acre Westmoreland Sugar Estate. The course is restricted to villa renters in high season (November 15 to April 30 each year); greens fees are $175 for 18 holes, $87.50 for 9 holes. In the off-season, greens fees for visitors are $125 for 18 holes and, for villa renters, $75 for either 18 or 9 holes. Greens fees include use of an electric cart; club rental is available.

HIKING Hilly but not mountainous, the northern interior and the east coast are ideal for hiking. The **Arbib Heritage & Nature Trail** (⊠ Speightstown, St. Peter ☎ 246/426–2421), maintained by the Barbados National Trust, is actually two trails—one offers a rigorous hike through gullies and plantations to old ruins and remote north-country areas; the other is a shorter, easier walk through Speightstown's side streets and past an ancient church and chattel houses. Guided hikes take place on Wednesday, Thursday, and Saturday at 9 AM (book by 3 PM the day before) and cost $7.50. The **Barbados National Trust** (⊠ Wildey House, Wildey, St. Michael ☎ 246/426–2421) sponsors free walks, called **Hike Barbados**, year-round on Sunday from 6 AM to about 9 AM and from 3:30 PM to 6 PM; once a month, a moonlight hike substitutes for the afternoon hike and begins at 5:30 PM (bring a flashlight). Experienced guides group you with others of similar levels of ability. Stop & Stare hikes go 5 to 6 mi; Here & There, 8 to 10 mi; and Grin & Bear, 12 to 14 mi. Wear loose clothes, sensible shoes, sunscreen, and a hat, and bring your camera and a bottle of water. Routes and locations change, but each hike is a loop, finishing in the same spot where it began. Check newspapers or call the Trust for the meeting place on a particular Sunday.

HORSE RACING   Horse racing is administered by the **Barbados Turf Club** (☎ 246/426–3980 ⊕ www.barbadosturfclub.com) and takes place on alternate Saturdays throughout the year at the Garrison Savannah, a six-furlong grass oval in Christ Church, about 3 mi (5 km) south of Bridgetown. The important races are the Sandy Lane Barbados Gold Cup, held in late February or early March, and the United Insurance Barbados Derby Day in August. Post time is 1:30 PM. General admission is $5 for grandstand seats and $12.50 for the Club House. (Prices are double on Gold Cup day.)

SEA EXCURSIONS   Minisubmarine voyages are enormously popular with families and those who enjoy watching fish but who don't wish to snorkel or dive. Party boats depart from Bridgetown's Deep Water Harbour for sightseeing and snorkeling or romantic sunset cruises. Prices are $60 to $80 per person for daytime cruises and $35 to $65 for three-hour sunset cruises, depending on the type of refreshments and entertainment included; transportation to and from the dock is provided.

⟲   The 48-passenger **Atlantis III** (✉ Shallow Draught, Bridgetown ☎ 246/436–8929 ⊕ www.atlantisadventures.net) turns the Caribbean into a giant aquarium. The 45-minute trip aboard the 50-foot submarine takes you to wrecks and reefs as deep as 150 feet.

A daytime cruise on the 57-foot catamaran **Heatwave** (☎ 246/429–9283) includes stops along the coast for swimming and snorkeling and a barbecue lunch. The sunset cruise includes dinner. The 44-foot CSY sailing yacht **Limbo Lady** (☎ 246/420–5418) sails along the captivating west coast, stopping for a swim, snorkeling, and a Bajan buffet lunch on board. Sunset cruises are another option. The 53-foot catamaran **Tiami** (☎ 246/430–0900 ⊕ www.tallshipscruises.com) offers a luncheon cruise to a secluded bay or a romantic sunset and moonlight cruise with special catering and live music. Four- and five-hour daytime cruises along

⟲   the west coast on the 100-foot MV **Harbour Master** (☎ 246/430–0900 ⊕ www.tallshipscruises.com) stop in Holetown and land at beaches along the way; evening cruises are shorter but add a buffet dinner and entertainment. Day or night you can view the briny deep from the ship's on-board 34-seat semisubmersible. The red-sail **Jolly Roger** (☎ 246/228–8142) "pirate" ship runs four-hour lunch-and-snorkeling sails along the south and west coasts. Be prepared for a rather raucous time, with rope swinging, plank walking, and other games—and plenty of calypso music and complimentary drinks. The sunset cruise, also four hours, includes a buffet dinner, drinks, and entertainment.

SURFING   The best surfing is on the east coast, at Bathsheba Soup Bowl, where the Independence Classic Surfing Championship (an international competition) is held every November—when the surf is at its peak. For information, call the **Barbados Surfing Association** (☎ 246/228–5117).

WINDSURFING   Barbados is on the World Cup Windsurfing Circuit and is one of the
★   best locations in the world for windsurfing. Winds are strongest November through April at the island's southern tip, at Silver Sand–Silver Rock Beach, which is where the Barbados Windsurfing Championships are held in mid-January. Use of boards and equipment is often among

the amenities included at larger hotels; equipment can usually be rented by nonguests.

Club Mistral (⊠ Oistins, Christ Church ☏ 246/428–7277) is a great place to learn to windsurf, because the waves here are usually flat. More-experienced windsurfers congregate at **Silver Rock Windsurfing Club** (⊠ Silver Rock Hotel, Silver Sands–Silver Rock Beach, Christ Church ☏ 246/428–2866), where the surf ranges from 3 to 15 feet and provides an exhilarating windsurfing experience.

Shopping

Areas & Malls

Bridgetown's **Broad Street** is the downtown shopping area. **DaCostas Mall,** in the historic Colonnade Building on Broad Street, has more than 25 shops that sell everything from Piaget to postcards; across the street, **Mall 34** has 22 shops where you can buy duty-free goods, souvenirs, and snacks. At the **Cruise Ship Terminal** shopping arcade, passengers can buy both duty-free goods and Barbadian-made crafts at more than 30 boutiques and a dozen vendor carts and stalls.

Holetown and St. Lawrence Gap each have a **Chattel House Village,** a cluster of brightly colored shops selling local products, fashions, beachwear, and souvenirs. Also in Holetown, **Sunset Crest Mall** has two branches of the Cave Shepherd department store, a bank, a pharmacy, and several small shops; at **West Coast Mall,** you can buy duty-free goods, island wear, and and groceries. In Rockley, Christ Church, **Quayside Shopping Center** houses a small group of boutiques, restaurants, and services.

Department Stores

Cave Shepherd (⊠ Broad St., Bridgetown, St. Michael ☏ 246/431–2121) offers a wide selection of clothing and luxury goods; branch stores are in Holetown, at the airport, and at the Cruise Ship Terminal. **Harrison's** (⊠ Broad St., Bridgetown, St. Michael ☏ 246/431–5500) has 11 locations—including its two large stores on Broad Street and one each at the airport and the Cruise Ship Terminal—offering luxury name-brand goods from the fashion corners of the world.

Specialty Items

ANTIQUES Although many of the private homes, greathouses, and museums in Barbados are filled with priceless antiques, you'll find few for sale—mainly British antiques and some local pieces, particularly mahogany furniture. Look especially for planters' chairs and the classic Barbadian rocking chair, as well as old prints, and paintings. **Greenwich House Antiques** (⊠ Greenwich Village, Trents Hill, St. James ☏ 246/432–1169) fills an entire plantation house with Barbadian mahogany furniture, crystal, silver, china, books, and pictures; it's open daily from 10:30 to 5:30.

CLOTHING **Dingolay** (⊠ Bay St., Bridgetown, St. Michael ☏ 246/436–2157 ⊠ Hwy. 1, Holetown, St. James ☏ 246/432–8709) sells tropical clothing designed and made in Barbados for ladies and girls as well as shoes, handbags, and accessories from around the world. Check out the colorful T-shirts from **Irie Blue** (⊠ Lower Broad St., Bridgetown, St. Michael ☏ 246/426–

Where de Rum Come From

A DAILY "TOT" OF RUM (2 ounces) has been duly administered to each sailor in the British Navy for more than 300 years—as a health ration. At times, rum has also played a less appetizing—but equally important—role. When Admiral Horatio Nelson died in 1805 aboard ship during the Battle of Trafalgar, his body was preserved in a cask of his favorite rum until he could be properly buried.

Hardly a Caribbean island doesn't have its own locally made rum, but Barbados is truly "where de rum come from." Mount Gay, the world's oldest rum distillery, has been in continuous operation on Barbados since 1703, according to the original deed for the Mount Gay Estate, which itemized two stone windmills, a boiling house, seven copper pots, and a still house. The presence of rum-making equipment on the plantation at the

time suggests that the previous owners were actually producing rum in Barbados long before 1703.

Today, much of the island's interior is still planted with sugarcane—where the rum really does come from—and several great houses, situated on historic sugar plantations, have been restored with period furniture and are open to the public.

To really fathom rum, however, you need to delve a little deeper than the bottom of a glass of rum punch. Mount Gay offers an interesting 45-minute tour of its Bridgetown plant, followed by a tasting. You can learn about the rum-making process from cane to cocktail, hear more rum-inspired anecdotes, and have an opportunity to buy bottles of its famous Eclipse or Extra Old rum at duty-free prices. Bottoms up!

8464), which are designed and made in Barbados. You can also find them in many gift shops. **Sandbox & Co.** (⊠ Bell House, Sunbury Plantation, St. Philip ☎ 246/423–0888) offers locally made and designed swimwear, resort wear, children's clothing, and home furnishings.

DUTY-FREE
GOODS
Duty-free luxury goods—china, crystal, cameras, porcelain, leather items, electronics, jewelry, perfume, and clothing—are found in Bridgetown's Broad Street department stores and their branches, at the Cruise Ship Terminal shops (for passengers only), and in the departure lounge shops at Grantley Adams International Airport. Prices are often 30% to 40% less than at home. To buy goods at duty-free prices, you must produce your outbound travel ticket and passport at the time of purchase—or you can have your purchases delivered free to the airport or harbor for pickup. Duty-free alcohol, tobacco products, and some electronic equipment *must* be delivered to you at the airport or harbor.

Little Switzerland (⊠ DaCostas Mall, Broad St., Bridgetown, St. Michael ☎ 246/431–0030) is the anchor shop at DaCostas Mall and has a branch at the Cruise Ship Terminal. Here you can find perfume, jewelry, cameras, audio equipment, Swarovski and Waterford crystal, and Wedgwood china. The **Royal Shop** (⊠ 32 Broad St., Bridgetown ☎ 246/

429–7072) carries fine watches and jewelry fashioned in Italian gold, Caribbean silver, diamonds, and other gems.

HANDICRAFTS Typical crafts include pottery, shell and glass art, wood carvings, handmade dolls, watercolors, and other artwork (both originals and prints). **Best of Barbados** (⊠ Worthing, Christ Church ☎ 246/421–6900), which has a total of seven locations, offers high-quality artwork and crafts in both "native" style and modern designs; everything is made or designed on Barbados. **Earthworks Pottery** (⊠ No. 2, Edgehill Heights
Fodor'sChoice Edgehill Heights, St. Thomas ☎ 246/425–0223) is a family-owned and
★ -operated pottery where you can purchase anything from a dish or knick-knack to a complete dinner service or one-of-a-kind art piece. You can find the characteristically blue or green pottery decorating hotel rooms or for sale in gift shops throughout the island, but the biggest selection (including some "seconds") is at Earthworks, where you also can watch the potters work. **Island Crafts** (⊠ 5 Pelican Craft Centre, Bridgetown, St. Michael ☎ 246/426–4391) offers locally made pottery, wood carvings, straw items, glass art, batik, and wire sculptures. Additional shops are at Harrison's Cave, the airport courtyard, and the airport departure lounge. **Pelican Craft Centre** (⊠ Princess Alice Hwy., Bridgetown, St. Michael ☎ 246/427–5350) is a cluster of workshops halfway between the Cruise Ship Terminal and downtown Bridgetown where craftspeople create and sell locally made leather goods, batik, basketry, carvings, jewelry, glass art, paintings, pottery, and other items. It's open weekdays 9 to 5 and Saturday 9 to 2, with extended hours during holidays or cruise-ship arrivals. In the chattel houses at **Tyrol Cot Heritage Village** (⊠ Codrington Hill, St. Michael ☎ 246/424–2074) you can watch local artisans make hand-painted figurines, straw baskets, clothing, paintings, and pottery—and, of course, buy their wares.

Nightlife & the Arts

Nightlife

When the sun goes down, the people come out to "lime" (which may be anything from a "chat-up" to a full-blown "jump-up"). Performances by world-renowned stars and regional groups are major events, and tickets can be hard to come by—but give it a try. Most resorts have nightly entertainment in season, and nightclubs often have live bands for listening and dancing. The busiest bars and dance clubs rage until 3 AM. On Saturday nights, some clubs—especially those with live music—charge a cover of about $15.

★ ☾ The **Oistins Fish Fry** is the place to be on weekend evenings, when the south-coast fishing village becomes a convivial outdoor street fair. Barbecued chicken and flying fish are served right from the grill and consumed at roadside picnic tables; servings are huge, and prices are inexpensive—about $5. Drinks, music, and dancing add to the fun.

BARS Barbados supports the rum industry with more than 1,600 "rum shops," simple bars where men (mostly) congregate to discuss the world (or life in general). In more sophisticated inns, you can find world-class rum drinks made with the island's renowned Mount Gay and Cockspur brands—and no shortage of Barbados's own Banks beer.

The **Boatyard** (⊠ Bay St., Bridgetown, St. Michael ☎ 246/436–2622) is a pub with both a DJ and live bands; from happy hour until the wee hours, the patrons are mostly local and visiting professionals. **Waterfront Cafe** (⊠ The Careenage, Bridgetown, St. Michael ☎ 246/427–0093) has live jazz in the evening, with a small dance floor for dancing. The picturesque location alongside the wharf is also a draw.

On the south coast, **Bubba's Sports Bar** (⊠ Hwy. 7, Rockley, Christ Church ☎246/435–8731) offers merrymakers and sports lovers live sports on three 10-foot video screens and a dozen TVs, along with a Bajan à la carte menu and, of course, drinks at the bar. **Champers** (⊠ Hwy. 1, Hastings, Christ Church ☎246/435–6644) is a waterfront wine bar where folks gather for good conversation, a great view, snacks, and a selection from the extensive wine list.

On the west coast, **Coach House** (⊠ Hwy. 1, Paynes Bay, St. James ☎ 246/432–1163) has live entertainment nightly and international sports via satellite TV. **Upstairs at Olives** (⊠ 2nd St., Holetown, St. James ☎ 246/432–2112) is a sophisticated watering hole. Enjoy cocktails and conversation seated amid potted palms and cooled by ceiling fans—either before or after dinner downstairs.

DANCE CLUBS **After Dark** (⊠ St. Lawrence Gap, Dover, Christ Church ☎246/435–6547) attracts mostly young people to live appearances of reggae, calypso, and *soca* (an upbeat, sexy variation of calypso) headliners such as Krosfyah. **Club Xtreme** (⊠ Main Rd., Worthing, Christ Church ☎ 246/228–2582) attracts a young crowd on Wednesday, Friday, and Saturday nights for the latest DJ-spun alternative, dance, R&B, reggae, and other party music. The open-air, beachfront **Harbour Lights** (⊠ Upper Bay St., Bridgetown, St. Michael ☎ 246/436–7225) claims to be the "home of the party animal" and has dancing under the stars most nights to live reggae and soca music. The **Ship Inn** (⊠ St. Lawrence Gap, Dover, Christ Church ☎ 246/435–6961) is a large, friendly pub with local band music every night for dancing.

THEME NIGHTS On Wednesday and Friday evenings at the **Plantation Restaurant and** ★ ☾ **Garden Theater** (⊠ St. Lawrence Main Rd., Dover, Christ Church ☎ 246/ 428–5048) the Tropical Spectacular calypso cabaret presents "Bajan Roots & Rhythms," a delightful extravaganza that the whole family will enjoy. The show includes steel-band music, fire eating, limbo, and dancing to the reggae, soca, and pop music sounds of popular Barbadian singer John King and the Plantation House Band. The fun begins at 6:30 PM. A Barbadian buffet dinner, unlimited drinks, transportation, and the show cost $75; for the show and drinks only, it's $37.50.

Exploring Barbados

The terrain changes dramatically from any one of the island's 11 parishes to the next, and so does the pace. Bridgetown, the capital, is a rather sophisticated city. West-coast resorts and private estates ooze luxury, whereas the small villages and vast sugar plantations found throughout central Barbados reflect the island's history. The relentless Atlantic surf shaped the cliffs of the dramatic east coast, and the northeast is called Scotland because of its hilly landscape. Along the lively south coast, the daytime hustle and bustle produce a palpable energy that continues well into the night—at countless restaurants, dance clubs, and nightspots.

Bridgetown

This bustling capital city is a major duty-free port with a compact shopping area. The principal thoroughfare is Broad Street, which leads west from National Heroes Square.

Numbers in the margin correspond to points of interest on the Bridgetown map.

WHAT TO SEE   **❶ Barbados Synagogue.** Providing for the spiritual needs of one of the oldest Jewish congregations in the western hemisphere, this synagogue was formed by Jews who left Brazil in the 1620s and introduced sugarcane to Barbados. The adjoining cemetery has tombstones dating from the 1630s. The original house of worship, built in 1654, was destroyed in an 1831 hurricane, rebuilt in 1833, and restored by the Barbados National Trust in 1992. Friday-night services are held during the winter months, but the building is open to the public year-round. Shorts are not acceptable during services but may be worn at other times. ⊠ *Synagogue La., St. Michael* ☎ *246/426–5792* ✆ *Donation requested* ⊙ *Weekdays 9–4.*

❷ The Careenage. Bridgetown's natural harbor and gathering place is where, in the early days, schooners were careened (turned on their sides) to be scraped of barnacles and repainted. Today the Careenage serves as a marina for pleasure yachts and excursion boats. A pedestrian boardwalk skirts the north side of the marina; the Chamberlain Bridge and the Charles Duncan O'Neal Bridge cross the Careenage.

❸ National Heroes Square. Across Broad Street from the Parliament Buildings and bordered by High and Trafalgar streets, this triangular plaza marks the center of town. Its monument to Lord Horatio Nelson (who was in Barbados only briefly in 1777 as a 19-year-old navy lieutenant) predates Nelson's Column in London's Trafalgar Square by 36 years. Also here are a war memorial and a fountain that commemorates the advent of running water on Barbados in 1865.

❹ Parliament Buildings. Overlooking National Heroes Square in the center of town, these Victorian buildings were built around 1870 to house the British Commonwealth's third-oldest parliament. A series of stained-glass windows depicts British monarchs from James I to Victoria. ⊠ Broad St., St. Michael ☎ 246/427–2019 ✆ Donations welcome ⊙ Tours weekdays at 11 and 2, when parliament isn't in session.

❻ Queen's Park. Northeast of Bridgetown, Queen's Park contains one of the island's two immense baobab trees. Brought to Barbados from Guinea, in West Africa, around 1738, this tree has a girth of more than 51 feet. Queen's Park Art Gallery, managed by the National Culture Foundation, is the island's largest gallery; exhibits change monthly. Queen's

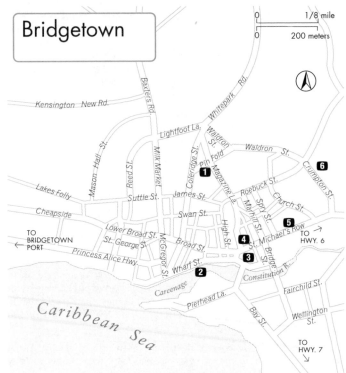

Park House, the historic home of the British troop commander, has been converted into a theater, with an exhibition room on the lower floor and a restaurant. ⊠ *Constitution Rd., St. Michael* ☎ *246/427–2345 gallery* ⌨ *Free* ☉ *Daily 9–5.*

❺ **St. Michael's Cathedral.** Although no one has proved it conclusively, George Washington, on his only trip outside the United States, is said to have worshipped here in 1751. The original structure was nearly a century old by then. Destroyed twice by hurricanes, it was rebuilt in 1784 and again in 1831. ⊠ *Spry St., east of National Heroes Sq., St. Michael.*

Southern Barbados

Christ Church Parish, which is far busier and more developed than the west coast, is chockablock with condos, high- and low-rise hotels, and beach parks and is also home to the St. Lawrence Gap and its many places to eat, drink, shop, and party. As you move southeast, the broad, flat terrain comprises acre upon acre of cane fields, interrupted only by an occasional oil rig and a few tiny villages hugging crossroads. Along the byways are colorful chattel houses, the property of tenant farmers. Historically, these typically Barbadian, ever-expandable houses were built to be dismantled and moved as required.

Numbers in the margin correspond to points of interest on the Barbados map.

WHAT TO SEE **Barbados Museum.** This intriguing museum, in the former British Military Prison (1815) in the historic Garrison area, has artifacts from Arawak days (around 400 BC) and galleries that depict 19th-century military history and everyday life. You can see cane-harvesting tools, wedding dresses, ancient (and frightening) dentistry instruments, and slave sale accounts kept in a spidery copperplate handwriting. The museum's Harewood Gallery showcases the island's flora and fauna; its Cunard Gallery has a permanent collection of 20th-century Barbadian and Caribbean paintings and engravings; and its Connell Gallery features European decorative arts. Additional galleries include one for children; the museum also has a gift shop and a café. ⊠ *Hwy. 7, Garrison Savannah, St. Michael* ☎ *246/427–0201 or 246/436–1956* ⊕ *www.barbmuse.org.bb* ⊠ *$4* ◎ *Mon.–Sat. 9–5, Sun. 2–6.*

16 Codrington Theological College. An impressive stand of royal palms lines the road leading to the coral-stone buildings and serene grounds of Codrington College, an Anglican seminary opened in 1745 on a cliff overlooking Consett Bay. You're welcome to tour the buildings and walk the nature trails. Keep in mind, though, that beachwear is not appropriate here. ⊠ *Sargeant St., Consett Bay, St. John* ☎ *246/423–1140* ⊕ *www.codrington.org* ⊠ *$2.50* ◎ *Daily 10–4.*

11 Emancipation Statue. This powerful statue of a slave—whose raised hands, with broken chains hanging from each wrist, evoke both contempt and victory—is commonly referred to as the Bussa Statue. Bussa was the man who, in 1816, led the first slave rebellion on Barbados. The work of Barbadian sculptor Karl Brodhagen was erected in 1985 to commemorate the emancipation of the slaves in 1834. The statue, in the middle of a busy intersection east of Bridgetown, overlooks a broad cane field—a setting that makes the depiction of Bussa all the more poignant. ⊠ *St. Barnabas Roundabout, intersection of ABC Hwy. and Hwy. 5, Haggatt Hall, St. Michael.*

15 Foursquare Rum Distillery & Heritage Park. A long road bisecting acres of cane fields brings you to the newest rum distillery built in Barbados. Situated on a 19th-century sugar plantation, the spotless, environmentally friendly, high-tech distillery produces ESA Field white rum and premium Alleyne Arthur varieties. Adjacent is the 7-acre Heritage Park, which showcases Bajan skills and talents in its Art Foundry and Cane Pit Amphitheatre; a row of shops and vendor carts has a diverse selection of local products, crafts, and foods. ⊠ *Foursquare Plantation, St. Philip* ☎ *246/420–1977* ⊠ *$7.50* ◎ *Daily 9–5.*

10 Graeme Hall Nature Sanctuary. This 35-acre oasis, a Barbados National Environmental Heritage Site, sits smack in the middle of the busy commercial area of the south coast. Opened in January 2004, the wildlife habitat includes the island's largest inland lake as well as ponds and wading pools, marshes and mangroves, two enormous walk-through aviaries, observation huts, and horticulture exhibits. It's interesting, educational, peaceful, and delightful for both adults and kids. ⊠ *Main Rd., Wor-*

thing, Christ Church ☎ *246/435–9727* ⊕ *www.barbadosbirds.com* 🎫 *$12.50* ⊙ *Daily 8–6.*

8 Harry Bayley Observatory. The headquarters of the Barbados Astronomical Society since 1963, the observatory has a 14-inch reflector telescope—the only one in the Eastern Caribbean. ⊠ *Off Hwy. 6, Clapham, St. Michael* ☎ *246/426–1317 or 246/422–2394* 🎫 *$5* ⊙ *Fri. 8:30* AM–*11:30* PM.

14 Sunbury Plantation House & Museum. Lovingly rebuilt after a 1995 fire destroyed everything but the thick flint-and-stone walls, Sunbury offers an elegant glimpse of the 18th and 19th centuries on a Barbadian sugar estate. Period furniture, old prints, and a collection of horse-drawn carriages have been donated to lend an air of authenticity. Luncheon is served in the back garden. ⊠ *Off Hwy. 5, Six Cross Roads, St. Philip* ☎ *246/423–6270* ⊕ *www.barbadosgreathouse.com* 🎫 *$7.50* ⊙ *Daily 10–5.*

9 Tyrol Cot Heritage Village. This interesting coral-stone cottage just south of Bridgetown was constructed in 1854 and has been preserved as an example of period architecture. In 1929 it became the home of Sir Grantley Adams, the first premier of Barbados and the namesake of its international airport. Part of the Barbados National Trust, the cottage is now filled with antiques and memorabilia of the late Sir Grantley and Lady Adams. It's also the centerpiece of an outdoor "living museum," where artisans and craftsmen have their workshops in a cluster of traditional chattel houses. The crafts are for sale, and refreshments are available at the "rum shop." ⊠ *Rte. 2, Codrington Hill, St. Michael* ☎ *246/424–2074 or 246/436–9033* 🎫 *$6* ⊙ *Weekdays 9–5.*

Central Barbados

On the west coast, in St. James Parish, Holetown marks the center of the Platinum Coast—so called for the vast number of luxurious resorts and mansions that face the sea. Holetown is also where British captain John Powell landed in 1625 to claim the island for King James. On the east coast, the crashing Atlantic surf has eroded the shoreline, forming steep cliffs and prehistoric rocks that look like giant mushrooms. Bathsheba and Cattlewash are favorite seacoast destinations for local folks on weekends and holidays. In the interior, narrow roads weave through tiny villages and along and between the ridges. The landscape is covered with tropical vegetation and is riddled with fascinating caves and gullies.

WHAT TO SEE   **Andromeda Gardens.** Beautiful and unusual plant specimens from around ★ **17** the world are cultivated in 6 acres of gardens that are nestled among streams, ponds, and rocky outcroppings overlooking the sea above the Bathsheba coastline. The gardens were created in 1954 with flowering plants collected by the late horticulturist Iris Bannochie. They're now administered by the Barbados National Trust. The Hibiscus Café serves snacks and drinks. ⊠ *Bathsheba, St. Joseph* ☎ *246/433–9261* 🎫 *$6* ⊙ *Daily 9–5.*

18 Barclays Park. Straddling the Ermy Bourne Highway on the east coast, just north of Bathsheba, this public park was donated by Barclays Bank (now First Caribbean International Bank). Pack a picnic or stop at the popular snack bar and enjoy lunch with a gorgeous ocean view.

19 **Chalky Mount.** This tiny east-coast village is perched high in the hills that yield the clay that has supplied local potters for 300 years. A number of working potteries are open daily to visitors. You can watch as artisans create bowls, vases, candleholders, and decorative objects—which are, of course, for sale.

★ 26 **Flower Forest.** It's a treat to meander among fragrant flowering bushes, canna and ginger lilies, puffball trees, and more than 100 other species of tropical flora in a cool, tranquil forest of flowers and other plants. A ½-mi-long (1-km-long) path winds through the 50 acres of grounds, a former sugar plantation; it takes about 30 to 45 minutes to follow the path, or you can wander freely for as long as you wish. Benches located throughout the forest give you a place to pause, sit down for a bit, and reflect. There's also a snack bar, a gift shop, and a beautiful view of Mount Hillaby. ✉ *Hwy. 2, Richmond Plantation, St. Joseph* ☎ *246/433–8152* 🎫 *$7* ⏲ *Daily 9–5.*

4

25 **Folkestone Marine Park & Visitor Centre.** On land and offshore, the whole family will enjoy this park just north of Holetown. The museum and aquarium illuminate some of the island's marine life; and for some first-hand viewing, there's an underwater snorkeling trail around Dottin's Reef (glass-bottom boats are available for nonswimmers). A barge sunk in shallow water is home to myriad fish, making it a popular dive site. ✉ *Church Point, Holetown, St. James* ☎ *246/422–2871* 🎫 *Free* ⏲ *Weekdays 9–5.*

12 **Francia Plantation House.** Built of large coral-stone blocks in 1913, this greathouse blends French, Brazilian, and Caribbean architectural influences. You can tour the house (descendants of the original owner still live here) and gardens. Most of the antique furniture was made in Barbados of local mahogany; 17th- and 18th-century maps, watercolors, and prints grace the walls. ✉ *Gun Hill, St. George* ☎ *246/429–0474* 🎫 *$5* ⏲ *Weekdays 10–4.*

★ 13 **Gun Hill Signal Station.** The 360-degree view from Gun Hill, 700 feet above sea level, was what made this location of strategic importance to the 18th-century British army. Using lanterns and semaphore, soldiers based here could communicate with their counterparts at the Garrison, on the south coast, and at Grenade Hill, in the north. Time moved slowly in 1868, and Capt. Henry Wilkinson whiled away his off-duty hours by carving a huge lion from a single rock—which is on the hillside just below the tower. Come for a short history lesson but mainly for the view; it's so gorgeous, military invalids were once sent here to convalesce. ✉ *Gun Hill, St. George* ☎ *246/429–1358* 🎫 *$4.60* ⏲ *Weekdays 9–5.*

28 **Harrison's Cave.** This limestone cavern, complete with stalactites, stalagmites, subterranean streams, and a 40-foot waterfall, is a rare find in the Caribbean—and one of Barbados's most popular attractions. The one-hour tours are conducted via electric trams, which fill up fast; reserve ahead of time. Hard hats are required and provided, but all that

Fodor's Choice ★

may fall on you is a little dripping water. ⊠ *Hwy. 2, Welchman Hall, St. Thomas* 🕾 *246/438–6640* 🖃 *$13* 🕙 *Daily 9–6; last tour at 4.*

㉙ Malibu Beach Club & Visitor Centre. Just north of Bridgetown, the fun-loving Malibu Rum people encourage those taking the distillery tour to make a day of it. The beach—which has a variety of water-sports options—is adjacent to the visitor center. Lunch and drinks are served at the beachside grill. ⊠ *Black Rock, Brighton, St. Michael* 🕾 *246/425–9393* 🖃 *$7.50, $27.50 with lunch, $37.50 day pass* 🕙 *Weekdays 9–5.*

㉚ Mount Gay Rum Visitors Centre. On this popular 45-minute tour you learn the colorful story behind the world's oldest rum—made in Barbados since the 18th century. Although the distillery is in the far north—in St. Lucy Parish—tour guides explain the rum-making procedure. Both historic and modern equipment is on display, and rows and rows of barrels are stored in this location. The tour concludes with a tasting and an opportunity to buy bottles of rum and gift items—and even have lunch. ⊠ *Spring Garden Hwy., Brandons, St. Michael* 🕾 *246/425–8757* ⊕ *www.mountgay.com* 🖃 *$6, $27.50 with lunch* 🕙 *Weekdays 9–4.*

㉗ Welchman Hall Gully. This 1-mi-long (2-km-long) natural gully is really a collapsed limestone cavern, once part of the same underground network as Harrison's Cave. The Barbados National Trust protects the peace and quiet here, making it a beautiful place to hike past acres of labeled flowers and stands of trees. You can see and hear some interesting birds—and, with luck, a native green monkey. ⊠ *Welchman Hall, St. Thomas* 🕾 *246/438–6671* 🖃 *$5.75* 🕙 *Daily 9–5.*

Northern Barbados

Speightstown, the north's commercial center and once a thriving port city, now relies on quaint local shops and informal restaurants. Many of Speightstown's 19th-century buildings, with typical overhanging balconies, have been or are being restored. The island's northernmost reaches, St. Peter and St. Lucy parishes, have a varied topography and are lovely to explore. Between the tiny fishing towns along the northwestern coast and the sweeping views out over the Atlantic to the east are forest and farm, moor and mountain. Most guides include a loop through this area on a daylong island tour—it's a beautiful drive.

WHAT TO SEE **Animal Flower Cave.** Small sea anemones, or sea worms, resemble jewellike flowers when they open their tiny tentacles. They live in small pools—some large enough to swim in—in this cave at the island's very northern tip. The view of breaking waves from inside the cave is magnificent. ⊠ *North Point, St. Lucy* 🕾 *246/439–8797* 🖃 *$2* 🕙 *Daily 9–4.*

㉑ Barbados Wildlife Reserve. The reserve is the habitat of herons, innumerable land turtles, screeching peacocks, shy deer, elusive green monkeys, brilliantly colored parrots (in a large walk-in aviary), a snake, and a caiman. Except for the snake and the caiman, the animals run or fly freely—so step carefully and keep your hands to yourself. Late afternoon is your best chance to catch a glimpse of a green monkey. ⊠ *Farley Hill, St. Peter* 🕾 *246/422–8826* 🖃 *$11.50* 🕙 *Daily 10–5.*

20 **Farley Hill.** At this national park in northern St. Peter, across the road from the Barbados Wildlife Reserve, the imposing ruins of a plantation greathouse are surrounded by gardens and lawns, along with an avenue of towering royal palms and gigantic mahogany, whitewood, and casuarina trees. Partially rebuilt for the filming of *Island in the Sun,* the classic 1957 film starring Harry Belafonte and Dorothy Dandridge, the structure was later destroyed by fire. Behind the estate, there's a sweeping view of the region called Scotland for its rugged landscape. ☒ *Farley Hill, St. Peter* ☎ *246/422–3555* ☒ *$2 per car, pedestrians free* ☉ *Daily 8:30–6.*

22 **Morgan Lewis Sugar Mill.** Built in 1727, the mill was operational until 1945. Today it's the only remaining windmill in Barbados with its wheelhouse and sails intact. No longer used to grind sugarcane, it was donated to the Barbados National Trust in 1962 and eventually restored to its original working specifications in 1998 by millwrights from the United Kingdom. The surrounding acres are now used for dairy farming. ☒ *Cherry Tree Hill, St. Andrew* ☎ *246/422–7429* ☒ *$5* ☉ *Weekdays 9–5.*

★ **23** **St. Nicholas Abbey.** There's no religious connection here at all. The island's oldest greathouse (circa 1650) was named after the British owner's hometown, St. Nicholas Parish near Bristol, and Bath Abbey nearby. Its stone-and-wood architecture makes it one of only three original Jacobean-style houses still standing in the western hemisphere. It has Dutch gables, finials of coral stone, and beautiful grounds. The first floor, fully furnished with period furniture and portraits of family members, is open to the public. Fascinating home movies, shot by the last owner's father, record Bajan life in the 1930s. The Calabash Café, in the rear, serves snacks, lunch, and afternoon tea. ☒ *Cherry Tree Hill, St. Peter* ☎ *246/422–8725* ☒ *$5* ☉ *Weekdays 10–3:30.*

BARBADOS ESSENTIALS

To research prices, get advice from other travelers, and book travel arrangements, visit www.fodors.com.

Transportation

BY AIR

Several international carriers offer frequent nonstop or direct flights between North America or Europe and Barbados (BGI), which is a regional hub. These include Air Canada, Air Jamaica, American Airlines (which also has connecting service through San Juan), British Airways, BWIA (which flies from both the U.S. and the U.K.), Continental, Delta, USAirways, and Virgin Atlantic.

Barbados is also well connected to other Caribbean islands via Caribbean Star, Caribbean Sun, and LIAT. Mustique Airways, SVG Air, and Trans Island Air (TIA) link Barbados with St. Vincent and the Grenadines.

⚑ Air Canada ☎ 246/428-5077 or 800/744-2472. **Air Jamaica** ☎ 246/428-1660 or 800/523-5585. **American Airlines** ☎ 246/428-4170. **British Airways** ☎ 246/436-6413. **BWIA** ☎ 800/538-2942. **Caribbean Star** ☎ 246/431-0540 or 800/744-7827. **Caribbean Sun** ☎ 246/431-0540 or 800/744-7827.

Continental Airlines ☎ 800/534-0089. **Delta** ☎ 800/221-1212. **LIAT** ☎ 888/844-5428. **Mustique Airways** ☎ 246/428-1638. **SVG Air** ☎ 784/457-5124. **Trans Island Air** ☎ 246/418-1654. **US Airways** ☎ 800/622-1015. **Virgin Atlantic** ☎ 246/228-4886 or 800/744-7477.

AIRPORTS: 🚹 Airport Information **Grantley Adams International Airport** BGI ☎ 246/428-7101.

BY BOAT

Half the annual visitors to Barbados are cruise passengers. Bridgetown's Deep Water Harbour is on the northwest side of Carlisle Bay, and up to eight cruise ships can dock at the Cruise Ship Terminal. Downtown Bridgetown is a ½-mi (1-km) walk from the pier; a taxi costs about $3 each way.

BY BUS

Bus service is efficient, inexpensive, and plentiful. Blue buses with a yellow stripe are public, yellow buses with a blue stripe are private, and private "Zed-R" vans (so called for their ZR license plate designation) are white with a maroon stripe. All buses travel frequently along Highway 1 (St. James Road) and Highway 7 (South Coast Main Road), as well as inland routes. The fare is Bds$1.50 (75¢) for any one destination; exact change in either local or U.S. currency is appreciated. Buses pass along main roads about every 20 minutes. Stops are marked by small signs on roadside poles that say TO CITY or OUT OF CITY, meaning the direction relative to Bridgetown. Flag down the bus with your hand, even if you're standing at the stop. Bridgetown terminals are at Fairchild Street for buses to the south and east and at Lower Green for buses to Speightstown via the west coast.

BY CAR

Barbados has nearly 975 mi (1,570 km) of paved roads that follow the coastline and meander through the countryside. A network of main highways facilitates traffic flow into and out of Bridgetown. The Adams-Barrow-Cummins (ABC) Highway bypasses Bridgetown, which saves time getting from coast to coast. Small signs tacked to trees and poles at intersections point the way to most attractions, and local people are helpful if you get lost. Remote roads are in fairly good repair, yet few are lighted at night—and night falls quickly at about 6 PM year-round. Even in full daylight, the tall sugarcane fields lining both sides of the road in interior sections can hinder visibility.

You can find gasoline stations in and around Bridgetown, on the main highways along the west and south coasts, and in most inland parishes. Although times vary, you can find most open daily with hours that extend into the evening; a few are open 24 hours a day.

Drive on the left, British style. Be mindful of pedestrians and occasional livestock walking on country roads. When someone flashes headlights at you at an intersection, it means "after you." Be especially careful negotiating roundabouts (traffic circles). The speed limit, in keeping with the pace of life and the narrow roads, is 30 mph in the country, 20 mph in town. Bridgetown actually has rush hours: 7 to 9 and 4 to 6. Park only in approved parking areas; downtown parking costs Bds75¢ to Bds$1 per hour.

To rent a car in Barbados, you must have a valid driver's license and major credit card. A local driver's permit, which costs $5, is obtained through the rental agency. More than 75 agencies rent cars, Jeeps, or minimokes (small, open-sided vehicles), and rates are expensive—about $55 per day for a minimoke to $85 or more per day for a four-wheel-drive vehicle (or $400 to $500 or more per week) in high season, depending on the vehicle and whether it has air-conditioning. Most firms also offer discounted three-day rates. The rental generally includes insurance, pickup and delivery service, maps, 24-hour emergency service, and unlimited mileage. Baby seats are usually available upon request.

🚹 **Coconut Car Rentals** ✉ Bay St., Bridgetown, St. Michael ☎ 246/437-0297. **Courtesy Rent-A-**

Car ✉ Grantley Adams International Airport, Christ Church ☎ 246/418-2500. **National Car Rentals** ✉ Lower Carlton, St. James ☎ 246/426-0603. **Sunny Isle Sixt Car Rentals** ✉ Worthing, Christ Church ☎ 246/435-7979. **Sunset Crest Car Rental** ✉ Sunset Crest, Holetown, St. James ☎ 246/432-2222.

BY TAXI

Taxis operate 24 hours a day. They aren't metered but charge according to fixed rates set by the government. They carry up to four passengers, and the fare may be shared. For short trips, the rate per mile (or part thereof) should not exceed $1.50. Drivers are courteous and knowledgeable; most will narrate a tour at an hourly rate of about $25 for up to three people. Be sure to settle the price before you start off and agree on whether it's in U.S. or Barbados dollars.

Contacts & Resources

BANKS & EXCHANGE SERVICES

Prices quoted throughout this chapter are in U.S. dollars unless otherwise noted.

The Barbados dollar is pegged to the U.S. dollar at the rate of Bds$1.98 to $1. U.S. paper currency, major credit cards, and traveler's checks are all accepted island-wide. Be sure you know which currency is being quoted when making a purchase.

Major credit cards readily accepted throughout Barbados include American Express, Diners Club, EnRoute, Eurocard, MasterCard, and Visa. You can use major credit cards, if you have a PIN, to obtain cash advances (in Barbadian dollars) from most ATM machines.

Barbados National Bank has a branch at Grantley Adams International Airport that's open every day from 8 AM until the last plane lands or arrives. First Caribbean International Bank has a network of operations on the Caribbean islands, including several branches and ATMs in Barbados. The Bank of Nova Scotia, or Scotiabank, is a major Canadian bank that is represented

throughout the Caribbean. Caribbean Commercial Bank has convenient Saturday morning hours at its branch at Sunset Crest Mall, in Holetown. ATMs are available 24 hours a day at bank branches, transportation centers, shopping centers, gas stations, and other convenient spots throughout the island.

BUSINESS HOURS

Banks are open Monday through Thursday from 8 to 3, Friday from 8 to 5 (some branches in supermarkets are open Saturday morning from 9 to noon). At the airport, the Barbados National Bank is open from 8 AM until the last plane leaves or arrives, seven days a week (including holidays). The General Post Office in Cheapside, Bridgetown, is open weekdays from 7:30 to 5; the Sherbourne Conference Center branch is open weekdays from 8:15 to 4:30 during conferences; and branches in each parish are open weekdays from 8 to 3:15. Most stores in Bridgetown are open weekdays from 8:30 or 9 to 4:30 or 5, Saturday from 8:30 to 1 or 2. Stores in shopping malls outside of Bridgetown may stay open later. Some supermarkets are open daily from 8 to 6 or later.

ELECTRICITY

Electric current on Barbados is 110 volts–50 cycles, U.S. standard. Hotels generally have plug adapters and transformers available for appliances made in countries that operate on 220-volt current.

EMBASSIES

🇦🇺 Australia **Australian High Commission** ✉ Bishop's Court Hill, Pine Rd., Bridgetown, St. Michael ☎ 246/435-2834.
🇨🇦 Canada **Canadian High Commission** ✉ Bishop's Court Hill, Pine Rd., Bridgetown, St. Michael ☎ 246/429-3550.
🇬🇧 United Kingdom **British High Commission** ✉ Lower Collymore Rock, Bridgetown, St. Michael ☎ 246/430-7800.
🇺🇸 United States **Embassy of the United States** ✉ Broad St., Bridgetown, St. Michael ☎ 246/436-4950.

EMERGENCIES

⚡ Emergency Services **Ambulance** ☎ 511. **Fire** ☎ 311. **Police** ☎ 211 emergencies, 242/430-7100 nonemergencies.

⚡ Hospitals **Bayview Hospital** ✉ St. Paul's Ave., Bayville, St. Michael ☎ 246/436-5446. **Queen Elizabeth Hospital** ✉ Martindales Rd., Bridgetown, St. Michael ☎ 246/436-6450.

⚡ Pharmacies **Grant's** ✉ Fairchild St., Bridgetown, St. Michael ☎ 246/436-6120 ✉ Main Rd., Oistins, Christ Church ☎ 246/428-9481. **Knight's** ✉ Lower Broad St., Bridgetown, St. Michael ☎ 246/426-5196 ✉ Super Centre Shopping Center, Main Rd., Oistins, Christ Church ☎ 246/428-6057 ✉ Suncrest Mall, Hwy. 1, Holetown, St. James ☎ 246/432-1290 ✉ Hwy. 1, Speightstown, St. Peter ☎ 246/422-0048.

⚡ Scuba-Diving Emergencies **Coast Guard Defence Force (24-hour hyperbaric chamber)** ✉ St. Ann's Fort, Garrison, St. Michael ☎ 246/427-8819 emergencies, 246/436-6185 nonemergencies. **Divers' Alert Network** ☎ 246/684-8111 or 246/684-2948.

HOLIDAYS

Public holidays are New Year's Day (Jan. 1), Errol Barrow Day (Jan. 21), Good Friday (Fri. before Easter), Easter Monday (day after Easter), National Heroes Day (Apr. 28), Labour Day (May 1), Whitmonday (7th Mon. after Easter), Emancipation Day (Aug. 1), Kadooment Day (1st Mon. in Aug.), Independence Day (Nov. 30), Christmas (Dec. 25), and Boxing Day (Dec. 26).

INTERNET, MAIL & SHIPPING

You'll find Internet cafés in and around Bridgetown, in Speightstown on the west coast, and at St. Lawrence Gap on the south coast. Rates range from $2 for 15 minutes to $8 or $9 per hour.

An airmail letter from Barbados to the United States or Canada costs Bds$1.15 per half ounce; an airmail postcard, Bds45¢. Letters to the United Kingdom cost Bds$1.40; postcards, Bds70¢. Letters to Australia and New Zealand cost Bds$2.75; postcards, Bds$1.75. When sending mail to Barbados, be sure to include the parish name in the address.

⚡ **Bean-n-Bagel Internet Cafe** ✉ St. Lawrence Gap, Dover, Christ Church ☎ 246/420-4604. **Clicks-N-Bytes Cafe** (✉ 144 Roebuck St., Bridgetown, St. Michael ☎ 246/427-8939. **Connect Internet Cafe** ✉ Shop #9, 27 Broad St., Bridgetown, St. Michael ☎ 246/228-8648. **ICS Internet Cafe** ✉ St. Lawrence Gap, Dover, Christ Church ☎ 246/428-1513. **Surf 'n' Lime** ✉ Road View, Main Rd., Speightstown, St. Peter ☎ 246/422-5871.

PASSPORT REQUIREMENTS

All visitors, including U.S. and Canadian citizens, must have a valid passport and a return or ongoing ticket. A birth certificate and photo ID are *not* sufficient proof of citizenship.

SAFETY

Crime isn't a major problem, but take normal precautions. Lock your room, and don't leave valuables in plain sight or unattended on the beach. Lock your rental car, and don't pick up hitchhikers.

TAXES & SERVICE CHARGES

At the airport, each adult passenger leaving Barbados must pay a departure tax of $12.50 (Bds$25), payable in either Barbadian or U.S. currency; children 12 and under are exempt. Although it may be included in cruise packages as a component of port charges, the departure tax is not included in airfare and must be paid in cash by each traveler prior to entering the secure area of the airport.

A 7.5% government tax is added to all hotel bills. A 10% service charge is often added to hotel bills and restaurant checks in lieu of a tip. At your discretion, tip beyond the service charge to recognize extraordinary service.

A 15% V.A.T. is imposed on restaurant meals, admissions to attractions, and merchandise sales (other than duty-free). Prices are often tax inclusive; if not, the V.A.T. will be added to your bill.

TELEPHONES

The area code for Barbados is 246.

Local calls are free from private phones; some hotels charge a small fee. For directory assistance, dial 411. Calls from pay phones cost Bds25¢ for five minutes. Pre-paid phone cards, which can be used throughout Barbados and other Caribbean islands, are sold at shops, attractions, transportation centers, and other convenient outlets.

Direct-dialing to the United States, Canada, and other countries is efficient and reasonable, but always check with your hotel to see if a surcharge is added. Some toll-free numbers cannot be accessed in Barbados. To charge your overseas call on a major credit card without incurring a surcharge, dial 800/744–2000 from any phone.

Depending on your carrier, you may find that you can use your cell phone in Barbados to call home; but be aware that the roaming charges can be extremely expensive—even for just a brief telephone call. Renting a cell phone while on vacation is a less expensive alternative than using your own—unless, of course, you've secured competitive international rates and roaming charges ahead of time. A cell phone can be rented for as little as $5 a day (minimum one-week rental); then pre-paid cards are available at several locations throughout the island and in varying denominations—$5, $10, $25, and $37.50. Reserve ahead; otherwise, it's first-come, first-served.

🎫 Cellphone Rental **Global Business Centre** ✉ West Coast Mall, Sunset Crest, Holetown, St. James ☎ 246/432-6508 ⊕ www.globalbizcentre. com

TIPPING

If no service charge is added to your bill, tip waiters 10% to 15% and maids $2 per room per day. Tip bellhops and airport porters $1 per bag. Taxi drivers appreciate a 10% tip.

TOUR OPTIONS

A sightseeing tour is a good way to get your bearings and to experience the rich Bajan culture. Taxi drivers will give you a personalized tour of Barbados for about $25 per hour for up to four people. Or you can choose a fascinating helicopter ride, an overland horseback or mountain bike journey, a 4x4 safari expedition, or a full-day bus excursion. The prices vary according to the mode of travel and the number and kind of attractions included. Ask your hotel to help you make arrangements.

Bajan Helicopters offers an eagle's-eye view of the island. The air-conditioned jet helicopters accommodate up to five people for a 30-mi "Discover Barbados Tour" or a 50-mi "Island Tour." Prices start at $97.50 per person. Highland Adventure Centre offers horseback or mountain bike tours for $50 per person, including transportation, guides, and refreshments. Whether it's your first time on a horse or you're an experienced rider, the chance to view plantation houses, three coastlines, and quaint villages astride a thoroughbred is a thrilling opportunity—don't forget your camera! The mountain bike tour is an exhilarating 12-km ride (15% uphill) through the picturesque heart of northern Barbados, ending up at Barclays Park on the east coast. Island Safari will take you to all the popular spots via a 4x4 Land Rover—including some gullies, forests, and remote areas that are inaccessible by conventional cars and buses. The cost is $45 to $65 per person, including snacks or lunch. L. E. Williams Tour Co. will pick you up at your hotel for a seven-hour narrated bus tour—an 80-mi circuit of the best of Barbados. The $62.50 per-person price includes a Bajan buffet lunch and beverages at Atlantis Inn on the rugged east coast.

🎫 **Bajan Helicopters** ✉ Bridgetown Heliport, Bridgetown, St. Michael ☎ 246/431-0069 ⊕ www. bajanhelicopters.com. 🐎 **Highland Adventure Centre** ✉ Cane Field, St. Thomas ☎ 246/438-8069 or 246/438-8928. 🐎 **Island Safari** ✉ Main Rd., Bush Hall, St. Michael ☎ 246/429-5337 ⊕ www.

barbadostraveler.com. **L. E. Williams Tour Co.**
✉ Hastings, Christ Church ☎ 246/427-1043.

VISITOR INFORMATION

🔲 Before You Leave **Barbados Tourism Authority** ✉ 800 2nd Ave., 2nd fl., New York, NY 10017
⊕ www.barbados.org ☎ 212/986-6516 or 800/
221-9831 🖷 212/573-9850 ✉ 150 Alhambra Circle, Suite 1000, Coral Gables, FL 33134 ☎ 305/442-
7471 🖷 305/567-2844 ✉ 3440 Wilshire Blvd.,
Suite 1215, Los Angeles, CA 90010 ☎ 213/380-2198
🖷 213/384-2763 ✉ 105 Adelaide St. W, Suite 1010,
Toronto, Ontario M5H 1P9, Canada ☎ 416/214-
9880 or 800/268-9122 🖷 416/214-9882 ✉ 263
Tottenham Court Rd., London W1T 7LA, U.K. ☎ 20/
7636-9448 🖷 20/7637-1496 ✉ 1 Bligh St., 10th fl.,
Sydney 2000 Australia ☎ 2/9221-9988 🖷 2/
9221-9800.

🔲 In Barbados **Barbados Tourism Authority**
✉ Harbour Rd., Bridgetown, St. Michael ☎ 246/
427-2623 🖷 246/426-4080 ✉ Grantley Adams
International Airport, Christ Church ☎ 246/428-5570
✉ Cruise Ship Terminal, Bridgetown, St. Michael
☎ 246/426-1718. **Barbados Hotel & Tourism Assn**
✉ 4th Ave., Belleville, St. Michael ☎ 246/426-
5041 🖷 246/429-2845 ⊕ www.bhta.org.

WEDDINGS

Barbados makes weddings relatively simple for nonresidents, as there are no minimum residency requirements. Most resorts, therefore, offer wedding packages
and have on-site wedding coordinators to
help you secure a marriage license and
plan a personalized ceremony and reception. Alternatively, you may wish to have
your wedding at a scenic historic site or
botanical garden, on the grounds of a
restored greathouse, or at sunset on a
quiet beach.

To obtain a marriage license, which often
can be completed in less than a half hour,
both partners must apply in person to the
Ministry of Home Affairs (in the General
Post Office building, Cheapside,
Bridgetown, and open 8:15–4:30 weekdays) by presenting valid passports. If either party was previously married and
widowed, you need to present a certified
copy of the marriage certificate and a
death certificate for the deceased spouse; if
either party is divorced, you need a certified copy of the official divorce decree.
Nonresidents of Barbados must pay a fee
of $75 (Bds$150) plus a stamp fee of
$12.50 (Bds$25). Finally, you must make
arrangements for an authorized marriage
officer (a magistrate or minister) to perform the ceremony.

Bonaire

Flamingos, Washington/Slagbaai National Park

WORD OF MOUTH

"The reason to go is the water. Bonaire is the best shore snorkeling island we have ever visited. . . . We often went to several per day, breaking off for lunch and then back out to the reef."
—slk230

"There is an excellent park on the North side of the island, Washington-Slagbaai. We spent most of the day driving around & stopping for views, walks & quick dips . . . [but] it's not paved."
—tully

www.fodors.com/forums

WELCOME TO BONAIRE

At the market in Kralendijk, hagglers vie for produce brought in by boat from lusher islands. But nature holds sway over human pursuits on this scrubby, cactus-covered landfall. Divers come to explore some of the best sites this side of Australia's Great Barrier Reef. Above the water are more than 15,000 flamingos—the biggest flock in the Western Hemisphere.

Boca Ko

Washington

Mt. Brandaris

Playa Funchi 🄽

Mai

Boca Slagbaai

🄱🄱 Washington/Slagb National Park

Gotomeer 🄲🄻

Landhuis Karpata 🄲🄳

Northern Scenic

Karpata

Rappel

Since Bonaire is relatively flat, it's easy to explore by mountain bike. A trail circumnavigates Washington/Slagbaai National Park, so you can explore on your own or on a guided trip.

TOP 4 REASONS TO VISIT BONAIRE

1. As locals say, you come here to dive, eat, dive, sleep, and dive.

2. You don't have to be a certified diver to appreciate Bonaire's reefs; snorkelers can see a lot of the beauty just below the surface of the water.

3. Tourists came to enjoy the tranquility of the island long before they started exploring offshore.

4. Dining is surprisingly good and varied for such a small island.

DIVER'S PARADISE

With just over 18,000 people, this little island (112 square mi/290 square km) has a real, small-town atmosphere. Kralendijk, the capital, has just 3,000 inhabitants. The entire coastline—from the high-water tidemark to a depth of 200 ft (61 m)—is protected as part of the Bonaire Marine Park, making it one of the best diving destinations in the western hemisphere.

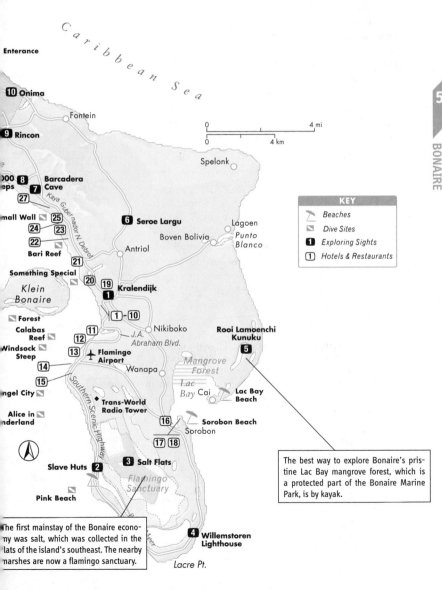

Caribbean Sea

Enterance

10 Onima

Fontein

9 Rincon

Spelonk

000 **8**
eps **7** **Barcadera Cave**

27

Kaya Gobernador N. Debrot

mall Wall **25**
24 **23**
22
Bari Reef

21

Seroe Largu 6

Boven Bolivia

Antriol

Lagoen

Punto Blanco

Something Special

20 **19** **Kralendijk**
1

Klein Bonaire

1 - **10**

Forest

Calabas Reef

11

Nikiboko

J.A. Abraham Blvd.

Rooi Lamoenchi Kunuku

5

Windsock Steep

12

13 **✈ Flamingo Airport**

Wanapa

14

15

Mangrove Forest

Lac Bay Cai

Lac Bay Beach

ngel City

Alice in nderland

Trans-World Radio Tower

16 **☂ Sorobon Beach**

Sorobon

17 **18**

Slave Huts 2

3 Salt Flats

Flamingo Sanctuary

Pink Beach

4 Willemstoren Lighthouse

Lacre Pt.

KEY

⩲	Beaches
🖾	Dive Sites
1	Exploring Sights
1	Hotels & Restaurants

Southern Scenic Highway

The best way to explore Bonaire's pristine Lac Bay mangrove forest, which is a protected part of the Bonaire Marine Park, is by kayak.

The first mainstay of the Bonaire economy was salt, which was collected in the flats of the island's southeast. The nearby marshes are now a flamingo sanctuary.

BONAIRE PLANNER

Getting to Bonaire

You can fly nonstop to Bonaire (BON) from Amsterdam, but only Continental flies nonstop from the U.S. (from Houston). Most flights connect in San Juan, Montego Bay, or Aruba if you are coming from North America. If you want to connect through Aruba, you'll more likely than not have to book your flight on a tiny island-hopper directly with an island-based airline.

Hassle Factor: Medium to High

On the Ground

Bonaire's Flamingo Airport is tiny but welcoming (the KLM 747 almost dwarfs the airport when it lands). Rental cars and taxis are available, but try to arrange for pickup through your hotel. A taxi will run between $9 and $12 (for up to four people) to most hotels; $18 to the Lac Bay Resort or Sorobon Beach Resort. Fares are 25% extra from 7 PM to midnight and 50% extra from midnight to 6 AM. If you anticipate having to change your flight details while on Bonaire, be mindful of the prospect that some airline counters may close at 5 PM. Many folks just use bicycles to get around, unless they are going more than a few miles.

Where to Stay

Where you stay will depend on whether or not you are a diver. Alongside the numerous lodges that offer only the basics, you can now find luxury resorts that provide more land-based amenities, so consider your own needs and budget when making your final decision. Families can find self-catering accommodations, and many places will appeal to budget travelers. The best resorts are often on decent beaches, but these are mostly man-made. Almost all the island's resorts are clustered around Kralendijk.

Hotel & Restaurant Costs

Assume that hotels operate on the European Plan (**EP**—with no meals) unless we specify that they use either the Continental Plan (**CP**—with a Continental breakfast), Breakfast Plan (**BP**—with full breakfast), or the Modified American Plan (**MAP**—with breakfast and dinner). Other hotels may offer the Full American Plan (**FAP**—including all meals but no drinks) or may be All-Inclusive (**AI**—with all meals, drinks, and most activities).

WHAT IT COSTS in Dollars					
	$$$$	**$$$**	**$$**	**$**	**¢**
Restaurants	over $25	$20–$25	$12–$20	$5–$10	under $5
Hotels	over $250	$150–$250	$75–$150	$50–$75	under $50

Restaurant prices are for a main course excluding the usual 10%–15% service charge. Hotel prices are for two people in a double room in high season, excluding 6% tax, $6.50 per night room surcharge, 10%–15% service charge, and meal plans.

Activities

Diving—both open-water reef dives and beach dives—is among the best in the world, so the sport figures centrally into most visitors' itineraries. But there is plenty for non-divers to do as well. **Day sails** are popular for snorkelers who want to see some of the ocean life but who are not certified. **Sport fishing** is also a popular activity, and several captains can take you out to search for big-game fish. Near-constant trade winds make Bonaire a popular **windsurfing** destination. Though things are pretty quiet at night, the island has some very good **restaurants**.

By Vernon
O'Reilly
Ramesar

THE WORLD UNDER THE SURFACE IS LIKE A BLUE-TINGED DREAM. Nearby, parrot fish meander through white coral caverns. Ahead, sharp-eyed barracuda move through the water like silver daggers. A manta glides overhead in slow motion like an alien spacecraft. But the enchanting undersea world of Bonaire, like a dream, is an experience done on borrowed time. Breaking the surface is your awakening. Warm air, arid vistas, and the startling gleam of sun on water are your reward.

Bonaire is widely regarded as one of the best destinations in the Caribbean for shore diving, and with good reason. The dry climate and coral composition of the island mean that there's little soil runoff, allowing near perfect visibility in the coastal waters. The islanders have exploited this advantage, and you can find local businesses that cater to virtually every diving need. Even though tourism is the backbone of the economy here, authorities try to ensure that the booming hotel industry does not damage the environment upon which it is based. Thankfully, the fact that most visitors to Bonaire come for the natural beauty has prevented the kind of tourism that has turned neighboring islands like Aruba into commercialized tourist magnets.

5

Islanders are serious about conserving Bonaire's natural beauty. All the coastal waters of the island were turned into a national park in 1979, and in 1999 Bonaire purchased the 1,500-acre privately owned outlying island of Klein Bonaire to prevent unwanted development. Anyone diving around the island must purchase a one-year permit, and park rangers patrol the waters, handing out hefty fines to people who violate park rules. Spear-fishing, removing coral, and even walking on coral are just some of the restricted activities. Rather than restricting legitimate divers, these rules have resulted in a pristine marine environment that makes for a supremely satisfying dive experience. Damage to the reefs caused by rare passing hurricanes is usually quickly repaired by the healthy ecosystem. Small wonder that even the license plates in Bonaire declare it a DIVER'S PARADISE.

Bonaire also offers a variety of experiences above the surface to those willing to explore its 112 square mi (290 square km). The southern salt flats give an interesting glimpse into the island's economic history. Washington National Park, in the north, has the island's highest peak (784 feet) and is a haven for some of the thousands of flamingos that make Bonaire their home. The near-perfect climate also makes Bonaire the ideal destination for working on a tan or just relaxing.

Although many islanders claim that the name Bonaire comes from the French for "good air," this explanation is unlikely, particularly since the island was never colonized by the French. The island was first inhabited by an Amerindian people (related to the Arawaks) called the Caquetios. Alonso de Ojeda and Amerigo Vespucci landed here in 1499 and claimed it for Spain. It seems likely that they adopted the Amerindian name for the island, which probably sounded very much like Bonaire and which meant "low country." Because the Spanish found little use for the island except as a penal colony, the original inhabitants were shipped off to work on the plantations of Hispaniola, and Bonaire remained largely undeveloped. When the Dutch seized the islands of Aruba, Bonaire, and Curaçao in 1633, they started building the salt industry in Bonaire, which fueled the economy then and which remains an important industry today.

The majority of the 12,000 inhabitants live in and around the capital, Kralendijk. The word almost universally applied to this diminutive city is "cute." It's probably one of the few major downtown areas in the world that can be traversed in under three minutes. Part of the Netherlands Antilles, Bonaire is actually governed from neighboring Curaçao.

Where to Stay

Although meal plans are available at most hotels, the island has many excellent—and often inexpensive—restaurants. If you're planning a dive holiday, look into the many attractive dive packages.

Rental Apartments

If you prefer do-it-yourself home-style comfort over the pampering and other services offered by a hotel, you can rent a fully furnished apartment. **Black Durgon Inn Properties** (☎ 599/717–5736, 800/526–2370 in U.S. ⊕ www.blackdurgon.com) is a small, noncommercial community with its own pier on the water, though no beach. **Bonaire Hotel & Tourism Association** (☎ 800/388–5951 ⊕ www.bonairestays.com) has information on a variety of properties ranging from budget to upscale. **Sun Rentals** (☎ 599/717–6130 ⊕ www.sunrentals.an) offers quite a range of accommodations. You can choose among private ocean-view villas in luxurious areas like Sabadeco, furnished oceanfront apartments (with a pool) in town, or bungalows in Lagoenhill, an inland community. The Sun Oceanfront Apartments are an excellent budget choice for families.

Hotels

⏺ **$$$$**   🏨 **Harbour Village Bonaire.** This luxury enclave of ochre-color buildings
Fodor'sChoice   is the benchmark for luxury accommodations on the island. The stan-
★   dard rooms are perfectly fine—though admittedly a bit small; much better are the one-bedroom beachfront villas, which are lavishly appointed and feature outlandishly large marble bathrooms. Room patios open onto either the private beach or the 4-acre tropical garden. Visiting celebrities make this hotel home as much for the beautifully furnished rooms and excellent beach as for the attentive and understated service offered by the well-trained staff. Those seeking a truly romantic experience can order a torch-lighted dinner on the beach. ⊠ *Kaya Gobernador N. Debrot 71, Kralendijk* ☎ *599/717–7500 or 800/424–0004* 🖷 *599/717–7507* ⊕ *www.harbourvillage.com* ⤻ *16 rooms, 14 1-bedroom suites* ⏢ *2 restaurants, room service, fans, in-room safes, minibars, some refrigerators, cable TV, Wi-Fi, 4 tennis courts, pool, gym, hair salon, beach, dive shop, snorkeling, boating, marina, bar, shops, babysitting, dry cleaning, laundry service, business services, meeting rooms, airport shuttle* ⊟ *AE, D, DC, MC, V* ⏤⏤ *EP.*

$–$$$ 🏨 **Bellafonte Chateau de la Mer.** Although it lacks the amenities of a large
Fodor'sChoice   resort—including a pool—the intimacy and exclusivity of this elegant
★   palazzo-style hotel near Kralendijk more than compensate. An arched

The Donkeys of Bonaire

VISITORS TO BONAIRE ARE often startled by the sight of donkeys lazily roaming about the landscape. In fact, these little equines are considered by islanders an integral part of the modern landscape of Bonaire.

Bonaire has no large indigenous species of mammals. Donkeys were imported to the island in the 1500s to serve the needs of Spanish colonists. They provided an effective means of transport and continued to be used for that purpose for the salt industry that eventually developed. With their minimal water requirements and ability to eat just about any vegetation, the animals proved well adapted to the arid environment. Later, when the salt industry became more mechanized and other forms of transport were introduced, the donkeys were left to wander. With no predators to deal with and little competition for the scrub and cactus

that cover the island, the donkeys have survived, and their numbers have even increased over the years.

Today there are more than 200 wild donkeys roaming the island, and they charm tourists. Islanders often have a more tarnished view. Roaming about in search of food, donkeys will often push through fences and munch and stomp through ornamental plants. There have also been numerous injuries and a few deadly automobile accidents caused by donkeys wandering on the roads at night.

However, Bonaire's relationship with the ubiquitous quadrupeds seems destined to remain close for the foreseeable future. A donkey sanctuary has been established in the interior to look after ill donkeys and care for orphaned youngsters. The center has more than 80 donkeys in its care.

passageway opens out to a breathtaking ocean vista complete with a jetty that seems to have jumped out of the pages of a design magazine. Rooms are chic, with teak and stainless-steel accents that create a clean and breezy feeling. Room balconies are large enough to host a cocktail party for 20 and are perfect for private sunbathing, but to truly experience this hotel, an ocean-view room is essential. Manager Sjoerd Vanderbrug is an amiable host and is always willing to offer guests helpful advice about the island over a cup of Dutch coffee. ⊠ *E. E. G. Blvd. 10, Belnem* ☎ *599/717–3333* 🖷 *599/717–8581* ⊕ *www. bellafontebonaire.com* ➪ *6 studios, 8 1-bedroom suites, 6 2-bedroom suites, 2 3-bedroom penthouse suites* ⌂ *Fans, some kitchens, some kitchenettes, cable TV, Wi-Fi, outdoor hot tub, dive shop, dock, boating, laundry service* ▤ *AE, MC, V* ⦿ *EP.*

★ **$$** ⊞ **Captain Don's Habitat.** Bonaire's first hotel catering to divers remains a favorite, with a PADI five-star dive center offering more than 20 specialty courses. For a small price difference over the cost of a standard room, studios offer a full kitchen and much more breathing space. Villa suites have spectacular ocean views; downstairs units have massive patios. Rum Runners restaurant serves excellent pizza made in its brick oven. There's little nightlife here other than the usual post-dive chatter before everyone heads off to bed to rest before the next day's activities, and the beach is tiny but fine for shore dives or snorkeling, with mesmerizing reef formations 90 feet from shore. ✉ *Kaya Gobernador N. Debrot 103, Box 88, Kralendijk* ☎ *599/717–8290 or 800/327–6709* 🖷 *599/717–8240* ⊕ *www.habitatdiveresorts.com* ⇆ *24 suites, 9 villas, 20 cottages* ⟍ *Restaurant, fans, in-room safes, some kitchens, refrigerators, cable TV, Wi-Fi, pool, beach, dive shop, 2 docks, snorkeling, bicycles, volleyball, bar, business services, meeting room* ▤ *AE, D, DC, MC, V* ¶⃝ *EP.*

$$ 🏨 **Plaza Resort Bonaire.** No other hotel in Bonaire can match the range of activities offered here, with everything from tennis to water sports, and a gorgeous beach. Rooms are exceptionally large and well furnished, with tile floors, but are otherwise unremarkable. This is a sprawling resort, so getting around can be a bit of a hike. Live entertainment on Tuesday nights is a big draw, as is the weekly beach barbecue. The hotel's resident iguanas are docile and friendly and are usually happy to provide guests with a photo opportunity. ✉ *J. A. Abraham Blvd. 80, Kralendijk* ☎ *599/717–2500 or 800/766–6016* 🖷 *599/717–7133* ⊕ *www.plazaresortbonaire.com* ⇆ *174 rooms, 48 villas* ⟍ *3 restaurants, room service, fans, in-room safes, some kitchens, refrigerators, cable TV, 4 tennis courts, pool, health club, massage, beach, dive shop, dock, windsurfing, boating, bicycles, 3 bars, shops, children's programs (ages 5–15), business services, convention center, meeting rooms* ▤ *AE, D, DC, MC, V* ¶⃝ *EP.*

☼ $$ 🏨 **Sand Dollar Condominium Resort.** This condo complex has family-friendly apartments ranging from studios to three-bedrooms, each of which is individually owned and decorated for a comfortable, lived-in feeling. Ocean views from the rooms are great, and the pool is a lovely oasis; the beach, however, is tiny and disappears at high tide. The nearby grocery and ice cream parlor are handy, and the Chat 'n' Browse cybercafé is a popular place to meet locals and visitors alike. ✉ *Kaya Gobernador N. Debrot 79, Box 262, Kralendijk* ☎ *599/717–8738 or 800/288–4773* 🖷 *599/717–8760* ⊕ *www.sanddollarbonaire.com* ⇆ *68 condos* ⟍ *Restaurant, kitchens, cable TV, Wi-Fi, 2 tennis courts, pool, beach, dive shop, bar, children's programs (ages 3–17), Internet room* ▤ *AE, D, DC, MC, V* ¶⃝ *EP.*

$$ 🏨 **Sorobon Beach Naturist Resort.** No need to worry about an extensive packing list for Bonaire's only naturist resort, which is on Lac Bay. Clothing is optional everywhere. The rooms are outfitted in an appropriately sparse style but are comfortable and include full kitchens. Rooms are air-conditioned but, inexplicably, only between 7 PM and 7 AM. The property offers Wi-Fi, so it is not unusual to witness the rather bizarre spectacle of guests sitting around getting up close and personal with their laptops. It's worth noting that guests using the beach here are fully visible from the most popular windsurfing beach on the island, which is right next door. This is definitely a family-oriented property, so those looking for a party center should look elsewhere. ✉ *Sorobon Beach* ⌂ *Box 14, Kralendijk* ☎ *599/717–8080 or 800/828–9356* 🖷 *599/717–6080* ⊕ *www.sorobonbeach.com* ⇆ *28 1-bedroom chalets, 1 2-bedroom chalet, 1 3-bedroom house* ⟍ *Restaurant, fans, in-room safes, kitchens,* *massage, beach, snorkeling, kayaks, Wi-Fi, Ping-Pong, bar, library, laundry service, airport shuttle; no room TVs* ☰ *AE, MC, V* ⚑ *EP.*

✪ $–$$ ⚏ **Buddy Dive Resort.** Well-equipped rooms, a nicely landscaped compound, and excellent dive packages keep guests coming back to this large resort. The former Lion's Dive rooms are slightly larger, are fully air-conditioned, and offer a greater degree of privacy than the original Buddy Dive rooms. All have the basics you'd expect in a Caribbean resort, including a private balcony or patio. Divers will appreciate the drive-through air-filling station for compressed air or Nitrox in the compound. There's a nice beach and a couple of decent restaurants too. ⊠ *Kaya Gobernador N. Debrot 85, Box 231, Kralendijk* ☎ *599/717–5080 or 866/462–8339* ⊟ *599/717–8647* ⊕ *www.buddydive.com* ⚑ *6 rooms, 72 apartments* ᕃ *2 restaurants, some kitchens, cable TV, 3 pools, beach, dive shop, bar, laundry facilities, children's programs (ages 5–15), car rental* ☰ *AE, D, MC, V* ⚑ *EP.*

$–$$ ⚏ **Den Laman Condominiums.** Though the exterior of Bonaire's newest hotel property will not win any design awards, the location and beautifully finished interior are definitely first-class. Rooms are spacious and tastefully done in rattan, teak, and stainless steel. The Ocean View rooms require contortions to see the ocean, so it is best to request an Oceanfront room. One of the island's best seafood restaurants, the Den Laman Restaurant & Bar, is in the building. ⊠ *Kaya Gobernador N. Debrot 77, Kralendijk* ☎ *599/717–1700* ⊟ *599/717–1710* ⊕ *www. denlaman.com* ⚑ *15 rooms* ᕃ *Restaurant, kitchens, cable TV, bar, car rental, fans, dive shop.* ☰ *AE, MC, V* ⚑ *EP.*

✪ $–$$ ⚏ **Divi Flamingo Resort.** The brightly colored buildings of this resort are a two-minute stroll from downtown, but the main draw is the combination of a top-notch dive program and the only casino on Bonaire. The property features some of the lushest landscaping to be found on this arid island. Rooms are immaculate, and lower-level oceanfront rooms have balconies about 2 feet from the water. Sunbathers will appreciate the beautiful sun pier that affords excellent views of downtown. Chibi Chibi restaurant serves scrumptious seafood dishes and treats guests to a nightly underwater light show. There is live entertainment nightly during high season. ⊠ *J. A. Abraham Blvd. 40, Box 143, Kralendijk* ☎ *599/ 717–8285 or 800/367–3484* ⊟ *599/717–8238* ⊕ *www.diviflamingo. com* ⚑ *129 rooms* ᕃ *2 restaurants, grocery, in-room safes, cable TV, 2 pools, gym, outdoor hot tub, spa, dive shop, dock, snorkeling, bar, casino, shops, meeting rooms, car rental* ☰ *AE, D, DC, MC, V* ⚑ *EP.*

Fodor'sChoice ★

★ $ ⚏ **Bruce Bowker's Carib Inn.** The island's first full-time dive instructor, Bruce Bowker, opened this inn in 1980 after moving to Bonaire from the United States. The cozy rooms and Bruce's personal touch have given his resort the highest return-visitor ratio on the island. Most apartment-style units have kitchens, and all bedrooms are air-conditioned. Bruce's background means that the emphasis here is on diving, diving, and more diving. Even though this is a PADI five-star lodge, novice divers can also benefit from the small class sizes. ⊠ *J. A. Abraham Blvd. 46, Box 68, Kralendijk* ☎ *599/ 717–8819* ⊟ *599/717–5295* ⊕ *www.caribinn.com* ⚑ *10 units* ᕃ *Fans, some kitchens, microwaves, refrigerators, cable TV, pool, beach, dive shop, snorkeling* ☰ *D, MC, V* ⚑ *EP.*

★ ☺ ¢–$ ▦ **Coco Palm Garden & Casa Oleander.** Three friends and neighbors have created a series of cozy cottages on adjoining properties, each fully equipped and individually decorated to the point where the hard part is choosing among them. The pool, restaurant, and bar are in the Coco Palm section, all awash with cheerful colors. The property caters primarily to Europeans, so the emphasis is on ambience and efficiency rather than luxurious amenities. This European flavor also means that topless sunbathing is acceptable even around the pool area. While most rooms have air-conditioning, there is a $10 daily charge for using it. Two larger villas (Nos Kas and BonHome) are down the road and are a good choice for families. This is probably your best value on the island for ambience, but keep in mind that the beach is a three-minute walk away. ⊠ *Kaya van Eps 9, Belnem* ☏ *Box 216, Kralendijk* ☎ *599/717–2108 or 599/790–9080* 🖷 *599/717–8193* ⊕ *www.cocopalmgarden.org* ⇗ *20 rooms, 2 villas* ☖ *Some BBQs, kitchens, pool, shop, laundry facilities; no TV in some rooms* ▭ *MC, V* ¶◎¶ *EP.*

¢ ▦ **Golden Reef Inn.** This new inn is located just a little inland but offers charmingly decorated, fully self-contained apartments at a very reasonable price. The larger units are fine for families. Amazingly, for the price, the rate includes free airport transfers and the kitchens are stocked with basic breakfast foodstuffs. ⊠ *Kaya Den Haag 7, Hato* ☎ *599/717–5759* 🖷 *599/717–5659* ⊕ *www.goldenreefinn.com* ⇗ *4 studios, 7 1-bedroom apartments, 5 villas* ☖ *Fans, in-room safes, kitchenettes, cable TV, pool, dive shop, babysitting, laundry facilities* ▭ *AE, MC, V* ¶◎¶ *EP.*

★ ¢ ▦ **Yachtclub Apartments.** Across from Harbour Village, these apartments may be the best budget lodging on the island. Large rooms are set in a pristine lemon-yellow compound. Kralendijk is a few minutes' walk away, yet peace and quiet are readily available around the (usually deserted) pool. Room configurations range from studios to a five-bedroom suite. ⊠ *Kaya Gobernador N. Debrot 52, Kralendijk* ☎ *599/717–7424* 🖷 *519/717–7372* ⊕ *www.yachtclubapartmentsbonaire.com* ⇗ *13 apartments* ☖ *In-room safes, kitchens, cable TV, car rental* ▭ *AE, D, MC, V* ⟳ *2-night minimum* ¶◎¶ *EP.*

Where to Eat

Dining on Bonaire is far less expensive than on Aruba or Curaçao, and you can find everything from Continental to Mexican to Asian fare. Many restaurants serve only dinner—only a few establishments not affiliated with hotels are open for breakfast, so check ahead.

ECLECTIC

★ $$–$$$$ ✕ **Zeezicht Bar & Restaurant.** Zeezicht (pronounced zay-*zeekt* and meaning "sea view") serves three meals a day. At breakfast and lunch you get basic American fare with an Antillean touch, such as a fish omelet; dinner is more Caribbean and mostly seafood, served either on the terrace overlooking the harbor or in the nautically themed homey, rough-hewn main room. Locals are dedicated to this hangout, especially for the ceviche, conch sandwiches, and the Zeezicht special soup with conch, fish, and shrimp. ⊠ *Kaya J. N. E. Crane 12, Kralendijk* ☎ *599/717–8434* ▭ *AE, MC, V.*

$$–$$$ ✕ **La Guernica.** Tapas—so popular everywhere else in the world—have finally made landfall on Bonaire. This trendy eatery overlooking the board-walk and the harbor is great for people-watching; there's outdoor seat-ing as well as a couch- and pillow-filled lounge area. The interior is done in hacienda style with terra-cotta tiles, clay decorations, and comfy lounge chairs. The lunch menu offers a range of sandwiches and salads. This is *the* place to sip a cocktail and be seen. ⊠ *Kaya Bonaire 4C, Kral-endijk* ☏ *599/717–5022* ⊟ *AE, MC, V.*

$$–$$$ ✕ **Mona Lisa Bar & Restaurant.** Here you can find Continental, Caribbean, and Indonesian fare. Popular bar dishes include Wiener schnitzel and fresh fish with curry sauce. The intimate stucco-and-brick dining room, presided over by a copy of the famous painting of the lady with the mys-tic smile, is decorated with Dutch artwork, lace curtains, and whirring ceiling fans. The colorful bar adorned with baseball-style caps is a great place for late-night schmoozing and noshing on light snacks or the catch of the day, which is served until 10 PM. There is a four-course fixed-price dinner on offer most evenings for about $40. ⊠ *Kaya Grandi 15, Kralendijk* ☏ *599/717–8718* ⌕ *Reservations essential* ⊟ *AE, MC, V* ⊘ *Closed Sun. No lunch.*

$$ ✕ **Kontiki Beach Club.** The dining room is a harmonious blend of terra-cotta tile floors and rattan furnishings around a limestone half-moon bar. There's also a brick terrace for alfresco dining. Chef-owners Miriam and Martin are especially proud of their Dutch *kibbeling* (fish in a beer batter served with chili sauce). There are frequent live jazz performances on the outdoor stage and a constantly changing display of local art on the walls. Although located quite far from downtown, it is definitely worth the drive. ⊠ *Kaminda Sorobon 64, Lac Bay* ☏ *599/717–5369* ⊟ *AE, D, MC, V.*

★ **$–$$** ✕ **Le Flamboyant.** This intimate restaurant offers good food at afford-able prices. The cozy historic house—conveniently downtown—also has a small gourmet food shop, espresso bar, and lovely cocktail bar. The main attraction is the tree-covered courtyard at the back. Lunch offers a selection of ample sandwiches and salads; dinner is mostly seafood and pastas. Vegetarians will not have to pick and hunt for suitable items, as there's a comprehensive vegetarian menu. ⊠ *Kaya Grandi 12, Kralendijk* ☏ *599/717–3919* ⊟ *AE, MC, V.*

¢–$$ ✕ **City Café/City Restaurant.** This busy waterfront eatery is also one of the most reliable nightspots on the island, so it's always hopping day or night. Breakfast, lunch, and dinner are served daily for very reason-able prices. Seafood is always featured, as are a variety of sandwiches and salads. The pita sandwich platters are a good lunchtime choice for the budget challenged. Weekends, there's always live entertainment and dancing. ⊠ *Hotel Rochaline, Kaya Grandi 7, Kralendijk* ☏ *599/717–8286* ⊟ *AE, MC, V.*

¢ ✕ **Wind & Surf Beach Bar.** Part of Bonaire Windsurf Place and located right on the beach, this fun eatery is probably the most casual dining experience on the island. Tables and chairs are set directly in the sand under a straw-roofed structure so that cooling winds sweep through the space. The food is simple but very good; the main offerings are sandwiches, salads, and burgers. The experience of dining with your toes in the sand is sure to leave lingering pleasant memories. The weekly barbecue night with live entertainment is well worth the drive. ⊠ *Sorobon Beach* ☎ *599/717–2288* ▤ *No credit cards.*

$$–$$$ ✕ **Salsa.** The newest and chicest eatery in downtown is owned by the same partners who own City Café/City Restaurant. The two-story palapa-covered structure features two totally different dining experiences. The downstairs garden and bar area offers a casual atmosphere with finger foods and tapas. Upstairs is a more elegant affair with a truly international menu and is designed for a real evening out. The adventurous diner may want to try the four-course "A Taste of the World" menu, where each course reflects a different world cuisine. ⊠ *Kaya Isla Riba, Kralendijk* ☎☎ *599/717–3558* ⌲ *Reservations essential* ▤ *AE, MC, V* ⊗ *No lunch.*

★ **$$–$$$$** ✕ **Den Laman Restaurant & Bar.** A longtime feature of the Bonaire dining landscape, the restaurant is now under new ownership and in fancy new digs at the Den Laman Condominiums. The lunch and dinner menus include everything from lobster thermidor to hamburgers, so almost everyone is likely to find something that appeals. The oceanfront setting is unbeatable, and the prix-fixe dinner menus are not a bad deal at all. ⊠ *Kaya Gobernador N. Debrot 77, Kralendijk* ☎ *599/717–4106* ▤ *AE, MC, V.*

$–$$
✕ **Bistro De Paris.** Any restaurant that welcomes you with a free glass of kir and a personal welcome from the owner should be taken very seriously. Patrice Rannou has transformed an unassuming house into a lovely bistro serving the best French food on the island. The low-key decor (complete with Perrier-bottle vases) belies the extraordinary food on offer. A beautifully presented carpaccio salad with blue cheese is an absolute treat. Lamb lovers will fall to pieces over the char-grilled chops served with haricots verts and asparagus. The dinner menu is very reasonably priced, but those on an extremely tight budget should at least explore the lunch offerings. Many patrons choose to dine on the newly built outdoor patio. ⊠ *Kaya Gobernador N. Debrot 46, Kralendijk* ☎ *599/717–7070* ▤ *MC, V* ⊗ *Closed Sun. No lunch Sat.*

$$–$$$$
✕ **Croccantino.** At this casual restaurant in a 19th-century Bonairean house you can indulge in authentic Italian food on the large outdoor terrace or in the air-conditioned indoor rooms—smoking or non. For an appetizer try fried calamari with hot marinara sauce, and follow it up with lobster fettuccine. If you're looking for a light and reasonably priced lunch, try the prix-fixe specials. ⊠ *Kaya Grandi 48, Kralendijk* ☎ *599/717–5025* ▤ *D, MC, V* ⊗ *Closed Sun. No lunch Sat.*

★ **$–$$$$** ✕ **Capriccio.** This splendid, family-run Italian eatery has plenty to boast about. The pastas are handmade daily, and fresh mozzarella is imported from Italy once a week. The wine cellar includes 200 labels and more than 7,000 bottles. You can opt for casual à la carte dining on the terrace or a romantic meal in the tonier, air-conditioned dining room. If your appetite is hearty, go for the five-course prix-fixe menu. Otherwise, choose one of the 50 regular offerings. ⊠ *Kaya Isla Riba 1, Kralendijk* ☎ *599/717–7230* ▤ *AE, D, MC, V* ⊗ *Closed Tues. No lunch Sun.*

★ **$–$$$** ✕ **Donna & Giorgio's.** Donna and her Sardinian-born husband serve delicious home-style meals in this charming restaurant on the main road just outside of Kralendijk. With Giorgio in the kitchen, Donna and her daughter greet diners and make them feel at home. Guests may choose to sit in the cozy interior near the bar or outside at one of the tables on the gravel-covered terrace, which is lovely on a cloudless night; however, it's only inches from the road, so there's occasional car noise. You can always find a selection of pizzas and pastas, as well as daily specials displayed on a blackboard outside. Live music on Sundays attracts a large crowd. ⊠ *Kaya Grandi 60, Kralendijk* ☎ *599/717–3799* ⊟ *MC, V* ⊘ *Closed Wed. and Sept.*

SEAFOOD ✕ **It Rains Fishes.** The mood is vivacious at this popular terrace restau-
$$$–$$$$ rant in a converted mansion overlooking the water. Fish dominates the menu, but tapas and satays are also available. The signature dish is fresh fish in a mustard sauce. Check out the mural of colorful underwater creatures near the bar; each was uniquely conceived and hand-painted by a member of the staff or one of the owners. ⊠ *Kaya J .N. E. Craane 24, Kralendijk* ☎ *599/717–8780* ⊟ *D, MC, V* ⊘ *Closed Sun. No lunch.*

★ **$$–$$$** ✕ **Richard's Waterfront Dining.** Animated, congenial Richard Beady and his partner, Mario, own this casually romantic waterfront restaurant, which has become one of the island's most recommended—a reputation that's well deserved. The daily menu is listed on large blackboards, and the food is consistently excellent. Fish soup is usually offered and is sure to please, as is the grilled wahoo. ⊠ *J. A. Abraham Blvd. 60, Kralendijk* ☎ *599/717–5263* ⊟ *AE, MC, V* ⊘ *Closed Mon. No lunch.*

$$–$$$ ✕ **Blue Moon Café.** Great ocean views, a relaxed atmosphere, and friendly and attentive staff are some of the advantages of this waterfront seafood restaurant. Chef Martin Bouwmeester creates a delectable creamy conch soup, which is delicately flavored and brimming with chunks of conch. The pool table and bar are excellent pre-dining diversions. ⊠ *Kaya C. E. B. Hellmund 5, Kralendijk* ☎ *599/717–8617* ⊟ *MC, V* ⊘ *Closed Wed. No lunch May–Nov.*

Beaches

Don't expect long stretches of glorious powdery sand. Bonaire's beaches are small, and though the water is blue (several shades of it, in fact), the sand isn't always white. In 2005, Bonaire's National Parks Foundation introduced a new "nature fee" that basically requires all nondivers to pay a $10 annual fee in order to enter the water anywhere around the island, even if you aren't diving.

Boca Slagbaai. Inside Washington–Slagbaai Park is this beach of coral fossils and rocks with interesting offshore coral gardens that are good for snorkeling. Bring scuba boots or canvas sandals to walk into the water, because the beach is rough on bare feet. The gentle surf makes it an ideal place for swimming and picnicking. Turn left at the "Y" intersection shortly after entering the national park and follow the signs. ⊠ *Off main park road, in Washington–Slagbaai National Park.*

Klein Bonaire. Just a water-taxi hop across from Kralendijk, this little island offers picture-perfect white-sand beaches. The area is protected, so absolutely no development has been allowed. Make sure to pack everything before heading to the island, including water and something to hide under, because there are no refreshment stands, no changing facilities, and almost no shade to be found. Boats leave from the Town Pier, across from the City Café, and the round-trip water-taxi ride costs roughly $14 per person.

Lac Bay Beach. Known for its festive music on Sunday nights, this open bay area with pink-tinted sand is equally dazzling by day. It's a bumpy drive (10 to 15 minutes on a dirt road) to get here, but you'll be glad when you arrive. It's a good spot for diving, snorkeling, and kayaking (as long as you bring your own), and there are public restrooms and a restaurant for your convenience. ⊠ *Off Kaminda Sorobon, Cai.*

★ **Pink Beach.** As the name suggests, the sand here has a pinkish hue that takes on a magical shimmer in the late-afternoon sun. The water is suitable for swimming, snorkeling, and scuba diving. Take the Southern Scenic Route (E. E. G. Boulevard) on the island's western side; the beach is close to the slave huts. It's a favorite Bonairean hangout on the weekend, but it's almost deserted during the week. Because of the coral that is thrown up on the beach, sandals are recommended. ⊠ *Southern Scenic Hwy., south of airport.*

Playa Funchi. This Washington–Slagbaai National Park beach is notable for the lagoon on one side, where flamingos nest, and the superb snorkeling on the other, where iridescent green parrot fish swim right up to shore. Turn right at the "Y" intersection after the entrance to the park and follow the signs. ⊠ *Off main park road, in Washington–Slagbaai National Park.*

Sorobon Beach. Adjacent to the Sorobon Beach Resort and its nude beach, this is *the* windsurfing beach on Bonaire. You can find a restaurant–bar next to the resort and windsurfing outfitters on the beach. The public beach area has restrooms and huts for shade, as well as a direct line of sight to the nude section. If driving, take E. E. G. Boulevard (this is the southern route out of Kralendijk) to Kaya I. R. Randolf Statuuis Van Eps then follow this route straight on to Sorobon Beach. ⊠ *Kaya IR. Randolf Statuuis Van Eps, Sorobon.*

Windsock Beach. Near the airport (just off E. E. G. Boulevard), this pretty little spot, also known as Mangrove Beach, looks out toward the north side of the island and has about 200 yards of white sand along a rocky shoreline. It's a popular dive site, and swimming conditions are also good. ⊠ *Off E. E. G. Blvd., near airport.*

Sports & the Outdoors

Bicycling

Bonaire is generally flat, so bicycles are an easy way to get around. Because of the heat it's essential to carry water if you're planning to cycle for any distance and especially if your plans involve exploring the deserted interior. There are more than 180 mi (290 km) of unpaved routes (as well as the many paved roads) on the island. For mountain bike rentals try **Captain Don's Habitat** (⊠ Kaya Gobernador N. Debrot 103, Kralendijk ☎ 599/717–8290 or 599/717–8913). Rates average around $15 to $20 per day, and a credit card or cash deposit is usually required. **Cycle Bonaire**

(⊠ Kaya Gobernador N. Debrot 77A, Kralendijk ☎ 599/717–2229) rents mountain bikes and gear (trail maps, water bottles, helmets, locks, repair and first-aid kits) for $15 a day or $75 for six days; half-day and full-day guided excursions start at $55, not including bike rental. **Tropical Travel** (⊠ K. A. Abraham Blvd. 80, Kralendijk ☎ 599/717–2500 Ext. 8199) at the Plaza Resort Bonaire offers bikes for $7 per day or $42 per week.

Day Sails & Snorkeling Trips

Regularly scheduled sunset sails and snorkel trips are popular (prices range from $25 to $50 per person), as are private or group sails (expect to pay about $425 per day for a party of four). The *Aquaspace* (⊠ Nautico Marina Pier, Kralendijk ☎ 599/717–2568) is a trimaran with an air-conditioned underwater observation deck that is 90% glass and provides incredible views. Regularly scheduled cruises cost between $35 and $69; most include a meal or snacks. **Bonaire Boating** (⊠ Divi Flamingo Resort, J. A. Abraham Blvd. 40, Kralendijk ☎ 599/790–5353) offers half- and full-day charters aboard a luxury 56-foot sailing yacht ($395 and $695, respectively), a 57-foot motor yacht ($455 for four hours), or the private charter of a 26-foot Bayliner day cruiser for $295 for three hours. Sunset sailings are also available with drinks for $32 per person. Glass-bottom boat trips, such as those offered by *Bonaire Dream* (⊠ Harbour Village Marina, Kaya Gobernador N. Debrot, Kralendijk ☎ 599/717–8239 or 599/717–4514), are popular in Bonaire: the 1½-hour trip costs $25 per person and leaves on Wednesday at 4 from the town pier. **Kantika di Amor Watertaxi** (⊠ Kaya J. N. E. Craane 24, opposite the restaurant It Rains Fishes, Kralendijk ☎ 599/560–7254 or 599/790–5399) provides daily rides to Klein Bonaire and drift snorkel and evening cruises with complimentary cocktails. The *Mushi Mushi* (☎ 599/790–5399) is a catamaran offering a variety of two- and three-hour cruises starting at $25 per person. It departs from the Bonaire Nautico Marina in downtown Kralendijk (opposite the restaurant It Rains Fishes). The *Oscarina* (☎ 599/790–7674 ⊕ www.bonairesailing.com/oscarina) is a 42-foot sloop offering a variety of day packages, including an all-day sail with a gourmet lunch for $425. If you want to do some sailing on your own, **Toucan Diving** (⊠ Plaza Resort Bonaire, Kralendijk ☎ 599/717–2500 ⊕ www.toucandiving.com) rents Boston Whalers for half or full days. *Tropical Travel* (⊠ Plaza Resort Bonaire, K. A. Abraham Blvd. 80, Kralendijk ☎ 599/717–2500 Ext. 8199) offers a variety of cruise packages starting at $30 per person. The *Woodwind* (☎ 599/786–7055 ⊕ www.woodwindbonaire.com) is a 37-foot trimaran that offers regular sailing and snorkeling trips as well as charters.

Diving & Snorkeling

Bonaire has some of the best reef diving this side of Australia's Great Barrier Reef. It takes only 5 to 25 minutes to reach many sites, the current is usually mild, and although some reefs have sudden, steep drops, most begin just offshore and slope gently downward at a 45-degree angle. General visibility runs 60 to 100 feet, except during surges in October and November. You can see several varieties of coral: knobby-brain, giant-brain, elkhorn, staghorn, mountainous star, gorgonian, and black. You can also encounter schools of parrot fish, surgeonfish, angelfish, eel, snapper, and grouper. Beach diving is excellent just about everywhere on the leeward side, so night diving is popular. There are sites here suitable for every skill level; they're clearly marked by yellow stones on the roadside.

Bonaire, in conjunction with *Skin Diver* magazine, has also developed the **Guided Snorkeling Program.** The highly educational and entertaining program begins with a slide show on important topics, from a beginner's look at reef fish, coral, and sponges to advanced fish identification and night snorkeling. Guided snorkeling for all skill levels can be arranged through most resort dive shops. The best snorkeling spots are on the island's leeward side, where you have shore access to the reefs, and along the west side of Klein Bonaire, where the reef is better developed. All snorkelers and swimmers must pay a $10 "nature fee," which allows access to the waters around the island and Washington–Slagbaai National Park for one calendar year. The fee can be paid at most dive shops.

Fodor'sChoice   In the well-policed **Bonaire Marine Park** (✉ Karpata ☎ 599/717–8444
★   ⊕ www.bmp.org), which encompasses the entire coastline around Bonaire and Klein Bonaire, divers take the rules seriously. Don't even *think* about (1) spearfishing; (2) dropping anchor; or (3) touching, stepping on, or collecting coral. You must pay an admission of $25 (used to maintain the park), for which you receive a colored plastic tag (to attach to an item of scuba gear) entitling you to one calendar year of unlimited diving. Checkout dives—dives you do first with a master before going out on your own—are required, and you can arrange them through any dive shop. All dive operations offer classes in free buoyancy control, advanced buoyancy control, and photographic buoyancy control. Tags are available at all scuba facilities and from the Marine Park Headquarters.

DIVE SITES   The *Guide to the Bonaire Marine Park* lists 86 dive sites (including 16 shore-dive-only and 35 boat-dive-only sites). Another fine reference book is the *Diving and Snorkeling Guide to Bonaire,* by Jerry Schnabel and Suzi Swygert. Guides associated with the various dive centers can give you more complete directions. It's difficult to recommend one site over another; to whet your appetite, here are a few of the popular sites.

★ **Angel City.** Take the trail down to the shore adjacent to the Trans-World Radio station; dive in and swim south to Angel City, one of the shallowest and most popular sites in a two-reef complex that includes Alice in Wonderland. The boulder-size green-and-tan coral heads are home to black margates, Spanish hogfish, gray snappers, stingrays, and large purple tube sponges.

Bari Reef. Catch a glimpse of the elkhorn and fire coral, queen angelfish, and other wonders of Bari Reef, just off the Sand Dollar Condominium Resort's pier.

★ **Calabas Reef.** Off the coast of the Divi Flamingo Resort, this is the island's busiest dive site. It's replete with Christmas-tree worms, sponges, and fire coral adhering to a ship's hull. Fish life is frenzied, with the occasional octopus putting in an appearance.

Bonaire Marine Park

THE BONAIRE MARINE PARK was founded in 1979 in an effort to protect the island's most precious natural resource. Covering an area of less than 700 acres, the park includes all the waters around the island from the high-water mark to the 60-meter depth. Legislation prevents collecting (or even walking on) coral, using spear guns, or removing marine life. It also means that boats may not drop anchor in most of the island's waters and that divers may not use gloves unless they're needed for ascending or descending a line.

Because the island has so zealously protected its marine environment, Bonaire offers an amazing diversity of underwater life. Turtles, rays, and fish of every imaginable color abound in the pristine waters of the park. The small ($10) charge for a diving tag allows unlimited use of the park for a year, and every cent goes toward the care and management of the Bonaire Marine Park. And it's money well spent, islanders and most visitors will tell you.

Forest. You need to catch a boat to reach Forest, a dive site off the southwest coast of Klein Bonaire. Named for the abundant black-coral forests found in it, the site gets a lot of fish action, including a resident spotted eel that lives in a cave.

Rappel. This spectacular site is near the Karpata Ecological Center. The shore is a sheer cliff, and the lush coral growth is the habitat of some unusual varieties of marine life, including occasional orange sea horses, squid, spiny lobsters, and spotted trunkfish.

Small Wall. One of Bonaire's three complete vertical wall dives (and one of its most popular night-diving spots), Small Wall is in front of the Black Durgon Inn, near Barcadera Beach. Because the access to this site is on private property, this is usually a boat-diving site. The 60-foot wall is frequented by squid, turtles, tarpon, and barracuda and has dense hard and soft coral formations; it also allows for excellent snorkeling.

Something Special. South of the marina entrance at Harbour Village Bonaire, this spot is famous for its garden eels. They wave about from the relatively shallow sand terrace looking like long grass in a breeze.

Town Pier. Known for shielding one of Bonaire's best night dives, the pier is right in town, across from the City Café. Divers need permission from the harbormaster and must be accompanied by a local guide.

Windsock Steep. This excellent shore-dive site (from 20 to 80 feet) is in front of the small beach opposite the airport runway. It's a popular place for snorkeling. The current is moderate, the elkhorn coral profuse; you may also see angelfish and rays.

DIVE OPERATORS Many of the dive shops listed below offer PADI and NAUI certification courses and SSI, as well as underwater photography and videography courses. Some shops are also qualified to certify dive instructors. Full certification courses cost approximately $370; open-water refresher courses run about $185; a one-tank boat dive with unlimited shore diving costs about $37; a two-tank boat dive with unlimited shore diving is about

$55. As for equipment, renting a mask, fin, and snorkel costs about $8.50 all together; for a BC and regulator, expect to pay about $16. Check out children's programs like Aquakids and Ocean Classroom—or inquire about their equivalents.

Most dive shops on Bonaire offer a complete range of snorkel gear for rent and will provide beginner training; some dive operations also offer guided snorkeling and night snorkeling. The cost for a guided snorkel session is about $25 and includes slide presentations, transportation to the site, and a tour. Gear rental is approximately $9 per 24-hour period.

Bonaire Dive & Adventure (⊠ Sand Dollar Condominium Resort, Kaya Gobernador N. Debrot 77A, Kralendijk ☎ 599/717–2229 ⊕ www. bonairediveandadventure.com) is probably the best choice for first-timers who want a stress-free introduction to the sport. **Bonaire Scuba Center** (⊠ Black Durgon Inn, Kaya Gobernador N. Debrot 145, Kralendijk ☎ 599/717–5736, 908/566–8866, 800/526–2370 for reservations in U.S. ⌂ Box 775, Morgan, NJ 08879). **Bruce Bowker's Carib Inn Dive Center** (⊠ J. A. Abraham Blvd. 46, Kralendijk ☎ 599/717–8819 ⊕ www. caribinn.com). **Buddy Dive Resort** (⊠ Kaya Gobernador N. Debrot 85, Kralendijk ☎ 599/717–5080 ⊕ www.buddydive.com). **Captain Don's Habitat Dive Shop** (⊠ Kaya Gobernador N. Debrot 103, Kralendijk ☎ 599/ 717–8290 ⊕ www.habitatdiveresorts.com). **Dee Scarr's "Touch the Sea"** (⌂ Box 369, Kralendijk ☎ 599/717–8529 ⊕ www.touchthesea.com). **Dive Inn** (⊠Kaya C. E. B. Hellmund, close to South Pier, Kralendijk ☎599/ 717–8761 ⊕ www.diveinn-bonaire.com). **Divi Dive Bonaire** (⊠ Divi Flamingo Beach Resort & Casino J. A. Abraham Blvd. 40, Kralendijk ☎ 599/717–8285 ⊕ www.diviflamingo.com). **Larry's Shore & Wild Side Diving** (☎ 599/790–9156 ⊕ www.larryswildsidediving.com) is run by a former army combat diver and offers a variety of appealing options ranging from the leisurely to downright scary. This company has become an extremely popular choice, so try to book as early as possible. **Photo Tours Divers** (⊠ Caribbean Court Bonaire, J. A. Abraham Blvd. 82, Kralendijk ☎ 599/717–3460 ⊕ www.bonphototours.com). **Toucan Diving** (⊠ Plaza Resort Bonaire, J. A. Abraham Blvd. 80, Kralendijk ☎ 599/717–2500 ⊕ www.toucandiving.com) offers the Aquakids program for children 5 to 12. **Wanna Dive** (⊠ Hotel Rochaline, Kaya Grandi 7, next to City Café, Kralendijk ☎ 599/790–8880 ⊕ www. wannadivebonaire.com).

Fishing

Captain Cornelis of **Big Game Sportfishing** (⊠ Kaya Krisolito 6, Santa Barbara ☎☎ 599/717–6500 ⊕ www.bonairefishing.com/biggame) offers deep-sea charters for those in search of wahoo, marlin, tuna, swordfish, and sailfish. His rates—which cover bait, tackle, and refreshments—average $325 for a half-day, $450 for a full day for as many as five people. **Multifish Charters** (☎ 599/717–3648 ⊕ www. bonairefishing.net) has day or night reef fishing on a 38-foot Bertram twin diesel; the cost for six hours is $335 (six-person maximum). A nine-hour day of deep-sea fishing costs $475 (six-person maximum), including refreshments. **Piscatur Charters** (⊠ Kaya H. J. Pop 3, Kralendijk ☎ 599/717–8774 ⊕ www.bonairetours.com/piscatur) offers light-tackle angler reef fishing for jackfish, barracuda, and snapper from a 15-foot skiff. Rates are $225 for a half-day. You can charter the 42-foot Sport Fisherman *Piscatur,* which carries up to six people, for $350 for a half-day, $500 for a full day. Bonefishing runs $200 for a half-day.

Horseback Riding

You can take hour-long trail rides at the 166-acre **Kunuku Warahama Ranch** (⊠ Kaya Guanare 11, east of Kralendijk, off road to Cai ☎ 599/717–7324) for $20. Guides take you through groves of cacti where iguanas, wild goats, donkeys, and flamingos reside. Reserve one of the gentle pintos or palominos a day in advance, and try to go early in the morning, when it's cool. The ranch, open Tuesday through Sunday from 10 to 6, also has an alfresco restaurant, a golf driving range, and two playgrounds.

Landsailing

This fast-paced activity is basically windsurfing on land using a sail and a three-wheeled apparatus (called a blokart). It can get pretty dusty but is definitely fun and worth a try. **Landsailing Bonaire** (⊠ Kaya Jupiter 4, Belnem ☎ 599/717–8122 or 599/786-8122 ⊕ www.landsailingbonaire. com) provides training, equipment, and safety clothing for $40 for the first hour and $15 for each additional hour.

Kayaking

Divers and snorkelers can use kayaks to reach otherwise inaccessible dive sites and simply tow the craft along during their dive. Nondivers can take advantage of the calm waters around the island to explore the coastline and the fascinating stands of mangrove around the Lac Bay area. The mangrove harbors myriad wildlife and acts as a hatchery for marine life. Almost all of the kayaks used are of the sit-on-top variety, which are able to negotiate shallow waters better.

Bonaire Dive & Adventure (⊠ Kaya Gobernador N. Debrot 79, Kralendijk ☎ 599/717–8738 or 800/288–4773 ⊕ www.discoverbonaire.com) rents kayaks and also operates guided trips. At **Jibe City** (⊠ Sorobon Beach ☎ 599/717–5233, 800/748–8733 in U.S. ⊕ www.jibecity.com), which is primarily a windsurfing outfit, kayaks go for $10 (single) and $15 (double) per hour; $25 and $30, respectively, per half-day (closed in September). **Mangrove Info & Kayak Center** (⊠ Kaminda Lac 141, on road to Lac Cai, Lac Bay ☎ 599/790–5353 ⊕ www.bonairekayaking.com) offers guided kayak tours of the mangrove forest at 9 AM and 11 AM daily, for $25 an hour and $43 for two hours. The center houses a unique mangrove aquarium designed to study the Lac Bay mangroves' effect on the global ecosystem as well as a photo gallery showing underwater existence within the forest like never before. The tours are pleasant even for the exercise-challenged and usually provide a great way to work on your tan.

Windsurfing

With near constant breezes and calm waters, Bonaire is consistently ranked among the best places in the world for windsurfing. Lac Bay, a protected cove on the east coast, is ideal for windsurfing. Novices will find it especially comforting, since there's no way to be blown out to sea. The island's windsurfing companies are headquartered there on Sorobon Beach.

★ The **Bonaire Windsurf Place** (⌧ Sorobon Beach ☎ 599/717–2288 ⊕ www.bonairewindsurfplace.com), commonly referred to as "the Place," rents the latest Hot Sails Maui, Starboard, and RRD equipment for $40 for half-day or $60 for a full day. A two-hour group lesson costs $45; private lessons are $75 per hour (these rates do not include equipment, which adds at least $35 to the price). A three-day group-lesson package is a bargain at $190, since it includes a one-hour lesson, one hour of practice, and equipment rental; groups are generally limited to four people. Elvis, Roger, and Constantine, who own the place, are all former windsurfing champs. **Jibe City** (⌧ Sorobon Beach ☎ 599/717–5233, 800/748–8733 in U.S. ⊕ www.jibecity.com) offers lessons for $45 (includes board and sail for beginners only); board rentals start at $20 an hour, $45 for a half-day. There are pickups at all the hotels at 9 AM and 1 PM; ask your hotel to make arrangements.

Shopping

You can get to know all the shops in Kralendijk in an hour or so, but sometimes there's no better way to enjoy some time out of the sun and sea than to go shopping (particularly if your companion is a dive fanatic and you're not). Almost all the shops are on the Kaya Grandi and adjacent streets and in tiny malls. Harbourside Mall is a pleasant, open-air mall with several fine air-conditioned shops. The most distinctive local crafts are fanciful painted pieces of driftwood and hand-painted *kunuku*, or little wilderness houses. One word of caution: buy as many flamingo T-shirts as you want, but don't take home items made of goatskin or tortoise shell; they aren't allowed into the United States. Remember, too, that it's forbidden to take sea fans, coral, conch shells, and *all* other forms of marine life off the island.

Specialty Items

CLOTHING **Benetton** (⌧ Kaya Grandi 29, Kralendijk ☎ 599/717–5107) claims that its prices for men's, women's, and children's clothes are 30% lower than in New York. **Best Buddies** (⌧ Kaya Grandi 32, Kralendijk ☎ 599/717–7570) stocks a selection of Indonesian batik shirts, pareus, and T-shirts. At **Island Fashions** (⌧ Kaya Grandi 5, Kralendijk ☎ 599/717–7565) you can buy swimsuits, sunglasses, T-shirts, and costume jewelry.

DUTY-FREE GOODS **Flamingo Airport Duty Free** (⌧ Flamingo Airport ☎ 599/717–5563) sells perfumes and cigarettes. **Perfume Palace** (⌧ Harborside Mall, Kaya Grandi 31, Kralendijk ☎ 599/717–5288) sells perfumes and makeup from Lancôme, Estée Lauder, Chanel, Ralph Lauren, and Clinique.

HANDICRAFTS **Bon Tiki** (⌧ Kaya C. E. B. Hellmund 3, Kralendijk ☎ 599/717–6877) sells unique works from Bonaire's finest artists. **JanArt Gallery** (⌧ Kaya Gloria 7, Kralendijk ☎ 599/717–5246), on the outskirts of town, sells unique watercolor paintings, prints, and art supplies; artist Janice Huckaby also hosts art classes. **Cinnamon Art Gallery** (⌧ Kaya A. P. L. Brion 1, Kralendijk ☎ 599/717–7103), on a side street off Kaya Grandi, offers a selection of fine art from local artists. Whatever you do, make a

★ point of visiting **Jenny's Art** (⊠ Kaya Betico Croes 6, near post office, Kralendijk ☎ 599/717–5004). Roam around her house, which is a replica of a traditional Bonaire town complete with her handmade life-size dolls and the skeletons of all her dead pets. Lots of fun (and sometimes kitschy) souvenirs made out of driftwood, clay, and shells are all handmade by Jenny. **Maharaj Gifthouse** (⊠ Kaya Grandi 11, Kralendijk ☎ 599/717–4402) has a vast assortment of Delft blue hand-painted china, local artwork, and stainless steel and crystal items that make great gifts.

JEWELRY **Atlantis** (⊠ Kaya Grandi 32B, Kralendijk ☎ 599/717–7730) carries a
★ large range of precious and semiprecious gems. The tanzanite collection is especially beautiful. You will also find Sector, Raymond Weil, and Citizen watches, among others, all at great savings. Since gold jewelry is sold by weight here, it's an especially good buy. **Littman's** (⊠ Kaya Grandi 33, Kralendijk ☎ 599/717–8160 ⊠ Harborside Mall, Kaya Grandi 31, Kralendijk ☎ 599/717–2130) is an upscale jewelry and gift shop where many items are handpicked by owner Steven Littman on his regular trips to Europe. Look for Rolex, Omega, Cartier, and Tag Heuer watches, fine gold jewelry, antique coins, nautical sculptures, resort clothing, and accessories.

Nightlife

Most divers are exhausted after they finish their third, fourth, or fifth dive of the day, which may explain why there are no full-time discos on Bonaire. Strange as it may sound, the most effective approach to finding the best hotspot is to stand downtown, listen for the loudest music, and then follow your ears. Most of the time nightlife consists of sitting on a quiet beach sipping a local Amstel Bright beer. Top island performers, including the Foyan Boys, migrate from one resort to another throughout the week. You can find information in the free magazines (published once a year) *Bonaire Affair* and *Bonaire Nights*. The twice-monthly *Bonaire Update Events & Activities* pamphlet is available at most restaurants.

Carnival, generally held in February, is the usual nonstop parade of steel bands, floats, and wild costumes, albeit on a much smaller scale than on some other islands. It culminates in the ceremonial burning in effigy of King Momo, representing the spirit of debauchery.

BARS The Thursday-night happy hour at **Captain Don's Habitat** (⊠ Kaya Gobernador N. Debrot 85, Kralendijk ☎ 599/717–8286) is popular. Downtown, **City Café** (⊠ Hotel Rochaline, Kaya Grandi 7, Kralendijk ☎ 599/ 717–8286) is a wacky hangout splashed in magenta, banana, and electric blue. Here you can find cocktails, snack food, live music on weekends, and karaoke on Wednesday nights. **Karel's** (⊠ Kaya J. N. E. Craane 12, Kralendijk ☎ 599/717–8434) sits on stilts above the sea and is *the* place for mingling—especially Friday and Saturday nights, when there's live island and pop music. **La Guernica** (⊠ Kaya Bonaire 4C, Kralendijk ☎ 599/717–5022), with an ultrachic bar and comfy-couch-lined terrace is the place to be seen on weekend nights.

CASINOS   **Divi Flamingo Resort** (✉ J. A. Abraham Blvd., Kralendijk ☎ 599/717–8285) is the only casino on the island and operates until 4 AM.

DANCE CLUBS   **City Café** (✉ Kaya Grandi 7, Kralendijk ☎ 599/717–8286) is the island's closest thing to a dance club. On weekend nights the restaurant moves the tables aside and it becomes an instant dance floor. On Sunday afternoon at **Lac Cai** (✉ Lac Cai) enjoy the festive Sunday Party, where locals celebrate the day with live music, dancing, and food from 3 to 11. Take a taxi, especially if you plan to imbibe a few rum punches.

★

Exploring Bonaire

Two routes, north and south from Kralendijk, the island's small capital, are possible on the 24-mi-long (39-km-long) island; either route will take from a few hours to a full day, depending on whether you stop to snorkel, swim, dive, or lounge. Those pressed for time will find that it's easy to explore the entire island in a day once stops are kept to a minimum.

Numbers in the margin correspond to points of interest on the Bonaire map.

What to See

KRALENDIJK   Bonaire's small, tidy capital city (population 3,000) is five minutes from ❶ the airport. The main drag, J. A. Abraham Boulevard, turns into **Kaya Grandi** in the center of town. Along it are most of the island's major stores, boutiques, and restaurants. Across Kaya Grandi, opposite the Littman jewelry store, is Kaya L. D. Gerharts, with several small supermarkets, a handful of snack shops, and some of the better restaurants. Walk down the narrow waterfront avenue called Kaya C. E. B. Hellmund, which leads straight to the **North and South piers.** In the center of town, the Harborside Mall has chic boutiques. Along this route is **Fort Oranje,** with its cannons. From December through April, cruise ships dock in the harbor once or twice a week. The diminutive ochre-and-white structure that looks like a tiny Greek temple is the **fish market;** local anglers no longer bring their catches here (they sell out of their homes these days), but you can find plenty of fresh produce brought over from Columbia and Venezuela. Pick up the brochure *Walking and Shopping in Kralendijk* from the tourist office to get a map and full listing of all the monuments and sights in the town.

SOUTH BONAIRE   The trail south from Kralendijk is chock-full of icons—both natural and man-made—that tell Bonaire's mini-saga. Rent a four-wheel-drive vehicle (a car will do, but during the rainy season of October through November the roads can become muddy) and head out along the Southern Scenic Route. The roads wind through dramatic desert terrain, full of organ-pipe cacti and spiny-trunk mangroves—huge stumps of saltwater trees that rise from the marshes like witches. Watch for long-haired goats, wild donkeys, and lizards of all sizes.

★ ☙ ❺   **Rooi Lamoenchi Kunuku.** Owner Ellen Herrera restored her family's homestead north of Lac Bay, in the Bonairean kadushi (cactus) wilderness, to educate tourists and residents about the history and tradition of authentic kunuku living and show unspoiled terrain in two daily tours.

You must make an appointment in advance and expect to spend a couple of hours. ✉ *Kaya Suiza 23, Playa Baribe* ☎ *599/717–8490* ⊕ *www. webpagecur.com/rooilamoenchi* ✍ *$12* ⊙ *By appointment only.*

➌ Salt Flats. You can't miss the salt flats—voluptuous white drifts that look something like mountains of snow. Harvested once a year, the "ponds" are owned by Cargill, Inc., which has reactivated the 19th-century salt industry with great success (one reason for that success is that the ocean on this part of the island is higher than the land—which makes irrigation a snap). Keep a lookout for the three 30-foot obelisks—white, blue, and red—that were used to guide the trade boats coming to pick up the salt. Look also in the distance across the pans to the abandoned solar saltworks that's now a designated **flamingo sanctuary.** With the naked eye you might be able to make out a pink-orange haze just on the horizon; with binoculars you will see a sea of bobbing pink bodies. The sanctuary is completely protected, and no entrance is allowed (flamingos are extremely sensitive to disturbances of any kind).

☝ ➋ Slave Huts. The salt industry's gritty history is revealed in Rode Pan, the site of two groups of tiny slave huts. The white grouping is on the right side of the road, opposite the salt flats; the second grouping, called the red slave huts (though they appear yellow), stretches across the road toward the island's southern tip. During the 19th century, slaves working the salt pans by day crawled into these huts to rest. Each Friday afternoon they walked seven hours to Rincon to weekend with their families, returning each Sunday. Only very small people will be able to enter, but walk around and poke your head in for a look.

➍ Willemstoren Lighthouse. Bonaire's first lighthouse was built in 1837 and is now automated (but closed to visitors). Take some time to explore the beach and notice how the waves, driven by the trade winds, play a crashing symphony against the rocks. Locals stop here to collect pieces of driftwood in spectacular shapes and to build fanciful pyramids from objects that have washed ashore.

NORTH BONAIRE The Northern Scenic Route takes you into the heart of Bonaire's natural wonders—desert gardens of towering cacti (kadushi, used to prepare soup, and the thornier *yatu,* used to build cactus fencing), tiny coastal coves, and plenty of fantastic panoramas. The road also weaves between eroded pink-and-black limestone walls and eerie rock formations with fanciful names like the Devil's Mouth and Iguana Head (you'll need a vivid imagination and sharp eye to recognize them). Brazil trees growing along the route were used by Indians to make dye (pressed from a red ring in the trunk). Inscriptions still visible in several island caves were made with this dye.

A snappy excursion with the requisite photo stops will take about 2½ hours, but if you pack your swimsuit and a hefty picnic basket (forget about finding a KFC), you could spend the entire day exploring this northern sector. Head out from Kralendijk on Kaya Gobernador N. Debrot until it turns into the Northern Scenic Route. Once you pass the Radio Nederland towers you cannot turn back to Kralendijk. The narrow road becomes one-way until you get to Landhuis Karpata, and you have to follow the cross-island road to Rincon and return via the main road through the center of the island.

➐ Barcadera Cave. Once used to trap goats, this cave is one of the oldest in Bonaire; there's even a tunnel that looks intriguingly spooky. It's the first sight along the northern route; watch closely for a yellow marker on your left before you reach the towering Radio Nederland antennas. Pull off across from the entrance to the Bonaire Caribbean Club, and you can discover some stone steps that lead down into a cave full of stalactites and vegetation.

➓ Gotomeer. This saltwater lagoon near the island's northern end is a popular flamingo hangout. Bonaire is one of the few places in the world where pink flamingos nest. The shy, spindly-legged creatures—affectionately called "pink clouds"—are magnificent birds to observe, and there are about 15,000 of them in Bonaire (more than the number of human residents). The best time to catch them at home is January to June, when they tend to their gray-plumed young. For the best view take the paved access road alongside the lagoon through the jungle of cacti to the parking and observation area on the rise overlooking the lagoon and Washington–Slagbaai National Park beyond.

➌ Landhuis Karpata. This mustard-color building was the manor house of an aloe plantation in the 19th century. The site was named for the *karpata* (castor bean) plants that are abundant in the area—you can see them along the sides of the road as you approach. Notice the rounded outdoor oven where aloe was boiled down before the juice was exported. Although the government has built a shaded rest stop at Karpata, there's still no drink stand.

➑ 1,000 Steps. Directly across the road from the Radio Nederland towers on the main road north, you'll see a short yellow marker that points to the location of these limestone stairs carved right out of the cliff. If you trek down the stairs, you can discover a lovely coral beach and protected cove where you can snorkel and scuba dive. Actually, you'll count only 67 steps, but it feels like 1,000 when you walk back up carrying scuba gear.

➓ Onima. Small signposts direct the way to the Indian inscriptions found on a 3-foot limestone ledge that juts out like a partially formed cave entrance. Look up to see the red-stained designs and symbols inscribed on the limestone, said to have been the handiwork of the Arawak Indians when they inhabited the island centuries ago. The pictographs date back at least to the 15th century, and nobody has a clue what they mean. To reach Onima, pass through Rincon on the road that heads back to Kralendijk, but take the left-hand turn before Fontein.

➒ Rincon. The island's original Spanish settlement, Rincon is where slaves brought from Africa to work the plantations and salt fields lived. Superstition and voodoo lore still have a powerful impact here, more so than in Kralendijk, where the townspeople work hard at suppressing old ways. Rincon is now a well-kept cluster of pastel cottages and 19th-century buildings that constitute Bonaire's oldest village. Watch your driving here—goats and dogs often sit right in the middle of the main drag.

⑥ Seroe Largu. Just off the main road, this spot, at 394 feet, is one of the highest on the island. A paved but narrow and twisting road leads to a magnificent daytime view of Kralendijk's rooftops and the island of Klein Bonaire. A large cross and figure of Christ stand guard at the peak, with an inscription reading *ayera* (yesterday), *awe* (today), and *semper* (always).

🖐 ⑪ Washington–Slagbaai National Park. Once a plantation producing divi-divi trees (the pods were used for tanning animal skins), aloe (used for medicinal lotions), charcoal, and goats, the park is now a model of conservation. It's easy to tour the 13,500-acre tropical desert terrain on the dirt roads. As befits a wilderness sanctuary, the well-marked, rugged routes force you to drive slowly enough to appreciate the animal life and the terrain. (Think twice about coming here if it has rained recently—the mud you may encounter will be more than inconvenient.) If you're planning to hike, bring a picnic lunch, camera, sunscreen, and plenty of water. There are two routes: the long one (22 mi [35½ km]) is marked by yellow arrows, the short one (15 mi [24 km]) by green arrows. Goats and donkeys may dart across the road, and if you keep your eyes peeled, you may catch sight of large iguanas camouflaged in the shrubbery.

Bird-watchers are really in their element here. Right inside the park's gate, flamingos roost on the salt pad known as **Salina Mathijs,** and exotic parakeets dot the foot of **Mount Brandaris,** Bonaire's highest peak, at 784 feet. Some 130 species of birds fly in and out of the shrubbery in the park. Keep your eyes open and your binoculars at hand. Swimming, snorkeling, and scuba diving are permitted, but you're requested not to frighten the animals or remove anything from the grounds. Absolutely no hunting, fishing, or camping is allowed. A useful guide to the park is available at the entrance for about $6. To get here, take the secondary road north from the town of Rincon. The Nature Fee for swimming and snorkeling also includes admission to this park. 🕾 *599/717–8444* ⊕ *www.bonairenature.com/washingtonpark* ✉ *$10* ⊙ *Daily 8–5; you must enter before 3.*

BONAIRE ESSENTIALS

To research prices, get advice from other travelers, and book travel arrangements, visit www.fodors.com.

Transportation

BY AIR
Continental Airlines offers once-weekly direct service to Bonaire (BON) from Houston. Canadians and Americans will usually have to change planes in San Juan or Aruba. Air Jamaica, American Eagle,

and BonairExpress provide connecting service. KLM offers daily direct flights from Amsterdam.

🖪 **Air Jamaica** 🕾 599/717-7747 or 800/523-5585. **American Eagle** 🕾 599/717-2005 or 800/433-7300. **BonairExpress** 🕾 599/717-3471, 800/374-7747 in U.S., 3120/4-747-747 in Netherlands. **KLM** 🕾 599/717-7447.

🖪 **Flamingo Airport** BON 🕾 599/717-3800. **Airport Taxi Stand** 🕾 599/717-8100.

BY BIKE & MOPED

Scooters are a great way to zip around the island. Rates are about $18 per day for a one-seater and up to $38 for a deluxe two-seater. A valid driver's license and cash deposit or credit card are required. Bonaire Motorcycle Shop rents Harley-Davidson motorcycles as well as scooters.

🏍 **Bonaire Motorcycle Shop** ✉ Kaya Grandi 64, Kralendijk ☎ 599/717-7790. **Macho! Scooter Rentals** ✉ J. A. Abraham Blvd. 80, Kralendijk ☎ 599/717-2500.

BY CAR

You'll need a valid U.S., Canadian, or international driver's license to rent a car, and you must meet the minimum and maximum age requirements (usually 21 and 70) of each rental company. There's a government tax of $3.50 per day per rental; no cash deposit is needed if you pay by credit card.

Gas costs about double what it does in the United States, and you can find stations in Kralendijk, Rincon, and Antriol. Main roads are well paved, but remember that there are also many miles of unpaved roads; the roller-coaster hills at the national park require a strong stomach, and during the rainy season (October through November) mud—called Bonairean snow—can be difficult to navigate. All traffic stays to the right, and there's not a single traffic light. Signs or green arrows are usually posted to leading attractions; if you stick to the paved roads and marked turnoffs, you won't get lost.

🚗 **Avis** ✉ Flamingo Airport, Kralendijk ☎ 599/717-5795. **Budget** ✉ Flamingo Airport, Kralendijk ☎ 599/717-7424. **Flamingo Car Rental** ✉ Kaya Grandi 86, Kralendijk ☎ 599/717-8888, 599/717-5588 at airport. **Hertz** ✉ Flamingo Airport, Kralendijk ☎ 599/717-7221. **Island Rentals** ✉ Kaya Industria 31, Kralendijk ☎ 599/717-2100. **National** ✉ Kaya Nikiboko Zuid 114, Kralendijk ☎ 599/717-7940 or 599/717-7907.

BY TAXI

Taxis are unmetered; they have fixed rates controlled by the government. A trip from the airport to your hotel will cost between $9 and $12 for up to four passengers. A taxi from most hotels into town costs between $5 and $8. Fares increase from 7 PM to midnight by 25% and from midnight to 6 AM by 50%. Drivers are usually knowledgeable enough about the island to conduct half-day tours; they charge about $30 for up to four passengers for half-day northern- or southern-route tours.

🚕 **Taxi Central Dispatch** ☎ 599/717-8100.

Contacts & Resources

BANKS & EXCHANGE SERVICES

There's no real need to convert your American dollars into the local currency, the NAf guilder. U.S. currency and traveler's checks are accepted everywhere, and the difference in exchange rates is negligible. Banks accept U.S. dollar banknotes at the official rate of NAf 1.78 to the U.S. dollar, traveler's checks at NAf 1.80. This rate is practically fixed. The rate of exchange at shops and hotels ranges from NAf 1.75 to NAf 1.80. The guilder is divided into 100 cents. You can find ATMs at the airport, in Kralendijk, and at Hato branches of MCB, as well as at the Sand Dollar Resort and the Plaza Resort; at the Tourism Corporation of Bonaire; and at Banco di Caribe on Kaya Grandi.

BUSINESS HOURS

Banks are generally open weekdays from 8:30 to 3:30. The bank at the airport has extended hours: weekdays from 7:30 to 10, weekends from 8 to 6. Stores in the Kralendijk area are generally open Monday through Saturday from 8 to noon and 2 to 6 but may open earlier or stay open later depending on the season.

ELECTRICITY

Bonaire runs on 120 AC/50 cycles. A transformer and occasionally a two-prong adapter are required. Note that some appliances may work slowly (60 cycles are typical in North America), hair dryers may overheat, and sensitive equipment may be damaged.

EMERGENCIES

🔲 Ambulance & Fire **Ambulance** ☎ 599/717–8900. **Fire** ☎ 599/717–8000.

🔲 Hospitals **St. Franciscus Hospital** ✉ Kaya Soeur Bartola 2, Kralendijk ☎ 599/717–8900. **Scuba-diving emergencies** ☎ 599/717–8187.

🔲 Pharmacies **Botika Bonaire** ✉ Kaya Grandi 27, by Harborside Mall, Kralendijk ☎ 599/717–8905.

🔲 Police **Police emergencies** ☎ 599/717–8000.

HOLIDAYS

Public holidays are New Year's Day, Carnival Monday (Mon. before Ash Wednesday), Good Friday (Fri. before Easter), Rincon Day and Queen's Birthday (Apr. 30), Labor Day (May 1), Bonaire Day (Sept. 6), Antilles Day (Oct. 21), Christmas and the day after (Dec. 25–26).

INTERNET, MAIL & SHIPPING

Bonaire is not the ideal place for Internet junkies, as most hotels do not offer even basic dial-up service in rooms, much less Wi-Fi. There are a few cybercafés, the best being Chat 'n' Browse at Sand Dollar Shopping Plaza. Downtown, Cyber City at City Café and Bonaire Access at Harbourside Mall are the most popular. Some hotels offer Wi-Fi, Sand Dollar Condominiums being one example.

Airmail postage to North America and Europe is NAf 2.25 for letters and NAf 1.10 for postcards. The main post office is at the southeast corner of Kaya Grandi and Kaya Libertador S. Bolivar in Kralendijk. The post office is open weekdays from 7:30 to noon and 1:30 to 4.

🔲 Internet Cafés **Bonaire Access** ✉ Harbourside Mall, Kralendijk ☎ No phone. **Chat 'n' Browse** ✉ Sand Dollar Shopping Plaza, Kaya Gobernador N. Debrot 79, Kralendijk ☎ 599/717–2281. **Cyber City** ✉ City Café, Kaya Grandi 7, Kralendijk ☎ 599/717–8286.

LANGUAGE

The official language is Dutch, but the everyday language is Papiamento, a mix of Spanish, Portuguese, Dutch, English, and French, as well as African tongues. You can light up your waiter's eyes if you can say *masha danki* (thank you very much) and *pasa un bon dia* (have a nice day). English is spoken by almost everyone on the island.

PASSPORT REQUIREMENTS

U.S. citizens must carry valid passports. In addition, everyone must have a return or ongoing ticket and is advised to confirm reservations 48 hours before departure. The maximum stay is 90 days.

SAFETY

Bonaire has a reputation for being friendly and safe, but petty crime exists. Divers who park their cars on the beach while offshore are at high risk of finding broken windows upon their return. The best, though admittedly strange, advice is to leave the vehicle unlocked and windows down when it is parked. The cost of replacing windows on a rental vehicle can be exorbitant, and if there's nothing to steal in the vehicle, the attraction for thieves is gone. Keep your money, credit cards, jewelry, and other valuables in your hotel's safety-deposit box.

TAXES

The departure tax when going to Curaçao is $5.75 (NAf 10.25). For all other destinations it's $20 (NAf 35.60). This tax must be paid in cash at the airport prior to departure. U.S. currency is accepted, but paying in NAf is usually faster. Hotels charge a room tax of $6.50 per person, per night in addition to the V.A.T. Many hotels add a 10% to 15% service charge to your bill. A V.A.T (value-added tax) of 6% is tacked on to dining and lodging costs. V.A.T. may or may not be included in your quoted room rates, so be sure to ask. It's almost always included in restaurant prices.

TELEPHONES

You can make international calls from hotel front desks or from the Telbo central phone company office (next to the tourism office in Kralendijk), which is open 24 hours a day. You can rent a cell phone

5

from CellularOne Bonaire or Chat 'n' Browse at the Sand Dollar Shopping Plaza; the phone will cost you about $3 rental a day (plus a deposit), and you can buy pre-paid phone cards—cell-call costs are about 75% cheaper than hotel calls.

The country code for Bonaire is 599; 717 is the exchange for every four-digit telephone number on the island. When making interisland calls, dial 717 plus the local four-digit number. Local phone calls cost NAf 50¢.

Phone cards from home rarely work on Bonaire. You can try AT&T by dialing 001–800/872–2881 from public phones. To call Bonaire from the United States, dial 011–599/717 plus the local four-digit number.

🔒 **CellularOne Bonaire** ✉ Kaya Grandi 26, Kralendijk ☎ 599/717-8787. **Chat 'n' Browse** ✉ Sand Dollar Shopping Plaza, Kaya Gobernador N. Debrot 79, Kralendijk ☎ 599/717-2281.

TIPPING
Most restaurants add a 10% to 12% service charge; if they don't, tip at the same level. Taxi drivers like a 10% tip, but it isn't mandatory. Bellhops should receive $1 per bag.

TOUR OPTIONS
Achie Tours has several half- and full-day options. Bonaire Tours & Vacations will chauffeur you around on two-hour tours of either the island's north or south or on a half-day city-and-country tour ($25), which visits sights in both regions. Or simply ask any taxi driver for an island tour (be sure to negotiate the price up front). Tropical Travel offers a variety of land- and water-based tours of various lengths starting at $27.

🔒 **Achie Tours** ✉ Kaya Nikiboko Noord 33, Kralendijk ☎ 599/717-8630. **Bonaire Tours & Vacations** ✉ Kaya Gobernador N. Debrot 79, Kralendijk

☎ 599/717-8738 ⊕ www.bonairetours.com. **Tropical Travel** ✉ Plaza Resort Bonaire, J. A. Abraham Blvd. 80, Kralendijk ☎ 599/717-2500.

VISITOR INFORMATION
🔒 Before You Leave **Tourism Corporation Bonaire** ✉ 10 Rockefeller Plaza, Suite 900, New York, NY 10020 ☎ 212/956-5913 or 800/266-2473 ⊕ www.infobonaire.com.

🔒 In Bonaire **Tourism Corporation Bonaire** ✉ Kaya Grandi 2, Kralendijk ☎ 599/717-8322 or 599/717-8649.

WEDDINGS
With scenic photo opportunities and peaceful surroundings, it's no wonder that couples swoon at the idea of tying the knot on Bonaire. Weddings can be arranged fairly quickly, but it's best to begin planning at least four to six weeks in advance. One member of the couple must apply for temporary residency. Official witnesses must also apply for temporary residency, but most wedding coordinators can arrange for local witnesses. Once temporary residency has been granted, the couple applies for a marriage license and certificate; after the marriage, an apostille (official seal) must be put on the documents. Blood tests are not required.

I Do Bonaire specializes in wedding planning, as does Marvel Tromp of Multro Travel & Tours. The Web site of the Bonaire Government Tourist Office has details if you want to do your own planning. Several resorts on the island have wedding planners, including Harbour Village Bonaire, the Buddy Dive Resort, Captain Don's Habitat, and Plaza Resort Bonaire.

🔒 **I Do Bonaire** ✉ Kaya L. D. Gerharts 22, Kralendijk ☎ 599/717-8778 ⊕ www.bonairetours.com. **Multro Travel & Tours** ✑ Box 237, Lighthouse Beach Resort 22 ☎ 599/717-8334 ⊕ www.bonaireweddings.com.

British Virgin Islands

The Baths

WORD OF MOUTH

"You'll love Tortola. My best advice is to rent a really good Jeep so you can get around the island. The roads are really steep and if you're not used to it, it can be a bit scary at first."

—Coconut

"The Baths at Virgin Gorda are truly a magical spot, but only if you're not sharing them. . . . If you can, choose to go very early in the morning, or in the late afternoon—before and after the crowds."

—Callaloo

WELCOME TO THE BRITISH VIRGIN ISLANDS

NATURE'S LITTLE SECRETS

Most of the 50-some islands, islets, and cays that make up the British Virgin Islands (BVI) are remarkably hilly and volcanic in origin, having exploded from the depths of the sea some 25 million years ago. The exception is Anegada, which is a flat, coral-limestone atoll. Tortola (about 10 square mi/ 26 square km) is the largest member of the chain.

KEY

🚢 Ferry
🚢 Cruise Ship Terminal

You can still find traces of a primeval rain forest at the top of Sage Mountain, the highest peak in the BVI.

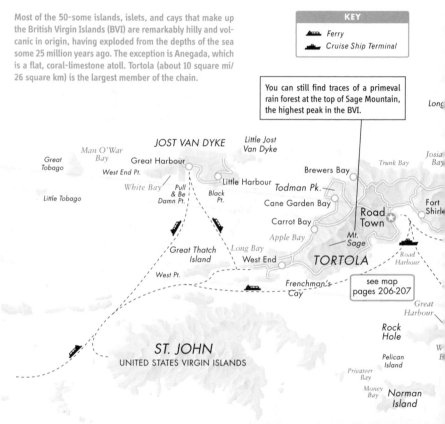

Long

JOST VAN DYKE
Little Jost Van Dyke

Man O'War Bay
Great Tobago
Great Harbour
West End Pt.
White Bay
Pull & Be
Damn Pt.
Little Harbour
Black Pt.
Todman Pk.
Brewers Bay
Trunk Bay
Josia Bay

Little Tobago
Cane Garden Bay
Carrot Bay
Apple Bay

Road Town
Mt. Sage

Fort Shirl

Great Thatch Island
Long Bay
West End
West Pt.
Frenchman's Cay
TORTOLA

Road Harbour

see map pages 206-207

Great Harbour

ST. JOHN
UNITED STATES VIRGIN ISLANDS

Rock Hole
Pelican Island
Privateer Bay
Money Bay
Norman Island
W B

The British Virgin Islands are mostly quiet and casual, so don't expect to party 'til dawn, and definitely leave the tux at home. Luxury here means getting away from it all rather than getting the trendiest state-of-the-art amenities. And the jackpot is the chance to explore the many islets and cays by sailboat.

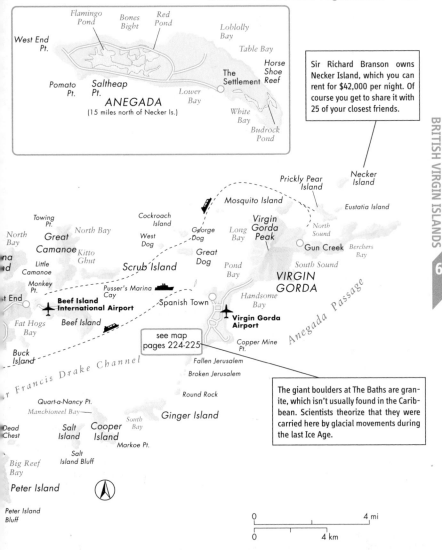

Sir Richard Branson owns Necker Island, which you can rent for $42,000 per night. Of course you get to share it with 25 of your closest friends.

The giant boulders at The Baths are granite, which isn't usually found in the Caribbean. Scientists theorize that they were carried here by glacial movements during the last Ice Age.

see map pages 224-225

TOP 4 REASONS TO VISIT THE BRITISH VIRGIN ISLANDS

1 With over 50 islands in the chain, sailors can drop anchor at a different, perfect beach every day.

2 Laid-back luxury resorts offer a full-scale retreat from your everyday life.

3 Diving and snorkeling doesn't get any easier than around Anegada, where vibrant reefs are often just feet from the shore.

4 Your trip isn't complete until you've chilled at the casual beach bars on Jost Van Dyke.

BRITISH VIRGIN ISLANDS PLANNER

Getting to the British Virgin Islands

There are no direct flights to the British Virgin Islands. To fly into Tortola (EIS), you must connect in San Juan or St. Thomas on a propeller-driven plane, regardless of where you are flying from. But it's sometimes just as easy and cheap to use one of the regularly scheduled ferries from either Charlotte Amalie or Red Hook on St. Thomas; these ferries also go to Virgin Gorda, but the only option for Anegada is a flight. The trip to Tortola takes less than an hour. If you're already in St. John, you can get to Tortola from there by ferry as well. Separate ferries go from Tortola to Jost Van Dyke and the other island retreats. You can take a tiny island-hopper flight to either Virgin Gorda (VIJ) or Anegada (NGD) from Tortola, but you'll have to book it directly with one of the small island-based airlines.

Hassle Factor: Medium to High

Activities

The BVI **sailing** scene is one of the best in the world, with Tortola as one of the major charter yacht centers of the Caribbean. It's no wonder that sailing is so popular; most of the best BVI **beaches** are on deserted islands and are accessible only by boat. The most famous beach in the chain is The Baths on Virgin Gorda, which is lined with giant, round boulders that provide for great off-the-beach snorkeling. The **nightlife** center of the region is actually a series of simple beach bars on Jost Van Dyke, but yachties in the know are happy to bop over for a drink and to hear Foxy Callwood sing at his eponymous bar and restaurant. **Diving** and **game-fishing** in these waters are also good.

On the Ground

At Tortola's Beef Island airport, taxis hover at the exit from customs. Fares are officially set but are lower per person for more than three passengers. Figure about $15 for up to three people and $5 for each additional passenger for the 20-minute ride to Road Town, and about $20 to $30 for the 45-minute ride to West End. Expect to share your taxi, and be patient if your driver searches for people to fill his cab—only a few flights land each day, and this could be your driver's only run.

On Virgin Gorda, if you're staying on North Sound, a taxi will take you from the airport to the dock, where your hotel launch will meet you, but be sure to make launch arrangements with your hotel before your arrival. If your destination is Leverick Bay, your land taxi will take you there directly. You can also take the North Sound Express directly from the Beef Island airport to Spanish Town or North Sound. On Anegada, your hotel will organize your transportation from the small airstrip.

Renting a Car

Both Tortola and Virgin Gorda have a number of car-rental agencies. Although taxi service is good, you may wish to rent a car to explore farther afield or try many different beaches (you may need to if you are staying at an isolated resort). On Anegada it's possible to rent a car, but most people rely on taxis for transportation. Jost Van Dyke has a single road, and visitors travel on foot or by local taxi.

Where to Stay

When to Go

Pick your island carefully because each is different, as are the logistics of getting there. Tortola gives you a wider choice of restaurants, shopping, and resorts. Virgin Gorda has fewer off-resort places to eat and shop, but the resorts themselves are often better, and the beaches are exquisite. Anegada is remote and better suited for divers. Jost Van Dyke has some classic Caribbean beach bars, along with fairly basic accommodations. When you want to be pampered and pampered some more, select a remote resort reached only by ferry, or even one of the appealing outer-island resorts that are still somewhat affordable for mere mortals. If you want to enjoy everything the BVI have to offer, charter a sailboat so you can drop anchor where and when you want.

The largest resort in the British Virgin Islands has 120-some rooms, and most have considerably fewer. Luxury here is more about personal service than over-the-top amenities. The best places are certainly comfortable, but they aren't showy. You'll find villas and condos in abundance, and they are a good option for families.

High season doesn't really get into full swing until Christmas and ends sooner (usually by April 1) than on most Caribbean islands. In the off-season, rates can be a third less.

In April, glimpse the colorful spinnakers as sailing enthusiasts gather for the internationally known **BVI Spring Regatta**. In August, try your hand at sport fishing, as anglers compete to land the largest catch at the **BVI Sportfishing Tournament**.

Hotel & Restaurant Costs

Assume that hotels operate on the European Plan (**EP**—with no meals) unless we specify that they use either the Continental Plan (**CP**—with a Continental breakfast), Breakfast Plan (**BP**—with full breakfast), or the Modified American Plan (**MAP**—with breakfast and dinner). Other hotels may offer the Full American Plan (**FAP**—including all meals but no drinks) or may be All-Inclusive (**AI**—with all meals, drinks, and most activities).

WHAT IT COSTS in Dollars

	$$$$	**$$$**	**$$**	**$**	**¢**
Restaurants	over $30	$20–$30	$12–$20	$8–$12	under $8
Hotels*	over $350	$250–$350	$150–$250	$80–$150	under $80
Hotels**	over $450	$350–$450	$250–$350	$125–$250	under $125

*EP, BP, CP   **AI, FAP, MAP
Restaurant prices are for a main course excluding 10% service charge. Hotel prices are for two people in a double room in high season and exclude 7% BVI hotel tax, 10% service charge, and meal plans (except at all-inclusives).

Updated by
Carol M.
Bareuther and
Lynda Lohr

WITH THE SAILS DOWN AFTER A SMOOTH TRIP across Sir Francis Drake Channel, our boat glided into White Bay at Jost Van Dyke for an afternoon of snorkeling and sun. A fresh-from-the-sea lobster dinner followed at a shoreside restaurant. The next day we anchored at Cane Garden Bay on Tortola's north shore for a dinghy ride ashore to listen to some hot music, and the day after that at a remote bay where we were the only boat. Traveling by sea is the way to hop around this archipelago of small islands and tiny cays. If a sailing trip isn't on your horizon, take one of the ferries that connect all the islands except Anegada.

The British Virgin Islands (BVI) are in the midst of transition. Once a collection of about 50 sleepy islands and cays, the British Virgin Islands—particularly the main island of Tortola—now sees huge cruise ships crowding its dock outside Road Town. Shoppers clog the downtown area on busy cruise-ship days, and traffic occasionally comes to a standstill. Even the second-largest island, Virgin Gorda, gets its share of smaller ships anchored off the main village of Spanish Town. Despite this explosive growth in the territory's tourism industry, it's still easy to escape the hubbub. Hotels outside Road Town usually provide a quiet oasis, and those on the other islands can be downright serene.

Each island has a different flavor. Want access to lots of restaurants and shopping? Make Tortola your choice. The largest of the BVIs, it covers 10 square mi and sits only a mile from St. John in the United States Virgin Islands (USVI). If you want to kick back at a small hotel or posh resort, try Virgin Gorda. Sitting nearly at the end of the chain, the 8-square-mi (21-square-km) island offers stellar beaches and a laidback atmosphere. If you really want to get away from it all, the outermost islands, including Anegada and Jost Van Dyke, will fill the bill. Some of the smallest—Norman, Peter, Cooper, and Necker—are home to just one resort or restaurant. Others remain uninhabited specks on the horizon.

No matter what your choice, the scenery is stunning, with lush mountains meeting sandy beaches on all but nearly flat and reef-fringed Anegada. The warm Caribbean Sea beckons no matter which island you choose. Visitors mainly come to relax, though the number of organized activities is growing. The territory stakes its reputation on sailing, and you will find a number of companies renting bare or crewed charter boats.

Visitors have long visited the BVI, starting with Christopher Columbus in 1493. He called the islands *Las Once Mil Virgines*—the 11,000 Virgins—in honor of the 11,000 virgin companions of St. Ursula, martyred in the 4th century AD. Pirates and buccaneers followed, and then came the British, who farmed the islands until slavery was abolished in 1834. The BVI are still politically tied to Britain, so the queen appoints a royal governor, but residents elect a local Legislative Council. Offshore banking and tourism share top billing in the territory's economy, but the majority of the islands' jobs are tourism-related. Despite the growth, you can usually find a welcoming smile.

American or British?

YES, THE UNION JACK FLUTTERS overhead in the tropical breeze, schools operate on the British system, place names have British spellings, Queen Elizabeth II appoints the governor—and the Queen's picture hangs on many walls. Indeed, residents celebrate the Queen's birthday every June with a public ceremony. You can overhear that charming English accent from a good handful of expats when you're lunching at Road Town restaurants, and you can buy British biscuits—which Americans call cookies—in the supermarkets.

But you can pay for your lunch and the biscuits with American money, because the U.S. dollar is legal tender here. The unusual circumstance is a matter of geography. The practice started in the mid-20th century, when BVI residents went to work in the nearby USVI. On trips home, they brought their U.S. dollars with them. Soon, they abandoned the barter system, and in 1959, the U.S. dollar became the official form of money. Interestingly, the government sells stamps for use only in the BVI that often carry pictures of Queen Elizabeth II and other royalty with the monetary value in U.S. dollars and cents.

The American influence continued to grow when Americans began to open businesses in the BVI because they preferred its quieter ambience to the hustle and bustle of St. Thomas. Inevitably, cable and satellite TV's U.S.-based programming, along with Hollywood-made movies, further influenced life in the BVI. And most goods are shipped from St. Thomas in the USVI, meaning you'll find more American-made Oreos than British-produced Peak Freens on the supermarket shelves.

6

TORTOLA

Updated by
Lynda Lohr

Once a sleepy backwater, Tortola is definitely on the busy side these days, particularly when several cruise ships drop anchor off Road Town. Passengers crowd the town's streets and shops, and open-air jitneys filled with cruise-ship passengers create bottlenecks on Tortola's byways. That said, most folks visit Tortola to relax on its deserted sands or linger over lunch at one of its many delightful restaurants. Beaches are never more than a few miles away, and the steep green hills that form Tortola's spine are fanned by gentle trade winds. The neighboring islands glimmer like emeralds in a sea of sapphire. It can be a world far removed from the hustle of modern life, but it simply doesn't compare to Virgin Gorda in terms of beautiful beaches—or even really nice resorts, for that matter.

Where to Stay

Luxury on Tortola is more about a certain state of mind—serenity, seclusion, gentility, and a bit of Britain in the Caribbean—than about state-of-the-art amenities and facilities. Indeed, don't let a bit of rust on the screen or a chip in the paint mar your appreciation of the ambience.

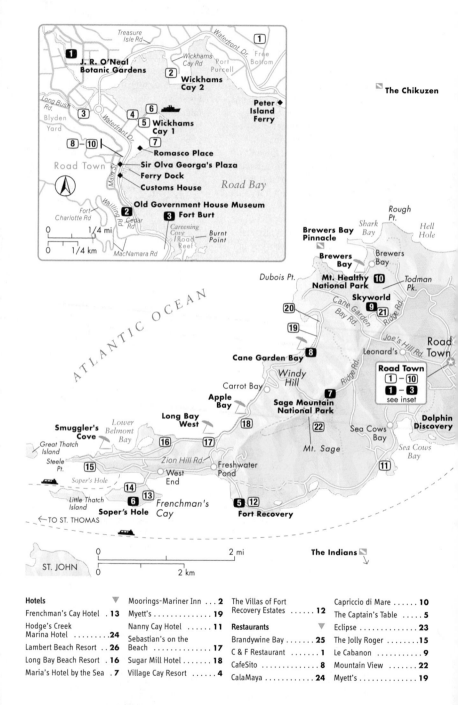

Tortola

TO ANEGADA ↗

Wash Ballock Pt.

Longman's Pt.

North Bay

Great Camanoe

Muskmellon Bay

Guana Island

Kitto Ghut

White Bay

Lee Bay

Scrub Island

Monkey Pt.
Elizabeth Beach

Little Camanoe

Marina Cay

Rogue's Pt.

26

Trellis Bay

Ridge Rd.

Long Bay, Beef Island

Buta Mt.

Long Look

East End

Beef Island International Airport

Mt. Belle-Vue

Parham Town

Long Swamp

23

Bluff Bay

Beef Island

Baughers Bay

Ft. Shirley

Wickhams Cay

Fat Hogs Bay

Road Harbour

24

25

Paraquita Bay

Buck Island

TO VIRGIN GORDA ↗

Sir Francis Drake Channel

Alice in Wonderland

KEY	
⚓	*Beaches*
◥	*Dive Sites*
⛴	*Ferry*
🚢	*Cruise Ship Terminal*
1	*Exploring Sights*
1	*Hotels & Restaurants*
....	*Trail*

Blonde Rock
Painted Walls
RMS Rhone

TO PETER ISLAND ↓

Instead, enjoy getting to know your fellow guests and staff at the island's cozy hotels. Hotels in Road Town don't have beaches, but they do have pools and are within walking distance of restaurants, nightspots, and shops. Accommodations outside Road Town are relatively isolated, but most are on beaches. The Tortola resorts are intimate—only a handful have more than 50 rooms. You will likely spend most of your time outside, so the location, size, or price of a hotel should be more of a factor to you than the decor of the rooms. Guests are treated as more than just room numbers, and many return year after year. This can make booking a room at popular resorts difficult, even off-season, despite the fact that more than half the island's visitors stay aboard their own or chartered boats.

A few hotels lack air-conditioning, relying instead on ceiling fans to capture the almost constant trade winds. Nights are cool and breezy, even in midsummer, and never reach the temperatures or humidity levels that are common in much of the United States in summer. You may assume that all accommodations listed here have air-conditioning unless we mention otherwise. Remember that some places may be closed during the peak of hurricane season—August through October—to give their owners a much-needed break.

Villas

Renting a villa is growing in popularity. Vacationers like the privacy, the room to get comfortable, and the opportunity to cook their own meals. As everywhere, location counts, so if you want to be close to the beach, opt for a villa on the North Shore. If you want to dine out in Road Town every night, a villa closer to town may be a better bet.

Prices per week during the winter season run from around $2,000 for a one- or two-bedroom villa up to $10,000 for a five-room beachfront villa. Rates in summer are substantially less. Most, but not all, villa managers accept credit cards.

Areana Villas (⌂ Box 263, Road Town ☎ 284/494–5864 🖷 284/494–7626 ⊕ www.areanavillas.com) represents top-of-the-line properties. Homes offer accommodations for 2 to 10 people in one- to five-bedroom villas decorated in soothing pastels. Many have pools, whirlpool tubs, and tiled courtyards.

The St. Thomas–based **McLaughlin-Anderson Luxury Villas** (⌂ 1000 Blackbeard's Hill, Suite 3, St. Thomas, VI 00802-6739 ☎ 240/776-0635 or 800/537–6246 ⊕ www.mclaughlinanderson.com) manages nearly three dozen properties spread over Tortola. Villas range in size from one to six bedrooms and come with full kitchens and stellar views. Most have pools. The company can hire a chef and stock your kitchen with groceries.

Purple Pineapple Villa Rentals (⌂ Box 305498-314, St. Thomas, VI 00803 ☎ 284/495–3100 🖷 305/723–0855 ⊕ www.purplepineapple.com) manages eight luxury homes in locations all over the island from its base in Tortola. Most have pools, hot tubs, and other amenities. Villas range in size from one to six bedrooms.

Hotels & Inns

ROAD TOWN
$$

Maria's Hotel by the Sea. Sitting near the water in busy Road Town, Maria's Hotel by the Sea is perfect for budget travelers who want to be near shops and restaurants but who don't need many frills. The least expensive rooms don't have ocean views, but all have bright tropical fabrics and rattan furniture to remind you that you're on an island. ⊠ *Waterfront Dr., Box 2364* ☎ *284/494–2595* 🖷 *284/494–2420* ⊕ *www. mariasbythesea.com* 🗪 *41 rooms* △ *Restaurant, refrigerators, cable TV, in-room data ports, pool, bar* ⊟ *AE, MC, V* ⦿| *EP.*

$$

Moorings-Mariner Inn. If you enjoy the camaraderie of a busy marina, this inn on the fringes of Road Town may appeal to you. It's a hot spot for charter boaters—usually a lively group—heading out for a week-or-more sail around the islands. Rooms are spacious and have balconies or porches that are perfect for an afternoon's relaxing. All have pastel accents that complement the peach exteriors. ⊠ *Waterfront Dr., Box 139* ☎ *284/494–2333 or 800/535–7289* 🖷 *284/494–2226* 🗪 *36 rooms, 4 suites* △ *Restaurant, some kitchenettes, refrigerators, cable TV, in-room data ports, pool, dive shop, dock, marina, volleyball, bar, shops, Internet room* ⊟ *MC, V* ⦿| *EP.*

$$

Village Cay Resort & Marina. If you want to be able to walk to restaurants and shops, you simply can't beat the prime location in the heart of Road Town. It's perfect for charter-yachters who want a night or two in town before heading out to sea, but land-based vacationers like it equally well. Rooms and suites are done in tropical style with tile floors, rattan furniture, and town or marina views. If you're planning on seeing more than Road Town, you'll need a car to explore and sun at the beach. Otherwise, a tiny pool will have to suffice for your morning swim. ⊠ *Wickham's Cay I, Box 145* ☎ *284/494–2771* 🖷 *284/494–2773* ⊕ *www. villagecay.com* 🗪 *21 rooms* △ *Restaurant, refrigerators, cable TV, in-room broadband, pool, spa, marina, bar, shops, Internet room* ⊟ *AE, MC, V* ⦿| *EP.*

OUTSIDE ROAD
TOWN
$$$$

Long Bay Beach Resort. Although the service draws complaints, the management has been addressing the frosty attitude of some staff members. Long Bay Beach Resort is still Tortola's only choice if you want all the resort amenities, including a beach, scads of water sports, tennis, and even a pitch-and-putt golf course. Accommodations range from traditional hotel rooms to three-bedroom villas, with lots of choices in between. All have a modern tropical feel with rattan furniture and brightly colored fabrics. Given its relative isolation on the northwest shore, you may not be inclined to make many excursions. Luckily, the Garden Restaurant serves romantic dinners. ⊠ *Long Bay* 🖈 *Box 433, Road Town* ☎ *284/495–4252 or 800/345–0271* 🖷 *284/495–4677* ⊕ *www. longbay.com* 🗪 *53 rooms, 37 suites* △ *2 restaurants, some in-room safes, some kitchens, some kitchenettes, cable TV, in-room data ports, 2 tennis courts, pool, gym, spa, beach, dive shop, snorkeling, 2 bars, shops, Internet room, meeting rooms* ⊟ *AE, D, MC, V* ⦿| *EP.*

$$$–$$$$
Fodor'sChoice
★

Sugar Mill Hotel. Though it's not a sprawling resort, this is our favorite resort on Tortola. The rooms are attractively decorated with more than the usual floral spreads and have balconies with good views, kitchens or kitchenettes, and even some sofa beds. The grounds get accolades for their attractive gardens, but many say the real reason to stay here is the easy access to the excellent Sugar Mill restaurant, which has both superb food and a stunning setting in the property's old sugar mill. Owners and food-and-travel writers Jeff and Jinx Morgan have brought all their expertise to this well-run small resort. The north-shore location puts you across the road from a nice beach, but you need a car to do anything more than enjoy the sun and sand. ⊠ *Apple Bay* ⌂ *Box 425, Road Town* ☎ *284/495–4355 or 800/462–8834* 🖷 *284/495–4696* ⊕ *www.sugarmillhotel.com* 🛏 *19 rooms, 2 suites, 1 villa, 1 cottage* 🖒 *2 restaurants, some kitchens, some kitchenettes, cable TV, in-room data ports, pool, beach, snorkeling, 2 bars, Internet room; no TV in some rooms* ▤ *AE, MC, V* ❘⊙❘ *EP.*

$$$–$$$$ ⊡ **The Villas of Fort Recovery Estates.** This is one of those small but special properties, distinguished by friendly service and the chance to get to know your fellow guests rather than the poshness of the rooms and upscale amenities. Villas come in several sizes, and all are quaint—though not fancy—and have good views across the water of St. John. A sandy beach stretches seaside, providing ample opportunity for relaxing. The emphasis on wellness is a welcome touch, and beachside yoga classes are a specialty. The staff is helpful and will arrange day sails and scuba-diving trips. ⊠ *Waterfront Dr., Box 239, Pockwood Pond* ☎ *284/495–4354 or 800/367–8455* 🖷 *284/495–4036* ⊕ *www.fortrecovery.com* 🛏 *29 suites, 1 villa* 🖒 *Kitchens, cable TV, in-room data ports, Wi-Fi, pool, fitness classes, gym, massage, beach, snorkeling, babysitting, laundry service, Internet room* ▤ *AE, MC, V* ❘⊙❘ *CP.*

$$–$$$$ ⊡ **Lambert Beach Resort.** Although this isolated location on the northeast coast puts you far from Road Town, Lambert Bay is one of the island's loveliest stretches of sand and the main reason to recommend this resort. Rooms are tucked back in the foliage, but you're just a few steps away from an afternoon of sunning and swimming. A handful of restaurants in and around nearby Fat Hogs Bay are within easy reach if you just have to get off that gorgeous beach. At this writing, condo construction was set to begin; ask about their progress if you fear construction noise will be a problem. ⊠ *Lambert Bay, Box 534, East End* ☎ *284/495–2877* 🖷 *284/495–2876* ⊕ *www.lambertbeachresort.com* 🛏 *38 rooms, 2 villas, 27 condos* 🖒 *Restaurant, some kitchens, refrigerators, some cable TV, some in-room data ports, tennis court, pool, spa, beach, snorkeling, boating, bar, shop, Internet room* ▤ *AE, D, MC, V* ❘⊙❘ *EP.*

$$$ ⊡ **Frenchman's Cay Hotel.** Tucked away down a narrow road near busy Soper's Hole, Frenchman's Cay provides a quiet oasis for folks who want the option of eating in or out and a bit more space than you'd find in a typical hotel room. All accommodations are villa style, with separate bedrooms and kitchens but no air-conditioning. We like this place for its get-away-from-it-all feel. That said, you can easily walk to Soper's Hole to expand your dining horizons and to do some shopping. ⊠ *Frenchman's Cay, Box 1054, West End* ☎ *284/495–4844 or 800/235–4077* 🖷 *284/495–4056* ⊕ *www.frenchmans.com* 🛏 *9 villas* 🖒 *Restaurant, fans, kitchenettes, tennis court, pool, beach, snorkeling, bar; no a/c, no room TVs* ▤ *AE, D, MC, V* ❘⊙❘ *EP.*

$$–$$$ 🏨 **Sebastian's on the Beach.** Sitting on the island's north coast, Sebastian's definitely has a beachy feel, and that's its primary charm. Rooms vary in amenities and price, with the remodeled beachfront rooms a bit more up-to-date than those that the hotel calls "beach rear." The beachfront rooms have the best views and put you right on the sand. The less expensive rooms are basic, across the street from the ocean, and lack views. Those nearest the intersection of North Coast Road and Zion Hill Road can also suffer from traffic noise. Although you can eat all your meals at the resort's enjoyable restaurant, the wonderful Sugar Mill Restaurant is just a short drive east. ⊠ *Apple Bay* 🕙 *Box 441, Road Town* ☎ *284/495–4212 or 800/336–4870* 🖷 *284/495–4466* ⊕ *www. sebastiansbvi.com* ☜ *26 rooms, 9 villas* ☖ *Restaurant, fans, refrigerators, some in-room data ports, beach, bar, Internet room; no TV in some rooms* ▤ *AE, D, MC* ❘⊙❘ *EP.*

$$ 🏨 **Hodge's Creek Marina Hotel.** Sitting marina-side out on the island's East End, this hotel puts you in the middle of the nautical action. If you're heading out on a chartered sailboat or if you especially enjoy the marine scene, this is definitely the place for you. Rooms are carpeted and have tiny balconies, but brightly colored spreads and curtains give the rooms a tropical feel. There's a small pool and the CalaMaya Restaurant in the complex, but you need a car to get out and about. ⊠ *Hodge's Creek* 🕙 *Box 663, Road Town* ☎ *284/494–5000* 🖷 *284/494–7676* ⊕ *www.hodgescreek.com* ☜ *24 rooms* ☖ *Restaurant, cable TV, pool, dock, boating, marina, shops, Internet room* ▤ *AE, MC, V* ❘⊙❘ *EP.*

$$ 🏨 **Myett's.** Tucked away in a beachfront garden, this tiny hotel puts you right in the middle of Cane Garden Bay's busy nightlife. The restaurant is one of the area's hottest spots. Rooms have a typical tropical feel, thanks to the tile floors and rattan furniture. If it's available, opt for the one room with a water view. Although you might be content to lounge at the beach and stroll around Cane Garden Bay, you'll need a car to get out and about. ⊠ *Cane Garden Bay* 🕙 *Box 556, Cane Garden Bay* ☎ *284/495–9649* 🖷 *284/495–9579* ⊕ *www.myettent.com* ☜ *3 rooms* ☖ *Restaurant, fans, refrigerators, no room TV, beach, shops, Internet room, car rental* ▤ *AE, MC, V* ❘⊙❘ *EP.*

$$ 🏨 **Nanny Cay Hotel.** This quiet oasis is far enough from Road Town to give it a secluded feel but close enough to make shops and restaurants convenient. You're just steps from the hotel's restaurant, boat charters, and the chance to stroll the busy boatyard to gawk at the yachts under repair, but you still have to drive a good 20 minutes to get to the closest beach at Cane Garden Bay. The rooms, which have tile floors, are cheerful, with lots of bright Caribbean colors. ⊠ *Nanny Cay* 🕙 *Box 281, Road Town* ☎ *284/494–2512 or 866/284–4683* 🖷 *284/494–0555* ⊕ *www.nannycay.com* ☜ *38 rooms* ☖ *2 restaurants, some kitchenettes, cable TV, tennis court, pool, dive shop, dock, boating, marina, shops, Internet room, meeting rooms* ▤ *MC, V* ❘⊙❘ *EP.*

Where to Eat

On Tortola local seafood is plentiful, and although other fresh ingredients are scarce, the island's chefs are a creative lot who apply genius to whatever the supply boat delivers. Contemporary American dishes prepared with a Caribbean influence are very popular. The fancier, more expensive restaurants have dress codes: long pants and collared shirts for men and elegant, casual resort wear for women.

Road Town

CARIBBEAN ✗ **C&F Restaurant.** Crowds head to this casual spot for the best barbe-
$$–$$$ cue in town (chicken, fish, and ribs), fresh local fish and lobster, and excellent curries. Sometimes there's a wait for a table, but it's worth it. The restaurant is just outside Road Town, on a side street past the Moorings and Riteway. ✉ *Off Canaan Rd., Purcell Estate* ☎ *284/494–4941* ⌣ *Reservations not accepted* ▭ *AE, D, MC, V* ☉ *No lunch.*

ECLECTIC ✗ **CafeSito.** Don't be put off by the pedestrian decor. The chef at this
$$$ shopping-center spot conjures up delicious dishes that run the gamut from burgers to lobster to chicken alfredo. It's the place to go for pizza smothered with everything from the standard cheese and tomato to the more unusual chicken and bacon. In winter, the staff will deliver anything from its menu straight to your hotel. ✉ *Wickham's Cay I, Waterfront Dr.* ☎ *284/494–7412* ▭ *D, MC, V.*

FRENCH ✗ **Le Cabanon.** Birds and bougainvillea brighten the patio of this breezy
$$–$$$$ French restaurant and bar, a popular gathering spot for locals and visitors alike. French onion soup and herring salad are good appetizer choices. From there, move on to roasted pigeon, monkfish in rosemary sauce, or beef tenderloin with green peppercorn sauce. Save room for such tasty desserts as chocolate cake, crème brûlée, or a platter of French cheeses. ✉ *Waterfront Dr.* ☎ *284/494–8660* ▭ *D, MC, V* ☉ *Closed Sun.*

ITALIAN ✗ **Spaghetti Junction at Beach Club Terrace.** Popular with the boating
★ $–$$$ crowd, this longtime favorite serves up delightful West Indian food like stewed lobster and fresh local fish along with Italian favorites like penne smothered in a spicy tomato sauce, spinach-mushroom lasagna, and angelhair pasta with shellfish. For something that combines a bit of both, try the spicy jambalaya pasta. ✉ *Blackburn Hwy., Baughers Bay* ☎ *284/494–4880* ▭ *AE, MC, V* ☉ *Closed Sun.*

★ $–$$ ✗ **Capriccio di Mare.** The owners of the well-known Brandywine Bay restaurant also run this authentic, little Italian outdoor café. Stop by for an espresso, fresh pastry, a bowl of perfectly cooked linguine, or a crispy tomato and mozzarella pizza. Drink specialties include a mango Bellini, an adaptation of the famous cocktail served at Harry's Bar in Venice. ✉ *Waterfront Dr.* ☎ *284/494–5369* ⌣ *Reservations not accepted* ▭ *D, MC, V* ☉ *Closed Sun.*

SEAFOOD ✗ **The Captain's Table.** Select the lobster you want from the pool, but
$–$$$ be careful not to fall in—it's in the floor right in the middle of the dining room. The menu also includes traditional escargots, filet mignon with blue cheese sauce, duckling with berry sauce, and creative daily specials that usually include freshly caught fish. Ceiling fans keep the dining room cool, but there are also tables on a breezy terrace overlooking the harbor. ✉ *Wickham's Cay I* ☎ *284/494–3885* ▭ *AE, MC, V* ☉ *No lunch Sat.*

Outside Road Town

AMERICAN–
CASUAL
☺ $$–$$$

✕ **Pusser's Landing.** Yachters flock to this waterfront restaurant. Downstairs, from late morning to well into the evening, belly up to the outdoor mahogany bar or sit downstairs for sandwiches, fish-and-chips, and pizzas. At dinnertime head upstairs for a harbor view and a quiet alfresco meal of grilled steak or local fish. ⊠ *Soper's Hole* ☎ 284/495–4554 ▤ *AE, MC, V.*

CARIBBEAN
$$–$$$$

✕ **Quito's Gazebo.** This rustic beachside bar and restaurant is owned and operated by Quito Rhymer, a multitalented BVI recording star who plays and sings solo on Tuesday and Thursday and performs with his reggae band on Friday and Saturday. The menu is Caribbean, with an emphasis on fresh fish. Try the conch fritters or the chicken roti. ⊠ *Cane Garden Bay* ☎ 284/495–4837 ▤ *AE, MC, V* ☺ *Closed Mon.*

$$–$$$

✕ **Myett's Garden & Grille.** Right on the beach, this bi-level restaurant and bar is hopping day and night. Chowder made with fresh Anegada lobsters is the specialty, though the menu includes everything from vegetarian dishes to grilled shrimp, steak, and tuna. There's live entertainment every night during the winter. ⊠ *Cane Garden Bay* ☎ 284/495–9649 ▤ *AE, MC, V.*

$–$$$
Fodor'sChoice
★

✕ **Roti Palace.** You might be tempted to pass this tiny spot on Road Town's Main Street when you see the plastic tablecloths and fake flowers, but owner Jean Leonard's reputation for dishing up fantastic roti is known far and wide. A flatbread is filled with curried potatoes, onions and lobster, chicken, beef, conch, goat, or vegetables. Ask for the bone out if you order the chicken to save yourself the trouble of fishing them out of your mouth. ⊠ *Main St., Road Town* ☎ 284/494–4196 ▤ *No credit cards* ☺ *Closed Sun.*

CONTEMPORARY
$$–$$$$

✕ **Palm Terrace Restaurant.** Relax over dinner in this open-air restaurant at Long Bay Beach Resort. Tables are well spaced, offering enough privacy for intimate conversation. The menu changes daily, but several dishes show up regularly. Good appetizers are garlicky escargots in a pastry shell, Caribbean-style fish chowder, and shrimp fritters. Entrées include tuna glazed with tamarind and honey, pan-roasted duck with a rosemary glaze, or a filet mignon served with mushrooms. There are always at least five desserts to choose from, which might include Belgian chocolate mousse, strawberry cheesecake, or a fluffy lemon and coconut cake. ⊠ *Long Bay Beach Resort, Long Bay* ☎ 284/495–4252 ▤ *AE, D, MC, V* ☺ *No lunch.*

$$–$$$$

✕ **Sebastian's Beach Bar & Restaurant.** The waves practically lap at your feet at this beachfront restaurant on Tortola's northern shore. The menu runs to seafood—especially lobster, conch, and local fish—but you can also find dishes like ginger chicken and filet mignon. It's a perfect spot to stop for lunch on your around-the-island tour. Try the grilled dolphinfish sandwich, served on a soft roll with an oniony tartar sauce. Finish off with a cup of Sebastian's coffee spiked with home-brewed rum. ⊠ *North Coast Rd., Apple Bay* ☎ 284/494–4212 ▤ *AE, D, MC.*

★ $$$

✕ **Eclipse.** This popular waterfront spot isn't much more than a terrace filled with tables, but you can be caressed by the soft ocean breezes while you are impressed with the cuisine. With dishes from all over the globe, the menu is certainly well traveled. Sample several small dishes—maybe the cracked calamari, chèvre salad, and tuna carpaccio—as you peruse the two-page grazing menu. Or if you prefer, dig into the spicy curries, shrimp with chestnuts, grilled swordfish, and vegetarian dishes on the regular menu. ⊠ *Fat Hog's Bay, East End* ☎ *284/495–1646* ▭ *MC, V* ⊗ *No lunch.*

🕐 **$$$** ✕ **Skyworld.** The top of a mountain is the location for this casually elegant dining room. The menu changes constantly, but look for imaginative dishes such as pork tenderloin medallions on a bed of red onion marmalade and rabbit with roasted vegetables. Other specialties include grilled local fish, roast duck, rack of lamb with a sauce du jour, and key lime pie. The lunch menu runs to hamburgers and sandwiches with some interesting additions such as a goat cheese tartlet. The restaurant can be crowded for lunch when cruise ships dock. ⊠ *Ridge Rd., Joe's Hill* ☎ *284/494–3567* ▭ *AE, D, DC, MC, V.*

$$$ ✕ **Turtles.** If you're touring the island, Turtles is a good place to stop for lunch or dinner. Sitting just back from the beach at Lambert Beach Resort, this casual place provides a relaxing respite from the rigors of navigating mountain roads. At dinner you might find tiger shrimp in a curry sauce or rack of lamb with a raspberry glaze. Lunch favorites include fried shrimp, fresh tuna on a bun, and pasta dishes. ⊠ *Lambert Beach Resort, Lambert Bay, East End* ☎ *284/495–2877* ▭ *AE, D, MC, V.*

$$–$$$ ✕ **CalaMaya.** Casual fare is what you'll find at this waterfront restaurant. You can always order a burger or lobster salad; the grilled Kaiser sandwich—shrimp, cheese, and pineapple on a crisp roll—is a tasty alternative. For dinner, try the snapper with onions, peppers, and thyme. ⊠ *Hodge's Creek Marina, Blackburn Hwy.* ☎ *284/495–2126* ▭ *AE, MC, V.*

$$–$$$ ✕ **Mountain View.** It's worth the drive up Sage Mountain for lunch or
Fodor'sChoice dinner at this casual restaurant. The view is spectacular—one of the best
★ on Tortola. The small menu includes dishes like veal with a ginger sauce and grilled mahimahi in a lime-onion sauce. The lobster salad sandwich is the house lunch specialty. If it's on the menu, don't pass up the chicken roti. ⊠ *Sage Mountain* ☎ *284/495–9536* ▭ *AE, MC, V.*

$$–$$$ ✕ **Sugar Mill Restaurant.** Candles gleam, and the background music is
Fodor'sChoice peaceful in this romantic restaurant inside a 17th-century sugar mill. Well-
★ prepared selections on the à la carte menu, which changes nightly, include some pasta and vegetarian entrées. Lobster bisque with basil croutons and a curried lobster patty are good starters. Favorite entrées include grilled swordfish with a lime-and-chive butter, beef curry with *poppadoms* (Indian popovers), pan-seared roast duck, and fresh fish with a spicy creole sauce. ⊠ *Sugar Mill Hotel, Apple Bay* ☎ *284/495–4355* ▭ *AE, MC, V* ⊗ *No lunch.*

ECLECTIC ✕ **The Jolly Roger Restaurant.** This casual, open-air restaurant near the
$–$$$ ferry terminal is as popular with locals as it is with visitors. The menu ranges from burgers to rib-eye steak to the island favorite, local lobster. Try the savory conch fritters filled with tender local conch and herbs for a good start to your dinner. End it with a slice of sweet key lime pie. ⊠ *West End* ☎ *284/495–4559* ▭ *D, MC, V.*

ITALIAN ╳ **Brandywine Bay.** Candlelit outdoor tables have sweeping views of neigh-
$$$ boring islands, and owner Davide Pugliese prepares foods the Tuscan
Fodor'sChoice way: grilled with lots of fresh herbs. The remarkable menu always in-
★ cludes duck with a berry sauce and often has homemade mozzarella,
beef carpaccio, grilled swordfish, and veal chop with ricotta and sun-
dried tomatoes. The wine list is excellent, and the lemon tart and the
tiramisu are irresistible. ⊠ *Sir Francis Drake Hwy., east of Road Town,
Brandywine Bay* ☎ *284/495–2301* ⌲ *Reservations essential* ▭ *AE, MC,
V* ⊗ *Closed Sun. No lunch.*

Beaches

Beaches in the BVI are less developed than those on St. Thomas or St.
Croix, but they are simply not as inviting. The best BVI beaches are on
deserted islands reachable only by boats, so take a snorkeling or sailing
trip at least once. Tortola's north side has several perfect palm-fringed,
white-sand beaches that curl around turquoise bays and coves, though
none really achieve greatness. Nearly all are accessible by car (preferably
one with four-wheel-drive), albeit down bumpy roads that corkscrew pre-
cipitously. Some of these beaches are lined with bars and restaurants as
well as water-sports equipment stalls; others have absolutely nothing.

Apple Bay. If you want to surf, the area including Little Apple Bay and
Capoon's Bay is the spot—although the white, sandy beach itself is nar-
row. Sebastian's, a very casual hotel, caters to those in search of the per-
fect wave. The legendary Bomba's Surfside Shack—a landmark festooned
with all manner of flotsam and jetsam—serves drinks and casual food.
Otherwise, there's nothing else in the way of amenities. Good surf is
never a sure thing, but you're more apt to find it in January and Feb-
ruary. If you're swimming and the waves are up, take care not to get
dashed on the rocks. ⊠ *North Shore Rd. at Zion Hill Rd.*

Brewers Bay. The water here is good for snorkeling, and you can find a
campground with showers and bathrooms and beach bar tucked in the
foliage right behind the beach. An old sugar mill and ruins of a rum dis-
tillery are just north of the beach along the road. The beach is easy to
find, but the paved roads leading down the hill to it can be a bit daunt-
ing. You can get there from either Brewers Bay Road East or Brewers
Bay Road West. ⊠ *Brewers Bay Rd. E off Cane Garden Bay Rd., or
Brewers Bay Rd. W off Ridge Rd.*

Cane Garden Bay. This enticing beach has exceptionally calm, crystalline
waters and a silky stretch of sand except when storms at sea turn the
water murky. Snorkeling is good along the edges. Casual guesthouses,
restaurants, bars, and even shops are just steps off the beach in the grow-
ing village of the same name. It's a laid-back, even somewhat funky place
to put down your beach towel. Water-sports shops rent equipment. It's
the closest beach to Road Town—one steep uphill and downhill drive—
and one of the BVI's best-known anchorages (unfortunately, it can be
very crowded when cruise ships are in town). ⊠ *Cane Garden Bay Rd.
off Ridge Rd.*

Elizabeth Beach. Home to Lambert Beach Resort, the palm-lined, wide,
and sandy beach has parking for nonguests on its steep downhill ac-

cess road. The undertow can be severe here in winter, but it's a nice place to spend a few hours. Other than at the hotel, which welcomes nonguests at its restaurant, there are no amenities aside from peace and quiet. Turn at the sign for Lambert Beach Resort. If you miss it, you wind up at Her Majesty's Prison. ⊠ *Lambert Rd. off Ridge Rd., on the eastern end of island.*

Long Bay, Beef Island. The scenery here is superlative: the beach stretches seemingly forever, and you can catch a glimpse of Little Camanoe and Great Camanoe islands. If you walk around the bend to the right, you can see little Marina Cay and Scrub Island. Long Bay is also a good place to find seashells. Swim out to wherever you see a dark patch for some nice snorkeling. There are no amenities, so come prepared with your own drinks and snacks. Turn left shortly after crossing the bridge to Beef Island. ⊠ *Beef Island Rd., Beef Island.*

Long Bay West. Have your camera ready to snap the breathtaking approach to this stunning, mile-long stretch of white sand. Although Long Bay Resort sprawls along part of it, the entire beach is open to the public. The water isn't as calm here as at Cane Garden or Brewers Bay, but it's still swimmable. Rent water-sports equipment and enjoy the beachfront restaurant at the resort. Turn left at Zion Hill Road; then travel about half a mile. ⊠ *Long Bay Rd.*

Smuggler's Cove. After bouncing your way down a pothole-filled dirt road to this beautiful, palm-fringed beach, you'll feel as if you've found a hidden piece of the island, although you probably won't be alone on weekends. There's a fine view of Jost Van Dyke, and the snorkeling is good as well. It's popular with Long Bay Resort guests who want a change of scenery, but there are no amenities. Follow Long Bay Road past Long Bay Resort, keeping to the roads nearest the water until you reach the beach. It's about a mile past the resort. ⊠ *Long Bay Rd.*

Sports & the Outdoors

CRICKET Fans of this sport are fiercely loyal and exuberant. Matches are held at the New Recreation Grounds, next to the J. R. O'Neal Botanic Gardens, weekends from February to April. Check local newspapers or ask at your hotel front desk for information on times and teams.

DIVING & SNORKELING Clear waters and numerous reefs afford some wonderful opportunities for underwater exploration. In some spots, visibility reaches 100 feet, but in many locations colorful reefs teeming with fish are just a few feet below the sea surface. The BVI's system of marine parks means the underwater life visible through your mask will stay protected. There are several popular dive spots around the islands. **Alice in Wonderland** is a deep dive south of Ginger Island with a wall that slopes gently from 15 feet to 100 feet. It's an area overrun with huge mushroom-shape coral, hence its name. Crabs, lobsters, and shimmering fan corals make their homes in the tunnels, ledges, and overhangs of **Blonde Rock,** a pinnacle that goes from just 15 feet below the surface to 60 feet deep. It's between Dead Chest and Salt Island. When the currents aren't too strong, **Brewers Bay Pinnacle** (20 to 90 feet down) teems with sea life. At the **Indians,** near Pelican Island, colorful corals decorate canyons and grottos created by four large, jagged pinnacles that rise 50 feet from the ocean floor. The **Painted Walls** is a shallow dive site where corals and sponges create a kaleidoscope of colors on the walls of four long gullies. It's northeast of Dead Chest.

The **Chikuzen,** sunk northwest of Brewers Bay in 1981, is a 246-foot vessel in 75 feet of water; it's home to thousands of fish, colorful corals, and big rays. In 1867 the **RMS Rhone,** a 310-foot royal mail steamer, split in two when it sank in a devastating hurricane. It's so well preserved that it was used as an underwater prop in the movie *The Deep.* You can see the crow's nest and bowsprit, the cargo hold in the bow, and the engine and enormous propeller shaft in the stern. Its four parts are at various depths from 30 to 80 feet (nearby Rhone Reef is only 20 to 50 feet down). Get yourself some snorkeling gear and hop a dive boat to this wreck, off Salt Island (across the channel from Road Town) and part of the BVI National Parks Trust. Every dive outfit in the BVI runs scuba and snorkel tours here, and if you go on only one trip, make it this one. Rates start at around $60 for a one-tank dive and $85 for a two-tank dive.

Your hotel probably has a dive company located right on the premises. If not, the staff can recommend one nearby. Using your hotel's dive company makes a trip to the offshore dive and snorkel sites a breeze. Just stroll down to the dock and hop aboard. All dive companies are certified by PADI, the Professional Association of Diving Instructors, which ensures your instructors are qualified to safely take vacationers diving. The boats are also inspected to make sure they're seaworthy. If you've never dived, try a short introductory dive, often called a resort course, which teaches you enough to get you under water. In the unlikely event you get a case of the bends, a condition that can happen when you rise to the surface too fast, your dive team will whisk you to the decompression chamber at Roy L. Schneider Regional Medical Center Hospital in nearby St. Thomas.

Blue Waters Divers (⊠ Nanny Cay ☎ 284/495–1200 ⊠ Soper's Hole, West End ☎ 284/294–1200 ⊕ www.bluewaterdiversbvi.com) teaches resort, open-water, rescue, and advanced diving courses and also makes daily trips. If you're chartering a sailboat, the company's boat will meet your boat at Peter, Salt, or CooperIsland for a rendezvous dive. Rates include all equipment as well as instruction. Make arrangements two days in advance. **Dive Tortola** (⊠ Prospect Reef ☎ 284/494–9200 ⊕ www. divetortola.com) offers beginner and advanced diving courses and daily trips. Trainers teach open-water, rescue, advanced diving, and resort courses. Dive Tortola also offers a rendezvous diving option for folks on charter sailboats.

FISHING Most of the boats that take you deep-sea fishing for bluefish, wahoo, swordfish, and shark leave from nearby St. Thomas, but local anglers like to fish the shallower water for bonefish. A half-day of bone fishing runs about $480, a full day around $850. Call **Caribbean Fly Fishing** (⊠ Nanny Cay ☎ 284/499–4797 ⊕ www.caribfllyfishing.com).

HIKING Sage Mountain National Park attacts hikers who enjoy the quiet trails that crisscross the island's loftiest peak. There are some lovely views and the chance to see rare species that grow only at higher elevations.

HORSEBACK
RIDING

If you've ever wanted to ride a horse along a deserted beach, through a rain forest, or if you want to head up to mountain ridges for spectacular views, **Shadow Stables** (⌧ Ridge Rd., Todman Peak ☎ 284/494–2262) offers small group rides for $100 per person per hour.

SAILING
★ ☺

The BVI are among the world's most popular sailing destinations. They're close together and surrounded by calm waters, so it's fairly easy to sail from one anchorage to the next. Most of the Caribbean's biggest sailboat charter companies have operations in Tortola. If you know how to sail, you can charter a bareboat (perhaps for your entire vacation); if you're unschooled, you can hire a boat with a captain. Prices vary depending on the type and size of the boat you wish to charter. In season, a weekly charter runs from $1,500 to $35,000. Book early to make sure you get the boat that fits you best. Most of Tortola's marinas have hotels, which give you a convenient place to spend the nights before and after your charter.

If a day sail to some secluded anchorage is more your spot of tea, the BVI has numerous boats of various sizes and styles that leave from many points around Tortola. Prices start at around $80 per person for a full-day sail, including lunch and snorkeling equipment.

BVI Yacht Charters (⌧ Inner Harbour Marina, Road Town ☎ 284/494–4289 or 888/615–4006 ⊕ www.bviyachtcharters.com) offers 31-foot to 56-foot sailboats for charter—with or without a captain and crew, whichever you prefer. **Catamaran Charters** (⌧ Nanny Cay Marina, Nanny Cay ☎ 284/494–6661 or 800/262–0308 ⊕ www.catamarans. com) charters catamarans with or without a captain. The **Moorings** (⌧ Wickham's Cay II, Road Town ☎ 284/494–2331 or 800/535–7289 ⊕ www.moorings.com), considered one of the best bareboat operations in the world, has a large fleet of well-maintained, mostly Beneteau sailing yachts. Hire a captain or sail the boat yourself. If you prefer a powerboat, call **Regency Yacht Vacations** (⌧ Wickham's Cay I, Road Town ☎ 284/495–1970 or 800/524–7676 ⊕ www. regencyvacations.com) for both bareboat and captained sail and power-boat charters. **Sunsail** (⌧ Hodge's Creek Marina, East End ☎ 284/495–4740 or 800/327–2276 ⊕ www.sunsail.com) offers a full fleet of boats to charter with or without a captain. **Voyages** (⌧ Soper's Hole Marina, West End ☎ 284/494–0740 or 888/869–2436 ⊕ www.voyagecharters. com) offers a variety of sailboats for charter with or without a captain and crew.

Aristocat Charters (⌧ West End ☎ 284/499–1249 ⊕ www. aristocatcharters.com) sets sail daily to the Indians and Peter Island aboard a 48-foot catamaran. **White Squall II** (⌧ Village Cay Marina, Road Town ☎ 284/495–2564 ⊕ www.whitesquall2.com) takes you on regularly scheduled day sails to the Baths at Virgin Gorda, Jost Van Dyke, or the Caves at Norman Island on an 80-foot schooner.

SURFING

Surfing is big on Tortola's north shore, particularly when the winter swells come in to Josiah's and Apple bays. Rent surfboards starting at $25 for a full day.

HIHO (⊠ Waterfront Dr., Road Town ☏ 284/494–7694 ⊕ www.go-hiho. com) has a good surfboard selection for sale or rent. The staff will give you advice on the best spots to put in your board.

WINDSURFING Steady trade winds make windsurfing a breeze. Three of the best spots for sailboarding are Nanny Cay, Slaney Point, and Trellis Bay on Beef Island. Rates for sailboards start at about $25 an hour or $75 for a full day.

Boardsailing BVI (⊠ Trellis Bay, Beef Island ☏ 284/495–2447 ⊕ www. windsurfing.vi) rents equipment and offers private and group lessons.

Shopping

The BVI aren't really a shopper's delight, but there are many shops show-casing original wares—from jams and spices to resort wear to excellent artwork.

Shopping Areas

Many shops and boutiques are clustered along and just off Road Town's **Main Street.** You can shop in Road Town's **Wickham's Cay I** adjacent to the marina. **Crafts Alive Market** on the Road Town waterfront is a collection of colorful West Indian–style buildings with shops that carry items made in the BVI. You might find pretty baskets or interesting pottery or perhaps a bottle of home-brew hot sauce. There's an ever-growing number of art and clothing stores at **Soper's Hole** in West End.

Specialty Stores

ART The **Gallery** (⊠ 102 Main St., Road Town ☏ 284/494–6680) carries photographs by local photographer Amanda Baker and paintings by other Tortola artists. **Sunny Caribbee** (⊠ Main St., Road Town ☏ 284/494–2178) has many paintings, prints, and watercolors by artists from throughout the Caribbean.

CLOTHES & **Arawak** (⊠ On the dock, Nanny Cay ☏ 284/494–5240 ⊠ Hodge's Creek
TEXTILES Marina, Hodge's Creek ☏ 284/495–1106) carries batik sundresses, sportswear, and resort wear for men and women. There's also a selection of children's clothing. **Latitude 18°** (⊠ Main St., Road Town ⊠ Soper's Hole Marina, West End ☏ 284/494–7807 for both stores) sells Maui Jim, Smith, Oakley, and Revo sunglasses; Freestyle, Quiksilver, and Roxy watches; and a fine collection of beach towels, sandals, sundresses, and sarongs. **Pusser's Company Store** (⊠ Main St. at Waterfront Rd., Road Town ☏ 284/494–2467 ⊠ Soper's Hole Marina, West End ☏ 284/495–4599) sells nautical memorabilia, ship models, marine paintings, an entire line of clothes for both men and women, and gift items bearing the Pusser's logo, handsome decorator bottles of Pusser's rum, Caribbean books, Cuban cigars, and luggage. **Sea Urchin** (⊠ Mill Mall, Road Town ☏ 284/494–4108 ⊠ Soper's Hole Marina, West End ☏ 284/495–4850) is the source for local books, jewelry, sunglasses, and resort wear—print shirts and shorts, colorful swimsuits, sandals, T-shirts—for the whole family. **Zenaida's of West End** (⊠ Soper's Hole Marina, West End ☏ 284/495–4867) displays the fabric finds of Argentine Vivian Jenik Helm, who travels through South America, Africa,

and India in search of batiks, hand-painted and hand-blocked fabrics, and interesting weaves that can be made into pareus (women's wraps) or wall hangings. The shop also sells unusual bags, belts, sarongs, scarves, and ethnic jewelry.

FOODSTUFFS **Ample Hamper** (✉ Inner Harbour Marina, Road Town ☎ 284/494–2494 ✉ Frenchman's Cay Marina, West End ☎ 284/495–4684 ⊕ www. amplehamper.com) has an outstanding collection of cheeses, wines, fresh fruits, and canned goods from the United Kingdom and the United States. You can have the management here provision your yacht or rental villa. **Best of British** (✉ Wickham's Cay I, Road Town ☎ 284/494–3462) has lots of nifty British food sitting cheek and jowl with more American fare. Shop here for Marmite, Vegemite, shortbread, frozen meat pies, and delightful Christmas crackers filled with surprises. **K-Marks** (✉ Waterfront Dr., at Port Purcell, Road Town ☎ 284/494–4649) carries the usual supermarket stuff—albeit a much smaller selection than you might find in your hometown supermarket.

GIFTS **Bamboushay** (✉ Nanny Cay Marina, Nanny Cay ☎ 284/494–0393) sells handcrafted Tortola-made pottery in shades that reflect the sea. In a brightly painted West Indian house, **Sunny Caribbee** (✉ Main St., Road Town ☎ 284/494–2178) packages its own herbs, teas, coffees, vinegars, hot sauces, soaps, skin and suntan lotions, and exotic concoctions—Arawak Love Potion and Island Hangover Cure, for example. There are also Caribbean books and art and hand-painted decorative accessories.

JEWELRY **Columbian Emeralds International** (✉ Wickham's Cay I, Road Town ☎ 284/494–7477), a Caribbean chain catering to the cruise-ship crowd, is the source for duty-free emeralds plus other gems, gold jewelry, crystal, and china. **D'Zandra's** (✉ Wickham's Cay I, Road Town ☎ 284/494–8330) carries mostly black coral items set in gold and silver. Many pieces reflect Caribbean and sea themes. **Samarkand** (✉ Main St., Road Town ☎ 284/494–6415) crafts charming gold-and-silver pendants, earrings, bracelets, and pins, many with an island theme: seashells, lizards, pelicans, palm trees. There are also reproduction Spanish pieces of eight (old Spanish coins worth eight reals) that were found on sunken galleons.

PERFUMES & **Flamboyance** (✉ Palm Grove Shopping Center, Waterfront Dr., Road Town COSMETICS ☎ 284/494–4099) carries designer fragrances and upscale cosmetics.

STAMPS The **BVI Post Office** (✉ Main St., Road Town ☎ 284/494–3701) is a philatelist's dream. It has a worldwide reputation for exquisite stamps in all sorts of designs. Although the stamps carry U.S. monetary designations, they can be used for postage only in the BVI.

Nightlife & the Arts

Nightlife
Like any other good sailing destination, Tortola has watering holes that are popular with salty and not-so-salty dogs. Many offer entertainment; check the weekly *Limin' Times* for schedules and up-to-date information. Bands change like the weather, and what's hot today can be old news tomorrow. The local beverage is the Painkiller, an innocent-

tasting mixture of fruit juices and rums. It goes down smoothly but packs quite a punch, so give yourself time to recover before you order another.

By day **Bomba's Surfside Shack** (⊠ Apple Bay ☎ 284/495–4148), which is covered with everything from crepe-paper leis to ancient license plates to colorful graffiti, looks like a pile of junk; by night it's one of Tortola's liveliest spots and one of the Caribbean's most famous beach bars. There's a fish fry and a live band every Wednesday and Sunday. People flock here from all over on the full moon, when bands play all night long. At the **Jolly Roger** (⊠ West End ☎ 284/495–4559) an ever-changing roster of local and down-island bands plays everything from rhythm and blues to reggae and rock every Friday and Saturday—and sometimes Sunday—starting at 8. Local bands play at **Myett's** (⊠ Cane Garden Bay ☎ 284/495–9649) every night, and there's usually a lively dance crowd. Courage is what people are seeking at **Pusser's Road Town Pub** (⊠ Waterfront St., Road Town ☎ 284/494–3897)—John Courage by the pint. Other nights try Pusser's famous mixed drinks—Painkillers—and snack on the excellent pizza. At the **Pub** (⊠ Waterfront St., Road Town ☎ 284/494–2608) there's a happy hour from 5 to 7 every day and live blues on Thursday. BVI recording star Quito Rhymer sings island ballads and love songs at **Quito's Gazebo** (⊠ Cane Garden Bay ☎ 284/495–4837), his rustic beachside bar-restaurant. Solo shows are on Tuesday and Thursday at 8:30; on Friday and Saturday nights at 9:30 Quito performs with his band. There's often live music at **Sebastian's** (⊠ Apple Bay ☎ 284/495–4212) on Sunday evenings, and you can dance under the stars.

The Arts

Musicians from around the world perform in the series **Classics in the Atrium** (⊠ H. Lavity Stoutt Community College, Paraquita Bay ☎ 284/494–4994 ⊕ www.hlscc.edu) from October to March each year. Past artists have included Britain's premier a cappella group, Black Voices; the Leipzig String Quartet; and Keith Lockhart and the Serenac Quartet (from the Boston Pops Symphony).

Every May, hordes of people head to Tortola for the three-day **BVI Music Festival** (⊠ Cane Garden Bay ☎ 284/495–3378 ⊕ www.bvimusicfest. com) to listen to reggae, gospel, blues, and salsa music by musicians from around the Caribbean and the U.S. mainland.

Exploring Tortola

Tortola doesn't have many historic sights, but it does have lots of beautiful natural scenery. Although you could explore the island's 10 square mi (26 square km) in a few hours, opting for such a whirlwind tour would be a mistake. There's no need to live in the fast lane when you're surrounded by some of the Caribbean's most breathtaking panoramas and beaches. Also, the roads are extraordinarily steep and twisting, making driving demanding. The best strategy is to explore a bit of the island at a time. For example, you might try Road Town (the island's main town) one morning and a drive to Cane Garden Bay and West End (a little town on, of course, the island's west end) the next afternoon. Or consider a visit to East End, a *very* tiny town located exactly where its name suggests. The north shore is where all the best beaches are found.

Numbers in the margin correspond to points of interest on the Tortola map.

What to See in Road Town

The bustling capital of the BVI looks out over Road Harbour. It takes only an hour or so to stroll down Main Street and along the waterfront, checking out the traditional West Indian buildings painted in pastel colors and with high-pitched, corrugated-tin roofs, bright shutters, and delicate fretwork trim. For hotel and sightseeing brochures and the latest information on everything from taxi rates to ferry-boat schedules, stop in the BVI Tourist Board office. Or just choose a seat on one of the benches in Sir Olva Georges Square, on Waterfront Drive, and watch the people come and go from the ferry dock and customs office across the street.

❸ **Fort Burt.** The most intact historic ruin on Tortola was built by the Dutch in the early 17th century to safeguard Road Harbour. It sits on a hill at the western edge of Road Town and is now the site of a small hotel and restaurant. The foundations and magazine remain, and the structure offers a commanding view of the harbor. ⊠ *Waterfront Dr., Road Town* ☎ *No phone* ⌘ *Free* ⊙ *Daily dawn–dusk.*

★ ❷ **Old Government House Museum.** The seat of government until 1987, this gracious building now displays a nice collection of items from Tortola's past. The rooms are filled with period furniture, hand-painted china, books signed by Queen Elizabeth II on her 1966 and 1977 visits, and numerous items reflecting Tortola's seafaring legacy. ⊠ *Waterfront Dr., Road Town* ☎ *284/494-3701* ⌘ *$3* ⊙ *Weekdays 9–2.*

★ ❶ **J. R. O'Neal Botanic Gardens.** Take a walk through this 4-acre showcase of lush plant life. There are sections devoted to prickly cacti and succulents, hothouses for ferns and orchids, gardens of medicinal herbs, and plants and trees indigenous to the seashore. From the Tourist Board office in Road Town, cross Waterfront Drive and walk one block over to Main Street and turn right. Keep walking until you see the high school. The gardens are on your left. ⊠ *Botanic Station, Road Town* ☎ *284/494-3904* ⌘ *$3* ⊙ *Mon.–Sat. 9–4:30.*

What to See Elsewhere on the Island

❽ **Cane Garden Bay.** Once a sleepy village, Cane Garden Bay is growing into one of Tortola's important destinations. Stay here at a small hotel or guesthouse or stop by for lunch, dinner, or drinks at a seaside restaurant. You can find a few small stores selling beachware and basics like suntan lotion, and, of course, one of Tortola's most popular beaches is at your feet. The roads in and out of this area are dauntingly steep, so use caution when driving.

★ ☺ ❹ **Dolphin Discovery.** Get up close and personal with dolphins as they swim in a spacious seaside pen. There are two different programs that provide a varying range of experiences. In the Royal Swim, dolphins tow participants around the pen. The less expensive Encounter allows you to touch the dolphins. ⊠ *Prospect Reef Resort, Road Town* ☎ *284/494–*

7675 ⊕ *www.dolphindiscovery.com* ⊠ *Royal Swim $129, Encounter $79* ☉ *Daily, by appointment only.*

❺ Fort Recovery. The unrestored ruins of a 17th-century Dutch fort, 30 feet in diameter, sit amid a profusion of tropical greenery on the Villas of Fort Recovery Estates grounds. There's not much to see here, and there are no guided tours, but you're welcome to stop by and poke around. ⊠ *Waterfront Dr., Road Town* ☎ *284/485–4467* ⊠ *Free.*

❿ Mount Healthy National Park. The remains of an 18th-century sugar plantation are here. The windmill structure has been restored, and you can see the ruins of a mill, a factory with boiling houses, storage areas, stables, a hospital, and many dwellings. It's also a nice place to picnic. ⊠ *Ridge Rd., Todman Peak* ☎ *No phone* ⊕ *www.bvinationalparkstrust. org* ⊠ *Free* ☉ *Daily dawn–dusk.*

★ ❼ Sage Mountain National Park. At 1,716 feet, Sage Mountain is the highest peak in the BVI. From the parking area, a trail leads you in a loop not only to the peak itself (and extraordinary views) but also to a small rain forest, sometimes shrouded in mist. Most of the forest was cut down over the centuries to clear land for sugarcane, cotton, and other crops; to create pastureland; or simply to utilize the stands of timber. In 1964 this park was established to preserve what remained. Up here you can see mahogany trees, white cedars, mountain guavas, elephant-ear vines, mamey trees, and giant bullet woods, to say nothing of such birds as mountain doves and thrushes. Take a taxi from Road Town or drive up Joe's Hill Road and make a left onto Ridge Road toward Chalwell and Doty villages. The road dead-ends at the park. ⊠ *Ridge Rd., Sage Mountain* ☎ *284/494–3904* ⊕ *www.bvinationalparkstrust.org* ⊠ *$3* ☉ *Daily dawn–dusk.*

★ ❾ Skyworld. Drive up here and climb the observation tower for a stunning 360-degree view of numerous islands and cays. On a clear day you can even see St. Croix (40 mi [64½ km] away) and Anegada (20 mi [32 km] away). ⊠ *Ridge Rd., Joe's Hill* ☎ *No phone* ⊠ *Free.*

❻ Soper's Hole. On this little island connected by a causeway to Tortola's western end, you can find a marina and a captivating complex of pastel West Indian–style buildings with shady balconies, shuttered windows, and gingerbread trim that house art galleries, boutiques, and restaurants. Pusser's Landing is a lively place to stop for a cold drink (many are made with Pusser's famous rum) and a sandwich and to watch the boats in harbor.

VIRGIN GORDA

Updated by
Lynda Lohr

Virgin Gorda, or "Fat Virgin," received its name from Christopher Columbus. The explorer envisioned the island as a pregnant woman in a languid recline with Gorda Peak being her big belly and the boulders of the Baths her toes. Different in topography from Tortola, with its arid landscape covered with scrub brush and cactus, Virgin Gorda has a slower pace of life, too. Goats and cattle own the right of way, and the unpretentious friendliness of the people is winning.

Virgin Gorda

Mountain Pt.

George Dog

Cockroach Island

West Dog

Great Dog

Nail Bay Point **12**

Mango Bay

2 Virgin Gorda Peak National Park

Sir Francis Drake Channel

Mahoe Bay **11**

13

Pond Bay

Savannah Bay

Little Dix Bay

Colison Pt.

9

10

Handsome Bay

St. Thomas Bay

Virgin Gorda Airport

6

1

8

← TO TORTOLA

Spanish Town
Fort Pt.

5 **7**

The Valley

Copper Mine Bay

1

3

Spring Bay Beach

Devil's Bay **3** **2**

The Baths

Crook's Bay

4 Copper Mine Point

4

Stoney Bay

Fallen Jerusalem

5 Coastal Islands

0 _____ 1 mi

0 _____ 1 km

Hotels ▼

Biras Creek Resort **19**

Bitter End
Yacht Club **17**

Fischer's Cove
Beach Hotel **5**

Guavaberry Spring Bay
Vacation Homes **3**

Leverick Bay
Resort & Marina **14**

Little Dix Bay **9**

Mango Bay Resort . . . **11**

Nail Bay Resort **12**

Olde Yard Village **10**

Saba Rock Resort **16**

Virgin Gorda
Villa Rentals **15**

Restaurants ▼

The Bath and Turtle **6**

Biras Creek **19**

The Clubhouse **17**

The Fat Virgins Cafe **18**

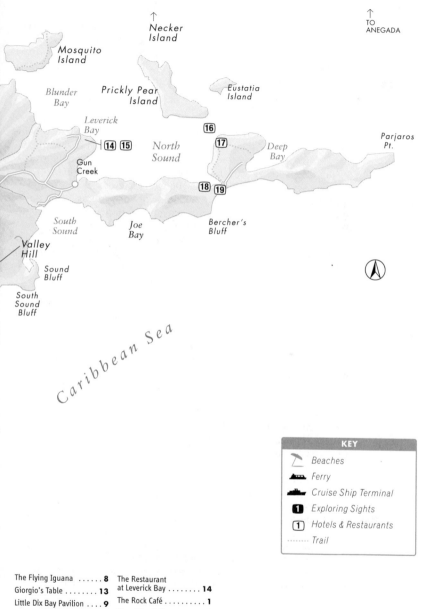

Where to Stay

Virgin Gorda's charming hostelries appeal to a select, appreciative clientele; repeat business is extremely high. Those who prefer Sheratons, Marriotts, and the like may feel they get more for their money on other islands, but the peace and pampering offered on Virgin Gorda are priceless to the discriminating traveler.

For approximate costs, *see* the lodging price chart *in* Tortola.

Hotels & Inns

$$$$ ☷ **Biras Creek Resort.** Although Biras Creek is tucked out of the way on the island's North Sound, the get-away-from-it-all feel is actually the major draw. Anyway, you're just a five-minute ferry ride from the dock at Gun Creek. There are a handful of other hotels in the area, but this resort's gourmet meal plan means you won't want to leave. A member of the exclusive Relais &Châteaux family of hotels, Biras Creek offers suites with separate bedroom and living areas, though only bedrooms have air-conditioning. Guests get around on complimentary bicycles. Rates are per couple, per night, and include everything but beverages. ⌂ *Box 54, North Sound* ☎ *284/494–3555 or 800/223–1108* ☒ *284/494–3557* ⊕ *www.biras.com* ⇆ *31 suites* ♨ *2 restaurants, in-room safes, refrigerators, in-room data ports, 2 tennis courts, pool, spa, beach, snorkeling, windsurfing, boating, bicycles, hiking, bar, shop, Internet room; no room TVs* ▭ *AE, MC, V* ⑩ *FAP.*

♨ **$$$$** ☷ **Bitter End Yacht Club.** Sailing's the thing at this busy hotel and marina in the nautically inclined North Sound, and since the use of everything from small sailboats to Windsurfers to kayaks is included in the price, you have no reason not to get out on the water. If you're serious about learning to sail, sign up for lessons with the acclaimed Nick Trotter Sailing School. Of course, if you just want to lounge about on the beachfront chaises or on your balcony, that's okay, too. There's a busy social scene, with guests gathering to swap sailing tales at the hotel's bars. Rooms are bright and cheery, with the decor leaning toward the blues and whites. You reach the Bitter End only by a free private ferry. ⌂ *Box 46, North Sound* ☎ *284/494–2746 or 800/872–2392* ☒ *284/494–4756* ⊕ *www.beyc.com* ⇆ *87 rooms* ♨ *3 restaurants, pool, beach, dive shop, snorkeling, windsurfing, boating, waterskiing, bar, children's programs (ages 6–18), Internet room; no a/c in some rooms, no room TVs* ▭ *AE, MC, V* ⑩ *AI.*

FodorśChoice ★

★ ♨ **$$$$** ☷ **Little Dix Bay.** This laid-back luxury resort offers something for everyone, which is why we like it. You can swim, sun, and snorkel on a gorgeous sandy crescent, play tennis or windsurf, or just relax with a good book. The hotel's restaurants serve stellar food, but you're only a five-minute drive from Spanish Town's less expensive restaurants and shopping. Rooms have rattan and wood furniture and a casual feel. The grounds are gorgeous, with lots of lush plantings kept snipped to perfection. Depending on when you visit, your fellow guests will be honeymooners or folks who've spent a week or two in the winter season for years. ⌂ *Box 70, Little Dix Bay* ☎ *284/495–5555* ☒ *284/495–5661* ⊕ *www.littledixbay.com* ⇆ *98 rooms, 8 suites, 2 villas* ♨ *3 restaurants,* *in-room safes, refrigerators, in-room data ports, Wi-Fi, 7 tennis courts, pool, gym, spa, beach, snorkeling, windsurfing, 2 bars, library, shops, children's programs (ages 3–16), Internet room, business services, car rental; no room TVs ⊟ AE, MC, V ⵏ◯⵿ EP.*

★ **$$–$$$$** 🖼 **Nail Bay Resort.** Rambling up the hill above the coast, this resort offers a wide selection of rooms and suites to fit every need. The beach is just a short walk away from the units at lower elevations, but if you're staying higher up the hill, you might want to drive to avoid the uphill trek back to your room. You get cooking facilities (at least microwave, fridge, toaster oven, and coffee maker) no matter how small your room. It's a bit of a drive down a miserable dirt road to reach the resort, but it offers lots of activities and a restaurant, so you won't need to leave unless you want to. The rooms and apartments have modern rattan furniture, tile floors, and nice views. There's some construction in the area, so check before you go if noise bothers you. ⌂ *Box 69, Nail Bay* ☎ *284/494–8000 or 800/871–3551* 📠 *284/495–5875* ⊕ *www.nailbay. com* ⥁ *9 rooms, 4 suites, 1 studio apartment, 7 villas* △ *Restaurant, fans, some kitchens, some kitchenettes, in-room VCRs, tennis court, beach, snorkeling, boccie, croquet, bar, Internet room* ⊟ *AE, MC, V* ⵏ◯⵿ *EP.*

$$–$$$$ 🖼 **Saba Rock Resort.** Reachable only by a free ferry or by your own yacht, this resort on its own tiny cay isn't for everyone. However, it's good for folks who want to mix and mingle with the sailors who drop anchor for the night. The bar and restaurant are busy with yachters gathering for sundowners, lunch, and dinner. The rooms are spacious, each with a different decor. All have tile floors, rattan or wood furniture, and colorful spreads and drapes. A resort boat will drop you off at nearby North Sound resorts if you need a change of pace. ⌂ *Box 67, North Sound* ☎ *284/495–7711 or 284/495–9966* 📠 *284/495–7373* ⊕ *www.sabarock. com* ⥁ *7 1-bedroom suites, 2 2-bedroom suites* △ *Restaurant, fans, some kitchens, refrigerators, cable TV, in-room data ports, Wi-Fi, beach, snorkeling, bar, recreation room, shop; no phones in some rooms* ⊟ *MC, V* ⵏ◯⵿ *CP.*

$$$ 🖼 **Olde Yard Village.** All the condos in this upscale complex have at least partial ocean views, and the location—a few minutes' drive outside Spanish Town—is ideal, close enough so that you can easily pop out to dinner but far enough out of town to make you feel as if you're more isolated than you are. You will need a car, though, to make those trips a breeze. The Olde Yard Village will be building new units over next five years, but construction is a bit removed from the existing accommodations. ⌂ *Box 26, The Valley* ☎ *284/495–5544 or 800/653–9273* 📠 *284/495–5986* ⊕ *www.oldeyardvillage.com* ⥁ *26 condos* △ *Kitchens, microwaves, refrigerators, cable TV, in-room data ports, pool, bar* ⊟ *AE, D, MC, V* ⵏ◯⵿ *EP.*

⟳ **$–$$** 🖼 **Fischer's Cove Beach Hotel.** The rooms are modest, the walls thin, and the owners in the midst of upgrading the chipped furniture and tired bedspreads, but you can't beat the location. Budget travelers should consider this hotel if they want a good beach just steps away. If you plan to stay put, you won't even need to rent a car. Spanish Town's handful of restaurants and shopping at Virgin Gorda Yacht Harbor are an easy 15-minute walk away. For better views, opt for the beachfront rooms.

⌂ Box 60, The Valley ☎ 284/495–5252 ⊟ 284/495–5820 ⊕ www. fischerscove.com ⤶ 12 rooms, 8 cottages ⌂ Restaurant, fans, some kitchenettes, refrigerators, beach, playground; no a/c in some rooms, no TV in some rooms ⊟ AE, MC, V ⫶◯⫶ EP.

$ ▦ **Leverick Bay Resort & Marina.** With its colorful buildings and bustling marina, Leverick Bay is a good choice, but the resort does not have a great beach. With easy access to various water-sports activities, a tasty on-site restaurant, and comfortable and spacious rooms, it's still a good deal. If you prefer an apartment, opt for one of the units stretching up the hillside above the marina. There's a one-week minimum stay in the apartments. All the accommodations have tile floors and pastel accents with a tropical feel. *⌂ Box 63, Leverick Bay ☎ 284/495–7421 or 800/848–7081 ⊟ 284/495–7367 ⊕ www.leverickbay.com ⤶ 14 rooms, 4 condos ⌂ 2 restaurants, grocery, fans, in-room safes, some kitchens, refrigerators, cable TV, tennis court, pool, hair salon, spa, beach, dive shop, dock, boating, marina, bar, shops, laundry facilities, Internet room ⊟ AE, D, MC, V ⫶◯⫶ EP.*

Villas

Those craving seclusion would do well at a villa. Most have full kitchens and maid service. Prices per week in winter run from around $2,000 for a one- or two-bedroom villa up to $10,000 for a five-room beachfront villa. Rates in summer are substantially less.

On Virgin Gorda, a villa in the North Sound area means you'll pretty much stay put at night unless you want to make the drive on narrow roads to the Valley's restaurants. If you opt for a spot near the Baths, it's an easy drive to town.

The St. Thomas–based **McLaughlin-Anderson Luxury Villas** (✉ 1000 Blackbeard's Hill, Suite 3, Charlotte Amalie, VI 00802-6739 ☎ 340/776–0635 or 800/537–6246 ⊕ www.mclaughlinanderson.com) handles nearly two dozen properties all over Virgin Gorda. Villas range in size from two bedrooms to six bedrooms and come with many amenities, including full kitchens, pools, and stellar views. The company can hire a chef and stock your kitchen with groceries. A seven-night minimum is required during the winter season.

Virgin Gorda Villa Rentals (⌂ Box 63, Leverick Bay ☎ 284/495–7421 or 800/848–7081 ⊕ www.virgingordabvi.com) manages more than 40 properties near Leverick Bay Resort and Mahoe Bay, so it's perfect for those who want to be close to activities. Many villas—from studios to houses with six or more bedrooms—have private swimming pools and air-conditioning, at least in the bedrooms; all have full kitchens, are well maintained, and have spectacular views.

★ $$–$$$ ▦ **Guavaberry Spring Bay Vacation Homes.** Rambling back from the beach, these hexagonal one- and two-bedroom villas give you all the comforts of home with the striking boulder-fringed beach just minutes away. The same company also manages 18 villas in the vicinity. The villas are best for independent travelers who want to be able to cook or simply head 10 minutes to Spanish Town for a night out. The popular Baths are a short walk away, and snorkeling is excellent. The rooms have dark-wood or white walls, tile floors, and tropical bright spreads and curtains. Not all have sea views. ⌂ *Box 20, The Valley* ☎ *284/495–5227* 🖨 *284/ 495–5283* ⊕ *www.guavaberryspringbay.com* ⇗ *12 1-bedroom units, 6 2-bedroom units, 18 villas* ⌂ *Grocery, fans, kitchens, beach, Internet room; no a/c, no room phones, no room TVs* ▤ *No credit cards* ⎟○⎟ *EP.*

$–$$$ 🖾 **Mango Bay Resort.** Sitting seaside on Virgin Gorda's north coast, this collection of contemporary duplex apartments will make you feel at home in the tropics. Each apartment is individually owned, so each has a different decor, but you can count on tile floors and tropical accents. The homes come with floats, kayaks, and snorkeling equipment, so you can find plenty to do when you're tired of lounging in the chaise. The popular Giorgio's Table restaurant is a short walk away. ⌂ *Box 1062, Mahoe Bay* ☎ *284/495–5672* 🖨 *284/495–5674* ⊕ *www.mangobayresort.com* ⇗ *18 condos, 2 villas* ⌂ *Fans, kitchens, cable TV, beach* ▤ *MC, V* ⎟○⎟ *EP.*

Where to Eat

Restaurants range from simple to elegant. Hotels that are accessible only by boat will arrange transport in advance upon request from nonguests who wish to dine at their restaurants. It's wise to make dinner reservations almost everywhere except really casual spots.

For approximate costs, *see* the dining price chart *in* Tortola.

AMERICAN– CASUAL **$$$–$$$$** ✕ **The Restaurant at Leverick Bay.** This bi-level restaurant looks out over North Sound. The fancier upstairs dining room is slightly more expensive, with a menu that includes steaks, pork chops, chicken, and fresh fish. There's a prime rib special on Saturday nights. Below, the bar offers light fare all day—starting with breakfast and moving on to hamburgers, salads, and pizzas until well into the evening. There's a children's menu downstairs. ⌧ *Leverick Bay Resort & Marina, Leverick Bay* ☎ *284/495–7154* ▤ *MC, V.*

☉ **$$–$$$$** ✕ **The Flying Iguana Restaurant & Bar.** Local artwork is displayed in this charming restaurant's comfortable lounge. The open-air dining room looks past the island's tiny airport to the sea. Enjoy classic eggs and bacon for breakfast; for lunch there are sandwiches and juicy hamburgers. The dinner menu includes fresh seafood, grilled chicken, steaks, and a pasta special. ⌧ *Virgin Gorda Airport, The Valley* ☎ *284/495–5277* ▤ *MC, V.*

$$$ ✕ **The Mine Shaft Café.** Perched on a hilltop that offers a 360-degree view of spectacular sunsets, this restaurant near Copper Mine Point serves simple yet well-prepared food, including grilled fish, chicken, steaks, and baby back ribs. Tuesday nights feature an all-you-can-eat Caribbean-style barbecue. The bar, as well as the monthly full-moon parties, draws a big local crowd. ⌧ *Copper Mine Point, The Valley* ☎ *284/495–5260* ▤ *AE, MC, V.*

$$–$$$ ✕ **The Bath & Turtle.** You can sit back and relax at this informal tavern with a friendly staff—although the noise from the television can be a bit much. Well-stuffed sandwiches, homemade pizzas, pasta dishes, and daily specials like conch gumbo round out the casual menu. Live musicians perform Saturday nights. ⌧ *Virgin Gorda Yacht Harbour, Spanish Town* ☎ *284/495–5239* ▤ *AE, MC, V.*

$$–$$$ ✕ **LSL Restaurant.** An unpretentious place along the road to the Baths, this small restaurant with pedestrian decor is a local favorite. You'll always find fresh fish on the menu, but folks with a taste for other dishes won't be disappointed. Try the veal with mushrooms and herbs in a white wine sauce or the breast of chicken with rum cream and nuts. ⊠ *Tower Rd., The Valley* ☎ *284/495–5151* ▭ *MC, V.*

☾ **$$–$$$** ✕ **Top of the Baths.** At the entrance to the Baths, this popular restaurant starts serving at 8 AM. Tables are on an outdoor terrace or in an open-air pavilion; all have stunning views of the Sir Francis Drake Channel. Hamburgers, sandwiches, and fish-and-chips are offered at lunch. Conch fritters and pumpkin soup are among the dinner appetizers. Entrées include fillet of yellowtail snapper, shrimp creole, and jerk chicken. For dessert, the mango raspberry cheesecake is excellent. The Sunday barbecue, with live music, is served from noon until 3 PM and is an island event. ⊠ *The Valley* ☎ *284/495–5497* ▭ *AE, MC, V.*

☾ **$–$$** ✕ **The Fat Virgins Café.** This casual beachfront eatery offers a straightforward menu of flying-fish sandwiches, baby back ribs, chicken roti, vegetable pasta, and fresh fish specials for lunch and dinner. Friday nights feature a special Chinese menu. There's a good selection of Caribbean beer. ⊠ *Biras Creek Resort, North Sound* ☎ *284/495–7052* ▭ *MC, V.*

CONTEMPORARY ✕ **Biras Creek Restaurant.** This hilltop restaurant at the Biras Creek
$$$$ Hotel has stunning views of North Sound. The four-course prix-fixe menu changes daily and includes several choices per course. For starters, there may be a five-spice duck salad drizzled with an orange-onion marmalade and beetroot dressing, or creamy leek and potato soup ribboned with thin strips of smoked salmon. Entrées may include pan-seared salmon wrapped in Parma ham, and the desserts, including a chocolate tart covered with caramelized bananas and warm chocolate sauce, are to die for. Dinner ends with Biras Creek's signature offering of cheese and port. ⊠ *Biras Creek Hotel, North Sound* ☎ *284/494–3555 or 800/223–1108* 🖷 *284/494–3557* ⊲ *Reservations essential* ▭ *AE, D, MC, V* ☾ *No lunch.*

$$$–$$$$ ✕ **Little Dix Bay Pavilion.** For an elegant evening, you can't do better than this—the candlelight in the open-air pavilion is enchanting, the daily-changing menu sophisticated, the service attentive. The dinner menu always includes a fine selection of superbly prepared seafood, meat, and vegetarian entrées—sugarcane-skewered tuna with a smoked shrimp-ginger salsa, rack of lamb with a fresh mint sauce, and red snapper fillet baked in a banana leaf. The Monday breakfast, lunch, and evening buffets shine. ⊠ *Little Dix Bay Resort, Spanish Town* ☎ *284/495–5555 Ext. 174* ⊲ *Reservations essential* ▭ *AE, D, MC, V.*

ITALIAN ✕ **Giorgio's Table.** Gaze out at the stars and listen to the water lap
$$$–$$$$ against the shore while dining on homemade ravioli, beef fillet in a brunello wine sauce, or truffle duck ragout over pappardelle pasta. House specialties include fresh lobster that you choose from a 5,000-gallon seawater pool. There's also a selection of 120 different wines kept in a temperature-controlled cellar. Lunch is more casual and includes pizzas and sandwiches. ⊠ *Mahoe Bay* ☎ *284/495–5684* ▭ *AE, D, MC, V.*

$$–$$$ ✕ **The Rock Café.** Surprisingly good Italian cuisine is served open-air among the waterfalls and giant boulders that form the famous Baths. For dinner, feast on spinach-and-ricotta gnocchi, spaghetti with lobster sauce, or fresh red snapper in a butter and caper sauces. For dessert, try the pear and chocolate pie with vanilla sauce. For lunch there's casual fare: pizza, burgers, and sandwiches. ⊠ *The Valley* ☎ *284/495–5482* ▭ *AE, D, MC, V.*

SEAFOOD ✕ **The Clubhouse.** The Bitter End Yacht Club's open-air waterfront
★ $$$$ restaurant is a favorite rendezvous for the sailing set—busy day and night. You can find lavish buffets for breakfast, lunch, and dinner as well as an à la carte menu. Dinner selections include grilled swordfish or tuna, chopped sirloin, scallops, shrimp, and local lobster. ⊠ *Bitter End Yacht Club, North Sound* ☎ *284/494–2745* ⌨ *Reservations essential* ▭ *AE, MC, V.*

Beaches

Although some of the best beaches are reachable only by boat, don't worry if you're a landlubber, because you can find plenty of places to sun and swim. Anybody going to Virgin Gorda must experience swimming or snorkeling among its unique boulder formations, which can be visited at several beaches along Lee Road. The most popular of these spots is the Baths, but there are several other similar places nearby that are easily reached.

The Baths. Featuring a stunning maze of huge granite boulders that extend into the sea, this national park beach is usually crowded midday with day-trippers. The snorkeling is good, and you're likely to see a wide variety of fish, but watch out for dinghies coming ashore from the numerous sailboats anchored just off the beach. Public bathrooms and a handful of bars and shops are close to the water and at the start of the path that leads to the beach. Beach lockers are available to keep belongings safe. ⊠ *About 1 mi (1½ km) west of Spanish Town ferry dock on Tower Rd., Spring Bay* ☎ *284/494–3904* ⌨ *$3* ☉ *Daily dawn–dusk.*
Nail Bay. Head to the island's north tip and you'll be rewarded with a trio of beaches within the Nail Bay Resort complex that are ideal for snorkeling. Mountain Trunk Bay is perfect for beginners, and Nail Bay and Long Bay beaches have coral caverns just offshore. The resort has a restaurant, which is an uphill walk but perfect for beach breaks. ⊠ *Nail Bay Resort, off Plum Tree Bay Rd., Nail Bay* ☎ *No phone* ⌨ *Free* ☉ *Daily dawn–dusk.*
Savannah Bay. For a wonderfully private beach close to Spanish Town, try Savannah Bay. It may not always be completely deserted, but it's a long stretch of soft, white sand. Bring your own mask, fins, and snorkel, as there are no facilities. The view from above is a photographer's delight. ⊠ *Off North Sound Rd., ¾ mi (1¼ km) east of Spanish Town ferry dock, Savannah Bay* ☎ *No phone* ⌨ *Free* ☉ *Daily dawn–dusk.*
Spring Bay Beach. Just off Tower Road, this national-park beach gets much less traffic than the nearby Baths, and has the similarly large, imposing boulders that create interesting grottos for swimming. The snorkeling is excellent, and the grounds include swings and picnic tables. ⊠ *Off*

Tower Rd., 1 mi (1½ km) west of Spanish Town ferry dock, Spring Bay ☎ *284/494–3904* ✉ *Free* ☉ *Daily dawn–dusk.*

Sports & the Outdoors

CRICKET   You can catch a match at the Recreation Grounds in Spanish Town February to April. The BVI Tourist Board at Virgin Gorda Yacht Harbor can give you information on game dates and times.

DIVING & SNORKELING   Where you go snorkeling and what company you pick depend on where you're staying. Many hotels have on-site dive outfitters, but if they don't, one won't be far away. If your hotel does have a dive operation, just stroll down to the dock and hop aboard—no need to drive anywhere. The dive companies are all certified by PADI. Costs vary, but count on paying about $75 for a one-tank dive and $95 for a two-tank dive. All dive operators offer introductory courses as well as certification and advanced courses. Should you get an attack of the bends, which can happen when you ascend too rapidly, the nearest decompression chamber is at Roy L. Schneider Regional Medical Center in St. Thomas.

There are some terrific snorkel and dive sites off Virgin Gorda, including areas around the Baths, the North Sound, and the Dogs. The Chimney at Great Dog Island sports a coral archway and canyon covered with a wide variety of sponges. At Joe's Cave, an underwater cavern on West Dog Island, huge groupers, eagle rays, and other colorful fish accompany divers as they swim. At some sites you can see 100 feet down, but divers who don't want to go that deep and snorkelers will find plenty to look at just below the surface.

☼ The **Bitter End Yacht Club** (✉ North Sound ☎ 284/494–2746 ⊕ www.beyc.com) offers a number of snorkeling trips day and night. **Dive BVI** (✉ Virgin Gorda Yacht Harbour, Spanish Town ☎ 284/495–5513 or 800/848–7078 ⊕ www.divebvi.com) offers expert instruction, certification, and day trips. **Sunchaser Scuba** (✉ Bitter End Yacht Harbor, North Sound ☎ 284/495–9638 or 800/932–4286 ⊕ www.sunchaserscuba.com) offers resort, advanced, and rescue courses.

FISHING   The sportfishing here is so good that anglers come from all over the world. **Charter Virgin Gorda** (✉ Leverick Bay, North Sound ☎ 284/495–7421 ⊕ www.chartervirgingorda.com) offers a choice of trips aboard its 46-foot Hatteras, the *Mahoe Bay*, for full-day marlin hunting. Plan to spend $800 to $1,200.

GOLF   The 9-hole minigolf course, **Golf Virgin Gorda** (✉ Copper Mine Point, The Valley ☎ 284/495–5260), is next to the Mine Shaft Café, delightfully nestled between huge granite boulders. There's no charge to play.

SAILING & BOATING   The BVI waters are calm, and terrific places to learn to sail. You can also rent sea kayaks, waterskiing equipment, dinghies, and power boats,
☼ or take a parasailing trip. The **Bitter End Sailing & Windsurfing School** (✉ Bitter End Yacht Club, North Sound ☎ 284/494–2746 ⊕ www.beyc.com) offers classroom, dockside, and on-the-water lessons for sailors of all levels. Private lessons are $60 per hour. If you just want to sit back, relax, and let the captain take the helm, choose a sailing or power yacht from

Double "D" Charters (✉ Virgin Gorda Yacht Harbour, Spanish Town ☎ 284/495–6150 ⊕ www.doubledbvi.com). Rates are $55 for a half-day trip and $90 for a full-day island-hopping excursion. Private full-day cruises or sails for up to eight people run $850. If you'd rather rent a Sunfish or Hobie Wave, check out **Leverick Bay Watersports** (✉ Leverick Bay, North Sound ☎ 284/495–7376 ⊕ www.watersportsbvi.com).

WINDSURFING The North Sound is a good place to learn to windsurf: it's protected, so you can't be easily blown out to sea. The **Bitter End Yacht Club** (✉ North Sound ☎ 284/494–2746 ⊕ www.beyc.com) gives lessons and rents equipment for $60 per hour for nonguests. A half-day Windsurfer rental runs $60 to $100.

Shopping

Most boutiques are within hotel complexes or at Virgin Gorda Yacht Harbour. Two of the best are at Biras Creek and Little Dix Bay. Other properties—the Bitter End and Leverick Bay—have small but equally select boutiques.

CLOTHING **Blue Banana** (✉ Virgin Gorda Yacht Harbour, Spanish Town ☎ 284/495–5957) carries a large selection of name-brand swimsuits plus cover-ups, T-shirts, and accessories. At **Dive BVI** (✉ Virgin Gorda Yacht Harbour, Spanish Town ☎ 284/495–5513), you can find books about the islands as well as snorkeling equipment, sportswear, sunglasses, and beach bags. **Fat Virgin's Treasure** (✉ Biras Creek Hotel, North Sound ☎ 284/495–7054) sells cool island-style clothing in tropical prints, a large selection of straw sun hats, and unusual gift items like island-made hot sauces, artistic cards, and locally fired pottery. **Margo's Boutique** (✉ Virgin Gorda Yacht Harbour, Spanish Town ☎ 284/495–5237) is the place to buy breezy, boldly printed sarongs and handmade accessories like shell and pearl jewelry. **Next Wave** (✉ Virgin Gorda Yacht Harbour, Spanish Town ☎ 284/495–5623) sells T-shirts, canvas tote bags, and locally made jewelry. The **Pavilion Gift Shop** (✉ Little Dix Bay Hotel, Little Dix Bay ☎ 284/495–5555) has the latest in resort wear for men and women, as well as jewelry, books, housewares, and expensive T-shirts. **Pusser's Company Store** (✉ Leverick Bay ☎ 284/495–7369) has a trademark line of sportswear, rum products, and gift items.

FOODSTUFFS The **Bitter End Emporium** (✉ Bitter End Yacht Harbor, North Sound ☎ 284/494–2745) is the place for such edible treats as local fruits, cheeses, baked goods, and gourmet prepared food to take out. **Buck's Food Market** (✉ Virgin Gorda Yacht Harbour, Spanish Town ☎ 284/495–5423 ✉ Gun Creek, North Sound ☎ 284/495–7368) is the closest the island offers to a full-service supermarket and has everything from an in-store bakery and deli to fresh fish and produce departments. The **Chef's Pantry** (✉ Leverick Bay ☎ 284/495–7677) has the fixings for an impromptu party in your villa or boat—fresh seafood, specialty meats, imported cheeses, daily baked breads and pastries, and an impressive wine and spirit selection. The **Wine Cellar & Bakery** (✉ Virgin Gorda Yacht Harbour, Spanish Town ☎ 284/495–5250) sells bread, rolls, muffins, cookies, sandwiches, and sodas to go.

GIFTS **Flamboyance** (✉ Virgin Gorda Yacht Harbour, Spanish Town ☎ 284/495–5946) has a large line of fragrances, including those inspired by the scent of tropical flowers. The **Palm Tree Gallery** (✉ Leverick Bay ☎ 284/495–7479) sells attractive handcrafted jewelry, paintings, and one-of-a-kind gift items, as well as games and books about the Caribbean. The **Reeftique** (✉ Bitter End Yacht Harbor, North Sound ☎ 284/494–2745) carries island crafts and jewelry, clothing, and nautical odds and ends with the Bitter End logo. **Thee Artistic Gallery** (✉ Virgin Gorda Yacht Harbour, Spanish Town ☎ 284/495–5104) has Caribbean-made jewelry, 14-karat-gold nautical charms, maps, collectible coins, crystal, and Christmas tree ornaments with tropical themes.

Nightlife

Pick up a free copy of the *Limin' Times*—available at most resorts and restaurants—for the most current local entertainment schedule.

The Bath & Turtle (✉ Virgin Gorda Yacht Harbour, Spanish Town ☎ 284/495–5239), one of the liveliest spots on Virgin Gorda, hosts island bands regularly in season from 8 PM until midnight. Local bands play at **Bitter End Yacht Club** (✉ North Sound ☎ 284/494–2746) nightly during the winter season. **Chez Bamboo** (✉ Across from Virgin Gorda Yacht Harbour, Spanish Town ☎ 284/495–5752) is the place on the island for live jazz on Friday nights. The bar at **Little Dix Bay** (✉ Little Dix Bay ☎ 284/495–5555) presents elegant live entertainment several nights a week in season. The **Mine Shaft Café** (✉ Copper Mine Point, The Valley ☎ 284/495–5260) has live bands on Tuesday and for Ladies Night on Friday from 7 PM to 9 PM. The **Restaurant at Leverick Bay** (✉ Leverick Bay Resort & Marina, Leverick Bay ☎ 284/495–7154) hosts live music on Saturday through Wednesday nights in season. The **Rock Café** (✉ The Valley ☎ 284/495–5177) has live bands Friday, Saturday, and Sunday nights.

Exploring Virgin Gorda

One of the most efficient ways to see Virgin Gorda is by sailboat. There are few roads, and most byways don't follow the scalloped shoreline. The main route sticks resolutely to the center of the island, linking the Baths at the tip of the southern extremity with Gun Creek and Leverick Bay at North Sound and providing exhilarating views. The craggy coast, scissored with grottoes and fringed by palms and boulders, has a primitive beauty. If you drive, you can hit all the sights in one day. The best plan is to explore the area near your hotel (either the Valley or North Sound) first, then take a day to drive to the other end. Stop to climb Gorda Peak, which is in the island's center.

Numbers in the margin correspond to points of interest on the Virgin Gorda map.

What to See

 The Baths. At Virgin Gorda's most celebrated sight, giant boulders are scattered about the beach and in the water. Some are almost as large as houses and form remarkable grottos. Climb between these rocks to swim in the many placid pools. Early morning and late afternoon are the best times to visit if you want to avoid crowds. If it's privacy you crave, follow the shore northward to quieter bays—Spring Bay, the Crawl, Little Trunk, and Valley Trunk—or head south to Devil's Bay. ⊠ *Off Tower Rd., The Baths* ☎ *284/494–3904* ⊕ *www.bvinationalparkstrust. org* ⊠ *$3* ⊙ *Daily dawn–dusk.*

❻ Coastal Islands. You can easily reach the quaintly named Fallen Jerusalem Island and the Dog Islands by boat. They're all part of the BVI National Parks Trust, and their seductive beaches and unparalleled snorkeling display the BVI at their beachcombing, hedonistic best. ☎ *No phone* ⊠ *Free.*

❹ Copper Mine Point. Here stand a tall stone shaft silhouetted against the sky and a small stone structure that overlooks the sea. These are the ruins of a copper mine established 400 years ago and worked first by the Spanish, then by the English, until the early 20th century. In April 2003 this historic site became the 20th park under the BVI National Parks Trust jurisdiction. ⊠ *Copper Mine Rd.* ☎ *No phone* ⊕ *www. bvinationalparkstrust.org* ⊠ *Free.*

❶ Spanish Town. Virgin Gorda's peaceful main settlement, on the island's southern wing, is so tiny that it barely qualifies as a town at all. Also known as the Valley, Spanish Town has a marina, some shops, and a couple of car-rental agencies. Just north of town is the ferry slip. At the Virgin Gorda Yacht Harbour you can stroll along the dock and do a little shopping.

★ ❺ Virgin Gorda Peak National Park. There are two trails at this 265-acre park, which contains the island's highest point, at 1,359 feet. Small signs on North Sound Road mark both entrances; sometimes, however, the signs are missing, so keep your eyes open for a set of stairs that disappears into the trees. It's about a 15-minute hike from either entrance up to a small clearing, where you can climb a ladder to the platform of a wooden observation tower and a spectacular 360-degree view. ⊠ *North Sound Rd., Gorda Peak* ☎ *No phone* ⊕ *www.bvinationalparkstrust. org* ⊠ *Free.*

JOST VAN DYKE

Updated by
Carol M.
Bareuther

Named after an early Dutch settler, Jost Van Dyke is a small island northwest of Tortola and is *truly* a place to get away from it all. Mountainous and lush, the 4-mi-long (6½-km-long) island—with fewer than 200 full-time residents—has one tiny resort, some rental houses and villas, a campground, a handful of cars and taxis, and a single road. Water conservation is encouraged, as the source of supply is rainwater collected in basement-like cisterns. Most lodgings will ask you to follow the Caribbean golden rule: "In the land of sun and fun, we never flush for number one." Jost is one of the Caribbean's most popular anchorages, and there's a disproportionately large number of informal bars and restaurants, which have helped earn Jost its reputation as the "party island" of the BVI.

The Laid-Back Lifestyle at Its Best

IT'S THE LAID-BACK ATTITUDE of Jost Van Dyke, which boasts a beach as its main street and has had electricity only since the 1990s, that makes the famous feel comfortable and everyday folk feel glorious. At no locale is this more so than at Foxy's Tamarind. Foxy Callwood, a seventh-generation Jost Van Dyker and calypsonian extraordinaire, is the star here, strumming and singing rib-tickling ditties full of lewd and laughable lyrics that attract a bevy of boaters and even celebrities like Tom Cruise, Kelsey Grammer, and Steven Spielberg.

What began in the 1970s as a lemonade-stand-size bar, albeit with "modern" fixtures like a galvanized roof and plywood walls, has evolved into a bona fide beach bar with sand floor, wattle walls, and thatched roof that defines the eastern end of the beach at Great Harbour. Without the glitz of St. Thomas, glamour of St. John, or grace of Tortola, islanders like Foxy knew they needed to carve out their own unique niche—and have done so by appearing to have done nothing at all. Unhurried friendliness and a slice of quintessential Caribbean culture flow freely here.

Foxy, who fished for a living before he started singing for his supper, has traveled the world and had the world come to him for endless parties for Halloween, for Labor Day weekend, and for the New Year. The *New York Times* named Foxy's one of its three top picks to ring in the millennium. What's the appeal? Foxy sums it up himself: "It's the quantity of people and the quality of the party. You can dance on the tables and sleep on the beach. No one is going to bother you."

Where to Stay

For approximate costs, *see* the lodging price chart *in* Tortola.

★ $$–$$$ ☒ **Sandcastle.** This six-cottage hideaway sits on a half-mile stretch of white-sand beach shared by a half dozen beach bars and restaurants. The peach-color cottages are simply furnished. Two-bedroom cottages have outdoor showers and no air-conditioning, but the one-bedroom cottages do have these conveniences. Either way, the Caribbean is no more than 20 feet from your doorstep. There's nothing to do here except relax in a hammock, read, walk the beach, swim, and snorkel. Unfortunately, you may find your serenity shattered between 11 AM and 3 PM by the bustle of charter-boat day-trippers who arrive on large catamarans for lunch and drinks at the Soggy Dollar Bar. At night, tuck into a casually elegant, four-course candlelight dinner at the Sandcastle Restaurant. For weeklong stays you have the option of a package that includes all breakfasts and most dinners. Long-time owners Debby Pearce and Bruce Donath sold the resort in 2005, but new owners Jerry and Tish O'Connell have maintained the same level of service. ☒ *White Bay* ☎ *284/495–9888* ☒ *284/495–9999* ⊕ *www.sandcastle-bvi.com* ➪ *4 1-bedroom cottages, 2 2-bedroom cottages* ᓱ *Restaurant, beach, bar, shops; no a/c in some rooms, no room TVs* ☰ *D, MC, V* ⦿ *EP, MAP.*

$–$$$ White Bay Villas & Seaside Cottages. There's no missing the beautiful sea views from the verandas of these hilltop one- to three-bedroom villas and cottages. Accommodations are open-air, with screenless doors and shuttered windows, although there's mosquito netting over the beds. Almost everything is provided, from linens and beach towels to an occasional bunch of fresh bananas or a ripe papaya from the trees outside. Although there are some small markets on the island, it's a good idea to buy groceries on St. Thomas or Tortola before arriving. White Bay and five beach bars are less than a five-minute walk downhill. A mile farther down the beach there's a small supermarket, half a dozen beach bars and restaurants, a souvenir shop, and water-sports rental. ⊠ *White Bay* ⌂ *Box 3368, Annapolis, MD 21403* ☎ *410/571–6692 or 800/778–8066* ⊕ *www.jostvandyke.com* ⇱ *3 villas, 3 cottages* ⟡ *Fans, kitchens, cable TV, in-room VCRs, beach; no a/c* ⦿ *EP.*

WHERE TO CAMP **Ivan's Stress-Free Bar & White Bay Campground.** If you don't mind roughing it a bit, Ivan's will give you a quintessential Caribbean experience. You can pitch your tent 6 feet from the sea or farther back under the sea-grape trees where there's an electric hookup and lamp. Or opt for a primitive cabin, where you can find just a bed, fan, and bucket of water to wash the sand off your feet. There's an outhouse, sun showers (basically a plastic sack hung from a tree branch), and a communal kitchen stocked with pots and pans. Thursday-night barbecues attract campers and noncampers alike. Ivan will happily conduct nature walks and arrange island tours, sailing, and diving trips, but he's a musician at heart. Impromptu jam sessions are always a highlight, and if you pack a musical instrument, you can join in, too. ⟡ *Flush toilets, drinking water, showers, picnic tables, food service, electricity, public telephone, swimming (ocean)* ⇱ *8 cabins, 5 tents, 15 campsites* ⊠ *White Bay* ☎ *284/495–9312* ⊕ *www. caribbeancruisingclub.com/ivan* ⌂ *Reservations essential* ⊟ *No credit cards.*

Where to Eat

Restaurants on Jost Van Dyke are informal (some serve meals family-style at long tables) but charming. The island is a favorite charter-boat stop, and you're bound to hear people exchanging stories about the previous night's anchoring adventures. Most restaurants don't take reservations, and in all cases dress is casual.

For approximate costs, *see* the dining price chart *in* Tortola.

$$$$ ✕ **Sandcastle.** Candles illuminate this tiny beachfront dining room during the four-course, prix-fixe affairs. The menu changes frequently but can include a West Indian pumpkin or curried-apple soup; curried shrimp or three-mustard chicken; and, for dessert, rum bananas or key lime pie. Reservations are required by 4 PM for the single dinner seating at 7 PM. For lunch, you can get flying-fish sandwiches, hamburgers, and conch fritters at the Soggy Dollar Bar, famous as the purported birthplace of the lethal drink called the Painkiller. ⊠ *Sandcastle, White Bay* ☎ *284/495–9888* ⌂ *Reservations essential* ⊟ *D, MC, V.*

$$–$$$$ ✕ **Foxy's Tamarind.** One of the true hot spots in the BVI—and a must-stop for yachties from the world over—Foxy's hosts the madcap Wooden

Boat Race every May and throws big parties on New Year's Eve, April Fools' Day, and Halloween. This lively place serves local food, has terrific barbecue dinners on Friday and Saturday nights, mixes its own rum punch, and now offers its own Foxy's brand beer. Famed calypso performer and owner Foxy Callwood plays the guitar and creates calypso ditties about diners. Reservations for dinner are required by 5 PM. ⊠ *Great Harbour* ☎ 284/495–9258 ⌂ *Reservations essential* ▭ *AE, MC, V* ⊗ *No lunch weekends.*

☼ **$$–$$$$** ╳ **Foxy's Taboo.** An oasis in the middle of uninhabited marshland at Diamond Cay, this simple, open-air eatery has plastic chairs and tiled wooden tables overlooking a "marina" (really a small dock). But the menu is definitely more upscale here than at Foxy's place in Great Harbour. The Taboo burger at lunch is a hand-formed mound of 100% beef, served with mango chutney and pepperjack cheese on ciabata bread. House-made pizzas have toppings ranging from jalapeño peppers to proscuitto and kalamata olives. Dinner selections include mango-tamarind chicken. There are a dozen or more wines available by the bottle or glass. Don't miss the tiramisu for dessert. Dinner reservations are required by 5 PM. ⊠ *Diamond Cay* ☎ 284/495–0218 ⌂ *Reservations essential* ▭ *AE, MC, V* ⊗ *Closed Mon. No dinner Sun.*

$$–$$$$ ╳ **Sydney's Peace & Love.** Here you can find great lobster, caught aboard owner Sydney Hendrick's own fishing boat, as well as barbecue chicken and ribs. All is served on an open-air terrace or an air-conditioned dining room at the water's edge. The find here is a sensational (by BVI standards) jukebox. The cognoscenti sail here for dinner, since there's no beach—meaning no irksome sand fleas. ⊠ *Little Harbour* ☎ 284/495–9271 ▭ *D, MC, V.*

$$–$$$ ╳ **Abe's by the Sea.** Specialties at this popular, informal seaside spot include fresh lobster, conch, and spareribs. During the winter season there's a pig roast every Wednesday evening. ⊠ *Little Harbour* ☎ 284/495–9329 ▭ *D, MC, V.*

★
☼ **$$–$$$** ╳ **Ali Baba's.** This sandy-floor eatery offers beach-bar dining at its best. Lobster and grilled local fish, including swordfish, kingfish, and wahoo, are a specialty. There's a pig roast on Monday night. Beware: Ali Baba's special rum punch is delicious but potent. Dinner reservations are required by 6 PM. ⊠ *Great Harbour* ☎ 284/495–9280 ⌂ *Reservations essential* ▭ *AE, MC, V.*

☼ **$$–$$$** ╳ **Corsairs Beach Bar & Restaurant.** This beach bar is easily recognized by the restored U.S. Army Jeep that adjoins the dining area. Tex-Mex and Caribbean cuisine star at lunch, with selections ranging from lobster quesadillas to jerk chicken wings. Northern Italian takes over at night, when you can find seafood pomodoro, which is chockful of shrimp, fish, squid, and lobster. Live music and a great drink menu keep things moving at night. ⊠ *Great Harbour* ☎ 284/495–9294 ▭ *MC, V.*

★
☼ **$$–$$$** ╳ **Harris' Place.** Cynthia Harris is famous for her hospitality, along with her family's famous pig-roast buffets and Monday-night lobster specials. This is the hot spot to rub elbows with locals and the charter-boat crowd for breakfast, lunch, or dinner. ⊠ *Little Harbour* ☎ 284/495–9302 ▭ *AE, D, MC, V.*

$$–$$$ ✕ **Rudy's Mariner's Rendezvous.** Hamburgers, cheeseburgers, and barbecue ribs are the specialties at this beachfront spot at the extreme western end of Great Harbour. There's a lobster buffet every Thursday night in season. You can also find a superette here where you can buy basic groceries. ⊠ *Great Harbour* ☎ *284/495–9282* ▭ *D, MC, V.*

Beaches & Activities

Jost Van Dyke Safari Services. Native Jost Van Dyker Dorsey Chinnery is expert at navigating the steep roads here in his big, red open-air safari cab. He knows all the best spots to visit on a sightseeing tour and can help you with everything from beach-hopping to barhopping. His tours cost $20 per person. ☎ *284/495–9267 or 284/443–3832* ⊕ *www. bviwelcome.com/jvdsafari.*

JVD Scuba. See the undersea world around the island with divemaster Colin Aldridge. One of the most impressive dives in the area is off the north of Little Jost Van Dyke island. Here you'll find the Twin Towers: a pair of rock formations rising an impressive 90-feet. A one-tank dive costs $60, two-tank dive $95, and four-hour beginner course $120. ⊠ *Great Harbour* ☎ *284/495–0271* ⊕ *www.jvdwatersports.com.*

Sandy Cay. Just offshore, the little islet known as Sandy Cay is a gleaming scimitar of white sand, with marvelous snorkeling.

★ ☾ **White Bay.** On the south shore, west of Great Harbour, this long stretch of white sand is especially popular with boaters who come ashore for a libation at one of the beach bars.

Nightlife

★ Jost Van Dyke is the most happening place to go bar-hopping in the BVI. In fact, yachties will sail over just to have a few drinks. All the spots are easy to find, congregated in two general locations: Great Harbour and White Bay (⇨ *see* Where to Eat, *above*). On the Great Harbour side you can find Foxy's, Rudy's, and Ali Baba's; on the White Bay side is the One Love Bar & Grill, where Seddy Callwood will entertain you with his sleight of hand, and the Soggy Dollar bar at the Sandcastle restaurant, where legend has it the famous Painkiller was first concocted. If you can't make it to Jost Van Dyke, you can have a Painkiller at almost any bar in the BVI.

ANEGADA

Updated by
Lynda Lohr

Fodor's Choice
★

Anegada lies low on the horizon about 14 mi (22½ km) north of Virgin Gorda. Unlike the hilly volcanic islands in the chain, this is a flat coral-and-limestone atoll. Nine miles (14 km) long and 2 mi (3 km) wide, the island rises no more than 28 feet above sea level. In fact, by the time you're able to see it, you may have run your boat onto a reef. (More than 300 captains unfamiliar with the waters have done so since exploration days; note that bareboat charters don't allow their vessels to head here without a trained skipper.) Although the reefs are a sailor's nightmare, they (and the shipwrecks they've caused) are a scuba diver's dream. Snorkeling, especially in the waters around Loblolly Bay on the north shore, is also a transcendent experience. You can float in shallow, calm, reef-protected water just a few feet from shore and see one coral formation after another, each shimmering with a rainbow of colorful fish. Such watery pleasures are complemented by ever-so-fine, ever-so-white sand (the northern and western shores have long stretches of the stuff) and the occasional beach bar (stop in for burgers, Anegada lobster, or a frosty beer). The island's population of about 150 lives primarily in a small south-side village called the Settlement, which has two grocery stores, a bakery, and a general store. Many local fisherfolk are happy to take visitors out bonefishing.

Where to Stay

For approximate costs, *see* the lodging price chart *in* Tortola.

$$ 🏨 **Anegada Reef Hotel.** This may be the busiest place on sleepy Anegada. Although boaters drop anchor in sheltered waters inside the reef and guests from other hotels stop by for lobster salad lunches, the resort itself remains a serene spot. Head here if you want to relax in the shade on a beach that stretches forever, enjoy the company of like-minded folks, and do nothing more strenuous than heading out once or twice to fish the nearby waters. Rooms are simple but fresh with pastel fabrics. ⊠ *Setting Point* ☎ *284/495–8002* 🖷 *284/495–9362* ⊕ *www.anegadareef. com* ⌨ *16 rooms* ⌂ *Restaurant, beach, bar; no room phones, no room TVs* ⊟ *MC, V* ⦿ *AI.*

☙ $ 🏨 **Neptune's Treasure.** Basic beachside rooms with simple but squeaky-clean furnishings are the hallmark of this family-owned guesthouse. If you're happy with a simple place to rest your head (there aren't even TVs in the rooms) while you swim in crystal-clear waters, sun at the round-the-island beach, enjoy fresh-from-the-sea dinners at the hotel's restaurant, and watch the sun go down, this is the place. If you must move out of the hammock, the hotel will organize an island tour or a fishing expedition. ⊠ *Between Pomato and Saltheap points* ☎ *284/495–9439* 🖷 *284/495–8060* ⊕ *www.neptunestreasure.com* ⌨ *9 rooms* ⌂ *Restaurant, beach; no room TVs* ⊟ *MC, V* ⦿ *EP.*

Where to Eat

There are between 6 and 10 restaurants open at any one time, depending on the season and on whim. Check when you're on the island.

For approximate costs, *see* the dining price chart *in* Tortola.

AMERICAN– ✕ **Big Bamboo.** Ice-cold beer, fruity drinks, burgers, fresh fish, crab
CASUAL cakes, and grilled lobsters entice a steady stream of barefoot diners to
$$–$$$$ this beach bar for lunch. Dinner is by request only. ⊠ *Loblolly Bay West* ☎ *284/495–2019* ⊟ *MC, V.*

SEAFOOD ✕ **Pomato Point Restaurant.** This relaxed restaurant-bar is on a narrow
$$$–$$$$ beach a short walk from the Anegada Reef Hotel. Entrées include steak, lobster, stewed conch, and freshly caught seafood. Owner Wilfred Creque displays various island artifacts, including shards of Arawak pottery and 17th-century coins, cannonballs, and bottles. ⊠ *Pomato Point* ☎ *284/495–9466* ⌕ *Reservations essential* ⊟ *D, MC, V* ⊘ *Closed Sept.*

$$–$$$$ ✕ **Anegada Reef Hotel Restaurant.** Seasoned yachters gather here nightly to share tales of the high seas. Dinner is by candlelight and always includes famous Anegada lobster, steaks, and chicken—all prepared on the large grill by the little open-air bar. ⊠ *Anegada Reef Hotel, Setting Point* ☎ *284/495–8002* ⌂ *Reservations essential* ▭ *MC, V.*

$$–$$$$ ✕ **Cow Wreck Bar & Grill.** Named for the cow bones that once washed up on shore, this open-air beachside eatery is a fun place to watch the antics of surfers and kite boarders skidding across the bay. Tuck into conch fritters or a lobster salad sandwich for lunch or freshly grilled lobster for dinner. ⊠ *Loblolly Bay East* ☎ *284/495–8057* ▭ *MC, V.*

♻ **$$–$$$$** ✕ **Neptune's Treasure.** The owners catch, cook, and serve the seafood (lobster is a specialty, as is garlic-studded shark, in season) at this casual bar and restaurant in the Neptune's Treasure guesthouse. ⊠ *Between Pomato and Saltheap points* ☎ *284/495–9439* ▭ *MC, V.*

Shopping

Anegada Reef Hotel Boutique (⊠ Setting Point ☎ 284/495–8062) has a bit of everything: resort wear, hand-painted T-shirts, locally made jewelry, books, and one-of-a-kind gifts. At **Dotsy's Bakery** (⊠ The Settlement ☎ 284/495–9667) you can find a tempting array of fresh-baked breads, cookies, and desserts. Dotsy sells pizza and hamburgers too. **Pat's Pottery** (⊠ Nutmeg Point ☎ 284/495–8031) sells bowls, plates, cups, candlestick holders, and original watercolors.

OTHER BRITISH VIRGIN ISLANDS

For approximate costs, *see* the dining and lodging price charts *in* Tortola.

Cooper Island

This small, hilly island on the south side of the Sir Francis Drake Channel, about 8 mi (13 km) from Road Town, Tortola, is popular with the charter-boat crowd. There are no roads (which doesn't really matter, as there aren't any cars), but you can find a beach restaurant, a casual hotel, a few houses (some are available for rent), and great snorkeling at the south end of Manchioneel Bay.

$$ ✕▥ **Cooper Island Beach Club.** Cooper Island is one of those Caribbean spots that hark back to an earlier era when frills were few but the peaceful atmosphere was sublime. You usually either love the quiet or hate the isolation. Once you arrive via a complimentary ferry ride from Prospect Reef, Tortola, there's nothing to do but relax, enjoy the sun and the sea, and visit with old and new friends. Rooms are really small suites with basic cooking facilities, but the hotel's restaurant is nearby if you don't want to lug groceries on the ferry. Don't pack your hairdryer or electric shaver, because the hotel's primitive electrical system can't handle it. Meals run to basics like fish, chicken, and steak. Reservations are essential for the restaurant if you're not a resort guest. ⊠ *Manchioneel Bay* ⌂ *Box 859, Road Town, Tortola* ☎ *413/863–3162 or 800/542–4624* 🖷 *413/863–3662* ⊕ *www.cooper-island.com* ⇨ *12 rooms*

FodorśChoice
★

6

⚐ *Restaurant, fans, kitchens, beach, dive shop, bar; no a/c, no room phones, no room TVs* ☰ *MC, V* ◎| *EP.*

Guana Island

Guana Island sits off Tortola's northeast coast. Sailors often drop anchor at one of the island's bays for a day of snorkeling and sunning. The island is a designated wildlife sanctuary, and scientists often come here to study its flora and fauna. It's home to a back-to-nature resort that offers few activities other than relaxation. Unless you're a hotel guest or a sailor, there's no easy way to get here.

$$$$ ▦ **Guana Island Resort.** Guana Island is a nature lover's paradise, and it's a good resort if you want to stroll the hillsides, snorkel around the reefs, and swim at its six beaches, and still enjoy some degree of comfort. Rooms are simple but charming, with rattan furniture and tile floors, and open to the tropical breezes. Once you're here, you're here. You can spend your time dining and socializing with the other guests or immersed in that book you never got around to reading. You can rent the entire 15-room resort if you'd like to vacation with a group of your friends or family. The hotel's launch picks you up at Terrence B. Lettsome Airport on Beef Island (Tortola's airport) for the short hop across the water to the resort. ⊠ *Guana Island* ⌂ *Box 32, Road Town, Tortola* ☏ *284/494–2354 or 800/544–8262* 🖨 *284/495–2900* ⊕ *www.guana.com* ⇥ *15 rooms* ⚐ *Restaurant, fans, Wi-Fi, beach, dock, snorkeling, windsurfing, boating; no a/c, no room phones, no room TVs* ☰ *AE, MC, V* ◎| *FAP.*

Marina Cay

☺ Beautiful little Marina Cay is in Trellis Bay, not far from Beef Island. Sometimes you can see it and its large J-shape coral reefs—a most dramatic sight—from the air soon after takeoff from the airport on Beef Island. With only 8 acres, this islet is considered small even by BVI standards. On it there's a restaurant, Pusser's Store, and a six-unit hotel. Ferry service is free from the dock on Beef Island.

Where to Stay & Eat

$$–$$$$ ▦ **Pusser's Marina Cay Hotel & Restaurant.** If getting away from it all is your priority, this may be the place for you, because there's nothing more to do on this beach-rimmed island but swim, snorkel, and soak up the sun—there's not even a TV to distract you. Rooms, decorated in simple wicker and wood with floral-print fabrics, are on a hilltop facing the trade winds; two villas look right out to the morning sunrise. The laid-back tempo picks up at 4 PM for happy hour when charter boaters come ashore to hear local musicians entertain in the bar. The restaurant, open for lunch and dinner, offers a menu that ranges from fish and lobster to steak, chicken, and barbecued ribs. Pusser's Painkiller Punch is the house specialty. There's free ferry service from the Beef Island dock for anyone visiting the island, though ferry times and frequency vary with the seasons. ⊠ *West side of Marina Cay* ⌂ *Box 76, Road Town, Tortola* ☏ *284/494–2174* 🖨 *284/494–4775* ⊕ *www.pussers.com* ⇥ *4 rooms, 2 2-bedroom villas* ⚐ *Restaurant, fans, beach, bar, shop; no a/c, no room phones, no room TVs* ☰ *AE, MC, V* ◎| *CP.*

Peter Island

Although Peter Island is home to the resort of the same name, it's also a popular anchorage for charter boaters and a destination for Tortola vacationers. The scheduled ferry trip from Peter Island's shoreside base outside Road Town runs $15 round-trip for nonguests. The island is lush, with forested hillsides sloping seaward to meet white sandy beaches. There are no roads other than those at the resort, and there's nothing to do but relax at the lovely beach set aside for day-trippers. You're welcome to dine at the resort's restaurants.

$$$$ ✕▥ **Peter Island Resort.** Total pampering and the prices to match are the ticket at this luxury resort. If you want to while away your days at the beach, enjoy a morning at the spa, stroll the lushly planted grounds, and relax over dinner with other like-minded guests—and have the money to afford the steep rates—this is a good place to do it. For more active types, there are tennis and water sports galore. Peter Island is a half-hour ferry ride from Tortola, but once you arrive, you're in another world. The rooms are gorgeous, with thoughtful touches like showers with a view. A couple of villas sit above the hotel rooms. ⊠ *Peter Island* ✍ *Box 211, Road Town, Tortola* ☎ *284/495–2000 or 800/346–4451* 🖷 *284/495–2500* ⊕ *www.peterisland.com* ⬐ *52 rooms, 2 villas* ⚒ *2 restaurants, fans, in-room safes, pool, gym, massage, spa, beach, dive shop, dock, snorkeling, windsurfing, boating, bar, shop, Internet room; no room TVs* ⊟ *AE, MC, V* ❙⦿❙ *FAP.*

6

BRITISH VIRGIN ISLANDS ESSENTIALS

To research prices, get advice from other travelers, and book travel arrangements, visit www.fodors.com.

Transportation

BY AIR

There's no nonstop service from the continental United States to the BVI; connections are usually made through San Juan, Puerto Rico, or St. Thomas. You can also fly to Anegada and Virgin Gorda; these flights may originate in San Juan, St. Thomas, or Tortola.

All three of the BVI's airports—on Tortola (TOV), Virgin Gorda (VIJ), and Anegada (no code)—are classic Caribbean and almost always sleepy. However, the Terrence B. Lettsome Airport terminal at Beef Island can get crowded when several departures are scheduled close together.

🛪 Airline Contacts **Air Sunshine** ☎ 284/495–8900 ⊕ www.airsunshine.com. **American Eagle** ☎ 284/495–2559 ⊕ www.aa.com. **Cape Air** ☎ 284/495–2100 ⊕ www.flycapeair.com. **Fly BVI** ☎ 284/495–1747 ⊕ www.fly-bvi.com. **LIAT** ☎ 284/495–2577 ⊕ www.liatairline.com.

🛪 Airport Contacts **BVI Taxi Association** ☎ 284/494–3942. **Mahogany Rentals & Taxi Service** ⊠ Virgin Gorda ☎ 284/495–5469.

BY BOAT & FERRY

Ferries connect the airport gateway of St. Thomas, USVI, with Tortola and Virgin Gorda. They leave from both Charlotte Amalie and Red Hook. Ferries also link St. John, USVI, with Tortola, Jost Van Dyke, and Virgin Gorda, as well as Tortola with Jost Van Dyke, Peter Island, and Virgin Gorda. Tortola has two ferry terminals—one at West End and one in

Road Town—so make sure you hop a ferry that disembarks closest to where you want to go.

There's huge competition among the Tortola-based ferry companies on the St. Thomas–Tortola runs, with boats leaving close together. As you enter the ferry terminal to buy your ticket, crews may try to convince you to take their ferry. Ferries to Virgin Gorda land in the Valley. All ferries from the BVI to Red Hook, St. Thomas, stop in St. John to clear U.S. customs. Ferry schedules vary by day, and not all companies make daily trips. The BVI Tourist Board Web site (⇨ *see* Visitor Information, *below*) has links to all the ferry companies, which are the best up-to-date sources of information for specific routes and schedules.

🗺 **Inter-Island Boat Services** ☎ 284/495-4166. **Native Son** ☎ 284/495-4617 ⊕ www.nativesonbvi. com. **New Horizon Ferry Service** ☎ 284/495-9477. **North Sound Express** ☎ 284/495-2138. *Nubian Princess* ☎ 284/495-4999. **Peter Island Ferry** ☎ 284/495-2000 ⊕ www.peterisland.com. **Smith's Ferry** ☎ 284/495-4495 ⊕ www.smithsferry.com. **Speedy's Ferries** ☎ 284/495-5240 ⊕ www. speedysbvi.com.

BY CAR

Driving in the BVI is on the left side of the road, British style—but your car will have left-hand drive like those used in the United States. Speed limits (rarely enforced) are 20 mph in town and 35 mph outside town. Gas tends to be expensive. Tortola's main roads are well paved, for the most part, but there are exceptionally steep hills and sharp curves; driving demands your complete attention. A main road circles the island, and several roads cross it, almost always through mountainous terrain. Virgin Gorda has a smaller road system, and a single, very steep road links the north and south ends of the island. Anegada's few roads are little more than sandy lanes.

You need a temporary BVI license, available at the rental-car company for $10

with a valid license from another country. The minimum age to rent a car is 25. Most agencies offer both four-wheel-drive vehicles and cars (often compacts).

🗺 **Avis** ⊠ Opposite Police Station, Road Town, Tortola ☎ 284/494-3322. **D&D** ⊠ Waterfront Dr., close to West End, Tortola ☎ 284/495-7676. **D. W. Jeep Rentals** ⊠ The Settlement, Anegada ☎ 284/495-9677. **Hertz** ⊠ West End, Tortola ☎ 284/495-4405 ⊠ Airport, Tortola ☎ 284/495-2763 ⊠ Road Town, Tortola ☎ 284/494-6228. **Itgo Car Rental** ⊠ Wickham's Cay I, Road Town, Tortola ☎ 284/494-2639. **L&S Jeep Rental** ⊠ South Valley, Virgin Gorda ☎ 284/495-5297. **Mahogany Rentals & Taxi Service** ⊠ Spanish Town, Virgin Gorda ☎ 284/495-5469. **Speedy's Car Rentals** ⊠ The Valley, Virgin Gorda ☎ 284/495-5240.

BY TAXI

Your hotel staff will be happy to summon a taxi for you. Rates aren't set, so you should negotiate the fare with your driver before you start your trip. It's cheaper to travel in groups because there's a minimum fare to each destination, which is the same whether you have one, two, or three passengers. The taxi number is also the license plate number. On Tortola, the BVI Taxi Association has stands in Road Town near the ferry dock. The Beef Island Taxi Association operates at the Beef Island–Tortola airport. You can also usually find a West End Taxi Association ferry at the West End ferry dock.

Andy's Taxi & Jeep Rental offers service from one end of Virgin Gorda to the other. Mahogany Rentals & Taxi Service provides taxi service all over Virgin Gorda.

🗺 **Andy's Taxi & Jeep Rental** ⊠ The Valley, Virgin Gorda ☎ 284/495-5511. **Beef Island Taxi Association** ⊠ Beef Island Airport, Tortola ☎ 284/495-1982. **BVI Taxi Association** ⊠ Near the ferry dock, Road Town, Tortola ☎ 284/494-2322. **Mahogany Rentals & Taxi Service** ⊠ The Valley, Virgin Gorda ☎ 284/495-5469. **West End Taxi Association** ⊠ West End ferry terminal, Tortola ☎ 284/495-4934.

Contacts & Resources

BANKS & EXCHANGE SERVICES
The currency is the U.S. dollar. On Tortola, banks are near the Waterfront at Wickham's Cay I. All have ATM machines. Look for First Caribbean International Bank, First Bank, and Scotia Bank, among others. On Virgin Gorda, First Caribbean International isn't far from the ferry dock in Spanish Town.

BUSINESS HOURS
Banking hours are usually Monday through Thursday from 9 to 2:30 and Friday from 9 to 2:30 and 4:30 to 6. Post offices are open weekdays from 9 to 5 and Saturday from 9 to noon. Stores are generally open Monday through Saturday from 9 to 5. Some may be open on Sunday.

ELECTRICITY
Electricity is 110 volts, the same as in North America, so European appliances will require adapters. The electricity is quite reliable.

EMERGENCIES
🛈 Ambulance, Fire & Police **General emergencies** ☎ 999.
🛈 Hospitals & Clinics **Anegada Government Health Clinic** ☎ 284/495-8049. **Jost Van Dyke Government Health Clinic** ☎ 284/495-9239. **Peebles Hospital** ✉ Road Town, Tortola ☎ 284/494-3497. **Virgin Gorda Government Health Clinic** ✉ The Valley ☎ 284/495-5337.
🛈 Marine Emergencies **VISAR** ☎ 767 from phone or Marine Radio Channel 16.
🛈 Pharmacies **Island Drug Centre** ✉ Spanish Town, Virgin Gorda ☎ 284/495-5449. **J. R. O'Neal Drug Store** ✉ Road Town, Tortola ☎ 284/494-2292. **Medicure Pharmacy** ✉ Road Town, Tortola ☎ 284/494-6189 ✉ Spanish Town, Virgin Gorda ☎ 284/495-5479.

HOLIDAYS
The following public holidays are celebrated in the BVI: New Year's Day, Commonwealth Day (Mar. 14), Good Friday (Fri. before Easter), Easter Sunday (usually Mar. or Apr.), Easter Monday (day after Easter), Whit Monday (1st Mon. in May), Sovereign's Birthday (June 16), Territory Day (July 1), BVI August Festival Days (usually 1st 2 wks in Aug.), St. Ursula's Day (Oct. 21), Christmas, and Boxing Day (day after Christmas).

INTERNET, MAIL & SHIPPING
There are post offices in Road Town on Tortola and in Spanish Town on Virgin Gorda. Postage for a first-class letter to the United States and Canada is 50¢. Postcards to the United States and Canada are 35¢. For a small fee, Rush It, in Road Town and in Spanish Town, offers most U.S. mail and UPS services (via St. Thomas the next day). If you wish to write to an establishment in the BVI, be sure to include the specific island in the address; there are no postal codes. Some businesses have a USVI postal address.
🛈 Shipping Contacts **Rush It** ✉ Road Town, Tortola ☎ 284/494-4421 ✉ Spanish Town, Virgin Gorda ☎ 284/495-5821.

PASSPORTS REQUIREMENTS
U.S. and Canadian citizens, as well as citizens of all other countries, need a valid passport.

SAFETY
Although crime is rare, use common sense: don't leave your camera on the beach while you take a dip or your wallet on a hotel dresser when you go for a walk.

TAXES
The departure tax is $5 per person by boat and $20 per person by plane. There's a separate booth at the airport and ferry terminals to collect this tax, which must be paid in cash in U.S. currency. Most hotels add a service charge ranging from 5% to 18% to the bill. A few restaurants and some shops tack on an additional 10% charge if you use a credit card. There's no sales tax in the BVI. However, there's a 7% government tax on hotel rooms.

TELEPHONES
Your mobile phone may or may not work in the BVI. If you are on the south side of

Tortola, you may be able to connect to Cingular and Sprint, but other islands are problematic. The BVI has local companies only. Even if your U.S. mainland company assures you that your phone will work, don't count on it.

The area code for the BVI is 284; when you make calls from North America, you need only dial the area code and the number. From the United Kingdom you must dial 001 and then the area code and the number. From Australia and New Zealand you must dial 0011 followed by 1, the area code, and the number.

To call anywhere in the BVI once you've arrived, dial all seven digits. A local call from a pay phone costs 25¢, but such phones are sometimes on the blink. An alternative is a Caribbean phone card, available in $5, $10, and $20 denominations. They're sold at most major hotels and many stores and can be used to call within the BVI, as well as all over the Caribbean, and to access USADirect from special phone-card phones. For credit card or collect long-distance calls to the United States, use a phone-card telephone or look for special USADirect phones, which are linked directly to an AT&T operator. USADirect and pay phones can be found at most hotels and in towns.

🛈 **USA Direct** ☎ 800/872-2881, 111 from a pay phone.

TIPPING

Tip porters and bellhops $1 per bag. Sometimes a service charge (10%) is included on restaurant bills; it's customary to leave another 5% if you liked the service. If no charge is added, 15% is the norm. Cabbies normally aren't tipped because most own their cabs; add 10% to 15% if they exceed their duties.

TOUR OPTIONS

Romney Associates/Travel Plan Tours can arrange island tours, boat tours, snorkeling and scuba-diving trips, dolphin swims, and yacht charters from its Tortola and Virgin Gorda bases.

🛈 **Romney Associates/Travel Plan Tours** ☎ 284/494-4000

VISITOR INFORMATION

🛈 **BVI Tourist Board** ⊠ Ferry Terminal, Road Town, Tortola ☎ 284/494-3134. **Virgin Gorda BVI Tourist Board** ⊠ Virgin Gorda Yacht Harbour, Spanish Town, Virgin Gorda ☎ 284/495-5181.

WEDDINGS

Getting married in the BVI is a breeze, but you must make advance plans. To make things go smoother, hire a wedding planner to guide you through the ins and outs of the BVI system. Many hotels also have wedding planners on staff to help organize your event. Hotels often offer packages that include the ceremony; accommodations for you, your wedding party and your guests; and extras like massages, sailboat trips, and champagne dinners.

You must apply in person for your license ($110) weekdays at the attorney general's office in Road Town, Tortola. You must wait three days to pick it up at the registrar's office in Road Town. If you plan to be married in a church, announcements (called *banns* locally) must be published for three consecutive Sundays in the church bulletin. Only the registrar or clergy can perform ceremonies. The registrar charges $35 at the office and $100 at another location. No blood test is required.

🛈 **BVI Wedding Planners & Consultants** ☎ 284/494-5306 ⊕ www.bviweddings.com.

Cayman Islands

Coral reef, Little Cayman Island

WORD OF MOUTH

"We love Eden Rock. We've seen things there we've never seen at any of the other places we snorkeled. Last year it was the biggest barracuda we'd ever seen . . . the year before it was several turtles."

—SuzieC

"Cayman Brac is VERY laid back. Hardly anyone there. Most tourists are divers. . . . The diving at Brac was the best dive vacation we have done."

—Kima

WELCOME TO THE CAYMAN ISLANDS

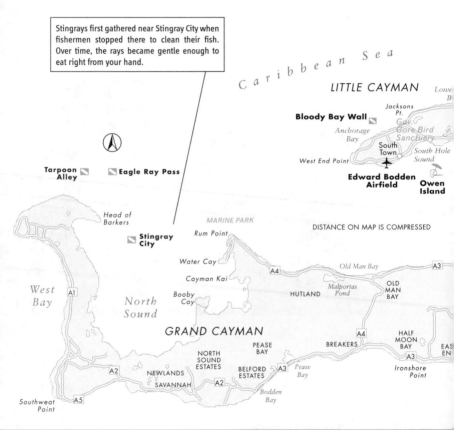

Stingrays first gathered near Stingray City when fishermen stopped there to clean their fish. Over time, the rays became gentle enough to eat right from your hand.

Caribbean Sea

LITTLE CAYMAN

Lowe B

Bloody Bay Wall

Jacksons Pt.

Gov.

Gore Bird Sanctuary

Anchorage Bay

South Town

South Hole Sound

West End Point

Edward Bodden Airfield

Owen Island

Tarpoon Alley

Eagle Ray Pass

Head of Barkers

MARINE PARK

DISTANCE ON MAP IS COMPRESSED

Stingray City

Rum Point

Water Cay

Old Man Bay

A3

A4

Cayman Kai

Malportas Pond

OLD MAN BAY

West Bay

A1

North Sound

Booby Cay

HUTLAND

GRAND CAYMAN

BREAKERS

A4

HALF MOON BAY

EAS EN

NORTH SOUND ESTATES

PEASE BAY

A3

A2

NEWLANDS

BELFORD ESTATES

A3

Pease Bay

Ironshore Point

SAVANNAH

A2

Southweat Point

A5

Bodden Bay

Grand Cayman may be the world's largest offshore finance hub, but other offshore activities have put the Caymans on the map. Pristine waters, breathtaking coral formations, and plentiful and exotic marine creatures beckon divers from around the world. Other vacationers are drawn by the islands' mellow civility.

FUN ON AND OFF SHORE

Grand Cayman, which is 22 mi (36 km) long and 8 mi (13 km) wide, is the largest of the three low-lying islands that make up this British colony. Its sister islands (Little Cayman and Cayman Brac) are almost 90 mi (149 km) north and east. The Cayman Trough between the Cayman Islands and Jamaica is the deepest part of the Caribbean.

Cayman Brac is named for its 140-foot bluff on the island's eastern end, which is the highest point in the Cayman Islands chain.

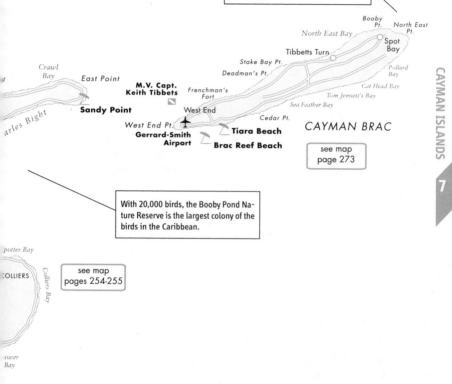

With 20,000 birds, the Booby Pond Nature Reserve is the largest colony of the birds in the Caribbean.

see map
page 273

see map
pages 254-255

CAYMAN ISLANDS

7

TOP 4 REASONS TO VISIT THE CAYMAN ISLANDS

1. Underwater visibility (about 120 feet) is among the best in the Caribbean, and nearby, healthy reefs make this one of the Caribbean's top dive destinations.

2. With no panhandlers, little crime, and excellent resorts and restaurants, it's an easy place to vacation.

3. A snorkeling trip to Sting Ray Sandbar is an experience you'll always remember.

4. Grand Cayman's Seven Mile Beach is one of the Caribbean's best sandy beaches.

CAYMAN ISLANDS PLANNER

Getting to the Cayman Islands

There are plenty of nonstop flights to Grand Cayman (GCM) from North America, the U.K., and Jamaica. There is also one weekly nonstop from Miami to Cayman Brac (CYB), though most people hop over to the Brac and Little Cayman (LYB) on a small plane from Grand Cayman. Flights land at Owen Roberts Airport (Grand Cayman), Gerrard-Smith Airport (Cayman Brac), or Edward Bodden Airstrip (Little Cayman).

Hassle Factor: Low for Grand Cayman; Medium for Little Cayman and Cayman Brac

Activities

Diving is a major draw to all three of the Cayman Islands; the Bloody Bay Wall, off the coast of Little Cayman, is one of the Caribbean's top dive destinations, but there are many sites convenient to Grand Cayman, where shore diving is also good. One of the most popular activities on Grand Cayman is a dive or snorkeling trip to **Stingray City** or Stingray Sandbar; petting and feeding the amazing creatures is a highlight of many Caribbean trips. On land, Grand Cayman has the most to offer, with plenty of tours and activities, including **semi-submersible tours** of the bay for those who want to see under the waves without getting wet. Grand Cayman's **Seven Mile Beach** is one of the Caribbean's finest long stretches of sand. **Rock climbers** have now discovered the Brac's limestone bluff.

On the Ground

In Grand Cayman you must take a taxi or rent a car at the airport since most hotels are not permitted to offer airport shuttles. Hotel pickup is more readily available on Cayman Brac and Little Cayman, and taxi service and car rentals are also available on the smaller islands as well.

Renting a Car

It's possible to get by without a car on Grand Cayman if you are staying in the Seven Mile Beach area, where there are both buses and plentiful—albeit fairly expensive—taxis. (You must call a taxi; they can't be hailed on the street.) You could even walk or ride a bike. If you want to explore the rest of the island or if you are staying in a condo, you'll probably want a car.

A car is less of a necessity on Cayman Brac or Little Cayman, but cars are available on both islands. Many resorts will loan or rent you a bicycle to get around, and that will often suffice, though Cayman Brac is large enough that a car can be a convenience.

To rent a car, bring your valid driver's license, and the car-rental firm will issue you a temporary permit ($7.50). Most firms offer everything from compacts to Jeeps to minibuses. Rates range from $40 to $85 a day. If you're staying in the Seven Mile Beach area of Grand Cayman, most agencies offer free pick-up, which is convenient if you don't want to rent a car immediately upon landing at the airport.

Where to Stay

Grand Cayman draws the bulk of Cayman Island visitors and is a well-developed destination with plenty to offer those looking to relax or dive the nearby reefs. It's expensive during the high season but offers the widest range of resorts, restaurants, and activities both in and out of the water; most resorts are on or near Seven Mile Beach, but a few are north in the West Bay Area, near Rum Point, or on the quiet East End. Both Little Cayman and Cayman Brac are more geared toward serving the needs of divers, who still make up the majority of visitors. Beaches on the Sister Islands, as they are called, don't measure up to Grand Cayman's Seven Mile Beach. Still, Cayman Brac has a fairly wide range of small, intimate resorts—several of them fairly upscale—as well as some independent restaurants, but the atmosphere is quiet. Little Cayman is quieter still, and you'll most likely eat where you stay. The smaller islands are cheaper than Grand Cayman, but with the extra cost of transportation, the overall cost is usually a wash.

TYPES OF LODGINGS

Grand Cayman:		**The Sister Islands:**
Grand Cayman has plenty of medium-sized resorts as well as a new Ritz-Carlton, a 7-story behemoth on Seven Mile Beach. The island also has a wide range of condos	and villas, many in resort-like compounds on or near Seven Mile Beach and the Cayman-Kai area. There are even a few small guest houses for budget-minded visitors.	Cayman Brac has mostly intimate resorts. Little Cayman has a mix of small resorts and condos, most appealing to divers.

Hotel & Restaurant Costs

Assume that hotels operate on the European Plan (**EP**—with no meals) unless we specify that they use either the Continental Plan (**CP**—with a Continental breakfast), Breakfast Plan (**BP**—with full breakfast), or the Modified American Plan (**MAP**—with breakfast and dinner). Other hotels may offer the Full American Plan (**FAP**—including all meals but no drinks) or may be All-Inclusive (**AI**—with all meals, drinks, and most activities).

WHAT IT COSTS in Dollars

	$$$$	**$$$**	**$$**	**$**	**¢**
Restaurants	over $30	$20–$30	$12–$20	$8–$12	under $8
Hotels*	over $350	$250–$350	$150–$250	$80–$150	under $80
Hotels**	over $450	$350–$450	$250–$350	$125–$250	under $125

*EP, BP, CP   **AI, FAP, MAP
Restaurant prices are for a main course at dinner. Hotel prices are for a double room in high season, excluding 10% tax, 10–15% service charges, and meal plans (escept at all-inclusives).

When to Go

High season begins in mid-December and continues through early to mid-April. During the low season, you can often get a substantial discount of as much as 40%.

Grand Cayman has two major events: the **Batabano Carnival** in April and **Pirates** Week in late October. Pirates Week is a Carnival-like celebration, when visitors and locals dress up as pirates and wenches; music, fireworks, parades, street dances, and competitions take place island-wide.

During the Cayman Islands **International Fishing Tournament** in April, fishermen can enjoy plenty of action and win big prizes.

7

Updated by
Cathy Church

THE SIGNPOST just past the airport–post office–fire station on Little Cayman reads IGUANAS HAVE THE RIGHT OF WAY. Many of these prehistoric-looking lizards lurk about the island, which is the smallest of the three Cayman Islands. According to Gladys, of Pirates Point, iguanas love grapes. She keeps extras on hand just so her guests can feed them to the beasts. That kind of hospitality is the norm on an island where the repeat guest list is high and the police officer has yet to use his siren. Each of the Cayman Islands has its own pace; from Grand Cayman to the Brac to Little Cayman, it's slow, slower, slowest.

This British colony, which consists of Grand Cayman, smaller Cayman Brac, and Little Cayman, is one of the Caribbean's most popular destinations. Columbus is said to have sighted the islands in 1503 and dubbed them Las Tortugas after seeing so many turtles in the sea. The name was later changed to Cayman, referring to the caiman crocodiles that once roamed the islands. The Cayman Islands remained largely uninhabited until the late 1600s, when England took them and Jamaica from Spain. Emigrants from England, Holland, Spain, and France arrived, as did refugees from the Spanish Inquisition and deserters from Oliver Cromwell's army in Jamaica; many brought slaves with them as well. The Caymans' caves and coves were also perfect hideouts for the likes of Blackbeard, Sir Henry Morgan, and other pirates out to plunder Spanish galleons. Many ships fell afoul of the reefs surrounding the islands, often with the help of Caymanians, who lured vessels to shore with beacon fires.

Today's Caymans are seasoned with suburban prosperity (particularly Grand Cayman, where residents joke that the national flower is the satellite dish) and stuffed with crowds (the hotels that line the famed Seven Mile Beach are often full, even in the slow summer season). Most of the 44,000 Cayman Islanders live on Grand Cayman, where the cost of living is at least 20% higher than in the United States, but you won't be hassled by panhandlers or feel afraid to walk around on a dark evening (the crime rate is very low). Add political and economic stability to the mix, and you have a fine island recipe indeed.

GRAND CAYMAN

Grand Cayman has long been known for two offshore activities: banking and scuba diving. With 349 banks, the capital, George Town, is relatively modern and usually bustles with activity, but never more so than when two to seven cruise ships are docked in the harbor, an increasingly common occurrence. Accountants in business clothes join thousands of vacationers in their tropical togs, jostling for tables at lunch. When they're not mingling in the myriad shops, vacationers delve into sparkling waters to snorkel and dive, but increasingly, couples are also coming to be married, or at least to enjoy their honeymoon.

In September 2004, Grand Cayman was hit hard by Hurricane Ivan, and the effects on the mangroves and large trees are still visible. There is a lot of new construction and plenty of traffic, so check with a local to plan driving time. It can take 45 minutes during rush hours to go 8 mi.

Where to Stay

The massive Ritz-Carlton complex on Seven Mile Beach is the first of several developments to build under new laws allowing seven-story buildings. It's the tallest and largest resort complex on Grand Cayman. Brace yourself for resort prices—there are few accommodations in the lower price ranges. You'll find no all-inclusive resorts on Grand Cayman, and very few offer a meal plan. Parking is always free at island hotels and resorts.

Hotels

★ �™ **$$$$** □ **Hyatt Regency Grand Cayman Beach Suites.** This impersonal resort has no garden area, so the setting is one of concrete and elevators. Nevertheless, the ocean-view suites are plush, with a living room and a kitchenette; the higher the room, the smaller the balcony, but your view gets more stunning. Furnishings are a bit formal. Nice Hyatt touches like bathtubs for two and canopied beach chairs do help to make you comfortable. At this writing, the fate of the main hotel building, which was damaged by Hurricane Ivan, was still undecided. ⊠ *West Bay Rd., Box 1698, Seven Mile Beach* ☎ *345/949–1234 or 800/233–1234* 🖷 *345/949–8528* ⊕ *grandcayman.hyatt.com* ⤴ *53 beach suites, 112 rooms and 10 suites in main hotel* ⚭ *2 restaurants, in-room safes, kitchenettes, cable TV with movies, in-room data ports, Wi-Fi, 9-hole golf course, pool, gym, hair salon, spa, beach, dive shop, snorkeling, windsurfing, boating, parasailing, waterskiing, bar, shops, children's programs (ages 3–12), concierge, car rental* ▤ *AE, D, DC, MC, V* ❙◎❙ *EP.*

☞ **$$$$** □ **Ritz-Carlton.** The Ritz-Carlton, Grand Cayman offers a level of luxury and service not available elsewhere in the Cayman Islands. The 144-acre resort is anchored by a seven-story behemoth that faces Seven Mile Beach on the west and the North Sound on the east. The amenities are luxurious and were designed by top professionals. Two of the five restaurants are headed by Eric Ripert of Le Bernardin, rated the finest in New York. The golf course was designed by Greg Norman; tennis is run by Nick Bellettieri (coach of great players like Andre Agassi); and the Ambassadors of the Environment children's program is run by none other than Jean-Michel Cousteau. The Ritz specialty is service: your caddy offers coaching and concierge services, the tennis courts have video cameras for interactive personal-play analysis, the masseuse will come to your room, and a personal chef can prepare your meal in the kitchen in your suite. ⚲ *Box 32348 SMB, Seven Mile Beach* ☎ *345/943–9000* 🖷 *345/943–9001* ⊕ *www.ritzcarlton.com* ⤴ *329 rooms, 12 suites, 24 condominiums* ⚭ *5 restaurants, in-room safes, some kitchens, minibars, cable TV, in-room DVDs, in-room data ports, Wi-Fi, 2 pools, spa, dive shop, bar, laundry facilities* ▤ *AE, D, MC, V* ❙◎❙ *BP.*

☞ **$$$–$$$$** □ **Cobalt Coast Resort & Suites.** This small hotel is perfect for divers who want a sparkling, spacious, stylish room or suite right on the ironshore, far from the busy beach. The management pays attention to the details and has succeeded in producing a wonderful place to get away and just dive. The dive operation, Dive Tech, runs smoothly, and the restaurant is surprisingly good for such a small hotel. Add great shore diving (espe-

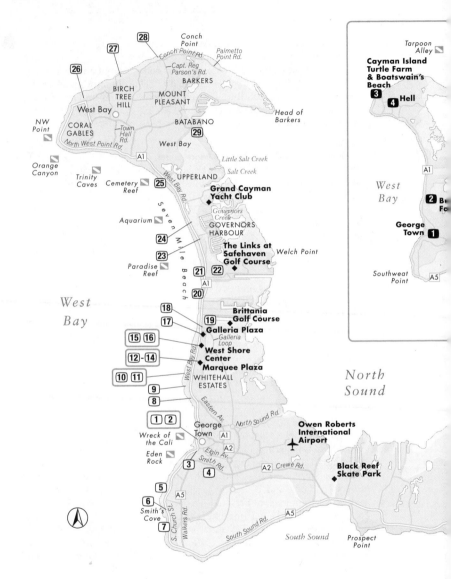

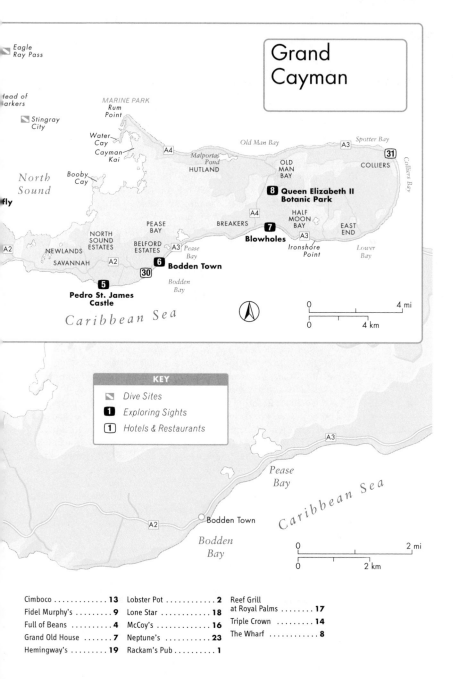

Grand
Cayman

KEY

Dive Sites

1 Exploring Sights

1 Hotels & Restaurants

cially in the calmer summer season) and this is a no-brainer. ☒ 18-A Sea Fan Dr., West Bay ☎345/946–5656 🖷345/946–5657 ⊕www.cobaltcoast. com ⤳7 rooms, 11 suites ⚘ Restaurant, in-room safes, some kitchens, refrigerators, cable TV, in-room data ports, Wi-Fi, pool, hot tub, dive shop, bar, laundry facilities, airport shuttle ⊟ AE, D, MC, V ⦿ BP.

🐚 **$$$–$$$$** 🏨 **Westin Casuarina Resort & Spa.** The Westin has something to offer everyone. You can walk a perfect beach, enjoy the sumptuous spa, dine in a great restaurant, or lounge in the pool with an ocean view. The sophisticated room decor includes rich wood furnishings and pampering showers. Many of the ocean-view rooms, which were remodeled in 2005, have better-than-advertised views. The kids' club offers games, swimming, and sand-castle building for ages 4 through 12. ☒ West Bay Rd., Box 30620, Seven Mile Beach ☎ 345/945–3800 or 800/228–3000 🖷 345/949–5825 ⊕ www.westin.com ⤳ 339 rooms, 8 suites ⚘ 3 restaurants, minibars, cable TV, in-room broadband, pool, gym, 2 hot tubs, beach, dive shop, 3 bars, shops, meeting rooms ⊟ AE, MC, V ⦿ EP.

🐚 **$$–$$$** 🏨 **Grand Cayman Marriott Beach Resort.** The airy, marble lobby has a high ceiling and opens onto a lovely courtyard filled with tropical plants. Large adjoining rooms are ideal for families, and all have balconies and new hardwood furniture. The beach, pool, beach bar, and dive center with water toys fills every waterside need. Add to this a lovely open-air restaurant that serves superb food, and you don't need to leave the property. When you do, it's a short walk to more restaurants and stores. This is a good value. ☒ West Bay Rd., Box 30371, Seven Mile Beach ☎345/949–0088 or 800/228–9290 🖷345/949–0288 ⊕ www.marriott.com ⤳ 309 rooms, 4 suites ⚘ Restaurant, in-room safes, some refrigerators, cable TV, pool, hair salon, hot tub, spa, beach, dive shop, snorkeling, windsurfing, bar, shops, dry cleaning, laundry facilities, Internet room, business services, meeting rooms, car rental ⊟ AE, D, DC, MC, V ⦿ EP.

★ **$$–$$$** 🏨 **Sunshine Suites Resort.** This friendly all-suites hotel is an impeccably clean money saver. The rooms don't have balconies, patios, or even much of a view, but each has a complete kitchen, and there's an outdoor grill you can use for picnics. It's a five-minute walk to Seven Mile Beach, where the resort provides beach chairs and towels near the Westin Resort. Breakfast is served poolside. Guests get free access to a local gym; the resort provides lockers for dive gear. ☒ West Bay Rd., George Town ☎ 345/949–3000 or 877/786–1110 🖷 345/949–1200 ⊕ www.sunshinesuites. com ⤳ 130 suites ⚘ Restaurant, kitchens, cable TV with movies, in-room data ports, Wi-Fi, pool, laundry facilities, business services, meeting room, car rental ⊟ AE, D, MC, V ⦿ CP.

★ 🐚 **$$** 🏨 **Courtyard by Marriott Grand Cayman.** If you can ignore the unattractive parking lot and the busy road between the hotel and the beach, this is a good hotel and a real value. The huge swimming pool behind the hotel has a relaxing, tropical setting. After a hard day snorkeling and lounging at the beach, you can visit the seaside beach-bar shack to watch the sunset. Up to two kids under 16 can stay free in their parents' room. The restaurant serves everything from burgers to a fine salmon with mustard sauce. ☒ West Bay Rd., West Bay ☎ 345/946–4433, 800/228–9290 reservations 🖷 345/946–4434 ⊕ www.marriott.com ⤳ 231 rooms, 1 2-bedroom suite ⚘ 2 restaurants, refrigerators, cable

TV, in-room broadband, pool, gym, beach, dive shop, 2 bars, dry cleaning, laundry facilities, laundry service, business services, meeting room, car rental ▭ AE, D, MC, V ¶ EP.

$$ **Sunset House.** This friendly seaside resort is on the ironshore south of George Town, close enough for a short trip to stores and restaurants yet far enough away to feel secluded. The rooms are simple, but good diving and a homey atmosphere are the main attractions. A 9-foot bronze mermaid, a small wreck, and friendly angel fish supplement a terrific reef just steps from the rooms. The thatched-roof My Bar is popular for a casual meal or a sunset drink. The world-famous Cathy Church's Underwater Photo Centre and Gallery is based here to round out the island's best diving services. ✉ *S. Church St., Box 479GT, George Town* ☎ *345/949–7111 or 800/854–4767* 📠 *345/949–7101* 🌐 *www.sunsethouse.com* *58 rooms, 2 suites* *Restaurant, cable TV, pool, dive shop, bar, laundry facilities, Internet room* ▭ *AE, D, MC, V* ¶ *EP.*

$–$$ **Spanish Bay Reef Resort.** Secluded on the remote northwest tip of the island, Grand Cayman's only all-inclusive resort is blessed with wonderful shore diving, especially during the calmer summer months. Boardwalks connect simple guest rooms. Though it's showing signs of age, the resort does offer a pleasant level of privacy. There's a sandy strip of beach between the sea wall and the pool area. ✉ *167 Conch Point Rd., Box 903, West Bay* ☎ *345/949–3765* 📠 *345/949–1842* *67 rooms* *Restaurant, cable TV, pool, hot tub, snorkeling, bar* ▭ *AE, D, MC, V* ¶ *AI.*

$–$$ **Turtle Nest Inn.** Fodor's Choice ★ This affordable, intimate seaside inn, with interesting art on the walls, has roomy one-bedroom apartments and a pool overlooking a narrow beach with good snorkeling. It's perched at the roadside in Bodden Town, the island's original capital, which was heavily damaged in Hurricane Ivan. Views that once included lush foliage now oversee (temporarily) a broken village. The closest grocery store is about 25 minutes away, so rent a car. ✉ *Red Bay Rd., Bodden Town* ☎ *345/947–8665* 📠 *345/947–6379* 🌐 *www.turtlenestinn.com* *8 apartments* *Kitchens, cable TV, in-room DVDs, pool, beach, laundry facilities* ▭ *AE, D, MC, V* ¶ *EP.*

Guesthouses

They may be some distance from the beach and short on style and facilities, but these guesthouses offer rock-bottom prices, a friendly atmosphere, and your best shot at getting to know the locals. Rooms are clean and simple, and most have private baths.

$–$$ **Eldemire's B&B Guest House.** You're about 15 minutes from Seven Mile Beach at this guesthouse south of George Town, but you're less than 1 mi (1½ km) north of Smith Cove Beach. Rooms, which have cheery walls and basic furniture, are homey and cozy. You only get breakfast with the regular rooms. ✉ *18 Pebbles Way, off S. Church St., Box 482, George Town* ☎ *345/949–5387* 📠 *345/949–6987* 🌐 *www.eldemire.com* *6 rooms, 2 studios, 3 apartments* *Fans, some kitchens, some kitchenettes, cable TV, pool; no room phones* ▭ *MC, V* ¶ *EP.*

$ **Rocky Shore Guest House.** Come here if you really want to connect with Cayman. Owner Chris is a Caymanian artist, a nice young man who will teach you about local crafts. His wife, Trina, offers complete massage services. Both will help you experience local foods, such as an evening together enjoying fish tea, a popular spicy fish soup. Since it's in an inland residential area—complete with kids and dogs a half-mile from Cobalt Coast Resort—you'll need a car. The two cheapest rooms share a bath. ⊠ *30 Grass Piece La., West Bay* ☎ *345/926–0119* 🖷 *345/946–0118* ⊕ *www.getaway.ky* 🛏 *4 rooms, 2 with private bath* ♨ *Fans, some kitchens, some kitchenettes, cable TV; no room phones* ▤ *MC, V* ⊙ *CP.*

Villas & Condominiums

Most condo complexes are very similar, with telephones, satellite TV, air-conditioning, living and dining areas, patios, and parking. Differences are amenities, proximity to town and beach, and the views. As with resorts, rates are higher in winter, and there may be a three- or seven-night minimum. The **Cayman Islands Department of Tourism** (⊕ www. caymanislands.ky) provides a list of condominiums and small rental apartments. There are dozens of large private villas available on the beach, especially on the North Side near Cayman Kai. There are several Web sites, including www.caymanvillas.com

★ **$$$$** ⊞ **Lacovia Condominiums.** The courtyard area of this handsome condo property could be a quiet park. Large shade trees somehow escaped hurricane Ivan in 2004, and thick, lush gardens full of flowers are everywhere. What's missing is the usual pressure of traffic, construction, and concrete walls so common in this area of Grand Cayman. That and perhaps the big, green iguanas, which we've heard about but haven't seen. The condos themselves are nicely kept and have contemporary decor. The beach here is wide and soft, with more wonderful shade trees and thatched gazebos. It is a short walk to a shopping center, a grocery store, restaurants, dive shops, and nightlife. ⊠ *Seven Mile Beach* ☎ *345/949–7599* 🖷 *345/949–0172* ⊕ *www.lacovia.com* 🛏 *35 1; 2; and 3-bedroom condos* ♨ *Kitchens, cable TV, in-room broadband, pool, tennis court, gym, hot tub, beach, laundry facilities* ▤ *AE, D, MC, V* ⊙ *EP.*

☾ **$$–$$$$** ⊞ **Discovery Point Club.** This complex of all oceanfront suites is at the north end of Seven Mile Beach, 6 mi (9½ km) from George Town. It has a fabulous beach and great snorkeling in the protected waters of nearby Cemetery Reef. Tennis courts, a pool, and screened-in private porches add to the high appeal here; kids six and under stay free. Studios—which are really hotel rooms—do not have full kitchens. ⊠ *West Bay Rd., Box 439, West Bay* ☎ *345/945–4724* 🖷 *345/945–5051* ⊕ *www.discoverypointclub.com* 🛏 *16 studios, 19 1-bedroom condos, 12 2-bedroom condos* ♨ *BBQs, some kitchens, some kitchenettes, cable TV, 2 tennis courts, pool, beach, laundry facilities* ▤ *AE, D, MC, V* ⊙ *EP.*

★ **$$–$$$$** ⊞ **Reef Resort.** This well-run time-share property on the less hectic east end of Grand Cayman offers good value. You'll need a car; it's a 45-minute drive to George Town. Each villa has a roomy terrace facing the sea. The famous "Barefoot Man" sings at Castro's Hideaway on Tuesday and Thursday; his lighthearted songs on scuba diving and Caribbean life are lots of fun. The beach is terrific and uncrowded. ⊠ *Queen's Hwy., Box 20865 SMB, East End* ☎ *345/947–3100, 800/221–8090, 954/485–5412 reservations* 🖷 *345/947–3191* ⊕ *www.thereef.com.ky* 🛏 *70 suites* ♨ *Restaurant, grocery, fans, some kitchens, some kitchenettes,* *refrigerators, cable TV, tennis court, pools, gym, hair salon, outdoor hot tub, spa, beach, dive shop, dock, snorkeling, boating, bicycles, bar, laundry facilities, concierge; no smoking* ⊟ *AE, MC, V* ⦿ *EP.*

Where to Eat

Grand Cayman dining is casual (even shorts are okay, but *not* beach-wear and tank tops, of course). Mosquitoes can be pesky when you are dining outdoors, especially at sunset, so plan ahead or ask for repellent. Winter can be chilly enough to warrant a light sweater. You should make reservations at all but the most casual places, particularly during the high season.

Prices are about 30% more than those in a major U.S. city. Many restaurants add a 10% to 15% service charge to the bill; be sure to check before leaving a tip. Alcohol with your meal can send the tab skyrocketing. Buy liquor duty-free before you leave the airport and enjoy a cocktail or nightcap from the comfort of your room or balcony. Cayman customs limits you to two bottles per person.

Don't hesitate to try the local cuisine. Turtle is the traditional specialty of the Cayman Islands and can be served in soup or stew or as a steak. Conch, the meat of a large pink mollusk, is ubiquitous in stews and chowders, fritters and panfried (cracked). Fish—including snapper, tuna, wahoo, and marlin—is served baked, broiled, steamed, or "Cayman-style" (with peppers, onions, and tomatoes). Caribbean lobster is available, but there are no other shellfish in local waters. Many of these dishes would suit any palate, while the unique flavors of codfish, ackee, or curried goat may appeal to the more adventurous diner.

AMERICAN
★ ☺ $–$$$ ✕ **McCoy's.** This is a good family restaurant, with an artistic Caribbean ambience. The food varies from roasted red-pepper hummus to Cayman burgers to seafood and steak dinners prepared with flavor. However, all the prices are nice and low, making this a good value. The bar is partitioned from the restaurant. A kids' menu and special late-night menu (served until midnight) are pluses. ⊠ *West Shore Centre, West Bay Rd., Seven Mile Beach* ☎ *345/945–2290* ⊟ *AE, MC, V.*

¢–$ ✕ **Chicken Chicken!** The delicious chicken is slow-roasted on a hardwood rotisserie to dine in at one of three tables or for take-out. There are lots of great sides, and it's bargain-priced. ⊠ *West Shore Centre, West Bay Rd., Seven Mile Beach* ☎ *345/945–2290* ⊟ *AE, MC, V.*

CAFÉS
★ ¢–$$ ✕ **Full of Beans Cafe.** If you want freshly squeezed juices, home-grown herbs, lots of vegetarian options, low prices, and three meals a day, seek out this strip-mall café. You can get take-out, delivery, and even catering if you're planning a party. A surprisingly large, eclectic menu includes everything from fresh banana bread and mango smoothies to cranberry Brie salad, a Thai chicken wrap, and steak au poivre. ⊠ *Pasadora Place, Smith Rd., George Town* ☎ *345/943–2326* ⊟ *No credit cards* ⊘ *Closed Sun.*

★ ¢ ✕ **Antica Gelateria.** Owner Carlo is a delight to watch as he excitedly caresses the gelato into each cup. He offers 24 incredible flavors at a time, but there is always something new; he makes 600 different flavors during the year! Eat it there or take home a kilo. Mix flavors for a real treat. ⊠ *Marquee Plaza, near the Cinema, Seven Mile Beach* ☎ *345/943–4343* 🖃 *No credit cards* ⊘ *Closed Mon.*

CARIBBEAN
$–$$$
✕ **Breezes by the Bay.** This cheerful restaurant overlooks the busy George Town harbor from across Harbor Drive, so go to the second floor to avoid traffic noise. Prices are a bargain, especially for peel-and-eat shrimp. The desserts are huge. The bar mixes great specialty drinks. Inside is no-smoking. ⊠ *Harbor Dr., George Town* ☎ *345/943–8469* 🖃 *AE, MC, V.*

CONTINENTAL
$$$–$$$$
Fodor's Choice
★
✕ **Grand Old House.** Classic European cuisine with a Caribbean influence is delicious (the potato-crusted tuna is my favorite), but it's the outdoor, romantic atmosphere—the best on the island—that justifies the high prices here. The setting is the Petra Plantation House, which dates from 1908 and is a favorite for weddings. Sparkling lights adorn the covered, oceanside gazebos and spacious patio, or you can dine indoors, where a pianist provides the perfect music. (It's sometimes difficult to talk, however, if you're close to the piano.) The service is stellar and the wine list noteworthy (though wine prices are high). ⊠ *S. Church St., George Town* ☎ *345/949–9333* 🍽 *Reservations essential* 🖃 *DC, MC, V* ⊘ *No lunch weekends.*

★ $$$–$$$$
✕ **Hemingway's.** Sea views and breezes attract diners to this elegant, open-air restaurant on the beach at the Hyatt Regency Grand Cayman. A small menu of creative Continental dishes should suit any taste. The wine prices will take your breath away, but the service is superb. ⊠ *Hyatt Regency Grand Cayman, West Bay Rd., Seven Mile Beach* ☎ *345/945–5700* 🖃 *AE, D, DC, MC, V.*

ECLECTIC
$$–$$$$
✕ **Calypso Grill.** Caribbean decor, a wonderful outdoor setting on the North Sound, and unique dishes make finding this restaurant worth the trouble. Menu choices include grilled ginger tuna, Jamaican-style escoveitch fish, and a roasted rack of lamb; there's always a blackened fresh catch of the day. Pay attention to the signs from the four-way stop in West Bay if you are trying to find it on your own. ⊠ *Morgan's Harbour, West Bay* ☎ *345/949–3948* 🖃 *AE, D, MC, V.*

$$–$$$$
✕ **Rackam's Pub.** This open-air bar and grill is built on a jetty north of George Town Harbor and is a great place to be at sunset. Boaters can tie up alongside. You can use a ladder to snorkel the wreck of the *Cali* and climb back up for a burger or fish-and-chips. Evening fare includes a Monday-night lobster fest. ⊠ *N. Church St., George Town* ☎ *345/945–3860* 🖃 *AE, MC, V.*

$–$$
✕ **Cimboco.** Don't let the small number of tables fool you. The food here is as wonderful as the prices are reasonable, and it's one of our favorite less expensive places on the island. Have the eggplant, feta, and pine-nut pizza; the grilled-vegetable "sun stack"; or consistently good pasta and fish dishes from the exhibition kitchen. Pastel colors on the walls add to the cheerful atmosphere. The location is conveniently next to the movie theater. ⊠ *Harquail Bypass, Seven Mile Beach* ☎ *345/947–2782* 🖃 *AE, MC, V.*

ENGLISH ✕ **Triple Crown.** This excellent pub offers a pleasant English-style atmo-
¢–$$ sphere. Popular dishes range from Lancashire hot pot (a baked lamb
stew with sliced potatoes on top) to sausage and mash and loads of Amer-
ican dishes too. Efficient smoke-eating machines keep the haze to a min-
imum; TVs are tuned into British and occasionally even U.S. sporting
events. The bar menu is served until midnight, but prices are generally
low—the Sunday carvery is only $16.25. ⊠ *Marquee Plaza, Seven Mile
Rd., Seven Mile Beach* ☎ *345/943–7821* ▭ *AE, MC, V.*

ITALIAN ✕ **Neptune's.** This friendly, not overly fancy restaurant has an unpreten-
★ $$–$$$$ tious but genuinely delicious and reasonably priced menu. Chef Raj is
quick to please and will deal with special dietary requirements, includ-
ing oil- and salt-free options. Grilled vegetables and salmon Provençal
(not on the menu) or whole wheat pasta served many ways can be wonderful, but you can order excellent fish dishes and filet mignon as well.
There's both indoor and outdoor seating. To get a free bruschetta, tell
Yunio that Fodor's sent you. ⊠ *Trafalgar Place, West Bay Rd., West
Bay* ☎ *345/946–8709* ▭ *AE, D, MC, V.*

SEAFOOD ✕ **Blue by Eric Ripert.** Delicate cuisine, impeccable service (even unused
$$$$ flatware is replaced between courses), soothing elegance (each plate and
glass is a work of art), and not a hint of pretense make this the finest
restaurant in Cayman. To top it off, the wine list is surprisingly reasonable, with many fine choices on the lower end. The cuisine is a blend of
Caribbean and New York styles. The baked red snapper in spicy-sour
sancocho broth (a complex, light meat sauce) with sweet potato, plantain, and avocado is among the best choices from the prix-fixe tasting
menu. Mahi-mahi with apple, cucumber, and caper salad with tomato-
verbena gazpacho is also excellent. Choose from a regular three-course
or the Chef's tasting menu. ⊠ *Ritz Carlton Grand Cayman, West Bay
Rd., Seven Mile Beach* ☎ *345/943–9000* ▭ *AE, D, MC, V* ☉ *Closed
Sun.–Mon. No lunch.*

★ $$$–$$$$ ✕ **Reef Grill at Royal Palms.** You can enjoy impeccable service and divine
food served in four different areas: an intimate dining room, the more
casual garden patio, the beach patio, or even upstairs in an open-air din-
ing room overlooking Seven Mile Beach. Sea bass is superb, as is the
tuna. The food is fresh and stunningly prepared, yet the prices for both
food and wine are eminently reasonable. ⊠ *West Bay Rd., Seven Mile
Beach* ☎ *345/945–6358* ▭ *AE, MC, V.*

$$$–$$$$ ✕ **The Wharf.** The popularity of this large restaurant can often lead to
impersonal service and mediocre food. The location at the edge of the
sea is enviable and is a tremendous part of the appeal. The Ports of Call
bar is a good place to watch the sunset, and tarpon feeding off the deck
is a nightly (9 PM) spectacle here. ⊠ *West Bay Rd., George Town*
☎ *345/949–2231* ▭ *AE, MC, V.*

$$–$$$$ ✕ **Lobster Pot.** The nondescript building belies the lovely decor and delicious seafood coming out of the kitchen of this small, second-story
restaurant overlooking the harbor. Enjoy lobster at least 12 different
ways along with reasonably priced wine. The cooking is creative both
on and off the menu, and the chef can happily provide delicious reduced-
oil and -fat alternatives. The balcony offers a great view of the 6:30 PM

7

tarpon feeding. ⊠ *245 N. Church St., George Town* ☎ *345/949–2736* ☰ *AE, MC, V.*

TEXMEX   ✕ **Lone Star Bar & Grill.** Everybody has a great time at this casual hang-
$–$$$ out, which is a favorite of local dive masters. Prices are low—even for
the wine. If you like burgers, steaks, Tex-Mex, and sports, this is the
place to be, with or without the kids. ⊠ *West Bay Rd., Seven Mile Beach*
☎ *345/945–5175* ☰ *AE, MC, V.*

Beaches

The island is blessed with many fine beaches. These are the very best.

★ **Conch Point.** Drive past Spanish Bay Reef and Papagallo until the road
starts to disappear, at which point you can see an often-deserted beach,
a great place to walk. Unfortunately, it's not so good for swimming be-
cause of the shallow water and rocky bottom, and it can be cluttered
at times with seaweed and debris. ⊠ *Conch Point Rd., Barkers.*

East End Beaches. Just drive along and look for any sandy beach. Park
your car and enjoy a stroll. The stretch by the Reef Resort is a good
one. ⊠ *Queen's Hwy., East End.*

Rum Point. This North Sound beach has shade, hammocks, a restaurant,
and snorkel gear rentals. Because it's protected by a barrier reef, snor-
keling is safe and the sand is soft. The bottom remains shallow for a
long way from shore, but the bottom is littered with small coral heads,
so kids shouldn't wrestle in the water here. Take the ferry from the Hyatt
or drive; it's especially popular on Sunday. Start from here for a fast trip
to Stingray City Sandbar. ⊠ *North Side.*

Fodor'sChoice **Seven Mile Beach.** Grand Cayman's west coast is dominated by the fa-
★ mous Seven Mile Beach—actually a 5½-mi-long (9-km-long) expanse
☾ of powdery white sand. The width of the beach varies with the season;
toward the south end it narrows and disappears altogether, leaving only
rock and ironshore. It starts to widen into its normal silky softness any-
where between Tarquyn Manor and the Reef Grill at Royal Palms. Free
of litter and peddlers, it's an unspoiled (though sometimes crowded) en-
vironment. Most of the island's resorts, restaurants, and shopping cen-
ters are along this strip. At the public beach toward the north end you
can find chairs for rent ($10 for the day, including a beverage) and plenty
of water toys, two beach bars, restrooms, and showers. ⊠ *West Bay
Rd., Seven Mile Beach.*

★ **Smith's Cove.** South of the Grand Old House, this small beach is a pop-
ular swimming and snorkeling spot and a wonderful location for a
beach wedding. The bottom drops off quickly enough to allow you to
swim and play close to shore. Although the beach can be a little rocky,
there's little to no debris or coral heads, and there are restrooms and
parking. ⊠ *Off S. Church St., George Town.*

South Sound Cemetery Beach. A narrow, sandy driveway takes you past
the small cemetery to a perfect beach. The dock here is primarily used
by dive boats during winter storms. You can walk in either direction;
the water is calm and clear, and the sand is soft and clean. You'll defi-
nitely find no crowds. ⊠ *S. Sound Rd., George Town.*

Water Cay. If you want an isolated, unspoiled beach, bear left at Rum Point on the North Side and follow the road to the end. When you see a soft, sandy beach, stop your car. Wade out knee deep and look for the large orange starfish. (Don't touch—just look.) ⊠ *North Side.*

Sports & the Outdoors

BIRD-WATCHING   **Silver Thatch** (☎ 345/945–6588 or 345/916–0678) is run by Geddes Hislop, who knows his birds and his island. He specializes in natural and historic heritage tours. The cost is $45 per person for 2 to 10 people, $50 for the early-morning bird-watching/botanic-park tour. Serious birders leave at the crack of dawn, but you can choose the time and leave at the crack of noon instead.

DIVING   Pristine clear water, breathtaking coral formations, and plentiful marine life mark the **North Wall**—a world-renowned dive area along the North Side of Grand Cayman. **Trinity Caves,** in West Bay, is a deep dive with numerous canyons starting at about 60 feet and sloping to the wall at 130 feet. Most dive operators offer scuba trips to **Stingray City,** in the North Sound. Widely considered the best 12-foot dive in the world, it's a must-see for adventurous souls. Here dozens of stingrays congregate—tame enough to suction squid from your outstretched palm. You can stand in 3 feet of water at **Stingray Sandbar** as the gentle stingrays glide around your legs looking for a handout. Don't worry—these stingrays are so used to thousands of tourist encounters that they are no danger, and the experience is often a highlight of a Grand Cayman trip.

If someone tells you that the minnows are in at **Eden Rock,** drop everything and make a scuba dive here (on South Church Street, south of George Town). The schools swarm around you as you glide through the grottos, and it's an unforgettable experience. The grottos themselves are safe—not complex caves—and the entries and exits are clearly visible at all times. Snorkelers can enjoy the outside of the grottos as the reef rises and falls from 10 to 30 feet deep. Avoid carrying fish food unless you know how not to get bitten by eager yellowtail snappers. The waters around Grand Cayman are varied, so if the water looks rough where you are, there's usually a side of the island that is wonderfully calm.

Other good shore-entry snorkeling spots include **West Bay Cemetery,** north of Seven Mile Beach, and the reef-protected shallows of the island's **north and south coasts.** Ask for directions to the shallow wreck of the *Cali* in George Town harbor area; there are several places to enter the water, including a ladder at Rackam's Pub. Among the wreckage you'll recognize the winch and, of course, lots of friendly fish.

As one of the Caribbean's top diving destinations, Grand Cayman is blessed with many top-notch dive operations offering diving, instruction, and equipment for sale and rent. A single-tank boat dive averages $50, a two-tank dive about $75. Snorkel-equipment rental is about $5 to $15 a day. Divers are required to be certified and possess a "C" card. To become fully certified takes three to six days, costs $350 to $400, and includes classroom instruction, pool and boat sessions, and check-out dives. To save time during your limited holiday, you can start the

Learn to Dive

ALMOST ANYONE CAN ENJOY scuba, and it's easy to try. If you take a three-hour resort course that costs about $80 to $100, you can start with an introduction to scuba as you stand in the shallow end of the swimming pool, learn how to use the mask and fins and how to breathe underwater with a regulator. In the deep you can practice a few simple skills that will help to keep you safe. The exciting part is the shallow dive in the ocean. The instructor stays close as you float above the reef, watching fish react to you. Don't worry—there are no dangerous fish here, and they don't bite, as long as you're not handling fish food. You can see corals and sponges, maybe even a turtle. It's an amazing world, and you can be in it with very little effort.

If you have any fear of diving, find an instructor who will allow you the time you need to be comfortable with each step. For more information on how to learn to enjoy snorkeling and diving even if it frightens you, go to ⊕ www.cathychurch.com/fearfuldiver.html.

Diving is a great experience that does not have to be strenuous. Almost anyone can enjoy being underwater. If you're not strong, have someone else carry your tank and don't go in rough water from shore. Dive from a boat in warm, clear Cayman water, where there's rarely a current or surge. But don't say you can't do it until you have tried. It can be one of the most rewarding activities in the world.

—Cathy Church

book and pool work at home and finish the open-water portion in warm, clear Cayman waters. Certifying agencies offer this referral service all around the world.

When choosing a dive operator, here are a few things to ask: Do they require that you stay with the group? Do they include towels? camera rinse water? protection from inclement weather? tank-change service? beach or resort pickup? or snacks between dives? Ask what dive options they have during a winter storm (called a nor'wester here). What kind of boat do they have? (Don't assume that a small, less crowded boat is better. Some large boats are more comfortable, even when full, than a tiny, uncovered boat without a marine toilet. Small boats, however, offer more personal service and less crowded dives.)

Strict marine protection laws prohibit you from taking any marine life from many areas around the island. Always check with the **Department of Environment** (☎ 345/949–8469) before fishing. To report violations, call **Marine Enforcement** (☎ 345/948–6002).

Cayman Aggressor IV (☎ 800/348–2628 ⊕ www.aggressor.com), a 110-foot live-aboard dive boat, offers one-week cruises. The food is basic, but the crew offers a great mix of diving, especially when weather allows the crossing to Little Cayman.

ᕣ **Divetech** (✉ Cobalt Coast Resort & Suites, 18-A Sea Fan Dr., West Bay ☎ 345/946–5658 or 888/946–5656 ⊕ www.divetech.com ✉ Turtle

Reef, near Turtle Farm, West Bay ☎ 345/949–1700) has opportunities for shore diving at its lush north-coast location, which provides loads of interesting creatures, a miniwall, and, of course, the North Wall. With quick access to West Bay, the boat is quite comfortable. The West Bay Express is a good deal: rent an underwater scooter, tour in one direction with a guide to the second location, and get a ride back in the van for only $75. Technical training is excellent, and the company offers good, personable service. Snorkel and diving programs are available year round for children ages eight and up.

Don Foster's Dive Cayman Islands (✉218 S. Church St., George Town ☎345/949–5679 or 800/833–4837 ⊕ www.donfosters.com) has a pool with a shower and also snorkeling along the ironshore. The shore diving includes a few interesting swim-throughs, or you can book a boat dive.

Eden Rock Diving Center (✉ 124 S. Church St., George Town ☎ 345/949–7243 ⊕ www.edenrockdive.com), south of George Town, provides easy access to Eden Rock and Devil's Grotto. It has full equipment rental, lockers, and shower facilities.

Ocean Frontiers (✉ Reef Resort, Austin Connelly Dr., East End ☎ 345/947–7500 ⊕ www.oceanfrontiers.com) is an excellent operation, offering friendly small-group diving and a technical training facility. Although dive sites may not have as much color as West Bay, the East End is beautifully rugged and picturesque. The water can be rough from the easterly trade winds, but during winter storms this is the lee side.

Red Baron Charters (✉Cayman Islands Yacht Club, C27, Seven Mile Beach ☎ 345/916–1293 ⊕ www.redbarondivers.com) has small boats and personalized service with beach pickup.

Red Sail Sports (☎ 345/949–8745 or 877/733–7245 ⊕ www.redsailcayman.com) offers daily trips from most of the major hotels. Dives are often run as guided tours, a perfect option for beginners. If you're experienced and if your air lasts a long time, discuss this with the boat captain to see if he requires that you come up with the group as determined by the first person who runs low on air. There is a full range of kids' dive options for ages 5 to 15. The company also operates dinner and sunset sails.

Sunset Divers (✉ Sunset House, 390 S. Church St., George Town ☎ 345/949–7111 or 800/854–4767 ⊕ www.sunsethouse.com), a full-service PADI teaching facility, has great shore diving and four dive boats to hit all sides of the island. Divers can be independent on their boats as long as they abide by the maximum time and depth standards.

FISHING   If you enjoy action fishing, Cayman waters have plenty to offer. Boats are available for charter, offering fishing options that include deep-sea, reef, bone, tarpon, light-tackle, and fly-fishing. June and July are good all-around months for fishing for blue marlin, yellow- and blackfin tuna, dolphinfish, and bonefish. Bonefish have a second season in the winter months, along with wahoo and skipjack tuna.

Black Princess Charters (☎ 345/916–6319 or 345/949–0400), owned by Capt. Chuckie Ebanks, fully equipped for deep-sea and reef fishing as well as snorkel trips.

Burton's Tourist Information & Activity Services (☎ 345/949–6598 or 345/926–8294) offers a concierge service that can provide information and book virtually any island services.

Captain Asley's Watersports (☎ 345/949–3054) prides itself on personable, flexible, and customized charter services for diving, snorkeling, and sportfishing.

★ **Sea Star Charters** (☎ 345/949–1016, 345/916–5234 after 8 AM) is run by Clinton Ebanks, a fine and very friendly Caymanian, who will do whatever it takes to make sure that you have a wonderful time on his small, 28-foot cabin cruiser, enjoying light-tackle, bone-, and bottom-fishing. He's a good choice for beginners and offers a nice cultural experience, as well as sailing charters. Only cash and traveler's checks are accepted.

White Rose Charters (☎ 345/949–1012, 345/325–1472, cell), owned by Capt. Alphonso Ebanks, has one of the highest catches in bone-, tarpon, reef, and drift fishing. He has two boats to choose from.

GOLF   The golf course at the new Ritz-Carlton Grand Cayman was designed by Greg Norman. Built on previously sacrosanct mangroves, its five long par-fours will play into the Caribbean trade winds, making a 470-yard hole play like 600. At this writing, the course was still being finished and was expected to open in mid-2006.

The **Grand Cayman–Britannia** (⊠ West Bay Rd., Seven Mile Beach ☎ 345/949–1234 ⊕ grandcayman.hyatt.com) golf course, next to the Hyatt Regency, was designed by Jack Nicklaus. The course is really three in one—a 9-hole, par-70 regulation course; an 18-hole, par-57 executive course; and a Cayman course played with a Cayman ball that goes about half the distance of a regulation ball. Windier, and therefore more challenging, than most other courses is the **Links at Safe Haven** (⊠ Off West Bay Rd., Seven Mile Beach ☎ 345/945–4155), which was designed by Roy Case; it's a par-71, 6,605-yard 18-hole course with lots of water and sand traps along undulating terrain and with ever-prevailing trade winds. Make sure that you wear shorts at least 14 inches long and 15 inches for ladies; no T-shirts are allowed, only collared shirts.

HIKING   The National Trust's **Mastic Trail** (⊠ Frank Sound Rd., entrance by fire station at botanic park, Breakers ☎ 345/949–0121 for guide reservations) is a rugged 2-mi (3-km) slash through woodlands, mangrove swamps, and ancient rock formations. In the 1800s this woodland trail was used as a direct path to and from the North Side. A comfortable walk depends on weather, winter being better because it is drier. Call the National Trust to determine suitability and to book a guide for $45; tours are run daily from 9 to 5 by appointment only. Or walk on your own with a $5 guidebook. The trip takes about three hours.

HORSEBACK   **Coral Stone Stables** (☎ 345/916–4799 ⊕ www.csstables.com) offers 1½-
RIDING   hour leisurely horseback rides along the white-sand beaches at Bodden Town and inland trails at Savannah; complimentary photos are included. **Pampered Ponies** (☎ 345/945–2262 or 345/916–2540 ⊕ www.ponies.ky) has horses trained to walk, trot, and canter along the beaches

and beach trails. You can do either private rides or a variety of guided trips, including early–morning, sunset, moonlight, and swim rides along the uninhabited beach from Conch Point to Morgan's Harbour on the north tip beyond West Bay.

KAYAKING **Surfside Aqua Sports** (☎ 345/916–2820) offers a leisurely paddle along the mangrove shore, then gives you the opportunity to snorkel from a platform at the barrier reef. You spend a total of two hours on the water at an easy pace, and no experience is needed. The trip costs $75, complete with snorkel gear.

SKATING & **Black Pearl Skate & Surf Park** (✉ Red Bay Rd., Grand Harbour ☎ 345/
SKATEBOARDING 947–4161 ⊕ www.blackpearl.ky), a great skating park (skate boards, in-line skates), is the size of a football field and has a flow course, a 60-foot vert ramp, and a standing wave-surf machine. You can rent anything you need.

SEA EXCURSIONS The most impressive sights in the Cayman Islands are on and underwater, and several submarinelike glass-bottom-boat trips will allow you to see these wonders. Sunset sails, dinner cruises, and other theme (dance, booze, pirate) cruises are available from $20 to $50 per person.

On Grand Cayman don't miss a trip with **Atlantis Submarines** (☎ 345/
949–7700, 866/546–7820 ⊕ www.atlantisadventures.net), which takes 48 passengers along the Cayman Wall down to 100 feet. Through its large windows you can see the reef first-hand without getting wet. At night, the lights show the underwater colors more brilliantly than during the day. Cost is $84 for 75-minute trip. A mini-sub takes two passengers down to 800 feet (for $395), where colorful sponges can grow to huge sizes in water too deep for damaging storm waves to reach.

For your own private submarine tour, take the **Bubble Sub** (☎ 345/916–
3483 ⊕ www.bubblesub.com). Two people sit in a large, clear dome with 360-degree visibility, so you can see everything up close and personal while your pilot in scuba gear drives you from the outside. You can take over the controls if you wish. This is the closest thing to scuba diving you're likely to find. Children four years and up can do this with one adult. At $400 per couple, it's a pricey, but memorable, excursion.

The *Jolly Roger* (☎ 345/945–7245 ⊕ www.jollyrogercayman.com) is a two-thirds replica of Christopher Columbus's 17th-century Spanish galleon *Nina*; the company also owns the *Valhalla*, a wooden Norwegian brig built in 1934 that holds over 100 passengers. On the afternoon cruise, you watch traditional pirate antics and enjoy a snorkel stop; the kids get to practice firing the cannon. There are also sunset and dinner cruises with music and dancing, or you can charter it for your wedding. Food is not gourmet, and it can be a touristy experience, but it's fun.

On the *Nautilus* (☎ 345/945–1355 ⊕ www.nautilus.ky) you can sit above deck or venture below, where windows allow you to see the reefs and marine life. A one-hour undersea tour is $39. Watch divers feed the fish, or take the tour that includes snorkeling.

For real sailing on a 39-foot sailing sloop, try **Red Baron Charters** (☎ 345/ 945–4744 or 345/916–4333). You can even help crew if you wish. A half-day charter costs $400 and accommodates up to eight passengers. A 46-foot boat is also available: $1,100 full day or $400 for a sunset sail. Try their ecotours to the mangroves, Rum Point, or Sting Ray City in their 33-foot rubber inflatable.

The *Spirits of Cayman, Poseidon,* and *Ppalu* (☎ 345/946–3362) offer day sails to Stingray City, happy-hour cruises, and sunset sails. All three are large catamarans and often carry large groups. Although the service may not be personal, it will be efficient.

SQUASH   The **South Sound Squash Club** (✉ S. Sound Rd., George Town ☎ 345/ 949–9469) has seven international courts, changing room, bar and lounge, and coaches.

SNORKELING   Stingray Sandbar is the most popular snorkeling destination by far, and dozens of boats head that way several times a day. It's a not-to-be-missed experience, which you will remember for years to come.

Bayside Watersports (☎ 345/949–3200 or 866/978–0022 reservations only, 10 AM to 3 PM weekdays ⊕ www.baysidewatersports.com) offers half-day snorkeling trips, North Sound Beach lunch excursions, Stingray City and full-day deep-sea fishing and dinner cruises. The company operates several popular boats.

Captain Marvin's (☎ 345/949–4590 ⊕ www.captainmarvins.com) offers multistop North Sound snorkel trips, which include Stingray Sandbar and a lunch on the beach. This popular company also offers fishing charters and land tours.

Shopping

On Grand Cayman the good news is that there's no sales tax *and* there's plenty of duty-free merchandise. Locally made items to watch for include woven mats, baskets, jewelry made of a marblelike stone called Caymanite (from the cliffs of Cayman Brac), and authentic sunken treasure, though the latter is never cheap. Cigar lovers take note: some shops carry famed Cuban brands, but you must enjoy them on the island; bringing them back to the United States is illegal.

Although you can find black-coral products in Grand Cayman, they're controversial. Most of the coral sold here comes from Belize and Honduras; Cayman Islands marine law prohibits the removal of live coral from its own sea (although most of it has been taken illegally). Black coral grows at a very slow rate (3 inches every 10 years) and is an endangered species. Consider buying other products instead.

Areas & Malls

The **Anchorage Center** across from the cruise-ship North Terminal has 10 of the most affordable stores and boutiques selling duty-free goods from such great brand names as John Hardy, Movado, and Concord, as well as designer ammolite jewelry. Downtown is the **Kirk Freeport Plaza,** known for its boutiques selling fine watches, duty-free china, Gucci goods, perfumes, and cosmetics. Just keep walking—there's plenty of shopping in all directions. Stores in the **Landmark** sell perfumes, treasure coins, and upscale beachwear; Breezes by the Bay restaurant is upstairs.

Specialty Items

ART The waterfront gallery **Artifacts** (⊠ Harbour Dr., George Town ☎ 345/949–2442) sells Spanish pieces of eight, doubloons, and Halcyon Days
★ enamels (hand-painted collectible pillboxes made in England). **Cathy Church's Underwater Photo Centre & Gallery** (⊠ S. Church St., George Town ☎ 345/949–7415) has a collection of Cathy's spectacular color and limited-edition black-and-white underwater photos. Framed prints are shipped to the United States at no extra charge. Have her autograph her latest coffee-table book. One of many local artists, Horacio Esteban,
★ from Cayman Brac, sculpts Caymanite at **Esteban Gallery** (⊠ AALL Trust Bank Bldg., ground floor, Waterfront, George Town ☎ 345/946–2787). His work is beautiful, uniquely Cayman, and worth a look. On the shore in George Town, **Island Glassblowing Studio** (⊠ N. Church St., George Town ☎ 345/946–1483) is run by the Zawitowski family of designers, who offer free demonstrations of their incredible skills. The **Kennedy Gallery** (⊠ West Shore Centre, West Bay Rd., George Town ☎ 345/949–8077) sells lithographs and prints depicting the Cayman Islands by local artists. The **National Gallery** (⊠ Waterfront, ground floor of Harbour Place, George Town ☎ 345/945–8111) always has an interesting exhibition of various visual arts. The small retail shop has great art and design objects
★ from around the world. **Pure Art** (⊠ S. Church St., George Town ☎ 345/949–9133) sells watercolors, wood carvings, lacework, and much more by local artists. It is about 1½ mi (2½ km) south of George Town. This is a great place to browse even if you aren't planning a purchase.

CAMERAS The **Camera Store** (⊠ Waterfront Centre, N. Church St., George Town
★ ☎ 345/949–4551) has friendly and knowledgeable service, lots of duty-free digital cameras, accessories, and fast photo printing from self-service kiosks.

FOODSTUFFS There are four modern, U.S.-style supermarkets for groceries and pharmaceutical needs. Ask for the closest one near you. All offer a full range of groceries and lots of fresh produce (except it's not so fresh at Hur-
★ ley's Grand Harbour). Each has an associated pharmacy. The **Tortuga Rum Company** (⊠ N. Sound Rd., George Town ☎ 345/949–7701 or 345/949–7867) has several rums available throughout the island as well as its world-famous, scrumptious rum cake (sealed fresh), which is sweet and moist and makes a great gift to take back to those who stayed behind. You can buy a fresh rum cake at the airport on the way home at the same prices asat the factory store.

HANDICRAFTS & The **Heritage Crafts Shop** (⊠ Harbour Dr., George Town ☎ 345/945–
SOUVENIRS 6041), near the harbor, sells local crafts and gifts. **Pirate's Grotto** (⊠ Harbor Dr., George Town ☎ 345/945–0244), basement level, below the Landmark, is a cute store with duty-free liquor and cigars (including Cubans) and Cayman Islands souvenirs.

JEWELRY The black-coral creations of **Bernard Passman** (⊠ Cardinal Ave., George Town ☎ 345/949–0123) have won the approval of the British royal family. You can find beautiful coral pieces at **Richard's Fine Jewelry** (✉ Harbour Dr., George Town ☎ 345/949–7156), where designers Richard Barile and Rafaela Barile attract celebrities. **24K-Mon Jewelers** (✉ Buckingham

★ Sq., Seven Mile Beach ☎ 345/949–1499) sells works of art from many jewelry makers, including Wyland, Merry-Lee Rae, and Stephen Douglas, as well as its own lovely designs.

Nightlife

Check the Friday edition of the *Caymanian Compass* for listings of music, movies, theater, and other entertainment. Bars are open during evening hours until 1 AM, and clubs are generally open from 10 until 3 AM, but none may serve liquor after midnight on Saturday and none can offer dancing on Sundays.

The **Attic** (✉ Queen's Court, West Bay Rd., Seven Mile Beach ☎ 345/949-7665) is a chic sports bar with three billiard tables and large-screen TVs; it's on the second floor above "O" Bar. **Bamboo Lounge** (✉ Hyatt Regency, West Bay Rd., Seven Mile Beach ☎ 345/947–8744) is a quiet, refined bar with adjacent sushi restaurant and a good selection of wine by the glass. For a casual drink, visit **Calico Jack's** (✉ West Bay Rd., Seven Mile Beach ☎ 345/945–7850), a friendly outdoor beach bar at the north end of Public Beach with a DJ on Monday and open-mike night on Tuesday, bands every Friday night, and parties during the full moon. You can sit at the bar or swing under a big tree at **Coconut Joe's** (✉ Across from Comfort Suites, Seven Mile Beach ☎ 345/943–5637) and watch the traffic go by. There's a Friday-night DJ. For a wild and rowdy good time, try the nightclub **Next Level** (✉ West Bay Rd., between the Hyatt and Westin, Seven Mile Beach ☎ 345/946–6398) or the adjacent Aqua Beach Bar, which has private tiki-hut booths and open mike on Thursday. Check on the live band schedule. The Next Level is a late-night hot spot offering dancing to everything from retro remixes to hip-hop.

★ **"O" Bar** (✉ Queen's Court, West Bay Rd., Seven Mile Beach ☎ 345/943–6227) is a trendy dance club with mixed music and flame-throwing, juggling bartenders. An upper-level private loft is available by reservation. You can watch tarpon feeding at **Rackam's Pub & Restaurant** (✉ N. Church St., George Town ☎ 345/945–3860), a happenin' bar on the water that has complimentary snacks on Friday and a cool misting spray during the

★ hot summer. **Royal Palms** (✉ West Bay Rd., George Town ☎ 345/945–6358) is where local bands play Friday and Saturday nights; it's an outdoor beach bar with plenty of room for dancing under the stars or a great Sunday-afternoon hangout to socialize, sit in the sun, and listen to music. Don't let the location of **Sapphire Lounge** (✉ Seven Mile Shops, Seven Mile Beach ☎ 345/925–7449)—in the back of a plain strip mall—fool you. This is a chic and trendy New York–style martini lounge and sushi bar with more than 30 different drinks, more martinis than I knew existed, and French-pressed coffee. The sushi is fresh. Choose from bar, tall tables, or sofas; there's new art on the walls every month. You can dance near the water to mellow music at the **Wharf** (✉ West Bay Rd., George

Town ☎ 345/949–2231) on Friday and Saturday evenings; there is salsa dancing and lessons on Tuesday.

Exploring Grand Cayman

The historic capital of George Town, on the southeast corner of Grand Cayman, is easy to explore on foot. If you're a shopper, you can spend days here; otherwise, an hour will suffice for a tour of the downtown area. To see the rest of the island, rent a car or scooter or take a guided tour. The portion of the island called West Bay is noted for its jumble of neighborhoods and a few attractions. It's about a half-hour to West Bay from George Town (over an hour during rush hours). The less developed East End has natural attractions from blowholes to botanical gardens, as well as the remains of the island's original settlements. Plan on at least 45 minutes for the drive out from George Town (more than an hour during rush hours). You need a day to explore the entire island—including a stop at a beach for a picnic or swim.

For a wonderful map of the natural attractions, go to the **National Trust** (⊠ S. Church St., north and across the street from Sunset House, George Town ☎ 345/949–0121 ⊕ nationaltrust.org.ky). The Trust sells books and guides to Cayman. The fabulous Web site hasmore than 50 information sheets on cultural and natural topics from iguanas to schoolhouses. Stop there first before you tour the island.

Numbers in the margin correspond to points of interest on the Grand Cayman map.

What to See

7 **Blowholes.** When the trade winds blow hard, crashing waves force water into caverns and send geysers shooting up through the ironshore. The blowholes were partially filled during Hurricane Ivan in 2004, so the water has to be pretty rough before they are dramatic. ⊠ *Frank Sound Rd., near East End.*

6 **Bodden Town.** In the island's original south-shore capital you can find an old cemetery on the shore side of the road. Graves with A-frame structures are said to contain the remains of pirates. There are also the ruins of a fort and a wall erected by slaves in the 19th century. A curio shop serves as the entrance to what's called the Pirate's Caves, partially underground natural formations that are more hokey (decked out with fake treasure chests and mannequins in pirate garb) than spooky.

2 **Butterfly Farm.** Your entry fee is good for your entire stay so that you can watch the life-stage changes of the butterflies. It's fun, easy, and interesting and makes a great photo op, particularly early in the morning or on a sunny afternoon. ⊠ *Lawrence Rd., across from cinema, Seven Mile Beach* ☎ *345/946–3411* ⊕ *www.thebutterflyfarm.com* ✉ *$15* ☻ *Mon.–Sat. 8:30–4, Sun. 8:30–noon.*

3 **Cayman Island Turtle Farm.** You can tour ponds with thousands of turtles in various stages of growth; some can be picked up from the tanks—a real treat for children and adults as the little creatures flap their fins and splash the water.&At this writing, **Boatswain's Beach,** a large marine theme park, had opened its first phase as an extension of the Cayman Island Turtle Farm. Further expansions were expected to open throughout 2006. ⊠ *West Bay Rd., West Bay* ☎ *345/949–3893* ⊕ *www. turtle.ky or boatswainsbeach.ky* ⊆ *$7.50* ☉ *Daily 8–4:30.*

❶ **George Town.** Begin exploring the capital by strolling along the waterfront, Harbour Drive to **Elmslie Memorial United Church,** named after the first Presbyterian missionary to serve in the Caymans. Its vaulted ceiling, wooden arches, and sedate nave reflect the religious nature of island residents. In front of the court building, in the center of town, names of influential Caymanians are inscribed on the **Wall of History,** which commemorates the islands' quincentennial in 2003. Across the street is the Cayman Islands Legislative Assembly Building, next door to the 1919 Peace Memorial Building.

In the middle of the financial district is the **General Post Office,** built in 1939. Let the kids pet the big blue iguana statues.

❹ **Hell.** The touristy stopover in West Bay is little more than a patch of incredibly jagged black rock formations. The attractions are the small post office and a gift shop where you can get cards and letters postmarked from Hell.

☾ **❺** **Pedro St. James Castle.** Built in 1780, the greathouse is Cayman's oldest stone structure and the only remaining late-18th-century residence on the island. The buildings are surrounded by 8 acres of natural parks and woodlands. You can stroll through landscaping of native Caymanian flora and experience one of the most spectacular views on the island from atop the dramatic Great Pedro Bluff. Don't miss the impressive multimedia theater show complete with smoking pots, misting rains, and two film screens where the story of Pedro's Castle is presented. The show plays on the hour; see it before you tour the site. ⊠ *S. Sound Rd., Savannah* ☎ *345/947–3329* ⊆ *$8* ☉ *Daily 8:30–5.*

❽ **Queen Elizabeth II Botanic Park.** This 65-acre wilderness preserve showcases a wide range of indigenous and nonindigenous tropical vegetation. Rare blue iguanas are bred and released in the gardens and are a common sight on the trails. If you're lucky, you'll see the brilliant green Cayman parrot—not just here but virtually anywhere in Cayman. ⊠ *Frank Sound Rd., Frank Sound* ☎ *345/947–9462, 345/947–3558 info line* ⊆ *$3* ☉ *Daily 9–6:30; last admission at 5:30.*

CAYMAN BRAC

Updated by
Cathy Church

Cayman Brac is named for its most distinctive feature, a rugged limestone bluff ("brac" in Gaelic) that runs up the center of the 12-mi (19-km) island, culminating in a sheer 140-foot cliff at its eastern end. The Brac, 89 mi (143 km) northeast of Grand Cayman, is accessible via Cayman Airways and Island Air. With only 1,800 residents—they call themselves Brackers—the island has the feel and easy pace of a small town. Brackers are known for their friendly attitude toward visitors, so it's easy to strike up a conversation.

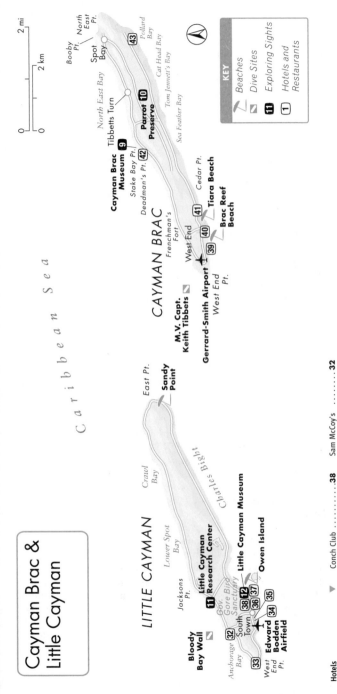

Where to Stay

Lodgings are small and intimate, and guests are often treated like family. Most resorts offer optional meal plans there are several restaurants, some of which provide free transport from your hotel. Most restaurants serve island fare (local seafood, chicken, and curries). On Friday and Saturday nights the spicy scent of jerk chicken fills the air; three roadside stands sell takeout dinners. A 1950s-style ice cream parlor is open on weekends. This is a nature and outdoor island; if the weather is bad, there are no indoor activities, so bring a good book just in case.

$$–$$$ ☒ **Divi Tiara Beach Resort.** Graceful palm trees fringe the white-sand beach—no crowds, no traffic, just trees, water, sand, and the ever-popular seaside bar. Valet-style, hassle-free diving and excellent buffet meals fill the divers' needs. The hotel is basic, but the rooms are nicely done. *⌂ Box 238 WPO, Cayman Brac ☎ 345/948–1553 or 800/ 801–5550 🖷 345/948–1316 ⊕ www.diviresorts.com ⇝ 59 rooms, 12 1-bedroom condos ⌂ Restaurant, in-room safes, some in-room hot tubs, cable TV, in-room data ports, tennis court, pool, beach, dive shop, dock, snorkeling, boating, bicycles, boccie, volleyball, bar, shops, laundry facilities, Internet room, business services, meeting room; no smoking ⊟ AE, MC, V ⎮⊙⎮ EP.*

★ $$ ☒ **Brac Caribbean and Carib Sands.** These neighboring complexes offer condos with one to four bedrooms. The Brac Caribbean balconies overlook the sea; Carib Sands' overlook the pool area. The poolside Captain's Table restaurant and bar at Brac Caribbean is a popular hangout for locals and visitors alike. *⌂ Box 4 SPO, Cayman Brac ☎ 345/948– 2265 or 866/843–2722 🖷 345/948–1111 ⊕ www.866thebrac.com ⇝ 42 condos ⌂ Restaurant, kitchens, cable TV, pool, beach, dive shop, fishing, bicycles, bar ⊟ AE, MC, V ⎮⊙⎮ CP.*

★ $$ ☒ **Brac Reef Beach Resort.** Popular with divers, this well-run resort features a beautiful sandy beach shaded by sea-grape trees, many complete with hammocks. The dock is illuminated nightly, attracting stingrays, tarpon, and other creatures to entertain you on your after-dinner stroll. The rooms are standard Caribbean rattan. *⌂ Box 56 WE, Cayman Brac ☎ 345/948–1323, 800/327–3835, 727/323–8727 in Florida 🖷 727/323– 8827 ⊕ www.bracreef.com ⇝ 40 rooms ⌂ Restaurant, cable TV, in-room data ports, tennis court, pool, gym, hot tub, spa, beach, dive shop, snorkeling, boating, kayaking, bicycles, bar, shop, laundry service, Internet room, business services, meeting rooms ⊟ AE, D, MC, V ⎮⊙⎮ AI.*

$–$$ ☒ **Walton's Mango Manor.** This beautifully restored traditional West Indian home has five rooms (all with bath), accented with lovely antique furnishings and architectural details, plus a spacious, private seaside cottage. The nearby ironshore beach is utterly tranquil and usually unoccupied. The engaging proprietors will gladly help you arrange fishing or diving excursions and other activities. Since only breakfast is included, you need a car to go out for other meals and explore the island. A tiny, exquisite synagogue is nestled between the house and the cottage. *⌂ Box 56 SPO, Cayman Brac ☎🖷 345/948–0518 ⊕ www. waltonsmangomanor.com ⇝ 5 rooms, 1 cottage ⌂ Fans; no room TVs ⊟ AE, MC, V ⎮⊙⎮ CP.*

$ 🏨 **Cayman Breakers.** This condo development sitting between the bluff and the ironshore on the southeast coast caters to climbers, who come to scale the sheer face of the bluff, as well as divers, who like to take advantage of the good shore diving right off the property. Spacious, two-bedroom units with tropical decor have full kitchens. ✍ *Box 202 SPO, Cayman Brac* 📠 *345/948–1463* ⊕ *www.caybreakers.com* ⤶ *18 2-bedroom condos* ♨ *BBQ, kitchens, cable TV, pool, laundry facilities* ▤ *AE, D, MC, V* ⧓⊙⧓ *EP.*

Beaches

Much of the Brac's coastline is ironshore, though there are several pretty sand beaches, mostly along the southwest coast (where swimmers will also find extensive beds of turtle grass). In addition to the hotel beaches, where everyone is welcome, there is a public beach with good access to the reef; it's well marked on tourist maps. The north-coast beaches, predominantly rocky ironshore, offer excellent snorkeling.

Sports & the Outdoors

DIVING & SNORKELING   Cayman Brac's waters have excellent sea life. The snorkeling off the **north coast** is spectacular, particularly at West End, where coral formations close to shore attract all kinds of critters. Many fish have colonized the Russian frigate—now broken in two—that was scuttled offshore from the site of the former Buccaneer's Inn. An artist named Foots has created an amazing underwater Atlantis. The island's three dive operators offer scuba and snorkeling training and PADI certification. Certified divers can purchase à la carte dive packages from either of the dive resorts.

Divi Dive Tiara (✉ Divi Tiara Beach Resort, Cayman Brac 📞 345/948–1553). **Reef Divers** (✉ Brac Reef Beach Resort, Cayman Brac 📞 345/948–1642 ⊕ www.bracreef.com). **Village Scuba School** (✉ Cayman Brac 📞 345/948–1509).

HIKING   Free printed guides to the Brac's many heritage and nature trails can be obtained from the **Brac Tourism Office** (✉ West End Community Park, west of the airport, Cayman Brac 📞 345/948–1649); you can also get the guides at the airport or at your hotel. Traditional routes across the Bluff have been cleared and marked; trailheads are identified with signs along the road. It's safe to hike on your own, though some trails are fairly hard going (wear light hiking boots) and others could be better maintained. For those who prefer less strenuous walking, **Christopher Columbus Gardens** (✉ Ashton Reid Dr. , just north of the Aston Rutty Centre) has easy trails and boardwalks. The park showcases the unique natural flora and features of the Bluff, including two cave mouths.

ROCK CLIMBING   If you are experienced and like dangling from ropes 140 feet above a rocky sea, the Brac is the place for you. Ropes and safety gear cannot be rented on the island—you need to bring your own. Through the years, climbers have attached permanent titanium bolts to the **Bluff** face, creating some 40 routes. The Cayman Breakers condo community has route maps and descriptions (⇨ *see* Cayman Breakers *in* Where to Stay).

Sculpting Cayman

A SCULPTOR NAMED FOOTS dreamed since childhood of creating his own version of Plato's lost city of Atlantis. Now 51 years old, he is seeing his dream fulfilled as he creates huge sculptures of concrete and sinks them in 45 feet of water off the north shore of Cayman Brac. The result is an astounding dive site and artificial reef with more than 100 sculptures covering several acres. The story starts at the Archway of Atlantis (each of the two bases weighs 21,000 pounds). The Elders' Way, lined with 5-foot temple columns, leads to the Inner Circle of Light, where there is a sundial large enough to sit in. Each Elder is modeled after an actual person who has contributed to the Cayman Islands. Foots creates a beautiful story with his creation and is doing this almost entirely on his own; he's made an incredible donation to the divers of the Brac. Foots plans to add a new phase every six months so that the story will go on for a long time before the project is finished.

SPELUNKING If you plan to explore Cayman Brac's caves, wear good sneakers or hiking shoes, as some paths are steep and rocky and some cave entrances reachable only by ladders. **Peter's Cave** offers a stunning aerial view of the picturesque northeastern community of Spot Bay. **Great Cave,** at the island's southeast end, has numerous chambers and photogenic ocean views. In **Bat Cave** you may see bats hanging from the ceiling (try not to disturb them). **Rebecca's Cave** houses the gravesite of a 17-month-old child who died during the horrific hurricane of 1932.

Exploring Cayman Brac

9 **Cayman Brac Museum.** Here you'll find a diverse, well-displayed collection of everyday implements used by previous generations of Brackers. A meticulously crafted scale model of the Caymanian schooner *Alsons* has pride of place. ✉ *Old Government Administration Bldg., Stake Bay* ☎ *345/948–2622 Ext. 4446* ✉ *Free* ☾ *Weekdays 9–noon and 1–4, Sat. 9–noon.*

10 **Parrot Preserve.** The likeliest place to spot the endangered Cayman Brac parrot—and other indigenous birds—is along this National Trust hiking trail off Major Donald Drive, a.k.a. Lighthouse Road. The 6-mi (9½-km) gravel road continues to the lighthouse at the Bluff's eastern end, where there's an astonishing view from atop the cliff to the open ocean— the best place to watch the sunrise.

LITTLE CAYMAN

The smallest of the three Cayman Islands, Little Cayman, often referred to as the gem of the Cayman Islands, has a full-time population of only 150, most of whom work in the tourism industry. This 12-square-mi (31-square-km) island is still pristine and has only a sand-sealed airstrip, no official terminal building, and few vehicles. With little commercial development, the island beckons to ecotourists who want to leave the bustle of city life behind. It's probably most well known for its spectacular diving on world-renowned Bloody Bay Wall and adjacent Jackson Marine Park.

Where to Stay

Accommodations are mostly in small lodges, many of which offer meal and dive packages. The meal packages are a good idea; the chefs in most places create wonderful meals.

Hotels

★ $$$$ ⬚ **Pirates Point Resort.** Nestled between sea grape and casuarina pine trees are 10 bungalow-style rooms, each with the feel of a guesthouse. Some of the rooms have air-conditioning, and others depend on the Caribbean breeze through louvered windows. You're likely to become fast friends with the effervescent owner, Texan-born Gladys Howard. Gladys, a chef who trained with Julia Child, oversees the scrumptious meals, which are served with fine wines and cocktails on a daily basis. She is a hardworking advocate for the environment but finds time to host weekly champagne parties on the veranda of her home just a few steps from the resort. Her dive staff are the best at finding rare creatures for the divers, and many of her guests are repeat clientele. *⬚ Box 43, Preston Bay* ☎ *345/948–1010* 🖷 *345/948–1011* ⊕ *www.piratespointresort.com* ⤶ *10 rooms ⌂ Restaurant, gym, dive shop, snorkeling, bicycles, bar, airport shuttle; no a/c in some rooms, no room TVs, no kids under 5* ▭ *MC, V* ⎢⊚⎢ *AI* ⊘ *Closed Sept.*

★ $$$$ ⬚ **Southern Cross Club.** Little Cayman's first resort was founded in the 1960s as a fishing club, and its focus is still on fishing and diving. Individual duplex cottages are on the most spectacular white-sand beach on Little Cayman, with views of the uninhabited Owen Island and romantic private outdoor showers. Rooms are decorated in hardwood furniture and bright, vivid colors. The atmosphere is friendly and restful. The dive services are superb—you set your gear up only once and the rest is done for you during your stay. Activities include horseshoes and badminton. *⬚ Box 44, South Hole Sound* ☎ *345/948–1099 or 800/899–2582* 🖷 *317/636–9503* ⊕ *www.southerncrossclub.com* ⤶ *9 rooms, 3 suites ⌂ Restaurant, bar, spa, dive shop, snorkeling, boating, fishing, bicycles, Wi-Fi, Internet room, fans, no room TVs, airport shuttle* ▭ *AE, MC, V* ⎢⊚⎢ *FAP.*

$$$ ⬚ **Little Cayman Beach Resort.** The largest resort on Little Cayman offers the most options for fun-seekers. The two-story hotel has modern facilities and brightly colored rooms that overlook either the pool area or the ocean (the ocean-facing rooms are quieter). A spa offers massages and hair and nail treatments. Meals are served buffet style. Diving and fishing packages are a good value. *⬚ Box 51, Blossom Village* ☎ *345/948–1033 or 800/327–3835* 🖷 *345/948–1040* ⊕ *www.littlecayman.com* ⤶ *40 rooms ⌂ Restaurant, bar, dive shop, boutique, tennis court, pool, gym, hot tub, spa, billiards, boating, windsurfing, fishing, bicycles, meeting rooms; cable TV, no smoking* ▭ *AE, MC, V* ⎢⊚⎢ *FAP.*

$$ 🏠 **Sam McCoy's Diving & Fishing Lodge.** This place is quiet, laid back, and rustic: you can relax in the hammock shed with owner Sam McCoy and listen to his stories. Authentic Caymanian meals are prepared by the family matriarch, Sam's wife, Mary, and served family-style in the large dining room overlooking the small pool and the ocean. Eight rooms are simple in decor and have private baths. McCoy's is a favorite for Saturday-evening barbecues under the stars at the beachside bar. 🏠 *Box 12, North Side* ☎ *345/948–0026 or 800/626–0496* 🖶 *345/948–0057* ⊕ *mccoyslodge.com.ky* ⤳ *8 rooms* ⚐ *Fans, cable TV, pool, dive shop, bar* ▭ *AE, MC, V* ▥ *AI.*

Villas & Condos

$$$$ 🏠 **Conch Club.** Two-story, two- and three-bedroom condos are brilliantly decorated and well equipped, ideal for families or small groups. The town house–style units have vaulted ceilings, full kitchens, private patios, and balconies that look out onto the pool and ocean. Diving is offered through Conch Club Divers. Guests can also enjoy the amenities at the Little Cayman Beach Resort (a sister property). 🏠 *Box 51, Blossom Village* ☎ *345/948–1033 or 800/327–3835* ⊕ *www.conchclub. com* ⤳ *8 2-bedroom condos, 4 3-bedroom condos* ⚐ *Kitchens, cable TV, pool, hot tub, spa, dive shop, bicycles, shop, laundry facilities, Internet room* ▭ *AE, MC, V* ▥ *EP.*

$$ 🏠 **The Club.** These ultramodern, luxurious condos are the newest and nicest units on Little Cayman. Each of the three-bedroom residences comes fully equipped, from kitchen to bedroom, with Turkish tiles and upscale furnishings. The complex has an outdoor pool and Jacuzzi along the beachfront. Guests can use the amenities of Little Cayman Beach Resort, which has the same owners; it's about a five-minute walk from the Club. You can sign up for a meal plan at the Little Cayman Beach Resort. Rates do not include housekeeping. 🏠 *Box 51, Blossom Village* ☎ *727/323–8727 or 800/327–3835* 🖶 *345/948–1040* ⊕ *www. theclubatlittlecayman.com* ⤳ *7 condos* ⚐ *Kitchens, cable TV, pool, hot tub, beach* ▭ *AE, MC, V* ▥ *EP.*

$$ 🏠 **Paradise Villas.** The cozy one-bedroom units have beach front terraces and hammocks. Rooms are simply but immaculately appointed with rattan furnishings and muted abstract fabrics. If you get tired of cooking for yourself in the well-equipped kitchen, delicious island-style food (not to mention the island's only bar) is steps away at the Hungry Iguana restaurant. Diving is done with the on-site dive shop. 🏠 *Box 48, Southern Hole Sound* ☎ *345/948–0001* 🖶 *345/948–0002* ⊕ *www. paradisevillas.com* ⤳ *12 1-bedroom villas* ⚐ *Kitchenettes, cable TV, pool, dive shop, bicycles, shop* ▭ *AE, MC, V* ▥ *EP.*

Beaches

★ **Owen Island.** This private island can be reached by rowboat, kayak, or an ambitious 200-yard swim. Anyone is welcome to come across and enjoy the deserted beaches.

Point o' Sand. On the easternmost point of the island, this secluded beach is great for wading, shell collecting, and snorkeling. On a clear day you can see 7 mi (11 km) across to Cayman Brac.

Sports & the Outdoors

BIRD-WATCHING
★

Booby Pond Nature Reserve is home for 5,000 pairs of red-footed boobies (the largest colony in the western hemisphere) and 1,000 magnificent frigate birds. You may catch black frigates and snowy egrets competing for lunch in dramatic dive-bombing battles. The sanctuary is near the airport, is open to the public, and has a gift shop and reading library.

DIVING &
SNORKELING
Fodor'sChoice
★

Bloody Bay Wall, on the NorthSide begins at a mere 18 feet and plunges to more than 1,000 feet, with visibility often reaching 150 feet—diving doesn't get much better than this. Expect to pay $60 to $75 for a two-tank boat dive. The island is small and susceptible to wind.

Paradise Divers (☎ 345/948–0001 ⊕ www.paradise-divers.com) runs a 46-foot boat from the north coast of Little Cayman to Bloody Bay and Jackson Bay. **Pirate's Point Dive Resort** (☎ 345/948–1010 ⊕ www.piratespointresort.com) has fully outfitted dive boats with dive masters who are great at finding odd and rare creatures. **Reef Divers** (☎ 345/948–1033), at Little Cayman Beach Resort, also offers a full-service photo and video center. **Sam McCoy's Diving & Fishing Lodge** (☎ 345/948–0026 or 800/626–0496 ⊕ www.mccoyslodge.com.ky) takes small groups on its dive boat. This is the closest dive operation to Bloody Bay (only 10 minutes away) and provides shore diving from Jackson's Point. The **Southern Cross Club** (☎ 800/899–2582 ⊕ www.southerncrossclub.com) limits each of its boats to 12 divers and has its own dock.

FISHING

Bloody Bay, off the north coast, is well known for fishing, and the shallows in South Hole Lagoon are a great spot for tarpon, bonefish, and permit (a large fish related to pompano). Sam McCoy, of **Sam McCoy's Diving & Fishing Resort** (☎ 345/948–0026 or 800/626–0496 ⊕ www.mccoyslodge.com.ky), is among the premier fishermen on the island. The **Southern Cross Club** (☎ 800/899–2582 ⊕ www.southerncrossclub.com) offers light-tackle and deep-sea fishing trips.

Exploring Little Cayman

⓬ **Little Cayman Museum.** The museum displays relics and artifacts that give a good introduction to the history and heritage of this small island. ⊠ *Across from Booby Pond Nature Reserve, Blossom Village* ☎ *No phone* ⊡ *Free* ⊙ *Tues. and Thurs. 3–5, by appointment only.*

⓫ **Little Cayman Research Centre.** Located near the Jackson Point marine reserve, this important research center supports visiting students and researchers and has a long list of projects under way studying the reef and ocean ecosystem of Little Cayman. It offers classes in tropical marine ecology for advanced students, a summer teachers' institute, and much more. The center is also soliciting funding through the parent U.S. non-profit organization Central Caribbean Marine Institute, so if you value the health of our reefs, which is only possible through understanding, go to the Web site and offer your help. ⊠ *North Side* ☎ *345/926–2789* ⊕ *www.reefresearch.org* ⊙ *By appointment only.*

CAYMAN ISLANDS ESSENTIALS

To research prices, get advice from other travelers, and book travel arrangements, visit www.fodors.com.

Transportation

BY AIR

All direct air service is to Grand Cayman and Cayman Brac, with connecting flights to Little Cayman on a small propeller plane. Cayman Airways offers nonstops from several destinations, including Boston, Chicago, Houston, Miami, and Tampa. British Airways flies from London–Gatwick via Nassau. Cayman Airways has multiple flights daily to both Cayman Brac and Little Cayman.

🛪 **Air Canada** ☎ 345/949-2309. **Air Jamaica** ☎ 345/949-2300. **American Airlines** ☎ 345/949-0666. **British Airways** ☎ 345/949-4118. **Cayman Airways** ☎ 345/949-2311. **Continental** ☎ 345/916-5545. **Delta** ☎ 345/945-8430. **US Airways** ☎ 345/949-7488.

AIRPORTS: 🛪 **Owen Roberts Airport** ⊠ Grand Cayman ☎ 345/943-7070. **Gerrard-Smith International Airport** ⊠ Cayman Brac ☎ 345/948-1222. **Edward Bodden Airstrip** ⊠ Little Cayman ☎ 345/948-0021.

BY BIKE & MOPED

When renting a motor scooter or bicycle, remember to drive on the left and wear sunblock and a helmet. Bicycles ($10 to $15 a day) and scooters ($30 to $35 a day) can be rented in George Town when cruise ships are in port. On Cayman Brac or Little Cayman your hotel can make arrangements for you. A few resorts also offer bicycles for local sightseeing.

BY BUS

On Grand Cayman, bus service, in mini-vans marked "Omni Bus," runs from 6 AM to midnight from West Bay to Rum Point. All routes branch from George Town near the library and are described in the phone book. The one-way fare from George Town to West Bay via Seven Mile Beach is $2.50. Some bus stops are well marked; others are flexible. Respond with a wave; then the driver toots his horn.

BY CAR

The major agencies have offices to the left as you depart the airport terminal in Grand Cayman; Andy's is to the right. All require that you walk outdoors for a hundred yards. Make sure your luggage is portable, because there's no shuttle; if there are two of you, one can watch the bags while the other gets the car. Many car-rental firms have free pickup and drop-off along Seven Mile Beach so you can rent just on the days you want to tour. Consider security when renting a Jeep that cannot be locked. Midsize cars here often mean sub-compact, so you may end up with a car that you wear unless you check the model. McLaughlin is the only agency on Little Cayman, though you probably won't need to rent a car there.

Traffic on West Bay Road and the road to Bodden Town in Grand Cayman is terrible, especially during the 7 to 9 AM and 4:45 to 6:30 PM commuting times, since these are the only thoroughfares to and from town. Exploring Cayman Brac on a scooter is easy and fun. You won't really need a car on Little Cayman, though there are a limited number of Jeeps for rent.

Gas is more expensive than in the United States. If you're touring Grand Cayman by car, there's a well-maintained road that follows the coast; it's hard to get lost except in West Bay. Driving in the Cayman Islands is on the left (as in the United Kingdom), so when pulling out into traffic, look to your right and drive defensively.

🚗 Grand Cayman Agencies **Ace Hertz** ☎ 345/949-2280 or 800/654-3131. **Andy's Rent a Car** ☎ 345/949-8111. **Avis** ☎ 345/949-2468 ⊕ www.aviscayman.com. **Budget** ☎ 345/949-5605 or 800/527-0700 ⊕ www.budgetcayman.com. **Coconut Car Rentals** ☎ 345/949-4377 ⊕ www.coconutcarrentals.com.

Dollar ☎ 345/949–4790. **Economy** ☎ 345/949–9550. **Marshall's** ☎ 345/949–2127 ⊕ www.cayman.com.ky. **Thrifty** ☎ 345/949–6640.

🚗 Cayman Brac & Little Cayman Agencies **B&S Motor Ventures** ⊠ Cayman Brac ☎ 345/948–1646. **CB Rent-a-Car** ⊠ Cayman Brac ☎ 345/948–2424. **Four D's Car Rental** ⊠ Cayman Brac ☎ 345/948–1599. **Rent-a-Car Ltd.** ⊠ Cayman Brac ☎ 345/948–1515. **McLaughlin Rentals** ⊠ Little Cayman ☎ 345/948–1000.

BY TAXI

Taxis offer 24-hour islandwide service. Call for a cab to be dispatched, as you generally cannot hail one on the street. Fares are set by the government and are not cheap, so ask ahead. The rate increases with the number of riders and bags. To travel in style by white limo, you can call A. A. Transportation or Elite Limousine Services.

🚗 **A. A. Transportation Services** ☎ 345/949–7222. **Charlie's Super Cab** ☎ 345/949–4748. **Elite Limousine Services** ☎ 345/949–5963. **Webster's Taxi Service** ☎ 345/947–1718.

Contacts & Resources

BANKS & EXCHANGE SERVICES

You should not need to change money in Grand Cayman, since U.S. dollars are readily accessible, though you may get some change in Cayman dollars, which are worth about 20% more than a U.S. dollar. If you do, ATMs accepting MasterCard and Visa with Cirrus affiliation are readily available in George Town; you usually have the option of U.S. or Cayman dollars. Traveler's checks and major credit cards are also widely accepted. The Cayman dollar (CI$) is divided into a hundred cents, with coins of 1¢, 5¢, 10¢, and 25¢ and notes of $1, $5, $10, $25, $50, and $100. There's no $20 bill.

All prices quoted in this book are in U.S. dollars unless otherwise noted.

BUSINESS HOURS

Banks are open Monday through Friday from 9 to 4. Post offices are open weekdays from 8:30 to 3:30 and Saturday from 8:30 to 11:30. Shops are open weekdays from 9 to 5 and Saturday in George Town from 10 to 2; in outer shopping plazas they are open from 10 to 5. Shops are usually closed Sunday except in hotels or when cruise ships are visiting.

ELECTRICITY

Electricity is reliable and is the same as the United States (110 volts/60 cycles).

EMBASSIES & CONSULATES

🚗 **U.S. Consular Representative** ⊠ Mrs. Gail Duquesney at Adventure Travel ☎ 345/945–1511.

EMERGENCIES

Although the quality of medical care is adequate on the island, air-ambulance service through Executive Air to Miami is available when necessary within two hours. Double-check the care that you are given and get second opinions when possible.

🚗 Emergency Services **Executive Air** ☎ 345/949–7775. **Medical and fire emergencies** ☎ 911. **Police emergencies** ☎ 911.

🚗 Hospitals **George Town Hospital** ⊠ Hospital Rd., George Town ☎ 345/949–8600. **Cayman Clinic** ☎ 345/949–4234.

🚗 Pharmacies **Cayman Drug** ⊠ Kirk Freeport Centre, George Town ☎ 345/949–2597. **Foster's Pharmacy** ⊠ Foster's Food Fair, Airport Rd., George Town ☎ 345/949–0505. **Health Care Pharmacy** ⊠ Photo-Pharm Centre, Walkers Rd., George Town ☎ 345/949–0442. **Kirk Pharmacy** ⊠ Kirk Supermarket, Eastern Ave., George Town ☎ 345/949–7180.

🚗 Diving Emergencies **Cayman Hyperbaric** ⊠ Hospital Rd., George Town ☎ 345/949–2989.

HOLIDAYS

Public holidays include New Year's Day, Ash Wednesday (46 days before Easter), Good Friday (Friday before Easter), Easter Sunday (usually Mar. or Apr.), Discovery Day (May 19), Queen's Birthday (June 16), Constitution Day (July 7), Christmas, and Boxing Day (Dec. 26). Boxing Day is a day to box up extra gifts for the poor—not a pugilistic day.

INTERNET, MAIL & SHIPPING

Many resorts offer Internet service, and some even offer wireless service throughout their property. You can find Internet cafés in almost all the shopping centers along Seven Mile Beach.

Sending a postcard to the United States, Canada, other parts of the Caribbean, or Central America costs CI 20¢. An airmail letter is CI 30¢ per half ounce. To Europe and South America, rates are CI 25¢ for a postcard and CI 40¢ per half ounce for airmail letters. When addressing letters to the Cayman Islands, be sure to include "BWI" (British West Indies) at the bottom of the envelope. Note that the islands don't use private addresses or postal codes; all mail is delivered to numbered post office boxes. For faster and reliable service to the United States, Federal Express, UPS, and DHL all have locations in the downtown area.

🚩 **Azzurro** ⊠ Buckingham Place, West Bay Rd., Seven Mile Beach **Café del Sol** ⊠ Marquee Plaza, Seven Mile Beach **PC Powerhouse** ⊠ West Shore Centre, West Bay Rd., Seven Mile Beach

PASSPORT REQUIREMENTS

U.S. citizens will have to carry a valid passport as of January 1, 2007; until then, a government-issued picture ID as well as an official birth certificate with a raised seal are acceptable. However, U.K. and Canadian citizens may enter the Cayman Islands with a certified birth certificate (with a raised seal) and a valid picture ID. Citizens of all other countries need a valid passport. Citizens of many countries, including Jamaica, must purchase expensive visas in advance.

SAFETY

The Cayman Islands are comparatively safe, but theft and muggings are becoming more common. Be smart: lock your room and car and secure valuables as you would at home. Don't wander alone late at night, especially in the George Town area. Purse snatching along the waterfront is still rather rare but not unknown.

TAXES

A 10% government tax is added to all accommodations fees. Otherwise, there's no tax on goods or services paid at the consumer level. There's a considerable import duty already paid for virtually everything brought onto the island with several exceptions, including cameras, books, and coffee.

TELEPHONE

Cable & Wireless (Cayman Islands) Ltd is the main provider. The area code for the Cayman Islands is 345. To make local calls (on or between any of the three islands), dial the seven-digit number. Credit cards and calling cards can be used to call worldwide from any phone and most hotels, though from the latter there's almost always a hefty surcharge, even to access toll-free access numbers for prepaid phone cards.

Almost everyone in the Cayman Islands has a cell phone. There are currently three suppliers of service: Cable & Wireless, Digicel, and Cingular. If you're bringing your own mobile phone and it's compatible with 850/1900 Mhz GSM network or TDMA digital network, you should be able to send and receive calls during your stay. Be sure, however, to check with your home provider to be sure that you have roaming service enabled. Mobile phone rental is also available from Cable & Wireless; you can stay connected for as little as CI$5 per day plus the cost of a calling card.

🚩 **Cable & Wireless** ☎ 345/949-7800 ⊕ www. candw.ky. **Cayman Online** ☎ 345/949-9777 ⊕ www.caymaninternet.com. **Cingular** ☎ 345/ 943-2273 ⊕ www.cingular.ky. **Digicel** ☎ 345/943-3444 ⊕ www.digicelcayman.com.

TIPPING

At large hotels a service charge is generally included and can be anywhere from 6% to 10%; smaller establishments and some villas and condos leave tipping up to you. Although tipping is customary at restaurants, note that some automatically include 15% on the bill—so check the tab carefully. Taxi drivers expect a 10% to 15% tip.

TOUR OPTIONS

Costs and itineraries for island tours are about the same regardless of the tour operator. Half-day tours average $30 to $50 a person and generally include a visit to the Turtle Farm and Hell in West Bay, as well as shopping downtown. Full-day tours ($55 to $75 per person) add lunch, a visit to Bodden Town, and the East End, where you visit blowholes (if the waves are high) on the ironshore and the site of the wreck of the *Ten Sails* (not the wreck itself—just the site). The Pirate graves in Bodden Town were destroyed during Hurricane Ivan, and the blowholes were partially filled. As you can tell, land tours here are low-key.

A. A. Transportation Services offers taxis and tour buses. Ask for Burton Ebanks. Majestic Tours offers West Bay group tours by bus. Tropicana Tours offers a Cayman highlights tour.

Cayman Island Helicopters offers amazing aerial tours on three itineraries: $65 for a flyover of Seven Mile Beach; $95 for a trip over Stingray City; and $265 for an island-wide aerial tour.

🚹 **A. A. Transportation Services** ☎ 345/949–7222 ⊕ www.burtons.ky. **Cayman Island Helicopters** ☎ 345/949-4354, 345/929-0116 cell. **Majestic Tours** ☎ 345/949-7773 ⊕ www.majestic-tours.com. **Tropicana Tours** ☎ 345/949-0944 ⊕ www.tropicana-tours.com.

VISITOR INFORMATION

🚹 Before You Leave **Cayman Islands Department of Tourism** ✉ 8300 N.W. 53rd St., Suite 103, Miami, FL 33166 ☎ 305/599-9033 ⊕ www.caymanislands.ky ✉ 2 Memorial City Plaza, 820 Gessner, Suite 170, Houston, TX 77024 ☎ 713/461-1317 ✉ 3 Park Ave., 39th fl., New York, NY 10016 ☎ 212/889-9009 ✉ 1 Lincoln Center, 18W 140 Butterfield Rd., Suite 920, Oakbrook Terrace, IL 60181 ☎ 630/705-1383 ✉ 234 Eglinton Ave. E, Suite 306, Toronto, Ontario, Canada, M4P 1K5 ☎ 416/485-1550 ✉ 6 Arlington St., London, U.K., SWIA 1RE ☎ 0207/491-7771.

🚹 In the Cayman Islands **Burton's Tourist Information & Activity Services** ☎ 345/949-6598 🖷 345/945-6222. **Department of Tourism** ✉ Regatta Office Park Leeward 2, W. Bay Rd., Box 67GT, George Town ☎ 345/949-0623 ✉ Owen Roberts Airport, Grand Cayman ☎ 345/949-3603.

WEDDINGS

Getting married in the Cayman Islands is a breeze, and many couples a year tie the knot on these islands. Most do so on lovely Seven Mile Beach with the sun setting into the azure sea as their picture-perfect backdrop. Underwater weddings in full scuba gear are also possible. Cathy Church can photograph your underwater wedding (see ⇨ Shopping, *above*).

Documentations can be prepared ahead of time or in one day while on the island. There's no on-island waiting period. In addition to the application, you need proof of identity, such as an original or certified birth certificate or passport; a Cayman Islands international embarkation/disembarkation card; and certified or original copies of divorce decrees/death certificates if you have been married before. You must list a marriage officer on the application, and you need at least two witnesses; if you haven't come with friends or family, the marriage officer can help you with that, too. A marriage license costs CI$160.

The best way to plan your wedding in the Cayman Islands is to contact a wedding coordinator, who will offer a wide variety of packages to suit every taste and budget. All of the logistics and legalities are properly handled, giving you time to relax and enjoy the wedding of your dreams. The Cayman Islands Department of Tourism keeps a list of wedding coordinators. Or you can order the brochure "Getting Married in the Cayman Islands" from Government Information Services. Vernon Jackson, of Cayman Weddings, is a wonderful marriage officer with a soft accent and a kind heart. You can choose from many different styles of services or rewrite one as you wish.

🚹 **Cayman Weddings** ☎ 345/949-8677 ⊕ www.caymanweddings.com.ky. **Deputy Chief Secretary** ✉ Government Administration Bldg., 3rd fl., George Town, Grand Cayman ☎ 345/949-7900. **Government Information Services** ✉ Cricket Sq., George Town ☎ 345/949-8092. **Heart of Cayman** ☎ 345/949-1343 ⊕ www.heartofcayman.com.

Curaçao

Playa Lagun

WORD OF MOUTH

"The best part about Curaçao is the culture and the local life. It truly provides many opportunities for the off-the-beaten-path vacation. It has not been overrun with tourism yet. . . ."

—Doug

"Curaçao is a windy arid island (will remind you of Arizona on the beach). . . . The beaches are wonderful and . . . you can "walk" out into the water and snorkel directly off the beach."

—John

www.fodors.com/forums

8

WELCOME TO CURAÇAO

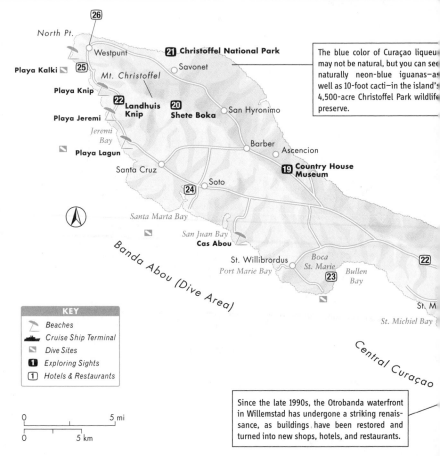

The blue color of Curaçao liqueur may not be natural, but you can see naturally neon-blue iguanas—as well as 10-foot cacti—in the island's 4,500-acre Christoffel Park wildlife preserve.

21 Christoffel National Park

North Pt.

Westpunt

Playa Kalki **25**

Mt. Christoffel

Playa Knip

22 Landhuis Knip

Playa Jeremi

Jeremi Bay

Playa Lagun

Santa Cruz

26

Savonet

20 Shete Boka

San Hyronimo

Barber

Ascencion

19 Country House Museum

Soto

24

Santa Marta Bay

San Juan Bay

Cas Abou

Banda Abou (Dive Area)

St. Willibrordus

Port Marie Bay

Boca St. Marie

23

Bullen Bay

22

St. M

St. Michiel Bay

Central Curaçao

KEY
- Beaches
- Cruise Ship Terminal
- Dive Sites
- **1** Exploring Sights
- 1 Hotels & Restaurants

0 ——————— 5 mi
0 ——————— 5 km

Since the late 1990s, the Otrobanda waterfront in Willemstad has undergone a striking renaissance, as buildings have been restored and turned into new shops, hotels, and restaurants.

Willemstad's fancifully hued, strikingly gabled townhouses glimmer across Santa Anna Bay, while vendors at the Floating Market sell tropical fruit from their schooners. Curaçao's diverse population mixes Latin, European, and African ancestries. Religious tolerance is a hallmark here. All people are welcome in Curaçao, and even tourists feel the warmth.

AN ISLAND REBORN AND REDISCOVERED

The largest and most populous of the Netherlands Antilles is 38 mi (61 km) long and no more than 7½ mi (12 km) wide. Its capital, Willemstad, has been restored and revived over the past few years and is a recognized UNESCO World Heritage Site. The colorful, waterfront townhouses are unique to the island.

Only one maker of the famous orange-flavored Curaçao liqueur is allowed to call itself "authentic": the Senior Curaçao distillery in Saliña Arriba. But the blue color is just an additive.

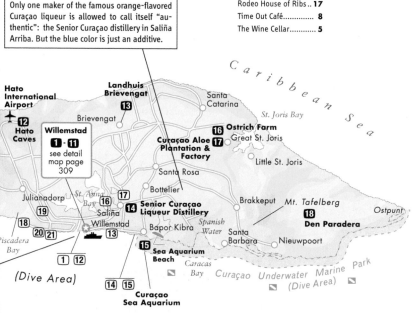

CURAÇAO

8

TOP 4 REASONS TO VISIT CURAÇAO

1. Since it sits below the hurricane belt, the weather in Curaçao is almost always alluring, even during the off-season.

2. Carnival is the year's biggest party, drawing an increasing crowd.

3. The island's cultural diversity is reflected in the good food from many different cultures.

4. Striking architecture and fascinating historic sights give you something to see when you're not shopping or lying on the charming beaches.

CURAÇAO PLANNER

Getting to Curaçao

The only nonstops to Curaçao (CUR) from North America are from Miami and Newark; your only other options at this writing are connections in San Juan, Montego Bay, or Aruba. There are direct flights from Amsterdam. If you want to connect through Aruba, you'll more likely than not have to book your flight on a tiny island-hopper directly with the island-based airline.

Hato International Airport has car-rental facilities, duty-free shops, and a restaurant. It takes about 20 minutes to get to the hotels in Willemstad by taxi.

Hassle Factor: Medium

Activities

The island has many good **beaches**, not to mention clear, blue water; however, a lot of the beaches on the southeast coast (even the hotel beaches) are a bit rocky. The softer, whiter beaches are on the west coast. Excellent **diving** has always been a draw in Curaçao, and a fair percentage of travelers are drawn by the teeming reefs and good shore-diving possibilities. **Day sails** are the most popular way to enjoy the water if you don't dive, and all of them offer opportunities for good snorkeling. Both sides of Willemstad—Punda and the revitalized Otrobanda—offer the shore bound plenty to occupy their time, making it well worth your while to check out the local **sights** and do some **shopping**. Do stop for a bite to eat at one of the many great restaurants. By night, you can gamble in a few **casinos** or check out some of the lively bars and dance clubs.

On the Ground

Taxis have meters, but drivers still use set fares when picking passengers up at the airport. Verify which method your driver will use before setting off. Fares from the airport to Willemstad and the nearby beach hotels run about $15 to $20, and those to hotels at the island's western end about $25 to $40.

Renting a Car

It's worthwhile to rent a car to explore the island, even if you don't take it for your entire stay. Many of the larger hotels have free shuttles into Willemstad, where you can shop and eat. Hotels in town usually provide a free beach shuttle. If you're planning to do country driving or rough it through Christoffel Park, a four-wheel-drive vehicle is best. All you need is a valid U.S., Canadian or British driver's license. You can rent a car from any of the major car agencies at the airport or have one delivered free to your hotel. Rates range from about $35 to $40 a day for a compact car to about $75 for a four-door sedan or four-wheel-drive vehicle; add 6% tax and required $12 daily insurance.

Where to Stay

Although Curaçao is the largest of the Dutch Antilles, resort development is still concentrated around the capital, Willemstad, so most resorts are within easy reach, either by shuttle or even by foot. As the island becomes more developed, visitors have a wider variety of options, and there are a few resorts farther removed as well, but it's the amenities that should drive your decision more than location. Those spending a bit more time—especially Europeans—gravitate to villas and bungalows.

TYPES OF LODGINGS

Resorts: Most of Curaçao's larger hotels are mid-sized resorts of 200 to 300 rooms, and many of them are within easy striking distance of town. There aren't any extravagantly luxurious resorts on the island—and none with mind-boggling nightly rates—but a few of the more atmospheric properties incorporate restored 18th-century buildings.

Dive Resorts: Most of the resorts catering to divers are smaller operations of under 100 rooms (often much smaller). While some of these are in and around Willemstad, there are also a few on the secluded west end of the island, and that's where shore diving is best.

Villas and Bungalows: Though they are marketed primarily to European travelers who have more time to spend on the island, self-catering accommodations are an option for anyone who has at least a week to spend in Curaçao.

When to Go

High season in Curaçao mirrors that in much of the Caribbean, basically from mid-December through mid-April. In the off-season, rates will be reduced at least 25% and often more.

The year's big event is **Carnival**, which concludes on Ash Wednesday; it's among the Caribbean's best parties and is beginning to draw visitors in larger numbers. The **Curaçao International Jazz Festival** is held in May; the **Salsa Festival** is held in June, July, or August.

8

Hotel & Restaurant Costs

Assume that hotels operate on the European Plan (**EP**—with no meals) unless we specify that they use either the Continental Plan (**CP**—with a Continental breakfast), Breakfast Plan (**BP**—with full breakfast), or the Modified American Plan (**MAP**—with breakfast and dinner). Other hotels may offer the Full American Plan (**FAP**—including all meals but no drinks) or may be All-Inclusive (**AI**—with all meals, drinks, and most activities).

WHAT IT COSTS in Dollars

	$$$$	$$$	$$	$	¢
Restaurants	over $30	$20–$30	$12–$20	$8–$12	under $8
Hotels*	over $350	$250–$350	$150–$250	$80–$150	under $80
Hotels**	over $450	$350–$450	$250–$350	$125–$250	under $125

*EP, BP, CP **AI, FAP, MAP
Restaurant prices are for a main course excluding 10%–15% service charge. Hotel prices are for two people in a double room in high season excluding 7% tax, customary 12% service charge, and meal plans (except at all-inclusives).

By Elise Rosen

THE FLOATING PONTOON BRIDGE swings open to let a giant freighter into Willemstad's historic harbor. For a few minutes there will be no crossing by foot from one side of the city to the other, so ferry passengers, chattering gleefully in a multitude of languages, gather at the landing on the Punda side and board for the quick trip across the bay to Otrobanda. Around the bend, a dozen Venezuelan schooners are anchored in the Waaigat Canal, their colorful cargo of fresh fish and produce laid out for sale. On the Handelskade, a man strolls along the harborfont with three iguanas draped over his shoulders, luring amused passersby to stop and have a picture taken with the creatures. Nearby, tourists sip frozen margaritas on the patio of an outdoor café under a giant red umbrella. In the background, the splendorous facades of Punda's waterfront town houses glisten in the sunlight.

The sun smiles down on Curaçao, which sits below the so-called hurricane belt, 35 mi (56 km) north of Venezuela and 42 mi (68 km) east of Aruba. The seat of government and the largest island of the Netherlands Antilles (at 38 mi [61 km] long and 3 mi [5 km] wide) Curaçao is infused with both Dutch and Caribbean influences everywhere, but you can also find touches of Latin America and the rest of the world, reflecting the island's ethnic diversity.

Gentle trade winds help keep the heat in check, and temperatures are generally in the 80s Fahrenheit. Water sports—including outstanding reef diving—attract enthusiasts from all over the world. Curaçao claims 38 beaches—some long stretches of silky sand, most smaller coves suitable for picture-postcards. In the countryside, the dollhouse look of plantation houses, or *landhuizen* (literally, "land houses"), makes a cheerful contrast to stark cacti and austere shrubbery.

The sprawling city of Willemstad is the island's capital. Its historic downtown and the natural harbor (*Schottegat*) around which it's built are included on UNESCO's World Heritage List, a coveted distinction reserved for the likes of the Palace of Versailles and the Taj Mahal. The "face" of Willemstad delights like a kaleidoscope—rows of sprightly painted town houses with gabled roofs sit perched alongside the steely blue Santa Anna Bay. Local lore has it that in the 1800s, the governor claimed he suffered from migraines and blamed the glare from the sun's reflection off the then-white structures. To alleviate the problem, he ordered the facades painted in colors.

Curaçao was discovered by Alonzo de Ojeda (a lieutenant of Columbus) in 1499. The first Spanish settlers arrived in 1527. In 1634 the Dutch came via the Netherlands West Indies Company. Eight years later Peter Stuyvesant began his rule as governor (in 1647, Stuyvesant became governor of New Amsterdam, which later became New York). Twelve Jewish families arrived in Curaçao from Amsterdam in 1651, and by 1732 a synagogue had been built; the present structure is the oldest synagogue in continuous use in the western hemisphere. Over the years the city built fortresses to defend against French and British invasions—the standing ramparts now house restaurants and hotels. The Dutch claim to Curaçao was recognized in 1815 by the Treaty of Paris. In 1954 Curaçao became—along with the other Antillean islands—an autonomous part of the Kingdom of the Netherlands, with a governor appointed by the queen, an elected parliament, and an island council.

The economy is based primarily on oil refining; tourism is the number two industry and becoming increasingly important, with a corresponding surge in hotel development in recent years. The opening of a mega pier has boosted cruise-ship passengers to record numbers. In addition, the government and private sources have invested millions of dollars to restore colonial buildings to their original stature.

Today Curaçao's population derives from nearly 60 nationalities—an exuberant mix of Latin, European, and African roots, who speak a Babel of tongues—resulting in superb restaurants and a flourishing cultural scene. Although Dutch is the official language, Papiamento is the vernacular of all the Netherlands Antilles and the preferred choice for communication among the locals. English and Spanish are also widely spoken. The island, like its Dutch settlers, is known for its religious tolerance, and tourists are warmly welcomed.

Where to Stay

You'll generally find hotels at all price levels provide friendly, prompt, detail-oriented service; however, the finer points of service are in some cases still in nascent stages. Many of the large-scale resorts east and west of Willemstad proper have lovely beaches and provide a free shuttle to the city, 5 to 10 minutes away; but you'll find utmost seclusion at hotels on the island's southwestern end, a 30- to 45-minute drive from town. Most hotels in town provide beach shuttles. At this writing, a 350-room Hyatt Regency resort (with an 18-hole golf course) was going up at Santa Barbara and was expected to open in mid-2007. Other major development projects include a Renaissance hotel and multipurpose entertainment and shopping complex to be built at the Riffort in Otrobanda (with projected completion in 2009), as well as new hotels to be built at Caracas Bay and Kontiki Beach (with projected openings in 2008); and at Piscadera Bay, a nearly completed Clarion Hotel & Suites with 150 to 200 rooms, scheduled to open in early 2006.

Villa and bungalow rentals are especially popular with divers and European visitors and are generally good options for large groups or longer stays. The **Curaçao Tourist Board** (see ⇨ Curaçao A to Z, *below*) has a complete list of rental apartments, villas, and bungalows on its Web site. The villas at **Livingstone Jan Thiel Resort** (⊠ Jan Thiel Beach z/n ☎ 5999/747–0332 ⊕ www.janthielresort.com) surround a swimming pool in a low-rise complex that offers a mini-market on-site, free access to the beach across the street, Internet access in the open-air lobby, and a special playground and programs for kids. Festive decor includes a large painted mural at the entrance and beaded shades on tabletop candleholders at the poolside restaurant.

The bungalows at **Papagayo Beach Resort** (⊠ Jan Thiel Beach z/n ☎ 5999/747–4333 ⊕ papagayo-beach.com) give you a unique option: on a whim you can open up a full wall so that your wraparound wooden terrace becomes part of your space and you're as close as it gets to living outdoors, while tucked under a roof and with all the amenities of a well-designed and nicely furnished home, including two bedrooms, a full kitchen with dishwasher, and bathroom (showers only). The restaurant menu changes seasonally; the pool bar is a cozy place to meet your neighbors. There's no beachfront, but you get free access to the beach across the street. Special programs and entertainment for kids are offered during school vacation periods.

$$$–$$$$ **Curaçao Marriott Beach Resort & Emerald Casino.** The cream of the crop
FodorśChoice of Curaçao's resorts beckons you to live it up from the moment you ar-
★ rive. The grand open-air lobby ushers you into a wonder-world—albeit carefree and unpretentious—embraced by a crescent beach that hugs the resort's edge. Towering palm trees and cheerful bursts of red hibiscus and oleander surround the panoply of laid-back luxury; attentive staff greet you with pleasantries at every turn. Indulge yourself with a holistic treatment at the spa, frolic at the swim-up bar, try your luck at the alluring—though small—casino, or kick back with a mojito at the Emerald Lounge, which turns into a disco nightly. Guest rooms, which are attractively outfitted but otherwise pretty standard-issue chain hotel rooms, all have balconies or patios. With myriad options, the breakfast buffet is among the island's best. An all-inclusive option is offered. *Box 6003, Piscadera Bay* ☎ *5999/736–8800* 🖨 *5999/462–7502* ⊕ *www.marriott. com* ➪ *237 rooms, 10 suites* ⚬ *3 restaurants, room service, in-room safes, cable TV, in-room broadband, in-room data ports, Wi-Fi, golf privileges, 2 tennis courts, pool, health club, hair salon, 2 outdoor hot tubs, spa, beach, dive shop, dock, snorkeling, windsurfing, 2 bars, casino, shops, babysitting, children's programs (ages 5–12), dry cleaning, laundry service, Internet room, business services, convention center, car rental, no-smoking rooms* ▤ *AE, D, DC, MC, V* ❘⊙❘ *EP.*

$$$ **Breezes Curaçao.** You might enjoy the conviviality at the island's biggest all-inclusive, but unless you venture off the lushly landscaped grounds, you won't get much taste of the real Curaçao. On the other hand, you won't have much reason to leave: Trapeze and trampoline clinics on the beach are among the highlights of the innumerable activities included in the room rate. Body-painting contests, beach volleyball, toga parties, karaoke, and much more add to the nonstop merriment. Water massages and pregnancy massages are among the latest additions to the full menu of destressing options at the spa. The casino is one of the island's largest. Don't hesitate to bring the kids, too; they'll find plenty of supervised action—like sand-castle building and circus workshops—and get lots of attention. ✉ *Martin Luther King Blvd. 8, Willemstad* ☎ *5999/736–7888 or 800/467–8737* 🖨 *5999/461–4131* ⊕ *www. breezes.com* ➪ *285 rooms, 54 suites* ⚬ *3 restaurants, in-room safes, cable TV, 2 tennis courts, 4 pools, health club, spa, beach, dive shop, dock, snorkeling, windsurfing, boating, bicycles, basketball, billiards, Ping-Pong, volleyball, 4 bars, piano bar, casino, nightclub, recreation room, video game room, shops, babysitting, children's programs (ages 2–16), complimentary weddings, dry cleaning, laundry service, Inter-*

net room, business services, convention center, meeting rooms, car rental, travel services, no-smoking rooms ▤ *AE, DC, MC, V* ⊠ *AI.*

★ $$–$$$ ▦ **Avila Beach Hotel.** The right blend of Old World touches, modern amenities, alluring beachfront, attentive managers and staff, and joie de vivre makes this resort the place of choice for the visiting Dutch royalty (well, all guests actually). This well-run hotel on a delightful beach has blossomed around the 18th-century mansion at its center. You'll find every comfort in the modern wings—the Blues Wing, so-called for the silhouettes of sax players on the guestroom doors, has waterside decks, jetted bathtubs, and well-stocked kitchenettes; a new wing and a pool were being constructed at this writing and were set to open in October 2006. The hotel retains traces of its Dutch heritage in the main lobby, which is dressed like a prim European parlor, with gilt mirrors and gas lamps. Dine under the bulb-lighted boughs of an enormous tree at the Belle Terrace restaurant or at Blues, a gem for its nightlife scene. A unique site for weddings, the Octagon Museum is housed in an 18th-century cupola on hotel grounds. ⊠ *Penstraat 130, Box 791, Willemstad* ☎ *5999/461–4377 or 800/747–8162* 🖷 *5999/461–1493* ⊕ *www.avilahotel.com* ⇨ *100 rooms, 8 suites* ⚲ *2 restaurants, café, in-room safes, kitchenettes, refrigerators, cable TV, in-room data ports, tennis court, spa, beach, 2 bars, Internet room, business services, convention center, meeting rooms* ▤ *AE, D, DC, MC, V* ⊠ *EP.*

$$–$$$ ▦ **Floris Suite Hotel.** Although aesthetically pleasing, the minimalist decor of the spacious suites and the stark open-air lobby of this modernist hotel give it a somewhat aloof feel, perhaps making it better suited for business travel than for a romantic getaway. The friendly staff, however, go out of their way to make your stay comfortable. Award-winning Dutch interior designer Jan des Bouvrie has used warm mahogany shades offset by cool, sleek stainless-steel adornments in the suites, all of which have a balcony or porch and a full kitchen. A lush tropical garden surrounds the pool, and the beach is across the street. ⊠ *J. F. Kennedy Blvd., Box 6246, Piscadera Bay* ☎ *5999/462–6111* 🖷 *5999/462–6211* ⊕ *www.florissuitehotel.com* ⇨ *71 suites* ⚲ *Restaurant, room service, fans, kitchens, minibars, cable TV, in-room broadband, in-room data ports, golf privileges, tennis court, pool, gym, dive shop, bar, babysitting, dry cleaning, laundry service, Internet room, business services, meeting rooms, no-smoking rooms* ▤ *AE, D, DC, MC, V* ⊠ *EP.*

★ $$–$$$ ▦ **Hotel Kurá Hulanda.** History comes to life at this quaint hotel, whose guest rooms are tucked into restored 18th-century houses built along pebblestone alleyways that diverge from a central courtyard. The pools and gardens are exquisite, especially at night, when lighting casts a romantic glow. Each room is uniquely decorated with Indian and Indonesian fabrics and furnishings; in-room perks include turn-down service, robes, Aveda toiletries, and CD players. The opulent Indian-style Bridal Suite is a work of art, with marble floors, hammered sterling silver furniture, and a large plasma TV. The only drawback is a lack of beachfront, but a private beach is accessible by a free shuttle, or you can visit the Lodge Kurá Hulanda & Beach Club. The revitalized Otrobanda neighborhood also has great dining within walking distance, and you're a stone's throw from the footbridge to cross over to the Punda for more shopping and sightseeing. The museum and excellent restaurants are worth a visit even if you don't stay here. ✉ *Langestraat 8, Otrobanda, Willemstad* 🖀 *5999/ 434–7700* 🖶 *5999/434–7701* ⊕ *www.kurahulanda.com* 🖙 *80 rooms, 12 suites* ⌂ *4 restaurants, coffee shop, room service, fans, in-room safes, refrigerators, cable TV, in-room broadband, in-room data ports, golf privileges, 2 pools, health club, spa, 2 bars, casino, shops, Internet room, business services, meeting room, free parking* ▭ *AE, D, MC, V* ⫿⊙⫿ *EP.*

★ **$$–$$$** 🏨 **Lodge Kurá Hulanda & Beach Club.** On the island's remote western tip, this sprawling resort with tranquil, lush gardens will make you feel far removed from the daily grind. Rooms in two-story villas offer home-style comforts, including kitchens, beautiful TVs (suites have a 29-inch TV with a DVD/CD player as well as a 21-inch TV in the bedroom), grand porches (many overlooking the ocean), and large, luxurious bathrooms. Cuddle up under 300-thread-count Egyptian cotton sheets and comforters. A free shuttle makes the 45-minute drive to and from town. You can explore the natural beauty of the area on hiking trails within the 350-acre property or on guided mountain bike or quad tours; an activity desk will help coordinate trips anywhere on the island. Or simply mingle with other guests at the outdoor lounge, where you might catch a guitar or sax player on some evenings. An all-inclusive option is available. ✉ *Playa Kalki 1, Westpunt* 🖀 *5999/839–3600* 🖶 *5999/ 839–3601* ⊕ *www.kurahulanda.com* 🖙 *42 rooms, 35 suites* ⌂ *3 restaurants, fans, in-room safes, kitchenettes, cable TV, in-room VCRs, in-room broadband, in-room data ports, tennis court, pool, fitness classes, gym, outdoor hot tub, massage, beach, dive shop, dock, snorkeling, boating, fishing, mountain bikes, hiking, bar, shop, dry cleaning, laundry service, Internet room, meeting room, car rental, some pets allowed* ▭ *AE, D, MC, V* ⫿⊙⫿ *EP.*

☪ **$$–$$$** 🏨 **Sunset Waters Beach Resort.** Serenity-seekers are sure to find what they want at this remote resort on a lusciously long stretch of beach. You can also find scheduled activities, and if you (or the kids) have a special request, the staff will try to accommodate you. The vibe is casual and carefree. Special events like a weekly beach barbecue and Sunday brunch with local food and a steel band engender camaraderie among guests; there's live music on most nights. Many guests are drawn by the excellent dive operation and the proximity to the west-end dive sites, including Mushroom Forest. Rooms are bright and airy, and many are ocean-facing, some with dramatic views through floor-to-ceiling windows. Be aware that a nude section of the beach can be seen from some rooms. Complimentary shuttles run to and from town. ✉ *Santa Marta Bay* 🖀 *5999/864–1233* 🖶 *5999/864–1237* ⊕ *www.sunsetwaters.com* 🖙 *70 rooms* ⌂ *Restaurant, some refrigerators, cable TV, miniature golf, tennis court, pool, health club, outdoor hot tub, beach, dive shop, snorkeling, boating, basketball, billiards, Ping-Pong, soccer, volleyball, 2 bars, shop, babysitting, children's programs (ages 2–16), playground, Internet room, meeting rooms, car rental, travel services; no phones in some rooms* ▭ *AE, D, MC, V* ⫿⊙⫿ *AI.*

☪ **$$** 🏨 **Holiday Beach Hotel & Casino.** Despite the large scale of everything around you, the Holiday Beach manages to offer a cheerful, welcoming ambience wherever you go that will put you immediately at ease.

One tradition is the whimsical main lobby display that changes themat-
ically according to season—like an island version of Macy's windows—
just before the entrance to Curaçao's largest casino. The crescent beach
is dotted with palm trees and palapas for shade. Rooms are airy and
bright, and each has a balcony or patio, although the dim interior hallways exude a dated motel feel. There's a 24-hour Denny's and a video
game arcade on-site, and the shops of Willemstad are within walking
distance. ⊠ *Pater Euwensweg 31, Box 2178, Otrobanda, Willemstad*
☎ *5999/462–5400 or 800/444–5244* 🖷 *5999/462–4397* ⊕ *www.hol-
beach.com* ⇨ *200 rooms, 1 suite* ⌂ *2 restaurants, in-room safes, refrigerators, cable TV, in-room broadband, 2 tennis courts, pool, gym, beach,
dive shop, snorkeling, billiards, volleyball, 2 bars, casino, video game
room, shops, playground, dry cleaning, laundry facilities, Internet room,
convention center, meeting rooms, car rental, some no-smoking rooms*
⊟ *AE, D, DC, MC, V* ⧠❘ *EP.*

🐾 **$$** ⊡ **Lions Dive & Beach Resort.** Divers are lured by the first-rate program
here, but this low-key resort has a lot to offer nondivers as well. The
location is great, right on the hip Sea Aquarium Beach strip, which is
bustling with activity, day and night. The open-air beach bar is a pop-
ular hangout. And best of all, there's plenty to do nearby, so you don't
have to rent a car or take taxis—at least eight eateries and bars are in
walking distance, and admission to the neighboring Sea Aquarium is
complimentary for hotel guests. Water sports (nonmotorized) are at your
doorstep. Ask for an ocean-view room, which is worth the extra cost.
All rooms have French doors opening onto a balcony or porch. The hotel
electrical current is 220 volts throughout, so Americans must bring an
adapter or borrow one at the front desk. The ride to town is about 10
to 12 minutes. ⊠ *Bapor Kibra z/n, Sea Aquarium Beach* ☎ *5999/434–
8888* 🖷 *5999/434–8889* ⊕ *www.lionsdive.com* ⇨ *105 rooms, 6 suites*
⌂ *Restaurant, fans, in-room safes, refrigerators, cable TV, in-room
data ports, pool, health club, spa, beach, dive shop, dock, snorkeling,
boating, marina, mountain bikes, bar, shop, babysitting, dry cleaning,
laundry service, Internet room, car rental* ⊟ *AE, D, DC, MC, V* ⧠❘ *EP.*

🐾 **$–$$** ⊡ **Habitat Curaçao.** R, R & R—rest, relaxation, and round-the-clock shore
diving—are what you can look forward to at this resort, which is near
a wildlife preserve in a secluded area blanketed by foliage. The dive center is top-notch and the house reef is pristine. The pool affords grand
vistas of the serene countryside setting, where nature lovers can explore
the nearby hiking trails. Willemstad is a half-hour drive away (a free
shuttle runs three times daily). Rooms are brightly outfitted with fabrics designed by local artist Nena Sanchez. Each room has a furnished
terrace or balcony. There's a shop for essentials, but a full grocery is
seven minutes away, so stock your fridge and stay awhile. The larger
lanai villas are an excellent value for families or groups. Various meal
and dive packages are available. ⊠ *Coral Estates, Rif St. Marie* ☎ *5999/
864–8800 or 800/327–6709* 🖷 *5999/864–8464* ⊕ *habitatcuracaoresort.
com* ⇨ *56 suites, 20 2-bedroom villas* ⌂ *Restaurant, in-room safes, some
kitchens, kitchenettes, cable TV, Wi-Fi, pool, health club, spa, beach,
dive shop, dock, billiards, bar, video game room, shop, Internet room,
meeting rooms* ⊟ *AE, DC, MC, V* ⧠❘ *EP.*

8

★ ☾ **$-$$** ▣ **Hilton Curaçao.** Two beautiful beaches of pillowy white sand beyond the open-air lobby make this hotel a jewel in its price range. Don't expect the glamorous life, but you can count on quality and service in both the rooms and the restaurants, which are kept up to high standards. Plenty of creature comforts—like coffeemakers, robes, and hair dryers—are provided in the rooms, which have balconies or patios. Luxuriate in everything from massage to aromatherapy at the spa, play chess on the oversize outdoor game board, or try your luck in the casino. A luminous free-form pool that seems to spill into the ocean invites you to take a dip before lounging with a piña colada. You can also walk over to the lively Hook's Hut for a drink or a meal, or to the neighboring Marriott. Downtown Willemstad is five minutes away by car. ⊠ *J. F. Kennedy Blvd., Box 2133, Piscadera Bay* ☎ *5999/462–5000* 🖷 *5999/462–5846* ⊕ *www. hiltoncaribbean.com* ⤵ *196 rooms, 12 suites* ⌕ *2 restaurants, room service, some in-room faxes, in-room safes, cable TV, some in-room broadband, in-room data ports, golf privileges, miniature golf, 2 tennis courts, 2 pools, health club, outdoor hot tub, spa, beach, dive shop, dock, snorkeling, boating, jet skiing, fishing, 2 bars, casino, babysitting, children's programs (ages 2–12), playground, dry cleaning, laundry service, concierge, Internet room, business services, meeting rooms, car rental, travel services, no-smoking rooms* ▤ *AE, D, DC, MC, V* ⦿ *EP.*

$ ▣ **Howard Johnson Plaza Hotel.** Everything the city has to offer is at your doorstep at this hotel on the main square of Otrobanda, an especially coveted location during the holidays and Carnival. At other times, despite the lack of beachfront, it's an acceptable choice for those on a budget, since you can jump in the pool to cool off or jump on a bus to head out for a day at the beach. Despite uninspiring decor, rooms are light-filled and well equipped with hair dryers and irons, and you can request a coffeemaker or refrigerator. Ask for a bay view, since those in the back look out over a murky puddle. ⊠ *Brionplein, Otrobanda, Willemstad* ☎ *5999/462–7800* 🖷 *5999/462–7803* ⊕ *www.hojo-curacao.com* ⤵ *50 rooms* ⌕ *Restaurant, café, room service, in-room safes, refrigerators, cable TV, in-room broadband, pool, bar, casino, babysitting, dry cleaning, laundry service, Internet room, car rental, free parking, no-smoking rooms* ▤ *AE, D, DC, MC, V* ⦿ *EP.*

$ ▣ **Plaza Hotel Curaçao.** At 14 stories high, this Curaçao "skyscraper" perched at the mouth of Willemstad's harbor affords striking views of the ocean and massive ships entering and leaving port. Although the hotel lacks beachfront, its pool area is a lively social hub. And you can walk into the city center—a definite plus. The enormous lobby—with marble floors, a winding wooden staircase, and a lagoon—is impressive. Hallways are a bit industrial—with pastel paint and tile floors—but rooms are tastefully furnished and accessorized. The honeymoon suites, with dark-wood furnishings, leather lampshades, bronze accents, and black-and-white photographs decorating the walls, have an abundance of charm. A free shuttle gives access to Kontiki Beach. ⊠ *Plaza Piar, Punda, Willemstad* ☎ *5999/461–2500* 🖷 *5999/461–6543* ⊕ *www. plazahotelcuracao.com* ⤵ *196 rooms, 24 suites* ⌕ *2 restaurants, snack bar, room service, in-room safes, cable TV, pool, billiards, 3 bars, casino, shops, playground, Internet room, business services, convention center,* *meeting rooms, car rental, free parking, no-smoking rooms* ⊟ *AE, MC, V* ❧❘ *EP.*

Where to Eat

Dine beneath the boughs of magnificent old trees, on the terraces of restored mansions and plantation houses, or on the ramparts of 18th-century forts. Curaçaoans partake of generally outstanding fare, with representation from a remarkable smattering of ethnicities. Outdoor or open-air sheltered dining is commonplace; note that most restaurants offer a smoking section or permit smoking throughout. Fine dining tends to be pricey, mostly because of the high cost of importing products to the island. For cheap eats with a local flair, drop by the Old Market for lunch, or stop at one of the snack bars or snack trucks you can find all over the island (have some guilders handy—many of them won't have change for dollars).

What to Wear

Dress in restaurants is almost always casual (though beachwear isn't acceptable). Some of the resort dining rooms and more elegant restaurants require that men wear jackets, especially in high season; ask when you make reservations.

CARIBBEAN
$$–$$$
✕ **Landhuis Daniel.** Dating from 1711, this mustard-colored landmark plantation house, which has seating on the outdoor patio, is near the narrow center of the island. The chef draws on creole, French, and Italian influences for his intriguing menu; many preparations use the plantation's own organically grown fruits, vegetables, and herbs, so it varies according to the seasonal crop yield. One option is the chef's prix-fixe "surprise menu"—just tell your waiter your preference for meat, fish, or vegetarian, and any dislikes. There's also a small inn here. ⊠ *Weg Naar, Westpunt* ☎ *5999/864–8400* ⊟ *AE, MC, V.*

★ $$–$$$
✕ **Jaanchi's Restaurant.** You'll be greeted by the owner, Jaanchi himself, a self-described "walking, talking menu," who will recite your choices of delectable dishes for lunch and maybe even a joke or two. The specialty at this sheltered, open-air restaurant is a hefty platter of fresh fish, typically wahoo. Jaanchi's iguana soup, touted in folklore as an aphrodisiac, is famous on the island. It's quite a sight when so-called sugar-thief birds flock to feeders outside the restaurant when the owner periodically fills them with sugar. Although predominantly a lunch spot, the restaurant will accommodate groups of four or more for dinner by prior arrangement. ⊠ *Westpunt 15, Westpunt* ☎ *5999/864–0126* ⊟ *AE, D, DC, MC, V.*

CONTINENTAL
★ $$$–$$$$
✕ **Astrolab Observatory.** Although the restaurant's name comes from the collection of astronomical instruments on display, you might leave thinking it comes from the out-of-this-world food. Among the stellar dishes is the grilled reef lobster in a vanilla butter sauce. Dine alfresco beneath a massive ficus tree in the gardens of the Kurá Hulanda compound or in the air-conditioned dining room. The extensive wine list is noteworthy. ⊠ *Kurá Hulanda, Langestraat 8, Otrobanda, Willemstad* ☎ *5999/434–7700* ⌁ *Reservations essential* ⊟ *AE, DC, MC, V* ☉ *Closed Sun. No lunch.*

8

$$$–$$$$ ✕ **Bistro Le Clochard.** Built into the 19th-century Riffort, this romantic
Fodor'sChoice   gem now anchors the entrance to the 21st-century Riffort Village com-
★   plex, the waterside terrace offering an enchanting view of the floating
bridge and harbor. Swiss and French are the key influences in the sub-
lime preparations; the chicken in curry sauce with exotic fruit is divine.
The signature dish is La Potence, a swinging, red-hot metal ball cov-
ered with bits of sizzling tenderloin and sausage, served with various
dipping sauces—a traditional bit of fun is to stake the cost of the meal
on not being the first person to drop a morsel. The cheese fondue def-
initely keeps diners coming back. Game lovers can have their fill from
the seasonal menu that's a perennial fixture. No matter what, leave room
for the sumptuous Toblerone chocolate mousse. ⊠ *Harborside Ter-
race, Riffort, Otrobanda, Willemstad* ☎ *5999/462–5666* ⚜ *Reserva-
tions essential* ⊟ *AE, DC, MC, V.*

$$$–$$$$ ✕ **The Wine Cellar.** Master Dutch chef Nico Cornelisse serves consistently
excellent meals in his Victorian-style dining room, which is adorned with
original paintings from the owner's collection. Several prix-fixe menus
are available, as well as a *menu romantique* for two that changes weekly.
A worldly wine list helps Curaçao's longest-standing eatery live up to
its name. The restaurant is wheelchair-accessible. ⊠ *Concordiastraat z/
n, Punda, Willemstad* ☎ *5999/461–2178* ⚜ *Reservations essential*
⊟ *AE, DC, MC, V* ⊘ *Closed Sun. No lunch Sat.*

★ $$$ ✕ **Fort Nassau Restaurant.** On a hill above Willemstad, this elegant restau-
rant is built into an 18th-century fort with a 360-degree view. For the
best perspective, sit beside the huge bay windows in the air-conditioned
interior; the terrace has a pleasant breeze, but the view is not quite optimal. Among the highlights of the diverse menu is the medley of
Caribbean seafood with mahimahi, shrimp, and grilled octopus. Scrumptious desserts will leave you feeling sated. ⊠ *Schottegatweg 82, near Juliana Bridge, Otrobanda, Willemstad* ☎ *5999/461–3450 or 5999/461–
3086* ⚜ *Reservations essential* ⊟ *AE, MC, V* ⊘ *No lunch weekends.*

ECLECTIC   ✕ **Blues.** Jutting out onto a pier over the ocean, this jazzy spot is an al-
★ $$–$$$ luring place for dinner. Menus are printed on LP record jackets—
descriptions of fish and meat dishes play on famous song lyrics. Live
music on Thursday and Saturday evenings features seductive vocalists
and top-notch musicians. If you'd rather be removed from the scene,
you can arrange for a cozy dinner on the beach—whether it's a table
for two or for a group, it will be nestled in the sand with colorful oversize pillows to sit on. There's also a terrific prix-fixe tapas buffet Friday nights. ⊠ *Avila Beach Hotel, Penstraat 130, Punda, Willemstad*
☎ *5999/461–4377* ⊟ *AE, D, DC, MC, V* ⊘ *Closed Mon. No lunch.*

$–$$$ ✕ **Gouverneur de Rouville Restaurant & Cafe.** Dine on the veranda of a
restored 19th-century Dutch mansion overlooking the Santa Anna Bay
and the resplendent Punda skyline. Intriguing soup options include
spicy gouda cheese soup, Cuban banana soup, and Curaçao-style fish
soup. *Keshi yena* (stuffed cheese) and spare ribs are savory entrées.
After dinner, you can stick around for live music at the bar, which stays
open until 1 AM. ⊠ *9 De Rouvilleweg, Otrobanda, Willemstad* ☎ *5999/
462–5999* ⊟ *MC, V.*

$–$$$ ✕ **Kontiki Beach.** Take respite from the sun in what looks like a rain forest burrowed in the sand. Each outdoor table offers shelter from the elements, enveloping you with large, leafy greenery and thatched roofs, giving you a sense of seclusion from fellow diners, too. At night, subtle lighting lends a romantic aura. There's something for everyone on the menu, with choices ranging from pastas and pizza to fish, mixed grilled meats, steak, soups, and salads. ✉ *Bapor Kibra z/n, Sea Aquarium Beach* ☎ *5999/465–1589* ▭ *MC, V.*

$–$$$ ✕ **La Bahia Seafood & Steakhouse.** As you dine on a sheltered terrace with a remarkable view of the harborfront, you're so close to the passing ships it seems you can almost touch them. For $9 you can buy a T-shirt touting: "I Had a Lobster at La Bahia," no matter what you order from the menu, which runs the gamut from burgers to pastas to *keshi yena* and other local specialties to surf and turf. ✉ *Otrobanda Hotel & Casino, Breedestraat, Otrobanda, Willemstad* ☎ *5999/462–7400* ▭ *AE, MC, V.*

¢–$$ ✕ **Time Out Café.** Tucked into an alley in the shopping heartland of Punda, this outdoor spot serves up light bites like tuna sandwiches and grilled cheese, as well as heartier fare, including chicken shwarma. You can also connect to friends and family via the Internet at reasonable rates. From Breedestraat facing Little Switzerland, take the alley to the left of the store (Kaya A. M. Prince) and walk about 20 yards, or look for the sign in Gomezplein Square and follow the arrow. ✉ *Keukenplein 8, Punda, Willemstad* ☎ *5999/524–5071* ▭ *No credit cards* ☾ *Closed Sun.*

FRENCH ✕ **Larousse.** Diners return time and again for old favorites from a menu
$$–$$$ of generally traditional French fare, peppered with variants like the chef's so-called Chinese-Russian tomato soup, which blends vodka and garlic in a sweet tomato base. The charming restaurant, with its nine cozy tables (including a tiny no-smoking section), is in a building that dates to 1742. Original paintings on the walls and white linen tablecloths accentuate the old-fashioned style that the owners lovingly cultivate. Asparagus is used with adoration when it is available on the island, and in season, wild game is prominent among the specials. Insiders come for the stockyard Chicago beef as well as the "salty" lamb (supposedly more tender), imported from Holland. Nothing comes out of a can here: even the ice cream, sauces, and sometimes the chocolate are homemade. ✉ *Penstraat 5, Punda, Willemstad* ☎ *5999/465–5418 or 5999/465–6503* ⚑ *Reservations essential* ▭ *AE, MC, V* ☾ *Closed Mon. No lunch.*

ITALIAN ✕ **La Pergola.** Built into the Waterfort Arches, this restaurant and its out-
$–$$$ door terrace are part of an adjoining strip of eateries in a coveted spot perched over the Caribbean. Listen to the rippling waves crash against the rocks as you sip wine and enjoy creative variations on homemade pastas and pizza. The pretty dining room looks like the interior of a Tuscan villa, with its arched, stuccoed ceiling, copper pots adorning the walls, and huge picture windows. ✉ *Waterfort Archesboog 12, Punda, Willemstad* ☎ *5999/461–3482* ▭ *AE, D, DC, MC, V* ☾ *No lunch Sun.*

PAN-ASIAN ✕ **Jaipur.** The subtle lighting and sound of the nearby waterfall seem to
★ **$$–$$$$** make the food even more sublime at this outdoor Pan-Asian restaurant—

8

with distinct Indian and Thai influences—that's part of the expansive Kurá Hulanda complex. The samosas filled with ground lamb make a great starter, and the tandoori mixed grill—*jugalbandhi*—with chicken, shrimp, and lamb, is a treat. ⊠ *Langestraat 8, Otrobanda, Willemstad* ☎ *5999/461–3482* ▤ *AE, DC, MC, V* ⊗ *Closed Mon. No lunch.*

STEAK   ✕ **Rodeo House of Ribs.** A haven for meat lovers, this family-owned
☾ **$$–$$$** restaurant has been in business since 1980. The staff (dressed in cowboy outfits) keeps the place lively. For kicks, ride the mechanical bull in the backyard: you could win a free meal if you stay up for more than two minutes. There's live music on Saturday nights. ⊠ *Fokkerweg 3, Salina* ☎ *5999/465–9465* ▤ *AE, MC, V.*

Beaches

While Curaçao might not be very green, it is surrounded by breathtaking blue. The island has 38 beaches, many of them quite striking, whether small inlets shielded by craggy cliffs or longer expanses of sparkling sand framing picture-perfect waters. Beaches along the southeast coast, even at the hotels, tend to be rocky in the shallow water (wear your reef shoes—some resorts loan them out for free); the west side has more stretches of smooth sand at the shoreline. Exploring the beaches away from the hotels is a perfect way to soak up the island's character. Whether you're seeking a lovers' hideaway, a special snorkeling adventure, or a great spot to wow the kids, you're not likely to be disappointed. There are snack bars and restrooms on many of the larger beaches, but it's at the smaller ones with no facilities where you might find utter tranquility, especially during the week. Note that most spots with entry fees offer lounge chairs for rent at an additional cost, typically $2 to $2.50 per chair.

East Side

★ ☾ **Sea Aquarium Beach.** This 1,600-foot stretch of sandy beach is divided into separate sections, each uniquely defined by a seaside resort or restaurant as its central draw. By day, no matter where you choose to enter the beach, you can find lounge chairs in the sand, thatched shelters, palm trees, and restrooms. The sections at Mambo and Kontiki beaches also have showers. There are two dive operators and water-sports centers (Ocean Encounters at Lion's Dive and Toucan Diving at Kontiki Beach), which cater to nearby hotel guests and walk-ins. Mambo Beach is always a hot spot and quite a scene on weekends, especially during the much-touted Sunday-night fiesta that's become a fixture of the island's nightlife. The ubiquitous beach mattress is also the preferred method of seating for the Tuesday-night movies at Mambo Beach (check the *K-Pasa* guide for listings—typically B-films or old classics—and reserve your spot with a shirt or a towel). At Kontiki Beach, you can find a spa, a hair braider, and a restaurant that serves refreshing piña colada ice cream. Unless you're a guest of a resort on the beach, the entrance fee to any section is $3 until 5 PM, then free. After 11 PM, you must be 18 or older to access the beach. ⊠ *Bapor Kibra, about 1 mi (1½ km) east of downtown Willemstad.*

West Side

☺ **Cas Abou.** This white-sand gem has the brightest blue water in Curaçao, a treat for swimmers, snorkelers, and sunbathers alike. You can take respite beneath the hut-shaded snack bar. The restrooms and showers are immaculate. The only drawback is the weekend crowds, especially Sunday, when local families come in droves; come on a weekday for more privacy. You can rent beach chairs, paddle boats, and snorkel and diving gear. The entry fee is $3. Turn off Westpunt Highway at the junction onto Weg Naar Santa Cruz; follow until the turnoff for Cas Abou, and then drive along the winding country road for about 10 minutes to the beach. ⊠ *West of St. Willibrordus, about 3 mi off Weg Naar Santa Cruz.*

Playa Jeremi. No snack bar, no dive shop, no facilities, no fee—in fact, there's nothing but sheer natural beauty. It's the kind of beach from which postcards are made. Quite a bit of development is planned for this beach, so have a look before it's too late. ⊠ *Off Weg Naar Santa Cruz, west of Lagun.*

Playa Kalki. Noted for its spectacular snorkeling, this beach is at the western tip of the island. The Ocean Encounters–West dive shop is here. ⊠ *Westpunt, near Jaanchi's.*

☺ **Playa Knip.** Two protected coves offer crystal-clear turquoise waters. Big (Groot) Knip is an expanse of alluring white sand, perfect for swimming and snorkeling. You can rent beach chairs and hang out under the palapas or cool off with ice cream at the snack bar. There are restrooms here but no showers. It's particularly crowded on Sunday or school holidays. Just up the road, also in a protected cove, Little (Kleine) Knip is a charmer, too, with picnic tables and palapas. Steer clear of the poisonous manchineel trees. There's no fee for these beaches. ⊠ *Banda Abou, just east of Westpunt.*

☺ **Playa Lagun.** This northwestern cove is caught between gunmetal-gray cliffs, which dramatically frame the Caribbean blue. Cognoscenti know this as one of the best places to snorkel—even for kids—because of the calm, shallow water. It's also a haven for fishing boats and canoes. There's a small dive shop on the beach, a snack bar (open weekends), and restrooms, but there's no fee. ⊠ *Banda Abou, west of Santa Cruz.*

★ **Playa Porto Mari.** Calm, clear water and a long stretch of white sand are the hallmarks of this beach, which is fine for swimming or just lounging. Without the commercial bustle of Sea Aquarium Beach, it's one of the best for all-around fun. A decent bar and restaurant, well-kept showers, changing facilities, and restrooms are all on-site; a nature trail is nearby. The double coral reef—explore one, swim past it, explore another—is a special feature that makes this spot popular with snorkelers and divers (there's a dive shop and a dock). The entrance fee (including one free beverage) is $2 on weekdays, $2.50 on Sunday and holidays. From Willemstad, drive west on Westpunt Highway for 7 km (4 mi); turn left onto Willibrordus Road at the Porto Mari billboard, and then drive 5 km (3 mi) until you see a large church; follow signs on the winding dirt road to the beach. ⊠ *Off Willibrordus Rd.*

8

Sports & the Outdoors

For the full gamut of activities in one spot, nature buffs (especially bird-watchers), families, and adventure seekers may want to visit **Caracas Bay Island** (☎ 5999/747–0777). Things to do here include hiking, mountain biking, canoeing, kayaking, windsurfing, jet-skiing, and snorkeling. There's a fully equipped dive shop, a restaurant, and a bar on premises. Admission to the scenic area is $3; activities cost extra.

BIKING & KAYAKING **Dutch Dream Adventures** (☎ 5999/864–7377 ⊕ www.dutchdreamcuracao.com) targets the action seeker with guided canoe and kayak safaris, mountain-bike excursions through Christoffel Park for groups of 10 or more, or custom-designed tours to suit your group's interests. So you wanna bike Curaçao? **Wanna Bike Curaçao** (☎ 5999/527–3720 ⊕ www.wannabike.net) has the fix: Kick into gear and head out for a guided mountain bike tour through the Caracas Bay peninsula and the salt ponds at the Jan Thiel Lagoon. Although you should be fit to take on the challenge, mountain-bike experience is not required. A two-hour tour runs about $29 and covers the bike, helmet, water, refreshments, park entrance fee, and the guide, but don't forget to bring a camera.

BOATING & WINDSURFING **Caribbean Sea Sports** (✉ Curaçao Marriott Beach Resort, Piscadera Bay ☎ 5999/462–2620 ⊕ www.caribseasports.com) runs a tight ship when it comes to all sorts of water sports, including kayaking, windsurfing, banana boats, tube rides, diving, and snorkeling. Captain "Good Life" at **Let's Go Watersports** (✉ Santa Cruz Beach 1 ☎ 5999/520–1147 or 5999/526–3362) will help you plan kayaking and other boat outings so you can live it up on the water.

DIVING & SNORKELING The **Curaçao Underwater Marine Park** includes almost a third of the island's southern diving waters. Scuba divers and snorkelers can enjoy more than 12½ mi (20 km) of protected reefs and shores, with normal visibility from 60 to 150 feet. With water temperatures ranging from 75°F to 82°F (24°C to 28°C), wet suits are generally unnecessary. No coral collecting, spearfishing, or littering is allowed. An exciting wreck to explore is the SS *Oranje Nassau,* which ran aground in 1906. The other two main diving areas are Banda Abou, along the southwest coast between Westpunt and St. Marie, and along central Curaçao, which stretches between Bullen Bay to the Breezes Curaçao resort. The north coast—where conditions are dangerously rough—is not recommended for diving.

Introductory scuba resort courses run about $45 to $100 (for one or two dives). Open-water certification courses run about $330 to $350 (excluding taxes) for the five-dive version. Virtually every operator charges $33 to $42 for a single-tank dive and $60 to $68 for a two-tank dive. One day of unlimited shore diving runs about $22 to $25. Snorkel gear commonly rents for $12 to $15 per day.

Easy Divers (✉ Habitat Curaçao, Coral Estates, Rif St. Marie ☎ 5999/864–8800 ⊕ www.habitatcuracaoresort.com) offers everything from introductory dives to advanced open-water courses. You are free to dive any time, night or day, in addition to the regularly scheduled dives, because the abundance of marine life at the house reef makes for easily accessible shore dives right from the resort.

★ ☾ **Ocean Encounters** (✉ Lions Dive & Beach Resort, Bapor Kibra z/n, Sea Aquarium Beach ☎ 5999/461–8131 ⊕ www.oceanencounters.com) is the largest dive operator on the island and also operates Toucan Diving at Kontiki Beach, which caters to walk-ins. Its operations cover the popular east-coast dive sites including the *Superior Producer* wreck, where barracudas hang out, and the tug boat wreck. Ocean Encounters has added west-end dive sites—including the renowned Mushroom Forest—to its repertoire with the acquisition of a dive outlet at Westpunt. Ocean Encounters offers a vast menu of scheduled shore and boat dives and packages, as well as certified PADI instruction. In July, the dive center sponsors a kids' sea camp in conjunction with the Sea Aquarium.

★ **Sunset Divers** (✉ Sunset Waters Beach Resort, Santa Marta Bay ☎ 5999/864–1708 ⊕ www.sunsetdiver.com), the closest full-service PADI operation to the famous Mushroom Forest, offers daily one- and two-tank dives, 24-hour shore diving, and custom dives. The friendly, expert staff concentrate in dive sites along the west-side reef system, which has gently sloping walls with lots of coral growth, soft and hard. Lesser known but no less spectacular sites they often visit include Harry's Hole and Boca Hulu. The house reef is incredible, too, with common sightings of octopus, eel, frogfish, and seahorses—plus there's a submerged small airplane that makes for a great snorkel. The operator has two boats, including a 44-foot yacht for up to 24 divers that's the largest dive boat on the island. Sunset Divers also rents photography gear.

FISHING **Let's Fish** (✉ Caracasbaaiweg 407N, Caracas Bay ☎ 5999/561–1812 or 5999/747–4489 ⊕ www.letsfish.net), a 32-foot fully rigged fishing boat, can accommodate groups of up to 11 people on half-day or full-day fishing trips to Klein Curaçao or Banda Abou in search of dolphin, marlin, wahoo, and more. With seven fishing vessels among the 14 yachts (and their captains) under his purview, Capt. J. R. Van Hutten, nicknamed Captain Jaro, of **Pro Marine Yacht Services** (✉ Warawaraweg 7, Van Engelen ☎ 5999/560–2081), is *the* man to see about deep-sea fishing excursions and other fishing trips or parties. Some deals offer free pickup at your hotel. Most boats keep your catch, so check in advance if you want it. You can book the 54-foot yacht *War Eagle,* captained by Jaro himself, and head out in search of marlin, barracuda, mahimahi, and wahoo.

GOLF In the mood to hit the green? Try the **Blue Bay Curaçao Golf and Beach Resort** (✉ Landhuis Blauw, Blue Bay z/n ☎ 5999/868–1755 ⊕ www.bluebaygolf.com). This 18-hole, par-72 course beckons experts and novices alike. Facilities include a golf shop, locker rooms, and a snack bar. Greens fees range from $75 to $95 in high season, and you can rent carts, clubs, and shoes. If you'd like to drive your game to a new level, take a lesson from the house pro ($28 for a half hour), or head for the driving range and putting green ($10 per person for unlimited range balls).

SEA EXCURSIONS Many sailboats and motorboats offer sunset cruises and daylong snorkel and picnic trips to Klein Curaçao, the uninhabited island between Curaçao and Bonaire, and other destinations. Prices are around $50 to $65 for a half-day trip (including food and drinks). The half-day "Taste of Curaçao" trip on the *Bounty* (☎ 5999/560–1887 ⊕ www. bountyadventures.com), a 90-foot schooner, features sailing, snorkeling, swimming, and rope swinging. It includes an open bar and barbecue lunch. One option aboard the 120-foot Dutch sailing ketch *Insulinde* (☎ 5999/560–1340 ⊕ www.insulinde.com) is a snorkeling and scenic tour combo for $30 (includes snacks and punch). The *Mermaid* (☎ 5999/ 560–1530 ⊕ www.mermaidboattrips.com) is a 66-foot motor yacht that carries up to 60 people to Klein Curaçao three times a week. A buffet lunch, beer, and soft beverages are provided at the boat's exclusive beach house, which has picnic tables, shade huts, and facilities. The 76-foot *Miss Ann* (☎ 5999/767–1579 ⊕ www.missannboattrips.com) motorboat offers snorkeling or diving, moonlight, and party trips for up to 100 people. For a unique vantage point, soak up the local marine life from the semi-submersible *Seaworld Explorer* (☎ 5999/461–0011 ⊕ www. atlantisadventures.net). An hour-and-a-half-long tour of the beautiful coral reefs is $40.

Shopping

From Dutch classics like embroidered linens, Delft earthenware, cheeses, and clogs to local artwork and handicrafts, shopping in Curaçao can turn up some fun finds. But don't expect major bargains on watches, jewelry, or electronics; Willemstad is not a duty-free port (the few establishments that claim to be "duty free" are simply absorbing the cost of some or all of the tax rather than passing it on to consumers); however, if you come prepared with some comparison prices, you might still dig up some good deals.

Areas

Willemstad's **Punda** is a treat for pedestrians, with most shops concentrated within a bustling area of about six blocks, giving you plenty of opportunity for people-watching to boot. Heerenstraat and Gomezplein are pedestrian malls, closed to traffic, and their roadbeds have been raised to sidewalk level and covered with pink inlaid tiles; other major shopping streets are Breedestraat and Madurostraat. Here you can find jewelry, cosmetics, perfumes, luggage, and linens—and no shortage of trinkets and souvenirs. Savvy shoppers don't skip town without a stop across the bay to **Otrobanda**, where the **Riffort Village Shopping Mall** houses a variety of retailers. However, the four-story waterfront complex will be undergoing major changes in coming years, as it becomes integrated into a multipurpose complex that will include a hotel and cinema that will be built next door. In the meantime, the shops and eateries within are in flux. There are also some retail shops in the Kurá Hulanda complex.

Specialty Items

ART GALLERIES   **Gallery Eighty Six** (✉ Scharlooweg 76, Punda, Willemstad ☎ 5999/461–3417) represents the work of local and international artists. The **Hortence Brouwn Gallery** (✉ Kaya Tapa Konchi 12, Brievengat ☎ 5999/ 737–2193) sells sculpted human forms (sometimes abstract) in bronze, cement, marble, and limestone. **Kas di Alma Blou** (✉ De Rouvilleweg 67, Otrobanda, Willemstad ☎ 5999/462–8896) is in a gorgeous 19th-century indigo town house and presents the top local artists; you can find shimmering landscapes, dazzling photographs, ceramics, even African-inspired Carnival masks. At either of the **Nena Sanchez Galleries** (⊠ Jan Kock Plantation, Weg Naar San Willibrordus z/n, San Willibrordus ☎ 5999/869–4965 ⊠ Bloempot Shopping Mall, Schottegatweg Oost 17, Bloempot ☎ 5999/738–2377), you can find this local artist's cheerful paintings in characteristically bright yellows, reds, greens, pinks, and blues. Her work depicting marine life and island scenes is available in various forms, including posters, mouse pads, and picture frames.

CIGARS   The smoky smell of success permeates **Cigar Emporium** (⊠ Gomezplein, Punda, Willemstad ☎ 5999/465–3955), where you can find the largest selection of Cuban cigars on the island, including H. Upmann, Romeo & Julieta, and Montecristo. Visit the climate-controlled cedar cigar room. However, remember that Cuban cigars cannot be taken back to the United States legally.

CLOTHING   **Bamali** (⊠ Breedestraat, Punda, Willemstad ☎ 5999/461–2258) sells funky, fabulous women's apparel, including Indonesian batik clothing; charming jewelry made of beads, shells, gemstones, and silver; handbags of leather and other fabrics; and lots of other unique accessories. Custom-made clothing is available here, too. Get suited up for the beach at the **Bikini Shop** (⊠ Bapor Kibra z/n, Sea Aquarium Beach z/n ☎ 5999/461–7343), where you can find women's bathing suits (Vix, Becca, La Goufe, etc.) and accessories including cover-ups, flip-flops, and sunglasses. You can find a large selection of Calvin Klein apparel and lingerie at **Janina** (⊠ Madurostraat 13, Punda, Willemstad ☎ 5999/461–1371), which also carries Levi's jeans. **Mayura** (⊠ Breedestraat 8, Punda, Willemstad ☎ 5999/461–7277) has T-shirts galore, plus souvenirs like Curaçao islandscape towels and key chains. **Tommy Hilfiger** (⊠ Breedestraat 20–21, Punda, Willemstad ☎ 5999/465–9963) carries the full designer line for men, women, and children. You can find a large selection of smart men's and women's wear at **Wulfsen & Wulfsen** (⊠ Wilhelminaplein 1, Punda, Willemstad ☎ 5999/461–2302), from European and American designers like Gant, Kenneth Cole, and Passport.

FOODSTUFFS **Centrum Supermarket** (⊠ Weg Naar Bullenbaai z/n, Piscadera ☎ 5999/869–6222) is one of the better markets in terms of variety and quality. A bakery is on premises, too. **Toko Zuikertuintje** (⊠ Zuikertuintjeweg, Santa Rosa ☎ 5999/737–0188), a supermarket built on the site of the original 17th-century Zuikertuintje Landhuis, carries all sorts of European and Dutch delicacies.

GIFTS   **Boolchand's** (⊠ Heerenstraat 4B, Punda, Willemstad ☎ 5999/461–6233) sells electronics, jewelry, Swarovski crystal, Swiss watches, and cameras behind a facade of red-and-white-checkered tiles. **Julius L. Penha & Sons** (⊠ Heerenstraat 1, Punda, Willemstad ☎ 5999/461–2266), in front of the Pontoon Bridge, sells French perfumes and cosmetics, clothing, and accessories, in a baroque-style building that dates from 1708. At **Little Switzerland** (⊠ Breedestraat 44, Punda, Willemstad ☎ 5999/461–2111) you can find jewelry, watches, crystal, china, and leather goods at significant savings.

8

HANDICRAFTS   **Caribbean Handcraft Inc.** (✉ Kaya Kakina 8, Jan Thiel ☎ 5999/767–1171) offers an elaborate assortment of locally handcrafted souvenirs. It's worth visiting just for the spectacular hilltop view. **Landhuis Groot Santa Martha** (✉ Santa Martha ☎ 5999/864–1323 or 5999/864–2969) is where artisans with disabilities fashion handicrafts, including ceramic vases, dolls, and leather products. There's a $3 entrance fee for adults. It's closed on weekends.

JEWELRY   **Clarisa** (✉ Gomezplein 10, Punda, Willemstad ☎ 5999/461–2006) specializes in cultured pearls and also carries European gold jewelry and watches. **Different Design** (✉ Gomezplein 7, Punda, Willemstad ☎ 5999/465–2944) offers gorgeous custom-made pendants and rings of precious gems and gold. **Freeport** (✉ Heerenstraat 13, Punda, Willemstad ☎ 5999/461–9500) has a fine selection of watches and jewelry (lines include David Yurman, Movado, and Maurice Lacroix). **Gandelman** (✉ Breedestraat 35, Punda, Willemstad ☎ 5999/461–1854) has watches by Cartier and Rolex, leather goods by Prima Classe, and Baccarat and Daum crystal. **Pieters Jewelers** (✉ Gomezplein, Punda, Willemstad ☎ 5999/465–4774) carries fine watches including Seiko, Tissot, and Swatch, as well as gold jewelry, gemstones, and glassware.

LINENS   **New Amsterdam** (✉ Gomezplein 14, Punda, Willemstad ☎ 5999/461–2437 ✉ Breedestraat 29, Punda, Willemstad ☎ 5999/461–3239) is the place to price hand-embroidered tablecloths, napkins, and pillowcases, as well as blue Delft.

PERFUMES &   The **Yellow House** (✉ Breedestraat 23, Punda, Willemstad ☎ 5999/461–
COSMETICS   3222) offers a vast selection of perfumes at low prices.

Nightlife

Friday is a big night out, with rollicking happy hours and live music at many bars and hotels. And although it might sound surprising, Sunday-night revelry into the wee hours is an island tradition. Pick up a copy of the weekly free entertainment listings, *K-Pasa,* available at most restaurants and hotels, or check out the Web site kikotakiko.com for current happenings around the island.

Fodor'sChoice   Outrageous costumes, blowout parades, pulsating Tumba rhythms, ★ miniprocessions known as jump-ups, and frenetic energy characterize **Carnival** on Curaçao. The season lasts longer here than on many other islands: the revelries begin at New Year's and continue until midnight the day before Ash Wednesday. One highlight is the Tumba Festival (dates vary), a four-day musical event featuring fierce competition between local musicians for the honor of having their piece selected as the official road march during parades. For the Grand Parade, space is rented along the route and people mark their territory by building wooden stands, some lavishly decorated and furnished.

BARS   Martinis are the specialty at **Avalon Social Club** (✉ Caracasbaaiweg 8, Saliña ☎ 5999/465–6375), where a perky crowd pours in for the daily happy hour from 6 to 7. Sushi is a popular choice for lunch or dinner; another standout feature is the Wednesday-night "tapas only" menu.

Live jazz electrifies the pier at **Blues** (✉ Avila Beach Hotel, Penstraat 130, Punda, Willemstad ☎ 5999/461–4377) on Thursday—*the* night to go—and Saturday. Wednesday-night jam sessions are hot at **De Gouverneur** (✉ 9 De Rouvilleweg, Otrobanda, Willemstad ☎ 5999/462–5999). **Fort Waakzaamheid Tavern & Restaurant** (✉ Seru Domi z/n ☎ 5999/462–3633)—the name means "Fort Alertness"—is a pleasant place for a cocktail day or night, complete with a panoramic view of the island. **Grand-café de Heeren** (✉ Zuikertuintjeweg, Bloempot ☎ 5999/736–0491) is a great spot to grab a locally brewed Amstel Bright and meet a happy blend of tourists and transplanted Dutch locals. By day **Hook's Hut** (✉ Next to Hilton Curaçao, Piscadera Bay ☎ 5999/462–6575) is a beach hangout for locals and tourists stationed at the nearby hotels. There's decent food for lunch and dinner, and the daily happy hour from 5 to 6 kicks off a lively nighttime scene. The outdoor pool table is in terrible shape, but it's one of the few bar tables around.

With giant green leaves and thatched roofs giving each table ultimate seclusion, **Kontiki Beach Club** (✉ Bapor Kibra z/n, Sea Aquarium Beach ☎ 5999/465–1589) is a great spot to tuck away and have a drink with your companion if you want to feel simultaneously alone yet part of all the action on the beach. If you capture the fun on camera anytime at **Tu Tu Tango** (✉ Plaza Mundo Merced, Punda, Willemstad ☎ 5999/465–4633), you can send in your photos for posting to its online gallery; there's a lively happy hour on Friday from 6 to 7 PM and silver-screen theme parties once a month, owing to the bar's location behind the cinema. The seaside outdoor deck at the **Waterfort Arches** (✉ Waterfortstraat Boog 1, Punda, Willemstad ☎ 5999/465–0769) comprises a connecting strip of several bars and restaurants that have live entertainment on various nights of the week. There's never a dull moment at **Wet & Wild Beach Club** (✉ Bapor Kibra z/n, Sea Aquarium Beach ☎ 5999/561–2477), where the name speaks for itself every weekend night—Friday happy hour features free barbecue snacks; on Saturday a DJ or live band jams until it's too late to care about the time; on Sunday things get charged starting with happy hour at 6; the fiesta goes on past midnight.

CASINOS Casino gambling is becoming ever more popular on Curaçao, and hotels are refurbishing their casinos or adding new ones to keep up. Still, the sass and sparkle of the Vegas-style casinos is virtually nonexistent on the island. Although you might hear some hoots and hollers from a craps table, some clanking of coins from the slot machines, and the perpetual din of money changing hands, don't expect bells and whistles, glitzy decor, or cocktail waitresses in thematic costumes. The following hotels have casinos that are open daily: the Curaçao Marriott Beach Resort & Emerald Casino, the Hilton Curaçao, the Plaza Hotel Curaçao, Holiday Beach Hotel & Casino, Howard Johnson Plaza Hotel & Casino, the Otrobanda Hotel & Casino, and the Breezes Curaçao. Even the biggest of these rooms offer only a few card games, and some are limited to slot machines. As for ambience, only the casino at the Marriott—which features pleasant live entertainment some nights—even approaches the class of a Bond-like establishment. The Holiday Beach Casino is the largest on the island and the only one with sports betting—you can watch the live action on TV in the multiscreen room. The Holiday also has Texas Hold'em tables. Around the island, slot machines open earlier than table games, between 10 AM and 1 PM. Most of the rooms have penny and nickel slots in addition to the higher-priced machines. Tables generally open at 3 PM or 4 PM. Casinos close about 1 AM or 2 AM weekdays; some stay open until 4 AM on weekend nights.

DANCE & MUSIC CLUBS **Baya Beach** (✉ Caracas Bay Island Park, Caracas Bay Island ☎ 5999/747–0777) is a festive place that lures dancers with its pulsating blend of salsa, merengue, and hip-hop. Saturday nights are the liveliest. **Living Room** (✉ Saliña 129, Saliña ☎ 5999/461–4443) is jamming on weekends. Dance into the wee hours in the chic, burnished-red interior. **Mambo Beach** (✉ Sea Aquarium Beach z/n ☎ 5999/461–8999), an open-air bar and restaurant, draws a hip, young crowd that flocks here to dance the night away under the stars. Popular with tourists and locals throughout the week, this is *the* place to be on Sunday night; come in time for happy hour and warm up for the night-long party with some beach volleyball.

Exploring Curaçao

Willemstad

What does the capital of Curaçao have in common with New York City? Broadway, for one thing. Here it's called Breedestraat, but the origin is the same. Dutch settlers came here in the 1630s, about the same time they sailed through the Verazzano Narrows to Manhattan, bringing with them original red-tile roofs, first used on the trade ships as ballast and later incorporated into the architecture of Willemstad.

The city is cut in two by Santa Anna Bay. On one side is the Punda—crammed with shops, restaurants, monuments, and markets—and on the other is Otrobanda (literally, the "other side"), with lots of narrow, winding streets full of private homes notable for their picturesque gables and Dutch-influenced designs. In recent years the ongoing regeneration of Otrobanda has been apparent, marked by a surge in development of new hotels, restaurants, and shops; the rebirth, concentrated near the waterfront, was spearheaded by the creation of the elaborate Kurá Hulanda complex.

There are three ways to cross the bay: by car over the Juliana Bridge; by foot over the Queen Emma Pontoon Bridge; or by free ferry, which runs when the pontoon bridge is swung open for passing ships. All the major hotels outside town offer free shuttle service to town once or twice daily. Shuttles coming from the Otrobanda side leave you at Riffort. From here it's a short walk north to the foot of the pontoon bridge. Shuttles coming from the Punda side leave you near the main entrance to Fort Amsterdam.

Numbers in the margin correspond to points of interest on the Willemstad map.

WHAT TO SEE **Curaçao Museum.** Housed in an 1853 plantation house, this small museum is filled with artifacts, paintings, and antiques that trace the is-

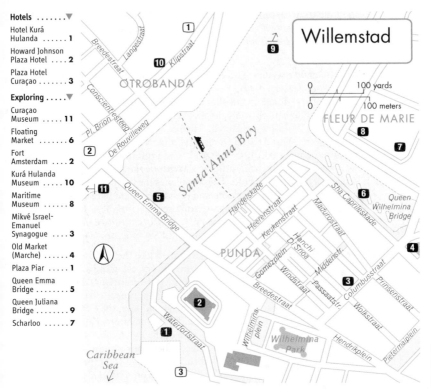

land's history. This is also a venue for art exhibitions that visit the island. ☒ *V. Leeuwenhoekstraat z/n, Otrobanda* ☎ *5999/462–3873* ☜ *$3* ☉ *Weekdays 9–noon and 2–5, Sun. 10–4.*

★ ❻ **Floating Market.** Each morning dozens of Venezuelan schooners laden with tropical fruits and vegetables arrive at this bustling market on the Punda side of the city. Mangoes, papayas, and exotic vegetables vie for space with freshly caught fish and herbs and spices. The buying is best at 6:30 AM—too early for many people on vacation—but there's plenty of action throughout the afternoon. Any produce bought here should be thoroughly washed or peeled before being eaten. ☒ *Sha Caprileskade, Punda.*

NEED A BREAK?

For a cooling break from your explorations, **Vienna Ice Café** (☒ Handelskade 14, Punda, Willemstad ☎ 5999/736–1086) serves up scrumptious homemade ice cream. Indulge your sweet tooth with such flavors as green apple, mango, and rum plum.

❷ **Fort Amsterdam.** Step through the archway and enter another century. The entire structure dates from the 1700s, when it was the center of the city and the island's most important fort. Now it houses the governor's residence, the Fort Church, the Council of Ministers, and government offices. Outside the entrance, a series of majestic gnarled *wayaka* trees are fancifully carved with human forms—the work of local artist Mac Alberto. ⊠ *Foot of Queen Emma Bridge, Punda* ☎ *5999/461–1139* 🎫 *$1.75, to church museum only* ⊙ *Weekdays 9–noon and 2–5, Sun. service at 10.*

⑩ Kurá Hulanda Museum. This fascinating museum of African history and other non-Western cultures is housed within the confines of a restored 18th-century village in Otrobanda. The museum is built around a former mercantile square (Kurá Hulanda means "Holland courtyard"), where slaves were sold by the Dutch. Themes of the exhibits include evolution, slavery, West African empires (you can actually play an ancient xylophone), and pre-Columbian gold. The profound "Black Holocaust" section, covering the transatlantic slave trade, includes a gut-wrenching replica of a slave-ship hold. The complex is the brainchild of Dutch philanthropist Jacob Gelt Dekker, and the museum grew from his personal collection of artifacts. An on-site conference center has state-of-the-art facilities for lectures and seminars. ⊠ *Klipstraat, Otrobanda* ☎ *5999/ 462–1400* ⊕ *www.kurahulanda.com* 🎫 *$6* ⊙ *Daily 10–5.*

FodorśChoice ★ (to the left of Kurá Hulanda Museum entry)

❽ Maritime Museum. The museum—designed like the interior of a ship— gives you a sense of Curaçao's maritime history, using ship models, maps, nautical charts, navigational equipment, and audiovisual displays. Topics explored in the exhibits include the development of Willemstad as a trading city, Curaçao's role as a contraband hub, the explosion of *De Alphen* in 1778, the slave trade, the development of steam navigation, the rise of cruise tourism, and the role of the Dutch navy on the island. The museum also offers a two-hour guided tour (Wednesday and Saturday, 2 PM) on its "water bus" through Curaçao's harbor—a route familiar to traders, smugglers, and pirates. The museum is wheelchair accessible. ⊠ *Van der Brandhofstraat 7, Scharloo* ☎ *5999/465–2327* 🎫 *Museum $6; museum and harbor tour $12* ⊙ *Mon.–Sat. 9–4.*

★ ❸ Mikvé Israel-Emanuel Synagogue. The temple, the oldest in continuous use in the western hemisphere, is one of Curaçao's most important sights and draws thousands of visitors a year. The synagogue was dedicated in 1732 by the Jewish community, which had grown from the original 12 families who came from Amsterdam in 1651. They were later joined by Jews from Portugal and Spain (via Amsterdam) fleeing persecution from the Inquisition. White sand covers the synagogue floor for two symbolic reasons: a remembrance of the 40 years Jews spent wandering the Sinai desert before being led by Moses out of the Diaspora; and a re-creation of the sand used by secret Jews, or "Conversos," to muffle sounds from their houses of worship during the Inquisition. The **Jewish Cultural Museum** (☎ 5999/461–1633), in back of the synagogue, displays antiques—including a set of circumcision instruments—and artifacts from around the world. Many of the objects are used in the synagogue, making it a "living" museum. English and Hebrew services are held Friday at 6:30 PM and Saturday at 10 AM. Men who attend should wear a jacket and tie. Yarmulkes are provided. ⊠ *Hanchi Snoa 29, Punda* ☎ *5999/461–1067* ⊕ *www.snoa. com* 🎫 *Synagogue free, donations accepted; Jewish Cultural Museum $5* ⊙ *Weekdays 9–11:45 and 2:30–4:45.*

❹ Old Market (Marche). Local cooks prepare hearty Antillean lunches in coal pots at this covered market behind the post office. Enjoy such Curaçaoan specialties as funchi (polenta), goat stew, fried fish, or stewed okra. Prices range from $4 to $7. ⊠ *De Ruyterkade, Punda.*

❶ Plaza Piar. This plaza is dedicated to Manuel Piar, a native Curaçaoan who fought for the independence of Venezuela under the liberator Simón Bolívar. On one side of the plaza is the Waterfort, built in the late1820s as part of a ring of defense around the old city. The original cannons are still positioned in the battlements. The foundation, however, now forms the walls of the Plaza Hotel Curaçao.

❺ Queen Emma Bridge. Affectionately called the Swinging Old Lady by the locals, this bridge connects the two sides of Willemstad—Punda and Otrobanda—across the Santa Anna Bay. The bridge swings open at least 30 times a day to allow passage of ships to and from sea. The original bridge, built in 1888, was the brainchild of the American consul Leonard Burlington Smith, who made a mint off the tolls he charged for using it: 2¢ per person for those wearing shoes, free to those crossing barefoot. Today it's free to everyone. The bridge was dismantled and completely repaired and restored in 2005.

❾ Queen Juliana Bridge. This 1,625-foot-long bridge was completed in 1974 and stands 200 feet above the water. It's the crossing for motor traffic between Punda and Otrobanda and affords breathtaking views (and photo ops) of the city, day and night.

❼ Scharloo. The Wilhelmina Drawbridge connects Punda with the once-flourishing district of Scharloo, where the early Jewish merchants first built stately homes. The architecture along Scharlooweg (much of it from the 17th century) is magnificent, and, happily, many of the colonial mansions that had become dilapidated have been meticulously renovated. The area closest to Kleine Werf is a red-light district and fairly run-down, but the rest is well worth a visit.

Elsewhere on Curaçao

The Weg Maar Santa Cruz road through the village of Soto winds to the island's northwest tip through landscape that Georgia O'Keeffe might have painted—towering cacti, flamboyant dried shrubbery, and aluminum-roof houses. Throughout this *cunucu*, or countryside, you can see fishermen hauling nets, women pounding cornmeal, and an occasional donkey blocking traffic. Land houses, large plantation houses from centuries past, dot the countryside. To explore the island's eastern side, take the coastal road—Martin Luther King Boulevard—from Willemstad about 2 mi (3 km) to Bapor Kibra. This is where you can find the Sea Aquarium and the Dolphin Academy. Farther east lies a nature park at Caracas Bay and the upscale Spanish Water neighborhood and marina. To the far northeast is Groot St. Joris, home of Curaçao's aloe plantation and one of the largest ostrich-breeding farms outside Africa.

Numbers in the margin correspond to points of interest on the Curaçao map.

★ **㉑**   **Christoffel National Park.** The 1,239-foot Mt. Christoffel, Curaçao's highest peak, is at the center of this 4,450-acre garden and wildlife preserve. There are eight hiking trails in the park, which take anywhere from 20 minutes to 2½ hours to complete. Start out early (by 10 AM the park starts to feel like a sauna), and if you're going without a guide, first study the *Excursion Guide to Christoffel Park*, sold at the visitor center. It outlines the various routes and identifies the indigenous flora and fauna. There's also a 20-mi (32-km) network of driving trails (use heavy-treaded tires), all of which traverse hilly fields full of prickly pear cacti, divi-divi trees, bushy-haired palms, and exotic flowers.

Watch for goats and small wildlife that might cross your path, and consider yourself lucky if you see any of the elusive white-tail deer. (Every day at 4 PM, guides lead 15-minute expeditions to track the protected herd of 150 to 200 of the deer in the park.) The whip snakes and minute silver snakes you may encounter aren't poisonous. White-tail hawks may be seen on the green route, white orchids and crownlike passionflowers on the yellow route. There are also caves—where you might hear the rustling of bat wings or spot scuttling nonpoisonous scorpions—and ancient Indian drawings. Spectacular bird-watching is abundant, and experts lead the way twice daily. The climb up Mt. Christoffel—an exhilarating challenge to anyone who hasn't grown up scaling the Alps—takes about two hours for a reasonably fit person who's not an expert hiker. The view from the peak, however, *is* thrilling—a panorama that includes Santa Marta Bay and the tabletop mountain of St. Hironimus. On a clear day you can even see the mountain ranges of Venezuela.

Guided nature walks, horseback rides, and jeep tours are all available and can be arranged through the main park office. Horseback tours are conducted from Rancho Alfin, which is in the park. Reservations are required. Additionally, most island sports outfitters offer some kind of activity in the park, such as kayaking, specialized hiking tours, and drive-through tours (see ⇨ Sports & the Outdoors, *above*). ⊠ *Savonet* ☎ *5999/864–0363 for information and tour reservations, 5999/462–6262 for jeep tours (Yellow Tourism Solutions), 5999/864–0535 for horseback tours* ☜ *$10* ☉ *Mon.–Sat. 8–4, Sun. 6–3; last admission 1 hr before closing.*

⓳ **Country House Museum.** The thatched-roof cottage is filled with antique furniture, farm implements, and clothing typical of 19th-century colonial life. Out back is a minifarm and vegetable garden. Look closely at the fence—it's made of living cacti. There's also a snack bar. A festival featuring live music and local crafts takes place here on the first Sunday of each month. ⊠ *Dokterstuin 27, on road to Westpunt from Willemstad, Westpunt* ☎ *5999/864–2742* ☜ *$2* ☉ *Tues.–Fri. 9–4, weekends 9–5.*

⓲ **Curaçao Aloe Plantation & Factory.** Drop in for a fascinating tour that takes you through the various stages of production of the aloe vera plant, renowned for its healing powers. You'll get a look at everything from the aloe fields to the final products. At the gift shop, you can buy CurAloe products, including homemade goodies like aloe wine, soap, pure aloe gel, and pure aloe juice, as well as sunscreen and other skin care products made off-site. The plantation is right on the way to the Ostrich Farm and run by the same owner. Tours begin every hour. ✉ *Weg Naar Groot St. Joris z/n, Groot St. Joris* ☎ *5999/767–5577* ⊕ *www. aloecuracao.com* ✍ *$4* ☉ *Mon.–Sat. 9–4; last tour at 3.*

★ ⓒ ⓯ **Curaçao Sea Aquarium.** You don't have to get your feet wet to get a bird's-eye view of the island's underwater treasures. The aquarium has about 40 saltwater tanks full of more than 400 varieties of marine life. For more up-close interaction, there are several mesmerizing options. You can hand-feed the sharks, stingrays, or sea turtles (or watch a diver do it) at the **Animal Encounters** section, which consists of a broad, 12-foot-deep open-water enclosure. Snorkelers and divers swim freely with tarpon, stingrays, and such. Diving instruction and equipment are part of the package, and novices are welcome. The cost includes admission to the Sea Aquarium, training, use of equipment, and food for the sea creatures. If you prefer to stay on your land legs, there's an underwater observatory in a stationary semi-submarine. Encounters, snorkels, and dives are also possible with the aquarium's six lovable sea lions from Uruguay. Kids as young as three can have their photo taken kissing a sea lion. Reservations for Animal Encounters, including sea lion programs, must be made 24 hours in advance. A restaurant, a snack bar, two photo centers, and souvenir shops are on-site.

At the **Dolphin Academy** (☎ 5999/465–8900 ⊕ www.dolphin-academy. com), you can watch a fanciful dolphin show (included in the price of Sea Aquarium admission). For more up-close interaction, you may choose from several special programs (extra charges apply and reservations are essential) to encounter the dolphins in shallow water, or to swim, snorkel, or dive with them. ✉ *Bapor Kibra z/n, Sea Aquarium Beach* ☎ *5999/461–6666* ⊕ *www.curacao-sea-aquarium.com* ✍ *$15; animal encounters $54 for divers, $34 for snorkelers; sea lion programs $39–$149; Dolphin Academy $69–$300* ☉ *Sea aquarium daily 8:30–5:30; Dolphin Academy daily 8:30–4:30.*

★ ⓒ ⓭ **Den Paradera.** Dazzle your senses at this organic herb garden, where guides will explain the origins of traditional folk medicines that can treat everything from stomach ulcers to diabetes. Owner Dinah Veeris is a renowned expert and author in the field. Top off your visit with a homemade beverage of aloe, ginger, and lemon. Shampoos made from plants like cactus, aloe vera, and calabash as well as ointments, oils, and potpourri are for sale at the gift shop. A special kids' garden was being developed with interactive play-and-learn programs. Reservations are essential for guided tours. ✉ *Seru Grandi Kavel 105A, Banda Riba* ☎ *5999/767–5608* ✍ *$4, $6 with guided tour* ☉ *Mon.–Sat. 9–6.*

★ ⓬ **Hato Caves.** Stalactites and stalagmites form striking shapes in these 200,000-year-old caves. Hidden lighting adds to the dramatic effect. Indians who used the caves for shelter left petroglyphs about 1,500 years ago. More recently, slaves from nearby plantations used the caves as a hideaway. Hour-long guided tours wind down to the water pools through various chambers. Keep in mind that there are 49 steps to climb up to

Curaçao Liqueur: The Bitter Smell of Success

SOME SAY THE FAMED CURAÇAO liqueur is what put this spirited island on the map. Oddly, the bitter oranges used to flavor the liqueur weren't recognized for their value until hundreds of years after they were introduced locally. The liqueur is made from the peels of the Laraha orange. In the 16th century, the Spaniards had brought over and planted Valencia oranges, but arid conditions rendered the fruit bitter, and the crops were left to grow in the wild. The plant became known as the Laraha, the so-called Golden Orange of Curaçao.

It was not until the mid-19th century that Edouard Cointreau of France came to appreciate the fragrance of the bitter fruit's dried peels, and he combined them with sweet oranges to make an aperitif. Eventually, the Senior family created a recipe of its own using the Laraha and began producing Curaçao liqueur commercially in 1896. Today, only Senior's Curaçao is allowed to use the "authentic" label, signifying it is made from the indigenous citrus fruit.

Laraha oranges are harvested twice a year, when the fruit is still green. The peels are sun-dried, then put in a copper still (the original!) with alcohol and water for several days, and finally mixed with Senior's "secret" ingredients and distilled some more. The final product is clear. Colorings (including the famous blue) are added but do not change the flavor. Bartenders, however, use the colorful varieties with great flourish to create fanciful drinks.

the entrance. To reach the caves, head northwest toward the airport, take a right onto Gosieweg, follow the loop right onto Schottegatweg, take another right onto Jan Norduynweg, a final right onto Roo-seveltweg, and follow signs. ⊠ *Rooseveltweg, Hato* ☎ *5999/868–0379* ⌨ *$7* ⊘ *Daily 10–5.*

⓭ Landhuis Brievengat. This mustard-colored plantation house is a fine example of a home from the island's past. You can see the original kitchen still intact, the 18-inch-thick walls, fine antiques, and the watchtowers once used for lovers' trysts. A Friday-night party is held on the wide wraparound terrace, with bands and plenty to drink ($6 cover charge). On the last Sunday of the month (from 6 PM to 7:30 PM), this estate holds an open house with crafts demonstrations and folkloric shows. It's a 15-minute drive northeast of Willemstad, near Centro Deportivo stadium. ⊠ *Brievengat* ☎ *5999/ 737–8344* ⌨ *$1* ⊘ *Mon.–Sat. 9:15–12:15 and 3–6.*

★ ☝ ⓰ Ostrich Farm. If you (and the kids) are ready to stick your neck out for an adventure, visit one of the largest ostrich-breeding farms outside Africa. Every hour, guided tours show the creatures' complete development from egg to mature bird. Kids enjoy the chance to hold an egg, stroke a day-old chick, and sit atop an ostrich for an unusual photo op. At the **Restaurant Zambezi** you can sample local ostrich specialties and other African dishes (reservations are recommended; closed Monday, no dinner Tuesday). The gift shop sells handicrafts made in southern Africa, including leather goods and wood carvings, as well as products made by local artisans. ⊠ *Groot St. Joris* ☎ *5999/747–2777* ⊕ *www. ostrichfarm.net* ⌦ *$10* ☉ *Tues.–Sun. 9–4.*

⓮ **Senior Curaçao Liqueur Distillery.** The famed Curaçao liqueur, made from the peels of the bitter Laraha orange, is produced at this mansion, which dates to the 1800s. Don't expect a massive factory—it's just a small showroom in an open-air foyer. There are no guides, but delightful old hand-painted posters explain the distillation process, and you can watch workers filling the bottles by hand. Assorted flavors are available to sample for free. If you're interested in buying—the orange-flavor chocolate liqueur is delicious over ice cream—you can choose from a complete selection in enticing packaging, including miniature Dutch ceramic houses. ⊠ *Landhuis Chobolobo, Saliña Arriba* ☎ *5999/461–3526* ⌦ *Free* ☉ *Weekdays 8–noon and 1–5.*

★ ⓴ **Shete Boka.** The name of this park means "Seven Inlets" in Papiamento. Indeed, the sea has carved out seven magnificent grottos (and a few less magnificent ones), the largest of which is Boka Tabla, where you can watch and listen to the waves crashing against the rocks beneath a limestone overhang. Boka Pistol is also spectacular, with thunderous waves smashing into the rocks and jetting up into towering plumes of spray, often leaving rainbows lingering in the mist. Several of the surrounding minicaverns serve as nesting places; watch flocks of parakeets emerge in formation, magnificent hawks soar and dip, and gulls dive-bomb for lunch. ⊠ *Westpunt Hwy., just past village center, Soto* ⌦ *$2.50* ☉ *Daily 8:30–5.*

CURAÇAO ESSENTIALS

To research prices, get advice from other travelers, and book travel arrangements, visit www.fodors.com.

Transportation

BY AIR

Continental Airlines offers a week nonstop flight (about five hours' flying time) to Curaçao from New York–Newark; flights depart Saturday mornings and return Saturday afternoons. You can also connect on American Airlines (via Miami or San Juan) or Air Jamaica (via Montego Bay). Nonstop flights are also available from Amsterdam (KLM), Caracas (Aeropostal), or Paramaribo, Suriname (SLM).

🛂 **Aeropostal** ☎ 5999/888-2818. **Air Jamaica** ☎ 800/523-5585 or 5999/888-2300. **American Airlines** ☎ 5999/869-5701. **Continental Airlines**

☎ 800/231-0856 **KLM** ☎ 5999/465-2747. **SLM** ☎ 5999/868-4360.
🛂 Airport Information **Hato International Airport** ☎ 5999/839-3201.

BY CAR

Most hotels outside Willemstad are just a few minutes away from the city center by taxi, keeping the fares relatively inexpensive for jaunts to go out to dinner or sightseeing in town. So if you don't plan on doing much independent exploring or beach-hopping and are not staying on a remote part of the island, you can get by without renting a car. There are many gas stations in the Willemstad area as well as in the suburban areas, including two on the main road as you head to the western tip of the island. Driving in the Nether-

8

lands Antilles is the same as in the United States, on the right-hand side of the road, though right turns on red are prohibited. Local laws require drivers and passengers to wear seat belts and motorcyclists to wear helmets. Children under age four must be in child safety seats.

🚹 **Avis** ☎ 5999/461-1255 or 800/228-0668. **Budget** ☎ 5999/868-3466 or 800/472-3325 **Hertz** ☎ 5999/888-0088 **National Car Rental** ☎ 5999/869-4433 **Thrifty** ☎ 5999/461-3089

BY TAXI

Meters have been added to taxi cabs, although rates are still fixed from point to point of your journey. The government-approved rates, which do not include waiting time, can be found in a brochure called "Taxi Tariff Guide," available at the airport, hotels, cruise-ship terminals, and at the Tourist Board. Rates are for up to four passengers. There's a 25% surcharge after 11 PM. Taxis are readily available at hotels and at taxi stands at the airport, in Punda, and in Otrobanda; in other cases, call Central Dispatch.

🚹 **Central Dispatch** ☎ 5999/869-0752.

Contacts & Resources

ADDRESSES

In street addresses that do not specify a house number, the "z/n" is actually a Dutch abbreviation for "zonder nummer" (no number).

BANKS AND EXCHANGE SERVICES

U.S. dollars—in cash or traveler's checks—are accepted nearly everywhere, so there's no need to worry about exchanging money. However, you may need small change for pay phones, cigarettes, or soda machines. The currency in the Netherlands Antilles is the florin (also called the guilder) and is indicated by "fl" or "NAf" on price tags. The florin is very stable against the U.S. dollar; the official rate of exchange at this writing was NAf 1.77 to US$1. There are more than 50 ATM locations on the island

that dispense money in the local currency. The airport has an ATM (it dispenses U.S. dollars), as do many bank branches.

Prices quoted throughout this chapter are in U.S. dollars unless otherwise indicated.
🚹 **Antilles Banking Corporation** ☎ 5999/461-2822. **Banco di Caribe** ☎ 5999/434-3800. **Maduro & Curiel's Bank** ☎ 5999/466-1100. **RBTT** ☎ 5999/763-8000.

BUSINESS HOURS

Banks are open weekdays from 8 to 3:30; the airport branch is open the same hours for all transactions but has extended hours for foreign exchange: 7 AM to 8 PM Monday through Saturday and 7:30 AM to 7 PM on Sunday. Post office hours are from 7:30 to 5 weekdays. The Groot Kwartier branch is open from 7 to 7 on weekdays and 7 to 3 on Saturday. Most shops are open Monday through Saturday from 8 to 6. Some are open on Sunday mornings and holidays when cruise ships are in port.

ELECTRICITY

The current is 110–130 volts/50 cycles, which is compatible with small North American appliances such as electric razors and hair dryers. Although most hotel rooms have both 110V and 220V outlets, you might need to borrow an adapter from the front desk if the appropriate outlets aren't situated to your convenience; it's advisable to bring your own.

EMBASSIES & CONSULATES

🚹 **Canada Consulate of Canada** ✉ Plaza Jojo Correa 2-4, Punda, Willemstad ☎ 5999/461-3515. 🚹 **United Kingdom British Consulate** ✉ Jan Sofat 38, Punda, Willemstad ☎ 5999/747-3322. 🚹 **United States United States Consulate** ✉ Roosevelthouse, J. B. Gorsira 1, Punda, Willemstad ☎ 5999/461-3066.

EMERGENCIES

🚹 **General Emergencies Ambulance & fire** ☎ 912. **On-call dentists** ☎ 8888. **On-call doctors** ☎ 1111. **Police** ☎ 911.

🔳 Hospitals **St. Elisabeth's Hospital** ✉ Breedestraat 193, Otrobanda, Willemstad ☎ 5999/462-4900 or 5999/462-5100.

🔳 Pharmacies **Botica Brion** ✉ Breedestraat 126, Otrobanda, Willemstad ☎ 5999/462-7027. **Botica Popular** ✉ Madurostraat 15, Punda, Willemstad ☎ 5999/461-1269.

🔳 Scuba-Diving Emergencies **St. Elisabeth's Hospital** ✉ Breedestraat 193, Otrobanda, Willemstad ☎ 5999/462-4900 or 5999/462-5100.

🔳 Sea Emergencies **Coast Guard** ☎ 113.

HOLIDAYS

Public holidays are New Year's Day, Carnival Monday, Good Friday, Easter Sunday, Easter Monday (day after Easter), the Queen's Birthday (not Beatrix, but rather her mother, Juliana; Apr. 30), Labor Day (May 1), Curaçao Flag Day (July 2), Antilles Day (Oct. 21), and Christmas holiday (Dec. 25 and 26).

LANGUAGE

Dutch is the official language, but the vernacular is Papiamento—a mixture of Dutch and many other tongues, including some African dialects. One theory holds that the language developed during the 18th century as a mode of communication between land owners and their slaves. Anyone involved with tourism generally speaks English. To guarantee a smile, wish someone *bon dia* (good day) or offer a warm *masha danki* (thank you very much) after someone has performed a service.

INTERNET, MAIL & SHIPPING

Internet service is widely available in Curaçao, with most hotels offering access in some form, whether through data ports, high-speed broadband, or Wi-Fi, if not in your hotel room, then in an Internet rooms or lobby area of your hotel. There are also several Internet cafés around Willemstad.

There are post offices in Punda, Otrobanda, and Groot Kwartier on Schottegatweg (Ring Road), as well as small branches at the Curaçao World Trade Center and the airport. Some hotels sell stamps and have letter drops; you can also buy stamps at some bookstores. An airmail letter to the United States, Canada, or Europe costs NAf 2.85, a postcard NAf 1.45.

🔳 Café Internet ✉ Handelskade 3B, Punda, Willemstad. **Dot Com** ✉ Saliña Galleries, Saliña. **Langames Cafe.com & Internet** ✉ Schottegatweg Oost 98A, Saliña. **Suya-Spot Internet C@fe** ☎ 5999/461-5388 ✉ Pietermaaiplein 13, Punda, Willemstad. **Wireless Internet Café** ✉ Hanchi Snoa 4, Punda, Willemstad.

PASSPORT REQUIREMENTS

Beginning on January 1, 2007, citizens of the U.S. are required to have a valid passport to travel to Curaçao; a birth certificate and photo ID will no longer be acceptable. Citizens of all other countries also must produce a passport. All visitors must be able to show an ongoing or return ticket as well as have proof of sufficient funds to support their stay on the island, although this is not routinely checked by customs.

SAFETY

Crime exists but is not rampant in Curaçao, so commonsense rules apply. Lock rental cars, and don't leave valuables in the car. Use in-room safes or leave valuables at the front desk of your hotel, and never leave bags unattended at the airport, on tours, or on the beach.

TAXES & SERVICE CHARGES

The airport international departure tax is $22 (including flights to Aruba), and the departure tax to other Netherlands Antilles islands is $7. This must be paid in cash, either florins or U.S. dollars. Hotels add a 12% service charge to the bill and collect a 7% government room tax; restaurants typically add 10% to 15%. Most goods and services purchased on the island will also have a 5% OB tax (a goods and services tax) added to the purchase price.

TELEPHONES

Phone service through the hotel operators in Curaçao has improved in recent years. Direct-dial service, both on-island and to elsewhere in the world, is fast and clear.

AT&T Direct service is available from most hotels; your hotel will likely add a surcharge. Dial access is also available at the AT&T calling center at the cruise-ship terminal and at the mega pier in Otrobanda. From other public phones, use phones marked LENSO; many more of these have been added around the island in recent years. You can also call direct from the air-conditioned Curaçao Telecom (CT) center using a prepaid phone card (open 8 AM to 5:30 PM, Monday through Saturday, the center also offers Internet access).

To place a local call on the island, dial the seven-digit local number. Pay phones charge NAf .50 for a local call—far less than the typical hotel charge. Whether for local or long-distance calling, it's common to use prepaid phone cards, which are widely available around the island, as many pay phones do not accept coins.

To call Curaçao direct from the United States, dial 011–5999 plus the number in Curaçao.

International roaming for most GSM mobile phones is available in Curaçao, so you can make and receive calls on your cell phone as long as your carrier has a roaming agreement. Local companies are UTS (United Telecommunication Services) and CT (Curaçao Telecom). You can also rent a mobile phone or buy a prepaid SIM card for your own phone; if you want to put a local SIM card in your cell phone, be sure to have it unlocked by your company before you travel overseas. Rentals are available at several outlets, including Rent-A-Fone, Speedy Cellular Rental Inc., and Bright Impex Wireless. Prepaid chips are available at UTS and CT.

📶 **AT&T Direct** ☎ 800/872-2881 **Bright Impex Wireless** ✉ Gosieweg 75, Gosie, Willemstad ☎ 5999/736-6234 or 5999/560-8294 **Curaçao Telecom** ✉ Brionplein H104, Otrobanda, Willemstad ☎ 5999/699-9518 ✉ Schottegatweg Oost 19, Bloempot ☎ 5999/736-1056 **Rent-A-Fone** ✉ Saliña Galleries Unit D-106, Saliña ☎ 5999/465-8844. **Speedy Cellular** ✉ Douwe Zalm Center 1-Q, Saliña ☎ 5999/736-7455. **UTS** ✉ Rigelweg 2, Groot Davelaar ☎ 5999/777-0101.

TIPPING

As service is usually included, tipping at restaurants isn't expected, though if you find the staff exemplary, you can add another 5% to 10% to the bill. A gratuity for taxi drivers is at your discretion, but about 10% is the standard. Tip porters and bellhops about $1 a bag, the hotel housekeeping staff $2 to $3 per day.

TOUR OPTIONS

Most tour operators have pickups at the major hotels, but if your hotel is outside the standard zone, there may be an additional charge of around $3. Tours are available in several languages, including English.

The so-called Trolley Train visits historic sites in Willemstad on a 1½-hour guided tour, one of the most popular run by Atlantis Adventures. This tour begins at Fort Amsterdam, and there's no hotel pickup. Peter Trips offers full-day island tours ($40, without lunch) departing from the hotels Tuesday, Friday, and Sunday at 9 AM, with visits to many points of interest, including Fort Amsterdam, Spanish Water, Scharloo, and Fort Nassau. A special eco-tour on Saturday features stops at Christoffel National Park, the Hato Caves, and Boka Tabla; the $35 fee includes park entrance. East- and west-side half-day tours are offered for $20. Among the favorites at Taber Tours is the Christoffel Park/Cas Abou Beach combo: Start the day with a guided hike up Mt. Christoffel followed by a tour of the park, and wind up at the beach to relax or snorkel. The newest addition to Curaçao's flock of tour companies, Yellow Tourism Solutions is a cut above the competition. It offers a full palette of half-day and full-day tours, whether you want to check out town, beaches, or historical sites, or head out with a group for a structured, guided activity (like horseback riding, quad rentals, diving, or snorkeling). The company's Yellow Jeep Safari takes you to Christoffel

National Park aboard a bright yellow 4x4 Land Rover, driven by a guide who will take you off the beaten (paved) path deep into the park's natural terrain.

Atlantis Adventures 🕾 5999/461-0011. **Peter Trips** 🕾 5999/561-5368 or 5999/465-2703 **Taber Tours** ✉ Dokway 🕾 5999/737-6637. **Yellow Tourism Solutions** ✉ Curaçao Marriott Beach Resort, Piscadera Bay 🕾 5999/462-6262 ⊕ www.tourism-curacao.com.

VISITOR INFORMATION

Curaçao Tourist Board ⊕ www.curacao-tourism.com ✉ Pietermaai 19, Punda, Willemstad 🕾 5999/434-8200 🕾 Hato International Airport 🕾 5999/868-6789.

WALKING TOURS

When making reservations for any tour, mention ahead that you speak English. Walking tours of historic Otrobanda, focusing on the unique architecture of this old section of town, are led by architect Anko van der Woude every Thursday (reservations are suggested), leaving from the central clock at Brionplein at 5:15 PM. Jopi Hart offers a walking tour that emphasizes the sociocultural aspects of Otrobanda; it begins at 5:15 PM on Wednesday and departs from the clock at Brionplein. The Talk of the Town tour with Eveline van Arkel will take you through historical Punda to visit sites including Fort Amsterdam, the restored Fort Church, the Queen Emma pontoon bridge, and the Mikvé Israel-Emanuel Synagogue (call for reservations; English tours are on Tuesdays at 9:30 AM). Gigi leads expert tours of Punda focusing on Jewish heritage, including an insider's look at the synagogue.

Anko van der Woude 🕾 5999/461-3554 **Jopi Hart** 🕾 5999/767-3798 **Eveline van Arkel** 🕾 5999/747-4349 or 5999/562-1861 **Gigi** 🕾 5999/697-0290

WEDDINGS

Curaçao's appeal as a destination wedding spot has been rising faster than you can say, "I do." Several resorts and event planners are equipped to help you with the legal requirements and procedures for the marriage itself in addition to arrangements for a reception and/or honeymoon. You and your partner must be living outside the Netherlands Antilles, and you must report to the Register's Office in person at least three days prior to your scheduled marriage. You must notify the Register's Office in writing (from abroad) at least two months ahead of your intended wedding day, stating more than one potential wedding day. You will need to include the following original documents: birth certificate; valid passport (a copy is acceptable at this stage); evidence that you are single; if applicable, evidence that you are divorced or a widow or widower. All of the documents must be current, that is, not more than six months old (with the exception of the passport and birth certificate). The Register's Office may request additional documents, depending on your personal circumstances. Once your documents are received, you will be notified within two weeks of a date and time for your marriage to be performed if everything is in order, of any documents that are lacking or not in order, and/or of any additional documentation you need to supply. A marriage certificate costs NAf 32.50 (about $20). A wedding package costs between NAf 350 (about $200) and NAf 750 (about $425).

Special Events Curaçao–Wedding & Party Planner can help you with the A-to-Zs of wedding logistics, including taking legal steps, booking hotel rooms, and finding the perfect location, caterer, florist, and photographer. Ban Kasa Wedding & Honeymoon Planner Curaçao offers personalized wedding services; a rep will pick you up at the airport and help with every detail from preliminary legal paperwork to your wedding video, and all the options in between (including fireworks, if you want them!).

Several hotels have wedding and honeymoon planners. Among the resorts that specialize in weddings are Avila Beach Hotel, Breezes Curaçao, Curaçao Marriott Beach Resort & Emerald Casino, Habitat Curaçao, Hotel Kurá Hulanda, and the

Lodge Kurá Hulanda & Beach Club. The hotels and independent party planners may require more time to assist you with the legal process and other arrangements than what the government requires.

🗗 **Ban Kasa Wedding & Honeymoon Planner Curaçao** ✉ Kaya Kashimiri 59, Curasol ☎ 5999/869-5670 ⊕ www.bankasa.com. **Office of the Register of Curaçao** ✉ Burgerlijke Stand Bevolkingsregister en Verkiezengen [BSB&V], A. M. Chumaceiro Blvd. 13, Punda, Willemstad ☎ 5999/461-1844 🖷 5999/461-8166. **Special Events Curaçao-Wedding & Party Planner** ✉ WTC Bldg., Piscadera Bay ☎ 5999/463-6139 ⊕ www.specialevents-curacao.com.

Dominica

Scotts Head

WORD OF MOUTH

"The ride was nice—through mountainous roads kissing the clouds, past green hills, banana fields, small towns and villages. Beautiful plants and flowers were everywhere."

—Mary

"If you are into nature stuff instead of shopping, this island is for you. Go snorkeling in the Champange area. Bubbles rise through geo-thermal vents as [you] swim underwater."

—cathy oberbeck

WELCOME TO DOMINICA

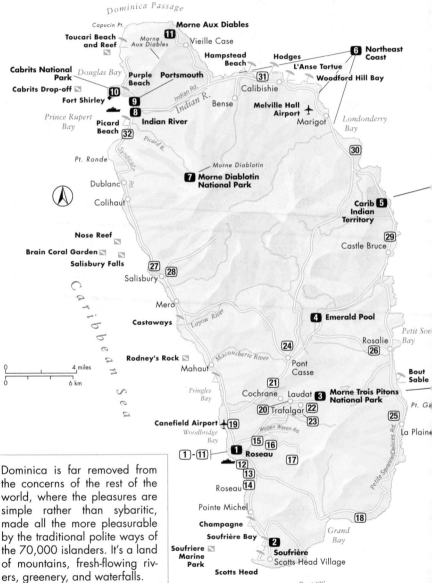

Dominica is far removed from the concerns of the rest of the world, where the pleasures are simple rather than sybaritic, made all the more pleasurable by the traditional polite ways of the 70,000 islanders. It's a land of mountains, fresh-flowing rivers, greenery, and waterfalls.

Dominica Passage

Capucin Pt.
Morne Aux Diables 11
Toucari Beach and Reef
Morne Aux Diables
Vieille Case
Hampstead Beach
Hodges
Northeast Coast 6
Cabrits National Park
Douglas Bay
Purple Beach
Portsmouth
L'Anse Tortue
Woodford Hill Bay
Cabrits Drop-off 10
9
31
Calibishie
Fort Shirley
8
Bense
Melville Hall Airport
Prince Rupert Bay
Indian River
Marigot
Londonderry Bay
Picard Beach 32
Indian Rd.
Indian R.
Picard R.
Pt. Ronde
Syndicate Rd.
30
Morne Diablotin
7 **Morne Diablotin National Park**
Dublanc
Colihaut
Carib Indian Territory 5
Nose Reef
29
Castle Bruce
Brain Coral Garden
Salisbury Falls
27 28
Salisbury
Mero
Layou River
4 **Emerald Pool**
Castaways
Rosalie
Petit Sor Bay
24
26
Rodney's Rock
Macoucherie River
Pont Casse
Bout Sable
Mahaut
21
Pt. G
Pringles Bay
Cochrane
Laudat
3 **Morne Trois Pitons National Park**
20
Trafalgar 22
Canefield Airport 19
Wotten Waven Rd.
23
25
La Plaine
Woodbridge Bay
15 16
1 - 11
Roseau
17
12
13
Roseau 14
Petite Savanne/Delices Rd.
Pointe Michel
18
Champagne
Grand Bay
Soufrière Bay
2
Soufriere Marine Park
Soufrière
Scotts Head Village
Scotts Head

Caribbean Sea

0   4 miles
0   6 km

Martinique Passage

THE NATURE ISLAND

The island is 29 mi (47 km) long and 16 mi (26 km) wide, with approximately 73,000 citizens. Since it was a British colony (achieving independence in 1978), you may wonder about the prevalence of French names. Although the English first claimed Dominica in 1627, the French controlled it from 1632 until 1759, when it passed back into English hands.

KEY

- Beaches
- Cruise Ship Terminal
- Dive Sites
- **1** Exploring Sights
- ① Hotels & Restaurants

Restaurants ....▼	Hotels ....▼
Cocorico..................... **10**	Anchorage Hotel **12**
Cornerhouse Café **6**	Beau Rive **29**
Creola **11**	Calibishie................... **31**
Crystal Terrace........... **14**	Castle Comfort Lodge.. **13**
Guiyave...................... **7**	Cocoa Cottage **23**
La Robe Creole **9**	Crescent Moon **24**
Miranda's Corner **21**	Evergreen Hotel **14**
O'Byrnes **4**	Exotica **17**
Pearl's Cuisine **2**	Fort Young Hotel **8**
Port of Call.................. **1**	Hummingbird Inn....... **19**
Rainforest Restaurant **22**	Habitation Chabert..... **30**
Waterfront Restaurant .. **5**	Itassi.......................... **16**
	Jungle Bay **25**
	Papillote **22**
	Picard Beach Cottages.................... **32**
	Roseau Valley Hotel.... **15**
	Roxy's Mountain Lodge........................ **20**
	Sunset Bay Club **27**
	Tamarind Tree **28**
	3 Rivers..................... **26**
	Zandoli **18**

The last few remaining Caribs, descendants of the fierce people who were among the earliest Caribbean residents—and for whom the sea is named—live on the northeast coast of Dominica.

Morne Trois Pitons National Park was the first UNESCO World Heritage Site in the Lesser Antilles (others are now in St. Kitts and St. Lucia).

DOMINICA

9

TOP 4 REASONS TO VISIT DOMINICA

1 The island's unspoiled natural environment is the major draw.

2 The hiking—particularly the hike around Boiling Lake—is exhilarating.

3 Diving pristine reefs full of colorful sea life or in bubbly, volcanic water is amazing.

4 For many, an island with no big beach resort is a minus, but if you are the type of person who's going to like Dominica, you know that's a plus.

DOMINICA PLANNER

Getting to Dominica

No airlines fly nonstop to Dominica from North America. You can transfer in San Juan to an American Eagle flight. Otherwise, it's a small island-hopper from Antigua, Barbados, Martinique, St. Lucia, or Guyana. There's also a 90-minute ferry from Guadeloupe or St. Lucia.

Canefield Airport (DCF), about 3 mi (5 km) north of Roseau, handles only small aircraft and daytime flights. It's convenient but served by only a few small Caribbean-based airlines. Melville Hall Airport (DOM) is on the northeast coast, 75 minutes from Roseau, and handles larger planes. That's where you'll probably arrive.

Hassle Factor: High, mostly because of the time it takes to travel here.

Hotel & Restaurant Costs

Assume that hotels operate on the European Plan (**EP**—with no meals) unless we specify that they use either the Continental Plan (**CP**—with a Continental breakfast), Breakfast Plan (**BP**—with full breakfast), or the Modified American Plan (**MAP**—with breakfast and dinner). Other hotels may offer the Full American Plan (**FAP**—including all meals but no drinks) or may be All-Inclusive (**AI**—with all meals, drinks, and most activities).

WHAT IT COSTS in Dollars					
	$$$$	**$$$**	**$$**	**$**	**¢**
Restaurants	over $30	$20–$30	$12–$20	$8–$12	under $8
Hotels	over $350	$250–$350	$150–$250	$80–$150	under $80

Restaurant prices are for a main course at. Hotel prices are per night for a double room in high season, excluding 5% tax, customary 10%–15% service charge, and meal plans (except at all-inclusives).

On the Ground

Cab fare from Canefield Airport to Roseau is about $20. The 75-minute drive from Melville Hall Airport to Roseau takes you through the island's Central Forest Reserve and is a tour in itself. The trip costs about $60 by private taxi or $20 per person in a shared taxi. The ferry drops you right in Roseau. If you're staying out on the island, you'll need to rent a car, and you may need a four-wheel-drive to reach some small resorts.

Activities

You don't come to Dominica to lie on the beaches because they aren't worth the trip. One of the things you do come for is **diving**, which can be tremendous, particularly in the protected Scotts Head Marine Reserve. **Whale-watching** is also spectacular during the season, and **hiking** in the island's completely undeveloped rain forest reserves is exciting any time of the year. Most **beaches** are just so-so, but Champagne, which has steam vents from an underwater volcano just offshore, is an experience—you'll feel as if you are swimming in warm, effervescent Champagne.

Updated by
Roberta
Sotonoff

IN DOMINICA, YOU GO TO MOTHER NATURE, or Mother Nature comes to you. Perhaps you will see nature's beauty in underwater silence, swimming in volcanic bubbles while millions of colors dash by; or perhaps you will discover its magnificence hiking steep and narrow stretches of red mud and lush forests on your climb up a mountain volcano. At the end of the day, when you emerge or descend, a rainbow will smile and you can sleep the sleep of the legendary explorer returning from the wild. Any way you choose to experience Dominica, her big and small wonders will inspire your awe.

With all this abundance of nature, there's also a lot of active watching to do—of birds flying, turtles hatching, and dolphins and whales jumping. Even when you're not looking, something is sure to capture your gaze. The sensory overload isn't just visual. Your soul may be soothed by the refreshing smell of clean river water and cleaner air; your taste buds will be tantalized by the freshest fruits and vegetables; and your skin will be caressed by the purest natural soaps.

Wedged between the two French islands of Guadeloupe and Martinique, Dominica (pronounced dom-in-*ee*-ka) is as close to the garden of Eden as you're likely to get. Wild orchids, anthurium lilies, ferns, heliconia, and myriad fruit trees sprout profusely. Much of the interior is still covered by luxuriant rain forest and remains inaccessible by road. Here everything grows more intensely: greener, brighter, and bigger. A natural fortress, the island protected the Caribs (the region's original inhabitants) against European colonization. The rugged northeast is still reserved as home to the last survivors of the Caribs, along with their traditions and mythology.

Dominica—29 mi (47 km) long and 16 mi (26 km) wide, with a population of 70,000—did eventually become a British colony; but it attained independence in November 1978 and now has a seat in the United Nations as the central Caribbean's only natural World Heritage Site. Its capital is Roseau (pronounced rose-*oh*); the official language is English, although most locals communicate with each other in Creole; roads are driven on the left; family and place names are a mélange of English, Carib, and French; and the religion is predominantly Catholic. It's a conservative society. Unlike neighboring Martinique and Guadeloupe, Dominica frowns on topless bathing, and swimsuits should never be worn on the street. The economy is still heavily dependent on agriculture.

With fewer than 100,000 overnight visitors annually, Dominica is a little-known destination with no major hotel chains, but the island's forestry service has preserved more national forests, marine reserves, and parks, per capita, than almost anywhere on earth.

Dominica is a popular "alternative" Caribbean experience. It's an ideal place to go if you want to really get away—hike, bike, trek, spot birds and butterflies in the rain forest, and explore waterfalls; experience a vibrant culture in Dominica's traditions; kayak, dive, snorkel, or sail in marine reserves; or go out in search of the many resident whale and dolphin species. To experience Dominica, from the Elfin Woodlands and dense rain forest to the therapeutic geothermal springs and world-class dive sites that mirror the terrestrial terrain, is really to know the earth as it was created.

Where to Stay

Many properties offer packages with dives, hikes, tours, and/or meal plans included, along with all the usual amenities. Some advertise winter rates with a discount for either summer or longer stays.

C $$ **Habitation Chabert.** French taste transformed this 17th-century mansion and former rum distillery into the poshest resort on the island. Surrounded by 1.4 acres of gardens, the common areas and rooms are elegant and plush in a regal blend of African and creole styles. You can rent a single air-conditioned room or the whole house, but it's particularly suited for a family or group of friends. The romantic tower room, which begs for a Juliet to call up a Romeo, is part of a two-level suite that includes a four-poster bed and bathroom with hand-painted French tiles. Authentic French cuisine is the fare at the hotel's restaurant. For an additional fee, you can get a car and driver and even a cook to help out with your meals. ⊠ *Hatton Garden* ☎ *767/445–7218* ⊕ *www.habitationchabert. com* ⇆ *5 rooms* ☖ *Restaurant, fans, in-room safes, pool, Internet room, airport shuttle; no room phones, no room TVs* ➟ *MC, V* ◉ *CP.*

★ $-$$ **Jungle Bay Resort & Spa.** Sweeping views of the untamed Atlantic dominate this new resort, which sits on 55 acres of the only developed section of the island's southeast. No matter where you are at this peaceful hideaway, you can always hear the sea. Hovering over the Atlantic and surrounded by lush greenery, you may feel as if you are a million miles away from the rest of the world. Exercise is a given, as the resort begins at sea level and climbs up to 1,000 feet. Many rooms are perched high on the cliff and have spectacular views. They are rustic with some very nice touches—coffeemaker, refrigerator, fresh fruit, flowers, and a delightful, enclosed outdoor shower. Overlooking the sea and the pool is the resort's restaurant, the Pavilion, which uses local spices and produce in preparing vegetarian, seafood, and chicken dishes as well as tasty cuisine like shrimp curry. The resort's plan that includes meals and activities is a superior value. It's about 2½ hours from the airport and 1 hour from Roseau. ⊠ *Delices* ✆ *Box 2352, Roseau* ☎ *767/446–1789 or 866/446-1789 in U.S. or Canada* ☎ *767/446–3344* ⊕ *www. junglebaydominica.com* ⇆ *35 cottages* ☖ *Restaurant, fans, pool, fitness classes, spa, game room, 2 bars, shop; no room phones, no room TVs, no kids,* ➟ *AE, D, MC, V* ◉ *CP.*

C $-$$ **Picard Beach Cottages.** Somewhat pricey by Dominica standards, these 18 cottages on the grounds of an old, 6-acre coconut plantation and its lovely landscaped gardens are just steps away from Dominica's longest grayish-sand beach. A white picket fence with private gates allows you access to the beach. Each one-bedroom cottage, which is only moderately maintained, accommodates two adults with two children or three adults and has a kitchenette, a living and dining area, and a verandah. The casual Le Flambeau Restaurant next door serves creole food. ⊠ *Prince Rupert Bay* ✆ *Box 34, Roseau* ☎ *767/445–5131* ☎ *767/445–5599* ⊕ *www.avirtualdominica.com/picard.htm* ⇆ *18 1-bedroom cot-*

tages ⏣ *Fans, kitchenettes, cable TV, some in-room data ports, beach, bar, Internet room* ▤ *AE, D, DC, MC, V* ⏘ *EP.*

★ $ ▦ **Beau Rive.** Owner Mark Steele puts Zen-like elegance and creative soul into every detail of this secluded B&B—natural soaps in the bath, music gently playing in the lobby, and delicious, freshly prepared food. All rooms are extraspacious and have verandahs with ocean views, but they omit things like TVs, phones, and air-conditioning. You can take quiet walks in the citrus and spice gardens or hike along the Richmond River. ⊠ *Near Castle Bruce* ⏚ *Box 2424, Roseau* ☏ 767/445–8992 ⊕ *www.beaurive.com* ↘ *8 rooms* ⏣ *Dining room, fans, pool, bar, library, Internet room; no a/c, no room phones, no room TVs, no kids under 16* ▤ *MC, V* ⏘ *CP.*

$ ▦ **Castle Comfort Lodge.** The boats anchored just off the pier, the telltale dive log, and the divers in the hot tub with mask imprints on their foreheads give it all away—this is the best dive lodge in Dominica. Located 1 mi (1½ km) south of Roseau, it offers good all-inclusive packages with top-notch diving and family-style dining. Nondivers who don't want or need fancy amenities will find the rooms adequate and can enjoy the property's pool, plus whale-watching cruises. ⊠ *Castle Comfort* ⏚ *Box 63, Roseau* ☏ 767/448–2188 or 888/414–7626 ⎙ 767/448–6088 ⊕ *www.castlecomfortdivelodge.com* ↘ *15 rooms* ⏣ *Restaurant, fans, cable TV, Wi-Fi, pool, hot tub, dive shop, boating, bar* ▤ *MC, V* ☾ *Closed Sept.* ⏘ *FAP.*

$ ▦ **Cocoa Cottages.** This eco-sensitive, hand-constructed wood-and-stone lodge has a cozy tree-house feel, and though very basic, it's also very comfortable. Many of the furnishings are made from recycled materials: bed frames from recycled spools, lamps from coconut shells, and flower pots from bamboo. All beds have colorful madras covers and mosquito nets. Some rooms have balconies and hammock chairs. You start your day with a cup of hot cocoa or tea made straight from the surrounding trees while you enjoy the melodious sounds of birds, then perhaps take a picnic at a nearby stream or a nature tour. ⊠ *Trafalgar* ⏚ *Box 288, Roseau* ☏ 767/448–0412 ⎙ 954/332–9540, Ext.1119 *in U.S.* ⊕ *www.cocoacottages.com* ↘ *6 rooms* ⏣ *Restaurant, fans, bar, game room, airport shuttle; no a/c, no room phones, no room TVs* ▤ *AE, MC, V* ⏘ *EP.*

★ ☙ $ ▦ **Crescent Moon Cabins.** In a hidden valley where waterfalls and a river run rampant, this small, family-run forest resort is so deep in the bush, you might genuinely believe you're camping—except you have the benefit of basic yet eco-friendly facilities with balconies and hammocks. All cabins have panoramic views; at night, you very well may look up to the stars in awe and wonder how it all began. What makes the property even more unique are hosts Ron and Jean Viveralli, who have pushed agri-tourism up a notch. Ron, a professionally trained chef, finds inspiration in the greenhouse, goats, chickens, and the fruits that are tenderly cared for by Jean. Ron makes his own coffee, goat cheese, and tofu from scratch. This is a great place for couples looking for romance or active families. But you'll definitely need a 4x4. ⊠ *Sylvania* ⏚ *Box 2400, Roseau* ☏ 767/449–3449 ⎙ 767/449–3449 ⊕ *www.crescentmooncabins.com* ↘ *4 cabins* ⏣ *Dining room,*

9

pool, hot tub, library, Internet room; no a/c, no room phones, no room TVs ⊟ *MC, V* ❙◎❙ *EP.*

$ 🖼 **Evergreen Hotel.** This family-run, modern oceanfront inn is a nondiver's oasis in diver-friendly Castle Comfort. Located 1 mi (1½ km) south of Roseau, it has spacious waterfront rooms with large showers and balconies—many with ocean views. A separate honeymoon cottage is in a charming, foliage-filled nook. The Crystal Terrace restaurant, just off the pool, has a creative creole menu. ⊠ *Castle Comfort* ✆ *Box 309, Roseau* ☎ *767/448–3288* 🖷 *767/448–6800* ⊕ *www.avirtualdominica. com/evergreen.htm* 🖘 *16 rooms, 1 cottage* ⚊ *Restaurant, some refrigerators, cable TV, pool, bar, Internet room, meeting rooms* ⊟ *AE, D, MC, V* ❙◎❙ *BP.*

$ 🖼 **Exotica.** After winding your way up the mountain through lush vegetation, you arrive at 1,600 feet, where you are immediately surrounded by beautiful landscape and then wrapped in mountains and water. Wooden bungalows have red roofs with solar panels for power; brightly furnished, each has a kitchen, bedroom with two (extralong) double beds, and a large living room with trundle beds. If you don't want to cook, Fae, a trained nutritionist, serves delicious creole food at the Sugar Apple Café, including produce from her organic garden. This is a great place to bird-watch, and the view of the distant ocean from your bungalow is stunning. It is so peaceful up here that many guests come for long stays. The newest addition to the property is Cassia House, a full-service restaurant. You may need to rent a jeep to get around. ⊠ *Giraudel* ✆ *Box 109, Roseau* ☎ *767/448–8839* 🖷 *767/448–8829* ⊕ *www. exotica-cottages.com* 🖘 *6 bungalows* ⚊ *2 restaurant, fans, kitchens; no a/c, no room TVs* ⊟ *AE, D, MC, V* ❙◎❙ *EP.*

$ 🖼 **Fort Young Hotel.** Sitting on the edge of a cliff just to the south of Roseau, on the site of a former 18th-century-era French fort, this hotel is probably the most urbanlike establishment on the island. Ample-size rooms have balconies with either a limited or full ocean view. Newly remodeled bathrooms have granite vanities. The spacious lobby is quite inviting, and an attached boardwalk has a variety of shops, including a few duty-free ones. The Waterfront Restaurant is one of the island's most upscale and romantic. ⊠ *Victoria St., Box 519, Roseau* ☎ *767/448– 5000* 🖷 *767/448–8065* ⊕ *www.fortyounghotel.com* 🖘 *70 rooms, 3 suites* ⚊ *3 restaurants, fans, cable TV, some in-room broadband, pool, 3 hot tubs, spa, marina, 2 bars, shops, business services, meeting rooms* ⊟ *AE, MC, V* ❙◎❙ *EP.*

$ 🖼 **Hummingbird Inn.** The ocean views, lushly fragrant garden, and naturally sensuous atmosphere at this hillside retreat provide a romantic setting for honeymooners and, needless to say, hummingbirds. Beds are dressed with handmade quilts. Shutters can be left open all night to let in breezes, soothing honeysuckle, and the sounds of the surf. The Honeymoon Suite has a stately mahogany four-poster bed, a kitchen, and a patio. The reception area, lounge, and dining terrace are all in the main house. Phones and TVs are optional. ⊠ *Morne Daniel* ✆ *Box 1901, Roseau* ☎☎ *767/449–1042* ⊕ *www.thehummingbirdinn.com* 🖘 *9 rooms, 1 suite* ⚊ *Restaurant, fans, some kitchens, bar; no a/c* ⊟ *AE, D, MC, V* ❙◎❙ *CP.*

★ ☾ $ ▦ **Papillote Wilderness Retreat.** Luxuriant vegetation abounds in this retreat's 4 acres of botanical gardens—all in the middle of the tropical forest. This family-friendly, welcoming destination has a mind-boggling collection of rare and indigenous plants and flowers that are planted among three secluded mineral pools and stone sculptures; suite 11 has its own hot tub. For activity out of doors, the river beckons you to take a dip, and the 200-foot Trafalgar Falls are a short hike from your room. The terrace-style Rainforest restaurant, which has spectacular mountain and valley views, serves excellent local cuisine. ⊠ *Trafalgar Falls Rd., Trafalgar* ⬦ *Box 2287, Roseau* ☎ *767/448–2287* ⊟ *767/448–2285* ⊕ *www.papillote.dm* ⊷ *3 rooms, 4 suites* ⬧ *Restaurant, fans, some in-room hot tubs, fitness classes, bar, shop; no a/c, no room phones, no room TVs* ⊟ *AE, D, MC, V* ⊙ *Closed Sept.–mid-Oct.* ⦶ *EP.*

☾ $ ▦ **Roseau Valley Hotel.** With tile floors and cheerful decor, this little inn is quite inviting. Some rooms have TVs and terraces, while others have a shared balcony and TV access. Internet service is available for $5 per day. The Waterhole Restaurant specializes in fresh locally grown food. ⊠ *2 mi (3 km) east of Roseau, Box 1876, Roseau* ☎ *767/449–8176 or 800/225–5872* ⊟ *767/449–8722* ⊕ *www.roseauvalleyhotel.com* ⊷ *10 rooms* ⬧ *Restaurant, fans, some kitchens, pool, bar, airport shuttle; no TVs in some rooms* ⊟ *AE, MC, V* ⦶ *BP.*

$ ▦ **Sunset Bay Club.** Sunset is a simple but comfortable beachfront resort on a stretch of Dominica's spectacular west coast. Lush gardens filled with scurrying wildlife are crisscrossed by pathways that meander from rooms to garden benches, to the pool, the sauna hut, and back to the beach and restaurant. You can get a TV in your room for an additional charge. The Four Seasons Restaurant is renowned for its seafood, wide selection of cocktails, and drop-dead views. Although most people opt for the all-inclusive plan, a breakfast-only plan is available. ⊠ *Batalie Beach, Coulibistrie* ☎ *767/446–6522* ⊟ *767/446–6523* ⊕ *www.sunsetbayclub.com* ⊷ *12 rooms, 1 suite* ⬧ *Restaurant, fans, in-room safes, pool, sauna, beach, dive shop, bar, airport shuttle; no a/c, no room phones* ⊟ *AE, MC, V* ⦶ *All-inclusive.*

☾ $ ▦ **Tamarind Tree Hotel & Restaurant.** The warmth and friendliness of owners Annette and Stefan Loerner-Peyer are this small inn's most valuable asset. Located 100 feet above the Caribbean, the intimate, no-frills hotel has awesome views. A very able Swiss chef produces fine steaks, German bread, and Continental and creole cuisine in its restaurant. The local beer, Kabuli, is on tap, made from plastic plumbing pipes. ⊠ *Salisbury* ⬦ *Box 754, Roseau* ☎ *767/449–7395* ⬦ *hotel@tamarindtree-dominica.com* ⊷ *9 rooms* ⬧ *Restaurant, fans, refrigerators, pool, bar* ⊟ *MC, V* ⦶ *BP.*

$ ▦ **3 Rivers Eco Lodge.** Nestled in a valley where three rivers meet, six comfortable cottages make up this ecofriendly B&B. Totally self-sustaining, the lodge generates its own electricity with river currents and uses solar heat for its hot water supply. You can hike and take dips in any of the three cool river ponds, or just relax and ponder nature from your hammock. You can also camp on the grounds, helping yourself to the fruits in the organic garden. This is also a place where you can work for room and board. You will need a four-wheel drive to get here, though. ⊠ *New*

9

Foundland Estate ✉ *Box 1292, Roseau* ☎ *767/446–1886* 🖷 *270/ 517–4588* ⊕ *www.3riversdominica.com* 🛏 *6 cottages* ⚒ *Restaurant, fans, badminton, billiards, bar; no a/c, no room phones, no room TVs* 🟰 *D, MC, V* ⊙⏐ *EP.*

★ $ 🏨 **Zandoli Inn.** Perched on an 80-foot cliff overlooking the southeast Atlantic coast, this small inn has an amazing view—water and then mountains—that is inspiring. You'll weave through 6 acres of luscious gardens and trails with benches along the way where you can sit and contemplate the scenery. Upstairs, rooms are elegant and comfortable. Downstairs is the dining room and bar, where hotel guests join owner Linda for scrumptious organic meals and rum-laced drinks. Farther down the cliff is the plunge pool—under a canopy of orchids; or you can go for a more adventurous swim from huge boulders in the aqua-blue Atlantic. ✉ *Roche Cassée, Stowe* ✉ *Box 2099, Roseau* ☎ *767/446–3161* 🖷 *767/ 446–3344* ⊕ *www.zandoli.com* 🛏 *5 rooms* ⚒ *Dining room, fans, pool, hiking, bar, laundry service; no a/c, no room phones, no room TVs, no kids under 12* 🟰 *AE, MC, V* ⊙⏐ *EP.*

¢–$ 🏨 **Calibishie Lodges.** New owners Chris and Linda Vinck have big plans for making these bright bamboo- and melon-color buildings even nicer than they are now. Emerging from behind the terraced lemongrass are the only lodgings so close to the beautiful beach and seaside village of Calibishie, one of Dominica's most picturesque. Six one-bedroom, self-contained units, with Scandinavian furnishings throughout, offer all the comforts of home except for air-conditioning. A small swimming pool and sun deck lead off from the bar. Meal plans are available. If the property is full, ask about Dominica Sea View Apartments, which the Vincks also own. ✉ *Calibishie Main Rd., Calibishie* ☎🖷 *767/445–8537* ⊕ *www.calibishie-lodges.com* 🛏 *6 apartments* ⚒ *Restaurant, fans, in-room safes, kitchenettes, cable TV, pool, bar, airport shuttle; no a/c,* 🟰 *D, MC, V* ⊙⏐ *EP.*

¢–$ 🏨 **Roxy's Mountain Lodge.** This simple mountain retreat is popular with nature enthusiasts as a gateway to the Morne Trois Pitons National Park. The rooms are comfortable enough, but the whole hotel needs some serious TLC. A restaurant that serves traditional Dominican cuisine opens onto a huge terrace that overlooks the gardens. The bar is a watering hole frequented by hikers fresh from the nearby trails. Laudat can get chilly during winter months, so be sure to pack something warm. The property's biggest asset is its genuinely warm and friendly manager, Gloria Anthony. ✉ *Laudat* ✉ *Box 265, Roseau* ☎🖷 *767/448–4845* ⊕ *www.avirtualdominica.com/eiroxys.htm* 🛏 *15 rooms, 1 suite* ⚒ *Restaurant, some kitchens, some kitchenettes, hiking, bar; no a/c, no room phones, no room TVs* 🟰 *AE, MC, V* ⊙⏐ *EP.*

¢ 🏨 **Anchorage Hotel.** Adventure seekers of every age come to this lodge for diving, whale-watching, or other tours led by the in-house tour company. This family-run operation is not unlike Castle Comfort Lodge next door—both offer simple rooms and top-notch activities. The Ocean Terrace Restaurant & Bar is open to dramatic sunsets with visiting yachts in the foreground. Both locals and visitors frequent the weekly buffet dinners with live music. ✉ *Castle Comfort* ✉ *Box 34, Roseau* ☎ *767/448–2638* 🖷 *767/448–5680* ⊕ *www.anchoragehotel.dm* 🛏 *32* *rooms ⌂ Restaurant, some refrigerators, cable TV, pool, dive shop, squash, bar ☰ AE, D, MC, V ⦿ EP.*

🐾 ¢ 🖼 **Itassi Cottages.** You forget how close these three cottages are to Roseau as you swing on your hammock overlooking the ocean. On beautifully landscaped grounds, the two-bedroom cottage can house as many as six people; the one-bedroom cottage accommodates up to four; and the studio cottage comfortably sleeps two. Each has a full kitchen and cable TV, and there's a shared laundry room. They are furnished with a mix of antiques, straw mats, handmade floral bedspreads, and calabash lamps. ⌂ *Morne Bruce* 🕾 *Box 2333, Roseau* ☎ *767/448–4313* 🖷 *767/448–3045* ⊕ *www.avirtualdominica.com/itassi* ⇥ *3 cottages* ⌂ *Fans, kitchens, cable TV, laundry facilities; no a/c ☰ AE, MC, V ⦿ EP.*

Where to Eat

You can expect an abundance of vegetables, fruits, and root crops to appear on menus around the island, for Dominica's economy, after all, is based on agriculture. Sweet ripe plantains, *kushkush* yams, breadfruit, dasheen (also called "taro"), fresh fish, and chicken prepared in at least a dozen different ways are among the staples. The locals drink a spiced rum—steeped with herbs such as anisette (called "nanny") and *pweve* (lemongrass). Dominican cuisine is also famous for its use of local game, such as the *manicou* (a small opossum) and the *agouti* (a large indigenous rodent), but you'll have to be an intrepid diner to go that route. At the time of this writing, the government had banned mountain chicken (a euphemism for a large frog called *crapaud*) because of problems with disease. Beware of menus that still include it.

What to Wear

Most Dominicans dress nicely but practically when eating out—for dinner it's shirts and trousers for men and modest dresses for women. During the day, nice shorts are acceptable at most places; beach attire is frowned upon, unless of course you're eating on the beach.

CARIBBEAN ✕ **Crystal Terrace Restaurant & Bar.** You can find classic local food with
$$–$$$ a very elegant twist at this restaurant in the Evergreen Hotel. Dine on a large, airy terrace perched right over the sea, or relax at the bar while sipping a tropical cocktail. Dinners are prix-fixe, with a choice of appetizer such as crab back, soup, or salad; entrées of chicken, fish, or other meats served with local produce; and a dessert of fresh fruit or homemade cake and ice cream. Breakfast and lunch are also served here, and reservations are advised. ⌂ *Evergreen Hotel, Castle Comfort* ☎ *767/448–3288* ⊕ *www.avirtualdominica.com/evergreen.htm* ☰ *AE, MC, V.*

★ **$$–$$$** ✕ **Rainforest Restaurant at Papillote.** Savor a lethal rum punch while lounging in a hot mineral bath in the Papillote Wilderness Retreat gardens. Then try the bracing callaloo soup, dasheen puffs, fish "rain forest" (marinated with papaya and wrapped in banana leaves), or the succulent freshwater prawns. This handsome Caribbean restaurant has quite possibly one of the best views in the region. Dine at an altitude cool enough to demand a throw and inspire after-dinner conversation.

✉ *Papillote Wilderness Retreat, Trafalgar Falls Rd., Trafalgar* ☎ *767/ 448-2287* ⌂ *Reservations essential* ▭ *AE, D, MC, V.*

★ **$-$$$** ✕ **La Robe Creole.** A cut-stone building only steps away from the Old Market Plaza houses one of Dominica's best restaurants. In a cozy dining room with wood rafters, ladder-back chairs, and colorful madras tablecloths, you can dine on a meal selected from an eclectic à la carte menu. Callaloo soup is one specialty, lobster crêpes and salads are others. The downstairs takeout annex, Mouse Hole, is an inexpensive and tasty place to snack when you're on the run. The restaurant makes its own delicious mango chutney and plantain chips, which you can buy in local shops. ✉ *3 Victoria St., Roseau* ☎ *767/448-2896* ▭ *D, MC, V* ☾ *Closed Sun.*

¢-$$ ✕ **Miranda's Corner.** Just past Springfield on the way to Pont Casse, you'll begin to see hills full of flowers. At a big bend, a sign on a tree reads MIRANDA'S CORNER, referring to a bar, rum shop, and diner all in one. Here Miranda Alfred is at home, serving everyone from Italian tourists to banana farmers. Many of her ingredients are grown in her adjacent garden. The specialties are numerous, including titri fish (when it is fresh and in season) and tropical juices. All are prepared with a potion of passion and a fistful of flavor. Miranda's is open for breakfast, lunch, and dinner and is an acceptable pit stop if you are in the area; call ahead to make sure it will be open when you're in the area. ✉ *Mount Joy, Springfield* ☎ *767/449-2509* ▭ *MC.*

¢-$ ✕ **Guiyave.** This popular lunchtime restaurant in a quaint Caribbean town house also has a shop downstairs serving a scrumptious selection of sweet and savory pastries, tarts, and cakes. These can also be ordered upstairs, along with more elaborate fare such as fish court bouillon or chicken in a sweet-and-sour sauce. Choose to dine either in the airy dining room or on the sunny balcony perched above Roseau's colorful streets—the perfect spot to indulge in one of the fresh-squeezed tropical juices. ✉ *15 Cork St., Roseau* ☎ *767/448-2930* ▭ *AE, D, MC, V* ☾ *Closed Sun. No dinner.*

¢-$ ✕ **Pearl's Cuisine.** In a creole town house in central Roseau, chef Pearl, with her robust and infectious character, prepares some of the island's best local cuisine. She offers everything—including *sousse* (pickled pigs' feet), blood pudding, and rotis—in typical Dominican style. When sitting down to lunch or dinner, ask for a table on the open-air gallery that overlooks Roseau, and prepare for an abundant portion, but make sure you leave space for dessert. If you're on the go, enjoy a quick meal from the daily varied menu in the ground-floor snack bar. You're spoiled for choice when it comes to the fresh fruit juices. ✉ *50 King George V St., Roseau* ☎ *767/448-8707* ▭ *AE, D, MC, V* ☾ *Closed Sun. No dinner.*

¢-$ ✕ **Port of Call Restaurant & Bar.** A haunt of middle-aged barristers and laid-back locals is ideally just around the corner from the bayfront in downtown Roseau. This breezy restaurant with a soothing gray-and-white color scheme occupies a traditional stone building. The layout is such that you can have your privacy and a relaxing meal. Management here is always ready to meet your needs for home-style local cuisine or a selection of à la carte dishes such as a hamburger and fries, or maybe just an exotic cocktail from the bar. ✉ *3 Kennedy Ave., Roseau* ☎ *767/448–2910* ▭ *AE, D, MC, V.*

¢ ✕ **Creola.** On one of the busiest streets in Roseau you can escape the bustle and step into a quaint, informal eatery, which is very similar to Pearl's Cuisine. Taking pride in age-old cooking traditions, the owner uses only the freshest local produce. Changing specials might include curried conch or callaloo (fragrant with cumin, coconut cream, lime, clove, and garlic). Don't miss the fresh fruit juices, ice creams, and desserts. ✉ *66 King George V St., Roseau* ☎ *767/440–2870* ▭ *No credit cards* ☺ *Closed Sun. No dinner.*

ECLECTIC ✕ **Waterfront Restaurant.** At the southern end of Roseau's bayfront, this
★ ☺ elegant and romantic restaurant overlooks the Caribbean coastline.
$$–$$$$ You can dine outdoors on the wraparound verandah while listening to the sound of the sea or indoors in the air-conditioned formal dining room. Executive chef Mark Rickett's menu includes spa-vegetarian choices alongside the traditional international and local dishes. Tropical desserts include cheesecake and guava tart. The menu dips into a wide range of cuisines, from creole specialties like callaloo soup to beef, lamb, duck, and even skewered shrimp with a Thai sauce. No matter what your choice, it will be served by a friendly and efficient waitstaff. The bar's happy-hour steel band adds a nice touch. ✉ *Fort Young Hotel, Victoria St., Roseau* ☎ *767/448–5000* ▭ *AE, MC, V.*

¢–$ ✕ **Cornerhouse Café.** Just off the Old Market Plaza in a historic, three-story stone-and-wood town house, this is Dominica's only true Internet café; the sign on the lattice verandah reads DOMINICA'S INFORMATION CAFÉ. An eclectic menu of meals and other treats is on offer to sustain you during your surfing: bagels with an assortment of toppings, delicious soups, sandwiches, salads, cakes, and coffee. Computers are rented by the half-hour; relax on soft chairs and flip through books and magazines while you wait. Wednesday is quiz night, and every night is game night—but arrive early, as there's always a full house. ✉ *Old and King George V Sts., Roseau* ☎ *767/449–9000* ⊕ *www.avirtualdominica.com/cornerhouse* ▭ *No credit cards* ☺ *Closed Sun.*

FRENCH ✕ **Cocorico.** It's hard to miss the umbrella-covered chairs and tables at
¢–$$ this Parisian-style café on a prominent bayfront corner in Roseau. Breakfast crêpes, croissants, baguette sandwiches, and piping-hot café au lait are available beginning at 8:30. Throughout the day you can relax indoors or out and enjoy any of the extensive menu's selections with the perfect glass of wine. In the cellar downstairs, the Cocorico wine store has a reasonably priced selection from more than eight countries. You can also choose from a wide assortment of pâtés and cheeses, crêpes, sausages, cigars, French bread, and chocolates. ✉ *Bayfront and Kennedy Aves., Roseau* ☎ *767/449–8686* ▭ *MC, V* ☺ *Closed Sun. No dinner.*

IRISH **O'Byrnes Pub & Grub.** You don't expect to find real Guinness and sham-
$–$$$ rocks in Dominica, but this Irish-style pub has both, along with grub like burgers, quesadillas, wings, pizza, and beer. TVs hang from ceilings of the stone-walled establishment so you can watch all the current sporting events. ✉ *Castle St., Roseau* ☎ *767/440–4337* ▭ *MC, V* ☺ *Closed Sun. and Mon.*

Beaches

As a volcanic island, Dominica offers many powder-fine black-sand beaches. Found mostly in the north and east, they are windswept, dramatic, and uncrowded, lending themselves more to relaxing than swimming because many have undercurrents. However, slightly farther north there are beautiful secluded white- or brown-sand beaches and coves. Although northeast-coast beaches offer excellent shallow swimming, their wind-tossed beauty can be dangerous; there are sometimes strong currents with the whipped-cream waves. From these beaches you can see the islands of Marie-Galante and Les Saintes and parts of Guadeloupe. On the southwest coast, beaches are fewer and mostly made of black sand and rounded volcanic rocks. Swimming off these rocky shores has its pleasures, too: the water is usually as flat as a lake, deep and blue, and is especially good for snorkeling. In general, the west coast is more for scuba diving and snorkeling than for beach-going.

★ **Champagne.** On the west coast, just south of the village of Pointe Michel, this stony beach is hailed as one of the best spots for swimming, snorkeling, and diving but not for sunning. It gets its name from volcanic vents that constantly puff steam into the sea, which makes you feel as if you are swimming in warm champagne. ⊠ *1 mi south of Pointe Michel.*

Hampstead Beach. This isolated shoreline on the northeast coast is one of the few really golden-sand beaches on the island. It actually encompasses three bays, of which Batibou Bay is sheltered and calm. Come here to relax, suntan, and swim. You need a 4x4 to get here, but it's worth the long drive and effort. There are no facilities. ⊠ *Off Indian Rd., west of Calibishie.*

L'Anse Tortue. This isolated, golden-sand beach on the northeast coast, which is also known as Turtle Bay, is a favorite for the somewhat adventurous who want to swim and tan and avoid other people without having to drive all the way out to Hampstead Beach. It sits on a cove just past Woodford Hill, and some days the odd surfer finds just the right wave. It's an easy walk down to it from the road. ⊠ *East of Calibishie.*

Mero Beach. This silver-gray stretch of beach is on the west coast, just outside of the village of Mero, where the entire community comes to party on Sunday. It's good for sunbathing and swimming. ⊠ *Mero.*

★ **Pointe Baptiste.** Extravagantly shaped, red-sandstone boulders surround this beautiful golden-sand beach. Access is a 15-minute walk, entering through private property, so the beach is quiet and unpopulated. Come here to relax, tan, take dips in the ocean, and climb these incredible rock formations. There are no facilities, but this is one of the nicest beaches on the island. It's near the Pointe Baptiste Guest House. ⊠ *Calibishie.*

Scotts Head. At the southernmost tip of the island, a small landmass is connected to the mainland by a narrow stretch of stony beach separating the Atlantic and the Caribbean. It's a fantastic spot for snorkeling, and you can have lunch at one of the village restaurants. ⊠ *Scotts Head Village.*

Sports & the Outdoors

ADVENTURE PARKS The **Rainforest Aerial Tram** (✉ Laudat ☎ 767/448–8775, 767/440–3266, or 866/759–8726 in U.S. ⊕ www.rainforestrams.com) gives you a bird's-eye view of a pristine forest aboard an open, eight-person gondola. For 90 minutes to two hours, you slowly skim the tree-top canopy while a guide provides scientific information about the flora and fauna. At the top, there is an optional walking tour, which is worth the steps. The price is about $55. It's popular with cruise-ship passengers, so it's a good idea to reserve ahead.

Wacky Rollers (✉ Front St., Roseau ⌂ Box 900 Roseau ☎ 767/440–4386 ⊕ www.wackyrollers.com) will make you feel as if you are training for the Marines as you swing on a Tarzan-style rope and grab onto a vertical rope ladder, rappel across zip lines and traverse suspended log bridges, a net bridge, and four monkey bridges (rope loops). It costs $60 and should take from 1½ to 3½ hours to conquer the 28 "games." There is also an abbreviated kids' course. Wacky Rollers also organizes adventure tours around the island. Although the office is in Roseau, the park itself is in Hillsborough Estate, about 20 to 25 minutes north of Roseau.

CYCLING Cyclists find Dominica's rugged terrain to be an exhilarating challenge, and there are routes suitable for all levels of bikers. **Nature Island Dive** (✉ Soufrière ☎ 767/449–8181 ⊕ www.natureislanddive.com) has a fleet of bikes in good condition. You can rent a mountain bike for $21, but if you prefer a knowledgeable guide to lead you through specific areas, the cost ranges from $30 to $65.

DIVING & SNORKELING

Fodor'sChoice ★

Dominica has been voted one of the top 10 dive destinations in the world by *Skin Diver* and *Rodale's Scuba Diving* magazines—and has won many other awards for its underwater sites that are truly awesome. There are numerous highlights all along the west coast of the island, but the best are those in the southwest—within and around **Soufrière/Scotts Head Marine Reserve.** This bay is the site of a submerged volcanic crater; the Dominica Watersports Association has worked along with the Fisheries Division for years to establish this reserve and has set stringent regulations to prevent the degradation of the ecosystem. Within a half-mile (¾ km) of the shore, there are vertical drops from 800 feet to more than 1,500 feet, with visibility frequently extending to 100 feet. Shoals of boga fish, creole wrasse, and blue cromis are common, and you might even see a spotted moray eel or a honeycomb cowfish. Crinoids (rare elsewhere) are also abundant here, as are giant barrel sponges. Other noteworthy dive sites outside this reserve are **Salisbury Falls, Nose Reef, Brain Coral Garden,** and—even farther north—**Cabrits Drop-Off** and **Toucari Reef.** The conditions for underwater photography, particularly macrophotography, are unparalleled. The going rate is between $50 and $80 for a two-tank dive or from about $85 for a resort course with one open-water dive. All scuba-diving operators also offer snorkeling; equipment rents for $10 to $20 a day; trips with gear begin at about $27. Princess Margaret Hospital now has a recompression chamber.

The **Anchorage Dive & Whale Watch Center** (⊠ Anchorage Hotel, Castle Comfort ☎ 767/448–2638 ⊕ www.anchoragehotel.dm) has two dive boats that can take you out day or night. It also offers PADI instruction (all skill levels), snorkeling and whale-watching trips, and shore diving. One of the island's first dive operations, it offers many of the same trips as Dive Dominica. **Cabrits Dive Center** (⊠ Portsmouth ☎ 767/445–3010 ⊕ www.cabritsdive.com) is the only PADI five-star dive center in Dominica. Nitrox courses are also available for $250. Since Cabrits is the sole operator on the northwest coast, its dive boats have the pristine reefs almost to themselves, unlike other operations, whose underwater territories may overlap. **Dive Dominica** (⊠ Castle Comfort Lodge, Castle Comfort ☎ 767/448–2188 ⊕ www.divedominica.com), one of the island's dive pioneers, conducts NAUI, PADI, and SSI courses as well as Nitrox certification. With four boats, it offers diving, snorkeling, and whale-watching trips and packages including accommodation at the Castle Comfort Lodge. Its trips are similar to Anchorage's. **Fort Young Dive Centre** (⊠ Fort Young Hotel, Victoria St., Roseau ☎ 767/448–5000 Ext. 333 ⊕ www.divefortyoung.com) conducts snorkeling, diving, and whale-watching trips departing from the hotel's own dock. **Nature Island Dive** (⊠ Soufrière ☎ 767/449–8181 ⊕ www.natureislanddive.com) is run by an enthusiastic crew. Some of the island's best dive sites are right outside its door, and it offers diving, snorkeling, kayaking, and mountain biking as well as resort and full PADI courses.

FISHING   Anglers will delight in the numerous banks and drop-offs, as well as in the year-round fair weather. **Game Fishing Dominica** (⊠ Mero ☎☎ 767/449–6638 ☎ 767/235–6638 ⊕ www.gamefishingdominica.com) works off the Castaways dock in Mero. Eight years ago they started the Annual International Sportfishing Tournament in Dominica. Francis Cambran will take you out for between $450 and $700 for five to eight hours, providing all equipment, bait, and refreshments. You can also do a coast-fishing trip for $50 per person, with a minimum of four persons, for about three hours. Whale-watching trips are also available.

HIKING   Dominica's majestic mountains, clear rivers, and lush vegetation con-
★   spire to create adventurous hiking trails. The island is crisscrossed by ancient footpaths of the Arawak and Carib Indians and the Nègres Maroons, escaped slaves who established camps in the mountains. Existing trails range from easygoing to arduous. To make the most of your excursion, you'll need sturdy hiking boots, insect repellent, a change of clothes (kept dry), and a guide. Hikes and tours run $25 to $50 per person, depending on destinations and duration. Some of the natural attractions within the island's National Parks require visitors to purchase a site pass. These are sold for varying numbers of visits. A single-entry site pass costs $2, a day pass $5, and a week pass $10. Local bird and forestry expert **Bertrand Jno Baptiste** (☎ 767/446–6358) leads hikes up Morne Diablotin and along the Syndicate Nature Trail; if he's not available, ask him to recommend another guide. Hiking guides can be arranged through the **Dominican Tourist Office** (⊠ Valley Rd., Roseau ☎ 767/448–2045 ⊕ www.dominica.dm). The **Forestry Division** (⊠ Dominica Botanical Gardens, between Bath Rd. and Valley Rd., Roseau

☎ 767/448–2401) is responsible for the management of forests and wildlife and has numerous publications on Dominica as well as a wealth of information on reputable guides.

WHALE-
WATCHING
★

Dominica records the highest species counts of resident cetacea in the southern Caribbean region, so it's not surprising that tour companies claim 90% sighting success for their excursions. Humpback whales, false killer whales, minke, and orcas are all occasionally seen, as are several species of dolphin. But the resident sperm whales (they calve in Dominica's 3,000-feet-deep waters) are truly the stars of the show. During your 3½-hour expedition, which costs about $50, you may be asked to assist in recording sightings, data that can be shared with local and international organizations. Although there are resident whales and dolphins and therefore year-round sightings, there are more species to be observed in November through February. Turtle-watching trips are also popular. **Game Fishing Dominica** also offers trips (see ⇨ Fishing, *above*). The **Anchorage Dive & Whale Watch Center** (⊠ Anchorage Hotel, Castle Comfort ☎ 767/448–2638 ⊕ www.anchoragehotel.dm) offers whale-watching trips. **Dive Dominica** (⊠ Castle Comfort Lodge, Castle Comfort ☎ 767/448–2188 ⊕ www.divedominica.com) is a major whale-watching operator.

Shopping

Dominicans produce distinctive handicrafts, with various communities specializing in their specific products. The crafts of the Carib Indians include traditional baskets made of dyed *larouma* reeds and water-proofed with tightly woven *balizier* leaves. These are sold in the Carib Indian Territory as well as in Roseau's shops. Vertivert straw rugs, screw-pine tableware, *fwije* (the trunk of the forest tree fern), and wood carvings are just some examples. Also notable are local herbs, spices, condiments, and herb teas. Café Dominique, the local equivalent of Jamaican Blue Mountain coffee, is an excellent buy, as are the Dominican rums Macoucherie and Soca. Proof that the old ways live on in Dominica can be found in the number of herbal remedies available. One stimulating memento of your visit is rum steeped with *bois bandé* (scientific name *Richeria grandis*), a tree whose bark is reputed to have aphrodisiacal properties. It's sold at shops, vendors' stalls, and supermarkets all over the island. The charismatic roadside vendors can be found all over the island bearing trays laden with local and imported souvenirs, T-shirts, and trinkets. Duty-free shopping is also available in specific stores around Roseau.

9

Dominican farmers islandwide bring their best crops to the Roseau Market, at the end of Dame Eugenia Boulevard and Lainge Lane, every Saturday from 6 AM to 1 PM. It may well be the largest farmers' market in the Caribbean. Vendors are usually out on roadsides when there are cruise ships in port.

Major Shopping Areas

One of the easiest places to pick up a souvenir is the Old Market Plaza, just behind the Dominica Museum, in Roseau. Slaves were once sold here, but today handcrafted jewelry, T-shirts, spices, souvenirs, batik, and lacquered and woven bamboo boxes and trays are available from a group of vendors in open-air booths set up on the cobblestones. These are usually busiest when there's a cruise ship berthed across the street. On these days you can also find a vast number of vendors along the bayfront.

Specialty Items

ART   Most artists work from their home studios, and it often takes the right contact to find them. You can usually see the work of the island's artists at the Old Mill Cultural Center (see ⇨ Nightlife & the Arts, *below*). The tree-house studio and café at **Indigo** (⊠ Bournes ☎ 767/445–3486) sells works by in-house artists Clem and Marie Frederick and also serves fresh sugarcane juice or bush teas.

CLOTHING   There's such a wide selection when it comes to clothing stores in Roseau that it really is best to walk around and explore for yourself. However, for classic Caribbean and international designer clothing, there are several reliable boutiques to try. **Ego Boutique** (⊠ 9 Hillsborough St., Roseau ☎ 767/448–2336) carries an extensive selection of designer clothing and exquisite crafts and home accessories from around the world.

GIFTS &   As cruise-ship visits have increased in frequency, duty-free shops are
SOUVENIRS   cropping up, including some name-brand stores, mostly within Roseau's bayfront. **Baroon International** (⊠ Kennedy Ave., Roseau ☎ 767/449–2888) sells unusual jewelry from Asia, the United States, and other Caribbean islands; there are also pieces that are assembled in the store, as well as personal accessories, souvenirs, and special gifts. **Jeweller's International** (⊠ Fort Young Hotel, Victoria St., Roseau ☎ 767/440–3319) carries perfumes; crystals; gold-and-silver jewelry alone or with emeralds, diamonds, and other gems; liquor; and other gift items. For quality leather goods and other personal accessories, try **Land** (⊠ 19 Castle St., Roseau ☎ 767/448–3394). **Smoke & Booze** (⊠ Cork St., Roseau ☎ 767/440–0789) has a large selection of duty-free cigarettes, cigars, and alcohol. On the second floor of Fort Young shopping area, **Mango Tango** (⊠ Fort Young Hotel, Victoria St., Roseau ☎ 767/448–2026) sells duty-free upscale and designer clothing. **Whitchurch Duty-Free** (⊠ Fort Young Hotel, Victoria St., Roseau ☎ 767/448–7177) offers a large assortment of items, including perfumes, leather goods, and designer sunglasses.

HANDICRAFTS   The **Crazy Banana** (⊠ 17 Castle St., Roseau ☎ 767/449–8091) purveys everything from earthenware to doorstops, as well as other Caribbean-made crafts, rums, cigars, jewelry, and local art. **Dominica Pottery** (⊠ Bayfront St. and Kennedy Ave., Roseau ☎ No phone) carries products made from various local clays and glazes. **Papillote Wilderness Retreat** (⊠ Trafalgar ☎ 767/448–2287) has an intimate gift shop with local handcrafted goods and particularly outstanding wood carvings by Louis Desire. **Tropicrafts** (⊠ Independence St. and Turkey La., Roseau ☎ 767/448–2747) has a back room where you can watch local ladies weave grass mats. You can also find arts and crafts from around the Caribbean, local wood carvings, rum, hot sauces, perfumes, and traditional Carib baskets, hats, and woven mats.

CLOSE UP

The Original Caribbeans

THE CARIBBEAN SEA GOT ITS name from the aboriginal inhabitants of the Lesser Antilles known as the Caribs, whose territory ranged as far as the Amazon and the Venezuelan-Columbian Andes. The Island Caribs were a warlike, maritime people who carried out raids on neighboring islands in expertly carved large canoes, thus gradually displacing other inhabitants—such as the Arawaks—from the region.

Linguistically, the name Carib is traced to the Arawak word for "cannibal." However, much of the anthropological data collected by European missionaries regarding actual cannibalism is believed to have been greatly exaggerated, distorting the Caribs' practices. (For that reason, the sequel to *Pirates of the Caribbean*, which was filmed in Dominica, was locally somewhat controversial.) What can't be contested is that the Caribs forcefully resisted European colonization but then dramatically lost power over the Lesser Antilles after

two major massacres in the 17th century. One of these incidents occurred in Dominica, where one Carib village is still called Massacre.

By the end of the 18th century, the Caribs, including those from other islands, had mostly retreated into the rugged mountains of northeastern Dominica. Island historian Lennox Honychurch observed: "It is a sad irony that this tribe of seafarers, after whom the waters of the Caribbean have been named, should end up in a corner of the island where access to the sea is almost impossible."

Today, roughly 3,000 Carib descendants live in what is known as the Carib Territory. This area, however, is visually indistinguishable from any other poor, rural community in Dominica. Echoes of their past civilization still glimmer in their baskets made of larouma reed and canoes hollowed out of a single gommier tree.

9

Nightlife & the Arts

The friendly, intimate atmosphere and colorful patrons at the numerous bars and hangouts will keep you entertained for hours. If you're looking for jazz, calypso, reggae, steel-band, soca (a variation of calypso), cadence-zouk, or jing ping—a type of folk music featuring the accordion, the *quage* (a kind of washboard instrument), drums, and a "boom boom" (a percussion instrument)—you're guaranteed to find it. Wednesday through Saturday nights are really lively, and during Carnival, Independence, and summer celebrations, things can be intense. Indeed, Dominica's Carnival, the pre-Lenten festival, is the most spontaneous in the Caribbean.

FodorśChoice ★ The annual **World Creole Music Festival** (⊕ www.dominica.dm/festivals) in late October or early November also packs in the action, with three days and nights of pulsating rhythm and music. Creole Music enthusiasts come from all over the world to listen to the likes of Kassav, Aswad, and Tabou Combo. Throughout the year, however, most larger hotels have some form of live evening entertainment.

In addition to the World Creole Music Festival, which is a big draw for the island, the other big cultural event in Dominica are the Emancipation celebrations hosted by the National Cultural Council each August.

Nightlife

Once Friday afternoon rolls around you can sense the mood change. Local bars crank up the music, and each village and community has its own particular nightly entertainment. If by this point in your trip you have made friends with some locals, they will be only too happy to take you to the current hot spot.

At **Cellars Bar** (⊠ Sutton Place Hotel, Old St., Roseau ☎ 767/449–8700), Wednesday night is Amateur Bartenders Soca Rum Night. Volunteer to be the bartender; taste tests of the featured cocktails are free. Friday is Kubuli Karaoke Night, with patrons competing for prize drinks; it's a real blast and perfect way to totally kick back. There's a $4 minimum on both nights. Relax with Robert James's piano and cross-over jazz at **Jazz Walk** (⊠ 9B Church St., Roseau ☎ 767/245–3633 or 767/448–2834). Poetry night is Wednesday, and the house trio plays on Friday. It's also open for lunch on Friday. **Symes Zee's** (⊠ 34 King George V St., Roseau ☎ 767/448–2494) draws a crowd on Thursday night from 10 until the wee hours of the morning, when there's a jazz/blues/reggae band. There's no cover, and the food, drinks, and cigars are reasonably priced. **Warehouse** (⊠ Canefield ☎ 767/449–1303), outside Roseau just past the airport, is *the* place to dance on Saturday night. DJs are brought in from other islands to ensure there's variety to all the vibrations. The entrance fee is $5.

The Arts

Arawak House of Culture (⊠ Kennedy Ave. near Government Headquarters, Roseau ☎ 767/449–1804), managed by Harry Sealy at the Cultural Division, is Dominica's main performing-arts theater. A number of productions are staged here throughout the year, including plays, recitals, and dance performances. The **Old Mill Cultural Center** (⊠ Canefield ☎ 767/449–1804) is one of Dominica's historic landmarks. The Old Mill was the island's first sugarcane processing mill and rum distillery. Today, it's a place to learn about Dominica's traditions. Performances and events—including art exhibits—take place here throughout the year.

Exploring Dominica

Despite the small size of this almond-shaped island, it can take a couple of hours to travel between the popular destinations. Many sights are isolated and difficult to find; you may be better off taking an organized excursion. If you do go it alone, drive carefully: roads can be narrow and winding. Plan on eight hours to see the highlights; to fully experience the island, set aside a couple of days and work in some hikes.

Numbers in the margin correspond to points of interest on the Dominica map.

WHAT TO SEE **Cabrits National Park.** Along with Brimstone Hill in St. Kitts, Shirley
⓾ Heights in Antigua, and Ft. Charlotte in St. Vincent, the Cabrits National Park's Ft. Shirley ruins are among the most significant historic
sites in the Caribbean. Just north of the town of Portsmouth, this 1,300-
acre park includes a marine park and herbaceous swamps, which are
an important environment for several species of rare birds and plants.
At the heart of the park is the Ft. Shirley military complex. Built by the
British between 1770 and 1815, it once comprised 50 major structures,
including storehouses that were also quarters for 700 men. With the help
of the Royal Navy (which sends sailors ashore to work on the site each
time a ship is in port) and local volunteers, historian Dr. Lennox Honychurch restored the fort and its surroundings, incorporating a small
museum that highlights the natural and historic aspects of the park and
an open canteen-style restaurant. ⊠ *Portsmouth* ☎ *No phone* ▧ *$2*
☉ *Museum daily 8–4.*

★ ☚ ❺ **Carib Indian Territory.** In 1903, after centuries of conflict, the Caribbean's
first settlers, the Kalinago (more popularly known as the Caribs), were
granted a portion of land (approximately 3,700 acres) on the island's
northeast coast, on which to establish a reservation with their own
chief. Today it's known as Carib Territory, clinging to the northeasterly
corner of Dominica, where a group of just over 3,000 Caribs, who resemble native South Americans, live like most other people in rural
Caribbean communities. Many are farmers and fishermen; others are
entrepreneurs who have opened restaurants, guesthouses, and little
shops where you can buy exquisite Carib baskets and other handcrafted
items. The craftspeople retain knowledge of basket weaving, wood
carving, and canoe building, which has been passed down from one generation to the next.

The Caribs' long, elegant canoes are created from the trunk of a single
gommier tree. If you're lucky, you may catch canoe builders at work.
The reservation's Catholic church in Salybia has a canoe as its unique
altar, which was designed by Dr. Lennox Honychurch, a local historian,
author, and artist. **L'Escalier Tête Chien** (literally "Snake's Staircase,"
it's the name of a snake whose head resembles that of a dog) is a hardened lava formation that runs down into the Atlantic. The ocean here
is particularly fierce, and the shore is full of countless coves and inlets.
According to Carib legend, at night the nearby Londonderry Islets meta-
morphose into grand canoes to take the spirits of the dead out to sea.
Though there's not currently much in the territory that demonstrates
the Caribs' ancient culture and customs, plans for a museum showing
early Carib life are in the works.

☚ ❹ **Emerald Pool.** Quite possibly the most-visited nature attraction on the island, this emerald-green pool fed by a 50-foot waterfall is an easy trip
to make. To reach this spot in the vast Morne Trois Pitons National Park,
you follow a trail that starts at the side of the road near the reception
center (it's an easy 20-minute walk). Along the way you can pass lookout points with views of the windward (Atlantic) coast and the forested
interior. If you don't want a crowd, check whether there are cruise ships
in port before going out, as this spot is popular with cruise-ship tour groups.

9

🐾 **8** **Indian River.** The mouth of the Indian River, which flows into the ocean in Portsmouth, was once a Carib Indian settlement. A gentle rowboat ride for wildlife spotting along this river lined with *terra carpus officinalis* trees, whose buttress roots spread up to 20 feet, is not only a relaxing treat but educational and most times entertaining. To arrange such a trip, stop by the visitor center in Portsmouth and ask for one of the "Indian River boys." These young, knowledgeable men are members of the Portsmouth Indian River Tour Guides Association (PIRTGA) and have for years protected and promoted one of Dominica's special areas. Most boat trips take you up as far as Rahjah's Jungle Bar. You can usually do an optional guided walking tour of the swamplands and the remnants of one of Dominica's oldest plantations. Tours last one to three hours, starting at $10 per person, but the actual price depends on your guide.

⓫ **Morne Aux Diables.** In the far north of Dominica, this peak soars 2,826 feet above sea level and slopes down to Toucari and Douglas bays and long stretches of dark-sand beach. To reach the mountain, take the road along the Caribbean coast. It twists by coconut, cocoa, and banana groves, past fern-festooned embankments, over rivers, and into villages where brightly painted shanties are almost as colorful as all the flora and fauna.

🐾 **7** **Morne Diablotin National Park.** The park is named after one of the region's highest mountains, Morne Diablotin—at 4,747 feet, Dominica's highest peak. The peak takes its name, in turn, from a bird, known in English as the black-capped petrel, that was prized by hunters in the 18th century. Though the mountain's namesake bird is now extinct on the island, Dominica is still a major birding destination. Of the island's many exotic—and endangered—species, the green-and-purple Sisserou parrot (*Amazona imperialis*) and the Jaco, or red-neck, parrot (*Amazona arausiaca*) are found here in greater numbers than anywhere else in Dominica. Before the national park was established, the Syndicate Nature Trail was protected with the help of some 6,000 schoolchildren, each of whom donated 25¢ to protect the habitat of the flying pride of Dominica, as well as countless other species of birds and other wildlife. The west-coast road (at the bend near Dublanc) runs through three types of forest and leads into the park. The trail offers a casual walk; just bring a sweater and binoculars. The five- to eight-hour hike up Morne Diablotin isn't for everyone. You need a guide, sturdy hiking shoes, warm clothing, and a backpack with refreshments and a change of clothes (including socks) that are wrapped in plastic to keep them dry. A good guide for Morne Diablotin is local ornithology expert **Bertrand Jno Baptiste** (☎ 767/446–6358).

3 **Morne Trois Pitons National Park.** A UNESCO World Heritage Site, this 17,000-acre swath of lush, mountainous land in the south-central interior (covering 9% of Dominica) is the island's crown jewel. Named after one of the highest 4,600-foot mountains on the island, it contains the island's famous "boiling lake," majestic waterfalls, and cool mountain lakes. There are four types of vegetation zones here. Ferns grow 30 feet tall, wild orchids sprout from trees, sunlight leaks through green canopies, and a gentle mist rises over the jungle floor. A system of trails has been developed in the park, and the Division of Forestry and Wildlife works hard to maintain them—with no help from the excessive rainfall and the profusion of vegetation that seems to grow right before your eyes. Access to the park is possible from most points of the compass, though the easiest approaches are via the small mountaintop villages of Laudat (pronounced low-*dah*) and Cochrane.

About 5 mi (8 km) out of Roseau, the Wotton Waven Road branches off toward Sulphur Springs, where you can see the belching, sputtering, and gurgling releases of volcanic hot springs. At the base of Morne Micotrin you can find two crater lakes: the first, at 2,500 feet above sea level, is **Freshwater Lake.** According to a local legend, it's haunted by a vindictive mermaid and a monstrous serpent. Farther on is **Boeri Lake,** fringed with greenery and with purple hyacinths floating on its surface. The undisputed highlight of the park is **Boiling Lake.** Reputedly the world's largest such lake, it's a cauldron of gurgling gray-blue water, 70 yards wide and of unknown depth, with water temperatures from 180°F to 197°F. Although generally believed to be a volcanic crater, the lake is actually a flooded fumarole—a crack through which gases escape from the molten lava below. As many visitors discovered in late 2004, the "lake" can sometimes dry up, though it fills again within a few months and, shortly after that, once more starts to boil. The two- to four-hour (one-way) hike up to the lake is challenging (on a very rainy day, be prepared to slip and slide the whole way up and back). You'll need attire appropriate for a strenuous hike, and a guide is a must. Most guided trips start early (no later than 8:30 AM) for this all-day, 7-mi (11-km) round-trip trek. On your way to Boiling Lake you pass through the **Valley of Desolation,** a sight that definitely lives up to its name. Harsh sulfuric fumes have destroyed virtually all the vegetation in what must once have been a lush forested area. Small hot and cold streams with water of various colors—black, purple, red, orange—web the valley. Stay on the trail to avoid breaking through the crust that covers the hot lava. During this hike you'll pass rivers where you can refresh yourself with a dip (a particular treat is a soak in a hot-water stream on the way back). At the beginning of the Valley of Desolation trail is the **TiTou Gorge,** where you can swim in the pool or relax in the hot-water springs along one side. If you're a strong swimmer, you can head up the gorge to a cave (it's about a five-minute swim) that has a magnificent waterfall; a crack in the cave about 50 feet above permits a stream of sunlight to penetrate the cavern.

Also in the national park are some of the island's most spectacular waterfalls. The 45-minute hike to **Sari Sari Falls,** accessible through the east-coast village of La Plaine, can be hair-raising. But the sight of water cascading some 150 feet into a large pool is awesome. So large are these falls that you feel the spray from hundreds of yards away. Just beyond the village of Trafalgar and up a short hill, there's the reception facility, where you can purchase passes to the national park and find guides to take you on a rain-forest trek to the twin **Trafalgar Falls;** the 125-foot high waterfall is called the Father, and the wider, 95-foot high one,

Fodor's Choice
★

the Mother. If you like a little challenge, let your guide take you up the riverbed to the cool pools at the base of the falls (check whether there's a cruise ship in port before setting out; this sight is popular with the tour operators). You need a guide for the arduous 75-minute hike to **Middleham Falls.** It's best if you start at Laudat (the turnoff for the trail-head is just before the village); the trip is much longer from Cochrane Village. The trail takes you to another spectacular waterfall, where water cascades 100 feet over boulders and vegetation and then into an ice-cold pool (a swim here is absolutely exhilarating). Guides for these hikes are available at the trailheads; still, it's best to arrange a tour be-fore even setting out.

❻ Northeast Coast. Steep cliffs, dramatic reefs, and rivers that swirl down through forests of mangroves and fields of coconut define this section of Dominica. The road along the Atlantic, with its red cliffs, whipped-cream waves, and windswept trees, crosses the Hatton Garden River be-fore entering the village of Marigot. In the northeastern region there are numerous estates—old family holdings planted with fruit trees. Beyond Marigot and the Melville Hall Airport is the beautiful Londonderry Es-tate. The beach here is inspiring, with driftwood strewn about its vel-vety black sands, which part halfway—where the Londonderry River spills into the Atlantic (swimming isn't advised because of strong cur-rents, but a river bath here is a memorable treat). Farther along the coast, beyond the village of Wesley (which has a gas station and a shop that sells wonderful bread) and past Eden Estate, there are still more beau-tiful beaches and coves. The swimming is excellent at Woodford Hill Bay, Hodges Beach, Hampstead Estate, Batibou Bay, and L'Anse Tortue. A stop in the charming community of Calibishie is a must; here you'll find bars and restaurants right on the beach, as well as laid-back villas and guest houses. At Bense, a village in the interior just past Calibishie, you can take a connector road to Chaud Dwe (pronounced show-*dweh*), a beautiful swimming spot in a valley; the only crowd you're likely to encounter is a group of young villagers frolicking in the 15-foot-deep pool and diving off the 25-foot-high rocks.

❾ Portsmouth. In 1782 Portsmouth was the site of the Battle of Les Saintes, a naval engagement between the French and the English. The English won the battle but lost the much tougher fight against malaria-carrying mosquitoes that bred in the nearby swamps. Once intended to be the capital of Dominica, thanks to its superb harbor on Prince Rupert Bay, it saw as many as 400 ships in port at one time in its heyday, but on ac-count of those swamps, Roseau, not Portsmouth, is the capital today. Maritime traditions are continued here by the yachting set, and a 2-mi (3-km) stretch of sandy beach fringed with coconut trees runs to the Pi-card Estate area.

❶ Roseau. Although it's one of the smallest capitals in the Caribbean, Roseau has the highest concentration of inhabitants of any town in the eastern Caribbean. Caribbean vernacular architecture and a bustling mar-ketplace transport visitors back in time. Although you can walk the en-tire town in about an hour, you'll get a much better feel for the place on a leisurely stroll.

For some years now, the Society for Historical Architectural Preservation & Enhancement (SHAPE) has organized programs and projects to preserve the city's architectural heritage. Several interesting buildings have already been restored. **Lilac House,** on Kennedy Avenue, has three types of gingerbread fretwork, latticed verandah railings, and heavy hurricane shutters. The **J. W. Edwards Building,** at the corner of Old and King George V streets, has a stone base and a wooden second-floor gallery; it's now the cozy Cornerhouse Café. **The old market plaza** is the center of Roseau's historic district, which was laid out by the French on a radial plan rather than a grid, so streets such as Hanover, King George V, and Old radiate from this area. South of the marketplace is the Fort Young Hotel, built as a British fort in the 18th century; the nearby state house, public library, and Anglican cathedral are also worth a visit. New developments at bayfront on Dame M. E. Charles Boulevard have brightened up the waterfront.

The 40-acre **Botanical Gardens,** founded in 1891 as an annex of London's Kew Gardens, is a great place to relax, stroll, or watch a cricket match. In addition to the extensive collection of tropical plants and trees, there's also a parrot aviary. At the Forestry Division office, which is also on the garden grounds, you can find numerous publications on the island's flora, fauna, and national parks. The forestry officers are particularly knowledgeable on these subjects and can also recommend good hiking guides. ⊠ *Between Bath Rd. and Valley Rd.* ☎ *767/448–2401 Ext. 3417* ✆ *$2* ☉ *Mon. 8–1 and 2–5, Tues.–Fri. 8–1 and 2–4.*

The old post office now houses the **Dominica Museum.** This labor of love by local writer and historian Dr. Lennox Honychurch contains furnishings, documents, prints, and maps that date back hundreds of years; you can also find an entire Carib hut as well as Carib canoes, baskets, and other artifacts. ⊠ *Dame M. E. Charles Blvd., opposite cruise-ship berth* ☎ *767/448–8923* ✆ *$2* ☉ *Weekdays 9–4 and Sat. 9–noon.*

❷ **Soufrière.** Tourism is quietly mingling with the laid-back lifestyle of the residents of this gently sunbaked village in the southwest, near one of the island's two marine reserves. Although it was first settled by French lumbermen in the 17th century, it's mainly fishermen you'll find here today. In the village you can find a historic 18th-century Catholic church built of volcanic stone, one of the island's prettiest churches; the ruins of the L. Rose Lime Oil factory; Sulfur Springs, with its hot mineral baths to the east; and the best diving and snorkeling on the island within the **Soufrière/Scotts Head Marine Reserve.** To the west you'll find Bois Cotlette (a historic plantation house) and to the south the Scotts Head Peninsula—at the island's southern tip—which separates the Caribbean from the Atlantic. So if there isn't enough treasure here to satisfy you, there's always the rain forest waiting to be challenged.

DOMINICA ESSENTIALS

To research prices, get advice from other travelers, and book travel arrangements, visit www.fodors.com.

Transportation

BY AIR

There are no nonstop flights from the United States, but you can connect through San Juan. Other, smaller Caribbean airlines fly from Antigua, Barbados, Martinique, St. Lucia, Trinidad, and Guyana. Caribbean Sun began service to and from San Juan, Trinidad, and St. Lucia in 2005.

🔲 Airline Information **Air Caraïbes** ☎ 767/448-2181. **American/American Eagle** ☎ 767/448-6680 or 800/433-7300. **Caribbean Sun Airlines** ☎ 800/744-7827, 866/864-6272 in U.S. ⊕ www.flycsa.com. **LIAT** ☎ 767/448-2421, 767/448-0628 or 888/844-5428 ⊕ www.liatairline.com. **Whitchurch Travel (for Caribbean Star Airlines)** ☎ 767/448-2181 or 767/445-8841.

🔲 Airport Information **Canefield Airport** ☎ 767/449-1199. **Melville Hall Airport** ☎ 767/445-7101.

BY BOAT & FERRY

Express des Isles has regularly scheduled interisland jet catamaran ferry service connecting Dominica to Guadeloupe, Martinique, and St. Lucia; during peak seasons additional arrivals and departures are added. Generally, though, the ferry arrives and departs at the Roseau Ferry Terminal on Monday, Wednesday, Friday, Saturday, and Sunday from Guadeloupe; it continues south to Martinique, as well as St. Lucia, on specific days. The crossing costs €64 to €99, takes approximately 90 minutes, and offers superb views of the other islands.

🔲 **Express des Isles** ☎ 767/448-2181 ⊕ www.express-des-iles.com.

BY CAR

Unless you are staying in Roseau or arranging to do extensive guided tours, a car may be a necessity, since cabs can be very expensive. Daily car-rental rates begin at $39 (weekly and long-term rates can be negotiated), though you can often pay more if you rent a car for only a day or two. Expect to add approximately another $7 to $17 a day for optional collision damage insurance. You'll need to buy a visitor's driving permit (EC$34) at one of the airports or at the Traffic Division office on High Street in Roseau. Most rental-car companies offer airport and hotel pickup and drop-off.

Roads can be narrow in places, and they meander around the coast and through mountainous terrain. Gasoline stations can be found all over the island. Gasoline is quite a bit more expensive than in the United States. Driving in Dominica is on the left side, though you can rent vehicles with a steering wheel on either the left or right.

🔲 **Best Deal Car Rental** ✉ 15 Hanover St., Roseau ☎ 767/449-9204 or 767/235-3325 ⊕ www.bestdealrentacar.com. **Courtesy Car Rentals** ✉ 10 Winston La., Goodwill ☎ 767/445-7677 📠 767/448-7733 ⊕ www.avirtualdominica.com/courtesycarrental. **Island Car Rentals** ✉ Goodwill Rd., Goodwill ☎ 767/255-6844 or 767/445-8789 ⊕ www.avirtualdominica.com/islandcarrentals.

TAXIS

Taxis and minibuses are available at the airports and in Roseau as well as at most hotels and guest houses. Rates are fixed by the government (from Melville Hall Airport to Roseau, the fare is $60) but if you opt for a co-op—sharing a taxi (and the fare) with other passengers going in the same direction—you will be able to negotiate a special price (as little as $20 per person from the airport to Roseau). Drivers also offer their services for tours anywhere on the island beginning at $25 to $30 an hour for up to four persons; a four- to five-hour island tour will cost approximately $150. It's best to get a recommendation from your hotel. You can recognize a taxi and/or minibus by the H, HA, and

HB plates; simply flag them down or make your way to the nearest bus stop. For more information on reputable taxi companies, contact the Dominica Taxi Association or Nature Island Taxi Association. **Dominica Taxi Association** ☎ 767/449-8533. **Nature Island Taxi Association** ☎ 767/448-1679.

Contacts & Resources

BANKS & EXCHANGE SERVICES

The official currency is the Eastern Caribbean dollar (EC$), but U.S. dollars are readily accepted. The exchange rate is EC$2.69 to the US$1, but, unless you ask, you'll usually get change in EC dollars. Most Americans will not need to exchange money, U.S. dollars being readily accepted except at the smallest places. Major credit cards are also widely accepted, as are traveler's checks. You can find ATMs in all the banks in Roseau—including Barclays International Bank on Old Street, the Royal Bank of Canada near the cruise-ship berth, Banque Française Commerciale on Queen Mary Street, and the Bank of Nova Scotia on Hillsborough Street—as well as some in larger villages such as Portsmouth. They dispense EC dollars only and accept international bank cards.

Prices throughout this chapter are quoted in U.S. dollars, unless indicated otherwise.

BUSINESS HOURS

Banks are open Monday through Thursday from 8 to 2, Friday from 8 to 5. Post offices are open Monday from 8 to 5, Tuesday through Friday from 8 to 4, and Saturday from 8 to 1. Businesses are generally open Monday from 8 to 5, Tuesday through Friday from 8 to 4, and Saturday from 8 to 1. Some stores have longer hours, but you should call ahead to confirm them.

ELECTRICITY

Electric voltage is 220–240 AC, 50 cycles. North American appliances require an adapter and transformer; however, many establishments provide these and often have dual-voltage fittings (110–120 and 220–240 volts).

EMBASSIES

Belgium Honorary Consul ☎ 767/447-2168. **France Honorary Consul** ☎ 767/448-0508. **Netherlands Honorary Consul** ☎ 767/448-3841. **Sweden Honorary Consul** ☎ 767/448-2181. **United Kingdom Honorary Consul** ☎ 767/448-7655 or 767/255-2417.

EMERGENCIES

General Emergencies Ambulance, Police & Fire ☎ 999. **Hospitals Grand Bay Hospital** ✉ Grand Bay ☎ 767/446-3706. **Marigot Hospital** ✉ Marigot ☎ 767/445-7091. **Portsmouth Hospital** ✉ Portsmouth ☎ 767/445-5237. **Princess Margaret Hospital** ✉ Federation Dr., Goodwill ☎ 767/448-2231 or 767/448-2233. **Pharmacies Bulls Eye Pharmacy** ✉ 6 Federation Dr., Goodwill ☎ 767/449-8600. **Jolly's Pharmacy** ✉ 12 King George V St., Roseau ☎ 767/448-3388. **New Charles Pharmacy** ✉ Cork St., Roseau ☎ 767/448-3198.

HOLIDAYS

Public holidays are New Year's, Merchant's Holiday (Jan. 2), Carnival Jump-Up Days (2 days before Ash Wednesday each year), Ash Wednesday, Labour Day (May 1), Whitmonday (May 24), Emancipation Day (early Aug.), Independence Day (Nov. 3), Community Service Day (Nov. 4), Christmas Day, and Boxing Day (Dec. 26).

INTERNET, MAIL & SHIPPING

Some hotels and inns have Internet service, but certainly not all. In addition to getting services at Cornerhouse Café, you can check your e-mail or go online at Cyber Land Internet Café, which has two branches in Rosea and one in Portsmouth. You'll pay about EC$2.50 for 30 minutes of Internet use.

First-class letters to North America cost EC95¢ and those to the United Kingdom cost EC90¢; postcards are EC55¢ to just about anywhere in the world. The general post office is opposite the ferry terminal in Roseau. Dominica is often confused with

9

the Dominican Republic, so when addressing letters to the island, be sure to write: The Commonwealth of Dominica, Eastern Caribbean. Islands in this part of the Caribbean do not use postal codes.

🚹 **Cornerhouse Café** ⊠ Old and King George V Sts., Roseau ☎ 767/449-9000. **Cyber Land Internet Café** ⊠ George St., Roseau ⊠ Woodstone Shopping Mall, Roseau ⊠ Grandby St., Portsmouth.

PASSPORT REQUIREMENTS
U.S. citizens must have a valid passport starting on January 1, 2007.

SAFETY
Petty crime can be a problem on Dominica, as with nearly all destinations in the world. It's always wise to secure valuables in the hotel safe and not carry too much money or many valuables around. Remember that if you rent a car to tour the island, you may have to park it in a remote area; don't leave valuables in your vehicle while you're off on a hike or a tour.

TAXES & SERVICE CHARGES
The departure-embarkation tax is US$22 or EC$55, payable in cash only at the airport at the time of departure from the island. Hotels collect a 10% government hotel occupancy tax, restaurants a 15% government V.A.T.

TELEPHONES
Your tri-band GSM mobile phone will work in Dominica, and if your provider will unlock your phone, you can purchase a local SIM card for $EC26.88 and use prepaid cell cards. You can also buy a prepaid cell phone for as little as EC$80.

The island has a somewhat adequate telecommunication system and accordingly efficient direct-dial international service. All pay phones are equipped for local and overseas dialing, accepting EC coins, credit cards, or phone cards, which you can buy at many island stores and at the airports. To call Dominica from the United States, dial the area code (767) and the local access code (44), followed by the five-digit local number. On the island, dial only the seven-digit number that follows the area code.

🚹 **AT&T Direct** ☎ 800/872-2881 does not always work. **MCI World Phone** ☎ 800/888-8000. **Sprint** ☎ 800/744-2250.

TIPPING
Most hotels and restaurants add a 10% service charge to your bill. A 5% tip for exceptionally good service on top of the service charge is always welcome; otherwise just tip accordingly.

TOUR OPTIONS
Since Dominica is such a nature-centered destination, there's no shortage of certified guides, as well as numerous tour and taxi companies. Ask the staff at your hotel for a recommendation. Generally tours start off in the Roseau area, but most operators will arrange convenient pickups. Prices range between $35 and $75 per person depending on the duration, amenities provided, and number of persons on the excursion. Johnathan Peter of Baggie Taxi &Tours offers private tours. Dominica Tours is one of the island's largest tour companies, offering a range of hikes and bird-watching trips. Ken's Hinterland Adventure Tours & Taxi Service offers a range of island tours and guided hikes, including some oriented specifically for families with children.

🚹 **Baggie Taxi &Tours** ☎ 767/616-0034 or 767/235-5091. **Dominica Tours** ⊠ Anchorage Hotel, Castle Comfort ☎ 767/448-2638 or 767/448-0990 ⊕ www.anchoragehotel.dm. **Ken's Hinterland Adventure Tours & Taxi Service** ⊠ Fort Young Hotel, Victoria St., Roseau ☎ 767/448-4850, or 767/448-1660, or 866/880-0508 ⊕ www.kenshinterlandtours.com.

VISITOR INFORMATION
🚹 Before You Leave **Dominican Tourist Office** ⊕ www.dominica.dm ⊠ 800 2nd Ave., Suite 1802, New York, NY 10017 ☎ 212/949-1711 🖷 212/949-1714. **The Dominica Tourist Office–U.K** ⊠ MKI Ltd., Mitre House, 66 Abbey Rd., Bush Hill Park, Enfield, Middlesex EN1 2QE, U.K. ☎ 208/350-1004 🖷 208/350-1011. **Office of the Dominica High Commission, London** ⊠ 1 Collingham Gardens, London SW5 0HW, U.K. ☎ 207/370-5194 🖷 207/373-8743.

In Dominica **Division of Tourism** ✉ Valley Rd., Roseau ☎ 767/448-2045 ✉ Old Post Office, Dame M. E. Charles Blvd., Roseau ☎ 767/448-2045 Ext. 118 ✉ Canefield Airport, Canefield ☎ 767/449-1242 ✉ Melville Hall Airport, Marigot ☎ 767/445-7051.

WEB SITES

The most comprehensive Web portal to all things Dominican is "A Virtual Dominica," which has links to hotels, shops, car-rental agencies, and a wealth of information about visiting the island. "Visit Dominica" is a tourism site that is supported by the fees of the many establishments that pay to appear on it, but it has a fairly comprehensive range of information. **A Virtual Dominica** ⊕ www.avirtualdominica.com. **Visit Dominica** ⊕ www.visit-dominica.com.

WEDDINGS

To get married in Dominica, prospective spouses must file an application at least two days prior to the ceremony, and at least one of the parties must have been on the island for a minimum of two days before the ceremony. Non-Dominicans must produce a valid passport and original birth certificate (not a baptismal certificate), and if one of the parties has been married before, a divorce decree or death certificate for the former spouse must be presented as well. The parties to the marriage must sign a statutory declaration on marital status, which must be obtained and sworn in Dominica in the presence of a local lawyer. The parties must also complete and sign an application form "G," which must be witnessed by a magistrate. At least two witnesses must be present at the marriage ceremony. If you marry in Dominica, the tourist office recommends that you deal with a local lawyer. The total cost for the marriage license, marriage ceremony at the Registrar's office, legal fees, and stamps will be approximately $316. There will be additional costs involved if the marriage takes place in a church or somewhere else on the island.

Fort Young offers wedding packages including bridal bouquet, a bottle of champagne, and a wedding cake, while Papillote and Exotica also have experience organizing weddings for guests. **Ministry of Community Development and Gender Affairs** ✉ Government Headquarters, Roseau ☎ 767/448-2401 Ext. 3250.

Dominican Republic

Strumming a merengue

WORD OF MOUTH

"In Punta Cana, walking on the beach with the only goal of "let's just walk until we get to that point over there" is a daily routine."

—kep

"The beaches in Cabarete or Sosúa are awesome. Caberete has one of the longest stretches of beach on the island & it is not the least bit narrow. Cabarete & Sosúa also have great nightlife & restaurants."

—BigBadTea

www.fodors.com/forums

WELCOME TO THE DOMINICAN REPUBLIC

Cofresí Beach
Luperón Beach
Montecristi
Guayubin
Puerto Plata 19
Playa Dorada
46 - 50
42 - 45
ATLANTIC OCEAN
Sosúa
18
Cabarete
Cabarete Beach
31 - 41
Cabo Francés Viejo
Cabrera
Laguna Grí-Grí
30
Mt. Isabel de Torres 20
Gregorie Luperón International Airport
Playa Grande
Bahía Escocesa
27 29
HAITI
Pico Duarte
51 52
Santiago
Moca
Las Terrenas
Nagua
Samaná 17
Santiago 21
La Vega Vieja
22
San Francisco de Macorís
Bahía de San
Jarabacoa 23
HISPANIOLA
Sabana de la Mar
← TO HAITI
Los Haitises National Park
San Juan
Monte Plata
Hato Maye
Lago Enriquillo
24
Neiba
Azua
San Cristóbal
San Pec de Maco
Las Américas International Airport
9
10
Duvergé
Bahía de Ocoa
Bani
Boca Chica
Juan Dolio
Barahona 25
Bahoruco Beach
Pto. Palenque
Santo Domingo
1 - 13
1 - 8
see detail map page 391
Oviedo
Cabo Beata

0   50 miles
0   75 km

Like the merengue seen on all the dance floors in Santo Domingo, the Dominican Republic is charismatic yet sensuous, energetic yet elegant. The charm of the people adds special warmth: a gracious wave of greeting here, a hand-rolled cigar tapped with a flourish there. Dazzling smiles just about everywhere will quickly beguile you.

LA ISLA ESPAÑOLA

The Dominican Republic covers the eastern two-thirds of the island of Hispaniola (Haiti covers the other third). At 18,765 square mi (48,730 square km), it's the second-largest Caribbean country (only Cuba is larger), and with over 8.8 million people, the second most populous country, too. It was explored by Columbus on his 1492 voyage to the New World.

KEY

↗ *Beaches*
◿ *Dive Sites*
1 *Exploring Sights*
⒈ *Hotels & Restaurants*

Cabo Samaná

ayo Levantado

Miches

El Seibo

Higüey

El Macao

Bavaro

Punta Cana

14 - **23**
see detail
map page 362

La Romana
International
Airport

Punta Cana
International
Airport

Punta
Cana

La Romana

Minitas

Bayahibe

Bahía
de Yuma

Isla Saona **16** **Isla Saona**

Mona Passage

Río Chavón

DOMINICAN REPUBLIC

10

TOP 4 REASONS TO VISIT THE DOMINICAN REPUBLIC

1. There are some 1,000 miles of excellent, pearl-white beaches.

2. Millions come each year to indulge themselves at the best-value all-inclusive resorts in the Caribbean.

3. Every imaginable activity—world-class golf, horseback riding, white-water rafting, surfing, diving, wind surfing, and more—is possible here.

4. The Dominicans love to party, dance, drink, and have a good time at happening bars and clubs.

DOMINICAN REPUBLIC PLANNER

Getting to the Dominican Republic

Every airline seems to be adding nonstops to one of the DR's five major airports; however, the best connections are usually to Santo Domingo (SDQ), Punta Cana (PUJ), and Puerto Plata (POP). Because of the number of all-inclusive resorts, many visitors still come in on charter flights from as far away as Germany and Italy, but also from Toronto and Cleveland. Plan your air travel carefully so you don't end up flying into Punta Cana when you are staying at Casa de Campo, a 2-hour-plus drive. Travel between the island's many developed tourism zones can be arduous and expensive.

Hassle Factor: Low for popular destinations, High for off-the-beaten-path places.

Activities

The biggest draw for tourists are powder-soft **beaches**, particularly in Punta Cana, but each of the resort areas has decent beaches. **Windsurfers** have found the breezes in Cabarete to be among the most favorable in the Caribbean. The D.R. also has several of the Caribbean's finest **golf courses**. **Adventure tours** are popular in the country's interior.

Nightlife is a highlight, particularly in Santo Domingo, where **historical sights** are also a major draw. However, with so many all-inclusive resorts, much of the activity is focused inward, and the majority of tourists never leave their resorts except to go on guided tours and excursions in the immediate vicinity of their hotel.

On the Ground

If you book a package trip, your airport transfers may be included in the price of your package, and a representative from your tour company should be waiting for you after baggage claim; otherwise, you can hire a taxi at the airport. Taxi prices are fairly consistent. Expect to pay $30 to $35 to get from Las Américas Airport to Santo Domingo, $20 to Boca Chica or Juan Dolio. The fare from Puerto Plata airport is about $20 to Playa Dorada and a bit more to Cabarete and a bit less to Sosúa. From Punta Cana airport, you'll pay $20 to $50 if you take a taxi to your resort, depending on distance.

Renting a Car

If you're staying at an all-inclusive resort, you will probably not need a car. If you're traveling around the D.R., a car can be handy. Both international and local companies rent cars in the D.R. Rates are quite expensive, averaging $75 and more per day for a basic ride. For lower rates you'll usually have to rent a car for a full week. The local outfits give substantially better rates than the majors; however, you may feel more confident in going with one of the name brands—there's more recourse, for example, in case of an accident. Booking online from home can give you better prices.

To rent a car here, you must have a valid driver's license from your own country, be more than 25 years old, and have a major credit card (or cash deposit). Your card will be used to secure a deposit of some $200. This should be torn up on safe return of the vehicle. Make certain that it is. If you do not receive insurance from your credit card (or if it is not included), you'll need to buy insurance, which is expensive.

Where to Stay

A hotel in **Santo Domingo** allows you to enjoy the capital's great restaurants, nightlife, and historical sights, but most travelers visit the busy, overwhelming city as a day-trip. **Boca Chica** and **Juan Dolio** offer some of the island's cheapest—but most mediocre—all-inclusives, along with crowded beaches. **La Romana** has Casa de Campo as well as a few resorts on other, better beaches; the region is within reasonable striking distance of Santo Domingo for those needing a taste of history to go with their platanos. The isolated, though beautiful, **Barahona** region offers a respite from development and overcrowding but is a four-hour drive from Santo Domingo. **Punta Cana** reigns supreme for its many reasonably priced all-inclusives, but it's better for those looking for a resort-based vacation than for the adventurous. **Samaná** is isolated, but its quiet beaches are attractive to those who can stomach the three-hour drive from Puerto Plata. **Playa Dorada**, the DR's original resort area, is still a land of decent all-inclusives and golf courses, but more independent-minded travelers (and all windsurfers) may prefer **Sosúa** and **Cabarete**, where you'll still find a few charming independent inns and small resorts.

Hotel & Restaurant Costs

Assume that hotels operate on the European Plan (**EP**—with no meals) unless we specify that they use either the Continental Plan (**CP**—with a Continental breakfast), Breakfast Plan (**BP**—with full breakfast), or the Modified American Plan (**MAP**—with breakfast and dinner). Other hotels may offer the Full American Plan (**FAP**—including all meals but no drinks) or may be All-Inclusive (**AI**—with all meals, drinks, and most activities).

WHAT IT COSTS in Dollars					
	$$$$	**$$$**	**$$**	**$**	**¢**
Restaurants	over $30	$20–$30	$12–$20	$8–$12	under $8
Hotels*	over $350	$250–$350	$150–$250	$80–$150	under $80
Hotels**	over $450	$350–$450	$250–$350	$125–$250	under $125

*EP, BP, CP **AI, FAP, MAP
Restaurant prices are for a main course at dinner and do not include 16% tax or cusomary 10% service charge. Hotel prices are per night for a double room in high season, excluding 16% tax, customary 10% service charge, and meal plans (except at all-inclusives).

When to Go

The D.R. is busy year-round. During the usually quiet summer season, Europeans flock to the lovely beaches, keeping rates high from mid-June through August. However, in late spring (after Easter until early June) and early fall (September to October) you can get good deals. Unlike many islands, where rain showers are usually a temporary passing thing, the rains in the D.R. can linger when they do come, especially from June through November.

The largest event in the country is the annual **Jazz Festival** in October, which draws enthusiasts from all over the world.

Carnival celebrations are held in Santiago and La Vega. The **Festival del Merengue** is held in Santo Domingo in late July and early August.

10

By Eileen
Robinson Smith

IT'S *TRANQUILLA* IN THE ZONA COLONIAL AT SIESTA TIME. Most Dominicans have never given up the habit of taking a siesta after their main midday meal, a vestige of their Spanish heritage. You hear the distinctive flutter of the pigeons' wings as they peck for crumbs among the dramatic ruins of the Bari Hospital. The little old tailor in his ancient shop closes the narrow doors from the inside. The coconut boys and the frying empanada men; the barbers in their gossipy, 1950s-vintage shops; the old women sitting on their white balconies adorned with fuchsia bougainvillea: they'll all be awake soon, but for now you can't help but love the stillness.

The vibrant lifestyle of this sun-drenched, Latin-Caribbean country, where Spanish is the national language and where the people are hospitable and good-natured, makes the Dominican Republic a different cultural experience. If you pick up the rhythm of life here, as freewheeling as the island's trademark merengue, this can be a beguiling tourist destination. And it's still one of the least expensive of the Caribbean islands.

Christopher Columbus first claimed the island for Spain on his first New World voyage in 1492 and wrecked his flagship, the *Santa Maria,* on its Atlantic shore on Christmas Eve; later, his brother Bartolomeo founded Santo Domingo de Guzman (1496), the first city in the New World. With some 300 examples of Spanish-colonial architecture, the Zona Colonial was declared a World Heritage Site by UNESCO in 1990. A throbbing microcosm, there are 100 square blocks of history, very much alive more than five centuries later. Its trendy restaurants, art galleries, boutique hotels, and late-night clubs help make Santo Domingo a superb urban vacation destination.

Dominicans will extend a gracious welcome, saying, "This is your home!" and indeed are happy to share what they have, which is a physically beautiful island bathed by the Atlantic Ocean to the north and the Caribbean Sea to the south. Among its most precious assets are 1,500 km (1,000 mi) of gorgeous beaches studded with coconut palms and sands ranging from pearl white to golden brown to volcanic black.

The Caribbean sun kisses this exotic land (warm temperatures average 82°F year-round), which occupies two-thirds, or 76,192 square mi (48,442 square km), of the island of Hispañola, sharing the remainder with the Republic of Haiti. Cuba is due west, and to the east is Puerto Rico. It's a fertile country blessed with resources, particularly cocoa, coffee, rum, tobacco, and sugarcane.

A land of contrasts, the island has alpine landscapes, brown rivers with white-water rapids, rain forests full of wild orchids, and fences of multicolor bougainvillea. Indigenous species from crocodiles to the green cockatoo, symbol of the island, live in these habitats. Bird-watchers, take note: there are 29 endemic species flying around here.

The contrasts don't stop with nature. You can see signs of wealth, for the upper strata of society lives well indeed. In the capital, the movers and shakers ride in chauffeur-driven silver Mercedes. On the country roads you'll be amazed that four people with sacks of groceries and a stalk of bananas can fit on a smoky old *motoconcho* (motor bike/taxi). Similarly, Dominicans can be fair-skinned with light eyes, or black, but mostly they are shades of brown. This is a land of *mestizos,* who are a centuries-old mix of native Indians, Spanish colonists, and African slaves, plus every other nationality that has settled here, from Italian to Arabic.

Accommodations now offer a remarkable range—surfers' camps, exclusive boutique hotels, and amazing megaresorts that have brought the all-inclusive hotel to the next level of luxury.

Most Dominican towns and cities are neither quaint nor particularly pretty; poverty still prevails. However, the standard of life has really come up along with the growth of North American tourism. With the weakness of the dollar, it's not the cheap date it has been; prices remain competitive, but a vacation in the D.R. can still be a relative bargain.

Islanders have an affinity for all things American: the people, language (more and more speak English), electronic products, fashions, and lifestyle. A great Dominican dream is to go to the States as a shortstop or pitcher and become the next Sammy Sosa, then return to be a philanthropist in one's own hometown.

Where to Stay

The Dominican Republic has the largest hotel inventory (at this writing some 67,000 rooms, with more than 15,000 under construction) in the Caribbean and draws large numbers of stateside visitors. That is a far cry from the mid-1990s, when most Americans thought it was a country in Latin America if they thought about it at all. Surfers can still find digs for $20 a night in Cabarete, while the new generation of luxurious all-inclusives in Playa de Uvero Alto, the new frontier of Punta Cana, is simply awesome.

Santo Domingo properties generally base their tariffs on the EP plan—though many now include breakfast—and maintain the same room rates year-round. Beach resorts have high winter rates, with prices reduced for the shoulder seasons of late spring and early fall but not as much now in summer, as that has become another strong season. All-inclusives dominate in Punta Cana. Cabarete was a stronghold of the small inn, but each year it's getting more all-inclusives. Villa rentals are gaining in popularity all over the island, with the new Guavaberry complex in Juan Dolio among the most popular and upscale offerings.

Santo Domingo

The seaside capital of the country is in the middle of the island's south coast. In Santo Domingo, most of the better hotels are on or near the Malecón, with several small, desirable properties in the trendy Colonial Zone, allowing you to feel part of that magical environment. The capital is where you will find some of the most sophisticated hotels and restaurants, not to mention nightlife. However, such an urban vacation is best coupled with a beach stay elsewhere on the island.

★ **$$$–$$$$** ⊡ **Sofitel Nicolas Ovando.** This luxury hotel, sculpted from the residence of the first Governor of the Americas, is the best thing to happen in the Zone since Diego Columbus's palace was finished in 1517. Colonial rooms have canopied king-size beds, tall ceilings, original stone window benches, and shutters. Some prefer the sunny (smaller) rooms in the contemporary annex; with the river views, these are smart examples of French minimalist style. The pool is shaded by trees and tropical plantings, and swimmers leave the sun for a fitness break in the gym. The bar is a social scene, particularly when the music men harmonize. The breakfast spread is lavish. ⊠ *Calle Las Damas, Zona Colonial* ☎ *809/685–9955 or 800/763–4835* 🖷 *809/685–9302* ⊕ *www.sofitel.com* ⤺ *100 rooms, 4 suites* ⌂ *Restaurant, room service, minibars, in-room safes, cable TV, pool, gym, 2 bars, shops, dry cleaning, laundry service, concierge, Internet room, business services, meeting rooms, parking (free), some pets allowed* ⊟ *AE, MC, V* ❏⊙❏ *BP.*

★ **$$–$$$** ⊡ **Sofitel Frances Santo Domingo.** Discerning business travelers, American vacationers, celebs, and other luminaries (including Oscar de la Renta) opt for the intimate, refined luxury of this small, well-run hotel. French and Dominican flags fly over the arched coral-stone entrance to this city landmark, a former French residence. Hacienda-like rooms with tall beamed ceilings, dark and soundproof (ask for second-floor corner rooms), overlook the courtyard, an urban refuge with cast-iron balustrades and hanging ferns. At night, the keyboard man plays many American faves. Service throughout is exceptional, with English spoken. A romantic hideaway, it's probably not the best place for children. Ask about various monthly soirees, art exhibits, cocktail parties, and theme nights. ⊠ *Calles Las Mercedes and Arzobispo Meriño, Zona Colonial* ☎ *809/685–9331 or 800/763–4835* 🖷 *809/685–1289* ⊕ *www.sofitel.com* ⤺ *19 rooms* ⌂ *Restaurant, room service, in-room safes, minibars, cable TV, massage, bar, meeting room* ⊟ *AE, MC, V* ❏⊙❏ *BP.*

$$ ⊡ **Renaissance Jaragua Hotel & Casino.** The sprawling, pink oasis is perennially popular, particularly with Americans, for its beautiful grounds and huge, free-form pool. Fountains splash and hot tubs gurgle. Saunas bake in what is the capital's largest fitness club—although not the best. Everything is bigger than life, from the rooms, where executive-size desks face the satellite TV, to the gigantic suites in the renovated main building to the generous lobby and huge, lively casino where bands heat up the action. Comfy European linens and duvets make sleeping a dream vision. Management and staff are professional and caring. Ask about the Pure Magic weekend package. ⊠ *Av. George Washington 367, El Malecón* ☎ *809/221–2222* 🖷 *809/686–0528* ⊕ *www.marriott.com* ⤺ *292 rooms, 8 suites* ⌂ *3 restaurants, in-room safes, some kitchens, minibars, cable TV, some in-room data ports, golf privileges, 4 tennis courts, pool, hot tub, gym, sauna, spa, 5 bars, casino, dance club, concierge, concierge floor, Internet room, business services* ⊟ *AE, D, MC, V* ❏⊙❏ *EP.*

$–$$ ⊡ **The Hilton Santo Domingo.** After years in the making, the brand-new Hilton premiered in the summer of 2005 and has become *the* address on the Malecón for businesspeople, convention attendees, and leisure travelers. The five luxurious executive floors are wired for business, each with three phones, Internet ports, and actual corner offices with imposing desks and ergonomic leather chairs. Creature comforts are satisfied with the plush duvets, rain showers, and surround sound in the bathrooms, oversize flat-screen TVs, and sea views. Service is right on the money, and rates surprisingly moderate, particularly with packages that include a lavish and healthy buffet breakfast. ✉ *Av. George Washington 500, Zona Colonial* ☎ *809/685–0000* 🖨 *809/685–0202* ⊕ *www. hiltoncaribbean.com* ⤶ *228 rooms, 32 suites* ⚒ *2 restaurants, in-room safes, minibars, cable TV, in-room data ports, golf privileges, pool, gym, spa, 3 bars, casino, concierge, concierge floor, Internet room, business services, conference center* ☰ *AE, D, MC, V* ▯⚬▯ *EP.*

$ 🏨 **Hodelpa Caribe Colonial.** When you leave this little Hernando's Hideaway, the caring staff will say, "Why so soon?" The art deco–style lobby makes clever use of blue objets d'art, as does the high-tech Internet center. Rooms have white-gauze canopies on king-size beds; an all-white honeymoon suite has a Jacuzzi. Splurge for a suite or a superior room (even those have tight bathrooms), rather than a subterranean standard. Sit out on your balcony and wave to the neighbors. On Friday nights a Mexican fiesta takes place on the side terrace, with dancers and tequila action. ✉ *Isabel La Católica 59, Zona Colonial* ☎ *809/683–1000 or 888/403–2603* 🖨 *809/683–2303* ⊕ *www.hodelpa.com* ⤶ *52 rooms, 2 suites* ⚒ *Restaurant, room service, in-room safes, minibars, cable TV, bar, laundry service, concierge, Internet room, free parking* ☰ *AE, MC, V* ▯⚬▯ *BP.*

$ 🏨 **InterContinental V Centenario.** For some years, this major Malecón property was not living up to the InterContinental image, and although it is still not one of the group's glamour resorts, it is now doing everything right. All rooms—not just the luxe ones on the Club Level with sea-view balconies—have been redone in subtle earth tones, more masculine than tropical cheery. It's international cuisine from the memorable breakfasts to meeting breaks and gastronomic dinners. Service is professional, and conferences run smoothly. Leisure time came be spent on the swanky pool deck, where discerning attendants dispense frosty drinks and plush, pastel towels, or at the classy casino. ✉ *Av. George Washington 218, Zona Colonial* ☎ *809/221–1578* 🖨 *809/221–2020* ⊕ *www. ichotelsgroup.com* ⤶ *165 rooms, 31 suites* ⚒ *2 restaurants, in-room safes, minibars, cable TV, some in-room data ports, golf privileges, tennis court, pool, hot tub, gym, spa, 2 bars, casino, concierge, concierge floor, Internet room, business services, conference center* ☰ *AE, MC, V* ▯⚬▯ *EP.*

Boca Chica–Juan Dolio

The Boca Chica–Juan Dolio resort area is immediately east of Las Americas International Airport. Boca Chica, a seasoned destination, is popular mainly with Dominicans and Europeans. Juan Dolio, a bit farther east from the capital, has a string of mid-rise hotels fronting its golden beach, although a few more Americans—often first-timers to the D.R.—visit here. A new condo and villa development called Guavaberry Golf & Country Club promises an upscale residential atmosphere with resort amenities to golfers in the Juan Dolio area; an expansion, which was expected at this writing to open in 2006, may eventually become an alternative to Casa de Campo.

10

$ ☒ **Barceló Capella Beach Resort.** Although this resort continues to get a mixed report card for both food and service, it is still the best on Juan Dolio Beach. The grounds are estatelike. Yellow stucco buildings have white fretwork and Moorish arches. Ask for one of the quieter sections (in the 1000s), which have a civilized British-colonial air, or for a newer (though smaller and not as quiet) room in the 4000s, smack on the beach. All are priced the same. The buffet has sea views and rotates 17 theme nights. The best à la carte option is the beach grill restaurant, adjacent to the tri-level palapa-top disco. ☒ *Juan Dolio* ☐ *Box 4750, Villas Del Mar, Santo Domingo* ☎ *809/526–1080* ☐ *809/526–1088* ⊕ *www.barcelo-hotels.com* ☞ *500 rooms, 8 junior suites, 1 suite* ☖ *5 restaurants, minibars, cable TV, 2 tennis courts, 2 pools, health club, massage, sauna, beach, dive shop, snorkeling, windsurfing, boating, 3 bars, dance club, miniature golf, recreation room, theater, shops, children's programs (ages 4–12), concierge, concierge floor, meeting rooms* ⊟ *AE, MC, V* ⧦ *AI.*

La Romana

La Romana is on the southeast coast, about a two-hour drive from Santo Domingo and the same distance southwest of Punta Cana. An international airport here has nonstop service to both the United States and Canada. Casa de Campo's Marina Chavón, with its Mediterranean design and impressive yacht club and villa complex, is as fine a marina facility as can be found anywhere. The shops and restaurants are a big draw for all tourists to the area, as is Altos de Chavón, the re-created 16th-century Mediterranean town on the grounds of Casa de Campo. In nearby Bayahibe Bay, which has an idyllic beach, the resorts have always been popular with *capitaleños* and Europeans. As it has become difficult to get a room in Punta Cana, North Americans are checking in here and really leaving satisfied. They don't miss the high density of Punta Cana. The actual town of La Romana is not pretty nor quaint, but it is a real slice of Dominican life.

★ ☾ **$$$$** ☒ **Casa de Campo.** At the country's most illustrious resort, golfers vie for tee-times at the three famed P. B. Dye–designed courses, while their offspring have a grand time. Family reunions in luxury villas are popular. The offerings are constantly evolving and at this writing included hot-rock massages and Tae Bo classes at the beach. Rooms are called casitas and are in two-story, nondescript blocks, but inside they are commodious, with down pillows, walk-in closets, and balconies overlooking the gardens. A drawback is Minetas Beach, which is relatively unremarkable, not to mention a long ride from most rooms. Each room comes with a four-person golf cart, and guests can rent electric bikes; there's an efficient shuttle. Booking a room on the EP plan is possible, but few do because the all-inclusive plan is a better value. ☐ *Box 140, La Romana* ☎ *809/523–3333 or 305/856–7083* ☐ *809/523–8548* ⊕ *www.casadecampo.com.do* ☞ *350 rooms, 150 villas* ☖ *9 restaurants, in-room safes, some kitchens, minibars, cable TV, in-room data ports, 3 18-hole golf courses, 13 tennis courts, 16 pools, health club, sauna, dive shop, snorkeling, windsurfing, fishing, bicycles, horseback riding, 4 bars, theater, shops, children's programs (ages 1–18)* ⊟ *AE, MC, V* ⧦ *AI.*

★ **$$** ⊞ **Iberostar Hacienda Dominicus.** Iberostar's reputation for excellent cuisine has helped to cement its popularity with families and incentive groups; An excellent beach doesn't hurt, either. Elaborate metal chandeliers in the open-air lobby illuminate a fascinating collection of sculptures, from yacht replicas to life-size horses and bulls. Although not as wildly creative, rooms are oversize (no extra charge for an ocean view, so ask). The gazebo wedding chapel is within a lagoon, the habitat for hot-pink flamingos. Lucy's Club makes kids feel, well, cool. The PADI five-star center has an excellent site at nearby Saona Island. A bike tour of Bayahibe helps you experience the country. ⊠ *Playa Bayahibe, Bayahibe* ☎ *809/688–3600 or 888/923–2722* 🖷 *809/221–0921* ⊕ *www.iberostar. com* ⇶ *460 rooms, 38 junior suites* ♨ *4 restaurants, in-room safes, minibars, cable TV, 2 tennis courts, 3 pools, health club, spa, dive shop, snorkeling, boating, billiards, 7 bars, dance club, showroom, shops, children's programs (ages 4–12), Internet room, business services, 2 meeting rooms, car rental* 🖃 *AE, MC, V* ¹⊙¹ *AI.*

☾ **$** ⊞ **Sunscape Casa del Mar La Romana.** With its whimsical Victorian fretwork, this resort is on an exceptional, palm-fringed ribbon of white sand protected by a coral reef, which makes for easy snorkeling. Since Sunscape's takeover in 2004, combined with a major renovation of all restaurants, guest rooms (ask for those with dramatic views of the sea, the spectacular pool, or both), and an enlarged lobby, guests are satisfied. A Metamorphosis Spa soothes adults, and the Explorer Club, which orchestrates sandcastle-building competitions, weekly campouts, and mini-safaris, raises the family profile substantially. Outside entertainers bring a professionalism to theater performances. And you're 15 minutes to Casa de Campo and its golf. ⊠ *Bayahibe Bay, La Romana* ☎ *809/ 221–8880* 🖷 *809/221–8881* ⊕ *www.sunscaperesorts.com* ⇶ *568 rooms* ♨ *4 restaurants, in-room safes, minibars, 4 tennis courts, 2 pools, gym, hot tub, beach, dive shop, snorkeling, windsurfing, boating, bicycles, archery, horseback riding, volleyball, 4 bars, dance club, theater, children's programs (ages 4–12), meeting rooms* 🖃 *AE, MC, V* ¹⊙¹ *AI.*

Punta Cana

The easternmost coast of the island has 25 mi (40 km) of incredible beach punctuated by coco palms; add to that a host of all-inclusive resorts, an atmospheric thatched-roof airport, and many more direct flights than any other D.R. resort area, and it's easy to see why this region—despite having almost 24,000 hotel rooms (more than on most other Caribbean islands)—is almost always sold out. It has become the Cancun of the D.R., and although you can usually get a room during hurricane season, booking far in advance is advisable. Look for coed Metamorphosis spas, which offer a soothing atmosphere and a litany of both therapeutic and fun body treatments, at many resorts.

Playa de Uvero Alto, a miraculous virgin beach shaded by idyllic coconut groves and unobstructed views of the sea, is amazing. Unfortunately, it's nearly an hour from the Punta Cana airport on a road that, despite repairs, it still a tough go. But there are now four resorts there. Sivory Punta Cana, a boutique hotel with an all-inclusive option, was about to open at this writing. This area also books up fast because the

10

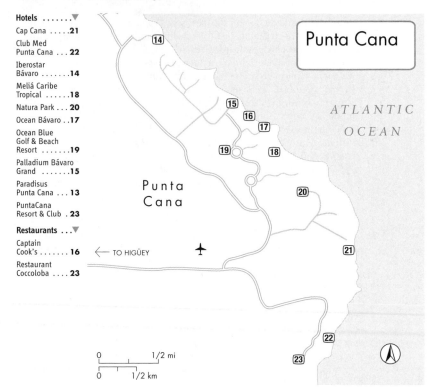

resorts tend to be less expensive and people don't seem to mind being away from the maddening crowds.

The **Cap Cana** (✉ Punta Cana ☎ 809/227–2262 or 800/785–2198 ⊕ www.capcana.com), a resort and villa complex about 15 minutes down the coast from the airport, was expected—at this writing—to open its first hotel by October 2006. Eventually, the complex will include three signature Jack Nicklaus golf courses, polo and horse-riding fields, and a yacht club. Already open is the exclusive Caletón Beach Club, with a high-tech architectural design and palapa roof, not to mention a spectacular pool. A Balinese-style restaurant is also open. The first phase of the marina, 500 slips, and one golf course were expected to open by May 2006. Some condos should be open by March 2006 and the Attabella Sanctuary Collection Hotel by October 2006.

🐚 **$$$$** ▥ **Meliá Caribe Tropical.** At this American-friendly resort, prices have escalated and are now higher than at some more luxurious new properties; guest complaints have also risen. Melia bought into the Flintstone theme for two mini-clubs to appeal more to families. Golf is not unlimited, although you can purchase a golf package. Golfers are pleased with the 27 holes that are at the adjacent Cocotal Golf Club, which has PGA award-winning teaching pros. The VIP Royal Service level costs even

CLOSE UP

Other D. R. Hotel Choices

THE DOMINICAN REPUBLIC IS awash in hotels. Those recommended in this chapter are our favorites, but the travel packages you see advertised in your local newspaper may include others, including the following places:

$$$ Iberostar Costa Dorada (✉ Playa Dorada ☎ 809/320–1000 or 888/923–2722 ⊕ www.iberostar.com) will dazzle you with its sprawling lobby with its hardwood benches and sculptures; the curvaceous pool with a central Jacuzzi is encircled by Roman pillars. Other all-inclusives could learn from its buffet.

$$ Barceló Bavaró Palace (✉ Playa Bavaro ☎ 809/686–5797 ⊕ www. barcelo.com), a minicity with more restaurants and shops than most towns, also has good tennis courts and golf courses, a lakefront church, Vegas-like shows, a shuttle train, and a contemporary convention center. In the same Punta Cana complex are four other hotels: Bavaro Golf, Beach, Garden, and Casino. Guest reviews are mixed here; some are vehement, but the complex is thriving.

Occidental El Embajador (✉ Av. Sarasota 65, Santo Domingo ☎ 809/221–2131, 800/858–2258 🖷 809/532–4494 ⊕ www.occidentalhotels.com) is a landmark in a quiet, upscale,

residential neighborhood, near to the Malecón. Continuing renovations keep it perenially popular. El Jardin, the laudable gourmet restaurant, has both indoor seating and tables set amid the tropical gardens.

$–$$ The Hodelpa Gran Almirante Hotel & Casino (✉ Av. Estrella Sadhal, Santiago ☎ 809/580–1992 ⊕ www.hodelpa.com), which now has a pool and sundeck, offers executive rooms and is the city's best hotel.

$ Barceló Gran Hotel Lina Spa & Casino (✉ Av. Máximo Gómez at 27 de Febrero, Santo Domingo ☎ 809/563–5000 ⊕ www.barcelo.com), a steadfast city landmark for decades, underwent a major renovation in 2004, so it's looking refreshed. The professional management and staff have earned the repeat business and a strong convention trade.

$ Catalonia Beach, Golf & Tennis Resort (✉ Cabeza de Toros, Playa Bavaro ☎ 809/412–0000 ⊕ www. cataloniabavaro.com), whose grounds are punctuated with fountain- and sculpture-filled gardens, lagoons, and a white-sand beach, feels virtually alone in its location; it has some age but is a well-oiled operation. Guests feel it is a good value for money.

10

more, but with high occupancy levels, the higher level of service at this sprawling resort is worth the extra price. The spa, with its Grecian columns and whirlpool surrounded by classical sculptures, is by Metamorphosis. ✉ *Punta Cana* ☎ *809/221–1290 or 800/336–3542* 🖷 *809/221–4595* ⊕ *www.solmelia.es* 📞 *1,044 junior suites* 🛏 *15 restaurants, room service, fans, in-room safes, minibars, cable TV, 27-hole golf course, 8 tennis courts, 2 pools, health club, spa, beach, snorkeling, windsurfing, boating, 6 bars, casino, dance club, showroom, children's programs (ages 4–11), Internet room, business services, convention center, meeting rooms* 🖶 *AE, DC, MC, V* 🍽 *AI.*

$$$$ ⊞ **Paradisus Punta Cana.** A kind of tropical paradise, with all the joys and toys, not to mention flamingos and herons roaming the lagoons and parklike grounds, Paradisus is struggling to keep up with the newer competition. The bi-level suites and the lagoonlike pool complex were renovated in 2003. Guests have some issues because they expect a lot for these prices. Unlimited golf, diving, horseback riding, and a climbing wall help to satisfy, as do couples' beach massages. Royal Service offers a VIP Lounge, concierge, and butler service. Americans compose 20% to 40% of the guest mix; listen for "God Bless America" at 5 PM sharp. ⊠ *Playa Bávaro* ☎ *809/687–9923 or 800/336–3542* 🖷 *809/687–0752* ⊕ *www.paradisuspuntacana.solmelia.com* ⇨ *527 suites* ♻ *11 restaurants, room service, in-room safes, minibars, cable TV, golf privileges, 4 tennis courts, pool, health club, spa, beach, dive shop, snorkeling, windsurfing, boating, bicycles, archery, 4 bars, casino, children's programs (ages 4–12)* ⊟ *AE, D, DC, MC, V* ⦿| *AI.*

♻ **$$$** ⊞ **Iberostar Bávaro Resort.** Like its sister resorts, this Spanish Doña has an elegance, evidenced in its lobby, an artistic showpiece. It's one of the most desirable Punta Cana properties. The dramatic public spaces segue into grounds criss-crossed with lagoons that lead to a broad, beautifully maintained white-sand beach. This complex actually consists of three resorts (there's also the Punta Cana and Dominicana). Although rooms don't compare with the public spaces, the Bávaro's are the sweetest, with a separate sitting area; rooms in the other two are similar but lack the living area. True to Iberostar's emphasis on quality food and beverages, there are now 11 restaurants. ⊠ *Playa Bávaro* ☎ *809/221–6500 or 888/923–2722* 🖷 *809/688–6186* ⊕ *www.iberostar.com* ⇨ *590 rooms, 8 apartments* ♻ *11 restaurants, ice cream parlor, snack bar, fans, in-room safes, minibars, cable TV, 3 tennis courts, pool, health club, hair salon, outdoor hot tub, spa, beach, dive shop, snorkeling, windsurfing, boating, volleyball, 3 bars, lounge, casino, dance club, showroom, video game room, shops, children's programs (ages 4–12), dry cleaning, laundry service, concierge, Internet room, business services, meeting rooms* ⊟ *AE, D, MC, V* ⦿| *AI.*

$$$ ⊞ **Ocean Bávaro Spa & Beach Resort.** A lot new is poppin' here, including a Japanese restaurant, a conference room, a glitzy casino, and soon a coffee house. A renovation was in order here and has begun with Building 7. A more active, international clientele are kept busy with yoga and tai-chi classes on the beach, as well as superior water sports. Marine-blue hammocks lull sportsters into siestas, but they come alive again at the bars. The three-pool complex—and even the gym—faces the sea and the white sands. The Metamorphosis Spa, with Vichy showers and soothing new-age music, is a great escape from the animation boys. ⊠ *Playa Bávaro* ☎ *809/221–0714* 🖷 *809/683–2303* ⊕ *www.oceanhotels. net* ⇨ *735 rooms, 14 suites* ♻ *7 restaurants, 2 snack bars, room service, in-room safes, some minibars, cable TV, 2 tennis courts, 3 pools, fitness classes, gym, 2 hair salons, 2 outdoor hot tubs, spa, beach, dive shop, dock, snorkeling, windsurfing, boating, fishing, billiards, Ping-Pong, volleyball, 3 bars, piano bar, sports bar, casino, dance club, shops, children's programs (ages 4–12), laundry service, concierge, Internet room, car rental* ⊟ *AE, MC, V* ⦿| *AI.*

$$$ 🏨 **Ocean Blue Golf & Beach Resort.** When this new-wave megaresort opened in 2005, it exceeded expectations. (Now the service has finally to catch up with the facilities.) You pay more to be near the pristine beach; otherwise, it's a hike. Suite options are many and worth the extra cost, offering marble bathrooms and Jacuzzi tubs. The main buffet, with handsome murals, is operated more like a food court and is exceptional; house wines are served from bottles. This is one resort that has an authentic Dominican restaurant and a cool, California-retro diner, called Route 66. Just a swing away from the White Sands Golf Course, it even has a modern bowling alley. ✉ *Arena Gorda, Bavaro, Punta Cana* 🕿 *809/476–2326* 🖷 *809/221–0814* ⊕ *www.oceanhotels.net* ⤴ *708 suites* ♿ *9 restaurants, in-room safe, in-room hot tub, cable TV, golf privileges, 2 pools, hair salon, 2 outdoor hot tubs, massage, sauna, beach, dive shop, snorkeling, windsurfing, boating, bicycles, billiards, bowling, 10 bars, nightclub, theater, shops, children's programs (ages 4–12), Internet room, car rental* ▭ *AE, MC, V* ⧠ *AI.*

★ **$$$** 🏨 **Secrets Excellence.** The only all-inclusive member of Preferred Hotels, this adults-only resort has that extra measure of romance and sensuality that makes it perfect for lovers. All the spacious suites have double Jacuzzis, separate showers, and coffeemakers. Excellence Club rooms have such extra perks as CD/DVD players and a concierge service; in swim-out suites the patio has immediate access to the pool. Either one is worth the extra money. A great spa and wellness center, fun casino, and premium-brand drinks are other upscale perks all guests enjoy. Topless bathing is allowed on the seemingly endless stretch of virgin beach. A black stretch limo can make the 50-minute drive from the airport almost pleasurable, albeit for a price; the isolation and distance from the airport are the only drawback here. ✉ *Playa de Uvero Alto* 🕿 *809/685–9880* 🖷 *809/688–1075* ⊕ *www.secretsresorts.com* ⤴ *446 rooms, 112 suites* ♿ *8 restaurants, 2 snack bars, room service, in-room safes, in-room hot tubs, minibars, cable TV, some in-room DVDs, in-room data ports, golf privileges, 3 tennis courts, 2 pools, gym, hair salon, spa, beach, snorkeling, windsurfing, boating, bicycles, archery, billiards, boccie, horseback riding, volleyball, 9 bars, casino, dance club, complimentary weddings, dry cleaning, laundry service, concierge, Internet room, convention center, car rental, travel services; no kids* ▭ *AE, MC, V* ⧠ *AI.*

★ **$$$** 🏨 **Sunscape The Beach.** This stellar addition to the distant Playa Uvero Alto frontier packs in the "wow" factor, raising the all-inclusive bar to a new level of luxury. Yet its prices are the same as at shabbier, decade-old resorts. Families are catered to here with good kids' programs, as are conference groups with extensive meeting facilities, and even honeymooners with the private outdoor Jacuzzi suites. Rooms have high-quality, light-hued furnishings, ceiling fans, and four-poster canopy beds. The Asian-inspired spa and fitness center is one of the best in the country. A river of pools with waterfalls meanders effortlessly to a white-sand beach from your oceanfront swim-out room. Is this paradise? The only negative: the Punta Cana airport and shopping plazas are at least an hour away. ✉ *Playa de Uvero Alto* 🕿 *809/682–0404* 🖷 *809/552–6183* ⊕ *www.sunscaperesorts.com* ⤴ *620 rooms, 102 suites* ♿ *7 restaurants, room service, in-room safes, some in-room hot*

10

tubs, minibars, cable TV, golf privileges, 2 tennis courts, 2 pools, health club, hair salon, spa, beach, dive shop, snorkeling, windsurfing, boating, bicycles, 7 bars, casino, nightclub, piano, theater, shops, children's programs (ages 4–17), concierge, Internet room, business services, convention center, car rental, travel services $=$ *AE, MC, V* ⬦ *AI.*

★ ☺ **$$** ⊡ **Club Med Punta Cana.** A lively bonhomie continues to make this family resort one of the best of Club Med's Caribbean offerings. It now has a festive, new paint job; interiors of the two-room suites are all clean and fresh. There's also a fabulous new inline skating complex and, underneath its palapa roof, a new teen center. The circus area, with a flying trapeze, is now well defined, and the Mini-Club offerings have never been better. The buffet exhibits marvelous creativity. A mix of international couples, singles, and families are all kept busy by the fun staffers, who do their best to bring everyone together. ⊠ *Punta Cana* ☎ *809/ 686–5500 or 800/258–2633* 🖷 *809/959–5287* ⊕ *www.clubmed.com* ⬦ *519 suites* ⬧ *2 restaurants, snack bar, in-room safes, minibars, cable TV, 3 pools, fitness classes, massage, beach, windsurfing, boating, waterskiing, archery, volleyball, 2 bars, nightclub, children's programs (ages 2–12), laundry service, Internet room* $=$ *AE, MC, V* ⬦ *AI.*

☺ **$$** ⊡ **PuntaCana Resort & Club.** Since its creation in 1970, this charismatic resort has never looked better, the food has never tasted so good, and the service has never been so slick. (If you saw service weaknesses on a previous visit, you can come back safely now.) A major renovation in 2005 has resulted in substantial all-around improvements. Specialty restaurants have been redecorated and are looking chic. La Choza, the beach restaurant, has been upgraded and can now host weddings; the new lookout tower is where you might spot winter whales. A Six Senses Spa housed in the gorgeous beach-golf club is open. The new Tortuga Bay Hotel, which includes 15 luxurious one- to four-bedroom villas, offers privacy, butler service, a separate check-in, and its own exclusive restaurant. ⊠ *Playa Punta Cana* ☎ *809/959–2262 or 888/442–2262* 🖷 *809/959– 3951* ⊕ *www.puntacana.com* ⬦ *175 rooms, 16 junior suites, 11 suites, 98 villas* ⬧ *9 restaurants, in-room safes, minibars, cable TV, Wi-Fi, 18-hole golf course, 6 tennis courts, 4 pools, 2 health clubs, spa, hair salon, beach, dive shop, snorkeling, windsurfing, boating, marina, fishing, horseback riding, 7 bars, dance club, theater, children's programs (ages 5–12), playground, laundry service, Internet room, business services, meeting rooms* $=$ *AE, MC, V* ⬦ *MAP.*

Fodor's Choice
★

☺ **$$** ⊡ **Sirenis Tropical Suites.** This young beauty, a siren of the Playa de Uvero Alto frontier, now allows children in both the Tropical Suites and Cocotel sections. Rooms are spacious but nothing special and have a generic look. The beach, however, is a gorgeous stretch of virgin sand. The Galaxy Club takes the little ones; the Rap Club is for the 7- to 12-year-olds. Couples gravitate to the spa, which has a 30-person whirlpool. You can also gamble in the casino or dance the night away; however, party animals have to pay for drinks in the disco. Remember that the airport is more than an hour away by a bumpy road. ⊠ *Playa de Uvero Alto* ☎ *809/688–6490* 🖷 *809/688–7999* ⊕ *www.sirenishotels.com* ⬦ *436 rooms, 364 junior suites, 16 suites* ⬧ *9 restaurants, 2 snack bars, minibars, 4 tennis courts, 4 pools, gym, hot tub, steam room, beach,*

*dive shop, snorkeling, windsurfing, boating, archery, Ping-Pong, volley-
ball, 3 bars, casino, theater, shops, children's programs (ages 4–12), Internet room, meeting room ⊟ AE, MC, V ⦿ AI.*

$–$$ ⛊ **Natura Park Eco-Resort & Spa.** You can feel good about being here as
you dine on meals made from wholesome, all-natural ingredients. Carved
from a former coconut plantation in 1997, the resort retains a mangrove
forest and a natural lake. The eco-sensitive architecture incorporated
the cut cane, coco palms, local wood, and unearthed stones into the furniture, walkways, and footbridges. Set amid tropical gardens, buildings
occupy only 10% of the property. Rooms have been repainted and
given new bedspreads, all in natural earth tones. Give your body a
treat, and take yourself off to the Health Center & Beauty Farm.
⊠ *Playa Bávaro* ☎ *809/221–2626* 📠 *809/221–6060* ⊕ *www.blau-
hotels.com* 🛏 *490 rooms, 20 suites ♨ 3 restaurants, in-room safes, minibars, 3 tennis courts, pool, outdoor hot tub, spa, beach, windsurfing,
boating, 6 bars, dance club, theater, children's programs (ages 4–11)*
⊟ *AE, DC, MC, V* ⦿ *AI.*

🌀 **$** ⛊ **Palladium Bávaro Grand Resort & Spa.** This is the standout in a smooth-
running triumvirate of resorts, which includes the Fiesta Palace and the
sportier Fiesta Beach. Though on a nice stretch of white sand surrounded
by a palm grove, few rooms have sea views; however, the Palladium's
deluxe rooms and junior suites have arches and pillars, marbleized coral
stone, and hydro-massage tubs. The lobby shines, and there is a central
sports complex as well as an entertainment complex with an indoor, 1,400-
seat theater. One of the most family-friendly resorts in Punta Cana, it
has exclusive family suites for up to eight persons. ⊠ *Playa Bávaro*
☎ *809/221–8149* 📠 *809/221–8150* ⊕ *www.fiesta-hotels.com* 🛏 *979
rooms, 384 suites ♨ 4 restaurants, in-room safes, minibars, cable TV, 2
tennis courts, 4 pools, gym, hair salon, 4 outdoor hot tubs, spa, beach,
dive shop, snorkeling, windsurfing, archery, badminton, 6 bars, dance
club, theater, shops, babysitting, children's programs (ages 3–12), playground, Internet room, car rental* ⊟ *AE, MC, V* ⦿ *AI.*

Samaná

Samaná is the name of both the peninsula that curves around the eponymous bay and of the largest town. Las Terrenas is at least a 2½-hour
drive from Cabarete. The nearest major international airport is Puerto
Plata International Gregorio Luperon, more than a three-hour drive away,
but a small domestic airline, Takeoff Destinations, now flies here from
Santo Domingo, as does AERODOMCA (see ⇨ *By Air under* Transportation *in* Dominican Republic Essentials).

$$$ ⛊ **Serenity House.** Serenity House is the new name for Villa Serenas, a
small, romantic hideaway on the coast of Las Galeras, in Samaná. Hap-
pily, new owner Starz Resorts—which also owns Victorian House in
Sosua—is keeping the intimate and tranquil atmosphere for which it has
been loved by lovers. At this writing, the lobby was being redecorated
in a Carib-Indonesian style, and a gazebo bar overlooking the sea was
being added. The restaurant, seemingly made for honeymooners, serves
fusion cuisine, with a menu for half-boarders and a supplemental gour-
met menu. Quoted rates include breakfast, but you should buy the

10

MAP, since the inn is secluded. ⊠ *Las Galleras, Samaná* ☎ *809/538–0000* 🖷 *809/538–0009* ⊕ *www.starzresorts.com* ⥲ *21 rooms* ♨ *Restaurant, pool, beach, bar; no a/c, no room TVs* ☰ *MC, V* ⦿ *BP.*

$–$$ 🖾 **Viva Wyndham Samaná.** When Viva took over the former Guatapanal Hotel in 2004, it underwent a dramatic expansion of facilities, with a new lobby bar, two new specialty restaurants (Asian and Mediterranean), a beach bar, kids' club, and a disco. Along the way came a dramatic rise in rates. Some former guests miss the simple yellow-and-white resort, but what is the same are the manicured gardens and the astounding beach, El Cosón. Accommodations are far more commodious, with new mattresses, yellow-and-blue bedspreads, and curtains. Americans gravitate toward the ocean-view superior rooms and the cabanas smack on the beach. ⊠ *Bahía de Cosón, Las Terrenas* ☎ *809/240–5050* 🖷 *809/240–5536* ⊕ *www.vivaresorts.com* ⥲ *144 rooms, 12 family rooms, 62 suites* ♨ *5 restaurants, in-room safes, cable TV, some kitchenettes, pool, gym, beach, dive shop, snorkeling, windsurfing, boating, 2 bars, dance club, shop, children's programs (ages 4–12), car rental* ☰ *AE, MC, V* ⦿ *AI.*

$ 🖾 **Hotel Bahía Las Ballenas.** What you get here is a charismatic taste of French bonhomie. Alas, Joel, the longtime manager, is no longer on board, so the fate of this place is still up in the air. Appealing especially to American Francophiles, the hotel has the kind of international sophistication you find in Bali. Individual bungalows with palapa roofs are spaced throughout the manicured tropical gardens; though few have real ocean views, several overlook the curvaceous pool. The artistic, open-air bathrooms have fascinating European tile work and decorative fixtures. Know that you'll find no air-conditioning or TVs and that new homes are planned for the space between the bungalows and the beachfront, which will block the sea views. ⊠ *Playa Bonita, Las Terrenas* ☎ *809/240–6066* 🖷 *809/240–6107* ⥲ *32 rooms* ♨ *Restaurant, pool, massage, beach, dive shop, bar, shop; no a/c, no room TVs* ☰ *AE, D, MC, V* ⦿ *CP.*

North Coast

The northern coast of the island, with mountains on one side, is also called the Amber Coast on account of the large quantities of amber found in the area. The sands on its 75 mi (121 km) of beach are also golden. Major resort areas are Playa Dorada, Cabarete, and Sosúa. Plan to fly into Puerto Plata International Gregorio Luperon Airport.

★ $$$$ 🖾 **Casa Colonial Beach & Spa.** Rivals say "over the top" isn't superlative enough to describe this exquisite, all-suite boutique hotel, the first in the D.R. to join the lofty Small Luxury Hotels of the World. White stucco buildings have columns and wrought-iron balustrades. Suites are outfitted with the finest Frette linens. The lobby feels more like a lounge, with a stellar bar; the designer gourmet restaurant specializes in fusion cuisine. Upscale spa devotees will savor the Baqua Spa, with its Vichy showers, body wraps, inventory of massages and facials, and refreshing juices. The rooftop sundeck is close to heaven—an infinity pool and four warm Jacuzzis provide several agreeable alternatives to the golden beach. ⊠ *Playa Dorada, Box 22, Puerto Plata* ☎ *809/320–3232* 🖷 *809/320–4017* ⊕ *www.vhhr.com* ⥲ *50 suites* ♨ *2 restaurants, minibars, cable TV, in-room data ports, golf privileges, pool, gym, 4 outdoor hot* *tubs, spa, beach, bar, piano bar, library, shops, babysitting, laundry service, concierge, meeting room* ⊟ *AE, MC, V* ⦿ *EP.*

$$$$ ▦ **Orchid Bay Estates.** A Caribbean dream, this small collection of fully staffed waterfront estates share an idyllic, mile-long beach, where aromatic almond trees bend low over pearlescent sand. Rugged cliffs frame this pretty postcard. Though originally thought of as remote (it's one hour from Cabarete), this area is now booming, with several restaurants within a five-minute walk and a shopping plaza open on the Cabrera road. Too expensive? Well, the largest Italian-style palazzo with its praiseworthy chef can sleep 16; when the rate is divided per person, it is quite affordable The experience is unforgettable, be it for a wedding, a conference, or a *Big Chill*–style reunion. ⊠ *Cabrera* ☎ *809/589–7773* 📠 *809/589–7447* ⊕ *www.orchidbay.com* ⇱ *7 villas* ⚄ *Kitchens, cable TV, tennis court, 7 pools, 2 gyms, beach, horseback riding* ⊟ *MC, V* ⦿ *EP.*

$$$$ ▦ **Sea Horse Ranch.** Celebrities and other bigwigs frequent this luxury residential resort, but with privacy paramount and security tight, you'll never get anyone to say whom you might see. The grandest villa, La Bandera (No. 124), has a private beach, six bedrooms, and a gourmet kitchen (with a staff of two) and a thatched-cana roof. The style is Hemingwayesque—shades of old Havana, lots of dark wood, rattan, and wide, palm-leaf fans. For couples only—though with four bedrooms—villa No. 2 is oceanfront on the cliffs. Various packages are available. Overlooking a cove, the beach club has an Italian-accented restaurant and offers deliveries to villas. This is called a thoroughbred community—and not just because of its international equestrian center. ⊠ *Cabarete* ☎ *809/571–3880 or 800/635–0991* 📠 *809/571–2374* ⊕ *www.sea-horse-ranch.com* ⇱ *75 villas* ⚄ *Restaurant, kitchens, cable TV, 5 tennis courts, beach, snorkeling, horseback riding, bar, babysitting* ⊟ *AE, MC, V* ⦿ *EP.*

$$$$ ▦ **Victorian House.** Roosted on a cliff above breathtaking Sosúa Bay, this

Fodor'sChoice boutique hotel is a delightful replica of a Victorian gingerbread house.
★ It's much more low-key and not as densely populated as its sister property, the Sosúa Bay Hotel, next door. (You can also pipe into its all-inclusive plan.) Check-in is at a white-pillared cottage, originally a settlement house for Jewish refugees in the 1940s. There, multilingual concierges pamper independent travelers; at 5 each afternoon you get luscious hors d'oeuvres and fresh mimosas. Now beds have dreamy new mattresses, European duvets, and six down pillows. Terraces have teak chaises and ever-changing knockout views. ⊠ *Calle Dr. Alejo Martinez 1, El Batey, Sosúa, Puerto Plata* ☎ *809/571–4000* 📠 *809/571–4545* ⊕ *www.starzresorts.com* ⇱ *32 rooms, 7 junior suites, 1 2-bedroom suite, 7 1-bedroom suites, 3 penthouses* ⚄ *5 restaurants, room service, in-room safes, some kitchenettes, refrigerators, cable TV, 2 pools, health club, beach, dive shop, snorkeling, windsurfing, boating, fishing, mountain bikes, 5 bars, dance club, children's programs (ages 4–12), laundry facilities, concierge, meeting room, car rental* ⊟ *MC, V* ⦿ *BP.*

$$ ▦ **Sosúa Bay Hotel.** Bellmen, who look snappy in their pith helmets, are stationed at the entrance of the handsome Carib-Indonesian lobby. The pools cascade into each other with awesome, panoramic views of Sosúa Bay; rooms in buildings 3 and 4 share those views. Although not the shining star it was initially, the hotel is still winning praise from Cana-

10

dian tour operators. The rotunda buffets are still better than the norm—particularly on Seafood Night—but now the specialty restaurants get the vote. Take the shuttle to Starz Azzurro Clubs to enjoy their primo beach, but first eat lunch here. At night, couples kiss under the gas lights to the sounds of "Besame mucho." ⊠ *Calle Dr. Alejo Martinez 1, El Batey, Sosúa, Puerto Plata* ☎ *809/571–4000* 🖷 *809/571–4545* ⊕ *www. starzresorts.com* ↙ *193 rooms* ♦ *5 restaurants, in-room safes, refrigerators, 2 pools, fitness classes, gym, hair salon, 2 hot tubs, beach, dive shop, snorkeling, windsurfing, boating, fishing, mountain bikes, 5 bars, cabaret, children's programs (ages 4–12), laundry facilities, Internet room, business services, meeting room* ☰ *MC, V* ▯◯▯ *AI.*

🕓 **$$** ▣ **Sun Village Resort & Spa.** Constructed like a sprawling Mediterranean hill town, this resort has moved up a notch in standing since its debut. It's no longer an isolated family resort catering to the adjacent Ocean World; now, it's a happening place for sophisticated couples and incentive groups. How? Quality restaurants, including Lemon Grass, an exotic Thai hideaway, and Teddy's Island BBQ, a fun, funky beach hangout created by Canadian celebrity chef Ted Reader, have reinvigorated the dining scene. Also added have been 205 luxury suites and an alluring spa with sea-view spa suites (most rooms, alas, have no view). ⊠ *Confresi Beach, Puerto Plata* ☎ *809/970–7538 or 888/446–4695* 🖷 *809/ 970–3156* ⊕ *www.sunvillageresorts.com* ↙ *289 rooms, 11 suites* ♦ *5 restaurants, in-room safes, minibars, cable TV, golf privileges, 2 tennis courts, 7 pools, health club, 2 outdoor hot tubs, spa, beach, dive shop, snorkeling, windsurfing, boating, bicycles, billiards, Ping-Pong, 8 bars, nightclub, theater, shops, children's programs (ages 4–12), Internet room, 2 meeting rooms* ☰ *AE, MC, V* ▯◯▯ *AI.*

🕓 **$–$$** ▣ **Gran Ventana Beach Resort.** This resort is characterized by a sophisticated style that sets it apart from the nearby competition. The lobby, with pottery and local drums suspended from the walls, is a contemporary study in Caribbean colors with a fountain. The beach is on a point with unobstructed views to the left. Families are a good share of the market, and this resort is solid as far as the tour operators are concerned, with service and food improving each season. Many couples prefer the larger rooms (sans good ocean views, unfortunately) that surround the quiet pool. A Victorian-style wedding gazebo is popular for nuptials. ⊠ *Playa Dorada, Box 22, Puerto Plata* ☎ *809/320–2111* 🖷 *809/320– 2112* ⊕ *www.vhhr.com* ↙ *499 rooms, 2 suites, 1 penthouse* ♦ *5 restaurants, in-room safes, minibars, golf privileges, tennis court, 2 pools, gym, hair salon, 2 hot tubs, sauna, beach, snorkeling, windsurfing, boating, bicycles, 7 bars, dance club, recreation room, theater, shops, children's programs (ages 4–12), playground, meeting rooms, car rental* ☰ *AE, MC, V* ▯◯▯ *AI.*

★ **$–$$** ▣ **Victoria Resort Golf & Beach.** Victoria has had a major face-lift, a total, amazing, multi-millon-dollar redo of the rooms and public spaces, including Indo-Caribbean furnishings, marble bathrooms, an enlarged lobby with a wooden deck, and a long concierge desk backed by two oversize mirrors. The gourmet room has been contemporized, the buffet extended and enhanced with ceramics. Coral stone and travertine can now be seen throughout. The gardens, too, have been redesigned, with a new boulevard between the two buildings; the beach club and its offerings have also been upgraded. Victoria's niche has been etched—couples, honeymooners, and golfers. Guests now can opt for a breakfast-only plan with beverages instead of the all-inclusive plan. ⊠ *Playa Dorada, Box 22, Puerto Plata* ☎ *809/320–1200* 📠 *809/320–4862* ⊕ *www.vhhr.com* 🛏 *164 rooms, 26 suites, 3 2-bedroom villas* 🖒 *4 restaurants, in-room safes, minibars, cable TV, golf privileges, tennis court, 2 pools, gym, outdoor hot tub, dive shop, snorkeling, windsurfing, boating, jet skiing, parasailing, horseback riding, 4 bars, nightclub* ☰ *AE, D, MC, V* ⍔ *AI.*

★ $ 🏨 **Natura Cabanas.** This oceanfront eco-paradise, which offers accommodations in thatched-roof cabanas, has grown up. Bungalows, such as the Africana, are becoming more sophisticated with bamboo, artistic brick, and stonework. The diverse clientele enhances this back-to-nature experience; you might find yourself next to a surfer, a young neurologist, or a yoga aficionado (there are classes and Pilates, too). Lole, the *dueña*, and her caring, bilingual staff promote camaraderie. Healthful breakfasts and lunches are served in one of the two seafront restaurants, where the mellow music is the backdrop for backgammon and international cuisine. The new, artistically designed Attabeyra Spa has upgraded services and classes. ⊠ *Playa Perla Marina, Cabarete* ☎ *809/571–1507* 📠 *809/ 571–1507* ⊕ *www.naturacabana.com* 🛏 *10 bungalows* 🖒 *2 restaurants, fans, some kitchenettes, refrigerators, pool, fitness classes, spa, beach, bar; no a/c, no room phones, no room TVs* ☰ *MC, V* ⍔ *CP.*

★ $ 🏨 **Velero Beach Resort.** Laze in the hammock swing on the palm that bends over the beach while you watch the kite surfers work to become airborne. They're the only thing between you and the horizon at this well-managed hotel and residential enclave with its own beachfront and manicured gardens studded with cacti, orchids, and pottery. Well-heeled Dominicans, hip Americans, and other international guests appreciate that it's removed from the noise of town yet just minutes down the sand from the happening bars. Spacious suites with full kitchens are the best deals and can be divided into smaller units. Guests in regular rooms (which have no kitchens) get a complimentary breakfast at the private beach club. ⊠ *Calle la Punta 1, Cabarete* ☎ *809/571–9727 or 866/383–5376* 📠 *809/571–9722* ⊕ *www.velerobeach.com* 🛏 *22 2-bedroom suites, 7 penthouses* 🖒 *Restaurant, in-room safes, some kitchens, refrigerators, cable TV, in-room data ports, pool, beach, shop, Internet room, business services, meeting room* ☰ *AE, MC, V* ⍔ *EP.*

$ 🏨 **Piergiorgio Palace Hotel.** Italian fashion designer Piergiorgio realized that his romantic, Victorianesque inn, with its wraparound veranda and intricate fretwork, had to evolve if it was to keep up with his newer, all-inclusive neighbors. And so he introduced new drapes and comforters from Europe to update the decor. Six new spacious rooms have been built cliffside; more spa-treatment rooms and an entertainment room have been added. The hotel's location is superlative for weddings—the gazebo has breathtaking bay views, as does the pizzeria (with the wood-burning oven) and the gourmet restaurant. Honeymooners love its romanticism, fostered by the charming, strolling guitarist. ⊠ *Calle La Puntilla 1, El Batey, Sosúa* ☎ *809/571–2626* 📠 *809/571–2786* ⊕ *www. piergiorgiohotel.com* 🛏 *49 rooms, 3 apartments, 2 penthouses* 🖒 *2 restau-*

10

rants, in-room safes, some kitchens, cable TV, 2 pools, hot tub, spa, beauty salon, 2 bars, $\rightleftharpoons$ *AE, MC, V* ⧉⧉ *BP.*

🌣 $ ⧉ **Windsurf Resort Hotel.** This small resort exemplifies the evolution of Cabarete since the late 1990s. Starting life as a cheap haunt for young board boys (guests enjoy complimentary water sports at the Bic Center across the road), it's evolved, offering larger and more attractive condos and adding a coral stone pool and a restaurant. It now also offers Wi-Fi and consequently attracts laptoppers. The crowd has shifted to couples, mostly baby boomers. There is still a fun quotient here, although units are showing some wear. If, as with the new Caberete crowd, your taste is more upscale, the Canadian owner, Gordon, is just completing Ocean Point, a three-story oceanfront complex designed in a tropical Asian style. ⊠ *Carretera Principal, Cabarete* ☎ *809/571–0718* 🖷 *809/ 571–0710* ⊕ *www.windsurfcabarete.com* ⇆ *48 rooms, 38 1-bedroom condos, 16 2-bedroom condos* ⎔ *Restaurant, picnic area, room service, fans, kitchenettes, cable TV, Wi-Fi, refrigerators, pool, windsurfing, boating, boccie, volleyball, 2 bars, shop* $\rightleftharpoons$ *MC, V* ⧉⧉ *EP.*

¢–$ ⧉ **Villa Taina.** Smack amid the action, steps down from the main drag, this small, German-owned inn encapsulates the original spirit of Cabarete. It caters to the independent traveler and the young and sporty who want more commodious digs than a surf camp. Enjoy an ample breakfast in the beachside restaurant, which is sheltered from the wind by translucent kite boards; your fellow coffee drinkers may be shielded by German and French newspapers. Barbecue night, which offers both cool sounds and a fun crowd, is an excellent value. Request the quiet rooms (the second floor up to the penthouses) that front the beach. ⊠ *Calle Principal, Cabarete* ☎ *809/571–0722* 🖷 *809/571–0883* ⊕ *www. villataina.com* ⇆ *55 rooms, 1 apartment* ⎔ *Restaurant, refrigerators, cable TV, pool, beach, massage, dive shop, windsurfing, bar, 2 shops* $\rightleftharpoons$ *MC, V* ⧉⧉ *BP.*

Where to Eat

The island's culinary repertoire includes Spanish, Italian, Middle Eastern, Indian, Japanese, and *nueva cocina Dominicana* (contemporary Dominican cuisine). If seafood is on the menu, it's bound to be fresh. The dining scene in Santo Domingo is the best in the country and probably as fine a selection of restaurants as you will find anywhere in the Caribbean. *Capitaleños* dress for dinner and dine late. The crowds pick up after 9:30 PM, when the Americans are already finishing dessert.

Among the best Dominican specialties are *queso frito* (fried cheese), *sancocho* (a thick stew usually made with five meats and served with rice and avocado slices), *arroz con pollo* (rice with beans and fried chicken parts), *pescado al coco* (fish in coconut sauce), and *plátanos* (plantains) in all their tasty varieties, including *tostones* (fried green plaintains). Shacks and stands that serve cheap eats are an integral part of the culture and landscape, but eat street food at your own risk—more like your peril. Presidente is the best local beer. Brugal rum is popular with the Dominicans, but Barceló *anejo* (aged) rum is as smooth as cognac, and Barcelo Imperial considered so special it's brought out only at Christmastime.

What to Wear

In resort areas, shorts and bathing suits under beach wraps are usually (but not always) acceptable at breakfast and lunch. For dinner, long pants, skirts, and collared shirts are the norm. Restaurants tend to be more formal in Santo Domingo, both at lunch and at dinner, with trousers required for men and dresses suggested for women. Ties aren't required anywhere, but jackets are (even at the midday meal) in some of the finer establishments.

Santo Domingo

ENGLISH
$$–$$$$

✕ **Coco's Restaurant.** In 1996, two gents from the United Kingdom had the courage to buy this colonial house and redecorate it with antiques, hanging plants, coral wainscoting, and vintage pics of English royalty. And a restaurant was born, offering British comfort food with Caribbean nuances: boneless chicken breasts in a ginger-mango sauce with red cabbage and perfectly sautéed potatoes. Yucca pancakes with lump fish roe and sour cream make a super appetizer, the blackberry cheesecake one fine finale. Inquire about Indian night. The guys have an ample liquor locker—lots of Scotch—and good sounds, like Elton John. ⊠ *Padre Billini 53, Zona Colonial* ☎ *809/687–9624* ▭ *MC, V* ☉ *Closed Mon.*

ITALIAN
$$–$$$$
Fodor'sChoice
★

✕ **Spaghettissimo.** This former private residence, with pool and terrace seating, has been renovated with a sense of elegant, minimalist style. And, yes, it's still the well-loved restaurant owned by Frederic Gollong, but with a new image and address. The contemporary menu exhibits such eclectic influences as Thai and Japanese, with shellfish a specialty. Classics like lamb osso buco with Milanese risotto as well as arugula salad with walnuts, proscuitto, and Roquefort are also on the menu. And as your table candle, filled with coffee beans, elicits a heady aroma, have a luscious dessert like vanilla galleta, with caramelized pecans and pralines. The revised lunch menu has artistic salads, pastas, and lighter fare at more moderate prices. ⊠ *Manuel de Jesús Troncoso 13, Piantini* ☎ *809/ 547–2650 or 809/334–6060* ▭ *AE, MC, V* ☉ *No dinner Sun.*

Boca Chica

SEAFOOD
$–$$

✕ **El Pelicano.** Begin with a mango daiquiri while you watch the sun drop behind the pier that extends into gin-clear water. Let a spicy ceviche jump-start your tastebuds. Regulars know to order the shellfish casserole and the paella, though the grilled lobster with garlic butter is also a perennial fave. On Wednesday night, the buffet often includes lobster. Fifteen minutes from Las Americas Airport, this is an ideal place to endure a long layover. Eat a delectable lunch, swim in the sea, sleep in the sun, and then shower in the clean locker rooms. Take a hazelnut piña colada in a plastic cup to go, and wave good-bye. ⊠ *Coral Hamaca Beach Hotel & Casino, Playa Boca Chica* ☎ *809/523–4611 Ext. 830* ▭ *AE, MC, V.*

Punta Cana

CONTEMPORARY
★ $$–$$$

✕ **Restaurant Coccoloba.** This elegant dining room in the country's most sophisticated resort clubhouse was decorated by Oscar de la Renta. The tableware is so chic and colorful—with geometric plates—that it makes the food, already stellar, taste even better. Begin the feast of the senses

10

with sea bass and crab-meat cakes with mango and papaya chutney. Then follow with a quality main course. Our suggestion: the lamb tenderloin with rosemary sauce atop a cassava cake; however, you might not be able to turn down lobster tempura with spinach sauce. The intelligent wine list complements the cuisine. An afterthought? Try the almond biscuit with chocolate sauce over caramelized pineapple. ⊠ *PuntaCana Resort & Club, Playa Punta Cana* ☎ *809/959–2262* ⌲ *Reservations essential* ▤ *AE, MC, V* ⊘ *No lunch.*

SEAFOOD   ✕ **Captain Cook's.** Although Punta Cana is the land of all-inclusives, this
$$$ landmark draws the crowds, who willingly pay a fixed price for drinks, boat transportation, and the *parrillada mixta* (a mix of seafood—mussels, baby lobsters, fresh fish, squid, shrimp) with fries and tomato salad, followed by coffee, fruit, and shots of fiery *mamajuana.* Sit in the sand at the water's edge and watch as the fishermen hang their catch up by the tail. It's wild and crazy as mariachis play *Ai, yai, yai,* vendors hawk Haitian art, and waiters sprint to the beach tables delivering sizzling metal cauldrons of the signature dish. ⊠ *Playa El Cortecito* ☎ *809/ 552–1061* ▤ *D, MC, V.*

The North Coast

The Cabarete area in particular—where all-inclusive resorts don't yet totally dominate the scene—has some fun, original restaurants, but these are often small places, so it's important that you make reservations in advance; otherwise, you may be turned away. However, expat residents complain that the prices in this town have now moved past the good-value-for-money mark. Also, more and more the restaurants are insisting on cash only, be it pesos, dollars, or euros.

AMERICAN   ✕ **Ali's Surf Camp.** You sit at long tables with a disparate group of
CASUAL   strangers from at least three different countries, surrounded by bullrushes
$ poking up from a lagoon. You can have a good feed for around 10 bucks. Try grilled, sweet barbecued ribs with fries, seafood with a Dominican salad and a baked potato, or the house-special churrasco—and always there's a shooter of mamajuana. The German owner, Ali, has designated Saturday as Sushi Night. The palapa roof gives the terrace shelter, and the wood-burning oven means flavorful pizza, but best douse yourself with mosquito repellent. You can even call now to make reservations, and you should if you have a large group. ⊠ *Procab Cabarete, Cabarete* ☎ *809/571–0733* ▤ *No credit cards* ⊘ *No lunch.*

¢–$ ✕ **EZE Bar & Restaurant.** This restaurant has a loyal following from breakfast to dinner, from wallet-watchin' windsurfers to wealthy capitaleño families. You can get an energy kick from yogurt and mango smoothies; you'll love the megasalads with shrimp, avocado, greens, and black olives. The chicken curry wrap and new Lebanese pitas are also tops, as is the cheeseburger with bacon. Frosty, tropical cocktails are excellent, yet the blenders also churn out healthy, organic veggie elixirs. The dinner menu now is priced similarly to lunch, with more refined specials, which might be calamari or even lobster. The manager, Christos, is Bulgarian and so is the mezze platter. ⊠ *Cabarete Beach, in front of Bic Center, Cabarete* ☎ *809/880–8779* ▤ *No credit cards.*

CONTEMPORARY ╳ **Miró Gallery & Restaurant.** There's now more of a scene at the bar here,
$–$$ as an English-speaking radio station does live broadcasts from the lounge and cranks up the crowd. Chef-owner Lydia Wazana, a Canadian of Moroccan descent, is a queen-pin among the art set, too, and her imaginative offerings include chicken tagine, Asian-seared tuna, and seafood curry served in a coconut shell. Cool it down with mixed greens, avocado, orange, and walnut salad with housemade breads. Grazers can share tapas such as the yucca fries or more Middle Eastern offerings like hummus, baba ghanoush, and grilled veggies. The chocolate mud pie is a "yes!" ⊠ *Cabarete Beach, next to O'Shay's, Cabarete* ☎ *809/571–0888* ▭ *MC, V* ☽ *No lunch.*

CONTINENTAL ╳ **L'Etoile d'Or.** Behind the French doors, this intimate restaurant is
★ **$$$$** draped with billowing white linen and displays enough candle power to be ecclesiastical. An elegant, artistically presented prix-fixe menu might include a pumpkin cream soup or fried camembert with a velouté sauce; a sorbet course; a petite but divine entrée like lobster medallions with dill sauce or something more substantial like the lamb chops with mango-mint chutney; and finally, a surprise dessert. Service is discreet and professional, the wine list upscale. This is an ideal place for a proposal. ⊠ *Victorian House, Sosua* ☎ *809/571–4000* ⏣ *Reservations essential* ▭ *AE, MC, V* ☽ *No lunch.*

$$$ ╳ **Joseph's Grill & Grape.** Anyone boating on Sosúa Bay would notice the blue and white gazebos perched on a cliff, like a set for the *Thousand Arabian Nights.* These rondellas are even sexier when you are seated in one, especially the primo cliff-hanger, with the sounds and sights of the waves below, that can house a celebratory group of eight. The concept is an ever-changing prix-fixe with original dishes and unexpected pairings, juxtaposed with thick U.S. steaks. Main courses come in petite and large; dessert might be inventive, like poached pears in a creamy Bailey's sauce or more classic, like chocolate fondue with mangoes. ⊠ *Sosúa by the Sea Sosúa* ☎ *809/571–3222* ⏣ *Reservations essential* ▭ *AE, MC, V* ☽ *No Lunch. No dinner Mon. or Tues.*

$$ ╳ **Castle Club.** A man's home is his castle. In this one, Doug Beers prepares creative lunches and dinners for guests who traverse the rocky driveway to enjoy this one-of-a-kind experience. His wife, Marguerite, is the gracious hostess, who shows patrons their home and artwork, strategically positioned between the many open-air arches. Served on antique lace tablecloths strewn with bougainvillea, the well-orchestrated dinner might consist of carrot-ginger soup, salad niçoise, snapper with a coconut–passion fruit sauce, rosemary potatoes, and chocolate mousse. After, Doug lights a fire in the great room and offers guests a liqueur to warm their interior. ⊠ *Mocha Rd., between Jamao and Los Brazos, 20 mins from Cabarete* ☎ *809/357–8334 or 809/223–0601* ⏣ *Reservations essential* ▭ *No credit cards.*

JAPANESE ╳ **Wabi Sabi.** With geometric plate presentation as aesthetically pleas-
★ **$–$$** ing as a Japanese garden, this new sushi restaurant could go up against its counterparts in Tokyo. An architect who has lived in Japan created all of the woodwork and settees, which are lined with red and orange pillows. The black-and-white modern art and the "chill" music are the

backdrop for beautifully executed, classic sashami and sushi, as well as some creations that include shrimp tempura rolls and string bean salad dressed with peanut sauce. Clad in a black kimono, the chef was trained by the legendary Nobu. ☒ *Kite Beach, in front of Hotel Aqualina, Cabarete* ☎ *809/571–0101 or 809/853–6848* ▭ *No credit cards.*

SEAFOOD
★ $–$$
✕ **Restaurant at Natura Cabanas.** Seafood is at the heart of the menu here, and appropriately so, for diners listen to the sounds of the waves crashing on coral rock as they choose between the catch of the day with a sauce of caramelized onions, nuts, and raisins and the paella. Start with the ceviche and then segue to the curried fish. It all tastes so fresh. For dessert, rum raisin mousse with vanilla sauce is *mmmm*. The wines are French, Spanish, and Chilean (go for the *reservas*), as is the chef. Regular guests sidle up to the bar to watch him work his magic to the beat of the hip, international CDs. ☒ *Natura Cabanas, Perla Marina, Cabarete* ☎ *809/858–5822 or 809/571–1507* ⌁ *Reservations essential* ▭ *No credit cards.*

¢–$$
✕ **Al Fresco.** International music, Euro-style furniture, an inviting terrace with hanging plants, and minimalist decor convey an upscale, modern atmosphere. Seafood, often coupled with pasta or risotto, is the focus on the menu. You can find live lobsters, a delicacy not often seen in the Dominican Republic, as well as sushi arranged artistically on white geometric plates. The Alfresco roll and the shrimp tempura–spinach roll will make ordinary sushi pale in comparison. As starters, shrimp carpaccio or fresh octopus with basil and tomato in fish sauce (here called "anguilla sauce") are appetizers that you won't find in your hometown. The De los Santos family, the caring owners, keep the doors open until 1 AM. ☒ *Playa Dorada Plaza, next to Hemingway's, Puerto Plata* ☎ *809/320–1137 or 809/320–2230* ▭ *AE, MC, V* ☾ *No lunch.*

Santiago

The D.R.'s second city, Santiago, has always been a lovely, provincial place; the draw nowadays is the new, world-class art gallery and museum, Centro León. Most people come from the Puerto Plata area as day-trippers, but a few spend the night, especially if they fly in directly from New York on Jet Blue. From Sosúa and Cabarete, it's about a 1½-hour drive on the scenic highway that passes through mountain villages; from Puerto Plata it's about 1 hour, from Santo Domingo 2½ hours. Those who come for the day can also enjoy lunch in one of Santiago's great restaurants.

CONTEMPORARY
$–$$
✕ **Maroma.** You might assume this is an Italian restaurant, and part of the menu is, including lobster ravioli and the porcini and portobello mushroom risotto. But you can also find Asian specialties and Dominican fusion food. Whatever you choose is sure to be well prepared. If you want a light lunch, try the Japanese ceviche with avocado in a ginger-soy sauce. A favorite is the Maroma Sampler, a platter with an empanada filled with Cabrales blue cheese over greens with a pear vinaigrette, and salt-fish croquettes with avocado dressing and fried yucca. *Tres leches* cake, swimming in guava sauce, is a true Dominican dessert. ☒ *1–3 Calle 15, Los Jardines Metropolitanos* ☎ *809/724–4643* ▭ *AE, MC, V* ☾ *No dinner Sun.*

ITALIAN ✕ **Il Pasticcio.** Everyone from college students to politicos packs this ec-
★ $ centrically decorated culinary landmark (check out the foil-wrapped Vespa
and the hand-stenciled border on the wall that reads LOVE–SEX–MONEY).
Chef-owner Paolo is a true *paisano,* and his fabulous creations are authentic and fresh. Try out the great antipasto selections or exotic Italian
mushrooms in oil, or you could commence with the delicious Pasticcio
salad with smoked salmon, mozzarrella, anchovies, capers, and baby
arugula. Paolo couples fresh pastas with unexpected sauces, like gnoc-
chi with puttanesca; the ravioli with spinach and ricotta is another fave.
Don't stop 'til you finish the chocolate salami! ⊠ *5, Calle 3, at Av. Del
Llano, Cerros de Gurabo* ☏ *809/582–6061 or 809/276–5466* ▭ *AE,
MC* ⊙ *Closed Mon.*

Beaches

The Dominican Republic has more than 1,000 mi (1,623 km) of beaches,
including the Caribbean's longest stretch of white sand: Punta Cana–
Bávaro. Many beaches are accessible to the public (in theory, all beaches
in this country, from the high-water mark down, are open to everyone)
and may tempt you to stop for a swim. That's part of the uninhibited
joy of this country. Do be careful, though: some have dangerously
strong currents, which may be the reason why they are undeveloped.

Fodor'sChoice **Playa Bahoruco.** This isolated, gorgeous stretch of virgin beach goes on
★ for miles in either direction, with rugged cliffs dropping to golden sand
and warm, blue water. It's the ideal wild, undeveloped Caribbean beach,
but many sections are pebbly, so you need surf shoes for swimming. Just
a little to the south, on the stretch of beach called San Rafael, are beach
shacks where you can buy meals of fresh fish, even whole coconut sea
bass. ⊠ *Carretera La Costa, Km 17, 8 mi (13 km) south of Barahona.*
Playa Boca Chica. Developed by wealthy industrialist Juan Vicini in the
early 1900s, the beach—an immaculate stretch of fine sand—was where
entire families moved their households for the summer. You can walk far
out into the gin-clear waters protected by coral reefs. Unfortunately, some
areas are now cluttered with plastic furniture, pizza stands, and cottages.
The old Hamaca Hotel (now the Coral Hilton Hamaca) was the place to
see and be seen; dictator Trujillo kept quarters here; unfortunately, its glory
days are long gone. The strip with the rest of the mid-rise resorts is kept
busy, particularly on weekends, mainly with Dominican families and
some Europeans. If you're staying in the capital, this is the closest good
beach, but best to go midweek. Take lunch at one of the larger beachfront restaurants like El Pelicano or Neptuno's Club and just hang out
on a chaise lounge. Pelicano is a great alternative to long layovers at the
airport, for the fine bathroom facilities with multiple showers. ⊠ *Autopista
Las Americas, 21 mi (34 km) east of Santo Domingo, Boca Chica.*
Playa Cabarete. If you follow the coastal road east from Playa Dorada,
you can find this beach, which has strong waves and ideal, steady wind
(from 15 to 20 knots), making it an integral part of the international
windsurfing circuit. Segments of this beach are strips of golden sand punctuated only by palm trees. In the most commercial area, restaurants and
bars are back-to-back, spilling onto the sand. The informal scene is young

10

and fun, with expats and tourists from every imaginable country. ⊠ *Sosúa–Cabarete Rd., Cabarete.*

Playa Dorada. On the north's Amber Coast, this is one of the D.R.'s most established resort areas. Each hotel has its own slice of the beach, which is soft beige sand, with lots of reefs for snorkeling. Gran Ventana Beach Resort, which is on a point, marks the end of the major hotel development. The Atlantic waters are great for windsurfing, waterskiing, and fishing. ⊠ *Off Autopista Luperon, 10 min east of Puerto Plata, Playa Dorada.*

Playa Grande. On the north coast, between the towns of Rio San Juan and Cabrera, this long stretch of powdery sand is slated for development—so go while you still can. The public entrance to the beach is about a mile after Playa Grande Golf Course, which is at Km 9. Here, the beach is on a lovely cove, with towering cliffs on both sides. In winter there are waves and some tricky currents, but in summer the water is flat. The only facilities are at the golf club and the not-so-wonderful Occidental Playa Grande Hotel atop a cliff, though a few beach shacks fry up fresh fish, garlicky shrimp, and keep the beer on ice. An outcropping separates this beach from Playa Precioso, which is lovely to walk in winter but more swimmable in warm months. During the week you'll have little company, but on Sunday afternoons (or during the entire Easter week), when the locals are here in full force, the scene is busy and inadvisable. ⊠ *Carretera Río San Juan–Cabrera, Km 11.*

Playa Las Terrenas. On the north coast of the Samaná Peninsula, tall palms list toward the sea, and the beach is extensive and postcard perfect, with crystalline waters and soft, golden sand. There's plenty of color—vivid blues, greens, and yellows—as well as colorful characters. Two hotels are right on the beach at Punta Bonita. To the west is Playa El Cosón, opposite Cayo Ballena, a great whale-watching spot (from January to April). Samaná has some of the country's best beaches and drop-dead scenery, the rough roads notwithstanding. ⊠ *Carretera Las Terrenas, Las Terrenas.*

Playa Sosúa. Sosúa Bay is a gorgeous, natural harbor, renowned for its coral reefs and dive sites, about a 20-minute drive from Puerto Plata. Here, calm waters gently lap at a shore of soft golden sand. Swimming is delightful, except after a heavy rain when litter floats in. From the beach you can see mountains in the background, the cliffs that surround the bay, and seemingly miles of coastline. Snorkeling from the beach can be good, but the best spots are offshore, closer to the reefs. (Don't bother going to "Three Rock"—save your $20 and snorkel off the beach.) Unfortunately, the backdrop is a string of tents where hawkers push souvenirs, snacks, drinks, and water-sports equipment rentals. Lounge chairs can usually be had for 50 pesos, so bargain. ⊠ *Carretera Puerto Plata–Sosúa, Sosúa.*

★ **Punta Cana.** One of the best and longest Caribbean beaches is 20 mi (32 km) of pearl-white sand shaded by swaying coconut palms; it forms the backdrop for the busiest of the D.R.'s tourist regions. The area encompasses Cabeza de Torres, Playa Bávaro, and continues all the way around the peninsula to Playa de Uvero Alto. Each hotel has its own strip of sand with rows of chaise lounges, and you can often arrange for a day pass if you call in advance. The stretch between Club Med and the Punta Cana

Resort & Club is one of the most beautiful. Few isolated stretches exist anymore. Playa El Corticito, where the restaurant Captain Cook's sits, is more how life used to be, with fishermen bringing in their catch, though even there you can find souvenir shops and strolling vendors. The public beach at Macao is no longer a good option, having been taken over for four-wheeler excursions, and soon a new Westin resort will rise from its sands. There are more deserted stretches in the Uvero Alto area, but that road is rough and, outside of the four resorts, has few services. ⊠ *Off Autopista Las Americas, east of Higüey, Punta Cana.*

Sports & the Outdoors

Although there's hardly a shortage of activities here, the resorts have virtually cornered the market on sports, including every conceivable water sport. In some cases facilities may be available only to guests of the resorts.

BASEBALL Baseball is a national passion, and Sammy Sosa is still a legend in his own time. But he is just one of many celebrated Dominican baseball heroes, including pitcher Odalis Revela. Triple-A Dominican and Puerto Rican players and some American major leaguers hone their skills in the D.R.'s professional Winter League, which plays from October through January. Some games are held in the Tetelo Vargas Stadium, in the town of San Pedro de Macorís, east of Boca Chica. As many as 20,000 fans often crowd the **Liga de Béisbol Stadium** (☎ 809/567–6371) in Santo Domingo. If your Spanish is good, you can call the stadium; otherwise, ask staff at your hotel to arrange tickets.

BIKING & HIKING Pedaling is easy on pancake-flat beaches, but there are also some steep hills in the D.R. Several resorts rent bikes to guests and nonguests alike. **Iguana Mama** (⊠ Calle Principal 74, Cabarete ☎ 809/571–0908 or 809/ 571–0228 ⊕ www.iguanamama.com) has traditional and mountain bikes and will take you on guided rides on the flats or test your mettle on the steep grades in the mountains. Downhill rides, which include a taxi up to the foothills, breakfast, and lunch, cost $85 for a full-day trip, $60 for a half-day trip. Advanced rides, on and off roads, are $40 to $50. Guided hikes cost $35 to $65.

BOATING Sailing conditions are ideal, with constant trade winds. Favorite excursions include day trips to Catalina Island and Saona Island—both in the La Romana area—and sunset cruises on the Caribbean. Prices for crewed sailboats of 26 feet and longer with a capacity of 4 to 12 people range from $120 to $700 a day. The **Carib BIC Center** (⊠ Cabarete ☎ 809/571–0640 ⊕ www.caribwind.com) is a renowned windsurfing center that also rents Lasers, 17-foot catamarans, Boogie boards, and sea kayaks. It now has an Olympic laser training center with a former racer instructing. **La Marina Chavon** (⊠ Casa de Campo, Calle Barlovento 3, La Romana ☎ 809/523–8646 ⊕ www.casadecampomarina.com) has much going on, from sailing to motor yachting and socializing at the Casa de Campo Yacht Club. The full-service marina **La Marina PuntaCana** (⊠ Punta Cana Resort & Club, Punta Cana ☎ 809/221–2262) rents small boats by the half- or full day.

10

DIVING Ancient sunken galleons, undersea gardens, and offshore reefs are among the lures here. Most divers head to the north shore. In the waters off Sosúa alone you can find a dozen dive sites (for all levels of ability) with such catchy names as Three Rocks (a deep, 163-foot dive), Airport Wall (98 feet), and Pyramids (50 feet). Some 10 dive schools are represented on Sosúa Beach; resorts have dive shops on-site or can arrange trips for you.

Northern Coast Aquasports (⊠ Sosúa ☎ 809/571–1028 ⊕ www. northerncoastdiving.com) is a five-star, Gold Palm PADI dive center; it's also the only National Geographic Center in the D.R. Professionalism is apparent from the initial classroom and pool practice to the legendary dive sites around beautiful Sosúa Bay, where you can explore the reefs, walls, wrecks, and swim-throughs, from 25 to 130 feet. Successful completion of a three-day course and $350 earns you a PADI Open Water Certification card. Classrooms have air-conditioning and DVDs.

Off Las Terrenas in 1979, three atolls disappeared following a seaquake, providing an opportunity to snorkel forever. **Viva Diving** (⊠ Viva Wyndham Samaná Resort, Las Terrenas ☎ 809/240–5050) offers catamaran snorkeling trips to El Burro or Playa Jackson along with a beach barbecue lunch. Italian dive master Mauro offers PADI and SSI instruction and certification. One close dive ($40) is Las Ballenas (i.e., "the Whales"), a cluster of four little islands. If you're willing to go farther away, the shop can organize a freshwater dive at Cueva Do Do, near Cabrera, where you can explore the underwater caves. It's $90 for the six-hour trip, which includes taxi, entrance, food, drink, and the dive.

FISHING Marlin and wahoo are among the fish that folks angle for here (fishing is best between January and June). **La Marina Chavon** (⊠ Casa de Campo, Calle Barlovento 3, La Romana ☎ 809/523–8646 ⊕ www. casadecampomarina.com) is the best charter option near La Romana. Costs to charter a boat—with a crew, refreshments, bait, and tackle—generally range from $592 to $1,616 for a half-day and from $790 to $3,191 for a full day. River fishing is just $46 for three hours. At **La Marina PuntaCana** (⊠ PuntaCana Resort & Club, Punta Cana ☎ 809/ 959–2262 ⊕ www.puntacana.com), which is on the southern end of the resort, half-day, deep-sea fishing excursions are available for $95 per person, with a minimum of two people, $70 for observers. For a Bertram 33-footer to go after tuna, marlin, dorado, and wahoo, it's $575 for four hours. It costs the same to charter a 45-foot Sportfisherman. Also, ask about the yolas fishing boats with outboards.

GOLF The D.R. has some of the best courses in the Caribbean, designed by the top golf architects. Prices listed are for the winter season; some, but not all, reduce their rates between April and October, so ask. The **Barceló Bávaro Beach Golf & Casino Resort** (⊠ Playa Bávaro ☎ 809/686–5797) has an 18-hole course, open to its own guests and those of other hotels. The rate for those not staying at Bávaro is $120, which includes greens fees, golf carts, and a day pass, which gives you food and drink for the day. **PuntaCana Resort & Club** (⊠ Punta Cana ☎ 809/959–2262 Ext. 101, 111, or 809/959–4653 ⊕ www.puntacana.com) has an 18-hole course by P. B. Dye, with spectacular views of the Caribbean. Greens fees (in-

Fodor'sChoice
★

cluding golf carts) are $61 for 9 holes, $88 for 18 holes, cart included, for resort guests; $100 for 9 holes, $144 for 18 holes (carts $30) for nonguests, who must reserve two weeks in advance from November through April. Multiple-round packages are available. At this writing, construction on a second course—designed by Tom Fazio—was under way in Corales, the private enclave of luxurious homes. Laid out along cliffs and coves, it was expected to open by 2008. Lessons and clinics are offered at Punta Cana Golf Academy. **White Sands Golf Course** (⊠ Near Ocean Blue Golf & Beach Resort, Playa Bávaro ☎ 809/688–2978) was designed by Pepe Gancedo, a six-time Spanish champion, who is often called the Picasso of golf-course designers. The cost for 9 holes is $125, but inquire first about packages. A second phase of the course should be open by the time this book appears, for a total of 18 holes.

Fodor'sChoice
★

Golf magazine has called "Teeth of the Dog" at **Casa de Campo** (⊠ La Romana ☎ 809/523–3333 ⊕ www.casadecampo.com.do) the finest golf resort in the Caribbean. Greens fees are $203; if you're an avid golfer, though, inquire about the resort's multiday passes and golf packages. Close to Altos de Chavón, "Dye Fore" ($203) hugs a cliff that overlooks the ocean, as well as Río Chávon and its palm groves. Pete Dye has designed a third, 18-hole inland course named "The Links" ($145). Tee times at all courses must be reserved at least a day in advance by resort guests, earlier for nonguests.

Although the 7,156-yard, par 72, 21-hole course at **Guvaberry Golf & Country Club** (⊠ Autovia del Este, Km 55, Juan Dolio ☎ 809/333–4653 ⊕ www.guavaberrygolf.com) has earned the reputation as one of the tops in the country. Gary Player, the architect, is a key factor. He designed it with an island hole and a wide putting area, beautifying it with bougainvillea and coral stone. Intimidating at first glance, it's a challenging but fair course with long fairways. Play costs $99, including a cart. The golf director is a PGA pro. A branch of the Montréal-based Golfologist Academy, which gives audiovisual analysis of your golf swing, opened in 2006. **Los Marlins Championshop Golf Course** (⊠ Juan Dolio ☎ 809/526–1359) is an 18-hole, 6,400-yard, par-72 course designed by Charles Ankrom. Its moderate cost is $30 for 9 holes with cart, $10 for a caddy; $59 for 18 holes, $17 for a caddy. Golfers get 10% off at the Metro Country Club. The adjacent Embassy Suites Hotel has added to the popularity of this established course, within 45 minutes of Santo Domingo hotels.

10

Golf Digest has named **Playa Dorada Golf Club** one of the top 100 courses outside the United States. Adjacent to the Victoria Resort, it's open to guests of all the hotels in the area. Greens fees for 9 holes are $50, 18 holes $75; caddies are mandatory for foursomes and will cost about $9 more; carts are optional, at $25. The club house was refurbished with contemporary style for the Salvatore Ferragamo Golf Tournament. **Playa Grande Golf Course** (⊠ Carretera Río San Juan–Cabrera, Km 9 ☎ 809/582–0860), between Río San Juan and Cabrera on the north coast, is described as the Pebble Beach of the Caribbean, with 10 holes along the Atlantic Ocean. Greens fees to play the 18-hole, par-72 are

$120, $68 for 9 holes, which includes mandatory carts. Caddies, also mandatory, are $10 for 18 holes, $5 for 9, plus tip.

HORSEBACK RIDING The 250-acre Equestrian Center at **Casa de Campo** (⊠ La Romana ☎ 809/523–3333 ⊕ www.casadecampo.com.do) has something for both Western and English riders—a dude ranch, a rodeo arena (where Casa's trademark "Donkey Polo" is played), guided trail rides, and jumping and riding lessons. Guided rides run about $35 an hour; lessons cost $56 an hour. There are early morning and sunset trail rides, too. Handsome, old-fashioned carriages are available for hire, as well. The **Equestrian Center** (⊠ PuntaCana Resort & Club, Punta Cana ☎ 809/959–2262 ⊕ www.puntacana.com) is across from the main entrance of the resort. The rate for a one-hour trail ride is $20; it winds along the beach, the golf course, and through tropical forests. The two-hour jungle trail ride, which costs $34, has a stopover at a lagoon fed by a natural spring, so wear your swimsuit under your long pants. You can also do a three-hour full-moon excursion. The stock are Paso Fino horses. **Guavaberry Equestrian Center** (⊠ Guavaberry Golf &Country Club, Autovia del Este, Km 55, Juan Dolio ☎ 809/333–4653) has a clean stable with professional European management, good stock, and English and western saddles. Delightful hour-plus trail rides throughout the extensive grounds of the resort cost $25; riding lessons, from beginning to advanced, are $50. Complimentary transportation is provided to all Juan Dolio hotels and to the Hamaca Coral by Hilton Hotel in Boca Chica. **Rancho Isabella** (⊠ Las Terrenas ☎ 809/847–4849), on the Samaná Peninsula, can give you either a western or English saddle for one of its 15 mounts. A 1½-hour ride along the beach is $10. The nocturnal full-moon ride to Boca de la Diablo will be remembered and includes drinks and a Domincan feast on the beach, with chicken, goat, and shrimp for $46. This is a simple, local operation, but it's fun, scenic, and priced right. The director of the upscale **Sea Horse Ranch** (⊠ Cabarete ☎ 809/571–3880), Marcos Streit, is a Swiss national who competed in Europe for 30 years at the highest levels. He has trained quality horses for jumping and dressage and added a new competition ring, built to international regulations. A jumping event, the first of the Annual Sea Horse Ranch Invitationals, was held in 2005. Lessons, including dressage instruction, start at $35 an hour. Streit has improved the quality of mounts and tack for the trail and endurance rides (starting at $38 for 90 minutes, $57 for three hours, including drinks and snacks—but make reservations). The most popular ride includes stretches of beach and a bridle path across a neighboring farm's pasture, replete with wild flowers and butterflies. Feel free to tie your horse to a palm tree and jump into the waves.

POLO Casa de Campo is a key place to play or watch the fabled sport of kings. The resort has always prided itself on the polo traditions it has kept alive since its opening in the 1970s. Matches are scheduled from October to June, with high-goal players flying in from France and Argentina. Private polo lessons ($60 an hour) and clinics are available for those who always wanted to give it a shot. Guvaberry Golf & Country Club in Juan Dolio is constructing two polo fields.

TENNIS There must be a million nets around the island, and most of them can be found at the large resorts. **La Terraza Tennis Club** (⊠ Casa de Campo, La Romana ☎ 809/523–3333) has been called the Wimbledon of the Caribbean. This 12-acre facility, perched on a hill with sea views, has 13 Har-Tru courts. Nonmembers are welcome (just call in advance); court time costs $28 an hour, and lessons are $55 an hour with an assistant pro, $69 with a pro. **Occidental Tennis Academy** (⊠ Occidental Club on the Green, Playa Dorada, Puerto Plata ☎ 809/320–1111 hotel's main switchboard ⊕ www.occidentalhotels.com) was the first tennis academy in the Caribbean. It's equipped with seven Har-Tru clay and hard courts (night-lighted), as well as a gym, pool, social club, and pro shop. Classes are given and supervised by pros. Programs are for adults and children five and over. You can get private ($13 an hour) or group classes ($8), in English or Spanish, for beginners to professionals. Courts can also be rented by nonguests. The **Playa Naco Resort & Spa** (⊠ Playa Dorada ☎ 809/320–6226 Ext. 2568) allows nonguests to play on its four clay courts for $10 an hour by day, $20 at night. Lessons from the pro cost $23 an hour plus the cost of the court. **PuntaCana Resort & Club** (⊠ Playa Punta Cana ☎ 809/959–2262 Ext. 7158) has six courts and tennis clinics on Tuesday and Thursday, as well as an exhibition stadium. Nonguests can play for two hours for $26, or $12 an hour from 6 PM to 7 PM; the courts close at 7 PM. **Sea Horse Ranch** (⊠ Cabarete ☎ 809/571–2902) has a tennis center with five clay courts, illuminated for night play and open to nonguests. Court time is $20 an hour, with a fee of $6 for night play; $20 to play with the European pro, Marko Srdic; and $1.50 for ball boys. Instructions, available in four languages, cost $20.

WIND- & KITE SURFING
Fodor'sChoice
★

Between June and October, Cabarete Beach has what many consider to be optimal windsurfing conditions: wind speeds at 20 to 25 knots (they come from the side shore) and 3- to-10-foot Atlantic waves. The Professional Boardsurfers Association has included Cabarete in its international windsurfing slalom competition. The novice is also welcome to learn and train on wider boards with light sails. **Carib BIC Center** (⊠ Cabarete ☎ 809/571–0640 ⊕ www.caribwind.com) offers equipment and instruction. Lessons are generally $30 to $35 an hour; boards rent for $20 an hour. A gem of a windsurfing club, this family-owned business has many repeat clients and is open year-round. It also operates a beach bar and a retail shop. **Kitexcite** (⊠ Kite Excite Hotel, Kite Beach, Cabarete ☎ 809/571–9509, 809/913–0827, or 809/914–9745 ⊕ www.kitexcite.com) operates the largest school for one of the Caribbean's newest popular sports. Your board—smaller than a windsurfing board—is attached to a parachutelike "kite." Those who are proficient can fly through the air.

10

Shopping

Cigars continue to be the hottest commodity coming out of the D.R. Many exquisite hand-wrapped smokes come from the island's rich Ciabo Valley, and Fuente Cigars—handmade in Santiago—are highly prized. Only reputable cigar shops sell the real thing, and many you will see sold on the street are fakes. You can also buy and enjoy Cuban cigars here, but they can't be brought back to the United States legally. Dominican rum and coffee are also good buys. *Mamajuana,* an herbal liqueur, is said to be the Dominican answer to Viagra. The D.R. is the homeland of designer Oscar de la Renta, and you may want to stop at the chic shops that carry his creations. La Vega is famous for its *diablos cajuelos* (devil masks), which are worn during Carnival. Look also for the delicate, faceless ceramic figurines that symbolize Dominican culture.

Though locally crafted products are often of a high caliber (and very affordable), expect to pay hundreds of dollars for designer jewelry made of amber and larimar. Larimar—a semiprecious stone the color of the Caribbean Sea—is found on the D.R.'s south coast. Prices vary according to the stone's hue; the rarest and most expensive gems have a milky haze, and the less expensive are solid blue. Amber has been mined extensively between Puerto Plata and Santiago. A fossilization of resin from a prehistoric pine tree, it often encases ancient animal and plant life, from leaves to spiders to tiny lizards. Beware of fakes, which are especially prevalent in street stalls. A reputable dealer can show you how to tell the difference between real larimar and amber and imitations.

Bargaining is both a game and a social activity in the D.R., especially with street vendors and at the stalls in El Mercado Modelo. Vendors are disappointed and perplexed if you don't haggle. They're also tenacious, so unless you really plan to buy, don't even stop to look.

Areas & Malls

SANTO DOMINGO The restored buildings of **La Atarazana,** which is across from Alcazar in the Colonial Zone, are filled with shops, art galleries, restaurants, and bars. One of the main shopping streets in the Zone is **Calle El Conde,** a pedestrian thoroughfare. With the advent of so many restorations, the dull and dusty stores with dated merchandise are giving way to some hip, new shops. However, many of the offerings, including local designer shops, are still of a caliber and cost that the Dominicans can afford. Some of the best shops are on **Calle Duarte** north of the Colonial Zone, between Calle Mella and Avenida de Las Américas. **El Mercado Modelo,** a covered market, borders Calle Mella in the Colonial Zone; vendors here sell a dizzying selection of Dominican crafts. The **Malecón Center,** adjacent to the equally new Hilton Santo Domingo, will house 170 shops, boutiques, and services plus several movie theaters. In the tower above are luxury apartments and Sammy Sosa, in one of the penthouses. **Plaza Central,** between Avenidas Winston Churchill and 27 de Febrero, is where you can find many top international boutiques. **Unicentro,** on Avenida Abraham Lincoln, is a major Santo Domingo mall.

PUNTA CANA **La Galleria,** a shopping and dining complex, has grown like topsy around the little town, church, and schools that have been built on the road to the airport for employees of PuntaCana Resort & Club. It's now a new day-trip destination for visitors in the area. Unique in the country, it has everything from an Oscar de la Renta shop to an art gallery to a Portugese restaurant.

PUERTO PLATA In Puerto Plata, a popular shopping street for costume jewelry and souvenirs is **Calle Beller. Playa Dorada Plaza,** on Calle Duarte at Avenida 30 de Marzo, is a shopping center in the American tradition; stores here sell everything from cigars, rum, coffee, and herbal remedies to ceramics, trinkets, and American clothing brands. The seven showrooms of the **Tourist Bazaar,** on Calle Duarte, are in an old mansion with a patio bar.

LA ROMANA   **Altos de Chavón** is a re-creation of a 16th-century Mediterranean village on the grounds of the Casa de Campo resort, where you can find art galleries, boutiques, and souvenir shops grouped around a cobbled square. Extraspecial are El Club de Cigaro and the rotating art exhibits at the Museo Arqueológico Regional. **La Marina Chavón** has some of the chicest shops in the entire country, including a Jenny Polanco boutique.

Specialty Items

ART   **Casa Jardin** (✉ Balacer Gustavo Medjía Ricart 15, Naco, Santo Domingo ☎ 809/565–7978) is the garden studio of abstract painter Ada Balacer. Works by other women artists are also shown; look for pieces by Yolarda Naranjo, known for her modern work that integrates everything from fiberglass, hair, rocks, and wood to baby dresses. **Galería de Arte Mariano Eckert** (✉ Av. Winston Churchill and Calle Luis F. Tomen, 3rd fl., Evaristo Morales, Santo Domingo ☎ 809/541–7109) focuses on the work of Eckert, an older Dominican artist who's known for his still lifes. **Galería de Arte Nader** (✉ Rafael Augusto Sanchez 22, between Ensanche Piantini and Plaza Andalucia II, Piantini, Santo Domingo ☎ 809/687–6674 or 809/544–0878) showcases top Dominican artists in various media. The gallery staff is well known in Miami and New York and works with Sotheby's. **Lyle O. Reitzel Art Contemporaneo** (✉ Plaza Andalucia II, Piantini, Santo Domingo ☎ 809/227–8361) has, since 1995, specialized in contemporary art and showcases mainly Latin artists, from Mexico, South America, and Spain, and some of the most controversial Dominican visionaries. **Mi Pais** (✉ Calle Villanueva at Antera Mota, Puerto Plata ☎ No phone) is an innovative gallery that showcases paintings and sculptures by such Dominican artists as Orlando Menicucci, Servio Certad, Pedro Terrero, and Celia Vargas Nadel. At **Miró Gallery & Restaurant** (✉ Cabarete Beach, next to O'Shay's, Cabarete ☎ 809/571–0888) you can find rotating exhibitions of contemporary art with an emphasis on Latino artists and photographers, especially from the Dominican Republic and Cuba. Opening soirees are social events; during October's Jazz Festival this is a music venue, too. **Plaza Toledo Bettye's Galeria** (✉ Isabel la Católica 103, Zona Colonial, Santo Domingo ☎ 809/688–7649) sells a fascinating array of artworks, including Haitian vodoo banners, metal sculptures, even souvenirs, chandeliers, and estate jewelry; the American ex-pat owner, Bettye Marshall, has a great eye and can also rent you a room in her B&B.

CLOTHING   **Inspirations** (✉ Calle Principal 1, Cabarete ☎ 809/571–9554) has racks of swimwear (mainly two-piece), cool sundresses, tropical capri pants, sexy sleepwear, and guy things like sandals and Jams. Gifts include Taino-made coasters and wooden boxes with primitive drawings etched on metal. **Plaza Central** (✉ Avs. Winston Churchill and 27 de Febrero, Piantini, Santo Domingo ☎ 809/541–5929) is a major shopping center with a Jenny Polanco shop (an upscale Dominican designer who has incredible white outfits, artistic jewelry, and purses) and other high-end stores.

10

DUTY-FREE ITEMS **Centro de los Héroes** (⊠ Av. George Washington, El Malecón, Santo Domingo) sells liquor, cameras, and the like.

HANDICRAFTS **Collector's Corner Gallery & Gift Shop** (⊠ Plaza Shopping Center, Calle Duarte at Av. 30 de Marzo, Puerto Plata ☎ No phone) has souvenirs, including many made of amber. **Felipe & Co.** (⊠ El Conde 105, Zona Colonial, Santo Domingo ☎ 809/689–5810) has a fascinating assortment of Dominican crafts and artwork, coffee, inexpensive "free spirit" jewelry, and some tropical clothing.

HOME FURNISHINGS **Motif** (⊠ Pedro Clisante 12, Sosúa ☎ 809/571–1999), a new second-floor boutique gallery owned by Lisa Kirkman, is a tasteful mix of high-quality Indonesian-Caribbean furniture and accessories and impressive local artwork. Much of the art and accessories could be carried on a plane, or shipping can be arranged. The exquisite **Nuovo Rinascimento** (⊠ Plazoleta Padre Billini, Zona Colonial, Santo Domingo ☎ 809/686–3387), replete with contemporary furniture and antiques, has a treasure trove of Venetian linens and towels. Shipping can be arranged. The wooden hacienda doors open to a world of white sculptures and an inner courtyard with a lily-pad-dotted pool. Café Bellini offers authentic Italian cuisine in a striking contemporary setting.

JEWELRY **Ambar Tres** (⊠ La Atarazana 3, Zona Colonial, Santo Domingo ☎ 809/688–0474) carries a wide selection of items including high-end jewelry made with amber and larimar, the country's other indigenous, semiprecious stone. If you tour the in-house museum, you'll have a deeper appreciation of the gem. **Harrisons** (⊠ Playa Dorada Plaza, Puerto Plata ☎ 809/586–3933) doesn't sell trinkets but rather high-end jewelry, most likely at better prices than in your hometown. For quality larimar and amber with well-designed settings, many in platinum, this is it. Branches can be found in many touristic zones.

TOBACCO **Cigar King** (⊠ Calle Conde 208, Baguero Bldg., Zona Colonial, Santo Domingo ☎ 809/686–4987) keeps Dominican and Cuban cigars in a temperature-controlled cedar room. **Santo Domingo Cigar Club** (⊠ Renaissance Jaragua Hotel & Casino, Av. George Washington 367, El Malecón, Santo Domingo ☎ 809/221–1483) is a great place to find yourself a good smoke.

Nightlife

★ Santo Domingo's nightlife is vast and ever-changing. Check with the concierges and hip *capitalen os.* Get a copy of the *Vacation Guide* and the newspaper *Touring*—both available free at the tourist office and at hotels—to find out what's happening. Look in the *Santo Domingo News* and the *Puerto Plata News* for listings of events. The Amber Coast—Playa Dorada, but particularly Cabarete—has more than its fair share of clubs, mostly on the beachfront.

Bars & Cafés

SANTO DOMINGO **bobos** (⊠ Calle Hostos 157, Zona Colonial ☎ 809/689–1183) is a happening scene, a contemporary concept in a 400-year-old edifice, with a lantern-lighted terrace. Inverted, colorful umbrellas hang high above

Annual Jazz

IT'S SHADES OF HAVANA in the 1950s, of New York's Harlem in the 1920s, with bearded jazz musicians in berets playing among *cubanos* with white Panama hats and Guayabera shirts. It's a fusion of African percussion and drums—bongos and congos, backed up by marimbas and maracas, sexy songbirds and their piano men. It's rotund tuba players and sweat-stained black shirts as trumpet and sax players blow it out.

Every October, the towns of Sosúa, Cabarete, Puerto Plata, and Santiago are transformed into music venues when the biggest names in Latin jazz hit the north coast, including such legends as Chuck Mangione, Sade, Carlos Santana, Mongo Santa Maria, Chu Cho Valdés, and Arturo Sandoval.

As hot as salsa, the pulsating tropical sounds draw thousands of aficionados, from poor students to black-tie patrons of the arts, who come for the music, the energy, the art exhibits, the educational workshops, the sun and the sea. This is one five-star event that is democratic—most tickets cost about $15.

Sizzling hot nights inevitably climax in impromptu jam sessions at such venues as Miro's Restaurant in Cabarete, the Voodoo Lounge in Sosúa, and Hemingway's Café in Playa Dorada Plaza. In short, the D.R. Jazz Fest is one of the best parties of the year.

Resorts book up early, especially those that are hotbeds of jazz activity, like Sosúa Bay Hotel–Victorian House and Sea Horse Ranch. Check out the festival's Web site for more information: ⊕ www. drjazzfestival.com.

the water sculpture in the front window. Waiters wear long, ochre Indian shirts. Patrons cuddle on the Cambodian bed with silk pillows, for this is a place to feel free—to dance, to sing out. A tapas menu offers sushi and Thai, Cambodian, and Dominican specialities. Jazz is heard on Wednesday night, and art exhibits are bimonthly. **Cigarro Café** (⊠ Grand Hotel Linda, Av. Máximo Gómez and Av. 27 de Febrero, Gazcue ☎ 809/563–5000 Ext. 7166) is the place to go for high-quality cigars, coffee, and cognac with an appealing assortment of gadgets for the smoker. Clients go between here and the hotel's piano bar, where you can still dance cheek-to-cheek. **Doubles** (⊠ Calle Arzobispo Meriño 54, Zona Colonial ☎ 809/688–3833) looks like a friend's place— that is, if you have a friend who has a hip sense of interior design and would mix rattan furniture, antiques, subdued lighting, and candles in a space that's centuries old. Spanish tiles add interest to this atmospheric piano bar. **Marrakesh Café & Bar** (⊠ Hotel Santo Domingo) is where a sophisticated after-work crowd gathers for its American and international music (jazz on Monday) and Casablanca style. Complimentary tapas come to the table, and you can get top-shelf liquors. Don't think of the sandwich when you visit **Monté Cristo** (⊠ Av. Jose Armado Soler at Av. Abraham Lincoln, Serralles ☎ 809/542–5000), although the crowds can sandwich you in at this pub. The clientele spans the decades, music crosses the Americas, and there's a small dance floor. Both hot

10

and cold tapas and sandwiches are served. It's open after work until whenever, usually 4 AM, and there's no cover. It's the only club where there's anything happening on a Tuesday night, which is a wine tasting. **Praia** (✉ Gustavo Mejia Ricart 74, Ensanche Naco ☎ 809/540–8753) is a bar and wine lounge, popular with rich Dominicans and tourists. The contemporary design utilizes glass and steel for a cool, minimalist decor. Music is modern and electronic; drinks are expensive. **Punto Y Corcho** (✉ Av. Abraham Lincoln at Gustavo Mejía Ricart, Piantini ☎ 809/683–0533), on Plaza Andalucia, is where wine (by the glass and bottle) and local and international liquors are the order of the night. This is a great date and late-night spot, and it tends to appeal to a more mature, sophisticated type. The **Trio Cafe** (✉ Av. Abraham Lincoln N 12A, at Plaza Castilla Ensanche, Naco ☎ 809/412–0964) is one of those places where the cool, older crowd comes to graze, drink, and dance, even though there's no real dance floor. They just stand around and groove, and chances are they will make new friends—as might you.

NORTH COAST **Hemingway's Cafe** (✉ Playa Dorada Plaza, Puerto Plata ☎ 809/320–2230) has long been the rockin' spot for the young in spirit who love to party. There's rock or reggae by DJs or live bands, but only big-name merengue bands elicit a cover charge. On Saturday night there's a Latin fiesta, and on Thursday the mike is taken over by karaoke singers. The kitchen closes at 2 AM and serves American-style, fun food and good burgers, with fajitas a specialty. **Lax** (✉ Cabarete Beach, Cabarete ☎ 809/710–0569) is a perennially popular open-air bar that really comes alive by night. You can sit in the sand in lounge chairs or jump into the action under the palapa, where a DJ will be spinning madly or a live band will be rockin'. There's good grazing chow, too, and drinks come from the blenders and in pitchers. **Voodoo Lounge & Voodoo Grill** (✉ In front of Sosúa Bay Hotel, Sosúa ☎ 809/571–3559) is an upscale spot in Sosúa, owned by Canadian pop singer Michael Behm, who performs here, and it's priced to attract a higher caliber of clientele. The super stereo system plays techno music, European hits, and retro sounds, and then there's karaoke night. TVs in the bar downstairs tune in to sporting events. Co-owner Ken Jones has inaugurated food service, including creative pastas as well as a litany of appetizers.

Casinos

Well into the wee small hours, casinos keep the action hot. Gambling here is more a sideline than a raison d'être. Most casinos are in the larger hotels of Santo Domingo, a couple in Playa Dorada, and more now in Punta Cana. All offer blackjack, craps, and roulette and are generally open daily from 3 PM to 4 AM. You must be 18 to enter, and jackets are required at the chic casinos in the capital. In Santo Domingo, several upscale hotels have casinos: Barceló Gran Hotel Lina Spa; Meliá Santo Domingo Casino; Hispaniola Hotel & Casino (attracts a younger crowd); Renaissance Jaragua Hotel; and the Hilton Santo Domingo.

On the north coast, the Jack Tar Village Hotel in Puerto Plata and Breezes in Cabarete both have big, busy casinos, as does the Occidental Allegro Playa Dorada.

SANTO DOMINGO **Atlantis World Casino** (✉ George Washington 218, El Malecón ☎ 809/688–808) is American-friendly with shiny new slots that accept dollars. Although there's no charge to enter the gaming room, the table minimums are higher than most, so the casino attracts a more upscale crowd.

LA ROMANA **Casino Santana Beach** (✉ Santana Beach, between La Romana and San Pedro Macoris ☎ 809/412–1104 or 809/412–1051) is surprisingly sophisticated for a touristy beachside casino. It's right on the beach; there's a tropical terrace and an aquarium behind the roulette wheel. Drinks are on the house while you play, be it blackjack, Caribbean stud poker, or the slots. The live music is nice, not crazy.

Dance Clubs

Dancing is as much a part of the culture here as eating and drinking. As in other Latin countries, after dinner it's not a question of *whether* people will go dancing but *where* they'll go. Move with the rhythm of the merengue and the pulsing beat of salsa (adopted from neighboring Puerto Rico). Among the young, the word is that there's no better place to party in the Caribbean than Santo Domingo's Colonial Zone. Almost every resort in Puerto Plata and Punta Cana has live entertainment, dancing, or both. Many clubs stay open until dawn or until the last couple gives it up.

SANTO DOMINGO **Loft** (✉ Tiradentes 44, Naco ☎ 809/732–4016) is a modern and exclusive lounge with a grazing menu that includes sushi, bruschetta, hot wings, and nachos; later on, it segues into a large and popular disco with a great sound system and lighting. **Moon** (✉ At Calle Hostos and Arzobispo Nouel, Zona Colonial ☎ 809/686–5176) is a smaller club dedicated to electronic music and reggae. It generally appeals to the younger 18- to 24-year-olds. **Nowhere Bar** (✉ Calle Hostos 205, Zona Colonial ☎ 809/685–8290) is hot and the crowd mostly young and affluent, but all ages stop by, like Americans in college here, who have adopted this place. They hang on the first level, where the latest music from the States—plus hip-hop and house—is played. A DJ playing Dominican music packs in the locals on the second floor. Thursday night is the infamous Ladies Night. You can party until 6 AM on Friday and Saturday, when local bands take the stage. The Kitchen is now serving, or you can have your meal—American and Dominican bar food as well as gourmet items—in a fanciful box, anywhere at Nowhere. An artistic renovation of a 16th-century, two-story mansion, this is the bar seen in the movie *Miami Vice* (2006).

NORTH COAST **Crazy Moon** (✉ Paradise Beach Club & Casino, Playa Dorada ☎ 809/320–3663) is a megaspace that's often filled to capacity. Latin music and hip-hop mixed with Euro sounds are popular. Rest up from time to time at the horseshoe bar, so that you can keep the pace until the wee small hours of the *mañana*. **Gravity** (✉ Playa Nacho Resort, Playa Dorada ☎ 809/320–6226) doesn't crank up until after midnight, but it keeps rolling until 4 AM. Locals and tourists hip-hop together. **Mangu** (✉ Jack Tar Village, Playa Dorada ☎ 809/320–3800) is the newest late-night disco in Playa Dorada, so all of the *turistas* check it out. What's novel is that choreographed dancers perform. **Onno's Bar** (✉ Cabarete Beach,

10

Cabarete ☎ 809/571–0461), a serious party place, is usually wall-to-wall and back-to-back as the young and fit pack the dance floor and groove to techno bands.

Exploring the Dominican Republic

Santo Domingo

Parque Independencia separates the old city from the modern Santo Domingo, a sprawling, noisy city with a population of close to 2 million. (Note: Hours and admission charges to sights are erratic.)

Numbers in the margin correspond to points of interest on the Santo Domingo map.

Fodor'sChoice ★ Spanish civilization in the New World began in Santo Domingo's 12-block **Zona Colonial.** As you stroll its narrow streets, it's easy to imagine this old city as it was when the likes of Columbus, Cortés, and Ponce de León walked the cobblestones, pirates sailed in and out, and colonists were settling themselves. Tourist brochures tout that "history comes alive here"—a surprisingly truthful statement. Every Thursday to Sunday night at 8:30, a typical folklorico show is staged at Parque Colón and Plaza Espana.

A fun horse and carriage ride throughout the Zone costs $20 for an hour. The steeds are no thoroughbreds, but they clip right along, though any commentary will be in Spanish. The drivers usually hang out in front of the Sofitel Nicolas Ovando. History buffs will want to spend a day exploring the many "firsts" of our continent. You can get a free walking-tour map and brochures in English at the Secretaria de Estado de Turismo office at Parque Colón (Columbus Park), where you may be approached by freelance, English-speaking guides, who will want to make it all come alive for you. They'll work enthusiastically for $20 an hour for four persons. Do wear comfortable shoes.

☾ ❹ **Alcazar de Colón.** The castle of Don Diego Colón, built in 1517, has 40-inch-thick coral-limestone walls. The Renaissance-style structure, with its balustrade and double row of arches, has strong Moorish, Gothic, and Isabelline influences. The 22 rooms are furnished in a style to which the viceroy of the island would have been accustomed—right down to the dishes and the viceregal shaving mug. ⊠ *Plaza de España, off Calle Emiliano Tejera at foot of Calle Las Damas, Zona Colonial* ☎ *809/687–5361* ☒ *RD$20* ☉ *Mon. and Wed.–Fri. 9–5, Sat. 9–4, Sun. 9–1.*

❼ **Calle Las Damas.** The Street of the Ladies was named after the elegant ladies of the court who, in the Spanish tradition, promenaded in the evening. Here you can see a sundial dating from 1753 and the Casa de los Jesuitas, which houses a fine research library for colonial history as well as the Institute for Hispanic Culture; admission is free, and it's open weekdays from 8 to 4:30.

❾ **Casa de Bastidas.** There's a lovely inner courtyard here with tropical plants and galleries for temporary exhibitions. ⊠ *Calle Las Damas off Calle El Conde, Zona Colonial* ☎ *No phone* ☒ *Free* ☉ *Tues.–Sun. 9–5.*

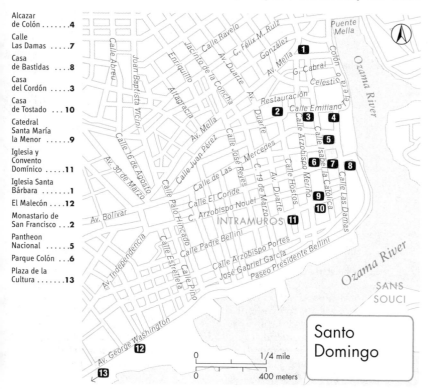

Santo
Domingo

❸ Casa del Cordón. This structure, built in 1503, is the western hemisphere's oldest surviving stone house. Columbus's son, Diego Colón, viceroy of the colony, and his wife lived here until the Alcazar was finished. It was in this house, too, that Sir Francis Drake was paid a ransom to prevent him from totally destroying the city. ✉ *Calle Emiliano Tejera and Calle Isabel la Católica, within the Banco Popular, Zona Colonial* ☎ *No phone* 💲 *Free* ⊙ *Weekdays 8:30–4:30.*

⓫ Casa de Tostado. The house was built in the early 16th century and was the residence of writer Don Francisco Tostado. Note its unique twin Gothic windows. It now houses the Museo de la Familia Dominicana (Museum of the Dominican Family), which has exhibits on well-heeled 19th-century Dominican society. The house, garden, and antiquities have all been restored. ✉ *22 Calle Padre Bellini, near Calle Arzobispo Meriño, Zona Colonial* ☎ *809/689–5000* 💲 *RD$50* ⊙ *Thurs.–Tues. 9–2.*

❿ Catedral Santa María la Menor. The coral-limestone facade of the first cathedral in the New World towers over the south side of the Parque Colón. Spanish workmen began building the cathedral in 1514, but left to search for gold in Mexico. The church was finally finished in 1540. Its facade is composed of architectural elements from the late Gothic to the lavish plateresque style. Inside, the high altar is made of hammered silver. At this writing, a museum was being built for the cathedral's treasures. ✉ *Calle Arzobispo Meriño, Zona Colonial* ☎ *809/689–1920* 📷 *Free* ☉ *Mon.–Sat. 9–4; Sun. masses begin at 6 AM.*

⑫ **Iglesia y Convento Domínico.** This graceful building with a rose window is still a Dominican Church and Convent, founded in 1510. In 1538, Pope Paul III visited here and was so impressed with the lectures on theology that he granted the church and convent the title of university, making it the oldest institution of higher learning in the New World. ✉ *Calle Padre Bellini and Av. Duarte, Zona Colonial* ☎ *809/682–3780* 📷 *Free* ☉ *Tues.–Sun. 9–6.*

❶ **Iglesia Santa Bárbara.** This combination church and fortress, the only one of its kind in Santo Domingo, was completed in 1562. ✉ *Av. Mella, between Calle Isabel la Católica and Calle Arzobispo Meriño, Zona Colonial* ☎ *809/682–3307* 📷 *Free* ☉ *Weekdays 8–noon; Sun. masses begin at 6 AM.*

⑬ **El Malecón.** Avenida George Washington, better known as the Malecón, runs along the Caribbean and has tall palms, cafés, hotels, and sea breezes.

❷ **Monasterio de San Francisco.** Constructed between 1512 and 1544, the San Francisco Monastery contained the church, convent, and hospital of the Franciscan order. Sir Francis Drake's demolition squad significantly damaged the building in 1586, and in 1673 an earthquake nearly finished the job, but when it's floodlit at night, the eerie ruins are dramatic indeed. The Spanish government has donated money to turn this into a beautiful cultural center, but work still had not yet begun at this writing. ✉ *Calle Hostos at Calle Emiliano, Zona Colonial* ☎ *809/687–4722.*

❺ **Pantheon Nacional.** The National Pantheon (circa 1714) was once a Jesuit monastery and later a theater. The real curiosity here is the military guard who stays as still as the statues, despite the schoolchildren who try to make him flinch. ✉ *Calle Las Damas, near Calle de Las Mercedes, Zona Colonial* ☎ *No phone* 📷 *Free* ☉ *Mon.–Sat. 10–5.*

❻ **Parque Colón.** The huge statue of Christopher Columbus in the park named after him dates from 1897 and is the work of French sculptor Gilbert. Like all the parks in the Zona Colonial, this one has been restored. ✉ *El Conde at Arzobispo Meriño, Zona Colonial.*

⑬ **Plaza de la Cultura.** Landscaped lawns, modern sculptures, and sleek buildings make up the Plaza de la Cultura. There are several museums and a theater here. The works of 20th-century Dominican and foreign artists are displayed in the **Museo de Arte Moderno** (☎ 809/682–8260). Native sons include Elvis Aviles, an abstract painter whose works have a lot of texture. His art combines Spanish influences with Taíno Indian and other Dominican symbols. Tony Capellan is one of the best-known artists, representing the D.R. in major international exhibitions. The **Museo del Hombre Dominicano** (☎ 809/687–3623) traces the migrations of Indians from South America through the Caribbean islands. The **Teatro Nacional** (☎ 809/687–3191) stages fascinating performances in Spanish only, but don't let that stop you. When in Rome, you would go to an Italian opera, right?. ✉ *Museo de Arte Moderno and Museo del Hombre Dominicano RD$20 each, Museo de Historia Natural RD$3* ⊙ *Tues.–Sun. 10–5.*

The East Coast

Las Américas Highway (built by the dictator Trujillo so his son could race his sports cars) runs east along the coast from Santo Domingo to La Romana—a two-hour drive. Midway are the well-established beach resorts, Juan Dolio, and Sammy Sosa's hometown, San Pedro de Macoris. East of La Romana are Punta Cana and Bávaro, glorious beaches on the sunrise side of the island. Along the way is Higüey, an undistinguished city notable only for its giant concrete cathedral and shrine (someone had a vision of the Virgin Mary here), which resembles a pinched McDonald's arch.

Numbers in the margin correspond to points of interest on the Dominican Republic map.

★ ⓯ **Altos de Chavón.** This re-creation of a 16th-century Mediterranean village sits on a bluff overlooking the Río Chavón, about 3 mi (5 km) east of the main facilities of Casa de Campo. There are cobblestone streets lined with lanterns, wrought-iron balconies, wooden shutters, and courtyards swathed with bougainvillea, and **Iglesia St. Stanislaus,** the romantic setting for many a Casa de Campo wedding. More than a museum piece, this village is a place where artists live, work, and play. Dominican and international painters, sculptors, and artisans come here to teach sculpture, pottery, silk-screen printing, weaving, dance, and music at the school, which is affiliated with New York's Parsons School of Design. They work in their studios and crafts shops selling their finished wares. The village also has an archaeological museum and five restaurants. A 5,000-seat **amphitheater** (☎ 809/523–2424 for Kandela tickets ⊕ www. kandela.com.do) now features *Kandela,* a spectacular musical extravaganza showcasing the island's sensuous Afro-Caribbean dance moves, music, and culture. Concerts and celebrity performances by such singers as Julio Iglesias, his son Enrique, and the Pet Shop Boys share the amphitheater's schedule of events.

⓰ **Isla Saona.** Off the east coast of Hispaniola lies this island, now a national park inhabited by sea turtles, pigeons, and other wildlife. Caves here were once used by Indians. The beaches are beautiful, and legend has it that Columbus once strayed ashore here. Getting here, on catamarans and other excursion boats, is half the fun.

⓮ **San Pedro de Macorís.** The national sport and the national drink are both well represented in this city, an hour or so east of Santo Domingo. Some of the country's best baseball games are played in Tetelo Vargas Stadium. Many Dominican baseball stars have their roots here, including George Bell, Tony Fernandez, Jose Río, and Sammy Sosa. The Macorís Rum distillery is on the eastern edge of the city. During the 1920s this was a very important town, and mansions from that era are being restored by the Office of Cultural Patrimony, as are some remaining vestiges of 16th-century architecture and the town's cathedral. Outside town is Juan Dolio, a beach and resort area popular with Dominicans and foreign visitors.

10

The North Coast

The Autopista Duarte ultimately leads (a three-to four-hour drive) from Santo Domingo to the north coast, sometimes called the Amber Coast because of its large, rich amber deposits. The coastal area around Puerto Plata, notably Playa Dorada, is a region of well-established, all-inclusive resorts and developments; the north coast has more than 70 mi (110 km) of beaches, with condominiums and villas going up fast. The farther east you go from Puerto Plata and Sosúa, the prettier and less spoiled the scenery becomes. The autopista runs past Cabarete, a village that's a popular windsurfing haunt, and Playa Grande, which has a miraculously unspoiled white-sand beach.

⑳ Mt. Isabel de Torres. Southwest of Puerto Plata, this mountain soars 2,600 feet above sea level and is notable for its a huge statue of Christ. Up there also are botanical gardens, which the government has promised to restore. Cable cars take you to the top for a spectacular view. Know that they usually wait until the cars are filled to capacity before going up—and that's cozy. ⊠ *Off Autopista Duarte, follow signs* ☎ *No phone* 🎫 *Cable car RD$100* ⊘ *Cable car Mon., Tues., and Thurs.–Sun. 9–5.*

⑲ Puerto Plata. Although sleeping for decades, this was a dynamic city in its heyday and it's coming back. You can get a feeling for this past in the magnificent Victorian gazebo in the central **Parque Independencia.** On Puerto Plata's own Malecón, the **Fortaleza de San Felipe** protected the city from many a pirate attack and was later used as a political prison. The nearby **lighthouse** has been restored. Big changes are afoot in this town, which is just realizing what it needs to do to become a tourist destination. The Office of Cultural Patrimony, which has done an admirable job of pulling the Zona Colonial from the darkness to a place to be seen, is at work on Puerto Plata. Simultaneously, a group of private business owners and investors have developed a long-term plan for beautifying this city, which has hundreds of classic, wooden gingerbread buildings. Mansions, including Casa Olivores and the Tapounet Family home, are being restored; a Victorian mansion on Calle Jose del Carmen is now a gallery and coffee shop. Nearby, the second floor of the Playa Dorada Plaza has been transformed into a 10,000-square-foot convention center and is hosting local and international conventions.

The **Museo de Ambar Dominicano** (Dominican Amber Museum) is in a lovely old galleried mansion. It both displays and sells the D.R.'s national stone, semiprecious, translucent amber, which is actually fossilized pine resin that dates from about 50 million years ago, give or take a few millennia. Shops on the museum's first floor sell amber, souvenirs, and ceramics. Dominican amber is considered to be the finest in the world. If you buy from street vendors for a low price, you're probably buying plastic. ⊠ *Calle Duarte 61* ☎ *809/586–2848* 🎫 *RD$15* ⊘ *Mon.–Sat. 9–5.*

Ocean World is a multimillion-dollar adventure park in Cofresi. It's a wonderful aquatic adventure with a sea lion show and snorkel reef tour, interactive dolphin programs, exotic birds, sharks, and even swimming tigers in their own grotto. Lunch, looking out to sea, is delightful. You no longer have to come on a tour, but you must make advance reservations and decide among various tour options, which can almost triple the regular admission cost. If you're staying in the Puerto Plata or Cabarete area, ask at your hotel for tour schedules. Children must be six to do the dolphin swim. A marina is soon coming. ✉ *In front of Hotel Sun Village, on autopista to Santiago, Confresi* ☎ *809/291–1000 or 809/291–1111* ⊕ *www.ocean-world.info* ✐ *$55–$145* ☉ *Daily 9–5.*

⑰ Samaná. Back in 1824, a sailing vessel called the *Turtle Dove*, carrying several hundred escaped American slaves, was blown ashore in Samaná. The survivors settled and prospered, and today their descendants number several thousand. The churches here are Protestant; the worshippers live in villages called Bethesda, Northeast, and Philadelphia; and the language spoken is an odd 19th-century form of English mixed with Spanish.

Sportfishing at Samaná is considered to be among the best in the world. In addition, about 3,000 humpback whales winter off the coast of Samaná from December to March. Major whale-watching expeditions are being organized and should boost the region's economy without scaring away the world's largest mammals. Postcard-perfect Playa Las Terrenas is a remote stretch of gorgeous, pristine Atlantic beaches on the north coast, attracting surfers and windsurfers, the young and offbeat. There's a strong French influence here, with modest seafood restaurants, a dusty but burgeoning main street in the town, a small airfield, a couple of all-inclusive resorts, and several congenial smaller hotels right on the beach. If you're happy just hanging out, drinking rum, and soaking up the sun, this is the place. A highway connecting Samaná to Santo Domingo and an airport were under construction at this writing.

⑱ Sosúa. This small community was settled during World War II by 600 Austrian and German Jews. After the war many of them returned to Europe or went to the United States, and most who remained married Dominicans. Only a few Jewish families reside in the community today, and there's only the original one-room wooden synagogue.

Sosúa is called Puerto Plata's little sister and consists of two communities—El Batey, the modern hotel development, and Los Charamicos, the old quarter—separated by a cove and one of the island's prettiest beaches. The sand is soft and white, the water crystal clear and calm. The walkway above the beach is packed with tents filled with souvenirs, pizzas, and even clothing for sale—a jarring note. The town had developed a reputation for prostitution, but much is being done to eliminate that and to clean up the more garish elements. Upscale condos and hotels are springing up, and the up-and-coming Dominican families are coming back to the big houses on the bay.

Museo Judío Sosúa chronicles the fascinating immigration and settlement of the Jewish refugees in the 1940s. The adjacent synagogoue sees many Jewish couples from abroad marry. ✉ *Calle Dr. Rosen at David Stern* ☎ *809/571–1386* ✐ *RD$75* ☉ *Weekdays 9–1 and 2–4.*

The Cibao Valley

The heavily trafficked four-lane highway north from Santo Domingo, known as the Autopista Duarte, cuts through the lush banana plantations, rice and tobacco fields, and royal poinciana trees of the Cibao Valley. Along the road are stands where for a few pesos you can buy pineapples, mangoes, avocados, *chicharrones* (fried pork rinds), and fresh-fruit drinks.

㉓ Jarabacoa. Nature lovers should consider a trip to Jarabacoa, in the mountainous region known rather wistfully as the Dominican Alps. There's little to do in the town itself but eat and rest up for excursions on foot, horseback, or by motorbike taxi to the surrounding waterfalls and forests—quite incongruous in such a tropical country. Other activities include adventure tours, particularly white-water rafting or canoe trips, jeep safaris, and paragliding. Accommodations in the area are rustic but homey.

㉒ La Vega Vieja. Founded in 1495 by Columbus, La Vega is the site of one of the oldest settlements in the New World. You may find the tour of the ruins of the original settlement, Old La Vega, rewarding. About 3 mi (5 km) north of La Vega is Santo Cerro (Holy Mount), site of a miraculous apparition of the Virgin and therefore many local pilgrimages. The Convent of La Merced is here, and the views of the Cibao Valley are breathtaking. The town's remarkable Concepción de la Vega Church was constructed in 1992 to commemorate the 500th anniversary of the discovery of America. The unusual modern Gothic style—all curvaceous concrete columns, arches, and buttresses—is striking.

La Vega is also celebrated for its Carnival, featuring haunting devil masks. These papier-mâché creations are intricate, fanciful gargoyles painted in surreal colors; spiked horns and real cows' teeth lend an eerie authenticity. Several artisans work in dark, cramped studios throughout the area; their skills have been passed down for generations.

㉑ Santiago. The second city of the D.R., where many past presidents were born, sits about 90 mi (145 km) northwest of Santo Domingo and is about an hour's drive from Puerto Plata and 90 minutes from Cabarete via the scenic mountain road. An original route from centuries past, the four-lane highway between Santiago and Puerto Plata is dotted with sugar mills. The Office of Cultural Patrimony is overseeing their restoration. This industrial center has a surprisingly charming, provincial feel; the women of Santiago are considered among the country's most beautiful. High on a plateau, a massive monument honoring the restoration of the republic guards the entrance to the city. Traditional yet progressive, Santiago is still relatively new to the tourist scene but already has several thriving restaurants. It's definitely worth setting aside some time to explore the city. Some colonial-style buildings—with wrought-iron details and tiled porticos—date from as far back as the 1500s. Many homes reflect a Victorian influence, with the requisite gingerbread latticework and fanciful colors. Santiago is the island's cigar-making center; the Fuente factory is here, though the cigars cannot be bought on the island (if you see them for sale on the streets, they are counterfeit).

You can gain an appreciation for the art and skill of Dominican cigar making by taking a tour of **E. León Jimenes Tabacalera** (⊠ Av. 27 de

Febrero, Villa Progresso ☎ 809/563–1111 or 809/535–5555). A tour takes approximately 90 minutes, and the factory is open daily from 9 to 5.

Fodor'sChoice
★ Without question, the **Centro León** is a world-class cultural center for the Dominican arts. A postmodern building with an interior space full of light from a crystal dome, the center includes several attractions, including a multimedia biodiversity show, a museum dedicated to the history of the D.R., a simulated local market, a dramatic showcase of Dominican art and sculpture, galleries for special exhibits, a sculpture garden, an aviary, classrooms, and a replica of the León family's first cigar factory, where a dozen cigar rollers are turning out handmade cigars. There's even a first-rate cafeteria. ⊠ *Ave. 27 de Febrero 146, Villa Progresso* ☎ *809/582–2315* ⊕ *www.centroleon.org.do* ☞ *RD$50, RD$150 guides in English* ⊙ *Exhibitions Tues.–Sun. 9–6, public areas daily 9–9.*

The Southwest

㉕ Barahona. The drive from Santo Domingo zigs and zags through small towns, passing coco and banana plantations until you get on Carretera Azua, a fine highway with mountain views and fences of bougainvillea hiding fields of peppers and flowers. You can bathe in the cascades of icy mountain rivers or in hot thermal springs surrounded by dense foliage, *llanai* vines, and fruit trees. Barahona can be a tropical Garden of Eden.

㉔ Lago Enriquillo. The largest lake in the Antilles is near the Haitian border. The salt lake is also the lowest point in the Antilles: 114 feet below sea level. It encircles wild, arid, and thorny islands that serve as sanctuaries for such exotic birds and reptiles as flamingoes, iguanas, and caimans—the indigenous crocodile. The area is targeted by the government for improvements and infrastructure designed for ecotourists, but progress continues to be slow.

DOMINICAN REPUBLIC ESSENTIALS

To research prices, get advice from other travelers, and book travel arrangements, visit www.fodors.com.

Transportation

BY AIR

INTERNATIONAL: The following airlines provide service from the United States: American Airlines/American Eagle, Continental, Copa (to Santo Domingo only, via Panama), Delta, Jet Blue (to Santiago and Santo Domingo only), Spirit (to Santo Domingo only), and US Airways. Providing service from Europe are Air Europa, Air France, Iberia, and Lufthansa. Pan Am flies to San Juan; Air Caraïbes connects to the French West Indies; LIAT goes down-island, mainly to the English-speaking isles. Air Canada flies to Toronto.

Many visitors to the D.R., particularly into Punta Cana, fly nonstop on charter flights direct from the East Coast, Midwest, and Canada. These charters are part of a package and can only be booked through a travel agent.

🛈 **Air Canada** ☎ 881/333-0111. **Air Caraïbes** ☎ 590/82-47-00 in Guadeloupe. **American Airlines/American Eagle** ☎ 809/200-5151. **Continental** ☎ 809/262-1060. **Copa** ☎ 809/472-2672. **Delta** ☎ 809/200-9191. **Iberia** ☎ 809/508-7979. **Jet Blue** ☎ 809/233-8239. **LIAT** ☎ 809/621-8888.

10

Lufthansa ☎ 809/689-9625. **Pan Am** ☎ 809/227-0330. **SPIRIT** ☎ 809/381-4111 or 212/599-1171. **US Airways** ☎ 809/540-0505 or 800/428-4322.

DOMESTIC: Aerodomar offers regular flights between Santo Domingo and Samaná. Air Century, flying out of Herrara Airport in Santo Domingo, offers charters, transfers, and sightseeing. Air Taxi has charter planes for trips around the island or to neighboring islands. Caribar has both planes and helicopters for charter and offers general air service, ambulance service, and aerial photography trips. Helidosa takes passengers where they want to go and has aerial sightseeing excursions, too. Takeoff Destination Service has flights between Santo Domingo (Herrera Airport) and Punta Cana, Puerto Plata, and Samaná, as well as a number of day-trip excursions.

⊠ **Aerodomar** ⊠ Herrera Airport, Santo Domingo ☎ 809/567-1195. **Air Century** ⊠ Herrara Airport, Santo Domingo ☎ 809/566-0888 ⊕ www.aircentury.com. **Air Taxi** ⊠ Herrera Airport, Santo Domingo ☎ 809/227-8333 or 809/567-1555. **Caribar** ⊠ Herrara Airport, Santo Domingo ☎ 809/567-3900 ⊠ La Romana–Casa de Campo Airport, La Romana ☎ 809/980-9906. **Helidosa Helicopters** ⊠ Punta Cana ☎ 809/688-0744, 809/552-6066, or 809/552-6069. **Takeoff Destination Service** ☎ 809/552-1333 ⊕ www.takeoffweb.com.

AIRPORTS & TRANSFERS: The Dominican Republic has five major airports. The busiest are Las Américas International Airport, about 20 mi (32 km) outside Santo Domingo; Puerto Plata International Gregorio Luperon Airport, about 7 mi (11 km) east of Playa Dorada; and Punta Cana International Airport. The La Romana–Casa de Campo International Airport and Cibao International Airport in Santiago are also getting an increasing number of international flights.

If you book a package through a travel agent, your airport transfers will almost certainly be included in the price you pay. Look for your company's sign as you exit baggage claim. If you book independently, then you may have to take a taxi or rent a car.

Anticipate long lines and be sure to give yourself a full two hours for international check-in.

✈ **Cibao International Airport** STI ⊠ Santiago ☎ 809/582-4894. **Las Américas International Airport** SDQ ⊠ Santo Domingo ☎ 809/549-0450. **Gregorio Luperon International Airport** POP ⊠ Puerto Plata ☎ 809/586-0107 or 809/586-0219. **Punta Cana International Airport** (PUJ) ☎ 809/686-8790. **La Romana/Casa de Campo International Airport** (LRM) ☎ 809/556-5565.

BY BUS

Privately owned air-conditioned buses are the cheapest way to get around the country. They make regular runs to Santiago, Puerto Plata, Punta Cana, and other destinations from Santo Domingo. You can make reservations for Metro Buses, Caribe Tours, and Espresso Bavaro. One-way bus fare from Santo Domingo to Puerto Plata is about $7.50, and it takes 3½ hours; the fare to Punta Cana (Bavaro) is also $7.50, and it takes about 3½ hours. Metro's deluxe buses have more of an upscale clientele; although the coffee and cookies are complimentary, there are no movies. Caribe sometimes shows bilingual movies, keeps the air-conditioning frigid, and is favored by locals and families; buses are often filled to capacity, especially on weekends and holidays. Espresso Bavaro buses depart from Avenida Máximo Gómez–Plaza Los Girasoles; the buses are not the best, but the price is right and the American movies current. If you're going to one of the Punta Cana resorts, you get off at the stop before the last and take a cab waiting at the taxi stand.

Frequent service from Santo Domingo to the town of La Romana is provided by Express Bus. Buses depart from Revelos Street in front of Enriquillo Park every hour on the hour from 5 AM to 9 PM; the schedule is exactly the same from La Romana, where they leave from Camino Avenue. In Santo Domingo, there's no office and no phone, but a ticket-taker will take your $4 just before departure. There's general chaos, a crazy kind of congestion (allow time in a taxi), horns blowing, and diesel fumes, but it all comes together. Don't be dismayed; remember that you're spending $4 instead of $120 on a taxi. Travel time is about 1¼ hours, and if luck is with you you'll get the larger bus, which will show a first-rate American movie. Once in town you can take a taxi from the bus stop to Casa de Campo ($9) or Sunscape Casa del Mar or Iberostar Dominicus ($12).

🚩 **Caribe Tours** ☎ 809/221-4422 ⊕ www.caribetours.com.do. **Espresso Bavaro** ☎ 809/682-9670. **Metro Buses** ☎ 809/566-7126 in Santo Domingo, 809/586-6062 in Puerto Plata, 809/587-4711 in Santiago.

BY CAR

Driving in the D.R. can be a harrowing experience; because of that (and also because of the high cost), we don't recommend that the typical vacationer rent a car. Many Dominicans drive recklessly, and their cars are often in bad shape (missing headlights, tail lights). It's best if you don't drive outside the major cities at night. If you must, use extreme caution, especially on narrow, unlighted mountain roads. Watch out for pedestrians, bicycles, motorbikes (some without headlights), and the occasional stray cow, goat, or horse.

Obtain a good road map from your rental agency, and consult the agent there or your hotel concierge about routes. Although some roads are still full of potholes, the route between Santo Domingo and Santiago is a four-lane divided highway, and the road between Santiago and Puerto Plata is a smooth blacktop. The highway from Casa de Campo to Punta Cana is also a fairly smooth ride. Surprisingly, many of the scenic secondary roads, such as the "high road" between Playa Dorada and Santiago, are in good shape. Driving is on the right. The 80-kph (50-mph) speed limit is enforced: there's even radar in areas like Punta Cana.

Fill up—and keep an eye on—the tank; gas stations are few and far between in rural areas. Gas prices are high by U.S. standards, nearly $4 a gallon. Make certain that attendants don't reach for the super pump. You don't need to be putting that expensive liquid in a rental car.

Most major companies have outlets at Las Américas Airport outside Santo Domingo and at Gregorio Luperon International Airport in Puerto Plata, the airports of choice for most independent travelers who are likely to rent cars. If you want to rent a car for a day of exploring, you can often do so at a car-rental desk at your resort and have it delivered to you there.

🚩 Major Agencies **Avis** ✉ Las Américas Airport ☎ 809/549-0468 ✉ Gregorio Luperon International Airport, Puerto Plata ☎ 809/586-0214. **Budget** ✉ Las Américas Airport ☎ 809/549-0351 ✉ Gregorio Luperon International Airport, Puerto Plata ☎ 809/586-0413. **Hertz** ✉ Las Américas Airport ☎ 809/549-0454 ✉ Puerto Plata ☎ 809/586-0200. **National** ✉ Las Américas Airport ☎ 809/549-0763 ✉ Gregorio Luperon International Airport, Puerto Plata ☎ 809/586-0285.

🚩 Local Agencies **McAuto Rental Car** ✉ Las Américas Airport ☎ 809/549-8911 ⊕ www.mccarrental.com. **McBeal** ✉ Santo Domingo ☎ 809/688-6518. **Nelly Rent-a-Car** ✉ Las Américas Airport ☎ 809/530-0036, 800/526-6684 in U.S.

BY PUBLIC TRANSPORTATION

Motoconchos are a popular, inexpensive mode of transportation in such areas as Puerto Plata, Sosúa, Cabarete, and Jarabacoa. You can flag down one of these motorbikes along rural roads and in town; rates vary from RD$35 per person for a short run, but have gone up to as much as RD$100 to RD$150 between Cabarete and Sosúa (double after 6 PM).

BY TAXI

Taxis, which are government-regulated, line up outside hotels and restaurants. They're unmetered, and the minimum fare within Santo Domingo is about $6, but you can bargain for less if you order a taxi away from the major hotels; albeit more ex-

10

pensive, hotel taxis are also the nicest and the safest option. Freelance taxis aren't allowed to pick up from hotels, so they hang out on the street in front of them. They can be half the cost per ride depending on the distance. By all means, avoid unmarked street taxis, particularly in Santo Domingo. Carry some small bills, because drivers rarely seem to have change.

Recommendable radio-taxi companies in Santo Domingo are Tecni-Taxi (which also operates in Puerto Plata) and Apolo. Tecni is the cheapest, quoting RD$80 as a minimum per trip, Apolo RD$90. Hiring a taxi by the hour—with unlimited stops and a minimum of two hours—is often a better option if you're doing a substantial sightseeing trip. Tecni charges RD$240 per hour but will offer hourly rates only before 6 PM; Apolo charges RD$280 per hour, day or night. When booking an hourly rate, be sure to establish clearly the time that you start. Prices in Punta Cana have become outrageous, however, and it's not unheard of to be charged US$150 for three hours if you book through your resort's concierge. At Plaza Bavaro shopping center, where many taxis are standing around and especially if you can negotiate in Spanish, you can get one for a fraction of that price.

You can use taxis to travel to out-of-town destinations at quoted rates. Check with your hotel or the dispatcher at the airport. For example, from Santo Domingo the price is $80 to go to Casa de Campo (though Tecni charges only $60). If you book through your hotel concierge, it will be $100 to $120.

Apolo Taxi ☎ 809/537-0000, 809/537-1245 for a limo, must be booked far in advance. **Tecni-Taxi** ☎809/567-2010, 809/566-7272 in Santo Domingo, 809/320-7621 in Puerto Plata.

Contacts & Resources

BANKS & EXCHANGE SERVICES

You may need to change some money, particularly if you're not staying in an all-inclusive resort, where dollars are usually accepted. Prices quoted in this chapter are in U.S. dollars unless noted otherwise. The coin of the realm is the Dominican peso (written RD$). At this writing, the exchange rate was approximately RD$32.50 to the US$1.

Independent merchants will willingly accept U.S. dollars, and these are sometimes better because the peso can fluctuate wildly in value. However, change will be in pesos. Always make certain you know in which currency any transaction is taking place and carry a pocket calculator. You can find *cambios* (currency exchange offices) at the airports, as well as on the street, and in major shopping areas throughout the island. A passport is usually required to cash traveler's checks, if they're taken. Save some of the official receipts with the exchange transaction, so if you end up with too many pesos when you are ready to leave the country, you can turn them in for dollars. Some hotels provide exchange services, but as a general rule hotels and restaurants will not give you favorable rates–casino cages are better. Major credit cards (American Express not as often) are accepted at most hotels, large stores, and restaurants. Banco Popular has many locations throughout the country; many with ATMs that accept international cards—but they spit out pesos.

BUSINESS HOURS

Banks are open weekdays from 8:30 to 4:30. Post offices are open weekdays from 7:30 to 2:30. Offices and shops are open weekdays from 8 to noon and 2 to 6, Saturday from 8 to noon. About half the stores stay open all day, no longer closing for a midday siesta.

ELECTRICITY

The current is 110–120 volts/60 cycles just as in North America. Electrical blackouts occur less frequently than in the past and tend to last only one to two minutes (when they're over, everyone claps), but most hotels and restaurants have generators.

EMBASSIES & CONSULATES

◪ Canada **Canadian Embassy** ✉ Capitan Eugenia de Marchena 39, Box 2054, La Esperilla, Santo Domingo ☎ 809/685-1136. **Canadian Consulate** ✉ Edificio Isabel de Torres, Suite 311C, Puerto Plata ☎ 809/586-5761.

◪ United Kingdom **British Embassy** ✉ Edificio Corominas Pepin, Av. 27 de Febrero 233, Naco, Santo Domingo ☎ 809/472-7671 or 809/472-7373.

◪ United States **United States Embassy** ✉ Leopoldo Navarro, at Cesar Nicolas Penson, Naco, Santo Domingo ☎ 809/221-5511.

EMERGENCIES

◪ Emergency Services **Ambulance & Fire** ☎ 911. **Police Emergencies** ☎ 809/586-2804 in Puerto Plata, 711 in Santo Domingo, 809/571-2233 in Sosúa.

◪ Medical Clinics **Centro Médico Sosúa** ✉ Av. Martinez, Sosúa ☎ 809/571-3949. **Centro Médico Universidad Central del Este** ✉ Av. Máximo Gómez 68, La Esperilla, Santo Domingo ☎809/221-0171. **Clínica Abreu** ✉ Calle Beller 42, Gazcue, Santo Domingo ☎ 809/688-4411. **Clínica Dr. Brugal** ✉ Calle José del Carmen Ariza 15, Puerto Plata ☎ 809/586-2519. **Clínica Gómez Patino** ✉ Av. Independencia 701, Gazcue, Santo Domingo ☎809/685-9131. **Hospiten Hospital Bávaro** ✉ Bávaro ☎ 809/686-1414. **Servi-Med** ✉ Plaza La Criolla, Sosúa ☎ 809/571-0964 ✉ Calle Principal, next to Helados Bon ☎ 809/571-0964.

◪ Pharmacies **Farmacia Deleyte** ✉ Av. John F. Kennedy 89, Puerto Plata ☎ 809/586-2583. **San Judas Tadeo** ✉ Av. Independencia 57, Gazcue, Santo Domingo ☎ 809/689-6664.

ETIQUETTE & BEHAVIOR

Wearing shorts, short skirts, and halter tops in churches is considered inappropriate. Men in Santo Domingo never wear shorts. Know that security at hotels and resorts is tight, particularly about having guests in your room, especially if they're Dominican and of the opposite sex.

HEALTH

Never assume that water in the D.R. is safe. Drink only bottled water; some people recommend brushing your teeth with bottled water as well. Food safety has been a recurring problem in the country, but each year hygiene standards are becoming more strict. If you are staying at an all-inclusive resort, try to arrive at the start of a buffet meal, before the food has sat out in the heat, or even in an air-conditioned dining room. Salads can be iffy, and you should avoid them in most cases unless you know that the greens have been washed in bottled or purified water. Don't buy from the street vendors. If you experience intestinal problems, see a doctor at the earliest opportunity, for it could even be salmonella. Some people bring prescribed antibiotics from home, and that's not a bad idea.

HOLIDAYS

Major public holidays are New Year's Day, Ephiphany—known also as Three Kings Day (Jan. 6), Our Lady of La Altagracia Day (Jan. 21), Duarte's Birthday (Jan. 26), Independence Day (Feb. 27), Good Friday, Labor Day (1st Mon. in May), Corpus Christi (June 14), Restoration Day (Aug. 16), Our Lady of Las Mercedes Day (Sept. 24), Constitution Day (Nov. 4), and Christmas.

LANGUAGE

Spanish is spoken in the D.R. Staff at major tourist attractions and front-desk personnel in most major hotels speak some English, but you may have difficulty making yourself understood. Outside the popular tourist establishments, restaurant menus are in Spanish, as are traffic signs everywhere. Using smiles and gestures will help, and though you can manage with just English, people are even more courteous if you try to speak their language.

INTERNET, MAIL & SHIPPING

Paid Internet access of some kind is available in almost every hotel, though you may sometimes have access to only one slow and old terminal in the lobby. Wi-Fi is becoming more prevalent in the better hotels; it is usually free but generally exists only in the lobby and some public areas, rather than in your room. In Santo Domingo, there are dozens of Internet

10

cafés, also several in centrally located parts of Cabarete, Sosua, and Playa Dorada.

Airmail postage to North America for a letter or postcard is RD$40, to Canada RD$35; letters may take more than two weeks to reach their destination or never make it. Or you can pay a whopping RD$250 for a "fast mail" stamp (which still takes a week) in a souvenir shop (outside Santo Domingo, post offices aren't easy to find). The main branch of the post office in Santo Domingo is on Calle Heroes del Luperon at Rafael Damiron La Ferla. If you need to send a package home, it's more reliable to use Fedex or DHL, even though the cost is a small fortune.

PASSPORTS & VISAS

Starting January 1, 2007, all U.S. citizens must carry a valid passport. Additionally, upon arrival most people must purchase a tourist card, which costs $10 in cash unless it's included in your package price (be sure to ask). You must return the receipt for this tourist card when you leave or you'll be charged another $10 fee.

PROSTITUTION

Although the D.R. has had a reputation for prostitution and sex tourism, officials are making efforts to curb the problem. In the late 1990s, Sosúa was like one big red-light district, with European male tourists coming specifically for sex tourism. Town fathers have made vigorous efforts to clean things up—and they have—but prostitution still exists in the now designated *Zona Rojas*. It's traditionally been a different story in Cabarete, where young, local surfer boys target northern European girls, who end up paying the freight. The real action goes down in Punta Cana, with the infamous "spanky hanky" boys—staffers, often waiters, bartenders, and activity staff—who prey on single female guests, especially older ones, lavishing attention on them, saying, "Meet me in the disco." Such a rendezvous often ends up in a seedy, drive-up, by-the-hour motel. What some unsuspecting ladies don't realize is

that not only will they have to ante up for the room but for the boy's services as well.

In Santo Domingo, prostitutes are alive and not always well (diseases are a real threat). They ply their trade, roaming casinos and hotels, but the top properties vigilantly thwart their efforts. Throughout the D.R., sex bars are usually called "gentlemen's clubs." And there's substantial gay prostitution as well.

SAFETY

Violent crime against tourists in the D.R. is rare, and the island has a history of being safe. It definitely is safer now that President Lionel Fernandez is back in power. Nevertheless, you should exhibit the same caution you would in any unfamiliar destination. Poverty is everywhere in the D.R., and petty theft (particularly of cell phones), pickpocketing, and purse snatching (thieves usually work in pairs) are most frequent in Santo Domingo. Pay attention, especially when leaving a bank, a *cambio*, or a casino around the Malecón, and alas, even in the Zona Colonial, despite the very visible Zone police. Crime has even come to Santiago, so be cautious at night, and lock the doors of your car or taxi. Armed private security guards are a common sight at clubs and restaurants.

Security at the all-inclusive resorts is good, but petty theft still occurs. Punta Cana remains one of the safest regions, Ulvero Alto even more so. In this region, a pot salesman is more often a boy hawking shiny, stainless-steel pots. However, should anyone approach you to buy drugs, know that the penalties in this country are extremely tough—jail (not pretty), fines, and no parole—and don't even think of bringing any from home. Take hotel-recommended taxis at night. When driving, always lock your car and never leave valuables in it, even when doors are locked. If you have a safe in your hotel room, use it; camouflage your laptop.

TAXES & SERVICE CHARGES

Departure tax—separate from the $10 tourist card you must purchase on entering the country—is $20 and almost always included in the price of your ticket. The government tax (IBIS) is a whopping 16% and is added to almost everything, to bills at restaurants, hotels, sports activities, rental cars, and even at the registers in the *supermercados* for any items that are not considered basic, including any imported goods.

TELEPHONES

To call the D.R. from the United States, dial 1, then the area code 809 and the local number. From the D.R. you can also use the same procedure to call a U.S. or Canadian number (i.e., just dial 1 plus the area code and number). Some U.S. toll-free numbers can be dialed from the D.R., but not all, by dialing 1-880. To make a local call, you must now dial 809 plus the seven-digit number (dial "1-809" if you are calling a cell phone). To the United Kingdom, dial 011, the country and city codes, and the number. Directory assistance is 1411.

Rates for local calls vary in hotels; some charge only a few pesos a minute, others a set rate for local calls and a higher set rate for calls to the U.S.—and that is above and beyond the per-minute charges. However, phone cards, which are sold at gift shops and supermarkets, can give you considerable savings if you're calling the United States or Canada, for which a hotel might charge $1 to $2 a minute. Verizon cards can be used in most hotels (but check to see if you still will incur a connection fee, etc.). The BLA BLA BLA card (I'm not kidding) by Tricom will work only in special telecommunications offices and from private homes, but it gives you the biggest bang for the peso. Verizon calling centers have equally good rates to the States and Canada, now about 35¢ a minute, but you will have to pay cash.

Orange and Verizon are the two major cell phone companies in the D.R. If you have a tri-band GSM phone, it will probably work on the island, but you can also get a local phone and SIM card. You cannot rent from Orange, but you can from Verizon; however, the cost makes it more economical to buy one for less than $50. You then buy prepaid phone cards of various denominations for your airtime. These are sold at numerous outlets, including most pharmacies and supermarkets. You can then call locally or long distance.

TIPPING

Generally, a 10% service charge is included in all hotel and restaurant bills; it's the Dominican law. In restaurants, the bill will say *propino incluido* or simply *servis*. When in doubt, ask. Even then it's still expected that you will tip an extra 5% to 10% if the service was up to your liking. In resorts, it's customary to leave at least a dollar per day for the hotel maid. Taxi drivers expect a 10% tip, especially if they've had to lift luggage or to wait for you. Skycaps and hotel porters expect at least $1 per bag.

Guests have started to tip at most all-inclusive resorts, even at those where tipping is supposed to be included. Bell boys, waiters, concierges, and bartenders (who may now have a tip cup) are starting to expect a dollar, and they tend to give far better service to those who tip. Bring a large supple of U.S. dollar bills for tips.

TOUR OPTIONS

Go Dominican Tours has representatives in the Playa Dorada hotels offering tours to Santiago with a visit to the Jimenes cigar factory, and to the mountain area, Jarabacoa, with a look-see at a cascade and horseback riding for $60. You can also take a 3½-hour rafting trip in Jarabacoa, including a Dominican lunch at a ranch, for $90. Various jeep safaris trek to flower, fruit, and coffee plantations. Iguana Mama was the first adventure tour company in the D.R.; it organizes biking, hiking, cascading (27 waterfalls for $60), and whale-watching trips to Samana, January to March, costing $100, $60 for children.

10

Hotel Residence Playa Colibri acts as a tour operator for excursions in Las Terrenas to such sights as the El Limón Cascades and Playa Moron. The staff can arrange jeep safaris and trips to Santi's Restaurant, and Casa Berca, which is accessible only on horseback.

Takeoff Destination Service, which operates domestic flights out of Punta Cana Airport, also offers day trips, including a Samaná Safari, with plane and speedboat rides, horseback riding, an island barbecue, winter whale-watching, and a visit to Los Haitises National Park, for $219; rafting in Jarabacoa, with a plane to Santiago, ranch breakfast, and mountain river rafting, costs $299; an ecotour of Barahona is $299; a Santo Domingo city tour prices out at $219; and a new and exciting hot-air balloon ride 3,000 feet above sugarcane fields costs $275, including breakfast with champagne.

Tropical Tours provides both transfers from Santo Domingo and Las Americas Airport to Casa ($38 per person one-way, $70 round-trip), as well as tours from Casa. One takes guests to the La Romana Maravillas Cave for a half-day for $25. The company also rents electric bikes for about $28 a day. Turinter offers a six-hour trip to Altos de Chavón ($73); a full day of swimming and boating with a beach barbecue on Saona Island ($84); a trip to Catalina Island ($76); and specialty trips (museums, shopping, fishing), all from Santo Domingo. It also operates from Punta Cana.

⛶ **Go Dominican Tours** ✉ Playa Dorada ☎ 809/586-5969. **Hotel Residence Playa Colibri** ✉ Las Terrenas ☎ 809/240-6434. **Iguana Mama** ✉ Cabarete ☎ 809/571-0908 ⊕ www.iguanamama.com. **Takeoff Destination Service** ✉ Punta Cana ☎ 809/552-1333. **Tropical Tours** ✉ Casa de Campo, La Romana ☎ 809/723-3008 ⊕ www.tropicaltourssa.com. **Turinter** ☎ 809/685-4020 ⊕ www.turinter.com.

VISITOR INFORMATION

⛶ Before You Leave **Dominican Republic Tourist Office** ⊕ www.dominicana.com.do ✉ 136 E. 57th St., Suite 803, New York, NY 10022 ☎ 212/588-1012 or 888/374-6361 ✉ 248 N.W. Le Jeune Rd., Miami, FL 33126 ☎ 305/444-4592 or 888/358-9594 ✉ 2080 Rue Crescent, Montréal, Québec H3G 288, Canada ☎ 514/499-1918 or 800/563-1611 ✉ 20 Hand Ct., High Holborn, London WC1, U.K. ☎ 207/242-7778.

⛶ In the Dominican Republic **Secretary of Tourism** ✉ Secretaria de Estado de Turismo, Edificios Guberbamentales, Av. México, at the corner of Av. 30 de Marzo, Gazcue, Santo Domingo ☎ 809/221-4660. **Puerto Plata tourist office** ✉ Jose del Carmen Ariza 45, Puerto Plata ☎ 809/586-3676.

WEDDINGS

The relative ease of getting married in the Dominican Republic has made it a major destination for Caribbean weddings. There are no residency requirements, nor are blood tests mandatory. As elsewhere in the Caribbean, civil ceremonies performed by a judge are easier and require less documentation than those performed in churches. They will be performed in Spanish unless you arrange for an English translator. Similarly, the legalized wedding certificate will be in Spanish and may not be delivered for a week or more. Most couples arrange their wedding ceremonies through the wedding coordinator at their resort. You must usually submit documents at least two weeks in advance of your wedding, and the cost for processing is usually about $70 per person.

A number of resorts cater to the wedding market and provide a gorgeous backdrop for the occasion. At Secrets Excellence in Punta Cana, weddings are free if you book a seven-day stay in an ocean-view junior suite or better, and they throw in an extra room for the groom on the night before the wedding.

Grenada
with Carriacou

Grand Anse Beach

WORD OF MOUTH

"I agree that Grenada is a fantastic, lush, and beautiful island and certainly not overcrowded. If you want to see the Caribbean as it used to be 30 years ago, Grenada is the answer."

—Sandcrab

"Grenada has very good hiking, with a number of rain-forest trails of different difficulty, as well as good beaches. Grand Anse is world class, and there are several others . . . that are quite nice."

—RAB

www.fodors.com/forums

WELCOME TO GRENADA

THE SPICE ISLAND

A relatively small island, Grenada is 21 mi (34 km) long and 12 mi (19 km) wide; much of the interior is lush rain forest. It's a major producer of spices and flavorings. Carriacou—23 mi (37 km) north of Grenada—is just 13 square mi (34 square km). Tiny Petite Martinique is 2 mi farther north.

Grand Étang Lake, in the center of the island's national park, fills the crater of an extinct volcano.

The *Bianca C.*, a cruise ship that caught fire in 1961, caught fire and sank in 100 feet of water west of St. George's. It's one of the island's most popular dive sites.

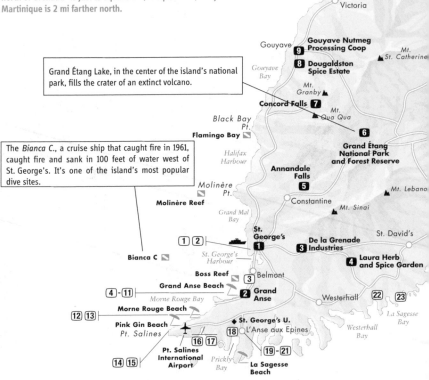

David Bay

Saute

St. Mark Bay

Carib's Lea

Victoria

Gouyave

Gouyave Nutmeg Processing Coop 9

Mt. St. Catherine

Gouyave Bay

8 **Dougaldston Spice Estate**

Mt. Granby

Concord Falls 7

Mt. Qua Qua

6

Black Bay Pt.

Flamingo Bay

Grand Étang National Park and Forest Reserve

Halifax Harbour

Annandale Falls

5

Mt. Lebano

Molinère Pt.

Constantine

Mt. Sinai

Molinère Reef

Grand Mal Bay

St. George's 1

St. David's

1 2

De la Grenade 3 **Industries**

Bianca C

St. George's Harbour

4 **Laura Herb and Spice Garden**

Boss Reef

3 Belmont

22 23

Grand Anse Beach

2 **Grand Anse**

Westerhall

4 - 11

Morne Rouge Bay

La Sagesse Bay

Morne Rouge Beach

12 13

♦ **St. George's U.**

Westerhall Bay

Pink Gin Beach

18 L'Anse aux Epines

Pt. Salines

16 17

14 15

Pt. Salines International Airport

Prickly Bay

19 - 21

La Sagesse Beach

These days the Isle of Spice busies itself cultivating nutmeg, cloves, and other spices, and vestiges of its once turbulent past have all but disappeared. Renowned for its natural beauty, its fragrant air, and its friendly people, Grenada has lovely beaches and plenty of outdoor and cultural activities.

KEY

- Beaches
- Cruise Ship Terminal
- Dive Sites
- **1** Exploring Sights
- ① Hotels & Restaurants

TOP 4 REASONS TO VISIT GRENADA

1 The scent of spices fills the air, perfumes the soap, improves the drinks, and even flavors the ice cream.

2 Nature abounds: Spot monkeys in the mountains, watch birds in the rain forest, join fish in the sea, and build sandcastles on the beach.

3 Friendliness isn't overrated: Grenadians go out of their way to make you feel welcome.

4 With no huge resorts, you really can get away from it all.

GRENADA PLANNER

Getting to Grenada & Carriacou

A few airlines have nonstop flights to Grenada (GND) from the U.S., U.K., and Canada, though that number does not include American Airlines, the Caribbean's dominant carrier. If you can't get a nonstop flight, then you'll have to connect through San Juan for an American Eagle flight or through another nearby island for the short hop on a Caribbean-based airline. Carriacou is connected by fairly frequent air service from Grenada on small hopper planes and by an inexpensive, 90-minute ferry ride.

Hassle Factor: Low to Medium for Grenada, Medium to High for Carriacou.

Activities

Grenada's **beaches** are beautiful, and Grand Anse is among the Caribbean's finest; little Carriacou has a few nice beaches, the best of which is on Sandy Island, which is just offshore from the major town, Hillsborough. It may be hard to pull yourself away from the beach, but be sure to spend a day or two exploring Grenada's lush scenery. The capital city of **St. George's** has a busy harbor, interesting shops, and several historic sites. A visit to a **spice plantation** and a nutmeg processing plant or, if you're adventurous, a guided **hike** in the rain forest, up a mountainside, or to a hidden waterfall is a highlight of most trips. **Sailing**, particularly to the Grenadine's, a small chain of islands north of Carriacou, is exceptional. **Diving, fishing**, and **snorkeling** opportunities are also good.

On the Ground

Point Salines International Airport, at the southwestern tip of Grenada, is a modern facility suitable for the largest jets. Best of all, it's no more than a 10-minute drive from nearly all hotels and resorts. On Carriacou, five minutes south of Hillsborough, Lauriston Airport is a lighted landing strip suitable only for small planes, with a small building for ticket sales and shelter.

On Grenada, taxis are always available for transportation between the Point Salines Airport and hotels. Fares to St. George's are $15; to the hotels of Grand Anse and L'Anse aux Épines, $10. Rides taken between 6 PM and 6 AM incur a $4 surcharge. At Carriacou's Lauriston Airport, taxis meet every plane; the fare to Hillsborough is $4.

Renting a Car

On Grenada, having a car or Jeep is a convenience—particularly if you're staying at a resort in a location other than Grand Anse, which has frequent minibus service. Otherwise, round-trip taxi rides can get expensive if you plan to leave the resort frequently for shopping, meals, or visiting other beaches. Driving is also a reasonable option if you want to explore the island on your own. To rent a car on Grenada, you need a valid driver's license and a local permit (available at the Central Police Station on the Carenage and at some car-rental firms), which costs $12 (EC$30). You can rent a car on Carriacou, but it's easier to take taxis.

Where to Stay

Grenada's tourist accommodations are, for the most part, in the southwest part of the island—primarily on or near Grand Anse Beach or overlooking small bays along the island's southern coast. Nearly all of the island's major beach resorts—including a few that were extensively damaged and then remodeled or even rebuilt after Hurricane Ivan in 2004—have recovered completely. Carriacou is a small island, and its guest houses are mostly in and around Hillsborough.

TYPES OF LODGING

Luxury Resorts:	**Modest Resorts & Apartment Complexes:**	**Guest Houses:**
Grenada has a handful of luxurious inns and resorts. The best resort on the island (and one of the best in the Caribbean), the Spice Island Beach Resort, reopened in December 2005 after a major renovation after Hurricane Ivan.	Most resorts and hotels on Grenada are small, and many are modest, but that is part of their charm.	Small guest houses predominate on Carriacou, where no property has more than 25 rooms.

Hotel & Restaurant Costs

Assume that hotels operate on the European Plan (**EP**—with no meals) unless we specify that they use either the Continental Plan (**CP**—with a Continental breakfast), Breakfast Plan (**BP**—with full breakfast), or the Modified American Plan (**MAP**—with breakfast and dinner). Other hotels may offer the Full American Plan (**FAP**—including all meals but no drinks) or may be All-Inclusive (**AI**—with all meals, drinks, and most activities).

WHAT IT COSTS in Dollars					
	$$$$	**$$$**	**$$**	**$**	**¢**
Restaurants	over $30	$20–$30	$12–$20	$8–$12	under $8
Hotels*	over $350	$250–$350	$150–$250	$80–$150	under $80
Hotels**	over $450	$350–$450	$250–$350	$125–$250	under $125

*EP, BP, CP   **AI, FAP, MAP
Restaurant prices are for a main course at dinner. Hotel prices are per night for a double room in high season, excluding 8% government tax, 10% service charge, and meal plans (except at all-inclusives).

When to Go

Outside of the high season, which stretches from December 15 to April 15, prices at most Grenada resorts are discounted by up to 40%. There are fewer seasonal changes on Carriacou, where the simple guest houses are all inexpensive to begin with. Grenada and Carriacou have some interesting festivals, but you won't find any of the big-scale events you find on many islands.

The **Spice Island Billfish Tournament** is held in late January. The **Grenada Sailing Festival** happens in late January or early February and includes six days of races and regattas. The **Grenada International Triathlon** is in late April. Grenada's **Carnival**, is a month-long celebration beginning the second week of August.

The Carriacou **Carnival** in mid-February is the small island's biggest celebration. The **Carriacou Regatta** in August draws yachts from around the Caribbean. The Big Drum Dance is the highlight of the **Carriacou Parang Festival**, a musical and cultural celebration held the week before Christmas.

By Jane E.
Zarem

WHILE I WAS WALKING ALONG A NARROW STREET IN ST. GEORGE'S during my first visit to Grenada, someone on the opposite side hollered, "Hey!" The young man was calling to me. "First time in Grenada?" he asked. Reflexively, though wary, I ever so slightly nodded yes. Then, in a big, friendly voice, he asked, "Are you enjoyin' it?" When I nodded again, his face broadened into a huge smile, and with a big wave he continued on his way. That, I can affirm, based on subsequent visits well into the double digits, is a typical encounter in visitor-friendly Grenada.

Grenada was on a roll. On February 2, 2004, the people on this lush, green, picturesque isle happily celebrated the nation's 30th year of independence. The divisive political events leading to the intervention by U.S. troops in October 1983 had been successfully placed on the back burner of people's minds. And over the last two decades, Grenada had developed a healthy tourism sector and a modern infrastructure, including welcoming hotels and resorts, good roads, up-to-date technology, and reliable utilities. Then, on September 7, 2004, Hurricane Ivan tore through the island, and Grenada was turned upside-down.

Grenada lies in the southeastern Caribbean, 12 degrees north of the equator. It is the southernmost of the Windward Islands. Considered outside the hurricane belt, Grenada experiences storm surges from time to time and occasional wind damage when major storms pass by or through its Caribbean neighbors to the north. When Hurricane Ivan's 120-mph winds blew through the island, most Grenadians had never experienced a major hurricane firsthand and, as a result, were taken completely by surprise. Prior to Ivan, the last hurricane to make a direct hit on Grenada was Janet in 1955.

Overnight, countless houses in the countryside were destroyed; roofs on residences and businesses around the island and on hotels and resorts along the southwestern coast were severely damaged or completely torn away; and untold numbers of trees, including those on which the island's lucrative nutmeg crop depends, were toppled. Roads, especially in the less densely populated north, were impassable for several weeks, while the lifelines of electricity, water, and communications were nonexistent for several months after the storm. One of the most heartbreaking losses was the near total destruction of the recently completed, multimillion-dollar National Stadium, on the north side of St. George's, where Grenadians passionately enjoyed cricket or soccer matches and Carnival festivities.

Although this event forced a sidestep in the island's forward motion, Grenada is once again on a roll. Grenadians stepped up to the plate, and the island is, to all appearances, mostly recovered. Mother Nature swiftly brought back the tropical beauty for which Grenada is renowned—although it may be 2010 or so before the nutmeg crop is back to normal. Throughout it all, the people of Grenada retained their friendliness and optimism, the beaches remained beautiful, the sea stayed warm and refreshing. All but a very few tourist facilities are either back to normal or bigger and better than before. And the government of China is helping Grenada rebuild the National Stadium in time for the World Cup

Cricket series in 2007. All told, horrific Hurricane Ivan and its aftermath couldn't damage the spirit of the Grenadian people.

The nation of Grenada actually consists of three islands: Grenada, the largest, with 120 square mi (311 square km) and a population of 102,000; Carriacou (*car*-ree-a-coo), 23 mi (37 km) north of Grenada, with 13 square mi (34 square km) and a population of about 9,000; and Petite Martinique, 2 mi (3 km) northeast of Carriacou, with just 486 acres and a population of only 900. Carriacou and Petite Martinique are popular for day trips, fishing adventures, or diving and snorkeling excursions, but most of the tourist activity is on Grenada. People interested in a really quiet, get-away-from-it-all vacation will, however, appreciate the simple pleasures of Carriacou during an extended stay.

The island of Grenada itself, just 21 mi (34 km) long and 12 mi (19 km) wide, has 45 beaches and countless secluded coves. Crisscrossed by nature trails and laced with spice plantations, its mountainous interior is mostly consumed by a natural rain-forest preserve. St. George's is still one of the most picturesque capital cities in the Caribbean, and Grand Anse is one of the region's finest beaches. Nicknamed Isle of Spice, Grenada has long been a major producer of nutmeg, cinnamon, mace, cocoa, and other spices and flavorings. The aroma of spices fills the air in markets, in restaurants, and throughout the countryside.

Although he never set foot on the island, Christopher Columbus sighted Grenada in 1498 and named it Concepción. Spanish sailors following in his wake renamed it Granada, after the city in the hills of their homeland. Adapted to Grenade by French colonists, the name transformation to Grenada was completed by the British in the 18th century.

Throughout the 17th century, Grenada was the scene of many bloody battles between indigenous Carib Indians and the French. Rather than surrender to the Europeans after losing their last battle in 1651, the Caribs committed mass suicide by leaping off a cliff in Sauteurs, at the island's northern tip. The French were later overwhelmed by the British in 1762, the beginning of a seesaw of power between the two nations. By the Treaty of Versailles in 1783, Grenada was granted to the British and, almost immediately, thousands of African slaves were brought in to work the sugar plantations. Slavery in Grenada actually began with the French colonization in 1650 and was finally abolished in 1834.

Forts that the French began to protect St. George's Harbour during their colonization of Grenada were later completed and used by the British during theirs. Today, Fort George and Fort Frederick are two of the most-visited sites in St. George's. Besides the historical interest, the two locations have magnificent views of the harbor, the capital city itself, and the distant mountains and countryside. Interestingly, not a single shot was fired from either fort for more than two centuries. Then in 1983, Prime Minister Maurice Bishop and several of his supporters were murdered at Fort George by political foes who had split off from Bishop's party. That event triggered the request from Grenada's governor general and the heads of state of neighboring islands for U.S. troops to intervene, which they did on October 25, 1983.

From that time forward, Grenada's popularity as a vacation destination has increased each year, notwithstanding the temporary effects of Ivan, as travelers continue to seek friendly, exotic islands to visit. Nearly all hotels, resorts, and restaurants in Grenada are family-owned and run by people (mostly Grenadians) whose guests often become their friends. Grenadians, in fact, have a well-deserved reputation for their friendliness, hospitality, and entrepreneurial spirit. You can be sure you'll be "enjoyin' it" when you visit Grenada.

Where to Stay

Lodging options range from simply furnished, inexpensive apartments to elegant suites or villas just steps from the sea. Hotels tend to be small and intimate, with friendly management and attentive staff. All guest rooms are equipped with air-conditioning, an in-room TV, and telephone unless indicated otherwise. During the off-season (April 15 to December 15), prices may be discounted up to 40%.

Villas & Private Homes

For information about renting a villa or home on Grenada, contact **Villas of Grenada** (⌂ Box 218, St. George's ☎ 473/444–1896 🖷 473/444–4529 ⊕ www.villasofgrenada.com). In-season rates range from about $1,600 a week for a two-bedroom home with a pool to $8,000 a week for a six-bedroom home on the beach.

For Carriacou rental information, contact **Down Island Villa Rentals** (✉ Craigston ☎ 473/443–8182 🖷 473/443–8290 ⊕ www.islandvillas.com). In-season rates range from $65 per day for a small cottage or in-town apartment suitable for two people to $185 per day for a villa with panoramic views and a swimming pool that accommodates up to six people.

Hotels on Grenada

★ $$$$ 🏨 **Calabash Hotel.** The elegant suites here are in 10 two-story cottages distributed in a horseshoe around 8 acres of gardens that hug a curved beach on Prickly Bay. Each suite has a spacious bedroom and sitting area with rattan and wicker furniture and a verandah, where breakfast is served daily by your maid. Two-thirds of the suites have whirlpool baths; eight have private plunge pools. Each room has a CD player and is wired for cable TV, which you may have on request. Complimentary fruit is served on the beach each morning; tea is served in the restaurant each afternoon; and canapés are delivered to your suite in the evening. Rhodes Restaurant serves memorable cuisine. ✉ *L'Anse aux Épines, St. George ⌂ Box 382, St. George's ☎ 473/444–4334 🖷 473/444–5050 ⊕ www.calabashhotel.com ⇨ 30 suites △ Restaurant, room service, fans, kitchenettes, cable TV, in-room data ports, golf privileges, tennis court, pool, gym, spa, beach, snorkeling, boating, billiards, shuffleboard, 2 bars, library, recreation room, shops, babysitting, dry cleaning, laundry service, concierge, Internet room, car rental* ⊟ *AE, MC, V* ¶⊙¶ *CP.*

★ $$$$ 🏨 **Laluna.** You may think you've landed on an island in the South Pacific, but this upscale enclave is hidden away on a remote, pristine beach near Grenada's Quarantine Point. Laluna's large thatched-roof cottages—each with its own plunge pool—line the beachfront and climb the wooded hillside. Bedrooms open onto large verandahs that serve as indoor-outdoor sitting areas. Bathrooms have showers that partially open to the natural environment. Guests congregate at the comfortable beachfront lounge, bar, and restaurant and have free access to a small CD and video library, a couple of bikes, and a kayak or two. The resort faces west, assuring a beautiful seaside sunset every evening. ⊠ *Morne Rouge, St. George* ⊡ *Box 1500, St. George's* ☏ *473/439–0001 or 866/452–5862* 🖷 *473/439–0600* ⊕ *www.laluna.com* ⤴ *16 cottages* ⟨ *Restaurant, fans, in-room safes, minibars, cable TV, in-room VCRs, in-room data ports, pool, gym, massage, beach, snorkeling, boating, mountain bikes, bar, library, shop, laundry facilities, concierge, Internet room, car rental; no kids under 14 mid-Dec.–mid-Apr.* ▤ *AE, MC, V* ⦿ *EP.*

$$$$ ▣ **Maca Bana Villas.** Clustered on a 2-acre hillside overlooking mile-**Fodor'sChoice** long Magazine Beach, each of Maca Bana's seven villas offers a breath-★ taking view—of the white-sand below, out to sea, up the coastline to pretty St. George's Harbour, and beyond to the rain-forest-covered, cloud-capped mountains. Each villa is named for a tropical fruit, a theme that carries through to the artistically inspired decor. And each has a spacious veranda with a private hot tub. A small but inviting infinity pool is centrally located and open to all guests. Villas accommodate two to six persons, but families with young children should be aware of the steep terrain. Roomy gourmet kitchens are equipped with every appliance, tool, utensil, and piece of crockery or glassware that you can imagine—including an espresso machine and groceries for your first breakfast. If you wish, request a personal chef from the restaurant below to create a meal in your own kitchen—or to give you a cooking lessons. Would-be artists can sign up for lessons with noted artist Rebecca Thompson, the owner's wife. Or perhaps a personal yoga or tai chi lesson on your own deck will do the trick. ⊠ *Point Salines, St. George* ☏☏ *473/535–5355* ⊕ *www.macabana.com* ⤴ *2 one-bedroom villas, 5 two-bedroom villas* ⟨ *Restaurant, fans, in-room safes, kitchens, cable TV, in-room VCRs, Wi-Fi, pool, hot tubs, beach, bar, laundry facilities* ▤ *AE, MC, V* ⦿ *EP.*

$$$$ ▣ **Spice Island Beach Resort.** After 15 months and $12 million worth **Fodor'sChoice** of rebuilding and renovations, Grenada's premier resort is back. Ex-★ quisite accommodations in dozens of gleaming white buildings extend along 1,600 feet of Grand Anse Beach. Beachfront "seagrape" suites are steps from the sand, and several luxury pool suites have private gardens and saltwater plunge pools. Two suites have been specifically designed to be accessible for people with mobility problems. Guest rooms are richly decorated with contemporary furniture imported from Asia and elegant fabrics in hues and patterns that reflect the "Isle of Spice." Bathrooms are enormous, with double-size whirlpool tubs and marble tiles. Breakfast and dinner are served at Oliver's, the open-air gourmet restaurant; lunch and cocktails, at the Sea & Surf Bar. Throughout the resort, the service is impeccable. Janissa's Spa, a full-service facility in a secluded setting, offers a full menu of beauty and therapeutic treatments, five treatment lounges (one in an outdoor garden setting), a salon, and an outdoor relaxation area. Kids enjoy all-day activities at the Nutmeg Pod, which includes a nap room and a four-seat Playstation room with kid-size recliner chairs. ⊠ *Grand Anse, St. George* ☎ *473/444–4258* 🖷 *473/444–4807* ⊕ *www.spiceislandbeachresort.com* 🖙 *64 suites* 🕭 *2 restaurants, room service, fans, in-room safes, minibars, cable TV, in-room broadband, Wi-Fi, golf privileges, tennis court, pool, gym, hair salon, outdoor hot tub, spa, beach, dive shop, snorkeling, boating, bicycles, bar, library, shops, children's program (ages 3–12), laundry service, Internet room, business services, meeting rooms* ▭ *AE, D, DC, MC, V* ¶⊙¶ *AI.*

★ **$$$–$$$$** 🖾 **Bel Air Plantation.** On an 18-acre peninsula on Grenada's southeastern coast, gaily painted gingerbread cottages dot a verdant hillside. Beautifully constructed by local craftsmen, the spacious cottages are luxuriously decorated in a country-casual style, with teak and wicker furniture, coordinated Caribbean colors, framed botanical prints, and the works of local artisans. Each one- or two-bedroom cottage has a fully equipped kitchen, Bose entertainment system, CD library, and private veranda. Arrange fishing and boating charters next door at Grenada Marina, or simply relax in style. The excellent Water's Edge restaurant is on-site; rent a car for sightseeing and going to town (a half-hour drive). ⊠ *St. David's Harbour, St. David* ☝ *Box 857, LB 125, St. George's* ☎ *473/444–6305* 🖷 *473/444–6316* ⊕ *www.belairplantation.com* 🖙 *11 cottages* 🕭 *Restaurant, café, grocery, room service, fans, in-room safes, kitchens, cable TV, in-room data ports, pool, beach, dock, snorkeling, boating, fishing, hiking, bar, shops, laundry facilities, concierge, Internet room, airport shuttle, car rental; no kids under 15* ▭ *AE, D, DC, MC, V* ¶⊙¶ *EP.*

$$$ 🖾 **Coyaba.** The Cherman family reopened a bigger and better version of the popular beachfront resort in December 2005 after it was closed for more than a year following Hurricane Ivan. Coyaba, which means "heaven" in the Arawak language, is situated in a 5½-acre garden of palm trees, hibiscus, frangipani, and bougainvillea. It is one of the few hotels located directly on beautiful Grand Anse Beach. The island's Amerindian heritage influenced the resort's architecture and interior design, which includes natural materials, colorful fabrics, and native artwork. But this is not a "rustic" environment. The accommodations are modern, and the decor is beautifully serene; all rooms have a view of the sea from the private patio or balcony. Three rooms are accessible for guests with disabilities. Arawakabana features gourmet dining on the terrace, and the poolside Carbet offers an à la carte menu. ⊠ *Grand Anse St. George* ☝ *Box 336, St. George's* ☎ *473/444–4129* 🖷 *473/444–4808* ⊕ *www.coyaba.com* 🖙 *80 rooms* 🕭 *2 restaurants, cable TV, in-room data ports, golf privileges, tennis court, pool, gym, massage, beach, dive shop, snorkeling, boating, croquet, 2 bars, library, laundry services, meeting room* ▭ *AE, MC, V* ¶⊙¶ *EP.*

☾ **$$** 🖾 **Blue Horizons Garden Resort.** A short walk from Grand Anse Beach, "Blue" is especially popular among divers, nature lovers, and those seeking attractive accommodations at an affordable price. All suites here have separate sitting-dining rooms and one or two beds; studios have dining alcoves and one bed. All units have kitchenettes and private terraces. Owner Arnold Hopkin recently poured $1.2 million into refurbishments, including contemporary-style furnishings, updated kitchen appliances, and gleaming tiles and fixtures in the bathrooms. Trees and plantings on the 6-acre property are home to 21 species of birds. Popular adventure packages focus on rain-forest hikes or scuba diving. La Belle Creole restaurant is renowned for its contemporary West Indian cuisine. ⊠ *Grand Anse, St. George* ☎ *Box 41, St. George's* 📞 *473/444–4316 or 473/444–4592* 📠 *473/444–2815* 🌐 *www.grenadabluehorizons. com* 🛏 *26 suites, 6 studios* ♿ *Restaurant, fans, in-room safes, kitchenettes, cable TV, in-room data ports, Wi-Fi, golf privileges, pool, outdoor hot tub, 2 bars, library, recreation room, babysitting, laundry service, meeting rooms, car rental* ▭ *AE, D, MC, V* ⦿| *EP.*

$$ 🏨 **Grenadian by Rex Resorts.** This massive beachfront resort on Tamarind Bay, particularly favored by Europeans, is minutes from the airport. Guest rooms are in a blocks of several two-story sun-yellow buildings—some along the beach and others on a bluff overlooking the sea. The pool, casual restaurant, and bar are in a beachfront complex but separated from the guest buildings by a large lawn and lake. Buffet breakfast and dinner are served at the International Restaurant; the Oriental serves Chinese cuisine at dinner. After dinner, guests gather at the spacious lounge area and enjoy nightly entertainment. ⊠ *Tamarind Bay, Point Salines St. George's* ☎ *473/444–3333* 🌐 *www.rexresorts.com* 🛏 *191 rooms, 21 suites* ♿ *3 restaurants, fans, cable TV, in-room data ports, 2 tennis courts, pool, gym, beach, snorkeling, 2 bars, shops, babysitting, children's program (ages 4–12), laundry service, business services, meeting rooms; no a/c in some rooms, no TV in some rooms, no smoking* ▭ *AE, D, DC, MC, V* ⦿| *EP.*

🐣 **$$** 🏨 **True Blue Bay Resort & Marina.** The lawns and gardens at this family-run resort, a former indigo plantation, slope down to True Blue Bay. Three cottages are near the pool, and four spacious apartments are perched on a cliff overlooking the bay. Each has a living room with a sofa bed, a dining area, and a fully equipped kitchen. Modern villa rooms, decorated in Caribbean colors, also have views of the bay. The restaurant specializes in Mexican and Caribbean cuisine. Two beaches are on the bay, and Grand Anse Beach is a five-minute drive away. Arrange yacht charters at the marina or dive excursions at the on-site dive center. This is a perfect place for families. ⊠ *Old Mill Ave., True Blue Bay, St. George* ☎ *Box 1414, St. George's* 📞 *473/443–8783 or 866/325–8322* 📠 *473/444–5929* 🌐 *www.truebluebay.com* 🛏 *24 rooms, 4 1-bedroom apartments, 3 2-bedroom cottages* ♿ *Restaurant, snack bar, fans, some kitchens, some kitchenettes, cable TV, in-room data ports, 2 pools, gym, 2 beaches, dive shop, snorkeling, boating, marina, fishing, bar, library, shop, babysitting, 2 playgrounds, laundry service, Internet room, business services, meeting room, car rental* ▭ *AE, MC, V* ⦿| *CP.*

$$ 🏨 **Twelve Degrees North.** Named for the latitude at which it sits, this small, secluded inn has one- and two-bedroom suites, all of which face the sea. Accommodations come with a personal housekeeper who cooks breakfast and lunch, cleans, and tends to your laundry. Groceries are stocked for your arrival, along with fresh-cut flowers, rum punch, and a spice basket. Apartments are bright and airy, with modern furniture and woven-grass rugs on the tile floors. The balcony or patio is perfect for breakfast (in the terry robes provided), a quiet lunch, sunset drinks, or a romantic dinner for two. Activities center on the private beach, pool, and tennis court. ⊠ *L'Anse aux Épines, St. George* 🕾 *Box 241, St. George's* 🕾🕾 *473/444–4580* ⊕ *www.twelvedegreesnorth.com* ⏴ *8 suites* ⚘ *Tennis court, pool, massage, beach, snorkeling, boating, library, laundry service; no a/c, no room TVs, no kids under 15* 🖃 *AE, V* ❑ *EP.*

🐾 **$–$$** ⊡ **Allamanda Beach Resort.** Right on Grand Anse Beach, this small hotel has some rooms with whirlpool baths; many rooms also have connecting doors, making it a good choice for families. All rooms have tile floors and a balcony or patio. The restaurant serves international cuisine, and a poolside snack bar has great fresh-fruit smoothies. At the water-sports center you can find Sunfish and snorkeling equipment. Shopping, restaurants, nightlife, and the minibus to town are right at the doorstep. An all-inclusive option is available, which also includes a massage. ⊠ *Grand Anse, St. George* 🕾 *Box 1025, St. George's* 🕾 *473/444–0095* 🖷 *473/444–0126* ⊕ *www.allamandaresort.com* ⏴ *50 suites* ⚘ *Restaurant, snack bar, fans, in-room safes, refrigerators, cable TV, in-room data ports, tennis court, pool, gym, massage, beach, snorkeling, boating, volleyball, babysitting, meeting room* 🖃 *AE, D, MC, V* ❑ *EP.*

🐾 **$–$$** ⊡ **Grenada Grand Beach Resort.** On 20 landscaped acres along a broad section of beautiful Grand Anse Beach, this resort offers comfortable rooms and extensive amenities. Freshwater swimmers enjoy the 300-foot pool with its waterfalls and swim-up bar. Besides couples and families, groups sometimes frequent this resort, which has Grenada's largest convention center. Guest rooms all have attractive mahogany furniture, king or twin beds, and a large balcony or patio. Two suites have double-size whirlpool tubs. The restaurant offers table d'hôte and à la carte menus—where you can get a delicious New York–style steak. ⊠ *Grand Anse, St. George* 🕾 *Box 441, St. George's* 🕾 *473/444–4371* 🖷 *473/444–4800* ⊕ *www.grenadagrand.com* ⏴ *238 rooms, 2 suites* ⚘ *2 restaurants, snack bar, room service, fans, in-room safes, cable TV, in-room data ports, 9-hole golf course, 2 tennis courts, 2 pools, 2 outdoor hot tubs, gym, hair salon, massage, beach, snorkeling, dive shop, boating, Ping-Pong, shuffleboard, 2 bars, shops, laundry service, business services, convention center, Internet room, meeting rooms, car rental, travel services; no-smoking rooms* 🖃 *AE, DC, MC, V* ❑ *BP.*

🐾 **$** ⊡ **Flamboyant Hotel & Villas.** Built on a steep hillside, the rooms at this popular, Grenadian-owned hotel have private verandas with panoramic views of Grand Anse Bay. One-bedroom suites and two-bedroom, two-bath cottages each have a fully equipped kitchen and sitting room with sofa bed, making this an excellent value for families. Be prepared for lots of stairs (about 100) to get to Grand Anse Beach. Meals are served at the Owl, a beachfront restaurant and bar. The crab races, after dinner on Monday nights, are legendary. ⊠ *Grand Anse, St. George* 🕾 *Box 214, St. George's* 🕾 *473/444–4247* 🖷 *473/444–1234* ⊕ *www.flamboyant.com* ⏴ *38 rooms, 20 suites, 2 cottages* ⚘ *Restaurant, grocery, room service, in-room safes, kitchenettes, minibars, cable TV, golf privileges, pool, beach, dive shop, snorkeling, billiards, bar, cabaret, recreation room, shop, babysitting, laundry service, meeting room, Internet room, car rental* 🖃 *AE, D, DC, MC, V* ❑ *EP.*

$ **Gem Holiday Beach Resort.** Owner Miriam Bedeau and her family operate this no-frills hotel on pretty Morne Rouge Beach. One- and two-bedroom self-catering apartments are small and simple, with kitchenettes, dining-living rooms with mahogany furniture, and private verandahs overlooking the sea. Only the bedrooms are air-conditioned. If you don't want to cook, the beachfront Sur La Mer restaurant specializes in seafood and West Indian dishes for lunch and dinner. Fantazia, Grenada's premier (soundproof) dance club, is also on the property. ✉ *Morne Rouge, St. George* 📫 *Box 58, St. George's* ☎ *473/444–2288* 📠 *473/444–1189* 🌐 *www.gembeachresort.com* *15 1-bedroom apartments, 4 2-bedroom apartments* *Restaurant, grocery, fans, kitchenettes, cable TV, in-room data ports, beach, snorkeling, bar, dance club, babysitting, laundry service, car rental* 💳 *AE, D, DC, MC, V* 🍽 *EP.*

$ **Mariposa Beach Resort.** Over the hill from Grand Anse Beach, this colony of colorful Mediterranean-style villas overlooks Morne Rouge Bay. Each stylishly decorated room has a water view, a covered veranda or garden, and an Italian-tile bathroom. It's a short walk downhill to Morne Rouge Beach and the resort's private jetty, where you can catch a water taxi to Grand Anse Beach or even to St. George's. The restaurant specializes in seafood and international dishes. ✉ *Morne Rouge, St. George* 📫 *Box 857, St. George's* ☎ *473/444–3171* 📠 *473/444–3172* 🌐 *www.mariposaresort.com* *31 rooms, 15 apartments* *2 restaurants, room service, fans, in-room safes, some kitchens, refrigerators, cable TV, pool, beach, dock, 2 bars, laundry service, Internet room* 💳 *AE, MC, V* 🍽 *BP.*

$ **La Sagesse Nature Centre.** Secluded on La Sagesse Bay—10 mi (16 km) east of the airport (about a 30-minute drive)—the grounds here include a salt-pond bird sanctuary, thick mangroves, nature trails, and ½ mi (¾ km) of tree-shaded beach. Five large guest rooms are in the historic manor house; a nearby beach cottage has two individually rented rooms; and a more modern beachfront building has two rooms and three suites, two of which are duplex. All accommodations are within 30 feet of the beach, and all except those in the manor house have screened verandahs. The restaurant is popular; the food, excellent. Be content to relax here and enjoy the natural surroundings; you'll probably need to rent a car. ✉ *La Sagesse, St. David* 📫 *Box 44, St. George's* ☎ *473/444–6458* 📠 *473/444–6458* 🌐 *www.lasagesse.com* *9 rooms, 3 suites* *Restaurant, fans, minibars, beach, snorkeling, boating, hiking, bar, babysitting, laundry service; no a/c in some rooms, no room TVs* 💳 *MC, V* 🍽 *EP.*

Hotels on Carriacou

¢–$ **Carriacou Grand View Hotel.** The view is lovely, particularly at sunset, from this perch high above Hillsborough Harbour. Though the building is four stories high, its hillside location provides entrances at three levels, making stair-climbing much less of an issue, even if you're on the top floor. Guest rooms are pleasant and comfortably furnished; suites have added sitting rooms (large enough for a roll-away bed) and full kitchens. Most bathrooms have showers only. The beach and the town are a 15-minute walk away—or rent a car and explore Carriacou during your stay. The friendly atmosphere extends to the restaurant, which attracts guests and locals alike. ✉ *Beausejour* ☎📠 *473/443–6348* 🌐 *www.carriacougrandview.com* *6 rooms, 7 suites* *Restaurant,* *fans, kitchenettes, cable TV, pool, piano bar, shop, Internet room, meeting room; no a/c in some rooms* ▤ MC, V ⑩ EP.

¢–$　▦ **Green Roof Inn.** This small inn operated by a Scandinavian family has just five rooms—three have private showers; two others share. All are individually decorated in a contemporary style, with richly painted walls and pure white fabrics. All rooms have access to a verandah and cooling sea breezes. Beds have mosquito netting for an undisturbed sleep with wide-open windows. You're guaranteed beautiful views of Hillsborough Bay and the offshore cays—and incredible sunsets night after night. This is a perfect venue for a scuba diving, snorkeling, or beachcombing vacation—or just total relaxation. ⊠ *Hillsborough Bay, Hillsborough* 📠 *473/443–6399* ⊕ *www.greenroofinn.com* ⟳ *5 rooms* ⌂ *Restaurant, fans, beach, bar, library; no a/c, no room TVs* ▤ MC, V ⑩ CP.

¢　▦ **Ade's Dream Guest House.** Adjacent to the jetty in Hillsborough, this small guest house is a convenient place to rest your weary head after a day touring Carriacou, snorkeling at Sandy Island, or scuba diving at some of Grenada's best dive spots. Enjoy a good meal at Sea Wave, the owner's restaurant across the street; next day, fall out of bed at your leisure to catch the boat back. Or hey, stay longer. The accommodations (7 of the 23 rooms have shared baths) are simple, with queen-size or twin beds and a writing table, but the view of the mountains, sea, neighboring islands, and all the harbor activity is great—and it's certainly priced right. ⊠ *Main St., Hillsborough* 📠 *473/443–7317* 📠 *473/443–8435* ⊕*grenadines.net/carriacou/ade.htm* ⟳*23 rooms, 16 with bath* ⌂*Restaurant, grocery, fans, kitchenettes, beach, laundry facilities, car rental; no a/c in some rooms, no room TVs* ▤ AE, MC, V ⑩ BP.

¢　▦ **Silver Beach Resort.** Choose between a self-catering cottage with sitting room and kitchenette or an oceanfront double room at this laid-back beachfront resort a short walk from the jetty in Hillsborough. All quarters have a patio or balcony; most have an ocean view. Enjoy the beach, arrange a dive trip, or plan a fishing excursion on the resort's 30-foot Chris-Craft. The open-air Shipwreck restaurant serves hearty breakfasts and Caribbean and seafood dinners. Those who purchase MAP may dine at other local restaurants. In-room cable TV is available for $2 extra per day. ⊠*Beausejour Bay, Hillsborough* 📠*473/443–7337* 📠*473/443–7165* ⊕ *www.silverbeachhotel.net* ⟳ *10 rooms, 6 cottages* ⌂ *Restaurant, fans, kitchenettes, cable TV, tennis court, dive shop, dock, snorkeling, windsurfing, boating, fishing, bar, shops, laundry service, airport shuttle, car rental, travel services; no a/c* ▤ AE, D, MC, V ⑩ EP.

Where to Eat

Grenada grows everything from lettuce and tomatoes to citrus, mangoes, papaya (called *pawpaw*), callaloo (similar to spinach), dasheen (a root vegetable), christophenes (like squash), breadfruit—the list is endless. And all restaurants prepare dishes with local produce and season them with the many spices grown here. Be sure to try the local flavors of ice cream: soursop, guava, rum raisin, coconut (the best), or nutmeg.

Soups—especially pumpkin and callaloo—are divine and often start a meal. Pepper pot is a savory stew of pork, oxtail, vegetables, and spices simmered for hours. Oildown, the national dish, is salted meat, breadfruit, onion, carrot, celery, dasheen, and dumplings all boiled in coconut milk until the liquid is absorbed and the savory mixture becomes "oily." A roti—curried chicken, beef, or vegetables wrapped inside a pastry turnover and baked—is more popular in the Caribbean than a sandwich.

Fresh seafood of all kinds, including lobster, is plentiful. Conch, known here as *lambi*, is popular and often appears curried or in a stew. Crab back, though, is not seafood—it's land crab. Most Grenadian restaurants serve seafood and at least some native dishes.

Rum punches are ubiquitous and always topped with grated nutmeg. Clarke's Court and Westerhall are locally produced and marketed rums. Carib, the local beer, is refreshing, light, and quite good. If you prefer a nonalcoholic drink, opt for fruit punch—a delicious mixture of freshly blended tropical fruit.

What to Wear

Dining in Grenada is casual. At dinner, collared shirts and long pants are appropriate for men (even the fanciest restaurants don't require jacket and tie) and sundresses or slacks are fine for women. Beachwear, of course, should be reserved for the beach.

Grenada

CARIBBEAN
$$–$$$

✕ **Coconut Beach Restaurant.** Take local seafood, add butter, wine, and Grenadian spices, and you have excellent French creole cuisine. Throw in a beautiful location on Grand Anse Beach, and this West Indian cottage—rebuilt by owner Dennot "Scratch" McIntyre after Hurricane Ivan ripped it to shreds—becomes a perfect spot for an alfresco lunch or oceanfront dinner. Lobster is a specialty, perhaps wrapped in a crepe, dipped in garlic butter, or added to pasta. Or try the Caribbean chicken, seafood platter, lambi, or even grilled steak. Homemade coconut pie is a winner for dessert. On Wednesday and Sunday nights in season, dinner is a beach barbecue with live music. ⊠ *Grand Anse St. George's* ☎ *473/444–4644* ☐ *AE, D, MC, V* ⊘ *Closed Tues.*

¢–$

✕ **The Nutmeg.** West Indian specialties, fresh seafood, great hamburgers, and a waterfront view make this a favorite with locals and visitors alike. It's upstairs on the Carenage (above Sea Change bookstore), with large, open windows from which you can watch the harbor activity as you eat. Try the callaloo soup, curried lambi, fresh seafood, or a steak— or just stop by for a rum punch and a roti, a fish sandwich and a Carib beer, or a hamburger and a Coke. ⊠ *The Carenage, St. George's, St. George* ☎ *473/440–2539* ☐ *AE, D, MC, V.*

CHINESE–CARIBB
EAN
¢–$$

✕ **Tropicana.** The chef-owner here hails from Trinidad and specializes in both Chinese and West Indian cuisine. Local businesspeople seem to be the best customers for the extensive menu of Chinese food, the tantalizing aroma of barbecued chicken notwithstanding. Eat in or take out— it's open from 7:30 AM to midnight. Tropicana is right at the Lagoon Road traffic circle, overlooking the marina. ⊠ *Lagoon Rd., St. George's, St. George* ☎ *473/440–1586* ☐ *AE, DC, MC, V.*

CONTEMPORARY   ✕ **La Belle Creole.** The marriage of contemporary and West Indian
$$$$ cuisines and a splendid view of distant St. George's are the delights of
this romantic hillside restaurant at the Blue Horizons Garden Resort.
The always-changing five-course table d'hôte menu is based on original recipes from the owner's mother, a pioneer in incorporating local
products into "foreign" dishes. Try, for instance, Grenadian caviar (roe
of the white sea urchin), cream-of-bread-nut (related to the breadfruit)
soup, lobster-egg flan, or callaloo quiche, followed by lobster à la creole or ginger pork chops. The inspired cuisine, romantic setting, and gracious service are impressive. ⊠ *Blue Horizons Garden Resort, Grand
Anse, St. George* 🕾 *473/444–4316 or 473/444–4592* ⌁ *Reservations
essential* ▤ *AE, D, MC, V.*

★ $$–$$$ ✕ **Rhodes Restaurant.** The open-air restaurant at the Calabash Hotel, named
for acclaimed British chef Gary Rhodes, is surrounded by palms, flowering plants, and twinkling lights. Past menus have featured seared yellowfin tuna Benedict and Waldorf salad cocktail with avocado and
grapefruit as starters, followed by fillet of red snapper on smoked
salmon potatoes, Caribbean pepper steak with sweet-potato *parmen-
tière* (pancake), or roast duck breast with leeks and pepperpot sauce.
The passion-fruit panna cotta, light as a soufflé and bathed in a fruity
sauce, is nothing short of divine. ⊠ *Calabash Hotel, L'Anse aux Épines,
St. George* 🕾 *473/444–4334* ⌁ *Reservations essential* ▤ *AE, MC, V*
🕘 *No lunch.*

★ $$–$$$ ✕ **Water's Edge.** At this Bel Air Plantation restaurant overlooking pris-
tine St. David's Harbour, the dining experience is as exquisite as the view
is mesmerizing. (The napkins are even folded into the shape of binoculars.) Tables are set on the covered verandah or on the garden patio.
The extensive menu includes fish and lobster from the surrounding waters, fresh produce from nearby farms and the resort's own gardens, and
imported meats—all delicately flavored with local herbs and spices.
Have drinks in the lounge before or after your meal to enjoy the 360-
degree view. ⊠ *Bel Air Plantation, St. David's Point, St. David* 🕾 *473/
443–2822* ⌁ *Reservations essential* ▤ *AE, D, MC, V.*

ECLECTIC   ✕ **The Beach House.** At this colorful restaurant next door to Laluna re-
$$–$$$ sort, the gleaming white sand and sea views are the perfect backdrop
for a salad or pasta luncheon on the deck. At dinner, excellent entrées—
sashimi tuna, rack of lamb, blackened fish, or prime rib—accompanied
by a superb wine give new meaning to the term "beach party." A kids'
menu is available, too. ⊠ *Airport Rd. Point Salines St. George's* 🕾 *473/
444–4455* ⌁ *Reservations essential* ▤ *AE, MC, V* 🕘 *Closed Sun.*

$–$$$ ✕ **Tout Bagay Restaurant & Bar.** Its name means "everything is possible,"
and the eclectic menu proves the point. At lunch, for example, you might
select a salad (lobster, shrimp, Caesar) or try a local specialty, such as
a roti, flying-fish sandwich, or creole-style fish. At dinner, the menu is
equally broad—lobster thermidor, cappellini with red-pepper pesto and
shrimp, curry goat, or sweet-and-sour lambi. Since it's on the water at
the northern end of the Carenage, the view (day or night) is spectacu-
lar. It's a popular lunch choice for businesspeople, as well as those tour-
ing the capital or shopping on adjacent streets. ⊠ *The Carenage, St.
George's, St. George* 🕾 *473/440–1500* ▤ *MC, V.*

¢–$$ ✕ **La Boulangerie.** This combination French bakery and Italian pizzeria, convenient to the hotels at Grand Anse, is a great place for an inexpensive breakfast or light meal—to eat in, take out, or have delivered. You'll find croissants and other specialty breads, focaccia and baguette sandwiches, pizza and pasta dishes, coffee and espresso, and homemade gelato. ⊠ *Le Marquis Complex Grand Anse St. George's* ☎ *473/444–1131* ⊟ *AE. MC, V.*

SEAFOOD
$$–$$$$ ✕ **The Red Crab.** Locals and expats love to gather at this pub, especially on Saturday night. The curried lambi and garlic shrimp keep the regulars coming back. Seafood, particularly lobster, and steak (imported from the U.S.) are staples of the menu; hot garlic bread comes with every order. Eat inside or under the stars, and enjoy live music Monday and Friday evenings in season. ⊠ *L'Anse aux Épines, near Calabash, St. George* ☎ *473/444–4424* ⌔ *Reservations essential* ⊟ *AE, MC, V* ⊗ *Closed Sun.*

$–$$ ✕ **Aquarium Restaurant.** As the name suggests, fresh seafood is the spe-
Fodor'sChoice cialty here. Visitors and locals alike flock to the Aquarium for delicious
★ dining in a relaxed, friendly atmosphere. Many spend the day at the adjacent beach (you can rent kayaks or snorkeling gear), breaking for a cool drink or satisfying lunch on the deck. The dining room is surrounded by lush plants and palms, and a waterfall adds romance. The dinner menu always includes fresh fish, grilled lobster, and specialties such as callaloo cannelloni. On Sunday there's a beach barbecue. A very congenial spot, it's even convenient to the airport for a preflight meal. ⊠ *LaSource Rd., Point Salines, St. George* ☎ *473/444–1410* ⌔ *Reservations essential* ⊟ *AE, D, DC, MC, V* ⊗ *Closed Mon.*

¢–$$ ✕ **La Sagesse Nature Centre.** The perfect spot to soothe a frazzled soul, La Sagesse's open-air seafood restaurant is on a secluded cove in a nature preserve about 30 minutes from Grand Anse. You can combine your lunch or dinner with a hike or a day at the beach. Select from sandwiches, salads, or lobster for lunch. Lambi, smoked marlin, tuna steak, and a daily vegetarian entrée may be joined on the dinner menu by specials like chicken française. Wash down your meal with a cold beer or a fresh-fruit smoothie. Transportation is available. ⊠ *La Sagesse, St. David* ☎ *473/444–6458* ⌔ *Reservations essential* ⊟ *AE, MC, V.*

Carriacou

CARIBBEAN ✕ **Callaloo by the Sea Restaurant & Bar.** On the main road, just south of
¢–$$ the town jetty in Hillsborough, diners enjoy extraordinary views of Sandy Island and Hillsborough Bay. The emphasis is on West Indian dishes and excellent seafood—including lobster, fried fish fingers, and lambi stew—plus sandwiches, salads, and curried chicken. The callaloo soup, of course, is outstanding. This is a perfect lunch stop for day-trippers. After you eat, step from the dining room onto the beach for a swim; then mosey back to the jetty to catch the ferry back to Grenada. ⊠ *Hillsborough* ☎ *473/443–8004* ⊟ *AE, MC, V* ⊗ *Closed Sept.*

SEAFOOD ✕ **Scraper's.** Scraper's serves up lobster, conch, and the fresh catch of
¢–$ the day. It's a simple spot seasoned with occasional calypsonian serenades (by owner Steven "Scraper" Gay, who's a pro). Order a rum

punch to really enjoy yourself. ✉ *Tyrrel Bay* ☎ *473/443–7403* ▤ *AE, D, MC, V.*

Beaches

Grenada

Grenada has some 80 mi (130 km) of coastline, 65 bays, and 45 white-sand (and a few black-sand) beaches—many in little coves. The best beaches are just south of St. George's, facing the Caribbean, where most resorts are also clustered.

★ **Bathway Beach.** A broad strip of sand with a natural reef that protects swimmers from the rough Atlantic surf on Grenada's far northern shore, this Levera National Park beach has changing rooms at the park headquarters. ✉ *Levera, St. Patrick.*

Fodor'sChoice **Grand Anse Beach.** In the southwest, about 3 mi (5 km) south of St. George's,
★ Grenada's loveliest and most popular beach is a gleaming 2-mi (3-km) semicircle of white sand lapped by clear, gentle surf. Sea-grape trees and coconut palms provide shady escapes from the sun. Brilliant rainbows frequently spill into the sea from the high green mountains that frame St. George's Harbour to the north. The Grand Anse Craft & Spice Market is at the midpoint of the beach. ✉ *Grand Anse, St. George.*

La Sagesse Beach. Along the southeast coast, at La Sagesse Nature Center, this is a lovely, quiet refuge with a strip of powdery white sand. Plan a full day of nature walks, with lunch at the small inn adjacent to the beach. ✉ *La Sagesse, St. David.*

Morne Rouge Beach. One mile (1½ km) south of Grand Anse Bay, this ½-mi-long (¾-km-long) crescent has a gentle surf that is excellent for swimming. Light meals are available nearby. ✉ *Morne Rouge, St. George.*

Carriacou

Anse La Roche. Like all the beaches on Carriacou, this one—about a 15-minute hike from the village of Prospect, in the north—has pure white sand, sparkling clear water, and abundant marine life for snorkelers. It's never crowded here. ✉ *Windward.*

Hillsborough Beach. Day-trippers can take a dip at this strip of sand adjacent to the jetty. The beach extends for quite a distance in each direction, so there's plenty of room to swim without interference from the boat traffic. ✉ *Hillsborough.*

Paradise Beach. This long, narrow stretch of sand between Hillsborough and Tyrrel Bay has calm, clear, inviting water, but there are no changing facilities. ✉ *L'Esterre.*

★ **Sandy Island.** This is a truly deserted island off Hillsborough—just a ring of white sand with a few palm trees, surrounded by a reef and crystal-clear waters. Anyone hanging around the jetty with a motorboat will provide transportation for about $10 per person, round-trip. Bring your snorkeling gear and, if you want, a picnic—and leave all your cares behind. ✉ *Hillsborough Bay.*

Tyrrel Bay Beach. This swath of sand is popular with the sailing set, who use the bay as an anchorage. But beware the manchineel trees here; they drop poisonous green "apples," and their foliage can burn your skin. ✉ *Harvey Vale.*

Sports & the Outdoors

BOATING &
SAILING
★

As the "Gateway to the Grenadines," Grenada attracts significant numbers of seasoned sailors to its waters. Large marinas are in the lagoon area of St. George's, at Prickly Bay and True Blue on Grenada's south coast, at St. David's in southeast Grenada, and at Tyrrel Bay in Carriacou. You can charter a yacht, with or without crew, for weeklong sailing vacations through the Grenadines or along the coast of Venezuela. Scenic half- or full-day sails along Grenada's coast cost $3 to $60 per person (with a minimum of four passengers), including lunch or snacks and open bar; a full-day cruise from Grenada to Carriacou may cost $350 to $700, depending on the boat, for up to six people.

Carib Cats (☎ 473/444–3222) departs from the lagoon area of St. George's for a full-day sail along the southwest coast, a half-day snorkel cruise to Molinère Bay, or a two-hour sunset cruise along the west coast. **Footloose Yacht Charters** (☎ 473/440–7949 ⊕ www.grenadasailing. com) operates from the lagoon in St. George's and has both sailing and motor yachts available for day trips around Grenada or longer charters to the Grenadines. **Horizon Yacht Charters** (☎ 473/439–1000 ⊕ www. horizonyachtcharters.com), at True Blue Bay Resort, will arrange bareboat or crewed charters, as well as day sails or three-day trips to the Grenadines. **Island Dreams** (☎ 473/443–3603) operates from Martin's Marina in L'Anse aux Épines and has a 45-foot sailing yacht available for private half- or full-day charters for up to 10 passengers or overnight sails around Grenada or to the Grenadines for two people.

DIVING &
SNORKELING

You can see hundreds of varieties of fish and some 40 species of coral at more than a dozen sites off Grenada's southwest coast—only 15 to 20 minutes by boat—and another couple of dozen sites around Carriacou's reefs and neighboring islets. Depths vary from 20 to 120 feet, and visibility varies from 30 to 100 feet.

Off Grenada: A spectacular dive is *Bianca C,* a 600-foot cruise ship that caught fire in 1961, sank to 100 feet, and is now encrusted with coral and serves as a habitat for giant turtles, spotted eagle rays, barracuda, and jacks. **Boss Reef** extends 5 mi (8 km) from St. George's Harbour to Point Salines, with a depth ranging from 20 to 90 feet. **Flamingo Bay** has a wall that drops to 90 feet and is teeming with fish, sponges, sea horses, sea fans, and coral. **Molinère Reef** slopes from about 20 feet below the surface to a wall that drops to 65 feet. It's a good dive for beginners, and advanced divers can continue farther out to view the wreck of the *Buccaneer,* a 42-foot sloop.

Off Carriacou: **Kick-em Jenny** is an active underwater volcano, with plentiful coral and marine life in the vicinity and, usually, visibility up to 100 feet; though you can't actually dive down 500 feet to reach the actual volcano. **Sandy Island**, in Hillsborough Bay, is especially good for night diving and has fish that feed off its extensive reefs 70 feet deep. For experienced divers, **Twin Sisters of Isle de Rhonde** is one of the most spectacular dives in the Grenadines, with walls and drop-offs of up to 185 feet and an underwater cave.

Most dive operators take snorkelers along on dive trips or have special snorkeling adventures. The best snorkeling in Grenada is at Molinère Point, north of St. George's; in Carriacou, Sandy Island is magnificent and just a few hundred yards offshore. Snorkeling trips cost about $25 per person.

The PADI-certified dive operators listed below offer scuba and snorkeling trips to reefs and wrecks, including night dives and special excursions to the *Bianca C.* They also offer resort courses for beginning divers and certification instruction for more experienced divers. It costs about $40 to $45 for a one-tank dive, $75 to $80 for a two-tank dive, $50 for trips to the *Bianca C,* $110 to $125 to dive Isle de Rhonde, and $55 to $60 for night dives. Discounted 5- and 10-dive packages are usually offered. Resort courses cost about $80 to $95 and open-water certification from $200 to $395.

Aquanauts Grenada (✉ Grand Anse Beach, Grand Anse, St. George's ☎ 473/444–1126 or 888/446–9235 in U.S. ✉ True Blue Bay Resort, True Blue ☎ 473/439–2500 ⊕ www.aquanautgrenada.com) has a multilingual staff, so instruction is available in English, German, Dutch, French, and Spanish. Two-tank dive trips, accommodating no more than eight divers, are offered each morning to both the Caribbean and Atlantic sides of Grenada. **Dive Grenada** (✉ Flamboyant Hotel, Morne Rouge, St. George ☎ 473/444–1092 ⊕ www.divegrenada.net) offers dive trips twice daily (at 10 AM and 2 PM), specializing in diving the *Bianca C.* **EcoDive** (✉ Grenada Grand Beach Resort, Grand Anse, St. George ☎ 473/444–7777 ⊕ www.ecodiveandtrek.com) offers two dive trips daily, both drift and wreck dives, as well as weekly trips to dive Isle de Rhonde. The company also runs Grenada's marine conservation and education center, which conducts coral-reef monitoring and turtle projects. **ScubaTech Grenada** (✉ Calabash Hotel, L'Anse aux Épines, St. George ☎ 473/439–4346 ⊕ www.scubatech-grenada.com) has two full-time diving instructors and, in addition to daily dive trips, offers the complete range of PADI programs, from discover scuba to divemaster.

Arawak Divers (✉ Tyrrel Bay, Carriacou ☎ 473/443–6906 ⊕ www. arawak.de) has its own jetty at Tyrrel Bay; it takes small groups on daily dive trips and night dives, offers courses in German and English, and provides pickup service from yachts. **Carriacou Silver Diving** (✉ Main St., Hillsborough, Carriacou ☎ 473/443–7882 ⊕ www.scubamax.com) accommodates up to 12 divers on one of its dive boats and up to 6 on another. The center operates two guided single-tank dives daily as well as individually scheduled excursions.

FISHING Deep-sea fishing around Grenada is excellent, with marlin, sailfish, yellowfin tuna, and dolphinfish topping the list of good catches. You can arrange sportfishing trips for $375 for a half-day to $580 for a full day that accommodate up to five people. **True Blue Sportfishing** (☎ 473/444–2048 ⊕ www.yesaye.com) offers big-game charters on its 31-foot *Yes Aye.* It has an enclosed cabin, fighting chair, and professional tackle. British-born Capt. Gary Clifford, who has been fishing since the age of six, has run the company since 1998. Refreshments and courtesy transport are included.

GOLF An 18-hole, 7,250-yard championship golf course has been under development for some time at Levera Beach, at the northeastern tip of Grenada, but it remains on hold due to the focus on rebuilding following Hurricane Ivan. Determined golfers might want to try the pleasant but not particularly challenging 9-hole course at the **Grenada Golf & Country Club** (☎ 473/444–4128), about halfway between St. George's and Grand Anse. Greens fees are EC$7, and club rental is available; your hotel can make arrangements for you. Popular with local businessmen, this course is convenient to most hotels and is the only public course on the island.

HIKING Mountain trails wind through **Grand Étang National Park & Forest Reserve**
Fodor'sChoice (☎ 473/440–6160); if you're lucky, you may spot a Mona monkey or
★ some exotic birds on your hike. There are trails for all levels—from a self-guided nature trail around Grand Étang Lake to a demanding one through the bush to the peak of Mt. Qua Qua (2,373 feet) or a real trek up Mt. St. Catherine (2,757 feet). Long pants and hiking shoes are recommended. The cost is $25 per person for a four-hour guided hike up Mt. Qua Qua, $20 each for two or more, or $15 each for three or more; the Mt. St. Catherine hike starts at $35 per person. **EcoTrek** (☎ 473/444–7777 ⊕ www.ecodiveandtrek.com) takes small groups on day trips to the heart of the rain forest, where you'll find hidden waterfalls and hot-spring pools. **Henry's Safari Tours** (☎ 473/444–5313 ⊕ www.spiceisle.com/safari) offers hiking excursions through rich agricultural land and rain forest to Upper Concord Falls and other fascinating spots. **Telfor Bedeau, Hiking Guide** (☎ 473/442–6200), affectionately referred to locally as the Indiana Jones of Grenada, is a national treasure. Over the years he has walked up, down, or across nearly every mountain, trail, and pathway on the island. In February 2005, he hit the incredible milestone of having hiked 10,000 miles throughout Grenada over 43 years. His experience and knowledge make him an excellent guide, whether it's an easy walk with novices or the most strenuous hike with experts.

Shopping

Grenada's best souvenirs or gifts for friends back home are spice baskets filled with cinnamon, nutmeg, mace, bay leaves, cloves, turmeric, and ginger. You can buy them for as little as $2 in practically every shop, at the open-air produce market at **Market Square** in St. George's, at the vendor stalls along the Carenage and at the port, and at the Vendor's Craft & Spice Market on Grand Anse Beach. Vendors also sell handmade fabric dolls, coral jewelry, seashells, and hats and baskets handwoven from green palm fronds. Bargaining is not appropriate in the shops and isn't customary with vendors—although most will offer you "a good price."

Here's some local terminology you should know. If someone asks if you'd like a "sweetie," you're being offered a candy. When you buy spices, you may be offered "saffron" and "vanilla." The saffron is really turmeric, a ground yellow root rather than the fragile pistils of crocus

Mr. Canute Caliste

SELF-TAUGHT FOLK ARTIST
Canute Caliste, certainly one of Grenada's national treasures, began painting at nine years of age in a colorful, primitive style that hardly changed for nearly 80 years. His charming, childlike paintings depict island life—boatbuilding, bread baking, wedding festivities, courting, farming, dancing, whaling, children's games, even a mermaid.

Born in Carriacou in 1914, Caliste painted in a tiny studio, a simple board building adjacent to his home in the village of L'Esterre. Surrounded by kids, grandkids, and barnyard animals, the artist—with apparently boundless energy—completed up to 16 paintings per day, always labeling, dating, then signing each one: "Mr. Canute Caliste."

A prolific family man, Caliste has 19 children and more than 100 grandchildren. Daughter Clemencia Caliste Alexander (his ninth child, with six kids of her own) has worked in the Carriacou Historical Museum, in Hillsborough, since 1978. Her teenage son, incidentally, inherited his grandfather's skill and style.

Over the years, the price of Caliste's works skyrocketed. In the early 1990s, visitors to his studio could purchase a barely dry painting for $10 to $25. Today Caliste paintings fetch hundreds of dollars at the museum in Carriacou and often thousands of dollars from private collectors. Caliste stopped painting at age 87 but continued to play the fiddle in a local quadrille band. He passed away in 2005, at the age of 91.

Caliste's amusing paintings are certainly delightful mementos of a visit to Grenada, but those finding them too dear can purchase inexpensive postcard-size prints or his book, *The Mermaid Wakes*, which is chock full of prints, at the museum. The book is also available in book and gift shops in Grenada.

flowers; the vanilla is an essence made from locally grown tonka beans, a close substitute but not the real thing. No one is trying to pull the wool over your eyes; these are common local terms.

Areas & Malls

In St. George's, the **Carenage** has several gift and souvenir shops. On the north side of the harbor, **Young Street** is a main shopping thoroughfare; it rises steeply uphill from the Carenage, then descends just as steeply to the market area.

In Grand Anse, a short walk from the resorts, the **Excel Plaza** has shops and services to interest locals and tourists alike, including a full-service health club and a three-screen movie theater. **Grand Anse Shopping Centre** has a supermarket and liquor store, a clothing store, a fast-food restaurant, a pharmacy, an art gallery, and several small gift shops. **Le Marquis Complex,** nearby but across the street, has restaurants, shops, an art gallery, and tourist services. **Spiceland Mall** has a modern supermarket with a liquor section, clothing and shoe boutiques for men and women, housewares stores, a wine shop, gift shops, a food court, a bank, and a video-game arcade.

Specialty Items

ART **Art Grenada** (⌂ Grand Anse Shopping Centre, Suite 7, Grand Anse, St. George ☎ 473/444–2317) sells paintings, drawings, and watercolors exclusively by Grenadian artists, among them Canute Caliste, Lyndon Bedeau, and Susan Mains. Exhibitions change monthly, and you can have your purchases shipped.

BOOKS A colorful souvenir picture book, a book on island culture and history, a charming local story for kids, a thick novel for the beach, or a paperback for the trip home–all are good reasons to drop into a bookstore. **Sea Change** (⌂ The Carenage, St. George's, St. George ☎ 473/440–3402) is nestled underneath the Nutmeg restaurant, right on the waterfront.

DUTY-FREE GOODS Duty-free shops at the airport sell liquor at impressive discounts of up to 50%, as well as perfumes, crafts, and Grenadian syrups, jams, and hot sauces. You can shop duty-free at some shops in town, but you must show your passport and outbound ticket to benefit from the duty-free prices. **Gitten's** (⌂ The Carenage, St. George's, St. George ☎ 473/440–3174 ⌂ Spiceland Mall, Grand Anse, St. George ☎ 473/439–0860 ⌂ Point Salines International Airport, St. George ☎ 473/444–2549) carries perfume and cosmetics at its three shops.

FOODSTUFFS **Marketing & National Importing Board** (⌂ Young St., St. George's, St. George ☎ 473/440–1791) stocks fresh fruits and vegetables, spices, hot sauces, and local syrups and jams at lower prices than you can find in most gift
★ shops. The open-air **Market Square** (⌂ Foot of Young St., St. George's, St. George) is a bustling produce market that's open mornings; Saturday is the best—and busiest—time to stock up on fresh fruit to enjoy during your stay. But it's a particularly good place to buy island-grown spices, perhaps the best such market in the entire Caribbean. Crafts, leather goods, and decorative objects are also for sale.

GIFTS **Figleaf** (⌂ Le Marquis Complex, Grand Anse, St. George ☎ 473/439–1824) is a small gift shop where you can find an interesting selection of Caribbean arts and crafts, aromatherapy and herbal bath products, and casual clothing. **Imagine** (⌂ Grand Anse Shopping Centre, Grand Anse, St. George ☎ 473/444–4028) specializes in island handicrafts, including straw work, ceramics, island fashions, and batik fabrics. **Pssst Boutique** (⌂ Spiceland Mall, Grand Anse, St. George ☎ 473/439–0787) will catch your eye; it's chock-full of unusual costume jewelry, colorful island clothing, and fascinating gift items for the home.

HANDICRAFTS **Art Fabrik** (⌂ 9 Young St., St. George's, St. George ☎ 473/440–0568) is a studio where you can watch artisans create batik before turning it into clothing or accessories. In the shop you can find fabric by the yard or fashioned into dresses, shirts, shorts, hats, and scarves. The **Vendor's Craft & Spice Market at Grand Anse** (⌂ Grand Anse, St. George ☎ 473/444–3780), managed by the Grenada Board of Tourism, is located between the main road and the beach. The facility has 82 booths for vendors who sell arts, crafts, spices, music tapes, clothing, produce, and refreshments. It's open daily from 7 to 7. **Tikal** (⊠ Young St., St. George's, St. George ☎ 473/440–2310) is known for its exquisite baskets, artwork, jewelry, batik items, and fashions, both locally made and imported from Africa and Latin America.

Nightlife & the Arts

Nightlife

Grenada's nightlife is centered on the resort hotels and a handful of nightspots in the Grand Anse area. During the winter season some hotels have a steel band or other local entertainment several nights a week.

BARS **Banana's Sports Bar** (⊠ True Blue, St. George ☎ 473/444–4662) is a casual restaurant and nightspot popular among the students at nearby St. George's University. There's music—Caribbean, salsa, oldies, alternative, pop—and dancing Wednesday through Saturday nights. On weekends, there's a EC$10 cover charge.

DANCE CLUBS **Dynamite Disco** (⊠ The Limes, Grand Anse, St. George ☎ 473/444–4056) has a party every weekend, with disco, reggae, and calypso music. **Fantazia** (⊠ Morne Rouge, St. George ☎ 473/444–4224) is a popular nightspot; disco, soca, reggae, and international pop music are played from 9:30 PM until the wee hours on weekends. There's a small cover charge of EC$10 to EC$20.

THEME NIGHTS **Rhum Runner** (⊠ The Carenage, St. George's, St. George ☎ 473/440–2198), a 60-foot twin-deck catamaran, leaves from the Carenage at 7:30 PM each Friday and Saturday for a moonlight cruise in the waters around St. George's and Grand Anse, returning about midnight. Tickets are $10, and reservations are recommended. On Wednesday from 6 to 9 there's a sunset dinner cruise for $40 per person; reservations must be made by 4:30 the day before. *Rhum Runner II*, a 72-foot sister ship, operates monthly moonlight cruises the Friday and Saturday nights nearest the full moon for $11 per person—add $2 for a barbecue dinner.

The Arts

ISLAND CULTURE **Marryshow Folk Theatre** (⊠ Herbert Blaize St., St. George's, St. George ☎ 473/440–2451) presents concerts, plays, and special cultural events. Call for a schedule.

Exploring Grenada

Numbers in the margin correspond to points of interest on the Grenada & Carriacou map.

Grenada

Grenada is divided into six parishes, including one named St. George, in which the communities of Grand Anse, Morne Rouge, True Blue, and L'Anse aux Épines, as well as the capital city of St. George's, are all located.

WHAT TO SEE **Annandale Falls.** A mountain stream cascades 40 feet into a pool sur-
❺ rounded by exotic vines, such as liana and elephant ear. A paved path leads to the bottom of the falls, and a trail leads to the top. This is a

lovely, cool spot for swimming and picnicking. ⊠ *Main interior road, 15 mins northeast of St. George's, St. George* ☎ *473/440–2452* ☒ *$1* ⊗ *Daily 9–5.*

❿ **Carib's Leap.** At Sauteurs (the French word for "leapers"), on the island's northernmost tip, Carib's Leap (or Leapers Hill) is the 100-foot vertical cliff from which the last of the indigenous Carib Indians flung themselves into the sea in 1651. After losing several bloody battles with European colonists, they chose to kill themselves rather than surrender to the French. A commemorative display recounts the event. ⊠ *Sauteurs.*

★ ❼ **Concord Falls.** About 8 mi (13 km) north of St. George's, a turnoff from the West Coast Road leads to Concord Falls—actually three separate waterfalls. The first is at the end of the road; when the currents aren't too strong, you can take a dip under the cascade. Reaching the two other waterfalls requires an hour's hike into the forest reserve. The third and most spectacular waterfall, at Fountainbleu, thunders 65 feet over huge boulders and creates a small pool. It's smart to hire a guide. The path is clear, but slippery boulders toward the end can be treacherous without assistance. ⊠ *Off West Coast Rd., St. John* ☒ *Changing room $2.*

❸ **De La Grenade Industries.** In the suburb of St. Paul's, five minutes outside St. George's, this company produces syrups, jams, jellies, and a liqueur from nutmeg and other homegrown fruits and spices. The liqueur "recipe" is a 19th-century formula and a family secret. The company was founded in 1960 by Sybil La Grenade as a cottage industry. Following her tragic death in a car accident in 1991, the company is now overseen by her daughter, Cécile, a U.S.-trained food technologist. You're welcome to watch the process and purchase gifts from the retail operation on-site. ⊠ *Morne Délice, St. Paul's, St. George* ☎ *473/440–3241* ⊕ *www.delagrenade.com* ☒ *Free* ⊗ *Weekdays 8–5, Sat. 9–12:30.*

☾ ❽ **Dougaldston Spice Estate.** Just south of Gouyave, this historic plantation, now primarily a living museum, still grows and processes spices the old-fashioned way. You can see cocoa, nutmeg, mace, cloves, and other spices laid out on giant racks to dry in the sun. A worker will be glad to explain the process (and will appreciate a small donation). You can buy spices for about $2 a bag. ⊠ *Gouyave, St. John* ☎ *No phone* ☒ *Free* ⊗ *Weekdays 9–4.*

★ ☾ ❾ **Gouyave Nutmeg Processing Cooperative.** Touring the nutmeg processing coop, in the center of the west-coast fishing village of Gouyave (pronounced *gwahve*), is a fragrant, fascinating way to spend half an hour. You can learn all about nutmeg and its uses, see the nutmegs laid out in bins, and watch the workers sort them by hand and pack them into burlap bags for shipping worldwide. The three-story plant turned out 3 million pounds of Grenada's most famous export each year prior to Hurricane Ivan's devastating effect on the crop in 2004. Locals estimate it will be 2010 before the nutmeg industry returns to that level. ⊠ *Gouyave, St. John* ☎ *473/444–8337* ☒ *$1* ⊗ *Weekdays 10–1 and 2–4.*

☾ ❷ **Grand Anse.** A residential and commercial area about 5 mi (8 km) south of downtown St. George's, Grand Anse is named for the world-renowned beach it surrounds. Grenada's tourist facilities—resorts, restaurants, some shopping, and most nightlife—are in this general area. **Grand Anse Beach** is a 2-mi (3-km) crescent of sand shaded by coconut palms and sea-grape trees, with gentle turquoise surf. A public entrance is at Camerhogne Park, just a few steps from the main road. Water taxis from the Carenage in St. George's pull up to a jetty on the beach. **St. George's University,** which for years held classes at its enviable beachfront location in Grand Anse, has a sprawling campus in True Blue, a nearby residential community. The university's Grand Anse property, from which the evacuation of U.S. medical students was a high priority of the U.S. Marines during the 1983 intervention, is currently used for administrative purposes. ⊠ *St. George.*

★ ⟡ ❻ **Grand Étang National Park & Forest Reserve.** Deep in the mountainous interior of Grenada is a bird sanctuary and forest reserve with miles of hiking trails, lookouts, and fishing streams. **Grand Étang Lake** is a 36-acre expanse of cobalt-blue water that fills the crater of an extinct volcano 1,740 feet above sea level. Although legend has it the lake is bottomless, maximum soundings are recorded at 18 feet. The informative **Grand Étang Forest Center** has displays on the local wildlife and vegetation. A forest manager is on hand to answer questions. A small snack bar and souvenir stands are nearby. ⊠ *Main interior road, between Grenville and St. George's, St. Andrew* ☎ *473/440–6160* ✒ *$1* ⊙ *Daily 8:30–4.*

⟡ ❹ **Laura Herb & Spice Garden.** The 6½-acre gardens are part of an old plantation in the village of Laura, in St. David Parish, just 6 mi (10 km) east of Grand Anse. On the 20-minute tour you can learn all about Grenada's indigenous spices and herbs—including cocoa, clove, nutmeg, pimiento, cinnamon, turmeric, and tonka beans (similar to vanilla)—and how they're used for flavoring and for medicinal purposes. ⊠ *Laura, St. David* ☎ *473/443–2604* ✒ *$2* ⊙ *Weekdays 8–4.*

⓫ **Levera National Park & Bird Sanctuary.** This portion of Grenada's protected parkland encompasses 450 acres at the northeastern tip of the island, where the Caribbean Sea meets the Atlantic Ocean. Facilities include a visitor center, changing rooms, a small amphitheater, and a gift shop. A natural reef protects swimmers from the rough Atlantic surf at Bathway Beach. Thick mangroves provide food and protection for nesting seabirds and seldom-seen parrots. Some fine Arawak ruins and petroglyphs are on display, and the first islets of the Grenadines are visible from the beach. Entrance and use of the beaches and grounds are free; there's a small charge to view the displays in the visitor center. ⊠ *Levera, St. Patrick* ☎ *473/442–1018* ✒ *Free* ⊙ *Weekdays 8:30–4.*

⓭ **Pearl's Airport.** Just north of Grenville, on the east coast, is the island's original airport, which was replaced in 1984 by Point Salines International Airport. Deteriorating Cuban and Soviet planes sit at the end of the old runway, abandoned after the 1983 intervention, when Cuban "advisors" helping to construct the airport at Point Salines were summarily removed from the island. There's a good view north to the Grenadines and a small beach nearby. ⊠ *Grenville, St. Andrew.*

River Antoine Rum Distillery. At this rustic operation, kept open primarily as a museum, a limited quantity of Rivers rum is produced by the same methods used since the distillery opened in 1785. The process begins with the crushing of sugarcane from adjacent fields in the River Antoine (pronounced an-*twine*) Estate. The result is a potent overproof rum, sold only in Grenada, that will knock your socks off. ✉ *River Antoine Estate, St. Patrick, St. Patrick* ☎ *473/442–7109* 💲 *$2* ☉ *Guided tours daily 9–4.*

St. George's. Grenada's capital is a bustling West Indian city, most of which remains unchanged from colonial days. Narrow streets lined with shops wind up, down, and across steep hills. Pastel-painted warehouses cling to the waterfront, while buildings and homes rise from the waterfront and disappear into steep green hills.

St. George's Harbour is the center of town. Schooners, ferries, and tour boats tie up along the seawall or at the small dinghy dock. On weekends a tall ship is likely to be anchored in the middle of the harbor, giving the scene a 19th-century flavor. The **Carenage** (pronounced car-a-*nahzh*), which surrounds horseshoe-shape St. George's Harbour, is the capital's main thoroughfare. Warehouses, shops, and restaurants line the waterfront. At the center of the Carenage, on the pedestrian plaza, sits the *Christ of the Deep* statue. It was presented to Grenada by Costa Cruise Line in remembrance of its ship *Bianca C,* which burned and sank in the harbor in 1961 and is now a favorite dive site.

The **Grenada National Museum** (✉ Young and Monckton Sts. ☎ 473/440–3725 💲 $1 ☉ Weekdays 9–4:30, Sat. 10–1), a block from the Carenage, is built on the foundation of a French army barracks and prison that was originally built in 1704. The small museum has exhibitions of news items, photos, and proclamations relating to the 1983 intervention, along with Empress Josephine's childhood bathtub and other memorabilia from earlier historical periods.

FodorsChoice
★
Fort George (✉ Church St.) is high on the hill at the entrance to St. George's Harbour. It's Grenada's oldest fort—built by the French in 1705 to protect the harbor. No shots were ever fired here until October 1983, when Prime Minister Maurice Bishop and some of his followers were assassinated in the courtyard. The fort now houses police headquarters but is open to the public daily; admission is free. The 360-degree view of the capital city, St. George's Harbour, and the open sea is spectacular. An engineering feat for its time, the 340-foot-long **Sendall Tunnel** was built in 1895 and named for an early governor. It separates the harbor side of St. George's from the Esplanade on the bay side of town, where you can find the markets (produce, meat, and fish), the cruise-ship terminal, and the public bus station.

Don't miss St. George's picturesque **Market Square** (✉ Granby St.), a block from the cruise-ship terminal. It's open every weekday morning but really comes alive on Saturday from 8 to noon. Vendors sell baskets, spices, brooms, clothing, knickknacks, coconut water, and heaps of fresh produce. Market Square is historically where parades and political rallies take place.

St. Andrew's Presbyterian Church (✉ Halifax and Church Sts.), also known as Scots' Kirk, was constructed with the help of the Freemasons in 1830. It was heavily damaged by Hurricane Ivan in 2004; only the steeple remains intact. Its future is uncertain. Built in 1825, the beautiful **St. George's Anglican Church** (✉ Church St.) is filled with statues and plaques depicting Grenada in the 18th and 19th centuries. **St. George's Methodist Church** (✉ Green St., near Herbert Blaize St.) was built in 1820 and is the oldest original church in the city. The Gothic tower of **St. George's Roman Catholic Church** (✉ Church St.) dates from 1818, but the current structure was built in 1884; the tower is the city's most visible landmark. **York House** (✉ Church St.), dating from 1801, is home to Grenada's Houses of Parliament and Supreme Court. It, the neighboring Registry Building (1780), and Government House (1802) are fine examples of early Georgian architecture.

Overlooking the city of St. George's and the inland side of the harbor, historic **Fort Frederick** (✉ Richmond Hill) provides a panoramic view of two-thirds of Grenada. The fort was started by the French and completed in 1791 by the British; it was also the headquarters of the People's Revolutionary Government during the 1983 coup. Today you can get a bird's-eye view of much of Grenada from here.

Carriacou

Carriacou, the land of many reefs, is a hilly island and (unlike its lush sister island, Grenada) has neither lakes nor rivers, so its drinking water comes from the falling rain, caught in cisterns and purified with bleach. It gets quite arid during the dry season (January through May). Nevertheless, pigeon peas, corn, and fruit are grown here, and the climate seems to suit the mahogany trees used for furniture making and the white cedar critical to the boatbuilding that has made Carriacou famous.

Hillsborough is Carriacou's main town. Just offshore, Sandy Island is one of the nicest beaches around (although the gradually rising sea is taking its toll on this tiny spit of land). Almost anyone with a boat can give you a ride out to the island for a small fee (about $10 round-trip), and you can leave your cares on the dock. Rolling hills cut a wide swath through the middle of Carriacou, from Gun Point in the north to Tyrrel Bay in the south.

Interestingly, tiny Carriacou has several distinct cultures. Hillsborough is decidedly English; the southern region, around L'Esterre, reflects French roots; and the northern town of Windward has Scottish ties. African culture, of course, is the overarching influence.

WHAT TO SEE   **Belair.** For a wonderful bird's-eye view of Hillsborough and Carriacou's
⑮ entire west coast, drive to Belair, 700 feet above sea level, in the north-central part of the island. On the way you can pass the photogenic ruins of an old sugar mill. The Belair lookout is adjacent to Princess Royal Hospital, where patients surely find the view of the harbor and endless sea to be restorative.

 Carriacou Museum. Housed in a building that once held a cotton gin, one block from the waterfront, the museum has exhibitions of Amerindian,

European, and African artifacts, a collection of watercolors by native folk artist Canute Caliste, and a gift shop loaded with local items. ⊠ *Paterson St., Hillsborough* ☎ *473/443–8288* 🖅 *$2* ⊙ *Weekdays 9:30–4, Sat. 10–4.*

⑰ Tyrrel Bay. Picturesque Tyrrel Bay is a large protected harbor in southwest Carriacou. The bay is almost always full of sailboats, powerboats, and working boats—coming, going, or bobbing at their moorings. Edging the bay is a beach with pure white sand; bars, restaurants, a guest house, and a few shops face the waterfront.

⑯ Windward. The small town of Windward, on the northeast coast, is a boatbuilding community. You can encounter a work-in-progress along the roadside in Windward, where Grenada's Ministry of Culture has set up a training ground for interested youngsters to learn boatbuilding skills from seasoned boatbuilders. Originally constructed for inter-island commerce, the boats are now built primarily for fishing and pleasure sailing.

Petite Martinique

⑱ Petite Martinique (pronounced *pit*-ty mar-ti-*neek*), 10 minutes north of Carriacou by boat, is tiny and residential, with a guesthouse or two but no tourist facilities or attractions—just peace and quiet. Meander along the beachfront and watch the boatbuilders at work. And if by chance there's a boat launch, sailboat race, wedding, or cultural festival while you're there, you're in for a treat. The music is infectious, the food bountiful, the spirit lively.

GRENADA ESSENTIALS

To research prices, get advice from other travelers, and book travel arrangements, visit www.fodors.com.

Transportation

BY AIR

Air Jamaica has nonstop flights from New York and connecting flights from its other gateway cities via Montego Bay, Jamaica, with a stop in St. Lucia. American Airlines has a daily flight via American Eagle from San Juan, Puerto Rico. BWIA flies from New York, Miami, Washington, D.C., Toronto, London, and Manchester via Trinidad. British Airways flies from London/Gatwick twice a week. US Airways has weekly flights from Philadelphia. Virgin Atlantic flies from London–Heathrow. Air Canada Vacations operates charter flights from Toronto.

Caribbean Star and LIAT both offer frequent scheduled service linking Grenada with neighboring islands. SVG Air flies between Grenada and Carriacou, with some flights continuing on to Union Island and connecting with flights to St. Vincent or Barbados.

The departure tax, collected at the airport, is $20 (EC$50) for adults and $10 (EC$25) for children ages 5–11, payable in cash in either currency. A $4 (EC$10) departure tax is collected when you depart Carriacou.

🖪 Airline Contacts **Air Jamaica** ☎ 473/444–5975 or 800/523–5585. **American Eagle** ☎ 473/444–2121. **British Airways** ☎ 473/439–0681 or 800/744–2997. **BWIA** ☎ 473/444–1221 or 800/538–2942. **Caribbean Star** ☎ 473/439–4444 or 473/439–4422. **LIAT** ☎ 473/440–5428. **SVG Air** ☎ 473/444–3549 or 800/744-7285, 473/ 443–8519 in Carriacou. **US Air-ways** ☎ 473/439–0681. **Virgin Atlantic** ☎ 473/ 439–7471 or 473/439–5024.

🔲 Airport Contacts **Lauriston Airport** ☎ 473/ 443–6306. **Point Salines Airport** ☎ 473/444–4101.

BY BOAT & FERRY

The high-speed power catamaran *Osprey Express* makes two round-trip voyages daily from Grenada to Carriacou and on to Petite Martinique. The fare for the 90-minute one-way trip between Grenada and Carriacou is $19 per person one-way, $35 round-trip. For the 15-minute trip between Carriacou and Petite Martinique, the fare is $6 each way. The boat leaves Grenada from the Carenage in St. George's.

If you're looking for adventure and economy rather than comfort and speed, cargo schooners from Grenada to Carriacou and Petite Martinique also take passengers. The *Alexia II, Alexia III,* and/or *Adelaide B* depart from the Carenage in St. George's early each morning (except Monday and Thursday) for the four-hour voyage to Carriacou; the return trip to Grenada departs Carriacou at various times each morning (except Tuesday and Friday), depending on the boat and the day. The *Adelaide B* continues on from Carriacou to Petite Martinique (about a 1½-hour trip) on Wednesday and Saturday afternoons, returning early on Monday and Thursday mornings. The fare between Grenada and Carriacou on these schooners is $7.50 one-way, $12 round-trip; between Carriacou and Petite Martinique, it's about $5 each way. Reservations aren't necessary, but get to the wharf at daybreak to be sure you don't miss the boat.

The mail boat between Carriacou and Petite Martinique makes one round-trip on Monday, Wednesday, and Friday, leaving Petite Martinique at 8 AM and returning from Windward, Carriacou, at noon. The fare is about $5 each way.

🔲 *Osprey Express* ☎ 473/440–8126 ⊕ www. ospreylines.com.

BY CAR

Driving is a constant challenge in the tropics; however, most of Grenada's 650 mi (1,050 km) of paved roads are kept in fairly good condition—albeit steep and narrow beyond the Grand Anse area. The main road between St. George's and Grand Anse winds along the coast and is heavily traveled—and kept in excellent condition. Directions are clearly posted, but having a map on hand is certainly a good idea when you are traveling in the countryside. Driving is on the left, British-style. Gas stations are in St. George's, Grand Anse, Grenville, Gouyave, and Sauteurs.

Some rental agencies impose a minimum age of 25 and a maximum age of 65 to rent a car. Rental cars (including four-wheel-drive vehicles) cost $55 to $75 a day or $285 to $375 a week with unlimited mileage. In high season there may be a three-day minimum rental. Rental agencies offer free pickup and drop-off at either the airport or your hotel.

🔲 On Grenada: **David's Car Rentals** ☎ 473/444–3399 ⊕ www.davidscars.com. **Dollar Rent-A-Car** ☎ 473/444–4788 ⊕ www.dollargrenada.com. **Indigo Car Rentals** ☎ 473/439–3300 ⊕ www. indigocarsgrenada.com. **McIntyre Bros. Ltd.** ☎473/ 444–3944 ⊕ www.caribbeanhorizons.com. **Y & R Car Rentals** ☎ 473/444–4448 ⊕ www.y-r.com.

On Carriacou: **Barba's Auto Rentals** ☎ 473/443–7454 or 473/407–5156.

BY TAXI

Taxis are plentiful, and rates are set by the government. The trip between Grand Anse and St. George's costs $10; between Point Salines and St. George's, $15. A $4 surcharge is added for rides taken between 6 PM and 6 AM. Taxis often wait for fares at hotels and at the welcome center at the cruise-ship terminal on the north side of St. George's. Taxis can be hired at an hourly rate of $20, as well.

Water taxis are available along the Carenage. For $4 (EC$10) a motorboat will transport you on a lovely cruise between St. George's and the jetty at Grand Anse

Beach. Water taxis are privately owned, unregulated, and don't follow any particular schedule—so make arrangements for a pickup time if you expect a return trip.

In Carriacou the taxi fare from Hillsborough to Belair is $4; to Prospect, $6; and to Tyrrel Bay or Windward, $8.

Contacts & Resources

BANKS & EXCHANGE SERVICES

Prices quoted in this chapter are in U.S. dollars unless otherwise indicated.

Grenada uses the Eastern Caribbean dollar (EC$). The official exchange rate is fixed at EC$2.67 to US$1; taxis, shops, and hotels sometimes have slightly lower rates (EC$2.50 to EC$2.60). You can exchange money at banks and hotels, but U.S. and Canadian paper currency, traveler's checks, and major credit cards are widely accepted. You will usually receive change in EC$. Major credit cards—including Access, American Express, Diners Club, Discover, Eurocard, MasterCard, and Visa—are widely accepted.

🛈 First Caribbean International Bank ⊠ Church and Halifax Sts., St. George's, St. George ☎ 473/440-3232 ⊠ Grand Anse, St. George ☎ 473/444-3322 ⊠ Grenville, St. Andrew ☎ 473/442-7733 ⊠ Carriacou ☎ 473/443-7232. National Commercial Bank ⊠ True Blue, St. George ☎ 473/444-2265 ⊠ Halifax St., St. George's, St. George ☎ 473/440-3566 ⊠ Grand Anse, St. George ☎ 473/444-2627 ⊠ Grenville, St. Andrew ☎ 473/442-7618 ⊠ Carriacou ☎ 473/443-7289. Scotiabank ⊠ Halifax St., St. George's, St. George ☎ 473/440-3274 ⊠ Grand Anse, St. George ☎ 473/444-1917 ⊠ Victoria St., Grenville, St. Andrew ☎ 473/442-5507.

BUSINESS HOURS

Banks are open Monday through Thursday from 8 to 3, Friday from 8 to 5. The main post office, at Burns Point by the port in St. George's, is open weekdays from 8 to 3:30. Each town or village has a post office branch. Stores are generally open weekdays from 8 to 4 or 4:30 and Saturday from 8 to 1; some close from noon to 1 during the week. Most are closed Sunday, although tourist shops usually open if a cruise ship is in port.

ELECTRICITY

Electric current on Grenada is 220 volts–50 cycles. Appliances rated at 110 volts (U.S. standard) will work only with a transformer and adapter plug. For dual-voltage computers or appliances, you'll still need an adapter plug; some hotels will loan adapters. Most hotels have 110 outlets for electric razors.

EMBASSIES

🛈 United Kingdom **British High Commission** ⊠ The Netherlands Bldg., Grand Anse, St. George ☎ 473/440-3536 or 473/440-3222 ⊕ www.britishhighcommission.gov.uk.
🛈 United States **Embassy of the United States** ⊠ L'Anse aux Épines Stretch, L'Anse aux Épines, St. George ☎ 473/444-1173 or 473/444-1177 ⊕ www.spiceisle.com/homepages/usemb_gd.

EMERGENCIES

🛈 Ambulance **Carriacou Ambulance** ☎ 774. **St. Andrew's Ambulance** ☎ 724. **St. George's, Grand Anse, and L'Anse aux Épines Ambulance** ☎ 434.
🛈 Coast Guard **Coast Guard** ☎ 399 emergencies, 473/444-1931 nonemergencies.
🛈 Hospitals **Princess Alice Hospital** ⊠ Mirabeau, St. Andrew ☎ 473/442-7251. **Princess Royal Hospital** ⊠ Belair, Carriacou ☎ 473/443-7400. **St. Augustine's Medical Services, Inc.** ⊠ St. Paul's, St. George ☎ 473/440-6173. **St. George's General Hospital** ⊠ St. George's, St. George ☎ 473/440-2051.
🛈 Pharmacies **Charles Pharmacy** ⊠ Sea View, Carriacou ☎ 473/443-7933. **Gitten's** ⊠ Halifax St., St. George's, St. George ☎ 473/440-2165 ⊠ Spiceland Mall, Grand Anse, St. George ☎ 473/439-0863. **Gitten's Drugmart** ⊠ Main Rd., Grand Anse, St. George ☎ 473/444-4954. **Mitchell's Pharmacy** ⊠ Grand Anse Shopping Centre, Grand Anse, St. George ☎ 473/444-3845. **Parris' Pharmacy Ltd.** ⊠ Victoria St., Grenville, St. Andrew ☎ 473/442-7330. **People's Pharmacy** ⊠ Church St., St. George's, St. George ☎ 473/440-3444.
🛈 Police & Fire **Emergencies** ☎ 911.

HEALTH

Insects can be a nuisance after heavy rains, when mosquitoes emerge, and on the beach after 4 PM, when tiny sand flies begin to bite. Use repellent, especially when hiking in the rain forest. Tap water in hotels and restaurants is perfectly safe to drink.

HOLIDAYS

Public holidays include New Year's Day (Jan. 1), Independence Day (Feb. 7), Good Friday, Easter Monday, Labour Day (May 1), Whitmonday (7th Mon. after Easter), Corpus Christi (8th Thurs. after Easter), Emancipation Holidays (1st Mon. and Tues. in Aug.), Carnival (2nd Mon. in Aug.), Thanksgiving Day (Oct. 25), Christmas, and Boxing Day (Dec. 26).

LANGUAGE

English is the official language in Grenada. Creole patois isn't commonly heard except, perhaps, among older folks in the countryside.

INTERNET, MAIL & SHIPPING

Many hotels and resorts in Grenada offer free or inexpensive Internet access to their guests. Java-Kool Internet Cafe, on the Carenage in St. George's, is open Monday through Saturday from 9 AM to 9 PM.

Airmail rates for letters to the United States, Canada, and the United Kingdom are EC$1 for a half-ounce letter or postcard; airmail rates to Australia or New Zealand are EC$1.60 for a half-ounce letter or EC$1 for a postcard. When addressing a letter to Grenada, simply write "Grenada, West Indies" after the local address.

🚩 **Java-Kool Internet Cafe** ✉ The Carenage, St. George's ☎ 473/435-3506.

PASSPORTS & VISAS

Beginning January 1, 2008, U.S. citizens must have a valid passport to reenter the United States. For entry to Grenada, a valid passport or an original birth certificate with raised seal and a valid, government-issued photo ID are acceptable for U.S., Canadian, and British citizens; everyone else must have a valid

passport. All visitors to Grenada must also have a return or ongoing ticket.

SAFETY

Crime isn't a big problem in Grenada, but it's a good idea to secure your valuables in the hotel safe and not leave articles unattended on the beach. Removing bark from trees, taking wildlife from the forest, and removing coral from the sea are all against the law.

TAXES & SERVICE CHARGES

The departure tax, collected at the airport, is $20 (EC$50) for adults and $10 (EC$25) for children ages 5–11, payable in cash in either currency. A $4 (EC$10) departure tax is collected when you are departing from Carriacou. An 8% government tax is added to all hotel and restaurant bills. A 10% service charge is generally added to hotel and restaurant bills.

TELEPHONES

The area code is 473 (easily remembered, because the numbers correspond on the dial to the first three letters of "Grenada"). Local calls are free from most hotels; for directory assistance, dial 411. Prepaid phone cards, which can be used in special card phones throughout the Caribbean for local or international calls, are sold in denominations of EC$20 ($7.50), EC$30 ($12), EC$50 ($20), and EC$75 ($28) at shops, attractions, transportation centers, and other convenient outlets. You can place direct-dial calls from Grenada to anywhere in the world using pay phones, card phones, most hotel room phones, and some mobile phones. For international calls using a major credit card, dial 111; to place a collect call or use a calling card, dial 800/225-5872 from any telephone. Pay phones are available at the airport, the cruise-ship welcome center, the Cable & Wireless office on the Carenage in St. George's, shopping centers, and other convenient locations. Pay phones accept EC25¢ and EC$1 coins, as well as U.S. quarters.

Your own cell phone may work in Grenada, but roaming charges may be prohibitively expensive. Local cell phones can be rented from the Cable & Wireless office in St. George's, or you can purchase a local prepaid card for your own cell phone at Cable & Wireless or from Digicel Grenada.

Cable & Wireless ⊠ The Carenage, St. George's ☎ 473/441-2202. **Digicel Grenada** ⊠ Granby St., St. George's ☎ 473/435-4947.

TIPPING

If the usual 10% service charge is not added to your hotel or restaurant bill, a tip at that amount is appropriate. Additional tipping is discretionary.

TOUR OPTIONS

Guided tours offer the sights of St. George's, Grand Étang National Park & Forest Reserve, spice plantations and nutmeg processing centers, rain-forest hikes and treks to waterfalls, snorkeling trips to local islands, and day trips to Carriacou. A full-day sightseeing tour costs $55 to $65 per person, including lunch; a half-day tour, $40 to $45; a guided hike to Mt. Qua Qua, $45. Grenada taxi drivers will conduct island sightseeing tours for $140 per day or $20 per hour for up to four people. Carriacou minibus drivers will take up to four people on a 2½-hour island tour for $60, and $20 per hour thereafter.

On Adventure Jeep Tour you ride in the back of a Land Rover, safari fashion, along scenic coastal roads, trek in the rain forest, lunch at a plantation, have a swim, and skirt the capital. Caribbean Horizons offers personalized tours of historic and natural island sites, market and garden tours, and excursions to Carriacou. Dennis Henry of Henry's Safari Tours knows Grenada like the back of his hand. He leads adventurous hikes and four-wheel-drive-vehicle nature safaris, or you can design your own tour. Mandoo Tours offers half- and full-day tours following northern, southern, or eastern routes, as well as hikes to Concord Falls and the mountains. Spiceland Tours

has several five- and seven-hour island tours, from the Urban–Suburban tour of St. George's and the south coast to the Emerald Forest tour, highlighting Grenada's natural beauty. Sunsation Tours offers customized and private island tours to all the usual sites and "as far off the beaten track as you want to go." From garden tours or a challenging hike to a day sail on a catamaran, it's all possible.

Adventure Jeep Tour ☎ 473/444-5337 ⊕ www.grenadajeeptours.com. **Caribbean Horizons** ☎ 473/444-1555 ⊕ www.caribbeanhorizons.com. **Henry's Safari Tours** ☎ 473/444-5313 ⊕ www.spiceisle.com/safari. **Mandoo Tours** ☎☎ 473/440-1428 ⊕ www.grenadatours.com. **Spiceland Tours** ☎ 473/440-5127. **Sunsation Tours** ☎ 473/444-1594 ⊕ www.grenadasunsation.com.

VISITOR INFORMATION

At the south end of the Carenage in St. George's, the Grenada Board of Tourism has its offices.

Before You Leave **Grenada Board of Tourism** ⊕ www.grenadagrenadines.com ⊠ 317 Madison Ave., New York, NY 10017 ☎ 212/687-9554 or 800/927-9554 🖷 212/573-9731 ⊠ 439 University Ave., Suite 920, Toronto, Ontario M5G 1Y8, Canada ☎ 416/595-1339 🖷 416/595-8278 ⊠ 1 Battersea Church Rd., London SW11 3LY, U.K. ☎ 020/7771-7016 🖷 020/7771-7181. **Grenada Hotel Association** ☎ 473/444-1353, 800/322-1753 in U.S. and Canada 🖷 473/444-4847 ⊕ www.grenadahotelsinfo.com.

In Grenada **Grenada Board of Tourism** ⊠ Burns Pt., St. George's, St. George ☎ 473/440-2001 or 473/440-2279 🖷 473/440-6637 ⊠ Pointe Salines, St. George ☎ 473/444-4140 ⊠ Main St., Hillsborough, Carriacou ☎ 473/443-7948 🖷 473/440-6637.

WEDDINGS

One appeal of marrying in Grenada is that you've already begun to enjoy a lovely island honeymoon before the wedding ceremony occurs. Nonresidents of Grenada must be on the island for a minimum of three working days prior to applying for a marriage license. Most resorts will organize your wedding for you and handle all the necessary legal arrangements once you've arrived in Grenada. Beachside weddings are popular, whether you choose a location on magnificent Grand Anse Beach or one on a tiny secluded cove. Or you may prefer a setting in a tropical garden with soft steel-pan music playing in the background, or in the rain forest, or even on a sailboat.

Your application for a marriage license is made at the Prime Minister's Office in St. George's, and the necessary stamp duty and license fees must be paid there. The process takes approximately two days—or slightly longer if either partner is divorced or there are legal issues. Documents you need to present are valid passports, birth certificates, affidavits of single status (from a clergyperson, lawyer, or registry on official letterhead), a divorce decree or former spouse's death certificate if applicable, and evidence of parental consent if either party is under the age of 21. All paperwork must be written in English (or translated and certified).

📌 **Prime Minister's Office** ✉ Ministerial Complex, Botanical Gardens, St. George's, St. George ☎ 473/440-2255.

Guadeloupe

Running on Plage Caravelle, Grande-Terre

WORD OF MOUTH

"Guadeloupe is France in the tropics. It is fantastic to get your coffee and croissants in the morning and have the aroma of baguettes in the air. It's best to speak a little French . . . since little English is spoken." —Rusalka

"The best place for diving and snorkeling is at Ile aux Pigeons (Pigeon Island) on Basse Terre—one of Jacques Cousteau's favorite diving spots. . . . You'll need a car to see it all."

—Paul

WELCOME TO GUADELOUPE

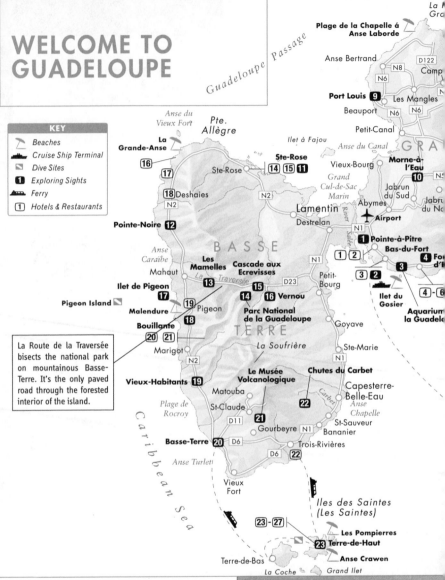

KEY

- Beaches
- Cruise Ship Terminal
- Dive Sites
- 1 Exploring Sights
- Ferry
- 1 Hotels & Restaurants

Guadeloupe Passage

Anse du Vieux Fort

Pte. Allègre

La Grande-Anse

16

17

18 Deshaies

N2

Pointe-Noire 12

BASSE

Anse Caraïbe

Mahaut

Les Mamelles

Cascade aux Ecrevisses

13

15

La Traversée

N1

D23

Petit-Bourg

Ilet de Pigeon 17

Pigeon Island

Malendure

Pigeon

19

18

14

16 Vernou

Parc National de la Guadeloupe

TERRE

Goyave

Bouillante

Marigot

N2

20

21

La Soufrière

La Route de la Traversée bisects the national park on mountainous Basse-Terre. It's the only paved road through the forested interior of the island.

Vieux-Habitants 19

Matouba

St-Claude

D11

21

Le Musée Volcanologique

Chutes du Carbet

22

Capesterre-Belle-Eau

Anse Chapelle

St-Sauveur

Ste-Marie

N1

Ste-Marie

Plage de Rocroy

Gourbeyre N1

Bananier

Basse-Terre 20

D6

Trois-Rivières

D6

22

Anse Turlet

Vieux Fort

Caribbean Sea

Iles des Saintes (Les Saintes)

23 - 27

Les Pompierres

23 Terre-de-Haut

Anse Crawen

Terre-de-Bas

La Coche

Grand Ilet

Plage de la Chapelle à Anse Laborde

Anse Bertrand

N8 D122

Camp

N6

Port Louis 9

Les Mangles

Beauport N6 N6

Petit-Canal

GRA

Ilet à Fajou

Anse du Canal

Ste-Rose

14 15 11

Vieux-Bourg

Morne-à-l'Eau

10

Grand Cul-de-Sac Marin

Abymes

Jabrun du Sud

Jabru du No

Lamentin

River Salée

Airport

Destrelan

N1

Pointe-à-Pitre

Bas-du-Fort

1 2

4 For d'I

3 2

3

Ilet du Gosier

4 - 6

Aquarium la Guadeloupe

A heady blend of French style and tropical delights, butterfly-shaped Guadeloupe is actually two islands divided by a narrow channel: smaller, flatter, and drier Grand-Terre (Large Land) and wetter and more mountainous Basse-Terre (Low Land). Sheltered by palms, the beaches are beguiling, and the sidewalk cafés are a bit like the Riviera.

THE BUTTERFLY ISLAND

Guadeloupe, annexed by France in 1674, is not really a single island but rather an archipelago. The largest parts of the chain are Basse-Terre and Grande-Terre, which together are shaped somewhat like a large butterfly. The other islands are the Iles des Saintes, La Désirade, and Marie-Galante.

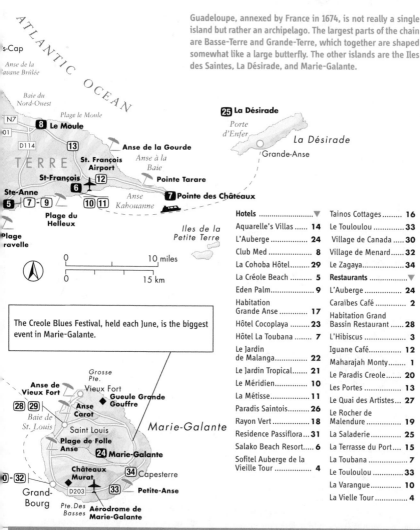

> The Creole Blues Festival, held each June, is the biggest event in Marie-Galante.

TOP 4 REASONS TO VISIT GUADELOUPE

1 Guadeloupe's restaurants highlight the island's fine Creole cuisine.

2 Small, inexpensive inns, called *relais*, give you a genuine island experience and may help you to improve your French.

3 Adventure sports—particularly on the wilder Basse-Terre's Parc National—keep the adrenaline pumping.

4 Remote La Désirade is a truly affordable, friendly island if you want an escape-from-it-all experience.

GUADELOUPE PLANNER

Getting to Guadeloupe

Only Air France offers a nonstop to Guadeloupe from the U.S. You can fly nonstop from Montréal as well, or connect through San Juan or one of the other Caribbean islands on a small island-hopper plane. There are also nonstops from Paris. Some travelers prefer the regularly scheduled ferry service from Dominica, St. Lucia, and Martinique, but the extra travel time certainly increases the hassle factor. The smaller islands are harder to reach; even with regular ferries and island-hoppers, you will almost always need to spend some time on Guadeloupe both coming and going. However, the rewards of these charming islands mean the hassles melt away the moment you step onto their sandy shores.

Most airlines fly into Aéroport International Pôle Caraïbes, 3 mi (5 km) from Pointe-à-Pitre (PTP), which is a fairly modern airport by Caribbean standards.

Hassle Factor: Medium for Guadeloupe to High for the smaller islands.

Activities

Guadeloupe's **beaches** can be good, but few resorts are on the best. Visitors come instead for good **diving**, the chance to **hike** and explore in Basse-Terre's wild national park, and **Creole cuisine**. Good **water sports** make up for sometimes mediocre beaches; windsurfing, sailing, fishing, and jet-skiing are all fun.

Biking isn't limited to the annual race. On the smaller islands, relaxing, sunbathing, and soaking up some old-time Caribbean **atmosphere** usually rank among the top activities. While shopping isn't the best, night owls will find plenty of **bars and clubs**, as well as a lively music scene.

On the Ground

Cabs meet flights at the airport if you decide not to rent a car. The metered fare is about $11 to Pointe-à-Pitre, $26 to Gosier, and $47 to St-François. Fares go up 40% on Sunday and holidays and from 9 PM to 7 AM. You can take a public bus from the airport to downtown Pointe-à-Pitre, though you'd never want to stay overnight there; a local bus then runs from the capital to Gosier. If you have a lot of luggage or aren't very patient, it's not an advisable alternative.

Renting a Car

If you're based in Gosier or at a large resort, you'll probably only need a car for a day or two of sightseeing. If driving is not your forte—you need to be a keen driver to maneuver the roundabouts, the mountain roads, and go up against the fast, aggressive drivers—leave it to an English-speaking taxi driver.

Your valid driver's license will suffice for up to 20 days. There are rental offices at Aéroport International Pôle Caraïbes and the major resorts. Count on spending between €40 and €60 a day for a small car (usually Korean or French) with standard shift, in the winter season. Automatics are considerably more expensive and normally have to be reserved in advance, but they are certainly available now. Many agencies, particularly the smaller ones, will insist on a substantial deposit being posted to your credit card; make sure that they tear that up upon your safe return. Others companies, including Europcar, charge a €20 drop-off fee for the airport, even if you pick the car up there. Allow at least 30 minutes to drop off your car at the end of your stay.

Where to Stay

Guadeloupe is actually not a single island but rather an archipelago of large and small islands that are connected through short flights and ferries, or in the case of Grand-Terre and Basse-Terre, a land bridge. Grand-Terre has the big package hotels that are concentrated primarily in four or five communities on the south coast, while wilder Basse-Terre has more individual resorts spread out around the island. More distant and much quieter are the Îles des Saintes, Marie-Galante, and La Désirade. On each of these smaller islands tourism is but a part of the economy and development is light, and any will give you a sense of what the Caribbean was like before the mega resorts took over.

TYPES OF LODGINGS

On Guadeloupe you can opt for a splashy **resort** with a full complement of activities or a small **relais** (inn) for more personal attention and a more authentic island experience. Many of the island's large chain hotels cater to French package groups, yet an increasing number of them are being renovated to the degree that they will cater more to the expectations of Americans. **Villas** are another option—particularly for families—but the language barrier is often a deterrent to Americans.

Hotel & Restaurant Costs

Assume that hotels operate on the European Plan (**EP**—with no meals) unless we specify that they use either the Continental Plan (**CP**—with a Continental breakfast), Breakfast Plan (**BP**—with full breakfast), or the Modified American Plan (**MAP**—with breakfast and dinner). Other hotels may offer the Full American Plan (**FAP**—including all meals but no drinks) or may be All-Inclusive (**AI**—with all meals, drinks, and most activities).

WHAT IT COSTS in Euros

	$$$$	$$$	$$	$	¢
Restaurants	over €30	€20–$30	€12–€20	€8–€12	under €8
Hotels*	over €350	€250–€350	€150–€250	€80–€150	under €80
Hotels**	over €450	€350–€450	€250–€350	€125–€250	under €125

*EP, BP, CP   **AI, FAP, MAP

Restaurant prices are for a main course at dinner and do not include the customary 10%–15% service charge. Hotel prices are per night for a double room in high season, excluding 7½% tax, customary 10% service charge, and meal plans (except at all-inclusives).

When to Go

The tourism industry thrives during the high season from mid-November through May but is quiet the rest of the year. Prices decline 25% to 40% in the off-season.

Carnival is one of the year's highlights, starting in early January and continuing until Ash Wednesday; the celebration finishes with a parade and a huge street party on Mardi Gras. June's **Creole Blues Festival** on Marie-Galante is gaining in fame and beginning to ensure that the small island's hotels fill up. In August, the **Tour Cycliste de la Guadeloupe**, which runs over 800 mi of both Grand-Terre and Basse-Terre, is the Caribbean's answer to the Tour de France.

On one Sunday in mid-August, Point-à-Pitre holds a Fête des Cuisinières to celebrate creole cuisine. A huge public lunch is followed by a grand ball.

In October, the Union des Arts Culinaires sponsors an upscale food festival.

12

By Eileen
Robinson Smith

OUR SMALL SQUADRON OF *SCOOTERS DE MER* is on a discovery mission. As we skim the ocean blue, the clouds are so low that we feel we may have to go right through them. We fly past the outline of a volcano to an uninhabited island, where we do lunch at a beach shack, in awe as a fisherman holds up a lobster and a long, animated octopus. Fueled by creole comfort food, we get on our Jet Skis and ride, only to gear down to a whisper in deference to the primeval stillness of the mangrove swamp. Skinny minutes later we pull alongside a foreign container ship, dodging the debris in Pointe-à-Pitre's harbor after a heavy rain—big bamboo, a corrugated roof, and even a kitchen sink!

Guadeloupe is a large island—629 square mi (1,629 square km)—that has been physically endowed with enviable topography and natural resources. You will be dazzled by its raw beauty, white-sand beaches that turn volcanic black in the west, looming mountains, riotous rain forests, a volcano shrouded in clouds, and scenery that changes by the mile, from tropical highlands to coastal seascapes with cliffs nicked by Atlantic waves. The verdant west coast of Basse-Terre could go up against any island in a Caribbean beauty contest. Guadeloupe has the advantages of a tropical, maritime climate, and you can bake in the sun at a seaside resort or be comfortably cool in the forest while you practice adventure sports.

It's no wonder that in 1493 Christopher Columbus welcomed the sight of this emerald paradise, where fresh, sweet water flows in cascades. And it's understandable why France annexed it in 1674 and why the British schemed to wrench it from them. In 1749 Guadeloupe mirrored what was happening in the Motherland. It, too, was an island divided, between royalists and those in favor of revolution.

Surprisingly, the resident British sided with the royalists, so Victor Hugues was sent to banish the Brits. While here, he sent to the guillotine more than 300 loyal-to-the-royal planters and freed the slaves, thus all but destroying the plantocracy. An old saying of the French Caribbean refers to *les grands seigneurs de la Martinique et les bonnes gens de la Guadeloupe* (the lords of Martinique and the bourgeoisie of Guadeloupe), and that still rings true. You'll find more aristocratic descendants of the original French planters on Martinique (known as *békés*) and also more "expensive" people, both living and vacationing there. That mass beheading is one of the prime reasons. Ironically, Napoléon—who ultimately ousted the royals—also ousted Hugues and reestablished slavery. It wasn't until 1848 that an Alsatian, Victor Schoelcher, abolished it for good.

Guadeloupe became one of France's *départements d'outremer* in 1946, meaning that it's a dependent of France. It was designated a region in 1983, making it a part of France, albeit a distant part. This brought many benefits to the islanders, from their fine highway systems to the French social services and educational system, as well as a high standard of living. However, certain tensions exist, including an anti-colonial resentment harbored by the older generations. Guadeloupe's young people realize the importance of tourism to the island's future, and you'll find them welcoming, smiling, and practicing the English and tourism skills they learn in school. Of course, some *français* is indispensable, though you may receive a bewildering response in creole patois.

Guadeloupe is a little bit of France, but far from the Metropole. Instead, this tropical paradise exudes an exoticism, one that has a primal quality to it. Its people, food, dance, and music are more Afro-influenced. Savor the spicy side of this life, exemplified by the wonderful potpourri of whole spices that floods the outdoor markets. The very aromas are heady.

Although Guadeloupe is thought of as an island, it is several, each entity with its own personality. "The mainland" consists of the two largest islands in the Guadeloupe archipelago: Basse-Terre and Grande-Terre, which look something like a butterfly. The outer islands—Les Saintes, Marie-Galante, Petite-Terre, and Désirade—are finally being acknowledged as the wonderfully unique travel destinations they are, still relatively unspoiled by the outside world. Tourism officials are now wisely marketing their country as Les Isles de Guadeloupe. See which one is your place in the sun. Vive les vacances!

Where to Stay

Most of the island's resort hotels are on Grande-Terre: Gosier, St-François, and Bas-du-Fort are generally considered major resort areas, as is Ste-Anne. Most hotels include buffet breakfast in their rates. Many smaller hotels do not accept American Express, so be sure to ask.

Villas

Aquarelle's Villas (✉ No. 1 Domaine de Nogent, Ste-Rose ☎ 0590/68–65–23 📠 0590/68–65–23 ⊕ www.aquarelles-villas.com) is the newest luxury address on Basse-Terre's north coast. The reception impresses guests with its paintings and wispy, flowing silk screens. In a gated community, these homes have private pools, and most have sea views; villas are directly on the beach or a pathway away. Furnishings are particularly stylish, kitchens expensively equipped, and the latest electronics (plasma TVs, DVD/CD systems) abundant. An on-site Franco-creole restaurant offers room service, or you can hire a personal chef. Villas have two to five bedrooms and are a surprisingly good value for families or small groups, costing between €296 and €566 per night.

French Caribbean International (☎ 800/322–22–23, 805/967–9850 in Santa Barbara, CA 📠 805/967–7798 ⊕ www.frenchcaribbean.com) handles private villa rentals, from charming cottages in Basse-Terre ($130 to $350 a night) to deluxe sea-view villas in Grande-Terre ($2,600 to $7,000 per week), all with pools. With decades of experience in the French Caribbean, the company has a reputation for honesty and professionalism.

Hotels on Grande-Terre

★ $$$$ 🏨 **Le Méridien La Cocoteraie.** This classy boutique hotel, with its new lobby decor of dark, rattan furnishings and walls of burnt orange and espresso, is a study in refinement. Yet it is genuinely convivial, thanks to the caring staff; the circular Indigo Bar, where American golfers get acquainted with European aristocracy; and a welcoming general manager, Fidel Montana, who has earned his devoted following from Monaco to Montreal.

Creole Dress

SINCE THE BEGINNING of the colonial period, the dress fashions on this island have played an important social role. In the 17th and 18th centuries, the French ladies always wore graceful fashions, and the female slaves who worked in the greathouses (*habitations*) on the plantations were the first of their color to have their own fashions. They tended to gravitate toward cottons—the white eyelet and muslin, and predominantly madras plaids of orange and green.

Most Guadeloupean women wore one of two basic styles: the *golle*—a white-cotton gathered dress, often of eyelet; and the *ti-collet*, a simple, everyday dress made from brightly colored cotton, usually a madras, tied at the waist with a scarf and worn without a petticoat, are the ones that prevailed. Turbans and eventually *chapeaux* (similar, but with corners) covered their dark hair. As this headgear evolved, one glance could tell you whether a woman was married or single by the number of peaked corners.

Female slaves were not allowed to wear jewelry, but after their liberation in 1848 they couldn't get enough of it. An array of creole-style jewelry, including rosette necklaces, gold beads, and large hoop earrings, became popular.

Until the late 1970s, women often dressed in traditional madras costumes with turbans, balancing pounds of produce on their heads. The turbans are gone now for everyday wear, as is the genuine madras, although a synthetic substitute is sold, mainly in tourist shops and as tablecloths and children's clothing. Happily, you will still see these colorful costumes at annual festivals, at folkloric dance performances, and sometimes on hotel staff. Alas, progress isn't always as pretty as the past.

Refurnished suites now have flat-screen TVs and dual, free-form bathroom sinks. Second-floor beachfront suites are idyllic. A room with a view of the glorious pool, which is traversed by a white latticework bridge and decorated with magnificent Asian urns, is the best-priced. At night there's entertainment—like a Brazilian jazz guitarist. ✉ *Av. de l'Europe, St-François 97118* ☎ *0590/88–79–81* 🖷 *0590/88–78–33* ⊕ *www. lemeridien.com* 🛏 *50 suites* ⚐ *Restaurant, room service, in-room safes, minibars, cable TV, golf privileges, 2 tennis courts, pool, massage, gym, beach, bar, babysitting, laundry service, car rental* ▤ *AE, DC, MC, V* ⊗ *Closed Sept. 15–Oct. 20* ⒪ *BP.*

$$$–$$$$
Fodor'sChoice
★

🏨 **Sofitel Auberge de la Vieille Tour.** An island classic fashioned around a historic sugar mill, this upscale hotel consistently renews itself, pleasing both business travelers and well-off vacationers. Everyone loves the initial welcome, the cool drink and scented towels dispensed by girls in white eyelet. After a day at the beach it's back to your deluxe bi-level room, with its glass-enclosed bathroom, to watch the lighthouse as it begins its nightly blink (request nos. 85 to 90). The lounge is a trip back in time, as patrons relax in planter chairs under whirling fans while the piano man plays. Talented folkloric dancers perform on Thursday at the authentic creole buffet. The Zagaya Restaurant serves creole cuisine and has laudable nightly entertainment. ⊠ *Rte. de Montauban, Gosier 97190* ☎ *0590/84–23–23* ⎙ *0590/84–33–43* ⊕ *www.sofitel.com* ⬎ *181 rooms, 32 deluxe rooms* ♨ *3 restaurants, room service, in-room safes, minibars, cable TV, 2 tennis courts, pool, hair salon, massage, beach, 2 bars, dance club, shops, Internet room, business services, meeting rooms, car rental* ⊟ *AE, MC, V* ⦿ *BP.*

★
☼ **$$–$$$** 🏨 **Club Med La Caravelle.** One of the first Caribbean Club Meds has been renovating again and will continue to upgrade. Situated on 50 secluded acres and on one of the island's best white-sand beaches, the resort is noted for its water-sports program, and kids adore the miniclub. Americans often pay to upgrade to the larger, seafront rooms in the Marie-Galante wing. A wonderful French élan pervades, but Americans will feel welcome (this July 4 at the beachside restaurant, a U.S. flag waved, and a red, white, and blue cake was served). ⊠ *Quartier Caravelle, Ste-Anne 97180* ☎ *0590/85–49–50 or 800/258–2633* ⎙ *0590/85–49–70* ⊕ *www. clubmed.com* ⬎ *329 rooms* ♨ *2 restaurants, in-room safes, cable TV, 6 tennis courts, pool, fitness classes, beach, windsurfing, boating, archery, volleyball, 3 bars, pub, nightclub, children's programs (ages 4–17), laundry service, Internet room, Wi-Fi* ⊟ *AE, MC, V* ⦿ *All-inclusive.*

$$ 🏨 **Eden Palm.** Set away from the tourist zones and brimming with sophisticated French style, this resort is especially noted for its personalized service. From the highway, you see a splash of blue and gold amid a pastoral landscape. Impressive, wrought-iron gates with a pair of dancing lions open to a centuries-old sugar mill bordered by ponds. A gentle fountain enhances the open-air lobby, with its stylish rattan furnishings. Each duplex bungalow houses two handsome rooms with tropical murals; suites are bi-level, and all have garden terraces. Breakfast is a highlight with fresh-squeezed juices and French cheeses served on blue-and-gold china. A virgin beach is two minutes away by golf cart, and guests love to hang out at the delightful pool. ⊠ *Lieu dit Le Helleux, Ste-Anne 97180* ☎ *0590/88–48–48* ⎙ *0590/88–48–49* ⊕ *www.edenpalm.com* ⬎ *40 rooms, 23 suites* ♨ *Restaurant, in-room safes, minibars, tennis court, pool, wading pool, gym, outdoor hot tub, sauna, beach, Ping-Pong, bar, cabaret, theater, playground, Internet room* ⊟ *AE, MC, V* ⦿ *BP.*

$$ 🏨 **Hôtel La Toubana.** If the ideal location is your primary motivator, then this be the place. Few hotels on Guadeloupe command such a panoramic view of the sea—spanning four islands, no less. Swimmers in the infinity pool feel that they can touch the surf hundreds of feet below. Guests can also bathe in the cove, dramatically lighted by night, adjacent to Club Med's beach. The cliffside balcony suite has the most dramatic vistas. A complete renovation was still under way at this writing, expected to be completed by fall 2006. The cigar and wine lounge offers some high-ticket vintages. With a roster of entertainment, this is now one of the island's "in" places. ⊠ *B. P. 63-Fonds Thezan, Ste-Anne 97180* ☎ *0590/88–25–57* ⎙ *0590/88–38–90* ⊕ *www.deshotelsetdesiles.com* ⬎ *32 bungalows, 1 suite* ♨ *Restaurant, kitchenettes, tennis court, pool, beach, jet skiing, meeting room* ⦿ *BP.*

$–$$ ⊞ **La Créole Beach Hotel.** This 10-acre complex, which also includes a residential development, offers hotel rooms with varying levels of comfort, making for a rather diverse clientele. What unites everyone is a fun atmosphere, whether you enjoy aqua-aerobics, playing petanque, or moving to a zouk band. The nicest accommodations are the two-bedroom, two-bath, bi-level Mahogany suites, which have a colorful, French minimalist style, gourmet kitchens, and enviable sea views from their terraces. The Créole Beach rooms are handsome, with crisp white bedspreads and contemporary artwork. The oversize rooms and suites at Les Palmes are like those on a teak-appointed yacht. ⊠ *Pointe de la Verdure, Box 61, Gosier 97190* ☎ *0590/90–46–46* 🖷 *0590/90–46–66* ⊕ *www. deshotelsetdesiles.com* ⇨ *353 rooms, 15 junior suites, 5 suites* ♢ *2 restaurants, some kitchens, cable TV, pool, 2 beaches, dive shop, snorkeling, windsurfing, boating, volleyball, bar, meeting rooms, car rental* ⊟ *AE, DC, MC, V* ⑪ *EP.*

♻ **$–$$** ⊞ **Salako Beach Resort.** The three hotels that make up this resort are marketed primarily to conference groups and French package tourists, but there's no reason why you can't come, too. On one of the best strips of Gosier Beach, the complex includes the Clipper, which has basic rooms below the standard acceptable to most Americans (though many have ocean views); the Salako, which has large, deluxe rooms with renovated bathrooms, most of which have sea views; and the Prao, which has two-room suites with terraces, kitchenettes, and two lovely bathrooms. Alas, although the most expensive, they have no sea views. The well-publicized club-disco draws patrons from outside too. ⊠ *Pointe de la Verdure, Gosier 97190* ☎ *0825/826–971 reservations, 0590/82–64–64* 🖷 *0590/84–72–72* ⊕ *www.karibea.com* ⇨ *211 rooms, 59 suites* ♢ *3 restaurants, in-room safes, some kitchenettes, some refrigerators, cable TV, Wi-Fi, 2 pools, gym, outdoor hot tub, beach, dive shop, snorkeling, jet skiing, 2 bars, shops, children's programs (ages 6–11), dry cleaning, laundry service, Internet room, meeting rooms, car rental, travel services, free parking* ⊟ *AE, MC, V* ⑪ *EP.*

★ ♻ **$** ⊞ **La Métisse.** Pretty as a postcard from a honeymoon couple, this pink stucco hotel, embellished with white-and-blue gingerbread, encircles a butterfly-shape pool with a raised hot tub. Sequestered in an upscale residential neighborhood, it's furnished with white wicker and is squeaky clean. Connecting rooms are ideal for families. The caring owners give guests rides to town, the beach, and the golf course, which makes a rental car a luxury but not a necessity. The best is that when you awake, you draw your drapes, and the breakfast fairy, who hides in the garden, delivers a lovely breakfast with fresh juice and house-made jam to your poolside terrace. ⊠ *66, les Hauts de St-François, St-François 97118* ☎ *0590/88–70–00* 🖷 *0590/88–59–08* ⊕ *www.im-caraibes.com/metisse* ⇨ *7 rooms* ♢ *In-room safes, minibars, cable TV, in-room data ports, pool, hot tub, playground* ⊟ *AE, MC, V* ⑪ *CP.*

Hotels on Basse-Terre

$$ ⊞ **Le Jardin de Malanga.** A former coffee plantation, this *hôtel de charme* is as close as you may ever get to a Garden of Eden; it's certainly an ideal place for any Adam to bring his Eve. Two intriguing guest rooms

FodorśChoice
★

and one suite are in the atmospheric, antiques-filled main house, built in 1927 of gorgeous red-hue hardwoods. This is the preferred environment. However, there is more privacy in the chic, contemporary creole-style cottages of courbaril wood; these have patios with hammocks, and monogrammed robes and towels hang in the bathrooms. An infinity pool looks out to the sea and to the mountains. In the terrace restaurant, expect a Carib-French cuisine that utilizes the bounty of the estate. You'll want a car, since the nearest beach, Grande-Anse, is 20 minutes away. ⊠ *Hermitage, Trois-Rivières 97114* ☎ *0590/92–67–57* 🖷 *0590/ 92–67–58* ⊕ *www.deshotelsetdesiles.com* ➾ *8 rooms, 1 suite* ⌂ *Dining room, fans, pool; no room TVs* ⊟ *AE, MC, V* ⧄ *CP.*

$$ ⌧ **Rayon Vert.** Small, homey, and romantic, this inn, which is managed by a bilingual French couple, has a private, noncommercial ambience. Exotic flowers proliferate in the hillside gardens and around the infinity pool, with its incomparable view of the Bay of Ferry and the tiny village below. You can swim in the infinity pool or lounge on a teak chaise under a white market umbrella. Opt for one of the larger bungalows (81, 82, 101, or 102), where the sea views are amazing, though alas, the decor is dated. The restaurant's Carib-French repast is both simple and delicious, as flavorful as the Marseilles fish soup and the crayfish with fresh orange juice. ⊠ *Le Coque Ferry, Deshaies 97126* ☎ *0590/ 28–43–23* 🖷 *0590/28–46–27* ⊕ *hotel.lerayonvert.free.fr* ➾ *10 rooms, 12 bungalows* ⌂ *Restaurant, minibars, cable TV, in-room VCRs, pool* ⊟ *MC, V* ⊘ *Closed May 28–July 8* ⧄ *BP.*

$$ ⌧ **Tainos Cottages.** Now this is a story. A Frenchman—a world traveler—goes to Indonesia, buys seven wooden cottages, and imports them *as well as* two Indonesians to reassemble them on a privileged site overlooking Grande-Anse Beach. He and his wife (an accomplished chef) give the raised, open-air bungalows exotic names, decorating them tastefully, if spartanly, with four-poster beds with mosquito netting (*les mosques* are a drawback here). The pool is steps from the sea, or if that's not enough, you can lounge like Asian royalty on elevated Indonesian beds, shaded by gazebos. Summer rates drop by half, and you get a discount by booking online. ⊠ *Plage de Grande-Anse, Deshaies 97126* ☎ *0590/ 28–44–42* 🖷 *0590/68–01–75* ⊕ *www.tainosvillage.com* ➾ *7 bungalows* ⌂ *Restaurant, in-room safes, minibars, pool, beach, bar, Internet room; no a/c, no room TVs* ⊟ *MC, V* ⧄ *CP.*

★ ☾ **$–$$** ⌧ **Habitation Grande Anse.** Although this simple, family-oriented hotel doesn't have the amenities and services of a big resort, it's perched on a hill overlooking one of the island's best beaches. It also has English-speaking Italian owners, brothers Claudio and Fulvio, who keep things running smoothly. A mix of bungalows, apartments, studios, and standard rooms have rattan furniture and even satellite TV; two-bedroom apartments accommodate four to six people and have the highest rates. A super Euro-style villa for seven people has the best sea views. A terrace restaurant-cum-bar, serving breakfast and lunch, is open from November through April. ⊠ *Localité Ziotte 97126* ☎ *0590/28–45–36* 🖷 *0590/28–51–17* ⊕ *www.grande-anse.com* ➾ *3 rooms, 39 studios, 3 apartments* ⌂ *Restaurant, in-room safes, kitchens, cable TV, pool, bar, car rental* ⊟ *AE, MC, V* ⧄ *EP.*

🖐 ¢ 🖼 **Le Jardin Tropical.** The setting is one pretty, tropical picture: white-and-blue bungalows with gingerbread trim and landscaped gardens that topple down the hillside. The cluster of terraced bungalows and the appealing L-shaped pool enjoy an exceptional view of the Caribbean, but you're still a mile from the closest beach. The largest accommodation can house 10 people (for 150 per night). This small property, built in the late 1990s, is immaculately maintained. There's an attractive, open-air common area furnished with white wicker; you'll also find a bar, breakfast area, billiards, and a wide-screen satellite TV. ⊠ *Rte. de Poirier, Pigeon-Bouillante 97125* ☎*0590/98–77–23* 🖨*0590/98–74–33* ⊕*www. rocher-de-malendure.gp* ⇌ *6 units* ⚲ *Fans, kitchenettes, pool, bar, Internet room; no room TVs* ⊟ *MC, V* ᐅ◯ *EP.*

Hotels on Iles des Saintes

★ $ 🖼 **L'Auberge les Petits Saints aux Anacardiers.** The fashionably eccentric, fun couples, hip families, and serious Caribbeanophiles gravitate to this charismatic inn. Admirably consistent attention from the hands-on owners ensures the madcap house-party atmosphere is a pleasure. The "lobby" is a wild mélange of treasures for sale, from Thai horse sculptures to Indonesian antiques to the artwork of co-owner Didier Spindler. The bar blends up healthy fruit and vegetable smoothies by day and perfect piña coladas and mango daiquiris at sunset. With enviable hillside views overlooking the pool and the bay, the main building has the charm of decades past, with dormers and gingerbread fretwork, but it's been upgraded to American standards. ⊠*La Savane, Terre-de-Haut 97137* ☎ *0590/99–50–99* 🖨 *0590/99–54–51* ⊕ *www.petitssaints.com* ⇌ *4 rooms, 3 suites, 1 guest house* ⚲ *Dining room, cable TV, in-room data ports, pool, bar, airport shuttle* ⊟ *AE, MC, V* ᐅ◯ *CP.*

$ 🖼 **Hôtel Cocoplaya.** Although the decor of your room may make you feel that you've been transported to faraway China or Africa, in reality you're on the waterfront, just minutes from the main square. Soundproof double windows block out even the annoying drone of the motor scooters. The minimalist open lobby, its bar, ice cream counter, and beach restaurant have been designed with characteristic French élan. English is spoken by the young, accommodating management. ⊠ *Terre-de-Haut 97137* ☎ *0590/92–40–00* 🖨 *0590/99–50–41* ⊕ *www.cocoplaya. com* ⇌ *10 rooms* ⚲ *Restaurant, ice cream parlor, some minibars, cable TV, beach, bar* ⊟ *MC, V* ᐅ◯ *CP.*

★ $ 🖼 **Paradis Saintois.** You can feel like the king of the hill as you lull yourself into a *sieste* in your hammock while watching the village and the Caribbean blue below. The apartments (suitable for four to six people) with kitchen terraces are appealing, clean, and well maintained. Couples should ask for the newest studios, which have handcrafted stone and tilework. Tri-color bougainvillea surrounds the pool; the beach is a 10-minute walk. Guests share the large barbecue and the picnic table, where convivial punch parties take place; fish, lobster, rum, wine, champagne, beer, and water can be purchased from the office. The longer you stay, the less you pay. ⊠ *Rte. des Pres Cassin–B.P.I., Terre-de-Haut 97137* ☎ *0590/99–56–16* 🖨 *0590/99–56–11* ⊕ *www.antilles-info-tourisme. com* ⇌ *5 apartments, 3 studios, 1 room* ⚲ *Fans, kitchenettes, 2 pools,*

bicycles, laundry service; no a/c, no room phones, no room TVs ⊟ *MC,*
V ¶⦿| *EP* ⌇ *2-night minimum.*

Hotels on Marie-Galante

Accommodations run the gamut from inexpensive, locally owned beachfront bungalows to complexes with Anglo owners. **Residence Passiflora**
(⊠ Grand-Bourg ☎ 0590/97–50–48 ⊕ www.charly-location.com) is
composed of two deluxe, duplex villas perched on a hillside overlooking the sea. The decor is chic French, and there's a Jacuzzi. **Le Touloulou**
(⊠ Plage de Petite-Anse, Capesterre ☎ 0590/97–32–63) has four stucco
bungalows with kitchenettes. Freshly painted, they're simple, but you can
roll out of your terrace hammock onto the beach. The good, creole
seafood restaurant is a happening place, with atmospheric music from
the beach bar vying with the slapping of the waves. The disco adjacent
to the restaurant warms up to hot at night. **Village de Menard** (⊠ Section
Canada ☎ 0590/97–09–45) consists of squeaky clean, colorfully decorated bungalows and studios with a pool in a pastoral setting. **Le Village
de Canada** (⊠ Section Canada ☎ 0690/50–55–50) has studios, bungalows, and apartments, some with sea views; there's a pool. **Le Zagaya**
(⊠ Capesterre ☎ 0590/97–37–84 ⊕ www.le-zagaya.com), which is decorated in blue and white with marine artifacts and ships' doors, offers
simple rooms with beds canopied with mosquito netting clustered around
a pool. Two bungalows with kitchens are available for longer stays. One
of the two owners, Nina, is an Italian chef; meals are celebratory.

🕊 **$** 🏨 **La Cohoba Hôtel.** The only full-service beach resort on island is owned
and managed by well-known Guadeloupeans, who have not forgotten
their culture. Woven branches add creole authenticity to the entrance
of the dining room, where reproduced cave paintings decorate the walls.
Each of the simple stucco units has two rooms and a terrace. You may
find a varied lot staying here, including city dwellers from Pointe-à-Pitre,
French package tourists, business groups, or others with a little jingle
in their pockets. A pool sits in the gardens, *and* the resort is on a beach,
although hidden from view by a tropical forest named for its discov-
erer, Christopher Columbus. ⊠ *Folle Anse, near St-Louis, 97112*
☎ *0590/97–50–50* 🖷 *0590/97–97–96* ⊕ *www.deshotelsetdesiles.com*
⌇ *100 suites* △ *Restaurant, cable TV, 2 tennis courts, pool, beach, windsurfing, boating, waterskiing, bicycles, volleyball, bar, meeting room,
car rental* ⊟ *AE, MC, V* ¶⦿| *CP.*

Hotels on La Désirade

Even more remote than Marie-Galante, tiny La Désirade has a few simple guest houses. **Armour D'Oliver** (☎ 0590/81–40–52 or 0690/69–66–45)
is small and immaculate, but you'll likely want a car if you stay here.
There's no beach, but there's a pool and a barbecue for grilling. **Club
Caravelle** (☎ 0590/20–04–00 🖷 0590/20–06–00 ⊕ www.desirade-
islands.com) is inland, but some of the apartments have two floors, and
most have sea views, though the best views are from the terrace restaurant. **Oualiri Beach Hotel** (☎ 0590/20–20–08 or 0690/71–24–76 🖷 0590/
85–51–51 ⊕ www.rendezvouskarukera.com), a feet-in-the-sand B&B,
is owned by an English-speaking hospitality veteran. New sling-back chairs

on the beach and other contemporary improvements have updated this simple six-room inn.

Where to Eat

Creole cooking is the result of a fusion of influences: African, European, Indian, and Caribbean. It's colorful, spicy, and made up primarily of local seafood and vegetables, including christophenes (like a squash), root vegetables, and plantains, always with a healthy dose of pepper sauce. Favorite appetizers are *accras* (salted codfish fritters), *boudin* (highly seasoned blood sausage), and *crabes farcis* (stuffed land crabs). *Langouste* (lobster) and *lambi* (conch) are widely available, as is *souchy* (like ceviche, it's fish "cooked" or marinated in lime juice).

You can find a diverse selection of dining options—from pizza to Vietnamese to haute French cuisine. What you won't find are many inexpensive places; however, menu prices *do* include tax and service. Look for fine dining restaurants that belong to the gastronomic association l'Union des Arts Culinaires (UAC). Conversely, for a quick and inexpensive bite to eat, visit a *boulangerie,* where you can buy luscious French pastries or basic sandwiches. Relatively inexpensive snack shops sell crepes, hamburgers, or simple sandwiches (look for the chain DeliFrance). *Moules et frites* (mussels in broth served with fries) can be found at cafés in Gosier and the Bas du Fort marina.

What to Wear

Dining is casual at lunch, but beach attire is a no except at the more laid-back marina and beach eateries. Dinner is slightly more formal. Long pants, collared shirts, and skirts or dresses are appreciated, although not required.

Grande-Terre

CAFÉS
¢–$

✕ **Caraïbes Café.** This sidewalk café straight out of Paris is the "in" place for lunch and also a spot for a quick breakfast, a fresh juice cocktail (try *corossel/mangue*), a cappuccino, a sundae (*un coupe*), or a Pernod while you watch the people and listen to French crooners. The *formule* (fixed-price menu) is always the best deal. There are both main course and dessert crêpes, sandwiches, and grilled sirloin steak (*entrecote*) with perfect *pommes frites*. Service is fast and friendly and can even be in English. ⊠ *Pl. de la Victoire, Pointe-à-Pitre* ☎ *0590/82–92–23* ▭ *MC, V* ☉ *Closed Sun. No dinner.*

CARIBBEAN
★ $$–$$$

✕ **L'Hibiscus Restaurant.** Silver serving domes conceal a happy marriage of Guadeloupean and classical French cuisine that utilizes local spices and produce in the best possible ways. The gracious chef-owner, Jocelyn Corvo, returned to his native Guadeloupe after 24 years of enviable posts in France; he is a master saucier, and his originality with the ubiquitous root vegetables is remarkable. Freshwater crayfish in a coconut cream sauce with saffron is dreamy. Reasonably priced prix-fixe menus have some fine choices, including paupiette of salmon with a ginger crustacean sauce. The waterfront restaurant is more cheery tropical than chichi, the ceremonious presentations notwithstanding. ⊠ *Bord de Mer, across from Zenith, Bas-du-Fort* ☎ *0590/91–13–61* ▭ *AE, V* ☉ *Closed mid-Sept.–mid-Oct.*

12

CONTEMPORARY ✕ **La Vieille Tour Restaurant.** Formal presentations on fine white china
★ **$$$–$$$$** serve as the perfect backdrop for the artistic creations of chef Denis
Schetrit. One of only 300 Master Chefs of the World, he is dedicated
to preserving, advancing, and perpetuating great French cuisine, even
as he bows to more recent culinary tastes. There is a succession of ap-
petizers, each better than the one before it, such as foie gras with spicy,
tropical fruit chutney. The creole bouillabaisse has a depth and com-
plexity that will remain in your culinary memory bank. Dessert presen-
tations are dazzling, with lots of puff pastry, towers, sauces, and glacés.
When reserving, ask for Leandre—he is the English-speaking waiter of
choice. ✉ *Sofitel Auberge de la Vieille Tour Hotel, Rte. de Montauban,
Gosier* ☎ *0590/84–23–23* 🚫 *AE, MC, V* ⊗ *Closed some days June–Nov.
No lunch.*

$$$ ✕ **Iguane Café.** A UAC member, this restaurant serves unquestionably
Fodor'sChoice original cuisine with Asian, Indian, and African influences. Iguanas are
★ indeed the theme, and you can spy them in unexpected places—juxtaposed with antique French cherubs and driftwood mirrors, for example. The chefs are constantly daring. Fresh seafood is always remarkable,
the presentations uniformly dramatic. Start with a tart of crab and
shrimp, pineapple, and two sauces; then go on to filet mignon with a
veal jus infused with marrow and truffles (petite fresh vegetables are served
in the marrow bone). Desserts are little marvels. The music is very
French, the service professional. ✉ *Rte. de La Pointe des Châteaux, ½
mi (¾ km) from airport, St-François* ☎ *0590/88–61–37* 🚫 *AE, MC*
⊗ *Closed Tues. No lunch Mon.–Sat.*

FRENCH ✕ **La Varangue.** Le Méridien fine-dining restaurant is as casually chic as
★ **$$$** it is poolside, open-air, and facing the lagoon. Begin, perhaps, with the
duo of fish fillets with avocado and saltfish or the Caribbean cucumber-
coconut soup, served icy cold. The duck breast with local honey, wine,
orange, and coriander is quite French. Lobster, my dear? Well, it's fresh
and grilled but also the most costly menu item. The wine and champagne
list is appropriately upscale. Lunch can be as caloric as the sinful salmon
ravioli or as light as a classic salade niçoise. The mango mousse with
mascarpone is a multiethnic delicacy. ✉ *Le Méridien La Cocoteraie, av.
de l'Europe, St-François* ☎ *0590/88–79–81* 🚫 *AE, MC, V.*

$$–$$$ ✕ **La Toubana Restaurant.** Fresh lobsters, a seemingly endless supply of
which swim in the canals that beautify the deck, draw many diners. The
cuisine here is more French than creole, except for Thursday's famous
buffet with tam-tam drummers and folkloric dancers. Chicken in coconut
sauce is the best main course. Anything chocolate is divine for dessert.
On Tuesday nights, the piano man plays in the handsome, open-air din-
ing room with its deep leather chairs, the same ones that are used in the
wine cave, which is also a cigar bar. Lunch patrons dine on the terrace
and love the infinity pool. With feet dangling and an exotic cocktail in
hand, you can watch the sea churn below. ✉ *Hotel La Toubana, B.P.
63-Fonds Thézan, Ste-Anne* ☎ *0590/88–25–57* 🚫 *AE, MC, V.*

INDIAN ✕ **Les Portes des Indes.** Eating here is like taking a trip to an exotic land:
★ **$$–$$$** the open-air pergola, the gates painted primary blue, the wooden stat-
uary, the Hindu music, the pungent aromas, and the bust of Ganesha.

Within the paisley-covered menu you can find authentic dishes and such innovations as boneless chicken Korma with crème fraîche, almonds, and raisins served with a beautiful white-and-yellow basmati rice tossed with cilantro, cashews, and fried onions. Children may never get past the incredible Indian cheese bread or the tamarind and mint chutneys. Cool down the heat with *kulfi*, Indian ice cream topped with ginger confit. The welcome here is always warm and the service dignified. ⊠ *Desvarieux, St-François* ☎ *0590/21–30–87* ▭ *V* ☉ *Closed Mon. No dinner Sun.*

$-$$$ ✕ **Maharajah Monty.** Ask directions at the tourism office, which is just a few blocks away. Climb the staircase to the second floor and open the door to a wildly ornate, red-and-gold dining experience. Here you can find all of your Indian faves with creole leanings. The owner, the lovely Madame Manjit Kaur, with her bejeweled forehead and traditional costume, is representative of the island's significant East Indian population. For mild palates she suggests the tandoori chicken, or you can heat things up with a *vindaloo* with coconut milk. If you want to splurge, look no further than curried shrimp or lobster. ⊠ *Rue A. René-Boisneuf, Angle Rue Jean Jaures, Pointe-à-Pitre* ☎ *0590/83–12–60* ▭ *MC, V* ☉ *No dinner Sun.*

Basse-Terre

CARIBBEAN ✕ **La Terrasse du Port** (Chez Mimi). Pink-stripe awnings lead patrons,
★ $-$$$ many of whom arrive in BMWs and Citroëns, to this unassuming second-story restaurant. Mimi, a Guadeloupean, reigns in the kitchen, while Bernard, her French husband, is on the floor. Seafood is the main event, with lobster creole a specialty. And you must love that coquille *lambi* (conch), the crayfish with reduced lobster bisque, and the shrimp flambéed in *vieux rhum*. Desserts? They're delectable, from the profiteroles with chocolate ganache and the white-chocolate mousse with coconut milk to the ginger sorbet with an apricot *tuile*. The atmosphere is fun, the music French. Bernard often hands out digestifs. ⊠ *Bd. Maritime, Ste-Rose* ☎ *0590/28–60–72* ▭ *MC, V* ☉ *Closed Mon. and Oct. 1–15. No dinner Sun.*

FRENCH ✕ **Le Rocher de Malendure.** Guests climb the yellow stairs for the panoramic
★ $$-$$$$ sea views but return for the food. If you arrive before noon, when the divers pull in, you might snag one of the primo tables in a gazebo, which literally hang over the Caribbean. Begin with a perfectly executed mojito. With such fresh fish, don't hesitate to try the sushi *antilliaise*, a mixed-fish ceviche. The house-made golden raisin rolls are perfect with the warm goat cheese salad with honey sauce perfumed by herbes de Provence. Grilled crayfish and lobster, octopus fricassee, shellfish bouillabaisse, and *dorade* (mahimahi) with a vanilla cream sauce have contemporary presentations and classic good flavor. Stone and steam cooking at the table are so guilt-free. UAC member. ⊠ *Bord de Mer, Malendure de Pigeon, Bouillante* ☎ *0590/98-70-84* ▭ *AE, MC, V* ☉ *Closed Wed. and Sept.*

★ $$-$$$ ✕ **Le Paradis Créole.** Begin at sunset with one of the *punches maisons* at the pool bar with its remarkable, 360-degree view of the sea. Billed as *gastronomic évolutive*, this is more than just fuel for the divers who populate this simple hilltop hotel. There are two moderate prix-fixes

12

plus a menu that is continually evolving to highlight the chef's global repertoire. Caribbean fish and crustaceans are complemented by original sauces of fruit and local spices and accompanied by creative takes on the local vegetables. Desserts with fresh tropical-fruit sauces are always originals and delectable. UAC member. ✉ *Le Paradis Créole hotel, Rte. de Poirier, Pigeon-Bouillante* ☎ *0590/98–71–62* ▭ *MC, V* ◷ *Closed Sun. and Mon. No lunch.*

Iles des Saintes

CAFÉS
¢–$

✕ **Le Quai des Artistes.** French hospitality veterans opened this artsy café in a choice waterfront location almost simultaneously with the unveiling of the renovated main dock. Arrivals stream out of the ferries and are immediately attracted to the colorful café–cum–art gallery, where they often take breakfast. Under the leather canopy, it's shades of Greenwich Village with books and newspapers, gourmet teas and coffees, wine, and, yes, liquor for those who want an icy rum cocktail. Contemporary art lines the walls, there for the buying. Tapas are the main food source and include Japanese sushi, smoked fish plates, salads, and creole snacks, such as really tasty accras. It's aperitifs at sunset and beyond, for the café closes by 8. ✉ *At the main dock, Terre-de-Haut* ☎ *0690/35–63–69* ▭ *MC, V* ◷ *No dinner.*

ECLECTIC
$$$

✕ **L'Auberge les Petits Saints aux Anarcadiers Restaurant.** Chef-owner Jean Paul Colas describes his cuisine as "clean and simple," but it often has a layered complexity. With no prix-fixe menu anymore, guests can now choose to eat lightly—the seared Tataki tuna coupled with a vegetarian salad, for example. Carnivores can now have a top-quality filet mignon with imported cèpe mushrooms. The fish could be a deep-water snapper with passion fruit sauce, and lobster will be grilled (for €40). Co-owner Didier Spindler makes superb desserts, or try the ti punch sorbet. On the veranda, the night sounds of the tropics vie with *musique* by Carla Bruni or Enya. ✉ *L'Auberge les Petits Saints aux Anarcadiers, La Savane, Terre-de-Haut* ☎ *0590/99–50–99* ⌨ *Reservations essential* ▭ *AE, MC, V.*

$–$$

✕ **La Saladerie.** The menu is a sophisticated mélange of light plates and the freshest of fish. You can make a meal of either the beef or fish carpaccio, or the assorted smoked fish and chilly gazpacho. Try the shrimp in coconut milk with rice, coupled with a salad that you compose. For dessert, a litany of sundaes showcases tropical ice creams and sorbets. The wine list is pleasantly varied; after dinner, you can indulge in a snifter of Calvados or Armagnac and just listen to the mellow jazz or walk the pier and give in to the inclination to be romantic. The French owner, an architect and artist, has hung his large, mixed-media collages. ✉ *Anse Mire, Terre-de-Haut* ☎ *0590/99–53–43* ◷ *Closed Tues. No dinner Mon.* ▭ *MC, V.*

Marie-Galante

SEAFOOD
$–$$$

✕ **Le Touloulou.** On the curve of Petite-Anse Beach, with tables in the sand, this ultracasual eatery serves the freshest seafood. Chef José—well, he's good. His standouts include fricassee of conch with breadfruit. You can also ask for conch in lemon-butter sauce. A lobster prix-fixe is a good deal. Set menus often include a shrimp and fish curry duo. José plays

DJ with his collection of French and international music. La Pergola's circular bar has the best in rum cocktails to sip while contemplating the sun's descent. ⊠ *Petite-Anse* ☎ *0590/97–32–63* ▭ *MC, V* ☉ *No dinner Sun. Closed mid-Sept.–mid-Oct.*

$$ ✕ **L'Habitation Grand Bassin Restaurant.** The table d'hôte menu is presented by a lovely island couple who purchased this guesthouse prior to their retirement. Now they enjoy welcoming guests to it and serving creole dishes like local snails in broth, fricassee of conch, fish in coconut or vanilla sauce, and fish stuffed with shellfish, along with dumplings, breadfruit, and gratin of cucumbers. For Christmas Eve day, they kill a fatted pig and hire musicians to play old-time music. The restaurant is open only when there are reservations. ⊠ *L'Habitation Grand Bassin, Section Grand Bassin, St-Louis* ☎ *0590/97–31–27* ⚓ *Reservations essential* ▭ *No credit cards.*

Beaches

Guadeloupe's beaches are generally narrow and tend to be cluttered with cafés and cars (when parking spots fill up, folks create impromptu lots on the sand). You're sure to find many long, sparsely visited stretches, and all beaches are free and open to the public; parking fees are rare. Most hotels allow nonguests to use changing facilities, towels, and beach chairs for a small fee. On the southern coast of Grande-Terre, from Ste-Anne to Pointe des Châteaux, you can find stretches of soft white sand. Along the western shore of Basse-Terre you can see signposts to many small beaches. The sand starts turning gray as you reach Ilet de Pigeon (Pigeon Island); it becomes volcanic black farther south. There's one official nudist beach, but topless bathing is common. The Atlantic waters on the northeast coast of Grande-Terre are too rough for swimming.

Grande-Terre Beaches

L'Autre Bord. The waves on this Atlantic beach give the long expanse of sand a wild look in contrast to the city's provincialism. Walking the seaside promenade fringed by flamboyant trees is a pleasant way to pass a day. The beach, which is protected by an extensive coral reef, is a magnet for surfers and windsurfers. Le Toussant Gwanda, a surfing festival, is generally held here during the first week in November. ⊠ *Le Moule.*

Plage Caravelle. Just southwest of Ste-Anne is one of Grande-Terre's longest and prettiest stretches of sand, the occasional dilapidated shack notwithstanding. Protected by reefs, it's also a fine snorkeling spot. Club Med occupies one end of this beach, where nude bathing is no longer permitted. Nonguests can enjoy its beach and water sports, as well as lunch and drinks, by buying a day pass. You can also have lunch at La Toubana, then descend the stairs to the beach below. ⊠ *Rte. N4, southwest of Ste-Anne.*

Plage de la Chapelle à Anse-Bertrand. If you want a delightful day trip to the northern tip of Grande-Terre, aim for this spot, one of the prettiest white-sand beaches, whose gentle midafternoon waves are popular with families. When the tide rolls in, it's equally popular with surfers, not to mention the site of numerous competitions. Several little terrace restaurants at the far end of the beach soothe your appetite, but you might want to bring your own shade, because none rent chaise lounges. Before hitting the beach, tour Anse Bertrand. This was where the Caribs made their last stand, and it was a major sugar center. ✉ *4 mi (6½ km) south of La Pointe de la Grand Vigie.*

Plage du Helleux. Except on Sunday, this long stretch of *sauvage* beach—framed by dramatic cliffs—is often completely deserted in the morning or early afternoon, but by 4 PM, you might find 70-odd young surfers, because that's when the waves are right. Cliffs rise dramatically to the right. Many locals take their young children here, but always use caution, for the current can be strong. The beach has no facilities, but you can get lunch and drinks at the Eden Palm Hotel. From Ste-Anne, take the St-François Road about 3 mi (5 km) until you reach the Hotel Eden Palm; pass the hotel on your left and take the next right. The beach is about two minutes farther along. ✉ *Rte. N4, Lieu-dit le Helleux, Ste-Anne.*

Pointe Tarare. This secluded, sandy strip just before the tip of Pointe des Châteaux is the island's only nude beach. If you don't feel comfortable with that, just keep walking and find your own white, sandy spot. A small bar-café is in the parking area, a four-minute walk away, but it's still best to bring some water and food; there's no place to rent beach chairs, though. What you do have is one of the most dramatic, wild beachscapes; looming above are rugged cliffs topped by a huge crucifix. When approaching St-François Marina, go in the direction of Pointe des Châteaux at the roundabout and drive for about 15 minutes. ✉ *Rte. N4, southeast of St-François.*

Basse-Terre Beaches

La Grande-Anse. One of Guadeloupe's widest beaches has soft beige sand sheltered by palms. To the west it's a round, verdant mountain. There's a large parking area, some food concessionaires, but no other facilities. The beach can be overrun on Sunday, not to mention littered. Right after the parking lot, you can see signage for the creole restaurant Le Karacoli; if you have lunch there (it's not inexpensive), you can *sieste* on their chaise lounges. ✉ *Rte. N6, north of Deshaies.*

Malendure. Across from Pigeon Island and the Jacques Cousteau underwater park, this long, gray volcanic beach on the Caribbean's calm waters has restrooms, a few beach shacks offering cold drinks and snacks, and a huge parking lot, where tour buses often line up. The lot and the beach can get littered, but the beach is cleaned regularly. There's no solitude to be found here, but it's the starting-off point for dive boats, sportfishing boats, glass-bottom boats, and whale-watching vessels. So if you're scheduled to do any of the above, you can hang here afterward for a full day of sea and sand. Snorkeling from the beach is good. Le Rocher Malendure, a fine seafood restaurant, is perched on a cliff over the bay. ✉ *Rte. N6, Bouillante.*

Beaches on Other Islands

Anse Crawen. This ½-mi (¾-km) stretch of white sand is secluded for nude sunbathing, but don't plan on shedding your suit on Sunday, which is family day. To reach it, go past the resort Bois Joli and continue straight until you see the beach. ✉ *Terre-de-Haut.*

Anse de Vieux Fort. This gorgeous Marie-Galante beach stretches alongside crystal-clear waters that border a large body of fresh water, which is ideal for canoeing. It's a surprising contrast from the nearby mangrove swamp you can discover on the hiking trails. The beaches in this area are wide due to the erosion of the sand dunes. It's known as a beach for lovers because of the solitude. Bring your own everything, because this is virgin territory. ⊠ *Rte. D205, just past Pointe Fleur d'Épée, Vieux Fort.*

Petite-Anse. This long, golden beach on Marie-Galante is punctuated with sea-grape trees. It's idyllic during the week, but on weekends the crowds of locals and urban refugees from the main island arrive. La Touloulou's great creole seafood restaurant provides the only facilities. The golden sands are ideal for shelling. ⊠ *6½ mi (10 km) north of Grand-Bourg via Rte. D–203, Petite-Anse.*

Les Pompierres. This beach is particularly popular with families with small children, as there's a gradual slope, no drop-off, and a long stretch of shallow water. To get here, go to the seamen's church near the main plaza, and then head in the direction of Marigot, then continue straight until you see a palm-fringed stretch of tawny sand. ⊠ *Terre-de-Haut.*

Sports & the Outdoors

BICYCLING The French are mad about *le cyclisme*. If you want to be part of this pedal power, take to two wheels. Cycling fever hits the island each August, when hundreds of cyclists converge for the 10-day Tour de Guadeloupe, which covers more than 800 mi (1,290 km). If you rent a bicycle, expect to be asked to leave a deposit, but the amount seems to vary; normally you can use a credit card to secure your rental (MasterCard or Visa). On Terre-de-Haut, there are a number of shops to the immediate left and right of the ferry dock; the farther from the dock they are, the lower the rates. And you can usually negotiate the price down—a little.

On Grande-Terre you can rent bikes at **Eli Sport** (⊠ Rond Point de Grand-Camp, Grand-Camp, Grande-Terre ☎ 0590/90–37–50), which has VTT racing bikes (and only VTTs) for adults; there are no children's bikes. The price is right at €10 a day, but reserve as far in advance as possible, or you may find yourself walking instead. **Rent-a-Bike of Ste. Anne** (⊠ Ste-Anne ☎ 0690/65–05–05) rents bikes out by the hour (€13 for adults, €8 for kids), or you can have a vigorous day (seven hours, with a lunch break, and different degrees of difficulty) of "green" tourism exploring the island with a group (€30). Scooters can be rented as well, and the company organizes hikes and camping trips. **Vert Intense** (⊠ Basse-Terre, Basse-Terre ☎ 0590/99–34–73 or 0690/55–40–47 ⊕ www.vert-intense.com) is your main Basse-Terre sports connection. The company is known for hiking excursions but puts together groups for VTT bike hikes as well. Prices depend on size, and the company prefers that you make a reservation four days in advance.

BOATING & If you plan to sail these waters, you should be aware that the winds and SAILING currents tend to be strong. There are excellent, well-equipped marinas in Pointe-à-Pitre, Bas-du-Fort, Deshaies, St-François, and Gourbeyre. You can rent a yacht (bareboat or crewed) from several companies. To make a bareboat charter, your navigational and seamanship skills will be tested. If you do not pass, you must hire a skipper or be left on land. **Cap Sud** (⊠ 3 pl. Créole, Bas-du-Fort, Grande-Terre ☎ 0590/90–76–70 ⊕ www.capsud-yachtcharter.com) has a fleet of eight yachts, including monohulls and catamarans. The sailboats are generally rented as bareboats by the week. The giant yacht-rental company **Sunsail** (⊠ Bas-du-Fort Marina, Bas-du-Fort, Grande-Terre ☎ 0590/90–92–02, 410/280–2553, 207/253–5400 in U.S. ☏ 0590/90–97–99 ⊕ www.sunsail.com) has a base on Guadeloupe. Although it's primarily a bareboat operation, you can hire skippers by the week if you have limited experience, or you can get expert instruction in sailing skills and the local waters. Ocean kayaks, Windsurfers, and kite boards can be rented, too, but these must be reserved in advance.

DIVING The main diving area at the **Cousteau Underwater Park,** just off Basse-Terre near Pigeon Island, offers routine dives to 60 feet. But the numerous glass-bottom boats and day-trippers make the site feel like a crowded marine parking lot. The underwater sights, however, are spectacular. Guides and instructors here are certified under the French CMAS (and some have PADI, but none have NAUI). Most operators offer two-hour dives three times per day for about €45 to €50 per dive; three-dive packages are €120 to €145. Hotels and dive operators usually rent snorkeling gear.

Chez Guy et Christian (⊠ Plage de Malendure, Basse-Terre ☎ 0590/98–82–43) has a good reputation and is well established among those who dive off Pigeon Island. One dive boat departs three times daily and charges €34 a dive. A second dive boat goes to Les Saintes, with two dives, one at a wreck, the other at a reef (€85 includes lunch). English-speaking dive masters are PADI-certified. Show your Fodor's guide and ask for a discount. After 10 years of experience, dive master Cedric Phalipon of **Club de Plongée Des Saintes, Pisquettes** (⊠ Le Mouillage, Terre-de-Haut, Iles des Saintes ☎ 0590/99–88–80) knows all the sites and islets and gives excellent lessons in English. Equipment is renewed frequently and is of a high caliber. Small tanks are available for kids, who are taken buddy diving. **Les Heures Saines** (⊠ Le Rocher de Malendure, Plage de Malendure, Bouillante, Basse-Terre ☎ 0590/98–86–63 or 0690/55–40–47 ⊕ www.plongee-guadeloupe.com) is the premier operator for dives in the Cousteau Reserve. Trips to Les Saintes offer one or two dives, for medium and advanced cardholders, with time for lunch and sightseeing. Wreck, night, and Nitrox diving are also available. The instructors, many English-speaking, are excellent with children. The company also offers sea kayaking and winter whale- and dolphin-watching trips with marine biologists as guides, all aboard a 60-foot catamaran equipped with hydrophones.

FISHING Not far offshore from Pigeon-Bouillante, in Basse-Terre, is a bounty of big game fish—bonito, dolphinfish, captain fish, barracuda, kingfish, and tuna—or you can thrill to the challenge of the big billfish like marlin and swordfish. Fishermen have been known to come back with as many as three blue marlins in a single day. For Ernest Hemingway wannabes, this is it. To reap this harvest, you'll need to charter one of the high-tech sportfishing machines with flying bridges, competent skippers, and mates. The boats charter for $430 to $600 a day, with lunch and drinks included. Rates depend on the number of persons (up to a maximum of six). It's more than half those prices for a half-day charter. This is a heavy dose of machismo for not much more than a C-note per person.

Centre de Peche Sportive (✉ Malendure de Pigeon, Bouillante, Basse-Terre ☎ 0590/98–70–84) has two state-of-the-art boats and is known for success in showing anglers where to pull in the big billfish. The per-day rate is €500, and often, the boat doesn't come back until sunset. You can also go night-fishing for swordfish, and the crew will cut the bills and fins off your catch. The company is affiliated with the restaurant Le Rocher de Malendure, which offers simple oceanfront bungalows. **Michel** (✉ Les Galbas, Ste-Anne, Basse-Terre ☎ 0590/85–42–17, 0690/55–21–35–) is a reliable big-fishing charter outfit that can usually pick anglers up at their hotel and allow them to charge their €150 to their hotel bill. Non-fishermen along for just the adrenaline rush are half-price. The mates will be happy to take your picture with your catch of the day.

GOLF **Golf Municipal St-François** (✉ St-François, Grande-Terre ☎ 0590/88–41–87), across from Le Méridien La Cocoteraie Hotel, is an 18-hole, par-71, Robert Trent Jones–designed course; it has an English-speaking pro, a clubhouse, a pro shop, and electric carts for rent. The greens fees are €40 for 9 holes, €50 for 18; carts rent for €34 for 9 holes and €50 for 18. Clubs can be rented for €25. The course is open daily from 7:30 AM to 6 PM. It's best to reserve tee times a day or two in advance. Cocoteraie guests enjoy a 30% discount.

HIKING With hundreds of trails and countless rivers and waterfalls, the **Parc Na-**
Fodor'sChoice **tional de la Guadeloupe** on Basse-Terre is the main draw for hikers.
★ Some of the trails should be attempted only with an experienced guide. All tend to be muddy, so wear a good pair of boots. Know that even the young and fit can find these outings arduous; the unfit may find them painful. Start off slowly, with a shorter hike, and then go for the gusto. Since June 2004, canyoning and all water sports—rafting, hot-dogging, hydrospeed, jet-skiing, and even canoeing and kayaking—were forbidden in the central zone of the park. Administrators, with the appropriate scientists, are still studying the impact on the park's ecosystem.

Les Heures Saines (✉ Le Rocher de Malendure, Plage de Malendure, Bouillante ☎ 0590/98–86–63), a professional operation that has distinguished itself at sea, has now come ashore to offer freshwater canyoning in a river outside the national park as well as hikes to La Randonnée. There are three different canyoning circuits, including one called "The Trail of the Three Waterfalls" (super, but six to seven hours in duration). On "The Bivouac" you spend 24 reality-show-like hours in the forest. For many of these excursions, you have to wait for a group to be assembled, so prices can depend on the numbers. Book as far in advance as you can.

Vert Intense (✉ Basse-Terre, Basse-Terre ☎ 0590/99–34–73 or 0690/55–40–47 ⊕ www.ecotourisme-guadeloupe.net) organizes hikes in the national park and to the volcano with fascinating commentary. You will move from steaming hot springs to an icy waterfall in the same hike. Guide Eric is patient and safe, and he can bring you to heights that you never thought you could reach, including the top of Le Soufriére. The volcano hike costs only €25 but must be booked four days in advance. A mixed-adventure package spanning three days costs €210. The French-speaking guides, who also know some English and Spanish, can take you to other tropical forests and rivers, where the sport of canyoning can still be practiced. If you are just two people, VI can put you together with a group.

JET SKIING   The young and sporty French are wild for their *scooters de mer,* but you can't rent a Jet Ski in France (or Guadeloupe) unless you have a special license. Instead, **Atmospheres** (☒ Pointe de la Verdure, Gosier ☎ 0690/49–47–28 ⊕ www.atmosphere.gp) organizes group excursions for two to four hours (costing €80 to €135). It's an exhilarating way to enjoy the sea, and you can experience a number of different sites speedily. If it's your first time out, you might first try the shorter, two-hour run. This is not for the tame or the frail; if you have knee and/or back problems (either driver or passenger), and speed frightens you, stay on your chaise lounge. Even the twentysomethings are sore afterward.

SEA EXCURSIONS   **Evasions** (☒ Le Rocher de Malendure, Pigeon ☎ 0590/92–74–24 or 0690/57–19–44 ⊕ www.evasiontropicale.org) operates daylong whale-watching cruises that are combined with a trip to the whale museum. With the help of the onboard sonar, whales are easy to find from December through March, the main season. Children and all ages adore observing, photographing, and listening to the whales. Trips cost €55 per person, but each person on the trip must also buy an annual membership to the Association for Study and Census of Turtles, Marine & Mammals of the Caribbean for €25. **Paradox** (☒ Marina, St-François ☎ 0690/83–62–35), a top-of-the-line catamaran, sails to Marie-Galante and Les Saintes for €75, attracting an upscale clientele. It's not your typical booze cruise. Rum bottles aboard? Sure, but the passengers are more likely to be in it for the marine experience and the stopover on nature preserve Petit Terre. The music is soothing and the lunch better, with vegetarian dishes, a cheesy bread, fresh fish, barbecue chicken, and ribs. **Tip Top Cruises** (☒ 35 Résidence de la Presqu'ile, Bas-du-Fort, Grande-Terre ☎ 0590/84–66–36 ☒ Av. de l'Europe/marina, St-François, Grande-Terre ☎ No phone) operates two large, safe catamarans that fly through the water to Les Saintes and other islands, including Marie-Galante and Dominica. It's a full day at sea, with snorkeling, kayaking, lunch (with a supplement for lobster), rum libations, and shore excursions, including the little islet of Petit Terre, with its resident population of sea turtles. Tip Top has been tops in the biz for years because it runs a clean and tight ship—fun but professional.

WIND- & KITE SURFING   Most beachfront hotels can help you arrange lessons and rentals. **Centre Nautique** (☒ Creole Beach Resort, Pointe de la Verdure, Gosier ☎ 0590/90–46–59) is open to anyone and run by former windsurfing champions who are instructors of the first degree; the company will rent Windsurfers for €20 an hour, Hobie Cats for €32 an hour, and can arrange fishing, catamaran, and motorboat excursions. **LCS** (☒ Ste-Anne Lagoon, Ste-

Anne, Grande-Terre ☎ 0590/88–15–17 ⊕ www.lookasurf.com), in business since the early 1980s, specializes in lessons for children six and older as well as adults and has boards for rent as well. Instructors are certified by the French National Federation of Sailing. LCS organizes offshore competitions and runs a retail surf shop too. Windsurfing buffs congregate at the **UCPA Hotel Club** (⊠ St-François, Grande-Terre ☎ 0590/88–64–80 ⊠ Terre-de-Haut, Les Saintes ☎ 0590/99–54–94), where for moderate weekly rates (€600) they sleep in hostel-style quarters, eat three meals a day, and windsurf. Lessons and boards (also available to nonguests) are included in the package, as are bikes to pedal to the lagoon. A sister club on Terre-de-Haut has a water-sports center in the middle of town, though the hotel itself is out on isolated Baie de Marigot.

Shopping

You can find good buys on anything French. Many stores offer a 20% discount on luxury items purchased with traveler's checks or, in some cases, major credit cards. As for local handicrafts, you can find fine wood carvings, madras table linens, island dolls dressed in madras, woven straw baskets and hats, and *salakos*—fishermen's hats made of split bamboo, some covered in madras—which make great wall decorations. Of course, there's the favorite Guadeloupean souvenir, rum. *Rhum vieux*, like fine cognac, is the best. For foodies, the market ladies sell aromatic fresh spices, crisscrossed with cinnamon sticks, in great little baskets lined with madras.

Areas & Malls

Grande-Terre's largest shopping mall, **Destrelland,** has more than 70 stores and is just minutes from the airport, which is a shopping destination in its own right. In **Pointe-à-Pitre** you can enjoy browsing in the street stalls around the harbor quay and at the two markets (the best is the Marché de Frébault). The town's main shopping streets are rue Schoelcher, rue de Nozières, and the lively rue Frébault. At the St-John Perse Cruise Terminal there's an attractive mall with about two dozen shops. **Bas-du-Fort**'s two shopping areas are the Cora Shopping Center and the marina, where there are 20 or so shops and quite a few restaurants. In **St-François** there are more than a dozen shops surrounding the marina, some selling sensual French lingerie, swimsuits, and fashions. A supermarket has incredibly good prices on French wines and cheeses, and if you pick up a fresh baguette, you have a picnic. (Then you can get go get lost at a secluded beach.)

Specialty Items

ART **Brigitte Boesch** (⊠St-François, Grande-Terre ☎0590/88–48–94), a German-born painter who has exhibited all over the world, lives in St-François, and her studio is worth a visit. Call for directions. **Pascal Foy** (⊠ Rte. à Pompierres, Terre-de-Haut, Iles des Saintes ☎ 0590/99–52–29) produces stunning homages to traditional creole architecture: paintings of houses that incorporate collage make marvelous wall hangings. As his fame has grown, his media attention has expanded, so prices have risen.

CHINA, CRYSTAL **Rosebleu** (⊠ 5 rue Frébault, Pointe-à-Pitre, Grande-Terre ☎ 0590/
& SILVER 82–93–43 ⊠ Aéroport International Pôle Caraïbes, Grande-Terre ☎ No

phone) sells china, crystal, and silver by top manufacturers, including Christofle.

CLOTHING **Côté Plage** (⊠ Place du Marché, Pointe-à-Pitre, Grande-Terre ☎ No phone) sells bikinis, sundresses, cartoon T-shirts, and straw beach totes in addition to other ideal island wares. To complement there's a line of simple jewelry—turtles, geckos, and sea horses—made of sand and resin. **DODY** (⊠ 31 rue Frébault, Pointe-à-Pitre, Grande-Terre ☎ 0590/ 82–18–59) is the place if you have wanted to purchase white eyelet (blouses, skirts, dresses, or even bustiers); the shop has a high-quality designer line, but you will pay upwards of €100 to €300 for a piece. There's lots of madras, too, which is especially cute in children's clothing. **U Gail** (⊠ La Marina La Coursive, St-François, Grande-Terre ⊕ www.legallclothing.com) handles a line of fashionable French resortware for women and children that has hand-painted figures like turtles and dolphins on cool cotton knits. There are several other outlets across the island.

COSMETICS & **L'Artisan Parfumeur** (⊠ Centre St-John Perse, Pointe-à-Pitre, Grande-
PERFUME Terre ☎ 0590/83–80–25) sells top French and American brands as well as tropical scents. **L'Atelier du Savon** (⊠ Terre-de-Haut, Iles des Saintes ☎ 0590/99–56–44) makes all of its soaps from vegetable products, in scents including marine spice and opium. Beautifully packaged gift baskets can include bath salts and aromatic oils. **Au Bonheur des Dames** (⊠ 49 rue Frébault, Pointe-à-Pitre, Grande-Terre ☎ 0590/82–00–30) sells several different lines of cosmetics and skin-care products in addition to its perfumes. **Phoenicia** (⊠ Bas-du-Fort, Grande-Terre ☎ 0590/90–85–56 ⊠ 8 rue Frébault, Pointe-à-Pitre, Grande-Terre ☎ 0590/83–50–36 ⊠ 121 bis rue Frébault, Pointe-à-Pitre, Grande-Terre ☎ 0590/82–25–75) sells mainly French perfumes. **Vendôme** (⊠ 8–10 rue Frébault, Pointe-à-Pitre, Grande-Terre ☎ 0590/83–42–84) is Guadeloupe's exclusive purveyor of Stendhal and Germaine Monteil cosmetics.

HANDICRAFTS **Almanda** (⊠ La Marina La Coursive, St-François, Grande-Terre ☎ 0590/ 88–63–32) carries artistic home furnishings but mostly items sized to carry home: tablecloths, place mats, pillow covers, runners, vases, and decorative accessories. "Out of Africa" bags can be bought to carry your new purchases. At **Kaz à Lorgé** (⊠ 25 rue Benoît Cassin, Terre-de-Haut, Iles des Saintes ☎ 0590/99–59–60) you can find an artistic jumble of handicrafts, both local and from around the world, that fills the two tiny rooms of this "gingerbread" shop: prints, mobiles, wall masks, Haitian woodcraft, miniature lobster traps, and cutesy things made from madras. The **Centre Artisanat** (⊠ Ste-Anne, Grande-Terre) offers a wide selection of local crafts, including art composed of shells, wood, and stone. One of the outlets sells authentic Panama hats.

Madras Bijoux (⊠ 115 rue Nozière, Pointe-à-Pitre, Grande-Terre ☎ 0590/ 82–88–03) specializes in replicas of authentic creole jewelry; it also cre-
★ ates custom designs and does repairs. At **Maogany Artisanat** (⊠ Terre-de-Haut, Iles des Saintes ☎ 0590/99–50–12), artist and designer Yves Cohen's shop has been redone like a yacht. He carries batiks and hand-painted T-shirts in luminescent seashell shades. Hand-loomed silk fab-

rics are embellished with gold thread; others are translucent, like his sensual women's collection. Silk shawls and scarves, hand-embroidered with tropical birds, and his children's collection make great gifts. From the Amazon, he has imported Indian jewelry of coconut and mother-of-pearl. For men, there are real Panama hats and buccaneer shirts.

LIQUOR & The airport duty-free stores have a good selection of rum and tobacco.
TOBACCO **Délice Shop** (⊠ 45 rue Achille René-Boisneuf, Pointe-à-Pitre, Grande-Terre ☎ 0590/82–98–24) is the spot for island rum and edibles from France—from cheese to chocolate.

Nightlife

Guadeloupeans maintain that the beguine began here, and, for sure, the beguine and mazurkas were heavily influenced by the European quadrille and orchestrated melodies. Their merging together is the origin of West Indian music and it gave birth to zouk (music with an African-influenced Caribbean rhythm) at the beginning of the 1980s. Still the rage here, it has spread not only to France but to other European countries. Many resorts have dinner dancing or offer regularly scheduled entertainment by steel bands and folkloric groups.

The island's performing arts scene is centered on the **Centre des Arts** (⊠ Place des Martyrs de la Liberté, Pointe-à-Pitre ☎ 0590/82–79–78), where each season is more exciting than the last. The litany of performances includes musical comedies, exceptional jazz and blues concerts, and even art exhibitions. American guitarists, hip hoppers and break dancers, classical musicians, and theatrical companies have all performed here. Prices are democratic. Ask for the special deals.

BARS & **Club Med** (⊠ Quartier Caravelle, Ste-Anne ☎ 0590/85–49–50) sells
NIGHTCLUBS night passes that include cocktails, dinner, a show in the theater, followed by admission to the disco (53, 57 on the weekends.) It's a good option for single women, who will feel comfortable and safe at the disco, where there are plenty of staff willing to be dance partners. Something is always happening at the **Creole Beach Hotel** (⊠ Pointe de la Verdure, Gosier ☎ 0590/90–46–46). Entertainment might be a vocalist on the keyboard and, often, live bands playing beguine and zouk, which are both very danceable. You should call in advance so that your name will
★ be at the security gate. On Tuesday nights, **Eden Palm Theater** (⊠ Hotel Eden Palm, Lieu-dit le Helleux, Ste-Anne ☎ 0590/88–48–48) presents a Cuban-influenced Caribbean musical review on Saturday nights. The show—like nothing else on the island—has plumage, imaginative costumes, and a bevy of dancers. On Friday, there's another spectacle, an indigenous Indian and African dance and music show. Prices are €50 a person for dinner and a show or €50 for two for a bottle of French champagne and appetizers. **Midway** (⊠ Marina, Pointe-à-Pitre ☎ 0590/90–03–49) looks like a hole-in-the-wall, but a lot of good sounds can be heard inside. The piano bar draws a crowd of locals and French tourists, as do the rock and local bands. **Le Palace** (⊠ Delair, Ste-Anne ☎ 0590/90–80–96), a fun spot, is a complex with a pool and musical bar and *le barrio latino*.

CASINOS Both of the island's casinos are on Grande-Terre and have American roulette, blackjack, and stud poker. The legal age for gambling is 18, and you need a photo ID to prove it. Jacket and tie aren't required, but "proper attire" means no shorts, T-shirts, jeans, flip-flops, or sneakers.

Casino de Gosier (⊠ Gosier, Grande-Terre ☎ 0590/84–79–69) has a bar, restaurant, and cinema. The higher-stakes gambling is behind a closed door. You'll have to pay €10 to be part of that action—or even to look on. It's open Monday to Sunday from 8:30 PM; slot machines open at 10 AM. **Casino de St-François** (⊠ Marina, St-François, Grande-Terre ☎ 0590/88–41–31) is not a handsome showplace, but the slots draw them in. A restaurant still bills itself as a piano bar, but there's no longer a piano or a player. The menu is appealing, however, and a good value. On Wednesday nights you can hear a Cuban salsa group and sometimes reggae or even karaoke. It's open daily from 7 PM.

DISCOS Night owls should note that carousing here isn't cheap. On the weekend and when there's live music, most discos charge a cover of at least €10, which might go up to as much as €20. Your cover usually includes a drink, and other drinks cost about €10 each. Most clubs are very smoky.

Acapulco (⊠ 1 rue Paul Finette, St-François, Grande-Terre ☎ 0590/20–79–18) is an intimate spot with local, zouk, and international music; it has different themes nightly. **Le Cheyenne** (⊠ Rte. de Montauban Gosier, Grande-Terre) is a dramatic, Native American–theme disco that's currently drawing the crowds. Look for the sculpture of a Cheyenne chief over the grand entrance. On weekends, there's a cover charge when the basement disco is open. **La Plantation** (⊠ Gourbeyre, Basse-Terre ☎ 0590/81–23–37) is the top spot on Basse-Terre; couples dance to zouk, funk, and house music on the immense mezzanine dance floor. **Zenith** (⊠ Bord de Mer, Bas-du-Fort, Grande-Terre ☎ 0590/90–72–04) is one of the island's better clubs, well located, featuring local creole salsa and good service; there's a view of the sea and a terrace with a pool.

Exploring Guadeloupe

To see each "wing" of the butterfly, you'll need to budget at least one day. They are connected by a bridge, and Grande-Terre has pretty villages along its south coast and the spectacular Pointe des Châteaux. You can see the main sights in Pointe-à-Pitre in a half day. Touring the rugged, mountainous Basse-Terre is a challenge. If time is a problem, head straight to the west coast; you could easily spend a day traveling its length, stopping for sightseeing, lunch, and a swim. You can make day trips to the islands, but an overnight works best.

Numbers in the margin correspond to points of interest on the Guadeloupe map.

Grande-Terre

❸ **Aquarium de la Guadeloupe.** Unique in the Antilles, this aquarium is a good place to spend an hour. The well-planned facility is in the marina near Pointe-à-Pitre and has an assortment of tropical fish, crabs, lobsters, moray eels, puffy coffers, a shark or two, and live coral. It's also a turtle rescue center. The retail shop has sea-related gifts, toys, and jewelry. ⊠ *Pl. Créole, off Rte. N4, Pointe-à-Pitre* ☎ *0590/90–92–38* ⌨ *€7.50* ⊘ *Daily 9–7.*

4 **Fort Fleur d'Épée.** The main attraction in Bas-du-Fort is this 18th-century fortress, which hunkers down on a hillside behind a deep moat. It was the scene of hard-fought battles between the French and the English in 1794. You can explore its well-preserved dungeons and battlements and take in a sweeping view of Iles des Saintes and Marie-Galante. ⊠ *Bas-du-Fort* ☎ *0590/90–94–61* ⌨ *€6* ⊘ *Mon. 10–5, Tues.–Sun. 9–5.*

2 **Gosier.** Taking its name from the brown pelicans that nest on the islet of Gosier and along the south coast of Grande-Terre, Gosier was still a tiny village in the 1950s, a simple stopping place between Pointe-à-Pitre and Ste-Anne. However, it grew rapidly in the 1960s, when the beauty of the southern coastline began to bring in tourists in ever-increasing numbers. Today Gosier is Guadeloupe's premier tourist resort while at the same time serving as a chic suburb of Pointe-à-Pitre. People sit at sidewalk cafés reading *Le Monde* as others flip-flop their way to the beach. The town has several hotels, nightclubs, shops, a casino, and a long stretch of sand.

10 **Morne-à-l'Eau.** This agricultural town of about 16,000 people has an amphitheater-shape cemetery, with black-and-white-checkerboard tombs, elaborate epitaphs, and multicolor (plastic) flowers. On All Saints' Day (November 1), it's the scene of a moving (and photogenic) candlelight service.

8 **Le Moule.** On the Atlantic coast, and once the capital city of Guadeloupe, this port city of 24,000 has had more than its share of troubles: it was bombarded by the British in 1794 and 1809 and by a hurricane in 1928. An important touristic center in past decades, it's experiencing a comeback. A large East Indian population, which originally came to cut cane, lives here. Canopies of flamboyant trees hang over the narrow streets, where colorful vegetable and fish markets do a brisk business. The town hall, with graceful balustrades, and a small 19th-century neoclassical church are on the main square. Le Moule's beach, protected by a reef, is perfect for windsurfing.

7 **Pointe des Châteaux.** The island's easternmost point offers a breathtaking view of the Atlantic crashing against huge rocks, carving them into pyramid like shapes. The majestic cliffs are reminiscent of the headlands of Brittany. There are spectacular views of Guadeloupe's south and east coasts and the island of La Désirade. The dramatic scene is marred by a parking lot filled with tour buses and makeshift bars and snack stands, but if you are spending hours at the beach, you will need the sustenance. On weekends locals come in numbers to walk their dogs, surf, or look for romance.

1 **Pointe-à-Pitre.** Although not the capital city, it is the island's largest, a commercial and industrial hub in the southwest of Grande-Terre. The isles of Guadeloupe have 450,000 inhabitants, 99.6% of whom live in the cities. Pointe-à-Pitre is bustling, noisy, and hot—a place of honking horns and traffic jams and cars on sidewalks for want of a parking place. By day its pulse is fast, but at night, when its streets are almost deserted, you don't want to be there.

The city has suffered severe damage over the years from earthquakes, fires, and hurricanes. It took heavy hits by Hurricanes Frederick (1979), David (1980), and Hugo (1989). On one side of rue Frébault you can see the remaining French colonial structures; on the other, the modern city. Some of the downtown area has been rejuvenated. The Centre St-John Perse has transformed old warehouses into a cruise-terminal complex that consists of the spartan Hotel St-John, restaurants, shops, and the port authority headquarters. An impressive terminal is within, for the ferries that depart for Iles des Saintes, Marie-Galante, Dominica, Martinique, and St. Lucia.

The heart of the old city is Place de la Victoire; surrounded by wooden buildings with balconies and shutters (including the tourism office) and by sidewalk cafés, it was named in honor of Victor Hugues' 1794 victory over the British. During the French Revolution, Hugues ordered the guillotine set up here so that the public could witness the bloody end of 300 recalcitrant royalists.

Even more colorful is the bustling marketplace, between rues St-John Perse, Frébault, Schoelcher, and Peynier. It's a cacophonous place, where housewives bargain for spices, herbs (and herbal remedies), and a bright assortment of papayas, breadfruits, christophenes, and tomatoes. For fans of French ecclesiastical architecture, there's the imposing **Cathédrale de St-Pierre et St-Paul** (⊠ rue Alexandre Isaac at rue de l'Eglise), built in 1807. Although battered by hurricanes, it has fine stained-glass windows and creole-style balconies and is reinforced with pillars and ribs that look like leftovers from the Eiffel Tower.

Anyone with an interest in French literature and culture won't want to miss the **Musée St-John Perse,** which is dedicated to Guadeloupe's most famous son and one of the giants of world literature, Alexis Léger, better known as St-John Perse, winner of the Nobel Prize for literature in 1960. Some of his finest poems are inspired by the history and landscape—particularly the sea—of his beloved Guadeloupe. The museum contains a complete collection of his poetry and some of his personal belongings. Before you go, look for his birthplace at 54 rue Achille René-Boisneuf. ⊠ *At rues Noizières and Achille René-Boisneuf* ☎ *0590/ 90–01–92* ⊠ *€2* ⏲ *Thurs.–Tues. 8:30–12:30 and 2:30–5:30.*

Musée Schoelcher celebrates Guadeloupe's native son Victor Schoelcher, a high-minded abolitionist from Alsace who fought against slavery in the French West Indies in the 19th century. The museum contains many of his personal effects, and exhibits trace his life and work. Come for the architecture, the works of art, and the music history. ⊠ *24 rue Peynier* ☎ *0590/82–08–04* ⊠ *€3* ⏲ *Weekdays 9–5.*

 Port Louis. This fishing village of about 7,000 is best known for the Souffleur Beach. It was once one of the island's prettiest, but it has become a little shabby. Still, the sand is fringed by flamboyant trees, and though the beach is crowded on weekends it's blissfully quiet during the week. There are also spectacular views of Basse-Terre.

❺ Ste-Anne. In the 18th century this town, 8 mi (13 km) east of Gosier, was a sugar-exporting center. Sand has replaced sugar as the town's most valuable asset. La Caravelle (where you can find the Club Med) and the other beaches here are among the best in Guadeloupe. On a more spiritual note, Ste-Anne has a lovely cemetery with stark-white tombs.

★ ❻ St-François. This was once a simple little village, primarily involved with fishing and harvesting tomatoes. The fish and tomatoes are still here, as are the old creole houses and the lively market with recommendable food stalls, but increasingly, the St-François marina district is overtaking Gosier as Guadeloupe's most fashionable tourist resort area. Le Méridien La Cocoteraie, one of the island's ritziest hotels, is just off Avenue de l'Europe, which runs between the marina and the rolling fairways and water obstacles of the 18-hole Robert Trent Jones–designed, municipal golf course. On the marina side, a string of shops, hotels, bars, restaurants and a casino—as well as funky food trucks selling pizza, crêpes, burgers, and Asian stir-fries—cater to tourists.

Basse-Terre

Basse-Terre (which translates as "Low-Land") is by far the highest and wildest of the two wings of the Guadeloupe butterfly, with the peak of the Soufrière Volcano topping off at nearly 59,055 feet. Basse-Terre, where you can find the island's national park, is an ecotourist's treasure, with lush, equatorial plant life and myriad adventurous opportunities for hikers and mountain-bikers on the old *traces,* routes that porters once took across the mountains. Yet this half of Guadeloupe has retained its authenticity, and you can still find numerous fishing villages and banana plantations, stretching as far as the eye can see. The northwest coast, between Bouillante and Grande-Anse, is magnificent; the road twists and turns up steep hills smothered in vegetation and then drops down and skirts deep-blue bays and colorful seaside towns. Constantly changing light, towering clouds, and frequent rainbows only add to the beauty.

⓴ Basse-Terre. Because Pointe-à-Pitre is so much bigger, few people suspect that this little town of 15,000 is the capital and administrative center of Guadeloupe. But if you have any doubts, walk up the hill to the state-of-the-art Théâtre Nationale, where some of France's finest theater and opera companies perform. Paid for by the French government, it's a sign that Basse-Terre is reinventing itself. Founded in 1640, it has endured not only foreign attacks and hurricanes but sputtering threats from La Soufrière as well. The last major eruption was in the 16th century, though the volcano seemed active enough to warrant evacuating more than 70,000 people in 1975.

For a guided tour of Basse-Terre, climb aboard the **Pom Pom** (☎ 0590/81–24–83), a trolley that does a circuit of the major sights. The ride costs €7 and lasts 2½ hours.

★ ℭ The **Jardin Botanique,** or the botanical garden, an exquisitely tasteful 10-acre park populated with parrots and flamingos, has a circuitous walking trail that takes you by ponds with floating lily pads, cactus gardens, and every kind of tropical flower and plant, including orchids galore. A restaurant, with surprisingly good meals, and a snack bar are housed in terraced gingerbread buildings, one overlooking a waterfall, the other the mountains. The garden has a children's park and nature-oriented playthings in the shop. ⊠ *Deshaies* ☎ *0590/28–43–02* 🖅 *€10* 🕐 *Daily 9–6.*

⑱ Bouillante. The name means "boiling," and so it's no surprise that hot springs were discovered here. However, today the biggest attraction is scuba diving on nearby Pigeon Island, which is accessed by boat from Plage de Malendure. There's a small information kiosk on the beach (Plage de Malendure) that can help you with diving and snorkeling arrangements.

⑮ Cascade aux Ecrevisses. Part of the Parc National de la Guadeloupe, Cray-fish Falls is one of the island's loveliest (and most popular) spots. There's a marked trail (walk carefully—the rocks can be slippery) leading to this splendid waterfall, which dashes down into the Corossol River—a good place for a dip. Come early, though; otherwise you definitely won't have it to yourself.

㉒ Chutes du Carbet. You can reach three of the Carbet Falls (one drops from 65 feet, the second from 360 feet, the third from 410 feet) via a long, steep path from the village of Habituée. On the way up you pass the Grand Étang (Great Pond), a volcanic lake surrounded by interesting plant life. For horror fans there's also the curiously named Étang Zombi, a pond believed to house evil spirits. If there have been heavy rains, *don't even think about it.*

⑰ Ilet de Pigeon. This tiny, rocky island a few hundred yards off the coast is the site of the Jacques Cousteau Marine Reserve, the island's best scuba and snorkeling site. Although the reefs here are good, they don't rank with the best Caribbean dive spots. Several companies conduct diving trips to the reserve, and it's on the itinerary of some sailing and snorkel-ing trips (see ⇨ Diving *and* ⇨ Sea Excursions *in* Sports & the Outdoors).

⑬ Les Mamelles. Two mountains—Mamelle de Petit-Bourg, at 2,350 feet, and Mamelle de Pigeon, at 2,500 feet—rise in the Parc National de la Guadeloupe. *Mamelle* means "breast," and when you see the mountains, you can understand why they are so named. Trails ranging from easy to arduous lace up into the surrounding mountains. There's a glorious view from the lookout point 1,969 feet up Mamelle de Pigeon. If you're a climber, plan to spend several hours exploring this area. Hark! If there have been heavy rainfalls, cancel the idea.

㉑ Le Musée Volcanologique. Inland from Basse-Terre, on the road to Ma-touba, is the village of St-Claude, where you can see this museum and learn everything you need to know about volcanoes. ⊠ *Rue Victor Hugo, St-Claude* ☎ *0590/78–15–16* 🖅 *€4* 🕐 *Daily 9–5.*

★ **⑭ Parc National de la Guadeloupe.** This 74,100-acre park has been recog-nized by UNESCO as a Biosphere Reserve. Before going, pick up a *Guide to the National Park* from the tourist office; it rates the hiking trails ac-cording to difficulty, and most are quite difficult indeed. Most mountain trails are in the southern half of the park. The park is bisected by the Route de la Traversée, a 16-mi (26-km) paved road lined with masses of tree ferns, shrubs, flowers, tall trees, and green plantains. It's the ideal point of entry to the park. Wear rubber-sole shoes and take along a swimsuit, a sweater, and perhaps food for a picnic. Try to get an early start to stay ahead of the hordes of cruise-ship passengers who are making a day of it. Check on the weather; if Basse-Terre has had a lot of rain, give it up. Last year, after intense rainfall, rock slides closed the Trace for months. ✉ *Administrative Headquarters, Rte. de la Traversée, St-Claude* ☎ *0590/80–86–00* ⊕ *www.guadeloupe-parcnational. com* 🖘 *Free* ⊙ *Weekdays 8–5:30.*

⑫ Pointe-Noire. Pointe-Noire is a good jumping-off point from which to explore Basse-Terre's little-visited northwest coast. A road skirts magnificent cliffs and tiny coves, dances in and out of thick stands of mahogany and gommier trees, and weaves through unspoiled fishing villages with boats and ramshackle houses as brightly colored as a child's finger painting. This town has two small museums devoted to local products. **La Maison du Bois** (☎ 0590/98–17–09) offers a glimpse into the traditional use of wood on the island. Superbly crafted musical instruments and furnishings are for sale. It's open Tuesday to Sunday from 9:30 to 5:30 and charges €1 admission. Across the road from La Maison du Bois is **La Maison du Cacao** (☎ 0590/98–21–23), which has exhibits on the operation of a cocoa plantation. Some antique implements are on display, and for your euros you get a hot chocolate. Chocolate bars and other goodies are for sale. It's open daily from 9 to 5 for a €6 admission fee.

⑪ Ste-Rose. In addition to a sulfur bath, there are two good beaches (Amandiers and Clugny) and several interesting small museums in Ste-Rose. **Domaine de Séverin** (☎ 0590/28–91–86), free and open daily from 8:30 to 5, is a historic rum distillery with a working waterwheel. Sadly, the fine restaurant in the colonial house is no longer serving, but there's a simple open-air lunch room that has a good menu. A *petit* train traverses the plantation from 9:30 to 10:45 and again from 3:30 to 5:30 from Sunday to Friday; this scenic tour costs €6. A gift shop sells rum, spices, and hot sauces.

★ ⑯ Vernou. Many of the old mansions in this area remain in the hands of the original aristocratic families, the *békés* (Creole for "whites"), who trace their lineage to before the French Revolution. Traipsing along a path that leads beyond the village through the forest, you come to an impressive waterfall at Saut de la Lézarde (Lizard's Leap). It is not always open in low season.

⑲ Vieux-Habitants. This was the island's first colony, established in 1635. Beaches, a restored coffee plantation, and the oldest church on the island ★ (1666) make this village worth a stop. From the riverfront **Musée du Café** (☎ 0590/98–54–96), dedicated to the art of coffeemaking, the tantalizing aroma of freshly ground beans reaches the highway. Plaques and photos tell of the island's coffee history. The shop sells excellent coffee and rum punches (liqueurs). Admission is €6. It's open daily from 9 to 5.

Iles des Saintes

The eight-island archipelago of Iles des Saintes, often referred to as Les Saintes, dots the waters off the south coast of Guadeloupe. The islands are Terre-de-Haut, Terre-de-Bas, Ilet à Cabrit, Grand Ilet, La Redonde, La Coche, Le Pâté, and Les Augustins. Columbus discovered them on November 4, 1493, and christened them Los Santos (Les Saintes in French) in honor of All Saints' Day.

Only Terre-de-Haut and Terre-de-Bas are inhabited, with a combined population of more than 3,000. Many of les Saintois are fair-haired, blue-eyed descendants of Breton and Norman sailors. Unless they are in the tourism industry, they tend to be taciturn and standoffish. Fishing still is their main source of income, and they take pride in their work. The shores are lined with their boats and *filets bleus* (blue nets dotted with burnt-orange buoys). For generations, the fishermen wore hats called *salakos,* which look like inverted saucers, patterned after a hat said to have been brought here by a seafarer from China or Indonesia. Now you're more likely to see visors and French sunglasses.

★ ㉓ **Terre-de-Haut.** With 5 square mi (13 square km) and a population of about 1,500, Terre-de-Haut is the largest and most developed of Les Saintes. Its "big city" is Bourg, with one main street, bistros, cafés, and shops. Clutching the hillside are trim white houses with bright red or blue doors, balconies, and gingerbread frills.

Terre-de-Haut's ragged coastline is scalloped with lovely coves and beaches, including the semi-nudist beach at Anse Crawen. The beautiful bay, complete with a "sugarloaf" mountain, has been called a mini Rio. There are precious few vehicles or taxis on island, so you'll often find yourself walking, despite the hilly terrain. Or you can add to the din and rent a motorbike. Take your time on these rutted roads. Around any bend there can be a herd of goats chomping on a fallen palm frond. Two traffic lights have brought a small amount of order to the motorbike hordes. A new ordinance has, too! When aggressively soliciting you, the scooter agencies will not tell you that it is now prohibited to scoot in town from 9 to noon, nor from 2 to 4.

This island makes a great day trip, but you can really get a feel for Les Saintes if you stay over. It's not unlike St. Barths, but for a fraction of the price.

Fort Napoléon. This gallery holds a collection of 250 modern paintings, influenced by cubism and surrealism. However, this museum is noted for its exhaustive exhibit of the greatest sea battles ever fought. You can also visit the well-preserved barracks and prison cells, or admire the botanical gardens, which specialize in cacti of all sizes and descriptions. ✉ *Bourg* ☎ *0590/37–99–59* 🎟 *€5* 🕘 *Daily 9–noon.*

Other Islands

㉕ **La Désirade.** *Desirable* is the operative word here. This small, somewhat remote island is an absolute find for those who prefer a road less traveled, who want their beaches long and white, who aren't interested in experiencing crime or traffic, and who don't mind that accommodations are simple if the price and quality are right. The Désirade populace (all 1,700 of them) welcome tourism, and these dear hearts have an old-fashioned sense of community that you will be welcomed into.

According to legend, the "desired land" was so named by the crew of Christopher Columbus, whose tongues were dry for want of fresh water when they spied the island; alas, it was the season for drought. The 8-square-mi (21-square-km) island, 5 mi (8 km) east of St-François, is a chalky plateau, with an arid climate, perennial sunshine, cacti, and iguanas. Rent a four-wheel-drive to climb the zigzag road that leads to the Grande Montagne. Make a photo stop at the diminutive white chapel, which offers a panorama of the sea below. Afraid that you might zig instead of zag down the precipice? Then take a fun, informative van tour that you join near the tourism office at the harbor, or hire the owner of Colibri Tours, Michel Pin, for a private tour in English. The ruins of the original settlement—a leper colony—are on the tour.

Only one road runs around the perimeter of the island, and if you're interested in visiting one of the many gorgeous beaches shaded by coco palms and sea grape trees, you can do that on a scooter. Driving is safer here than anywhere.

NEED A BREAK?

La Désirade has a few cute and casual spots to grab a bite to eat. The goats and their kids that you pass on your island tour may end up in a curry at **Chez Nounoune** (✉ La Providence ☎ 0590/20–03–59). If you're on the beach, you might want to stop by **La Payotte** (✉ Plage de Beauséjour ☎ 0590/20–01–29) for the fresh catch, conch, or lobster, or the French owner's famous chicken with a sauce of *noix de cajou* and some sweet potato gratin. Mind you, avoid it when there is a tour group on the island.

★ ㉔ **Marie-Galante.** An authentic island, it resonates with history. Columbus sighted this 155-square-km (60-square-mi) island on November 3, 1493, named it after his flagship, the *Maria Galanda,* and sailed on. It's dotted with ruined 19th-century sugar mills, and sugar is still its major product. Honey and 59-proof rum are its other favored harvests. With its rolling hills of green cane still worked by oxen and men with broad-brim straw hats, it's like traveling back in time to when all of Guadeloupe was still a giant farm.

Although it's only an hour by high-speed ferry from Pointe-à-Pitre, the country folk here are still sweet and shy. You can see swarms of yellow butterflies, and maybe a marriage carriage festooned with flowers, with a replica of a windmill as its coach, pulled by two white oxen. A daughter of the sea, Marie-Galante has some of the archipelago's most gorgeous, uncrowded beaches. Take time to explore the dramatic coast. You can find soaring cliffs—such as the Gueule Grand Gouffre (Mouth of the Giant Chasm) and Les Galeries (where the sea has sculpted a natural arcade)—and enormous sun-dappled grottos, such as Le Trou à Diable, whose underground river can be explored with a guide. Port Louis, the island's "second city," is the new hip spot. The ferry dock is in Port Louis, and it's also on the charts for yachts and regattas. After sunset, the no-see-ums and mosquitoes can be a real irritation, so always be armed with repellent. As this is still a rural island, with 40% of the population of 12,000 over 40, the bar and disco scene is active mainly during holidays.

The **Château Murat** (✉ Grand-Bourg, Marie-Galante ☎0590/97–94–41) is a restored 17th-century sugar plantation and rum distillery housing exhibits on the history of rum making and sugarcane production and an admirable *ecomusée,* whose displays celebrate local crafts and customs. It's open daily from 9:15 to 5; admission is free. **Le Moulin de Bézard** (✉ Chemin de Nesmond, off D202, Marie-Galante) is the only rebuilt windmill in the Caribbean. There are two gift shops and a café housed in replicated slave quarters with wattle walls. Admission is €4; it's open daily from 10 to 2. You should make it a point to see one of the distilleries, especially **Père Labat** (✉ Section Poisson, Grand-Bourg, Marie-Galante ☎ 0590/97–03–79), whose rum is considered some of the finest in the Caribbean and whose atelier turns out lovely pottery; admission is free, and it's open daily from 7 to noon.

GUADELOUPE ESSENTIALS

To research prices, get advice from other travelers, and book travel arrangements, visit www.fodors.com.

Transportation

BY AIR

American Airlines is the only U.S. carrier that flies to Guadeloupe (PTP), offering connecting service on American Eagle from San Juan. Air France flies nonstop from Paris and also has direct service from Miami and San Juan. Air Canada has nonstop flights from Montréal. Air Caraïbes connects St. Maarten, Martinique, Santo Domingo in the D.R., and Havana, Cuba. LIAT flies from several other Caribbean islands.

⑭ Air Canada ☎ 0590/21-12-77. **Air Caraïbes** ☎ 0590/82-47-00 or 590/64-47-00. **Air France** ☎ 0590/21-11-80 or 0820-820-820. **American Airlines/American Eagle** ☎ 0590/21-13-66. **LIAT** ☎ 0590/21-13-93.

AIRPORTS & TRANSFERS: The airport here, usually called the Pointe-à-Pitre airport (PTP) after the capital and closest major city, is one of the largest and most modern in the Caribbean, but it is still small enough to be manageable. It's clean with

good signage, shops, restaurants, and car-rental agencies. There is a tourism information booth in the terminal with bilingual staffers, ATMs (CBs), and a currency exchange. Ask your resort if airport transfers can be supplied; they are almost always cheaper than taking a taxi, but with the absence of any kind of public transit, that or a rental car may be your only option. Taxi fare to Pointe-à-Pitre is about €15, to Gosier resorts you'll pay about €30, and to St-François it's more than €50.

⑭ Aéroport International Pôle Caraïbes ☎ 0590/21-14-72 or 0590/21-14-00.

BY BOAT & FERRY

Ferry schedules and fares often change (expect them to go up as gas prices sky-rocket) especially on weekends, so phone first or check them at the tourist office or ferry terminal. Children usually pay a reduced price, but there's usually not a charge for infants.

You can travel to the outlying islands in the Guadeloupe archipelago usually in the morning, returning in the afternoon. Brudey Frères ferries travel between Pointe-à-Pitre and Terre-de-Haut (in Les Saintes) and Marie-Galante. A Brudey Frères ferry travels from Trois-Rivières on Basse-Terre to Terre-de-Haut. Comatrile ferries travel from St-François on Grande-Terre to both La Désirade and Marie-Galante. These ferries usually leave in the early morning and again in the afternoon. Both Comatrile and Express des Isles operate ferries between Terre-de-Haut and Marie-Galante. Note: In the low season, because of the hike in gas prices, you may have to take a complimentary bus from the Pointe-à-Pitre terminal to the ferry dock in Basse-Terre, which can take nearly an hour. That crossing is shorter but rougher.

Brudey Frères also runs ferries to Dominica, Martinique, and St. Lucia as does Express des Iles. Any of these trips is going to cost in the neighborhood of €60, and the crossings take between three and four hours, even five sometimes. Most of these services are daily, with extra departures on weekends, but be sure to call and confirm schedules and prices. The services can be crowded on weekends and after music festivals and other events.

🛈 **Brudey Frères Transport Maritime** ☎ 0590/90−04−48, 0590/91−60−87 in Pointe-à-Pitre, 0590/92−69−74 in Trois Rivières, 0590/88−66−67 in St-François, 0590/97−77−82 in Marie-Galante ⊕ www.brudey-freres.fr. **Comatrile** ☎ 0590/91−02−45. **Express des Isles** ☎ 0825/35−90−00 or 0590/91−98−53 ⊕ www.express-des-iles.com.

BY CAR

Providing you consider yourself a good driver, and you heed the following tips, it is fun to explore this island by rental car. Guadeloupe has 1,225 mi (1,976 km) of fine highways, marked as in Europe, and driving (which is on the right, as in the United States and France) around Grande-Terre is relatively easy. Basse-Terre requires more skill to navigate the hairpin bends in the mountains and around the eastern shore; at night these scenic roads are poorly lighted and treacherous. Guadeloupeans are skillful, fast, and oftentimes impatient drivers. When the fearless mo-

torcycle boys—called hornets—come at you, pull over to the side. Avoid morning and evening rush hours, especially around Pointe-à-Pitre. If you're lost, know that the people on the side of the road are waiting for a lift and if you stop they'll jump in. Try to find a gas station and have your map ready, for chances are the attendants speak more Creole than French. Inside, the manager or other customers usually speak French and maybe English. Make certain that attendants don't put Super in your tank. Return your vehicle with the same amount of gas or you'll be charged some exorbitant rate. Inquire whether you can rent a car that takes diesel (*gazole*); as in Europe, diesel is considerably cheaper than gasoline. Also, if you have too much fun and bring the car back dirty (inside), you might have to pay for cleaning it—Hertz threatens to charge €77. Sixt, which provides excellent service in three languages, is increasing its fleet of high-end automatics for its American clients.

🛈 **Avis** ☎ 0590/21−13−54. **Budget** ☎ 0590/21−13−49. **Europcar** ☎ 0590/21−13−52. **Hertz** ☎ 0590/21−13−46. **Jumbo Car** ☎ 0590/21−13−50. **Rent A Car** ☎ 0590/21−13−62 **Sixt** ☎ 0590/ 21−13−44.

BY MOPED

The only places in Grande-Terre where tourists can drive scooters relatively safely are around St-Anne, St-François, and right around Gosier. You can rent a Vespa scooter at Eli Sport or Equator Moto for about $29 per day, including insurance. You'll need to put down nearly €150 for a deposit. There are numerous vendors by the ferry dock in Terre-de-Haut, Les Saintes, where you can rent mopeds, so search for the best price, but beware that moped traffic in town is restricted during the day; you may find it easier to simply walk. Marie-Galante has Loca Sol and Magaloc, and this is now the best island for scooting.

🛈 **Eli Sport** ✉ Grand Camp, Grande-Terre ☎ 0590/90−37−50. **Equator Moto** ✉ Gosier, Grande-Terre ☎ 0590/90−36−77. **Loca Sol** ✉ Rue du Fort, Grand-Bourg, Marie-Galante ☎ 0590/97−76−58. **Magaloc** ✉ Grand-Bourg, Marie-Galante ☎ 0590/72−91−33.

BY TAXI

Taxis are metered and fairly pricey, and fares increase by 40% between 9 PM and 7 AM and on Sunday and holidays. Tourist offices or your hotel can arrange for an English-speaking taxi driver and even organize a small group for you to share the cost of a tour. Nicho—of Nicho's Reliable Taxi—speaks perfect English and knows every back way when the traffic backs up on the main highways. Call Narcisse Taxi for an English-speaking, professional taxi driver and tour guide with a minivan. If your French is in order, you can call Radio Cabs.

🚖 **Narcisse Taxi** ☎ 0690/35-27-29, 0590/94-55-95 on Grande-Terre. **Nicho's Reliable Taxi** ☎ 0590/74-86-85. **Radio Cabs** ☎ 0590/82-00-00, 0590/83-09-55, or 0590/20-74-74.

Contacts & Resources

BANKS & EXCHANGE SERVICES

A few places accept U.S. dollars, but you should plan to change some dollars into euros (prices quoted throughout the chapter are in euros unless otherwise noted). It's best to change your money at a bank, although a *bureau de change,* such as Change Caraïbe, which is near both the tourist office and market in Pointe-à-Pitre, advertises rates as good as those in the bank, though they usually take a larger commission.

You can find ATMs (*Distributeurs Automatiques* or CBs) that accept Visa and MasterCard at the airport and at most major banks. There's an ATM at the ferry dock in Pointe-à-Pitre and one at the dock in Les Saintes. As you might expect, they all dole out euros. If it's a Plus card, your ATM card should work, but you'll not be able to check your balance; you must have a four-digit PIN. However, ATMs don't always work with foreign bank cards, particularly in smaller towns, and don't always work, period. Have a back-up plan. On Les Saintes, where there's no longer a bank, the post office (when open) will cash traveler's checks.

BUSINESS HOURS

Banks are open weekdays from 8 to noon and 2 to 4; Crédit Agricole, Banque Populaire, and Société Générale de Banque aux Antilles have branches that are open Saturday. In summer most banks are open from 8 to 3. Banks close at noon the day before a legal holiday that falls during the week. Post offices are open weekdays from 8 to noon and 2 to 4, on Saturday from 8 to noon. Shops are open weekdays from 8 or 8:30 to noon and 2:30 to 6.

ELECTRICITY

Electricity is 220 volts, and plugs have two round prongs. So if you're visiting from North America, you'll need both an adapter and a converter to use any appliances you bring with you. If you bring a laptop, it's sometimes possible to buy a cord with a European plug at a local computer store, though your adapter will usually be dual-voltage already (be sure to check your manual or ask an expert if you have any questions).

EMERGENCIES

Pharmacies alternate in staying open around the clock. The tourist offices or your hotel can help you locate a pharmacist who is on duty and/or find an English-speaking doctor. SAMU is a medical service where you can get to see a doctor fast. However, the receptionists generally do not speak English. SOS Taxi Ambulance can get you to a hospital quickly, but you may need to have a French-speaking person make the call. SMUR is both an ambulance service and an emergency room.

🚨 Emergency Services **Ambulance** ☎ 15. **Fire** ☎ 18. **Police emergencies** ☎ 17. **Police nonemergencies on Basse-Terre** ☎ 0590/81-11-55. **Police nonemergencies on Grande-Terre** ☎ 0590/82-13-17. **SAMU** ☎ 0590/89-11-00. **SMUR Ambulance of Basse-Terre** ☎ 0590/80-54-01. **SOS Taxi Ambulance** ☎ 0590/82-89-33.

🏥 Hospitals **Centre Hôpitalier de Pointe-à-Pitre** ✉ Pointe-à-Pitre, Abymes, Grande-Terre ☎ 0590/89-10-10. **Centre Hôpitalier** ✉ Basse-Terre, Basse-Terre ☎ 0590/80-54-00.

ETIQUETTE & BEHAVIOR

Guadeloupeans are deeply religious and traditional, particularly the older generations, who, unfortunately, often still harbor an anticolonial resentment. Don't offend them by wearing short shorts or swimwear off the beach, and ask before taking a picture of any islander. Finally, observe the courtesy of saying "bonjour" or "bon soir" before asking a question; such social niceties are still practiced throughout the Caribbean and are expected.

HOLIDAYS

Among the public holidays are New Year's Day, Ash Wednesday (beginning of Lent, usually Feb.), Good Friday, Easter Monday, Labor Day (May 1), Bastille Day (July 14), Assumption Day (Aug. 15), All Saints' Day (Les Toussaints, Nov. 1), Armistice Day (Nov. 11), and Christmas.

INTERNET, MAIL & SHIPPING

Pointe-à-Pitre has several Internet cafés, mainly on back streets; the tourist office can point you in their direction. In Gosier, there is one across from the hotel Sofitel Auberge de la Vielle Tour. At the marina, there is a good one in the cluster of shops across the street from where you enter the marina.

Postcards to the United States cost about €.75 and to Canada €.90; letters up to 20 grams, €.90. Stamps can be purchased at post offices, *café-tabacs,* hotel newsstands, and souvenir shops. When writing to Guadeloupe, be sure to include the name of the specific island in the archipelago (e.g., Grande-Terre, Basse-Terre, Iles des Saintes) as well as the postal code, then "Guadeloupe" followed by "French West Indies."

🗝 **Le Caméléon** ✉ Mare-gaillard, Gosier ☎ 0690/58-84-50. **Le Cibercafé** ✉ Montauban, Gosier ☎ 0590/82-92-06. **Poly Info** ✉ 29 rue Barbes, Pointe-à-Pitre ☎ 0590/20-38-95.

LANGUAGE

The official language is French, though most of the islanders also speak Creole, a lyrical patois that you won't be able to understand even if you're fluent in French. Most of the staff in hotels know some English, but communicating is decidedly more difficult in the countryside and in stores. Some taxi drivers speak a little English. Arm yourself with a phrase book, a dictionary, patience, and a sense of humor.

PASSPORTS REQUIREMENTS

All arriving passengers must have a valid passport as well as a return or ongoing ticket to enter Guadeloupe. A birth certificate and valid picture ID are *not* sufficient.

SAFETY

Put your valuables in the hotel safe. Don't leave them unattended in your room or on the beach. If you rent a car, always lock it, with luggage and valuables—be it designer sunglasses or a laptop—stashed out of sight. It's not safe to walk around Pointe-à-Pitre at night.

TAXES & SERVICE CHARGES

The *taxe de séjour* (room tax), which varies from hotel to hotel, is usually €.76 but never exceeds €1.80 per person per day. Most hotel prices include a 10% to 15% service charge; if not, it'll be added to your bill. A 15% service charge is included in all restaurant prices, as are taxes.

TELEPHONES

If you need to make many calls outside of your hotel, purchase a *télécarte* at the post office or other outlets marked TÉLÉCARTE EN VENTE ICI. Télécartes look like credit cards and are used in special booths labeled TÉLÉCOM. Local and international calls made with these cards are cheaper than operator-assisted calls. It's difficult, but not impossible, to put collect or credit-card calls through to the United States from Guadeloupe. Many Guadeloupeans have cell phones as their primary telephone service. In a pinch, you can ask someone to make a call for you from his or her "Orange" (the name of the major cellular company) and offer a euro in return.

To make on-island calls, you now have to dial 0590 and the six-digit phone number.

12

To call Guadeloupe from the United States, dial 011–590, another 590, and then the local number. For cell phone numbers, dial 011–590-690. If in one of the other French West Indies, you dial 0590 and the six-digit local number, 0690 if it is a cell.

It's possible to buy (but not rent) a cell phone in Guadeloupe; however, be prepared to pay cash, as the main Orange office in Pointe-à-Pitre does not take credit cards. Better to use the Boutique Orange at the airport, but no one there speaks English. You will probably not be able to buy a local SIM card to use in your own mobile phone.

🗎 **Boutique Orange Aéroport** ✉ Aéroport International Pôle Caraïbes, Abymes ☎ 0590/21-13-36.

TIPPING

Restaurants are legally required to include a 15% service charge in the menu price, and no additional gratuity is necessary (although appreciated if service is particularly good). Tip skycaps and porters about €1 a bag. Many cab drivers own their own taxis and don't expect a tip. You won't have any trouble ascertaining if a 10% tip is expected. It's a look. Leaving the chamber maid a euro a night is always good form.

TOUR OPTIONS

Guadeloupe has a number of fun, professional tour operators. However, much happens only in French. Air Tropical has two twin-engine planes (five-passenger capacity) and organizes day trips to the neighboring islands; the most far-ranging is the Archipelago Air Cruise, which goes to Les Saintes in the morning and Marie-Galante or Désirade in the afternoon. Emeraude Guadeloupe offers everything from hikes up the volcano to botanical tours and visits to creole homes; guides are certified by the state, but you'll probably need some French to understand them. GMG Voyage tours can usually be booked through your hotel. The company runs

buses out to the north of Basse-Terre, to Carbet, and to the Severine Distillery, traversing the Route des Mamelles through the park—with commentary and lunch on Petite Anse for €75. The company also schedules trips that include a half-day sail. Marius Voyages offers excursions to the south and north coasts of Basse-Terre; the latter can include a visit to the Botanical Gardens and a glass-bottom boat ride to Pigeon Island. Excursions go throughout Grande-Terre, providing transport to the ferries for Marie-Galante and Les Saintes; they can even get you to Martinique or Dominica for a couple of nights. *Best of all,* the company offers airport transfers to hotels in Ste-Anne and St-François for a mere €45 for one or two persons (€80 round-trip). This beats taxi prices and can eliminate the need for a rental car.

🗎 **Air Tropical** ✉ St-François, Grande-Terre ☎ 0590/88-89-90 or 0690/35-05-15 ⊕ www.air-tropical.com. **Emeraude Guadeloupe** ✉ St-Claude ☎ 0590/81-98-28. **GMG Voyage** ✉ Gosier ☎ 0590/21-08-08. **Marius Voyages** ✉ Main St., Ste-Anne ☎ 0590/88-19-80.

VISITOR INFORMATION

🗎 **Comité du Tourisme des Isles de Guadeloupe** ✉ 5 sq. de la Banque, Pointe-à-Pitre ☎ 0590/82-09-30. **French Government Tourist Office** ⊕ www.franceguide.com ✉ 9454 Wilshire Blvd., Beverly Hills, CA 90212 ☎ 310/276-2835 ✉ 645 N. Michigan Ave., Chicago, IL 60611 ☎ 312/337-6339 ✉ 1981 McGill College Ave., Suite 490, Montréal, Québec H3A 2W9, Canada ☎ 514/288-4264 ✉ 30 St. Patrick St., Suite 700, Toronto, Ontario M5T 3A3, Canada ☎ 416/593-6427 ✉ 178 Piccadilly, London W1V 0AL, U.K. ☎ 0171/499-6911. **Office du tourisme de Marie-Galante** ✉ Rue du Port, BP 15, Grand-Bourg, Marie-Galante ☎ 0590/97-56-51. **Syndicats d'Initiatives** ✉ Av. de l'Europe, St-François ☎ 0590/88-48-74 ✉ Marie-Galante ☎ 0590/97-56-51 ✉ La Capitainerie, La Désirade ☎ 0590/85-00-86.

WEDDINGS

Since getting married in Guadeloupe has a long residency requirement, it's not really feasible to plan a wedding on the island.

Jamaica

Kayaks on the beach at Montego Bay

WORD OF MOUTH

"To me Jamaica has, for lack of a better word, a 'soul,' something that I find lacking in some of the more 'antiseptic' islands."

—Patty

"Thank God so many people get scared out of Jamaica trips or I would never be able to get a room and would have missed out on the best vacations of my life."

—MoniqueU

WELCOME TO JAMAICA

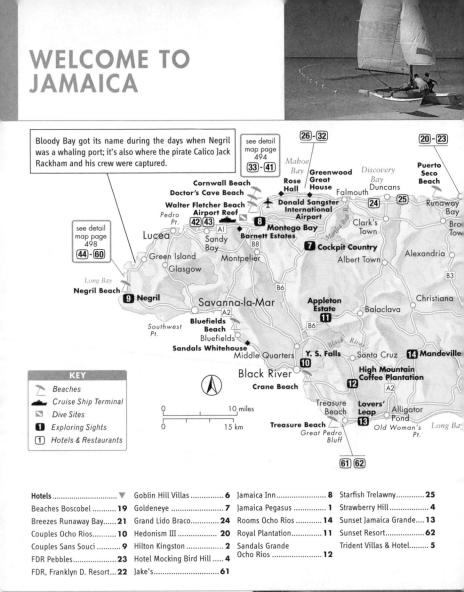

Bloody Bay got its name during the days when Negril was a whaling port; it's also where the pirate Calico Jack Rackham and his crew were captured.

see detail map page 494
33 - 41

26 - 32

20 - 23

Mahoe Bay
Greenwood Great House
Discovery Bay
Duncans
Puerto Seco Beach

Rose Hall
Falmouth

Cornwall Beach
Doctor's Cave Beach
Walter Fletcher Beach
Airport Reef

24
25
Runaway Bay
Bro Tow

Pedro Pt.
42 43

Donald Sangster International Airport

Clark's Town

see detail map page 498
44 - 60

Lucea
8
Montego Bay
7 Cockpit Country
Albert Town
Alexandria

A1
Sandy Bay
Barnett Estates
B8

B3

Green Island
Montpelier

Glasgow
B6

Long Bay
Negril Beach
9 Negril
A2
Savanna-la-Mar
Appleton Estate
11
Balaclava
Christiana

Southwest Pt.
Bluefields Beach
Bluefields
B6

Black River

Sandals Whitehouse
Middle Quarters
Y. S. Falls
10
Santa Cruz
14 Mandeville

Black River
Crane Beach
High Mountain Coffee Plantation
12
A2

KEY

⌐ Beaches
🚢 Cruise Ship Terminal
◥ Dive Sites
1 Exploring Sights
① Hotels & Restaurants

0   10 miles
0   15 km

Treasure Beach
Lovers' Leap
13
Alligator Pond
Old Woman's Pt.
Long Ba

Treasure Beach
Great Pedro Bluff

61 62

Chances are you will never fully understand Jamaica in all its delightful complexity, but you will probably have a good time trying. You can party in Negril, shop in Montego Bay, or simply relax at one of the island's many all-inclusive resorts, but you'll also discover culture and delicious island cuisine.

OUT OF MANY, ONE

The third-largest island in the Caribbean (after Cuba and Hispaniola), Jamaica is 146 mi (242 km) long and is slightly smaller than the state of Connecticut. It has a population of 2.7 million. With about 800,000 people, the capital, Kingston, is the largest English-speaking city south of Miami (in the Western Hemisphere, at least). The highest point is Blue Mountain Peak at 7,402 feet.

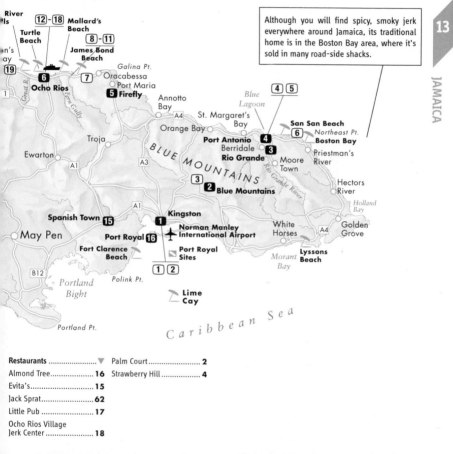

Although you will find spicy, smoky jerk everywhere around Jamaica, its traditional home is in the Boston Bay area, where it's sold in many road-side shacks.

13

JAMAICA

Restaurants .... ▼	Palm Court **2**
Almond Tree **16**	Strawberry Hill **4**
Evita's **15**	
Jack Sprat **62**	
Little Pub **17**	
Ocho Rios Village Jerk Center **18**	

TOP 4 REASONS TO VISIT JAMAICA

1 The all-inclusive resort was invented here, and the sprawling beachfront properties are among the best in the Caribbean.

2 Golfers will be delighted by the many wonderful courses, primarily in the Montego Bay area.

3 Families will find every conceivable activity, great beaches, and many child-friendly resorts.

4 Jamaica has rich cultural traditions exhibited particularly in local music, art, and cuisine.

JAMAICA PLANNER

Getting to Jamaica

Several major airlines fly nonstop to Montego Bay from North America, so if you need to make connections, it will usually be at a U.S. airport rather than San Juan. It's even possible to fly nonstop from Los Angeles. From the U.K., there are nonstop flights from London.

Donald Sangster International Airport (MBJ), in Montego Bay, is the most efficient point of entry for travelers destined for MoBay, Ocho Rios, Runaway Bay, and Negril. Norman Manley International Airport (KIN), in Kingston, is the best arrival point for travelers headed to the capital or Port Antonio.

Hassle Factor: Low to High, depending on how far you are from the MoBay airport.

Activities

Negril has the island's best beach, but there are also some spectacular wild **beaches** along the southwest coast, not to mention the famous Doctor's Cave beach in Montego Bay. If you tire of lying on the sand, tour operators will pick you up from your resort for a wide range of activities. The dive sites near Jamaica aren't spectacular, but there is good **diving** from any of the island's major resort areas. Jamaica has some spectacular **golf courses**, the best of which are near Montego Bay. You can go **rafting** on the Rio Grande, Martha Brae, or Black rivers; these slow, lazy floats on small rafts. Tour operators are coming up with new activities all the time. Chukka Cove in Ocho Rios operates an **ATV** course and a **canopy tour**, as well as **horseback riding**; Chukka Blue is the company's outlet in MoBay.

On the Ground

If your hotel doesn't offer a shuttle, you can get shared-van service from the airport in Montego Bay to Negril, Ocho Rios, and Runaway Bay—not to mention the hotels in and around Montego Bay. This service isn't inexpensive, but it's usually easier than trying to drive in an unfamiliar country with sometimes questionable roads and bad signage.

Renting a Car

The average traveler should not rent a car in Jamaica. With high prices, hectic traffic, and bad signage, it's usually easier—and cheaper—to use a taxi or take tours. This is particularly true if you are staying in an all-inclusive.

Although Jamaica has dozens of car-rental companies (you'll find branches at the airports and the resorts among other places), rentals can be difficult to arrange once you've arrived. Make reservations and send a deposit before your trip. (Cars are scarce, and without either a confirmation number or a receipt you may have to walk.) You must be at least 25 years old, have a valid driver's license (from any country), and have a valid credit card. You may be required to post a security of several hundred dollars before taking possession of your car; ask about it when you make the reservation. Rates are quite expensive, averaging $70 to $120 a day after the addition of the compulsory insurance, which you must purchase even if your credit card offers it.

Where to Stay

Montego Bay has the largest concentration of resorts on the island, all near the main airport; **Negril** is a more relaxed haven on the west coast but requires an hour-plus drive once you land. Both offer a mix of large and small resorts, plus good nightlife. In Negril, the resorts tend to be larger along the northern stretches of Negril Beach and Bloody Bay. **Runaway Bay** and **Ocho Rios** are more than an hour east of MoBay. Runaway Bay's all-inclusives are isolated and on fairly mediocre beaches; Ocho Rios has a real town atmosphere—albeit a busy one—with resorts lining decent beaches, though a few hotels are right in town. **Port Antonio**, a sleepy, laid-back haven, has a few resorts and a quiet atmosphere but is several hours from both the MoBay or Kingston airports. The **Southwest Coast** has a few small resorts, uncrowded beaches, and little development aside from the enormous new Sandals Whitehouse. Few vacationers choose to stay in the capital, **Kingston**, but the immediate area also includes the **Blue Mountains** and the luxe Strawberry Hill resort.

TYPES OF LODGINGS

Jamaica was the birthplace of the Caribbean **all-inclusive resort**, which is still the most popular vacation option here. Several of these are open only to male-female couples. Particularly in Negril, you'll find smaller, more **unique hotels** and inns that aren't part of the big chains; however, they aren't always cheap. The Island Outpost company operates several upscale **boutique resorts** all over Jamaica. Inexpensive **inns**, though marketed primarily to European travelers who have more time to spend on the island, are often much less isolated than the big resorts.

Hotel & Restaurant Costs

Assume that hotels operate on the European Plan (**EP**—with no meals) unless we specify that they use either the Continental Plan (**CP**—with a Continental breakfast), Breakfast Plan (**BP**—with full breakfast), or the Modified American Plan (**MAP**—with breakfast and dinner). Other hotels may offer the Full American Plan (**FAP**—including all meals but no drinks) or may be All-Inclusive (**AI**—with all meals, drinks, and most activities).

WHAT IT COSTS in Dollars

	$$$$	$$$	$$	$	¢
Restaurants	over $30	$20–$30	$12–$20	$8–$12	under $8
Hotels*	over $350	$250–$350	$150–$250	$80–$150	under $80
Hotels**	over $450	$350–$450	$250–$350	$125–$250	under $125

*EP, BP, CP **AI, FAP, MAP
Restaurant prices are for a main course at dinner and do not include the 10% service charge. Hotel prices are per night for a double room in high season, excluding 10% service charge, and meal plans (except at all-inclusives).

When to Go

High season in Jamaica runs roughly from mid-December through April. From May through mid-December, you can save from 20% to as much as 40% on rates, more if you use value-oriented travel packagers.

There are several annual events in Jamaica that draw huge numbers of visitors. **Air Jamaica's Jazz & Blues Festival** is in Montego Bay each January. **Reggae Sumfest** is usually in late July or early August. The **International Marlin Tournament** is held in Port Antonio every October.

The largest island-wide festival is **Carnival,** which is held in Kingston, Ocho Rios, and MoBay every March and April and in Negril every May.

13

By Paris
Permenter and
John Bigley

"DO YOU SEE THE ACKEE?" We were strolling the banks of the Black River on Jamaica's south coast when we heard the call of a man from a nearby car. He gestured up at an ordinary-looking tree we were near. Between its green leaves peeked small, red fruit, bursting open to reveal large, black seeds like eyes looking out at us. "That's ackee," he said. "We make our national dish from that fruit. You must try some while you are here!"

Jamaicans define enthusiasm. Whether the topic is ackee or dominoes, politics or carnival, the spirit of this island comes out in every interaction. Although the island is well known for its tropical beauty, reggae music, and cuisine, you may find that your interactions with local residents are what you truly remember.

Although 95% of the population traces its bloodlines to Africa, Jamaica is a stockpot of cultures, including those of other Caribbean islands, Great Britain, the Middle East, India, China, Germany, Portugal, and South America. The third-largest island in the Caribbean (after Cuba and Hispaniola), Jamaica enjoys a considerable self-sufficiency based on tourism, agriculture, and mining.

The island is rich in beauty, but a quick look around reveals widespread poverty and a land where the disparity between the lives of the resort guests and the resort employees is often staggering. High unemployment rates and poor economic opportunities have created a crime problem, one that the tourism board and the government constantly work to resolve. Most safety concerns center on Kingston, with its gang violence. In truth, serious crimes against tourists are rare, but petty theft is sometimes a problem. Property theft is a problem across the island, and there are high rates of burglary and robbery almost everywhere. It's rare to find a middle-class home anywhere without burglar bars.

Where vacationers opt to make their Jamaican home away from home depends on factors ranging from the length of their vacation to personal interests. With its direct air connections to many cities in the U.S., Montego Bay (or MoBay) is favored by Americans taking short trips; many properties are just minutes from the airport. Two hours east of the airport lies Ocho Rios (often just Ochi), a lush destination that's favored by honeymooners for its tropical beauty and myriad couples-only resorts. Ocho Rios is also a popular cruise port and where you can find one of the island's most recognizable attractions: the stair-step Dunn's River Falls, which invites travelers to climb in daisy-chain fashion, hand-in-hand behind a sure-footed guide.

As you continue east from Ocho Rios (although many travelers opt to fly into Kingston and take a short flight), Port Antonio is considered the most beautiful, untouched area of Jamaica, a hideaway for the rich and famous since Errol Flynn first lived there.

Nearly two hours west of MoBay lies Negril, once a hippy haven and now a growing destination that still hangs on to its laid-back roots despite the addition of several expansive all-inclusive resorts in recent years.

The south coast is more attractive to those travelers looking for funky fun in small, one-of-a-kind resorts and an atmosphere that encourages them to get out and mingle in the community, whether that means a game of dominoes in a local rum shop or a bicycle trip to buy the day's catch from local fisherman. Although the beaches here don't have the white-sand beauty of their northern cousins, this area is uncrowded and still largely undiscovered, although it's now home to a large couples-only all-inclusive resort.

Jamaica's capital city, Kingston, is a sharp contrast to the beach destinations. The largest English-speaking city in the western hemisphere south of Miami (with some 800,000 residents), this sprawling metropolis is primarily visited by business travelers or by those who want to learn more about the cultural side of Jamaica thanks to its numerous galleries, theaters, and cultural programs. But if you really want to understand Jamaica, you can't ignore Kingston.

Where to Stay

Jamaica was the birthplace of the Caribbean all-inclusive resort, a concept that started in Ocho Rios and has spread throughout the island, now composing the lion's share of hotel rooms. Package prices usually include airport transfers, accommodations, three meals a day, snacks, all bar drinks (often including premium liquors) and soft drinks, a full menu of sports options (including scuba diving and golf at high-end establishments), nightly entertainment, and all gratuities and taxes. At most all-inclusive resorts, the only surcharges are for such luxuries as spa and beauty treatments, telephone calls, tours, and weddings or vow-renewal ceremonies (though even these are often included at high-end establishments).

The all-inclusive market is especially strong with couples and honeymooners (although some properties restrict their clientele to male-female couples only). To maintain a romantic atmosphere (no Marco Polo games by the pool), some resorts have minimum age requirements ranging from 12 to 18. Other properties court families with tempting supervised kids' programs, family-friendly entertainment, and in-room amenities especially for young travelers.

Kingston

Visited by few vacationers but a frequent destination for business travelers and visitors with a deep interest in Jamaica heritage and culture, the sprawling city of Kingston is home to some of the island's finest business hotels. Skirting the city are the Blue Mountains, a completely different world from the urban frenzy of the capital city.

★ $$$–$$$$ **Strawberry Hill.** A 45-minute drive from Kingston—but worlds apart in terms of atmosphere—this exclusive resort was developed by Chris Blackwell, former head of Island Records (the late Bob Marley's label). Perched in the Blue Mountains, it's where the rich and famous go to retreat and relax. The resort has a pool, though this is one Jamaican property not for beach buffs but for those in search of gourmet dining, Aveda spa treatments, and pure relaxation in Georgian-style villas. The villas survey the Blue Mountains from expansive porches, most with an oversize hammock. Every bed has an electric mattress pad to warm things up on chilly evenings; mosquito nets surround you because there's no air-conditioning. ✉ *New Castle Rd., Irishtown* ☎ *876/944–8400* 🖷 *876/944–8408* 🌐 *www.islandoutpost.com* ➶ *12 villas* ⚐ *Restaurant, room service, fans, in-room safes, some kitchens, some kitchenettes, minibars, cable TV, in-room VCRs, pool, sauna, spa, mountain bikes, croquet, bar, laundry service, meeting rooms, airport shuttle; no a/c* ▭ *AE, D, MC, V* ⵘ *CP.*

$$ ⌸ **Hilton Kingston.** With all the standard amenities travelers expect to see at a high-rise chain hotel, this property ranks as a favorite with business travelers. The expansive marble lobby leads to attractive, well-appointed rooms. The concierge floors offer complimentary cocktails, hors d'oeuvres, and Continental breakfast. Extras include secured-access elevators and in-room coffee and tea setups. ✉ *77 Knutsford Blvd., Box 112* ☎ *876/926–5430* 🖷 *876/929–7439* 🌐 *www.hiltoncaribbean.com* ➶ *290 rooms, 13 suites* ⚐ *2 restaurants, in-room safes, cable TV, in-room data ports, Wi-Fi, 2 tennis courts, pool, health club, massage, sauna, 3 bars, nightclub, recreation room, shops, concierge, business services* ▭ *AE, D, DC, MC, V* ⵘ *EP.*

$–$$ ⌸ **Jamaica Pegasus.** In the heart of the financial district, this 17-story high-rise is popular with business travelers due to its location and business amenities. Popular with locals, the hotel's restaurant offers plenty of Jamaican favorites such as braised oxtail and grilled snapper. All rooms have balconies and large windows that face the Blue Mountains, the pool, or the Caribbean. There's an excellent business center, duty-free shops, and 24-hour room service. ✉ *81 Knutsford Blvd., Box 333* ☎ *876/926–3690* 🖷 *876/929–5855* 🌐 *www.jamaicapegasus.com* ➶ *300 rooms, 15 suites* ⚐ *Restaurant, coffee shop, room service, in-room safes, minibars, cable TV, in-room broadband, Wi-Fi, 2 tennis courts, pool, wading pool, gym, hair salon, basketball, 2 bars, shops, playground, laundry service, concierge, Internet room, business services* ▭ *AE, D, DC, MC, V* ⵘ *EP.*

Port Antonio

If you've had your fill of Jamaica's bustling resorts in Montego Bay and Ocho Rios, there's a sure antidote to the tourist scene: Port Antonio. This quiet community is on Jamaica's east end, 133 mi (220 km) west of Montego Bay, and is favored by those looking to get away from it all. Don't look for mixology classes or limbo dances here; this end of Jamaica is quiet and relaxed. The fun is usually found outdoors, followed by a fine evening meal. The area's must-do activities include rafting Jamaica's own Rio Grande, snorkeling or scuba diving in the Blue Lagoon, exploring the Nonsuch Caves, and stopping at the classy Trident for lunch or a drink.

$$–$$$ ⌸ **Hotel Mocking Bird Hill.** With only 10 rooms, some overlooking the sea and all with views of lush hillsides, Mocking Bird Hill is much more like a cozy B&B than a hotel. We are especially pleased at the way owners Barbara Walker and Shireen Aga run an environmentally sensitive operation: you can find bamboo instead of hardwood furniture, solar-heated water, meals made with local produce in the Mille Fleurs dining terrace, locally produced toiletries and stationery sets, and 7 naturally landscaped acres. There's a free shuttle to Frenchman's Cove Beach, about a five-minute drive away. Wedding packages are available. ⊠ *N. Coast Hwy., Point Ann, Box 254, Port Antonio* ☎ *876/993–7267* 📠 *876/993–7133* ⊕ *www.hotelmockingbirdhill.com* 🛏 *10 rooms* ⟁ *Restaurant, in-room safes, pool, massage, bar, laundry service, no-smoking rooms; no a/c, no room phones* ⊟ *AE, MC, V* ⦶ *MAP.*

$$–$$$ 🏨 **Trident Villas & Hotel Jamaica.** This slightly dated hotel maintains the "old Caribbean" atmosphere, complete with afternoon tea and antique furnishings seen at a dwindling number of resorts these days, a style some will favor and others may consider stuffy. You can have breakfast served on your private patio and watch peacocks strut the manicured lawns. Many of the pastel and floral rooms feature turrets and bay windows, as well as balconies or verandahs; however, they do not have TVs or clocks, and only some rooms have air-conditioning. ⊠ *N. Coast Hwy., Point Ann, Box 119, Port Antonio* ☎ *876/993–2602* 📠 *876/993–2960* ⊕ *www. tridentvillas.netfirms.com* 🛏 *8 rooms, 1 suite, 14 villas* ⟁ *Restaurant, in-room safes, minibars, 2 tennis courts, pool, fitness classes, massage, beach, snorkeling, boating, croquet, bar, library, laundry service, concierge; no a/c in some rooms, no room TVs* ⊟ *AE, D, MC, V* ⦶ *MAP.*

$–$$ 🏨 **Goblin Hill Villas at San San.** This lush 12-acre estate atop a hill overlooking San San Bay is best suited for travelers looking for a home-away-from-home atmosphere, not a bustling resort. Each attractively appointed villa comes with its own dramatic view, plus a staff member to do the grocery shopping, cleaning, and cooking for you. Villas come equipped with cable TV, ceiling fans (with a/c in the bedrooms only), and tropical furnishings; it's sometimes possible to rent the bedroom of one of the two-bedroom villas for a lower per-night cost. The beach is a 10-minute walk away. Excellent car-rental packages are available. ⌖ *Box 26, San San* ☎ *876/925–8108* 📠 *876/925–6248* ⊕ *www.goblinhill.com* 🛏 *28 1- and 2-bedroom villas* ⟁ *Fans, kitchens, cable TV, 2 tennis courts, pool, beach, bar, library; no room phones* ⊟ *AE, D, MC, V* ⦶ *EP.*

Ocho Rios

Ocho Rios lies on the north coast, halfway between Port Antonio and MoBay. Rivers, waterfalls, fern-shaded roads, and tropical lushness fill this fertile region. It's a favorite with honeymooners as well as Jamaicans, who like to escape crowded Kingston for the weekend. The area's resorts, hotels, and villas are all a short drive from the frenetic, traffic-clogged downtown, which has a crafts market, boutiques, duty-free shops, restaurants, and several scenic attractions. The community lies 67 mi (111 km) east of Montego Bay, a drive which, because of road conditions, takes about two hours. At this writing, a major road improvement project was under way.

★ ☾ $$$$ 🏨 **Beaches Boscobel Resort & Golf Club.** Although this resort is for anyone—including singles and couples—it's best suited for families, whose children enjoy supervised activities in one of five kids' clubs divided by age, from infants to teens. Some rooms have pull-out sofas, and there are also connecting rooms for large families. Children under age 2 stay free, and special rates cover children under age 16 sharing a room with a parent. ⊠ *N. Coast Hwy., Box 2, St. Ann* ☎ *876/975–7777* 📠 *876/*

975–7641 ⊕ *www.beaches.com* ⇆ *120 rooms, 110 suites* ⚹ *5 restaurants, fans, in-room safes, cable TV, golf privileges, 4 tennis courts, 4 pools, gym, hair salon, spa, beach, dive shop, snorkeling, 6 bars, video game room, babysitting, children's programs (ages infant–17), laundry service* ☞ *2-night minimum* ☰ *AE, MC, V* ¶⊙¶ *AI.*

$$$$ ⊡ **Couples Ocho Rios.** Renovations in 2004 spiffed up the guest rooms of Jamaica's first all-inclusive resort, which allows only male-female couples. Though similar to a Sandals in its creation of a romantic, cozy atmosphere, this Couples resort isn't quite as upscale and tends to draw a somewhat older repeat clientele. Connected by long hallways, rooms are a short walk from the beach; a handful of villa suites are tucked back in the gardens with private plunge pools or hot tubs. The resort is on a nice stretch of beach, and there's also a private island where you can sunbathe in the buff if you want. Weddings are included in the package, as are five off-site excursions. ⊠ *Tower Isle* ☎ *876/975–4271* 🖷 *876/975–4439* ⊕ *www.couples.com* ⇆ *189 rooms, 17 suites* ⚹ *4 restaurants, room service, in-room safes, cable TV, 5 tennis courts, pool, 5 outdoor hot tubs, massage, sauna, beach, dive shop, snorkeling, windsurfing, horseback riding, squash, 4 bars, complimentary weddings; no kids* ☞ *3-night minimum* ☰ *AE, D, MC, V* ¶⊙¶ *AI.*

★ $$$$ ⊡ **Goldeneye.** Whether you're a James Bond buff or just a fan of luxury getaways, this exclusive address 20 minutes east of Ocho Rios holds special appeal. Once the home of Bond author Ian Fleming, the estate is now one of the unique Island Outpost properties. The resort consists of Fleming's home, with three bedrooms and three outdoor baths, as well as a media room, kitchen, and its own private pool and beach. Also on the 15-acre property, four villas are tucked into the lush gardens, each with outdoor showers and lots of privacy. ⊠ *N. Coast Hwy., Oracabessa* ☎ *876/ 975–3354* 🖷 *876/975–3620* ⊕ *www.islandoutpost.com* ⇆ *1 house, 4 villas* ⚹ *Restaurant, cable TV, tennis court, pool, massage, beach, snorkeling, windsurfing, jet skiing* ☰ *AE, D, MC, V* ¶⊙¶ *AI.*

$$$$ ⊡ **Jamaica Inn.** Start a conversation about elegant Jamaican resorts, and this quietly sophisticated hotel will surely be mentioned. A historic favorite with the rich and famous (one suite is named for guest Winston Churchill), this pricey, genteel resort is known for its attentive staff. Each suite has its own verandah (larger than most hotel rooms) on the private cove's powdery, champagne-colored beach. The clifftop spa is known for its ayurveda and Fijian treatments. ⊠ *N. Coast Hwy., east of Ocho Rios, Box 1* ☎ *876/974–2514* 🖷 *876/974–2449* ⊕ *www. jamaicainn.com* ⇆ *49 rooms, 4 suites* ⚹ *Restaurant, room service, golf privileges, pool, gym, spa, beach, snorkeling, boating, croquet, 2 bars, library, dry cleaning, laundry service, meeting room; no room TVs, no kids under 12* ☰ *AE, D, MC, V* ¶⊙¶ *EP.*

★ $$$$ ⊡ **Royal Plantation.** Formerly the Royal Plantation at Beaches, this small, adults-only resort now operates independently. More exclusive than any of its sister properties in the Sandals or Beaches chains, the resort puts an emphasis on personal service, fine dining, and a refined atmosphere and does not offer an all-inclusive plan. Built high atop a bluff, it has a feel of exclusivity; all rooms, which are suites, have ocean views, not to mention luxurious bedding, fully stocked in-room bars, CD players, ma-

13

CLOSE UP

Other Sandals Resorts on Jamaica

THE SANDALS COMPANY has the most hotels of any company on Jamaica. Sandals resorts are open only to couples and are all-inclusive in their pricing. In addition to our favorites, which are reviewed in full in this chapter, the following resorts are also available.

Sandals Dunn's River Villaggio Golf Resort & Spa (⊠ N. Coast Hwy., 2 mi [3 km] east of Ocho Rios, Mammee Bay ☎ 876/972–1610 🖷 876/972–1611 ⊕ www.sandals.com). Renovated in 2005, this resort lacks extensive facilities, but it has a nice spa and allows guests to shuttle over to other Ocho Rios-area Sandals properties. *243 rooms, 16 suites.*

Sandals Inn (⊠ Kent Ave., Montego Bay ☎ 876/952–4140 🖷 876/952–6913 ⊕ www.sandals.com) is right in MoBay. This small hotel, renovated in 2005, is at the end of Doctor's Cave Beach. Guests can catch a shuttle to the other MoBay properties. *52 rooms.*

Sandals Montego Bay (⊠ Kent Ave., Montego Bay ☎ 876/952–5510 🖷 876/952–0816 ⊕ www.sandals.com). Minutes from the airport, this resort is on the largest stretch of beach in MoBay. The almond block of rooms and extensive beach are the resort's best features. *244 rooms.*

Sandals Negril Beach Resort & Spa (⊠ Norman Manley Blvd., Negril ☎ 876/957–5216 🖷 876/957–5338 ⊕ www.sandals.com) is at the top of Seven Mile Beach. *137 rooms, 86 suites.*

Sandals Whitehouse European Village & Spa (⊠ Whitehouse ☎ 876/957–5216 🖷 876/957–5338 ⊕ www.sandals.com) is the newest Sandals resort in Jamaica. It opened in spring 2005 on the south coast, consisting of several "villages." *304 rooms, 54 suites.*

---

hogany furniture, and marble baths, many with whirlpool tubs. The most expensive suites have special check-in and luggage services; optional butler service is also available. Steps lead to the beach, where the luxury continues with the services of a beach butler. ⊠ *N. Coast Hwy., Box 2* ☎ *876/974–5601* 🖷 *876/974–5912* ⊕ *www.royalplantation.com* 🛏 *77 suites* ⌂ *4 restaurants, room service, in-room safes, some in-room hot tubs, minibars, cable TV, in-room VCRs, in-room data ports, golf privileges, 2 tennis courts, pool, health club, outdoor hot tub, spa, beach, dive shop, windsurfing, concierge; no kids under 18* ⌒ *2-night minimum* ⊟ *AE, MC, V* ⦿ *EP.*

$$$$ ▣ **Sandals Grande Ocho Rios Beach & Villa Resort.** The largest resort in the Sandals chain encompasses the former Sandals Ocho Rios and Beaches Grande Sport, and it remains a couples-only retreat. On the "manor" side, you can find the greathouse and villas; the "riviera" side has easy beach access. Guests on both sides can hop a trolley to the beach club or Jamaica's largest pool complex, which is directly behind the manor house. Villas, some fairly far from the public areas, have their own private pools; some villas have as many as four individual guest suites, each with its own kitchen and living area, that share a single pool. Butler service is available in some classes; couples can also opt for the chef to prepare a special meal in their villa for an additional fee. ✉ *N. Coast Hwy., Box 2* ☎ *876/974–1027* 🖷 *876/974–5838* ⊕ *www.sandals.com* ⤵ *285 rooms, 244 villas* ♨ *8 restaurants, in-room safes, kitchens, minibars, refrigerators, cable TV, golf privileges, 4 tennis courts, 96 pools, health club, hair salon, 4 saunas, 2 spas, beach, dive shop, snorkeling, windsurfing, boating, billiards, 10 bars, 2 dance clubs, complimentary weddings, concierge, meeting rooms, airport shuttle; no kids* ⌨ *2-night minimum* 🖃 *AE, MC, V* ⦿ *AI.*

$$$$ ⊞ **Couples Sans Souci Resort & Spa.** This pampering all-inclusive emphasizes relaxation with complimentary spa treatments for guests staying four nights or longer (you get one 55- or two 25-minute treatments plus two treatments at the beauty salon). Rooms—all of which are suites—are soothing, with tile floors, plush linens, large balconies, and a style more Mediterranean than Caribbean. Bathrooms are particularly large and luxurious. Romantic oceanfront suites have oversize whirlpool tubs. Guests have their choice of beaches (one clothing-optional), though both have pebbly sand, and neither is as appealing as the pools. Though the resort is open to couples only, they do not have to be male-female couples. ✉ *N. Coast Hwy., Box 103, Mammee Bay, 2 mi (3 km) east of Ocho Rios* ☎ *876/994–1206* 🖷 *876/994–1544* ⊕ *www.couples. com* ⤵ *146 suites* ♨ *4 restaurants, room service, in-room safes, minibars, cable TV, 2 tennis courts, 4 pools, health club, 2 hot tubs, outdoor hot tub, spa, beach, 4 bars, library, complimentary weddings, laundry service, concierge, airport shuttle; no kids under 16* ⌨ *3-night minimum* 🖃 *AE, D, DC, MC, V* ⦿ *AI.*

$$–$$$ ⊞ **Sunset Jamaica Grande Resort& Spa.** Jamaica's largest conference hotel (formerly the Renaissance Jamaica Grande), which is right in Ocho Rios, bustles with groups thanks to its expansive conference center. Following an extensive renovation (finished it in 2005), it now welcomes a larger percentage of leisure travelers. Rooms, brightened with tropical colors, are divided between two high-rise towers; the best views are found in the north tower. Many guests spend their time at the pool complex, which is built as a replica of Dunn's River Falls and includes a meandering river. Kids are kept busy in the complimentary Club Mongoose activity program, and parents can play in an 80-machine slot and video blackjack room. Teens can head to the Jamrock Teen Center. ✉ *Main St., Box 100* ☎ *876/974–2201* 🖷 *876/974–5378* ⊕ *www. sunsetjamaicagrande.com* ⤵ *715 rooms, 15 suites* ♨ *5 restaurants, in-room safes, some refrigerators, cable TV, in-room data ports, 2 tennis courts, 5 pools, gym, 2 outdoor hot tubs, massage, sauna, spa, beach, snorkeling, windsurfing, 8 bars, children's programs (ages 2–12), playground, laundry facilities, laundry service, concierge, convention center* 🖃 *AE, D, DC, MC, V* ⦿ *AI.*

$ ⊞ **Rooms Ocho Rios.** Adjacent to Sunset Jamaica Grande Resort, this SuperClubs-owned hotel, as its name suggests, sells a rooms-only plan (though with Continental breakfast). Formerly Club Jamaica, the family-friendly hotel offers wireless Internet access. It's favored by business travelers and vacationers who plan to explore the region rather than make a resort their primary destination. Rooms have ocean views and all the basics, decorated in tropical tones. The beach is adequate but not exceptional. It's an economical choice for independent-minded travelers who would rather sample the town's many restaurants than be tied to an all-inclusive plan. ☒ *Main St.* ☎ *876/974–6632* 🖷 *305/666–5536* ⊕*www.roomsresorts.com* ↪*83 rooms, 10 suites* ⚓ *Restaurant, in-room safes, some kitchenettes, cable TV, Wi-Fi, pool, beach, bar, Internet room* ▭ *AE, D, MC, V* ⊖¶ *CP.*

Runaway Bay

The smallest of the resort areas, Runaway Bay, 50 mi east of Montego Bay and about 12 mi west of Ocho Rios, has a handful of modern hotels, a few all-inclusive resorts, and an 18-hole golf course.

$$$$ ⊡ **Grand Lido Braco.** If you want to experience a Jamaican village almost Disney-style, this resort's for you. Fifteen minutes west of Runaway Bay, the resort is built around a "village" complete with a town square with a fruit lady and peanut man. You can also find the island's largest clothing-optional facilities, which include a pool, hot tub, grill, and tennis courts. The beach—both clothed and nude sides—is expansive, although not Jamaica's best strip of sand; the large pool complex provides a popular option. Rooms are nice and have all the basic amenities but are not very large. ☒ *Trelawny, between Duncans and Rio Bueno* ☎ *876/954–0000* 🖷 *876/954–0021* ⊕ *www.superclubs.com* ↪ *226 rooms, 58 suites* ⚓ *5 restaurants, café, room service, in-room safes, cable TV, driving range, 9-hole golf course, 3 tennis courts, 2 pools, health club, 4 hot tubs, spa, beach, dive shop, snorkeling, windsurfing, fishing, hiking, soccer, 8 bars, dance club, shops, complimentary weddings, dry cleaning, laundry service, concierge, meeting rooms, airport shuttle; no kids under 16* ☞ *2-night minimum* ▭ *AE, D, DC, MC, V* ⊖¶ *AI.*

★ $$$$ ⊡ **Hedonism III.** Like its more spartan cousin in Negril, Hedonism is an adults-only hotel for travelers looking for unsubdued fun that includes a circus clinic and waterslide (through the disco, no less). Unlike its Negril equivalent, however, Hedonism III offers luxurious rooms and Jamaica's first swim-up rooms. The guest rooms, each with mirrored ceilings, have Jacuzzi tubs and CD players. The beach is divided into "nude" and "prude" sides, although a quick look shows that most people leave the suits at home. Scheduled activities include nude body painting and volleyball; the resort even holds Jamaica's only nude weddings. ☒ *Main Rd., Box 250, Runaway Bay* ☎ *876/973–4100* 🖷 *876/973–5402* ⊕ *www. superclubs.com* ↪ *225 rooms* ⚓ *5 restaurants, in-room safes, in-room hot tubs, some minibars, cable TV,*

TAKING IT OFF
Both Grand Lido Braco and Hedonism III give you an opportunity to go nude. In fact, an entire section of each resort is set aside for nudists. At Grand Lido Braco, the nude rooms are actually all suites that were originally planned as family rooms. In most places in Jamaica, letting it all hang out comes at a premium of up to 20% above the regular rates. You can also take it off at Hedonism II, Couples Ocho Rios, Couples San Souci, Sunset Beach Resort & Spa, and others.

2 tennis courts, 3 pools, health club, 3 outdoor hot tubs, beach, dive shop, snorkeling, windsurfing, boating, 6 bars, dance club, complimentary weddings, airport shuttle; no kids ☞ *2-night minimum* ☲ *AE, D, DC, MC, V* ⫮⊙⫯ *AI.*

★   ⚏ **FDR, Franklyn D. Resort.** A favorite for families with very young chil-
☾ **$$$–$$$$**   dren, this relaxed resort goes a step beyond the usual supervised kids' programs, assigning you a professional caregiver who will assist you throughout your stay. Kids can take part in a supervised club, but the nanny also assists with in-room help from washing out bathing suits to supervising naps. Guests enjoy spacious one-, two-, and three-bedroom suites. Children under six stay and eat free when staying in a room with their parents. ⌖ *Box 201, Runaway Bay* ☎ *876/973–4591* 🖷 *876/973–6987* ⊕ *www.fdrfamily.com* ⇛ *76 suites* ⚘ *4 restaurants, fans, kitchens, cable TV, in-room broadband, Wi-Fi, tennis court, pool, gym, beach, dive shop, snorkeling, bicycles, 3 bars, video game room, babysitting, children's programs (ages newborn–16), airport shuttle* ☲ *AE, D, MC, V* ⫮⊙⫯ *AI.*

☾ **$$$–$$$$**   ⚏ **FDR Pebbles.** A slightly more grown-up version of its sister resort, FDR, Pebbles bills itself as a soft-adventure experience for families. Although you're still assigned a vacation nanny for personalized babysitting if you have young kids, the family experience is taken a step further here with many more supervised programs for teens, including campouts. Located 30 minutes east of Montego Bay, the resort has the feel of a campground, with wooden room blocks, which are not as big or amenity-filled as those as FDR. Each junior suite is paneled with cedar and pine, highlighted with trim in tropical colors. Up to three children under age 16 can share a room with two parents; kids under 6 stay and eat free when sharing a room with parents. ⊠ *N. Coast Hwy., New Ct.* ☎ *876/617–2500* 🖷 *876/617–2512* ⊕ *www.fdrfamily.com* ⇛ *96 junior suites* ⚘ *3 restaurants, refrigerators, cable TV, Wi-Fi, pool, hair salon, beach, snorkeling, bar, video game room, children's programs (ages newborn–16), airport shuttle* ☲ *AE, D, MC, V* ⫮⊙⫯ *EP.*

$$–$$$ ⚏ **Breezes Runaway Bay.** This moderately priced SuperClubs resort emphasizes an active, sports-oriented vacation—including golf (at the resort's own course), a circus workshop, tennis, horse-and-carriage rides, and an array of water sports. Expert instruction and top-rate equipment are part of the package. Guests—often Germans, Italians, and Japanese—flock here to dive and snorkel around the reef off the beach, which also makes the bay superbly smooth for swimming. There's also a good golf school. ⊠ *N. Coast Hwy., Box 58, Runaway Bay* ☎ *876/973–2436* 🖷 *876/973–2352* ⊕ *www.superclubs.com* ⇛ *234 rooms* ⚘ *4 restaurants, in-room safes, driving range, 18-hole golf course, 4 tennis courts, pool, 3 outdoor hot tubs, beach, dive shop, snorkeling, windsurfing, 4 bars, complimentary weddings, airport shuttle; no kids under 14* ☞ *2-night minimum* ☲ *AE, D, DC, MC, V* ⫮⊙⫯ *AI.*

★ ☾ **$**   ⚏ **Starfish Trelawny.** A real bargain, this all-inclusive resort is operated by SuperClubs but with fewer extras than you find in the company's other resorts. Some motorized water sports, for example, including waterskiing, the banana boat ride, snorkeling trips, and scuba diving, are not included in the all-inclusive price. For beach lovers, the best option would be the garden-level cottages (especially popular with larger groups), which are just off the beach, but most guest rooms are found in high-rise towers. The resort is family-friendly from restaurants to nightly entertainment, although the late-night disco is aimed at adults. The resort has a rock-climbing wall, a circus workshop, "ice-skating" on a special plastic surface, and for an additional cost unlimited trapeze sessions. ⊠ *N. Coast Hwy., Falmouth* ☎ *876/954–2450* 📠 *876/954–9923* ⊕ *www.starfishresorts.com* 🛏 *350 rooms* ♿ *6 restaurants, in-room safes, minibars, cable TV, 4 tennis courts, 4 pools, 3 outdoor hot tubs, beach, dive shop, snorkeling, windsurfing, waterskiing, 6 bars, dance club, babysitting, children's programs (ages 6 months–12), meeting rooms, airport shuttle* ☞ *2-night minimum* 🖃 *AE, D, DC, MC, V* ⊙I *AI.*

Montego Bay

MoBay has miles of hotels, villas, apartments, and duty-free shops. Although without much cultural stimulus, it presents a comfortable island backdrop for the many conventions it hosts. And it has the added advantage of being the closest resort area to the island's main airport.

★ **$$$$** 🏨 **Half Moon.** With its many room categories, massive villas (with three to seven bedrooms), shopping village, hospital, school, dolphin swims, golf course, and equestrian center, Half Moon almost seems more like a town than a mere resort. What started out in 1954 as a group of private beach cottages offered for rent during off-season months has blossomed into one of Jamaica's most extensive resorts. Those beach cottages are still available and—just steps away from the sand as well as public areas—remain a great choice. Some rooms are a long walk from public areas, although a call can arrange for a golf cart pickup. The villas come with a private golf cart for your use. ⊠ *N. Coast Hwy., 7 mi (11 km) east of Montego Bay, Box 80* ☎ *876/953–2211* 📠 *876/953–2731* ⊕ *www.halfmoon-resort.com* 🛏 *52 rooms, 163 suites, 34 villas* ♿ *7 restaurants, room service, in-room safes, minibars, cable TV, 18-hole golf course, 13 tennis courts, 51 pools, fitness classes, gym, outdoor hot tub, sauna, spa, beach, dive shop, snorkeling, windsurfing, bicycles, badminton, croquet, horseback riding, Ping-Pong, squash, 3 bars, theater, shops, dry cleaning, laundry service, concierge, Internet room, convention center* 🖃 *AE, D, DC, MC, V* ⊙I *EP.*

$$$$ 🏨 **Ritz-Carlton Golf & Spa Resort, Rose Hall, Jamaica.** A favorite with conference groups, golfers, and anyone demanding the highbrow service for which the chain is known, this expansive resort lies across the road from the historic Rose Hall estate. Although the luxury hotel is elegant and has solid service, little here sets the mood of a Caribbean resort except its beachfront location and water-sports offerings. And the hotel's beach is small, so most water fun takes place at the nearby Rose Hall Beach Club, with free transportation provided to guests. If you like high tea, it's offered daily. Along with a full-service spa, there's a fully supervised children's club, making it a popular choice for families. ⊠ *1 Ritz Carlton Dr., St. James* ☎ *876/953–2800* 📠 *876/953–2501* ⊕ *www.ritzcarlton. com* 🛏 *427 rooms* ♿ *4 restaurants, in-room safes, cable TV, 18-hole golf course, pool, health club, spa, beach, dive shop, snorkeling, wind*

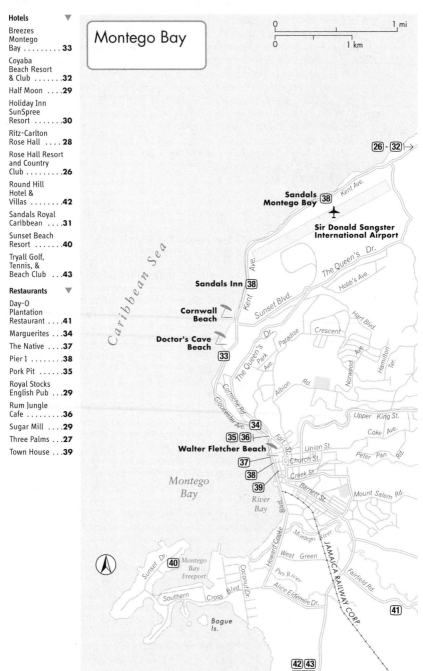

Montego Bay

0   1 mi
0   1 km

Caribbean Sea

26 - 32 →

Sandals Montego Bay 38

Kent Ave.

Sir Donald Sangster International Airport

The Queen's Dr.

Hobb's Ave.

Sandals Inn 38

Cornwall Beach

Kent

Sunset Blvd.

Hart Blvd.

Crescent

Doctor's Cave Beach

33

The Queen's Dr.

Paradise

Park Ave.

Albion Rd.

Norwood Ave.

Hamilton Ter.

Upper King St.

Corniche Rd.

Gloucester Ave.

Fort St.

34

35 36

Walter Fletcher Beach

37

38

39

Union St.

Church St.

Creek St.

Barnett St.

Coke Ave.

Peter Pan Rd.

Mount Salem Rd.

Montego Bay

River Bay

40

Montego Bay Freeport

Sunset Dr.

Southern Cross Blvd.

Coconut Dr.

Howard Cooke

Montego River

West Green

Pres River

Alice Eldemire Dr.

Fairfield Rd.

JAMAICA RAILWAY CORP.

41

Bogue Is.

42 43
↓

surfing, 3 bars, shops, children's programs (ages 5–12), concierge, meeting rooms ⊟ *AE, D, DC, MC, V* ¶⊙¶ *EP.*

★ **$$$$** ⊞ **Round Hill Hotel & Villas.** A favorite of celebrities thanks to its private and elegant villas, this peaceful resort 8 mi (13 km) west of MoBay also offers 36 traditional hotel rooms in the Pineapple House. In 2004, the hotel rooms were redecorated in a refined Ralph Lauren style—done by the designer himself, who owns one of the 27 villas that dot the resort's 98 acres. Each villa includes a personal maid and a cook to make your breakfast, and most have private pools. It's a fairly quiet place, with a small beach and limited dining options, but most guests return again and again because of the personal service and excellent management. ⊠ *N. Coast Hwy., Box 64* ☎ *876/956–7050* 📠 *876/956–7505* ⊕ *www. roundhilljamaica.com* ↪ *36 rooms, 27 villas* ♿ *Restaurant, room service, refrigerators, cable TV, 5 tennis courts, pool, health club, hair salon, spa, beach, dive shop, snorkeling, windsurfing, bar, shops, concierge, helipad* ⊟ *AE, D, DC, MC, V* ¶⊙¶ *EP.*

★ **$$$$** ⊞ **Sandals Royal Caribbean Resort & Private Island.** Four miles (6½ km) east of the airport, this elegant resort—the most upscale of the three Sandals properties in MoBay—consists of Jamaican-style buildings arranged in a semicircle around attractive gardens. Less boisterous than Sandals Montego Bay, it offers a few more civilized touches, including afternoon tea. In the evenings, a colorful "dragon boat" transports you to Sandals's private island for meals at an Indonesian restaurant. ⊠ *N. Coast Hwy., Box 167* ☎ *876/953–2231* 📠 *876/953–2788* ⊕ *www.sandals. com* ↪ *176 rooms, 14 suites* ♿ *4 restaurants, in-room safes, cable TV, 3 tennis courts, 4 pools, fitness classes, hair salon, 5 outdoor hot tubs, sauna, beach, dive shop, snorkeling, windsurfing, 5 bars, complimentary weddings, concierge, airport shuttle; no kids* ↪ *2-night minimum* ⊟ *AE, D, MC, V* ¶⊙¶ *AI.*

$$$–$$$$ ⊞ **Coyaba Beach Resort & Club.** Owners Joanne and Kevin Robertson live on the grounds of this small resort, interacting with guests and giving the intimate property a relaxing, welcoming ambience. From the plantation-style greathouse to the guest rooms, which are decorated with colonial prints and hand-carved mahogany furniture, you feel the graciousness and comforting atmosphere, which is reminiscent of a country inn. ⊠ *Montego Bay, Little River* ☎ *876/953–9150* 📠 *876/953–2244* ⊕ *www.coyabaresortjamaica.com* ↪ *50 rooms* ♿ *3 restaurants, fans, in-room safes, some refrigerators, cable TV, tennis court, pool, gym, outdoor hot tub, massage, spa, beach, snorkeling, windsurfing, billiards, volleyball, 3 bars, library, recreation room, playground, airport shuttle* ⊟ *AE, D, MC, V* ¶⊙¶ *EP.*

★ **$$$–$$$$** ⊞ **Tryall Club.** Well known among golfers, Tryall lies 15 mi (24 km) west of MoBay. The sumptuous villas—each of which has a private pool—and pampering staff lend a home-away-from-home atmosphere. The beautiful seaside golf course is considered one of the meanest in the world and hosts big-money tournaments. Golfers are more than willing to accept the relative isolation for easy access to the great course, but this resort is even farther out than Round Hill. ⊠ *N. Coast Hwy., Box 1206, Sandy Bay* ☎ *876/956–5660* 📠 *876/956–5673* ⊕ *www.tryallclub.com* ↪ *56 villas* ♿ *Restaurant, kitchens, cable TV, driving range, 18-hole*

*golf course, 9 tennis courts, pool, massage, beach, snorkeling, windsurf-
ing, 4 bars, children's programs (ages 5–12)* ☰ *AE, D, DC, MC, V* ⏃❏*EP.*

$$ ☷ **Breezes Montego Bay.** A good choice for those on more of a budget,
this active resort near the airport is especially favored by young travel-
ers. Right on Montego Bay's "Hip Strip," the resort places you steps
away from nearby nightclubs and shops. The beach is the great Doc-
tor's Cave, a public strand with a beach-club atmosphere, so you aren't
sealed off from the locals (whether that's a plus or a minus is up to you).
Rooms have white-tile floors, cozy love seats, carved wooden headboards,
and big marble bathrooms. A popular circus workshop and free wed-
dings are also part of the package. ⊠ *Gloucester Ave.* ☏ *876/940–1150*
🖷 *876/940–1160* ⊕ *www.superclubs.com* ⇆ *124 rooms* ⌂ *3 restau-
rants, in-room safes, cable TV, in-room VCRs, tennis court, pool, beach,
dive shop, snorkeling, windsurfing, 4 bars, complimentary weddings,
airport shuttle; no kids under 14* ⏃ *2-night minimum* ☰ *AE, D, DC,
MC, V* ⏃❏ *AI.*

$$ ☷ **Holiday Inn SunSpreeResort.** Family fun is tops here, although many
couples and singles are also drawn to the moderate prices and good lo-
cation, 6 mi (9½ km) east of the airport. You can find seven room blocks
spread along the long beach and large public areas that can, at times,
feel a bit overrun with kids and their noise. Adults can find some peace
in the quiet pool, which has its own swim-up bar. On the other side of
the grounds, a lighted 9-hole miniature golf course offers night play. Shoppers will be happy with the moderately priced shopping mall directly
across the street. Children under 11 stay and eat free, and an all-inclusive
plan—which most people choose—is available. ⊠ *N. Coast Hwy., Box
480* ☏ *876/953–2485* 🖷 *876/953–2840* ⊕ *www.montegobayjam.
sunspreeresorts.com* ⇆ *497 rooms, 27 suites* ⌂ *4 restaurants, 2 snack
bars, room service, in-room safes, cable TV, in-room data ports, miniature golf, 4 tennis courts, 3 pools, beach, dive shop, snorkeling, windsurfing, 4 bars, children's programs (ages 6 months–12), playground,
dry cleaning, laundry facilities, laundry service, concierge, airport shuttle, no-smoking rooms* ☰ *AE, D, DC, MC, V* ⏃❏ *AI.*

ⓒ **$$** ☷ **Sunset Beach Resort & Spa.** Often packed with charter groups, this ex-
pansive resort is a very good value if you don't mind mass tourism. With
one of Jamaica's best (and most used) lobbies, a waterpark, and excel-
lent beaches on a peninsula jutting out into the bay, the facilities here
help to redeem the motel-basic rooms. You can choose among three
beaches (one nude) or, when it's time to take a break from the sun, hit
the spa or slots-only casino. ⊠ *Freeport, Box 1168, Montego Bay*
☏ *876/979–8800* 🖷 *876/953–6744* ⊕ *www.sunsetbeachresort.com*
⇆ *420 rooms* ⌂ *4 restaurants, in-room safes, cable TV, 4 tennis courts,
3 pools, spa, beach, snorkeling, 5 bars, babysitting, children's programs
(ages 2–12)* ☰ *AE, MC, V* ⏃❏ *AI.*

ⓒ **$-$$** ☷ **Rose Hall Resort & Country Club.** Popular with conference groups as
well as families, this self-contained resort 4 mi (6½ km) east of the air-
port is on the grounds of the 400-acre Rose Hall Plantation. Kids love
the huge waterpark, complete with lagoons and lazy rafting river, while
golfers head across the street to the course. The lack of good swimming
beach is the biggest drawback; the waters here are sometimes better for

sailing. However, the expansive pool complex is a good alternative. ⊠ *N. Coast Hwy., Box 999* ☎ *876/953–2650* 🖷 *876/518–0203* ⊕ *www. rosehallresort.com* ⤳ *470 rooms, 19 suites* ⚭ *5 restaurants, room service, in-room safes, cable TV, in-room data ports, 18-hole golf course, 6 tennis courts, 3 pools, fitness classes, gym, massage, beach, dive shop, snorkeling, windsurfing, basketball, volleyball, 3 bars, nightclub, children's programs (ages 4–12), playground, meeting rooms* 🍴 *AE, D, DC, MC, V* ⦵ *AI.*

13

Negril

Some 50 mi (80 km) west of MoBay, Negril was once a hippie hangout, favored for its inexpensive mom-and-pop hotels and laid-back atmosphere. Today there's still a bohemian flair, but the town's one of the fastest-growing tourism communities in Jamaica, with several large all-inclusives along Bloody Bay, northeast of town. The main strip of Negril Beach and the cliffs are still favored by vacationers who like to get out and explore.

$$$$ 🏨 **The Caves.** Although set on 2 tiny acres, this petite resort packs a lot of punch in its cliffside location, drawing the Hollywood set as well as travelers looking for boutique-style pampering. Thatch-roof cottages are individually designed with vivid colors and hand-carved furniture, every one offering spectacular sunset views. The cottages are built above the natural sea caves that line the cliffs, one of which is used for private romantic dinners. TVs are available, but only if you ask. ⊠ *Lighthouse Rd., Negril* ☎ *876/975–3354* 🖷 *876/975–3620* ⊕ *www.islandoutpost. com* ⤳ *10 villas* ⚭ *Restaurant, minibars, in-room data ports, saltwater pool, hot tub, massage, spa, snorkeling, bicycles; no a/c, no kids under 16* 🍴 *AE, D, MC, V* ⦵ *AI.*

$$$$ 🏨 **Couples Negril.** Allowing only male-female couples, this resort emphasizes romance and relaxation and is a more laid-back alternative to the nearby Sandals Negril. The resort has a good beachfront along Bloody Bay, north of the funkier Negril Beach, although Negril's bohemian nature is still reflected throughout the nine low-rise buildings. The property is decorated by a rainbow of colors, and lively art by local craftspeople peppers public spaces. Rooms are similarly bright and roomy but are not luxurious. All land and water activities, selected excursions, and weddings are included in the rates. ⊠ *Norman Manley Blvd.* ☎ *876/957–5960* 🖷 *876/957–5858* ⊕ *www.couples.com* ⤳ *216 rooms, 18 suites* ⚭ *3 restaurants, room service, in-room safes, cable TV, 4 tennis courts, 2 pools, fitness classes, health club, 2 outdoor hot tubs, spa, beach, dive shop, snorkeling, windsurfing, 5 bars, complimentary weddings, concierge, airport shuttle; no kids* ⤳ *3-night minimum* 🍴 *AE, D, MC, V* ⦵ *AI.*

$$$$ 🏨 **Couples Swept Away Negril.** Sports-minded adults (including same-sex couples and singles, unlike at other Couples locations) are welcomed to this all-suites resort known for its expansive menu of sports offerings, top-notch facilities (the best in Jamaica and among the best in the Caribbean), and emphasis on healthy cuisine. If you're looking for an active vacation that is still sprinkled with a hint of romance, it's your best option in Negril. The suites are in 26 two-story tropical villas—

FodorsChoice ★

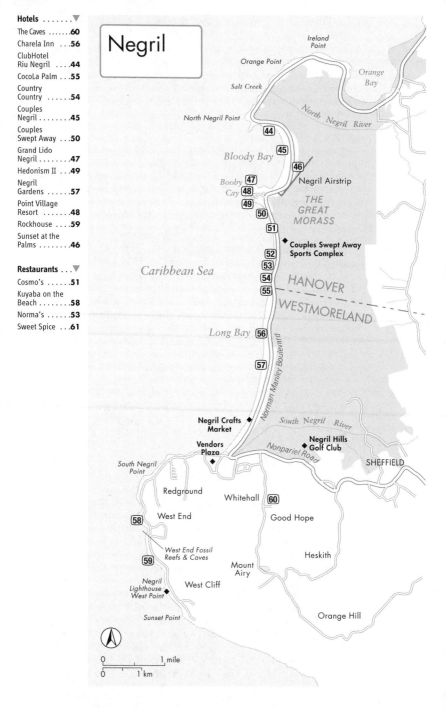

Negril

Ireland
Point
Orange Point
Orange
Bay
Salt Creek
North Negril River
North Negril Point
44
45
Bloody Bay
46
47
Negril Airstrip
Booby 48
Cay 49
THE
GREAT
50
MORASS
51
◆ Couples Swept Away
52 Sports Complex
53
Caribbean Sea
54 HANOVER
55
WESTMORELAND
Long Bay 56
Norman Manley Boulevard
57
Negril Crafts ◆
Market South Negril River
Vendors Negril Hills
Plaza ◆ Golf Club
South Negril Nonpariel Road
Point SHEFFIELD
Redground Whitehall 60
58 West End Good Hope
West End Fossil
Reefs & Caves
59 Heskith
Mount
Negril Airy
Lighthouse ◆ West Cliff
West Point
Sunset Point
Orange Hill

0   1 mile
0   1 km

each with a private garden atrium—spread out along a ½-mi (¾-km) stretch of gorgeous beach. Across the road lies one of Jamaica's best sports complexes, with classes and top-notch equipment and instruction. ⊠ *Norman Manley Blvd., Long Bay* ☎ *876/957–4061* 🖷 *876/957–4060* ⊕ *www.couples.com* 🛏 *134 suites* 🖒 *2 restaurants, fans, in-room safes, some minibars, cable TV, golf privileges, 10 tennis courts, 2 pools, health club, 2 outdoor hot tubs, spa, beach, dive shop, snorkeling, windsurfing, racquetball, squash, 4 bars, complimentary weddings, concierge, airport shuttle; no kids* 🕿 *3-night minimum* ▭ *AE, D, DC, MC, V* ¶◎¶ *AI.*

$$$$
Fodor'sChoice
★

Grand Lido Negril. A cursory look around the marble-clad lobby decorated with fine art and elegant columns might give the impression that this upscale all-inclusive is a tad stuffy. But fancy touches are balanced by an expansive nude beach (including its own hot tub, bar, and grill), giving you one of Jamaica's best resorts, where it's fun to dress for dinner but equally good to strip down for a day of fun in the sun. The nonnude beach is one of the best strips of sand in Negril. Appealing to an upscale crowd of all stripes, the mood here is quiet and relaxing—much different than at Hedonism II, which is just next door. Low-rise rooms, both oceanfront and garden suites, are stylish; many offer French doors just steps from the sand. ⊠ *Norman Manley Blvd., Box 88* ☎ *876/957–5010* 🖷 *876/957–5517* ⊕ *www.superclubs.com* 🛏 *210 suites* 🖒 *6 restaurants, room service, in-room safes, minibars, 4 tennis courts, 2 pools, health club, 5 outdoor hot tubs, spa, beach, dive shop, snorkeling, windsurfing, 9 bars, library, shops, complimentary weddings, laundry service, concierge, meeting rooms, airport shuttle, no-smoking rooms; no kids under 16* 🕿 *2-night minimum* ▭ *AE, D, DC, MC, V* ¶◎¶ *AI.*

★ **$$$$**
Hedonism II. Promising a perpetual spring break for adults, who are drawn to the legendary party atmosphere, this resort gets a lot of repeat business. Although you can find "prude" activities ranging from a rock-climbing wall to an expansive new gym, it's the nude side that's perpetually sold out. Guest rooms received a makeover in 2004, and although they don't match the opulence of those at Hedonism III, they now include TVs, multihead showers, and (of course) mirrors over the beds. Singles must allow the resort to match them with a same-sex roommate or pay a hefty supplement. Many nude travel groups plan vacations en masse here several times a year; another peak time is Halloween, when guests celebrate the resort's anniversary with wild costumes and decorated guest rooms. ⊠ *Norman Manley Blvd., Ruthland Point, Box 25* ☎ *876/957–5200* 🖷 *876/957–5289* ⊕ *www.superclubs. com* 🛏 *280 rooms* 🖒 *6 restaurants, in-room safes, miniature golf, 6 tennis courts, 4 pools, fitness classes, gym, health club, 4 outdoor hot tubs, massage, sauna, spa, beach, dive shop, snorkeling, windsurfing, boating, bicycles, basketball, billiards, paddle tennis, squash, volleyball, 6 bars, piano bar, dance club, shops, complimentary weddings, concierge, Internet room, airport shuttle, travel services; no kids* 🕿 *2-night minimum* ▭ *AE, D, DC, MC, V* ¶◎¶ *AI.*

$$$–$$$$
Sunset at the Palms Resort & Spa. Formerly Negril Cabins, this relaxed all-inclusive is a favorite with ecotourists. It was the world's first hotel to receive Green Globe Certification for environmentally sustainable

13

tourism, and the management works to maintain that status. Rooms here are in tree-house-like cottages amid towering royal palms. Open and airy, rooms have floral bedspreads, gauzy curtains, natural-wood floors, and high ceilings. The beach is across the street, along with activities including nonmotorized water sports. Nature buffs can also take a walk with the resort's resident gardener. ⊠ *Norman Manley Blvd., Box 118* ☎ *876/957–5350* 🖷 *876/957–5381* ⊕ *www.sunsetatthepalms.com* ⇰ *82 rooms, 3 suites ♢ 2 restaurants, in-room safes, some minibars, tennis court, pool, gym, spa, beach, snorkeling, windsurfing, volleyball, 2 bars, recreation room* ▤ *AE, D, MC, V* ⦿ *AI.*

$$–$$$$ 🖾 **ClubHotel Riu Negril.** This massive but beautiful resort, which opened in early 2004, is far north of Negril on Bloody Bay and has a decent, sandy beachfront. Don't expect much personalized service, but you do get your money's worth here—with good food and an extensive array of activities and facilities—and the prices are a bargain to boot. Rooms are attractive and offer the usual amenities, as well as a liquor dispenser, but those in the second and third blocks are a *very* long walk from everything, with no resort shuttle to help your weary feet. The programs for kids are slightly better here than at the Riu Tropical Bay, which is equally large and next door. ⊠ *Norman Manley Blvd.* ☎ *876/957–5700* 🖷 *876/957–5020* ⊕ *www.riu.com* ⇰ *420 rooms, 18 junior suites ♢ 4 restaurants, fans, in-room safes, minibars, cable TV, 2 tennis courts, 2 pools, wading pool, health club, indoor hot tub, hot tub, sauna, spa, beach, dive shop, snorkeling, windsurfing, boating, jet skiing, parasailing, volleyball, 3 bars, dance club, showroom, shops, babysitting, children's programs (ages 4–12), playground, laundry service, Internet room, meeting rooms, airport shuttle, car rental* ▤ *AE, D, MC, V* ⦿ *AI.*

$$–$$$ 🖾 **Point Village Resort.** Feeling more like an apartment complex than a beach resort, Point Village can make you feel as if you're planting some roots in Negril. With both an all-inclusive and room-only plan, you have the option of having it all or not. Kitchens help out those who must keep an eye on their budget. Though it's at the north end of Negril, which is mostly adults-only (Hedonism II and Grand Lido Negril are neighbors), this resort is fairly family-friendly. Rooms have tile floors and basic furnishings, and each is individually decorated. The sprawling complex has two small crescent beaches, rocky grottos to explore, and fine snorkeling offshore. One child age 13 and under stays free when sharing a room with parents. ⊠ *Norman Manley Blvd., Box 105* ☎ *876/957–5170* 🖷 *876/957–5113* ⊕ *www.pointvillage.com* ⇰ *99 studios, 66 1-, 2-, and 3-bedroom apartments ♢ 3 restaurants, grocery, kitchens, cable TV, tennis court, pool, outdoor hot tub, massage, beach, snorkeling, windsurfing, 4 bars, children's programs (ages newborn–12), playground* ▤ *AE, D, MC, V* ⦿ *AI.*

$–$$ 🖾 **Coco La Palm.** This quiet, friendly hotel on the beach has oversize rooms (junior suites average 525 square feet) in octagonal buildings around the pool. Some junior suites have private patios or terraces; most of these overlook the gardens (only seven rooms have ocean views). The resort makes a good home base from which to explore Negril Beach, or you can just relax under one of the tall coconut palms. The beachside restaurant is open-air and casual. ⊠ *Norman Manley Blvd.* ☎ *876/957–*

4227 🖷 876/957–3460 ⊕ *www.cocolapalm.com* ⤵ *76 rooms* △ *2 restaurants, refrigerators, cable TV, pool, outdoor hot tub, beach, bar* ⊟ *AE, DC, MC, V* |◎| *EP.*

$–$$ 🏨 **Negril Gardens Beach Resort.** This long-established, brightly colored, low-rise resort epitomizes the relaxed and funky style for which Negril has long been known. Guests are always just a quick walk from Negril's 7-mi-long beach. Rooms are fairly basic, but those beach-side get some noise from nearby clubs until the wee hours. The resort is under Sandals management but operates separately from either the Sandals or Beaches chain, welcoming couples, singles, and families. Children under two stay free, but each room has a maximum occupancy of three persons. ⊠ *Norman Manley Blvd., Box 3058* ☎ *876/957–4408* 🖷 *876/957–4374* ⊕ *www.negrilgardensresort.com* ⤵ *65 rooms* △ *Restaurant, in-room safes, cable TV, pool, beach, snorkeling, windsurfing, bars* ⚐ *2-night minimum* ⊟ *AE, D, MC, V* |◎| *AI.*

$ 🏨 **Charela Inn.** Directly on Negril beach, this quiet hotel is understated but elegant in a simple way and has a widely praised French-Jamaican restaurant. Each quiet room has a private balcony or a covered patio. You can opt for a room-only plan if you want to explore neighboring restaurants along the beach, but most guests go all-inclusive. Children up to 9 years old can stay in the parents' room for no additional charge; there's an $18 per-night charge for kids 10 to 15 years, although no children are permitted in deluxe guest rooms. The Saturday-night folkloric show draws guests from all over Negril. ⊠ *Norman Manley Blvd., Box 3033* ☎ *876/957–4277* 🖷 *876/957–4414* ⊕ *www.charela.com* ⤵ *49 rooms* △ *Restaurant, in-room safes, cable TV, pool, beach, windsurfing, boating, bar, laundry service* ⚐ *5-night minimum in high season, 3-night minimum summer* ⊟ *D, MC, V* |◎| *AI.*

$ 🏨 **Country Country.** Owned by Kevin and Joanne Robertson, who also own Montego Bay's Coyaba, this small hotel carries the same home-away-from-home feel of its north-coast cousin but with a distinct Negril charm. Rooms are housed in brightly painted cottages designed by Jamaican architect Ann Hodges (known for her work at Goldeneye and Strawberry Hill); the cottages come alive with country-style touches like gingerbread trim. The oversize rooms all have a private patio. ⊠ *Norman Manley Blvd.* ☎ *876/957–4341* 🖷 *876/957–4342* ⊕ *www.countryjamaica.com* ⤵ *14 rooms* △ *Restaurant, room service, in-room safes, refrigerators, cable TV, beach, bar* ⊟ *AE, MC, V* |◎| *FAP.*

$ 🏨 **Rockhouse Hotel.** With a spectacular cliffside location like that of the Caves—but without the high price tag—the small and trendy Rockhouse delivers both resort comforts and funky style. Rooms and suites are built from rough-hewn timber, thatch, and stone and filled with furniture that echoes the nature theme. Although double the price of a regular room, villas ($$$), which have outdoor showers and private sundecks above the cliffs, are worth the splurge. Studios have outdoor showers but are otherwise like the regular rooms, which seem pleasantly rustic. You can ask for a TV—but only to watch videos. To be honest, you're far better off enjoying the sunsets, for which Negril's known. There's a thatch-roof Jamaican restaurant, a spa, yoga, kayaking, and a clifftop infinity pool and bar. ⊠ *West End Rd., Box 3024* ☎ *876/957–4373* 🖷 *876/*

Fodor's Choice
★

13

957–0557 ⊕ *www.rockhousehotel.com* ⇖ *16 rooms, 18 villas* △ *Restaurant, fans, in-room safes, minibars, pool, snorkeling, 2 bars; no room TVs, no kids under 12* ▭ *AE, MC, V* ◉ *EP.*

South Coast

In the 1970s, Negril was Jamaica's most relaxed place to hang out. Today that distinction is held by the south coast, a long stretch of coastline ranging from Whitehouse to Treasure Beach. Here local residents wave to cars, and travelers spend their days exploring local communities and their nights in local restaurants. Until recently, the south coast was exclusively the home to a few small hotels, but then Sandals Whitehouse, which opened in February 2005, became the first big resort in the south. The best way to reach the south coast is from Montego Bay, driving overland, a journey of 90 minutes to two hours, depending on the destination.

$–$$$ ▦ **Jake's.** The laid-back, neighborly feel of the south coast is epitomized by Jake's, a relaxed place that's fun, funky, and friendly. Co-owner Jason Henzell, now president of Island Outpost, is active in community development and encourages his guests to get out and mingle in the area, whether that means fishing with the locals or hitting a rum shop. Each villa here (designed by Jason's mother, a theatrical designer) is unique, but some are not especially roomy. ⊠ *Calabash Bay, Treasure Beach* ☎ *876/965–3000* ᐧ *876/965–0552* ⊕ *www.islandoutpost.com* ⇖ *15 villas* △ *2 restaurants, in-room safes, minibars, saltwater pool, massage, beach, snorkeling, fishing, bicycles, Internet room; no room phones, no room TVs* ▭ *AE, D, MC, V* ◉ *EP.*

$–$$$ ▦ **Sunset Resort &Villas.** Next door to Jake's, this resort lacks the style of its attention-getting neighbor, but it still offers a friendly getaway that's lovingly owner-managed. Rooms are unique and oversize, although some of the decor strikes us as a bit too fussy and frilly. The owners are happy to advise guests about local fun and activities. The open-air restaurant serves beside a large, Astroturf-covered pool area. ⊠ *Calabash Bay, Treasure Beach* ☎ *876/965–0143* ᐧ *876/965–0555* ⊕ *www.sunsetresort.com* ⇖ *12 rooms* △ *Restaurant, minibars, cable TV, pool, beach* ▭ *AE, D, MC, V* ◉ *EP.*

Where to Eat

Although many cultures have contributed to Jamaica's cuisine, it has become a true cuisine in its own right. It would be a shame to travel to the heart of this complex culture without having at least one typical island meal.

Probably the most famous Jamaican dish is jerk pork—the ultimate island barbecue. The pork (purists cook a whole pig) is covered with a paste of Scotch bonnet peppers, pimento berries (also known as allspice), and other herbs and cooked slowly over a coal fire. Many aficionados believe the best jerk comes from Boston Beach, near Port Antonio. Jerk chicken and fish are also seen on many menus. The ever-so-traditional rice and peas, also known as "coat of arms," is similar to the *moros y cristianos* of Spanish-speaking islands: white rice cooked with red kidney beans, coconut milk, scallions, and seasonings.

CLOSE UP

Barbecue, Jamaica-Style

JAMAICA IS WELL KNOWN for its contributions to the world of music, but the island is also the birthplace of a cooking style known as jerk. Modern jerk originated in the 1930s along Boston Beach, east of Port Antonio. Here the first wayside stands sprang up on the side of the road, offering fiery jerk served in a casual atmosphere. Today jerk stands are everywhere on the island, but many aficionados still return to Boston Beach for the "real thing."

The historic origins of jerk are unknown (some say the Maroons brought the practice from Africa; others say the cooking style came to the island with the Caribs and the Arawaks). The practice of jerking meat was first recorded in 1698 by a French priest, who wrote of a jerk pit made with four forked sticks with crosspieces covered with a grill made of sticks. On the grill was placed a whole pig, stuffed with lime juice, salt, pimento, and spices that helped preserve the meat in the hot climate.

Today jerk is still cooked in a pit that contains a fire made from pimento wood. The meat, which is primarily pork but can also be chicken, goat, or fish, is marinated with jerk sauce. Every cook has his own favorite recipe, but most include allspice (pimento) berries, cloves, garlic, onion, ginger, cinnamon, thyme, and peppers. Commercial jerk sauces are also available. Once the jerk is cooked to perfection, it's served up with side dishes such as breadfruit, rice and peas, and a bread called festival.

The Sunset Beach Resort in Montego Bay holds an annual jerk cook-off each September, where prizes are given out for the best jerk in several different categories.

13

The island's most famous soup—the fiery pepper pot—is a spicy mixture of salt pork, salt beef, okra, and the island green known as callaloo. Patties (spicy meat pies) elevate street food to new heights. Although patties actually originated in Haiti, Jamaicans excel at making them. Curried goat is another island standout: young goat is cooked with spices and is more tender and has a gentler flavor than the lamb for which it was substituted by immigrants from India. Salted fish was once the best that islanders could do between catches. Out of necessity, a breakfast staple (and the national dish of Jamaica) was invented. It joins seasonings with salt fish and ackee, a red fruit that grows on trees throughout the island. When cooked in this dish, ackee reminds most people of scrambled eggs.

There are fine restaurants in all the resort areas, many in the resorts themselves, though the Kingston area has the widest selection. Many restaurants outside the hotels in MoBay and Ocho Rios will provide complimentary transportation.

WHAT TO WEAR   Dinner dress is usually casual chic (or just plain casual at many local hangouts, especially in Negril). There are a few exceptions in Kingston and at the top resorts; some require semiformal wear (no shorts, collared shirts for men) in the evening during high season. People tend to dress up for dinner; men might be more comfortable in nice slacks, women in a sundress.

Kingston

CONTINENTAL   ✕ **Palm Court.** On the mezzanine floor of the Hilton Kingston, the ele-
$$–$$$ gant Palm Court is open for lunch and dinner. The menu is Continental; the rack of lamb, sautéed snapper amandine, and grilled salmon are delicious. ⊠ *Hilton Kingston, 77 Knutsford Blvd.* ☎ *876/926–5430* ⊟ *AE, DC, MC, V.*

★ **$$$–$$$$**   ✕ **Strawberry Hill.** A favorite with Kingstonians for its elegant Sunday brunch, Strawberry Hill is well worth the drive from the city. The open-air terrace has a spectacular view of Kingston and the countryside. Entrées range from steamed snapper with coconut-scented rice to jerk-marinated chicken with rice and peas. ⊠ *New Castle Rd., Irishtown* ☎ *876/944–8400* ⊰ *Reservations essential* ⊟ *AE, D, MC, V.*

Ocho Rios

ECLECTIC   ✕ **Evita's Italian Restaurant.** Just about every celebrity who has visited Ocho
$$–$$$ Rios has dined at this hilltop restaurant, and Evita has the pictures to
Fodor'sChoice   prove it. Guests feel like stars themselves, with attentive waitstaff help-
★   ing to guide them through a list of about 30 kinds of pasta, ranging from lasagna Rastafari (vegetarian) and fiery jerk spaghetti to *rotelle colombo* (crabmeat with white sauce and noodles). Kids under 12 eat for half-price, and light eaters will appreciate half portions. The restaurant offers free transportation from area hotels. ⊠ *Mantalent Inn, Eden Bower Rd.* ☎ *876/974–2333* ⊟ *AE, D, MC, V.*

$–$$$ ✕ **Almond Tree.** One of the most popular restaurants in Ocho Rios, the Almond Tree has a menu of Jamaican and Continental favorites: pumpkin soup, pepper pot, and wonderful preparations of fresh fish, veal *piccata,* and fondue. The swinging rope chairs of the terrace bar and the tables perched above a Caribbean cove are great fun. ⊠ *Hibiscus Lodge Hotel, 83 Main St.* ☎ *876/974–2813* ⊰ *Reservations essential* ⊟ *AE, D, DC, MC, V.*

¢–$$ ✕ **Little Pub.** Relaxed alfresco dining awaits you at this charming restaurant, which also has a bustling sports bar and an energetic Caribbean revue several nights a week. Jamaican standards (jerk or curried chicken, baked crab, sautéed snapper) accompany surf-and-turf, lobster thermidor, pasta primavera, seafood stir-fry, crêpes suzette, and bananas flambé. Burgers and other standard pub fare are also available. ⊠ *59 Main St.* ☎ *876/974–2324* ⊟ *AE, D, MC, V.*

JAMAICAN   ✕ **Ocho Rios Village Jerk Centre.** This blue-canopied, open-air eatery is
¢   a good place to park yourself for frosty Red Stripe beer and fiery jerk
Fodor'sChoice   pork, chicken, or seafood. Milder barbecued meats, also sold by weight
★   (typically, ¼ or ½ pound makes a good serving), turn up on the fresh daily chalkboard menu posted on the wall. It's lively at lunch, especially when passengers from cruise ships swamp the place. ⊠ *DaCosta Dr.* ☎ *876/974–2549* ⊟ *D, MC, V.*

Montego Bay

CARIBBEAN   ✕ **Rum Jungle Cafe.** Decorated like an indoor jungle, this expansive
$$–$$$ restaurant in the Coral Cliff is casual and fun. Large buffets feature

Caribbean dishes ranging from escovitch fish to jerk chicken, while the large bar pours from a selection of Caribbean and worldwide rums. Sunday brunch is popular. ⊠ *Coral Cliff, 165 Gloucester Ave.* ☎ *876/952–4130* ☐ *AE, D, MC, V.*

¢–$$ ✕ **The Native.** Shaded by a large poinciana tree and overlooking Gloucester Avenue, this open-air stone terrace serves Jamaican and international dishes. To go native, start with smoked marlin, move on to the *boonoonoonoos* platter (a sampler of local dishes), and round out with coconut pie or *duckanoo* (a sweet dumpling of cornmeal, coconut, and banana wrapped in a banana leaf and steamed). Live entertainment and candlelight tables make this a romantic choice for dinner on weekends. ⊠ *29 Gloucester Ave.* ☎ *876/979–2769* ⌕ *Reservations essential* ☐ *AE, MC, V.*

CONTINENTAL ✕ **Three Palms.** Across the North Coast Highway from the Rose Hall Re-
$$–$$$$ sort & Country Club, this elegant restaurant is adjacent to the Cinnamon Hill golf course. Diners enjoy terrace views of the sea and select from a menu that includes good grilled seafood and steaks as well as local favorites such as herb-roasted chicken with plantains, and grouper rundown (which is cooked slowly in seasoned coconut broth until the fish just falls apart, or "runs down"). Guests under the Wyndham's all-inclusive plan pay a surcharge to dine here. This place tends to be a bit dressier than most others in MoBay. ⊠ *Rose Hall Resort & Country Club, N. Coast Hwy.* ☎ *876/953–2650* ⌕ *Reservations essential* ☐ *AE, D, MC, V.*

ECLECTIC ✕ **Day-O Plantation Restaurant.** Transport yourself back in time with a
$$–$$$ fine meal served on the garden terrace of this Georgian-style plantation house. You might start with smoked marlin and then segue into seafood ragout, broiled rock lobster with lemon butter, or beef fillet with béarnaise sauce. Sweeten things up with one of the traditional Jamaican desserts (rum pudding, sweet cakes, or fruit salad). After dinner, tour the house. ⊠ *Next door to Barnett Estate Plantation, Fairfield* ☎ *876/952–1825* ☐ *AE, D, MC, V* ☉ *Closed Mon.*

★ $$–$$$ ✕ **Sugar Mill.** Seafood is served with flair at this terrace restaurant on the Half Moon golf course. Caribbean specialties, steak, and lobster are usually offered in a pungent sauce that blends Dijon mustard with Jamaica's own Pickapeppa sauce. Otherwise, choices are the daily à la carte specials and anything flame-grilled. Live music and a well-stocked wine cellar round out the experience. ⊠ *Half Moon Golf, Tennis & Beach Club, N. Coast Rd., 7 mi (11 km) east of Montego Bay* ☎ *876/953–2228* ⌕ *Reservations essential* ☐ *AE, MC, V.*

$$–$$$ ✕ **Town House.** Most of the rich and famous who have visited Jamaica over the decades have eaten here. You find daily specials, delicious variations of standard dishes (red snapper papillote, with lobster, cheese, and wine sauce, is a specialty), and many Jamaican favorites (curried chicken with breadfruit and ackee). The 18th-century Georgian house is adorned with original Jamaican and Haitian art. There's alfresco dining on the stone patio. ⊠ *16 Church St.* ☎ *876/952–2660* ⌕ *Reservations essential* ☐ *AE, D, DC, MC, V.*

★ $–$$ ✕ **Royal Stocks English Pub & Steakhouse.** In Half Moon's Shopping Village, this pub brings a slice of jolly old England to Jamaica, from its dark decor to its menu featuring shepherd's pie, bangers and mash, and plenty of fish-and-chips. Umbrella-shaded tables out in the courtyard are the most popular, except on the hottest of days, when visitors retreat to the dark-panel pub. ⊠ *Half Moon Shopping Village, N. Coast Rd., 7 mi (11 km) east of Montego Bay* ☎ *876/953–9770* ⊟ *AE, MC, V.*

JAMAICAN ✕ **The Pork Pit.** A favorite with many MoBay locals, this no-frills eatery
¢ serves Jamaican specialties including some fiery jerk, which we must warn is spiced to local tastes, not watered down for tourist palates. Many get their food to go, but you can also find picnic tables just outside. ⊠ *27 Gloucester Ave.* ☎ *876/952–3663.*

SEAFOOD ✕ **Marguerites.** At this romantic pier-side dining room, flambé is the op-
$$–$$$ erative word. Lobster, shrimp, fish, and several desserts are prepared in dancing flames as you sip an exotic cocktail. The Caesar salad, prepared table-side, is also a treat. ⊠ *Gloucester Ave.* ☎ *876/952–4777* ⌲ *Reservations essential* ⊟ *AE, D, MC, V* ☉ *No lunch.*

$$–$$$ ✕ **Pier 1.** After tropical drinks at the deck bar, you'll be ready to dig into the international variations on fresh seafood; the best are the grilled lobster and any preparation of island snapper. Several party cruises leave from the marina here, and on Friday night the restaurant is mobbed by locals who come to dance. ⊠ *Off Howard Cooke Blvd.* ☎ *876/952–2452* ⊟ *AE, MC, V.*

Negril

CARIBBEAN ✕ **Norma's.** Although it's in the modest boutique hotel Sea Splash, make
$$–$$$ no mistake: this is Jamaican dining at some of its finest. Norma is Norma Shirley, one of Jamaica's best-known culinary artists, often called the Julia Child of the Caribbean. Opt for terrace or candlelight dining. Her dressed-up Jamaican fare is prepared with a creative flair. Try callaloo-stuffed chicken breast or jerk chicken pasta. ⊠ *Sea Splash Hotel, Norman Manley Blvd.* ☎ *876/957–4041* ⊟ *AE, MC, V.*

¢ ✕ **Sweet Spice.** For true Jamaican food in a no-frills atmosphere, this is the place to go. This mom-and-pop eatery run by the Whytes serves inexpensive, generous plates of conch, fried or curried chicken, freshly caught fish, oxtail in brown stew sauce, and other down-home specialties. The fresh juices are quite satisfying. Drop by for breakfast, lunch, or dinner. ⊠ *1 White Hall Rd.* ☎ *876/957–4621* ⊟ *D, MC, V.*

ECLECTIC ✕ **Kuyaba on the Beach.** This charming thatch-roof eatery has an inter-
¢–$$ national menu—including curried conch, kingfish steak, grilled lamb with sautéed mushrooms, and several pasta dishes—plus a lively ambience, especially at the bar. There's a crafts shop on the premises, and chaise lounges line the beach; come prepared to spend some time, and don't forget a towel and bathing suit. ⊠ *Norman Manley Blvd.* ☎ *876/957–4318* ⊟ *AE, D, MC, V.*

SEAFOOD ✕ **Cosmo's Seafood Restaurant & Bar.** Owner Cosmo Brown has made this
★ $–$$$ seaside open-air bistro a pleasant place to spend the afternoon—and maybe stay on for dinner. Fish is the main attraction, and the conch soup—a house specialty—is a meal in itself. You can also find lobster (grilled or curried), fish-and-chips, and the catch of the morning. Customers often drop cover-ups to take a dip before coffee and dessert and return to lounge

in chairs scattered under almond and sea-grape trees (there's an entrance fee of $1.50 for the beach). ✉ *Norman Manley Blvd.* ☎ 876/957–4784 ⊟ *AE, MC, V.*

South Coast

ECLECTIC
★ $–$$$

✕ **Jack Sprat Restaurant.** It's no surprise that this restaurant shares its home resort's bohemian style (it's the beachside dining spot at Jake's). From the casual outdoor tables to the late-night dancehall rhythm, it's a place to come and hang loose. Jerk crab joins favorites like pizzas and jerk chicken on the menu, all followed by Kingston's Devon House ice cream (try the coconut). ✉ *Jake's, Calabash Bay, Treasure Beach* ☎ 876/965–3583 ⊟ *AE, MC, V.*

13

Beaches

With its 200 mi (325 km) of beaches, it's no surprise that Jamaica's stretches of sand range in quality, atmosphere, and crowds. Some of the best beaches are private, owned by the resorts and accessible only to resort guests or travelers who have purchased a day pass to gain access to the facilities. Other beaches are public, although many include a small admission charge.

In general, a few beautiful beaches are found on the north coast, the sand growing lighter and finer as you travel west to Negril, which, with a 7-mi stretch of some of the Caribbean's finest coastline, ranks as one of the region's top beaches. As you head south, you find the beaches become smaller and often rockier, but also less crowded with both tourists and resorts.

Many resort beaches (especially those at adults-only properties) offer nude or clothing-optional sections. However, nudity (or even topless-ness) is not tolerated on public beaches. Jamaica is a very conservative, religious country, and public beaches where locals visit do not accept less than a full bathing suit.

PORT ANTONIO
Blue Lagoon. Though the beach is small, the large lagoon has to be seen to be believed. The cool, spring-fed waters cry out to swimmers and are a real contrast to the warmer sea waters. Floating docks encourage you to sun a little, or you can lie out on the small beach. After a swim, try some Jamaican dishes in the casual lagoon-side restaurant. Just how deep is the Blue Lagoon? You might hear it's bottomless (Jacques Cousteau verified that it is not), but the lagoon has been measured at a depth of 180 feet. ✉ *9 mi (13 km) east of Port Antonio, 1 mi (1½ km) east of San San Beach.*

Boston Bay. Considered the birthplace of Jamaica's famous jerk-style cooking, it's the beach where some locals make the trek just to buy dinner. You can get peppery jerk pork at any of the shacks spewing scented smoke along the beach. While you're there, you'll also find a small beach perfect for an after-lunch dip. ✉ *11 mi (18 km) east of Port Antonio.*

San San Beach. This small beach has beautiful blue water. Just offshore, Monkey Island is a good place to snorkel (and, sometimes, surf). ✉ *5 mi (8 km) east of Port Antonio.*

OCHO RIOS **Dunn's River Falls Beach.** You'll also find a crowd (especially if there's a cruise ship in town) at the small beach at the foot of the falls. Although tiny—especially considering the crowds that pack the falls—it's got a great view, as well as a beach bar and grill. Look up from the sands for a spectacular view of the cascading water, whose roar drowns out the sea as you approach. ⊠ *Rte. A1, between St. Ann's and Ocho Rios.*

James Bond Beach. Another alternative near Ocho Rios—if you don't mind the drive—is in the community of Oracabessa. This beach, on the estate of James Bond's creator, the late Ian Fleming, is owned by former Island Records producer Chris Blackwell, so it's no surprise that it often rocks with live music performances on the bandstand. Guests of Goldeneye enjoy it for free; visitors must pay $5 per person. ⊠ *Orcabessa.*

Turtle Beach. One of the busiest beaches in Ocho Rios is not the prettiest, but it's usually lively, with a mix of both residents and visitors. It's next to the Sunset Jamaica Grande and looks out over the cruise port. ⊠ *Main St.*

RUNAWAY BAY **Puerto Seco Beach.** This public beach looks out on Discovery Bay, the location where, according to tradition, Christopher Columbus first came ashore on this island. The explorer sailed in search of fresh water but found none, naming the stretch of sand Puerto Seco, or "dry port." Today the beach is anything but dry; concession stands sell Red Stripe and local food to primarily a local beach crowd. ⊠ *Discovery Bay, 5 mi (8 km) west of Runaway Bay.*

MONTEGO BAY **Doctor's Cave Beach.** Montego Bay's tourist scene has its roots right on the Hip Strip, the bustling entertainment district along Gloucester Avenue. Here a sea cave's waters were said to be curative and drew many travelers to bathe here. Though the cave was destroyed by a hurricane generations ago, the beach is always busy and has a perpetual spring break feel. It's the best beach in Jamaica outside one of the more developed resorts thanks to its plantation-style clubhouse with changing rooms, showers, gift shops, bar, grill, and even a cybercafé. There's a fee for admission; beach chairs and umbrellas are also for rent. It's also a good spot for snorkeling, as it's within the Montego Bay Marine Park, with protected corals and marine life. More active travelers can opt for parasailing, glass-bottom boat rides, or jet skiing.

Walter Fletcher Beach. Though not as pretty as Doctor's Cave Beach—or as tidy—it's home to Aquasol Theme Park. Along with a large beach (which includes lifeguards and security), the park offers water trampolines, Jet Skis, banana boat rides, Wave Runners, glass-bottom boats, snorkeling, tennis, go-cart racing, a disco at night, a bar, and a grill. Twice a week—on Wednesday and Friday—the park offers a beach bash with a live reggae show and all-around beach party. The beach is near the center of town, and there's protection from the surf on a windy day, so you can find unusually fine swimming here; the calm waters make it a good bet for children.

NEGRIL **Negril Beach.** Stretching for 7 mi (11 km), the long, white-sand beach
Fodor'sChoice in Negril is arguably Jamaica's finest. It starts with the white sands of
★ Bloody Bay north of town and continues along Long Bay all the way to the cliffs on the southern edge of town. Some stretches remain undeveloped, but there are increasingly few. Along the main stretch of beach,

the sand is public to the high-water mark, so a nonstop line of visitors and vendors parade from end to end. The walk is sprinkled with many good beach bars and open-air restaurants, some which charge a small fee to use their beach facilities. Bloody Bay is lined with large all-inclusive resorts, and these sections are mostly private. Jamaica's best-known nude beach, at Hedonism II, is always among the busiest; only resort guests or day-pass holders may sun here. ⊠ *Norman Manley Blvd.*

THE SOUTH COAST If you're looking for something off the main tourist routes, head for Jamaica's largely undeveloped southwest coast. These isolated beaches are some of the island's safest, because the population in this region is sparse and hasslers are practically nonexistent. That may change now that Sandals has built a giant new resort here. You should, however, use common sense; never leave valuables unattended on the beach.

Fodor'sChoice ★ **Treasure Beach.** The most atmospheric beach in the southwest is in the community of Treasure Beach. It comprises four long stretches of sand as well as many small coves, and though it isn't as pretty as those to the west or north—it has more rocks and darker sand—the idea that you might be discovering a bit of the "real" Jamaica more than makes up for the small negatives. Both locals and visitors use the beaches here, though you're just as likely to find it completely deserted except for a friendly beach dog.

Sports & the Outdoors

The tourist board licenses all recreational activity operators and outfitters, which should ensure you of fair business practices as long as you deal with companies that display its decals.

BIRD-WATCHING Jamaica is a major bird-watching destination, thanks to its varied habitat. The island is home to more than 200 species, some seen only seasonally or in particular parts of the island. Generally the early-morning and late-afternoon hours are the best time for spotting birds. Many birdwatchers flock here for the chance to see the vervian hummingbird (the second-smallest bird in the world, larger only than Cuba's bee hummingbird) or the Jamaican tody (which nests underground).

A great place to spot birds is the **Rocklands Bird Sanctuary & Feeding Station** (⊠ Anchovy ☎ 876/952–2009), which is south of Montego Bay. The station was the home of the late Lisa Salmon, one of Jamaica's first amateur ornithologists. Here you can sit quietly and feed birds—including the doctor bird, recognizable by its long tail—from your hand. A visit costs $10. About 10 minutes from Negril, **Royal Palm Reserve** (⊠ Springfield Rd., Sheffield ☎ 876/957–3736) is home to 50 bird species, including the West Indian whistling duck, which comes to feed at the park's Cotton Tree Lake. The park is also home to the Jamaican woodpecker, Jamaican oriole, Jamaican parakeet, and spectacular streamertail hummingbirds, who flit among the thick vegetation. Admission to the reserve is $10.

DIVING & SNORKELING Jamaica isn't a major dive destination, but you can find a few rich underwater regions, especially off the north coast. MoBay, known for its wall dives, has **Airport Reef** at its southwestern edge. The site is known for its coral caves, tunnels, and canyons. The first marine park in Jamaica, the **Montego Bay Marine Park**, was established to protect the natural resources of the bay; a quick look at the area and it's easy to see the treasures that lie beneath the surface. The north coast is on the edge of the Cayman Trench, so it boasts a wide array of marine life.

With its murkier waters, the southern side of the island isn't as popular for diving, especially near Kingston. **Port Royal**, which is near the airport, is filled with sunken ships that are home to many different varieties of tropical fish.

Prices on the island range from $45 to $80 for a one-tank dive. All the large resorts have dive shops, and the all-inclusive places sometimes include scuba diving in their rates. To dive, you need to show a certification card, though it's possible to get a small taste of scuba diving and do a shallow dive—usually from shore—after taking a one-day resort diving course, which almost every resort with a dive shop offers. A couple of places stand out.

Jamaqua Dive Centre (⊠ Club Ambiance, Runaway Bay ☎ 876/973–4845 ⊕ www.jamaqua.com) is a five-star PADI facility specializing in small dive groups. Along with dives, Jamaqua Dive Centre has a large menu of instructional courses ranging from snorkeling to rescue dive courses. You can also find underwater cameras for rent here. **Scuba Jamaica** (⊠ Half Moon, N. Coast Hwy., Montego Bay ☎ 876/973–4910 ⊕ www. scuba-jamaica.com) offers serious scuba facilities for dedicated divers. This operator is a PADI and NAUI operation and also offers Nitrox diving and instruction as well as instruction in underwater photography, night diving, and open-water diving. There's a pickup service for the Montego Bay, Runaway Bay, Discovery Bay, and Ocho Rios areas.

DOLPHIN SWIM PROGRAMS
Dolphin lovers find two well-run options in both Montego Bay and Ocho Rios. **Dolphin Cove** (⊠ N. Coast Hwy., adjacent to Dunn's River Falls, Ocho Rios ☎ 876/974–5335 ⊕ www.dolphincovejamaica.com) offers dolphin swims as well as lower-priced dolphin encounters for ages eight and up; dolphin touch programs for ages six and over; or simple admission to the grounds, which also includes a short nature walk. Programs cost between $39 and $155, depending on your depth of involvement with the dolphins. Advance reservations are required. **Half Moon** (⊠ N. Coast Hwy., Montego Bay ☎ 876/953–2211 ⊕ www. halfmoon-resort.com) is the Caribbean's only resort with a private dolphin experience. The Dolphin Lagoon is home to dolphins available for swims and encounters with resort guests only.

FISHING
Port Antonio makes deep-sea-fishing headlines with its annual Blue Marlin Tournament, and MoBay and Ocho Rios have devotees who exchange tales (tall and otherwise) about sailfish, yellowfin tuna, wahoo, dolphinfish, and bonito. Licenses aren't required, and you can arrange to charter a boat at your hotel. A chartered boat (with captain, crew, and equipment) costs about $500 to $900 for a half day or $900 to $1,500 for a full-day's excursion, depending on the size of the boat.

The *Glistening Waters Marina* (✉ N. Coast Hwy., Falmouth ☎ 876/954–3229 ⊕ www.glisteningwaters.com) offers charter trips from the Falmouth area. Thirty boats moored at the Glistening Waters Marina offer deep-sea fishing charters; the marina also has nighttime pontoon boat trips for a look at the lagoon, whose iridescence is caused by microscopic dinoflagellates that become luminescent when they move. For less serious anglers, Jamaica has several fishing parks. These offer lake fishing as well as nature walks, picnics, birding, and a family-friendly atmosphere. The easiest to reach is **Royal Palm Reserve** (✉ Springfield Rd., Sheffield ☎ 876/957–3736), about 10 minutes from Negril. Visitors can rent gear and try their luck at catching African perch or tarpon in Cotton Tree Lake. There's an admission price of $10 to visit the park and a $5 charge for fishing; you can also purchase any fish you catch to take back to your villa or resort for the night's dinner if you like.

GOLF Golfers appreciate both the beauty and the challenges offered by Jamaica's courses. Caddies are almost always mandatory throughout the island, and rates are $15 to $45. Cart rentals are available at all courses except Constant Spring and Manchester Country Club; costs are $20 to $35. Some of the best courses in the country are found near MoBay.

The Runaway Bay golf course is found at **Breezes Runaway Bay** (✉ N. Coast Hwy., Runaway Bay ☎ 876/973–7319). This 18-hole course has hosted many championship events (greens fees are $80 for nonguests; guests play for free).

The golf course at **Sandals Golf & Country Club** (✉ Ocho Rios ☎ 876/975–0119) is 700 feet above sea level (greens fees for 18 holes are $100, or $70 for 9 holes for nonguests). East of Falmouth, try **Grand Lido Braco Golf Club** (✉ Trelawny ☎ 876/954–0010), between Duncans and Rio Bueno, a 9-hole course with lush vegetation (nonguests should call for fee information). Caddies are not mandatory on this course.

★ **Half Moon** (✉ Montego Bay ☎ 876/953–2560), a Robert Trent Jones–designed 18-hole course 7 mi (11 km) east of town, is the home of the Red Stripe Pro Am (greens fees are $105 for guests, $150 for nonguests). In 2004 the course received an upgrade and once again draws international attention. **Ironshore SuperClubs Golf Club** (✉ Montego Bay ☎ 876/953–3681), 3 mi (5 km) east of the airport, is an 18-hole links-style course (greens fees are $50).

The newest course in Jamaica, which opened in January 2001, is the
★ White Witch course at the **Ritz-Carlton Golf & Spa Resort, Rose Hall** (✉ 1 Ritz Carlton Dr., Rose Hall, St. James ☎ 876/518–0174). The greens fees at this 18-hole championship course are $159 for resort guests, $179 for nonguests, and $99 for a twilight round. **Tryall Golf, Tennis & Beach Club** (✉ N. Coast Hwy., Sandy Bay ☎ 876/956–5681), 15 mi (24 km) west of Montego Bay, has an 18-hole championship course on the site of a 19th-century sugar plantation (greens fees are $85 for guests, $125 for nonguests). The **Rose Hall Resort & Country Club** (✉ N. Coast Hwy., Montego Bay ☎ 876/953–2650), 4 mi (6½ km) east of the airport, hosts several invitational tournaments (greens fees run $115 for guests, $150 for nonguests).

FodorsChoice

Great golf, rolling hills, and a "liquor mobile" go hand in hand at the 18-hole **Negril Hills Golf Club** (✉ Sheffield Rd., Negril ☎ 876/957–4638), the only golf course in Negril, which is east of town; the greens fees are $28.75 for 9 holes or $57.50 for 18 holes. In the hills, the 9-hole **Manchester Club** (✉ Caledonia Rd., Mandeville ☎ 876/962–2403) is the Caribbean's oldest golf course and charges greens fees of about $17.

HORSEBACK RIDING
Riders with an interest in history can combine both loves on a horseback tour at **Annandale Plantation** (✉ Ocho Rios ☎ 876/974–2323). The 600-acre plantation is high above Ocho Rios and today serves as a working farm, although in its glory days it hosted dignitaries such as the Queen Mother. Ocho Rios has excellent horseback riding, but the best of the

Fodor'sChoice ★
operations is **Chukka Cove Adventure Tours** (✉ Llandovery, St. Ann's Bay ☎ 876/972–2506 ⊕ www.chukkacaribbean.com), which is adjacent to the polo field, just west of town. The trainers here originally exercised the polo ponies by taking them for therapeutic rides in the sea; soon there were requests from visitors to ride the horses in the water. The company now offers a three-hour beach ride that ends with a bareback swim on the horses in the sea from a private beach. It's a highlight of many trips to Jamaica. **Hooves** (✉ Windsor Rd., St. Ann ☎ 876/972–0905 ⊕ www.hoovesjamaica.com) has several guided tours along beach, mountain, and river trails. One of the most interesting offerings is the Bush Doctor Mountain Ride, which takes visitors back into rural Jamaica for a two-hour look at the countryside, whose residents still often depend on the services of bush doctors who utilize local plants for treatments. Rather than be part of a guided group ride, you can opt to rent a horse by the hour at **Prospect Plantation** (✉ Ocho Rios ☎ 876/994–1058), which offers horseback riding for $48 per hour; advance reservations are required.

In the Braco area near Trelawny (between Montego Bay and Ocho Rios), **Braco Stables** (✉ Duncans ☎ 876/954–0185 ⊕ www.bracostables.com) offers guided rides including a bareback romp in the sea. Two rides are offered a day, and riders are matched to horses based on riding ability. The trip also includes complimentary refreshments served poolside at the Braco Great House.

MOUNTAIN BIKING
Jamaica's hilly terrain makes the island a fun challenge for mountain bikers although beginners can also find easier rides, especially near the beaches and on the western end of the island. Heavy, unpredictable traffic on the North Coast Highway makes it off limits for bikers, but country roads and hilly trails weave a network through the countryside.

Blue Mountain Bicycle Tours (✉ 121 Main St., Ocho Rios ☎ 876/974–7075 ⊕ www.bmtoursja.com) takes travelers on guided rides in the spectacular Blue Mountains. The excursion, an all-day outing, starts high and glides downhill, so all levels of riders can enjoy the tour. The trip ends with a dip in a waterfall; the package price includes transportation from Ocho Rios, brunch, lunch, and all equipment. From its location outside of Montego Bay, **Chukka Blue Adventure Tours** (✉ Sandy Bay, Hanover ☎ 876/953–5619 ⊕ www.chukkablue.com) offers both biking and ATV tours. There's a minimum age of 16 on the ATV tours.

The noisy ATVs jostle and splash their way along trails on a 10-mi ride through the hills before returning so visitors can take a dip in the sea. **Chukka Cove Adventure Tours** (⊠ Llandovery, St. Ann's Bay ☎ 876/972–2506 ⊕ www.chukkacaribbean.com) offers a 3½-hour bike tour through St. Ann and the village of Mount Zion with several stops and even snorkeling at the end. There is also an ATV tour. There's a minimum age of 6 for bikes, 16 for ATVs.

RIVER RAFTING   Jamaica's many rivers mean a multitude of freshwater experiences, from mild to wild. Relaxing rafting trips aboard bamboo rafts poled by local boatmen are almost a symbol of Jamaica and the island's first tourist activity outside the beaches. Recently soft-adventure enthusiasts have also been able to opt for white-water action as well with guided tours through several operators.

Fodor'sChoice ★   Bamboo rafting in Jamaica originated on the **Rio Grande,** a river in the Port Antonio area. Jamaicans had long used the bamboo rafts to transport bananas downriver; decades ago actor and Port Antonio resident Errol Flynn saw the rafts and thought they'd make a good tourist attraction. Today the slow rides are a favorite with romantic travelers and anyone looking to get off the beach for a few hours. The popularity of the Rio Grande's trips spawned similar trips down the **Martha Brae River,** about 25 mi (40 km) from MoBay. Another possibility from MoBay is the **River Lethe,** about 12 mi (19 km) southwest; the trip takes about 50 minutes. Near Ocho Rios, the **White River** has lazy river rafting in the daytime, followed by romantic river floats at night with the passage lit by torches. On the south coast, the **Black River** is the destination for gentle river rafting.

Jamaica Tours Limited (⊠ Providence Dr., Montego Bay ☎ 876/953–3700) conducts trips down the River Lethe, approximately 12 mi (19 km; a 50-minute trip) southwest of MoBay; the four-hour excursion costs about $54 per person, includes lunch, and takes you through unspoiled hill country. Bookings can also be made through hotel tour desks. **Martha Brae River Rafting** (⊠ Claude Clarke Ave., Montego Bay ☎ 876/952–0889 ⊕ www.jamaicarafting.com) leads trips down the Martha Brae River, about 25 mi (40 km) from most hotels in MoBay. The cost is $45 per person for the 1½-hour river run. **Rio Grande Tours** (⊠ St. Margaret's Bay ☎ 876/993–5778 ⊕ www.jamaicatoursltd.com) guides raft trips down the Rio Grande; the cost is $52 per raft. **South Coast Safaris Ltd.** (⊠ 1 Crane St., Black River ☎ 876/965–2513) takes visitors on slow cruises up the river to see the birds and other animals, including crocodiles, which, unlike their cousins on the Nile, are not aggressive.

For white-water buffs, several operators offer guided tours of varying levels ranging from tubing to kayaking. **Chukka Cove** and its sister company, Chukka Blue, offer white-water tubing on the White River, a soft adventure that doesn't require any previous rafting experience. Rafters travel in a convoy along the river and through some gentle rapids. ⊠ *Ocho Rios* ☎ *876/972–2506* ⊕ *www.chukkacove.com* ⊠ *Chukka Blue* ⊠ *Montego Bay* ☎ *876/953–5619* ⊕ *www.chukkablue.com.*

If you're looking for a more rugged adventure, then consider a white-water rafting trip with **Caliche Rainforest** (✉ Montego Bay ☎ 876/940–1745 ⊕ www.whitewaterraftingmontegobay.com); you must be 14 years old for this trip. The company also offers a less strenuous rafting trip for all ages.

TENNIS Many hotels have tennis facilities that are free to their guests, but a few will allow nonguests to play for a fee. Court fees generally run $5 to $8 per hour for nonguests; lessons start at $12 an hour.

The most extensive tennis center in the area, **Half Moon** (✉ Montego Bay ☎ 876/953–2211) offers tennis buffs the use of 13 Laykold courts (7 lighted for night play) and has a resident pro and a pro shop. You need to buy a membership card if you're not a guest; purchase of a day pass is $40.

Shopping

Shopping is not really one of Jamaica's high points, though you will certainly be able to find things to buy. Good choices include Jamaican crafts, which range from artwork to batik fabrics to baskets. Wood carvings are one of the top purchases; the finest carvings are made from the Jamaican national tree, lignum vitae, or tree of life, a dense wood that requires a talented carver to transform the hard, blond wood into dolphins, heads, or fish. Bargaining is expected with crafts vendors. Naturally, Jamaican rum is another top souvenir; there's no shortage of opportunities to buy it at gift shops and liquor stores, as is Tia Maria, the Jamaican-made coffee liqueur. Coffee (both Blue Mountain and the less expensive High Mountain) is sold at every gift shop on the island as well. The cheapest prices are found at the local grocery stores, where you can buy beans or ground coffee.

Areas & Malls

In **MoBay** the crafts market on **Market Street** is a compendium of stalls, each selling much the same thing. Come prepared to haggle over prices and to be given the hard sell; if you're in the right mood, though, the whole experience can be a lot of fun and a peek into Jamaican commerce away from the resorts. Montego Bay is also home to some traditional shopping malls where prices are set; you can shop in air-conditioned comfort. **Holiday Inn Shopping Centre** is one of the best. It's located directly across the street from the Holiday Inn and has jewelry, clothing, and crafts stores. The most serious shopping in town is at **Half Moon Village,** east of Half Moon resort. The bright yellow buildings are filled with the finest and most expensive wares money can buy, but the park benches and outdoor pub here make the mall a fun stop for window-shoppers as well.

With the laid-back atmosphere of **Negril,** it's no surprise that most shopping involves straw hats, baskets, and T-shirts, all plentiful at the **Rutland Point** crafts market on the north edge of town. For more serious shopping, head to **Time Square,** known for its luxury goods ranging from jewelry to cigars to watches. The gated shopping area has air-conditioned stores with high-dollar items.

Seeing the Real Jamaica

AN EXCELLENT WAY TO GET OUT to see more of the real Jamaica (and to meet down-to-earth Jamaicans) is by signing up for the Jamaica Tourist Board's free program called **Meet the People** (⌧ 62 Ward Ave., Mandeville ☎ 876/962–3725). Through the program, teachers might opt to visit a local school, parents to meet a Jamaican family for a day of fun on the beach, or flower lovers to go on a stroll through local gardens with a fellow botanist. You should make a call to the tourist board in advance of your trip so the office can match you with a volunteer, but this is an ideal opportunity to find out that Jamaica is about more than just beaches and fruity rum drinks.

13

Ocho Rios has several malls, and they are less hectic than the one in MoBay. Shopping centers include **Pineapple Place, Ocean Village,** the **Taj Mahal, Coconut Grove,** and **Island Plaza.** A fun mall that also serves as an entertainment center is **Island Village,** near the cruise port. The open-air mall includes ReggaeXplosion, shops selling Jamaican handicrafts, duty-free goods and clothing, a Margueritaville restaurant, and a small beach area with a water trampoline.

A shopping tour of the **Kingston** area should include **Devon House,** the place to find things old and new made in Jamaica. The greathouse is now a museum with antiques and furniture reproductions; boutiques and an ice cream shop—try one of the tropical flavors (mango, guava, pineapple, and passion fruit)—now fill what were once the stables.

Specialty Items

COFFEE Java lovers will find beans and ground coffee at gift shops throughout the island as well as at the airport. The lowest prices are found in local supermarkets; check the **Hi-Lo Supermarket** (⌧ West End Rd., Negril ☎ 876/957–4546). But if the store is out of Blue Mountain, you may have to settle for High Mountain coffee, the locals' second-favorite brand.

HANDICRAFTS **Gallery of West Indian Art** (⌧ 11 Fairfield Rd., Montego Bay ☎ 876/952–4547) is the place to find Jamaican and Haitian paintings. A corner of the gallery is devoted to hand-turned pottery (some painted) and beautifully carved and painted birds and animals. **Wassi Art Pottery Works** (⌧ Bougainvillea Dr., Great Pond, Ocho Rios ☎ 876/974–5044) produces one-of-a-kind works of art in terra cotta. Visitors can stroll through the studio, watching local artists produce colorful pots in an array of shapes and sizes. ★ **Harmony Hall** (⌧ Hwy. A1, Ocho Rios ☎ 876/975–4222), an eight-minute drive east of the main part of town, is a restored greathouse, where Annabella Proudlock sells her unique wooden boxes (their covers are decorated with reproductions of Jamaican paintings). Also on sale—and magnificently displayed—are larger reproductions of paintings, lithographs, and signed prints of Jamaican scenes and hand-carved wooden combs. In addition, Harmony Hall is well known for its shows by local artists. **Things Jamaican** (⌧ Devon House, 26

Hope Rd., Kingston ☎ 876/926–1961 ✉ Sangster International Airport, Montego Bay ☎ 876/952–4212) sells some of the best Jamaican crafts—from carved wooden bowls and trays to reproductions of silver and brass period pieces.

LIQUOR & TOBACCO As a rule, only rum distilleries, such as Appleton's and Sangster's, have better deals than the airport stores. Best of all, if you buy your rum at the airport stores, you don't have to tote all those heavy, breakable bottles to your hotel and then to the airport. There are several good cigar shops in Negril. Fine handmade cigars are available at the Montego Bay airport or at one of the island's many cigar stores. You can also buy Cuban cigars almost everywhere, though they can't be brought legally back to the United States. **Cigar King** (✉ 7 Time Square Mall, Negril ☎ 876/957–3315) has a wide selection of cigars, along with a walk-in humidor.

RECORDS & CDS The **Bob Marley Experience & Theatre** (✉ Half Moon Shopping Village, Montego Bay ☎ 876/953–3449) has a 68-seat theater where you can watch a documentary on the life and works of the reggae great, but it's mostly a huge shop filled with Marley memorabilia: CDs, books, and T-shirts. **Reggae Yard & Island Life** (✉ N. Coast Hwy., Island Village, Ocho Rios ☎ 876/675–8795 ☺ Daily 9–5), the largest music store in Ocho Rios, is adjacent to Reggae Xplosion. The offerings include an extensive selection of reggae CDs as well as other types of Caribbean music.

Nightlife

Nightlife includes both on-property shows at the all-inclusive resorts and nightclubs ranging from indoor clubs to beach bashes. For starters, there's reggae, popularized by the late Bob Marley and the Wailers and performed today by son Ziggy Marley, Jimmy Tosh (the late Peter Tosh's son), Gregory Isaacs, Jimmy Cliff, and many others. If your experience of Caribbean music has been limited to steel drums and Harry Belafonte, then the political, racial, and religious messages of reggae may set you on your ear; listen closely and you just might hear the heartbeat of the people. Dancehall is another island favorite, as is soca.

ANNUAL EVENTS
FodorsChoice
★ Those who know and love reggae should visit between mid-July and August for the **Reggae Sumfest** (⊕ www.reggaesumfest.com). This four-night concert—at the Bob Marley Performing Center (a field set up with a temporary stage), in the Freeport area of MoBay—showcases local talent and attracts such big-name performers as Third World and Ziggy Marley and the Melody Makers.

CASINOS Unlike on some Caribbean islands, you won't find a lot of casinos in Jamaica, although some resorts have slots-only gaming rooms. The largest of these is the **Coral Cliff** (✉ 165 Gloucester Ave., Montego Bay ☎ 876/952–4130), right on the Hip Strip, which has more than 120 slot machines. Weekly slot tournaments and complimentary drinks keep you playing. The gaming room is open 24 hours daily.

DANCE & MUSIC CLUBS For the most part, the liveliest late-night happenings throughout Jamaica are in the major resort hotels, with the widest variety of spots probably in Montego Bay. Some of the all-inclusives offer a dinner and disco pass from about $50 to $100; to buy a pass, call ahead the afternoon before to check availability and be sure to bring a photo ID with you. Pick up a copy of the *Daily Gleaner,* the *Jamaica Observer,* or the *Star* (available at newsstands throughout the island) for listings on who's playing when and where. In Negril, trucks with loudspeakers travel through the streets in the afternoon announcing the hot spot for the evening.

Live jazz performances are offered on Saturday evenings at the **Blue Lagoon Restaurant** (✉ San San Beach, Port Antonio ☎ 876/993–7791).

The **Little Pub** (✉ Main St., Ocho Rios ☎ 876/795–3169) produces Caribbean revues several nights a week. **Silks** (✉ Shaw Park Beach Hotel, Shaw Park Ridge Rd., Ocho Rios ☎ 876/974–2324), 1½ mi (2½ km) south of town, has long been a favorite on the dance scene.

The **Brewery** (✉ Shop 4, Miranda Ridge, Gloucester Ave., Montego Bay ☎ 876/940–2433) is a popular sports bar. With its location right on what's
★ deemed the Hip Strip, the colorful **Margueritaville Caribbean Bar & Grill** (✉ Gloucester Ave., Montego Bay ☎ 876/952–4777 ✉ Norman Manley Blvd., Negril ☎ 876/957–4467 ✉ Island Village, Ocho Rios ☎ 876/675–8800) boasts a spring-break crowd during the season with a fun-loving atmosphere any night of the year; there are also locations in Negril, Ocho Rios, and even at the Montego Bay airport. **Hurricanes Disco** (✉ Breezes Montego Bay Resort, Gloucester Ave., Montego Bay ☎ 876/940–1150) is packed with locals and visitors from surrounding small hotels thanks to a $50 night pass (which includes dinner and drinks). **Walter's** (✉ 39 Gloucester Ave., Montego Bay ☎ 876/952–9391) is a downtown favorite.

★ You can find Negril's best live music at **Alfred's Ocean Palace** (✉ Norman Manley Blvd., Negril ☎ 876/957–4669), with live performances
★ right on the beach. The sexy, always packed disco at **Hedonism II** (✉ Norman Manley Blvd., Negril ☎ 876/957–5200) is the wildest dance spot on the island; Tuesday (pajama night) and Thursday (toga night) are tops. For nonguests, night passes are $75 and cover everything from 6 PM to 3 AM; bring a photo ID to obtain a pass, but you should call ahead for a reservation. The **Jungle** (✉ Norman Manley Blvd., Negril ☎ 876/957–4005) is the hottest nightspot in Negril, with two raised bars and a circular dance floor.

Exploring Jamaica

Touring Jamaica can be both thrilling and frustrating. Rugged (albeit beautiful) terrain and winding (often potholed) roads make for slow going. Before you set off to explore the island by car, *always* check conditions prior to heading out, but especially in the rainy season from June through October, when roads can easily be washed out. Primary roads that loop around and across the island are two-lanes but are not particularly well marked. Numbered addresses are seldom used outside major townships, locals drive aggressively, and people and animals seem to have a knack for appearing on the street out of nowhere. That said, Jamaica's scenery shouldn't be missed. The solution? Stick to guided tours and licensed taxis—to be safe and avoid frustration.

If you're staying in Kingston or Port Antonio, set aside at least one day for the capital's highlights and another for a guided excursion to the Blue Mountains. If you have more time, head for Mandeville. You can find at least three days' worth of activity right along MoBay's boundaries; you should also consider a trip to Cockpit Country or Ocho Rios. If you're based in Ocho Rios, be sure to visit Dunn's River Falls; you may also want to stop by Firefly or Port Antonio. If Negril is your hub, take in the south shore, including Y. S. Falls and the Black River.

Numbers in the margin correspond to points of interest on the Jamaica map.

Southeast

❷ **Blue Mountains.** Best known as the source of Blue Mountain coffee, these mountains rising out of the lush jungle north of Kingston are a favorite destination with adventure travelers, hikers, and birders as well as anyone looking to see what lies beyond the beach. You can find guided tours to the mountains from the Ocho Rios and Port Antonio areas as well as from Kingston. Unless you're traveling with a local, don't try to go on your own; the roads wind and dip, hand-lettered signs blow away, and you could easily get lost. It's best to hire a taxi (look for red PPV license plates to identify a licensed taxi) or to take a guided tour. One place worth a visit—especially if you're interested in coffee—is **Mavis Bank** (✉ Mavis Bank ☎ 876/977–8005) and its Jablum coffee plant. An hour-long guided tour is $8; inquire when you arrive at the main office.

❶ **Kingston.** Few leisure travelers—particularly Americans—take the time to visit Kingston, because it's not reachable on a day trip from anywhere on the island besides Ocho Rios or the Blue Mountains. It's also a tough city to love. It's big and, all too often, bad, with gang-controlled neighborhoods that are known to erupt into violence, especially near election time.

However, if you've seen other parts of the island and yearn to know more about the heart and soul of Jamaica, Kingston is worth a visit despite big-city security concerns. The government and business center is also a cultural capital, home to numerous dance troupes, theaters, and museums. Indeed, Kingston seems to reflect more of the true Jamaica—a wonderful cultural mix—than do the sunny havens of the north coast. As one Jamaican put it, "You don't really know Jamaica until you know Kingston." It's also home to the University of the West Indies, one of the Caribbean's largest universities. In 2007 Kingston will play host to cricket's World Cup, serving as the site of the opening ceremonies and drawing the attention of the world to the island.

Kingston sprawls in every direction. To the west, coming in from Spanish Town, lie some of the city's worst slums, in the neighborhoods of Six Miles and Riverton City. Farther south, Spanish Town Road skirts through a high-crime district that many Kingstonians avoid. In the heart of the business district, along the water, the pace is more peaceful, with a lovely walk and parks on Ocean Boulevard. Also here is the Jamaica Convention Centre, home of the U.N. body that creates all laws for the world's seas. From the waterfront you can look across Kingston

Harbour to the Palisadoes Peninsula. This narrow strip is where you can find Norman Manley International Airport and, farther west, Port Royal, the island's former capital, which was destroyed by an earthquake. Downtown Kingston is considered unsafe, particularly at night, so be careful whenever you go.

Most travelers head to New Kingston, north of downtown. This is the home to hotels and offices as well as several historic sites. New Kingston is bordered by Old Hope Road on the east and Half Way Tree Road (which changes to Constant Spring Road) on the west. The area is sliced by Hope Road, a major thoroughfare that connects this region with the University of the West Indies, about 15 minutes east of New Kingston.

North of New Kingston, the city gives way to steep hills and magnificent homes. East of here, the views are even grander as the road winds into the Blue Mountains. Hope Road, just after the University of the West Indies, becomes Gordon Town Road and starts twisting up through the mountains—it's a route that leaves no room for error.

Devon House, built in 1881 and bought and restored by the government in the 1960s, is filled with period furnishings, such as Venetian crystal chandeliers and period reproductions. You can take a guided tour of the two-story mansion (built with a South American gold miner's fortune) only on a guided tour. On the grounds you can find some of the island's best crafts shops as well as one of the few mahogany trees to have survived Kingston's ambitious but not always careful development. ✉ *26 Hope Rd.* ☎ *876/929–6602* ✉ *House tour $5* ☉ *House Mon.–Sat. 9:30–4:30, shops Mon.–Sat. 10–6.*

The artists represented at the **National Gallery** may not be household names in other countries, but their paintings are sensitive and moving. You can find works by such Jamaican masters as intuitive painter John Dunkley, and Edna Manley, a sculptor who worked in a cubist style. Among other highlights from the 1920s through 1980s are works by the artist Kapo, a self-taught painter who specialized in religious images. Reggae fans should look for Christopher Gonzalez's controversial statue of Bob Marley (it was slated to be displayed near the National Arena but was placed here because many Jamaicans felt it didn't resemble Marley). ✉ *12 Ocean Blvd., Kingston Mall, near waterfront* ☎ *876/922–1561* ✉ *$2* ☉ *Tues.–Thurs. 10–4:30, Fri. 10–4, Sat. 10–3.*

★ At the height of his career, Bob Marley built a recording studio—painted Rastafarian red, yellow, and green—which now houses the **Bob Marley Museum.** The guided tour takes you through the medicinal herb garden, his bedroom, and other rooms wallpapered with magazine and newspaper articles that chronicle his rise to stardom. The tour includes a 20-minute biographical film on him; there's also a reference library if you want to learn more. Certainly there's much here that will help you to understand Marley, reggae, and Jamaica itself. A striking mural by Jah Bobby, *The Journey of Superstar Bob Marley,* depicts the hero's life from its beginnings, in a womb shaped like a coconut, to enshrinement in the hearts of the Jamaican people. ✉ *56 Hope Rd.* ☎ *876/927–9152* ⊕ *www.bobmarley-foundation.com* ✉ *$10* ☉ *Mon.–Sat. 9:30–4.*

⑯ Port Royal. Just south of Kingston, Port Royal was called "the wickedest city in Christendom" until an earthquake tumbled much of it into the sea in 1692. The spirits of Henry Morgan and other buccaneers add energy to what remains. The proudest possession of St. Peter's Church, rebuilt in 1726 to replace Christ's Church, is a silver communion set said to have been donated by Morgan himself (who probably obtained it during a raid on Panama).

A ferry from the square in downtown Kingston goes to Port Royal at least twice a day, but most visitors arrive by road, continuing past the airport to this small community. If you drive out to Port Royal from Kingston, you pass several other sights, including remains of old forts virtually overgrown with vegetation, an old naval cemetery (which has some intriguing headstones), and a monument commemorating Jamaica's first coconut tree, planted in 1863 (there's no tree there now, just plenty of cactus and scrub brush). You can no longer down rum in Port Royal's legendary 40 taverns, but two small pubs remain in operation.

You can explore the impressive remains of **Fort Charles,** once the area's major garrison. Built in 1662, this is the oldest surviving monument from the British occupation of Jamaica. On the grounds are a maritime museum and the old artillery storehouse, Giddy House, which gained its name after being tilted by the earthquake of 1907: locals say its slant makes you giddy. ☎ 876/967–8438 ✍ $1.50 ☼ Daily 9–5.

⑮ Spanish Town. Twelve miles (19 km) west of Kingston on A1, Spanish Town was the island's capital when it was ruled by Spain. The town has Georgian Antique Square, the Jamaican People's Museum of Crafts and Technology (in the Old King's House stables), and St. James, the oldest cathedral in the western hemisphere. Spanish Town's original name was Santiago de la Vega, meaning St. James of the Plains.

East Coast

❹ Port Antonio. The first Port Antonio tourists arrived in the early 20th century seeking a respite from New York winters. In time, the area became fashionable among a fast-moving crowd that included everyone from Rudyard Kipling to Bette Davis; today celebs such as Tom Cruise, Eddie Murphy, Brooke Shields, and Denzel Washington dodge the limelight with a getaway in this quiet haven. Although the action has moved elsewhere, the area can still weave a spell. Robin Moore wrote *The French Connection* here, and Broadway's tall and talented Tommy Tune found inspiration for the musical *Nine* while being pampered at Trident.

Port Antonio has also long been a center for some of the Caribbean's finest deep-sea fishing. Dolphin (the delectable fish, not the lovable mammal) is the likely catch here, along with tuna, kingfish, and wahoo. In October the weeklong Blue Marlin Tournament attracts anglers from around the world. By the time they've all had their fill of beer, it's the fish stories—rather than the fish—that carry the day.

A good way to spend a day in Port Antonio is to laze in the deep-azure water of the **Blue Lagoon** (✉ 1 mi [1½ km] east of San San Beach). Although there's not much beach to speak of, you can find a water-sports center, changing rooms, and a soothing mineral pool. Good, inexpensive Jamaican fare is served at a charming waterside terrace restaurant; it's open daily for lunch and dinner and has live jazz music on Saturday night. **DeMontevin Lodge** (✉ 21 Fort George St. ☎ 876/993–2604), on Titchfield Hill, is owned by the Mullings family. The late Gladys Mullings was Errol Flynn's cook, and you can still get great food here. The lodge, and a number of structures on nearby Musgrave Street (the crafts market is here), is built in a traditional seaside style that's reminiscent of New England. **Queen Street,** in the residential Titchfield area, a couple of miles north of downtown Port Antonio, has several fine examples of Georgian architecture. A short drive east from Port Antonio puts you at Boston Bay, which is popular with swimmers and has been enshrined by lovers of jerk pork. The spicy barbecue was originated by the Arawaks and perfected by the Maroons. Eating almost nothing but wild hog preserved over smoking coals enabled them to survive years of fierce guerrilla warfare with the English.

Some 6 mi (9½ km) northeast of Port Antonio are the **Athenry Gardens,** a 3-acre tropical wonderland including the Nonsuch Caves, whose underground beauty has been made accessible by concrete walkways, railed stairways, and careful lighting. ✉ *Nonsuch* ☎ *876/779–7144* 💲 *$6* ☼ *Daily 10–4.*

❸ **Rio Grande.** The Rio Grande (yes, Jamaica has a Rio Grande, too) is a granddaddy of river-rafting attractions: an 8-mi-long (13-km-long) swift, green waterway from Berrydale to Rafter's Rest (it flows into the Caribbean at St. Margaret's Bay). The trip of about three hours is made on bamboo rafts pushed along by a raftsman who is likely to be a character. You can pack a picnic lunch and eat it on the raft or on the riverbank; wherever you lunch, a Red Stripe vendor will appear at your elbow. A restaurant, a bar, and souvenir shops are at Rafter's Rest. The trip costs about $40 per two-person raft. (For more information on companies that arrange river-rafting excursions, *see* ⇨ River Rafting *in* Sports & the Outdoors, *above.*)

North Coast

❽ **Montego Bay.** Today many explorations of MoBay are conducted from a reclining chair—frothy drink in hand—on Doctor's Cave Beach. As home of the north-shore airport, Montego Bay, or MoBay, is the first taste most visitors have of the island. It's the second-largest city in Jamaica and has the busiest cruise pier. Travelers from around the world come and go in this bustling community year-round. The name Montego is derived from *manteca* ("lard" in Spanish). The Spanish first named this Bahía de Manteca, or Lard Bay. Why? The Spanish once shipped hogs from this port city. Jamaican tourism began here in 1924, when the first resort opened at Doctor's Cave Beach so that health-seekers could "take the waters." If you can pull yourself away from the water's edge and brush the sand off your toes, you can find some very interesting colonial sights in the surrounding area.

Fodor'sChoice ★ In the 1700s **Rose Hall** may well have been the greatest of greathouses in the West Indies. Today it's popular less for its architecture than for the legend surrounding its second mistress, Annie Palmer. As the story goes, Annie was born in 1802 in England to an English mother and Irish father. When she was 10, her family moved to Haiti, and soon her parents died of yellow fever. Annie was adopted by a Haitian voodoo priestess and soon became skilled in the practice of voodoo. Annie moved to Jamaica, married, and built Rose Hall, an enormous plantation spanning 6,600 acres with more than 2,000 slaves. According to legend, Annie murdered several of her husbands and her slave lovers. To know more about the tales of Rose Hall, read *The White Witch of Rose Hall,* a novel sold across the island. There's a pub on-site. It's across the highway from the Rose Hall Resort & Country Club. ⊠ *N. Coast Hwy.* ☎ *876/953–9982* 💲 *$15* ⊙ *Daily 9–6.*

★ The **Greenwood Great House** has no spooky legend to titillate, but it's much better than Rose Hall at evoking life on a sugar plantation. The Barrett family, from whom the English poet Elizabeth Barrett Browning descended, once owned all the land from Rose Hall to Falmouth; they built this and several other greathouses on it. (The poet's father, Edward Moulton Barrett, "the Tyrant of Wimpole Street," was born at nearby Cinnamon Hill, the estate of the late country singer Johnny Cash.) Highlights of Greenwood include oil paintings of the Barretts, china made for the family by Wedgwood, a library filled with rare books from as early as 1697, fine antique furniture, and a collection of exotic musical instruments. There's a pub on-site as well. It's 15 mi (24 km) east of Montego Bay. ⊠ *Greenwood* ☎ *876/953–1077* ⊕ *www.greenwoodgreathouse.com* 💲 *$12* ⊙ *Daily 9–6.*

❼ **Cockpit Country.** Fifteen miles (24 km) inland from MoBay is one of the most untouched areas in the West Indies: a terrain of pitfalls and potholes carved by nature in limestone. For nearly a century after 1655 it was known as the Land of Look Behind, because British soldiers nervously rode their horses through here on the lookout for the guerrilla freedom fighters known as Maroons. Former slaves who refused to surrender to the invading English, the Maroons eventually won their independence. Today their descendants live in this area, untaxed and virtually ungoverned by outside authorities. Most visitors to the area stop in Accompong, a small community in St. Elizabeth Parish. You can stroll through town, take in the historic structures, and learn more about the Maroons—considered Jamaica's greatest herbalists.

The **Martha Brae River,** a gentle waterway about 25 mi (40 km) southeast of Montego Bay, takes its name from an Arawak Indian who killed herself because she refused to reveal the whereabouts of a local gold mine to the Spanish. According to legend, she agreed to take them there and, on reaching the river, used magic to change its course, drowning herself and the greedy Spaniards with her. Her *duppy* (ghost) is said to guard the mine's entrance. Rafting on this river is a very popular activity. Martha Brae River Rafting (*see* ⇨ River Rafting *in* Sports & the Outdoors, *above*) arranges trips.

❺ **Firefly.** About 20 mi (32 km) east of Ocho Rios in Port Maria, Firefly was once Sir Noël Coward's vacation home and is now maintained by the Jamaican National Heritage Trust. Although the setting is Eden-like, the house is surprisingly spartan, considering that he often entertained jet-setters and royalty. He wrote *High Spirits, Quadrille,* and other plays here, and his simple grave is on the grounds next to a small stage where his works are occasionally performed. Recordings of Coward singing about mad dogs and Englishmen echo over the lawns. Tours include time in the photo gallery and a walk through the house and grounds, the viewing of a video on Coward, and a drink in the gift shop. ⊠ *Port Maria* ☎ *876/960–8134* ⊡ *$10* ☉ *Mon.–Thurs. 9–5, Sat. 9–5.*

6 **Ocho Rios.** Although Ocho Rios isn't near eight rivers as its name would seem to indicate, it does have a seemingly endless series of cascades that sparkle from limestone rocks along the coast. (The name Ocho Rios came about because the English misunderstood the Spanish *las chorreras*—"the waterfalls.")

The town itself isn't very attractive and can be traffic-clogged, but the area has several worthwhile attractions, including Dunn's River Falls and Prospect Plantation. A few steps from the main road in Ocho Rios are some of the most charming inns and oceanfront restaurants in the Caribbean. Lying on the sand of what seems to be your very own cove or swinging gently in a hammock while sipping a tropical drink, you'll soon forget the traffic that's just a stroll away.

The original "defenders" stationed at the Old Fort, built in 1777, spent much of their time sacking and plundering as far afield as St. Augustine, Florida, and sharing their booty with the local plantation owners who financed their missions. Fifteen miles (24 km) west is Discovery Bay, where Columbus landed and where there's a small museum of artifacts and such local memorabilia as ships' bells and cannons and iron pots used for boiling sugarcane. Don't miss a drive through Fern Gully, a natural canopy of vegetation filtered by sunlight. (Jamaica has the world's largest number of fern species, more than 570.) To reach the stretch of road called Fern Gully, take the A3 highway south of Ocho Rios.

FodorśChoice ★ **Dunn's River Falls** is an eye-catching sight: 600 feet of cold, clear mountain water splashing over a series of stone steps to the warm Caribbean. The best way to enjoy the falls is to climb the slippery steps: don a swimsuit, take the hand of the person ahead of you, and trust that the chain of hands and bodies leads to an experienced guide. The leaders of the climbs are personable fellows who reel off bits of local lore while telling you where to step; you can hire a guide's service for a tip of a few dollars. After the climb, you exit through a crowded market, another reminder that this is one of Jamaica's top tourist attractions. If you can, try to schedule a visit on a day when no cruise ships are in port. ⊠ *Off A1, between St. Ann's and Ocho Rios* ☎ *876/974–2857* ⊡ *$10* ☉ *Daily 8:30–5.*

To learn about Jamaica's former agricultural economy, a trip to **Prospect Plantation,** just west of Ocho Rios, is a must. But it's not just a place for history lovers or farming aficionados; everyone seems to enjoy the views over the White River gorge and the tour by jitney (a canopied open-air cart pulled by a tractor). The grounds are full of exotic fruits and tropical trees, some planted over the years by such celebrities as Winston Churchill and Charlie Chaplin. You can also go horseback riding on the plantation's 900 acres or play miniature golf, grab a drink in the bar, or buy souvenirs in the gift shop. If you want more time to really explore, you can rent one of the on-site villas. ⊠ *Hwy. A1, west of Ocho Rios* ☎ *876/994–1058* 🖾 *$29* ☉ *Daily 8–5; tours Mon.–Sat. at 10:30, 2, and 3:30.*

Jamaica's national motto is "Out of Many, One People," and at the **Coyaba River Garden & Museum** you can see exhibits on the many cultural influences that have contributed to the creation of the one. The museum covers the island's history from the time of the Arawak Indians up to the present day. A guided 45-minute tour through the lush 3-acre garden, which is 1½ mi (2½ km) south of Ocho Rios, introduces you to the flora and fauna of the island. The complex includes a crafts and gift shop and a snack bar. ⊠ *Shaw Park Estate, Shaw Park Ridge Rd.* ☎ *876/974–6235* ⊕ *www.coyabagardens.com* 🖾 *$5* ☉ *Daily 8–5.*

You enjoy the north-coast rivers and flowers without the crowds at **Cranbrook Flower Forest**, filled with blooming orchids, ginger, and ferns. This park is the private creation of Ivan Linton, who has pampered the plants of this former plantation since the early 1980s. Today Linton proudly points out the bird of paradise, croton, ginger, heliconia, and begonias as if they were his dear children. The grounds are perfect for a picnic followed by a hike alongside a shady Laughlin's Great River. The path climbs high into the hills to a waterfall paradise. Donkey rides, picnicking, croquet, wading, and volleyball are also available here. The complex includes a snack shop and restrooms. ⊠ *5 mi (8 km) east of Runaway Bay, 1 mi (1½ km) off N. Coast Hwy.* ☎ *876/770–8071* ⊕ *www.cranbrookff.com* 🖾 *$6* ☉ *Daily 9–5.*

An especially good choice for rainy days, **Green Grotto Caves** offers guided 45-minute tours of the cave, including a look at a subterranean lake. The cave has a rich history as a hiding place for everyone from pirates to runaway slaves to the Spanish governor, when he was on the run from the British. It's a good destination if you want to see one of Jamaica's caves without really going off the beaten path. You'll feel a little like a spelunker, though, because you wear hard hats throughout the tour. ⊠ *2 mi (3 km) east of Discovery Bay, 1 mi (1½ km) off N. Coast Hwy.* ☎ *876/973–2841* ⊕ *www.greengrottocaves.com* 🖾 *$20* ☉ *Daily 9–4.*

★ In the open-air Island Village shopping and entertainment center, which is owned by Island Records tycoon Chris Blackwell, **Reggae Xplosion** traces the history of Jamaican music. Ska, mento, dancehall, reggae, and more are featured in a series of exhibits spanning two stories. Special sections highlight the careers of some of Jamaica's best-known talents, including Bob Marley, Peter Tosh, and Bunny Wailer. The museum also includes an extensive gift shop with recordings and collectibles. ⊠ *N. Coast Hwy., Island Village* ☎ *876/974–8353* ⊕ *www.islandjamaica.com* 🖾 *$10* ☉ *Daily 9–5.*

If you want to combine a cultural experience with lunch, a stop by **Faith's Pen** is an interesting experience. Here, rows of food stands offer real Jamaican specialties with home-cooked taste. For just a few dollars, buy a streetside lunch of jerk or callaloo served at a picnic table. Faith's Pen stalls include such names as Johnny Cool No. 1 and Shut's Night and Day. Look for jerk chicken, curried goat, roast fish, and mannish water (a soup—and reported aphrodisiac—made from a goat's head). You can expect to fill up on traditional dishes for less than $10 per person. The facilities are spartan: each stall has a small area with stools. ☒ *12 mi south of Ocho Rios on A3 to intersection of A1, continue south on A1 about 4 mi.*

Travelers with an interest in Bob Marley won't want to miss Nine Mile, the community where the reggae legend was born and is buried. Today his former home is the **Bob Marley Centre & Mausoleum.** Tucked behind a tall fence, the site is marked with green and gold flags. Tours are led by Rastafarians, who take visitors through the house and point out the single bed that Marley wrote about in "Is This Love." ☒ *Rhoden Hall, Nine Mile* ☎ *876/995–1763* 💲 *$7* ☉ *Daily 9–5.*

West Coast

❾ **Negril.** In the 18th century, English ships assembled here in convoys for dangerous ocean crossings. The infamous pirate Calico Jack and his crew were captured right here while they guzzled rum. All but two of them were hanged on the spot; Mary Read and Anne Bonney were pregnant at the time, so their executions were delayed.

On the winding coast road 55 mi (89 km) southwest of MoBay, Negril was once Jamaica's best-kept secret, but it's begun to shed some of its bohemian, ramshackle atmosphere for the attractions and activities traditionally associated with MoBay. One thing that hasn't changed around this west-coast center (whose only true claim to fame is a 7-mi [11-km] beach) is a casual approach to life. As you wander from lunch in the sun to shopping in the sun to sports in the sun, you can find that swimsuits and cover-ups are common attire. Want to dress for a special meal? Slip on a caftan over your swimsuit.

Negril stretches along the coast south from horseshoe-shape Bloody Bay (named when it was a whale-processing center) along the calm waters of Long Bay to the Lighthouse. Nearby, divers spiral downward off 50-foot-high cliffs into the deep green depths as the sun turns into a ball of fire and sets the clouds ablaze with color. Sunset is also the time when Norman Manley Boulevard, which intersects West End Road, comes to life with bustling bistros and ear-splitting discos.

Even nonguests can romp at **Hedonism II** (☒ Norman Manley Blvd., Ruthland Point ☎ 876/957–5200). The resort beach is divided into "prude" and "nude" sides; a quick look around reveals where most guests pull their chaise lounges. Nude volleyball, body-painting contests, and shuffleboard keep daytime hours lively; at night most action occurs in the high-tech disco or in the hot tub. Your day pass (which gives you access from 10 to 5 for $65) includes food and drink and participation in water sports, tennis, squash, and other activities. Night passes ($75) cover dinner, drinks, and entrance to the disco. Day or night, reservations are a must; bring a photo ID as well. Negril's only structure of historical significance is the **Lighthouse** (✉ West End Rd.), which has guided ships past Jamaica's rocky western coast since 1895. You can stop by the adjacent caretaker's cottage from 11 to 7 (except Tuesday) and, for the price of a tip, climb the spiral steps to the best view in town.

South Coast

⓫ Appleton Estate. On a guided tour, you learn about the history of rum making. After a bit of rum history, starting with the days when sugarcane was crushed by donkey power, tours then progress into the modern factory, where one of Jamaica's best-known products is bottled. After the tour, samples flow freely. There's also a good restaurant here serving genuine Jamaican dishes. ✉ *Siloah* ☎ *876/963–9215* ⊕ *www. appletonrum.com* ✇ *Free* ◷ *Mon.–Sat. 9–4.*

Fodor's Choice
★

⓬ High Mountain Coffee Plantation. Free tours show how coffee beans are turned into one of the world's favorite morning drinks. After Blue Mountain coffee, High Mountain is Jamaica's best variety. ✉ *Williamsfield* ☎ *876/963–4211* ◷ *Weekdays, by appointment only.*

⓮ Mandeville. At 2,000 feet above sea level, Mandeville is considerably cooler than the coastal areas 25 mi (40 km) to the south. Its vegetation is also lusher, thanks to the mists that drift through the mountains. But climate and flora aren't all that separate it from the steamy coast: Mandeville seems a hilly tribute to all that's genteel in the British character. The people here live in tidy cottages with gardens around a village green; there's even a Georgian courthouse and a parish church. The entire scene could be set down in Devonshire, were it not for the occasional poinciana blossom or citrus grove.

★ **⓾ Y. S. Falls.** This waterfall is a quiet alternative to Dunn's River Falls in Ocho Rios. Most often seen as a half-day trip from Negril, the falls are tucked in a papaya plantation and reached via motorized jitney. If you aren't staying on the south coast, companies in Negril offer half-day excursions. ✉ *2 Market St., Black River* ☎ *876/997–6055* ⊕ *www.ysfalls. com* ✇ *$15* ◷ *Tues.–Sun. 9:30–4.*

⓭ Lovers' Leap. As legend has it, two slave lovers chose to jump off this 1,700-foot cliff rather than be recaptured by their master. Today it's a favorite stop with travelers, who enjoy a drink at the bar (try the lover's punch) and a view of the coastline. Tours of local cacti are available, and a miniature farm demonstrates the dry-farming technique used in this area. ✉ *Yardley Chase, Treasure Beach* ☎ *876/965–6634* ✇ *Free* ◷ *Daily.*

EN ROUTE

Although the constant roar of speeding trucks keeps the site from being idyllic, **Bamboo Avenue,** the section of Route A1 between Middle Quarters and Lacovia, is an often-photographed stretch of highway that's completely canopied with tall bamboo. At the side of the road, vendors sell chilled young coconuts, cracking them with a quick machete chop to reveal the jelly inside.

JAMAICA ESSENTIALS

To research prices, get advice from other travelers, and book travel arrangements, visit www.fodors.com.

Transportation

BY AIR

AIR TRAVEL TO JAMAICA: Jamaica is well served by major airlines. From the United States, Air Jamaica, American Airlines, ATA, Continental, Northwest, Spirit, and US Airways offer nonstop and connecting service. Air Canada offers service from major airports in Canada. Air Jamaica and British Airways offer service from the United Kingdom. Copa offers service between Miami and Kingston. Cayman Airways connects Jamaica to Grand Cayman and Cayman Brac; BWIA connects Jamaica to Antigua, Barbados, and Trinidad.

🛪 **Air Canada** ☎ 876/952-5160 in Montego Bay, 876/942-8211 in Kingston. **Air Jamaica** ☎ 876/952-4300 in Montego Bay, 888/359-2475. **American Airlines** ☎ 800/744-0006. **ATA** ☎ 800/521-5267 or 800/435-9282. **British Airways** ☎876/929-9020 in Kingston. **BWIA** ☎ 876/924-8364 in Kingston. **Cayman Airways** ☎ 876/924-8092 in Kingston. **Continental** ☎ 800/231-0856. **Copa** ☎ 876/926-1762 in Kingston. **Northwest Airlines** ☎ 800/225-2525. **Spirit Airlines** ☎ 586/791-7300 or 800/772-7117. **US Airways** ☎ 800/622-1015.

AIR TRAVEL AROUND JAMAICA: Air Jamaica Express, a subsidiary of Air Jamaica, provides shuttle services on the island. Be sure to reconfirm your departing flight a full 72 hours in advance. Tim Air offers quick flights between resort areas as well as to Kingston.

🛪 **Air Jamaica Express** ☎ 876/952-5401 in Montego Bay, 888/359-2475. **Tim Air** ☎ 876/952-2516 in Montego Bay ⊕ www.timair.com.

AIRPORTS & TRANSFERS: Many all-inclusive resorts include the cost of airport transfers in their rates. If yours doesn't you will have to book a shared-van service at the airport. It's not a cheap transfer to most resort

areas from MoBay because of the distances involved. Expect to pay $18 per person one-way from Montego Bay to Negril, $25 to Ocho Rios, and $35 to Boscobel.

🛪 Major Airports **Donald Sangster International Airport** ✉ Montego Bay ☎ 876/952-3124. **Norman Manley International Airport** ✉ Kingston ☎ 876/924-8452 ⊕ www.manley-airport.com.jm.

🛪 Minor Airports **Boscobel Aerodrome** ✉ Oracabessa, 8 mi [14 km] east of Ocho Rios ☎ 876/975-3101. **Negril Aerodrome** ✉ Negril ☎ 876/924-8452.

BY CAR

Driving in Jamaica can be an extremely frustrating chore. You must constantly be on guard—for enormous potholes, people, and animals darting out into the street, as well as aggressive drivers. With a one-lane road encircling the island, local drivers are quick to pass other cars—and sometimes two cars will pass simultaneously (inspiring the "undertakers love overtakers" signs seen throughout the island). Gas stations are open daily but accept cash only. Gas costs roughly double the price found in the United States. Remember that driving in Jamaica is on the left, British-style.

🛪 **Budget** ☎ 876/952-3838 in Montego Bay, 876/924-8762 in Kingston. **Hertz** ☎ 876/952-4250 in Montego Bay, 876/924-8028 in Kingston. **Island Car Rentals** ☎876/952-7225 in Montego Bay, 876/924-8075 in Kingston. **Jamaica Car Rental** ☎ 876/952-5586 in Montego Bay.

BY TAXI

Some but not all of Jamaica's taxis are metered. If you accept a driver's offer of his services as a tour guide, be sure to agree on a price before the vehicle is put into gear. (Note that a one-day tour should run about $150 to $180, depending on distance traveled.) All licensed taxis display red Public Passenger Vehicle (PPV) plates. Cabs can be summoned by phone or flagged down on the street. Rates are per car, not per passen-

13

ger, and 25% is added to the metered rate between midnight and 5 AM. Licensed minivans are also available and bear the red PPV plates. JUTA is the largest taxi franchise and has offices in all resort areas.

🚗 JUTA ☎ 876/974-2292 in Ocho Rios, 876/957-9197 in Negril, 876/952-0813 in Montego Bay ⊕ www.jutatoursnegrillltd.com.

Contacts & Resources

BANKS & EXCHANGE SERVICES

Currency exchange is available at the major airports, in hotels, and in area banks, but few Americans bother to exchange money, since American dollars are widely accepted. ATM machines in Jamaica do not accept American ATM cards, although cash advances can be made using credit cards—provided that you have a PIN. Major credit cards are widely accepted throughout the island, although cash is required at gas stations, in markets, and in many small stores. Discover and Diners Club are accepted at many resorts.

The official currency is the Jamaican dollar. At this writing the exchange rate was about J$64.43 to US$1. Prices quoted throughout this chapter are in U.S. dollars, unless otherwise noted.

BUSINESS HOURS

Banks are generally open Monday through Thursday from 9 to 2, Friday 9 to 4. Post office hours are weekdays from 9 to 5. Normal business hours for stores are weekdays from 8:30 to 4:30, Saturday 8 to 1.

ELECTRICITY

Like the electrical current in North America, the current in Jamaica is 110 volts but only 50 cycles, with outlets that take two flat prongs. Some hotels provide 220-volt plugs as well as special shaver outlets. If you plan to bring electrical appliances with you, it's best to ask when making your reservation.

EMBASSIES & CONSULATES

🏛 Canada **Canadian High Commission** ⊠ 3 W. King's House Rd., Kingston ☎ 876/926-1500.

🏛 United Kingdom **British High Commission** ⊠ Trafalgar Rd., Kingston ☎ 876/926-9050.
🏛 United States **U.S. Embassy** ⊠ 2 Oxford Rd., Kingston ☎ 876/929-4850.

EMERGENCIES

🏥Emergency Services **Ambulance and Fire Emergencies** ☎ 110. **Police Emergencies & Air Rescue** ☎ 119. **Scuba-Diving Emergencies** ⊠ St. Ann's Bay Hospital, St. Ann's Bay ☎ 876/972-2272.
🏥 Hospitals **Cornwall Regional Hospital** ⊠ Mount Salem, Montego Bay ☎ 876/952-5100. **Mo Bay Hope Medical Center** ⊠ Half Moon, Montego Bay ☎ 876/953-3981. **Port Antonio Hospital** ⊠ Naylor's Hill, Port Antonio ☎ 876/993-2646. **St. Ann's Bay Hospital** ⊠ St. Ann's Bay ☎ 876/972-2272. **University Hospital of the West Indies** ⊠ Mona, Kingston ☎ 876/927-1620.
🏥 Pharmacies **Great House Pharmacy** ⊠ Brown's Plaza, DaCosta Dr., Ocho Rios ☎ 876/974-2352. **Jamaica Pegasus** ⊠ 81 Knutsford Blvd., Kingston ☎ 876/926-3690.

HOLIDAYS

Public holidays include New Year's Day, Ash Wednesday (beginning of Lent, 6 wks before Easter), Good Friday, Easter Monday, Labor Day (May 23), Independence Day (1st Mon. in Aug.), National Heroes Day (Oct. 15), Christmas, and Boxing Day (Dec. 26).

INTERNET, MAIL & SHIPPING

Internet service is becoming far more widespread, and most hotels offer at least limited service, either at public terminals (often free at the all-inclusive resorts) to Wi-Fi.

Postcards may be mailed anywhere in the world for J$40. Letters to the United States and Canada cost J$40, to Europe J$45, to Australia J$60, and to New Zealand J$60. Due to costly and slow airshipping service, most travelers carry home packages, even large wood carvings.

LANGUAGE

The official language of Jamaica is English. Islanders usually speak a patois among themselves, a lyrical mixture of English, Spanish, and various African languages.

PASSPORT REQUIREMENTS

Starting January 1, 2007, U.S. citizens must carry a valid passport to reenter the United States. Canadian citizens must have proof of citizenship, either a passport (not expired beyond one year) or an original birth certificate (with a raised seal) or a naturalization certificate along with a government-issue photo ID.

SAFETY

Crime in Jamaica is, unfortunately, a persistent problem, so don't let the beauty of the island cause you to abandon the caution you would practice in any unfamiliar place. Many of the headlines are grabbed by murders in Kingston, often gang-related; violent crimes are, for the most part, largely a problem for residents who live in the city. Visitors should be extremely cautious about visiting many of the neighborhoods in Kingston that are outside the business district of New Kingston.

Property crime is an islandwide problem. Utilize your in-room safe and be sure to lock all doors—including balconies—when you leave your room or villa. Traveler's checks are a good idea in Jamaica, being safer than cash (just keep a record of the check numbers in a secure place so they can be replaced if necessary). Never leave a rental car unlocked, and never leave valuables in a locked car. Ignore efforts, however persistent, to sell you *ganja* (marijuana), which is illegal across the island.

TAXES

The departure tax is $27 and must be paid in cash if it's not added to the cost of your airline tickets; this policy varies by carrier, although most ticket prices now include the departure tax. Jamaica has replaced the room occupancy tax with a V.A.T. of 15% on most goods and services, which is already incorporated into the prices of taxable goods. Start in May 2005, incoming air passengers were charged a US$10 tourism enhancement fee; incoming cruise passengers pay a $2 fee; both these fees are almost always included in the price of your airline ticket or cruise passage.

TELEPHONES

Cellular service is expanding throughout Jamaica, especially in Kingston and in the resort areas (service remains sporadic in the mountainous regions). GSM cell phones equipped with tri-band or world-roaming service will find coverage throughout much of the coastal region. Cellular service averages about $1.50 per minute on the island. Prepaid SIM cards are a more economical way for travelers who plan to make a large number of local calls; rates for local calls start about 15¢ per minute, and incoming calls are free. Outgoing international calls to the U.S. start about 27¢ per minute. Prepaid SIM cards cost about $60 and usually include a $20 airtime credit. Cellular-phone rentals are also available starting about $20 per week.

Most hotels offer direct-dial telephone services with a substantial service change; local businesses provide fax services for a fee. Pay phones are available in most communities, but be aware that on the island calls from town to town are long-distance.

To dial Jamaica from the United States, just dial 1 + the area code 876. Some U.S. phone companies, such as MCI, won't permit credit-card calls to be placed from Jamaica because they've been victims of fraud. The best option is to purchase Jamaican phone cards, sold in most stores across the island.

TIPPING

Most hotels and restaurants add a 10% service charge to your bill. When a service charge isn't included, a 10% to 20% tip is expected. Tips of 10% to 20% are customary for taxi drivers as well. However, many all-inclusives have a strict no-tipping policy.

TOUR OPTIONS

Because most vacationers don't rent cars for both safety and cost reasons, guided

13

tours are a popular option if you're ready to take a break from the beach and explore. Check with your hotel concierge for information on half- and full-day tours that offer pickup at your resort. Jamaica's size and slow roads mean that you can't expect to see all the island on any one trip; even a full-day tour will concentrate on just one part of the island. Most of the tours are similar in both content and price. If you're in Montego Bay, tours often include one of the plantation houses in the area. Several Negril-based companies offer tours to Y.S. Falls on the south coast. Tours from Ocho Rios might include any of the area's top attractions, including Dunn's River Falls, a Black River Safari, Cockpit Country, Kingston, Mayfield Falls, or the Blue Lagoon. In almost all cases, you'll arrange your tour through the tour desk of your resort. However, a few of these tours are quite unique, including the following.

Visitors to Mandeville and Kingston areas can experience more of the real Jamaica through Countrystyle, which offers unique, personalized tours of island communities. You're linked with community residents based on your interests; tours can include anything from bird-watching in Mandeville to nightlife in Kingston.

Maroon Attraction Tours Co. leads full-day tours from MoBay to Maroon headquarters at Accompong, giving you a glimpse of the society of Maroons who live in Cockpit Country. The cost is $50 per person.

Reggae buffs visiting the Ocho Rios area enjoy the Zion Bus Line, which includes a visit to Bob Marley's boyhood home. Travelers ride a country-style bus painted in bright colors to the island's interior and the village of Nine Mile. The tour includes a look at the simple home where Marley was born and is now buried.

Countrystyle ✉ 62 Ward Ave., Mandeville ☎ 876/962-7758. **Maroon Attraction Tours Co.** ☎ N. Coast Hwy., Montego Bay ☎ 876/952-4546. **Zion Bus Line** ✉ Chukka Cove Adventure Tours, Llandovery ☎ 876/972-2506 ⊕ www.chukkacove.com.

VISITOR INFORMATION

Before You Leave Jamaica Tourist Board ⊕ www.visitjamaica.com ✉ 5201 Blue Lagoon Dr., Suite 670, Miami, FL 33146 ☎ 305/665-0557 ✉ 303 Eglinton Ave. E, Suite 200, Toronto, Ontario M4P 1L3, Canada ☎ 416/482-7850 ✉ 1-2 Prince Consort Rd., London SW7 2BZ, U.K. ☎ 0441/207-225-9090.

In Jamaica Jamaica Tourist Board ✉ 64 Knutsford Blvd., Kingston ☎ 876/929-9200, 888/995-9999 on-island help line ✉ Cornwall Beach, Montego Bay ☎ 876/952-4425 ✉ City Centre Plaza, Port Antonio ☎ 876/993-3051.

WEDDINGS

Thanks to its accommodating marriage laws, tropical beauty, and bountiful couples-only resorts, Jamaica is one of the top wedding destinations in the Caribbean. Several all-inclusive resorts, including SuperClubs and Couples, offer free wedding ceremonies, including the officiant's fee, marriage license, tropical flowers, a small wedding cake, champagne, and more.

Most couples work with their resort's wedding coordinator in advance of their visit to handle the legal paperwork. You can marry after only 24 hours on the island if you've applied for your license and supplied all necessary forms beforehand. You need to supply proof of citizenship (a passport or certified copy of the birth certificate signed by a notary public), written parental consent for couples under age 18, proof of divorce with the original or certified copy of the divorce decree if applicable, and copy of the death certificate if a previous marriage ended in death. Blood tests are not required.

Martinique

The swaying palms of Les Salines

WORD OF MOUTH

"The only drawback to Martinique I found is that not many Americans go there and very few people speak English, so brush up on your French."
　　　　　　　　　　　　　　　　　　　　　　　—john

"St. Pierre was at one time the social capital of Martinique. It is beautifully situated . . . in the shadow of Mt. Pelee. And that was its undoing. The entire town was destroyed by a volcano. . . ."
　　　　　　　　　　　　　　　　　　　　　　　—Sandy

WELCOME TO MARTINIQUE

PARIS IN THE TROPICS

The largest of the Windward Islands, Martinique is 425 square mi (1,101 square km). The southern part of the island is all rolling hills and sugarcane fields; it's also where you'll find the best beaches and most development. In the north are craggy cliffs, lush vegetation, and one of the Caribbean's largest volcanoes, Mont Pelée.

At 4,600 feet, Mont Pelée is one of the tallest volcanoes in the Caribbean. It last erupted in 1902, killing some 30,000 people in just two minutes.

The impressionist painter Paul Gauguin lived in Carbet after he was dismissed from a job working on the Panama Canal.

Martinique Passage

Maco 12
Grand-Rivière
Anse-Céron 11 Habitation Céron
Mont Pelée
Le Prêcheur 10
Le Morne Rouge 9
N2
Rade de St-Pierre
8 St-Pierre
D1
Musée Gauguin 7
Neisson Distillery 7
Carbet 6
Aqualand 5 Morne Vert
N2
Bellefontaine 3
Case-Pilot

Caribbean Sea

0 _____ 5 mi
0 _____ 5 km

KEY

- Beaches
- **1** Exploring Sights
- **1** Hotels & Restaurants

Joie de vivre is the credo in this French enclave, which is often characterized as a Caribbean suburb of Paris. Exotic fruit grows on the volcanoes' forested flanks amid a profusion of wild orchids and hibiscus. The sheer lushness of it all inspired the tropical paintings of one-time resident Paul Gauguin.

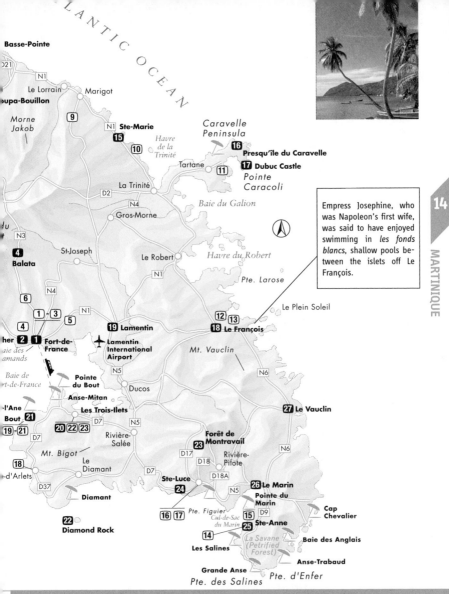

Basse-Pointe

ATLANTIC OCEAN

N1
Le Lorrain — Marigot
upa-Bouillon
D21

⑨

Morne
Jakob

N1 Ste-Marie
⑮
⑩

Havre
de la
Trinité

La Trinité

D2

N4

Gros-Morne

du
N3

⑷
Balata

St-Joseph

N4

⑥

Le Robert

N1

① - ③
⑤

N1

⑷

her ② ① Fort-de-
aie des France
amands

Baie de
rt-de-France

Pointe
du Bout

Anse-Mitan

l'Ane
Bout ㉑

⑲ - ㉑

D7

Mt. Bigot

⑱
-d'Arlets

D37

⑲ Lamentin
✈ Lamentin
International
Airport

N5

Ducos

Les Trois-Ilets

⑳ ㉒ ㉓

Rivière-
Salée

Le
Diamant

Diamant

㉒
Diamond Rock

Caravelle
Peninsula

⑯ Presqu'île du Caravelle

Tartane ⑰ Dubuc Castle
⑪ Pointe
Caracoli

Baie du Galion

Havre du Robert

Pte. Larose

Empress Josephine, who
was Napoleon's first wife,
was said to have enjoyed
swimming in *les fonds
blancs*, shallow pools between the islets off Le
François.

Le Plein Soleil

⑫ ⑬
⑱ Le François

Mt. Vauclin

N6

㉗ Le Vauclin

Forêt de
㉓ Montravail

D17

D18

Rivière-
Pilote

D7

Ste-Luce
㉔

D18A

⑯ ⑰ Pte. Figuier

N5

㉖ Le Marin

Pointe du
Marin

⑮ D9

Cap
Chevalier

Cul-de-Sac
du Marin ㉕ Ste-Anne

⑭

Les Salines

Grande Anse

Pte. des Salines

La Savane
(Petrified
Forest)

Baie des Anglais

Anse-Trabaud

Pte. d'Enfer

14

MARTINIQUE

TOP 4 REASONS TO VISIT MARTINIQUE

❶ A magical sensuality infuses
everything; it will awaken dormant
desires and fuel existing fires.

❷ A full roster of beautiful beaches will
let you enjoy sun and sand.

❸ Excellent French food, not to mention
French music and fashion make the
island a paradise for Francophiles.

❹ Hospitable, stylish, small hotels
abound, but there are big resorts,
too, if you want that scene.

MARTINIQUE PLANNER

Getting to Martinique

Getting to Martinique is still neither easy nor cheap. However, you now have several more options than in years past. American Eagle now flies daily from San Juan, and you can even go nonstop from New York–JFK (this flight is a weekly Club Med charter flight) or from Paris, of course. Connections are still available through St. Lucia, St. Maarten, and Guadeloupe on smaller island-hopper planes. It's also possible to get to Martinique by ferry from Dominica, Guadeloupe, or St. Lucia, a less desirable—though afford-able—option because of the travel time.

The modern Lamentin International Airport (FDF) is about a 15-minute taxi ride from Fort-de-France and some 40 minutes from Les Trois-llets peninsula.

Hassle Factor: Medium to High.

Activities

Martinique has plenty of **beaches** for relaxing, including some nice white-sand beaches south of Fort-de-France. However, you'll get a better taste of the island if you take part in the myriad activi-ties, which range from **sailing trips** to **wind-surfing**, from **fishing** to **canopy tours. Shoppers** will enjoy the fresh-from-France fashions available in Fort-de-France's bou-tiques and inexpensive French wines. Most hotels have entertain-ment during the high season, but there are also plenty of **night-spots** for dancing, though the crowds tend to be younger. Enjoying fine French and Creole **cuisine** is also at the top of many people's lists; the island has many won-derful restaurants.

On the Ground

Taxis in Martinique are expensive, so airport transfer costs must become a part of your vacation budget. From the airport to Fort-de-France you'll pay at least €30; from the airport to Pointe du Bout, about €35; and to Tartane, about €40. A 40% surcharge is levied between 7 PM and 6 AM and on Sunday. This means that if you arrive at night, depending on where your hotel is, it may be cheaper (although not safer) to rent a car from the airport and keep it for 24 hours than to take a taxi to your hotel.

Renting a Car

It's worth the hassle to rent a car—if for only a day or two—so that you can explore more of the island. Just be pre-pared for a manual shift. Traffic jams often occur on steep mountainous inclines that will necessitate the deft use of clutch, gas pedal, and emergency brake, and then it will inevitably rain. Renting a car is also expensive, about €70 per day or €330 per week (unlimited mileage) for a manual shift; the cost can be as much as €84 per day for an automatic, particularly during the high season. Automatics are usually in short supply, so they should be reserved in advance. You may save money by waiting to book your car rental on the island for a reduced weekly rate from a local agency. There's an extra charge if you drop the car off at the airport, having rented it somewhere else on the island.

A valid U.S. driver's license is needed to rent a car for up to 20 days. After that, you'll need an International Driver's Permit. U.K. citizens can use their EU licenses, since Martinique is a départe-ment of France.

Where to Stay

Martinique's accommodations range from tiny inns called relais créoles to splashy tourist resorts—some all-inclusive—and restored plantation houses. Several hotels are clustered in Point du Bout on Les Trois-Îlets peninsula, which is connected to Fort-de-France by ferry. Other clusters are in Ste-Luce and Le François, but other hotels and relais can be found all over the island. Since Martinique is the largest of the Windward Islands, this can mean a substantial drive to your hotel after a long flight or ferry trip. You may want to stay closer to the airport on your first night.

TYPES OF LODGINGS

There are only a few **deluxe properties** on the island. Those that lack megastar ratings offer an equally appealing mixture of charisma, hospitality, and French style. **Larger hotels** have the busy, slightly frenetic feel that the French seem to like. Groups and large families can save money by renting a **villa**, but the language barrier and need for a car can make this a less desirable option.

Hotel & Restaurant Costs

Assume that hotels operate on the European Plan (**EP**—with no meals) unless we specify that they use either the Continental Plan (**CP**—with a Continental breakfast), Breakfast Plan (**BP**—with full breakfast), or the Modified American Plan (**MAP**—with breakfast and dinner). Other hotels may offer the Full American Plan (**FAP**—including all meals but no drinks) or may be All-Inclusive (**AI**—with all meals, drinks, and most activities).

WHAT IT COSTS in Euros

	$$$$	$$$	$$	$	¢
Restaurants	over €30	€20–$30	€12–$20	€8–$12	under €8
Hotels*	over €350	€250–€350	€150–€250	€80–€150	under €80
Hotels**	over €450	€350–€450	€250–€350	€125–€250	under €125

*EP, BP, CP **AI, FAP, MAP
Restaurant prices are for a main course at dinner and include tax and a 15% service charge. Hotel prices are per night for a double room in high season, excluding taxes, 10% service charge, and meal plans (except at all-inclusives).

When to Go

High season runs from mid-November through May, and the island can be quiet the rest of the year, with some hotels closing down for months, particularly in September and October. Those places that remain open offer significant discounts.

14

Martinique's **Carnival** begins in January and runs until Lent, not unlike Mardi Gras in New Orleans. About 20 days into Lent there's a mini-Carnival called **Mi-carême;** this one-day hiatus from abstinence of parties and dances before sober times return until Easter. Early August sees the **Tour des Yoles Rondes** point-to-point yawl race. In odd-numbered years, the early-December **Jazz à la Martinique** festival usually draws a wide range of international talent, including such top performers as Branford Marsalis.

By Eileen
Robinson Smith

I AM FASCINATED BY THE INGENUITY of the sculpture configured from a rum cask. Classical music plays as a heady aroma comes from the distillery's wooden barrels, where the aged *rhum doré* I sip has been for 12 years. Here on Martinique's lush north coast, rum is produced like vintage wine, thanks in part to the volcanic soil. Cloud-capped Mount Pelée looms behind the plantation's greathouse, which for centuries existed peacefully under the shadow of the Caribbean's most impressive volcano. In 1902, when the mountain erupted violently, its molten lava destroyed the estate, but the cane fields were replanted and the operation lived on. This *habitation* is not just a history lesson but a stirring example of human tenacity in the face of adversity, of how to pull yourself up by the bootstraps. *Salud!*

Numerous scattered ruins and other historical monuments reflect the richness of Martinique's sugarcane plantocracy, of *rhum* and the legacy of slavery. The aristocratic planters are gone, but some things haven't changed so much. The island's economy depends on *les bananes* (bananas), *l'ananas* (pineapples), cane sugar, rum, fishing, and even— *voilà*—tourism, though it is not the lifeblood of the island. Martinicans will be glad you came, but there's no gushing welcome. Most islanders just go about their business, with thousands employed in government jobs offering more paid holidays than most Americans can imagine. Martinicans enjoy their time off, celebrating everything from *le fin de la semaine* (the weekend) to Indian feast days, sailboat races, carnival, and even All Saints' Day, which is fast becoming like our Halloween.

Christopher Columbus first sighted this gorgeous island in 1502, when it was inhabited by the fierce Caraïbes, who had terrorized the peace-loving Arawaks. The Arawaks called their home Madinina (the Isle of Flowers), and for good reason. Exotic wild orchids, frangipani, anthurium, jade vines, flamingo flowers, and hundreds of vivid varieties of hibiscus still thrive here.

Though the actual number of French residents does not exceed 15% of the total population, Martinique is still a part of France, an overseas *département* to be exact, and French is the official language, though the vast majority of the residents also speak Creole. In colonial days, Martinique was the administrative, social, and cultural center of the French Antilles, a rich, aristocratic island, famous for its beautiful women. The island even gave birth to an empress, Napoléon's Joséphine. It saw the full flowering of a plantocracy, with servants and soirees, wine cellars and snobbery. Islanders still enjoy a fairly high standard of living, and the per-capita GNP is the highest of any island in the French Antilles.

Martinique is the largest stronghold of the *békés*—the descendants of the original French planters—and they are still the privileged class on any of the French-Caribbean islands. Many control Martinique's most profitable businesses from banana plantations and rum distilleries to car dealerships. The island's élite dress in designer outfits straight off the Paris runways. In the airport waiting room, you can almost always tell the *Martiniquaises* by the well-tailored cut of their fashionable clothes.

Located between the Caribbean and the Atlantic, Martinique is 425 square mi (1,101 square km) in size and 72 mi (120 km) south of sister island Guadeloupe. English-speaking Dominica is Martinique's nearest neighbor, 15 mi (25 km) to the north. South is St. Lucia, 22 mi (37 km) away.

Of the island's 392,000 inhabitants, 100,000 live in Fort de France and its environs. Martinique has 34 separate municipalities; some little fishing villages on the lush north coast seem to be stuck in time.

If you believe in magic, Martinique has it, as well as a sensuality that fosters romance. It has become known as the island of *revenants*, those who always return. *Et pourquoi non?*

Where to Stay

14

Larger hotels usually include a large buffet breakfast of eggs, fresh fruit, cheese, yogurt, croissants, baguettes, jam, and café au lait. Smaller *relais* (inns) often have open-air terrace kitchenettes. Almost all have both smoking and no-smoking rooms, so ask if this is important to you. Also, most do not have elevators and many are built on hillsides, so if you have issues with stair-climbing, be sure to ask about that, too. A number of resorts translate their euro-based rates into dollars to the benefit of Americans, who then save about 20%. Be sure to ask about this islandwide promotion, which was ongoing at this writing.

VILLAS &
CONDOMINIUMS

If you're staying a week or longer, you can often save money by taking a self-catering vacation to Martinique, renting a villa or apartment by the sea, but don't forget to add in the cost of a car rental to your vacation budget. The more upscale rentals come with French-speaking maids and/or cooks. **French Caribbean International** (☎ 800/322–2223 ⊕ www.frenchcaribbean.com), an English-speaking reservation service operated for decades by Gerard Hill, can help you with both villa rentals and hotel rooms. At the **Villa Rental Service** (☎ 0596/71–56–11 🖷 0596/63–11–64) an English-speaking staffer can help you find a home, a villa, or an apartment to rent for a week or a month. Most properties are in the south of the island near good beaches.

South of Fort-de-France

★ $$$$ Cap Est Lagoon Resort & Spa. A member of the Relais & Châteaux group, Martinique's most exclusive resort has brought the wealthy, international set back. However—and despite some genial staff members—it's more beautiful than it is warm and hospitable. Contemporary villas (some bi-level) have a Franco-Caribbean design, with Southeast Asian influences; most have a view of the shallow, green, crystalline lagoon. Tip: The less expensive garden rooms have a water view from their second-floor bedrooms but not from the ground floor. All suites have CD/DVDs and plasma TVs; 36 have private plunge pools. Discriminating guests (and nonguests) can self-indulge at the elegant Spa by Guerlain; from the music to the minimalist decor, it's a soothing place to enjoy professional treatments. ⊠ *Quartier Cap Est, Le François 97240* ☎ *0596/54–80–80 or 800/735–2478* 🖷 *0596/54–96–00* ⊕ *www.capest.com* ⇲ *50 suites* ⚒ *2 restaurants, room service, minibars, cable TV,*

CLOSE UP

A How-To for Dining in Martinique

DINING IN MARTINIQUE is a delightful culinary experience, but as with driving here, it is best to get some directions before you head out. First of all, as in France, *entrées* are appetizers; the main courses will usually be labeled as follows: *poissons* (fish); *viandes* (meat); or *principal plats* (literally, main courses). You will notice that the appetizers are almost as expensive as the mains—and if the appetizer is foie gras you'll pay just as much as for a main course, but it is oh so worth it.

Entrecote is a sirloin steak, usually cut too thin. A filet mignon is a rarity, but you will see *filet mignon du porc*, which is pork tenderloin. *Ouassous* are incredible freshwater crayfish. Don't be alarmed when they are served with their heads on. Similarly, if a fish dish does not specify fillet, you will be looking into its eyes while carving flesh from its bones.

Every respectable restaurant has an admirable wine *carte*, and the offerings will be almost completely French, with few half bottles. Wines by the glass are often swill and are best avoided.

Finally, don't ever embarrass yourself by asking for a doggie bag: you will be considered gauche. The exception is at Sapori d'Italia, where pasta portions are magnanimous. Owner Valentina has purchased microwaveable doggie boxes for her esteemed American clients!

---

in-room DVD, in-room data ports, tennis court, pool, gym, spa, beach, dock, snorkeling, windsurfing, boating, fishing, 2 bars, laundry service, concierge, Internet room, meeting room, car rental, helipad ⊟ *AE, MC, V* ❍ *BP.*

$$$$ 🏨 **Sofitel Bakoua Martinique.** Impressive wrought-iron gates open to what is, undoubtedly, still one of Martinique's best resorts. Formerly an estate, the original structure has that East Indian Company look with cane and teak plantation-style furnishings and terra-cotta tiles. From the circular bar and the adjacent pool, the hillside view of the yachts in the bay and Fort-de-France is magical. Plush new down pillows, duvets, and European linens, as well as comfy window seats, have made the rather small beach-level rooms commodious; the same updates were being made to all rooms at this writing. The patios now have classy teak furniture. Employee attitudes, including those of the long-termers, have substantially improved, and management is working hard on weaknesses on the service end. Laudible nightly entertainment makes this one of the island's social centers. ⊠ *Pointe du Bout, Les Trois-Ilets 97229* ☎ *0596/66–02–02* 🖶 *0596/66–00–41* ⊕ *www.sofitel.com* ↘ *133 rooms, 6 suites* ⌂ *3 restaurants, minibars, cable TV, 2 tennis courts, pool, beach, snorkeling, boating, 2 bars, shops, babysitting, Internet room, business services, meeting rooms* ⊟ *AE, DC, MC, V* ❍ *BP.*

$$$ 🏨 **Club Med Buccaneer's Creek.** After a year's closure, one of the Caribbean's oldest Clubs has reopened with a huge splash after a renovation that cost more than $50 million. What had been a spartan, outdated resort has been reborn as one of the most upscale villages in the French chain. Its renaissance is key to Club Med's new strategy of meeting the more refined demands of both American and international travelers. Everything is plush and more plush. The expansion added 44 suites, a full-service spa, a floating bar, and a huge seaside pool. Situated on one of the island's best beaches, this Club was once adults-only; now children are welcomed, although there is no Mini-Club. ⊠ *Pointe du Marin, Ste-Anne 97227* ☎ *0596/76–72–72* 🖷 *0596/76–83–36* ⊕ *www. clubmed.com* ↪ *249 rooms, 44 suites* ⌂ *3 restaurants, in-room safes, minibars, cable TV, Wi-Fi, 6 tennis courts, pool, health club, spa, beach, windsurfing, boating, waterskiing, volleyball, bar, nightclub, laundry service, Internet room* ⊟ *AE, MC, V* ⦿| *AI.*

14

★ **$$** 🖾 **Le Plein Soleil.** This chic hideaway, long one of our favorites, closed in April 2006 and will not reopen until November 1. The existing accommodations in creole *cases* (cottages) will be enlarged and the terraces expanded; all bathrooms will be renovated. The decor throughout will be enlivened with the latest offerings from France, Bangkok, and Miami. Within the hibiscus, ferns, and yellow ginger of the lush grounds will be four new deluxe, bi-level bungalows. The terrace restaurant will also be expanded. ⊠ *Villa Lagon Sarc, Pointe Thalemont, Le François 97240* ☎ *0596/38–07–77* 🖷 *0596/65–58–13* ⊕ *www.sasi.fr/pleinsoleil* ↪ *16 bungalows* ⌂ *Restaurant, pool, Internet room* ⊟ *MC, V* ⦿| *EP.*

$–$$ 🖾 **Manoir de Beauregard.** Built in the 18th century, this plantation house has thick stone walls, mullioned windows, and loads of character. The three original rooms upstairs in the manor house are the best: Room 1 is lovely, with toile fabrics, but Room 3 is a huge space, with wood-beam ceilings, an antique wicker chaise, rockers, and a four-poster bed. The rooms in the modern annex lack charisma but are freshly painted. The new bungalows, built of rich, Brazilian hardwood, are far better. The restaurant is well regarded. The hotel, which is owned by the St. Cyr family, hosts many local weddings and art exhibits. ⊠ *Chemin des Salines, Ste-Anne 97227* ☎ *0596/76–73–40* 🖷 *0596/76–93–24* ⊕ *www. manoirdebeauregard.com* ↪ *11 rooms, 3 bungalows* ⌂ *Restaurant, pool, bar* ⊟ *MC, V* ⦿| *CP* ☉ *Closed Sept. and Oct.*

⟳ **$** 🖾 **Amandiers Resort.** This complex of three once-independent hotels, which share facilities, is on a nice stretch of beach and offers rooms at the right price. Amyris—the best, with creative sponge painting in the lobby and a new tropical color for each building—is all junior suites; with enviable views of the idyllic cove, superior rooms are just that and have kitchenettes to boot. Also on the beach are the more simple Amandiers rooms (if you go this route, choose a superior room). The comfy Caribia apartments, across the street from the two beachfront hotels, have one bedroom and sofa beds, with terrace kitchens and garden views, and a small but well-stocked commissary. ⊠ *Quartier Désert, Ste-Luce 97228* ☎ *0596/62–12–00* 🖷 *0596/62–12–10* ⊕ *www.karibea.com* ↪ *116 rooms, 108 junior suites, 75 apartments* ⌂ *2 restaurants, in-room safes, some kitchenettes, refrigerators, cable TV, Wi-Fi, tennis court, 3 pools, beach, snorkeling, 2 bars, children's programs (ages 4–11), Internet room, meeting rooms, car rental* ⊟ *AE, MC, V* ⦿| *EP.*

☪ $ 🗒 **Pierre & Vacances.** Family-oriented, this self-contained village is a happening place, with good music and tropical flowers in the pillared lobby. Energetic (but not annoying) staffers make the sports really enjoyable, whether it's *aqua gym* or scuba diving. If you overexert yourself, have a reflexology massage with essential oils. The amphitheater is the setting for many *serious* parties and concerts—P.V. has a large fun quotient. All the apartments, which are soundproof and have kitchenettes on the terrace, are attractive but not luxurious. The best are those on the higher floors; although there are no elevators, it's worth the climb for the knockout views. ✉ *Pointe Philippeau, Lieu-dit "Pavillon," Ste-Luce 97228* ☎ *0596/62–12–62* 📠 *0596/62–12–63* 🌐 *www.pierrevacances.com* ↳ *337 apartments* 🍴 *3 restaurants, grocery, in-room safes, kitchenettes, cable TV, tennis court, pool, 2 beaches, dive shop, snorkeling, jet skiing, 3 bars, shop, children's programs (ages 3–12), car rental* ═ *AE, MC, V* 🍽 *EP* ⊘ *Closed Sept.–Oct. 12.*

Fort-de-France & Points North

$$ 🗒 **La Valmenière Hôtel.** This high-rise, perched on a hillside overlooking Fort-de-France, is the closest to the airport (5 mi [8 km]) and the port and is ideal for first- or last-night stays. It's French moderne, wired for work, has an efficient and caring staff and management, and is constantly upgrading. Consequently, it stays well occupied with business travelers and sojourners. The staff is efficient and caring. Leisure time can be spent in the fun bar-brasserie, and you can loll in the infinity pool and mock the traffic below or bubble in the Jacuzzi on the solarium level. Friday night is particularly convivial with a piano man playing. Inquire about the weekend leisure packages. ✉ *Av. des Arawaks, Fort-de-France 97200* ☎ *0596/75–75–75* 📠 *0596/75–69–70* 🌐 *www.karibea.com* ↳ *116 rooms, 4 suites* 🍴 *2 restaurants, room service, in-room safes, minibars, satellite TV, in-room data ports, Wi-Fi, pool, gym, bar, shop, dry cleaning, laundry service, Internet room, business services, meeting rooms, car rental* ═ *AE, MC, V* 🍽 *EP.*

$ 🗒 **Le Domaine St. Aubin.** A "pick" that is destined to be a hit, this former estate, which has reopened under new ownership, is perched on a hilltop overlooking the sea. At first glance, it is a breathtaking sight. An interesting couple, who gave up Paris for the husband's homeland, has lovingly restored the 19th-century creole manor house with six guest rooms; five more rooms are in a historic building adjacent to the big house. Nine others were being carved out of the original stables at this writing and were slated for completion in November 2006. The restaurant is elegant, with fine china and a fixed-price menu that is one of Martinique's best culinary options. This may be the only island inn with wheelchair-accessible rooms, even a special hydraulic chair for the pool. €=$. ✉ *Petite Rivière Salée, off Rte. 1, La Trinité, 97220* ☎ *0596/69–34–77 or 0696/40–99–59* 📠 *0596/69–41–14* 🌐 *www.ledomainesaintaubin.com* ↳ *11 rooms* 🍴 *Restaurant, pool, meeting room; no room TVs* ═ *MC, V* 🍽 *EP.*

$ 🗒 **Engoulevent.** This small B&B in the suburbs about 10 minutes from Fort-de-France has two deluxe suites with contemporary decor; all have private baths, Wi-Fi, and private telephone lines. Breakfast is lovely, and you can also add dinner, a gastronomic table d'hôte with wine, sometimes for as little as €20. Personalized service is a hallmark; indeed, Madame is sometimes *overly* attentive. The best news for Americans: the use of a late-model, *automatic* Citroën can be included in the deal for €38. ✉ *22 rte. de l'Union Didier, Fort-de-France 97200* ☎ *0596/64–96–00* 🖷 *0596/64–97–84, 0696/45–56–36* ⊕ *www.engoulevent.com* ⤶ *5 suites* ⟡ *Dining room, minibars, cable TV, Wi-Fi, in-room data ports, pool, gym, hot tub, billiards, airport shuttle* ▭ *MC, V* ⟲ *3-night minimum* ⎮◎⎮ *BP.*

$ ▦ **La Plantation Leyritz.** A 17th-century sugar estate on 16 lush acres is a restful retreat that hasn't looked this good since its glory days. Rushing water cascades over the old wheel at the rear of the fieldstone restaurant, which now houses a conference room, too. Low-budget groups can triple up in the renovated single-male former slave quarters. Better digs are the simple cottages with rough-wood beams and (some) mahogany four-posters. A museum showcases Leyritz's famous banana figurines and vignettes of how rooms would have looked in centuries past. Tour groups create a buzz when they come for lunch in the restaurant, where the menu reflects fresh local produce. The resort is isolated and more than an hour from the airport, so you will need a car to explore the lush north coast. ✉ *Basse-Pointe 97218* ☎ *0596/78–53–92* 🖷 *0596/78–92–44* ⊕ *www.karibea.com* ⤶ *50 rooms* ⟡ *Restaurant, cable TV, tennis court, pool, bar* ▭ *AE, MC, V* ⎮◎⎮ *EP.*

$ ▦ **Squash Hôtel.** This well-run, suburban business hotel is ideally located if you need to sleep close to the airport (15 minutes away), and it's a good base for "doing" Fort-de-France (about 10 minutes by car, or there's a bus just down the hill for €1). The lobby is done in blue and white, with attractive wicker furnishings. Front-desk staff is efficient and bilingual. Although rooms aren't luxurious, they are cheery and bright, with a fresh look and white wicker furnishings. Breakfast is a bountiful buffet at the terrace restaurant by the pool. Afterward you may be tempted to stay put and enjoy the panorama of the sea and the city. ✉ *3 bd. de la Marne, Fort-de-France 97200* ☎ *0596/72–80–80* 🖷 *0596/63–00–74* ⊕ *www.karibea.com* ⤶ *102 rooms, 2 suites, 1 business suite* ⟡ *Restaurant, some minibars, cable TV, Wi-Fi, pool, gym, squash, bar, Internet room, business services, meeting rooms, car rental* ▭ *AE, DC, MC, V* ⎮◎⎮ *BP.*

¢–$ ▦ **La Caravelle.** The Mahler family have transformed this simple hotel with their energy and talents, their furnishings, and their artwork from Africa, where patriarch Jean-Paul worked for several decades as a hotel manager. Rooms now have TVs and a/c. The new, one-bedroom suite above the restaurant is handsome; several "family" rooms connect; and the refurbished apartment conveniently has two baths. There is a feel-good breakfast, with fresh local bread and yogurt that is served—as is dinner—in the terrace restaurant, with its awesome view of mountains and ocean. New teak chairs and tables there look smart, as does the new overhanging red tin roof. ✉ *Anse L'Etang, Tartane, La Trinité 97220* ☎ *0596/58–07–32* 🖷 *0596/58–07–90* ⊕ *www.hotel-la-caravelle-martinique.com* ⤶ *14 studios, 1 1-bedroom apartment* ⟡ *Restaurant, kitchenettes, satellite TV* ▭ *MC, V* ⎮◎⎮ *CP.*

14

Where to Eat

Martinique cuisine is a fusion of African and French and is certainly more international and sophisticated than that of its immediate island neighbors. The influx of young chefs, who favor a contemporary, less-caloric approach, has brought exciting innovations to the table. This *haute nouvelle creole* cuisine also emphasizes local products, predominantly starchy tubers like malanga, plaintains, white yams, and island sweet potatoes and vegetables like breadfruit, yucca, christophene, and taro leaves. Many creole dishes have been Franco-fied, transformed into mousselines, terrines, and gratins, with creamy sauces. And then there's the bountiful harvest of the sea—*lambi* (conch), *langouste* (clawless Caribbean lobster), and dozens of species of fish predominate, but you can also see *ouassous* (freshwater crayfish, which are like jumbo prawns).

Some local creole specialties are *accras* (cod or vegetable fritters), *crabes farcis* (stuffed land crab), and *feroce* (avocado stuffed with saltfish and farina). You can fire up fish and any other dish with a hit of hot *chien* (dog) sauce. Not to worry—it's made from onions, shallots, hot peppers, oil, and vinegar. To cool your jets, have a 'ti punch—four parts white rum and one part sugarcane syrup.

Finding a cheap American-style bite for lunch is not impossible. The supermarkets often have snack bars that serve sandwiches, as do the bakeries and larger gas stations like Esso and Total. *Les supermarchés,* such as Champion, have deli sections that have sinful French *fromages* and luscious pâtés, as well as French wines for significantly less than at home; add a long, thin baguette, and you have lunch. DeliFrance, the French deli chain, has locations in most tourist areas. And there are crêperies and pizza shacks, even an African pizza place in Le François. Menu prices in general will seem high but do include tax and service. Prix-fixe menus, sometimes with wine, can be a relative bargain.

WHAT TO WEAR For dinner, casual resort wear is appropriate. Generally, men do not wear jackets and ties, as they did in decades past, but they do wear collared shirts. Women typically wear light cotton sundresses, short or long. At dinnertime, beach attire is too casual for most restaurants. Nice shorts are okay for lunch, depending on the venue, but jeans and shorts aren't acceptable at dinner. Keep in mind that in Martinique lunch is usually a wonderful three-course, two-hour affair.

South of Fort-de-France

CARIBBEAN ✕ **Chez Carole.** Carole, who spent eight years in Toulouse, now cooks
¢–$ her island's creole specialties in Fort-de-France, across from the market. Tourists often pass by the loud hawkers to settle here, where they will be welcomed in English and may feel confident in their choice, as suggested by the tourism awards on display. Creole specialties include accras, fricassee of octopus and lambi (just say "*no plus salé*" to reduce the excess saltiness), crayfish, chicken Columbo, and grilled whole fish. Cruise-ship passengers love the fresh squeezed juices (with rum, if you like) and coconut milk shakes. Dollars and traveler's checks work

equally well here. ⊠ *Le Grand Marché, Rue Isambert, Fort-de-France* ☎ *0696/44–12–31* 🖃 *No credit cards* ⊗ *Closed Sun. No dinner.*

FRENCH
$$–$$$

✕ **Le Bleu Salé.** In a centuries-old house just before the harbor, Alain Cherkaoui, who once owned 'Tí Plage, is now presenting a fine-dining experience at a moderate price. The shadowy light cast by the Moroccan lanterns plays against the dark wood tables, with white linen runners, candlesticks, and white geometric plates creating an elegant atmosphere. Appetizers are delicious and inexpensive: cream of pumpkin soup, sashimi with ginger sauce, and mussels in garlic butter. Save room for the mains, including duck breast with honey and thyme sauce or, my favorite, prawns flambéed in pastis. On Sunday nights it's all about bouillabaisse creole. ⊠ *11 rue Félix Eboué, Anse-d'Arlets* ☎ *0596/ 68–62–79* 🖃 *V* ⊗ *Closed Mon. No lunch.*

BARBECUE
☾ $$

✕ **Le Grange Inn.** Nearly every item is cooked over the open grill: top-quality meats, jumbo crayfish (fresh and saltwater), scallops (St-Jacques), and fresh fish, with a choice of sauces, from a smoky *chien* to Provençale, with sides like garlicky haricots verts or a plantain gratin. Start with the house-made foie gras with onion jam. The wine list is inviting, and the grilled gingerbread with coconut dressing is an original dessert. Owner Phillipe loves kids, and their menu is fun. This is all about terrace dining, although there is now an air-conditioned dining room too. If you don't want to eat, just order a glass of champagne at the circular brick bar and listen to the hip music. ⊠ *Village Créole, Pointe du Bout, Les Trois-Ilets* ☎ *0596/66–01–66* 🖃 *AE, MC, V.*

ECLECTIC
$$

✕ **Les Passagers du Vent.** For years now rotating shows of art naïf paintings and creative contemporary cuisine have drawn a rather young and artsy, mostly French crowd. You can listen to cool music while you dine in the atmospheric red-brick bistro with an open-air terrace, shuttered windows, and wooden ceilings and floors. The proprietor is its stability, as is Jean-Claude, the superwaiter, but the chef has changed again. The menu continues to be creative, but on the whole, appetizers are better than main courses, particularly the meat. The seafood is the best, like curried *mérou* (grouper) poached in coconut milk and ginger. The dessert choices are laudable, including delicious profiteroles with mango sorbet. A prix-fixe lunch is a good deal. ⊠ *27 rue de l'Impératrice Joséphine, Les Trois-Ilets* ☎ *0596/68–42–11* 🖃 *AE, MC, V* ⊗ *Closed Sun. No lunch Mon. or Sat.*

FRENCH
★ $$$$

✕ **Le Plein Soleil Restaurant.** An original, contemporary menu cements this restaurant's well-deserved reputation. At lunch, the terrace has a hilltop sea view, and by night the mood is romantic, the service fine, the music heady—direct from Paris. The appetizer might be the freshest fish marinated in coconut milk with dashes of pureed avocado. A special *plat* is sliced duck breast draped over pear poached in a port wine sauce; a trilogy of pureed vegetable quenelles decorates the plate. Your finale might be an artistic cheese plate: goat, brie, and genuine Roquefort, encircled by a fan of fruit and bursts of pink peppercorns. ⊠ *Hôtel Le Plein Soleil, Villa Lagon Sarc, Pointe Thalemont, Le François* ☎ *0596/ 38–07–77* 🖄 *Reservations essential* 🖃 *MC, V* ⊗ *No dinner Sun.*

14

★ **$$$-$$$$** ✕ **Le Béleme.** This is the special-occasion restaurant for well-heeled residents and visitors who come to enjoy innovative French cuisine served in a contemporary setting. Alas, be prepared for sticker shock and, often, petite portions. A complementary *amuse-bouche* (literally, "mouth amuser," meaning a small morsel) may save you an appetizer, although the lobster ravioli is luscious. The *tatin de foie gras* and caramelized green bananas with a shallot-and-lime confit can still be had with 24 hours' notice. The menu changes seasonally and features such creations as roast guinea hen with foie gras and morrel mushrooms, dramatically presented by a bevy of servers. Lunch here or at the newly expanded beach restaurant is special, too, and provides a more affordable alternative. ✉ *Cap Est Lagoon Resort & Spa, Quartier Cap Est, Le François* ☎ *0596/ 54–80–80* ⚲ *Reservations essential* ▭ *AE, MC, V.*

ITALIAN ✕ **Sapori d'Italia.** The quality of the imported ingredients at this authen-
★ **$-$$$** tic Italian restaurant, from the beef carpaccio to the mussels gratiné, is significant. You'll need two people to finish off the "tasting" of three pastas, which can include raviolis with walnut sauce and the homemade tagliatelle with smoked salmon, cream, and crème fraîche. The wine list is a good mix of Italian and French vintages, with many half-bottles. Finish with an espresso and a perfect tiramisu or the warm apple tart made by the caring Milanese owner, Valentina, who sings like an angel in Italian and Creole. And she loves the American people! ✉ *Village Créole, Pointe du Bout, Les Trois-Ilets* ☎ *0596/66–15–85* ▭ *AE, MC, V* ☾ *Closed Wed. and 3 wks in June. No lunch Tues. July–Oct.*

THAI ✕ **La Case Thai.** This restaurant is as soothing as a spa, with a lily pond,
★ **$$** tumbled pottery, orchids suspended from the trees, and sophisticated music. Not so the bumpy dirt road. But all is forgotten when you join the animated crowd for a house cocktail of lychee liqueur, passion fruit, and two rums. Stagger multiple small courses of all your Thai favorites, making sure that someone orders something that comes in a pineapple. If something doesn't make your mouth go zing, you can ask the Thai chefs to heat it up. Afterward, explore the fascinating boutique with everything from Southeast Asian furnishings to silver jewelry. ✉ *Les Trois-Ilets* ☎ *0596/48–13–25* ⚲ *Reservations essential* ▭ *AE, MC, V* ☾ *Closed Sun. and Mon.*

Fort-de-France & Points North

CAFÉS ✕ **Mille Et Une Brindilles.** At this trendy salon you can order an aromatic
★ **$$** pot of tea in flavors like vanilla or mango, or a glass of wine. You'll find a litany of tapenades, olive cakes, flans, couscous, and other items for lunch. Fred, the bubbly Parisian who is both chef and proprietor, is the queen of terrines and can make a delicious tart (like Roquefort and pear) or pâté out of any vegetable or fish. Saturday brunch is very social and even includes a beverage for €20. The best-ever desserts, like the Amadéus—as appealing as the classical music that plays—and *moelleux au chocolat* (a rich chocolate and coffee pudding), are what you would want after your last supper on Earth. ✉ *27 rte. de Didier, Didier, Fort-de-France* ☎ *0596/71–75–61* ▭ *No credit cards* ☾ *Closed Sun. and Mon. No dinner.*

CARIBBEAN
★ $–$$

✕ **Le Colibri.** Gregarious Joel Paladino is lovingly continuing a family culinary tradition with this little local spot in the island's northeastern reaches with picturesque ocean views. You'll be impressed by the cuisine his lovely twin sisters prepare. Begin with deep-green callaloo soup with crab or delicious conch pie; then move on to grilled lobster with a christophene gratin (assuming you don't mind the splurge), or the rabbit baked with prunes (if you do). Some of the traditional creole dishes, like pigeon stuffed with coconut sauce, lambi fricassee, and *cochon au lait* (suckling pig), are favorites on Sunday. There's always a lower-price plat du jour. ⊠ *4 rue des Colibris, Morne-des-Esses, Ste-Marie* ☎ *0596/ 69–91–95* ▭ *AE, MC, V* ☾ *Closed Mon.*

FRENCH
$$–$$$$
FodorsChoice
★

✕ **La Belle Epoque.** In a wealthy suburb high above Fort-de-France, this antiques-filled dining room offers a truly fine-dining experience, from the professional service to the sparkling crystal stemware. The food is divine, and now a young, talented chef reigns who has modernized a menu steeped in classical French tradition. The quality of meat is excellent, particularly the lamb and even such hard-to-find cuts as sweetbreads. Also, the menu has an entire page devoted to foie gras, including an incredibly delicious portion encrusted in blue poppy seeds with red vine-leaf caramel. The prix-fixe can help keep costs down; check the daily offering and its price. Owner Martine, a statuesque blonde, makes this a personality palace. ⊠ *97 rte. de Didier, Didier, Fort-de-France* ☎ *0596/ 64–41–19* ▭ *MC, V* ☾ *Closed Sun. No lunch Mon. or Sat.*

14

$$–$$$

✕ **Le Dôme.** Sepia lithographs of St-Pierre in its glory days adorn the walls of this gourmet restaurant with a panoramic view of Fort-de-France. The prix-fixe can be an especially good value, but the most intriguing dishes are à la carte. Cream of breadfruit soup with bacon, marinated salmon with Cythère plums, and shredded christophene rémoulade are all excellent starters. Main courses include grilled black salmon with a velvety asparagus sauce and a quality veal filet mignon with a rich morrel sauce. Ask about the specially priced designated wine of the month. Gents can finish with a stogie from *la cave à cigares* poolside. ⊠ *Hôtel Valmeniegre, top fl., av. des Arawaks, Fort-de-France* ☎ *0596/75–75–75* ▭ *AE, MC, V.*

$$–$$$

✕ **La Table de Mamy Nounou.** If you looked at its business card, you'd expect a creole menu served by an elderly island lady. Not! It is owned by a French family. The elegant Madame Mahler will greet you; her husband, Jean-Paul, presides as chef; and her son, Bastien, eloquently describes the menu in the king's English. Have an aperitif while you admire the view from the lounge decorated with fascinating African antiques. Savor the pumpkin velouté, and go on to the house-made foie gras with sauterne jelly. A main choice is a combination of fish, shrimp, and scallops with a cinnamon-cider sauce. Finish with the *marquise au chocolat*, with rum-soaked chestnuts, and a quality cigar. ⊠ *Anse L'Etang, Tartane, La Trinité* ☎ *0596/58–07–32* ▭ *MC, V.*

SEAFOOD
$–$$

✕ **Chez Les Pecheurs.** This is the kind of beach restaurant you search for but seldom find. It began when owner Palmont still made his living fishing. Now the pink-and-blue boat-of-the-boss is the best one bobbin'. People come for the fisherman's platter (the fresh catch) with a special red sauce, ripe tomatoes, and perfect red beans and rice too. Fresh shrimp on the barbie can usually be had by ordering a day in advance. Bottles of Neisson rum are plunked in front of a table of, say, French doctors taking a time-out from their medical conference. On Friday nights, local bands play, and on Saturday a DJ gets everyone up and dancing in the sand. ⊠ *Le Bord de Mer, Carbet* ☎ *0696/23–95–59* ⊟ *No credit cards.*

Beaches

All of Martinique's beaches are open to the public, but hotels charge a fee for nonguests to use changing rooms and facilities. There are no official nudist beaches, but topless bathing is prevalent. Unless you're an expert swimmer, steer clear of the Atlantic waters, except in the area of Cap Chevalier and the Caravelle Peninsula. The soft white-sand beaches are south of Fort-de-France; to the north, the beaches are silvery black volcanic sand. Some of the most pleasant beaches are around Ste-Anne, Ste-Luce, and Havre du Robert.

Anse Corps de Garde. On the southern Caribbean coast, this is one of the island's best long stretches of white sand. The public beach has picnic tables, restrooms, sea-grape trees, and crowds, particularly on weekends, when you can find plenty of wandering food vendors but no chairs for rent. The water is calm, with just enough wave action to remind you it's the sea. Farther down the beach are hotels, including Pierre & Vacances and the Amandiers Resort, but none rent chairs to the nonguests. To reach this public beach from Fort-de-France, you take a right exit before you get to the town of Ste-Luce. You first see signs for the Karibéa Hotels and then one for Corps de Garde, which is on the right. At the stop sign take a left. ⊠ *Ste-Luce.*

Anse-Mitan. This is not the French Riviera, though there are often yachts moored offshore, but it can be particularly fun on Sunday. Small, family-owned seaside restaurants are half hidden among palm trees and are footsteps from the lapping waves. Nearly all offer grilled lobster and some form of music, perhaps a zouk band or something you might hear in a Parisian park. Inexpensive waterfront hotels line the clean, golden beach, which has excellent snorkeling just offshore. Chaise lounges are available for rent from hotels for about €5. When you get to Pointe du Bout, take a left at the yellow office of Budget Rent-A-Car, then the next left up a hill, and park near the simple little white church. ⊠ *Pointe du Bout, Les Trois-Ilets.*

Anse Tartane. This patch of sand is on the wild side of the Caravelle Peninsula, where the cliffs meet the blue ocean. It's what the French call a *sauvage* (virgin) beach, and the only people you are likely to see are brave surfers who ride the high waves or (on the first half) some local families. The surf school here has taught many kids the ropes. Résidence Océane looks down on all of this action but doesn't have a restaurant. Turn right before you get to La Trinité, and follow the Route de Château past the Caravelle Hotel. Instead of following the signs to Résidence Oceane, veer left and go downhill when you see the ocean. The road runs right beside the beach. There are several bays and *pointes* here, but if you keep heading to the right, you can reach the surf school. ⊠ *Tartane.*

Diamant Beach. The island's longest beach has a splendid view of Diamond Rock, but the waters are rough, with lots of wave action. Often the beach is deserted, especially midweek, which is more reason to bathe with prudence. Happily, it's a great place for picnicking and beachcombing; there are shade trees aplenty and parking is abundant and free. The hospitable, family-run Diamant les Bains hotel is here, so you can drop by for food, water, and rum; if you eat lunch there, the management may let you wash off in the pool that looks out onto the beach. From Les Trois-Ilets, go in the direction of Rivière Salée, taking the secondary road to the east, toward Le Diamant. A coastal route, it leads to the beach. ⊠ *Le Diamant.*

Pointe du Bout. The beaches here are small, man-made, and lined with resorts, which include the Sofitel Bakoua. Each little strip is associated with its resident hotel, and security guards and gates make access difficult. However, across from the main pedestrian entrance to the marina, if you take a left—between the taxi stand and the Kalenda Hotel—then go left again, you will reach the Sofitel beach, which has especially nice facilities. If things are quiet—particularly during the week—one of the beach boys may rent you a chaise; otherwise, just plop your beach towel down, face forward, and enjoy the delightful view of the Fort-de-France skyline. The water is dead calm and quite shallow, but it eventually drops off if you swim out a bit. The Sofitel has several nice options for lunch and drinks. ⊠ *Pointe du Bout, Les Trois-Ilets.*

Pointe du Marin. Stretching north from Ste-Anne, this is a good windsurfing and waterskiing spot as well as a family beach, with restaurants, campsites, and clean facilities; a small fee is charged. Club Med is on the northern edge, and you can purchase a day pass. From Le Marin, take the coastal road to Ste-Anne. Make a right before town, toward Domaine de Belfond. You can see signs for Pointe du Marin. ⊠ *Marin.*

★ **Les Salines.** A short drive south of Ste-Anne brings you to a mile-long-plus cove lined with soft white sand and coconut palms. The beach is awash with families and children during holidays and on weekends but quiet and uncrowded during the week. The far end—away from the makeshift souvenir shops—is most appealing. The calm waters are safe for swimming, even for the kids. You can't rent chaise lounges, but there are showers. Food vendors roam the sand. From Le Marin, take the coastal road toward Ste-Anne. You will see signs for Les Salines. If you see the sign for Pointe du Marin, you have gone too far. ⊠ *Ste-Anne.*

Sports & the Outdoors

BOATING & SAILING   Don't even consider striking out on the rough Atlantic side of the island unless you're an experienced sailor. The Caribbean side is much calmer—more like a vast lagoon. You can rent Hobie Cats, Sunfish, and Sailfish by the hour from most hotel beach shacks. As for larger crafts, bareboat charters can be had for $1,900 to $7,000 a week, depending on the season and the size of the craft. The Windward Islands are a joy for experienced sailors, but the channels between islands are often windy and have high waves. You must have a sailing license or be able to prove your nautical prowess. You can always hire a skipper and crew. Prior to setting out, you can get itinerary suggestions; the safe ports in

Martinique are many. If you charter for a week, you can go south to St. Lucia or Grenada or north to Dominica, Guadeloupe and Les Saintes. One-way sailing to St. Martin or Antigua is a popular choice.

Moorings Antilles Françaises (⊠ Le Marin ☎ 0596/74–75–39, 888/952–8420 in U.S., 727/535–1446 outside U.S. 🖷 0596/74–76–44 ⊕ www. moorings.com), one of the largest bareboat operations in the world, has downsized its fleet to some 10 boats in Martinique, both catamarans and monohulls. Boats can be rented fully crewed and/or fully provisioned. **Punch Croisières** (⊠ Bd. Allègre, Le Marin ☎ 0596/74–89-18 🖷 0596/74–88–08 ⊕ www.punch-croisieres.com) is a local, French-owned charter company with a fleet of 15 sailboats, 13 of which are catamarans from 38 to 57 feet; they go out bareboat or crewed. **Sunsail** (⊠ Le Marin ☎ 0596/74–77–61, 800/327–2276, 888/350–3568 in U.S. ⊕ www.sunsail.com) has joined with Stardust Yacht Charters to form one of the largest yacht-charter companies in the world. Although it's primarily a bareboat operation, those with limited experience can hire skippers by the week. Ocean kayaks can be rented too and must be reserved in advance. Check the Web site for discount deals even in the winter. **Windward Island Cruising Company** (⊠ Le Marin ☎ 0596/74–31–14 ⊕ www.sailing-adventure.com) has sailboats from 30 to 70 feet.

CANOPY TOURS Canopy tours—also known as tree-topping tours—are relatively new to Martinique, but even younger kids can join in the fun on some courses. However, if your body parts—particularly knees and elbows—are not as supple as they once were, or if you're afraid of heights, stay back at the hotel pool. The "tour" consists of a series of wooden ladders and bridges suspended from the trees, connected with zip lines. Participants are secured in harnesses and ropes that hitch to them like dog leashes. You connect to a cable and then fly and bellow like Tarzan until you get to the other side. Advanced reservations are usually required.

Mangofil (⊠ Domaine de Château Gaillard, Les Trois-Ilets ☎ 0596/68–08–08) is a professionally run operation, overseen by two young Frenchmen with national certifications, who managed a similar park in France. All of the platforms, ladders, and stations were installed by members of a special union in France, who do nothing but this task. Safety is key here, but there's also a lot of fun, and the boys have a sense of humor. Their full-moon parties are a hoot. The cost is €20. **Mohawk Aventures** (⊠ Domaine de Sigy, Le Vauclin ☎ 0696/92–20–19 or 0696/28–07–76) is next to a banana-packing facility. Although not as high or as professionally run as Mangofil (nor is English spoken as much), it's much more convenient to Le François. There are three adult courses and two appealing courses for children (based on age), as well as picnic tables. The cost is €20, and the facility is closed on Monday. At this writing, the owners were putting the finishing touches on an attractive snack bar.

CANYONING Canyoning, which involves hiking the canyons of the rain forests, usually along and through rivers, sliding over the rocks, then plunging down the cascades into icy pools, is relatively new to Martinique. It's ordinarily a costly sport, but members of **Club d'Escalade et Montagne**

(☎ 0596/52–64–04 for Pascal Gall, 0596/61–48–41 for Patrick Picard, 0696/26–07–78 for Olivier Motton), who can be called directly at their homes, will guide those wanting to experience this wet adventure for €25 for a four- to six-hour trek.

CYCLING Mountain biking is popular in mainland France, and now it has reached Martinique. You can rent a VTT (*Vélo Tout Terrain*), a bike specially designed with 18 speeds to handle all terrains for €15 with helmet, delivery, and pickup from your hotel, although it requires a €150 credit card deposit. **V. T. Tilt** (⌧ Les Trois-Ilets ☎ 0596/66–01–01 or 0596/76–67–25) has an English-speaking owner who loves to put together groups for fun tours, either half-day or full, which includes lunch. They can be beach, river, or mountain rides; tours of plantations or horse ranches; and historic, adventure, or nature experiences.

DAY SAILS The *Coconasse* (⌧ Pointe du Bout Marina, Les Trois-Ilets ☎ 0696/23–83–51 ⊕ www.coconasse.com) is a classic charter yacht that offers an upscale sailing experience for 2 to 10 persons. The seasoned skipper (15 transatlantic crossings) is 100% Italian, as are the lunch and Chianti he serves. A full day is €72, a half day €38. Both include drinks. Coconasse "flies" under sail and also offers a two-day passage to St. Lucia for €270. *Kata Mambo* (⌧ Pointe du Bout Marina, Les Trois-Ilets ☎ 0696/81–90–O8), a catamaran, offers a variety of options for half-day (€36) or full-day (€69) sails to St-Pierre. For €75.50, you also get a 4x4 adventure through sugarcane and banana plantations. The full-day trip includes unlimited rum libations; a good, multicourse lunch (half-lobsters are €10 extra) with wine; and great CD sounds in four languages. This is a fun day. The fact that they've been in the biz since the early 1990s attests to their professionalism.

DIVING & Martinique's underwater world is decorated with multicolor coral, crus-
SNORKELING taceans, turtles, and sea horses. Expect to pay €40 to €45 for a single dive; a package of three dives is around €110. **Okeanos Club** (⌧ Pierre & Vacances, Ste-Luce ☎ 0596/62–52–36 ⊕ www.okeanos-club.com) has a morning trip close to shore; in the afternoon, the boats go out into open water. Lessons (including those for kids 8 to 12) with a PADI-certified instructor can be held in English. It's always a fun experience. The dive shop looks out to Diamant Rock, which has wonderful underwater caves and is one of the preferred dives on the island. **Planète Bleue** (⌧ Pointe du Bout Marina, Les Trois-Ilets ☎ 0596/66–08–79 ⊕ www.planete-bleue.mq) has a big new dive boat, hand-painted with tropical fish and waves, so it's impossible to miss. The English-speaking international crew are proud they've been in business since the early 1990s. The company hits 20 sites, including the Citadel and Salomon's Pool. A boat goes out mornings and afternoons. Thursday is a full day on the north coast, with breakfast, lunch, and all drinks included. Half-day dives include gear and a 'ti punch, but no rum for the children, who are otherwise welcome. Sunday is a day of rest, except for the first one in the month, when it's off to Diamant Rock.

FISHING Deep-sea fishing expeditions in these waters hunt down tuna, barracuda, dolphinfish, kingfish, and bonito, and the big ones—white and blue marlins. You can hire boats from the bigger marinas, particularly in Pointe du Bout, Le Marin, and Le François; most hotels arrange these Hemingwayesque trysts but will often charge a premium. If you call several days in advance, they can also put you together with other anglers to keep costs down. The **Centre de Peche** (⊠ Marina du Marin, Le Marin ☎ 0596/76–24–20 or 0596/28–80–58), a fully loaded Davis 47-foot fishing boat, is like a sportsfisherman's dream. It goes out with a minimum of five anglers for €150 per person for a half day, or €260 per person for a full day, including lunch. Nonanglers can come for the ride for €70 and €130, respectively. Captain Yves speaks English fluently and is a fun guy.

GOLF   The **Golf Country Club de la Martinique** (⊠ Les Trois-Ilets ☎ 0596/68–32–81) has a par-71, 18-hole Robert Trent Jones course with an English-speaking pro, pro shop, bar, and restaurant. The club offers special greens fees to cruise-ship passengers. Normal greens fees are €53; an electric cart costs another €53. For those who don't mind walking while admiring the Caribbean view between the palm trees, club trolleys are €8. There are no caddies.

HIKING   Two-thirds of Martinique is designated as protected park land. Trails, all 31 of them, are well marked and maintained. At the beginning of each, a notice is posted advising on the level of difficulty, the duration of a hike, and any interesting points to note. The **Parc Naturel Régional de la Martinique** (⊠ 9 bd. Général de Gaulle, Fort-de-France ☎ 0596/73–19–30) organizes inexpensive guided excursions year-round. If there have been heavy rains, though, give it up. The tangle of ferns, bamboo trees, and llanai vines is dramatic, but during rainy season, the springs and waterfalls and wet, muddy trails will negate any enthusiasm.

HORSEBACK   Horseback riding excursions can traverse scenic beaches, palm-shaded
RIDING   forests, sugarcane fields, or a variety of other tropical landscapes. Trained guides often include running commentaries on the history, flora, and fauna of the island. At **Black Horse Ranch** (⊠ Les Trois-Ilets ☎ 0596/68–37–80), one-hour trail rides (€25) go into the countryside and across waving cane fields; two hours on the trail (€35) bring riders near a river. Only western saddles are used for adults; children can ride English. Semiprivate lessons in French or English are €40 a person, less for kids if they can join a group. **Habitation Cerón** (⊠ Anse Cerón ☎ 0596/52–94–53 or 0596/52–97–03), a 600-acre former plantation, has horse trails that run through the rain forest. A 90-minute ride is just €35. A new equestrian center offers private lessons, with either English or western saddles, for €30 an hour. Pony rides for the kidlets range from €6 to €15.

☾ **Ranch Jack** (⊠ Anse-d'Arlets ☎ 0596/68–37–69) has trail rides (English style) across the countryside for €22 an hour; half-day excursions (€43) go through the country and forests to the beach, beverages included. And the lessons for kids are recommendable. Some guides are English-speaking at **Ranch de Caps** (⊠ Cap Macré, Le Marin ☎ 0596/74–70–65 or 0696/23–18–18), where you can take a half-day ride (western) on the wild southern beaches and across the countryside for €45. Rides go out in the morning (8:30 to noon) and afternoon (1:30 to 5) every day but Monday. If you can manage a full day in the saddle, it costs €75. A real memory is the full-moon ride. Most of the mounts are Anglo-Arabs. Riders are encouraged to help cool and wash their horses at day's end. Reserve in advance. Riders of all levels are welcomed.

KAYAKING   Ecofriendly travelers will love skimming the shallow bay while paddling to bird and iguana reserves. Rent colorful fiberglass kayaks to explore the crystalline Havre du Robert, with its shallow pools (called *fonds blanc*) petite beaches, and islets such as Iguana Island. You can receive one of the island's warmest welcomes at **Les Kayaks du Robert** (⌧ Pointe Savane, Le Robert ☏ 0596/65–33–89); after a memorable paddle through shallow lagoons and mangrove swamps chasing colorful fish, you can enjoy a complimentary planter's punch, all for €16 per person for a half-day; a guided group trip costs slightly more.

WINDSURFING   At **Bliss** (⌧ Anse Bonneville Trinité, near Résidence Oceane, Tartane ☏ 0596/58–00–96 ⊕ www.surfmartinique.com), individual (€30) or group (€20) lessons are given to ages five and up. English and Spanish are spoken. Surf- and bodyboards (with fins) can also be rented for three hours for €14, or €24 for the day. **UPCA** (⌧ Le Plage, Le Vauclin ☏ 0596/74–33–68) rents out windsurfing boards at slightly better prices than most other outfitters.

14

Shopping

★   French fragrances and designer scarves, fine china and crystal, leather goods, wine (amazingly inexpensive at supermarkets), and liquor are all good buys in Fort-de-France. Purchases are further sweetened by the 20% discount on luxury items when paid for with traveler's checks or certain major credit cards. Among local items, look for creole gold jewelry, such as hoop earrings and heavy bead necklaces; white and dark rum; and handcrafted straw goods, pottery, and tapestries.

Areas & Malls

The area around the cathedral in Fort-de-France has a number of small shops that carry luxury goods. Of particular note are the shops on rue Victor Hugo, rue Moreau de Jones, rue Antoine Siger, and rue Lamartine. The **Galleries Lafayette** department store on rue Schoelcher in downtown Fort-de-France sells everything from perfume to pâté. On the outskirts of Fort-de-France, the **Centre Commercial de Cluny, Centre Commercial de Dillon, Centre Commercial de Bellevue**, and **Centre Commercial la Rond Point** are among the major shopping malls.

You can find more than 100 thriving businesses—from shops and department stores to restaurants, pizzerias, fast-food outlets, a superb supermarket, and the Galleria Hotel—at **La Galleria** in Le Lamentin. In Pointe du Bout there are a number of appealing tourist shops and boutiques, both in and around **Village Créole.**

Specialty Items

CHINA & CRYSTAL   **Cadet Daniel** (⌧ 72 rue Antoine Siger, Fort-de-France ☏ 0596/71–41–48) sells Lalique, Limoges, and Baccarat. **Roger Albert** (⌧ 7 rue Victor Hugo, Fort-de-France ☏ 0596/71–71–71) carries designer crystal.

CLOTHING   **Bisous Sucrés** (⌧ Village Créole, Pointe du Bout, Les Trois-Ilets ☏ 0596/74–77–04) offers a unique children's collection, including jewelry, madras dollies, and teeny underwear. If you adore cool Parisian fashions, **Cap Cod** (⊠ Pointe du Bout, Les Trois-Ilets) deals in names like Pilou des Partants, La Fée, and Maraboutée, the top dogs in cotton French-designer resort wear that will have you opening your wallet wide. Hope for a *solde* (sale). **Coté Plage Sarl** (⊠ Village Créole, Pointe du Bout Les Trois-Ilets ☎ 0596/66–13–00) stocks French sailor jerseys in creative colors, youthful straw purses in bold hues, fun teenage jewelry, and ladies' bathing suits. **Mounia** (⊠ Rue Perrinon, near the old House of Justice, Fort-de-France ☎ 0596/73–77–27), owned by a former Yves Saint Laurent model, carries the top French designers for women and men.

HANDICRAFTS   Following the signs advertising ATELIERS ARTISANALES (art studios) can yield unexpected treasures, many of them reasonably priced. The work of **Antan Lontan** (⊠ 213 rte. de Balata, Fort-de-France ☎ 0596/64–52–72) has to be seen. Sculptures, busts, statuettes, and artistic lamps portray the creole women and the story of the Martiniquaise culture. **Art et Nature** (⊠ Ste-Luce ☎ 0596/62–59–19) carries Joel Gilbert's unique wood paintings, daubed with 20 to 30 shades of earth and sand. **Artisanat & Poterie des Trois-Ilets** (⊠ Les Trois-Ilets ☎ 0596/68–18–01) allows you to watch the creation of Arawak- and Carib-style pots, vases, and jars. **Atelier Céramique** (⊠ Le Diamant ☎ 0596/76–42–65) displays the ceramics, paintings, and miscellaneous souvenirs of owners and talented artists David and Jeannine England, members of the island's ★ small British expat community. **Bois Nature** (⊠ La Semair, Le Robert ☎ 0596/65–77–65) is all about mood and mystique. The gift items begin with scented soap, massage oil, aromatherapy sprays, and perfumes. Then there are wind chimes, mosquito netting, and sun hats made of coconut fiber. The big stuff includes natural wood-frame mirrors and furniture à la Louis XV. **Centre des Métiers d'Art** (⊠ Rue Ernest Deproge, Fort-de-France ☎ 0596/70–25–01) exhibits authentic local arts and crafts.

Domaine Château Gaillard (⊠ Rte. des Trois-Ilets, Les Trois-Ilets ☎ 0596/68–15–68), a large two-story shopping complex, sells both handicrafts and tropical floral compositions. You can find pottery, jewelry, toys, paintings, and gifts. Coffee and chocolate are also for sale, as are antique creole and French women's costumes—a sexy bustier or empire-cut vest—for high prices. At **Galerie Jecy** (⊠ Pointe du Bout Marina, Les Trois-Ilets ☎ 0596/66–04–98), owner Stephanie designs fanciful, colorful metalwork, artistic enough to be called sculpture; her island themes include starfish, octopus, geckos, and impressive billfish. She also sells more portable souvenirs like colorful wooden napkin rings, fruit plates, and trivets. **Galerie de Sophen** (⊠ Pointe du Bout, Les Trois-Ilets ☎ 0596/66–13–64), across from the Village Créole, is a combination of Sophie and Henry, both in name and content. This art gallery showcases the work (originals and limited prints) of a French couple who live aboard their sailboat and paint the beauty of the sea and the island, from exotic birds to banana trucks. **Galerie d'Art du Village Créole** (⊠ Village Créole, Pointe du Bout, Les Trois-Ilets ☎ 0596/66–15–75) has affordable watercolors, oil paintings, and other mixed media (reproductions too) by local and Haitian artists as well as by the gallery owner.

PERFUMES **Roger Albert Nosibe** (✉ 7 rue Victor Hugo, Fort-de-France ☎ 0596/ 71–71–71) stocks such popular scents as those by Dior, Chanel, and Guerlain.

Nightlife & the Arts

Martinique is dotted with lively discos and nightclubs, but a good deal of the fun is to had by befriending Martinicans, French residents, and other expats so they will invite you to their private parties.

CASINOS The **Casino Batelière Plaza** (✉ Schoelcher ☎ 0596/61–73–23), a clean and classy casino on the outskirts of Fort-de-France, is built in a striking nouveau–plantation house style. It has both slot machines and table games. Slots open at 10 AM, but table games don't start until after 7:30 PM. You'll have to fork over a €10 admission (includes a drink), bring your passport (18 is the legal gambling age), and be properly attired (jacket and tie for men, dresses for women for table games; dressy casual for slots). There's usually some kind of entertainment on weekends, and it's open on Sunday, when most other places are closed tight.

DANCE CLUBS Your hotel or the tourist office can put you in touch with the current "in" places. It's also wise to check on opening and closing times and cover charges. For the most part, the discos draw a mixed crowd—Martinicans and tourists, and although predominantly a younger crowd, all ages go dancing here.

L'Amphore (✉ Pointe du Bout, Les Trois-Ilets ☎ 0596/66–03–09 or 0696/80–79–40) is a hot dance spot, with funk, soul, and disco plus international music from the 1970s and '80s. The dress code is strict: no shorts, bandanas, or sandals. To find the club, follow the road to Anse Mitan; it's on the left before the little church on the right. On weekends you need a reservation for a table; the VIP room is bottle-service only. It's open weekends only during the low season, often more during the high season. There's often a cover. **Crazy Nights** (✉ Ste-Luce ☎ 0596/ 68–56–68) remains popular because it's all about having one crazy night. With upward of 1,000 partying people, your chances are good here. Live concerts are frequent, but dancing and hip-swinging are the priorities. **Le Top 50** (✉ Zone Artisanale, La Trinité ☎ 0596/58–61–43) is one of the few night spots in the area where tourists, surfers, and locals all come together to party. **Yucca Bar** (✉ Zac de Rivière Roche, Fort-de-France ☎ 0596/60–48–36), with a Mexican motif and Tex-Mex food, is known for showcasing innovative bands, usually on Wednesday. Take a taxi, go with local friends, or get good directions, because the area is deserted at night. It's especially popular on the weekend. If you go early for the Tex-Mex buffet, you can avoid the cover charge.

FOLKLORIC PERFORMANCES Most leading hotels offer nightly entertainment in season, including the marvelous **Les Grands Ballets de Martinique,** one of the finest folkloric dance troupes in the Caribbean. Consisting of a bevy of musicians and dancers dressed in traditional costume, the ballet revives the Martinique of yesteryear through dance rhythms such as the beguine or the mazurka. This folkloric group appears Friday at the Hotel Sofitel Bakoua and Monday at the Novotel Diamant. Both have a set price for the dinner performance. **Tche Kreyal,** another folkloric ballet group, which has some 20 performers—many of them children—performs at Les Almandiers in Ste-Luce on Saturday. At the Hotel Amyris, the **Kalenda Ballet** dances on Wednesday nights. In addition, many restaurants offer live entertainment, usually on weekends. **Tikadoo** is a talented, energetic group whose members waltz, do the beguine, and even do Martinique-style country dancing (not unlike square dancing). They perform at the Hotel Le Pagerie in Pointe du Bout on Monday nights.

MUSIC CLUBS   Jazz musicians, like their music, tend to be informal and independent. They rarely hold regular gigs. Zouk mixes Caribbean rhythm and an Occidental tempo with creole words. Jacob Devarieux is the leading exponent of this style and is occasionally on the island. Otherwise, you're likely to hear one of his followers.

Calembasse Café (✉ 19 bd. Allègre, Le Marin ☎ 0596/74–69–27) pleases a diverse—though mostly older—crowd. Jazz is the norm, and often it's background for a talented local singer. Funky and hip, the interior is a bit rough, but civilized. Lunch and dinner are served, and on Saturday night, if you don't make a reservation, you will not have a seat. The food isn't wonderful, but if you have the conch tart and the grilled lobster, you'll leave satisfied and avoid the cover charge. There's sometimes a beach party. It's closed on Monday. **Le Molokoi** (✉ Le Diamant ☎ 0596/76–48–63) is a hot spot for zouk and pop music. **Le Ponton** (✉ On the point, behind the Sofitel Bakoua, Pointe du Bout, Les Trois-Ilets ☎ 0596/66–05–45) is a fun, youthful waterfront restaurant that attracts a lot of boating types, especially when the DJ cranks it up and particularly when live bands play on the weekends; music is local—French, reggae, and Latin. When owner Valentina of **Sapori d'Italia** (✉ Village Créole, Pointe du Bout, Les Trois-Ilets ☎ 0596/66–15–85) turns her talents to the microphone, she switches on the electronic keyboard and sings like a diva in Italian, French, and even Creole. **La Villa Créole** (✉ Anse Mitan ☎ 0596/66–05–53) is a restaurant whose French owner, Guy Bruere-Dawson, has been singing and strumming the guitar since the mid-1980s—everything from François Cabrel to Elton John, some Italian ballads, and original ditties. Other singers perform on weekends, but it's closed Sunday. In order to see the show, you must order dinner, lobster being the best option (reserve on weekends). There's also a small dance floor. In season you can find one or two combos playing at clubs and hotels, but it's only at **West Indies** (✉ Bd. Alfassa, across from Air Caraïbes, Fort-de-France ☎ 0596/63–63–77) where there are regular jazz sessions. But only go with lots of company, preferably Martinicans.

ISLAND CULTURE   **L'Atrium** (✉ Bd. Général de Gaulle, Fort-de-France ☎ 0596/70–79–29 or 0596/60–78–78), Martinique's cultural center, is where large-scale theater, dance, and musical performances take place. **Palais des Congrès de Madiana** (✉ Schoelcher 97233 ☎ 0596/72–15–15) is a major convention center and theater complex. The Palais de Congres showcases diverse events from international, classical guitar competitions to performances by the Glamour Boys, France's Chippendales. A multiplex cinema (10 screens), with custom seats, shows top-flight movies from

France and the states; many are rated for children. The brasserie is also a brewery, plus there's fast food.

Exploring Martinique

The north of the island will appeal to nature lovers, hikers, and mountain climbers. The drive from Fort-de-France to St-Pierre is particularly impressive, as is the one across the island, via Morne Rouge, from the Caribbean to the Atlantic. This is Martinique's wild side—a place of waterfalls, rain forest, and mountains. The highlight is Mont Pelée. The south is the more developed half of the island, where the resorts and restaurants are, as well as the beaches.

Numbers in the margin correspond to points of interest on the Martinique map.

14 Ajoupa-Bouillon. This flower-filled 17th-century village amid pineapple fields is the jumping-off point for several sights. The Saut Babin is a 40-foot waterfall, a half-hour walk from Ajoupa-Bouillon. The Gorges de la Falaise is a river gorge where you can swim. **Les Ombrages** botanical gardens has marked trails through the rain forest. ⊠ *Ajoupa-Bouillon* 🖭 €4 ⊙ *Daily 9–5:30.*

5 Aqualand. This U.S.-style water park is a great place for families to have a wet, happy day. The large wave pool is well tended; little ones love it, as they do the pirate's galleon in their own watery playground. Older kids may prefer to get their thrill from the slides, including the hairpin turns of the Giant Slalom, the Colorado slide, and the Black Hole, which winds around in total darkness. In the best French tradition, fast-food options are attractive, including crêpes, salads, and even beer. Inquire about catching a weekend Somatour shuttle boat. Nouvelle Frontier organizes tours that include the park. ⊠ *Rte. des Pitons, Carbet* 🕿 *0596/78-40-00* ⊕ *www.aqualand-martinique.fr* 🖭 €16 ⊙ *Daily 10–6.*

4 Balata. This quiet little town has two sights worth visiting. Built in 1923 to commemorate those who died in World War I, **Balata Church** is an exact replica of Paris's Sacré-Coeur Basilica. The **Jardin de Balata** (Balata Gardens), has thousands of varieties of tropical flowers and plants. There are shaded benches from which to take in the mountain view. You can order anthurium and other tropical flowers to be delivered to the airport. ⊠ *Rte. de Balata, Balata* 🕿 *0596/64-48-73* 🖭 €7 ⊙ *Daily 9–5.*

13 Basse-Pointe. On the route to this village on the Atlantic coast at the island's northern end you pass many banana and pineapple plantations. Just south of Basse-Pointe is a **Hindu temple** built by descendants of the East Indians who settled in this area in the 19th century. The view of of Mont Pelée from the temple is amazing.

★ The highlight of Basse-Pointe is the estimable **Leyritz Plantation,** which has been restored as a hotel. When tour groups aren't swarming, the rustic setting, complete with sugarcane factory and gardens, is delightful. A fascinating new museum includes vignettes of rooms from the plantation era plus *des figurines végétales* by local artisan Will Fenton. He has used bananas, *balisier* (a tall grass), and other local plants to make dolls of famous French women—from Marie-Antoinette to Madame Curie—in period costumes. Admission is waived if you have lunch. ⊠ *Leyritz Plantation, Basse-Pointe* ☎ *0596/78–53–92* ✉ *€3* ⊙ *Daily 10–6.*

❸ Bellefontaine. This colorful fishing village has pastel houses on the hillsides and beautifully painted *gommiers* (fishing boats) bobbing in the water. Look for the restaurant built in the shape of a boat.

㉒ Diamond Rock. This volcanic mound is 1 mi (1½ km) offshore from the small, friendly village of Le Diamant and is one of the island's best diving spots. In 1804, during the squabbles over possession of the island between the French and the English, the latter commandeered the rock, armed it with cannons, and proceeded to use it as a strategic battery. The British held the rock for nearly a year and a half, attacking any French ships that came along. The French got wind that the British were getting cabin fever on their isolated island and arranged for barrels of rum to float up on the rock. The French easily overpowered the inebriated sailors, ending one of the most curious engagements in naval history.

⑰ Dubuc Castle. At the eastern tip of the Presqu'île du Caravelle are the ruins of this castle, once the home of the Dubuc de Rivery family, who owned the peninsula in the 18th century. According to legend, young Aimée Dubuc de Rivery was captured by Barbary pirates, sold to the Ottoman Empire, became a favorite of the sultan, and gave birth to Mahmud II. You can park your car right after the turnoff for Résidence Oceane and walk the dirt road to the ruins.

㉓ Forêt de Montravail. A few miles north of Ste-Luce, this tropical rain forest is ideal for a short hike. Look for the interesting group of Carib rock drawings.

❶ Fort-de-France. With its historic fort and superb location beneath the towering Pitons du Carbet on the Baie des Flamands, Martinique's capital—home to about one-third of the island's 360,000 inhabitants—should be a grand place. It isn't. However, the aim of an ambitious redevelopment project, now under way, is to make it one of the most attractive cities in the Caribbean. It includes the renovation of the Savane Park, the construction of a spectacular waterfront promenade, and the Pointe Simon Business and & Tourist Center, which will have a 200-room Marriott Hotel and a large new shopping center. Alas, the tourist office, formerly on the waterfront, has moved to temporary quarters in the suburb of Schoelcher, so it's not readily accessible to the car-less.

The most pleasant districts of Fort-de-France—Didier, Bellevue, and Schoelcher—are up on the hillside, and you need a car (or taxi) to reach them. But if you try to drive here, you may find yourself trapped in gridlock in the warren of narrow streets downtown. Parking is difficult, and it's best to try for one of the garages or—as a second choice—outdoor public parking areas. A taxi or ferry may be a better alternative.

There are some good shops with Parisian wares (at Parisian prices) and lively street markets that sell, among other things, human hair for wigs, though the latter is not cheap. Near the harbor is a marketplace where local crafts, souvenirs, and spices are sold. Town can be fun, and you probably should just do it. But the heat, exhaust fumes, and litter tend to make exploring here a chore rather than a pleasure. At night the city feels dark and gloomy, with little street life except for the extravagantly dressed prostitutes who openly parade around after 10 PM. If you plan to go out, it's best to go with a group.

The heart of Fort-de-France is **La Savane,** a 12½-acre park filled with trees, fountains, and benches. It's a popular gathering place and the scene of promenades, parades, and impromptu soccer matches. Along the east side are numerous snack wagons. Alas, it's no longer a desirable oasis, what with a lot of litter and other negatives often found in urban parks. A statue of Pierre Belain d'Esnambuc, leader of the island's first settlers, is unintentionally upstaged by Vital Dubray's vandalized—now headless—white Carrara marble statue of the empress Joséphine, Napoléon's first wife. Diagonally across from La Savane, you can catch the ferries for the 20-minute run across the bay to Pointe du Bout and the beaches at Anse-Mitan and Anse-à-l'Ane. It's relatively cheap as well as stress-free—much safer, more pleasant, and faster than by car.

The most imposing historic site in La Savane (and in Fort-de-France) is **Fort St-Louis,** which runs along the east side of La Savane. It's open Monday through Saturday from 9 to 3, and admission is €4.

The **Bibliothèque Schoelcher** is the wildly elaborate Romanesque public library. It was named after Victor Schoelcher, who led the fight to free the slaves in the French West Indies in the 19th century. The eye-popping structure was built for the 1889 Paris Exposition, after which it was dismantled, shipped to Martinique, and reassembled piece by ornate piece. ⊠ *At rue de la Liberté, runs along west side of La Savane, and rue Perrinon* ☏ *0596/70–26–67* ✆ *Free* ⊙ *Mon. 1–5:30, Tues.–Fri. 8:30–5:30, Sat. 8:30–noon.*

★ **Le Musée Régional d'Histoire et d'Ethnographie** is a learning experience that is best undertaken at the beginning of your vacation, so you can better understand the history, background, and people of the island. Housed in an elaborate former residence (circa 1888) with balconies and fretwork, it has everything from displays of the garish gold jewelry that prostitutes wore after emancipation to reconstructed rooms of a home of proper, middle-class Martinicans. There's even a display of madras, creole headdresses with details of how they were tied to indicate if a woman was single, married, or otherwise occupied. ⊠ *10 bd. Général de Gaulle* ☏ *0596/72–81–87* ✆ *€3* ⊙ *Mon. and Wed.–Fri. 8:30–5, Tues. 2–5, Sat. 8:30–noon.*

Rue Victor Schoelcher runs through the center of the capital's primary shopping district, a six-block area bounded by rue de la République, rue de la Liberté, rue Victor Severe, and rue Victor Hugo. Stores sell Paris fashions and French perfume, china, crystal, and liqueurs, as well as local handicrafts. The Romanesque **St-Louis Cathedral** (⊠ Rue Victor Schoelcher), with its lovely stained-glass windows, was built in 1878, the sixth church on this site (the others were destroyed by fire, hurricane, and earthquake).

The Galerie de Biologie et de Géologie at the **Parc Floral et Culturel,** in the northeastern corner of the city center, will acquaint you with the island's exotic flora. There's also an aquarium. The park contains the island's official cultural center, where there are sometimes free evening concerts. ⊠ *Pl. José-Marti, Sermac* ☏ *0596/71–66–25* 🖃 *Grounds free; aquarium €5.60; botanical and geological gallery €1.12* ⊙ *Park daily dawn–10 PM; aquarium daily 9–7; gallery Tues.–Fri. 9:30–12:30 and 3:30–5:30, Sat. 9–1 and 3–5.*

⑱ Le François. With some 16,000 inhabitants, this is the main city on the Atlantic coast. Many of the old wooden buildings remain and are juxtaposed with concrete structures. The classic West Indian cemetery, with its black-and-white tiles, is still here, and a marina is at the end of town. Two of Martinique's best hotels are in this area, as well as some of the most upscale residences. Le François is also noted for its snorkeling. Offshore are the privately owned Les Ilets de l'Impératrice. The islands received that name because, according to legend, this is where Empress Joséphine came to bathe in the shallow basins known as *fonds blanc* because of their white-sand bottoms. Group boat tours leave from the harbor and include lunch and drinks. Prices vary (see ⇨ Sightseeing Tours *in* Sports & the Outdoors). You can also haggle with a fisherman to take you out for a while on his boat. There's a fine bay 6 mi (9½ km) farther along the coast at Le Robert, though the town is lackluster.

★ The **Habitation Clément** offers a glimpse into Martinique's colonial past, into the elegance and privilege of plantation society, and is complete with creole ladies in traditional dresses moving about the grounds. The Palm Grove is delightful, with an avenue of palms and park benches. It was all built with the wealth generated by its rum distillery, and its 18th-century splendor has been lovingly preserved. There's fine art displayed and classical music plays. Framed vintage labels from rum bottles track the changes in the marketing of rum and the island over the centuries. Enjoy the free tastings at the bar and wander into the retail shop. Consider the Canne Bleu, *Grappe Blanche* or aged rum, some bottled as early as 1952. ⊠ *Domaine de l'Acajou, Le François* ☏ *0596/54–62–07* ⊕ *www.rhum-clement.com* 🖃 *€7* ⊙ *Daily 8:30 AM–5:30 PM.*

⑪ Habitation Céron. This area has had many lives since its first in 1658 as a sugar plantation, or *habitation*. The owners, Louis and Laurence des Grottes, continue to create new options for visitors to their 600-acre property, the latest of which is a fleet of "quads" (off-road, four-wheelers) to provide a racy alternative to hiking through the rain forest. And you can now opt for the same run on horseback from the new equestrian center. Self-guided or guided tours through the plantation buildings include a video that describes when the factory was still producing sugar, rum, and manioc (yucca). Admission is waived if you buy lunch, which you can carry to the nearby beach if you like, though it's nicer to sit on the terrace. ⊠ *Anse Céron* ☏ *0596/52–94–53 or 0596/52–97–03* 🖃 *€6; quad tours €25–€40* ⊙ *Daily 9:30–5.*

⑲ Lamentin. There's nothing pretty about Lamentin; the international airport is its most notable landmark. The rest of the town is a sprawling industrial and commercial zone. But you come here for shopping in the big, fancy shopping mall Euromarché. La Galleria, a second megamall of roughly 100 shops and boutiques, offers everything from pâté de foie gras and Camembert to CDs and sunglasses.

⑫ Macouba. Named after the Carib word for "fish," this village was a prosperous tobacco town in the 17th century. Today its clifftop location affords magnificent views of the sea, the mountains, and—on clear days—the neighboring island of Dominica. The **JM Distillery** (☎ 0596/78–92–55) produces some of the best *vieux rhum* on the island here, though it's now owned by Habitation Clément. A tour and samples are free. Macouba is the starting point for a spectacular drive, the 6-mi (9½-km) **route to Grand' Rivière** (☎ 0596/55–72–74 for Syndicat d'Initiative Riverain) on the northernmost point. This is Martinique at its greenest: groves of giant bamboo, cliffs hung with curtains of vines, and 7-foot tree ferns that seem to grow as you watch them. Literally at the end of the road is Grand' Rivière, a colorful, sprawling fishing village at the foot of high cliffs. The Syndicat d'Initiative Riverain, or tourist office, in Macouba can arrange hiking and small-boat excursions.

㉖ Le Marin. The yachting capital of Martinique is also known for its colorful August carnival and its Jesuit church, circa 1766. From Le Marin a narrow road leads to picturesque Cap Chevalier (Cape Knight), about 1 mi (1½ km) from town. Most of the buildings are white and very Euro. The marina is lively, and there are waterfront restaurants and clubs.

⑨ Le Morne Rouge. This town sits on the southern slopes of the volcano that destroyed it in 1902. Today it's a popular resort spot and offers hikers some fantastic mountain scenery. From Le Morne Rouge you can start the climb up the 4,600-foot **Mont Pelée** volcano. But don't try it without a guide unless you want to get buried alive under pumice stones. Instead, drive up to the Refuge de l'Aileron. From the parking lot it's a mile (1½ km) up a well-marked trail to the summit. Bring a sweatshirt, because there's often a mist that makes the air damp and chilly. From the summit follow the route de la Trace (Route N3), which winds south of Le Morne Rouge to St-Pierre. It's steep and winding, but that didn't stop the *porteuses* of old: balancing a tray, these women would carry up to 100 pounds of provisions on their heads for the 15-hour trek to the Atlantic coast.

⑦ Musée Gauguin. Martinique was a brief station in Paul Gauguin's wanderings but a decisive moment in the evolution of his art. He arrived from Panama in 1887 with friend and fellow painter Charles Laval and, having pawned his watch at the docks, rented a wooden shack on a hill above Carbet. Dazzled by the tropical colors and vegetation, Gauguin developed a style, his Martinique period, that directly anticipated his Tahitian paintings. Disappointingly, this modest museum has only reproductions and some original letters and documents relating to the painter. Also remembered here is the writer Lafcadio Hearn. In his endearing book *Two Years in the West Indies* he provides the most exten-

14

sive description of the island before St-Pierre was buried in ash and lava. ✉ *Anse-Turin, Carbet* ☎ *0596/78–22–66* ⬛ *€6* ⊙ *Daily 9–5:30.*

6 **Neisson Distillery.** The "Mercedes" of Martinique rum brewers is a small, family-run operation whose rum is produced from pure sugarcane juice rather than molasses. It's open for tours and tastings, and the shop sells *Rhum Extra-Vieux* (45% alcohol content) that truly rivals cognac. You can now order online from Edward Hamilton, a dedicated rum guru in Chicago. ✉ *Carbet* ☎ *0596/78–07–90* ⊕ *www.neisson. com* ⬛ *Free* ⊙ *9–4.*

21 **Pointe du Bout.** This tourist area has resort hotels, among them the Sofitel Bakoua, and a marina. The ferry to Fort-de-France leaves from here. A cluster of boutiques, ice cream parlors, and rental-car agencies forms the hub from which restaurants and hotels of varying caliber radiate, but it's a pretty quiet place in the low season. The beach at Anse-Mitan, which is a little west of Pointe du Bout proper, is one of the best on the island. There are also numerous small restaurants and inexpensive guest houses here.

10 **Le Prêcheur.** This quaint village, the last on the northern Caribbean coast, is surrounded by volcanic hot springs. It was the childhood home of Françoise d'Aubigné, who later became the Marquise de Maintenon and the second wife of Louis XIV. At her request, the Sun King donated a handsome bronze bell, which still hangs outside the church. The Tomb of the Carib Indians commemorates a sadder event. It's a formation of limestone cliffs, from which the last of the Caribs are said to have flung themselves to avoid capture by the Marquise's forebears.

16 **Presqu'île du Caravelle.** Much of the Caravelle Peninsula, which juts 8 mi (13 km) into the Atlantic Ocean, is under the protection of the Regional Nature Reserve and offers places for trekking, swimming, and sailing. This is also the site of Anse-Spoutourne, an open-air sports and leisure center operated by the reserve. Tartane has a popular surfing beach with brisk Atlantic breezes.

25 **Ste-Anne.** A lovely white-sand beach and a Catholic church are the highlights of this town on the island's southern tip. There are a bevy of small, inexpensive cafés offering seafood and creole food, pizza parlors, produce markets, and barbecue joints—it's fun and lively. To the south of Ste-Anne is Pointe des Salines, the southernmost tip of the island and site of Martinique's best beach. Near Ste-Anne is **La Savane des Pétrifications,** the Petrified Forest. This desertlike stretch was once swampland and is a veritable geological museum.

24 **Ste-Luce.** This quaint fishing village has a sleepy main street with tourist shops and markets, and you can see some cool types taking a Pernod. From the sidewalk cafés there are panoramic sea views of St. Lucia. Nearby are excellent beaches and several resorts. To the east is Pointe Figuier, an excellent spot for scuba diving.

15 **Ste-Marie.** The winding, hilly route to this town of some 20,000 offers breathtaking views of the rugged Atlantic coastline. Ste-Marie is the commercial capital of the island's north. Look for a picturesque mid-

19th-century church here. The **Musée du Rhum,** operated by the St. James Rum Distillery, is housed in a graceful, galleried creole house. Guided tours take in displays of the tools of the trade and include a visit and tasting at the distillery. It can be a somewhat wild scene when some dozen tour buses pull in, though. ⊠ *Ste-Marie* ☎ *0596/69–30–02* 🎫 *Free* ⊙ *Weekdays 9–5, weekends 9–1, except during harvest period, Feb.–June; call first.*

After navigating the narrow road, you probably won't find more cordial hostesses than those here at **Le Musée de la Banane.** Excellent graphics and beautiful prints tell the story of the banana (Martinique's primary export) as it makes its way from the fields to your table. A vintage creole cottage serves as a well-stocked retail shop, and there's a bar and lunch counter with lots of edibles made from bananas. ⊠ *Habitation Limbé* ☎ *0596/69–45–52* 🎫 *€6* ⊙ *Daily 9–5.*

❽ St-Pierre. The rise and fall of St-Pierre is one of the most remarkable stories in the Caribbean. Martinique's modern history began here in 1635. By the turn of the 20th century St-Pierre was a flourishing city of 30,000, known as the Paris of the West Indies. As many as 30 ships at a time stood at anchor. By 1902 it was the most modern town in the Caribbean, with electricity, phones, and a tram. On May 8, 1902, two thunderous explosions rent the air. As the nearby volcano erupted, Mont Pelée split in half, belching forth a cloud of burning ash, poisonous gas, and lava that raced down the mountain at 250 mph. At 3,600°F, it instantly vaporized everything in its path; 30,000 people were killed in two minutes. One man survived. His name was Cyparis, and he was a prisoner in an underground cell in the town's jail, locked up for public drunkenness. Later, he went on the road with Barnum & Bailey Circus as a sideshow attraction.

An Office du Tourisme is on the *moderne* seafront promenade. Stroll the main streets and check the blackboards at the sidewalk cafés before deciding where to lunch. At night some places have live music. Like stage sets for a dramatic opera, there are the ruins of the island's first church (built in 1640), the imposing theater, the toppled statues. This city, situated on its naturally beautiful harbor and with its narrow, winding streets, has the feel of a European seaside hill town. Although many of the historic buildings need work, stark modernism has not invaded this burg. As much potential as it has, this is one town in Martinique where real estate is cheap—for obvious reasons. The **Cyparis Express,** a small tourist train, will take you around to the main sights with running narrative (in French) for €9.

★ For those interested in the eruption of 1902, the **Musée Vulcanologique Frank Perret** is a must. Established in 1932, it houses photographs of the old town, documents, and a number of relics—some gruesome—excavated from the ruins, including molten glass, melted iron, and contorted clocks stopped at 8 AM. ⊠ *Rue Victor Hugo* ☎ *0596/78–15–16* 🎫 *€3* ⊙ *Daily 9–5.*

★ An excursion to **Depaz Distillery** is one of the island's nicest treats. For four centuries it has been at the foot of the volcano. In 1902 the great house was destroyed in the eruption, but soon after it was courageously rebuilt and the fields replanted. A self-guided tour includes the workers' gingerbread cottages and an exhibit of art and sculpture made from wooden casks and parts of distillery machinery. The tasting room sells their rums, including golden and aged rum (notably Rhum Doré) and distinctive liqueurs made from ginger and basil. ⊠ *MontPelée Plantation* ☎ *0596/78–13–14* 🎟 *Free* ☉ *Mon.–Sat. 9–5.*

② **Schoelcher.** Pronounced "shell-*share*," this upscale suburb of Fort-de-France is home to the University of the French West Indies and Guyana, as well as Martinique's largest convention center, Madiana.

⑳ **Les Trois-Ilets.** Named after the three rocky islands nearby, this lovely little village (population 3,000) has unusual brick-and-wood buildings roofed with antique tiles. It's known for its pottery, straw, and woodwork but above all as the birthplace of Napoléon's empress Joséphine. In the square, where there's also a market and a fine *mairie* (town hall), you can visit the simple church where she was baptized Marie-Joseph Tascher de la Pagerie. The Martinicans have always been enormously proud of Joséphine, even though her husband reintroduced slavery on the island and most historians consider her to have been rather shallow.

★ A stone building that held the kitchen of the estate where Joséphine grew up houses the **Musée de la Pagerie.** It contains an assortment of memorabilia pertaining to her life and rather unfortunate loves, including a marriage certificate, a love letter written straight from the heart by Napoléon in 1796, and various antiques. The main house blew down in the hurricane of 1766, when she was three, and the family lived for years above the sugarcane factory, a hot, odiferous, and fly-ridden existence. At 16 she was wed (an arranged marriage because her father was a gambling man in need of money) to Alexandre de Beauharnais. After he was assassinated during the Revolution she married Napoléon, but despite his love for her, he divorced her, as she was unable to produce children. She was, however, able to keep her titles, various castles, and the equivalent of millions of dollars. ⊠ *Les Trois-Ilets* ☎ *0596/68–34–55* 🎟 *€5* ☉ *Tues.–Fri. 9–5:30, weekends 9–1 and 2:30–5:30.*

Down a dirt road, a Martinican has called up the past with his **La Savane des Esclaves** (the Savannah of the Slaves), a re-created slave village. The labor of love was begun in 2000 by Gilbert Larose, who has had a fascination with the simple island life of his ancestors. This is an in-depth look at that major element in Martinique's history and culture. ⊠ *Quartier La Ferme, Les Trois-Ilets* ☎ *0696/22–79–05, 0596/–68–33–9* 🎟 *€5* ☉ *Daily 10–noon and 2–5.*

㉗ **Le Vauclin.** The return of the fishermen at noon is the big event in this important fishing port on the Atlantic. There's also the 18th-century Chapel of the Holy Virgin. Nearby is the highest point in the south, Mont Vauclin (1,654 feet). A hike to the top rewards you with one of the best views on the island.

MARTINIQUE ESSENTIALS

To research prices, get advice from other travelers, and book travel arrangements, visit www.fodors.com.

Transportation

BY AIR

Air France, which flies several times a week from Miami with a stopover in Guadeloupe or Haiti, has service between the United States and Martinique. Air Antilles Express goes between Martinique, Guadeloupe, and St. Maarten. Air Caraïbes flies from Guadeloupe, St. Maarten, St. Barths, and Santo Domingo. American Eagle now flies to Martinique from San Juan on Thursday, Friday, Saturday, and Monday, making air connections from the United States much easier. LIAT connects Martinique with the English-speaking "down islands." It code-shares with Air Caraïbes.

A nonstop Club Med 757 charter flight leaves New York–JFK weekly on Saturday morning, from December through April, and may be continued through the low season as well.

🛫**Air Antilles Express** ☎0890/64-86-48 ⊕www.airantilles.com. **Air Caraïbes** ☎ 0596/42-16-52 or 0890/64-47-00 ⊕www.aircaraibes.com. **Air France** ☎ 0820/820-820. **American Eagle** ☎ 0590/21-13-66 in Guadeloupe. **LIAT** ☎ 0596/42-16-11, 0590/21-13-93 in Guadeloupe, 888/844-5428 in U.S. ⊕ www.liatairline.com.

AIRPORTS & TRANSFERS: Lamentin International Airport is a clean, contemporary airport, small enough to be managed easily; short- and long-term parking are immediately in front of the terminal. The airport is in the commercial area of Lamentin, a 15-minute taxi ride from Fort-de-France, and some 40 minutes from Les Trois-Ilets peninsula. A public bus stop is diagonally across the highway from the airport. The bus to Fort-de-France costs €1. However, there are no recommendable hotels in the downtown area, so take a taxi or rental car directly to your hotel, unless transfers are provided.

🛫 **Lamentin International Airport** ☎ 0596/42-16-00.

BY BOAT & FERRY

Weather permitting, *vedettes* (ferries) operate daily between Quai d'Esnambuc in Fort-de-France and the marinas in Pointe du Bout, Anse-Mitan, and Anse-à-l'Ane. Any of the three trips takes about 20 minutes, and the ferries operate about every 30 minutes on weekdays, with long waits in the low season. Two companies, Madinina and Caribéenne de Transport Maritime, operate these ferries. If you buy a round-trip you must use the return ticket for the same ferry company. The ferry is the best way to go into the capital, where traffic and parking are a tropical nightmare.

Express des Îles operates ferries to Dominica, Guadeloupe, and St. Lucia. Any of these trips costs in the neighborhood of €60 one-way, and the crossings generally take between three and four hours, even five on a bad day. Most of these services are daily, with extra departures on weekends, but be sure to call and confirm schedules and prices. The services can be crowded on weekends and after music festivals and other events.

🛥**Express des Îles** ☎ 0596/63-12-11. **Madinina** ☎0596/63-06-46. **Caribéenne de Transport Maritime** ☎ 0596/42-41-25.

BY CAR

It is worth the hassle to rent a car, even if it is just for a day or two, so that you can explore this beautiful island at your own pace.

The main highways, about 175 mi (280 km) of well-paved and well-marked roads, are excellent, but only in a few areas are they lighted at night. Many hotels are on roads that are barely passable, so get wherever you're going by nightfall or prepare to be lost. Then tell a stranger: "*Je suis perdu!*" (I am lost). It elicits sympathy. Drive defensively; although Martinicans are polite and lovely people, they drive with aggressive abandon.

Martinique, especially around Fort-de-France and environs, has become plagued with heavy traffic. Streets in the capital are narrow and choked with cars during the day. It's wiser to visit it on the weekends, since almost every weekday from October through late spring is a cruise-ship day. Absolutely avoid the Lamentin Airport area and Fort-de-France during weekday rush hours, roughly 7 to 10 AM and 4 to 7:30 PM, and on Sunday nights. Even the smaller towns like Trinité have rush hours. Pay particular attention late on Friday and Saturday nights. Martinicans love to party and those are the big nights out. Watch, too, for *dos d'ânes* (literally, donkey backs), speed bumps that are hard to spot—particularly at night—though if you hit one, you'll know it. Gas is costly, nearly $5 per gallon.

Of the many agencies, Jumbo is the most likely to cut a deal, but few staffers speak English. Europcar will deliver the car to you and later pick it up, and its rates are usually among the lowest.
🚗 **Avis** ☎ 0596/42-11-00. **Budget** ☎ 0596/42-04-04. **Europcar** ☎ 0596/42-42-42. **Hertz** ☎ 0596/51-01-01. **JumboCar** ☎ 0596/42-22-22 or 0820/22-02-30.

BY TAXI
Taxis, which are metered, are expensive, though you can try bargaining by offering to pay a flat rate to your destination. Drivers of M. Nartial Mercedes Taxis speak English, Spanish, and German as well as French. At Taxi de Place you will find some English-speaking drivers, lots of courtesy, and new SUVs.

Locals take *collectifs* (vans that take up to 10 passengers), which cost just a few euro and depart from the waterfront in Fort-de-France to all the main areas of the island. Don't be shy, because it can mean the difference between paying €3 and, say, €60 for a taxi to reach the same destination. Drivers don't usually speak English. Buses

also are an option and are even cheaper (for example, there's a bus that runs from Trinité to Tartane). The tourist offices can help with maps and information.
🚕 **M. Narital Mercedes Taxis** ☎ 0596/64-20-24, 0696/45-69-07 mobile. **Regular taxis** ☎ 0596/63-63-62 or 0596/63-10-10. **Taxi de Place** ☎ 0696/31-91-05.

Contacts & Resources

BANKS & EXCHANGE SERVICES
Prices quoted in this chapter are in euros, unless otherwise indicated.

The euro is the official currency in Martinique. U.S. dollars are accepted in some hotels but generally at an unfavorable rate. You can usually get the best rate by taking your euros from ATMs on the island (they are marked "CB"), but you will usually not be able to check your balance and will need a four-digit PIN. Go to a bank if you want to exchange dollars, but some smaller banks won't even cash U.S. traveler's checks or change dollars, including the Crédit Agricole, the only bank in Pointe du Bout. Change Caraïbes—which has offices at the airport and in Fort-de-France—usually offers decent rates.

You can find ATMs at the airport and at branches of the Crédit Agricole bank, which is on the Cirrus and Plus systems and also accepts Visa and MasterCard.

Having a certain amount of cash on hand is important, because some restaurants accept neither credit cards nor traveler's checks. Major credit cards are accepted in hotels and restaurants in Fort-de-France and Pointe du Bout, but few establishments in the countryside accept them. Many establishments don't accept American Express in any case.

BUSINESS HOURS
Banks are open weekdays from 7:30 to noon and 2:30 to 4. Post offices are generally open weekdays from 7 AM to 6 PM, Saturday from 8 AM until noon. Stores that cater to tourists are generally open weekdays from 8:30 to 6, Saturday 8:30

to 1. Many stores in Fort-de-France close from 12:30 to 2 for lunch.

ELECTRICITY

Most tourist locations are equipped with 220-volt electrical outlets. If you're coming from North America and plan to use your own appliances, bring a converter and an adapter.

EMERGENCIES

Emergency Services **Ambulance** ☎ 0596/70-36-48 or 0596/71-59-48. **Fire** ☎18. **Police** ☎17. **Hospitals** **Hôpital Maison Retraite** ⊠ Les Trois-Ilets ☎ 0596/66-30-00. **CHG Louis Domergue** ⊠ R Strade, Trinité ☎ 0596/66-46-00. **Hôpital du Marin** ⊠ Bd. Allègre, Marin ☎ 0596/74-92-05. **Hôpital de St-Pierre** ⊠ Rue Percée, St-Pierre ☎ 0596/78-18-24. **Hôpital Pierre Zabla Quitman** ⊠ Lamentin ☎ 0596/55-20-00.

Pharmacies **Pharmacie Cypria** ⊠ Bd. Général de Gaulle, Fort-de-France ☎0596/63-22-25. **Pharmacie de la Paix** ⊠ At rue Victor Schoelcher and rue Perrinon, Fort-de-France ☎ 0596/71-94-83.

HEALTH

The water in Martinique is safe, but *no one* drinks from the tap. Follow suit and go with bottled water; buy it cheap at a supermarket rather than take it from the minibar. If you develop stomach bloating and pain, the pharmacies have some good over-the-counter, antispasmodic medicine. If it persists more than a week, then it's probably time for a doctor and a round of antibiotics. Always come armed with mosquito repellent; there have been some dengue fever scares during rainy season.

HOLIDAYS

Public holidays are New Year's Day, Ash Wednesday (6 weeks before Easter), Good Friday, Easter Monday, Labor Day (May 1), Bastille Day (July 14), Assumption Day (Aug. 15), All Saints' Day (Nov. 1), Armistice Day (Nov. 11), and Christmas.

INTERNET, MAIL & SHIPPING

In Fort-de-France there's the Cyber Café Blénac, open weekdays from 10 AM to 1 PM and Saturday 6 PM to 1 AM. In Pointe du Bout, Prolavnet is both an Internet café

and a laundrette. There's also Internet service at the main post office and in some of the branches in other towns like Le François. In Le Marin, the Calebasse Café, a music venue by night, has an Internet station; it's closed Monday but opens early on other days, at 7 AM.

Airmail letters to the United States cost €.75 for up to 20 grams; postcards, €.50. For Canada the costs are €.90 and €.50; for Great Britain €.90 and €.50 respectively, yet France is only €.50 for letters. Stamps may be purchased from post offices, café-tabacs, and hotel newsstands. Letters to Martinique should include the name of the business, street (if available), town, postal code, island, and French West Indies. Be forewarned, however, that mail is extremely slow, both ways.

Calebasse Café ⊠ 19 bd. Allègre, Le Marin ☎ 0596/74-84-20. **Cyber Café Blénac** ⊠ Rue Blénac, Fort-de-France ☎ 0596/70-31-62. **Prolavnet** ⊠ Village Créole, Pointe du Bout ☎ 0596/66-07-79.

LANGUAGE

Martinicans speak a lovely French, and many speak Creole, a mixture of Spanish, French, and some African languages. However, even if you do speak French fluently, you may not understand. In major tourist areas you can find people who speak English, but using a few French words—even if it's only to say "*Parlez-vous anglais?*"—will be appreciated. But rest assured that these people are typically courteous and will work with you on your French—or lack thereof. Know that most menus are written in French.

PASSPORT REQUIREMENTS

All visitors must have a valid passport and a return or ongoing ticket. A birth certificate and picture ID are *not* sufficient.

SAFETY

Martinique is a reasonably safe island, and generally you will not feel threatened here. In Fort-de-France, however, exercise the same safety precautions you would in any large city. It's best not to be downtown at night unless you're with a group, preferably of Martinicans. And never leave jewelry, money, or designer sunglasses unattended on the beach or in your car. Keep your laptop "under wraps," even in your hotel room, and put valuables in hotel safes. Except for the area around Cap Chevalier and the Caravelle Peninsula, the Atlantic waters are rough and should be avoided by all but expert swimmers.

TAXES & SERVICE CHARGES

A resort tax varies from city to city. Each has its own tax, with most between €.76 and €1.25 per person per day; the maximum is €2.25. Rates quoted by hotels usually include a 10% service charge; however, some hotels add 10% to your bill.

TELEPHONES

There are no coin-operated phone booths. Public phones use a *télécarte*, which you can buy at post offices, café-tabacs, hotels, and *bureaux de change*.

To place a local or interisland call you have to dial all 10 numbers, beginning with 0596 and then the six-digit number. To call Martinique from the United States, dial 011 + 596 + 596 plus the local six-digit number (yes, you must dial 596 *twice*). If calling from Guadeloupe, dial 0596 and the six digits. Numbers with the 0696 prefix are for cell phones. To call the States from Martinique, dial 00 + 1, the area code, and the local number. You can now make collect calls to Canada through the Bell operator; you can get the AT&T or MCI operator from blue special service phones at the cruise ports and in town, such as at the Super Sumo snack bar, on rue de la Liberté, near the library. Or you can call the access numbers from your hotel phone. To call Great Britain from Martinique, dial 00 + 44, the area code (without the first zero), and the number. 🖪 **AT&T** ☎ 800/99-00-11. **Bell** ☎ 800/99-00-16. **MCI** ☎ 800/99-00-19.

TIPPING

All restaurants include a 15% service charge in their menu prices. You can al-

ways add to this if you feel that service was particularly good, especially if it is a place you intend to frequent. They will remember the generous Americans.

TOUR OPTIONS

Your hotel front desk can help you arrange a personalized island tour with an English-speaking driver. It's also possible to hire a taxi for the day or half day; there are set rates for certain itineraries, and if you share the ride with others the per-person price will be whittled down. La Belle Kréole runs one of the most fun excursion boats to *les fonds blanc*, also known as Empress Joséphine's baths. You can experience the unique Martinican custom of eating accras, drinking planter's punch, and smoking cigarettes in waist-deep water. Madinina Tours offers half- and full-day jaunts (lunch included) by sea and air. You can go by boat to St-Pierre on the north coast or by air to the Grenadines or St. Lucia. Madinina has tour desks in most of the major hotels. 🖪 ✉ Baie du Simon ☎ 0596/54-96-46 or 0696/29-93-13. **Madinina Tours** ✉ 111-113 rue Ernest Deproge, Fort-de-France ☎ 0596/70-65-25.

VISITOR INFORMATION

🖪 Before You Leave **Martinique Promotion Bureau** ✉ 444 Madison Ave., New York, NY 10022 ☎ 800/391-4909 ⊕ www.martinique.org ✉ 9454 Wilshire Blvd., Beverly Hills, CA 90212 ☎ 310/271-6665 ✉ 676 N. Michigan Ave., Chicago, IL 60611 ☎ 312/751-7800 ✉ 1981 McGill College Ave., Suite 490, Montréal, Québec H3A 2W9, Canada ☎ 514/288-4264 ✉ 1 Dundas St. W, Suite 2405, Toronto, Ontario M5G 1Z3, Canada ☎ 416/593-4723 or 800/361-9099 ✉ 178 Piccadilly, London W1V 0AL, U.K. ☎ 0181/124-4123. 🖪 In Martinique **Comité Martinique du Tourisme** ✉ Immeuble Le Beaupré, rue Schoelcher, Fort-de-France ☎ 0596/61-61-77 🖶 0596/61-09-59 ⊕ www.martinique.org.

WEDDINGS

Since getting married in Martinique requires a long residency requirement, it's not really feasible to plan a wedding on the island.

Montserrat

St. Patrick's Day Festival

WORD OF MOUTH

"I read three full books while I was there . . . the pace is wonderfully relaxed. Let me just say this, if your idea of your vacation is an island resort, this is probably not the place for you. If you want to experience a different type of place on this planet of ours, meet some genuinely friendly people, relax, and actually become a little more educated . . . this may be what you are looking for."

—SAnParis

WELCOME TO MONTSERRAT

It's been more than a decade since the Soufrière Hills Volcano erupted, and Montserrat is slowly coming back to life. Though the volcano continues to rumble, the island is otherwise as peaceful as the Caribbean gets, almost a throwback to another time, with the occasional modern convenience (and convenience store) thrown in. Montserrat draws eco-tourists, divers, and those who simply want to experience the Caribbean as it once was.

Hotels ▼	Restaurants ▼
Erindell Villa **5**	Gourmet Gardens **7**
Gingerbread Hill **4**	Jumping Jack's **10**
Grand View **3**	Tina's **2**
Travellers Palm **8**	Vue Pointe Restaurant **9**
Tropical Mansion **1**	
Vue Pointe Hotel **9**	Ziggy's **6**

> The island's best beach (the sole white-sand beach on the island) is accessible only by boat—or a very steep trail that we don't recommend.

> You can visit the Daytime Entry Zone from 6 AM to 6 PM daily, depending on how active the volcano is on any particular day.

KEY

1 *Exploring Sights*
1 *Hotels & Restaurants*

TOP 4 REASONS TO VISIT MONTSERRAT

1 Volcano lovers and other eco-tourists will experience a landscape that's been pretty much left alone for a decade, a rarity in the Caribbean.

2 You'll find tranquillity in abundance; if you want to lay back and relax, this is the place for you.

3 It's a buyer's market. Until the tourists come thundering back, value abounds here.

4 There's virtually no crime, and locals will welcome you with open arms. You won't find a friendlier place in the Caribbean.

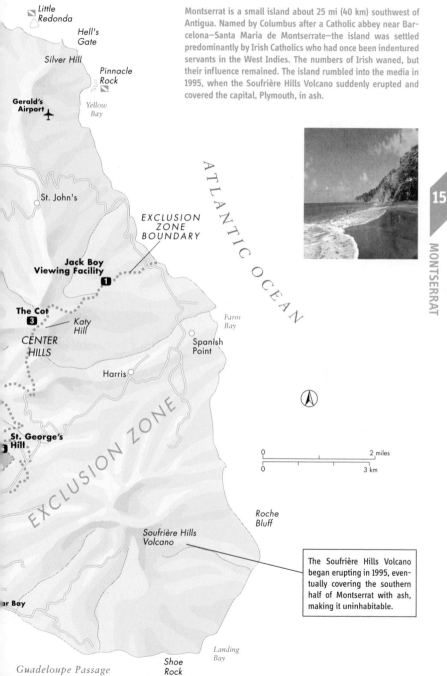

THE EMERALD ISLE OF THE CARIBBEAN

Montserrat is a small island about 25 mi (40 km) southwest of Antigua. Named by Columbus after a Catholic abbey near Barcelona—Santa Maria de Montserrate—the island was settled predominantly by Irish Catholics who had once been indentured servants in the West Indies. The numbers of Irish waned, but their influence remained. The island rumbled into the media in 1995, when the Soufrière Hills Volcano suddenly erupted and covered the capital, Plymouth, in ash.

Little Redonda

Hell's Gate

Silver Hill

Pinnacle Rock

Gerald's Airport

Yellow Bay

St. John's

EXCLUSION ZONE BOUNDARY

ATLANTIC OCEAN

Jack Boy Viewing Facility **1**

The Cot **3**

Katy Hill

Farm Bay

CENTER HILLS

Spanish Point

Harris

St. George's Hill

EXCLUSION ZONE

0 —————————————— 2 miles

0 —————————————— 3 km

Roche Bluff

Soufrière Hills Volcano

The Soufrière Hills Volcano began erupting in 1995, eventually covering the southern half of Montserrat with ash, making it uninhabitable.

ar Bay

Landing Bay

Guadeloupe Passage

Shoe Rock

MONTSERRAT PLANNER

Getting to Montserrat

There are no nonstop flights to Montserrat from North America. You can transfer on either Antigua or St. Maarten for a Winair flight (most departures are scheduled to coincide with the international flight schedule into the two islands) into the small but well-designed Gerald's Airport.

At one time, there was also ferry service from Antigua, but it had been discontinued at this writing; check with the Montserrat Tourist Board for the latest information.

Hassle factor: Medium

When to Go

The year's big event is the mid-March **St. Patrick's Day,** which ushers in a week of festivities, highlighted by musical concerts and masquerades à la Carnival. **Tourism Week,** usually late September or early October, encourages village competitions in music, dance, crafts, and food—with visitors eagerly welcomed. Late October's **Police, Fire, Search, and Rescue Services Community Week** also explodes with sound and color, as jump-ups, concerts, and barbecues lure hundreds of revelers. Mid-December into the New Year sees **Christmas Festival Celebrations,** from Calypso competitions to pageants and parades.

On the Ground

Though you can take taxis everywhere, you'll best appreciate Montserrat's quiet beauty if you rent a car and do some exploring on your own. Rates start at around $35 a day, but gas is expensive. Prepare to drive on your left, break for rambling goats and chickens, and negotiate some steep, winding roads. Otherwise, the fixed taxi fare from the airport ranges from $6 (for Tropical Mansions) to $22 (for the Vue Pointe Hotel).

Hotel & Restaurant Costs

Assume that hotels operate on the European Plan **(with no meals)** unless we specify that they use either the Continental Plan **(with a Continental breakfast),** Breakfast Plan **(with full breakfast),** or the Modified American Plan **(with breakfast and dinner).** Other hotels may offer the Full American Plan **(including all meals but no drinks)** or may be All-Inclusive **(with all meals, drinks, and most activities).**

WHAT IT COSTS in Dollars

	$$$$	$$$	$$	$	¢
Restaurants	over $30	$20–$30	$12–$20	$8–$12	under $8
Hotels*	over $350	$250–$350	$150–$250	$80–$150	under $80
Hotels**	over $450	$350–$450	$250–$350	$125–$250	under $125

*EP, BP, CP   **AI, FAP, MAP

Restaurant prices are for a main course at dinner, excluding the customary 10% service charge. Hotel prices are per night for a double room in high season, excluding 10% tax (7% for guesthouses and villas), service charges, and meal plans (except for all-inclusives).

Activities

You come to Montserrat for ecotourism, including **volcano viewing.** There's surprisingly varied **diving** in amazingly pristine waters. **Hiking** through unspoiled rain forest is another attraction, and intrepid travelers can even enter the Caribbean Pompeii, **Plymouth.** The showcase **beach** is Rendezvous Bay, a cliff-shadowed cove accessible only by boat or vigorous hike.

By Jordan
Simon

A POLICE ESCORT WAITS PATIENTLY as I stroll the ash-blanketed streets of Montserrat's capital, Plymouth. Behind me, cattle surreally meander through a vast gray expanse—the hardened mud flows that Montserrat's volcano spewed like nature's spittle—flanked by startlingly emerald greensward. Before me, a seemingly endless, pristine beach glistens like black pearls in the sun. The graceful Georgian buildings I fondly recall from my first visit in 1991 poke up like restless sprites: the bell turret of the War Memorial, the gables of Government House. Suddenly I stop short to avoid plunging through a collapsed roof. Spears of sunlight illuminate a droll yet dreamlike store display: untouched rows of sneakers and Swatches in a former shop—a good 15 feet underground.

Aficionados have always regarded Montserrat as an idyllic, fairy-tale island. But in 1995, Grimm turned grim when the Soufrière Hills Volcano erupted, literally throwing the island into the fire. The frilly Victorian gingerbreads of the capital, Plymouth, were buried, much of the tourism infrastructure was wiped out, and more than half the original 11,000 residents departed and have not been able to return. Though the volcano still belches (plumes of ash are visible from as far as Antigua), plucky locals joke that new beachfront is being created. The volcano itself is an ecotourism spot drawing travelers curious to see the awesome devastation. Ironically, other fringe benefits exist. Volcanic deposits enriched the already fertile soil; locals claim their fruit and vegetable crops have increased and improved. The slightly warmer waters have attracted even more varied marine life for divers and snorkelers to appreciate, along with new underwater rock formations.

Although an "Exclusion Zone" covers half the island, the rest is safe; in fact, the zone was slightly retracted after the volcano's lava dome partially collapsed during a pyroclastic flow in July 2003. Seismologists and vulcanologists conduct regular risk analyses and simulation studies (a new dome was growing at this writing, albeit very slowly, likely posing little danger). Visitors expecting mass devastation are in for a surprise; Montserrat ranks among the region's most pristine, serene destinations, its luxuriant vegetation and jagged green hills justifying the moniker Emerald Isle (most locals are descended from Irish settlers, whose influence lingers in place and family names, folklore, jigs, even a wispy brogue). The combined Carnival and Christmas festivities go on for nearly a month, when the island is awash with color, from calypso competitions to parades and pageants.

Other than the volcano, the steamiest activities are the fiercely contested domino games outside rum shops. That may soon change. The government speaks optimistically of building a new golf course, developing spa facilities to offer volcanic mud baths, even running tours—pending safety assessments—of Plymouth as a haunting Caribbean answer to Pompeii. An airport has been constructed, partly in the hope of recapturing the villa crowd that once frequented the island. But these developments—as well as debates over the new capital and threatened lawsuits against the British government for restricting access and utility service to homesites—will simmer for quite some time. One thing won't change: the people, whether native-born or expat, are among the warmest anywhere. Chat them up, and don't be surprised if you're invited to a family dinner or beach picnic.

Where to Stay

Currently, the island primarily offers villas (housekeepers and cooks can be arranged) or guesthouses, the latter often incorporating meals by request in the rate (ask if the 7% tax and 10% service charge are included), as well as two small hotels. In the pre-volcano (and Hurricane Hugo) days, when an international roster of celebrity musicians (Elton to Eric, the Rolling Stones to Sting) recorded at Sir George Martin's Air Studios, Montserrat was a favored spot for many rich and famous Britons (and the occasional American) to vacation. Today you can luxuriate in one of the handsome villas they called home when visiting and do so for comparatively affordable rates.

The leading villa rental company in Montserrat is **Tradewinds Real Estate** (⌂ Box 365, Old Towne ☎ 664/491–2004 ⊕ www.tradewindsmontserrat.com). Many of its 40-plus deluxe properties, ranging from one to four bedrooms, have plunge pools, ultramodern conveniences from DVD players and Internet access to gourmet kitchens, and amazing water vistas. Recommended properties with beach access and/or strategic hillside locations include Mango Falls, Casa del Sol, Fairwinds, and Vest View. Caring owners Susan Edgecombe and her mother, Betty Dix, really try to match guest to villa, remaining available throughout your stay to make any additional arrangements and offer touring and activity suggestions. Rates run from $750 to $3,000 per week in high season.

$ ▦ **Tropical Mansion Suites.** Despite the grandiose name, this is little more than a motel with neocolonial architectural pretensions, though a slight soullessness pervades the space, which lacks the warmth of family-run guesthouses. Nonetheless, it's the most "modern" hotel on island and quite comfortable. Rooms are clean and fairly spacious, with an upscale motor-lodge look, but balconies (save for Room 202, where Prince Philip stayed) regrettably face the interior courtyard, rather than the verdant sweep of hills undulating down to the sea. Though the institutional basement restaurant has received a face-lift, insist on patio seating. Meals are mostly buffet and adequate, if overpriced. ⊠ *Sweeney's* ☎ *664/491–8767* 🖷 *664/491–8275* ⊕ *www.tropicalmansion.com* ↳ *17 rooms, 1 suite* ⚭ *Restaurant, fans, some kitchenettes, refrigerators, cable TV, Wi-Fi, pool, bar, shops, Internet room, meeting rooms; no a/c in some rooms* ▭ *AE, D, MC, V* ¹⊙¹ *CP.*

★ **$** ▦ **Vue Pointe Hotel.** Montserrat's oldest, classiest hostelry keeps rising—literally—like a phoenix from the ashes, thanks to its gracious hosts, the Osborne family. Carol, American by birth, is as fiercely proud as any island native and a font of local lore and information. The bar and restaurants always percolate with life in season. Comfy, hexagonal rondavels sit amid grounds ablaze with red hibiscus, yellow allamanda, and pink oleander. Traditionally furnished rooms enlivened by local photos bear out the hotel's name with extraordinary volcano and/or water vistas (numbers 7 and 24 are the winners). Those with kitchenettes are particular bargains: experience true tranquility sipping a rum punch on your terrace as the sun fireballs across the long, gray ribbon of Old Road Bay. 🖰 *Box 65, Old Road Bay* ☎ *664/491–5210* 🖷 *664/491–4813* ⊕ *www.vuepointe.com* ☞ *27 rooms* ⚓ *2 restaurants, bar, fans, some kitchenettes, refrigerators, cable TV, 2 tennis courts, dive shop, snorkeling, pool, bar, library, shops, meeting rooms; no a/c* ⊟ *MC, V* ⦿ *CP.*

$ 🏨 **Grand View Bed & Breakfast.** The basement of this welcoming inn holds a radio station, but contented guests send the most powerful broadcast signal. Energetic, enthusiastic owner Theresa Silcott prides herself on being Monserrat's best hostess. She can take you to beaches and local shindigs, even brew bracing bush tea (ingredients are coaxed from her lovingly tended botanical-vegetable-herb garden, replete with mini-nature trail). Locals justly laud her traditional cuisine (she cooks by reservation only): the intensely flavored goat water, mountain chicken, and baked goods are cherished family recipes, while Theresa's homemade hot sauces and preserves make splendid souvenirs. Units are plain but clean and cheerful, and the hotel's name doesn't exaggerate. ✉ *Box 350, Baker Hill* ☎ *664/491–2284* 🖷 *664/491–6876* ⊕ *www.grandviewmni.com* ☞ *3 rooms, 3 suites* ⚓ *Restaurant, fans, some kitchenettes, some refrigerators, bar, Internet room, meeting rooms; no a/c in some rooms* ⊟ *No credit cards* ⦿ *CP.*

★ ¢–$ 🏨 **Gingerbread Hill.** This secluded mountainside retreat offers remarkable value, splendid views, utter tranquility, and exquisite grounds, where you can pluck your breakfast straight from the mango, banana, citrus, papaya, and coconut trees. Owners David and Clover Lea laughingly call themselves "unrepentant but well-done hippies," and they are—in the best sense of respecting nature, supporting local culture, and being self-sufficient. This Renaissance couple built the villas themselves, utilizing recycled or indigenous materials wherever possible. Clover is an artist and trained masseuse (ladies only); David is a documentary videographer, who'll give you fascinating perspectives on the volcano. Oldest son Jesse conducts tours and records island music. Two villas have such clever creative touches as trompe-l'oeil window frames, hand-painted tiles, as well as wraparound verandas with extraordinary views. The cozy Backpacker's Special has a microwave, CD player, and fridge. Reasonably priced meals are available (daughter-in-law Kristina Mae is a mean baker), utilizing fixings from the hydroponic gardens and fresh eggs from the family's chickens. 🖰 *Box 246, St. Peter's* ☎ *664/491–5812* 🖷 *786/524–4692* ⊕ *www.volcano-island.com* ☞ *1 2-bedroom villa, 1 1-bedroom villa, 2 rooms* ⚓ *Fans, some kitchens, some refrigerators, some microwaves, mountain bikes, laundry facilities, Internet room, airport shuttle; no a/c, no TV in some rooms* ⊟ *No credit cards* ⦿ *EP.*

¢ 🏨 **Erindell Villa Guesthouse.** This tranquil rain-forest retreat is a photo album in the making, overflowing with character and characters. Memorable snapshots run from lush gardens framed by emerald hills and azure sea to colorful cocktail hours brimming with bonhomie and island gossip. Warm and witty Lou and Shirley Spycalla treat you like family (offering such little extras as meet-and-greet airport service, snack baskets, and a cell phone loaner when hiking or beachcombing), separate entrances guarantee privacy in the two snug, self-contained units (the poolside room

15

is larger). If you'd rather not cook, you can feast *en famille* in the kitchen on enticing themed meals. ⊠ *Gros Michel Dr., Woodlands* ☎ *664/491–3655* ⊕ *www.erindellvilla.com* ⇥ *2 rooms* ⚑ *Restaurant, fans, microwaves, refrigerators, cable TV, pool, laundry service, complimentary airport transfers, Internet room; no a/c* ⊟ *No credit cards* ⦿ *CP.*

¢ ⊡ **Travellers Palm.** English expats Roy and Lottie McDonald simply couldn't enjoy their semi-retirement without sharing their island home. Whether breakfasting on the breeze-swept veranda or luxuriating by the pool, you're treated to invigorating views of the Caribbean (and Nevis and Redonda). Best of all is the extraordinarily lush landscaping, with plenty of hammocks and benches, all perfumed by ylang-ylang (locals stop by and ask for a handful to use as car deodorant) and Hawaiian frangipani; pick your own mangos, limes, coconuts, oranges, guavas, or papayas and ask Lottie to make a smoothie. Lottie also cooks family-style dinner upon request (try her chicken Kiev using Stilton). The McDonalds might even invite you to go barhopping or beachcombing. Two rooms are in the main house, and a snugger one is by the pool; all are decorated with Caribbean crafts and soft furnishings from bedspreads to slipcovers made by Lottie herself, enhancing the homey feel. ⊠ *Olveston* ☎ *664/491–4861* ⊕ *www.travellerspalmmontserrat.com* ⇥ *3 rooms* ⚑ *Fans, some refrigerators, pool, Internet room, airport shuttle; no a/c; no TV in some rooms* ⊟ *No credit cards* ⦿ *CP.*

Where to Eat

Restaurants are casual affairs indeed, ranging from glorified rum shops to hotel dining rooms. Most serve classic Caribbean fare, including such specialties as goat water (a thick stew of goat meat, tubers, and vegetables that seems to have been bubbling for days), the increasingly hard-to-find mountain chicken (giant frogs' legs), saal-fish kiac (codfish fritters), home-brewed ginger beer, and freshly made juices from soursop, mango, blackberry (different from the North American species), guava, tamarind, papaya, and gooseberry.

What to Wear

Dress is informal even at dinner, though skimpy attire is frowned upon by the comparatively conservative islanders. Long pants are preferred, albeit not required, for men in the evening.

CARIBBEAN ✗ **Vue Pointe Hotel Restaurant.** As former regulars slowly return to
$$–$$$ Montserrat, this attractive, semi-alfresco poolside restaurant–bar once again erupts with lively discussions among locals, expats, and an international clientele. Soft jazz on the sound system smokes around the bleached wood rafters and aquamarine pillars. You'll savor well-prepared, reasonably priced theme buffets and local specialties (baked chicken, lamb curry, kingfish creole). Seemingly the whole island packs the place for Chinese Friday dinners, Sunday Family Buffets, and the wildly popular Wednesday BBQ and Cultural Evening (including a shorter version of the regular folkloric performance by the Emerald Community Singers in enchanting national dress). ⊠ *Old Towne* ☎ *664/491–5210* ⊟ *MC, V.*

Luck of the Irish

MONTSERRAT'S FIRST EUROPEAN SETTLERS were persecuted English and Irish Catholics brought from Protestant St. Kitts by Englishman Thomas Warner in 1632. Seventeen years later, Oliver Cromwell sentenced many Irish political prisoners to work in the island's lucrative sugarcane fields. A 1678 census recorded that more than half the islanders were Irish. Their influence lingers today, starting with the shamrock passport stamp. The national flag bears a crest of the legendary Irish figure of Erin with a harp, while the names of both towns (Galway, Bunkum) and inhabitants (Maloney, Frith) hark back to Eire. The national dish, goat water, recalls a traditional Irish stew, while the rollicking *Bam-chick-a-lay* wouldn't be out of place in *Riverdance*. Montserrat is the only country outside Ireland where St. Patrick's Day is a public holiday; March 17 ushers in a week of celebrations across the island, the wearing of the green assuming a distinctly Caribbean beat with live calypso, reggae, and iron band music. Indeed, Montserrat's true African heritage is just as pronounced: many newborns are still given "jumbie" nicknames to fool those evil spirits, and the related jumbie dances, designed to propitiate or ward them off, are lusty and vibrant. The two traditions happily merge in the engaging people, such as Rootsman (aka Murphy), proprietor of the eponymous Carr's Bay bar, fervently discussing his homemade herbal remedies in a lyrical, lilting brogue.

$–$$$ ╳ **Tina's.** This pretty, seafoam-green-and-white wooden building is garlanded year-round with Christmas lights, a harbinger of the good vibes within, as off-duty cops flirt shyly with young women in curlers picking up the surprisingly good take-away pizza. It's the best place to eavesdrop on island gossip, as government functionaries file in for lunch (at least when day-trippers don't take over). Dine either in a trim room or on a breezy veranda (admittedly sans view). Occasionally you'll find old-time dishes like souse, but the menu is generally more upscale: specialties include velvety pumpkin soup, proper escargots, and tender lobster in sultry creole sauce or (even better) tangy garlic sauce; entrées are served with heaping helpings of salads and sides. Fine desserts (moist carrot cake and wonderfully textured coconut pie) end the meal. ⊠ *Brades* ☎ *664/491–3538* ▱ *No credit cards.*

ECLECTIC **$$$** ╳ **Ziggy's.** Vivacious owners John and Marcia Punter literally hacked Montserrat's most elegant eatery from the rain forest. They poured a concrete floor and dressed it with a white rectangular tent, palm fronds, potted plants, hardwood chairs, candlesticks, and colorful Moroccan-inspired table settings. The menu (posted on a blackboard) changes daily. Generally well executed dishes lean more toward bistro fare (emphasizing beef entrecôte or grilled marinated lamb over such island staples as chicken and fish); the signature butterfly shrimp usually precede entrées. A decent wine list enhances the meal; save room for the Chocolate Sludge. Though the schedule is erratic (reconfirm reservations), the location hard to find, and the service too relaxed, the ambience is appealingly serene and upscale. ⊠ *Mahogany Loop, Woodlands* ☎ 664/491-8282 ⌂ *Reservations essential* ▭ *No credit cards* ⊙ *No lunch, no dinner some nights.*

$–$$ ✕ **Gourmet Gardens.** This tranquil, secluded spot—a classic gingerbread chattel-house replica echoing the adjacent historic buildings of the former Olveston estate—fulfills more than half the name's promise. There are few more delightful experiences than relaxing on Mariet's veranda amid a virtual botanical garden or beneath the huge, shady tamarind tree. Lunches are excellent value, but Sunday brunch is the winner (scrumptious eggs Benedict). "Gourmet" is a slight exaggeration, but the global menu more than satisfies most palates and wallets. Specialties include stroganoff, chicken cordon bleu, and any dessert (try the chocolate mousse or cheesecake). ⊠ *Olveston* ☎ 664/491–7859 ⌂ *Reservations essential* ▭ *No credit cards* ⊙ *No dinner Wed.*

★ $–$$ ✕ **Jumping Jack's Beach Bar & Restaurant.** Danny and Margaret Sweeney's beachfront eatery certainly jumps Friday nights as one of the islands' most popular liming spots. Their trim, sky-blue-and-mauve shack is a delightful lunch spot as well. The decor—fishnets, Danny's tournament trophies, and photos of him displaying his prize catches—reflects the specialty: tuna, wahoo, and other freshly caught fish. But Margaret utilizes whatever ingredients are available. You might luck into chicken satay, lasagna, or flaky, flavorful chicken-and-mushroom, pork, and steak-and-kidney pies that elevate traditional English pub grub to an art form. And the sublime sticky toffee pudding, mango-ginger crumble, and pear tart justify Margaret's declaration, "I'd rather make desserts than clean the house!" ⊠ *Vue Pointe Hotel, Old Road Bay* ☎ 664/491–5645 ▭ *No credit cards* ⊙ *No lunch Mon. or Tues., no dinner Sat.–Thurs.*

Beaches

Montserrat's beaches are public and, with one exception, composed of soft, light to dark gray volcanic sand.

Foxes Bay. The ravages of volcanic ash and hurricanes are visible at this deserted taupe crescent in the Daytime Entry Zone: the former bird sanctuary and mangrove swamp with denuded tree trunks, and the ruin of a former Rotary Club refreshment booth. However, nature has impressively revivified itself, allowing Bob Hunt of the U.K. PGA to conduct feasibility studies for a 9-hole golf course (expandable to 18), which awaits funding on a verdant 60-acre site. The beach lacks facilities and shade. There are plans to rebuild the coastal main road, but for now the only access is via the old Belham Valley Road. ⊠ *Belham Valley Rd., 1½ mi (2½ km) south of Old Towne.*

Little Bay. Boats chug in and out of the port at the northern end of this otherwise comely crescent with calm waters. Several beach bars—Log-On (get passionate owner Arthur Brokes talking about the environment) and Shizzle ma Nizzle—provide cool shade and cooler drinks. Carlton's Fish Net Bar in the Festival Village specializes in barbecued stuffed trunkfish (a shellfish delicacy); the Good Life also offers fine food. You may see locals casting lines for their own dinner. ⊠ *Approx. 1½ mi (2½ km) north of Brades off the main road; look for turnoffs to Little Bay.*

Old Road Bay. Follow signs to Old Towne's Vue Pointe Hotel to reach this mile-long pearl-gray beauty, a favorite swimming beach. There's little shade other than what's provided by palapas set up by the hotel (request beach chairs if you buy lunch or drinks there or at Jumping Jack's Beach Bar & Restaurant). ⌧ *Old Road Bay.*

★ **Rendezvous Bay.** The island's sole white-sand beach is a perfect cove tucked under a forested cliff whose calm, unspoiled waters are ideal for swimming and offer remarkable snorkeling. It's accessibleonly via the sea or a steep trail that runs over the bluff to adjacent Little Bay (you can also negotiate boat rides from the fishermen who congregate there). There are no facilities or shade, but its very remoteness and pristine reef teeming with marine life lend it exceptional charm. ⌧ *Rendezvous Bay.*

Woodlands/Bunkum Bays. The only drawback to this secluded strand is the occasionally rough surf (children should be closely monitored). The breezy but covered picnic area on the cliff is one of the best vantage points to watch migratory humpback whales in spring, nesting green and hawksbill turtles in early fall. (From here, hike north then down across a wooden bridge to even less trammeled Bunkum Bay; the food and ambience at 4B'S are quintessentially Caribbean.) ⌧ *At turnoff just outside Woodlands Village.*

Sports & the Outdoors

Biking

Mountain biking is making a comeback, with a wide network of trails through the lush Centre Hills and, to the north, Silver Hill. Eco-centric expats James Naylor and David Lea run **Imagine Peace Bicycles** (⌧ BBC Complex, Main Rd., Brades ☎ 664/491–5812 or 664/493–1520), which rents state-of-the-art equipment from Cygnal and Mongoose ($10 to $15 per day) and conducts tours through the countryside.

Diving

More than 30 practically pristine dive sites surround Montserrat. The even more bountiful marine life has had time to recover from the predations of human activities, while the pyroclastic flows formed boulders, pinnacles, ledges, and walls that anchor new coral reefs. **Carr's Bay** is a favorite for shore dives, with arrow crabs, basket stars, turtles, and shimmering blue tang darting about hulking boulders and a small, colorful cave; night dives are particularly memorable as millions of bioluminescent microorganisms glow when disturbed. The shallow reefs surrounding **Woodlands Bay** feature varied underwater topography, including a small, colorful cave and thousands of banded coral shrimp, copper sweepers, sergeant majors, four-eyed butterfly fish, jacknife, attenuated trumpetfish, and turtles. **Rendezvous Bay** may be the finest spot for both snorkeling and diving, thanks to a sheltered reef and lack of ash or silt. You come face-to-face with spotted morays, porcupine fish, snake eels, octopi, and more. You can even hang out with thousands of (harmless) fruit bats in partly submerged caves. Other top dive sites include **Lime Kiln Bay** and **Off um Bay,** as well as the spectacular submarine rock formations around **Little Redonda** and the **Pinnacles** off the rougher, more challenging northeastern shores.

15

⟳ Dive master Bryan Cunningham took over Wolf Krebs's **Sea Wolf Diving School** (✉ Vue Pointe Hotel, Old Bay Rd., Old Towne ☎ 664/491–7807 ⊕ www.seawolfdivingschool.com), which offers PADI certification; shore, kayak, and boat dives; snorkeling trips; Plymouth excursions via boat (including a beach lunch); and even underwater photography classes utilizing state-of-the-art SeaLife equipment. Bryan and wife Tish are particularly good with kids: the shop stocks underwater Frisbees and torpedoes, as well as specialized children's gear.

Fishing

Deep-sea fishing (wahoo, bonito, shark, marlin, and yellowfin tuna) is superb, since the waters aren't disturbed by leviathan cruise ships. Affable **Danny Sweeney** (✉ Olveston ☎ 664/491–5645) has won several regional tournaments, including Montserrat's Open Fishing Competition. Half-day charters (up to four people) are $250. Though schools of game fish amazingly cavort just 2 to 3 mi (3 to 5 km) offshore, Danny's depth sounder picks up action in deeper waters. An extra bonus on the open sea are the gripping views of the volcanic devastation.

Hiking

Montserrat's lush, untrammeled rain forest teeming with exotic flora, fauna, and birdlife is best experienced on foot. The tourist office provides lists of hiking trails, from easy to arduous. Nine of the most dramatic routes are gradually being upgraded as part of the Montserrat Tourism Development Project; in addition to improving their definition, the government will also be building viewing platforms and providing interpretative information at strategic points. Still, if you're not experienced or fit, go with a guide; always wear sturdy shoes and bring water. Most marked trails run through the biologically diverse, scenic Centre Hills region, offering stirring lookouts over the volcano's barren flanks, surrounding greenery, and ash-covered villages in the Exclusion Zone. The rain forest is home to many regionally endemic wildlife species (tree frogs, dwarf geckos, anoles, mountain chicken—actually a type of frog, and the half-snake/half-lizard galliwasp), as well as most of the 34 resident birds, from red-billed tropic birds to the rare national bird, the Montserrat oriole, with its distinctive orange-and-black plumage. The Silver Hills in the north are vastly different, with dry and deciduous forests and open plains blanketing a defunct, heavily faulted and eroded volcano; views here might provide a glimpse of how southern Montserrat will look millions of years from now.

Scriber Tours (☎ 664/491–2546, or 664/491–3412, or 664/492–2943) is run by James "Scriber" Daley (but "a describer since I was little"), an employee of the Agricultural Department legendary for his uncanny bird calls. He leads nature hikes through the rain forest for $20 to $40; he'll hire additional guides if there are more than 10 people per group, ensuring personal attention. Scriber also explains indigenous flora, from 42 fern species (kids love when he "tattoos" them with silver fern leaves) to others prized for medicinal properties (you might collect the makings of bush tea for back pain or menstrual cramps). He also conducts a memorable, if brief, evening mountain-chicken tour, distributing flashlights to find the foot-long frogs.

Shopping

Montserrat offers a variety of local crafts and does a brisk trade in vulcanological mementos (many shops sell not only postcards and striking photographs but small bottles of gray ash capped by colorful, homemade cloth).

David Lea (✉ Gingerbread Hill, St. Peter's ☎ 664/491–5812) has chronicled Montserrat's volcanic movements in a fascinating eight-part video series, *The Price of Paradise,* each entry a compelling glimpse into the geological and social devastation—and regeneration. These, as well as rollicking local-music CDs by his son and other musicians, are available at his studio. **Jus' Looking** (✉ Gerald's Airport, Gerald's ☎ 664/491–2752) is a terrific last-minute stop for high-quality local arts and crafts, from photos to ceramics and painted gourds, high-test treats like Volcano Rum and homemade Gingerbread Liqueur (with a slice of gingerbread pickling inside the bottle), and low-priced souvenirs. **Luv's Cotton Store** (✉ Salem ☎ 664/491–3906) is the best source for sportswear made from Sea Island cotton, celebrated for its softness and high quality. Also occupying the National Trust building, the **Montserrat Philatelic Bureau** (✉ Salem ☎ 664/491–2042) sells a wealth of unusual stamps, including handsome first-day covers. **Oriole Gift Shop** (✉ Salem ☎ 664/491–3086), run by the Montserrat National Trust, is an excellent source for books on Montserrat (look for the *Montserrat Cookbook* and works by the island's former acting governor, Sir Howard Fergus), as well as handicrafts and locally made food products. **Woolcock's Craft & Photo Gallery** (✉ BBC Building, Brades ☎ 664/491–2025) promotes the work of local artists like Donaldson Romeo and sells spectacular photos of the volcano as well as of indigenous birds and other wildlife.

Nightlife

Although Montserrat is better known for another kind of wildlife, Friday-night revelers lime in roadside rum shops scattered around the island, often spilling out on the street as part of the informal evening culture. There's no closing time, and many bars serve yummy, authentic local food. **Bunkum Bay Beach Bar** (✉ St. Peter's ☎ 664/491–6077), also known as 4B's, is hip-hopping and happening Fridays and Saturdays with a DJ spinning the latest Caribbean hits; the fried chicken and grilled fish are succulent any time of day or night. **Garry Moore's Wide Awake Bar** (✉ Salem ☎ 664/491–7156) is a perennial favorite that doesn't close as long as customers are thirsty. Don't be afraid to wake Garry to pay your tab: he often naps at the bar (when he isn't complaining—mostly humorously—about a plumber's hard life and long hours). Mild-mannered restaurant by day, **Good Life** (✉ Little Bay ☎ 664/491–4576) often transforms on weekends into a strobing disco blasting the latest Caribbean and Euro-house mixes, attracting every young single ready to mingle. **Howe's Rum Shop** (✉ St. John's ☎ 664/491–3008) is the best spot for shooting pool and the breeze over luscious fried and barbecued chicken, liberally daubed with mouth- and eye-watering homemade sauces and seasonings. Harriette Weekes runs a hugely entertaining **Let's Go Limin' Rumshop Tour**

(☎ 664/491–5371) on most Friday nights, bopping among five (weekly changing) watering holes in a comfortable van, including stops for dinner, dancing, and a game of darts or dominoes. Lydia, the owner of the **Treasure Spot** (✉ Cudjoe Head ☎ 664/493–2003), often books the island's up-and-coming musicians (usually One Man Band but also Pops Morris, Hero, and Basil) to play weekends.

Exploring Montserrat

Though the more fertile—and historic—southern half of Montserrat has been destroyed by the volcano, emerald hills still reward explorers. Hiking and biking are the best ways to experience this island's unspoiled rain forest, glistening black-sand beaches, and lookouts over the devastation.

Numbers in the margin correspond to points of interest on the Montserrat map.

❸ The Cot. A fairly strenuous Centre Hills trail leads to one of Montserrat's few remaining historic sites—the ruins of the once-influential Sturges family's summer cottage—as well as a banana plantation. Its Duck Pond Hill perch, farther up the trail, dramatically overlooks the coastline, Garibaldi Hill, Old Towne, abandoned villages, and Plymouth.

❶ Jack Boy Viewing Facility. This vantage point—replete with telescope, barbecue grill, and tables for picnickers, landscaped grounds, and washrooms—provides bird's-eye views of the old W. H. Bramble airport and eastern villages damaged by pyroclastic flows. ✉ *Jack Boy Hill.*

★ ❹ **Montserrat National Trust.** The MNT's Natural History Centre aims to conserve and enhance the island's natural beauty and cultural heritage. The center has exhibits on Arawak canoe building, colonial sugar and lime production (the term "limey" was first applied here to English sailors trying to avoid scurvy), indigenous marine life, West Indian cricket, the Calypso monarchs, and the history of Sir George Martin's Air Studios, which once lured top musicians from Dire Straits to Stevie Wonder and Paul McCartney. Eventually one archival exhibit will screen videos of Montserrat's oral history related by its oldest inhabitants. The lovingly tended botanical gardens in back make for a pleasant stroll. ✉ *Main Rd., Olveston* ☎ *664/291–3086* ⊕ *www.montserratnationaltrust.com* ▧ *$2 suggested donation* ☉ *Mon.–Sat. 10–4.*

❺ Montserrat Volcano Observatory. The island's must-see sight occupies capacious, strikingly postmodern quarters with stunning vistas of the Soufrière Hills Volcano—a lunarscape encircled by brilliant green—and Plymouth in the distance. The MVO staff runs half-hour tours that explain monitoring techniques on sophisticated computerized equipment in riveting detail and describe the various pyroclastic surge deposits and artifacts on display. A new room re-creates the sensation of being there through 3-D interactive volcano cams, a high-impact film with IMAX footage, working seismometers (kids can jump up and down to manufacture vibrations), and other real-time monitoring instruments. ✉ *Flemings* ☎ *664/491–5647* ⊕ *www.mvo.ms* ▧ *Observatory free,*

Fodor'sChoice
★

tours $4 ✆ *Weekdays 8:30–4:30. Tours Tues. and Thurs. at 2; call ahead for other times.*

D&D Bar and Grocery (✉ Flemings ☏ 664/491–9730) is an unprepossessing shack, just downhill off the first right turn from the MVO. Owner Dawn Davis mastered mixology while working at Nisbet Plantation on Nevis, and she proudly offers more than 100 libations at her Lilliputian bar (and accepts challenges). She also bakes sublime bread and serves delectable, cheap local fare (souse, fishwater, baked chicken) on weekends.

❽ Plymouth. The adventuresome can stroll through Montserrat's former capital, albeit at their own risk. Once one of the Caribbean's loveliest towns, facing the vividly hued sea, it now resembles a dust-covered lunarscape, with elegant Georgian buildings buried beneath several feet of ash, mud, and rubble (though rain is slowly washing layers away). Entry is officially possible only with a police escort (lest you fall through a rickety roof), but this can be arranged with the Police Headquarters in Brades or through the Montserrat Tourist Board. A hazard allowance of EC\$150 is charged per individual or group. ✉ *Plymouth* ☏ *664/491–2230 (Tourist Office)* 🎫 *Police escort EC\$150* ✆ *Daily during daylight hours with police escort.*

❼ Richmond Hill. If you're not feeling overly daring (or would rather not pay the hazard allowance), this formerly affluent suburb of Plymouth, which is within the Daytime Entry Zone, is just north of the former capital and also offers a riveting panorama. You can see the 18th-century sugar mill that once housed the Montserrat Museum and poke around the abandoned (for now) Montserrat Springs Hotel, where a few items remain just as they were left on the front desk during the mass exodus in 1997. You might encounter a goat or cow nibbling mushrooms growing through the cracks in the pool and tennis court. The hot springs of the hotel are down the hill by the beach, which has grown substantially and become a favorite liming spot of locals and expats. ✉ *Richmond Hill* ✆ *Daylight hours.*

❷ Runaway Ghaut. Montserrat's *ghauts* (pronounced guts) are deep ravines that carry rainwater down from the mountains to the sea. This natural spring, a short, well-marked walk into the hilly bush outside Woodlands, was the site of bloody colonial skirmishes between the British and French. The legend is more interesting than the trail: "Those that drink its water clear they spellbound are, and the Montserrat they must obey." If you don't want to hike or picnic, a drink from the roadside faucet should ensure that you return to Montserrat in your lifetime. ✉ *Main road, just south of Woodlands.*

❻ St. George's Hill. The only access to this incredible Daytime Entry Zone vantage point over the devastation is across the Belham Valley, once a beautiful golf course but now totally covered by volcanic mudflow. Routes aren't signposted on the rough road, which is often impassable after heavy rains, so it's best to hire an experienced guide. You'll drive through Cork Hill and Weekes, villages for the most part spookily in-

15

tact (there's no way to provide utilities, though some enterprising souls are slowly installing solar power and water cisterns). Close to the summit, the equally eerie, abandoned, stark-white wind generator project and the giant satellite dishes of the Gem and Antilles radio stations resemble abstract art installations awaiting completion by Christo. At the top, Fort St. George contains sparse ruins, including a few cannons, but the overwhelming sight is the panorama of destruction, an unrelenting swath of gray offset by vivid emerald fields and turquoise Caribbean. ⊠ *St. George's Hill* ☽ *Daylight hours.*

MONTSERRAT ESSENTIALS

To research prices, get advice from other travelers, and book travel arrangements, visit www.fodors.com.

Transportation

BY AIR

The $18.5 million Gerald's Airport opened in July 2005. Winair offers several daily 20-minute flights on 19-seat Twin Otters from Antigua and St. Maarten.

🛈 **Winair** ☎ 664/491-262 or 664/491-2533, 888/255-6889 in U.S. ⊕ www.fly-winair.com.

BY CAR & TAXI

Temporary driving licenses are available for $20 at the police headquarters in Brades, which is open 24 hours weekdays. You can rent Jeeps and cars starting at $35 to $40 per day.

One main road—twisting up, down, and around many steep hills—runs from the north, down each side of the island, with little unnamed side roads streaming inland. Most addresses don't have street names or house numbers, but just ask anyone to direct you. You're best off initially with local guides, who will know where the best views are—and which parts of the island are off-limits due to volcanic activity. Respect the signs and closed gates that indicate the Exclusion Zone boundaries; though the Daytime Entry Zone is now open 24/7, you should avoid it at night.

Driving is on the left; the well-paved main road zigs, zags, climbs, and plummets precipitously, while many equally winding side roads are pocked with potholes. There are no traffic lights but a few zebra pedestrian crossings (without beacons); beware wandering pigs and goats. Gasoline in Montserrat tends to be quite expensive.

Taxis are unmetered but most rates are fixed; sample fares from the airport include $6 to Tropical Mansions and $22 to Vue Pointe.

🛈 Car Rentals **Jefferson Car Rental** ⊠ Palm Loop ☎ 664/491-2126. **Montserrat Enterprises** ⊠ Old Towne ☎ 664/491-2431. **Neville Bradshaw Agencies** ⊠ Olveston ☎ 664/491-5270.

Contacts & Resources

BANKS & EXCHANGE SERVICES

Local currency is the Eastern Caribbean dollar (EC$), which is tied to the U.S. dollar and fluctuates only slightly. US$1 is worth approximately EC$2.70; you get a slightly better rate if you exchange money at a bank than at your hotel (the exchange is sometimes rounded down to EC$2.50 in simpler transactions). American dollars are readily accepted, although you can usually receive change in EC$.

Most hotels, restaurants, and shops take major credit cards; all accept traveler's checks. An ATM (dispensing EC$) is available at one bank (a second ATM may open at the Bank of Montserrat).

Prices quoted throughout this chapter are in U.S. dollars unless otherwise indicated.

Bank of Montserrat ⊠ Brades ☎ 664/491-3843. **Royal Bank of Canada** ⊠ Brades ☎ 664/491-2426.

BUSINESS HOURS

Banks are open generally Monday through Thursday from 8 to 2 and Friday 9 to 3. Most shops open 8 to 4 Monday through Saturday, often closing early Wednesday and Saturday.

ELECTRICITY

Montserrat runs on 220 volts, but most lodgings also utilize 110 volts, permitting use of small North American appliances. Outlets may be either two- or three-pronged, so bring an adaptor.

EMERGENCIES

🚑 Ambulance & Fire **Ambulance** ☎ 411 or 664/491-2802. **Fire** ☎ 911.

🏥 Hospitals **Glendon Hospital** ⊠ St. John's ☎ 664/491-2552 or 664/491-7404.

💊 Pharmacies **Lee's Pharmacy** ⊠ Brades ☎ 664/491-3444

👮 Police **Police** ☎ 999.

HOLIDAYS

Public holidays are New Year's Day, St. Patrick's Day, Good Friday (usually late Mar. or Apr.), Easter Monday (usually late Mar. or Apr.), Labor Day (1st Mon. in May), Whitmonday (usually late May or early June), Queen's Birthday (June 12), Emancipation Day (Aug. 1), Christmas, Boxing Day (Dec. 26), Festival Day (Dec. 31).

INTERNET, MAIL & SHIPPING

There is one Internet café in Brades, which is open weekdays from 8 to 4.

Airmail letters to North America and the United Kingdom cost EC$1.50; postcards, EC$1.20. Letters to Australia and New Zealand cost EC$1.50; postcards, EC$1.20. The main post office is in the Government House in Brades. Note that there are no postal codes; when addressing letters to the island, you need only indicate the address and "Montserrat, West Indies."

Andy's Internet Cafe ⊠ BBC Bldg., Main Rd., Brades ☎ 664/491-9768 ⊕ www.andysinternetcafe.com.

PASSPORTS REQUIREMENTS

Even if visiting on a day trip, U.S. and Canadian citizens need proof of identity in the form of a passport or a birth certificate with a raised seal and government-issued photo identification. All others need passports. Beginning January 1, 2007, U.S. citizens will need to carry a valid passport to reenter the United States, as will Canadians. All visitors must present a return or ongoing ticket.

SAFETY

Montserrat is quite safe, but you should still take such normal precautions as locking valuables in the hotel safe; don't leave them unattended in a room, on a beach, or in a rental car.

TAXES & SERVICE CHARGES

The departure tax is $21, payable in cash only—either U.S. or E.C. currency. Day-trippers from Antigua spending less than 24 hours on Montserrat pay only a EC$10 "security charge" and no departure tax on Antigua. Hotels collect a 10% government room tax, guesthouses and villas 7%. Hotels and restaurants also usually add a 10% service charge to your bill.

TELEPHONES

Most accommodations have direct-dial phones; others can easily make connections through the switchboard. You can use the Cable & Wireless Phone Card (available in $5, $10, and $20 denominations in most hotels and post offices) for local and long-distance calls. Phone-card phones work much better than the regular coin-operated phones. Currently, mobile phones can't be rented, though one can be purchased for an average cost of EC$300 from Cable & Wireless.

To place a local call, simply dial the local seven-digit number. To call Montserrat from the United States, dial 1 + 664 + the local seven-digit number.

15

To call the United States and Canada, dial 1 + the area code + the seven-digit number, or use the phone card or one of the "CALL USA" phones, which are available at several locations, including the airport departure lounge, the cruise terminal at St. John's, and the English Harbour Marina. These take credit cards and, supposedly, calling cards (though Cable & Wireless tacks on a fee).

🏠 **Cable & Wireless** ✉ Sweeney's ☎ 268/491-1000

TIPPING

In restaurants it's customary to leave 5% beyond the regular service charge added to your bill if you're pleased with the service. Taxi drivers expect a 10% tip, porters and bellmen about $1 per bag. Maids are rarely tipped, but if you think the service exemplary, figure $2 to $3 per night.

TOUR OPTIONS

Jenny's Tours arranges day trips to Montserrat—including transportation from Antigua, an island tour, breakfast, and lunch—starting at $180 per person.

Joe "Fergus" Phillip, who operates Avalon Tours, often e-mails updates on Montserrat to visitors. Jadine Collins-Glitzenhirn (a wild woman in the best sense, who can take you on impromptu adventures) runs JIG Promotions. Both are friendly, knowledgeable, reliable taxi and tour drivers.

🏠 **Avalon Tours** ✉ Manjack ☎ 664/491-3432. **Jenny's Tours** ✉ Woods Centre, Box W471, St. John's ☎ 268/461-9361. **JIG Promotions** ✉ Davy Hill ☎ 664/491-2752.

VISITOR INFORMATION

The Montserrat Tourist Board lists accommodations, restaurants, activities, car rental agencies, and tours available on the island.

🏠 **Montserrat Tourist Board** ✉ Olveston ☎ 664/491-2230 ⊕ www.visitmontserrat.com ✉ Montserrat Government Office, 7 Portland Pl., London W1B 1PP, U.K. ☎ 0207/486-7073.

Puerto Rico

Fuerte San Cristóbal, San Juan

WORD OF MOUTH

"San Juan is one of my favorite cities, period. Old San Juan has great shopping, restaurants, picturesque streets, historic sites, etc. . . . [C]heck out the ruins of El Morro and San Cristobal. . . ."

—swimmr

". . . Vieques has the largest (and supposedly best) bioluminescent bay in the world and it is a very very cool sight. You have to do the trek with a group . . . and wait for the bay to light up. It's not to be missed." —dswl

WELCOME TO PUERTO RICO

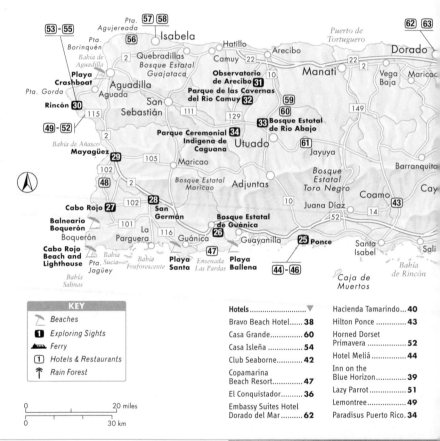

Mother Spain is always a presence here—on a sun-dappled cobblestone street, in the shade of a colonial cathedral or fort. Yet multifaceted Puerto Rico pulses with New World energy. The rhythms of the streets are of Afro-Latin salsa and bomba. And the U.S. flag flaps in the salty breezes wherever you go.

SPANISH AMERICAN

Puerto Rico is 110 mi (177 km) long and 35 mi (56 km) wide. With a population of almost 4 million, it's among the biggest Caribbean islands. The first Spanish governor was Juan Ponce de León in 1508; he founded Old San Juan in 1521. The United States won the island in the Spanish-American War in 1917 and made it a commonwealth in 1952.

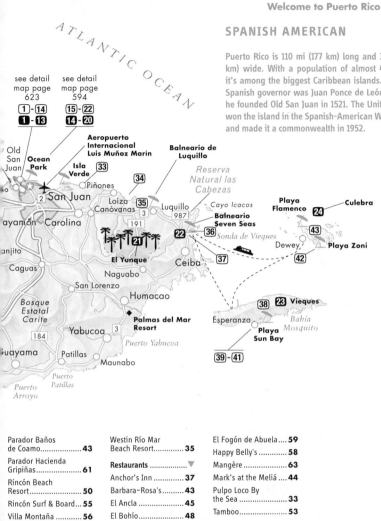

16

PUERTO RICO

TOP 4 REASONS TO VISIT PUERTO RICO

1 Happening clubs and discos make San Juan one of the Caribbean's nightlife capitals, rivaling even Miami.

2 Great restaurants run the gamut from elegant places in San Juan to simple spots serving delicious *comida criolla*.

3 Beaches—both developed and wild—suit the needs of surfers, sunbathers, and families.

4 Nature abounds, from the underground Río Camuy to El Yunque, the only Caribbean national forest.

PUERTO RICO PLANNER

Getting to Puerto Rico

San Juan (SJU) is a major hub for American Airlines, the dominant carrier to the Caribbean, making it an easy flight from almost anywhere in the U.S. Several other major airlines also fly to San Juan. But in the past few years, discount airlines like Jet Blue and Spirit have begun flying to San Juan, making it a relatively inexpensive destination as well. The island also has airports in Aguadilla (BQN), Fajardo (FAJ), Ponce (PSE), and Mayagüez (MAZ), and on the islands of Vieques (VQS) and Culebra (CPX), but there are few (if any) direct flights to any of these. Culebra and Vieques can also be reached by ferry.

Hassle Factor: Low for San Juan, Medium to High for areas outside of San Juan.

On the Ground

San Juan taxis have fixed zones, and fares from the airport to either the cruise-ship pier or a local hotel should cost between $10 and $19. Car services will take you to the well-established Dorado area for a set fee of around $25; you can usually get set-rate van service to major resorts east of San Juan or to Fajardo if you are catching the ferry for Vieques or Culebra. Many hotels will offer transportation, either free or for a set fee, so be sure to ask about that. Otherwise, you'll need to rent a car.

Renting a Car

It's not really worthwhile to rent a car if you are staying in San Juan. Traffic is heavy enough and parking difficult enough that it may be more of a hindrance than a help. And taxis will usually be a more cost-effective option to get around town. However, if you want to explore the island for a day or two, then a car is a necessity, as it is if you are staying somewhere else on the island, with the possible exception of a large resort that you don't plan to leave except on a guided tour. A car can also be a help if you are staying on Vieques or Culebra and want to explore the island or visit a distant beach.

Activities

Because of its size, Puerto Rico supports virtually any activity you might imagine. The west coast is one of the Caribbean's major **surfing** destinations; the north-central region has one of the world's largest underground river systems for **spelunking**; El Yunque is the only Caribbean entry in the national forest system and a mecca for **hikers** and **mountain bikers**; large resorts support several excellent **golf** courses and **tennis** facilities; and the surrounding waters are good for **fishing** and **diving**. Puerto Rico is also lined with several excellent **beaches**, including a few on Vieques that are only now open to the public after many long years. The island is dotted with interesting **historical sights**, and San Juan itself is not only one of the oldest cities in the Western Hemisphere, but also one of the most vibrant, with excellent **restaurants**, happening **night clubs**, and great **shopping**.

Where to Stay

If you want easy access to shopping, dining, and nightlife, then you should stay in San Juan, which also has decent beaches. Most of the other large, deluxe resorts are along the north coast, either in Dorado (west of San Juan) or between San Juan and Fajardo (east of the city). There are also a few resorts along the southern coast. Rincón, in the northwest, also has a concentration of resorts and great surfing. Look to the more isolated islands of Vieques and Culebra if you want to find excellent beaches and little development. Other small inns and hotels are around the island in the interior, including a few around El Yunque. Beware of "resort fees," which will add to your hotel costs.

TYPES OF LODGING

Big Hotels: San Juan's beaches are lined with large-scale hotels offering all the amenities, including happening restaurants and splashy casinos. The majority are spread out along Condado and Isla Verde beaches.	**Upscale Beach Resorts:** All over the island—but particularly along the north coast—large tourist resorts offer all the amenities along with a hefty dose of isolation.	**Paradores:** Small inns (many offering home-style comida criolla cooking) are spread out around the island, though they are rarely on the beach.

Hotel & Restaurant Costs

Assume that hotels operate on the European Plan (**EP**—with no meals) unless we specify that they use either the Continental Plan (**CP**—with a Continental breakfast), Breakfast Plan (**BP**—with full breakfast), or the Modified American Plan (**MAP**—with breakfast and dinner). Other hotels may offer the Full American Plan (**FAP**—including all meals but no drinks) or may be All-Inclusive (**AI**—with all meals, drinks, and most activities).

WHAT IT COSTS in Dollars

	$$$$	$$$	$$	$	¢
Restaurants	over $30	$20–$30	$12–$20	$8–$12	under $8
Hotels*	over $350	$250–$350	$150–$250	$80–$150	under $80
Hotels**	over $450	$350–$450	$250–$350	$125–$250	under $125

*EP, BP, CP   **AI, FAP, MAP

Restaurant prices are for a main course at dinner. Hotel prices are for a double room during the high season and do not include 7%–11% room tax, 5%–12% customary service charge, and meal plans (except at all-inclusives).

When to Go

San Juan in particular is very expensive during the busy tourist season from mid-December through mid-April; during the off-season, you can get good deals all over the island, with discounts of up to 40% off high-season rates.

Week-long **patron saint's festivals** happen throughout the year all over the island, so you can almost always find a celebration going on somewhere in Puerto Rico.

Of course, the pre-Lenten **Carnival** is celebrated in Puerto Rico, as it is on so many islands. Ponce's is the most famous, but several towns and regions have parades, music competitions, beauty pageants, and other parties.

Easter week sees spring breakers and Puerto Ricans filling up every beach.

The **Pablo Casals Festival** in early June is a popular event in San Juan itself.

In November the annual Festival of Puerto Rican music takes place in San Juan and other venues.

16

Updated by
Mark Sullivan

SUNRISE AND SUNSET are both worth waiting for when you're on Puerto Rico. The pinks and yellows that hang in the early-morning sky are just as compelling as the sinewy reds and purples that blend into the twilight. It's easy to compare them, as Puerto Rico is the smallest of the Greater Antilles. At 110 mi (177 km) long and 35 mi (56 km) wide, you can easily have breakfast in Fajardo, looking eastward over the boats headed to enchanted islands like Vieques and Culebra, then settle down for a lobster dinner in Rincón as the sun is sinking into the inky-blue water. That leaves you plenty of time in between to explore the southern coast, perhaps stopping to see the fanciful firehouse in Ponce or the charming colonial chapel in San Germán.

Known as the Island of Enchantment, Puerto Rico will surely put you under its spell. Here, traffic actually leads you to a "Road to Paradise," whether you're looking for a pleasurable, sunny escape from the confines of urbanity or a rich supply of stimulation to quench your cultural and entertainment thirst. On the island you have the best of both worlds, natural and urban thrills alike; and although city life is frenetic enough to make you forget you're surrounded by azure waters and warm sand, traveling a few miles inland or down the coast can easily make you forget you're surrounded by development.

Puerto Rico was populated primarily by Taíno Indians when Columbus landed in 1493. In 1508 Ponce de León established a settlement and became the first governor; in 1521 he founded what is known as Old San Juan. For centuries, while Africans worked on the coastal sugarcane fields, the French, Dutch, and English tried unsuccessfully to wrest the island from Spain. In 1898, as a result of the Spanish-American War, Spain ceded the island to the United States. In 1917 Puerto Ricans became U.S. citizens, and in 1952 Puerto Rico became a semiautonomous commonwealth.

Since the 1950s, Puerto Rico has developed exponentially, as witnessed in the urban sprawl, burgeoning traffic, and growing population (estimated at nearly 4 million); yet, *en la isla* (on the island) a strong Latin sense of community and family prevails. *Puertorriqueños* are fiercely proud of their unique blend of heritages.

Music is another source of Puerto Rican pride. Like wildflowers, *vellonera* (jukeboxes) pop up almost everywhere, and when one is playing, somebody will be either singing or dancing along—or both. Cars often vibrate with *reggaetón,* a hard, monotonous beat with lyrics that express social malaise. Salsa, a fusion of West African percussion, jazz, and other Latin beats, is the trademark dance. Although it may look difficult to master, it's all achieved by just loosening your hips. You may choose to let your inhibitions go by doing some clubbing *a la vida loca* espoused by pop star Ricky Martin. Nightlife options are of the variety available in any metropolitan environment—and then some.

By day you can take in the culture of the Old World; one of the richest visual experiences in Puerto Rico is Old San Juan. Originally built as a fortress by the Spaniards in the early 1500s, the old city has myriad attractions that include restored 16th-century buildings and 200-year-old houses with balustraded balconies of filigreed wrought iron that over-look narrow cobblestone streets. Spanish traditions are also apparent in the countryside festivals celebrated in honor of small-town patron saints. For quiet relaxation or more adventures off the beaten track, visit coffee plantations, colonial towns, or outlying islets where nightlife is virtually nonexistent.

And of course you don't come to a Caribbean island without taking in some of the glorious sunshine and natural wonders. In the coastal areas, the sun mildly toasts your body, and you're immediately healed by soft waves and cool breezes. In the misty mountains, you can wonder at the flickering night flies and the star-studded sky while the *coquís* (local tiny frogs) sing their legendary sweet lullaby. On a moonless night, watch the warm ocean turn into luminescent aqua-blue speckles on your skin. Then there are the island's many acres of golf courses, numerous tennis courts, rain forests, and hundreds of beaches that offer every imaginable water sport.

Where to Stay

The proximity of Isla Verde high-rise beachfront hotels to the airport appeals to those on business or for short-term stays, while you may find Condado a better location if you intend to drive around or leave the hotel premises often. Due to traffic, Old San Juan is for the less-hurried traveler who either stays in or out of San Juan most of the day. Smaller properties in the metro area offer personal hospitality often without compromising business amenities. Outside San Juan, particularly on the east coast, you can find self-contained luxury resorts that cover hundreds of acres. In the west, southwest, and south—as well as on the islands of Vieques and Culebra—smaller inns, villas, and condominiums for short-term rentals are the norm. Some government-sponsored paradores are rural inns, others offer no-frills apartments, and some are large hotels located close to either an attraction or beach.

Most hotels operate on the EP, although larger establishments often offer other meal plans or even all-inclusive packages. There's but a single, true all-inclusive resort, Paradisus Puerto Rico, on the eastern end of the island. In the off-season, or summer months, rates at some hotels can drop 20% or more. For hotels outside of San Juan rates most often don't include airport transfers. Be sure to ask when you book.

For information on paradores, contact the **Puerto Rico Tourism Company** (⌂ Box 902–3960, Old San Juan Station, San Juan 00902-3960 ☎ 787/721–2400 or 800/866–7827 ⊕ www.gotopuertorico.com/parames/paradores). **Small Inns & Hotels of Puerto Rico** (✉ 954 Av. Ponce de León, Suite 702, 00907 ☎ 787/725–2901 ⊕ www.prhtasmallhotels.com), a branch of the Puerto Rico Hotel & Tourism Association, is a marketing arm for some 25 small hotels island-wide.

Island West Properties & Beach Rentals (✉ Rte. 413, Km 1.3, Box 700, Rincón 00677 ☎ 787/823–2323 🖶 787/823–3254 ⊕ www.rinconrealestateforsale.com) can help you rent condos in Rincón by the

16

week or the month. **Puerto Rico Vacation Apartments** (✉ Calle Marbella del Caribe Oeste S-5, Isla Verde 00979 ☎ 787/727–1591 or 800/266–3639 🖶 787/268–3604 ⊕ www.sanjuanvacations.com) represents some 200 properties in Condado and Isla Verde. For condos or villas on Vieques, contact **Rainbow Realty** (☎ 787/741–4312 ⊕ www.enchanted-isle.com/rainbow).

Old San Juan

★ $$$$ 🏨 **El Convento.** Carmelite nuns once inhabited this 350-year-old convent, but they never had high-tech gadgets like in-room broadband connections or plasma TVs. The accommodations here beautifully combine the old and the new. All the guest rooms have hand-hewn wood furniture, shuttered windows, and mahogany-beamed ceilings, but some have a little extra. Room 508 has two views of the bay, while Rooms 216, 217, and 218 have private walled patios. Guests gather for the complimentary wine and hors d'oeuvres that are served before dinner. The streetside Café Bohemio, the second-floor El Picoteo, and the courtyard Café del Níspero are all good dining choices. ✉ *100 Calle Cristo, Old San Juan* 🗃 *Box 1048, 00902* ☎ *787/723–9020 or 800/468–2779* 🖶 *787/723–9260* ⊕ *www.elconvento.com* 🛏 *63 rooms, 5 suites* 🍴 *3 restaurants, in-room safes, cable TV, in-room DVD players, in-room broadband, Wi-Fi, pool, gym, 2 bars, library, shop, dry cleaning, laundry service, concierge, Internet room, business services, meeting room, parking (fee), no-smoking rooms* ▤ *AE, D, DC, MC, V* ¶◎¶ *EP.*

★ $$–$$$ 🏨 **Gallery Inn.** You can shop from your bed at this 200-year-old mansion, as owner Jan D'Esopo has filled the rooms with her own artworks. And not just the rooms, either; the hallways, the staircases, and even the roof are lined with her fascinating bronze sculptures. Even if you aren't a guest, D'Esopo is pleased to show you around and may even offer you a glass of wine. (Just make sure that Campeche, one of her many birds, doesn't try to sneak a sip.) No two rooms are alike, but all have four-poster beds, hand-woven tapestries, and quirky antiques filling every nook and cranny. There are views of the coastline from several of the rooms, as well as from the spectacular rooftop terrace. The first-floor Galería San Juan displays artwork by D'Esopo and others. There's no restaurant, but meals for groups can be prepared upon request. ✉ *204–206 Calle Norzagaray, Old San Juan 00901* ☎ *787/722–1808* 🖶 *787/724–7360* ⊕ *www.thegalleryinn.com* 🛏 *13 rooms, 10 suites* 🍴 *Dining room, some refrigerators, hot tub, piano, no-smoking rooms; no a/c in some rooms, no room TVs* ▤ *AE, DC, MC, V* ¶◎¶ *CP.*

$$–$$$ 🏨 **Sheraton Old San Juan Hotel.** This hotel's triangular shape subtly echoes the cruise ships docked nearby. Rooms facing the water have dazzling views of these behemoths as they sail in and out of the harbor. Others have views over the rooftops of Old San Juan. The rooms have been plushly renovated and have nice touches like custom-designed beds. On the top floor you'll find a sunny patio with a pool and whirlpool bath, as well as a spacious gym with the latest equipment; the concierge level provides hassle-free check-ins, Continental breakfasts, and evening hors d'oeuvres. ✉ *100 Calle Brumbaugh, Old San Juan 00901* ☎ *787/721–5100 or 866/376–7577* 🖶 *787/289–1910* ⊕ *www.sheratonoldsanjuan.com* 🛏 *200 rooms, 40 suites* 🍴 *Restaurant, room*

service, in-room safes, some minibars, cable TV with movies, in-room broadband, Wi-Fi, pool, gym, hot tub, bar, casino, dry cleaning, laundry service, concierge floor, business services, Internet room, meeting rooms, travel services, parking (fee), car rental, no-smoking rooms ⊟ *AE, D, DC, MC, V* ⧠ *EP.*

Greater San Juan

★ ⟳ $$$$ Ⓣ **Ritz-Carlton San Juan Hotel, Spa & Casino.** The elegance of marble floors and gushing fountains won't undermine the feeling that this is a true beach getaway. The hotel's sandy stretch is lovely, as is the cruciform pool, which is lined by statues of the hotel's signature lion. Works by Latin American artists adorn the lobby lounge and the hallways leading to the well-equipped business center. Rooms have a mix of traditional wooden furnishings and wicker pieces upholstered in soft fabrics. A full-service spa begs to pamper you with aloe body wraps and *parcha* (passion-fruit juice) massages. Though most room windows are sealed shut to muffle airport noise, many suites open onto terraces. Tastefully so, the casino has its own separate entrance. ⊠ *6961 Av. Los Gobernadores, Isla Verde 00979* ☎ *787/253–1700 or 800/241–3333* ⊟ *787/253–1777* ⊕ *www.ritzcarlton.com* ⤳ *403 rooms, 11 suites* ⟳ *3 restaurants, room service, minibars, cable TV, in-room broadband, Wi-Fi, 2 tennis courts, pool, fitness classes, gym, hair salon, hot tub, massage, sauna, spa, 3 bars, casino, nightclub, babysitting, children's programs (ages 4–12), dry cleaning, laundry service, concierge, concierge floor, business services, meeting rooms, parking (fee), no-smoking floor* ⊟ *AE, D, DC, MC, V* ⧠ *EP.*

⟳ $$$–$$$$ Ⓣ **Caribe Hilton San Juan.** How many hotels can claim to have their own fort? Fuerte San Gerónimo, which once guarded the entrance to San Juan Bay, is on the grounds of this sprawling resort, which also has a private beach, a luxurious spa, and one of the best-developed kids' programs on the island. (There's even an hour of free babysitting so you can have a grown-up meal at Morton's or one of the other restaurants.) Unfortunately, the guest rooms are a little past their prime, and the open-air lobby is crowded, noisy, and free of any charm whatsoever. The staff can seem disorganized at times. ⊠ *Calle Los Rosales, Puerta de Tierra, 00901* ☎ *787/721–0303 or 877/464–4586* ⊟ *787/725–8849* ⊕ *www.hiltoncaribbean.com* ⤳ *602 rooms, 44 suites* ⟳ *76 restaurants, room service, in-room safes, minibars, cable TV with movies and video games, in-room broadband, Wi-Fi, 3 tennis courts, pool, wading pool, health club, hair salon, outdoor hot tub, spa, beach, bar, video game room, shops, children's programs (ages 4–12), dry cleaning, laundry service, concierge, business services, meeting rooms, parking (fee), no-smoking floors* ⊟ *AE, D, DC, MC, V* ⧠ *EP.*

$$$ Ⓣ **Normandie Hotel.** One of the Caribbean's finest examples of art-deco
FodorśChoice architecture, this ship-shaped hotel hosted high-society types back in the
★ 1930s. After a stem-to-stern renovation, it's ready to sail again. Egyptian motifs in the grand ballroom and other period details have been meticulously restored. Guest rooms, many of them as big as suites, are decorated in sensuous shades of cream and oatmeal. Business travelers will appreciate the huge desks outfitted with broadband access. Those in search of relaxation need look no further than the sparkling pool or

16

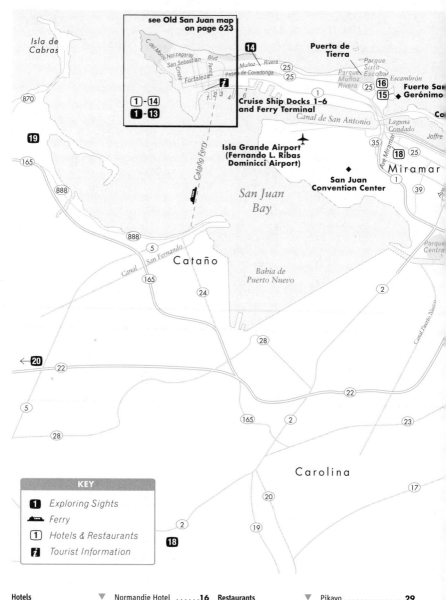

KEY

- **1** Exploring Sights
- Ferry
- **1** Hotels & Restaurants
- **i** Tourist Information

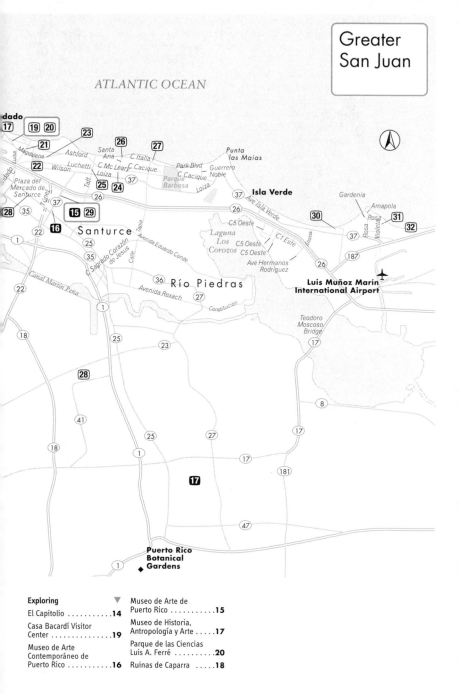

Greater San Juan

ATLANTIC OCEAN

the compact spa with its massage area overlooking the ocean. N Bar, on the second floor, has quickly become a see-and-be-seen place for the city's trendy crowd. ☒ *499 Av. Muñoz Rivera, Puerta de Tierra 00901* ☎ *787/729–2929* 🖷 *787/729–3083* ⊕ *www.normandiepr.com* 🖘 *58 rooms, 117 suites ⚑ 2 restaurants, in-room safes, minibars, cable TV, in-room broadband, Wi-Fi, pool, gym, massage, spa, beach, 2 bars, shop, babysitting, dry cleaning, laundry service, business services, convention center, Internet room, meeting rooms, car rental, parking (fee), no-smoking rooms* ⊟ *AE, MC, V* ⦿ *EP.*

$$–$$$ 🏨 **Courtyard by Marriott Isla Verde Beach Resort.** This 12-story hotel tries to be all things to all people—and succeeds to a great degree. Harried business executives appreciate its location near the airport and high-tech offerings like high-speed Internet connections. Families prefer the many dining options and the fact that the city's best beach is just outside. The place is buzzing during the day, especially around the three swimming pools. At night the action centers on the lobby bar, where live salsa music often has people dancing. (If you don't know how, you can take lessons.) The best part is the price: it's undoubtedly one of the best values in San Juan. ☒ *7012 Boca de Cangrejos, Isla Verde 00979* ☎ *787/791–0404 or 800/791–2553* 🖷 *787/791–1460* ⊕ *www.sjcourtyard.com* 🖘 *260 rooms, 33 suites ⚑ 3 restaurants, room service, in-room safes, refrigerators, cable TV, in-room VCRs, in-room broadband, Wi-Fi, 3 pools, gym, hot tub, beach, bar, lounge, casino, shop, dry cleaning, coin laundry, laundry service, playground, Internet room, business services, meeting rooms, parking (fee)* ⊟ *AE, D, DC, MC, V* ⦿ *BP.*

$$–$$$ 🏨 **The Water Club.** There's water everywhere at this boutique hotel, from the droplets that decorate the reception desk to the deluge that runs down the glass walls of the elevators. Guest rooms, all of which are decorated in a minimalist style, have an under-the-sea feel because of the soft glow of blue neon. Four rooms are equipped with telescopes for stargazing or people-watching along the beach. No matter which room you choose, you'll have a view of the ocean. The lobby's Liquid lounge is a popular stop along the party trail for hipsters. Wet, the rooftop bar, lets you recline on white leather sofas as you take in the view of the skyline. ☒ *2 Calle Tartak, Isla Verde 00979* ☎ *787/728–3666 or 888/265–6699* 🖷 *787/728–3610* ⊕ *www.waterclubsanjuan.com* 🖘 *84 rooms ⚑ Restaurant, room service, in-room safes, minibars, cable TV, in-room VCRs, in-room data ports, pool, gym, hot tub, massage, beach, 2 bars, dry cleaning, laundry service, concierge, Internet, meeting rooms, parking (fee), no-smoking floors* ⊟ *AE, D, DC, MC, V* ⦿ *EP.*

$–$$ 🏨 **Hostería del Mar.** This small hotel manages to charm you before you even walk in the door. You'll probably pause, as most people do, to admire the pond filled with iridescent goldfish before continuing into the wood-paneled lobby. The decor might be described as South Seas meets South Beach. The spacious guest rooms continue the tropical theme, aided by colorful fabrics and rattan furnishings. Many rooms have views of the beach, which is only a few feet away. Make sure to enjoy the kitchen's creative cuisine, either in the dining room or at a table on the sand. The staff is courteous and helpful. ☒ *1 Calle Tapia, Ocean Park 00911* ☎ *787/727–3302 or 877/727–3302* 🖷 *787/268–0772* ⊕ *www.*

hosteriadelmarpr.com ⌁ *8 rooms, 5 suites* ⚘ *Restaurant, some kitchenettes, cable TV, beach, bar, free parking; no smoking* ⊟ *AE, D, DC, MC, V* ⦿⧲ *EP.*

$–$$ ⌨ **Numero Uno.** The name refers to the address, but Numero Uno is also how this small hotel rates with its guests. It's not unusual to hear people trading stories about how many times they've returned to this relaxing retreat. Behind a whitewashed wall is a patio where you can catch some rays beside the pool, dine in the restaurant, or enjoy a cocktail at the bar. A few steps away, a sandy beach beckons; guests are provided with beach chairs and umbrellas. Rooms are decorated in sophisticated shades of cream and taupe; several have ocean views. ⊠ *1 Calle Santa Ana, Ocean Park 00911* ☎ *787/726–5010* 🖷 *787/727–5482* ⊕ *www.numero1guesthouse.com* ⌁ *11 rooms, 2 apartments* ⚘ *Restaurant, fans, some kitchenettes, refrigerators, cable TV, in-room broadband, pool, beach, bar* ⊟ *AE, MC, V* ⦿⧲ *CP.*

$ ⌨ **At Wind Chimes Inn.** Hidden behind a whitewashed wall covered with bougainvillea, this Spanish-style villa has the feel of an exclusive retreat. So much about the place invites you to relax: the patios shaded by royal palms, the terra-cotta-tiled terraces, and the small pool with a built-in whirlpool spa. And there's the soft, ever-present jingling of wind chimes, reminding you that the beach is just a block away. The spacious guest rooms have a tropical feel. The Boat Bar, open only to guests, serves a light menu from 7 AM to 11 PM. ⊠ *1750 Av. McLeary, Condado 00911* ☎ *787/727–4153 or 800/946–3244* 🖷 *787/728–0671* ⊕ *www.atwindchimesinn.com* ⌁ *17 rooms, 5 suites* ⚘ *Some kitchenettes, cable TV, pool, bar, Internet, parking (fee), no-smoking rooms* ⊟ *AE, D, MC, V* ⦿⧲ *EP.*

$ ⌨ **Coral Princess.** This art deco building—one of the few left in Condado—has personality to spare. The ample guest rooms subtly reflect the hotel's heritage with crisp lines and simple furnishings. The hotel is a block from the neighborhood's main drag, so you don't have to fight the crowds every time you walk out the front door. The beach is five minutes away, but you can always take advantage of the swimming pool on the palm-shaded terrace or the hot tub on the rooftop. ⊠ *1159 Av. Magdalena, Condado 00911* ☎ *787/977–7700* 🖷 *787/722–5032* ⊕ *www.coralpr.com* ⌁ *25 rooms, 1 apartment* ⚘ *Some kitchenettes, cable TV, in-room broadband, pool, hot tub, bar* ⊟ *AE, D, DC, MC, V* ⦿⧲ *CP.*

☾ $ ⌨ **El Prado Inn.** The multilingual staff at this quiet inn is as capable of satisfying your business and leisure needs as a large hotel. Like a secret garden, this 1930s art deco–style former mansion sits across a park two blocks south of the Condado beach (a three-minute walk) and four blocks north of the Plaza del Mercado. It's close to all the action, yet placidly removed from it. Each room is individually decorated with furniture and fabrics from Southeast Asia and Morocco. This inn welcomes about 50% American and 50% international repeat guests who have found themselves a sort of home base. ⊠ *1350 Calle Lucchetti, Condado 00907* ☎ *787/728–5925* 🖷 *787/725–6978* ⊕ *www.elpradoinn.net* ⌁ *22 rooms* ⚘ *Fans, in-room safes, some kitchens, some refrigerators, cable TV, pool, free parking* ⊟ *AE, MC, V* ⦿⧲ *CP.*

16

Eastern Puerto Rico

$$$$ **Paradisus Puerto Rico.** Puerto Rico's first all-inclusive resort, to the east of Río Mar, is on an enviable stretch of pristine coastline. The open-air lobby, with its elegant floral displays, resembles a Japanese garden, while the swimming pool's columns call to mind ancient Greece. If it sounds like there's an identity crisis here, you're right. But the hotel, run by Sol Meliá, does fairly well at being all things to all people. The 500 suites, many with their own hot tubs, are spread among two-story bungalows. Many look out onto the pair of 18-hole golf courses, which were still partly unfinished in late 2005. The staff is friendly and accommodating. ⊠ *Rte. 968, Km 5.8, Coco Beach* 🕾 *787/657–1026 or 800/336–3542* 🖶 *787/657–1055* ⊕ *www.solmelia.com* ⟿ *500 suites, 5 villas* ⚫ *6 restaurants, fans, in-room safes, some in-room hot tubs, minibars, cable TV with movies, 2 18-hole golf courses, 3 tennis courts, pool, wading pool, health club, spa, beach, dive shop, snorkeling, windsurfing, boating, waterskiing, fishing, 4 bars, casino, dance club, showroom, shops, children's programs (ages 4–12), dry cleaning, laundry service, concierge, Internet, business services, convention center, meeting room, car rental, travel services* ⊟ *AE, D, MC, V* ¶◯¶ *AI.*

$$$$ **Westin Río Mar Beach Golf Resort & Spa.** On more than 500 acres, this
Fodor'sChoice sprawling resort is geared toward outdoor activities. Many people come
★ to play the championship golf courses or hike in the nearby rain forest, but the biggest draw is the 2-mi-long stretch of sand just steps from the door. There's a kiosk near the swimming pools that rents sailboats and other equipment; a dive shop organizes excursions to nearby sites. Even the extensive programs for children are mostly outdoors. The seven-story hotel, which wraps around lush gardens, never feels overwhelming. The rooms are on the small side but are cleverly designed to make use of all the available space. The newest addition is a Mandara Spa, which transports you to the South Pacific with its hand-carved wood furnishings from Bali. ⊠ *6000 Río Mar Blvd., Río Grande 00745* 🕾 *787/888–6000* 🖶 *787/888–6235* ⊕ *www.westinriomar.com* ⟿ *528 rooms, 72 suites, 59 villas* ⚫ *7 restaurants, café, in-room safes, cable TV with movies and video games, in-room VCRs, in-room broadband, Wi-Fi, 2 18-hole golf courses, 13 tennis courts, 2 pools, health club, spa, beach, dive shop, windsurfing, boating, fishing, bicycles, 4 bars, casino, dance club, game room, shop, children's programs (ages 4–12), dry cleaning, laundry service, concierge, business services, convention center, Internet room, meeting rooms, airport shuttle, car rental, no-smoking rooms* ⊟ *AE, D, DC, MC, V* ¶◯¶ *EP.*

★ **$$$–$$$$** **El Conquistador Resort & Golden Door Spa.** The name means "The Conqueror," and this sprawling resort has claimed the northeastern tip of the island for itself. Perched on a bluff overlooking the ocean, it certainly is one of Puerto Rico's loveliest lodgings. Arranged in five "villages," the whitewashed buildings have a colonial-era feel. Cobblestone streets and fountain-filled plazas tie everything together. The resort's beach is on Palomino Island, just offshore; a free shuttle boat takes you there in about 15 minutes. A branch of the Japanese-influenced Golden Door Spa is widely considered among the Caribbean's best spas. The staff prides itself on its attentive service. ⊠ *1000 Av. El Conquistador, Box 70001, 00738*

☎787/863–1000 or 800/468–0389 🖷787/863–6500 ⊕*www.elconresort.
com* ➦ *750 rooms, 17 suites, 155 villas ♧ 17 restaurants, in-room
safes, minibars, cable TV with movies and video games, in-room VCRs,
in-room broadband, Wi-Fi, 18-hole golf course, 4 tennis courts, 8 pools,
hot tub, health club, hair salon, spa, beach, dive shop, snorkeling, windsurfing, boating, jet skiing, marina, 5 bars, casino, nightclub, shop, children's programs (ages 4–12), dry cleaning, laundry service, business
services, convention center, meeting rooms, airport shuttle, parking (fee),
car rental, no-smoking rooms* ▭ *AE, MC, V* ⊚�‖ *EP.*

Vieques & Culebra

$$–$$$$ 🏨 **Inn on the Blue Horizon.** This inn, consisting of six Mediterranean-style
villas, was the tiny island's first taste of luxury. It's still one of the most
sought-after accommodations, mostly because of its breathtaking set-
ting on a bluff overlooking the ocean. The entire place is often booked
months in advance by weddings and other big groups. Everything is geared
toward upping the romance quotient, from the intimate guest rooms to
the open-air bar, where the staff will make any cocktail you can name—
or create a new one and name it after you. Sadly, the popular Blue Macaw
restaurant closed for good in 2005. ⊠ *Rte. 996, Km 4.2, Esperanza,
Vieques* ⌂ *Box 1556, Vieques 00765* ☎ *787/741–3318* 🖷 *787/741–
0522* ⊕*www.innonthebluehorizon.com* ➦*10 rooms ♧ Restaurant, fans,
pool, massage, beach, bicycles, bar, library; no room phones, no room
TVs, no kids under 14* ▭ *AE, MC, V* ⊚�‖ *BP.*

$$ 🏨 **Bravo Beach Hotel.** If this boutique hotel were plopped down into the
Fodor'sChoice middle of South Beach, no one would raise an eyebrow. What was once
★ a private residence has been expanded to include four different buildings, all with views of nearby Culebra from their balconies. The guest
rooms have a minimalist flair, brightened by splashes of red and yellow.
High-tech offerings include a Sony Playstation in every room. If you're
traveling with an entourage, the two-bedroom villa has plenty of space
to entertain. One of the pools is the setting for the Palms, a chic lounge;
the other is the backdrop for the not-to-be-missed tapas bar. The hotel
is on a pretty stretch of beach, several blocks north of the ferry dock in
Isabel Segunda. ⊠ *North Shore Rd., Isabel Segunda, Vieques 00765*
☎ *787/741–1128* 🖷 *787/741–3908* ⊕ *www.bravobeachhotel.com* ➦*9
rooms, 1 villa ♧ Restaurant, minibars, cable TV with movies and
games, Wi-Fi, 2 pools, bar; no room phones, no kids under 14* ▭ *AE,
D, MC, V* ⊚❖ *BP.*

$$ ✕🏨 **Club Seaborne.** The prettiest place to stay in Culebra, this cluster
of plantation-style cottages sits on a hilltop overlooking Fulladoza Bay.
The place feels completely isolated, but it is only a mile or so from the
center of town. Opt for one of the rooms surrounding the pool or one
of the spacious villas. The largest sleeps five, making it a favorite of fam-
ilies. Specializing in seafood, the terrace restaurant ($$–$$$) is one of
the best on the island. The friendly staff is happy to help you set up snor-
keling and diving trips. The beaches, including Playa Flamenco, are a
few miles away. ⊠ *Calle Fulladoza, Km 1.5, Box 357, Culebra 00775*
☎ *787/742–3169* 🖷 *787/742–3176* ⊕ *www.clubseabourne.com* ➦*3
rooms, 8 villas, 1 cottage ♧ Restaurant, some kitchens, cable TV, pool,
bar, library* ▭ *AE, MC, V* ⊚❖ *CP.*

16

★ **$–$$**   ⊡ **Hacienda Tamarindo.** The century-old tamarind tree rising through the center of the main building gives this place its name. The plantation-style house, with its barrel-tile roof and wood-shuttered windows, is one of the most beautiful on the island. It's easy to find a spot all to yourself, whether it's on a shady terrace or beside the spectacular pool. The guest rooms were individually decorated by Linda Vail, who runs the place along with her husband, Burr. "Caribbean chic" might be the best way to describe her effortless way of combining well-chosen antiques, elegant wicker furniture, and vintage travel posters. The nicest room might be Number One, which is in a separate building and has a private terrace overlooking the ocean. The beach is nearby, but you'll need a car to get there. ⊠ *Rte. 996, Km 4.5, Esperanza, Vieques* ⬦ *Box 1569, Vieques 00765* ☎ *787/741–8525* 🖷 *787/741–3215* ⊕ *www. haciendatamarindo.com* ⇘ *16 rooms* ⚘ *Fans, cable TV, Wi-Fi, pool; no room phones, no room TVs, no kids under 15* ▭ *AE, MC, V* ¶◎¶ *BP.*

Southern Puerto Rico

★   ⊡ **Copamarina Beach Resort.** Without a doubt the most beautiful resort
☾ **$$–$$$**   on the southern coast, the Copamarina is set on 16 palm-shaded acres facing the Caribbean Sea. Fruit trees and other plants are meticulously groomed, especially around the pair of swimming pools (one popular with kids, the other mostly left to the adults). All the guest rooms are generously proportioned, especially in the older building. Wood shutters on the windows and other touches lend a tropical feel. New in 2005 was a small spa whose Asian-influenced design blends seamlessly with the rest of the hotel. The red snapper is a must at the elegant Alexandra restaurant. ⊠ *Rte. 333, Km 6.5, Box 805, Guánica 00653* ☎ *787/ 821–0505 or 800/468–4553* 🖷 *787/821–0070* ⊕ *www.copamarina. com* ⇘ *104 rooms, 2 villas* ⚘ *Restaurant, café, room service, in-room safes, refrigerators, cable TV, Wi-Fi, 2 tennis courts, 2 pools, 2 wading pools, gym, 2 hot tubs, massage, spa, 2 steam rooms, beach, dive shop, snorkeling, windsurfing, boating, volleyball, 2 bars, playground, coin laundry, business services, meeting rooms* ▭ *AE, MC, V* ¶◎¶ *EP.*

$$–$$$ ⊡ **Hilton Ponce Golf & Casino Resort.** The south coast's biggest resort sits on a black-sand beach about 6 km (4 mi) south of Ponce. Everything on this 80-acre property is massive, beginning with the open-air lobby. Constructed of reinforced concrete, like the rest of the hotel, it requires huge signs to point you in the right direction. All of its bright, spacious rooms are decorated in a lush, tropical motif and have balconies overlooking the sea. A large pool is surrounded by palm trees and has a spectacular view of the Caribbean. Golf lovers will appreciate the 27-hole course at the adjacent Costa Caribe Resort, which has a clubhouse with its own restaurant and lounge. ⊠ *1150 Av. Caribe, La Guancha* ⬦ *Box 7419, Ponce 00732* ☎ *787/259–7676 or 800/445–8667* 🖷 *787/259– 7674* ⊕ *www.hiltoncaribbean.com* ⇘ *253 rooms* ⚘ *4 restaurants, room service, in-room safes, some in-room hot tubs, minibars, cable TV with movies and video games, Wi-Fi, 3 9-hole golf courses, driving range, 4 tennis courts, pool, gym, hot tub, sauna, spa, beach, bicycles, basketball, Ping-Pong, volleyball, 3 bars, casino, dance club, video game room, shops, babysitting, children's programs (ages 8–12), play-*

ground, business services, convention center, meeting rooms, parking (fee) ⊟ AE, D, DC, MC, V ⭢⊙⊣ EP.

$ ☷ **Parador Baños de Coamo.** On weekends musicians play in the central courtyard of this rustic country inn. Rooms—in four modern two-story buildings—have soaring ceilings and open onto latticed wooden verandas. Thermal water flows from natural springs into a swimming pool a few steps away from a cool-water pool, where you can still see walls dating from 1843. The oldest building still standing is the 19th-century dining room, which serves huge portions of tasty *churrasco* (skirt steak) along with rice and beans. The open-air bar is popular in the afternoons. ⊠ *Rte. 546, Km 1, Box 1867, Coamo 00769* ☎ *787/825–2186 or 787/825–2239* 🖷 *787/825–4739* ⇌ *48 rooms* ♢ *Restaurant, cable TV, 2 pools, bar, video game room* ⊟ *AE, D, MC, V* ⭢⊙⊣ *EP.*

★ $ ☷ **Hotel Meliá.** In the heart of the city, this family-owned hotel has long been a local landmark. Its neoclassical facade, with flags from a dozen countries waving in the breeze, will remind you of the small lodgings in Spain. The lobby, with wood-beamed ceilings and blue-and-beige tile floors, is well worn but extremely charming. The best rooms have French doors leading out to small balconies; the six suites have terrific views of the main square. Breakfast is served on the rooftop terrace, which overlooks the mountains. A waterfall drops into the beautiful tiled swimming pool. The restaurant, Mark's at the Meliá, is one of the best on the island. ⊠ *75 Calle Cristina, Ponce Centro* ⊕ *Box 1431, Ponce 00733* ☎ *787/842–0260 or 800/448–8355* 🖷 *787/841–3602* ⊕ *www.hotelmeliapr.com* ⇌ *72 rooms, 6 suites* ♢ *Restaurant, cable TV, pool, bar, Internet room, parking (fee)* ⊟ *AE, MC, V* ⭢⊙⊣ *CP.*

Western & Central Puerto Rico

$$$$ ☷ **Horned Dorset Primavera.** This is, without a doubt, one of the two or
Fodor'sChoice three finest hotels on the island. The 22 whitewashed villas scattered
★ around throughout the tropical gardens are designed so you have complete privacy whether you are relaxing in your private plunge pool or admiring the sunset from one of your balconies. The furnishings in each of the two-story suites are impeccable, from the hand-carved mahogany table in the downstairs dining room to the four-poster beds in the upstairs bedroom. The marble bathroom has a footed porcelain tub that's big enough for two. (There's a second bath downstairs that's perfect for showering off after a walk on the beach.) Breakfast is served in your room, while lunch is available on a terrace overlooking the ocean. ⊠ *Rte. 429, Km 3, Box 1132, Roncón 00677* ☎ *787/823–4030, 787/823–4050, or 800/633–1857* 🖷 *787/725–6068* ⊕ *www.horneddorset. com* ⇌ *22 villas* ♢ *Restaurant, fans, 2 in-room safes, kitchenettes, 2 pools, gym, massage, beach, croquet, library, bar; no room TVs, no kids under 12* ⊟ *AE, MC, V* ⭢⊙⊣ *EP.*

$$$ ☷ **Villa Montaña.** This secluded cluster of villas, situated on a deserted stretch of beach between Isabela and Aguadilla, feels like a little town. You can pull your car into your own garage, then head upstairs to your airy studio or one-, two-, or three-bedroom suite with hand-carved mahogany furniture and canopy beds. Studios have kitchenettes, while the larger villas have full-size kitchens and laundry rooms. Eclipse ($$–$$$$),

16

the open-air bar and restaurant, serves Caribbean-Asian fusion cuisine. Dishes include a tasty seafood risotto. Playa de Shacks, a popular beach, is nearby. ⊠ *Rte. 4446, Km 1.9, Box 530, Isabela 00662* ☎ *787/872–9554 or 888/780–9195* 🖷 *787/872–9553* ⊕ *www.villamontana.com* ⟿ *56 villas* ♨ *Restaurant, cable TV, in-room DVD players, 2 tennis courts, 2 pools, beach horseback riding, gym, laundry facilities, business services, meeting rooms* ⊟ *AE, D, MC, V* ⦿ *EP.*

$$–$$$ 🏨 **Rincón Beach Resort.** It's a bit off the beaten path, and that's part of the allure of this oceanfront hotel. The South Seas–style decor begins in the high-ceilinged lobby, where hand-carved chaises invite you to enjoy the view through the almond trees. The rooms continue the theme with rich fabrics and dark-wood furnishings. A variety of activities are available, including whale- and turtle-watching in season. At the end of the infinity pool a boardwalk leads down to the sand. Unlike at many of the beaches just a few miles north, the waters here are calm—not great for surfing, but perfect for a dip. The resort is tucked away in Añasco, about halfway between Rincón to the north and Mayagüez to the south. ⊠ *Rte. 115, Km. 5.8, Añasco 00610* ☎ *787/589–9000* 🖷 *787/589–9010* ⊕ *www.rinconbeach.com* ⟿ *112 rooms* ♨ *Restaurant, room service, fans, in-room safes, some kitchenettes, refrigerators, cable TV, in-room data ports, pool, gym, beach, dive shop, snorkeling, boating, 2 bars, babysitting, business services, Internet room, free parking* ⊟ *AE, D, DC, MC, V* ⦿ *EP.*

♨ **$$** 🏨 **Embassy Suites Dorado del Mar Beach & Golf Resort.** Kids love the freeform pool that shimmers in the courtyard of this beachfront resort, a favorite with families because of its reasonable rates and spacious accommodations. All the suites have separate bedrooms and living rooms but are otherwise undistinguished. Golfers can take in the mountains and the sea at the same time while playing the course designed by the legendary Chi Chi Rodríguez. The Paradise Café serves Caribbean favorites such as crusted sea bass with mango butter. ⊠ *201 Dorado del Mar Blvd., Dorado 00646* ☎ *787/796–6125* 🖷 *787/796–6145* ⊕ *www.embassysuitesdorado.com* ⟿ *174 suites, 35 condos* ♨ *2 restaurants, room service, kitchenettes, cable TV with movies, in-room data ports, 18-hole golf course, 2 tennis courts, pool, gym, hot tub, bar, video game room, shop, dry cleaning, laundry facilities, laundry service, meeting rooms* ⊟ *AE, D, DC, MC, V* ⦿ *BP.*

$–$$ 🏨 **Casa Isleña.** With its barrel-tiled roofs, wall-enclosed gardens, and open-air dining room, Casa Isleña might remind well-traveled souls of a villa on the coast of Mexico. The secret of its charm is that this little inn retains a simplicity without compromising the romantic flavor of its setting. Several of the terra-cotta-floored rooms have balconies that overlook the pool and the palm-shaded stretch of beach. Others have terraces that face the courtyard. There's also a hot tub and an indoor patio with a soothing, burbling fountain. ⊠ *Rte. 413, Km 4.8, Barrio Puntas, Rincón 00677* ☎ *787/823–1525 or 888/289–7750* 🖷 *787/823–1530* ⊕ *www.casa-islena.com* ⟿ *9 rooms* ♨ *Restaurant, some refrigerators, cable TV, pool, hot tub, beach, snorkeling, shop, free parking* ⊟ *AE, MC, V* ⦿ *EP.*

$–$$ 🏨 **Villas del Mar Hau.** The accommodations here aren't luxurious, but if you're looking for an unpretentious atmosphere, you'll have a hard time doing better than this small, beachfront resort. One-, two-, and three-bedroom cottages are painted in cheery pastels and trimmed with gingerbread. If you are planning on cooking, you should consider one of the studios, all of which have full kitchens. Otherwise, the open-air Olas y Arena is known for its excellent fish and shellfish; the paella is especially good. The hotel also has a stable of horses reserved for guests. ✉ *Rte. 4466, Km 8.3, Box 510, Isabela 00662* ☎ *787/872–2045 or 787/872–2627* 📠 *787/872–0273* 🌐 *www.paradorvillasdelmarhau.com* 🛏 *40 rooms* �’ *Restaurant, fans, some kitchens, tennis court, pool, basketball, horseback riding, laundry facilities* 🖶 *AE, MC, V* ⦿ *EP.*

★ **$** 🏠 **Casa Grande Mountain Retreat.** This isn't sleeping in a tree house, but it's close. The guest rooms here are in five wooden buildings that sit on platforms high above the varied vegetation. When you lie in the hammock on your private porch, all you can see is the mountains in every direction. The furnishings couldn't be simpler—little more than a bed and a dresser—but that's part of the rustic charm. Leave the windows open at night to hear the chorus of tiny tree frogs sing cantatas. If this doesn't relax you, yoga classes are offered every morning. Even people who aren't staying here stop to dine on the terrace at Jungle Jane's restaurant ($$–$$$), which features Puerto Rican specialties such as *pollo guisado* (chicken stew). ✉ *Rte. 612, Km 0.3, Box 1499, Utuado 00641* ☎ *787/894–3939 or 800/343–2272* 📠 *787/894–3900* 🌐 *www.hotelcasagrande.com* 🛏 *20 rooms* �’ *Restaurant, fans, pool, fitness classes, hiking; no a/c, no room phones, no room TVs, no smoking* 🖶 *AE, MC, V* ⦿ *EP.*

$ 🏠 **Lazy Parrot.** Painted an eye-popping shade of pink, this mountainside hotel doesn't take itself too seriously. Colorful murals of the eponymous bird brighten the open and airy lobby. The accommodations are a bit more subdued, though they continue the tropical theme. (The Dolphin Room has—what else?—a stuffed dolphin.) Each has a balcony where you can enjoy the view. There are two restaurants that share a similar theme—Sloppy Joe's on the lower level serves sandwiches and other light fare, while Smilin' Joe's upstairs serves red snapper and other excellent seafood dishes. At the bar you can sample a parrot-themed concoction. ✉ *Rte. 413, Km 4.1, Rincón 00677* ☎ *787823–5654 or 800/294–1752* 📠 *787/823–0224* 🌐 *www.lazyparrot.com* 🛏 *11 rooms* �’ *2 restaurants, refrigerators, cable TV, pool, hot tub, 2 bars, shop* 🖶 *AE, D, MC, V* ⦿ *CP.*

$ 🏠 **Lemontree Waterfront Cottages.** Sitting right on the beach, these two buildings hold six apartments of various sizes. Choose from one three-bedroom unit, one two-bedroom unit, two one-bedroom units, or two studios. All have kitchenettes and private balconies with views of the coastline. Ted and Jane Davis, who bought the place in 2005, have added amenities not so common in this price range, such as plasma televisions. There is a dive shop on the premises and a massage therapist on call. This is one of the few gay-friendly places in Rincón. ✉ *Rte. 429, Km 4.1, Box 200, Rincón 00677* ☎ *787/823–6452* 🌐 *www.lemontreepr.com* 🛏 *6 apartments* �’ *Kitchenettes, cable TV, beach, massage* 🖶 *MC, V* ⦿ *EP.*

$ 🏠 **Parador Hacienda Gripiñas.** Built on the grounds of a coffee plantation, this 19th-century inn is surrounded on all sides by mountain peaks.

16

Several of the clapboard-walled rooms in the red-roofed manor house have private balconies overlooking lush gardens and the spring-fed pool; the nicest are numbers 4 and 5. There are plenty of small parlors where you can relax with a drink from the bar. The dining area, which meanders through three different rooms, serves criolla fare such as chicken with rice and beans; all meals are included in the rate. Nonguests are welcome for dinner. One hiking trail near the property leads to Cerro de Punta, about a 2½-hour climb. ⊠ *Rte. 527, Km 2.7, Box 387, Jayuya 00664* ☎ *787/828–1717* 🖶 *787/828–1719* ⊕ *www.haciendagripinas. com* ⇆ *19 rooms* ◊ *Restaurant, cable TV, 2 pools, hiking, bar* ☰ *AE, MC, V* 🍴 *FAP.*

¢–$ 🛏 **Rincón Surf & Board.** All the rooms have surfboard racks, which should give you a clue as to who is drawn to this out-of-the-way lodging. Two hostel-type rooms with bunk beds—remains of the original lodging concept—are available at $20 per person. One- to three-bed private rooms are ample in size and have a clean and fresh feel; some are like small apartments. All rooms have their own surf racks. Common areas are fun and friendly but not conducive to late-night partying, as the best surfing is for the early birds. ⊠ *Off Rte. 413, Barrio Puntas, Rincón 00677* ☎ *787/ 823–0610* 🖶 *787/823–6440* ⊕ *www.surfandboard.com* ⇆ *13 rooms, 2 hostel rooms* ◊ *Restaurant, some refrigerators, cable TV, pool, hot tub, beach, snorkeling, shop, free parking* ☰ *AE, MC, V* 🍴 *EP.*

Where to Eat

Your palate will be pleasantly amused by the range of dining choices available in Puerto Rico. In San Juan you can find more than 200 restaurants serving everything from Italian to Thai, as well as superb local eateries serving *comida criolla* (traditional creole food). All of San Juan's large hotels have fine restaurants, but some of the city's best eateries are stand-alone, and smaller hotels also often present good options. There's also a mind-boggling array of U.S. chain restaurants. No matter your price range or taste, San Juan is a great place to eat.

Mesónes gastronómicos are restaurants recognized by the government for preserving culinary traditions. There are more than 40 islandwide. (Although there are fine restaurants in the system, the *mesón gastronómico* label is not an automatic symbol of quality.) Wherever you go, it's *always* good to make reservations in the busy season, from mid-November through April, in restaurants where they're accepted.

Puerto Rican cooking uses a lot of local vegetables: plantains are cooked a hundred different ways—as *tostones* (fried green), *amarillos* (baked ripe), in *mofongo* (mashed, fried plantains), and as chips. Rice and beans with tostones or amarillos are accompaniments to almost every dish. Locals cook white rice with *habichuelas* (red beans), *achiote* (annatto seeds), or saffron; brown rice with *gandules* (pigeon peas); and *morro* (black rice) with *frijoles negros* (black beans). Yams and other root vegetables, such as yucca and *yautía* (yams), are served baked, fried, stuffed, boiled, and mashed. *Sofrito*—a garlic, onion, sweet pepper, coriander, oregano, and tomato puree—is used as a base for practically everything.

Beef, chicken, pork, and seafood are rubbed with *adobo,* a garlic-oregano marinade, before cooking. *Arroz con pollo* (chicken with rice), *sancocho* (beef or chicken and tuber soup), *asopao* (a soupy rice gumbo with chicken or seafood), and *encebollado* (steak smothered in onions) are all typical plates. Also look for fritters served along highways and beaches. You may find *empanadillas* (stuffed fried turnovers), *sorullitos* (cheese-stuffed corn sticks), *alcapurrias* (stuffed green-banana croquettes), and *bacalaítos* (codfish fritters). Caribbean lobster, available mainly at coastal restaurants, is sweeter and easier to eat than Maine lobster, and there's always plentiful fresh dolphinfish and red snapper. Conch is prepared in a chilled ceviche salad or stuffed with tomato sauce inside fritters.

Puerto Rican coffee is excellent black or *con leche* (with hot milk). The origin of the piña colada is attributed to numerous places, from the Caribe Hilton to a Fortaleza Street bar. Puerto Rican rums range from light mixers to dark, aged liqueurs. Look for Bacardí, Don Q, Ron Rico, Palo Viejo, and Barrilito.

What to Wear

Dress codes vary greatly, though a restaurant's price category is a good indicator of its formality. For less expensive places, anything but beachwear is fine. Ritzier eateries will expect collared shirts for men (jacket and tie requirements are rare) and chic attire for women. When in doubt, do as the Puerto Ricans often do and dress up.

16

Old San Juan

CAFÉS
$$

✕ **Café Berlin.** A handful of tables spill out onto the sidewalk at this unpretentious place overlooking Plaza Colón. There's something on the menu for everyone, from turkey breast in a mustard-curry sauce to salmon in a citrus sauce. There are even several good vegetarian dishes, including tofu in a mushroom sauce. Inside is a small bar, one of the few places in Puerto Rico that serve draft beer. ⊠ *407 Calle San Francisco, Old San Juan* ☎ *787/722–5205* ▭ *AE, MC, V.*

CARIBBEAN
$–$$

✕ **La Fonda del Jíbarito.** Sanjuaneros have favored this casual, family-run restaurant for years. The conch ceviche and chicken fricassee are among the specialties on the menu of *comida criolla* dishes. The back porch is filled with plants, and the dining room is filled with fanciful depictions of life on the street outside. The ever-present owner, Pedro J. Ruiz, is filled with the desire to ensure that everyone is happy. ⊠ *280 Calle Sol, Old San Juan* ☎ *787/725–8375* ⌿ *Reservations not accepted* ▭ *AE, MC, V.*

CONTEMPORARY
$$–$$$

✕ **Amadeus.** Facing Plaza San José, this bright and airy restaurant often throws open the doors and lets its tables spill into the square. If you want a little more privacy, there's also an interior courtyard and an intimate dining room with whitewashed walls, linen tablecloths, and lazily turning ceiling fans. Try nouvelle Caribbean appetizers such as dumplings with guava-rum sauce or plantain mousse with shrimp and entrées such as ravioli with a goat-cheese and pork with mango and sugarcane. ⊠ *106 Calle San Sebastián, Old San Juan* ☎ *787/722–8635* ▭ *AE, MC, V* ☺ *Closed Sun. No lunch Mon.*

$$–$$$ ✕ **Barú.** The well-traveled menu has earned Barú a solid reputation among sanjuaneros, so it's often crowded. The dishes, all served in medium-size portions so you can order several and share, range from Middle Eastern to Asian to Caribbean. Favorites include oysters in a soy-citrus sauce, risotto with green asparagus, and carpaccio made from beef, tuna, or salmon. More substantial fare includes filet mignon with horseradish mashed potatoes and pork ribs with a ginger-tamarind glaze. The dining room, in a beautifully renovated colonial house, is dark and mysterious. ✉ *150 Calle San Sebastián, Old San Juan* ☎ *787/977–7107* ▤ *AE, MC, V* ☾ *Closed Mon. No lunch.*

$$–$$$ ✕ **Parrot Club.** Loud and lively, this place is intent on making sure everyone is having a good time. You're likely to strike up a conversation with the bartender as you enjoy a passion-fruit cocktail or with the couple at the next table on the covered courtyard. Something about the atmosphere—ear-splitting salsa music and murals of swaying palm trees—makes it easy. The menu has contemporary variations of Caribbean classics. You might start with mouthwatering crab cakes or tamarind-barbecued ribs, followed by blackened tuna in a dark rum sauce or seared sea bass with lobster, leek, and scallop confit. ✉ *363 Calle Fortaleza, Old San Juan* ☎ *787/725–7370* ⌔ *Reservations not accepted* ▤ *AE, DC, MC, V.*

ECLECTIC   ✕ **La Ostra Cosa.** This restaurant's succulent prawns, grilled and served
★ **$$**   with garlic butter, are supposed to be aphrodisiacs. Well, everything on the menu is rated for its love-inducing qualities. (Look out for those labeled "Ay, ay, ay!") There are some seats indoors, but opt for one in the walled courtyard; with brilliant purple bougainvillea tumbling down and moonlight streaming through the trees, it's one of the city's prettiest alfresco dining spots. The gregarious owner, Alberto Nazario, brother of pop star Ednita Nazario, genuinely enjoys seeing his guests satisfied. He'll sometimes take out a guitar and sing old folk songs. Don't be surprised if the locals sing along. ✉ *154 Calle Cristo, Old San Juan* ☎ *787/722–2672* ▤ *AE, MC, V.*

FRENCH   ✕ **La Chaumière.** With black and white floor tiles, wood-beamed ceil-
$$$–$$$$ ing, and floral-print curtains, this two-story restaurant evokes provincial France. It has been under the same management since 1969, and with all that experience the service is smooth. Daily specials augment a menu of stellar French classics, including breast of duck with a cassis glaze and veal with a mustard cream sauce. If you want to go all out, there's the huge chateaubriand for two. ✉ *367 Calle Tetuan, Old San Juan* ☎ *787/722–3330* ▤ *AE, DC, MC, V* ☾ *Closed Sun. No lunch.*

ITALIAN   ✕ **Sofia.** Ignore the tongue-in-cheek recordings of "That's Amore."
$$–$$$ Everything else in this red-walled trattoria is the real deal, from the gleaming vegetables on the antipasto table to the interesting vintages on the small but well-chosen wine list. Start with the squid stuffed with sweet sausage; then move on to the linguine with clams and pancetta or the cannelloni filled with roasted duck and topped with mascarpone cheese. The plates of pasta are huge, so you might want to consider a half order (which is more the size of a three-quarter order). Save room for—what else?—a tasty tiramisu. ✉ *355 Calle San Francisco, Old San Juan* ☎ *787/721–0396* ▤ *AE, MC, V.*

PAN-ASIAN
$$$–$$$$

✕ **Kudetá.** The name is an inside joke—it's pronounced like coup d'é-tat, the French term for "revolution." A bit of an exaggeration, perhaps, but the kitchen has scored more than a few victories with dishes that blend Caribbean main dishes with Asian cooking methods. That's why the steak is covered with a wasabi demi-glace and the oysters are submerged is tasty green curry. The minimalist dining room is also a triumph, especially the sage-colored banquettes covered with aubergine-and-gold pillows. The black-clad staff couldn't be friendlier and is happy to help you negotiate the menu. ⊠ *314 Calle La Fortaleza* ☎ *787/977–5023* ▭ *AE, MC, V.*

$$–$$$

✕ **Dragonfly.** It's not hard to find this little restaurant—it's the one with crowds milling about on the sidewalk. If you can stand the wait—as you undoubtedly will, as reservations aren't accepted—then you'll get to sample chef Roberto Trevino's Latin-Asian cuisine. (For the best chance of avoiding a line, come at 6 PM, which is opening time.) The *platos* (plates) are meant to be shared, so order several for your table. Favorites include pork-and-plantain dumplings with an orange dipping sauce, smoked salmon pizza with wasabi salsa, and lamb spareribs with a tamarind glaze. The dining room, all done up in Chinese red, resembles an opium den. ⊠ *364 Calle La Fortaleza, Old San Juan* ☎ *787/977–3886* ⊗ *Reservations not accepted* ▭ *AE, MC, V* ⊘ *Closed Sun. No lunch.*

SEAFOOD
$$–$$$$
Fodor'sChoice
★

✕ **Aguaviva.** The name means "jellyfish," which explains why this ultra-cool, ultramodern place has lighting fixtures shaped like that sea creature. Elegantly groomed oysters and clams float on cracked ice along the raw bar. The extensive menu is alive with inventive ceviches, some with tomato or roasted red peppers and olives, and fresh takes on classics like paella. For something more filling, try dorado served with a shrimp salsa or tuna accompanied by seafood enchiladas. You could also empty out your wallet for one of the *torres del mar,* or towers of the sea, a gravity-defying dish that comes hot or cold and includes oysters, mussels, shrimp—you name it. Oh, and don't pass up the lobster mashed potatoes; those alone are worth the trip. ⊠ *364 Calle La Fortaleza, Old San Juan* ☎ *787/722–0665* ⊗ *Reservations not accepted* ▭ *AE, D, MC, V.*

SPANISH
$$$

✕ **El Picoteo.** You could make a meal of the small dishes that dominate the menu at this tapas bar. You won't go wrong with the sweet sausage in brandy or the turnovers stuffed with lobster. Small plates are best passed shared. If you're not into sharing, there are five different kinds of paella that arrive on huge plates. There's a long, lively bar inside; one dining area overlooks a pleasant courtyard, while the other takes in the action along Calle Cristo. Even if you have dinner plans elsewhere, consider stopping here for a nightcap. ⊠ *El Convento Hotel, 100 Calle Cristo, Old San Juan* ☎ *787/723–9621* ▭ *AE, D, DC, MC, V.*

Greater San Juan

CAFÉS
★ $

✕ **Kasalta.** Those who think coffee can never be too strong will be very happy at Kasalta, which has an amazing inky-black brew that will knock your socks off. Make your selection from the display cases full of luscious pastries and other tempting treats. Walk up to the counter

16

and order a sandwich, such as the savory Cubano, or such items as the meltingly tender octopus salad. ⊠ *1966 Calle McLeary, Ocean Park* ☎ 787/727–7340 ☰ *AE, MC, V.*

CARIBBEAN
★ $$–$$$$ ✕ **Ajili-Mójili.** In a plantation-style house, this elegant dining room sits on the edge of Condado Bay. Traditional Puerto Rican food is prepared with a flourish, though for high prices. Sample the fried cheese and *bolitas de yautía y queso* (cheese and yam dumplings); then move on to the *gallinita rellena* (stuffed cornish hen). The plantain-crusted shrimp in a white-wine herb sauce is delicious, as is the paella overflowing with shrimp, octopus, mussels, chicken, and spicy sausage. ⊠ *1006 Av. Ashford, Condado* ☎ 787/725–9195 ☰ *AE, DC, MC, V.*

★ $$–$$$ ✕ **Pamela's.** For the ultimate tropical dining experience, make a beeline here, the only city restaurant that offers outdoor seating on the sand, just steps away from the ocean, though it's also possible to dine indoors in air-conditioned comfort. The contemporary Caribbean menu is as memorable as the alfresco setting; daily specials might include blackened salmon glazed with a Mandarin honey sauce or Jamaican jerk shrimp and coconut corn *arepas* (pancakes, of sorts) with guava coulis. ⊠ *Numero Uno Guesthouse, 1 Calle Santa Ana, Ocean Park* ☎ 787/726–5010 ☰ *AE, D, MC, V.*

CONTEMPORARY
$$$$ ✕ **Pikayo.** Chef Wilo Benet is clearly the star here—a plasma television lets diners watch everything that's going on in his kitchen. The Puerto Rico native artfully fuses Caribbean cuisine with influences from around the world. Veal is served in a swirl of sweet-pea couscous, for example, and beef medallions are covered with crumbled blue cheese and a red wine reduction. The regularly changing menu is a feast for the eye as well as the palate and might include perfectly shaped tostones stuffed with oven-dried tomatoes or mofongo topped with saffron shrimp. A changing selection of paintings wraps around the minimalist dining room—the restaurant is, after all, inside a museum. ⊠ *Museo de Arte de Puerto Rico, 299 Av. José de Diego, Santurce* ☎ 787/721–6194 ☰ *AE, MC, V* ☺ *Closed Sun. and Mon.*

★ $$$–$$$$ ✕ **Chayote.** Slightly off the beaten path, this chic eatery is definitely an "in" spot. The chef gives haute international dishes tropical panache. Starters include chayote stuffed with prosciutto and corn tamales with shrimp in a coconut sauce. Half the entrées are seafood dishes, including pan-seared tuna with a ginger sauce and red snapper served over spinach. The ginger flan is a must for dessert. The sophisticated dining room is hung with works by local artists. ⊠ *Hotel Olimpo Court, 603 Av. Miramar, Miramar* ☎ 787/722–9385 ☰ *AE, MC, V* ☺ *Closed Sun.–Mon. No lunch Sat.*

$$–$$$$ ✕ **Mi Kasa.** Inspired in blending Japanese and Latin flavors, the dishes created here by chef José Aponte, former sous-chef at Nobu New York, elude labels. The ripe plantain halves topped with shrimp and scallops are a favorite among loyal customers. Other great dishes include salmon over baby spinach and baby back ribs coated with a spicy miso sauce. Don't leave without a taste of bar master Yuki's sake mojito. ⊠ *176 Duffaut St., Plaza del Mercado, Santurce* ☎ 787/725–3518 ⊲ *Reservations essential* ☰ *AE, MC, V* ☺ *Closed Mon.*

$$–$$$ ✕ **Zabó.** In a restored plantation surrounded by a quiet garden, this inventive restaurant seems as if it's out on the island somewhere rather than just off bustling Avenida Ashford. Make sure to order several of the tasty appetizers—such as breaded calamari in a tomato-basil sauce—so you can share them your dinner companions. Of the notable main courses, try the veal chops stuffed with provolone and pancetta or the miso-marinated salmon served over lemony basmati rice. ✉ *14 Calle Candida, Condado* ☎ *787/725–9494* ▭ *AE, D, DC, MC, V* ☾ *Closed Sun. and Mon. No lunch Tues.–Thurs. or Sat.*

SEAFOOD ✕ **La Dorada.** This fine seafood establishment, in the middle of Condado's
$$–$$$$ restaurant row, is surprisingly affordable. A grilled seafood platter is the specialty, but there are plenty of other excellent dishes, including mahimahi in caper sauce and codfish in green sauce. The friendly staff makes you feel genuinely welcome. ✉ *1105 Av. Magdalena, Condado* ☎ *787/722–9583* ▭ *AE, D, MC, V.*

SPANISH ✕ **Urdin.** The name of this restaurant comes from the Basque word for
$$–$$$ blue, which also happens to be the dining room's dominant color. The menu here consists mostly of Spanish dishes, but Caribbean touches abound. The soup and seafood appetizers are particularly good, and a highly recommended entrée is *chillo urdin de lujo* (red snapper sautéed with clams, mussels, and shrimp in a tomato, herb, and wine sauce). ✉ *1105 Av. Magdalena, Condado* ☎ *787/724–0420* ▭ *AE, MC, V.*

Eastern Puerto Rico

SEAFOOD ✕ **Anchor's Inn.** Seafood is the specialty at this restaurant perched high
$$–$$$ on a bluff overlooking the ocean. This is a great place to sample specialties such as *chillo entero* (fried whole red snapper). The convenient location, down the road from El Conquistador Resort, lures travelers who have had enough hotel food. ✉ *Rte. 987, Km 2.7, Fajardo* ☎ *787/863–7200* ⌂ *Reservations not accepted* ▭ *AE, MC, V* ☾ *Closed Tues.*

$–$$ ✕ **Pulpo Loco by the Sea.** Talk about truth in packaging—the Crazy Octopus has its palm-shaded tables planted firmly in the sand just a few yards from the ocean. As you might guess, octopus, oysters, mussels, and crab lead the lineup at this colorful seafood shack, though you can always munch on local favorites like fried codfish fritters. If your thirst is greater than your hunger, you can opt for a beer served in a plastic cup. The staff is friendly and seems to know all the customers on a first-name basis. ✉ *Rte. 187, Km 4.5, Piñones* ☎ *787/791–8382* ▭ *AE, MC, V.*

Vieques & Culebra

CARIBBEAN ✕ **Café Media Luna.** Tucked into a beautifully restored building in Isabel
$$–$$$ Segunda, this eatery has been a favorite for many years. Its popularity might be due to the convenient downtown location, or the intimate tables on the balconies that surround the second-floor dining room. More likely, however, it's the creativity of the cooks. (You can watch all the action, as the kitchen is in full view.) Try the cornish hen in a sweet-spicy coconut sauce or the seared yellowfin tuna served with vegetable tempura. Not so hungry? Then share one of the tasty pizzas. Half a dozen are on offer at any given time. ✉ *351 Calle Antonio Mellado, Isabel*

16

Segunda, Vieques ☎ *787/741–2594* ⌘ *Reservations essential* ▤ *AE, MC, V* ⊘ *Closed Mon. and Tues. No lunch.*

¢–$ ✕ **Barbara-Rosa's.** Her husband is on hand to chat with the customers, but Barbara Petersen does everything else: takes your order, cooks it up, and serves it with a flourish. You won't find better food anywhere on the island, and that includes the places that charge twice as much. Locals swear by her tender, flaky fish-and-chips. (The secret, her husband happily points out, is using red snapper.) Finish with key lime pie or peach and pineapple cobbler. ⊠ *Calle Escudero, Dewey, Culebra* ☎ *787/ 742–3271* ▤ *MC, V* ⊘ *Closed Sun. and Mon.*

Southern Puerto Rico

CONTEMPORARY ✕ **Mark's at the Meliá.** Hidden behind an etched-glass door, this discreet
$$–$$$$ restaurant is one of the best on the island. Chef Mark French has won
Fodor'sChoice praise for his creative blend of European cooking techniques and local
★ ingredients. That skill results in appetizers like terrine of foie gras with dried cherry compote and smoked salmon topped with caramelized mango. The menu changes often, but you're likely to see such entrées as plantain-crusted dorado and rack of lamb with a goat cheese crust. The chocolate truffle cake draws fans from as far away as San Juan. This is a family-run business, so Mark's wife, Melody, is likely to greet you at the door. ⊠ *Hotel Meliá, 75 Calle Cristina, Ponce Centro, Ponce* ☎ *787/ 284–6275* ⌘ *Reservations essential* ▤ *AE, MC, V* ⊘ *Closed Mon.–Tues.*

SEAFOOD ✕ **El Ancla.** Families favor this laid-back restaurant, whose dining room
☺ **$–$$$** sits at the edge of the sea. The kitchen serves generous and affordable plates of fish, crab, and other fresh seafood with tostones, french fries, and garlic bread. Try the shrimp in garlic sauce, salmon fillet with capers, or the delectable mofongo. Finish your meal with one of the fantastic flans. The piña coladas—with or without rum—are exceptional. ⊠ *9 Av. Hostos Final, Ponce Playa, Ponce* ☎ *787/840–2450* ▤ *AE, MC, V.*

$$ ✕ **El Bohío.** Watch seagulls dive for their dinner while you dine on a covered deck extending out into the bay. The long list of seafood is prepared in a variety of ways: shrimp comes breaded, stewed, or skewered; conch is served as a salad or cooked in a butter and garlic sauce. And the lobster can be prepared in just about any way you can imagine. ⊠ *Rte. 102, Km 9.7, Joyuda* ☎ *787/851–2755* ▤ *AE, DC, MC, V.*

Western & Central Puerto Rico

CARIBBEAN ✕ **El Fogón de Abuela.** This rustic restaurant on the edge of Dos Bocas
$–$$$ Lake would make any Puerto Rican grandmother envious. The menu features stews, red snapper (whole or filleted), and fricassees, including pork chop, goat, and rabbit. You arrive by taking the public boat from El Embarcadero on Route 612, by calling the restaurant from the dock and requesting a boat be sent to pick you up (free of charge), or by driving to the south side of the lake. From Utuado, take Route 111 to Route 140 to Route 612 and follow that to its end. ⊠ *Lago Dos Bocas* ☎ *787/894–0470* ▤ *MC, V* ⊘ *Closed Mon.–Thurs.*

ECLECTIC ✕ **Happy Belly's.** If you're in the mood for a hamburger or club sand-
$–$$$ wich, this laid-back restaurant is a good choice. The seating is in comfortable wooden booths that overlook Playa Jobos—the wind that

whips up the waves may also blow away your napkin. In the evening the menu changes to more substantial fare, with everything from shrimp scampi to baby back ribs. But many people just come for the socializing and the sunsets. ⊠ *Rte. 4466, Km 7.5, Isabela* ☎ 787/872–6566 ▭ *AE, MC, V.*

¢–$ ✕ **Tamboo.** This is a bar and grill that doesn't fall too much into either category. The open-air kitchen prepares any number of unusual items, from king crab sandwiches to chicken and basil wraps. The bar, also open to the elements, serves a mean margarita. Happy hour sometimes starts dangerously early—at 10 AM on Saturday. The deck is a great place to watch the novice surfers wipe out on the nearby beach. ⊠ *Rte. 413, Km 4.7, Rincón* ☎ 787/823–3210 ▭ *MC, V.*

ITALIAN   ✕ **Mangére.** Any night of the week you're likely to find this place packed
$$–$$$$ with locals who come for the convivial atmosphere as much as the delicious Italian fare. The glassed-in dining room gets noisy, so you may have to shout when you order the veal medallions with portobello and porcini mushrooms or the salmon with capers. Unusual for these parts, there's even a good selection of vegetarian options, including a hearty broccoli alfredo. The wine list, which naturally focuses on Italian vintages, is impressive. ⊠ *Rte. 693, Km 8.5* ☎ 787/796–4444 ▭ *AE, D, MC, V.*

16

Beaches

A visit to Puerto Rico isn't complete without at least a few splashes in the warm ocean followed by toasting yourself dry in the sun. By law, the island's *playas* (beaches) are all open to the public. Resort hotels may imply that the stretch in front of the hotel is private, but anyone is free to walk across that well-manicured sand. *Balnearios,* which are government-run beaches, are equipped with restrooms, changing areas, water fountains, lifeguards, and parking lots. In many cases there are also picnic tables, playgrounds, and camping facilities. Sometimes there are cheap food stands where you can find freshly caught fish. Admission is free, and parking is usually $2 or $3. Hours vary, but most balnearios are open from daily 9 to 5. Because of all these amenities, balnearios attract families and children. Often this results in noise, strong-smelling foods, and trash. For quiet relaxation, as a general rule, avoid them on the weekends. Better yet, bring your own picnic lunch and head out to one of the lesser-known beaches.

GREATER SAN   The city's beaches can get crowded, especially on weekends. There's free
JUAN AREA   access to all of them, but parking can be an issue in the peak sun hours—arriving early or in the late afternoon is a safer bet.

★   **Balneario de Carolina.** When people talk of "beautiful Isla Verde beach," this is the one they're talking about. A government-maintained beach, this balneario east of Isla Verde is so close to the airport that the leaves rustle when planes take off. The long stretch of sand, which runs parallel to Avenida Los Gobernadores, is shaded by palms and almond trees. There's plenty of room to spread out and lots of amenities: lifeguards, restrooms, changing facilities, picnic tables, and barbecue grills. ⊠ *Carolina* ▧ *Parking $2* ☉ *Daily 8–6.*

★ **Balneario de Escambrón.** In Puerta de Tierra, this government-run beach is just off Avenida Muñoz Rivera. This patch of honey-colored sand has shade provided by coconut palms and surf that's generally gentle. There are also lifeguards, bathhouses, bathrooms, and restaurants. ⊠ *Puerta de Tierra* 🚘 *Parking $3* ⊙ *Daily 7–7.*

Playa del Condado. East of Old San Juan and west of Ocean Park, this long, wide beach is overshadowed by an unbroken string of hotels and apartment buildings. Beach bars, water-sports outfitters, and chair-rental places abound. You can access the beach from several roads off Avenida Ashford, including Calle Cervantes and Calle Candina. The protected water at the small stretch of beach west of the Condado Plaza hotel is particularly calm and popular with families; surf elsewhere in Condado can be a bit strong. The stretch of sand near Calle Vendig (behind the Atlantic Beach Hotel) is especially popular with the gay community. If you're driving, on-street parking is your only option. ⊠ *Condado* ⊙ *Daily dawn to dusk.*

Playa de Ocean Park. The residential neighborhood east of Condado and west of Isla Verde is home to this 1-mi-long (1½-km-long) stretch of golden sand. The waters are often choppy but still swimmable—take care, however, as there aren't any lifeguards are on duty. Windsurfers say the conditions here are nearly perfect. The beach is popular with young people, particularly on weekends, as well as gay men. Parking is a bit difficult, as many of the streets are gated and restricted to residents. ⊠ *Ocean Park* ⊙ *Daily dawn to dusk.*

EASTERN
PUERTO RICO
ⓒ
Fodor'sChoice
★

Balneario de Luquillo. A magnet for families, this government-maintained beach is well equipped with changing areas and restrooms, lifeguards, food stands and picnic areas, and even stands where you can order a cocktail. It's most distinctive facility, though, is the Mar Sin Barreras (Sea Without Barriers), a low-sloped ramp leading into the water that allows wheelchair users to take a dip. The beach is off Route 3 as you head toward Fajardo. ⊠ *Off Route 3, Luquillo* 🚘 *Parking $2* ⊙ *Tues.–Sun. 9–5.*

ⓒ **Balneario Seven Seas.** This long stretch of powdery sand near the Reserva Natural Las Cabezas de San Juan may turn out to be the best surprise of your trip. Facilities include food kiosks, picnic tables, changing areas, restrooms, and showers. On weekends, the beach attracts crowds keen on its calm, clear waters—perfect for swimming and other water sports. ⊠ *Route 987, Fajardo* 🚘 *Parking $3* ⊙ *Daily 8–6.*

VIEQUES &
CULEBRA
Fodor'sChoice
★

Playa Flamenco. On Culebra's north coast is an amazingly lovely stretch of white sand. This beach, with its almost perfect half-moon shape, is consistently ranked as one of the two or three best in the world. Once you see it, you'll know why. Mountains rise up on all sides, making it feel miles away from civilization. It's only when the propeller planes fly low over the beach that you remember that the airport is just over the ridge. During the week Playa Flamenco is pleasantly uncrowded; on the weekend, though, it fills up fast with day-trippers. This is the only beach on Culebra with amenities such as restrooms, showers, and kiosks selling simple fare. ⊠ *Off Rte. 251, west of the airport, Culebra* ⊙ *Daily dawn to dusk.*

Playa Soni. On Culebra's northeastern end, this beach is far more isolated than Playa Flamenco, and it's just as beautiful. From the shore you can catch a glimpse of St. Thomas and St. Croix. To get here, take Route 250 east until you reach the end. ⊠ *Route 250, 11 km (7 mi) northeast of Dewey, Culebra* ⊙ *Daily dawn to dusk.*

Fodor's Choice ★ **Playa Sun Bay.** East of Esperanza this is easily the most popular of the dozens of beaches that ring Vieques. Its white sands skirt a mile-long, crescent-shape bay. You'll find food kiosks, picnic tables, and changing facilities. On weekdays, when the crowds are thin, you might also find wild horses grazing among the palm trees. There's often nobody at the gate to take your money. ⊠ *Route 997, Vieques* 🚗 *Parking $3* ⊙ *Daily dawn to dusk.*

SOUTHERN PUERTO RICO 🖐 **Balneario Boquerón.** This broad beach of hard-packed sand is fringed with coconut palms. You can find changing facilities, cabins, showers, restrooms, and picnic tables. Nearby, Playa Santa and Ballena golden sand beaches are often deserted. ⊠ *Boquerón* 🚗 *Parking $3* ⊙ *Daily 8 AM–10 PM.*

★ 🖐 **La Playuela.** At the very southwesternmost tip of the island, there are breathtaking views of salt mines and the stretches of white sand at the foot of the Cabo Rojo Lighthouse, which are part of a protected reserve. Getting to this beach is a bit of an adventure but bliss upon arrival. Access is via a very bumpy road; a 4x4 is recommended. ⊠ *End of Rte. 301* ⊙ *Dawn to dusk.*

16

WESTERN & CENTRAL PUERTO RICO **Playa de Jobos.** Isabela beaches are mostly rough and suitable for surfers, but some sections of this beach are safe and swimmable. On the same stretch, there are a couple of restaurants with oceanfront decks serving light fare and drinks. Down the road, the dunes and long stretches of golden sand are gorgeous for walks or running. Route 466 runs parallel and there are narrow accesses to the beach scattered throughout. ⊠ *Off Route 466, Isabela* ⊙ *Dawn to dusk.*

Playa Crashboat. This beach near Aguadilla is famous for the colorful fishing boats docked on its shores; its long, beautiful stretch of golden yellow sand; and its clear water, which is perfect for swimming. Named after rescue boats used when Ramey Air Force Base was in operation, this balneario has picnic huts, showers, parking, and restrooms. There's a modest food stand run by local fishermen where the catch of the day is served with cold beer. ⊠ *1 mi (1½ km) west of Rte. 107, Aguadilla* ⊙ *Dawn to dusk.*

Sports & the Outdoors

BOATING & SAILING **Aqua Frenzy Kayaks** (⊠ At dock area below Calle Flamboyán, Esperanza, Vieques ☎ 787/741–0913) rents kayaks and arranges kayak tours of Bahía Mosquito and other areas. Reservations for the excursion to glowing Bahía Mosquito cost $30. Make reservations at least 24 hours in advance. **Blue Caribe Kayaks** (⊠ 149 Calle Flamboyán, Esperanza, Vieques ☎ 787/741–2522 ⊕ www.enchanted-isle.com/bluecaribe) offers kayak trips to Bahía Mosquito for about $30, as well as trips to deserted parts of the coast and to nearby islets. You can also rent a kayak and set off on your ★ own. **Island Adventures** (⊠ Rte. 996, Esperanza, Vieques ☎ 787/741–0720

⊕ www.biobay.com), owned by former school teacher Sharon Grasso, will take you to Bahía Mosquito aboard nonpolluting, electrically powered pontoon boats. The best part is leaping into the water, where the outline of your body will be softly illuminated. The cost is about $30 per person. **Las Tortugas Adventures** (✉ Cond. La Puntilla, 4 Calle La Puntilla, Apt. D1-12, Old San Juan, San Juan ☎787/725–5169 ⊕www.kayak-pr.com) organizes group-kayaking trips to the Reserva Natural Las Cabezas de San Juan and the Bahía Mosquito in eastern Puerto Rico.

CYCLING Selected areas lend themselves to bike travel. Avoid main thoroughfares, as the traffic is heavy and the fumes are thick. The Paseo Piñones is an 11-mi bike path that skirts the ocean east of San Juan. The entire southwest coast of Cabo Rojo also makes for good biking, particularly the broad beach at Boquerón. Parts of oceanside Route 466 in Isabela that are still development-free make gorgeous rides with breathtaking views. Road bike events are organized year-round by the **Federación Puertorriqueña de Ciclismo** (☎ 787/721–8755 ⊕ www.federacionciclismopr.com).

At **Hot Dog Cycling** (✉ 5916 Av. Isla Verde, Isla Verde, San Juan ☎ 787/982–5344 ⊕ www.hotdogcycling.com), Raul del Río and his son Omar rent mountain bikes for $30 a day. They also organize group excursions to El Yunque and other places out on the island. If you want to bike the Paseo Piñones, you can rent bikes for about $5 an hour from **Dos Locos** (✉ Rte. 187, Km 5, Piñones ☎ 787/565–2537). This little kiosk sits beside Pulpo Loco By the Sea.

DIVING &   The diving is excellent off Puerto Rico's south, east, and west coasts, as
SNORKELING   well as its nearby islands. Particularly striking are dramatic walls created by a continental shelf off the south coast near La Parguera and Guánica. There's also some fantastic diving near Fajardo and around Vieques and Culebra, two small islands off the east coast. It's best to choose specific locations with the help of a guide or outfitter. Escorted half-day dives range from $45 to $95 for one or two tanks, including all equipment; in general, double those prices for night dives. Packages that include lunch and other extras start at $100.

Snorkeling excursions, which include transportation, equipment rental, and sometimes lunch, start at $50. Equipment rents for about $5 to $10.

Near Gate 5 of the old Ramey Air Force Base, **Aquatica Underwater Adventures** (✉ Rte. 110, Km 10, Aguadilla ☎ 787/890–6071) offers scuba-diving certification courses as well as snorkeling and surfing trips. You can also rent any gear you need. It's open Monday through Saturday from 9 to 5, Sunday from 9 to 3. **Culebra Divers** (✉ 4 Calle Pedro Marquez, Dewey, Culebra ☎ 787/742–0803 ⊕ www.culebradivers.com), run by Monica and Walter Rieder, caters to those who are new to scuba diving. You travel to dive sites on one of the company's pair of 26-foot cabin cruisers. One-tank dives are $60, while two-tank dives are $95. You can also rent a mask and snorkel to explore on your own. The office is in downtown Dewey, across from the ferry terminal. **Parguera Divers** (✉ Posada Porlamar, Rte. 304, Km 3.3, La Parguera ☎ 787/899–4171 ⊕ www.pargueradivers.com) offers scuba and snorkeling expeditions and basic instruction on the southwest coast. At **Sea Ventures Pro Dive**

Center (✉ Puerto del Rey Marina, Rte. 3, Km 51.4, Fajardo ☎ 787/863–3483 ⊕ www.divepuertorico.com) you can get PADI certified, arrange dive trips to 20 offshore sites, or organize boating and sailing excursions. A two-tank dive for certified divers, including equipment, is $99. **Taíno Divers** (✉ Black Eagle Marina, off Rte. 413, Rincón ☎ 787/823–6429 ⊕ www.tainodivers.com) has daily snorkeling and diving fishing trips. The cost is $55 and $99, including lunch. It also has daily trips to Desecheo Island, charters to Mona Island, and scuba PADI certification courses.

FISHING   Puerto Rico's waters are home to large game fish such as marlin, wahoo, dorado, tuna, and barracuda; as many as 30 world records for catches have been set off the island's shores. Half-day and full-day excursions can be arranged through **Mike Benítez Sport Fishing** (✉ Club Náutico de San Juan, Miramar, San Juan ☎ 787/723–2292 ⊕ www.mikebenitezfishing.com). From the 45-foot *Sea Born* you can fish for sailfish, white marlin, and blue marlin. You can arrange fishing trips with Capt. Francisco "Pochy" Rosario, who runs **Light Tackle Adventure** (✉ Boquerón ☎ 787/849–1430 ⊕ www.lighttackleadventure.8k.com). His specialty is tarpon, which are plentiful in these waters. **Shiraz Charters** (✉ Palmas del Mar Resort, Rte. 906, Humacao ☎ 644–5786 ⊕ www.charternet.com/fishers/shiraz) specializes in deep-sea fishing charters in search of tuna. Eight-hour trips start at about $150 per person, including equipment and snacks.

GOLF   Aficionados may know that Puerto Rico is the birthplace of golf legend Chi Chi Rodríguez—and he had to hone his craft somewhere. Currently, you can find nearly 20 courses on the island, including many championship links. Be sure to call ahead for tee times; hours vary, and several hotel courses give preference to guests. Greens fees start at about $20 and go up as high as $150. The **Puerto Rican Golf Association** (✉ 58 Calle Caribe, San Juan ☎ 787/721–7742 ⊕ www.prga.org) is a good source for information on courses and tournaments.

The 18-hole Arthur Hills–designed course at **El Conquistador Resort & Golden Door Spa** (✉ 1000 Av. El Conquistador, Fajardo ☎ 787/863–6784) is famous for its 200-foot changes in elevation. The trade winds make every shot challenging. **Palmas del Mar Country Club** (✉ Rte. 906, Humacao ☎ 787/285–2256 ⊕ www.palmascountryclub.com) has two good golf courses: the Rees Jones–designed Flamboyán course, named for the nearly six dozen flamboyant trees that pepper its fairway, winds around a lake, over a river, and to the sea before turning toward sand dunes and wetlands. The older, Gary Player–designed Palm course has a challenging par 5 that scoots around wetlands. Originally sketched out by Robert Trent Jones, Sr., the four 18-hole golf courses at the **Puerto Rico Golf Resort at Hyatt** (✉ Rte. 693, Km 10.8, Dorado ☎ 787/796–1234), formerly the Hyatt Dorado, all got a face-lift in 2005. Six new holes and six redesigned holes mean that the Pineapple and the Sugar Cane courses feel completely different. Jack Nicklaus has said that the 4th hole at the East Course is one of the top 10 holes in the world. The West Course is buffeted by constant breezes off the Atlantic, making it tough to negotiate. The spectacular **Westin Río Mar Country Club** (✉ Westin

Río Mar Beach Golf Resort & Spa, 6000 Río Mar Blvd., Río Grande ☎ 787/888–6000 ⊕ www.westinriomar.com) has a clubhouse with a pro shop and two restaurants set between two 18-hole courses. The River Course, designed by Greg Norman, has challenging fairways that skirt the Mameyes River. The Ocean Course has slightly wider fairways than its sister; iguanas can usually been spotted sunning themselves near its fourth hole. If you're not a resort guest, be sure to reserve tee times at least 24 hours in advance. Greens fees range from $100 to $165 for hotel guests and $135 to $190 for nonguests, depending on tee time.

HORSEBACK RIDING — Horseback riding is a well-establised family pastime in Puerto Rico, with *cabalgatas* (group day rides) frequently organized on weekends through mountain towns. **Gaby's World** (⊠ Rte. 127, Km 5.1, Yauco ☎ 787/856–2609) is a 204-acre horse ranch that conducts half-hour, one-hour, and two-hour rides through the hills surrounding Yauco. There are also pony rides for children. **Hacienda Carabali** (⊠ Rte. 992, Km 4, Río Grande ☎ 787/889–5820 or 787/889–4954), a family-run operation, is a good place to jump in the saddle and ride one of Puerto Rico's Paso Fino horses. Riding excursions include a one-hour jaunt along Río Mameyes and the edge of El Yunque and a two-hour ride along Balneario de Luquillo. Across from Casa Grande Mountain Retreat, **Rancho de Caballos** (⊠ Rte. 612, Km 0.3, Utuado ☎ 787/894–0240) offers three- to four-hour horse rides through mountain forests. West of Hyatt Hacienda del Mar, **Tropical Paradise Horse Back Riding** (⊠ Off Rte. 690, Dorado ☎ 787/720–5454) arranges rides along the beach on beautiful Paso Fino horses.

SURFING — The very best surfing beaches are along the northwestern coast from Isabela south to Rincón, which gained notoriety by hosting the World Surfing Championship in 1968. Today the town draws surfers from around the globe, especially in winter, when the waves are at their best.

Although the west-coast beaches are considered *the* places to surf, San Juan was actually where the sport got its start on the island, back in 1958, thanks to legendary surfers Gary Hoyt and José Rodríguez Reyes. In San Juan many surfers head to La Punta, a reef break behind the Ashford Presbyterian Hospital, or the Sheraton, a break named after the hotel (it's now the Marriott) with either surfboards or Boogie boards. In Isla Verde, white water on the horizon means that the waves are good at the beach break near the Ritz-Carlton, known as Pine Grove.

East of the city, in Piñones, the Caballo has deep- to shallow-water shelf waves that require a big-wave board known as a gun. Playa La Pared, near Balneario de Luquillo is a surfer haunt with medium-range waves. Numerous local competitions are held here throughout the year.

Not far from Playa La Pared, **La Selva Surf Shop** (⊠ 250 Calle Fernández Garcia, Luquillo ☎ 787/889–6205 ⊕ www.rainforestsafari.com/selva.html) has anything a surfer could need, including news about current conditions. The family-run shop also sells sunglasses, sandals, bathing suits, and other beach necessities. **Rincón Surf School** (⊠ Rte. 413, Rincón ☎ 787/823–0610 ⊕ www.surfandboard.com) offers full-day lessons that include board rental and transportation. You can also arrange two-, three-, and five-day surfing seminars. Boards can be rented for $20 without lesson. **West Coast Surf Shop** (⊠ 2E Calle Muñoz Rivera, Rincón ☎ 787/823–3935) is a good place to pick up new and used surfboards, body boards, kayaks, and snorkeling equipment or rent equipment. Surfboards rent for $20 per day; lessons are $35 per hour.

TENNIS If you'd like to use courts at a property where you aren't a guest, call in advance for information. Hotel guests usually get first priority, and you're likely to have to pay a fee. Courts at the following hotels are open to nonguests: Caribe Hilton, Condado Plaza, El San Juan Hotel, and San Juan Marriott in San Juan, Copamarina Beach Resort in Guánica, Hilton Ponce, Westin Río Mar Beach Resort and El Conquistador in eastern Puerto Rico. Of these the El Conquistador has some of the best facilities in the Caribbean. The four lighted courts of the **Isla Verde Tennis Club** (⊠ Calles Ema and Delta Rodriguez, Isla Verde, San Juan ☎ 787/727–6490) are open for nonmember use at $4 per hour, daily from 8 AM to 10 PM. The **Parque Central de San Juan** (⊠ Calle Cerra, exit on Rte. 2, Santurce, San Juan ☎ 787/722–1646) has 17 lighted courts. Fees are $3 per hour from 8 AM to 6 PM and $4 per hour from 6 PM to 10 PM.

WINDSURFING Lisa Penfield, a former windsurfing competitor, gives beginner lessons at **Blue Dolphin Watersports** (⊠ Hyatt Hacienda del Mar, Rte. 693, Km 10.8, Dorado ☎ 787/796–2188). You can get the best windsurfing advice and equipment from Jaime Torres at **Velauno** (⊠ 2430 Calle Loíza, Punta Las Marías, San Juan ☎ 787/728–8716 ⊕ www.velauno.com), one of the largest windsurfing centers in the U.S. It has rentals, repair services, and classes. It also sells new and used gear and serves as a clearinghouse for information on windsurfing events throughout the island.

16

Shopping

San Juan has the island's best range of stores, but it isn't a free port, so you won't find bargains on electronics and perfumes. You can, however, find excellent prices on china, crystal, fashions, and jewelry. Shopping for local crafts can also be gratifying: you'll run across a lot that's tacky, but you can also find treasures, and in many cases you can watch the artisans at work. Popular items include *santos* (small carved figures of saints or religious scenes), hand-rolled cigars, handmade *mundillo* lace from Aguadilla, *vejigantes* (colorful masks used during Carnival and local festivals) from Loíza and Ponce, and fancy men's shirts called guayaberas.

Areas & Malls

In Old San Juan—especially on Calles Fortaleza and Cristo—you can find everything from T-shirt emporiums to selective crafts stores, bookshops, art galleries, jewelry boutiques, and even shops that specialize in made-to-order Panama hats. Calle Cristo is lined with factory-outlet stores, including Coach and Ralph Lauren.

With many stores selling luxury items and designer fashions, the shopping spirit in the San Juan neighborhood of Condado is reminiscent of that in Miami. Avenida Condado is a good bet for souvenirs and curios as well as art and upscale jewelry or togs. Avenida Ashford is considered the heart of San Juan's fashion district. There's also a growing fashion scene in the business district of Hato Rey.

Right off the highway east of San Juan, the **Belz Factory Outlet World** (⊠ Rte. 3, Km 18.4, Canóvanas ☎ 787/256–7040 ⊕ www.belz.com) has more than 75 stores, including Nike, Guess, and Tommy Hilfiger. There's also a large food court and multiplex cinema showing first-run Hollywood movies, many in English. Just outside of the southern city of Ponce, **Plaza del Caribe Mall** (⊠ Rte. 2, Km 224.9, Ponce ☎ 787/259– 8989), one of the island's largest malls, has stores such as Sears and Gap. For a mundane albeit complete shopping experience, head to **Plaza Las Américas** (⊠ 525 Av. Franklin Delano Roosevelt, Hato Rey, San Juan ☎ 787/767–5202), which has 200 shops, including the world's largest JCPenney store, Macy's, Godiva, and Armani Exchange, as well as restaurants and movie theaters. About 20 minutes from Dorado via Highway 22 at Exit 55 is Puerto Rico's first factory-outlet mall. **Prime Outlets Puerto Rico** (⊠ Rte. 2, Km 54.8, Barceloneta ☎ 787/846–9011) is a pastel village of more than 40 stores selling discounted merchandise from such familiar names as Liz Claiborne, Calvin Klein, Brooks Brothers, and Reebok.

Specialty Items

ART **Galería Botelli** (⊠ 208 Calle Cristo, Old San Juan, San Juan ☎ 787/723– ★ 9987), a gorgeous gallery, displays the works of the late Angel Botelli, who as far back as 1943 was hailed as the "Caribbean Gaugin." His work, which often uses the bright colors of the tropics, often depicts island scenes. His work hangs in the Museo de Arts de Puerto Rico. There are works on display here by other prominent local artists as well.

★ **Galería Raíces** (⊠ 314 Av. José de Diego, Santurce, San Juan ☎ 787/723– 8909), half a block from the Museo de Arte de Puerto Rico, has works by emerging Puerto Rican artists. **Treehouse Studio** (⊠ Off Rte. 3, Río Grande ☎ 787/888–8062), a picturesque gallery not far from El Yunque, sells vibrant watercolors by Monica Laird, who also gives workshops. Call for an appointment and directions.

CLOTHES **Clubman** (⊠ 1351 Av. Ashford, Condado, San Juan ☎ 787/722–1867), after many years of catering to a primarily local clientele, is still the classic choice for gentlemen's clothing. **Otto** (⊠ 69 Av. Condado, Condado, San Juan ☎ 787/722–4609), owned by local designer Otto Bauzá, stocks his own line of casual wear for younger men.

The window displays at **Nativa** (⊠ 55 Calle Cervantes, Condado, San ★ Juan ☎ 787/724–1396) are almost as daring as the clothes its sells. **Nono Maldonado** (⊠ 1051 Av. Ashford, Condado, San Juan ☎ 787/ 721–0456) is well known for his high-end, elegant linen designs for men and women.

HANDICRAFTS **Artesanías Castor Ayala** (⊠ Rte. 187, Km 6.6 ☎ 787/876–1130) offers, ★ among other crafts, coconut-shell festival masks dubbed "Mona Lisas" because of their elongated smiles. Craftsman Raul Ayala Carrasquillo has been making these pieces for more than 40 years, following in the footsteps of his late father. These wild masks, most with tentacle-like horns, are prized by collectors. At the **Convento de los Dominicos** (⊠ 98 Calle Norzagaray, Old San Juan, San Juan ☎ 787/721–6866)—the Dominican Convent on the north side of the old city that houses the offices of the

Instituto de Cultura Puertorriqueña—you can find baskets, masks, the famous *cuatro* guitars, santos, and reproductions of Taíno artifacts.

JEWELRY For a wide array of watches and jewelry, visit the two floors of **Bared** (⊠ 154 Calle Fortaleza, Old San Juan, San Juan ☎ 787/722–2172), with a charmingly old-fashioned ambience. **Joyería Cátala** (⊠ Plaza de Armas, Old San Juan, San Juan ☎ 787/722–3231) is distinguished for its large selection of pearls. **Joyería Riviera** (⊠ 257 Fortaleza St., Old San Juan, San Juan ☎ 787/725–4000) sells fine jewelry by David Yurman and Rolex watches.

N. Barquet Joyeros (⊠ 201 Calle Fortaleza, Old San Juan, San Juan ☎ 787/721–3366), one of the bigger stores in Old San Juan, has Fabergé jewelry, pearls, and gold as well as crystal and watches. **Portofino** (⊠ 250 Calle San Francisco, Old San Juan, San Juan ☎ 787/723–5113) has an especially good selection of watches.

SOUVENIRS For almost two decades, Robert and Sharon Bartos of **El Alcázar**
★ (⊠ 103 Calle San José, Old San Juan, San Juan ☎ 787/723–1229) have been selling antiques and objets d'art from all over the world. Exotic *mariposas* cover the walls of **Butterfly People** (⊠ 257 Calle de la Cruz, Old San Juan, San Juan ☎ 787/732–2432). It's a lovely place, with clear plastic cases holding everything from a pair of common butterflies to dozens of rarer specimens. You can find a world of unique spices and sauces from around the Caribbean, kitchen items, and cookbooks at **Spicy Caribbee** (⊠ 154 Calle Cristo, Old San Juan, San Juan ☎ 787/ 625–4690).

16

Buy a recording of the tree frog's song, pick up a coffee-table book about the rain forest, and check out the books for eco-minded children at the large, lovely **Caribbean National Forest Gift Shop** (⊠ Rte. 191, Km 4.3, El Yunque ☎ 787/888–1880). Tucked among the rain-forest gifts are other Puerto Rican goods, including note cards, maps, soaps, jams, and
★ coffee. In a wooden shack painted vivid shades of yellow and red, **Fango** (⊠ Calle Castelar s/n, Dewey, Culebra ☎ 787/556–9308) is Culebra's best place for gifts. Jorge Acevedo paints scenes of island life, while Hannah Staiger designs sophisticated jewelry. The shop is no bigger than a walk-in closet, but you could easily spend an hour or more browsing among their one-of-a-kind works. Chocolate-loving Laurie Humphrey had trouble finding a supplier for her sweet tooth, so she opened the **Paradise Store** (⊠ Hwy. 194, Km 0.4, Fajardo ☎ 787/863–8182). Lindt and other gourmet chocolates jam the shop, which also sells flowers and such gift items as Puerto Rican–made soaps.

Nightlife & the Arts

Qué Pasa, the official visitor's guide, has listings of events in San Juan and out on the island. For daily listings, pick up a copy of the English-language edition of the *San Juan Star.* The Thursday edition's weekend section is especially useful. For the gay scene, check out the monthly *Puerto Rico Breeze;* the free newspaper is found in many businesses, especially in the Condado area.

Nightlife

In Old San Juan, Calle San Sebastián is lined with bars and restaurants. Salsa music blaring from jukeboxes in cut-rate pool halls competes with mellow Latin jazz in top-flight nightspots. Evenings begin with dinner and stretch into the late hours at the bars of the more upscale, so-called SoFo (south of Fortaleza) end of Old San Juan. Well-dressed visitors and locals alike often mingle in the lobby bars of large hotels, many of which have bands in the evening. An eclectic crowd heads to the Plaza del Mercado off Avenida Ponce de León at Calle Canals in Santurce after work to hang out in the plaza or enjoy drinks and food in one of the small establishments skirting the farmers' market. Condado and Ocean Park have their share of nightlife, too. Most are restaurant-and-bar environments.

Just east of San Juan along Route 187, funky Piñones has a collection of open-air seaside eateries that are popular with locals. On weekend evenings, many places have merengue combos, Brazilian jazz trios, or reggae bands. In the southern city of Ponce, people embrace the Spanish tradition of the *paseo,* an evening stroll around the Plaza las Delicias. The boardwalk at La Guancha in Ponce is also a lively scene. Live bands often play on weekends. Elsewhere *en la isla,* nighttime activities center on the hotels and resorts.

Wherever you are, dress to impress. Puerto Ricans have flair, and both men and women love getting dressed up to go out. Bars are usually casual, but if you have on jeans, sneakers, and a T-shirt, you may be refused entry at nightclubs and discos.

BARS & MUSIC CLUBS
The wildly popular **El Batey** (⌂ 101 Calle Cristo, Old San Juan, San Juan ☎ 787/725–1787) won't win any prizes for its decor. Grab a marker to add your own message to the graffiti-covered walls, or add your business card to the hundreds that cover the lighting fixtures. At **Liquid** (⌂ Water Club, 2 Calle Tartak, Isla Verde ☎ 787/725–4664 or 787/725–4675), the lobby lounge of San Juan's chicest boutique hotel, glass walls are filled with undulating water, and the fashionable patrons drink wild cocktails to pounding music. With a large dance and stage area and smokin' Afro-Cuban bands, **Rumba** (⌂ 152 Calle San Sebastián, Old San Juan, San Juan ☎ 787/725–4407) is one of the best parties in town.

CASINOS
By law, all casinos are in hotels, primarily in San Juan. The government keeps a close eye on them. Dress for the larger casinos is on the formal side, and the atmosphere is refined, particularly in the Isla Verde resorts. Casinos set their own hours but are generally open from noon to 4 AM. In addition to slot machines, typical games include blackjack, roulette, craps, Caribbean stud (a five-card poker game), and *pai gow* poker (a combination of American poker and the Chinese game pai gow). Hotels with casinos have live entertainment most weekends, as well as restaurants and bars. The minimum age to gamble is 18.

You may feel as if you're in Las Vegas when you step into the **Inter-Continental San Juan Resort & Casino** (⌂ 5961 Av. Isla Verde, Isla Verde, San Juan ☎ 787/791–6100). A torch singer warms up the crowd at a lounge-bar just outside the gaming room. Inside, a garish chandelier, dripping with strands of orange lights, runs the length of a mirrored ceiling. The casino at the **Ritz-Carlton San Juan Hotel, Spa & Casino** (⊠ Av. Las Gobernadores, Isla Verde, San Juan ☎ 787/253–1700) is refined by day or night. There's lots of activity, yet everything is hushed. The only place to gamble in Old San Juan is at the **Sheraton Old San Juan Hotel & Casino** (⊠ 101 Calle Brumbaugh, Old San Juan, San Juan ☎ 787/ 721–5100). Light bounces off the Bahía de San Juan and pours through its many windows; passengers bound off their cruise ships and pour through its many glass doors.

DANCE CLUBS   A long line of well-heeled patrons usually runs out the door of **Babylon** (⊠ El San Juan Hotel, 6063 Av. Isla Verde, Isla Verde, San Juan ☎ 787/ 791–1000). Those with the staying power to make it inside step out of the Caribbean and into the ancient Middle East. Those who tire of waiting often head to El Chico Lounge, a small room with live entertainment right off the hotel lobby. **Candela** (⊠ 110 San Sebastián, Old San Juan, San Juan ☎ 787/977–4305), a lounge–art gallery housed in a historic building, hosts some of the most innovative local DJs on the island and often invites star spinners from New York or London. This is the island's best showcase for experimental dance music. The festive late-night haunt is open Tuesday through Saturday from 8 PM onward, and the conversation can be as stimulating as the dance floor. No, there's no place to splash around at the **Pool Palace** (⊠ 330 Calle Recinto Sur, Old San Juan, San Juan ☎ 787/725–8487). The name refers to the 15 pool tables that are the centerpiece of this cavernous club. If a game of eight ball isn't your thing, there's also a dance floor the size of an airplane hanger and a lounge area with clusters of cozy leather sofas.

16

GAY & LESBIAN   The oceanfront deck bar of the **Atlantic Beach Hotel** (⊠ 1 Calle Vendig,
CLUBS   Condado, San Juan ☎787/721–6100) is famed for its early-evening happy hours, with pulsating tropical music, a wide selection of exotic drinks, and ever-pleasant ocean breezes. **Nuestro Ambiente** (⊠ 1412 Av. Ponce de León, Santurce, San Juan ☎ 787/724–9083) offers a variety of entertainment for women Wednesday through Sunday. The new kid on the block, **Starz** (⊠ 365 Av. de Diego, at Av. Ponce de León, Santurce, San Juan ☎ 787/721–8645) has dancing on Friday and Saturday nights, as well as a popular after-the-beach party on Sunday evening.

Catering mostly to a gay crowd, **Backstage** (⊠ Off Rte. 123, Ponce ☎ 787/448–8112) has a huge dance floor surrounded by intimate lounges where groups of friends inevitably gather. Don't get here before midnight, or you might arrive before the staff.

The Arts

If you're in Old San Juan on the first Tuesday of the month, take advantage of **Noches de Galerias** (☎ 787/723–6286). Galleries and select museums open their doors after-hours for viewings that are accompanied by refreshments and music.

There's something going on nearly every night at the **Centro de Bellas Artes Luis A. Ferré** (⊠ Av. José de Diego and Av. Ponce de León, Santurce, San Juan ☎ 787/725–7334), from pop or jazz concerts to plays, opera, and ballet. It's also the home of the San Juan Symphony Orchestra. Named for Puerto Rican playwright Alejandro Tapia, **Teatro Tapia** (⊠ Calle Fortaleza at Plaza Colón, Old San Juan, San Juan ☎ 787/722–0247) hosts theatrical and musical productions.

The **Museo de Arte de Ponce** (✉ 2325 Av. Las Américas, Sector Santa María, Ponce ☎ 787/848–0505) occasionally sponsors chamber music concerts and recitals by members of the Puerto Rico Symphony Orchestra. Check for theater productions and concerts at the **Teatro La Perla** (✉ Calle Mayor and Calle Cristina, Ponce Centro, Ponce ☎ 787/843–4322).

Exploring Puerto Rico

Old San Juan

Old San Juan, the original city founded in 1521, contains carefully preserved examples of 16th- and 17th-century Spanish colonial architecture. More than 400 buildings have been beautifully restored. Graceful wrought-iron balconies with lush hanging plants extend over narrow streets paved with *adoquines* (blue-gray stones originally used as ballast on Spanish ships). The Old City is partially enclosed by walls that date from 1633 and once completely surrounded it. Designated a U.S. National Historic Zone in 1950, Old San Juan is chockablock with shops, open-air cafés, homes, tree-shaded squares, monuments, and people. You can get an overview on a morning's stroll (bear in mind that this "stroll" includes some steep climbs). However, if you plan to immerse yourself in history or to shop, you'll need two or three days.

SIGHTS TO SEE   *Numbers in the margin correspond to points of interest on the Old San Juan Exploring map.*

⓫ **Alcaldía.** The city hall was built between 1604 and 1789. In 1841 extensive renovations were done to make it resemble Madrid's city hall, with arcades, towers, balconies, and a lovely inner courtyard. A tourist information center and an art gallery are on the first floor. ✉ *153 Calle San Francisco, Plaza de Armas, Old San Juan* ☎ *787/724–7171* ⌚ *Free* ☉ *Weekdays 8–4.*

❽ **Capilla del Cristo.** According to legend, in 1753 a young horseman named Baltazar Montañez got carried away during festivities in honor of St. John the Baptist, raced down the street, and plunged over the steep precipice. A witness to the tragedy promised to build a chapel if the young man's life could be saved. Historical records maintain the man died, though legend contends he lived. ✉ *End of Calle Cristo, Old San Juan* ☎ *No phone* ⌚ *Free.*

❺ **Casa Blanca.** The original structure on this site was a frame house built in 1521 as a home for Ponce de León; he died in Cuba without ever having lived in the house. His descendants occupied it for 250 years. From the end of the Spanish-American War in 1898 to 1966 it was the home of the U.S. Army commander in Puerto Rico. Several rooms decorated with colonial-era furnishings and an archaeology exhibit are on display. The lush garden is a quiet place to unwind. ✉ *1 Calle San Sebastián, Old San Juan* ☎ *787/725–1454* ⊕ *www.icp.gobierno.pr* ⌚ *$2* ☉ *Tues.–Sat. 8:30–4:20.*

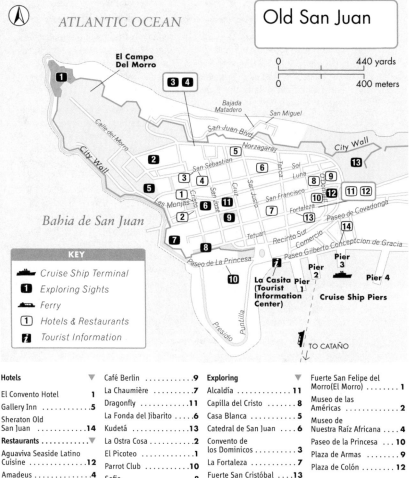

Old San Juan

ATLANTIC OCEAN

El Campo Del Morro

0 — 440 yards
0 — 400 meters

Bajada Matadero
San Miguel
Calle del Morro
City Wall
San Juan Blvd.
Norzagaray
City Wall
San Sebastián
Tanca
Sol
Luna
Cruz
San Justo
San Francisco
Fortaleza
Paseo de Covadonga
Bahia de San Juan
Las Monjas
Cristo
San José
Tetuan
Recinto Sur
Comercio
Paseo Gilberto Conceptcion de Gracia
Paseo de La Princesa
Presidio
Puntilla

KEY

🚢 Cruise Ship Terminal
1️⃣ Exploring Sights
⛴ Ferry
1 Hotels & Restaurants
ℹ Tourist Information

La Casita (Tourist Information Center)
Pier 1
Pier 2
Pier 3
Pier 4
Cruise Ship Piers

TO CATAÑO

Hotels ▼
El Convento Hotel **1**
Gallery Inn **5**
Sheraton Old San Juan **14**

Restaurants .... ▼
Aguaviva Seaside Latino Cuisine **12**
Amadeus **4**
Barú **3**

Café Berlin **9**
La Chaumière **7**
Dragonfly **11**
La Fonda del Jibarito **6**
Kudetá **13**
La Ostra Cosa **2**
El Picoteo **1**
Parrot Club **10**
Sofia **8**

Exploring ▼
Alcaldía **11**
Capilla del Cristo **8**
Casa Blanca **5**
Catedral de San Juan **6**
Convento de los Dominicos **3**
La Fortaleza **7**
Fuerte San Cristóbal **13**

Fuerte San Felipe del Morro(El Morro) **1**
Museo de las Américas **2**
Museo de Nuestra Raíz Africana **4**
Paseo de la Princesa ... **10**
Plaza de Armas **9**
Plaza de Colón **12**

Peaceful Music

CELLIST PABLO CASALS was one of the 20th century's most influential musicians. Born in Catalonia in 1876, he studied in Spain and Belgium, settled for a time in Paris, then returned to Barcelona. Tours in Europe, the United States, and South America brought him artistic and financial success and opportunities to collaborate with other prominent musicians.

By the advent of the Spanish Civil War, he was an internationally famous musician, teacher, and conductor. He was also an outspoken supporter of a democratic Spain. Forced into exile by Franco's regime, Casals arrived in Puerto Rico, his mother's birthplace, in 1956. There, the 81-year-old maestro continued to work and teach. He established the Casals Festival of Classical Music, making it a home for

sublime orchestral and chamber works. During two weeks each June, the Puerto Rico Symphony Orchestra is joined by musicians from all over the world.

In Catalan, Casal's first name is "Pau," which appropriately enough means "peace." He and his friend Albert Schweitzer appealed to the world powers to stop the arms race, and he made what many experts say is his greatest work—an oratorio titled "The Manger"—his personal message of peace. Casals died in Puerto Rico in 1973, but his many legacies live on. His favorite instruments, his recordings, and some of his many awards are preserved at the Museo Pablo Casals.

–Karen English

❻ Catedral de San Juan. The Catholic shrine of Puerto Rico had humble beginnings in the early 1520s as a thatch-topped wooden structure. Hurricane winds tore off the thatch and destroyed the church. It was reconstructed in 1540, when the graceful circular staircase and vaulted Gothic ceilings were added, but most of the work was done in the 19th century. The remains of Ponce de León are in a marble tomb near the transept. The trompe l'oeil work on the inside of the dome is breathtaking. Too bad that many of the other frescos are suffering from water damage. ⊠ *151 Calle Cristo, Old San Juan* ☎ *787/722–0861* ⊕ *www.catedralsanjuan.com* ⊠ *$1 donation suggested* ☉ *Mon.–Sat. 8–5, Sun. 8–2:30.*

❸ Convento de los Dominicos. Built by Dominican friars in 1523, this convent often served as a shelter during Carib Indian attacks and, more recently, as headquarters for the Antilles command of the U.S. Army. Now home to some offices of the Institute of Puerto Rican Culture, the beautifully restored building contains religious manuscripts, artifacts, and art. The institute also maintains a crafts store and bookstore here. Classical concerts are occasionally held here. ⊠ *98 Calle Norzagaray, Old San Juan* ☎ *787/721–6866* ⊠ *Free* ☉ *Mon.–Sat. 9–5.*

★ **❼ La Fortaleza.** Sitting on a hill overlooking the harbor, La Fortaleza was built as a fortress in 1533. it was not a very good fortress, mind you. It was attacked numerous times and taken twice, by the British in 1598 and by the Dutch in 1625. When the city's other fortifications were finished, La Fortaleza was transformed into a palace. Numerous changes to the original primitive structure over the past four centuries have resulted in the present collection of marble and mahogany, medieval towers, and stained-glass galleries. Guided tours of the extensive gardens and the circular dungeon are conducted on the hour in English, on the half hour in Spanish; both include a short video presentation. Call ahead, as sometimes tours are canceled because of official functions. The tours begin near the main gate in a yellow building called the Real Audiencia. ⊠ *Calle Recinto Oeste, Old San Juan* ☎ *787/721–7000 Ext. 2211* ⊕ *www.fortaleza.gobierno.pr* ⊠ *Free* ☉ *Weekdays 9–3:30.*

⓭ Fuerte San Cristóbal. This 18th-century fortress guarded the city from land attacks. Even larger than El Morro, San Cristóbal was known in its heyday as the Gibraltar of the West Indies. Five freestanding structures are connected by tunnels, and restored units include an 18th-century barracks. ⊠ *Calle Norzagaray, Old San Juan* ☎ *787/729–6960* ⊕ *www. nps.gov/saju* ⊠ *$3; $5 includes admission to El Morro* ☉ *Daily 9–5.*

❶ Fuerte San Felipe del Morro. On a rocky promontory at the Old City's northwestern tip is El Morro, which was built by the Spaniards between 1540 and 1783. Rising 140 feet above the sea, the fort is composed of six massive levels. It's a labyrinth of dungeons, barracks, towers, and tunnels. Its museum traces the history of the fortress. Tours and a video show are available in English. ⊠ *Calle Norzagaray, Old San Juan* ☎ *787/729–6960* ⊕ *www.nps.gov/saju* ⊠ *$3; $5 includes admission to Fuerte San Cristóbal* ☉ *Daily 9–5.*

 Fodor'sChoice ★

❷ Museo de las Américas. On the second floor of the imposing former military barracks, Cuartel de Ballajá, the museum's permanent exhibit, "Las Artes Populares en las Américas," focusing on the popular and folk art of Latin America, contains religious figures, musical instruments, basketwork, costumes, and farming and other implements. ⊠ *Calle Norzagaray and Calle del Morro, Old San Juan* ☎ *787/724–5052* ⊕ *www. museolasamericas.org* ⊠ *Free* ☉ *Tues.–Sun. 10–4.*

❹ Museo de Nuestra Raíz Africana. The Institute of Puerto Rican Culture created this museum to celebrate African influences in island culture. Musical instruments, documents relating to the slave trade, and a list of African words that have made it into Puerto Rican popular vocabulary are on display. ⊠ *101 Calle San Sebastián, Plaza de San José, Old San Juan* ☎ *787/724–4294* ⊕ *www.icp.gobierno.pr* ⊠ *Free* ☉ *Tues.–Sat. 8:30–4:20.*

❿ Paseo de la Princesa. This street down at the port is spruced up with flowers, trees, benches, street lamps, and a striking fountain depicting the various ethnic groups of Puerto Rico. At the west end of the paseo, beyond the fountain, is the beginning of a shoreline path that hugs Old San Juan's walls and leads to the city gate at Caleta de San Juan.

❾ Plaza de Armas. This is the original main square of Old San Juan. The plaza, bordered by Calles San Francisco, Fortaleza, San José, and

16

Cruz, has a lovely fountain with 19th-century statues representing the four seasons.

⑫ **Plaza de Colón.** A statue of Christopher Columbus stands atop a high pedestal in this bustling Old San Juan square. Bronze plaques on the statue's base relate various episodes in the life of the great explorer.

Greater San Juan

You'll need to resort to taxis, buses, *públicos* (shared vans), or a rental car to reach the points of interest in "new" San Juan. Avenida Muñoz Rivera, Avenida Ponce de León, and Avenida Fernández Juncos are the main thoroughfares that cross Puerta de Tierra, east of Old San Juan, to the business and tourist districts of Santurce, Condado, and Isla Verde. Dos Hermanos Bridge connects Puerta de Tierra with Miramar, Condado, and Isla Grande. Isla Grande Airport, from which you can take short hops, is on the bay side of the bridge. On the other side, the Condado Lagoon is bordered by Avenida Ashford, which threads past the high-rise Condado hotels and Avenida Baldorioty de Castro Expreso, which barrels east to the airport and beyond. Due south of the lagoon is Miramar, a residential area with fashionable turn-of-the-20th-century homes and a few hotels and restaurants. South of Santurce is the Golden Mile—Hato Rey, the financial hub. Isla Verde, with its glittering beachfront hotels, casinos, discos, and public beach, is to the east, near the airport.

Numbers in the margin correspond to points of interest on the Greater San Juan map.

WHAT TO SEE **El Capitolio.** The white-marble Capitol, a fine example of Italian Renais-
⑭ sance style, dates from 1929. The grand rotunda, which can be seen from all over San Juan, was completed in the late 1990s. Fronted by eight Corinthian columns, it's a very dignified home for the commonwealth's constitution. Guided tours, which take 45 minutes and include visits to the Rotunda and other parts of the building, are by appointment only. ⊠ *Av. Ponce de León, Puerta de Tierra* ☎ *787/977–4929* 💲 *Free* ⊙ *Weekdays 9–5, Sat. 9–1.*

⑯ **Museo de Arte Contemporáneo de Puerto Rico.** This Georgian-style structure, once a public school, displays a dynamic range of works by both established and up-and-coming Puerto Rican artists. Many of the works on display have strong political messages, including pointed commentaries on the island's status as a commonwealth. Only a small part of the permanent collection is on display at any time, but it might be anything from an exhibit of ceramics to a screening of videos. ⊠ *Av. Ponce de León at Av. R. H. Todd, Santurce* ☎ *787/977–4030* ⊕ *www. museocontemporaneopr.org* 💲 *Free* ⊙ *Tues.–Sat. 10–4, Sun. 1–4.*

⊙ **Museo de Arte de Puerto Rico.** One of the biggest museums in the
Fodor'sChoice Caribbean, this 130,000-square-foot building was once known as San
★ Juan Municipal Hospital. The beautiful neoclassical building, dating from
⑮ the 1920s, proved to be too small to house the museum's permanent collection of Puerto Rican art dating from the 17th century to the present. The solution was to build a new east wing, which is dominated by a five-story-tall stained-glass window, the work of local artist Eric Ta-

bales. The collection starts with works from the colonial era, most of them commissioned for churches. Here you'll find works by José Campeche, the island's first great painter. Also well represented is Francisco Oller y Cestero, who was the first to move beyond religious subjects to paint local scenes. There's much more to the museum, including a beautiful garden filled with a variety of native flora and one of the city's best and most expensive restaurants, Pikayo. ⊠ *299 Av. José de Diego, Santurce* ☎ *787/977–6277* ⊕ *www.mapr.org* ⊠ *$6* ۞ *Tues. and Thurs.–Sat. 10–5, Wed. 10–8, Sun. 11–6.*

⑰ Museo de Historia, Antropología y Arte (Museum of History, Anthropology and Art). The Universidad de Puerto Rico's museum has archaeological and historical exhibits that deal with the Native American influence on the island and the Caribbean, the colonial era, and the history of slavery. Art displays are occasionally mounted; the museum's prize exhibit is the painting *El Velorio* (*The Wake*), by the 19th-century artist Francisco Oller. ⊠ *Av. Ponce de León, Río Piedras* ☎ *787/764–0000 Ext. 5852* ⊕ *www.uprrp.edu* ⊠ *Free* ۞ *Weekdays 9–4:30, Thurs. 9–9, weekends 9–3.*

San Juan Environs

Numbers in the margin correspond to points of interest on the Puerto Rico map.

16

WHAT TO SEE

⑲ Casa Bacardí Visitor Center. Exiled from Cuba, the Bacardí family built a small distillery here in the 1950s. Today it's one of the world's largest, with the capacity to produce 100,000 gallons of spirits a day and 221 million cases a year. You can hop on a little tram to take a 45-minute tour of the bottling plant, distillery, and museum. Yes, you'll be offered a sample. If you don't want to drive, you can reach the factory by taking the ferry from Pier 2 for 50¢ each way and then a *público* (shared van) from the ferry pier to the factory for about $2 or $3 per person. ⊠ *Rte. 888, Km 2.6, Cataño* ☎ *787/788–1500 or 787/788–8400* ⊕ *www.casabacardi.org* ⊠ *Free* ۞ *Mon.–Sat. 8:30–5:30, Sun. 10–5. Tours every 15–30 mins.*

☾ ⑳ Parque de las Ciencias Luis A. Ferré. The 42-acre Luis A. Ferré Science Park contains a collection of intriguing activities and displays. The Transportation Museum has antique cars and the island's oldest bicycle. In the Rocket Plaza, children can experience a flight simulator, and in the planetarium, the solar system is projected on the ceiling. Also on-site are a small zoo and a natural-science exhibit. It's a long drive from central San Juan, though. ⊠ *Rte. 167, Bayamón* ☎ *787/740–6878* ⊠ *$5* ۞ *Wed.–Fri. 9–4, weekends 10–6.*

⑱ Ruinas de Caparra. In 1508 Ponce de León established the island's first settlement here. The Caparra Ruins—a few crumbling walls—are what remains of an ancient fort. The small Museo de la Conquista y Colonización de Puerto Rico (Museum of the Conquest and Colonization of Puerto Rico) contains historical documents, exhibits, and excavated artifacts, though you can see the museum's contents in less time than it takes to say the name. ⊠ *Rte. 2, Km 6.6, Guaynabo* ☎ *787/781–4795* ⊕ *www.icp.gobierno.pr* ⊠ *Free* ۞ *Tues.–Sat. 8:30–4:20.*

Eastern Puerto Rico

🅒 ㉑ **El Yunque.** The 28,000-acre Caribbean National Forest (known as El
FodorśChoice Yunque after the benevolent spirit Yuquiyú) didn't gain its "rain for-
★ est" designation for nothing. More than 100 billion gallons of precip-
itation fall here annually, spawning rushing streams and cascades, 240
tree species, and oversize impatiens and ferns. In the evening, millions
of inch-long *coquís* (tree frogs) begin their calls. El Yunque is also home
to the *cotorra*, Puerto Rico's endangered green parrot, as well as 67 other
types of birds.

Your best bet is to visit with a tour. If you'd rather drive here yourself,
take Route 3 east from San Juan. After 25 mi (40 km), turn south on
Route 191. The forest's 13 hiking trails are well maintained; many of
them are easy to walk and less than a mile long. Before you begin exploring, check out the high-tech interactive displays—explaining rain forests
in general and El Yunque in particular—at **El Portal** (⊠ Rte. 191, Km
4.3 ☎ 787/888–1880 ⊕ www.fs.fed.us/r8/caribbean), the information
center near the northern entrance. This is also a good place to pick up a
map of the park and talk to rangers about which trails are open. You
can also stock up on water, snacks, film, and souvenirs at the small gift
shop. The center is open daily from 9 to 5; admission is $3.

㉒ **Fajardo.** Founded in 1772, Fajardo has historical notoriety as a port where
pirates stocked up on supplies. It later developed into a fishing community and an area where sugarcane flourished. (There are still cane fields
on the city's fringes.) Today it's a hub for the yachts that use its marinas; the divers who head to its good offshore sites; and for the day-
trippers who travel by catamaran, ferry, or plane to the out-islands of
Culebra and Vieques. With the most significant docking facilities on the
island's eastern side, Fajardo is often congested and difficult to navigate.

Vieques & Culebra

㉔ **Culebra.** Culebra is known around the world for its curvaceous coastline. Playa Flamenco, the tiny island's most famous stretch of sand, is
considered one of the two or three best beaches in the world. If Playa
Flamenco gets too crowded, as it often does around Easter and Christmas, there are many other beaches that will be nearly deserted. There's
archaeological evidence that Taíno and Carib peoples lived on Culebra
long before the arrival of the Spanish in the late 15th century. The
Spanish didn't bother laying claim to it until 1886; its dearth of freshwater made it an unattractive location for a settlement. Although the
island now has modern conveniences, its pace seems little changed from
a century ago. There's only one town, Dewey, named after U.S. Admiral George Dewey. When the sun goes down, Culebra winds down as
well. But during the day it's a delightful place to stake out a spot on
Playa Flamenco or Playa Soni and read, swim, or search for shells. So
what causes stress on the island? Nothing.

㉓ **Vieques.** This island off Puerto Rico's east coast is famed for its Playa
Sun Bay, a gorgeous stretch of sand with picnic facilities and shade trees.
In May 2003, the U.S. Navy withdrew from its military operations and
turned over two-thirds of Vieques to the local government, which is trans-

forming it into the Vieques National Wildlife Refuge. Vieques has two communities—Isabel Segunda, where the ferries dock, and the smaller Esperanza. Both have restaurants and hotels that will surprise you with their sophistication. In addition to great beaches, Vieques has one attraction that draws visitors from all over the world. **Bahía Mosquito** (Mosquito Bay) is best experienced on moonless nights, when millions of bioluminescent organisms glow when disturbed—it's like swimming in a cloud of fireflies. If you're on the island, this is a not-to-be-missed experience.

Fodor'sChoice
★

Southern Puerto Rico

26 The 9,900-acre **Bosque Estatal de Guánica** (Guánica State Forest), a United Nations Biosphere Reserve, is a great place for hiking expeditions. It's an outstanding example of a tropical dry coastal forest, with some 700 species of plants ranging from the prickly pear cactus to the gumbo limbo tree. It's also one of the best places on the island for bird watching, as there are more than 100 types of bird, including the pearly-eyed thrasher, the lizard cuckoo, and the nightjar. One of the most popular hikes is the Ballena Trail, which begins at the ranger station on Route 334. This easy 1.2-mi (2-km) walk, which follows a partially paved road, takes you past a mahogany plantation to a dry plain covered with stunted cactus. A sign reading GUAYACÁN CENTENARIO leads you to an extraordinary guayacán tree with a trunk that measures 6 feet across. ✉ *Rte. 334, 333, or 325* ☎ *787/821–5706* 💲 *Free* 🕙 *Daily 9–5.*

Fodor'sChoice
★

16

27 **Cabo Rojo.** Named for the pinkish cliffs that surround it, Cabo Rojo was founded in 1771 as a port for merchant vessels—and for the smugglers and pirates who inevitably accompanied ocean-going trade. Today the region is known as a family resort destination, and many small, inexpensive hotels line its shores. Seaside settlements such as Puerto Real and Joyuda—the latter has a strip of more than 30 seafood restaurants overlooking the water—are found along the coast. Although you can hike in wildlife refuges at the outskirts of the town of Cabo Rojo, there aren't any area outfitters, so be sure to bring along water, sunscreen, and all other necessary supplies. The neoclassical Cabo Rojo Lighthouse marks the southwesternmost tip of the island.

25 **Ponce.** The island's second-largest urban area, Ponce shines in 19th-century style with pink-marble-bordered sidewalks, painted trolleys, and horse-drawn carriages. Stroll around the main square, the Plaza las Delicias, with its perfectly pruned India-laurel fig trees, graceful fountains, gardens, and park benches. View the Catedral de Nuestra Señora de la Guadalupe (Our Lady of Guadalupe Cathedral), perhaps even attend the 6 AM mass, and walk down Calles Isabel and Cristina to see turn-of-the-20th-century wooden houses with wrought-iron balconies.

★ You haven't seen a firehouse until you've seen the **Parque de Bombas,** a structure built in 1882 for an exposition and converted to a firehouse the following year. Today it's a museum tracing the history—and glorious feats—of Ponce's fire brigade. ✉ *Plaza las Delicias, Ponce Centro* ☎ *787/284–3338* 💲 *Free* 🕙 *Wed.–Mon. 9:30–6.*

Two superlative examples of early-20th-century architecture house the **Museo de la Historia de Ponce** (Ponce History Museum), where 10 rooms of exhibits vividly re-create Ponce's golden years, providing fascinating glimpses into the worlds of culture, high finance, and journalism in the 19th century. Hour-long tours in English and Spanish are available, but there's no set time when they start. ✉ *51–53 Calle Isabel, Ponce Centro* 🕾 *787/844–7071 or 787/843–4322* 🎫 *$3* ⊙ *Tues.–Fri. 9–5, weekends 10–6.*

The **Museo de Arte de Ponce** (Ponce Museum of Art) is easily identified by the hexagonal galleries on the second floor. It has one of the best art collections in Latin American, which is why residents of San Juan frequently make the trip down to Ponce. The 3,000-piece collection includes works by famous Puerto Rican artists such as Francisco Oller, represented by a lovely landscape called *Hacienda Aurora*. The highlight of the collection is the mesmerizing *Flaming June*, by Frederick Leighton, which has become the museum's unofficial symbol. ✉ *2325 Av. Las Américas, Sector Santa María* 🕾 *787/848–0505* ⊕ *www. museoarteponce.org* 🎫 *$5* ⊙ *Daily 10–5.*

The **Castillo Serrallés** is a splendid Spanish Revival mansion on Vigía Hill. This former residence of the owners of the Don Q rum distillery has been restored with a mix of original furnishings and antiques that recalls the era of the sugar barons. A short film details the history of the sugar and rum industries; tours are given every half-hour in English and Spanish. You can also just stroll through the gardens for a reduced admission fee. The 100-foot-tall cross (La Cruceta del Vigía) behind the museum has a windowed elevator, which you can ascend for views of Ponce. ✉ *17 El Vigía, El Vigía* 🕾 *787/259–1774* ⊕ *www.castilloserralles. net* 🎫 *$6, $9 includes admission to Cruceta El Vigía* ⊙ *Tues.–Thurs. 9:30–5, Fri.–Sun. 9:30–5:30.*

★ ⓒ Just outside Ponce, **Hacienda Buena Vista** is a 19th-century coffee plantation. It's a technological marvel—water from the nearby Río Canas was funneled into narrow brick channels that could be diverted to perform any number of tasks, including turning the waterwheel. (Seeing the two-story-tall wheel slowly begin to turn is thrilling, especially for kids.) Nearby is the two-story manor house, filled with furniture that gives a sense of what it was like to live on a coffee plantation nearly 150 years ago. The tours are by reservation only, so make sure to call several day ahead. ✉ *Rte. 123, Km 16.8, Sector Corral Viejo* 🕾 *787/ 722–5882 weekdays, 787/284–7020 weekends* ⊕ *www.fideicomiso. org* 🎫 *$5* ⊙ *Fri.–Sun., by reservation only.*

ⓒ At the **Centro Ceremonial Indígena de Tibes** (Tibes Indian Ceremonial Center), you can find pre-Taíno ruins and burials dating from AD 300 to 700. Some archaeologists, noting the symmetrical arrangement of stone pillars, surmise the cemetery may have been of great religious significance. The complex includes a detailed re-creation of a Taíno village and a museum. ✉ *Rte. 503, Km 2.8, Barrio Tibes* 🕾 *787/840– 2255 or 787/840–5685* ⊕ *ponce.inter.edu/tibes/tibes.html* 🎫 *$2* ⊙ *Tues.–Sun. 9–4.*

28 San Germán. Around San Germán's (population 39,000) two main squares—Plazuela Santo Domingo and Plaza Francisco Mariano Quiñones (named for an abolitionist)—are buildings done in every conceivable style of architecture found on the island, including Mission, Victorian, creole, and Spanish colonial. The city's tourist office offers a free guided trolley tour. Students and professors from the Inter-American University often fill the center's bars and cafés.

★ One of the oldest Christian religious structures in the Americas, the **Capilla de Porta Coeli** (Heaven's Gate Chapel) overlooks the long, rectangular Plazuela de Santo Domingo. It's not a grand building, but its position at the top of a stone stairway gives it a noble demeanor. It was Queen Isabel Segunda who decreed that the Dominicans should build a church and monastery in San Germán. A rudimentary structure was built in 1609, replaced in 1692 by the structure that can still be seen today. (Sadly, the monastery was demolished in 1866, leaving only a vestige of its facade.) The chapel now functions as a museum of religious art, displaying painted wooden statuary by Latin American and Spanish artists. ⊠ *East end of Plazuela Santo Domingo* ☎ *787/892–5845* ⊕ *www.icp.gobierno. pr* ⊡ *Free* ☉ *Wed.–Sun. 8:30–noon and 1 to 4:15.*

Western & Central Puerto Rico

The Puerto Rico Tourism Company calls the western side of the island Porta del Sol and maintains a separate Web site to highlight travel options in the region (see ⇨ Visitor Information *in* Puerto Rico Essentials, *below*).

33 Bosque Estatal de Río Abajo. In the middle of karst country—a region of limestone deposits that is peppered with fissures, caves, and underground streams—the Río Abajo State Forest spans some 5,000 acres and includes huge bamboo stands and silk-cotton trees. Walking trails wind through the forest, which is one of the habitats of the rare Puerto Rican parrot. An information office is near the entrance, and a recreation area with picnic tables is farther down the road. ⊠ *Rte. 621, Km 4.4* ☎ *787/ 817–0984* ⊡ *Free* ☉ *Daily dawn–dusk.*

29 Mayagüez. With a population of slightly more than 100,000, this is the largest city on Puerto Rico's west coast. Although bypassed by the mania for restoration that has spruced up Ponce and Old San Juan, Mayagüez is graced by some lovely turn-of-the-20th-century architecture, such as the landmark Art Deco Teatro Yagüez and the Plaza de Colón.

Founded in 1901 on a 235-acre farm on the outskirts of Mayagüez, the **Estación Experimental de Agricultura Tropical** (Tropical Agriculture Research Station) is run by the U.S. Department of Agriculture and contains a tropical plant collection that has been nurtured for more than a half century. More than 2,000 plant species from all over the tropical world are found here, including teak, mahogany, cinnamon, nutmeg, rubber, and numerous exotic flowers. Free maps are available for self-guided tours. ⊠ *Hwy. 2 and Rte. 108* ☎ *787/831–3435* ⊡ *Free* ☉ *Weekdays 7–4.*

16

★ **③** **Observatorio de Arecibo.** Hidden among pine-covered hills is the world's largest radar-radio telescope. Operated by the National Astronomy and Ionosphere Center of Cornell University, the 20-acre dish lies in a 563-foot-deep sinkhole in the karst landscape. If the 600-ton platform hovering eerily over the dish looks familiar, it may be because it can be glimpsed in scenes from the movie *Contact.* (And, yes, the dish has been used to search for extraterrestrial life.) You can walk around the viewing platform and explore two levels of interactive exhibits on planetary systems, meteors, and weather phenomena in the visitor center. ⊠ *Rte. 625, Km 3.0* ☎ *787/878–2612* ⊕ *www.naic.edu* ⊠ *$5* ⊗ *Wed.–Fri. noon–4, weekends 9–4.*

★ **③** **Parque Ceremonial Indígena de Caguana.** The 13 acres of this park were used more than 800 years ago by the Taíno tribes for worship and recreation, including a game—thought to have religious significance—that resembled modern-day soccer. Today you can see 10 *bateyes* (courts) of various sizes, large stone monoliths (some with petroglyphs), and re-creations of Taíno gardens. ⊠ *Rte. 111, Km 12.3* ☎ *787/894–7325* ⊠ *$2* ⊗ *Daily 8:30–4:30.*

☾ **③** **Parque de las Cavernas del Río Camuy.** This 268-acre park contains an enormous cave network and the third-longest underground river in the world. A tram takes you down a trail shaded by bamboo and banana trees to Cueva Clara, where the stalactites and stalagmites turn the entrance into a toothy grin. Hour-long guided tours in English and Spanish lead you on foot through the 180-foot-high cave, which is teeming with wildlife. You're likely to find blue-eyed river crabs and long-legged tarantulas. More elusive are the more than 100,000 bats that make their home in the cave. They don't come out until dark, but you can feel the heat they generate at the cave's entrance. Tours are first-come, first-served; plan to arrive early on weekends, when local families join the crowds. ⊠ *Rte. 129, Km 18.9* ☎ *787/898–3100* ⊠ *$10* ⊗ *Wed.–Sun. 8–4; last tour at 3:45.*

FodorsChoice ★

③ **Rincón.** Jutting out into the ocean along the rugged western coast, Rincón, meaning "corner" in Spanish, may have gotten its name because of how it is nestled in a corner of the coastline. The town jumped into the surfing spotlight after hosting the World Surfing Championship in 1968. Although the beat here picks up from October through April, when the waves are the best, Rincón, basically laid-back and unpretentious, is seeing a lot of development. If you visit between December and February you might get a glimpse of the humpback whales that winter off the coast. Because of its unusual setting, Rincón's layout can be a little disconcerting. The main road, Route 413, loops around the coast, and many beaches and sights are on dirt roads intersecting it.

PUERTO RICO ESSENTIALS

To research prices, get advice from other travelers, and book travel arrangements, visit www.fodors.com.

Transportation

BY AIR

San Juan's busy Aeropuerto Internacional Luis Muñoz Marín is the Caribbean hub of American Airlines, which flies nonstop from Baltimore, Boston, Chicago, Dallas, Fort Lauderdale, Miami, Newark, New York–JFK, Orlando, Philadelphia, Tampa, and Washington, D.C.–Dulles. Continental Airlines flies nonstop from Houston and Newark. Delta flies nonstop from Atlanta, Orlando, and New York–JFK. JetBlue flies nonstop from New York–JFK. Spirit Air flies nonstop from Fort Lauderdale and Orlando. United flies nonstop from Chicago, New York–JFK, Philadelphia, and Washington, D.C.–Dulles. US Airways flies nonstop from Baltimore, Boston, Charlotte, Chicago, Philadelphia, and Washington, D.C.–Dulles. International carriers serving San Juan include Air Canada from Toronto, Air France from Paris, Iberia from Madrid, and British Airways from London.

San Juan is no longer the only gateway into Puerto Rico. If you're headed to the western part of the island, you can fly directly into Aguadilla. Continental flies here from Newark, and JetBlue flies here from New York–JFK. If the southern coast is your goal, Continental flies to Ponce from Newark.

Air Flamenco, Isla Nena Air Service, and Vieques Air Link offer daily flights from San Juan to Vieques and Culebra. American Eagle and Cape Air fly between the international airport and Vieques.

Puerto Rico is also a good spot from which to hop to other Caribbean islands. American Eagle serves most islands in the Caribbean; Cape Air connects San Juan to St. Thomas and St. Croix. Seaborne Airlines has seaplanes departing from San Juan Piers 6 and 7 to St. Thomas and St. Croix.

🛪 Major Airlines **Air Canada** ☎ 888/247-2262 ⊕ www.aircanada.com. **Air France** ☎ 800/237-2747 ⊕ www.airfrance.com. **American Airlines/ American Eagle** ☎ 800/433-7300 ⊕ www.aa. com. **British Airways** ☎ 800/247-9297 ⊕ www. britishairways.com. **Continental** ☎ 800/231-0856 ⊕ www.continental.com. **Delta** ☎ 800/221-1212 ⊕ www.delta.com. **Iberia** ☎ 787/725-7000 ⊕ www.iberia.com. **JetBlue** ☎ 800/538-2583 ⊕ www.jetblue.com. **Spirit Air** ☎ 800/772-7117 ⊕ www.spiritair.com. **United Airlines** ☎ 800/864-8331 ⊕ www.united.com. **US Airways** ☎ 800/428-4322 ⊕ www.usairways.com.

🛪 Regional Airlines **Air Flamenco** ☎ 787/724-1818 ⊕ www.airflamenco.net **Cape Air** ☎ 800/525-0280 ⊕ www.flycapeair.com. **Isla Nena Air Service** ☎ 787/741-6362 or 877/812-5144 ⊕ www. islanena.8m.com. **Seaborne Airlines** ☎ 888/359-8687 ⊕ www.seaborneairlines.com. **Vieques Air Link** ☎ 787/722-3736 or 888/901-9247 ⊕ www. vieques-island.com/val.

AIRPORTS & TRANSFERS: Aeropuerto Internacional Luis Muñoz Marín (SJU) is 20 minutes east of Old San Juan in the neighborhood of Isla Verde. San Juan's other airport is the small Fernando L. Ribas Dominicci Airport in Isla Grande (SIG), near the city's Miramar section. From either airport you can catch flights to Culebra, Vieques, and other destinations on Puerto Rico and throughout the Caribbean. (Note that although the Dominicci airport was still operating at this writing, its future was uncertain.) A taxi to most parts of San Juan should cost $8 to $16. If you are staying in a hotel outside of San Juan, check with your resort to see if it offers transfers; taxi rides outside of the San Juan metro area can be very expensive.

Other Puerto Rican airports include Aeropuerto Internacional Rafael Hernández (BQN) in the northwestern town of

16

Aguadilla, Aeropuerto Eugenio María de Hostos (MAZ) in the west-coast community of Mayagüez, Mercedita (PSE) in the south-coast town of Ponce, Aeropuerto Diego Jiménez Torres (FAJ) in the east-coast city of Fajardo, Antonio Rivera Rodríguez (VQS) on Vieques, and Aeropuerto Benjamin Rivera Noriega (CPX) on Culebra.

⛴ **Aeropuerto Antonio Rivera Rodríguez** VQS ✉ Vieques ☎ 787/741-8358. **Aeropuerto Benjamin Rivera Noriega** CPX ✉ Culebra ☎ 787/742-0022. **Aeropuerto Diego Jiménez Torres** FAJ ✉ Fajardo ☎ 787/860-3110. **Aeropuerto Eugenio María de Hostos** MAZ ✉ Mayagüez ☎ 787/833-0148. **Aeropuerto Fernando L. Ribas Dominicci** SIG ✉ Isla Grande, San Juan ☎ 787/729-8711. **Aeropuerto Mercedita** PSE ✉ Ponce ☎ 787/842-6292. **Aeropuerto Rafael Hernández** BQN ✉ Aguadilla ☎ 787/891-2286. **Aeropuerto Internacional Luis Muñoz Marín** SJU ✉ Isla Verde, San Juan ☎ 787/791-3840.

BY BOAT & FERRY

The Autoridad de los Puertos (Port Authority) ferry between Old San Juan (Pier 2) and Cataño costs a mere 50¢ one-way. It runs every half hour from 6 AM to 10 PM and every 15 minutes during peak hours.

The Fajardo Port Authority's 400-passenger ferries run between that east-coast town and the out-islands of Vieques and Culebra; both trips take 90 minutes. The vessels carry cargo and passengers to Vieques three times daily ($2 one-way) and to Culebra twice a day Sunday through Friday and three times a day on Saturday ($2.25 one-way). Get schedules for the Culebra and Vieques ferries by calling the Port Authority in Fajardo, Vieques, or Culebra. You buy tickets at the ferry dock. Be aware that there may be a line if you are taking a car over, particularly on the weekend.

There's also Island Hi-Speed Ferry, which leaves Pier 2 in Old San Juan for Vieques and Culebra. During high season, the ferry makes one daily round-trip (leaving in the morning, returning in the afternoon).

Travel time is 1 hour 45 minutes to Culebra, 2 hours 15 minutes to Vieques. Round-trip fares are $68 to Culebra, $78 to Vieques. Reservations are recommended.

⛴ **Autoridad de los Puertos** ☎ 787/788-1155 in San Juan, 787/863-4560 in Fajardo, 787/742-3161 in Culebra, 787/741-4761 in Vieques. **Island Hi-Speed Ferry** ☎ 787/724-6600 ⊕ www.islandhighspeedferry.com.

BY CAR

If you are staying in San Juan, it's more trouble than it's worth to rent a car. However, if you are staying elsewhere on the island, a car is probably a necessity. If you rent a car, a good road map will be helpful in remote areas. A valid driver's license from your country of origin can be used in Puerto Rico for three months. Rates start as low as $39 a day.

You can find offices for dozens of agencies at San Juan's airports, and a majority of them have shuttle service to and from the airport and the pickup point. Most rental cars are available with automatic or standard transmission. Four-wheel-drive vehicles aren't necessary unless you plan to go way off the beaten path or along the steep, rocky roads of Culebra or Vieques; in most cases a standard compact car will do the trick. Always opt for air-conditioning, though.

Several well-marked multilane highways link population centers. Route 26 is the main artery through San Juan, connecting Condado and Old San Juan to Isla Verde and the airport. Route 22, which runs east–west between San Juan and Camuy, and the Luis A. Ferré Expressway (Route 52), which runs north–south between San Juan and Ponce, are toll roads (35¢–50¢). Route 2, a smaller highway, travels along the west coast, and Routes 3 and 53 traverse the east shore. Distances are posted in kilometers (1⁶⁄₁₀ km to 1 mi), whereas speed limits are posted in miles per hour. Some roads in the mountains are very curvy and take longer to cover than the distance on a map might suggest. Not every road is marked, but most Puerto Ricans are happy to help with directions. Most gas stations have both full- and self-service. Hours vary, but stations generally operate daily from early in the morning until 10 or 11 PM; in metro areas many are open 24 hours. Stations are few and far between in the central mountains and other rural areas; plan accordingly.

🚗 Major Agencies **Avis** ☎ 787/721–4499 in San Juan, 787/890–3311 in Aguadilla, 787/863–2735 in Fajardo, 787/833–7070 in Mayagüez. **Budget** ☎787/791–3685 in San Juan. **Hertz** ☎ 787/791–0840 in San Juan, 787/890–5650 in Aguadilla, 787/832–3314 in Mayagüez, 787/843–1658 in Ponce. **National** ☎787/791–1805 in San Juan. **Thrifty** ☎787/253–2525 in San Juan.

🚗 Local Agencies **AAA Car Rental** ☎ 787/726–7355 in San Juan ⊕ www.charliecars.com. **Charlie Car Rental** ☎787/728–2418 in San Juan ⊕www.charliecars.com. **Island Car Rental** ☎ 787/741–1666 in Vieques. **L&M Car Rental** ☎ 787/791–1160 in San Juan, 787/831–4740 in Mayagüez.

BY PUBLIC TRANSIT

The Autoridad Metropolitana de Autobuses (AMA) operates buses that thread through San Juan, running in exclusive lanes on major thoroughfares and stopping at signs marked PARADA. Destinations are indicated above the windshield. Bus B-21 runs through Condado all the way to Plaza Las Américas in Hato Rey. Bus A-5 runs from San Juan through Santurce and the beach area of Isla Verde. Fares are 50¢ or 75¢, depending on the route, and are paid in exact change upon entering the bus. Most buses are air-conditioned and have wheelchair lifts and lock-downs.

There is no bus system covering the rest of the island. If you do not have a rental car, your best bet is to travel by *públicos* (shared vans), which usually hold 17 passengers. They have yellow license plates ending in "P" or "PD," and they scoot to towns throughout the island, stopping in each community's main plaza. They operate primarily during the day; routes and fares are fixed by the Public Service Commission, but schedules aren't set, so you have to call ahead.

In San Juan, the main terminals are at the airport and at Plaza Colón in Old San Juan. San Juan–based público companies include Blue Line for trips to Aguadilla and the northwest coast, Choferes Unidos de Ponce for Ponce, Línea Caborrojeña for Cabo Rojo and the southwest coast, Línea Boricua for the interior and the southwest, Línea Sultana for Mayagüez and the west coast, and Terminal de Transportación Pública for Fajardo and the east.

🚌 **AMA** ☎ 787/767–7979. **Blue Line** ☎ 787/891–4550. **Choferes Unidos de Ponce** ☎ 787/764–0540. **Línea Boricua** ☎ 787/896–6755. **Línea Caborrojeña** ☎ 787/851–1252. **Línea Sultana** ☎ 787/765–9377.

BY TAXI

The Puerto Rico Tourism Company has instituted a well-organized taxi program. Taxis painted white and displaying the *garita* (sentry box) logo and TAXI TURISTICO label charge set rates depending on the destination; they run from the airport or the cruise-ship piers to Isla Verde, Condado/Ocean Park, and Old San Juan, with fixed "zone" rates ranging from $6 to $16. If you take a cab going somewhere outside the fixed "zones," insist on setting the meter. If the cab driver refuses, you can get out of the cab and report it to the taxi authority or negotiate the rate at your own level of comfort. City tours start at $30 per hour. Metered cabs authorized by the Public Service Commission start at $1 and charge 10¢ for every additional $\frac{1}{13}$ mi, 50¢ for every suitcase. Waiting time is 10¢ for each 45 seconds. The minimum charge is $3, and there is an extra $1 night charge between 10 PM and 6 AM.

In other Puerto Rican towns, you can flag down cabs on the street, but it's easier to have your hotel call one for you. Either way, make sure the driver is clear on whether he or she will charge a flat rate or use a meter to determine the fare. In most places, the cabs are metered.

Linéas are private taxis you share with three to five other passengers. There are

16

more than 20 companies, each usually specializing in a certain region. Most will arrange door-to-door service. Check local Yellow Pages listings under *Líneas de Carros*. They're affordable and are a great way to meet people, but be prepared to wait: they usually don't leave until they have a full load.

🚖 **Atlantic City Taxi** ☎ 787/268–5050 in San Juan. **Fajardo Taxi Service** ☎ 787/860–1112. **Lolo Felix Tours** ☎ 787/485–5447 on Vieques. **Major Taxicabs** ☎ 787/723–2460 in San Juan. **Ponce Taxi Association** ☎787/842–3370. **Public Service Commission** ☎ 787/751–5050. **Ruben's Taxi** ☎ 787/405–1209 on Culebra. **White Taxi** ☎ 787/832–1115 in Mayagüez.

Contacts & Resources

BANKS & MONEY

Puerto Rico, as a commonwealth of the United States, uses the U.S. dollar as its official currency. Credit cards, including Diners Club and Discover, are widely accepted, especially in tourist areas. Automated Teller Machines (ATMs; known as ATHs here) are readily available and reliable in the cities; many are attached to banks, but you can also find them on the streets and in supermarkets. ATMs are found less frequently in rural areas. Look to local banks such as Banco Popular and First Bank. Citibank also has branches in San Juan, including a convenient Condado branch across from the Radisson Hotel.

🏦 **Banco Popular** ✉ 206 Calle Tetuán, Old San Juan, San Juan ☎ 787/725–2636 ✉ 1060 Av. Ashford, Condado, San Juan ☎ 787/725–4197 ✉ 115 Muñoz Rivera, Isabel Segunda, Vieques ☎787/741–2071 ✉ Rte. 3, Km 42.4, Fajardo ☎ 787/860–1570 ✉ Plaza las Delicias, Ponce ☎ 787/843–8000 or 787/848–2410 ✉ Mayagüez Mall, Rte. 2, Km 159.4, Mayagüez ☎ 787/834–4750. **Citibank** ✉ 206 Calle Tanca, Old San Juan ☎ 787/721–0108 ✉ 1358 Av. Ashford, Condado ☎ 787/721–5656.

BUSINESS HOURS

Bank hours are generally weekdays from 8 to 4 or 9 to 5, though a few branches are open Saturday from 9 to noon or 1. Post offices are open weekdays from 7:30 to 4:30 and Saturday from 8 to noon. Government offices are open weekdays from 9 to 5. Most gas stations are open daily from early in the morning until 10 or 11 PM. Numerous stations in urban areas are open 24 hours. Street shops are open Monday through Saturday from 9 to 6 (9 to 9 during Christmas holidays); mall stores tend to stay open to 9 or so. Count on convenience stores staying open late into the night, seven days a week. Supermarkets are often closed on Sunday, although some remain open 24 hours, seven days a week.

ELECTRICITY

Puerto Rico uses the same electrical current as the U.S. mainland, namely 110 volts.

EMERGENCIES

🚑 **Ambulance, police, and fire** ☎ 911. **Air Ambulance Service** ☎ 800/633–3590 or 787/756–3424. **Dental emergencies** ☎ 787/722–2351 or 787/795–0320. **San Juan Tourist Zone Police** ☎ 787/726–7020, 787/726–7015 for Condado, 787/728–4770, 787/726–2981 for Isla Verde. **Travelers' Aid** ☎ 787/791–1054 or 787/791–1034.

🏥 Hospitals **Ashford Presbyterian Memorial Community Hospital** ✉ 1451 Av. Ashford, Condado, San Juan ☎ 787/721–2160. **General Hospital Dr. Ramón Emeterio Betances** ✉ 410 Av. Hostos, Mayagüez ☎ 787/834–8686. **Hospital de la Concepción** ✉ Calle Luna 41, San Germán ☎ 787/892–1860. **Hospital Damas** ✉ 2213 Ponce Bypass Rd., Ponce ☎ 787/840–8686. **Hospital Dr. Dominguez** ✉ 300 Font Martello, Humacao ☎787/852–0505. **Hospital Gubern** ✉ 11 Antonio R. Barcelo, Fajardo ☎ 787/863–0669.

HOLIDAYS

Public holidays in Puerto Rico include New Year's Day, Three Kings Day (Jan. 6), Eugenio María de Hostos Day (Jan. 8), Dr. Martin Luther King Jr. Day (3rd Mon. in Jan.), Presidents' Day (3rd Mon. in Feb.), Palm Sunday, Good Friday, Easter Sunday, Memorial Day (last Mon. in May), Independence Day (July 4), Luis Muñoz Rivera Day (July 16), Constitution Day (July 25), José Celso Barbosa Day (July 27), Labor Day (1st Mon. in Sept.), Columbus Day (2nd Mon. in Oct.), Veterans' Day (Nov.

11), Puerto Rico Discovery Day (Nov. 19), Thanksgiving Day, and Christmas.

LANGUAGE

Puerto Rico is officially bilingual, but Spanish predominates, particularly outside of the tourist areas of San Juan. Although English is widely spoken, you'll probably want to take a Spanish phrase book along on your travels about the island.

INTERNET, MAIL & SHIPPING

In Puerto Rico, Internet cafés are few and far between. If that weren't bad enough, many hotels have yet to install high-speed Internet access in their rooms. Your best bet is to use your hotel business center if you need to send an email. Puerto Rico uses the U.S. postal system, and all addresses on the island carry zip codes. You can buy stamps and aerograms and send letters and parcels in post offices. Stamp-dispensing machines can occasionally be found in airports, office buildings, and drugstores. Major post-office branches can be found in most major cities and towns.

U.S. Postal Service ✉153 Calle Fortaleza, Old San Juan, San Juan ✉163 Av. Fernández Juncos, San Juan ✉102 Calle Garrido Morales, Fajardo ✉94 Calle Atocha, Ponce ✉60 Calle McKinley, Mayagüez.

PASSPORT REQUIREMENTS

Puerto Rico is a commonwealth of the United States, so U.S. citizens don't need passports to visit the island since it's technically part of the U.S. (they must have a valid photo ID, however). You will not pass through immigration, as you do in the U.S. Virgin Islands, though there is an agriculture inspection before you check in for your flight home.

SAFETY

San Juan, like any other big city, has its share of crime, so guard your wallet or purse on the city streets. Puerto Rico's beaches are open to the public, and muggings can occur at night even on the beaches of the posh Condado and Isla Verde tourist hotels; however, you'll see people walking along Avenida Ashford in Condado until the wee hours. Although you certainly can—and should—explore the city and its beaches, use common sense. Don't leave anything unattended on the beach. Leave your valuables in the hotel safe, and stick to the fenced-in beach areas of your hotel. Always lock your car and stash valuables and luggage out of sight. Avoid deserted beaches at night.

TAXES

Accommodations incur a tax: for hotels with casinos it's 11%, for other hotels it's 9%, and for government-approved paradores it's 7%. Ask your hotel before booking. The tax, in addition to the standard 5% to 12% service charge or resort fee applied by most hotels, can add a hefty 20% or more to your bill. There's no sales tax in Puerto Rico.

TELEPHONES

Most U.S. mobile phone users will not pay any roaming charges to use their phones in Puerto Rico, though you should confirm that with your company. Puerto Rico's area codes are 787 and 939. Toll-free numbers (prefix 800, 888, or 877) are widely used in Puerto Rico, and many can be accessed from North America (and vice versa). For North Americans, dialing Puerto Rico is the same as dialing another U.S. state or a Canadian province. To make a local call in Puerto Rico you must dial 1, the area code, and the seven-digit number. For international calls, dial 011, the country code, the city code, and the number. Dial 00 for an international long-distance operator. Phone cards are not required but can be useful and are widely available (most drug stores carry them). The Puerto Rico Telephone Company sells its "Ring Cards" in various denominations.

TIPPING

Tips are expected, and appreciated, by restaurant waitstaff (15% to 20% if a service charge isn't included), hotel porters ($1 per bag), maids ($1 to $2 a day), and taxi drivers (15% to 18%).

16

VISITOR INFORMATION

The Puerto Rico Tourism Company has offices at the airports in San Juan and Aguadilla, as well as downtown offices in San Juan, Cabo Rojo, and Ponce.

🗐 Before You Leave **Puerto del Sol Tourism** ⊕ www.gotoportadelsol.com. **Puerto Rico Tourism Company** ⊕ www.gotopuertorico.com ☐ Box 902–3960, Old San Juan Station, San Juan, PR 00902–3960 ☎ 787/721–2400 or 800/866–7827 ✉ 666 5th Ave., 15th fl., New York, NY 10103 ☎ 212/586–6262 or 800/223–6530 ✉ 3575 W. Cahuenga Blvd., Suite 560, Los Angeles, CA 90068 ☎ 213/874–5991 or 800/ 874–1330 ✉ 901 Ponce de León Blvd., Suite 101, Coral Gables, FL 33134 ☎ 305/445–9112 or 800/815–7391.

🗐 In Puerto Rico **Culebra Tourism Office** ✉ 250 Calle Pedro Marquez, Dewey, Culebra ☎ 787/742–3521. **Fajardo Tourism Office** ✉ 6 Av. Muñoz Rivera ☎ 787/863–4013 Ext. 274. **Mayagüez City Hall** ☎ 787/834–8585. **Ponce Municipal Tourist Office** ✉ 2nd fl. of Citibank, Plaza las Delicias, Box 1709, Ponce 00733 ☎ 787/841–8160 or 787/841–8044. **Puerto Rico Tourism Company** ✉ Plaza Dársenas, near Pier 1, Old San Juan ☎ 787/722–1709 ✉ Aeropuerto Internacional Luis Muñoz Marín ☎ 787/791–1014 or 787/791–2551 ✉ Rte. 101, Km 13.7, Cabo Riojo ☎ 787/851–7070 ✉ 291 Vallas Torres, Ponce ☎ 787/843–0465 ✉ Rafael Hernández Airport, Aguadilla ☎ 787/890–3315. **Vieques Tourism Office** ✉ 449 Calle Carlos Lebrón, Isabel Segunda, Vieques ☎ 787/741–5000.

WEDDINGS

If you wish to get married in Puerto Rico, you must get an application from the Demographic Registry. There are no special residency requirements, but U.S. citizens must produce a driver's license and non-U.S. citizens must produce a valid passport for identification purposes. If either the bride or groom was previously married, certified copies of a divorce decree or death certificate must be produced as well as a medical certificate. The filing cost is $20.

Blood tests are required and must be done within 10 days of the marriage ceremony. The results must be certified and signed by a doctor or hotel physician in Puerto Rico. The cost for the laboratory test in Puerto Rico is about $15 to $25.

Both the bride and groom must appear in person to file the application at the Marriage License Bureau of the Demographic Registry, which is open weekdays from 7:30 AM to 3:30 PM.

Marriages may be performed by a judge or any clergyman. The marriage fee is usually between $150 and $350. Two stamps must be obtained from the Internal Revenue Office (Colecturia) for about $30.

Most large hotels on the island have marriage coordinators, who can explain the necessary paperwork and help you complete it on time for your marriage ceremony.

🗐 **Demographic Registry** ✉ 171 Calle Quisqueya, Hato Rey, San Juan 00917 ☐ Box 11854, San Juan 00910 ☎ 787/728–7080.

Saba

Yellow goatfish

WORD OF MOUTH

"I have been to Saba four times, each time for a week, and have not been bored. . . . There is very little nightlife, no beaches, not many organized things to do. It's perfect for me."

—Howard

"The hike to the top of Saba's mountain is very very strenuous. . . . The hike was worth it though—beautiful rain forest, lots of exotic trees and birds."

—Sally

WELCOME TO SABA

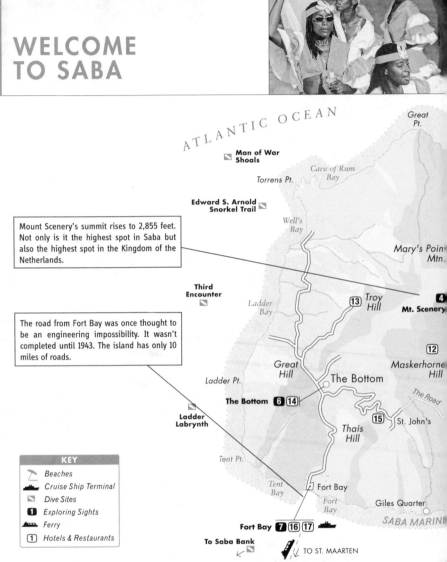

ATLANTIC OCEAN

Great Pt.

Man of War Shoals

Torrens Pt.

Cave of Rum Bay

Edward S. Arnold Snorkel Trail

Well's Bay

Mary's Point Mtn.

> Mount Scenery's summit rises to 2,855 feet. Not only is it the highest spot in Saba but also the highest spot in the Kingdom of the Netherlands.

Third Encounter

Ladder Bay

[13] Troy Hill

[4] Mt. Scenery

[12] Maskerhorne Hill

> The road from Fort Bay was once thought to be an engineering impossibility. It wasn't completed until 1943. The island has only 10 miles of roads.

Great Hill

The Bottom

Ladder Pt.

The Bottom [6] [14]

The Road

[15] St. John's

Ladder Labrynth

Thais Hill

Tent Pt.

KEY
- Beaches
- Cruise Ship Terminal
- Dive Sites
- [1] Exploring Sights
- Ferry
- [1] Hotels & Restaurants

Tent Bay

Fort Bay

Giles Quarter

SABA MARIN

Fort Bay

Fort Bay [7] [16] [17]

To Saba Bank

TO ST. MAARTEN

Mountainous Saba's precipitous terrain allows visitors to choose between the heights and the depths. The Bottom, the island's capital, was once thought to be the crater of an extinct volcano, from which a trail of 400 rough-hewn steps drops to the sea. Divers can take a different plunge to view the pristine reefs.

THE UNSPOILED QUEEN

Tiny Saba—an extinct volcano that juts out of the ocean to a height of 2,855 feet—is just 5 square mi (13 square km) in size and has a population of about 1,500. One of the Netherlands Antilles, it's 28 mi (45 km) south of St. Maarten and surrounded by some of the richest dive sites in the Caribbean.

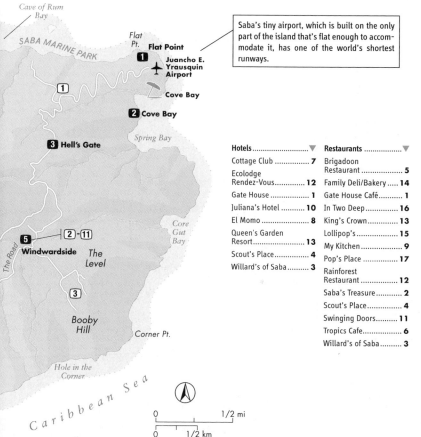

Saba's tiny airport, which is built on the only part of the island that's flat enough to accommodate it, has one of the world's shortest runways.

Hotels .... ▼	Restaurants .... ▼
Cottage Club **7**	Brigadoon Restaurant **5**
Ecolodge Rendez-Vous............. **12**	Family Deli/Bakery **14**
Gate House **1**	Gate House Café.......... **1**
Juliana's Hotel **10**	In Two Deep.............. **16**
El Momo **8**	King's Crown............. **13**
Queen's Garden Resort...................... **13**	Lollipop's **15**
Scout's Place.............. **4**	My Kitchen **9**
Willard's of Saba......... **3**	Pop's Place **17**
	Rainforest Restaurant **12**
	Saba's Treasure............ **2**
	Scout's Place............... **4**
	Swinging Doors.......... **11**
	Tropics Cafe................. **6**
	Willard's of Saba......... **3**

17

SABA

TOP 4 REASONS TO VISIT SABA

① Divers flock to Saba for the clear water and spectacular ocean life.

② Hikers can climb the island's pinnacle, Mount Scenery, but even the less intense trails offer just as many sweeping vistas.

③ Saba reminds you of what the Caribbean used to be: locals are genuine and the tourist traps nonexistent.

④ Several hotels, whose resident nature pros can tell you everything about local flora and fauna cater to ecotourists.

SABA PLANNER

Getting to Saba

Only one airline (Winair) flies to Saba (SAB), and then only from St. Eustatius and St. Maarten. Getting to St. Maarten isn't difficult as it is blessed with many nonstop and connecting flights from the U.S., Canada, and Europe.

You can also take a ferry from St. Maarten; the trip, which takes over an hour, can be rough and costs $57 round-trip. Because the limited schedule is geared to day-trippers, the ferry isn't an option unless you want to spend time both before and after your Saba stay on St. Maarten.

Hassle Factor: Medium

Where to Stay

Saba's few hotel rooms are primarily in a handful of friendly, tidy inns, or guesthouses perched on ledges or tucked into tropical gardens. Because the island is so small, nothing is very isolated, so it doesn't much matter where you stay. Among the choices are one luxury boutique hotel and a couple of splendid, small eco-resorts. There are also more than a dozen apartments, cottages, and villas for rent.

Hotel & Restaurant Costs

Assume that hotels operate on the European Plan (**EP**—with no meals) unless we specify that they use either the Continental Plan (**CP**—with a Continental breakfast), Breakfast Plan (**BP**—with full breakfast), or the Modified American Plan (**MAP**—with breakfast and dinner). Other hotels may offer the Full American Plan (**FAP**—including all meals but no drinks) or may be All-Inclusive (**AI**—with all meals, drinks, and most activities).

WHAT IT COSTS in Dollars					
	$$$$	**$$$**	**$$**	**$**	**¢**
Restaurants	over $30	$20–$30	$12–$20	$8–$12	under $8
Hotels*	over $350	$250–$350	$150–$250	$80–$150	under $80
Hotels**	over $450	$350–$450	$250–$350	$125–$250	under $125

*EP, BP, CP   **AI, FAP, MAP
Restaurant prices are for a main course and do not include customary 10%–15% service charge. Hotel prices are for two people in a double room in high season and do not include 8% tax, 10%–15% service charge, or meal plans.

On the Ground

The taxi fare from the airport to Hell's Gate is $6; to Windwardside it's $8; and to the Bottom it's $12.50. If you dare to drive the hairpin turns of Saba's one and only road, you can rent a car (about $45 a day with a full tank of gas and unlimited mileage). The only gas station is in Fort Bay.

Activities

Forget the beach because there isn't one. Abundant reefs, however, are a different story altogether. The island is surrounded by—and zealously preserves—myriad extraordinary **dive** sites. If you don't dive, there are plenty of shallow reefs you can explore by **snorkel**. If you're not into the briny deep, there's always the **hike** to the top of Mount Scenery, a breathtaking trip to an even better view, assuming the top isn't shrouded in cloud cover. Otherwise, it's a very quiet and peaceful place and not a half-bad destination if all you want to do is relax and chat with the ever-friendly locals.

By Katherine
Dykstra

THE SUN IS STILL LOW when I set out to conquer the 1,064 steps that spiral up Mount Scenery to Saba's summit, with a peak cloaked in a dense, gray haze. The island is so wet that it creates its own clouds, and the crest of Mount Scenery is almost always overcast. As I climb, the humidity intensifies, and the moss-covered stairs get steeper. It takes me nearly an hour to reach the top, and then something amazing happens. As I look down on the cloud, it miraculously parts, and I find the entire island stretched out before me: sweeping precipices, red roofs huddled together in each of the four villages, the single road that snakes between them, the steeple on the little yellow church. And just as quickly as the cloud parted, it rolls over again. I am left with the feeling that I've seen something very special. It's the very same feeling most people get upon discovering this remote Caribbean island.

One of the Netherlands Antilles, tropical Saba (pronounced *say*-ba) explodes out of the Caribbean Sea just south of St. Maarten (if you've seen the original *King Kong,* you'll recognize its majestic silhouette from the beginning of the film), but the island couldn't be more different. While St. Maarten is all beaches, gambling, and duty-free shopping, Saba is ecotourism, diving, and hiking.

Nearly half of Saba's 5 square mi (13 square km) are covered in verdant tropical rain forest; the other half is sprinkled with petite hamlets composed of white, green-shuttered houses trimmed in gingerbread, roofed in red, and built on grades so steep they seem to defy physics. Flower-draped walls and neat picket fences border narrow paths among the bromeliads, palms, hibiscus, orchids, and Norfolk Island pines. The land dips and climbs à la San Francisco and eventually drops off into sheer cliffs that drop right into the ocean, the fodder for some of the world's most striking dive sites and the primary reason for Saba's cultlike following. Divers seem to relish the fact that they're in on Saba's secret.

17

But word is slowly getting out. Every year more and more tourists are turned on to Saba's charms and make the 11-minute, white-knuckle flight from St. Maarten into the tiny airport (barely the size of an aircraft carrier's, the airstrip is one of the shortest in the world). Indeed, traffic jams along the winding, narrow road (yes, there's really just one) are no longer unheard of. The past few years have seen the opening of a day spa, as well as more restaurants and a Pilates and yoga studio (big advances considering around-the-clock electricity was established only in 1970). But don't fear you will find a booming metropolis; even as it changes, Saba retains an old-world charm.

A major point of local pride is that many Saban families can be traced all the way back to the island's settlement in 1640 by the Dutch (the surnames Hassell, Johnson, and Peterson fill the tiny phone book). And Sabans hold their traditions dear. Saba lace—a genteel art that dates back to the 1870s—is still hand-stitched by local ladies who, on the side, also distill potent, 151-proof Saba Spice, which is for sale in most of the island's mom-and-pop shops. Families follow the generations-old tradition of burying their dead in their neatly tended gardens.

Like the residents of most small towns, the Sabans are a tight-knit group; nothing happens without everyone hearing about it, making crime pretty much a nonissue. But they are eager to welcome newcomers and tend to make travelers feel less like tourists and more like old friends. After all, they're proud to show off their home, which they lovingly call "the unspoiled queen."

Where to Stay

Cable TV is common, but air-conditioning is a rarity.

$$$$ ⊡ **Willard's of Saba.** Getting to this lavish cliffside hotel, which literally clings to the mountain 2,000 feet straight up, is no small feat (many a car has had to give up halfway and roll right back down, and most cabs won't even attempt it). However, you may take heart, because once here, you'll have little reason to leave. Among the terraced bungalows, two of which were added in 2005, you'll find a massage room, hot tub, solar-heated pool, and the only tennis court on the island, not to mention the most stunning views on Saba. We're talking more than 180 degrees. Happily, it's worth almost every penny of the pricey rates. ⌂ *Box 515, Windwardside* ☎ *599/416–2498* ≞ *599/416–2482* ⊕ *www.willardsofsaba. com* ⤚ *9 rooms* ⌁ *Restaurant, fans, Wi-Fi, tennis court, pool, gym, hot tub, bar; no a/c, no room TVs* ⊟ *AE, D, MC, V* �︎◯︎ *EP.*

★ **$$–$$$** ⊡ **Queen's Garden Resort.** If romance is on the agenda, this is your resort. A quaint wooden stairway winds up past the largest pool on the island, all the way to the patio in front of the main building, which houses the King's Crown restaurant. Each night, tiki torches flicker and dense foliage gives everything an air of intimacy. That's if you can bear to leave your room: all 12 are decorated dreamily with Dutch colonial and Indonesian furnishings and bestowed with four-poster beds. Be sure to request one of the nine hot tub suites that open up to panoramic vistas of the village below. ⊠ *1 Troy Hill Dr., Box 4, Troy Hill* ☎ *599/416–3494 or 599/416–3496* ≞ *599/416–3495* ⊕ *www.queenssaba.com* ⤚ *12 suites* ⌁ *Restaurant, fans, in-room safes, some in-room hot tubs, kitchens, cable TV, pool, hot tub, bar; no a/c* ⊟ *AE, MC, V* ︎◯︎ *EP.*

★ **$–$$** ⊡ **Juliana's Hotel.** Aesthetics meets affordability here, and this applies to more than just the reasonable room rates. Everything seems to encompass both practicality and pampering. On one side of the hotel, there's the hill that leads to Windwardside's bustling Main Street; on the other, sweeping views of tropical flora end in glimmering blue. Rooms have Wi-Fi service to keep you in touch and balcony hammocks to make you wonder why you want to be. Air-conditioning (Juliana's is one of the only places on the island that have it), is the icing on the cake. ⊠ *Windwardside* ☎ *599/416–2269* ≞ *599/416–2389* ⊕ *www.julianas-hotel.com* ⤚ *9 rooms, 1 apartment, 2 cottages* ⌁ *Restaurant, fans, refrigerators, cable TV, Wi-Fi, pool; no a/c in some rooms* ⊟ *DC, MC, V* ︎◯︎ *BP.*

$ ⊡ **Cottage Club.** Form follows function at these gingerbread bungalows, where the price is right and the proximity to downtown is ideal. Bungalows sprawl down the side of the mountain, affording a bird's-eye view of the surf crashing into the rocks hundreds of feet below. (Nos. 1, 2, and 6 have the most striking vistas.) And the pool is tucked away in the trees, giving it the feel of a true tropical hideaway. Inside, queen-size beds hang out in scarcely decorated rooms, which come complete with kitchens. ✉ *Windwardside* ☎ *599/416–2486 or 599/416–2386* 🖷 *599/416–2476* ⊕ *www.cottage-club.com* ↴ *10 cottages* ⚷ *Kitchens, cable TV, pool; no a/c* ▤ *MC, V* ⏏ *EP.*

$ 🏨 **Ecolodge Rendez-Vous.** If you're serious about getting back to nature, this inn, buried deep in the rain forest, is for you. Just off the Crispeen Track via the Mount Scenery Trail, the lodge is solar-powered, which means sun showers, no television, and candlelight after dark. The 12 cottages contain only the basics (their charm comes from ornate nature-theme wall paintings done by local artist and owner Heleen Cornet). Interspersed among them are herb and vegetable gardens, whose produce is used in the Rainforest Restaurant. In 2005, a swimming pool—cleaned, of course, with an environmentally sensitive process—joined the on-site sweat lodge as just one more means of relaxation. ✉ *Crispeen Track, Windwardside* ☎ *599/416–3348* 🖷 *599/416–3299* ⊕ *www.ecolodge-saba.com* ↴ *12 cottages* ⚷ *Restaurant, some kitchenettes; no a/c, no room phones, no room TVs* ▤ *MC, V* ⏏ *EP.*

$ 🏨 **Gate House.** Aptly named, the Gate House rests in Lower Hell's Gate, the Saban equivalent of the suburbs. The rooms are as good an option as any in their price range but are relatively nondescript. The hotel's two high points, however, come in the form of a great French restaurant (the Gate House Café has fare so fine you won't want to eat anywhere else, though the prices might force you to) and the villa, an eight-person enclave nestled among banana trees just down the hill from the main house. The rustic hideaway has a spacious, comfortable living area and its own private pool. ✉ *Hell's Gate* ☎ *599/416–2416* 🖷 *599/416–2550* ⊕ *www.sabagatehouse.com* ↴ *5 rooms, 1 cottage, 1 villa* ⚷ *Restaurant, pool; no a/c, no TV in some rooms* ▤ *D, MC, V* ⏏ *CP.*

$ 🏨 **Mountain Spring Villas.** In 2005, El Momo's owners branched out and up by opening three villas just a short drive up Booby Hill from their original establishment. Though the villas boast the same views as their sibling, with modern amenities like cable TV, ceiling fans, and full kitchens you won't feel quite as far from home. The three bedrooms sleep six and are priced both by day and by week for longer sojourns. Visitors have access to El Momo's pool, snack bar, and hammocks. ✉ *Booby Hill* ✑ *Box 542, Windwardside* ☎☎ *599/416–2265* ⊕ *www.mountainspringvillas.com* ↴ *3 villas* ⚷ *Snack bar, fans, kitchens, microwaves, refrigerators, cable TV, pool, shop; no a/c* ▤ *D, MC, V* ⏏ *EP.*

$ 🏨 **Scout's Place.** Owned by German dive masters Wolfgang and Barbara Tooten, this all-in-one, no-frills dive resort is especially good for the diver on a tight budget. The finned set will find everything they need: simple and basic accommodations, expert instruction, special packages with Saba Divers, decent grub, and a little late-night fun (people come in droves for Friday-night karaoke)—and all for exactly the right price. ✉ *Windwardside* ☎ *599/416–2740* 🖷 *599/416–2741* ⊕ *www.sabadivers.com* ↴ *13 rooms* ⚷ *Restaurant, fans, some refrigerators, cable TV, in-room data ports, pool, dive shop, bar, shop; no a/c* ▤ *MC, V* ⏏ *CP.*

¢–$ 🏨 **El Momo.** If you want to feel as if you're doing your ecological part without giving up every modern convenience—as you might feel if you stay at the Ecolodge Rendez-Vous—then consider these tiny cottages. They're hidden among tropical flora 1,500 feet up Booby Hill. All but two have their own bathrooms. Take in the view from a hammock in the snack bar, or lounge by the pool, which has the only bridge on the island. And be sure to pick up a bottle of the homemade banana rum on your way out; it makes a great gift, or sedative for the flight home. ⊠ *Booby Hill* ☎ *Box 542, Windwardside* ☎☎ *599/416–2265* ⊕ *www. elmomo.com* ⇱ *7 cottages, 5 with bath* ⌂ *Snack bar, some kitchens, pool, shop; no a/c, no room TVs* ⊟ *D, MC, V* ⑩ *EP.*

Where to Eat

The island might be petite, but there's no shortage of mouthwatering fare from French to fresh seafood to Caribbean specialties. Reservations are necessary, as most of the restaurants are quite small. In addition, some places provide transportation.

What to Wear

Restaurants are informal. Shorts are fine during the day, but for dinner you may want to put on pants or a casual sundress. Just remember that nights in Windwardside can be cool due to the elevation.

CARIBBEAN
$–$$$

✕ **Lollipop's.** The expansive view from the floor-to-ceiling windows more than makes up for the restaurant's drab decor. At dinnertime you'll find a decently priced menu that consists primarily of seafood and vegetarian dishes. For Sunday brunch, the best reason to venture here, there are eggs benedict, saltfish, johnnycakes, crabmeat, ribs, chicken—the list goes on and on. And it all goes for $10. The restaurant offers both takeout and longer weekend hours (9 PM–2 AM) than most other eateries on the island, but late-night is party time, and the place is likely to be packed to the gills. No reservations are necessary, but if you call, someone will pick you up and drop you off—a sweet touch, indeed. ⊠ *St. John's* ☎ *599/416–3330* ⊟ *MC, V.*

$–$$

✕ **Family Deli/Bakery.** If you can get past its rather unimpressive name, you'll find that this local favorite is beloved for a reason. From the veranda, which overlooks the bustling main drag, you can get a flavor for the Bottom at night as you sip Heineken, the island's unofficial beer, and sup on just-caught seafood. Coconut shrimp and conch stew are two of the specialties. Or visit during the day for fresh breads, cakes, and pastries. ⊠ *The Bottom* ☎ *559/416–3858* ⊟ *MC, V.*

¢–$

✕ **Pop's Place.** Directly on the water overlooking the pier in Fort Bay is this itty-bitty come-as-you-are, Caribbean-flavored shack. Inside you'll find three tables, a tiny bar, and reggae music to really put you in the mood. Watch the divers come in as you dine on lobster sandwiches, the absolute best on the island. ⊠ *Fort Bay* ☎ *599/416–3480* ☉ *Closed Mon.*

CONTEMPORARY
$$–$$$

✕ **My Kitchen/Mijn Keuken.** This relaxed, rooftop restaurant in the heart of town has undergone a complete culinary transformation since it changed hands in 2005. The new owner—straight from Holland—has concocted a seafood-heavy menu complete with a rotating list of specials determined by the season and whether the supply boat from St. Maarten was able to dock that week. The seared spicy tuna, the grouper in creamy garlic sauce, and the escargots stand out. ⌧ *Windwardside* ☎ *599/416–2539* ▭ *MC, V.*

★ **$–$$** ✕ **Rainforest Restaurant.** You need a flashlight for the 10-minute hike down the Crispeen Track, by way of the Mount Scenery Trail, to find this restaurant in the middle of the rain forest. It's worth every bit of the trouble, though. Fresh seafood is always available, vegetables are picked fresh from the restaurant's own garden, and the steaks are huge. On Wednesday you can enjoy a guided ecological tour of the island via slideshow while you sup. There's no need for music—the lilting sound of the tree frogs is concert enough. ⌧ *Ecolodge Rendez-Vous, Crispeen Track, Windwardside* ☎ *599/416–3888* ▭ *MC, V.*

$–$$ ✕ **Tropics Cafe.** Three meals a day are served beside the pool at Juliana's or in the cabana-style, open-air dining room. The café, no longer strictly vegetarian, is owned by the same couple that owns the hotel. Sandwiches, salads, and fresh fish dominate the menu. Go on Friday night and for $10 you can bite into a burger and catch a screening of a recently released movie, romantically projected onto a sheet strung up just beyond the pool. ⌧ *Windwardside* ☎ *599/416–2469* ▭ *MC, V* ◷ *Closed Mon.*

ECLECTIC ✕ **Willard's of Saba.** Saba's most expensive restaurant has views of the
$$$–$$$$ sea at a dizzying 2,000 feet below. An enthusiastic, charming cook, Corazon de Johnson fuses international and Asian cuisine. If you miss the sunset, ask to see her photos of the famous green flash. (She loves to share when she has time.) Access to the restaurant is up a steep drive; only a few taxis will make the climb, but you can call the restaurant to arrange transport. ⌧ *Willard's of Saba, Windwardside* ☎ *599/416–2498* ▭ *AE, D, MC, V.*

$$–$$$ ✕ **King's Crown.** This dimly lighted, highly romantic restaurant has ditched its one-entrée-a-night offering in favor of a little variety. And what variety: Spanish gazpacho, French pâté, Caribbean barbecue, and New York strip steak are just a few of the international items that grace the menu. After dinner you can dance under the stars. Poolside parties, musical events, and theme nights with international flavors spice things up. ⌧ *Queen's Garden Resort, 1 Troy Hill Dr., Troy Hill* ☎ *599/416– 3623* ▭ *AE, MC, V* ◷ *Closed Tues.*

★ **$–$$$** ✕ **Brigadoon.** Just as many people visit this local favorite for the exceptional fare as for the entertaining atmosphere, which stars eccentric co-owner Trish Chammaa, who entertains with jokes and brassy banter. Trish's husband slaves over supper in the back, and the result is a perfect gastronomic experience. The varied menu includes fresh lobster and a well-priced schwarma plate. Don't miss the (by reservation only) sushi on Saturday night or one of the other nightly specials. The homemade desserts are great. ⌧ *Windwardside* ☎ *599/416–2380* ▭ *AE, DC, MC, V* ◷ *Closed Tues. No lunch.*

$–$$$ ✕ **Scout's Place.** The food here, which runs the gamut from goat stew to spit-roasted chicken, serves its purpose: It'll fill you up but isn't going to win any awards. That said, there's a great reason to come here, and it's called atmosphere. Locals flock here on Friday for karaoke, and there's bound to be a group looking for fun on every other night of the week.

17

Sit on the outdoor veranda, which has stunning views of the water, the tiny houses, and the lush forest that make Saba so picturesque. ⊠ *Scout's Place, Windwardside* ☎ *599/416–2740* ▭ *MC, V.*

$–$$ ✕ **Swinging Doors.** A cross between an English pub and an Old West saloon (yes, there are swinging doors), this lively watering hole serves not-to-be-missed barbecue on Tuesday and Friday nights. Pick from ribs or chicken, and don't forget to ask for peanut sauce—you'll be glad you did. Expect plenty of conversation, including some local gossip. ⊠ *Windwardside* ☎ *599/416–2506* ▭ *No credit cards.*

$ ✕ **In Two Deep.** The owners of the Saba Deep dive shop run this lively harborside spot, with its stained-glass window and mahogany bar. The soups and sandwiches (especially the Reuben) are excellent, and the customers are usually high-spirited—most have just come from a dive. Dinner is occasionally served, but only on holidays. ⊠ *Fort Bay* ☎ *599/416–3438* ▭ *MC, V* ⊘ *No dinner.*

¢–$ ✕ **Saba's Treasure.** Right in the heart of Windwardside sits this relaxed restaurant whose interior is crafted to look like the interior of a ship. Outside you practically sit on the street (grab one of these chairs for maximum local flavor). Go for a quick meal of stone-oven pizza or beer-battered shrimp, or linger over a drink at the tiny bar. ⊠ *Windwardside* ☎ *599/416–2819* ▭ *AE, MC, V* ⊘ *Closed Sun.*

FRENCH ✕ **Gate House Café.** It's well worth the trip to this out-of-the-way loca-
★ **$$–$$$$** tion to sample self-taught chef Michel Job's delicious French cuisine. To complement his entrées, from both land and sea, choose from the extensive wine list, winner of awards from *Wine Spectator* for four years running. Go early for cocktails on the verandah overlooking the ocean and stay late to enjoy Job's flourless Death by Chocolate, every inch of which he made with his own two hands. Lunch and dinner are served seven days a week, and pickup service is available. ⊠ *Gate House Hotel, Hell's Gate* ☎ *599/416–2416* ▭ *D, MC, V.*

Sports & the Outdoors

DIVING & Saba is one of the world's premier scuba-diving destinations. Visibility
SNORKELING is extraordinary, and dive sites are alive with corals and other sea crea-
Fodor'sChoice tures. Within ½ mi (¾ km) of shore, sea walls drop to depths of more
★ than 1,000 feet. The Saba National Marine Park, which includes shoals, reefs, and sea walls alive with corals and other sea creatures, is dedicated to preserving its marine life.

Divers have a pick of 28 sites, including **Third Encounter,** a top-rated pinnacle dive (usually to about 110 feet) for advanced divers, with plentiful fish and spectacular coral; **Man of War Shoals,** another hot pinnacle dive (70 feet), with outstanding fish and coral varieties; and **Ladder Labyrinth,** a formation of ridges and alleys (down to 80 feet), where likely sightings include grouper, sea turtles, and sharks.

Snorkelers need not feel left out: the marine park has several marked spots where reefs or rocks sit in shallow water. Among these sites is **Torrens Point** on the northwest side of the island. Waterproof maps are available from the marine park, the Saba Conservation Foundation, or dive shops.

Expect to pay about $50 for a one-tank dive, around $90 for a two-tank dive. Here are some dive operators that can help get you started. Owned by German divers, **Saba Divers** (⊠ Windwardside ☎ 599/416–2740 ⊕ www.sabadivers.com) offers multilingual instruction, making this a great option for anyone interested in meeting international divers or in practicing their language skills. It's the only outfit on the island that allows its customers to dive Nitrox for free. The crew at **Sea Saba** (⊠ Windwardside ☎ 599/416–2246 ⊕ www.seasaba.com) is both knowledgeable and jovial, making a day on the boat an illuminating and enjoyable experience for any diver. If you're looking for a more intimate dive experience, try **Saba Deep** (⊠ Fort Bay ☎ 599/416–3347 🖷 599/416–3497 ⊕ www.sabadeep.com), which tends to take out smaller groups. The company offers PADI- and/or NAUI-certified instructors.

Since 2003, local dive operator Lynn Costenaro, of Sea Saba, orchestrates an event that has become an international attraction. **Sea and Learn** (☎ 599/416–2246 ⊕ www.seaandlearn.org) is when pharmacologists, biologists, and other nature experts from all over the world descend on Saba during the month of October to give presentations, lead field trips, and show off research projects, all of which are designed to increase environmental awareness. Past events have included monitoring undersea octopus checkpoints and studying the medicinal value of indigenous plants. There are even special events for kids. And best of all, it's free. You can sign up online.

HEALTH CLUBS & DAY SPAS If huffing it up and down the mountains—not to mention just back to your hotel—isn't enough for you, swing over to **Vitality** (⊠ Windwardside ☎ 599/416–2751) to work out, take Hatha yoga or Pilates classes, or get a Thai massage. Private sessions are offered by appointment. It's closed on Thursday. **Saba Day Spa** (⊠ Windwardside ☎ 599/416–3488) has cozy facilities above Swinging Doors in Windwardside. Owner Sally Myers' expert hands (she was certified in the U.S.) more than make up for the small size of the establishment. Get a 50-minute massage or mini-facial for $60. Appointments are necessary.

HIKING On Saba you can't avoid some hiking, even if you just go to mail a postcard. The big deal, of course, is Mount Scenery, with 1,064 steps leading to its top. For information about Saba's 18 recommended botanical hikes, check with the **Saba Conservation Foundation** (⊠ Fort Bay ☎ 599/416–3295 ⊠ Trail Shop, Windwardside ☎ 599/416–2630 ⊕ www.sabapark.org), which maintains trails, or at the foundation's shop in Windwardside. Botanical tours are available on request. Crocodile James (James Johnson) will explain the local flora and fauna. A guided, strenuous full-day hike through the undeveloped back side of Mount Scenery costs about $50.

Shopping

The history of Saba lace, one of the island's most popular purchases, goes back to the late 19th century. Gertrude Johnson learned lace making at a Caracas convent school. She returned to Saba in the 1870s and taught the art that has endured ever since. Saban ladies display and sell their creations at the community center in Hell's Gate and from their houses; just follow the signs. Collars, tea towels, napkins, and other small articles are relatively inexpensive; larger ones, such as tablecloths, can be pricey. The fabric requires some care—it's not drip-dry. Saba Spice is another island buy. Although it *sounds* as delicate as lace and the aroma is as sweet as can be, the base for this liqueur is 151-proof rum. You can find souvenirs, gifts, and *Saban Cottages: A Book of Watercolors,* in almost every shop.

El Momo Folk Art (⊠ Windwardside ☎ 599/416–2518) has silk-screen T-shirts and souvenirs. **Jobean Glass** (☎ 599/416–2490) sells intricate handmade glass-bead jewelry as well as sterling silver and gold pieces by artist-owner Jo Bean. She also offers workshops in beadwork. The **Lynn Gallery** (⊠ Windwardside ☎ 599/416–2435) is open by appointment or by chance. It sells artwork by the multitalented Lynn family, which also has a gallery in St. Martin's Grand Case. From watercolors

★ of local houses to ocean-inspired sculpture, the **Peanut Gallery** (⊠ Windwardside ☎ 599/416–2509) offers the island's best selection of local and Caribbean art. Take time to browse through the offerings, and you might just walk away with something better than a refrigerator magnet with

★ which to remember your trip. The **Saba Artisan Foundation** (⊠ The Bottom ☎ 599/416–3260) turns out hand-screened fabrics that you can buy by the yard or that are already made into resort clothing. It's also a central location where you can buy the famous Saba lace as well as T-shirts and spices. **Sea Saba** (⊠ Windwardside ☎ 599/416–2246) carries T-shirts, diving equipment, clothing, and books. The **Yellow House & Around the Bend** (⊠ Windwardside ☎ 599/416–2334) sells local books, souvenirs, gift items, and lace.

Nightlife

Check the bulletin board in each village for a list of events, which often include parties. From 8 PM until late night on weekends, Caribbean DJs spin House music at the lively **Hypnotik** (⊠ The Bottom ☎ 599/416–3780). Wednesday is ladies' night, when women can drink the house-made rum punch for free. **Scout's Place** (⊠ Windwardside ☎ 599/416–2740) is a popular evening gathering place. The convivial bar can get crowded, and sometimes there's dancing. Go on Friday for karaoke night, when people swarm the spacious dining area.

Exploring Saba

Getting around the island means negotiating the narrow, twisting roadway that clings to the mountainside and rises from sea level to almost 2,000 feet. Although driving isn't difficult, just be sure to go slowly and cautiously. If in doubt, leave the driving to a cabbie so you can enjoy the scenery.

Numbers in the margins refer to points of interest on the Saba map.

The Bottom. Sitting in a bowl-shape valley 820 feet above the sea, this town is the seat of government and the home of the lieutenant governor. The gubernatorial mansion, next to Wilhelmina Park, has fancy fret-

Engineering Feats

TO VIEW SABA FROM A DISTANCE is to be baffled—the island soars out of the Caribbean Sea, cone-shape like the volcano that formed it, with steep, rocky shores providing a seemingly impassable barrier to the outside world. How anyone saw this land as inhabitable is a mystery. But Sabans are a tenacious lot, and they were bound and determined to make this island theirs.

Among the sheer rock walls that surround Saba, at what is now Fort Bay, settlers found a tiny cove where entrance was possible. They navigated rowboats in between the crashing waves, steadied themselves against the swell, and then, waist-deep in water, pulled the boats to shore. Nothing got onto the island without coming this way, not a person, nor set of dishes, nor sofa. From there, supplies were hauled up a steep path composed of more than 200 steps (all of different heights and widths) in the hands or on the heads of Sabans. The trail had been carved into the mountain and climbed 820 feet above sea level to the Bottom through a grand crevice. Visitors who were unable to climb were carried to the top at a cost of 30 guilders.

For nearly 300 years after Saba was settled, this was how it was done. Then, in the early 1900s, the locals decided to build a road. They first approached the Dutch government for help. Legend has it that the Dutch said the grade was too steep, that it could not be done. But the Sabans would not be deterred. They took the matter into their own hands and, with no trained engineers among them, began construction in 1938. The road took five years to complete and now climbs 653 feet out of Fort Bay.

The next feat of engineering came in 1956, when the Technical Economic Counsel of Netherlands Antilles deemed tourism Saba's only marketable resource and decided a pier and an airport had to be built. With only one place flat enough for an airstrip, the airport was built on Flat Point, a solidified lava flow. In 1959, the first conventional single-engine aircraft landed on the 1,300-foot airstrip, one of the smallest in the world. The airport itself opened in 1963. Engineers first tried to build a pier in 1934, but the perpetual waves destroyed it almost immediately. In 1972, the Sabans tried again and were able to build a short, 277-foot-long pier (the sea was simply too deep for anything longer), which was unfortunately too small to accommodate large cruise ships, a major thorn in the tourism industry's side.

17

work, a high-pitched roof, and wraparound double galleries. Saba University School of Medicine runs a **medical school** in the Bottom, at which about 250 students are enrolled.

On the other side of town is the Wesleyan Holiness Church, a small stone building with white fretwork. Though it's been renovated and virtually reconstructed over the years, its original four walls date from 1919; go inside and look around. Stroll by the church, beyond a place called the Gap, to a lookout point where you can see the 400 rough-hewn steps leading down to Ladder Bay. This and Fort Bay were the two landing sites from which Saba's first settlers had to haul themselves and their possessions up to the heights. Sabans sometimes walk down to Ladder Bay to picnic. Think long and hard before you do: climbing back requires 400 steps.

2 **Cove Bay.** Near the airport on the island's northeastern side, a 20-foot-long strip of rocks and pebbles laced with gray sand is really the only place for sunning. There's also a small tide pool here for swimming.

1 **Flat Point.** This is the only place on the island where planes can land. The runway here is one of the world's shortest, with a length of approximately 1,300 feet. Only STOL (short takeoff and landing) prop planes dare land here, as each end of the runway drops off more than 100 feet into the crashing surf below.

7 **Fort Bay.** The end of the Road is also the jumping-off place for all of Saba's dive operations and the location of the St. Maarten ferry dock. The island's only gas station is here, as is a 277-foot deep-water pier that accommodates the tenders from ships. On the quay are a decompression chamber, one of the few in the Caribbean, and three dive shops. In Two Deep and Pop's Place are two good places to catch your breath while enjoying some refreshments and the view of the water.

Established in 1987 to preserve and manage the island's marine resources, the **Saba National Marine Park** encircles the entire island, dipping down to 200 feet, and is zoned for diving, swimming, fishing, boating, and anchorage. One of the unique aspects of Saba's diving is the submerged pinnacles at about the 70-foot depth mark. Here all forms of sea creatures rendezvous. The information center offers talks and slide shows for divers and snorkelers and provides literature on marine life. (Divers are requested to contribute $3 a dive to help maintain the park facilities.) Before you visit, call first to see if anyone is around. ⊠ *Saba Conservation Foundation/Marine Park Visitors Center, Fort Bay* ☎ *599/416–3295* ⊕ *www.sabapark.org* ☺ *Weekdays 8–4.*

3 **Hell's Gate.** The Road makes 14 hairpin turns up nearly 2,000 vertical feet to Hell's Gate. Holy Rosary Church, on Zion's Hill, is a stone structure that looks medieval but was built in 1962. In the community center behind the church, village ladies sell their intricate lace. The same ladies make the potent rum-based Saba Spice, each according to her old family recipe. The intrepid can venture to Lower Hell's Gate, where the Old Sulphur Mine Walk leads to bat caves (with a sulfuric stench) that can—with caution—be explored.

4 **Mount Scenery.** Stone and concrete steps—1,064 of them—rise to the top

FodorsChoice
★

of Mount Scenery. En route to the mahogany grove at the summit, the steps pass giant elephant ears, ferns, begonias, mangoes, palms, and orchids; there are six identifiable ecosystems in all. The staff at the trail shop in Windwardside can provide a field guide. Have your hotel pack a picnic lunch, wear sturdy shoes, and take along a jacket and a canteen of water. The round-trip excursion will take about three hours and is best begun in the early morning.

5 Windwardside. The island's second-largest village, perched at 1,968 feet, commands magnificent views of the Caribbean. Here amid the oleander bushes are rambling lanes and narrow alleyways winding through the hills, and clusters of tiny, neat houses and shops as well as the Saba Tourist Office. At the village's northern end is the Church of St. Paul's Conversion, a colonial building with a red-and-white steeple.

★ Small signs mark the way to the **Saba Museum.** This 150-year-old house, surrounded by lemongrass and clover, was once a sea captain's home. Period pieces on display include a handsome mahogany four-poster bed, an antique organ, and, in the kitchen, a rock oven. You can also look at old documents, such as a letter a Saban wrote after the hurricane of 1772, in which he sadly says, "We have lost our little all." Don't miss the delightful stroll to the museum down the stone-walled Park Lane, one of the prettiest walks in the Caribbean. ✉ *Windwardside* ☎ *No phone* 🖃 *$1 suggested donation* ☉ *Weekdays 10–4.*

SABA ESSENTIALS

To research prices, get advice from other travelers, and book travel arrangements, visit www.fodors.com.

Travel

BY AIR
The approach to Saba's tiny airstrip is as thrilling as a roller-coaster ride. The strip is one of the shortest in the world, but no need to worry, because Britton-Norman Islander aircraft are built for it. In fact, the pilot needs only half of the length of the runway to land properly. If you're nervous, don't sit on the right. The wing seems almost to scrape against the cliff side on the approach.) Once you've touched down on the airstrip, the pilot taxis an inch or two, turns, and deposits you just outside a little shoe box from 1963 called Juancho E. Yrausquin Airport. After a new terminal was added, the airport had its grand reopening in 2002.

Winair is the only airline that flies to Saba—from St. Eustatius and St. Maarten. You must pay a $6 departure tax when leaving Saba by plane for either St. Maarten or St. Eustatius, or $20 if you're continuing on an international flight. (Note: When flying home through St.

Maarten from here, list yourself as "in transit" and avoid repaying the tax in St. Maarten, which is $20.)
🛫 Airline Contact **Winair** ☎ 599/416-2255 or 800/634-4907 ⊕ www.fly-winair.com.
🛫 Airport Contact **Juancho E. Yrausquin Airport** ☎ 599/416-2255.

BY BOAT & FERRY
The Edge, a high-speed ferry, leaves St. Maarten's Pelican Marina in Simpson Bay for Fort Bay on Saba every Wednesday through Sunday at 9 AM and boards for the return trip at about 3:45 PM. The trip, which can be rough, takes just over an hour each way. Round-trip fare is $60, plus 5% extra if you pay by credit card.

Other options for a trip to or from St. Maarten are the *Voyager I,* a large catamaran that holds 150 people and runs on Tuesday and Thursday between Marigot or Philipsburg and Fort Bay, and the *Voyager II,* a large powerboat that can take 100 people and runs on Tuesday and Thursday between Marigot, Philipsburg, and Fort Bay. The fare on either *Voyageur* boat is $57, port fees included, from Marigot. Call ahead to check current schedules.

🚹 *The Edge* ☎ 599/544-2640. *Voyager I and II*
☎ 599/542-4096 ⊕ www.voyager-st-barths.com.

BY CAR

You won't need long to tour the island by
car—you can cover the entire circuitous
length of the Road in the space of a
morning. If you want to shop, have
lunch, and do some sightseeing, plan on a
full day. If you rent a car, remember that
the island's only gas station in Fort Bay
closes at 3 PM.

Carless Sabans get around the old-
fashioned ways—walking and hitchhiking
(very popular and safe). If you choose to
thumb rides, you'll need to know the rules
of the Road. To get a lift from the Bottom
(which actually is near the top of the island), sit on the wall opposite the Anglican
church; to catch one in Fort Bay, sit on the
wall opposite the Saba Deep dive center,
where the road begins to twist upward.
🚹 Car Rentals **Caja's Car Rental** ⊠ The Bottom
☎ 599/416-2388.

BY TAXI

Taxis charge a set rate for up to four people per taxi, with an additional cost for
each person more than four. The fare
from the airport to Hell's Gate is $6, to
Windwardside it's $8, and to the Bottom
it's $12.50. The fare from the Fort Bay
ferry docks to Windwardside is $9.50. A
taxi from Windwardside to the Bottom
is $6.50.

Contacts & Resources

BANKS & EXCHANGE SERVICES

Prices quoted throughout the chapter are
in U.S. dollars unless otherwise noted.

U.S. dollars are accepted everywhere, but
Saba's official currency is the Netherlands
Antilles florin (NAf; also called the
guilder). The exchange rate is fixed at NAf
1.80 to US$1. Both First Caribbean Inter-
national Bank and the Royal Bank of
Trinidad & Tobago are in Windwardside
and provide foreign-exchange services.
RBTT has the only ATM on the island.

BUSINESS HOURS

The island's two banks open weekdays at
8:30. First Caribbean International Bank
closes at 2:30, the Royal Bank of Trinidad
& Tobago (RBTT) at 3 (4 on Friday).
There's one post office in Windwardside,
open weekdays from 8 to 4. Shops are
open weekdays and Saturday from 8 to 5.

ELECTRICITY

Saba's current is 110 volts/60 cycles, and
visitors from North America should have
no trouble using their travel appliances.

EMERGENCIES

🚹 Emergency Services **Ambulance** ☎ 599/416-
3288 or 599/416-3289. **Fire** ☎ 599/416-2222. **Po-
lice** ⊠ The Bottom ☎ 599/416-3237 or 599/416-3448.
🚹 Hospitals **A. M. Edwards Medical Center** ⊠ The
Bottom ☎ 599/416-3289.
🚹 Pharmacies **Pharmacy** ⊠ A. M. Edwards Med-
ical Center, The Bottom ☎ 599/416-3289.
🚹 Scuba Diving Emergencies **Saba Marine Park
Hyperbaric Facility** ⊠ Fort Bay ☎ 599/416-3295.

INTERNET, MAIL & SHIPPING

An airmail letter to North America or Europe costs NAf 2.25; a postcard, NAf
1.10. Book reservations through a travel
agent or over the phone; mail can take a
week or two to reach the island. The post
office is in Windwardside, near Scout's
Place, and offers express mail service.
When writing to Saba, don't worry about
addresses without post-office box numbers
or street locations—on an island this size,
all mail finds its owner. However, do make
sure to include "Netherlands Antilles" and
"Caribbean" in the address.

For $5 you can get 30 minutes of Internet
access on one of three computers at the Island Communication Services Business
Center, which is open weekdays from 10
to 7, on Saturday from 10 to 5.
🚹 Island Communication Services Business Center ⊠ Windwardside ☎ 599/416-2881.

LANGUAGE

Saba's official language is Dutch, but
everyone on the island speaks English.

Sabans are always willing to help, and they enjoy conversation. If you're open to chatting, you may get some good local advice.

MEDIA

For most Sabans, news comes from other islands. You can pick up the *Daily Herald*, St. Maarten's daily paper, complete with local and national news, or tune in to SXM TV 6, St. Maarten's television station. Saba does, however, have its own radio station, PJF-1, "The Voice of Saba," which is broadcast from the Bottom. Tune in to catch anything from "Devotional Hour" to "Night Grooves."

PASSPORTS & VISAS

U.S. and Canadian citizens need proof of citizenship. A valid passport is preferred, but a birth certificate with a raised seal along with a government-issue photo ID will do. British citizens must have a British passport. All visitors must have an ongoing or return ticket.

SAFETY

Crime is generally not a problem in Saba. Take along sunscreen and sturdy, no-nonsense shoes that get a good grip on the ground. You may encounter the harmless racer snake while hiking. Don't be alarmed; these snakes lie on rocks to sun themselves but skitter off when people approach.

TAXES & SERVICE CHARGES

You must pay a $6 departure tax when leaving Saba by plane for either St. Maarten or St. Eustatius, or $20 if you're continuing on an international flight. (Note: When flying home through St. Maarten from here, list yourself as "in transit" and avoid repaying the tax in St. Maarten, which is $20.) There's no departure tax when you leave by boat. Several of the larger hotels will tack on a 10% to 15% service charge; others will build it into the rates. Call ahead to inquire about service charges. Hotels add a 5% government tax plus a 3% turnover tax to the cost of a room (sometimes it's tacked on to your bill, and other times it's built into the room rate). Restaurants on Saba usually add a service charge of 10% to 15%.

TELEPHONES

Telephone communications are excellent on the island, and you can dial direct long-distance. There are public phone booths in the Bottom and Windwardside. Phones take prepaid phone cards, which can be bought at stores throughout the island, or local coins. To call Saba from the United States, dial 011 + 599 + 416, followed by the four-digit number.

TIPPING

Even if service charges have been added to your bill, it's customary but not necessary to tip hotel personnel and restaurant waitstaff; you should tip taxi drivers, as well. About 10% to 15% should do it.

TOUR OPTIONS

The taxi drivers who meet the planes at the airport or the boats at Fort Bay conduct tours of the island. Tours can also be arranged by dive shops or hotels. A full-day trek costs $40 for one to four passengers and $10 per person for groups larger than four. If you're in from St. Maarten for a day trip, you can do a full morning of sightseeing, stop off for lunch (have your driver make reservations before starting), complete the tour afterward, and return to the airport in time to make the last flight back to St. Maarten. Guides are available for hiking; arrangements may be made through the tourist office or the trail shop in Windwardside. Or check out the island in a guided boat tour available for groups of up to 10 on Tuesday and Wednesday. In an hour and a half you will circle the island while learning about its history, its indigenous sea-bird population, and its coral reefs.

VISITOR INFORMATION

🅵 **Saba Tourist Office** ⊕ www.sabatourism.com ⌚ Box 527, Windwardside ☎ 599/416-2231 or 599/416-2322 🖷 599/416-2350.

WEDDINGS

It isn't difficult to get married on Saba, but it does take a little preparation. A couple months before you travel, register via e-mail to secure a date and obtain all the necessary information, including the paperwork you need to submit beforehand. Include a letter requesting permission to be married on the island, addressed to the lieutenant governor of Saba. If you choose to be married somewhere other than in the Court Room at the Government Building, you must submit a written request to the lieutenant governor. Weddings are popular on Saba, and most of the hotels are willing to accommodate and cater provided you plan ahead. (Queen's Garden Resort is a particularly romantic spot.) The actual cost of the wedding ranges from $42 to $62, depending on when and where the ceremony is performed.

🏛 **Lt. Governor of Saba** 📖 Government Offices, The Bottom.

St. Barthélemy

Luxuriating in the surf at Anse à Colombier

WORD OF MOUTH

"The best dinner we had on St. Barths was the pâté, baguette, brie, and wine that we bought at a French deli and ate at sunset on a totally deserted beach! So romantic!"

—chicgeek

"Don't miss Saline beach! The water is pure turquoise blue and white sand beach—looks like the South Pacific."

—Ashley

www.fodors.com/forums

WELCOME TO ST. BARTHÉLEMY

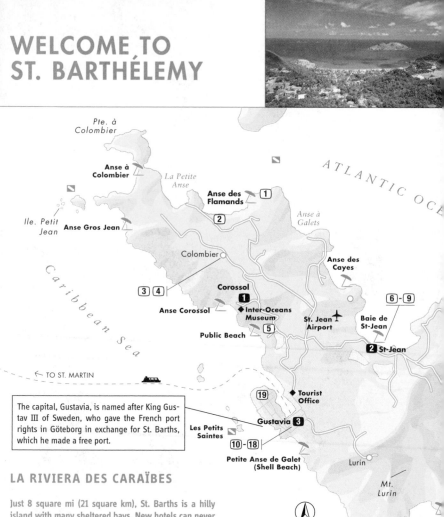

Pte. à Colombier

Anse à Colombier

La Petite Anse

Anse des Flamands 1

2

Anse à Galets

ATLANTIC OCE

Ile. Petit Jean

Anse Gros Jean

Colombier

Anse des Cayes

3 4

Corossol
1

Anse Corossol

◆ Inter-Oceans Museum

St. Jean ✈ Airport

Baie de St-Jean

6 - 9

Public Beach

5

2 St-Jean

← TO ST. MARTIN

◆ Tourist Office

19

The capital, Gustavia, is named after King Gustav III of Sweden, who gave the French port rights in Göteborg in exchange for St. Barths, which he made a free port.

Les Petits Saintes

Gustavia 3

10 - 18

Petite Anse de Galet (Shell Beach)

Lurin

Mt. Lurin

LA RIVIERA DES CARAÏBES

Just 8 square mi (21 square km), St. Barths is a hilly island with many sheltered bays. New hotels can never have more than 12 rooms, so you will find no high-rise resorts to spoil your views. The French, who had controlled the island since the late 17th century, gave it to Sweden in 1784 but finally reclaimed it in 1877.

Anse Gouver

Grande Pt.

Chic travelers put aside their cell phones long enough to enjoy the lovely beaches—long, surf-pounded strands; idyllic crescents crowded by cliffs or forests; glass-smooth lagoons perfect for windsurfing. Nothing on St. Barths comes cheap. But on a hotel's awning-shaded terrace, St. Barths' civilized ways seem worth every penny.

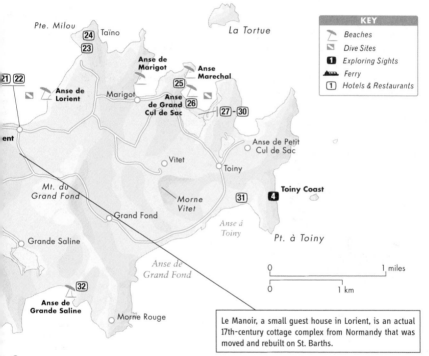

KEY

> Beaches
◣ Dive Sites
1 Exploring Sights
⛴ Ferry
① Hotels & Restaurants

ST. BARTHÉLEMY

18

Le Manoir, a small guest house in Lorient, is an actual
17th-century cottage complex from Normandy that was
moved and rebuilt on St. Barths.

TOP 4 REASONS TO VISIT ST. BARTHÉLEMY

❶ The island is active, sexy, hedonistic, and hip, with plenty of attractive young people as scenery.

❸ Shopping for stylish clothes and fashion accessories is better nowhere else in the Caribbean.

❷ If food and wine are your true loves, then you'll find your bliss here.

❹ Windsurfing and other water sports make going to the beach more than just a sun-tanning experience.

ST. BARTHÉLEMY PLANNER

Getting to St. Barths

There are no direct flights to St. Barths (SBH). No, not even on your private Gulfstream. You must fly to another island and then catch a smaller plane for the hop over. Most Americans fly first to St. Maarten, and then take the 10-minute flight to St. Barths, but you can also connect through St. Thomas or San Juan. There are also ferries from St. Martin, but their schedules are really geared for day-trippers.

Hassle Factor: Medium

Where to Stay

Most top hotels are on the northern beaches, but in the nearby hills are a number of relatively reasonable small hotels and guesthouses. Many visitors stay in villas, which can be simple bungalows or extravagantly decorated homes with infinity pools, but few of these are directly on the beach. More hotels and restaurants here have seasonal closings (at least some part of August through October) than on other islands. If you're on a "budget," rates can drop by 50% after mid-April.

On the Ground

Many hotels offer free airport transfers. Otherwise, there's a taxi stand at the airport; unmetered taxis cost about €10 to €25, depending on distance. Settle on a fare before you get in. Taxis virtually disappear at night, so you'll probably need to rent a car during your stay; it's an absolute necessity if you are staying in a villa. You might be able to rent a car directly from your hotel; otherwise, you should reserve one in advance of your trip. Some automatics are available, but you'll most likely get a small, manual four-wheel-drive vehicle. Charges average about $55 a day; automatics usually cost at least a third more.

Activities

St. Barths is about relaxing and reviving in high style. The most popular activity is **fine-dining,** and the most popular sport is **shopping.** Most other activities are on the water; the **yachting** scene is strong, as is **windsurfing. Beaches** are numerous and mostly good, though almost never truly great, but you'll definitely want to explore a few of them. The **diving** is good, though not excellent.

Hotel & Restaurant Costs

WHAT IT COSTS in Euros

	$$$$	$$$	$$	$	¢
Restaurants	over €30	€20–€30	€12–€20	€8–€12	under €8
Hotels*	over €350	€250–€350	€150–€250	€80–€150	under €80
Hotels**	over €450	€350–€450	€250–€350	€125–€250	under €125

*EP, BP, CP   **AI, FAP, MAP
Restaurant prices are for a main course at dinner and include a 15% service charge. Hotel prices are per night for a double room in high season, excluding taxes, 10%–15% service charge, and meal plans.

Updated by
Elise Meyer

STEPPING ONTO THE VILLA PATIO, I watch the sun rise over the volcanic mountain, glittering on the cobalt sea, and bathing the hills in a golden light. I stretch lazily, detecting the aroma of freshly brewed coffee. Should breakfast be an almond croissant? Or should we just have the ethereal brioche we discovered yesterday? I decide that a walk to the *boulangerie* is in order, especially in light of that new bikini. Ahhh, another perfect day in paradise. I make a mental note to book another Thai massage for Friday and grab my sunglasses. Is there any way this could be any better?

St. Barthélemy blends the respective essences of the Caribbean and France in perfect proportions. A sophisticated but unstudied approach to relaxation and respite prevails: you can spend the day on a beach, try on the latest French fashions, and watch the sun set while nibbling tapas over Gustavia Harbor, then choose from nearly 100 excellent restaurants for an elegant evening meal. You can putter around the island, scuba dive, windsurf on a quiet cove, or just admire the lovely views.

A mere 8 square mi (21 square km), St. Barths is a hilly island, with many sheltered inlets providing visitors with many opportunities to try out picturesque, quiet beaches. The town of Gustavia wraps itself neatly around a lilliputian harbor lined with impressive yachts and rustic fishing boats. Red-roofed bungalows dot the hillsides. Beaches run the gamut from calm to "surfable," from deserted to packed. The cuisine is tops in the Caribbean, part of the French *savoir vivre* that prevails throughout the island.

Longtime visitors speak wistfully of the old, quiet St. Barths. Development has quickened the pace of life here, that's true, but the island hasn't yet been overbuilt, and a 1982 ordinance limited new tourist lodgings to 12 rooms. The largest hotel—the Guanahani—has fewer than 100 rooms; the island's other rooms are divided among some 40 small hotels and guesthouses. About half the island's visitors stay in private villas. The tiny planes that arrive with regularity still land at the tidy airport only during daylight hours. And although "nightlife" usually means a leisurely dinner and a stargazing walk on the beach, something of a renaissance is under way, and a couple of hot new clubs might give you a reason to pack a pair of dancing shoes.

Christopher Columbus discovered the island—called "Ouanalao" by its native Carib Indians—in 1493; he named it for his brother Bartholomé. The first group of French colonists arrived in 1648, drawn by the ideal location on the West Indian Trade Route, but they were wiped out by the Caribs, who dominated the area. Another small group from Normandy and Brittany arrived in 1694. This time the settlers prospered—with the help of French buccaneers, who took advantage of the island's strategic location and protected harbor. In 1784 the French traded the island to King Gustav III of Sweden in exchange for port rights in Göteborg. The king dubbed the capital Gustavia, laid out and paved streets, built three forts, and turned the community into a prosperous free port. The island thrived as a shipping and commercial center until the 19th century, when earthquakes, fires, and hurricanes brought financial ruin.

Many residents fled for newer lands of opportunity, and Oscar II of Sweden decided to return the island to France. After briefly considering selling it to America, the French took possession of Saint-Barthélemy again on August 10, 1877.

Today the island is still a free port and is part of an overseas department of France. Arid, hilly, and rocky, St. Barths was unsuited to sugar production and thus never developed an extensive slave base. Most of the 3,000 current residents are descendants of the tough Norman and Breton settlers of three centuries ago. They are feisty, industrious, and friendly—but insular. However, you will find many new, young French arrivals, predominantly from northwestern France and Provence, who speak English well.

Where to Stay

There's no denying that hotel rooms and villas on St. Barths carry high prices, and the current weakness of the dollar makes for a costly respite. You're paying primarily for the privilege of staying on the island, and even at $500 a night the bedrooms tend to be small. Still, if you're flexible—in terms of timing and in your choice of lodgings—you can enjoy a holiday in St. Barths and still afford to send the kids to college.

The most expensive season falls during the holidays (mid-December to early January), when hotels are booked far in advance, usually require a 10- or 14-day stay, and can be double the high-season rates. A controversial tax on hotel and villa rental rates has been abandoned, so you should not have any surcharge on your bill.

VILLAS & CONDOMINIUMS
On St. Barths, the term "villa" is used to describe anything from a small cottage to a luxurious, modern estate. Today almost half of St. Barths' accommodations are in villas, and we recommend considering this option, especially if you're traveling with friends or family. An advantage to Americans is that villa rates are usually quoted and confirmed in dollars, thus bypassing unfavorable euro fluctuations. Most villas have a small private swimming pool and maid service daily except Sunday. They are well furnished with linens, kitchen utensils, and such electronic playthings as CD and DVD players, satellite TV, and broadband Internet connections. In-season rates range from $1,400 to $40,000 a week. Most villa-rental companies are based in the United States and have extensive Web sites so you can see pictures of the place you're renting; their local offices oversee maintenance and housekeeping and provide concierge services to clients. Just be aware that there are few beachfront villas, so if you have your heart set on "toes in the sand" and a cute waiter delivering your kir royale, stick with the hotels.

St. Barth Properties, Inc. (☎ 508/528–7727 or 800/421–3396 🖷 508/528–7789 ⊕ www.stbarth.com), owned by American Peg Walsh—a regular on St. Barths since 1986—represents more than 120 properties here and can guide you to the perfect place to stay. Weekly peak-season rates range from $1,400 to $40,000 depending on the property's size, location, and amenities. The excellent Web site offers virtual tours of most of the villas and even details of availability. An office in Gustavia can take care

Bliss & More

VISITORS TO ST. BARTHS can enjoy more than the comforts of home by taking advantage of any of the myriad spa and beauty treatments that are now available on the island. In 2005 two major hotels opened beautiful and comprehensive spas. Both the Isle de France and Guanahani hotels offer their guests an extensive array of spa treatments—for both men and women—either à la carte or as part of a package. Visitors to the island who are not staying at these hotels may also book treatments, depending on availability. In addition, scores of independent therapists will come to your hotel room or villa and provide any therapeutic discipline you can think of, including yoga, Thai massage, shiatsu, reflexology, and even manicures, pedicures, and hairdressing.

of any problems you may have and offers some concierge-type services. **Wimco** (☎ 800/932–3222 ☎ 401/847–6290 ⊕ www.wimco.com), which is based in Rhode Island, oversees bookings for more than 230 properties on St. Barths that are represented by SiBarth Real Estate. Rents range from $2,000 to $10,000 for two- and three-bedroom villas; larger villas rent for $7,000 per week and up. Properties can be previewed and reserved on Wimco's Web site, or you can obtain a catalog by mail. Wimco's Web site lists occasional last-minute specials. The company will arrange for babysitters, massages, chefs, and other in-villa services for clients, as well as private air-charters.

Hotels

When it comes to booking a hotel on St. Barths, the reservation manager can be your best ally. Rooms within a property can vary greatly. It's well worth the price of a phone call or the time investment of an e-mail correspondence to make a personal connection, which can mean much in arranging a room that meets your needs or preferences. Details of accessibility, views, recent redecorating, meal options, and special package rates are topics open for discussion. Most quoted hotel rates are per-room, not per-person, and include service charges and airport transfers.

$$$$ 🏨 **Carl Gustaf.** This luxurious hotel right in Gustavia is an acceptable option if you don't want to do much driving—it's even within walking distance to everything in town if you don't mind climbing the hill. One- and two-bedroom suites with private decks and plunge pools spill down a hill overlooking quaint Gustavia Harbor. High ceilings and white rooms are decorated with nautical prints, marble baths, tiny kitchens, and such welcome extras as fax machines, two satellite TVs, DVD players, computers with Internet connections, and stereos. Summer rates and an excellent honeymoon package are offered. The Carl Gustaf restaurant, known for its classic French cuisine, is spectacular for sunset cocktails and dinner over the twinkle of the harbor lights. ⊠ *Rue des Normands, Box 700, Gustavia 97099* ☎ *0590/29–79–00* ☎ *0590/ 27–82–37* ⊕ *www.hotelcarlgustaf.com* 🛏 *14 suites* ⚐ *Restaurant,*

18

kitchenettes, minibars, refrigerators, cable TV, in-room VCRs, in-room broadband, pool, health club, sauna, piano bar ⊟ *AE, MC, V* ⊠ *CP.*

☼ **$$$$** ⊡ **Le Christopher.** With oversize rooms, sunset views, and an especially gracious staff—plus a full, American-style breakfast—this is one of the island's relative bargains, the only hotel listed whose rates are lower this year. Two-story buildings in exceptional gardens house spacious, nicely furnished—if simple—rooms with tiled baths and either a balcony or terrace. The hotel's infinity pool, which hangs over the ocean, is the largest on the island and has a wading area. The well-equipped gym also has occasional yoga and fitness classes. There's also resort-wide Wi-Fi service. Two on-site restaurants serve contemporary, tasty cuisine if you don't want to make the 15-minute drive to town. ⊠ *Pointe Milou 97133* ☎ *0590/27–63–63* 📠 *0590/27–92–92* ⊕ *www.saint-barths. com/christopherhotel* 🛏 *41 rooms, 2 suites* ☖ *2 restaurants, room service, fans, in-room safes, minibars, cable TV, in-room VCRs, Wi-Fi, pool, health club, bar, shop, laundry service, airport shuttle, car rental* ⊟ *AE, DC, MC, V* ⊠ *BP* ⊗ *Closed late Aug.–late Oct.*

$$$$ ⊡ **Eden Rock.** St. Barths' first hotel opened in the 1950s on the craggy
Fodor'sChoice bluff that splits Baie de St-Jean. Extensive renovations and an expan-
★ sion in 2005 have raised it into the top category of St. Barth properties. Each of the hotel's 29 unique rooms, suites, and villas is tastefully decorated and luxuriously appointed with plasma satellite TV and high-speed Internet. New, large bathrooms have either deep soaking tubs or walk-in showers; all have loads of fluffy towels and Bulgari suds. The six beachfront villas built on the former Filao Beach property are magnificent and sleep up to four, with full kitchens and beautifully appointed modern living areas. Stunning bay views and great service are uniform. The breakfast buffet, included in the room rate, is terrific, and the on-site restaurants are first-rate and deserving of a visit (Sand Bar for lunch and Eden Rock for a tapas-style dinner menu and drinks). ⊠ *Baie de St-Jean 97133* ☎ *0590/29–79–99, 877/563–7015 in U.S.* 📠 *0590/ 27–88–37* ⊕ *www.edenrockhotel.com* 🛏 *29 rooms* ☖ *2 restaurants, minibars, cable TV, in-room broadband, pool, snorkeling, windsurfing, 2 bars, library* ⊟ *AE, MC, V* ⊠ *BP.*

$$$$ ⊡ **François Plantation.** A colonial-era graciousness pervades this intimate, exquisite hillside complex of West Indian–style cottages. The rooms have queen-size mahogany four-poster beds and colorful fabrics. Two larger rooms can accommodate an extra bed. The pool is atop a very steep hill with magnificent views. A new incarnation of the on-site restaurant, called La Table de Plantation, features Mediterranean-nuanced French cuisine. Good-value low-season packages include a car. Villa Plantation, a new one-bedroom house on the property, is lovely and quite reasonable, with amazing views. ⊠ *Colombier 97133* ☎ *0590/29–80–22* 📠 *800/207–8071* ⊕ *www.francois-plantation.com* 🛏 *12 rooms* ☖ *Restaurant, in-room safes, minibars, refrigerators, cable TV with movies, pool* ⊟ *AE, MC, V* ⊠ *CP* ⊗ *Closed Sept. and Oct.*

★ ☼ **$$$$** ⊡ **Hotel Guanahani & Spa.** The only full-service resort on the island has lovely rooms and suites (14 of which have private pools) and impeccable personalized service, not to mention one of the only children's programs (though it's more of a nursery). Rooms, all of which have large bathrooms with Bulgari toiletries, were redecorated in 2004 in a hip and attractive grape-and-kiwi color scheme; at the same time, a stunningly serene Clarins Spa and Leonor Greyl hair salon were added. Units vary in price, privacy, view, and distance from activities, so make your preferences known. The new Wellness Suite, which is at the top of the property, becomes your own hedonistic domain after the spa closes at night. Flat-screen TVs and DVDs are new in all rooms, as is resortwide Wi-Fi service; the well-equipped gym will be expanded for 2006. also here are two well-regarded restaurants, poolside L'Indigo and dramatic Bartolomeo, which has a lively lounge with music every night until 1 AM. ⊠ *Grand Cul de Sac 97133* ☎ *0590/27–66–60* 🖷 *0590/27–70–70* ⊕ *www.leguanahani.com* ↪ *38 rooms, 33 suites, 1 3-bedroom villa* ⚒ *2 restaurants, room service, cable TV, in-room DVDs, Wi-Fi, 2 tennis courts, 2 pools, hair salon, windsurfing, boating, piano bar, shop, children's programs (ages 2–12), meeting room* ▭ *AE, MC, V* ⏀❙ *CP.*

$$$$
Fodor$Choice
★
Hôtel St-Barth Isle de France. An obsessively attentive management team ensures that every detail at this intimate, casually refined resort keeps it on the list of the very best places in St. Barths—if not the entire Caribbean. It's not hard to understand why the property boasts a 72% high-season return rate, because it gets better each season. A general technology upgrade includes a reception-area computer for guests and a broadband connection for your laptop in all rooms. Huge, luxurious rooms furnished with modern four-posters, French fabrics, and fine art have superb marble baths (all with a tub or Jacuzzi tub, both rare on the island). The beachside La Case de l'Isle restaurant serves nouvelle cuisine. The spa is by Molton Brown. The beautiful white-sand beach remains pristine. Good off-season and honeymoon packages are offered. ⊠ *Baie des Flamands 97098* ☎ *0590/27–61–81* 🖷 *0590/ 27–86–83* ⊕ *www.isle-de-france.com* ↪ *26 rooms, 7 suites* ⚒ *Restaurant, minibars, refrigerators, cable TV, in-room VCRs, in-room broadband, tennis court, 2 pools, gym, squash, bar, Internet room* ▭ *MC, V* ⏀❙ *CP* ⊘ *Closed Sept.–Oct. 15.*

$$$$
Hotel La Banane. If you're seeking that beachy-sunny Caribbean look, you should look further. The high-style and hard-edged luxury of this intimate resort should please fans of Starwood's "W" brand. However, ebony walls, chunky modern wood furniture, and sisal rugs give private bungalows unusually chic-simple serenity. Private baths have every upscale amenity. The hotel's location behind a small shopping center may either be construed as a bother or a convenience, but Lorient Beach is a two-minute walk away. Breakfast is served around the palm-shaded pool. K'fe Massaï, the African-theme restaurant, is very popular. ⊠ *Quartier Lorient 97133* ☎ *0590/52–03–00* 🖷 *0590/27–68–44* ⊕ *www.labanane.com* ↪ *9 rooms* ⚒ *Restaurant, cable TV, in-room VCRs, 2 pools, bar* ▭ *AE, MC, V* ⏀❙ *CP.*

★ **$$$$**
Les Îlets de la Plage. On the far side of the airport, tucked away at the far corner of Baie de St-Jean, these well-priced, comfortably furnished island-style one-, two-, and three-bedroom bungalows (four right on the beach, seven up a small hill) have small kitchens, pleasant open-air sitting areas, and comfortable bathrooms. This is a good choice if you want to be right on the beach with the space and convenience of a villa but

18

the feel of a small resort. Crisp white linens and upholstery, lovely verandas, and daily deliveries of fresh bread from a nearby bakery add to the pleasantness of the surroundings, though only the bedrooms are air-conditioned. ⊠ *Plage de St-Jean, 91733* ☎ *0590/27–88–57* 🖷 *0590/27–88–58* ⊕ *www.lesilets.com* ⥹ *11 bungalows* ⚲ *Fans, in-room safes, kitchens, pool, gym, beach, concierge* ▭ *AE, MC, V* ⊙ *Closed Sept. 1–Nov. 1* ¶Ⅼ *EP.*

★ **$$$$** 🖬 **Le Toiny.** When perfection is more important than price, choose Le Toiny's romantic villas with mahogany furniture, yards of colored toile, and heated private pools. Rooms have every convenience of home: lush bathrooms, fully equipped kitchenettes, and either a stair-stepper or stationary bike. High-tech amenities include several flat-screen LCD TVs, stereos, fax machines, and Bang & Olufsen phones. Each suite has an outdoor shower. Breakfast comes to your terrace each morning, and spa services can be delivered as well. If ever you want to leave your villa, Sunday brunch and haute cuisine can be had at the alfresco Le Gaiac overlooking the Italian-tile pool. ⊠ *Anse à Toiny 97133* ☎ *0590/27–88–88* 🖷 *0590/27–89–30* ⊕ *www.hotelletoiny.com* ⥹ *15 1-bedroom villas, 1 3-bedroom villa* ⚲ *Restaurant, in-room faxes, in-room safes, minibars, cable TV, in-room DVDs, pool, exercise equipment, bar, laundry service* ▭ *AE, DC, MC, V* ¶Ⅼ *CP* ⊙ *Closed Sept.–late Oct.*

★ **$$$$** 🖬 **Le Sereno.** A St. Barth classic on a beautiful stretch of beach was reborn as an ultrachic retreat in 2005 (designed by superhot Parisian architect Christian Liaigre). Cutting-edge modern decor and techno amenities create a spare but luxurious sense of serenity. The suites are large by St. Barth standards and have spacious living areas and private sundecks. Large bathrooms, some with "steeping tubs," have roomy showers and vessel sinks of solid black granite. Other perks include linens and robes from Porthault, Parisian Ex Voto toiletries, high-speed Internet, plasma TVs, and a speaker dock for iPods (yours or their fully loaded ones to borrow). Bedlike poolside lounges for two set the romantic tone for the hip all-day lounge party. ⊠ *B.P. 19 Grand-Cul-de-Sac, 27113* ☎ *0590/29–83–00* 🖷 *0580/27–75–47* ⊕ *www.lesereno.com* ⚲ *Restaurant, in-room safes, minibars, cable TV, in-room DVDs, in-room broadband, pool, gym, bar, laundry service* ▭ *AE, MC, V* ¶Ⅼ *EP.*

$$$$ 🖬 **Le Tom Beach Hôtel.** Carole Gruson and Thierry de Badereau, of hot spot Ti St. Barth, own this boutique hotel on the St-Jean beach, and it continues to raise its level of chic. A garden winds around the brightly painted suites, over the pool via a small footbridge, into the hopping, open-air restaurant La Plage. The nonstop house party often spills out onto the terraces and lasts into the wee hours. Big, plantation-style rooms have high ceilings, cozy draped beds, nice baths, a TV with DVD player, direct-dial phones, and patios. Oceanfront suites are the most expensive, but all the rooms are clean and cozy. ⊠ *Plage St-Jean 97133* ☎ *0590/27–53–13* 🖷 *0590/27–53–15* ⊕ *www.st-barths.com/tom-beach-hotel* ⥹ *12 rooms* ⚲ *Restaurant, in-room safes, minibars, refrigerators, cable TV, in-room DVDs, pool, beach, bar, Internet room* ▭ *AE, MC, V* ¶Ⅼ *CP.*

$$$–$$$$ 🖬 **Emeraude Plage.** Right on the beach of Baie de St-Jean, this small resort consists of modern and clean bungalows and villas with fully equipped outdoor kitchenettes on small patios; nice bathrooms add to the comfort. The complex is convenient to nearby restaurants and shops. Hotel guests often gather to socialize in the comfortable library-lounge. The beachfront two-bedroom villas are something of a bargain, especially off-season. ⊠ *Baie de St-Jean 97133* ☎ *0590/27–64–78* 🖷 *0590/27–83–08* ⊕ *www.emeraudeplage.com* ⇨ *21 bungalows, 4 suites, 2 cottages, 1 villa* ⌂ *Fans, in-room safes, kitchenettes, cable TV, beach, bar, library, laundry service, Internet room* ▤ *MC, V* †◯| *EP* ⊘ *Closed Sept. 1–Nov. 1.*

☼ **$$$–$$$$** ▦ **Hôtel Baie des Anges.** Everyone is treated like family at this casual retreat. Ten clean, fresh, and nicely decorated—if somewhat plain—rooms are right on serene Flamands Beach; each has a kitchenette and private terrace. There's also a small pool. The food at La Langouste, the hotel's restaurant, is tasty and reasonably priced. The proprietor also manages a four-bedroom, three-bath villa a bit farther up the hill. ⊠ *Flamands 97095* ☎ *0590/27–63–61* 🖷 *0590/27–83–44* ⊕ *www.hotelbaiedesanges. com* ⇨ *10 rooms* ⌂ *Restaurant, fans, in-room safes, kitchenettes, cable TV, pool, beach, car rental* ▤ *AE, MC, V* †◯| *EP.*

★ **$$$–$$$$** ▦ **La Paillote.** Perched high above the glittering crescent of Grand Cul de Sac, which is home to some lively restaurants, and some of the most expensive hotels on the island, this tiny compound of five private and meticulously maintained bungalows has been built by Christine and Hubert Bonnet, two young entrepreneurs and avid gardeners with an appreciation for the architecture and drama of the Greek Islands. Accommodations vary from a tiny studio to a spacious two-bedroom villa with a private pool, but all have white-draped platform beds, sitting areas, and private patios—and the comfort and elegance of much more costly island digs. ⊠ *Grand Cul de Sac 97133* ☎ *0590/27–57–95* ⊕ *www.lapaillote-st-barth.com* ⇨ *5 bungalows* ⌂ *Kitchenettes, cable TV, pool* ▤ *AE, MC, V* †◯| *EP.*

☼ **$$$–$$$$** ▦ **St-Barth's Beach Hotel & Les Residences Saint-Barths.** Active Europeans and families love this simple, budget-friendly hotel for its location on a wide, calm beach ideal for wind-borne water sports (such as kite surfing or windsurfing), a complete gym (free for guests), nice boutique, and excellent restaurant, Le Rivage. The very favorably priced hillside villas (one with a private pool) can accommodate up to seven guests and include a car. There is no Internet service for guests here. ⌂ *Box 580, Grand Cul de Sac 97098* ☎ *0590/27–60–70* 🖷 *0590/27–75–57* ⊕ *www. saintbarthbeachhotel.com* ⇨ *36 rooms, 8 villas* ⌂ *Restaurant, some kitchens, refrigerators, cable TV, pool, gym, beach, windsurfing, airport shuttle* ▤ *MC, V* ⊘ *Closed Sept.–early Oct.* †◯| *EP.*

★ **$$–$$$$** ▦ **Hôtel le Village St-Jean.** A guest checking in for his 23rd visit simply asked us, "Is there any other place to stay?" And why wouldn't he? For two generations, the Charneau family has offered friendly service and reasonable rates at its small hotel, making guests feel like a part of the family. Handsome, spacious, and comfortable, the airy stone-and-redwood cottages have high ceilings, sturdy furniture, modern baths, open-air kitchenettes, and lovely terraces with hammocks; one has a Jacuzzi. You get the advantages of a villa and the services of a hotel here. The regular rooms have refrigerators, and most have king-size beds. Reg-

18

ulars are invited to store beach equipment. The location is great—you can walk to the beach and town from here—and most rooms and cottages have gorgeous views. See if Room 12, 15, or 10, perched on the edge of the hillside, is available when you book. A lounge with a plasma TV and Internet access is a popular gathering spot. Rooms (but not cottages) include Continental breakfast in the rates. Very reasonable summer rates for cottages include a car. ⌂ *Box 623, Baie de St-Jean 97133* ☎ *0590/27–61–39 or 800/651–8366* 🖷 *0590/27–77–96* ⊕ *www.villagestjeanhotel.com* ↪ *5 rooms, 20 cottages, 1 3-bedroom villa* ♨ *Restaurant, grocery, some kitchenettes, pool, hot tub, bar, library, shops; no room TVs* 🖃 *AE, MC, V* ⊖I *EP.*

$$ 🔲 **Le P'tit Morne.** Each of the modestly furnished but freshly decorated and painted mountainside studios has a private balcony with panoramic views of the coastline. The small kitchenettes are adequate for creating picnic lunches and other light meals. The snack bar serves breakfast. It's relatively isolated here, however, and the beach is a 10-minute drive away, but the young and friendly management is eager to help you enjoy your stay. ⌂ *Box 14, Colombier 97133* ☎ *0590/52–95–50* 🖷 *0590/27–84–63* ⊕ *www.timorne.com* ↪ *14 rooms* ♨ *Snack bar, kitchenettes, cable TV, pool, library* 🖃 *AE, MC, V* ⊖I *CP.*

$–$$ 🔲 **Les Mouettes.** This guesthouse offers clean, simply furnished, and economical bungalows that open directly onto the beach. They're also quite close to the road, which can be either convenient for a quick shopping excursion or bothersome on account of the noise. Each air-conditioned bungalow has a bathroom with a shower only, a kitchenette, a patio, two double beds, and a twin bed or fold-out sofa, making this place a good bet for families on a budget. ✉ *Quartier Lorient 97133* ☎ *0590/27–77–91* 🖷 *0590/27–68–19* ✑ *www.st-barths.com/hotel-les-mouettes* ↪ *7 bungalows* ♨ *Kitchenettes, beach, shops, car rental* 🖃 *No credit cards* ⊖I *EP.*

Where to Eat

Dining on St. Barths compares favorably to almost anywhere in the world. Varied and exquisite cuisine, a French flair in the decorations, sensational wine, and attentive service make for a wonderful epicurean experience. St. Barths' style is expressed in more than 80 charming restaurants, from beachfront grills to serious establishments serving five-course meals. On most menus, freshly caught local seafood mingles on the plate with top-quality provisions that arrive regularly from Paris.

Most restaurants offer a chalkboard full of daily specials that are usually a good bet. But even the pickiest eaters will find something on every menu. The weakness of the dollar means that many restaurants have become frightfully expensive. However, you can dine superbly at a number of the island's better restaurants without breaking the bank if you watch your wine selections and share appetizers or desserts. Lunch is usually less costly than dinner.

Reservations are strongly recommended and, in high season, essential. However, except during Christmas–New Years it's not usually necessary to book far in advance. A day's—or even a few hours'—notice is usually sufficient. If you enter a restaurant without a reservation, you may not be seated, even if there are empty tables. Restaurant owners on St. Barths take great pride in their service as well as in their food, and they would rather turn you away than slight you on an understaffed evening. At the end of the meal, as in France, you must request the bill. Until you do, you can feel free to linger at the table and enjoy the complimentary vanilla rum that's likely to appear.

Check restaurant bills carefully. A service charge (*service compris*) is always added by law, but you should leave the server 5% to 10% extra in cash. You'll usually come out ahead if you charge restaurant meals on a credit card in euros instead of paying with American currency, as your credit card will offer a better exchange rate than the restaurant. Many restaurants serve locally caught lobster (*langouste*); priced by weight, it's usually the most expensive item on a menu and, depending on its size and the restaurant, will range in price from $40 to $60. In menu prices below, it has been left out of the range.

What to Wear

A bathing suit and *pareu* (sarong) are acceptable at beachside lunch spots. Most top it off with a tee or tank. Jackets are never required and rarely worn, but people dress fashionably for dinner. Casual chic is the idea; women wear whatever is hip, current, and sexy. You can't go wrong in a tank dress or a ruffly skirt and top. Nice shorts (not beachy ones) at the dinner table may label a man *américain,* but many locals have adopted the habit, and nobody cares much. Pack a light sweater or shawl for an after-dinner beach stroll.

BARBECUE ✕ **Bar B.Q.** New on the St. Barths restaurant scene in 2004, this friendly
$$–$$$ restaurant combines real Spanish-style tapas starters, such as coriander-garlic shrimp, and a generous Serrano ham and chorizo plate, followed by huge wood platters heaped with real American-style barbecue ribs and other grilled meats. If you're hungry, go for the mixed grill platter—literally a sword-full of grilled chicken, beef, lamb, and more. A plasma TV in the bar, which mixes the best mojitos in the immediate vicinity, is usually tuned to satellite sports. ⊠ *Rue du Roi Oscar II, Gustavia* ☎ *0590/51–00–05* ▭ *AE, MC, V.*

CARIBBEAN ✕ **Pipiri Palace.** Tucked into a tropical garden, this popular in-town
★ **$$–$$$$** restaurant known for its barbecued ribs, beef fillet, and rack of lamb is consistently one of our absolute favorites. Fish-market specialties like red snapper cooked in a banana leaf or grilled tuna are good here, as are grilled duck with mushroom sauce and a skewered surf-and-turf with a green curry sauce. The blackboard lists daily specials that are usually a great choice, like a salad of tomato, mango, and basil. Pierrot, the friendly owner, is sure to take good care of you. ⊠ *Rue Général-de-Gaulle, Gustavia* ☎ *0590/27–53–20* ⌂ *Reservations essential* ▭ *MC, V* ☉ *Closed mid-June and July.*

$$–$$$ ✕ **La Gloriette.** This friendly, down-to-earth beachside spot serves delicious local creole dishes, such as crunchy accras and a cassoulet of local lobster, grilled fresh fish, meats, and light salads. Daily tasting menus, both creole and French, feature lobster specialties. This restaurant is open

18

on Sunday nights, when some other restaurants close. ✉ *Grand Cul de Sac* ☎ *0590/27–75–66* ▭ *AE, MC, V* ☉ *Closed Wed.*

★ **$$–$$$** ✕ **Le Rivage.** This popular, affordable restaurant received a needed face-lift in 2004, and it's a good choice for a beachside lunch or a casual seaside dinner. Huge salads, such as warm chèvre with bacon, cold mixed seafood, and classic salade niçoise (with tuna, olives, green beans, and hard-boiled eggs), are always good, but the menu also includes pastas, creole specialties, grilled fresh seafood, and steaks. This is a good place to try some creole specialties; there is a tasting platter that includes the classics. Save room for the warm apple pastry or warm chocolate cake with vanilla sauce for dessert. If you come for lunch, you can spend the rest of the afternoon sunning or taking windsurfing lessons on the beautiful beach. ✉ *St. Barths Beach Hôtel, Grand Cul de Sac* ☎ *0590/ 27–82–42* ▭ *AE, MC, V.*

CONTEMPORARY ✕ **Taïno.** This restaurant on the pretty pool terrace of the Christopher
$$$–$$$$ features traditional French cuisine with a lightened touch. First-course salads are often interestingly (and healthfully) garnished with dried fruit, *pignolis,* or marinated local seafood. Lemongrass coconut soup with tiger prawns, and tomato and mozzarella mousse are nice starters. Light, fresh pastas, and main courses like Angus beef in a coffee-bean sauce and monkfish in a coriander and lemon *confit* show off the versatility of the talented chef. Don't miss the Kahlua tiramisu. ✉ *Pointe Milou* ☎ *0590/27–63–63* ◔ *Reservations essential* ▭ *AE, MC* ☉ *Closed Sept.–late Oct.*

$$–$$$$ ✕ **La Mandala.** Owner Boubou has a couple of popular restaurants on the island, all of which are cute, fun, and have of-the-moment menus and friendly staff. This one offers tasty Thai-influenced food on a sweeping terrace over Gustavia Harbor. A wonderful sushi bar was added in 2006 and has become a huge hit with the celebrities that flock here. It's also great for a sunset cocktail. Try the vegetable-curry spring rolls, fish tempura with kimchee sauce, Peking-style duck, or the Thai-scented sea bass steamed in foil. ✉ *Rue de la Sous-Préfecture, Gustavia* ☎ *0590/ 27–96–96* ▭ *AE, MC, V.*

ECLECTIC ✕ **Do Brazil.** At this cozy restaurant nestled at the cliff side of Gustavia's
$$$–$$$$ Shell Beach, you'll be able to sample more of restaurateur Boubou's fusion creations. The menu is more French-Thai than Brazilian, although at dinner there are usually a couple of Brazilian specialties. The decor is vaguely jungle-chic—romantic at night, lively at lunch. Grilled sandwiches at the snack bar on the beachfront level are the perfect lunch. For dinner, choose between varied salads, raw fish, hand-chopped steak tartares, and a variety of fresh-caught grilled fish. The service has been known to be a little "relaxed." ✉ *Shell Beach, Gustavia* ☎ *0590/ 29–06–66* ◔ *Reservations essential* ▭ *AE, MC, V.*

★ **$$$–$$$$** ✕ **Maya's.** New Englander Randy Gurly and his French chef-wife, Maya, provide a warm welcome and a very pleasant dinner on their cheerful dock decorated with big, round tables and crayon-color canvas chairs, all overlooking Gustavia Harbor. A market-inspired menu of good, simply prepared and garnished dishes like mahimahi in creole sauce, shrimp gumbo, pepper-marinated beef fillet changes daily, assuring the ongoing popularity of a restaurant that seems to be on everyone's list of favorites. ⊠ *Public, Gustavia* ☎ *0590/27–75–73* ⌲ *Reservations essential* ⊟ *AE, MC, V.*

★ **$$$** ✕ **Le Ti St. Barth Caribbean Tavern.** Chef-owner Carole Gruson captures the funky, sexy spirit of the island in her wildly popular hilltop hot spot. We always come here to dance to great music with the attractive crowd lingering at the bar, lounge at one of the pillow-strewn banquettes, or chat on the torchlight terrace. By the time your appetizers arrive, you'll be best friends with the next table. The menu includes Thai beef salad, lobster ravioli, rare grilled tuna with Chinese noodles, and the best beef on the island. Provocatively named desserts, such as Nymph Thighs (airy lemon cake with vanilla custard) and Daddy's Balls (passionfruit sorbet and ice cream) end the meal on a fun note. Around this time someone is sure to be dancing on top of the tables. There's an extensive wine list. The famously raucous full-moon parties are legendary. ⊠ *Pointe Milou* ☎ *0590/27–97–71* ⌲ *Reservations essential* ⊟ *MC, V.*

$$–$$$ ✕ **Le Repaire.** This friendly brasserie overlooks Gustavia's harbor and is a popular spot from its early-morning opening at 7 AM to its late-night closing at midnight. Its flexible hours are great if you arrive mid-afternoon and need a good snack before dinner. Grab a cappuccino, pull a captain's chair to the streetside rail, and watch the pretty girls. The menu ranges from cheeseburgers, which are served only at lunch along with the island's best fries, to simply grilled fish and meat. The composed salads always please. Wonderful ice cream sundaes round out the menu. Try your hand at the billiards table or show up on weekends for live music. ⊠ *Quai de la République, Gustavia* ☎ *0590/27–72–48* ⊟ *MC, V.*

★ **$$–$$$** ✕ **Wall House.** The food can be really good—and the service is always friendly—at this restaurant on the far side of Gustavia harbor. The menu has been changed to emphasize the dishes that Frank, the amiable chef, does best, and the quality of everything continues to rise. Some of the best choices are specialties cooked on the elaborate gas rotisserie, including spit-roasted grouper, stuffed saddle of lamb, or five-spice honey pineapple duck. The pesto gnocchi are out of this world. Local businesspeople crowd the restaurant for the bargain prix-fixe lunch menu. The daily €25 dinner menu is a pretty good deal, too. An old-fashioned dessert trolley showcases some really yummy sweets. ⊠ *La Pointe, Gustavia* ☎ *0590/27–71–83* ⌲ *Reservations essential* ⊟ *AE, MC, V* ☉ *Closed Sept. and Oct.*

FRENCH ✕ **François Plantation.** A St. Barths favorite came under new management
$$$$ in 2006. Nothing about the lovely setting, on a sparkling white veranda, has changed, nor has the emphasis on serious wine. The food is experimental and somewhat esoteric, like a duck-and-foie-gras burger, rack of lamb in blood-orange and violet-mustard sauce, and wild lobster skewers on artichoke salad with zucchini-seed oil. Serious foodies take note. ⊠ *François Plantation, Colombier* ☎ *0590/29–80–22* ⌲ *Reservations essential* ⊟ *AE, MC, V* ☉ *Closed Sept. and Oct. No lunch.*

$$$–$$$$ ✕ **Le Gaïac.** If you are in the mood to dress up, this is the elegant, sophisticated restaurant at which to do it. Everything is taken very seriously here. Starched napery and impeccable service complement the blue bay view. Lunch includes chilled, spicy mango soup, salads, and grilled

18

seafood. The dinner menu showcases really serious food: guinea hen, wood pigeon, free-range chicken baked in a clay shell, fresh tuna with Japanese seaweed in a eucalyptus sauce, baby sole stuffed with scallops and mushrooms served in a scallop mousse: are you salivating? Tableside crêpes suzette are de rigueur. There's a €43 buffet brunch on Sunday. ⊠ *Le Toiny, Anse à Toiny* ☎ *0590/29–77–47* ▭ *AE, DC, MC, V* ⊘ *Closed Sept.–mid-Oct.*

★ $$$–$$$$ ╳ **Le Sapotillier.** The romantic brick walls, hand-painted wooden chairs, exquisite white-linen tablecloths, and vivid creole paintings evoke an old-style private island home. The service reminds us of dinner in the "best" homes, but this is not the cooking of your *maman*. Classic French food like rack of lamb and roasted Bresse chicken with potato gratin anchors the menu. Caramelized foie gras with pineapple is not to be missed. The sumptuous chocolate mousse and raspberry soufflé are longtime favorites. At a time when St. Barths cuisine is more and more casual, dinner here is a special treat. ⊠ *Rue du Centenaire, Gustavia* ☎ *0590/27–60–28* ⌕ *Reservations essential* ▭ *MC, V* ⊘ *Closed mid-May–late Oct. No lunch.*

★ $$$–$$$$ ╳ **Le Tamarin.** A leisurely lunch here en route to Grand Saline beach is a St. Barths *must*. Delicious French and creole cuisine is served at this sophisticated open-air restaurant. Get to know the parrot, or relax in a hammock after the house-special carpaccios of salmon, tuna, and beef. The lemon tart deserves its excellent reputation. ⊠ *Salines* ☎ *0590/27–72–12* ▭ *AE, MC, V* ⊘ *Open erratically May–Nov. Call to confirm.*

$$–$$$$ ╳ **Lafayette Club.** This true St. Barths classic is famous for its fabulous, if not irrational, priciness for down-to-earth cuisine, but lunch in the pale pink pavilion beside the turquoise lagoon inspires loyal patronage from those who don't object to spending a fortune for the chance to nibble on country-French specialties like ratatouille, lobster bisque, grilled duck breast, and tarte tatin in the company of whichever celebrities might be in residence on the island. Informal modeling of fashions from the on-site boutique provides a great cover for not-so-discreet people-peering. ⊠ *Grand Cul de Sac* ☎ *0590/27–75–69* ⌕ *Reservations essential* ▭ *AE, DC, MC, V* ⊘ *Closed Sept. and Oct.*

$$–$$$ ╳ **La Marine.** This St. Barths harborside classic was taken over in 2005 by Carole Gruson, and it has been spiffed up to match and meld into her hot next-door nightclub, Le Yacht Club. The traditional Thursday-night mussels remain, along with lots of other seafood choices. It's a good choice for lunch, too. ⊠ *Rue Jeanne d'Arc, Gustavia* ☎ *0590/ 27–68–91* ▭ *AE, MC, V.*

ITALIAN ╳ **PaCrì.** An adorable, young husband-and-wife team (she is the chef)
★ $$–$$$ serve delicious, huge portions of housemade pasta, wood-oven-fired pizza, and authentic Italian main courses, like Pugliese mahimahi, succulent meatballs, and sautéed veal *saltimbocca* on a breezy open terrace right near Saline Beach. The menu changes daily. Don't miss the *burrata,* a softball-size hunk of the best artisanal mozzarella you've ever had, flown in from Italy and garnished with prosciutto. Unusual desserts like lemon profiteroles are definitely worth the calories. Gorgeous waitstaff of both sexes add to the general air of voluptuousness. ⊠ *Route de Saline* ☎ *0590/29–35–63* ⌕ *Reservations essential* ▭ *AE, MC, V.*

SEAFOOD ✕**La Langouste.** This tiny beachside restaurant in the pool-courtyard of
$$–$$$ Hôtel Baie des Anges is run by Anny, the hotel's amiable, ever-present pro-
prietor. It lives up to its name by serving fantastic, fresh-grilled lobster at
a price that is somewhat gentler than at most other island venues. Simple, well-prepared fish, pastas, and an assortment of refreshing cold soups
are also available. Be sure to try the warm goat cheese in pastry served
on a green salad. ⌂ *Hôtel Baie des Anges, Flamands Beach* ☎ *0590/
27–63–61* ⚓ *Reservations essential* ▭ *MC, V* ✆ *Closed May–Oct.*

Beaches

There are many *anses* (coves) and nearly 20 *plages* (beaches) scattered
around the island, each with a distinctive personality and each open to
the general public. Even in season you can find a nearly empty beach.
Topless sunbathing is common, but nudism is forbidden—although
both Grande Saline and Gouverneur are de facto nude beaches. Bear in
mind that the rocky beaches around Anse à Toiny are not swimmable.

Anse à Colombier. The beach here is the least accessible, thus the most
private, on the island; to reach it you must take either a rocky footpath
from Petite Anse or brave the 30-minute climb down (and back up) a
steep, cactus-bordered—though clearly marked—trail from the top of
the mountain behind the beach. Appropriate footgear is a must, and you
should know that once you get to the beach, the only shade is a rock
cave. Boaters favor this beach and cove for its calm anchorage. ⌂ *Anse
à Colombier.*

Anse des Flamands. This is the most beautiful of the hotel beaches—a
roomy strip of silken sand. We love to come here for lunch and then
spend the afternoon sunning, taking a long beachwalk and a swim in
the turquoise water. From the beach, you can take a brisk hike to the
top of the now-extinct volcano believed to have given birth to St. Barths.
⌂ *Anse des Flamands.*

★ **Anse du Gouverneur.** Because it's so secluded, nude sunbathing is popular here; the beach is truly beautiful, with blissful swimming and views
of St. Kitts, Saba, and St. Eustatius. Venture here at the end of the day,
and watch the sun set behind the hills. The road here from Gustavia also
offers spectacular vistas. Legend has it that pirates' treasure is buried
in the vicinity. ⌂ *Anse du Gouverneur.*

Anse de Grand Cul de Sac. The shallow, reef-protected beach is especially
nice for small children, fly fishermen, kayakers, and windsurfers; it has
excellent lunch spots, water-sports rentals, and lots of the amusing
pelican-like frigate birds that dive-bomb the water fishing for their
lunch. ⌂ *Grand Cul de Sac.*

Fodor'sChoice **Anse de Grande Saline.** Secluded, with its sandy ocean bottom, this is
★ just about everyone's favorite beach and great for swimmers, too. Without any major development, it's an ideal Caribbean strand, though it
can be a bit windy here, so you can enjoy yourself more if you go on a
calm day. In spite of the prohibition, young and old alike go nude. The
beach is a 10-minute walk up a rocky dune trail, so be sure to wear sneakers or water shoes. The big salt ponds here are no longer in use, and the
place looks a little desolate. ⌂ *Grande Saline.*

18

Anse de Lorient. This beach is popular with St. Barths families and surfers, who like its rolling waves. Be aware of the level of the tide, which can come in very fast. Hikers and avid surfers like the walk over the hill to Point Milou in the late afternoon sun when the waves roll in. ⊠ *Lorient.*

Baie de St-Jean. Like a mini Côte d'Azur—beachside bistros, bungalow hotels, bronzed bodies, windsurfing, and lots of day-trippers—the reef-protected strip is divided by Eden Rock promontory, and there's good snorkeling west of the rock. ⊠ *Baie de St-Jean.*

Sports & the Outdoors

BOATING & SAILING
St. Barths is a popular yachting and sailing center, thanks to its location midway between Antigua and St. Thomas. Gustavia's harbor, 13 to 16 feet deep, has mooring and docking facilities for 40 yachts. There are also good anchorages available at Public, Corossol, and Colombier. You can charter sailing and motor boats in Gustavia Harbor for as little as a half-day. Stop at the Tourist Office in Gustavia for an up-to-the-minute list of recommended charter companies.

Marine Service (⊠ Gustavia ☎ 0590/27–70–34 ⊕ www.st-barths.com/marine.service) offers full-day outings on a 40-foot catamaran to the uninhabited Ile Fourchue for swimming, snorkeling, cocktails, and lunch; the cost is $100 per person. An unskippered motor rental runs about $260 a day. Marine Service can also arrange an hour's cruise ($32) on the glass-bottom boat *L'Aquascope.*

FISHING
Most fishing is done in the waters north of Lorient, Flamands, and Corossol. Popular catches are tuna, marlin, wahoo, and barracuda. There's an annual St. Barths Open Fishing Tournament, organized by Ocean Must, in mid-July.

Jicky Marine Center (⊠ Gustavia ☎ 0690/30–58–73) has a fishing boat for year-round marlin fishing and offers private dive trips, too. **Marine Service** (⊠ Gustavia ☎ 0590/27–70–34 ⊕ www.st-barths.com/marine.service) arranges ocean-fishing excursions. **Océan Must Marina** (⊠ Gustavia ☎ 0590/27–62–25) arranges deep-sea fishing expeditions as well as boat charters.

HORSEBACK RIDING
Two-hour horseback trail-ride excursions in the morning or the afternoon led by Coralie Fournier are about $40 per person at **St. Barth Equitation** (⊠ Ranch des Flamands, Anse des Flamands ☎ 0690/62–99-30). Instruction is also available.

DIVING & SNORKELING
Several dive shops arrange scuba excursions to local sites. Depending on weather conditions, you may dive at **Pain de Sucre, Coco Island,** or toward nearby **Saba.** There's also an underwater shipwreck to explore, plus sharks, rays, sea tortoises, coral, and the usual varieties of colorful fish. The waters on the island's leeward side are the calmest. For the uncertified who still want to see what the island's waters hold, there's an accessible shallow reef right off the beach at Anse de Cayes if you have your own mask and fins. Most of the waters surrounding St. Barths are protected in the island's **Réserve Marine de St-Barth** (⊠ Gustavia ☎ 0590/

27–88–18), which also provides information at its office in Gustavia. The diving here isn't nearly as rich as in the more dive-centered destinations like Saba and St. Eustatius, but the options aren't bad either, and none of the smaller islands offer the ambience of St. Barths.

Big Blue Diving (📷🖥 0590/27–83–74) has a following for its underwater electric-powered scooters, which remind fans of Lloyd Bridges in *Seahunt*. **Plongée Caraïbe** (📷🖥 0590/27–55–94) is recommended for its up-to-the-minute equipment and dive boat. Away from Gustavia, scuba and snorkeling trips, and small-boat charter can be arranged through **Mermaid** (✉ Grand Cul de Sac 📷 0690/76–79–55). **Splash** (✉ Gustavia 📷 0690/56–90–24) does scuba, snorkeling, and fishing, too Marine Service operates the only five-star, PADI-certified diving center on the island, called **West Indies Dive** (📷 0590/27–70–34 ⊕ www.st-barths.com/west-indies-dive). Scuba trips, packages, resort dives, and certifications start at $50, gear included.

GOLF There is now an **aqua-driving range** (✉ Grand Cul de Sac 📷 0690/37–46–45) open most afternoons at Grand Cul de Sac, where a bucket of balls costs a few euros, clubs included. Very well-heeled golf fanatics will be quite pleased with **Fly & Golf** (📷 0690/30–58–73 ⊕ www.flygolf.net), which debuted in 2003. PGA pro and former champion Emmanuel Dussart will arrange tee times and fly you in his private plane from St. Barths to one of the excellent golf courses on St. Thomas, Nevis, or another nearby island. The maximum number of golfers per trip is three. Call about pricing; if you have to think about it, you probably can't afford it.

WINDSURFING Windsurfing fever has definitely caught on in St. Barths. Gentle, constant trade winds make conditions ideal on some beaches, such as Anse de Grand Cul de Sac or Baie de St-Jean. You can rent boards for about €20 an hour at water-sports centers on the beaches. Lessons are offered for about $40 an hour at **Eden Rock Sea Sport Club** (✉ Eden Rock Hotel, Baie de St-Jean 📷 0590/27–74–77), which also rents boards. **Wind Wave Power** (✉ St. Barth Beach Hotel, Grand Cul de Sac 📷 0590/27–82–57) offers an extensive, six-hour training course. For €60, you can have a one-hour introductory lesson, along with the use of the Windsurfer for as long as you can stand up.

Shopping

Fodor'sChoice ★ St. Barths is a duty-free port, and with its sophisticated crowd of visitors, shopping in the island's 200-plus boutiques is a definite delight, especially for beachwear, accessories, jewelry, and casual wear. It would be no overstatement to say that shopping for fashionable clothing, accessories, and decorative items for the home is better in St. Barths than anywhere else in the Caribbean. New shops open all the time, so there's always something new to discover. Stores often close for lunch from noon to 2, and many on Wednesday afternoon as well, but they are open until about 7 in the evening. A popular afternoon pastime is strolling about the two major shopping areas in Gustavia and St-Jean.

18

Areas

In Gustavia, boutiques line the three major shopping streets. Quai de la République, nicknamed rue du Couturier, which is right on the harbor, rivals New York's Madison Avenue or Paris's avenue Montaigne for high-end "designer" retail, including brand-new shops for **Dior, Louis Vuitton, Tod's, Bulgari, Cartier, Chopard** and **Hermès**. These shops often carry items that are not available in the United States. The Carré d'Or plaza is great fun to explore. Shops are also clustered in **La Savane Commercial Center** (across from the airport), **La Villa Créole** (in St-Jean), and **Espace Neptune** (on the road to Lorient). It's worth working your way from one end to the other at these shopping complexes—just to see or, perhaps, be seen. Boutiques in all three areas carry the latest in French and Italian sportswear and some haute couture. You probably are not going to find any bargains as long as the euro remains high, but you might be able to snag that *pochette* that is sold out stateside, and in any case you will have a lot of fun hunting around.

Specialty Items

BOOKS **Funny Face Bookstore** (✉ Quai de la République, Gustavia ☎ 0590/29–60–14) is a full-service bookstore with hundreds of English titles for adults and kids, plus armchairs, coffee, and Internet access.

CLOTHING Shopping for up-to-the-minute fashions is as much a part of a visit to St. Barths as going to the beach. Shops change all the time, both in ownership and in the lines that are carried. Current listings are just a general guide. The best advice is simply to go for a long stroll and check out all the shops on the way. The following list is of shops that have an interesting variety of current and fun items, but it's by no means an exhaustive one.

Black Swan (✉ Le Carré d'Or, Gustavia ☎ 0590/27–65–16 ✉ La Villa Créole, St-Jean) has an unparalleled selection of bathing suits. The wide range of styles and sizes is appreciated. **Boutique Lacoste** (✉ Rue Du Bord de Mer, Gustavia ☎ 0590/27–66–90) has a huge selection of the once-again-chic alligator logo wear, as well as a shop next door with a complete selection of the Petit Bateau line of T-shirts popular with teens. **Cafe Coton** (✉ Rue du Bord du Mer, Gustavia ☎ 0590/52–48–42) is a great shop for men, especially for long-sleeve linen shirts in a rainbow of colors and Egyptian cotton dress shirts. Right next door to Cafe Coton, **Cachemire Crème** (✉ Rue du Bord du Mer, Gustavia ☎ 0590/52–48–42) stocks, as the name suggests, deliciously fine cashmere in unusual styles and a whole tiny line for very lucky children. **Calypso** (✉ Le Carré d'Or, Gustavia ☎ 0590/27–69–74) carries resort wear for women by D. Squared, Balenciaga, Lucien Pellat Finet, and Chloè. **Dovani** (✉ Rue de la République, Gustavia ☎ 0590/29–84–77) has elegant leather goods and Baccarat jewelry. Fans of Longchamp handbags and leather goods will find a good selection at about 20% off stateside prices at **Elysée Caraïbes** (✉ Le Carré d'Or, Gustavia ☎ 0590/52–00–94). **Hip Up** (✉ Rue Général-de-Gaulle, Gustavia ☎ 0590/27–69–33) stocks a wonderful line of swimwear for all ages; tops and bottoms are sold separately for a practically custom fit, with cute matching accessories like sandals, cargo skirts, and T-shirt tops to complete the look. **Jenny** (✉ La Villa Créole, St-Jean

✆ 0590/27–53–74) carries the sophisticated Sarah Pacini line of dressier clothes that transcend resort wear. **Indigos** (✉ La Villa Créole, St-Jean ✆ 0590/27–59–40) carries Ann Fontaine shirts and very wearable linen separates. **Kustom** (✉ Rte. de Saline, next door to Lili Belle, St-Jean ✆ 0590/87–95–92) carries Von Dutch and up-to-the-minute trends for the cynical fashionista. **Laurent Effel** (✉ Rue Général-de-Gaulle, Gustavia) now has four shops in Gustavia for beautiful leather belts, colorful linen shirts, bags, and shoes. One shop is devoted entirely to exotic leather accessories. Check out **Lili Belle** (✉ Pelican Plage St-Jean ✆ 0590/87–46–14), for hippie-chic drapey tops, drop-dead bikinis by D nu D, and Stella Forest T-shirts and blouses. Don't miss **Lolita Jaca** (✉ Le Carré d'Or, Gustavia ✆ 0590/27–59–98) for trendy, tailored sportswear by Paul & Joe and other fresh names from Paris like Donalé, not to mention Ailanto from Spain. **Mia Zia** (✉ Rue du Roi Oscar II, Gustavia ✆ 0590/27–55–48), which has relocated to big, new purple quarters in Gustavia, imports wonderful accessories from Morocco, including multicolored, tassled silk and cotton shawls, caftans, and colorful 6-foot-long silk cords to wrap around your wrists, waist, or neck. **Morgan's** (✉ La Villa Créole, St-Jean ✆ 0590/27–57–22) has a line of popular and wearable casual wear in the trendy vein.

Paradoxe (✉ La Villa Créole, St-Jean ✆ 0590/27–84–98 ✉ Rue de la Républic, Gustavia ✆ 0590/29–21–86) stocks flattering patterned stretch jeans by TARK'1 and pretty chiffon tops. **Pati de Saint Barth** (✉ Passage de la Crémaillière, Gustavia ✆ 0590/29–78–04) is the largest of the three shops that stock the chic, locally made T-shirts that have practically become the "logo" of St. Barths. The newest styles have hand-done graffiti-style lettering. At **Poupette** (✉ Rue de la République, Gustavia ✆ 0590/27–94–49), all the brilliant colored-silk and chiffon batik and embroidered peasant skirts and tops are designed by the owner. There also are great belts and beaded bracelets. **Raffia** (✉ Rte. de Saline, St-Jean ✆ 0590/27–78–39) has great handbags, resort accessories, and current fashions, including chic infant wear. **Stéphane & Bernard** (✉ Rue de la République, Gustavia ✆ 0590/27–69–13) stocks a well-edited, large selection of superstar French fashion designers, including Rykiel, Tarlazzi, Kenzo, Feraud, and Mugler. Look to **St. Tropez KIWI** (✉ St-Jean ✆ 0590/27–57–08 ✉ Gustavia ✆ 0590/27–68–97) for resort wear. **SUD SUD.ETC.Plage** (✉ Galerie du Commerce, St-Jean ✆ 0590/27–98–75) stocks everything for the beach: inflatables, mats, bags, and beachy shell jewelry. **Terra** (✉ Pelican Plage ✆ 0590/27–57–50) has pretty, classic styles of resort wear you can even wear back home.

COSMETICS Don't miss the superb skin-care products made on-site from local tropical plants by **Ligne de St. Barths** (✉ Rte. de Saline, Lorient ✆ 0590/27–82–63).

FOODSTUFFS **A.M.C** (✉ Quai de la République, Gustavia) is a bit older than Match but able to supply anything you might need for housekeeping in a villa, or for a picnic. **Match** (✉ St-Jean), a fully stocked supermarket across from the airport, has a wide selection of French cheeses, pâtés, cured meats, produce, fresh bread, wine, and liquor. **JoJo Supermarché** (✉ Lorient) is the well-stocked counterpart to Gustavia's two supermarkets and gets daily deliveries of bread and fresh produce. Prices are lower here than at the larger markets. **Maya's to Go** (⊠ Galleries du Commerce, St. Jean ☎ 0590/29–83–70) is the place to go for prepared picnics, meals, salads, rotisserie chickens, and more from the kitchens of the popular restaurant. For exotic groceries or picnic fixings, stop by St. Barths' gourmet *traiteur* (takeout) **La Rotisserie** (⊠ Rue du Roi Oscar II, Gustavia ☎ 0590/27–63–13 ⊠ Centre Vaval, St-Jean ☎ 0590/29–75–69) for salads, prepared meats, groceries from Fauchon, and Iranian caviar.

HANDICRAFTS   The ladies of Corossol produce intricate straw work, wide-brim beach hats, and decorative ornaments by hand. Call the tourist office, which can provide information about the studios of other island artists: Christian Bretoneiche, Robert Danet, Nathalie Daniel, Patricia Guyot, Rose Lemen, Aline de Lurin, and Marion Vinot.

Look for Fabienne Miot's unusual gold jewelry at **L'Atelier de Fabienne** (⊠ Rue de la République, Gustavia ☎ 0590/27–63–31). **Chez Pompi** (⊠ On the road to Toiny ☎ 0590/27–75–67) is a cottage whose first room is a gallery for the naive paintings of Pompi (also known as Louis Ledée). **Kayali** (⊠ Rue de la République, Gustavia ☎ 0590/27–64–48) shows varied works by local artists. Local works of art, including paintings, are sold in the bright **Made in St-Barth La Boutique** (⊠ La Villa Créole, St-Jean ☎ 0590/27–56–57). Find local stoneware, raku pottery, and other crafts at **St. Barth Pottery** (⊠ Gustavia ☎ 0590/27–69–81), next to the post office on the harbor.

JEWELRY   **Carat** (⊠ Quai de la République, Gustavia) has Chaumet and a large selection of Breitling watches. A good selection of watches, including Patek Phillippe and Chanel, can be found at **Diamond Genesis** (⊠ Rue Général-de-Gaulle, Gustavia). Next door to Cartier, **Oro del Sol** (⊠ Quai de la République, Gustavia) carries beautiful fine accessories by Bulgari, Ebel, and others. **Sindbad** (⊠ Carré d'Or, Gustavia ☎ 0590/27–52–29), at the top, is a tiny shop with funky, unique "couture" fashion jewelry by Gaz Bijou of St. Tropez, crystal collars for your pampered pooch, chunky ebony pendants on silk cord, Nomination bracelets, and other reasonably priced, up-to-the-minute styles.

LIQUOR &   **La Cave du Port Franc** (⊠ Rue de la République, Gustavia ☎ 0590/
TOBACCO   27–65–27) has a good selection of wine, especially from France. At **M'Bolo** (⊠ Rue Général-de-Gaulle, Gustavia ☎ 0590/27–90–54), be sure to sample the various varieties of infused rums, including lemongrass, ginger, and, of course, the island favorite, vanilla. Bring home some in the beautiful hand-blown bottles. **La Cave de Saint-Barths** (⊠ Marigot ☎ 0590/27–63–21) has an excellent collection of French vintages stored in temperature-controlled cellars. **Le Comptoir du Cigare** (⊠ Rue Général-de-Gaulle, Gustavia ☎ 0590/27–50–62), run by Jannick and Patrick Gerthofer, is a top purveyor of cigars. The walk-in humidor has an extraordinary selection. Try the Cubans while you are on the island, and take home the Davidoffs. Refills can be shipped stateside. Be sure to try on the genuine Panama hats. **Couleur des Isles Cuban Cigar** (⊠ Rue Général-de-Gaulle, Gustavia ☎ 0590/27–79–60) has many rare varieties of smokeables and good souvenir T-shirts too.

Nightlife

"In" clubs change from season to season, so you might ask around for the hot spot of the moment. There's more nightlife than ever in recent memory, and a late (10 PM or later) reservation at one of the club-restaurants will eventually become a front-row seat at a party. **Bar de l'Oubli** (⊠ Rue du Roi Oscar II, Gustavia ☎ 0590/27–70–06) is where young locals gather for drinks. **Carl Gustaf** (⊠ Rue des Normands, Gustavia ☎ 0590/27–82–83) lures a more sedate crowd, namely those in search of quiet conversation and sunset watching. **Le Feeling** (⊠ Lurin ☎ 0590/52–84–09) is a cabaret and disco in the Lurin Hills that has special theme nights on Thursday. It opens nightly at midnight for a cabaret show. **Le Nikki Beach** (⊠ St-Jean ☎ 0590/27–64–64) rocks on weekends during lunch, when the scantily clad young and beautiful lounge on the white canvas banquettes. **Le Repaire** (⊠ Rue de la République, Gustavia ☎ 0590/27–72–48) lures a crowd for cocktail hour and its pool table. **Le Santa Fé** (⊠ Lurin ☎ 0590/27–61–04), in the Lurin Hills, features a rowdy crowd, billiards, and satellite-TV sports. **Le Sélect** (⊠ Rue du Centenaire, Gustavia ☎ 0590/27–86–87) is St. Barths' original hangout, commemorated by Jimmy Buffet's "Cheeseburger in Paradise." The boisterous garden is where the barefoot boating set gathers for a brew. At this writing the hot spot was **Le Yacht Club** (⊠ Rue Jeanne d'Arc, Gustavia ☎ 0690/49–23–33); although ads call it a "private club," you can probably get in anyway.

Exploring St. Barthélemy

With a little practice, negotiating St. Barths' narrow, steep roads soon becomes fun. Free maps are everywhere, roads are well marked, and painted signs will point you where the tourist office has annotated maps with walking tours that highlight sights of interest. Starting in December 2005, some of the parking congestion on the island was alleviated by the **St-Barth Shuttle,** a fleet of four air-conditioned minibuses with round-trip routes between Gustavia, Flamands, Lorient, and Grand Cul de Sac. The round-trip ticket costs €10.

Numbers in the margin correspond to points of interest on the St. Barthélemy map.

❶ **Corossol.** The island's French-provincial origins are most evident in this two-street fishing village with a little rocky beach. Older local women weave lantana straw into handbags, baskets, hats, and delicate strings of birds. Ingenu Magras's **Inter Oceans Museum** has more than 9,000 seashells and an intriguing collection of sand samples from around the world. You can buy souvenir shells. ⊠ *Corossol* ☎ *0590/27–62–97* 💬 €3 🕙 *Tues.–Sun. 9–12:30 and 2–5.*

❸ **Gustavia.** You can easily explore all of Gustavia during a two-hour stroll. Street signs in both French and Swedish illustrate the island's history. Most shops close from noon to 2, so plan lunch accordingly. A good spot to park your car is rue de la République, where catamarans, yachts, and sailboats are moored. The **tourist office** (☎ 0590/27–87–27) on the pier can provide maps and a wealth of information. It's open Monday from 8:30 to 12:30, Tuesday through Friday from 8 to noon and 2 to 5, and Saturday from 9 to noon. On the far side of the harbor known as La Pointe is the charming **Municipal Museum,** where you can find watercolors, portraits, photographs, and historic documents detailing the island's history as well as displays of the island's flowers, plants, and marine life. ☎ 599/29–71–55 ⌖ €2 ⊗ *Mon., Tues., Thurs., and Fri. 8:30–12:30 and 2:30–6, Sat. 9–12:30.*

❷ **St-Jean.** The half-mile-long crescent of sand at St-Jean is the island's most popular beach. Windsurfers skim along the water here, catching the strong trade winds. A popular activity is watching and photographing the hair-raising airplane landings. You'll also find some of the best shopping on the island here, as well as several restaurants.

❹ **Toiny coast.** Over the hills beyond Grand Cul de Sac is this muchphotographed coastline. Stone fences crisscross the steep slopes of Morne Vitet, one of many small mountains on St. Barths, along a rocky shore that resembles the rugged coast of Normandy. It's one island beach that's been nicknamed the "washing machine" because of its turbulent surf. Even expert swimmers should beware of the strong undertow here; swimming is generally not recommended.

ST. BARTHS ESSENTIALS

To research prices, get advice from other travelers, and book travel arrangements, visit www.fodors.com.

Transportation

BY AIR

There are no direct flights to St. Barths. Most North Americans fly first into St. Maarten's Queen Juliana International Airport, from which the island is only 10 minutes away by air. Flights leave at least once an hour between 7:30 AM and 5:30 PM on Winair. Air Caraïbes, based in Guadeloupe, flies among the French West Indies and to the Dominican Republic. St. Barth Commuter is a small, private charter company that can also arrange service.

You must confirm your return interisland flight, even during off-peak seasons, or you may very well lose your reservation. Do not be upset if your luggage has not made the trip with you. It frequently will arrive on a later flight, and your hotel will send a porter to receive it; villa-rental

companies may also help you retrieve luggage from the airport, but you may have to beg. It's a good idea to pack a change of clothes, required medicines, and a bathing suit in your carry-on.

🛫 Airlines **Air Caraïbes** ☎ 0590/27-71-90, 877/772-1005 in U.S. ⊕ www.aircaraibes.com. **St. Barth Commuter** ☎ 0590/27-54-54 ⊕ www.stbarthcommuter.com. **Winair** ☎ 0590/27-61-01 or 800/634-4907 ⊕ www.fly-winair.com.

🛫 Airports **Aéroport de St-Jean** ☎ 0590/27-75-81.

BY BIKE & MOPED

Several companies rent motorbikes, scooters, mopeds, and mountain bikes. Motorbikes go for about $30 per day and require a $100 deposit. Helmets are required. Scooter and motorbike rental places are located mostly along rue de France in Gustavia and around the airport in St-Jean. They tend to shift locations slightly.

🚲 **Barthloc Rental** ⊠ Rue de France, Gustavia ☎ 0590/27-52-81. **Chez Béranger** ⊠ Rue de France, Gustavia ☎ 0590/27-89-00. **Ets Denis Dufau** ⊠ St-Jean ☎ 0590/27-54-83.

BY BOAT & FERRY

Voyager offers ferry service for day trips between St. Barths, St. Martin (Marigot), and Saba. Round-trips are offered for about $60 per person. All service is from Quai de la République. Private boat charters are also available. Rapide Explorer is a superfast catamaran service with several daily 45-minute crossings between St. Maarten's Chesterfield Marina and St. Barths. The fare is €75 for the round-trip, and you need to make reservations.

⚑ **Voyager** ☎ 0590/27-54-10 ⊕ www.voyager-st-barths.com. **Rapid Explorer** ☎ 0590/27-60-33 ⊕ www.st-barths.com/rapid-explorer.

BY CAR

Most travelers to St. Barths rent a car. The new St-Barth Shuttle service can be convenient and much less expensive than a taxi if you are just one or two people, but it still doesn't completely negate the need for a car.

You'll find major rental agencies at the airport. You must have a valid driver's license and be 25 or older to rent, and in high season there may be a three-day minimum. During peak periods, such as Christmas week and February, be sure to arrange for your car rental ahead of time. When you make your hotel reservations, ask if the hotel has its own cars available to rent; some hotels provide 24-hour emergency road service—something most rental companies don't offer.

Roads are sometimes unmarked, so be sure to get a map. Instead of road signs, look for signs pointing to a destination. These will be nailed to posts at all crossroads. Roads are narrow and sometimes very steep, so check the brakes and gears of your rental car before you drive away, and make a careful inventory of the existing dents and scrapes on the vehicle. Maximum speed on the island is 50 kph. Driving is on the right, as in the United States and Europe. St. Barths drivers often seem to be in an unending grand prix and thus tend to keep their cars maxed out, especially and inexplicably when in reverse. Parking is an additional challenge.

There are two gas stations on the island, one near the airport and one in Lorient. They aren't open after 5 PM or on Sunday, but you can use the one near the airport at any time with some credit cards, including Visa, JCB, or Carte Blanche. Considering the short distances, a full tank of gas should last you most of a week.

⚑ **Avis** ☎ 0590/27-71-43. **Budget** ☎ 0590/27-66-30. **Europcar** ☎ 0590/27-73-34 ⊕ www.st-barths.com/europcar/index.html. **Gumbs** ☎ 0590/27-75-32. **Hertz** ☎ 0590/27-71-14. **Turbe** ☎ 0590/27-71-42 ⊕ www.saint-barths.com/turbecarrental/.

BY TAXI

Taxis are expensive and not particularly easy to arrange, especially in the evening. There's a taxi station at the airport and another in Gustavia; from elsewhere you must contact a dispatcher in Gustavia or St-Jean. Technically, there's a flat rate for rides up to five minutes long. Each additional three minutes is an additional amount. In reality, however, cabbies usually name a fixed rate—and will not budge. Fares are 50% higher from 8 PM to 6 AM and on Sunday and holidays.

⚑ **Gustavia taxi dispatcher** ☎ 0590/27-66-31. **St-Jean taxi dispatcher** ☎ 0590/27-75-81.

Contacts & Resources

BANKS & EXCHANGE SERVICES

Banks and ATMs are well located throughout the island, so getting money is rarely a problem. The official currency in St. Barths is the euro; however, dollars are accepted in almost all shops and in many restaurants, though you will probably receive euros in change. Credit cards are accepted at most shops, hotels, and restaurants. In general, American Express charges in dollars; MasterCard charges in euros.

Prices quoted in this chapter are in euros, unless otherwise noted.

18

BUSINESS HOURS

Banks are generally open weekdays from 8 to noon and 2 to 3:30, but most have 24-hour ATMs. The main post office on rue Jeanne d'Arc in Gustavia is open Monday, Tuesday, Thursday, and Friday from 8 to 3, on Wednesday and Saturday until noon. The branch in Lorient is open weekdays from 7 AM to 11 AM and Saturday from 8 AM to 10 AM. The post office in St-Jean is open on Monday and Tuesday from 8 to 2 and on Wednesday through Saturday from 8 to noon. Stores are generally open weekdays from 8:30 to noon and 2 to 5, Saturday from 8:30 to noon. Some of the shops across from the airport and in St-Jean stay open on Saturday afternoon and until 7 PM on weekdays. A few around St-Jean even stay open on Sunday afternoon during the busy season. Although some shops are closed on Wednesday afternoon, most are open from 8:30 to noon and 3 to 6.

ELECTRICITY

Voltage is 220 AC/60 cycles, as in Europe. You can sometimes use American appliances with French plug converters and transformers. Most hotel rooms are conveniently supplied with hair dryers, and most have a shaver plug in the bathroom into which you can plug various rechargeables.

EMERGENCIES

🆘 Emergency Services **Ambulance & Fire** ☎ 18. **Police** ☎ 17 or 0590/27-66-66.
🆘 Hospitals **Hospital De Bruyn** ✉ Gustavia ☎ 0590/27-60-35.
🆘 Pharmacies **Island Pharmacie** ✉ Centre Commercial Vaval, St-Jean ☎ 0590/29-02-12 🖶 0590/29-06-17 is closed on Sunday. **Para-Pharmacie Physea** ✉ Rue de la République, Gustavia ☎ 0590/87-92-6 carries naturopathic cosmetics, herbal remedies, supplements, and a small selection of organic groceries and is open every day. **Pharmacie de L'Aéroport** ✉ St-Jean ☎ 0590/27-66-61 🖶 0590/27-73-21 is open every day. **Pharmacie St. Barth** ✉ Quai de la République, Gustavia ☎ 0590/27-61-82 🖶 0590/27-75-44 is closed on Sunday.

HOLIDAYS

Public holidays include New Year's Day, Easter weekend (Mar. or Apr.), Labor Day (May 1), Pentecost (mid- to late May), Bastille Day (July 14), Pitea Day (commemorates the joining of St. Barths with Pitea in Sweden, Aug. 15), All Saints' Day (Nov. 1), Armistice Day (Nov. 11), and Christmas.

LANGUAGE

French is the official language, so it can't hurt to pack a phrasebook and/or French dictionary. If you speak any French at all, don't be shy. You may also hear Creole, the regional French dialect called patois, and even the Creole of Guadeloupe. Most hotel and restaurant employees speak some English—at least enough to help you find what you need.

INTERNET, MAIL & SHIPPING

Most hotels provide Internet and e-mail access for guests at the front desk, if not right in the room, but if yours does not, make a visit to the Internet Service at Centre Alizes, which has fax service and 10 computers online. It's open weekdays from 8:30 to 12:30 and 2:30 to 7, as well as on Saturday morning. France Télécom can provide you with temporary Internet access that may let you connect your laptop. If you have a Wi-Fi-equipped laptop, there are hot spots at the port area, the Guanahani, and in the parking lot of the Oasis Shopping Center in Lorient; service is provided by Antilles Référencement, an excellent computer shop that can set you up with a temporary Internet account or provide other computer support.

Mail is slow. Correspondence between the United States and the island can take up to three weeks to arrive. The main post office is in Gustavia, but smaller post offices are in St-Jean and Lorient. When writing to an establishment on St. Barths, be sure to include "French West Indies" at the end of the address. Because of the slow mail service, faxes are widely used.

🖪 Internet Cafés **Antilles Référencement** ☒ Oasis Shopping Centre, Lorient ☏ 0590/58-97-97. **Centre Alizes** ☒ Rue de la République, Gustavia ☏ 0590/29-89-89. **France Télécom** ☒ Espace Neptune, St-Jean ☏ 0590/27-67-00.
🖪 Post Offices **Main post office** ☒ Rue Jeanne d'Arc, Gustavia ☏ 0590/27-62-00.

PASSPORT REQUIREMENTS
All foreign citizens need a passport and a return or ongoing ticket.

SAFETY
There's relatively little crime on St. Barths. Visitors can travel anywhere on the island with confidence. Most hotel rooms have minisafes for your valuables. As anywhere, don't tempt loss by leaving cameras, laptops, or jewelry out in plain sight in your hotel room or villa.

TAXES & SERVICE CHARGES
The island charges a $5 departure tax when your next stop is another French island, $10 if you're off to anywhere else. This is payable in cash only, dollars or euros, at the airport. At this writing, some hotels added an additional 10% to 15% service charge to bills, though most include it in their tariffs. There are no other additional taxes on either hotels or villa rentals.

TELEPHONES
MCI and AT&T services are available. Public telephones do not accept coins; they accept *télécartes*, prepaid calling cards that you can buy at the gas station next to the airport and at post offices in Lorient, St-Jean, and Gustavia. Making an international call using a télécarte is much less expensive than making it through your hotel.

If you bring a cell phone to the island and wish to activate it for local use, visit St. Barth Eléctronique across from the airport. You can also buy an inexpensive cell phone with prepaid minutes for as little as €20, including some initial air time. Many hotels will rent you a local-service cell phone; ask the manager or concierge.

The country code for St. Barths is 590. Thus, to call St. Barths from the U.S., dial 011 + 590 + 590 and the local six-digit number. Some cell phones use the prefix 690, in which case you would dial 590 + 690. For calls on St. Barths, you must dial 0590 + the six-digit local number; for St. Martin dial just the six-digit number for the French side, for the Dutch side (Sint Maarten) dial 00-599-54 + the five-digit number, but remember that this is an international call and will be billed accordingly. To call the United States from St. Barths, dial 001 + the area code + the local seven-digit number.
🖪 **France Télécom** ☒ Espace Neptune, St-Jean ☏ 0590/27-67-00. **St. Barth Eléctronique** ☒ St-Jean ☏ 0590/27-50-50.

TIPPING
Restaurants include a 15% service charge in their published prices, but it's common French practice to leave 5% to 10% *pourboire* (a tip; literally," for a drink")—in cash, even if you have paid by credit card. When your credit-card receipt is presented to be signed, the tip space should be blank—just draw a line through it—or you could end up paying a 30% service charge. Most taxi drivers don't expect a tip.

TOUR OPTIONS
You can arrange island tours by minibus or car at hotel desks or through any of the island's taxi operators in Gustavia or at the airport. The tourist office runs a variety of tours with varying itineraries that run about €46 for a half-day for up to eight people. Mat Nautic can help you arrange to tour the island by water on a Jet Ski or Waverunner. St-Barth Tours & Travel will customize a tour of the island. Wish Agency can arrange customized tours as well as take care of airline ticketing, event planning, maid service, and private party arrangements.
🖪 **Mat Nautic** ☒ Quai du Yacht Club, Gustavia ☏ 0690/49-54-72 **St-Barth Tours & Travel** ☒ Rue Jeanne d'Arc, Gustavia ☏ 0590/27-52-14. **Wish Agency** ☏ 0590/29-83-74.

18

VISITOR INFORMATION

A daily news sheet called *News* lists local happenings like special dinners or music and is available at markets and newsstands. Also, the free weekly *Journal de Saint-Barth*—mostly in French—is useful for current events. The small *Ti Gourmet Saint-Barth* is a free pocket-size guidebook that's invaluable for addresses and telephone numbers of restaurants and services. Look for the annual *Saint-Barth Tables* for full restaurant menus.

🛈 Before You Leave **French West Indies Tourist Board** ⊕ www.franceguide.com ✉ 610 5th Ave., New York, NY 10020. **French Government Tourist Office** ✉ 444 Madison Ave., 16th fl., New York, NY 10022 ☎ 900/990-0040, charges a fee ✉ 9454 Wilshire Blvd., Suite 303, Beverly Hills, CA 90212 ☎ 213/272-2661 ✉ 645 N. Michigan Ave., Suite 3360, Chicago, IL 60611 ☎ 312/337-6301 ✉ 1981 McGill College Ave., Suite 490, Montréal, Québec H3A 2W9, Canada ☎ 514/288-4264 ✉ 30 St. Patrick St., Suite 700, Toronto, Ontario M5T 3A3, Canada ☎ 416/593-4723 ✉ 178 Piccadilly, London W1V OAL, U.K. ☎ 0171/629-9376.

🛈 In St. Barths **Office du Tourisme** ✉ Quai Général-de-Gaulle ☎ 0590/27-87-27 🖶 0590/27-74-47 is an invaluable source for any reliable up-to-the-minute information you may need.

WEDDINGS

Since getting married in St. Barths has a long residency requirement, it's not really feasible to fly off to St. Barths for a wedding.

St. Eustatius

Fort Oranje, Oranjestad

WORD OF MOUTH

"[C]rime is almost non-existent. . . . Everyone you pass will wave at you, whether they know you or not, and one always enters a shop or place of business with a pleasant . . . greeting."

—Statia

"Although climbing the Quill was a little arduous, it was kind of fun since there was not a soul around except an occasional crab or snake (just one little guy who slithered away as fast as he could)."

—Doug

WELCOME TO ST. EUSTATIUS

Hotels

- Country Inn **12**
- Golden Era Hotel **3**
- King's Well Hotel **2**
- The Old Gin House **4**

Restaurants

- Blue Bead Bar & Restaurant **10**
- Chinese Bar & Restaurant **8**
- Golden Era Hotel Restaurant **3**
- Grillhouse/San Yen Chinese Bar & Restaurant **7**
- Happy City Chinese Bar & Restaurant **6**
- King's Well Restaurant **2**
- Ocean View Terrace **5**
- The Old Gin House **4**
- The Seaside Bar & Grill **4**
- Smoke Alley Bar & Grill **1**
- Stone Oven **9**
- Superburger **11**

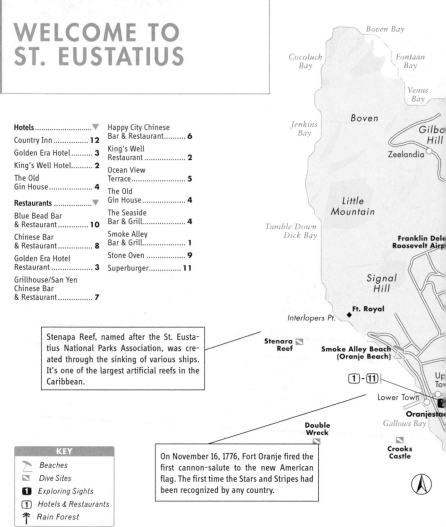

Stenapa Reef, named after the St. Eustatius National Parks Association, was created through the sinking of various ships. It's one of the largest artificial reefs in the Caribbean.

Boven Bay
Cocoluch Bay
Fontaan Bay
Venus Bay
Boven
Jenkins Bay
Gilbo Hill
Zeelandia
Little Mountain
Tumble Down Dick Bay
Franklin Dele Roosevelt Airp
Signal Hill
Ft. Royal
Interlopers Pt.
Stenara Reef
Smoke Alley Beach (Oranje Beach)
1 - 11
Up To
Lower Town
Oranjesta
Gallows Bay
Double Wreck
Crooks Castle
Barracuda Reef

On November 16, 1776, Fort Oranje fired the first cannon-salute to the new American flag. The first time the Stars and Stripes had been recognized by any country.

KEY

- Beaches
- Dive Sites
- Exploring Sights
- Hotels & Restaurants
- Rain Forest

Like Saba, tiny Statia is another quiet Caribbean haven for scuba divers and hikers. When the island was called the Emporium of the Western World, warehouses stretched for a mile along the quays, and 200 merchant ships could anchor at its docks. These days it's the day-trippers from St. Martin who walk the quays.

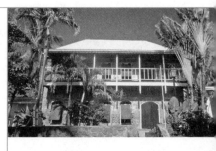

FRIENDLY TRANQUILLITY

A tiny part of the Netherlands Antilles, St. Eustatius (often just called "Statia") is just under 12-square-mi (30-square-km), making it twice as large as Saba. The island, which is 38 mi (63 km) south of St. Maarten, has a population of 2,900. Although there are three beaches, they are better for strolling than swimming.

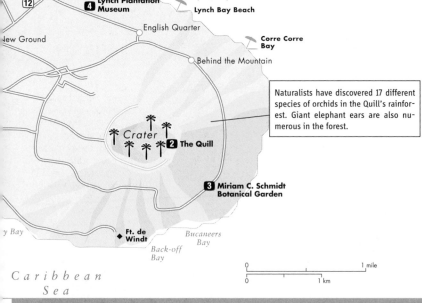

Naturalists have discovered 17 different species of orchids in the Quill's rainforest. Giant elephant ears are also numerous in the forest.

TOP 4 REASONS TO VISIT ST. EUSTATIUS

1. Diving—particularly to its modern and archaeological wrecks—is a highlight in Statia's protected waters.

2. Hiking the Quill, an extinct volcano that holds a primeval rain forest, is the top activity for landlubbers.

3. When you're not diving, you'll be overwhelmed by the genuine friendliness of the people.

4. For anyone interested in 18th-century history, even a day-trip from St. Maarten is a very satisfying experience.

ST. EUSTATIUS PLANNER

Getting to St. Eustatius

The only way to get to Statia (EUX) is on one of the regularly scheduled Winair flights from Saba, St. Maarten, or San Juan; you'll have to book this flight yourself, directly with Winair. There is no regularly scheduled ferry service, but flights from St. Maarten and San Juan are fairly frequent and are timed to coincide with the arrival of international flights there.

Hassle Factor: Medium-High

On the Ground

You could literally walk from the airport runway into town, but if you want to take a taxi, one or two will be waiting for arriving passengers at the airport, and you'll be whisked into Oranjestad.

To explore the island (and there isn't very much of it), car rentals, which cost about $40 to $45 a day, do the job. Statia's roads, somewhat pocked with potholes, are undergoing resurfacing, so the going can be slow and bumpy, and you'll sometimes encounter animals on the roads. The island has two gas stations—one at the south end of Lower Town on the waterfront and Godfrey's in Upper Town.

Where to Stay

Statia has only four hotels and a couple of B&Bs, each with 20 rooms or less; all are right in Oranjestad, within walking distance from everything in town. The island's 65 rooms are comfortable, though none could be considered luxurious. Sometimes the decor, like the redecorated 55-gallon drums turned TV stands at King's Well Hotel, is quite original.

Hotel & Restaurant Costs

Assume that hotels operate on the European Plan (**EP**—with no meals) unless we specify that they use either the Continental Plan (**CP**—with a Continental breakfast), Breakfast Plan (**BP**—with full breakfast), or the Modified American Plan (**MAP**—with breakfast and dinner). Other hotels may offer the Full American Plan (**FAP**—including all meals but no drinks) or may be All-Inclusive (**AI**—with all meals, drinks, and most activities).

WHAT IT COSTS in Dollars					
	$$$$	**$$$**	**$$**	**$**	**¢**
Restaurants	over $25	$20–$25	$12–$20	$5–$10	under $5
Hotels	over $250	$150–$250	$75–$150	$50–$75	under $50

Restaurant prices are for a main course excluding 3% tax and 10% service charge. Hotel prices are for two people in a double room in high season, excluding 7% tax and meal plans.

Activities

Statia has **beaches**, but they are fairly rocky, better suited for walking and beach-combing than for swimming and sunning. The more interesting action is below the waves. Along with Saba, which helps to administer its dive sites as part of the Saba Marine Park, Statia is a major **dive** destination. It has good wreck diving as well as reef diving. If you want to keep your head above water, then the Quill, Statia's extinct volcano, which holds a primeval rain forest, is well worth your time; a guided **hike** here will bring you face to face with all manner of exotic tropical flora and even some fauna.

By Roberta
Sotonoff

THE STARS ARE ABLAZE, but it's dark and empty on the road from the Blue Bead Restaurant to the Gin House Hotel. A chicken running across the road comprises all the traffic, and except for the sound of crickets, there is silence. No need to worry about walking alone. The island of Statia (pronounced *stay-sha*) is safe. How safe? The scuttlebutt is that a St. Maarten police officer sent to serve on the island thinks he is being punished because there is nothing for him to do.

With a population of about 2,700, it's difficult for someone to commit a crime—or do most anything else—without everyone finding out. Everyone knows everyone, and that's also a blessing. Statians are friendly; they beep their horns and say hello to anyone they see. Even day-trippers are warmly welcomed as friends. There are no strangers here.

Think of the tiny Netherland Antillean island of St. Eustatius, commonly called Statia, and think quiet times, strolls through history, and awesome diving and hiking. While many of its neighbors are pursuing the tourist business big-time, Statia just plods along. That's its charm.

The 12-square-mi (31-square-km) island in the Dutch Windward Triangle, 150 mi (241 km) east of Puerto Rico and 38 mi (61 km) south of St. Maarten, was the hub for commerce between Europe and the Americas during the 18th century. When ships carrying slaves, sugar, cotton, ammunition, and other commodities crowded its harbor, it was known as the Emporium of the Western World and the Golden Rock.

With an 11-gun salute to the American "Stars and Stripes" on the brig-of-war *Andrew Doria* on November 16, 1776, Statia's golden age ended. Statia's noteworthy role as the first country to recognize U.S. independence from Great Britain was not a gesture appreciated by the British. In 1781, British Admiral Rodney looted and economically destroyed the island. It has never really recovered.

Indeed, chaos ensued between 1781 and 1816 as the Dutch, English, and French vied for control of the island and it changed hands 22 times. The Netherlands finally won out, and Statia has been a Dutch possession since 1816.

Remnants of those bygone days are evident around the island. Hanging off the cliff at the only village, Oranjestad, is the nearly 370-year-old Fort Oranje, the site from where the famous shots were fired. The original Dutch Reformed Church, built in 1776, sits in its courtyard. Oranjestad itself, on a ridge above the sea, is lush with greenery and bursting with bougainvillea, oleander, and hibiscus. The rest of the island is rather pristine. The eastern side, bordered by the rough waters of the Atlantic, has an untamed quality to it, while extinct volcanoes and dry plains anchor the north end. Statia's crown is the Quill, a 1,968-foot extinct volcano, its verdant crater covered with a primeval rain forest. Hiking to the peak is a popular pastime.

Beaches on the island come and go as the waters see fit, but first-class dive sites lure most visitors to the island. Wrecks and old cannons are plentiful at archaeological dive sites, and modern ships, such as the cable-laying *Charles L. Brown,* have been sunk into underwater craters.

19

Stingrays, eels, turtles, and barracudas live in the undersea Caribbean neighborhood where giant pillar coral, giant yellow sea fans, and reef fingers abound. The sea has reclaimed the walls of Dutch warehouses that have sunk into the sea over the past several hundred years, but these underwater ruins serve as a day-care center for abundant schools of juvenile fish.

On land, beachcombers hunt for blue beads. The 17th-century baubles, found only on Statia, were used to barter for rum, slaves, tobacco, and cotton. The chance of finding one is slim unless you visit the St. Eustatius Historical Foundation Museum. Pre-Columbian artifacts dating back to 500 BC are also on display there.

Besides relying on tourism and the University of St. Eustatius School of Medicine, an accredited, two-year medical school, Statia's economy depends on oil. On the northern end of the island is a way-station for liquid gold, with a 16-million-barrel storage bunker encased in the Boven, an extinct volcano. It's not unusual to see the hovering tankers loading or unloading oil.

Statia is mostly a day-trip destination from nearby St. Maarten, where tourists come to explore historical sights and maybe take a quick hike or dive, and that might be just enough for some tourists. But those who stay longer will come to appreciate the unspoiled island, its history, and its peacefulness. Most of all they will come to enjoy the locals, who make a visit to the island special.

Where to Stay

Renting an apartment is an alternative to staying in a hotel. Although Statia has only a handful of them, several are available for $50 or less per night, but don't expect much beyond a bathroom and kitchenette. Check with the tourist office for options.

★ $–$$$ ▦ **The Old Gin House.** Built from 17th- and 18th-century cobblestones, this quaint old cotton warehouse turned hotel offers the island's nicest accommodations. Comfortable though not lavish rooms face the gardens and pool of the courtyard. The four across the street are oceanside. Chef Marc-Clovis Bertucchi oversees the hotel's Seaside Bar & Grill across the street as well as the main dining room. Internet service is free. ✉ *Bay Rd., Lower Town, Oranjestad* ☎ *599/318–2319* 📠 *599/318–2135* ⊕ *www.oldginhouse.com* ⤤ *18 rooms, 2 suites* ♨ *2 restaurants, some refrigerators, cable TV, some in-room DVDs, pool, bar, Internet room* ▭ *AE, MC, V* ¶⊙¶ *EP.*

$ ▦ **King's Well Hotel.** Win and Laura Piechutzki, along with their macaws, iguanas, cats, and Great Dane, warmly welcome visitors to their little inn. Perched on the wooded cliffs between Upper and Lower Town, the inn has eclectic furnishings, such as TV stands made of decorated oil barrels. All the rooms have balconies, and four have king-size water beds and French doors that face the sea. A cliffside patio is a pleasant place to watch the sunset. The King's Well Restaurant is probably the only place on the island to get authentic Weiner schnitzel. Weekly rates are

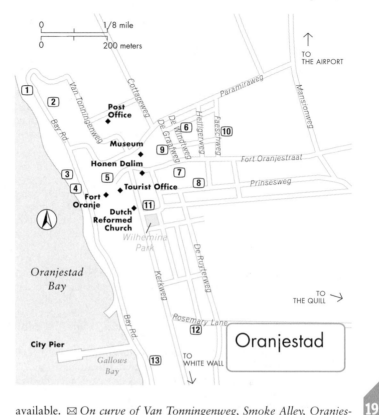

available. ⊠ *On curve of Van Tonningenweg, Smoke Alley, Oranjestad* ☎☎ *599/318–2538* ⊕ *www.kingswellstatia.com* ➳ *12 rooms* △ *Restaurant, refrigerators, cable TV, pool, hot tub, bar* ⊟ *D, MC, V* ⏍ *BP.*

$ ⊞ **Ruby's Inn.** In late 2005, the finishing touches were put on Statia's newest lodging. Rooms are small but adequate, with nice touches like air-conditioning. The property also includes a bar and a restaurant serving local fare. ⊠ *Rosemary Laan, Oranjestad* ☎ *599/318–4497 or 599/524–0644* ➳ *13 rooms* ᐣ *Restaurant, bar* ⊟ *No credit cards* ⏍ *CP.*

¢–$ ⊞ **Golden Era Hotel.** This hotel across the street from the Gin House has a funky, retro-1960s look. Only half the rooms have a view, but all have tile floors and little terraces. The oceanfront property offers friendly service and a restaurant with great creole food. ⊠ *Bay Rd., Lower Town, Box 109, Oranjestad* ☎ *599/318–2345, 800/223–9815 in U.S.* ᐣ *599/318–2445* ➳ *19 rooms, 1 suite* △ *Restaurant, refrigerators, cable TV, saltwater pool, bar* ⊟ *AE, D, MC, V* ⏍ *EP.*

¢ ⊞ **Country Inn.** Facing Zeelandia Bay and not far from the oil terminal and the airport, this folksy little inn is surrounded by a lush, tropical garden. Rooms are clean and comfortable but otherwise pretty basic.

Owner Iris Pompier prepares lunch and dinner on request. ✉ *3 Passion-fruit Rd., Concordia* ☎☎ *599/318–2484* ⬦ *6 rooms* ⟐ *Cable TV* ▭ *No credit cards* ¶◯| *EP.*

Where to Eat

It's surprising that on such a small island, you can find such a wide range of cuisines: Italian, German, French, Chinese, Indonesian, International and, of course, Caribbean are all represented here. What you won't find is anything very fancy. As with most everything on the island, low-key and casual is the name of the game.

ASIAN
$–$$
✕ **Chinese Bar & Restaurant.** Unless you're into Formica, don't expect to be wowed by the atmosphere at this simple spot. What you will find are large portions of dishes like *bami goreng* (Indonesian-style noodles with bits of beef, pork, or shrimp as well as tomatoes, carrots, bean sprouts, cabbage, soy sauce, and spices); or you can have pork chops with spicy sauce. It's do-it-yourself table hauling if you want to eat outside. ✉ *Prinsesweg, Upper Town, Oranjestad* ☎ *599/318–2389* ▭ *No credit cards.*

$–$$
✕ **Grillhouse/San Yen Chinese Bar & Restaurant.** Here is yet another Chinese restaurant that is short on decor—a few tables and a bar—but long on taste. Its special—a dish combining chicken, scallops, shrimp, beef, and sausage with vegetables—is delicious, filling, and well worth the trip. ✉ *Fort Oranjestad, Upper Town, Oranjestad* ☎ *599/318–2915* ▭ *No credit cards.*

¢–$$
✕ **Happy City Chinese Bar & Restaurant.** In the island's only strip mall, this tidy restaurant offers more than just Chinese fare. The locals frequent it to sup on Indonesian dishes such as *nasi goreng* (fried rice). ✉ *De Windtweg, Upper Town, Oranjestad* ☎ *599/318–2389* ▭ *No credit cards* ◷ *Closed Wed.*

CAFÉS
¢
Intermezzo. Statia's newest contribution to the dining scene is a coffee shop with just a handful of tables. It is the place to grab an espresso, cappuccino, or latte. There are also sandwiches and other light fare. An added bonus is the shop's wireless Internet service. Get here early, as it closes at 1 PM on Sunday and 3 PM the rest of the week. ✉ *Heyligerweg St., Ornajestad* ☎ *599/318–2520* ▭ *No credit cards* ◷ *No dinner.*

¢
Sand Box Tree Bakery. This is the perfect spot to grab a quick sandwich or satisfy your sweet tooth. This is also the place to get a wedding, birthday, or other special-occasion cake. It's in Oranjestad, opposite the Dutch Reformed Church. ✉ *Kerweg, Upper Town, Oranjestad* ☎ *599/ 318–2469* ▭ *No credit cards.*

CARIBBEAN
$$
✕ **Stone Oven.** At this cozy restaurant, you can eat inside a little dining room or outside on the patio. The kitchen specializes in local specialties like goat water (a hearty goat stew). Sometimes there is live music. ✉ *16A Feaschweg, Upper Town, Oranjestad* ☎ *599/318–2809* ▭ *No credit cards.*

$–$$
✕ **Golden Era Hotel Restaurant.** Don't pass up this restaurant because it is completely nondescript. Concentrate instead on the delicious seafood and fine creole food. It has another thing going for it: it's alongside the

water, so the sound of the Caribbean is always playing in the background. ✉ *Golden Era Hotel, Bay Rd., Lower Town, Box 109, Oranjestad* ☎ *599/ 318–2345* 🖃 *AE, D, MC, V.*

¢ ✕ **Superburger.** Statia's version of fast food comes from this little hang- out, which serves burgers and shakes as well as some West Indian dishes. It's a local favorite for breakfast and lunch. ✉ *Graaffweg, Upper Town, Oranjestad* ☎ *599/318–2412* 🖃 *No credit cards* ⊘ *No dinner.*

ECLECTIC ✕ **The Old Gin House Main Dining Room.** Though the setting—a comfort-
$$–$$$$ able dining room that borders a flower-filled courtyard—remains the same, this bistro has reinvented itself. With the arrival of chef Marc- Clovis Bertucchi, it now serves French cuisine with a West Indian and West African flair. Specialties include Drambuie steak, crusted roast beef, and a fanciful "floating island" dessert. This is the most upscale restau- rant on the island. ✉ *Old Gin House, Bay Rd., Lower Town, Oran- jestad* ☎ *599/318–2934* ⊘ *Closed Wed. No lunch.*

★ $$–$$$ ✕ **Blue Bead Bar & Restaurant.** This friendly little restaurant is the per- fect place to watch the sunset. Its cheerful blue-and-yellow decor and the friendly staff and congenial owners, Gilbert Bussald and Maryclaire Uldry, make the homemade French breads and pastries taste even bet- ter. There are always daily specials, but you shouldn't pass up the tasty garlic shrimp. ✉ *Bay Rd., Gallows Bay, Lower Town, Oranjestad* ☎ *599/318–2873* 🖃 *AE, D, MC, V* ⊘ *Closed Mon.*

$$–$$$ ✕ **King's Well Restaurant.** It's like watching Mom and Dad make dinner to see owners Win and Laura Piechutzki scurry around their open kitchen preparing the night's meal. And don't expect to eat alone, be- cause a meal at this breezy terrace overlooking the sea makes you part of the family. The *rostbraten* (roast beef) and schnitzels are authentic, as Win is German. The fresh lobster is another good choice. ✉ *King's Well Hotel, Bay Rd., Lower Town, Oranjestad* ☎☎ *599/318–2538* 🖃 *D, MC, V.*

$–$$$ ✕ **The Seaside Bar & Grill.** Set across the street from the Old Gin House, this place is more casual that the hotel's main dining room. The food is just as good, as it's also overseen by chef Marc-Clovis Bertucchi. His simple menu includes great scrambled eggs for breakfast; sandwiches and salads for lunch; and dinner specials that you can bet will always include something from the sea. A snack menu features crab ball and jalapeño poppers. On Wednesday evening there's a barbecue with live music. ✉ *Old Gin House Hotel, Bay Rd., Lower Town, Oranjestad* ☎ *599/318–2319* 🖃 *AE, MC, V.*

$–$$$ ✕ **Smoke Alley Bar & Grill.** Owner Michelle Balelo cooks Tex-Mex, Ital- ian, Caribbean, and American food to order at this beachfront hangout. The open-air eatery is the only place on the island where you can get draft beer. There's live music and barbecued meats every Friday night. ✉ *Lower Town, Gallows Bay* ☎ *599/318–2002* 🖃 *MC, V* ⊘ *Closed Sun.*

$–$$ ✕ **Ocean View Terrace.** This spot in the courtyard overlooking the his- toric Fort Oranje is a favorite for those who like to watch the sunset. Owner Lauris Redan serves sandwiches and burgers for lunch and local cuisine—baked snapper with shrimp sauce, spicy chicken, tenderloin steak—at dinner. You can get breakfast here too, and every now and

19

then there's a succulent barbecue. ⊠ *Oranjestraat, Upper Town, Oranjestad* ☏ *599/318–2934* ▭ *No credit cards* ⊗ *No lunch Sun.*

Beaches

If you lust after a white sandy beach, calm waters, and a place to cool yourself off with a quick dip, you're looking at the wrong island. Statia's beaches are mostly deserted, rocky stretches of pristine shoreline. Many of the beaches on the Caribbean side are here today and reclaimed by the sea tomorrow, while the Atlantic side is untamed with wild swells and a vicious undertow. Walking, shelling, and searching for the elusive blue beads are popular pastimes for beachgoers. It's likely, however, that the only place you will find real blue beads is in the St. Eustatius Historical Foundation.

Lynch Bay Beach. Just two bends north of Corre Corre Bay, light-brown sand covers this small beach on the island's Atlantic side. Opt for walking instead of swimming here. There are turbulent swells and an undertow. ⊠ *Lynch Bay.*

Smoke Alley Beach (Oranje Beach). The colors of the sands vary from light beige to black at this rocky beach on the Caribbean side near Gallows Bay. The waters are sometimes calm, so snorkeling is possible, but it's usually a better place for a walk than a swim. ⊠ *Oranjestad, north end.*

Zeelandia Beach. Walking, shelling, and sunbathing are popular pastimes on this 2-mi (3-km) stretch of black-and-tan sand. Its Atlantic-side location makes it a dangerous place even to put one piggy in the water. ⊠ *Oranjestad.*

Sports & the Outdoors

DIVING &
SNORKELING
Fodor'sChoice
★

The island's three dive shops along Bay Road in Lower Town rent all types of gear (including snorkeling gear for about $20 a day), offer certification courses, and organize dive trips. One-tank dives start at $40; two-tank dives are about $75. Both the Saba Marine Park and Quill National Park are under the supervision of **Statia National Parks** (☏ 599/318–2884 ⊕ www.statiapark.org). The marine tag fee, which all divers must buy, is used to help offset the costs of preserving the coral and other sea life here; the cost is $3 per day or $15 annually. There are two decompression chambers on the island, and the University of St. Eustatius, a medical school, offers technical training in undersea and hyperbaric medicine.

Dive Statia (⊠ Bay Rd., Lower Town, Oranjestad ☏ 599/318–2435 or 866/614–3491 ⊕ www.divestatia.com), a fully equipped and PADI-certified dive shop, has earned PADI's five-star Gold Palm designation. Owners Rudy and Rinda Hees operate the shop out of an old warehouse. In addition to the standard courses, Dive Statia also offers underwater photography courses, Nitrox diving, and DVPs—diver propulsion vehicles—for diving or snorkeling. **Golden Rock Dive Center** (⊠ Old Gin House, Bay Rd., Lower Town, Oranjestad ☏ 599/318–2964 or 800/311–6658 ⊕ www.goldenrockdive.com), operated by Glenn and Michele Faires, is one of several facilities with PADI's Gold Palm designation.

CLOSE UP

Diving on Statia

FORGET ABOUT GLITZ, GLAMOUR, and nightlife. Statia is the quintessential low-key island. Finding an illusive *iguana delicatissima* on the Quill is probably the most exciting thing you can do on land. Statia's real thrills are underwater.

Long ago, the ocean reclaimed the original sea wall built by the Dutch in the 1700s. The sunken walls, remnants of old buildings, cannons, and anchors are now part of an extensive reef system populated by reef fingers, juvenile fish, and other sea creatures.

Statia has more than 30 dive sites protected by the St. Eustatius Marine Park, which has an office on Bay Road in Lower Town. Barracuda swim around colorful coral walls at **Barracuda Reef,** off the island's southwest coast. At **Double Wreck,** just offshore from Lower Town, you can find two tall-masted ships that date from the 1700s. The coral has taken on the shape of these two disintegrated vessels, and the site attracts spiny lobsters, stingrays, moray eels, and large schools of fish. About 100 yards west of Double Wreck is the Japanese ship **Cheng Tong,** which sank in 2004. Off the south end of the island, the sinking of the **Charles L. Brown,** a 1957 cable-laying vessel, which was once owned by AT&T, created another artificial reef when it was sunk in a 135-foot underwater crater. Off the island's western shore, **Stenapa Reef** is an artificial reef created from the wrecks of barges, a harbor boat, and other ship parts. Large grouper and turtles are among the marine life you can spot here. For snorkelers, **Crooks Castle** has several stands of pillar coral, giant yellow sea fans, and sea whips just southwest of Lower Town.

In addition to certification courses, the company offers a National Geographic program that emphasizes conservation. A former Swiss pilot, Ronald Metrox, operates **Scubaqua** (⊠ Golden Era Hotel, Bay Rd., Lower Town, Oranjestad ☎ 599/318–2345 ⊕ www.scubaqua.com), which attracts Europeans as well as Americans. Dive courses are offered in various languages.

FISHING By and large, deep-sea fishing is not a major activity off Statia's shores. But it's nice to be out on the water. **Dive Statia** (⊠ Bay Rd., Lower Town, Oranjestad ☎ 599/318–2435 or 866/614–3491 ⊕ www.divestatia. com) offers a professional fishing charter that is advanced enough to be used for tournament fishing. A half-day tour, which includes bait, equipment, and refreshments, costs $350. **Golden Rock Dive Center** (⊠ Bay Rd., Lower Town, Oranjestad ☎ 599/318–2964 ⊕ www.goldenrockdive.com) offers half- and full-day trips on its dive boat for $400 and $600, respectively. All your gear and bait are included.

HIKING Trails range from the easy to the "Watch out!" The big thrill here is the Quill, the 1,968-foot extinct volcano with its crater cradling a rain forest. Give yourself two to four hours to complete the hike. The tourist office has a list of 12 marked trails and can put you in touch with a guide. Quill National Park includes a trail into the crater, which is a long, winding, but safe walk. Maps and the necessary $3 permit, which is good for a year, are available at the Saba Marine Park headquarters on Bay Road. Wear layers: it can be cool on the summit and steamy in the interior.

Shopping

The very limited shopping here is all duty-free. But other than the predictable souvenirs, there's not much to buy. Several shops carry delicious Dutch cheeses and chocolates and an interesting book by Heleen Cornett called *St. Eustatius: Echoes of the Past.* **Mazinga Gift Shop** (⊠ Fort Oranjestreet, Upper Town, Oranjestad ☎ 599/318–2245) is a small department store that sells the basic necessities. The **Paper Corner** (⊠ Van Tonningenweg, Upper Town, Oranjestad ☎ 599/318–2208) sells magazines, a few books, and stationery supplies.

Nightlife

Statia's nightlife consists of local bands playing weekend gigs and quiet drinks at hotel bars. The island's oldest bar, tiny **Cool Corner** (⊠ Wilhelminaweg, Upper Town, Oranjestad ☎ 599/318–2523), across from the St. Eustatius Historical Foundation Museum, is a lively after-work and weekend hangout. **Smoke Alley Bar & Grill** (⊠ Lower Town, Gallows Bay ☎ 599/318–2002) has live music on Friday night.

Exploring St. Eustatius

Statia is an arid island consisting of a valley between two mountain peaks. Most sights lie in the valley, making touring the island easy. From the airport you can rent a car or take a taxi and be in historic Oranjestad in minutes; to hike the Quill, Statia's highest peak, you can drive to the trailhead in less than 15 minutes from just about anywhere.

Numbers in the margin correspond to points of interest on the St. Eustatius map.

❹ Lynch Plantation Museum. Also known as the Berkel Family Plantation, this museum consists of two one-room buildings that show what life was like almost 100 years ago. A remarkable collection preserves this family's history—pictures, eyeglasses, original furnishings, and farming and fishing implements give a detailed perspective of life on Statia. Call ahead to arrange a private tour. Since it's on the northeast side of the island, you need either a taxi or a car to get there. ⊠ *Lynch Bay* ☎ *599/ 318–2338* ▣ *Free.*

❶ Oranjestad. Statia's capital and only town sits on the west coast facing the Caribbean. Both Upper Town and Lower Town are easy to explore on foot. With its three bastions, **Fort Oranje** has clutched these cliffs since 1636. In 1976 Statia participated in the U.S. bicentennial celebration by restoring the fort, and now the black cannons point out over the ramparts. In the parade grounds a plaque, presented in 1939 by Franklin D. Roosevelt, reads, HERE THE SOVEREIGNTY OF THE UNITED STATES OF AMERICA WAS FIRST FORMALLY ACKNOWLEDGED TO A NATIONAL VESSEL BY A FOREIGN OFFICIAL.

Built in 1775, the partially restored **Dutch Reformed Church,** on Kerkweg (Church Way), has lovely stone arches that face the sea. Ancient tales can be read on the gravestones in the adjacent 18th-century cemetery where people were often buried atop one another. On Synagogepad (Synagogue Path), off Kerkweg, is **Honen Dalim** ("She Who Is Charitable to the Poor"), one of the Caribbean's oldest synagogues. Dating from 1738, its exterior is partially restored.

Lower Town sits below Fort Oranjestraat (Fort Orange Street) and some steep cliffs and is reached from Upper Town on foot via the zigzagging, cobblestone Fort Road or by car via Van Tonningenweg. Warehouses and shops that were piled high with European imports in the 18th century are either abandoned or simply used to store local fishermen's equipment. Along the waterfront is a lovely park with palms, flowering shrubs, and benches—the work of the historical foundation. Peeking out from the shallow waters are the crumbling ruins of 18th-century buildings, from Statia's days as the merchant hub of the Caribbean. The sea has slowly advanced since then, and it now surrounds many of the stone-and-brick ruins, making for fascinating snorkeling.

In the center of Upper Town is the **St. Eustatius Historical Foundation Museum,** former headquarters of Lord George Rodney, a British admiral during the American Revolution. While here, Rodney confiscated everything from gunpowder to wine in retaliation for Statia's gallant support of the fledgling country. The completely restored house is Statia's most important intact 18th-century dwelling. Exhibits trace the island's history from the pre-Columbian 6th century to the present. Statia is the only island thus far where ruins and artifacts of the Saladoid, a newly discovered tribe, have been excavated. ⊠ *Doncker House, 3 Wilhelminaweg, Upper Town, Oranjestad* ☎ *599/318–2693* 🖃 *$2* ☯ *Weekdays 9–5, weekends 9–noon.*

❷ **The Quill.** This extinct, perfectly formed, 1,968-foot volcano has a primeval rain forest in its crater. If you like to hike, you'll want to head here to see giant elephant ears, ferns, flowers, wild orchids, fruit trees, and the endangered *iguana delicatissima* (a large—sometimes several feet long—greenish-gray creature with spines down its back). The volcanic cone rises 3 mi (5 km) south of Oranjestad on the main road. Local boys go up to the Quill by torchlight to catch delectable land crabs. The tourist board or Statia Marine Park will help you make hiking arrangements. Figure on two to four hours to hike the volcano. Make sure to purchase the required $3 permit at the park office before you begin.

Fodor's Choice

❸ **Miriam C. Schmidt Botanical Garden.** As if Statia is not tranquil enough, now comes this new, peaceful 52-acre park. The botanical park is a place of relaxation and quiet. The park has a greenhouse, a palm garden, a kitchen garden, and an observation bird trail. Its location, on the Atlantic side of the Quill on a plot called Upper Company, reveals a superb view of St. Kitts. For a picnic, there's no better place, but the only way to get there is by car or taxi.

19

ST. EUSTATIUS ESSENTIALS

To research prices, get advice from other travelers, and book travel arrangements, visit www.fodors.com.

Transportation

BY AIR

There are no nonstop flights to Statia from the U.S., but short hops to and from St. Maarten are frequently scheduled. Winair makes the 16-minute flight from St. Maarten to Statia's Franklin Delano Roosevelt Airport several times a day, the 10-minute flight from Saba once a day, and the 15-minute flight from St. Kitts twice a week in high season. Caribbean Sun, which code shares with US Airways, recently announced service from St. Maarten and San Juan, Puerto Rico. Reconfirm your flight, because schedules can change abruptly. The departure fee from the island is $5.65 within the Dutch Caribbean and $20 to all other destinations. If flying out of St. Maarten, check to see if the international departure fee has already been added into your airline ticket.

📞 Airline Contacts **Caribbean Sun Airlines** 📞 599/318-3020 ⊕ www.flycsa.com. **Winair** 📞 599/318-2303 or 800/634-4907 ⊕ www.fly-winair.com.

📞 Airport Contacts **Franklin Delano Roosevelt Airport** 📞 599/318-2887.

BY CAR

Driving in Statia is not difficult, mostly because there are not that many places to go. Street signs are not plentiful, but anyone you ask for directions will be more than happy to help you. The roads are generally in good condition.

If you are renting a car, daily rates range from $35 to $45.

📞 **ARC Car Rental** ⊠ Oranjestad 📞 599/318-2595. **Brown's** ⊠ White Wall Rd. 8, Oranjestad 📞 599/318-2266. **Rainbow Car Rental** ⊠ Statia Mall, Oranjestad 📞 599/318-2811. **Walter's** ⊠ Chapel Piece, Oranjestad 📞 599/318-2719.

BY TAXI

Taxis meet all flights from Franklin Delano Roosevelt Airport and charge about $5 per person for the drive into town.

Contacts & Resources

BANKS & CURRENCY EXCHANGE

Prices quoted throughout this chapter are in U.S. dollars, unless noted otherwise.

U.S. dollars are accepted everywhere, but legal tender is the Netherlands Antilles florin (NAf), also referred to as the guilder, and you shouldn't be surprised to receive change in them. The exchange rate fluctuates slightly but was about NAf1.88 to US$1 at this writing. The island's two banks in Upper Town provide foreign-exchange services. There is now an ATM at Windward Islands Bank.

📞 **FirstCaribbean International Bank** 📞 599/318-2392. **Windward Islands Bank** 📞 599/318-2846, 599/318-2845, or 599/318-2857.

BUSINESS HOURS

Banks have varying hours: FirstCaribbean International Bank is open weekdays from 8:30 to 3:30; Windward Islands Bank is open weekdays from 8:30 to noon and 1:30 to 3:30. Post offices are open weekdays from 7:30 to noon and 1 to 4 or 5. Shops are open from 8 to 6, and grocery stores are open from 7:30 to 7.

EMERGENCIES

📞 Emergency Services **Fire** 📞 699/318-2360 or 919. **Ambulance** 📞 599/318-2371, 599/318-2211, or 912. **Police** 📞 599/318-2333 or 911.

📞 Hospitals **Queen Beatrix Medical Center** ⊠ 25 Prinsesweg, Oranjestad 📞 599/318-2211 or 599/318-2371.

📞 Pharmacies **Pharmacy** ⊠ Queen Beatrix Medical Center, 25 Prinsesweg, Oranjestad 📞 599/318-2211 or 599/318-2371.

📞 Scuba Diving Emergencies **St. Eustatius School of Medicine** ⊠ Fort Bay 📞 599/318-2600.

HOLIDAYS

Public holidays for the year are New Year's Day, Good Friday, Easter Monday (Mar. or Apr.), Coronation Day and the Queen's Birthday (celebrating the birthday and coronation of Holland's Queen Beatrix, Apr. 30), Labor Day (May 1), Ascension Day (Apr. or May, 3 days after Easter), Emancipation Day (July 1), Statia-America Day (commemorating events of 1776, when Statia became the first foreign government to salute the American flag, Nov. 16), Christmas, and Boxing Day (Dec. 26).

LANGUAGE

Statia's official language is Dutch (it's used in government documents), but everyone speaks English. Dutch is taught as the primary language in the schools, and street signs are in both Dutch and English.

INTERNET, MAIL & SHIPPING

Intermezzo, on Heyligerweg Street in Ornajestad, has a Wi-Fi connection, as does the St. Eustatius Jubilee Library in the heart of Oranjestad across from the Government Administration Building.

The post office is in Upper Town, on Cottageweg. Airmail letters to North America and Europe are NAf 2.25; postcards, NAf 1.10. When sending letters to the island, be sure to include "Netherlands Antilles" and "Caribbean" in the address.

PASSPORTS & VISAS

U.S. and Canadian citizens must have proof of citizenship: either a passport or a birth certificate with a raised seal along with a government-authorized photo ID will do. Everyone else needs a valid passport. All visitors need a return or ongoing ticket. At this writing, a valid passport was expected to become a requirement for all U.S. citizens traveling to St. Eustatius beginning January 1, 2007, but one should have one anyway.

SAFETY

Statia is relatively crime-free, but common sense should prevail. Lock your rental car when leaving it, store valuables in the hotel safe, and lock your hotel-room door behind you. When driving, particularly at night, be on the lookout for goats and other animals that have wandered onto the road. While hiking, you might see the harmless racer snake sunning itself. These snakes are afraid of people and will promptly leave when you arrive.

TAXES & SERVICE CHARGES

The departure tax is $5.65 for flights to other islands of the Netherlands Antilles and $12 to foreign destinations, payable in cash only. Note: When flying home through St. Maarten, list yourself as "in transit" and avoid paying the $20 tax levied in St. Maarten if you are there for less than 24 hours. Hotels collect a 7% government tax and 3% turnover tax. Restaurants charge a 3% government tax and a 10% service charge.

TELEPHONES

Statia has microwave telephone service to all parts of the world. Direct dial is available. There are two pay phones on the island, one near the airport and one in Landsradio. They work with phone cards that you can buy at stores throughout the island. To call Statia from North America, dial 011 + 599 + 318, followed by the four-digit number. To call the United States using an AT&T card, the access number is 001–800/872–2881. To call within the island, dial only the five-digit number that starts with an 8.

TIPPING

Although your hotel or restaurant might add a 10% to 15% service charge, it's customary to tip maids, waitstaff, and other service personnel, including taxi drivers. About 10% for taxi drivers should do it; hotel maids will appreciate about a dollar or two per day, and members of the waitstaff will be grateful for an extra 5% to 10%.

TOUR OPTIONS

Statia's five taxis, a minibus, and two large buses are available for island tours. A

19

2½-hour outing costs $40 per vehicle for five people (extra persons are $5 each), usually including airport transfer. One of the better taxi tour operators is historian Josser Daniel, who is happy to show you his citation from President Bill Clinton for rescuing an American tourist from drowning.

The St. Eustatius Historical Foundation Museum sells a booklet detailing a walking tour of the sights for $3. The tour begins in Lower Town at the marina and ends at the museum. You can take it on your own using the booklet (numbered blue signs on most of the sights correspond to signs in the booklet), but a guide may prove more illuminating.

🔳 **Josser Daniel** ☎ 599/318-2358 **St. Eustatius Historical Foundation Museum** ✉ 3 Wilhelminaweg, Oranjestad ☎ 599/318-2693.

MEDIA

The *Daily Herald* is the newspaper for the Dutch islands. Each island—Statia, Saba, and St. Maarten/St. Martin—has a local edition. Radio Statia, the island's only radio station, broadcasts on 91.5 FM.

VISITOR INFORMATION

At the tourist office, right in the charming courtyard of the recently renovated government offices, you can pick up maps, brochures, advice, and a listing of 12 marked trails and arrange for guides and tours.

🔳 In St. Eustatius **Tourist Office** ⊕ www.statiatourism.com ✉ Fort Oranjestraat, Oranjestad ☎ 599/318-2433 or 599/318-2107 🖷 599/318-2433 ⊗ Weekdays 8-noon and 1-5.

WEDDINGS

Marriages in St. Eustatius follow the same rules as on other Netherland Antilles islands. Couples must be at least 18 years old and submit their documents at least 14 days prior to the wedding date. The application requires notarized original documents to be submitted to the registrar, including birth certificates, passports (for non-Dutch persons), divorce decrees from previous marriages, and death certificates of deceased spouses; six witnesses must be present if the ceremony is to take place outside of the Marriage Hall. The documents must be submitted in the Dutch or English language or else be translated into Dutch. The cost for this process is $276.

St. Kitts & Nevis

WORD OF MOUTH

"When we went to St. Kitts . . . we were looking for a laid back vacation without feeling the pressure of 'we need to do this and this and this' mentality. It was perfect for just that."

—paulalou

"Nevis is a terrific island if you don't mind dark sand beaches. . . . There are . . . scores of old ruins . . ., hiking trails, and small intimate plantation inns where you will be treated like the guest of honor."

—Sunnyboy

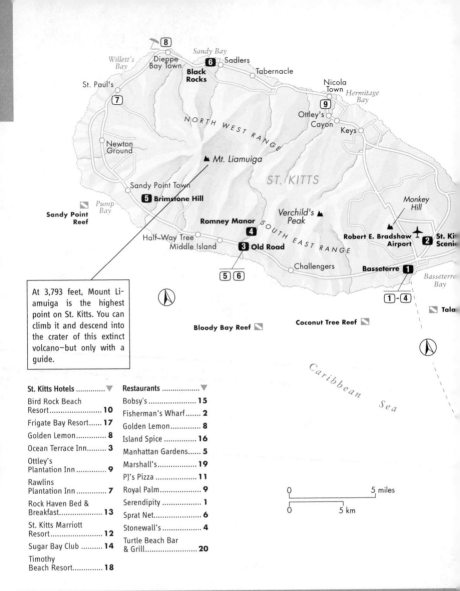

At 3,793 feet, Mount Liamuiga is the highest point on St. Kitts. You can climb it and descend into the crater of this extinct volcano—but only with a guide.

TOP 4 REASONS TO VISIT ST. KITTS & NEVIS

1. Both St. Kitts and Nevis are steeped in history; Brimstone Hill Fortress is the Eastern Caribbean's sole man-made UNESCO World Heritage site

2. Luxurious, restored plantation inns can be found on both islands.

3. Both islands have extinct volcanoes and luxuriant rainforests ideal for hikes, as well as fine diving and snorkeling sites.

4. You'll find less development—particularly on Nevis—and more cordial and courteous islanders than on more touristy islands.

WELCOME TO ST. KITTS & NEVIS

THE MOTHER COLONY AND HER SISTER

St. Kitts, a 65-square-mi (168-square-km) island is 2 mi (3 km) from smaller Nevis, about 40 square mi (121 square km). The two former British colonies are joined in a sometimes strained independence. St. Kitts is often called "The Mother Colony," because it was the first permanent English settlement in the Caribbean.

KEY

- Beaches
- Dive Sites
- **1** Exploring Sights
- Ferry
- **1** Hotels & Restaurants

Alexander Hamilton, the first U.S. Secretary of the Treasury, was born in Charlestown, on Nevis, where he spent his first five years.

see map on page 724

A yucca watches over North Friar's Bay on St. Kitts's narrow peninsula as the island trails off to Nevis, its diminutive companion just 2 mi distant. On both islands, green fields of sugarcane run to the sea, once-magnificent plantation houses are now luxurious inns, and lovely stretches of uncrowded beach stretch before you.

ST. KITTS & NEVIS PLANNER

Getting to St. Kitts & Nevis

There are no nonstop flights to Nevis since the airport can't support large jets. Americans will usually find it easier to connect in San Juan, but there are a few flights on small, Caribbean airlines from other islands. Americans can fly non-stop to St. Kitts, but British and Canadian travelers usually fly first to Antigua and then make the short hop over on a small plane. Depending on where you are flying from, it may be easier to take a nonstop to Antigua, San Juan, St. Maarten, or St. Thomas and then connect to either St. Kitts or Nevis. In truth, it's usually going to be cheaper to fly into St. Kitts and then take a sea taxi or regularly scheduled ferry to Nevis, but check the schedules or book your sea taxi in advance; a water taxi costs between $20 and $25 one-way, and can take as long as 45 minutes.

Robert L. Bradshaw Golden Rock Airport on St. Kitts (SKB, newly expanded and modernized) and the smaller, simpler Vance W. Armory International Airport on Nevis (NEV), are still fairly sleepy.

Hassle Factor: Low to Medium for St. Kitts, Medium for Nevis.

On the Ground

Taxis meet every ferry and flight to St. Kitts or Nevis. The taxis are unmetered, but fixed rates, in EC dollars, are posted at the airport and at the jetty. Note that rates are the same for one to four passengers. On St. Kitts the fares range from EC$18 to Basseterre, to EC$72 for the farthest point from the airport. From the airport on Nevis it costs EC$24 to Nisbet Plantation, EC$49 to the Four Seasons, and EC$67 to Montpelier. Before setting off in a cab, be sure to clarify whether the rate quoted is in EC or U.S. dollars. There's a 50% surcharge for trips made between 10 PM and 6 AM.

Renting a Car

If you'd like to dine at the various inns and sight-see for more than one day in St. Kitts, then you should rent a car. If you're staying in the Frigate Bay–Basseterre area, you can get by using taxis and doing a half-day island tour. On Nevis, if you deviate from Main Street in Charlestown, you're likely to have trouble finding your way. You can rent a car for a day or two of exploring if you want, but a tour with a guide is usually easier. On either island, you must get a temporary driving permit (EC$50 on St. Kitts, $24 on Nevis) and drive on the left.

Activities

Both St. Kitts and Nevis have good but not great **beaches** (Friar's or Frigate Bay on St. Kitts, Pinney's or Oualie Beach on Nevis). St. Kitts offers a wider range of activities, including good **diving, horseback riding, hiking** tours in the rain forest, and boat rides; the Royal St. Kitts Golf Club was renovated in 2004 and another **golf** course is being developed at this writing. Nevis has fewer organized activities, but they run the gamut from **wind surfing** to **deep-sea fishing** to **kayaking** to horse back riding. The Four Seasons Nevis has one of the Caribbean's finest golf courses. **Dining** at one of the fine plantation inn restaurants is always a highlight of any trip to Nevis or St. Kitts.

Where to Stay

St. Kitts has a wide variety of places to stay—beautifully restored plantation inns, full-service affordable hotels, simple beachfront cottages, and all-inclusive resorts. One large resort—the Marriott—is more mid-range than upscale and attracts large groups and package tourists. Choose St. Kitts if you want a wider choice of activities and accommodations (you can always do Nevis as a day-trip). Nevis is a small island with no large resorts, and most accommodations are upscale—primarily plantation inns and the luxurious Four Seasons. It's much quieter than St. Kitts, so choose it if you want to get away from the hectic island scene and simply relax in low-key comfort and surprisingly high style.

TYPES OF LODGING

Four Seasons Nevis: Really in a class by itself, the Four Seasons is the only lavish, high-end property on either island. If you can afford it, the resort is certainly one of the Caribbean's finest.	**Plantation Inns:** Unique to St. Kitts and Nevis are renovated, historic plantation houses that have been turned into upscale inns. On Nevis, the inns are the dominant form of lodging and the main draw. They are usually managed by hands-on owner-operators and offer	fine cuisine and convivial hospitality; though not usually on a beach, most of these inns have beach clubs with free private shuttle service.

Hotel & Restaurant Costs

Assume that hotels operate on the European Plan (**EP**—with no meals) unless we specify that they use either the Continental Plan (**CP**—with a Continental breakfast), Breakfast Plan (**BP**—with full breakfast), or the Modified American Plan (**MAP**—with breakfast and dinner). Other hotels may offer the Full American Plan (**FAP**—including all meals but no drinks) or may be All-Inclusive (**AI**—with all meals, drinks, and most activities).

WHAT IT COSTS in Dollars					
	$$$$	**$$$**	**$$**	**$**	**¢**
Restaurants	over $30	$20–$30	$12–$20	$8–$12	under $8
Hotels*	over $350	$250–$350	$150–$250	$80–$150	under $80
Hotels**	over $450	$350–$450	$250–$350	$125–$250	under $125

*EP, BP, CP **AI, FAP, MAP

Restaurant prices are for a main course at dinner and do not include the customary 10% service charge. Hotel prices are per night for a double room in high season, excluding 10% tax, customary 10%–15% service charge, and meal plans (except at all-inclusives).

When to Go

The high season is relatively short, starting in mid-December and stretching into early or mid-April. The shoulder season (roughly April to mid-June and November to mid-December) offers lower rates. Rates are lower still from mid-June through November, but as this coincides with hurricane season, things are usually quiet.

Carnival on St. Kitts is celebrated during the 10 days right after Christmas.

The **St. Kitts Music Festival** in late June or early July is the biggest event on the island and draws international singing stars.

September on St. Kitts is devoted to independence festivals.

Nevis calls its summer carnival **Culturama**, and it's celebrated in late July and early August. In mid-September, **Heritage Week** celebrates the island's history with several celebrations.

The **Nevis Culinary Heritage Exposition** brings in guest chefs for cooking demonstrations and wine tastings the last week of October.

20

By Jordan
Simon

AS I RAMBLE THROUGH THE RAIN FOREST, its pristine wildness envelops me like a warm quilt: a banyan tree with roots like the bannisters I slid down as a child, bromeliads and orchids strangling mahogany trees in their embrace, green vervet monkeys stealthily clutching fallen, overripe mangoes like treasure, iridescent butterflies and hummingbirds competing for prize blooms. But when the trail suddenly disappears into the lush, fragrant undergrowth, I panic momentarily. Then a shifting breeze carries tinkling laughter and clinking cups. Following the sound, I emerge within minutes, sun-blinded, onto a vast, immaculately groomed lawn rolling down to the sea. A quartet of casual yet worldly Brits waves from a table set by a restored 18th-century sugar factory. "You look like you could use a drink," one trills. As I approach, a smiling staffer intercepts me with a tray bearing a cool mint-scented towel and iced bush tea "to calm da nerves."

Variations on that scene are played out on both St. Kitts and Nevis. These idyllic sister islands, just 2 mi (3 km) apart at their closest point, offer visitors a relatively authentic island experience. Both have luxuriant mountain rain forests, uncrowded beaches, historic ruins, towering, long-dormant volcanoes, charming if slightly dilapidated Georgian capitals in Basseterre (St. Kitts) and Charlestown (Nevis), intact cultural heritage, friendly if shy people, and restored, 18th-century sugar plantation inns run by elegant, if sometimes eccentric, expatriate British and American owners.

The islands' history follows the usual Caribbean route: Amerindian settlements, Columbus's voyages, fierce colonial battles between the British and French, a boom in sugar production second only to that of Barbados. St. Kitts became known as the mother colony of the West Indies: English settlers sailed from there to Antigua, Barbuda, Tortola, and Montserrat, while the French dispatched colonists to Martinique, Guadeloupe, St. Martin, and St. Barths.

St. Kitts and Nevis, in addition to Anguilla, achieved self-government as an associated state of Great Britain in 1967. Anguillians soon made their displeasure known, separating immediately, while St. Kitts and Nevis waited until 1983 to become an independent nation. The two islands, despite their superficial similarities, have taken increasingly different routes regarding tourism. Nevis received an economic boost from the Four Seasons, which helped establish it as an upscale destination. St. Kitts, however, has yet to define its identity at a time when most islands have found their tourism niche. A fierce sibling rivalry has ensued.

Though its comparative lack of development is a lure, the Kittitian government is casting its economic net in several directions. Golf, ecotourism, and scuba diving are being aggressively promoted. The 648-room Marriott, triple the size of any previous hotel, has raised its profile somewhat. This has revived talk of chains like Ritz-Carlton and SuperClubs invading the islandscape (the ultraritzy Auberge Resorts will debut its first Caribbean property in 2008), alongside upmarket villa compounds, a major marine theme park, several golf courses, and the $17 million Beaumont Park horse-racing venue (itself part of a megadevelopment on the island's northwest end). The government hopes the number of available rooms will increase to more than 2,000 (from the current 1,439—including villas and condos), according to the "build it and they will come" philosophy. At this writing, a second, longer, and much-delayed cruise pier was slated for completion in late 2006, which would permit the largest ships to dock and disgorge passengers. But is St. Kitts ready to absorb all this? The island offers a surprisingly diverse vacation experience while retaining its essential Caribbean flavor. Divers have yet to discover all its underwater attractions, while nature lovers will be pleasantly surprised by the hiking. There's now every kind of accommodation, as well as gourmet dining, golf, and gaming.

Meanwhile, Nevis seems determined to stay even more unspoiled (there are still no traffic lights). Its natural attractions and activities certainly rival those of St. Kitts, from mountain biking and ecohiking to windsurfing and deep-sea fishing, though lying in a hammock and dining on romantic candlelit patios remain cherished pursuits. Pinneys Beach, despite occasional hurricane erosion, remains a classic Caribbean strand. Its historic heritage, from the Caribbean's first hotel to Alexander Hamilton's childhood home, is just as pronounced, including equally sybaritic plantation inns that seem torn from the pages of a romance novel.

Perhaps it's a warning sign that many guests call the catamaran trip to Nevis the high point of their stay on St. Kitts—and many Kittitians build retirement and second homes on Nevis. The sister islands' relationship remains outwardly cordial if slightly contentious. Nevis papers sometimes run blistering editorials advocating independence, though one plebiscite has already failed. St. Kitts and Nevis may separate someday, but their battles are confined to ad campaigns and political debates. Fortunately, well-heeled and barefoot travelers alike can still happily enjoy the many energetic and easygoing enticements of both blissful retreats.

ST. KITTS

Where to Stay

20

St. Kitts has an appealing variety of places to stay—beautifully restored plantation inns (where MAP is encouraged, if not mandatory), full-service affordable hotels, simple beachfront cottages, and all-inclusive resorts. There are also several guesthouses and self-serve condos. Increasing development has been touted (or threatened) for years. The island's first large hotel, the St. Kitts Marriott Resort, is now well established, but despite rumors, any upcoming developments—many quite upscale and primarily residential—are all under 300 units. On these islands, where breezes generally keep things cool, many, but not all, hotels, have air-conditioning.

$$$$ **Rawlins Plantation Inn.** Civilized serenity awaits at this remote plantation inn between verdant Mount Liamuiga and the cobalt Caribbean. Twelve acres of lavish, lovingly landscaped grounds are ablaze with hibiscus, oleander, and plumbago and dotted with the original copper syrup vats. Rooms occupy restored estate buildings (including the sugar mill) and trellised, gingerbread cottages charmingly decorated with local art-works and mahogany furnishings. Days are spent relaxing in one of the many strategically slung hammocks, perhaps contemplating the egrets stalking the palms or the views of St. Maarten and St. Eustatius. Expat artist Kate Spencer's studio is on-site; her husband, Philip, a keen sailor, might be building or restoring classic boats. The refined dining room, given a contemporary edge by a quietly sexy lounge, has always been an island favorite. With new owners having taken over in spring 2005, changes, including decor and the potentially questionable addition of vernacular-style "Carib Cottages," continue. ⌂ *Box 340, St. Paul's* ☎ *869/465–6221 or 800/346–5358* ▤ *869/465–4954* ⊕ *www. rawlinsplantation.com* ↪ *10 rooms* ⚬ *Restaurant, fans, tennis court, pool, bar, croquet, laundry service, Internet room; no a/c, no room phones, no room TVs* ▭ *MC, V* ☻ *Closed Aug. and Sept.* ⦿ *MAP.*

★ **$$$–$$$$** ▦ **Golden Lemon.** Perched at the northwest tip of St. Kitts, this serene, scintillating retreat was one of the Caribbean's first true luxury hide-aways. Arthur Leaman, a former decorating editor for *House and Garden,* rescued a decaying, 17th-century French plantation house in the early 1960s; his style and panache enliven the entire property. Greathouse rooms (opt for Nos. 1 through 4 and 10) feature wrought-iron canopy or four-poster beds and funky touches like leopard-print rugs. One- and two-bedroom soaring, duplex townhouses (some with private plunge pools) are equally stylish, painted in luscious colors from pumpkin to blueberry, their eclectic yet harmonious blend of artworks and an-tiques culled from Arthur and partner Martin Kreiner's travels. Repeat guests cherish the tranquility and sterling service; the only caveats are the remote location and rare reports of villagers harassing Americans. EP rates are available, but the location means the all-inclusive pack-ages are the better value. ⌂ *Box 17, Dieppe Bay* ☎ *869/465–7260 or 800/633–7411* ▤ *869/465–4019* ⊕ *www.goldenlemon.com* ↪ *9 rooms, 17 villas* ⚬ *Restaurant, fans, in-room data ports, pool, beach, bar, shop; no a/c in some rooms, no room TVs, no kids* ☻ *Closed Sept.–mid-Oct.* ▭ *AE, MC, V* ⦿ *BP.*

$$$–$$$$
★

▦ **Ottley's Plantation Inn.** You're treated like a beloved relative rather than a commercial guest at this quintessential Caribbean inn, formerly a sugar plantation at the foot of Mount Liamuiga: historic yet contem-porary, elegant yet unpretentious. The 18th-century greathouse (opt for top-floor rooms) and stone cottages hold commodious lodgings with hard-wood floors, Laura Ashley–esque trimmings, and wicker and antique furnishings. "Supreme" cottages have plunge pools and whirlpool tubs. You can wander the exquisitely landscaped ornamental gardens, which brilliantly counterpoint the wild adjacent rain forest, where the rustic-chic spa offers exotic treatments. Thoughtful extras include beach and town shuttles, as well as TVs and DVD players for rent. Art and Ruth Keusch and their family set the warm, fun-loving, yet cultured tone. Staff are professional, knowing their business but not yours, providing posh pampering without pomp. ⊠ *Ottley's, southwest of Nicola Town, Box 345* ☎ *869/465–7234 or 800/772–3039* ▤ *869/465–4760* ⊕ *www. ottleys.com* ↪ *24 rooms* ⚬ *Restaurant, fans, in-room safes, some in-*

room hot tubs, some minibars, tennis court, pool, spa, croquet, bar, shop, Internet room; no TV in some rooms $\boxminus$ *AE, D, MC, V* |O| *EP.*

$$$–$$$$ ⛄ **St. Kitts Marriott Resort.** There's no question that this flashy, big, bustling beachfront resort offers something for everyone, from families to conventioneers, golfers to gamblers. Unfortunately, it's all monumentally overscaled for tiny, quiet St. Kitts and is almost devoid of real Caribbean charm and flair. The staff is diligent, but service is inconsistent and often impersonal. Little things go wrong: phone cards don't work, bills show unwarranted minibar or dining charges, the glorious free-form pools are often surprisingly chilly, breakfast rush hour can mean interminable waits, furnishings are already showing wear. The property is so vast that only blocks 600–800 and 1300–1500 can claim true beachfront status; oceanview rooms often show only a speck of blue. One advantage of its size is that the resort rarely feels crowded (though DJs often blast music to create a party atmosphere). The Marriott scores points for its genuinely soothing Emerald Mist Spa; a splendid kids' area from fully loaded arcade to Club Mongoose (which tries to instill island flavor through nature hikes, limbo lessons, treasure hunts, and crafts classes); urbane cigar and lobby bars (great sushi); and a fine golf course. Suites are huge and a good value during the off-season, as are the many packages. $\boxtimes$ *Box 858, Frigate Bay* ☎ *869/466–1200 or 800/228–9290* 🖷 *869/466–1201* ⊕ *www.stkittsmarriott.com* ⇦ *523 rooms, 113 suites* 🛆 *8 restaurants, room service, in-room safes, refrigerators, cable TV, in-room broadband, in-room data ports, 18-hole golf course, 5 tennis courts, 3 pools, health club, spa, 2 outdoor hot tubs, beach, snorkeling, boating, 6 bars, piano bar, casino, nightclub, video game room, shops, babysitting, children's programs (ages 5–12), laundry service, Internet room, business services, convention center, meeting rooms, car rental* $\boxminus$ *AE, D, MC, V* |O| *EP.*

$$–$$$ ⛄ **Ocean Terrace Inn.** Referred to by locals as OTI, this is a rarity: a smart, intimate business hotel that nonetheless appeals to vacationers. The hillside location, convenient to downtown Basseterre, guarantees marvelous bay views from virtually every room. Luxuriant gardens, room blocks, and a split-level free-form waterfall pool tumble down to the sea. Island touches from masks to murals animate nooks and crannies. Handsomely decorated but tired rooms vary widely in size and style; many deluxe rooms and junior suites (which have a 1960s bachelor-pad look) have kitchenettes or whirlpool tubs. The condos are closer to the water and have great views. The urbane hilltop Waterfalls Restaurant (a definite comer) entices island powerbrokers. With regular shuttle to Turtle Beach, courteous helpful staff, and an on-site gym and mini-spa, peaceful OTI promotes rest, not revelries. $\boxtimes$ *Wigley Ave, Box 65, Fortlands* ☎ *869/465–2754 or 800/524–0512* 🖷 *869/465–1057* ⊕ *www.oceanterraceinn.com* ⇦ *71 rooms, 8 condominiums* 🛆 *3 restaurants, some fans, some in-room safes, some kitchens, some kitchenettes, refrigerators, cable TV, in-room data ports, 3 pools, health club, hair salon, 2 outdoor hot tubs, massage, sauna, dock, windsurfing, boating, waterskiing, 4 bars, shop, Internet room, business services, meeting rooms* $\boxminus$ *AE, D, MC, V* |O| *EP.*

$$–$$$ ⛄ **Sugar Bay Club.** This sprawling all-inclusive borders Frigate Bay's wild Atlantic side, offering varied accommodations in an architectural

20

mishmash ranging from creole-style cottages to cinderblock eyesores. Enormous rooms with the only true ocean views are in the newest buildings just steps from the beach but aren't worth the price (even-numbered rooms in Block G are the best); however, the odd-numbered garden-view rooms are a terrific buy and are just a few steps from the sand. Spacious poolside cottages have separate living rooms, while even cheaper, regular poolside rooms have cleverly segmented alcoves that contain additional single beds. Parents will appreciate the kids' club, extensive children's menus, separate adult-only pool, and warm staffers who double as babysitters. New management has slowly implemented "soft refurbishment," including brightening the mostly drab rooms. But the property's few stylish touches—art deco–style piano bar, waterfall pool, attractively designed restaurants—don't compensate for the lack of water-sports facilities, a major drawback for an all-inclusive. ⌂ *Box 341, Frigate Bay* ☎ *869/465–8037 or 800/858–4618* 🖷 *869/465–6745* ⊕ *www.eliteislandresorts.com* ⟿ *78 rooms, 22 1-bedroom cottages* ⌂ *2 restaurants, grocery, fans, some in-room safes, cable TV, tennis court, 2 pools, wading pool, gym, massage, beach, 2 bars, shops, children's programs (ages 4–12), Internet room, meeting rooms* ▭ *AE, MC, V* ⏉⏉ *AI.*

$–$$ ▦ **Frigate Bay Resort.** This cheery property's combination of location, value, and polite service compensates for dowdy decor and dire need for minor repairs throughout. Though a shuttle whisks you to nearby Caribbean and Atlantic beaches, you can walk to South Frigate Bay's many restaurants, bars, and water-sports operators. Poolside studios with kitchens are an excellent bargain for self-caterers but tend to be noisier than other rooms. If a water view is paramount, request higher-numbered units in buildings B and C (third-floor units have sweeping vistas over the golf course and Atlantic). The swim-up bar and the thatched, split-level, octagonal restaurant are uncommonly comely drinks spots (though the Continental-Caribbean fare is undistinguished). Best of all are weekly rates that can reduce tariffs by up to 25% per night. ⌂ *Box 137, Frigate Bay* ☎ *869/465–8935 or 800/266–2185* 🖷 *869/465–7050* ⊕ *www.frigatebay.com* ⟿ *40 rooms, 24 studios* ⌂ *Restaurant, fans, some kitchens, refrigerators, cable TV, in-room data ports, golf privileges, pool, bar, shop, Internet room, meeting rooms* ▭ *AE, D, MC, V* ⏉⏉ *EP.*

★ $–$$ ▦ **Timothy Beach Resort.** The only St. Kitts resort sitting directly on a Caribbean beach is incomparably located and restful. Smiling service and simple but sizable apartments make this a great budget find. Comfortable town-house-style units can be blocked off to form standard rooms. The oldest buildings right on the beach are larger and airier, with predictably better views. Third-floor suites also have breathtaking vistas, but beware the steep climb. It's an authentic island experience, from the verdant hillside setting to the line-drying sheets flapping in the breeze. Though you get ants on the march during damp weather (don't leave food out!), you also get bananaquits and bullfinches sharing your patio breakfast. Only rattling air-conditioners detract from the tranquil atmosphere—and you can always walk to the Marriott if you crave activity. On the beach is the decent Sunset Café, an unaffiliated water-sports concession, and several boisterous beach bars. ⌂ *Box 1198, Frigate Bay* ☎ *869/465–8597 or 800/288–7991* 🖷 *869/466–7085* ⊕ *www.timothybeach.com* ⟿ *60 apart-*

ments ☼ *Restaurant, some kitchens, refrigerators, cable TV, pool, beach, bar, shop, Internet room* ☰ *AE, MC, V* ⊙*| EP.*

$ ⊡ **Bird Rock Beach Resort.** This basic, well-maintained hotel crowns a bluff above Basseterre, delivering amazing views of the town, the sea, and the mountains from every vantage point. Two-story buildings in Carnival colors wind through small, pretty gardens. The newer rooms are spiffier, with vivid throw rugs and mahogany two-poster beds; studios with kitchenettes and pull-out sofas offer real bargains for families (an additional connecting room costs just $50). Avoid only the 700 block; most other rooms have jaw-dropping panoramas. The tiered sundeck and pool, replete with swim-up bar, and attractive Diana's restaurant rank among the island's top sunset perches. The minuscule man-made beach (a complimentary shuttle drops guests at Frigate Bay), irregular hours, and occasional plumbing problems are a small price to pay and don't seem to bother the laid-back divers and young Europeans who give Bird Rock an appealing international flavor. ⊠ *Basseterre Bay* ⌂ *Box 227, Basseterre* ☎ *869/465–8914 or 800/621–1270* 🖷 *869/465–1675* ⊕ *www.birdrockbeach.com* ⇖ *31 rooms, 19 studios* ☼ *2 restaurants, fans, some kitchenettes, cable TV, in-room broadband, tennis court, 2 pools, beach, dive shop, snorkeling, volleyball, 2 bars, library, shops, Internet room, meeting rooms* ☰ *AE, D, MC, V* ⊙*| EP.*

$ ⊡ **Rock Haven Bed & Breakfast.** This restful, cozy B&B, a two-minute drive from Frigate Bay beaches, provides truly local warmth, courtesy of Judith and Keith Blake. Their gingerbread house is lovely: the living and dining rooms have carved mahogany doors, crystal chandeliers, English rugs, and hardwood floors. The extensive, breezy veranda seduces with white-wicker chaise lounges, hammocks, and majestic sea views. Two rooms have brass beds draped with mosquito netting. The larger, preferable one has a full kitchen and its own patio and entrance. Judith prepares lavish breakfasts of banana pancakes and pumpkin fritters. Islanders also cherish her homemade ice creams, which you can sample on-site. ⌂ *Box 821, Frigate Bay* ☎ *869/465–5503* 🖷 *869/466–6130* ⊕ *www.rock-haven.com* ⇖ *2 rooms* ☼ *Fans, some kitchens, cable TV, laundry service; no a/c* ☰ *No credit cards* ⊙*| BP.*

20

Where to Eat

St. Kitts restaurants range from funky beachfront bistros to elegant plantation dining rooms (most with prix-fixe menus); most fare is tinged with the flavors of the Caribbean. Many restaurants offer West Indian specialties such as curried mutton, pepper pot (a stew of vegetables, tubers, and meats), and Arawak chicken (seasoned and served with rice and almonds on breadfruit leaf).

What to Wear
Throughout the island, dress is casual at lunch (but no bathing suits). Dinner, although not necessarily formal, definitely calls for long pants and sundresses.

CARIBBEAN ✕**Bobsy's.** Locals flock to this semi-alfresco terrace eatery for lively happy
$$–$$$ hours and on weekends for karaoke, sizzling salsa, live bands, and a DJ

spinning favorite dance tunes. Vivid colors (scarlet linens, orange walls with mauve and lime trim, turquoise rafters), African masks, autographed photos of reggae stars) attest to the authentic island ambience, as do such fine specialties as pumpkin soup, glazed passion-fruit ribs, and mango-ginger chicken (you can also get hefty burgers and such Continental standbys as lobster thermidor, chicken fettucine alfredo, and rack of lamb). ⊠ *Sugar's Complex, Frigate Bay* ☎ *869/466–6133* ⊟ *AE, MC, V* ⊘ *No lunch Sun. or Mon.*

$$ ✕ **Manhattan Gardens.** Even the tangerine, peach, and blueberry exterior of this 17th-century gingerbread creole house looks appetizing. Inside, you feel as if you're dining in owner-chef Rosalind Walters's home, with batik hangings, lace tablecloths, and wood carvings. The rear garden overlooking the sea comes alive for Saturday's Caribbean Food Fest and Sunday's barbecue. The regular menu includes lobster in lemon butter (the one pricey entrée), mahimahi in lemon-thyme sauce; local specials might consist of goat water (goat stew), souse (pickled pigs' trotters), and curried mutton. It's open for lunch (and some dinners) only when there are reservations. ⊠ *Old Road Town* ☎ *869/465–9121* ⊰ *Reservations essential* ⊟ *No credit cards* ⊘ *No dinner Sun.*

CONTEMPORARY   ✕ **Golden Lemon.** Evenings at the Golden Lemon hotel's restaurant begin
★ **$$$$** with cocktails and hors d'oeuvres on the bougainvillea-draped flagstone patio. A set three-course dinner is served in a tasteful room with crystal and white wrought-iron chandeliers, highback cane chairs, Delft porcelain, and arched doorways. Tempting dishes range from breadfruit puffs in peanut sauce to lobster cakes with passion-fruit mayonnaise to grilled tilapia with eggplant-and-sweet-pepper relish. Sunday brunch packs the patio for such offerings as banana pancakes and legendary beef stew made with rum. Owners Arthur Leaman and Martin Kreiner hold clever court (cajole them for anecdotes about conducting business in the Caribbean). ⊠ *Golden Lemon, Dieppe Bay* ☎ *869/465–7260* ⊰ *Reservations essential* ⊟ *AE, MC, V.*

★ **$$$$**   ✕ **Royal Palm.** A 65-foot spring-fed pool stretches from the remaining walls of the sugar factory bisecting the elegant restaurant at Ottley's Plantation Inn into a semi-enclosed lounge with sea views and breezy alfresco stone patio. Four-course extravaganzas (dishes are also available à la carte) blend indigenous ingredients with Pacific Rim, Mediterranean, southwestern, and Latin touches: for example, chili-shrimp corn cakes with chipotle pepper mayonnaise, ginger-grilled swordfish with watermelon relish and couscous, or turmeric-garlic crusted breast of chicken with pineapple-guava relish and pimento-honey raisin sauce. Finish with simple yet sinful indulgences such as coconut cream cheesecake or mango mousse with raspberry coulis. The combination of superb food, artful presentation, romantic setting, and warm bonhomie here is unbeatable. ⊠ *Ottley's Plantation Inn, Ottley's, southwest of Nicola Town* ☎ *869/465–7234* ⊰ *Reservations essential* ⊟ *AE, D, MC, V.*

$$–$$$$ ✕ **Marshall's.** The pool area of Horizons Villa Resort is transformed into a stylish eatery thanks to smashing ocean views, potted plants, serenading tree frogs, and elegant candlelighted tables. Jamaican chef Verral Marshall fuses ultrafresh local ingredients with global influences. Recommended offerings include pan-seared duck breast with raspberry-ginger sauce or portobello-stuffed tortellini with shrimp in creamy tomato-basil sauce. Most dishes are regrettably more orthodox, and the execution is increasingly uneven. ⊠ *Horizons Villa Resort, Frigate Bay* ☎ *869/466–8245* ⚑ *Reservations essential* ⊟ *AE, D, MC, V.*

$$–$$$ ✕ **Stonewall's.** Affable owners Garry and Wendy Steckles practically built this lush, tropical courtyard restaurant by hand. "Our sweat is varnished into the bar," Garry swears. Banana trees, bougainvillea, and bamboo—filled with a virtual orchestra of chirping tree frogs—grow everywhere. Selections depend on what's fresh and the cook's mood: most popular are the rib-eye steaks, barbecue ribs, and specialties such as pan-seared ginger wasabi tuna or cornish hen stuffed with orange-lime rice in a banana-raisin-cognac jus. The next-door boutique has a fantastic selection of West Indian items, from hand-painted Jamaican pottery to flowing resort wear by noted island designer John Warden. Try the house drink, Stone Against the Wall, concocted from Cavalier rum, amaretto, coconut rum, triple sec, pineapple and orange juices, and grenadine. ⊠ *5 Princes St., Basseterre* ☎ *869/465–5248* ⊟ *AE, D, MC, V* ☽ *Closed weekends. No lunch.*

ECLECTIC ✕ **Serendipity.** This stylish restaurant occupies an old Creole home
$$–$$$$ whose deck offers lovely views of Basseterre and the bay. As charming as the enclosed patio is, the interior lounge is more conducive to romantic dining, with cushy sofas, patterned hardwood floors, porcelain lamps, and African carvings. The menu reflects co-owner–chef Alexander James's peripatetic postings: you might start with fried Brie with blackberry sauce or beautifully presented spring rolls with plum-soy dipping sauce. Poached salmon with lobster brandy cream sauce and bacon-wrapped beef tenderloin topped with pâté, black truffle slice, and Port sauce typify the ambitious main courses. The wine list is well-considered, vegetarians will be delighted by the many creative options, and very affordable lunches feature gargantuan tapas-style selections. ⊠ *3 Wigley Ave., Fortlands, Basseterre* ☎ *869/465–9999* ⊟ *AE, D, MC, V* ☽ *Closed Mon. No lunch weekends.*

★ **$$–$$$** ✕ **Island Spice.** Though owner-chef Lynn Williams had worked in relative anonymity at various hotels for 20 years, he'd gained the respect of his peers, as well as a loyal local following. He finally opened his own marvelous eatery in a nondescript space (gussied up with handsome rotating artworks—all for sale, hurricane lamps, exhibition kitchen, and trellis-patterned ceiling). When pressed, he'll shyly describe his fare as "refined Caribbean fusion." It's that and more. The food is perfectly cooked, beautifully presented, and sensuously textured, especially the silken sauces. Witness melting conch in garlic butter, lemon-scented beer-batter grouper with tamarind-tomato essence, ribeye with mango red wine reduction, peanut-crusted chicken breast with banana curry, or New Zealand lamb chops in Merlot cane-sugar syrup. Desserts dissapoint somewhat—but you won't have room. ⊠ *Sugar's Complex, Frigate Bay* ☎ *869/465–0569* ⊟ *AE, MC, V* ☽ *No lunch.*

★ **$$–$$$** ✕ **Turtle Beach Bar & Grill.** Treats at this popular daytime watering hole at the south end of S.E. Peninsula Road include honey-mustard ribs, coconut-shrimp salad, grilled lobster (a best-buy special Friday nights), decadent bread pudding with rum sauce, and an array of tempting trop-

20

ical libations. Business cards and pennants from around the world plaster the bar; the room is decorated with a variety of nautical accoutrements. You can snorkel here, spot hawksbill turtles, feed the tame monkeys that boldly belly up to the bar (they adore green bananas and peaches), serve Wilbur the pig a beer, laze in a palm-shaded hammock, or rent a kayak or snorkel gear. Locals come Sunday afternoons for dancing to live bands and for fun but fiercely contested volleyball. ⊠ *S.E. Peninsula Rd., Turtle Beach* ☎ *869/469–9086* ▭ *AE, D, MC, V* ⊗ *No dinner Mon.–Thurs.*

ITALIAN   ✕ **PJ's Pizza.** "Garbage pizza"—topped with everything but the kitchen
$–$$$ sink—is a favorite, or you can create your own pie. Sandwiches, simple but lustily flavored pastas (try the goat cheese ravioli in sun-dried tomato sauce or spaghetti with humongous meatballs), and Mamma-mia classics (eggplant Parmesan to chicken rollantini) are also served. Finish your meal with delicious, moist rum cake. This casual spot, bordering the golf course and open to cooling breezes, is always boisterous, despite—or perhaps because of—its ironic location beside the Frigate Bay police station. ⊠ *Frigate Bay* ☎ *869/465–8373* ▭ *AE, D, MC, V* ⊗ *Closed Mon. and Sept. No lunch.*

SEAFOOD   ✕ **Fisherman's Wharf.** Part of the Ocean Terrace Inn, this extremely ca-
$$–$$$ sual waterfront eatery is decorated in swaggering nautical style, with rustic wood beams, rusty anchors, cannons, and buoys. Try the excellent conch chowder, followed by fresh grilled lobster or other shipshape seafood, and finish off your meal with a slice of the memorable banana cheesecake. The tables are long, wooden affairs, and the place is generally hopping, especially on weekend nights (alas, those seeking romance at the wharf's end are subject to fierce breezes). ⊠ *Ocean Terrace Inn, Fortlands, Basseterre* ☎ *869/465–2754* ▭ *AE, D, MC, V* ⊗ *No lunch.*

★ **$–$$**   ✕ **Sprat Net.** This simple cluster of picnic tables, sheltered by a brilliant turquoise corrugated-tin roof and decorated with driftwood, life preservers, photos of coastal scenes, and fishnets, sits on a sliver of sand. Nonetheless, it's an island hot spot. There's nothing fancy on the menu: just grilled fish, lobster, ribs, and chicken—served with mountains of coleslaw and peas and rice. But the fish is amazingly fresh: the fishermen-owners heap their catches on a center table, where you choose your own dinner, as if you were at market, watch it grilled to your specification, then dine family-style on paper plates. Sprat Net offers old-style Caribbean flavor, with the cheapest drinks and best bands on weekends. No wonder cars line up along the road, creating an impromptu jump-up. ⊠ *Old Road Town* ☎ *869/466–7535* ▭ *No credit cards* ⊗ *Closed Sept. and Sun. No lunch.*

Beaches

Beaches on St. Kitts are free and open to the public (even those occupied by hotels). The best beaches, with powdery white sand, are in the Frigate Bay area or on the lower peninsula. The Atlantic waters are rougher, and many black-sand beaches northwest of Frigate Bay double as garbage dumps, though locals bodysurf at Conaree Bay.

Banana/Cockleshell Bays. These twin connected eyebrows of glittering champagne-colored sand with majestic views of Nevis are backed by lush vegetation and shaded by coconut palms, stretching nearly 2 mi total (3 km) at the southeastern tip of the island. The sole development is Lion Rock Beach Bar, but Turtle Beach Bar & Grill is practically around the corner. Locals often come here weekends, throwing bonfire parties at night. The water is generally placid, ideal for swimming. The downside is irregular maintenance, with seaweed (particularly after rough weather) and occasional litter. Follow Simmonds Highway to the end and bear right, ignoring the turnoff for Turtle Beach. Beach aficionados should check out Majors Bay, the cove just to the west, where you can see locals fishing. ⊠ *Banana Bay.*

★ **Friar's Bay.** Locals consider Friar's Bay, on the Caribbean (southern) side, the island's finest beach. It's a long, tawny scimitar where the water always seems warmer and clearer. Unfortunately, the new Marine World development has coopted nearly half the strand. Still, several hopping, happening bars, including Shipwreck and Sunset Grill, serve terrific, inexpensive local food and cheap, frosty drinks. Chair rentals cost around $3, though if you order lunch you can negotiate a freebie. You can haggle with fishermen here to take you snorkeling off the eastern point, though live coral reefs protect both ends. The waters on the Atlantic (northern) side are rougher, but the beach has a wild, desolate beauty with some good surfing (wind, body, board), though seaweed often washes ashore. Friar's is the first major beach along S.E. Peninsula Drive (a.k.a. Simmonds Highway), approximately a mile southeast of Frigate Bay. ⊠ *Friar's Bay.*

Frigate Bay. The Caribbean side offers talcum-powder-fine beige sand fringed framed by coconut palms and sea grapes, while the Atlantic side (a 15-minute stroll), the 4-mi-wide (6½-km-wide) stretch—sometimes called North Frigate Bay—is a favorite with horseback riders. South Frigate Bay is bookended by Sunset Café and Oasis. In between are several other lively beach spots, including Cathy's (fabulous jerk ribs), the Monkey Bar, and Mr. X Shiggidy Shack. Most charge $3 to $5 to rent a chair, though they'll often waive the fee if you ask politely and buy lunch. Locals barhop late into Friday and Saturday nights. Waters are generally calm for swimming; the rockier eastern end offers fine snorkeling. The incomparably scenic Atlantic side is—regrettably—dominated by the Marriott (plentiful dining options), attracting occasional pesky vendors. The surf is choppier and the undertow stronger here. On cruise-ship days, groups stampede both sides. Frigate Bay is easy to find, just under 3 mi (5 km) from downtown Basseterre. ⊠ *Frigate Bay.*

Sand Bank Bay. A dirt road, nearly impassable after heavy rains, leads to a long mocha crescent on the Atlantic. The shallow coves are protected here, making it ideal for families, and it's usually deserted. Brisk breezes lure the occasional windsurfer, but avoid the rocky far left area due to fierce sudden swells and currents. This exceptionally pretty beach lacks facilities and shade (the ultraluxurious 1,700-acre Auberge Sandy Bank Bay Resort—with spa and golf course—will break ground here in anticipation of a 2008 opening). As you drive southeast along Simmonds Highway, approximately 10 mi (16 km) from Basseterre, look for an unmarked dirt turnoff to the left of the Great Salt Pond. ⊠ *Sand Bank Bay.*

20

White House Bay. The beach is rocky, but the snorkeling, taking in several reefs surrounding a sunken tugboat, as well as a recently discovered 18th-century British Troop ship, is superb. It's usually deserted, though the calm water (and stunning scenery) makes it a favorite anchorage of yachties. There are no facilities and little shade or seaweed. A dirt road skirts a hill to the right off Simmonds Highway approximately 2 mi (3 km) after Friar's. ⊠ *White House Bay.*

Sports & the Outdoors

BIKING　Mountain-biking is growing in popularity, with several peaks soaring more than 800 feet. **Fun Bikes** (☎ 869/466–3202 or 869/662–2088 ⊕ www.stkittsactivities.com) provides several three-hour excursions daily on all-terrain quad bikes that hold two people. You'll wind through cane fields, rain forest, abandoned plantation ruins, and local villages. Free taxi transfers from Frigate Bay and Basseterre and a complimentary drink at the historic Lodge Estate Great House headquarters (which also contains a bar and occasional disco) are included in the $65 rate.

BOATING &　Most operators are on the Caribbean side of Frigate Bay, known for its
FISHING　gentle currents. Turtle Bay offers stronger winds and stunning views of Nevis. Though not noted for big-game fishing, several steep offshore drop-offs do lure wahoo, barracuda, shark, tuna, yellowtail snapper, and mackerel. Rates are occasionally negotiable; figure approximately $350 for a four-hour excursion with refreshments. The knowledgeable Todd Leypoldt of **Leeward Island Charters** (⊠ Basseterre ☎ 869/465–7474 ⊕ www.leewardislandcharters.com) takes you out on his charter boat, *Island Lore*. He's also available for snorkeling charters, beach picnics, and sunset-moonlight cruises. **Mr. X Watersports** (⊠ Frigate Bay ☎ 869/465–0673) rents small craft, including motorboats (waterskiing and jet-skiing are available). Paddleboats are $15 per hour, sailboats (with one free lesson) $20 to $25 per hour. Mr. X and his cohorts are usually hanging out at the adjacent open-air Monkey Bar. **Turtle Beach Bar & Grill** (⊠ Turtle Beach ☎ 869/469–9086 ⊕ www.turtlebeach1.com) rents kayaks from the restaurant and can also arrange fishing trips.

DIVING &　Though unheralded as a dive destination, St. Kitts has more than a dozen
SNORKELING　excellent sites, and the government hopes to increase their visibility by creating several new marine parks. The surrounding waters feature shoals, hot vents, shallows, canyons, steep walls, and caverns at depths from 40 to nearly 200 feet. The St. Kitts Maritime Archaeological Project, which surveys, records, researches, and preserves the island's underwater treasures, has charted several hundred wrecks of galleons, frigates, and freighters dating back to the 17th century. **Bloody Bay Reef** is noted for its network of underwater grottos daubed with purple anemones, sienna bristle worms, and canary-yellow sea fans that seem to wave you in. **Coconut Tree Reef,** one of the largest in the area, includes sea fans, sponges, and anemones, as well as the Rocks, three enormous boulders with impressive multilevel diving. The only drift dive site, **Nags Head** has strong currents, but experienced divers might spot gliding rays, lobsters, turtles, and reef sharks. Since it sank in 50 feet of water in the early 1980s, the *River Taw* makes a splendid site for less-

experienced divers. **Sandy Point Reef** has been designated a National Marine Park, including Paradise Reef, with swim-through 90-foot sloping canyons, and Anchors Away, where anchors have been encrusted with coral formations. The 1985 wreck of the *Talata* lies in 70 feet of water; barracudas, rays, groupers, and grunts dart through its hull.

Dive St. Kitts (⊠ Frigate Bay, 2 mi [3 km] east of Basseterre ☎ 869/465–1189 ⊕ www.divestkitts.com), a PADI-NAUI facility, offers competitive prices; friendly, laid-back dive masters; and a more international clientele. The Bird Rock location features superb beach diving: common sightings 20 to 30 feet out include octopi, nurse sharks, manta and spotted eagle rays, and sea horses. Shore dives are unlimited when you book packages. Kenneth Samuel of **Kenneth's Dive Center** (⊠ Bay Rd., Newtown ☎ 869/465–2670 ⊕ www.kennethsdivecenter.com) is a PADI company takes small groups of divers with C cards to nearby reefs. Rates average $40 for single-tank dives, $75 for double-tank dives; add $10 to $15 for equipment. Night dives, including lights, are $60, and snorkeling trips (four-person minimum) are $35, drinks included. After 25 years' experience, former fisherman Samuel is considered an old pro and strives to keep groups small and prices reasonable. Austin Macleod, a PADI-certified dive master–instructor and owner of **Pro-Divers** (⊠ Ocean Terrace Inn, Basseterre ☎ 869/466–3483 ⊕ www.prodiversstkitts.com), offers resort and certification courses. He offers free introductory scuba courses twice weekly at Ocean Terrace Inn. He also takes groups to snorkeling sites accessible only by boat.

GOLF   St. Kitts hopes to market itself as a golf destination with the remodeling of the Royal St. Kitts Golf Course (completed in late 2004) and the anticipated opening of the 18-hole, La Vallee Golf Course, on the island's western side between Sandy Point and Newton Ground, a stunning layout experiencing financing problems. Two upcoming resort and villa developments include 18-hole courses. The **Royal St. Kitts Golf Club** (⊠ St. Kitts Marriott Resort, Frigate Bay ☎ 869/466–2700 ⊕ www. royalstkittsgolfclub.com) is an 18-hole, par-71 links-style championship course that underwent a complete redesign by Thomas McBroom to maximize Caribbean and Atlantic views and increase the challenge (there are now 12 lakes and 83 bunkers). Holes 15 through 17 actually skirt the Atlantic in their entirety, lending new meaning to the term sand trap. The sudden gusts, wide but twisting fairways, and extremely hilly terrain demand pinpoint accuracy and finesse, yet holes such as 18 require your power game. Greens fees are $130 for Marriott guests in high season, $170 for nonguests. The development includes practice bunkers, putting green, and a short-game chipping area. The Marriott expects to open a branch of the Nick Faldo Golf Institute here by late 2006.

HIKING   Trails in the central mountains vary from easy to don't-try-it-by-yourself. Monkey Hill and Verchild's Peak aren't difficult, although the Verchild's climb will take the better part of a day. Don't attempt Mount Liamuiga without a guide. You'll start at Belmont Estates on horseback, then proceed on foot to the lip of the crater, at 2,600 feet. You can go down into the crater—1,000 feet deep and 1 mi (1½ km) wide, with a small freshwater lake—clinging to vines and roots and scaling rocks,

20

even trees. Expect to get muddy. There are several fine operators (each hotel recommends its favorite); tour rates range from $35 for a rainforest walk to $65 for a volcano expedition and usually include round-trip transportation from your hotel and picnic lunch.

Earl of **Duke of Earl's Adventures** (☎ 869/465–1899) is as entertaining as his nickname suggests—and his prices are slightly cheaper. He genuinely loves his island and conveys that enthusiasm, encouraging hikers to swing on vines or sample unusual-looking fruits during his rain-forest trip. He also conducts a thorough volcano tour to the crater's rim. Greg Pereira of **Greg's Safaris** (☎ 869/465–4121 ⊕ www.gregssafaris.com), whose family has lived on St. Kitts since the early 19th century, takes groups on half-day trips into the rain forest and on full-day hikes up the volcano and through the grounds of a private 18th-century greathouse. The first includes visits to sacred Carib sites, abandoned sugar mills, and an excursion down a 100-foot coastal canyon containing a wealth of Amerindian petroglyphs. The Sugar Plantation Heritage Tour provides a thorough explanation of the role sugar and rum played in the Caribbean economy and colonial wars. He and his staff relate fascinating historical, folkloric, and botanical information. Oliver Spencer of **Off the Beaten Path** (☎ 869/465–6314) leads rainforest treks to the ruins of an abandoned coffee plantation taken over by spreading banyan trees, explaining folklore and flora, including herbal remedies, along the way.

HORSEBACK RIDING   Wild North Frigate Bay and desolate Conaree Beach are great for riding, as is the rain forest. Guides from **Trinity Stables** (☎ 869/465–3226) offer beach rides ($35) and trips into the rain forest ($45). The latter is intriguing as guides discuss plants' medicinal properties along the way (such as sugarcane to stanch bleeding) and pick oranges right off a tree to squeeze fresh juice. Otherwise, the staffers are cordial but shy, and this isn't a place for beginners' instruction.

SEA EXCURSIONS   In addition to the usual snorkeling, sunset, and party cruises (ranging in price from $35 to $75), most companies offer whale-watching excursions during the winter migrating season, January through April. **Banana Boat Tours** (⊠ Basseterre, St. Kitts ☎ 869/465–0645 ⊕ www.bananaboattours.com) provides snorkeling and sunset cruises from Turtle Beach on its 34-foot inflatable, Coast Guard–certified Scarib boat replete with state-of-the-art GPS tracking system. Private charters, Nevis–St. Kitts shuttles, and deep-sea fishing can be arranged. **Blue Water Safaris** (⊠ Basseterre, St. Kitts ☎ 869/466–4933 ⊕ www.bluewatersafaris.com) offers half-day snorkeling trips or beach barbecues on deserted cays, as well as sunset and moonlight cruises on its 65-foot catamaran *Irie Lime*. **Leeward Island Charters** (⊠ Basseterre, St. Kitts ☎ 869/465–7474) offers day and overnight charters on two 70-foot catamarans—the *Eagle* and *Spirit of St. Kitts*. Day sails are from 9:30 to 4:30 and include a barbecue, an open bar, and use of snorkeling equipment. The Nevis trip stops at Pinney's Beach for a barbecue and at Shooting Bay, a tiny cove in the bullying shadow of a sheer cliff, where petrels and frigate birds inspect your snorkeling skills. The crews are mellow, affable, and knowledgeable about island life.

Shopping

St. Kitts has limited shopping, but there are a few small duty-free shops with good deals on jewelry, perfume, china, and crystal. Several galleries sell excellent paintings and sculptures. The batik fabrics, scarves, caftans, and wall hangings of Caribelle Batik are well known. British expat Kate Spencer is an artist who has lived on the island for years, reproducing its vibrant colors on everything from silk pareus (beach wraps) to note cards to placemats. Other good island buys include crafts, jams, and herbal teas. Don't forget to pick up some CSR (Cane Spirit Rothschild), which is distilled from fresh sugarcane right on St. Kitts. The Brinley Gold company has made a splash among spirits connoisseurs for its coffee, mango, and vanilla rums (there is a tasting room at Port Zante).

Areas & Malls

Most shopping plazas are in downtown Basseterre, on the streets radiating from the Circus. **All Kind of Tings,** a peppermint-pink edifice on Liverpool Row at College Street Ghaut, functions as a de facto vendors' market, where several booths sell local crafts and cheap T-shirts. Its courtyard frequently hosts folkloric dances, fashion shows, poetry readings, and steel-pan concerts. The **Pelican Mall**—a shopping arcade designed to look like a traditional Caribbean street—has 26 stores, a restaurant, tourism offices, and a bandstand near the cruise-ship pier. Directly behind Pelican Mall, on the waterfront, is **Port Zante,** the deep-water cruise-ship pier; a much-delayed upscale shopping-dining complex is on its way to becoming a 25-shop area (including the usual large jewelry concerns), and a second pier is under construction in hopes of luring even larger cruise ships. If you're looking for inexpensive, island-y T-shirts and souvenirs, check out the series of vendors' huts behind Pelican Mall to the right of Port Zante as you face the sea. **Shoreline Plaza** is next to the Treasury Building, right on Basseterre's waterfront. **TDC Mall** is just off the Circus in downtown.

Specialty Items

ART **Booyork's Gallery** (⊠ College St., Basseterre ☎ 869/466–9159) is the atelier of Dennis Richards, who works in a remarkable range of media from pastels to papier-mâché, ceramics to collages: creative Carnival-inspired accessories (incorporating coconut husks, painted ostrich feathers, spangles, and beads), paintings on packed black sand, and wondrous watercolors, both figurative and abstract. Call ahead for appointments. **Flamboyant Art Gallery** (⊠ Sands Complex, #C7, Basseterre ☎ 869/466–3620) carries works by promising local artists, sculptors, and potters, as well as such renowned Caribbean masters as Heather Doram and Roland Richardson. **Spencer Cameron Art Gallery** (⊠ 10 N. Independence Sq., Basseterre ☎ 869/465–1617) has historical reproductions of Caribbean island charts and prints, in addition to owner Rosey Cameron's popular Carnevale clown prints and a wide selection of exceptional artwork by Caribbean artists. The gallery will mail anywhere.

HANDICRAFTS **Caribelle Batik** (⊠ Romney Manor, Old Road ☎ 869/465–6253) sells batik wraps, kimonos, caftans, T-shirts, dresses, wall hangings, and the like. The **Crafthouse** (⊠ Bay Rd., Southwell Industrial Site, ½ mi [1 km]

20

east of Shoreline Plaza, Basseterre ☎ 869/465–7754) is one of the best sources for local dolls, wood carvings, and straw work. **Glass Island** (✉ 4–5 Princes St., Basseterre ☎ 869/466–6771) sells frames, earrings, and hand-blown glass vases, bowls, and plates in sinuous shapes and seductive colors. **Island Hopper** (✉ The Circus, Basseterre ☎ 869/465–2905) is a good place for island crafts, especially wood carvings, pottery, textiles, and colorful resort wear, as well as humorous T-shirts and trinkets. **Kate Design** (✉ Bank St., Basseterre ☎ 869/465–5265) showcases the highly individual style of Kate Spencer, whose original paintings, serigraphs, note cards, and other pieces that she regularly introduces are also available from her studio outside the Rawlins Plantation. **Linen 'n' Things** (✉ The Circus, Basseterre ☎ 869/465–5636) specialize in beautifully textured clothing, accessories, and tableware, as well as local ceramics. The **Potter's House** (✉ Camps Estate Great House, Camps Estate ☎ 869/465–5947) is the atelier-home of Carla Astaphan, whose beautifully glazed ceramics and masks celebrate the Afro-Caribbean heritage.

Nightlife

Most nightlife revolves around the hotels, which host folkloric shows and calypso and steel bands of the usual limbo-rum-and-reggae variety. Look for such hard-driving local exponents of soca as Nu-Vybes, Grand Masters, and Small Axe, and the "heavy dancehall" reggae group, House of Judah. The Marriott has a large, glitzy casino (the island's only one) with table games and slots.

BARS **Bambu's** (✉ Bank St. off the Circus, Basseterre ☎ 869/466–5280) incorporates bamboo everywhere to create an outdoorsy interior: in the ceiling, railings, bar, lamps, mirrors, benches. The rest is splashed in wild hues such as lemon, tangerine, and raspberry. Local artworks adorn the walls, and the split-level warren of rooms accommodates those who seek intimate conversation, rooting for teams on the big-screen TV, and dancing on a tiny floor weekends. You can order both sophisticated single-malt scotches and down-home island food amid the Peace Corps–hip ambience. A favorite happy-hour watering hole is the **Circus Grill** (✉ Bay Rd., Basseterre ☎ 869/465–0143), a second-floor eatery whose veranda offers views of the harbor and the activity on the Circus. **Keys Cigar Bar** (✉ St. Kitts Marriott Resort, Frigate Bay ☎ 869/466–1200) is a surprisingly low-key, classy hangout, with cushy sofas, highback straw chairs, chess-set tables, and superlative selection of aged rums and *cubanos* (as well as top Dominican and Nicaraguan brands). **Mr. X Shiggidy Shack** (✉ Frigate Bay ☎ 869/762–3983) is known for its sizzling music at Thursday-night bonfire parties, raucous karaoke Saturdays (be sure to listen—or watch out—for notorious regular Bar Hopper, who'd put the worst *American Idol* contestants to shame), and Sunday dinners accompanied by the MRT band; it's also a must-stop on locals' unofficial Friday night liming circuit of Frigate Bay bars.

DANCE & MUSIC CLUBS Popular local DJ Ronnie Rascal entertains at his own night spot, **Club Atmosphere** (✉ Canada Estate ☎ 869/465–3655), on most Friday and Saturday nights. **Tigers** (✉ St. Kitts Marriott Resort, Frigate Bay ☎ 869/466–1200) is unintentionally retro-1990s, blaring cheesy early hip-hop and rap. But locals and tourists who want to get better acquainted pose strategically at the fiber-optically lighted central bar, on black leather sofas, or against a vast blood-red wall.

Exploring St. Kitts

You can explore Basseterre, the capital city, in a half hour or so; allow three to four hours for an island tour. Main Road traces the northwestern perimeter through seas of sugarcane and past breadfruit trees and stone walls. Villages with tiny pastel-color houses of stone and weathered wood are scattered across the island, and the drive back to Basseterre around the island's other side passes through several of them. The most spectacular stretch of scenery is on Dr. Kennedy Simmonds Highway to the tip of the Southeast Peninsula. This ultrasleek modern road twists and turns through the undeveloped grassy hills that rise between the calm Caribbean and the windswept Atlantic, past the shimmering pink Great Salt Pond, a volcanic crater, and seductive beaches. Major developments are under way, including the Beaumont Park Racetrack near Dieppe Bay, part of an anticipated massive luxury enclave called Kittitian Heights (itself part of the Whitegate Development Project). As this writing, construction continued on Marine World at South Friar's Bay, a 4-acre theme park with dolphin encounter, stingray lagoon, eco-friendly watersports center, beach bar and restaurant, nature trail, and aviary.

Numbers in the margin correspond to points of interest on the St. Kitts map.

❶ Basseterre. On the south coast, St. Kitts's walkable capital is graced with tall palms, and although many of the buildings appear run-down, there are interesting shops, excellent art galleries, and some beautifully maintained houses. Duty-free shops and boutiques line the streets and courtyards radiating from the octagonal **Circus,** built in the style of London's famous Piccadilly Circus. There are lovely gardens on the site of a former slave market at **Independence Square** (✉ Off Bank St.). The square is surrounded on three sides by 18th-century Georgian buildings. **St. George's Anglican Church** (✉ Cayon St.) is a handsome stone building with a crenellated tower originally built by the French in 1670 and called Nôtre-Dame. The British burned it down in 1706 and rebuilt it four years later, naming it after the patron saint of England. Since then it has suffered a fire, an earthquake, and hurricanes and was once again rebuilt in 1869. **Port Zante** (✉ Waterfront, behind the Circus) is an ambitious 27-acre cruise-ship pier and marina in an area that has been reclaimed from the sea. The domed welcome center is an imposing neoclassical hodgepodge, with columns and stone arches, shops, walkways, fountains, and West Indian–style buildings housing luxury shops, galleries, and restaurants. Construction on a second pier, 1,434 feet long with a draught to accommodate even leviathan cruise ships, should be completed by late 2006. Supposedly, the selection of shops and restaurants will expand as well.

In the restored former Treasury Building, the **National Museum** presents an eclectic collection reflecting the history and culture of the island—as

20

a collaboration of the St. Christopher Heritage Society and the island government. ⊠ *Bay Rd., Basseterre* ☎ *869/465–5584* ✉ *EC$1 residents, U.S.$1 nonresidents* ⊙ *Mon. and Sat. 9:30–1, Tues.–Fri. 9–1 and 2–5.*

NEED A BREAK?

The second-floor terrace eatery, **Ballahoo** (⊠ Fort St. ☎ 869/465–4197) draws a crowd for breakfast, lunch, and dinner. Specialties include chili shrimp, Madras beef curry, and a toasted rum-and-banana sandwich topped with ice cream. At lunchtime, you can watch the bustle of the Circus, and specials such as rotis bursting with curried chicken or vegetables slash prices nearly in half. Grab fresh local juices (tamarind, guava) if you can. Though the service is lackadaisical bordering on rude, the food is at least plentiful, the daiquiris killer, and the people-watching delightful.

❻ Black Rocks. This series of lava deposits was spat into the sea ages ago when the island's volcano erupted. It has since been molded into fanciful shapes by centuries of pounding surf. ⊠ *Atlantic coast, outside town of Sadlers, Sandy Bay.*

★ ❺ Brimstone Hill. The well-restored 38-acre fortress, a UNESCO World Heritage Site, is part of a national park dedicated by Queen Elizabeth in 1985. The steep walk up the hill from the parking lot is well worth it if military history and/or spectacular views interest you. After routing the French in 1690, the English erected a battery here, and by 1736 the fortress held 49 guns, earning it the moniker Gibraltar of the West Indies. In 1782, 8,000 French troops laid siege to the stronghold, which was defended by 350 militia and 600 regular troops of the Royal Scots and East Yorkshires. When the English finally surrendered, the French allowed them to march from the fort in full formation out of respect for their bravery (the English afforded the French the same honor when they surrendered the fort a mere year later). A hurricane severely damaged the fortress in 1834, and in 1852 it was evacuated and dismantled. The beautiful stones were carted away to build houses.

The citadel has been partially reconstructed and its guns remounted. A seven-minute orientation film recounts the fort's history and restoration. You can see what remains of the officers' quarters, the redoubts, the barracks, the ordinance store, and the cemetery. Its museum collections were depleted by hurricanes, but some pre-Columbian artifacts, objects pertaining to the African heritage of the island's slaves (masks, ceremonial tools, etc.), weaponry, uniforms, photographs, and old newspapers remain. The view from here includes Montserrat and Nevis to the southeast; Saba and St. Eustatius to the northwest; and St. Barths and St. Maarten to the north. Nature trails snake through the tangle of surrounding hardwood forest and savanna (a fine spot to catch the green vervet monkeys—inexplicably brought by the French and now outnumbering the residents—skittering about). ⊠ *Main Rd., Brimstone Hill* ☎ *869/465–2609* ⊕ *www.brimstonehillfortress.org* ✉ *$8* ⊙ *Daily 9:30–5:30.*

❸ Old Road. This site marks the first permanent English settlement in the West Indies, founded in 1624 by Thomas Warner. Take the side road toward the interior to find some Carib petroglyphs, testimony of even earlier habitation. The largest depicts a female figure on black volcanic rock, presumably a fertility goddess. Less than a mile east of Old Road along Main Road is **Bloody Point,** where French and British soldiers joined forces in 1629 to repel a mass Carib attack; reputedly so many Caribs were massacred that the stream ran red for three days. ⊠ *Main Rd., west of Challengers.*

★ ❹ **Romney Manor.** The ruins of this somewhat restored house (reputedly once the property of Thomas Jefferson) and surrounding cottages that duplicate the old chattel-house style are set in 6 acres of glorious gardens, with exotic flowers, an old bell tower, and an enormous, gnarled 350-year-old *saman* tree (sometimes called a rain tree). Inside, at **Caribelle Batik,** you can watch artisans hand-printing fabrics by the 2,500-year-old Indonesian wax-and-dye process known as batik. Look for signs indicating a turnoff for Romney Manor near Old Road.

❷ **St. Kitts Scenic Railway.** The old narrow-gauge train that had transported sugarcane to the central sugar factory since 1912 is all that remains of the once thriving industry, now that the St. Kitts Sugar Manufacturing Corporation has closed permanently. New two-story cars bedecked in bright Kittitian colors circle the island in just under four hours. Each passenger gets a comfortable, downstairs air-conditioned seat fronting vaulted picture windows and an upstairs open-air observation spot. The conductor's running discourse embraces not only the history of sugar cultivation but the railway's construction, island folklore, island geography, even other agricultural mainstays from papayas and pineapples to pigs. You can drink in complimentary tropical beverages (including luscious guava daiquiris) along with the sweeping rain-forest and ocean vistas. You can also savor sugar cakes and an a cappella choir's renditions of hymns, spirituals, and predictable standards like "I've Been Workin' on the Railroad." There's a break at the halfway point (La Vallee), where cruise-ship passengers disembark. By then, the trip may seem slow as molasses, but it's certainly uniquely Caribbean. ⊠ *Needsmust* ☎ *869/465–7263* ⊕ *www.StKittsScenicRailway.com* ⊠ *$89* ⊗ *Departures Mon. at 1 PM and Wed. at 9:30 AM; additional trips vary according to cruise-ship schedules (call ahead).*

20

NEVIS

Where to Stay

Most lodgings are in restored manor or plantation houses scattered throughout the island's five parishes (counties). The owners often live at these inns, and it's easy to feel as if you've been personally invited down for a visit. Before dinner you may find yourself in the drawing room having a cocktail and conversing with the family, other guests, and visitors who have come for a meal. Most inns operate on the MAP plan (including afternoon tea in addition to breakfast and dinner) and offer a free shuttle service to their private stretch of beach. If you require TVs and air-conditioning, you're better off staying at hotels and simply dining with the engaging inn owners.

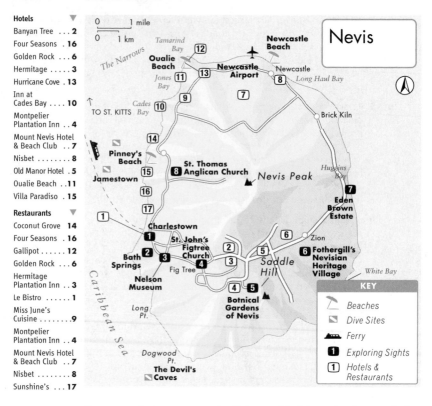

For approximate costs, *see* the dining and lodging price chart at the beginning of this chapter.

★ ☺ **$$$$** 🏨 **Four Seasons Resort Nevis.** This beachfront beauty impeccably combines world-class elegance with West Indian hospitality, magically appealing to everyone while scrupulously maintaining and upgrading facilities. Though the public spaces and guest rooms dazzle with mahogany, marble, and crystal, nothing feels overwhelming or overdone. Indeed, consummate taste prevails, redefining the term "understated luxury." Service is smiling and solicitous (aside from an occasionally harried front desk). A beach concierge dispenses everything from books to CDs, circulating regularly with fruit kebabs, Popsicles, and Evian spray. Yes, sometimes it seems overrun by noisy families and conventioneers. And yes, it's pricey. Since all rooms are spacious and elegantly appointed (and the buildings set fairly far back from the water), only those splurging will book the beachfront (or second-floor oceanview rooms—actually a superior value). Among the amenities here are a state-of-the-art business center, sybaritic spa, and 18-hole Robert Trent Jones, Jr. golf course, as well as a model children's club. Good-value packages—and complimentary extras such as nonmotorized water sports and twice-weekly golf clinics—help reduce the sting from the high rates. ⊠ *Pinney's*

Beach ⟡ *Box 565, Charlestown* ☏ *869/469–1111, 800/332–3442 in U.S., 800/268–6282 in Canada* ⎙ *869/469–1112* ⊕ *www.fourseasons. com* ⟳ *179 rooms, 17 suites, 61 villas* ⚘ *4 restaurants, room service, fans, in-room safes, minibars, cable TV, in-room DVDs, in-room broad-band, 18-hole golf course, 10 tennis courts, pro shop, 3 pools, health club, hair salon, hot tub, spa, beach, dive shop, snorkeling, windsurf-ing, boating, bicycles, 3 bars, pub, library, video game room, shops, babysitting, children's programs (ages 2–12), laundry facilities, laundry service, Internet room, business services, meeting rooms, car rental* ⊟ *AE, D, MC, V* ⦿ *EP.*

★ **$$$$** 🏨 **Montpelier Plantation Inn.** This Nevisian beauty epitomizes under-stated elegance and graciously updated plantation living, courtesy of the congenial, cultured Hofmann family. The fieldstone greathouse repli-cates the 18th-century original; water lilies float serenely in antique cop-per syrup pots; and the mill now houses an intimate restaurant. Hillside cottages, each with private verandas and sea views, dot 30 acres of rav-ishing gardens. The public spaces and guest rooms adopt a chicly min-imalist, Asian-inspired aesthetic. Bamboo is brilliantly employed: joined into rustic valances, woven as wall mats, or split for headboards. Each room is distinctive, though all have sisal rugs, Phillippine hemp chairs, louvered windows, bowls of fresh flowers, large bathrooms, and a sin-gle breathtaking tube filled with orchids and grass hanging above a custom-made canopy platform or mahogany four-poster bed. Attention to detail exemplifies Montpelier: guests register at their leisure once they've set-tled in; if you pre-ship your bags, they will be unpacked and your clothes pressed before you arrive. Accommodating, longtime staffers (nearly three per room) almost psychically intuit your needs. All you need to do is relax in a hammock contemplating the sea, enjoy compli-mentary tea by the 60-foot pool bedecked with marvelous local murals, or laze on Montpelier's secluded stretch of Pinney's (a 20-minute com-plimentary shuttle ride). ⊠ *Montpelier Estate* ⟡ *Box 474, Charlestown* ☏ *869/469–3462* ⎙ *869/469–2932* ⊕ *www.montpeliernevis.com* ⟳ *17 rooms* ⚘ *3 restaurants, fans, tennis court, pool, beach, snorkeling, 2 bars, game room, library, shop, Internet room; no room TVs, no kids under 8* ⊟ *AE, D, MC, V* ⊘ *Closed late Aug.–early Oct.* ⦿ *BP.*

★ **$$$$** 🏨 **Nisbet Plantation Beach Club.** At this beachfront plantation inn, pale yellow cottages face a regal, palm-lined grass avenue that sweeps like a dowager's train to the champagne-hued beach. The three categories of faultlessly maintained rooms were completely redone in late 2005 as part of a property-wide upgrade; all have vaulted ceilings, graceful patios, and gleaming tile floors. The best buys are the so-called superior units, set back amid the banyan trees. They're nearly as spacious as top-of-the-line rooms and cost $170 less. Affable service is smoothly unobtru-sive (look for special staffers' workshops in traditional Nevisian crafts) while convivial managers Bev and Wally Plachta welcome guests as if they were coming home. In addition to the soigné greathouse restau-rant, you'll find two casual beach eateries and a brilliantly painted deck bar with fantastic sunset views. A small gym, outdoor hot tub, and spa-treatment room were recently added. Laundry, afternoon tea, and smiles are complimentary. ⊠ *Newcastle Beach* ☏ *869/469–9325 or 800/742–*

20

6008 ≜ *869/469–9864* ⊕ *www.nisbetplantation.com* ⤳ *36 rooms* ⌂ *3 restaurants, fans, in-room safes, refrigerators, in-room data ports, tennis court, pool, gym, hot tub, massage, beach, snorkeling, croquet, 2 bars, library, shop, laundry service, Internet room; no room TVs* ⊟ *AE, D, MC, V* ⦿| *BP.*

★ $$$$ **Villa Paradiso.** These lavish three- and four-bedroom villas, run by Abercrombie & Kent's boutique luxury resort division, spill down a verdant hillside to a secluded stretch of Pinney's Beach. World-renowned designer Adam Tihany created the Balinese-inspired look (replete with handwoven thatched roofing, hand-carved timbers, and private courtyard gardens), which blends harmoniously with the natural setting. Interiors are spectacular, straddling classic and contemporary elements: carved mahogany and teak furnishings, sunken marble tubs and separate rainfall showers, plasma TV/DVDs, free-standing gourmet kitchens, and eclectic decor embracing Buddhas, model sailboats, African carvings, and huge earthenware or glazed urns. Each villa has 30-foot beamed ceilings and a vine-swaddled duplex balcony with stunning sea views and private plunge pool with waterfall. Needless to say, only the finest products—Anichini linens to Molton Brown toiletries—will do. Butlers and chefs can be arranged. It's still a work in progress: five more villas, two restaurants, and a water-sports center are slated to open sometime in 2007. There's a five-day minimum rental. ⊠ *Pinney's Beach* ⓓ *Box Newcastle* ☎ *869/469–7900 or 888/666–4282* ⊕ *www. villaparadisonevis.com* ⤳ *10 villas* ⌂ *Fans, kitchens, cable TV, in-room VCRs, Wi-Fi, 10 pools, gym, beach, snorkeling, boating, kayaking, bar* ⊟ *AE, D, MC, V* ⦿| *EP.*

★ $$$–$$$$ **Hermitage Plantation Inn.** A snug 1670 greathouse—reputedly the Caribbean's oldest surviving wooden building—forms the heart of this breeze-swept hillside hideaway. Maureen and Richard "Lupi" Lupinacci and their family are its vivacious soul and will introduce you to everyone who's anyone on Nevis. Lively, literate, and laid-back, it attracts a smart (in every sense) set, yet the ambience remains down-to-earth, and kids are definitely welcome—rare for such a refined retreat. The owners' passion for all things Caribbean, from heirloom antiques to vernacular architecture, is apparent. Stone-and-gingerbread cottages are either painstakingly restored originals or meticulous re-creations, with hardwood floors, four-poster canopy beds, and hammock-slung patios or balconies. Families and honeymooners adore the two-story Blue Cottage, but the Loft, Pink House, and Goosepen Cottage are equally sybaritic; the three-bedroom Manor House has its own pool and wraparound porches. The 17th-century stone terraces are embroidered with Maureen's wild English Romantic-style gardens (pluck your own fruit, or ask the kitchen to prepare a homeopathic bush tea); in genuine plantation fashion, the inn has its own stable, piggery, and livestock. ⊠ *Gingerland* ☎ *869/ 469–3477 or 800/682–4025* ≜ *869/469–2481* ⊕ *www.hermitagenevis. com* ⤳ *8 rooms, 8 cottages, 1 house* ⌂ *Restaurant, fans, in-room safes, some kitchens, refrigerators, tennis court, pool, horseback riding, bar, shops; no a/c, no TV in some rooms* ⊟ *AE, D, MC, V* ⦿| *BP.*

★ $$$–$$$$ **Mount Nevis Hotel & Beach Club.** The personable, attentive Meguid family blends the intimacy of the plantation inns, contemporary amenities

CLOSE UP

Off to the Races

ONE OF THE CARIBBEAN'S MOST festive, endearingly idiosyncratic events is the Nevis Turf & Jockey Club's "Day at the Races," held 10 to 12 times a year on the wild and windswept Indian Castle course. I first experienced the event in the mid-1990s, when I met club president Richard "Lupi" Lupinacci, owner of the Hermitage Plantation Inn. Before even introducing himself, Richard sized me up in the driveway: "You look about the right size for a jockey. How's your seat?" His equally effervescent wife, Maureen, then interceded, "Darling, if you loathe horses, don't worry. In fact, Lupi and I have an agreement about the Jerk and Turkey Club. I get major jewels for every animal he buys."

Since my riding skills were rusty, it was decided that I should be a judge (despite questionable vision, even with glasses). "If it's really by a nose, someone will disagree with you either way," I was reassured. The next day presented a quintessential Caribbean

scene. While a serious cadre of aficionados (including the German consul) talked turf, the rest of the island seemed more interested in liming and enjoying lively music. Local ladies dished out heavenly barbecued chicken and devilish gossip. Sheep and cattle unconcernedly ambled across the course. But when real horses thundered around the oval, the wooden stands groaned under the weight of cheering crowds, and bookies hand-calculated the payouts.

The irregularly scheduled races continue, albeit now on a properly sodded track, as does the equine hospitality. The **Hermitage Stables** (✉ Gingerland ☎ 869/469-3477) arrange everything from horseback riding to jaunts in hand-carved mahogany carriages. The **Nevis Equestrian Centre** (✉ Clifton Estate, Pinney's Beach ☎ 869/469-9118) offers leisurely beach rides as well as more demanding canters through the lush hills.

20

of the Four Seasons, and typical Nevisian warmth in this hilltop aerie. The former lime plantation (the wild trees' scent wafts on the breeze) affords sterling views from most rooms (request upper floors, which also have marvelous sloped hardwood cathedral ceilings). There's a well-equipped business center, a gym with inspiring water views, Jacuzzis on nearly every outdoor suite deck, and complimentary cell phones (you pay only for calls). Other upscale touches include granite counters, Italian-tile baths, ultramodern kitchens in the superior suites, and CD and DVD players. Standard rooms or junior suites (which have a sitting area and kitchenette) can be combined with the superior suites (whose sofa beds make them good family buys). You can luxuriate in a poolside hammock, catch the free shuttle to the beach club and its worthy pizzeria-grill, or take an invigorating hike to the ruins of Thomas Cottle Church, an unusual historic site because both slave owners and slaves worshiped there. ✉ *Shaw's Rd., Mount Nevis* ⌂ *Box 494, Newcastle* ☎ *869/ 469-9373 or 800/756-3847* 📠 *869/469-9375* ⊕ *www.mountnevishotel. com* ⇥ *16 suites, 8 junior suites, 8 rooms, 1 villa* ♿ *2 restaurants, fans, some in-room hot tubs, some kitchens, some kitchenettes, refrigerators, cable TV, some in-room DVDs, tennis courts, pool, gym, bar, Internet room, business services, meeting rooms* ⊟ *AE, MC, V* ⧫❍⧫ *BP.*

★ **$$–$$$$** ⊞ **Hurricane Cove Bungalows.** These dramatically set one-, two-, and three-bedroom bungalows cling like glorified tree houses to a cliff overlooking several glittering beaches. Enormous enclosed patios open onto the island's most glorious vistas; monkeys and pelicans often drop by informally. Every cottage has a full kitchen; many have outdoor gas grills and private swimming pools (those with no pool are especially good buys); it's a short if precipitous walk to Oualie and Lover's beaches. The tiny hotel pool sits in the foundation of a 250-year-old fort, shaded by a magnificent baobab tree. The bungalows are beautifully designed and decorated with beamed ceilings, batik wall hangings, terra-cotta floors, Thai teak furnishings, striking abstract art naïf, and beds swaddled in mosquito netting. Most coveted, especially by honeymooners, are Baobab, Williwaw, Sea Biscuit, and the ultraprivate Monkey cottages. ⊠ *Hurricane Hill* ⊕ *www.hurricanecove.com* ⊠⊠ *869/469–9462* ⊲⊐ *13 cottages* ⚬ *Fans, kitchens, pool, laundry service; no a/c, no room TVs* ⊟ *AE, D, MC, V* ⊗ *Closed Sept.* ⧫❍⧫ *EP.*

$$$ ⊞ **Old Manor Hotel.** Physically, this inn best evokes the old-time plantation atmosphere on Nevis, thanks to creative restoration (the original cistern is now the pool, and stone outbuildings hold public spaces and guest rooms). Yet it lacks personality. The setting is exceptionally pretty, with Mount Nevis looming in the background, apricot-and-jade buildings enveloped by tropical landscaping, and cannons and rusting sugar-factory equipment forming a virtual abstract sculpture garden. Despite occasional half-hearted renovations (TVs are still promised), large rooms remain a hodgepodge. The best have exposed wood beams, stone walls, polished hardwood floors, marble double vanities, and four-poster beds. Others are gloomy (reading lights are a chronic problem) or resemble a garage sale, contrasting tatty madras settees with contemporary curved white sofas and soiled rugs. The respected Cooperage restaurant features a top-notch nouvelle Continental menu and sensational sea views. ⊲⊐ *Box 70, Charlestown* ⊠ *869/469–3445 or 800/892–7093* ⊠ *869/469–3388* ⊕ *www.oldmanornevis.com* ⊲⊐ *14 rooms* ⚬ *2 restaurants, fans, refrigerators, pool, 2 bars, library, shops, Internet room; no a/c, no room TVs* ⊟ *AE, D, MC, V* ⧫❍⧫ *BP.*

$$–$$$ ⊞ **Golden Rock Plantation Inn.** Pam Barry's great-great-great-grandfather built this hillside estate in the early years of the 19th century, and Pam imbues the inn with her love of Nevisian heritage and nature. The old cistern was converted into a spring-fed swimming pool and the sugar mill into a honeymoon haven with gorgeous winding bamboo staircase. Cannons placed about the grounds contribute to the historic ambience, as do Pam's family silver and the extraordinary Eva Wilkin mural in the bar. An avid environmental activist, Pam hacked out nature trails throughout the mountainous, 96-acre property. Green vervet monkeys dash about the premises (they often congregate outside Cottage 1). Gingerbread cottages painted in pastels from coral to canary yellow have dazzling ocean views from their patios. Most rooms continue the island theme, with locally carved four-poster beds, native grass mats, antique rocking chairs, and hand-painted tables. Free transportation accesses the inn's beach bar (phenomenal rum punches) on Pinney's Beach and a windward strand ideal for seclusion and bodysurfing. New partners (from New York's art world) may upgrade the facilities (and prices). ☒ *Gingerland* ✉ *Box 493, Charlestown* ☎ *869/469–3346* 🖷 *869/469–2113* ⊕ *www.golden-rock.com* ➥ *16 rooms, 1 suite* ♨ *2 restaurants, fans, tennis court, pool, hiking, bar, Internet room; no a/c, no room TVs* ▤ *AE, D, MC, V* ☺ *Closed Sept.–mid-Oct.* ⑪ *EP.*

$$–$$$ 🏨 **Oualie Beach Hotel.** These cozy creole-style gingerbread cottages daubed in cotton-candy colors sit just steps from a taupe beach overlooking St. Kitts and are carefully staggered to ensure sea views from every room. Deluxe rooms have mahogany canopy four-poster beds and granite vanities, while studios have full kitchen and sofa beds. Unfortunately, many older rooms are slightly musty, with chipped furnishings and faded fabrics. Happily, eco-centric Oualie is noted for its wealth of on-site recreational opportunities from mountain biking to diving, windsurfing to turtle-watching, so you won't spend much time in your room anyway. It's also fairly hopping for a small Nevisian property. The informal restaurant—greatly improved by the addition of talented, enthusiastic chef Jason Bishop—is popular for its West Indian–theme Saturday nights, with live music. Dive packages and numerous Internet specials including early-bird discounts make Oualie excellent value. ☒ *Oualie Beach* ☎ *869/469–9735 or 800/682–5431* 🖷 *869/469–9176* ⊕ *www.oualiebeach.com* ➥ *32 rooms* ♨ *Restaurant, fans, in-room safes, some kitchens, refrigerators, cable TV, some in-room VCRs, Wi-Fi, spa, beach, dive shop, snorkeling, windsurfing, boating, fishing, mountain bikes, bar, Internet room, meeting room* ▤ *AE, D, MC, V* ⑪ *EP.*

$$ 🏨 **Inn at Cades Bay.** This relaxed beachfront complex offers excellent value (check for Internet deals and occasional special "low" high-season rates in January and February). Little touches compensate for the noise from Main Road traffic, lack of a restaurant now that the on-site Tequila Sheila's has closed, and slightly rocky, seaweed-strewn beach (snorkeling, at least, is superior). The carefully groomed grounds include 10 varieties of palm trees and a garden of succulents from aloe to cacti. A tiny lawn adorns every cozy peach-colored cottage with sage-green gabled roof, conch shells line the walkways, and vine-draped trellises ensure privacy for each ocean-view terra-cotta patio. Spacious rooms have high wooden tray ceilings, bleached-wood paneling, and stylish appointments including rattan beds, plantation antiques, and teak patio furnishings. Ask mellow owner Eddy Williams to procure some of mom Eulalie's hot sauce as a souvenir. At this writing, Eddy and ex-wife Sheila were considering selling the property. ☒ *Cades Bay* ☎ *869/469–8139* 🖷 *869/469–8129* ⊕ *www.cadesbayinn.com* ➥ *16 rooms* ♨ *Restaurant, fans, minibars, cable TV, pool, bar* ▤ *AE, MC, V* ⑪ *CP.*

$–$$ 🏨 **Banyan Tree Bed & Breakfast.** Jonathan and Anne Rose originally conceived their retirement haven as a working farm, but then they created this unique retreat tucked into the hilly, verdant countryside. Wild monkeys and psychedelically hued birds and butterflies claim the 6 acres of remarkably varied, vibrant gardens, from namesake banyan to bamboo stand, bromeliads to begonias, as their own. The utter peace and un-

20

spoiled natural setting inspire many guests to take up sketching with accomplished architect-artist Jonathan (or gardening with Anne). Breakfast and twice-weekly family-style buffet dinners creatively utilize the extensive array of fruits, vegetables, and herbs from the gardens. The lava-stone Guest House contains two comfortable rooms, each with private patio. The yellow Bamboo House, gloriously furnished with antique mahogany pieces, stands alone with stimulating mountain and sea views from its wraparound porch. The Roses often take guests on nature hikes or kayaking trips, eager to share their adopted paradise. ✉ *Morningstar* ☎ *869/469–3449 or 800/639–6109* ⊕ *www. banyantreebandb.com* ⤴ *2 rooms, 1 cottage* ⌂ *Fans, kitchenette, boating; no a/c, no room TVs* ▭ *MC, V* ☞ *3-night minimum* ◎ *Closed Aug.–mid-Nov.* ❙◎❙ *BP.*

Where to Eat

Dinner options range from intimate meals at plantation guesthouses (where the menu is often prix-fixe) to casual eateries. Seafood is ubiquitous, and many places specialize in West Indian fare. The island is trying to raise its profile as a fine-dining destination by holding NICHE (Nevis International Culinary Heritage Exposition), a gastronomic festival with guest chefs and winemakers offering cooking seminars and tastings during the last week of October.

What to Wear

Dress is casual at lunch, although beach attire is unacceptable. Dress pants and sundresses are appropriate for dinner.

For approximate costs, *see* the dining and lodging price chart at the beginning of this chapter.

CARIBBEAN
★ $$$$

✕ **Miss June's Cuisine.** Dinner with Miss June Mestier, a dynamo originally from Trinidad, could never be called ordinary. The all-inclusive evening begins with cocktails in the ornate living room, followed by dinner in an elegant dining room where tables are set with mismatched china and crystal. Hors d'oeuvres and three courses, including soup and fish, are served. "Now that you've had dinner," Miss June proclaims, "let's have fun," presenting a grand multi-dish feast highlighting her Trinidadian curries, local vegetable preparations, and meats. "I invite people into my home for dinner and then my manager has the audacity to charge them as they leave!" quips Miss June, who joins guests (who have included Oprah Winfrey, John Grisham, and members of Aerosmith) after dinner for coffee and brandy. Miss June won't kick you out, but she may ask you to turn the lights out as you leave. ✉ *Jones Bay* ☎ *869/469–5330* ⤴ *Reservations essential* ▭ *MC, V.*

$$$

✕ **Golden Rock Plantation Inn.** The romantic, dimly lighted room's vine-draped fieldstone walls date from the Golden Rock Inn's plantation days. Enchanting Eva Wilkin originals grace the walls, copper sugar-boiling pots are used as planters, and straw mats, turtle shells, and unglazed local pottery provide island interest. The prix-fixe menu might include house favorites like velvety pumpkin soup, raisin curry chicken, christophene (chayote) and green papaya pie, and grilled local snapper with *tannia* (a type of tuber) fritters. Don't miss the homemade juices, such as passion fruit, papaya, soursop, and ginger beer; do order the luscious lobster salad for lunch. During high season, a local string band jazzes up the popular Saturday-night Caribbean buffet, though crickets and tree frogs always provide fitting background music. ⊠ *Gingerland* ☎ *869/469–3346* ⚒ *Reservations essential* ▭ *AE, D, MC, V* ⊗ *Closed Sun.*

★ **$–$$$** ✕ **Sunshine's.** Everything about this beach shack is larger than life, including the Rasta man Llewelyn "Sunshine" Caines himself. Flags from around the world drape the lean-to and complement the international patrons (including an occasional movie star), who wander over from the adjacent Four Seasons. Picnic tables are splashed with bright sunrise-to-sunset colors; even the palm trees are painted. Fishermen cruise up with their catch—you might savor lobster rolls or snapper creole. Don't miss the lethal house specialty, Killer Bee rum punch. As Sunshine boasts, "One and you're stung, two you're stunned, three it's a knockout." ⊠ *Pinney's Beach* ☎ *869/469–1089* ▭ *No credit cards.*

CONTEMPORARY ✕ **Nisbet Plantation Beach Club.** The now blissfully air-conditioned
$$$$ greathouse—an oasis of polished hardwood floors, mahogany and cherrywood furnishings, equestrian bronzes, antique hurricane lamps, wicker furnishings, and stone walls—has long been a popular dinner spot. Tables on the veranda look down the palm-tree-lined fairway to the sea. The five-course menu combines Continental, Pacific Rim, and Caribbean cuisines with local ingredients. Sumptuous choices include chicken and coconut dumpling soup, red snapper on plantain and potato mash with tomato-ginger broth, followed by lemon and vanilla mascarpone mousse with hazelnut praline. Enjoy an impressively cosmopolitan selection of cocktails or coffee with silky-soft live music in the civilized front bar. Witty, dapper maître d' Patterson Fleming ensures a smooth, swank experience. ⊠ *Newcastle Beach* ☎ *869/469–9325* ⚒ *Reservations essential* ▭ *AE, D, MC, V.*

★ **$$$–$$$$** ✕ **Four Seasons Dining Room.** The main restaurant at the Four Seasons is imposing yet romantic: a beamed cathedral ceiling, imported hardwood paneling, parquet floors, ornate white-iron chandeliers, flagstone hearth, china-filled cabinets, hand-carved mahogany chairs, towering floral arrangements, and picture windows overlooking the sea. French-born chef Cyrille Pannier produces a Continental-inspired menu utilizing Caribbean ingredients, such as a ginger-poached lobster tail with Jamaican run and orange sauce, foie gras glazed with Nevisian honey topped with caramelized bananas and pineapple–vanilla bean sauce, or New Zealand rack of lamb with an eggplant tomato gratin and bacon-wrapped haricots verts. Desserts feature a variety of nightly soufflés, from chocolate to mango. The hotel can arrange a unique interactive dive-and-dine experience, plunging you into the deep with Cyrille to pluck lobster and other marine creatures that he'll cook for you later. The wine list is admirably comprehensive with surprisingly fair prices. The adjacent Neve (which counterpoints with aggressively contemporary decor) specializes in Italian grills and bountiful breakfast buffets. The Friday-night beach barbecues are deliciously hedonistic. ⊠ *Four Seasons Re-*

20

sort, *Pinney's Beach* ☎ 869/469–1111 ⚐ *Reservations essential* ▭ *AE, D, DC, MC, V* ☾ *No lunch.*

$$$ ✕ **Mount Nevis Hotel & Beach Club.** The hotel's airy dining room opens onto the terrace and pool with a splendid view of St. Kitts. The elegant yet light menu deftly blends local ingredients with a cornucopia of Caribbean-Continental cuisines, artfully presented by Puerto Rican–born chef Alberto Rodriguez. Sterling starters are sesame tempura shrimp with tamarind oyster sauce or salted fish cake Napoleon layered with fresh baby spinach, chorizo, and avocado salsa. Worthy if less innovative main courses include charcoal-grilled filet mignon with lentil-mushroom ragout or almond-encrusted snapper with balsamic tomato salad. Savor cocktails in the distinctive lounge (accented by sisal rugs, mosaic and painted tiles, artworks in fevered fauvist hues, towering bamboo stalks, and flowers floating in crystal bowls). Then repair to the sublime open-air dining room, where a pianist holds forth in an illuminated "stage" by the pool ✉ *Shaws Rd., Mt. Nevis Estates* ☎ 869/469–9373 ⚐ *Reservations essential* ▭ *AE, MC, V.*

★ **$$$** ✕ **Coconut Grove.** This thatched-palm roof and rough timber structure sports a sensuous South Seas look, best appreciated on the deck as the sun fireballs across the Caribbean. Inside, handsome teak furnishings are animated by Buddhas, parrot-hued throw pillows, batik hangings, and gauzy curtains. The fine Pacific Rim–Mediterranean fusion fare seems designed to complement the admirable wine selection—second on the sister islands only to that of the Four Seasons—rather than the other way around. Owners Gary and Karin Colt often bring winemaker friends in from Europe for tastings and dinners. Nonetheless, serious foodies won't be disappointed by the likes of plantain rolls with diced tiger shrimp in Colombo (curry) mango coulis or sliced flank beef steak in cabernet sauvignon butter garnished with truffled mashed potatoes. Happy hour 11 PM–midnight often ushers in impromptu dancing, continuing the "Bali high" theme. ✉ *Nelson's Spring, Pinney's Beach* ☎ 869/469–1020 ⚐ *Reservations essential* ▭ *MC, V* ☾ *No lunch.*

★ **$$$** ✕ **Hermitage Plantation Inn.** After cocktails in the inn's antiques-filled parlor (incomparable bartender Shaba's knockout rum punches are legendary), dinner is served on the veranda. Many ingredients are harvested from the inn's herb garden, fruit trees, piggery and livestock collection; the scrumptious cured meats, baked goods, preserves, and ice creams are homemade. Sumptuous three- and five-course set menus lovingly prepared by a team of local chefs might include conch cakes with lobster sauce, breadfruit-cheddar soufflé, mahimahi with lemongrass ginger and tamarind, and white-chocolate-ginger cheesecake. Bon mots and bonhomie serve as prelude, intermezzo, and coda for a lively evening. ✉ *Gingerland* ☎ 869/469–3477 ⚐ *Reservations essential* ▭ *AE, D, MC, V.*

$$$ ✕ **Montpelier Plantation Inn.** Owners Tim and Meredith Hoffman preside over a scintillating evening, starting with canapés and cocktails in the civilized Great Room. Dinner is served on the breezy west veranda, which gazes serenely upon the lights of Charlestown and St. Kitts. The inventive chef, Mark Roberts, utilizes the inn's herb gardens and fruit trees and occasionally even hauls in the day's catch. The changing three-course menu might present lobster tail on black bean cake with

FodorśChoice
★

scotch bonnet beurre blanc, seared swordfish in papaya–black bean salsa, and a proper herb-crusted rack of lamb in rosemary mustard jus. Meredith has crafted an exemplary wine list perfectly matched to the cuisine. The Mill opens on certain nights with sufficient reservations, offering a different set four-course menu accompanied by champagne and sorbets. Torches light cobblestone steps up to this theatrical faux sugar mill with crystal sconces, floating candles, and an antique mahogany gear wheel suspended from the ceiling. Simpler lunches (order the lobster salad) are served on the refreshing patio. ⊠ *Montpelier Estate* ☎ *869/469–3462* ♨ *Reservations essential* ▭ *AE, D, MC, V* ⊗ *Closed late Aug.–early Oct.*

ECLECTIC $$ ✕ **Le Bistro.** Known informally as Matt's, after owner–chef Matt Lloyd (former chef at Montpelier), this minuscule boîte, in a 1930s chattel house, is wildly popular, especially during Friday-night happy hour. Fare ranges from quiches to curries; coconut chicken's a standout, but opt for the fresh-fish specials (Matt usually hauls in the catch himself on his 30-footer, *Deep Venture,* which is available for rent). The impeccable presentation is as colorful as the quintessentially West Indian decor. Local chefs flock here on their nights off—always a promising sign. ⊠ *Chapel St., Charlestown* ☎ *869/469–5110* ▭ *MC, V* ⊗ *Closed weekends. No lunch.*

$–$$ ✕ **Gallipot.** A two-family venture, Gallipot, with its octagonal bar and casual atmosphere, attracts locals with ultrafresh seafood at reasonable prices, marvelous views of St. Kitts from the beach, and sensational sunsets. Large Sunday lunches with ample portions (only one dish per week, usually classic roast beef and Yorkshire pudding) are a big draw. The Fosberys built the bar as an addition to their small beach house on quiet Tamarind Bay, while their daughter and son-in-law, Tracy and Julian Rigby, provide fish through Nevis Water Sports, a charter-fishing company. Aside from their local customers, Gallipot attracts sailors with its moorings, showers, garbage-collection service, and laundry. ⊠ *Tamarind Bay* ☎ *869/469–8230* ▭ *MC, V* ⊗ *Closed Mon.–Wed. No dinner Sun.*

Beaches

All beaches are free to the public (the plantation inns cordon off "private" areas on Pinney's Beach for guests), but there are no changing facilities, so wear a swimsuit under your clothes.

Newcastle Beach. This broad swath of soft ecru sand shaded by coconut palms sits at the northernmost tip of the island near Nisbet Plantation, on the channel between St. Kitts and Nevis. It's popular with snorkelers, but beware stony sections and occasional strong currents that kick up seaweed and roil the sandy bottom. You can watch planes take off like sea birds: it's only a three- to four-minute drive east of the airport along the Main Road. ⊠ *Newcastle Beach.*

Oualie Beach. South of Mosquito Bay and north of Cades and Jones bays, this beige-sand beach lined with palms and sea grapes is where the folks at Oualie Beach Hotel can mix you a drink and fix you up with watersports equipment. There's excellent snorkeling amid calm water and fantastic sunset views with St. Kitts silhouetted in the background. Several beach chairs and hammocks ($3 rental if you don't have lunch) line the sand and the grassy "lawn" behind it (this beach expands and erodes constantly). Oualie is at the island's northwest tip, approximately 3 mi (5 km) west of the airport. ⊠ *Oualie Beach.*

★ **Pinney's Beach.** The island's showpiece has almost 4 mi (6½ km) of soft, golden sand on the calm Caribbean, lined with a magnificent grove of palm trees. The Four Seasons Resort is here, as is the beach pavilion of the Golden Rock Plantation Inn, and casual beach bars such as Sunshine's and the Double Deuce. Regrettably, the waters can be murky and filled with kelp if the weather has been inclement anywhere within a hundred miles, depending on the currents. You can't miss Pinney's: the Main Road hugs it, starting just north of Charleston (just take any of the short dirt turnoffs with signage for bars). ⊠ *Pinney's Beach.*

Sports & the Outdoors

BIKING **Windsurfing Nevis** (⊠ Oualie Beach ☎ 869/469–9682 ⊕ www. mountainbikenevis.com) offers mountain-bike rentals as well as specially tailored tours on its state-of-the-art Gary Fisher, Trek, and Specialised bikes. The tours ($50–$55), led by Winston Crooke, a master windsurfer and competitive bike racer, encompass lush rain forest, majestic ruins, and spectacular views. Rates vary according to itinerary and ability level but are aimed generally at experienced riders. Winston and his team delight in sharing local knowledge, from history to culture. For those just renting, Winston and Reggie determine your performance level and suggest appropriate routes.

DAYSAILS **Sea Nevis Charters** (⊠ Tamarind Bay, Nevis ☎ 869/469–9239) offers its 44-foot *Sea Dreamer* for snorkeling and island sunset cruises. Capt. Les Windley takes you to less trammeled sites and is a font of information on marine life.

DIVING & The **Devil's Caves** are a series of grottos where divers can navigate tun-
SNORKELING nels, canyons, and underwater hot springs while viewing lobsters, sea fans, sponges, squirrel fish, and more. The village of **Jamestown,** which washed into the sea around Fort Ashby, just south of Cades Bay, makes for superior snorkeling and diving. Reef-protected Pinney's Beach offers especially good snorkeling. Single-tank dives are usually $65, two-tank dives $95.

Scuba Safaris (⊠ Oualie Beach ☎ 869/469–9518 ⊕ www.scubanevis. com) is a PADI five-star facility, NAUI Dream Resort, and NASDS Examining Station, whose experienced dive masters offer everything from a resort course to full certification. They also provide a snorkeling learning experience that enables you not only to see but to listen to sea-
★ ☾ life, including whales and dolphins. **Under the Sea** (⊠ Oualie Beach ☎ 869/469–1291 ⊕ www.undertheseanevis.com) is the brainchild of Barbara Whitman, a marine biologist from Connecticut. Barbara's mission is to orient snorkelers and divers of all ages about sea life and various ecosystems so they'll appreciate—and respect—what they see. Using hands-on "touch tanks," videos, and self-painted marine murals

as familiarization tools, she then offers snorkeling lessons and tours to see the creatures in the wild. Her programs range from $25, and profits go toward educating local school children about their precious natural environment and increasing ecological awareness.

FISHING   Fishing here focuses on kingfish, wahoo, grouper, tuna, and yellowtail snapper, with marlin occasionally spotted. The best areas are Monkey Shoals and around Redonda. Charters cost approximately $350 per half-day, $675 per full day, and include open bar. *Deep Venture* (⌧ Oualie Beach ☎ 869/469–5110), run by fisherman-chef Matt Lloyd of Le Bistro, does day-fishing charters, providing a real insight into both commercial fishing and the Caribbean kitchen. **Nevis Water Sports** (⌧ Oualie Beach ☎ 869/469–9060 ⊕ www.fishnevis.com) offers sportfishing aboard the 31-foot *Sea Brat* under the supervision of tournament-winning captains Julian Rigby and Ian Gonzaley. Julian, originally from England, and wife Tracy organize the annual Nevis Yacht Club Sports Fishing Tournament, which reels in competitors from all over the Caribbean.

GOLF   Duffers doff their hats to the beautiful, impeccably maintained Robert Trent Jones, Jr.–designed 18-hole, par-72, 6,766-yard championship **Four**

Fodor'sChoice ★   **Seasons Golf Course** (⌧ Four Seasons Resort Nevis, Pinney's Beach ☎ 869/469–1111): the virtual botanical gardens surrounding the fairways almost qualify as a hazard in themselves. The front 9 holes are fairly flat until the 8th hole, which climbs uphill after your tee shot. Most of the truly stunning views are along the back 9. The signature hole is the 15th, a 660-yard monster that encompasses a deep ravine; other holes include bridges, steep drops, rolling pitches, extremely tight and unforgiving fairways, sugarmill ruins, and fierce doglegs. Attentive attendants canvas the course with beverage buggies, handing out chilled, peppermint-scented towels. Greens fees are $110 per person for 9 holes, $175 for 18.

HIKING   The center of the island is Nevis Peak—also known as Mount Nevis—which soars 3,232 feet and is flanked by Hurricane Hill on the north and Saddle Hill on the south. If you plan to scale Nevis Peak, a daylong affair, it's highly recommended that you go with a guide. Your hotel can arrange it (and a picnic lunch) for you. The **Upper Round Road Trail** is a 9-mi (14½-km) road constructed in the late 1600s and cleared and restored by the Nevis Historical and Conservation Society. It connects the Golden Rock Hotel, on the east side of the island, with Nisbet Plantation Beach Club, on the northern tip. The trail encompasses numerous vegetation zones, including pristine rain forest, and impressive plantation ruins. The original cobblestones, walls, and ruins are still evident in many places.

Herbert Heights Village Experience (☎ 869/469–2856 ⊕ www. herbertheights.com) is run by the Herbert family, who have fashioned their own unique activities. They lead four-hour nature hikes up to panoramic Herbert Heights, where you drink in fresh local juices and the views of Montserrat; the powerful telescope makes you feel as if you're staring right into that island's simmering volcano. The trail formed part of an escape route for runaway slaves. Numerous hummingbirds,

20

doves, and butterflies flit and flutter through the rain forest. The Herberts painstakingly reconstructed thatched cottages that offer a glimpse of village life a century ago at Nelson's Lookout. The price is $15; for $35 you can ride one of their donkeys. The festive activities include crab races, refreshments, rock climbing, and whale-watching in season through a telescope donated by Greenpeace. **Sunrise Tours** (☎ 869/469–2758 ⊕ www.nevisnaturetours.com), run by Lynell and Earla Liburd, offers a range of hiking tours, but their most popular is Devil's Copper, a rock configuration full of ghostly legends. Local people gave it its name because at one time the water was hot—a volcanic thermal stream. The area features pristine waterfalls and splendid bird-watching. They also do a Nevis village walk, a Hamilton Estate Walk, an Amerindian walk along the wild southeast Atlantic coast, and trips to the rain forest and Nevis Peak. They love highlighting Nevisian heritage, explaining time-honored cooking techniques, the many uses of dried grasses, and medicinal plants. Hikes range from $20 to $40 per

★ person, and you receive a certificate of achievement. **Top to Bottom** (☎ 869/469–9080 ⊕ www.walknevis.com), run by Jim and Nikki Johnston, offers eco-rambles (slow tours) and hikes that emphasize Nevis's volcanic and horticultural heritage (including pointing out folkloric herbal medicines). The Johnstons are also keen star- and bird-watchers (their Nevis Nights magically explain nocturnal biology, astronomy, even astrology). Three-hour rambles or hikes are $20 per person (snacks and juice included); it's $30 to $35 for more strenuous climbs (two offered) up Mount Nevis.

KAYAKING **Turtle Tours Nevis** (✉ Oualie Beach, Nevis ☎ 869/465–8503) offers sea kayaking along the Nevis coast, stopping at an otherwise inaccessible beach underneath a towering cliff for snorkeling and at Pinney's for refreshments and a refreshing view of St. Kitts.

WINDSURFING Waters are generally calm and northeasterly winds steady yet gentle, mak-
★ ing Nevis an excellent spot for beginners and intermediates. **Windsurfing Nevis** (✉ Oualie Beach ☎ 869/469–9682 ⊕ www.windsurfingnevis.com) offers top-notch instructors (Winston Crooke is one of the best in the islands) and equipment for $25 per half hour. Groups are kept small (eight maximum), and the equipment is state-of-the-art from Mistral North and Tushingham.

Shopping

Nevis is certainly not the place for a shopping spree, but there are some unusual and wonderful surprises, notably the island's stamps, batik, and hand-embroidered clothing. Honey is another buzzing biz. Quentin Henderson, the amiable head of the **Nevis Beekeeping Cooperative,** will even arrange trips by appointment to various hives for demonstrations of beekeeping procedures. Other than a few hotel boutiques and isolated galleries, virtually all shopping is concentrated on or just off Main Street in Charlestown. The lovely old stonework and wood floors of the waterfront Cotton Ginnery Complex make an appropriate setting for stalls of local artisans.

Specialty Items

ART Nevis has produced one artist of some international repute, the late Dame Eva Wilkin, who for more than 50 years painted island people, flowers, and landscapes in an evocative art naïf style. Her originals are now quite valuable, but prints are available in some local shops. The **Eva Wilkin Gallery** (✉ Clay Ghaut, Gingerland ☎ 869/469–2673) occupies her former atelier. If the paintings, drawings, and prints are out of your price range, consider buying the lovely note cards based on her designs. **Robert Humphreys** (✉ Zetlands ☎ 869/469–3326) sells his work, flowing bronze sculptures of pirouetting marlins and local birds and animals at Café des Arts, where it's possible to watch the artist at work in his studio.

CLOTHING Most hotels have their own boutiques. **Island Fever** (✉ Main St., Charlestown ☎ 869/469–0867) has become the island's classiest boutique, with an excellent selection of everything from bathing suits and dresses to straw bags and jewelry. You can find colorful Caribelle Batik clothing and painted coconut bags as well as T-shirts and other Nevis souvenirs at **Island Hopper** (✉ Main St., Charlestown ☎ 869/469–5430).

HANDICRAFTS Cheryl "Cherrianne" Liburd's **Bocane Ceramics** (✉ Main St., Stoney
★ Grove ☎ 869/469–5437) stocks beautifully designed and glazed local pottery, such as platters painted with marine life, pineapple tea sets, and coffee tables topped with mosaic depictions of chattel houses. **The Craft-House** (✉ Pinney's Rd., Charlestown ☎ 869/469–5505) is a marvelous source for local specialties from vetiver mats to leather moccasins; there's a smaller branch in the Cotton Ginnery. **Knick Knacks** (✉ Main St., Hanfield Bldg. near Ferry Dock, Charlestown ☎ 869/469–5784) showcases top local artisans, including Marvin Chapman (stone-and-wood carvings) and Jeannie Rigby (exquisite dolls). The **Nevis Handicraft Co-op Society** (✉ Main St., Charlestown ☎ 869/469–1746), next to the tourist office, offers works by local artisans (clothing, ceramic ware, woven goods) and locally produced honey, hot sauces, and jellies
★ (try the guava and soursop). **Newcastle Pottery** (✉ Main Rd., Newcastle ☎ 869/469–1746), a cooperative, has continued the age-old tradition of hand-built red-clay pottery fired over burning coconut husks. It's possible to watch the potters and purchase wares at their small Newcastle factory. Stamp collectors should head for the **Philatelic Bureau** (✉ Off
★ Main St., Charlestown ☎ 869/469–0617), opposite the tourist office. St. Kitts and Nevis are famous for their decorative, and sometimes valuable, stamps. Real beauties include the butterfly, hummingbird, and marine-life series. **Tropical Interiors** (✉ Main Rd., Clifton Estate, Cotton Ground ☎ 869/469–0578) carries marvelous items from peripatetic owner Gillian Smith's wanderings: Indonesian teak furnishings, Turkish kilims and antique copper pots, Greek ceramics, and the like.

Nightlife

In season it's usually easy to find a local calypso singer or a steel or string band performing at one of the hotels, notably the Four Seasons and Oualie Beach (which also features string musicians on homemade instruments Tuesday evenings). Scan the posters plastered on doorways announcing

20

informal jump-ups. Though Nevis lacks high-tech discos, many restaurants and bars have live bands or DJs on weekends. **Double Deuce** (✉ Pinney's Beach ☎ 869/469–2222) enjoys a local following for its great simple food (Montpelier's Mark Roberts consults), creative cocktails, and Hemingway-esque feel (the shack is plastered with sailing and fishing pictures, as well as Balinese masks, Sabrett's hot dog umbrellas, and windchimes). **Eddy's Bar & Restaurant** (✉ Main St., Memorial Sq., Charlestown ☎ 869/469–5958) has traditionally been the place to go on Wednesday nights for a raucous West Indian happy hour. Burgers, shepherd's pie, quesadillas, and a variety of well-prepared food will get you prepared for the long night ahead. The evening will go on and on to the wee hours with karaoke and dancing to a local DJ. **Mango** (✉ Four Seasons Resort, Pinney's Beach ☎ 869/469–1111) has become the latest hot spot for locals and visitors alike, thanks to a gorgeous outdoor lounge, sizzling music, fab drinks, and inventive, fairly reasonable menu. The **Water Department Barbecue** (✉ Pump Rd., Charlestown ☎ No phone) is the informal name for a lively Friday-night jump-up that's run by two fellows from the local water department to raise funds for department trips. Friday afternoons the tents go up and the grills are fired. Cars line the streets and the guys dish up fabulous barbecue ribs and chicken—as certain customers lobby to get their water pressure adjusted. It's a classic Caribbean scene.

Exploring Nevis

Nevis's main road makes a 21-mi (32-km) circuit through the five parishes; various offshoots of the road wind into the mountains. You can tour Charlestown, the capital, in a half hour or so, but you'll need three to four hours to explore the entire island. Part of the island's charm is its rusticity: there are no traffic lights, goats still amble through the streets of Charlestown, and local grocers announce whatever's in stock on a blackboard (anything from pig snouts to beer).

Numbers in the margin correspond to points of interest on the Nevis map.

② **Bath Springs.** The Caribbean's first hotel, the Bath Hotel, built by businessmann John Huggins in 1778, was so popular in the 19th century that visitors, including such dignitaries as Samuel Taylor Coleridge and Prince William Henry, traveled two months by ship to "take the waters" in the property's hot thermal springs. It suffered extensive hurricane and probably earthquake damage over the years and languished in disrepair until recently. Local volunteers have cleaned up the spring and built a stone pool and steps to enter the waters; now, residents and visitors enjoy the springs, which range from 104°F to 108°F, though signs still caution that you bathe at your own risk, especially if you have heart problems. Upon completion, this promising development will house the Nevis Island Administration offices, massage huts and changing rooms, a restaurant, and a cultural center and historic exhibit on the original hotel property. Follow Main Street south from Charlestown. ✉ *Charlestown outskirts.*

★ **⑤** **Botanical Gardens of Nevis.** In addition to terraced gardens and arbors, this remarkable 7.8-acre site in the glowering shadow of Mount Nevis has natural lagoons, streams, and waterfalls, superlative bronze mermaids, egrets and herons, and extravagant fountains. You can find a proper rose garden, sections devoted to orchids and bromeliads, cacti, and flowering trees and shrubs—even a bamboo garden. The entrance to the Rain Forest Conservatory—which attempts to include every conceivable Caribbean ecosystem and then some—duplicates an imposing Maya temple. A splendid re-creation of a plantation-style greathouse contains a tearoom with sweeping sea views (a lovely lunch and sunset tapas spot, thanks to consulting chef Jason Bishop from Oualie Beach) and a souvenir shop. ⊠ *Montpelier Estate* ☎ *869/469–3509* 🖃 *$9* ⊙ *Mon.–Sat. 9–4:30.*

★ ❶ **Charlestown.** About 1,200 of Nevis's 10,000 inhabitants live in the capital. The town faces the Caribbean, about 12½ mi (20 km) south of Basseterre on St. Kitts. If you arrive by ferry, as most people do, you'll walk smack onto Main Street from the pier. It's easy to imagine how tiny Charlestown, founded in 1660, must have looked in its heyday. The weathered buildings still have their fanciful galleries, elaborate gingerbread fretwork, wooden shutters, and hanging plants. The stonework building with the clock tower (1825, but mostly rebuilt after a devastating 1873 fire) houses the courthouse and the second-floor **library** (a cool respite on sultry days). The little park next to the library is Memorial Square, dedicated to the fallen of World Wars I and II. Down the street from the square, archaeologists have discovered the remains of a Jewish cemetery and synagogue (Nevis reputedly had the Caribbean's second-oldest congregation), but there's little to see. The **Alexander Hamilton Birthplace**, which contains the Museum of Nevis History, is on the waterfront, covered in bougainvillea and hibiscus. This Georgian-style house is a reconstruction of what is believed to have been the American patriot's original home, built in 1680 and thought to have been destroyed during an earthquake in the mid-19th century. Hamilton was born here in 1755 and moved to St. Croix when he was about 12. A few years later, at 17, he moved to the American colonies to continue his education; he became Secretary of the Treasury to George Washington and died in a duel with political rival Aaron Burr. The Nevis House of Assembly occupies the second floor of this building, and the museum downstairs contains Hamilton memorabilia, documents pertaining to the island's history, and displays on island geology, politics, architecture, culture, and cuisine. The gift shop is a wonderful source for historic maps, crafts, and books on Nevis. ⊠ *Low St., Charlestown* ☎ *869/469–5786* ⊕ *www.nevis-nhcs.org* 🖃 *$5 ($7 includes admission to Nelson Museum)* ⊙ *Weekdays 9–4, Sat. 9–noon.*

20

NEED A BREAK?

The front rooms of **Café des Arts** (⊠ Main St. and Samuel Hunkins Dr., Charlestown ☎ 869/469–7098) show the works of Caribbean artists, as well as handicrafts from pareus to pottery. Breakfast, lunch, dinner, and a proper espresso are served daily except Sunday in a delightful courtyard enclosed by stone wall sand overlooking Charlestown harbor. The globetrotting fare is as eclectic as the art: guava-glazed ribs, creamy chicken potpie, spiced Moroccan lamb shank, coq au vin, Thai curried fish cakes, tannia fritters, crab quesadillas. By night, they screen vintage Hollywood, Bollywood, and foreign flicks.

7 Eden Brown Estate. This government-owned mansion, built around 1740, is known as Nevis's haunted house, or haunted ruins. In 1822 a Miss Julia Huggins was to marry a fellow named Maynard. However, on the day of the wedding, the groom and his best man had a duel and killed each other. The bride-to-be became a recluse, and the mansion was closed down. Local residents claim they can feel the presence of "someone" whenever they go near the eerie old house with its shroud of weeds and wildflowers. You're welcome to drop by; it's always open, and it's free. ⌧ *East Coast Rd., between Lime Kiln and Mannings, Eden Brown Bay* ☏ *No phone.*

6 Fothergill's Nevisian Heritage Village. On the grounds of a former sugar plantation–cotton ginnery, this ambitious, ever-expanding project traces the evolution of Nevisian social history, from the Caribs to the present, through vernacular dwellings. Several huts re-create living conditions over the centuries. The Carib chief's thatched hut includes actual relics such as weapons, calabash bowls, clay pots, and cassava squeezers. Wattle-and-daub structures reproduce slave quarters; implements on display include coal pots and sea fans (used as sieves). A post-emancipation chattel house holds patchwork quilts. There's a typical sharecropper's garden, a blacksmithy, and a traditional rum shop (replete with domino players). Management hopes to establish a working still and a small restaurant dispensing authentic Nevisian fare. ⌧ *Gingerland, St. Georges* ☏ *869/469–5521 or 869/469–7037* ⌧ *EC$8* ☉ *Mon.–Sat. 9–4.*

3 Nelson Museum. This collection merits a visit for its memorabilia of Lord Horatio Nelson, including letters, documents, paintings, and even furniture from his flagship. Historical archives of the Nevis Historical and Conservation Society are housed here and are available for public viewing. Nelson was based in Antigua but on military patrol came to Nevis, where he met and eventually married Frances Nisbet, who lived on a 64-acre plantation here. Half the space is devoted to often provocative displays on island life, from leading families to vernacular architecture to the adaptation of traditional African customs, from cuisine to Carnival. ⌧ *Bath Rd., outside Charlestown* ☏ *869/469–0408* ⊕ *www.nevis-nhcs.org* ⌧ *$5 ($7 includes admission to Museum of Nevis History)* ☉ *Weekdays 9–4, Sat. 9–noon.*

4 St. John's Figtree Church. Among the records of this church built in 1680 is a tattered, prominently displayed marriage certificate that reads: HORATIO NELSON, ESQUIRE, TO FRANCES NISBET, WIDOW, ON MARCH 11, 1787. ⌧ *Church Ground* ☏ *No phone.*

8 St. Thomas Anglican Church. The island's oldest church was built in 1643 and has been altered many times over the years. The gravestones in the old churchyard have stories to tell, and the church itself contains memorials to Nevis's early settlers. ⌧ *Main Rd., Jessups, Just south of Cotton Ground* ☏ *No phone.*

ST. KITTS & NEVIS ESSENTIALS

To research prices, get advice from other travelers, and book travel arrangements, visit www.fodors.com.

Transportation

BY AIR

There are nonstop flights to St. Kitts from the United States but none to Nevis. American offers five weekly flights to St. Kitts from Miami most of the year. American Eagle has several daily flights into St. Kitts and two daily flights to Nevis from San Juan. US Airways flies nonstop on Saturday from both Philadelphia and Charlotte to St. Kitts. Other major domestic airlines fly from their eastern hubs either into Antigua, St. Maarten, San Juan, or St. Thomas, where connections to St. Kitts (and, less frequently, to Nevis) can be made on LIAT, Caribbean Star, Caribbean Sun, BWIA, Carib Aviation, and Winair. If you are traveling from the United Kingdom or Canada, you will probably fly into Antigua before connecting on a smaller aircraft to St. Kitts or Nevis.

🔏 Airline Information **American/American Eagle** ☎ 869/465-2273 or 869/469-8995. **BWIA** ☎ 869/465-2286 or 800/538-2942. **Carib Aviation** ☎ 869/469-9185 in Nevis. **Caribbean Star** ☎ 869/466-2562 or 866/864-6272. **Caribbean Sun** ☎ 869/465-2690 or 866/864-6272. **LIAT** ☎ 869/465-1330. **US Airways** ☎ 800/428-4322. **Winair** ☎ 869/465-8010, 869/469-9583 on Nevis.

🔏 Airport Information **Robert L. Bradshaw Golden Rock Airport** ✉ Golden Rock, St. Kitts ☎ 465-8013. **Vance W. Amory International Airport** ✉ Newcastle, Nevis ☎ 869/469-9343.

BY BOAT & FERRY

There are several ferry services between St. Kitts and Nevis, all with byzantine schedules that are subject to abrupt change. Most companies make two or three daily trips. All the ferries take about 30 to 45 minutes and cost $4 to $9. You can get up-to-date information about all

the options from a central number or a Web site (click on FERRY SCHEDULE).

Sea-taxi service between the two islands is operated by Kenneth Samuel, Nevis Water Sports, Leeward Island Charters, and Austin Macleod of Pro-Divers for $20 one-way in summer, $25 in winter; discounts can be negotiated for small groups. There's an additional EC$1 tax for port security, paid separately upon departure.

FARES & SCHEDULES: 🔏 **Ferry information** ☎ 869/466-4636 or 869/469-9373 ⊕ www.leytonms.com. **Kenneth's Dive Centre** ☎ 869/465-2670. **Leeward Island Charters** ☎ 869/465-7474. **Nevis Water Sports** ☎ 869/469-9060. **Pro-Divers** ☎ 869/465-3223.

BY CAR

You can get by without a car if you are staying in the Frigate Bay–Basseterre area, but if you are staying elsewhere on the island (and if you wish to get out and dine around), you'll need to rent a car. On Nevis, you may wish to rent a car for a day or two of exploring, but roads are so poorly marked that it's often easier to just take taxis and guided tours.

On St. Kitts, present yourself, your valid driver's license, and EC$50 at the police station on Cayon Street in Basseterre to get a temporary driving permit (on Nevis the car-rental agency will help you obtain a local license for $24 at the police station). The license is valid for three months on both islands. On either island, car rentals start at about $40 per day for a compact; expect to pay a few extra bucks for air-conditioning. Most agencies offer substantial discounts when you rent by the week.

Agencies include Avis, which has the best selection of Suzuki and Daihatsu four-wheel-drive vehicles on St. Kitts. Delisle Walwyn also provides an excellent selection and the option of a replacement car for one day on Nevis if you rent for three

20

days or more on St. Kitts. Agencies such as Noel's Courtesy Garage and Striker's Car Rentals offer a wide variety of cars and jeeps for exploring Nevis. TDC/Thrifty Rentals has a wide selection of vehicles and outstanding service; it offers a three-day rental that includes a car on both islands.

One well-kept main road circumnavigates St. Kitts and is usually clearly marked, making it difficult to get lost, though the northeast can get a bit bumpy, and the access roads to the plantation inns are notoriously rough. The roads on Nevis are new and beautifully smooth, at least on the most-traveled north, west, and south sides of the island. The east coast has some potholes, and pigs, goats, and sheep still insist on the right-of-way all around the island. Drivers on both islands tend to travel at a fast clip and pass on curves, so drive defensively. Driving is on the left, British-style, though you will probably be given an American-style car.

🚗 **Avis** ⊠ S. Independence Sq., Basseterre, St. Kitts ☎ 869/465-6507. **Delisle Walwyn** ⊠ Liverpool Row, Basseterre, St. Kitts ☎ 869/465-8449. **Nevis Car Rentals** ⊠ Newcastle, Nevis ☎ 869/469-9837. **Noel's Courtesy Garage** ⊠ Farms Estate, Nevis ☎ 869/469-5199 ⊕ www.noelcarrental.com. **Striker's Car Rental** ⊠ Hermitage Rd., Gingerland, Nevis ☎ 869/469-2634. **TDC/Thrifty Rentals** ⊠ Central St., Basseterre, St. Kitts ☎ 869/465-2991 🚗 Bay Rd., Charlestown, Nevis ☎ 869/469-5690 or 869/469-1005 ⊕ www.tdcltd.com.

BY TAXI

Taxi rates are government-regulated and are posted at the airport, the dock, and in the free tourist guide. There are fixed rates to and from all the hotels and to and from major points of interest. In St. Kitts you can call the St. Kitts Taxi Association. In Nevis, taxi service is available at the airport, by the dock in Charlestown, and through arrangements made at your hotel. Sample fares from the dock: EC$43 to Nisbet Plantation, EC$21 to the Four Seasons, and EC$29 to Hermitage.

🚕 **St. Kitts Taxi Association** ☎ 869/465-8487, 869/465-4253, 869/465-7818 after hrs. **Nevis taxi**

service ☎ 869/469-5631, 869/469-1483, 869/469-9790 for the airport, 869/469-5515 after dark.

Contacts & Resources

BANKS & EXCHANGE SERVICES

Legal tender is the Eastern Caribbean (EC) dollar. The rate of exchange at this writing was EC$2.68 to US$1. U.S. dollars are accepted practically everywhere, but you'll usually get change in EC currency. Americans will not usually need to exchange money in St. Kitts and Nevis, though you may get EC curency as change if you pay for something in U.S. dollars. Most large hotels, restaurants, and shops accept major credit cards, but small inns and shops often do not. MasterCard and Visa are the most frequently accepted credit cards. The Royal Bank of St. Kitts has an ATM. There are ATMs on Nevis at the airport, at the Bank of Nova Scotia, at FirstCaribbean International Bank, and at the St. Kitts-Nevis National Bank. They all accept CIRRUS and PLUS cards but dispense only EC dollars.

Prices quoted throughout this chapter are in U.S. dollars unless otherwise noted.

BUSINESS HOURS

Hours vary somewhat for banks but are typically Monday through Thursday from 8 to 2 and Friday from 8 to 4. The Bank of Nevis is also open Saturday from 8:30 to 11 AM. There are now numerous ATM machines located around both islands. Post offices on St. Kitts are open Monday and Tuesday from 8 to 4, Wednesday through Friday from 8 to 3:30, and occasionally Saturday from 8 to noon. The Nevis post office opens Monday through Friday from 8 to 3:30. Although shops used to close for lunch from noon to 1, more and more establishments are remaining open Monday through Saturday from 8 to 4.

ELECTRICITY

St. Kitts and Nevis hotels function on 110 volts, 60 cycles, making all North American appliances safe to use.

EMERGENCIES

There are no 24-hour pharmacies on St. Kitts or Nevis, but several pharmacies are open seven days a week, usually until at least 5 PM. Call ahead if it's late in the afternoon.

Ambulance & Fire Ambulance ☎ 911. **Fire emergencies on St. Kitts** ☎ 869/465–2515. **Fire emergencies on Nevis** ☎ 869/469–3444.

Hospitals Joseph N. France General Hospital ✉ Cayon St., Basseterre, St. Kitts ☎ 869/465–2551. **Alexandra Hospital** ✉ Government Rd., Charlestown, Nevis ☎ 869/469–5473.

Pharmacies City Drug ✉ Fort St., Basseterre, St. Kitts ☎ 869/465–2156 ✉ Rex Papillon, Frigate Bay, St. Kitts ☎ 869/465–1803. **Claxton Medical Centre Pharmacy** ✉ Main St., Charlestown, Nevis ☎ 869/469–5357. **Evelyn's Drugstore** ✉ Main St., Charlestown, Nevis ☎ 869/469–5278. **Parris Super Drugs** ✉ Central St., Basseterre, St. Kitts ☎ 869/465-8569.

Police Police emergencies ☎ 911, 869/465–2241 on St. Kitts, 869/469–5391 on Nevis.

HOLIDAYS

Public holidays are New Year's Day, Ash Wednesday (usually Feb.), Easter Monday (usually Mar. or Apr.), Labour Day (1st Mon. in May), Whitmonday (usually mid-May to late June), Emancipation Day (1st Mon. in Aug.), Independence Day (Sept. 19), Christmas Day, and Boxing Day (Dec. 26).

INTERNET, MAIL & SHIPPING

Some hotels provide Internet service to their guests (sometimes for a fee, sometimes not), but you'll find Internet cafés in Basseterre, St. Kitts, and Charlestown, Nevis.

Airmail letters to the United States and Canada cost EC$.90 per half ounce; postcards require EC$.80; to the United Kingdom letters cost EC$1.20, postcards EC$1; to Australia and New Zealand, letters cost EC$1.60, postcards EC$1.20. Mail takes at least 7 to 10 days to reach the United States. St. Kitts and Nevis issue separate stamps, but each honors the other's.

Leyton's Sun Surf Internet Cafe ✉ TDC Mall, Fort St., Basseterre, St. Kitts ☎ 869/465–5925.

Downtown Cybercafe ✉ Main St., Charlestown, Nevis ☎ 869/469-1999.

PASSPORT REQUIREMENTS

U.S. citizens must have a valid passport starting January 1, 2007. Canadian citizens need a valid passport or must prove citizenship with a birth certificate (with a raised seal) accompanied by a government-issue photo ID. Everyone else must have a passport. A return or ongoing ticket is mandatory. We strongly urge all Caribbean travelers to carry a valid passport, whether or not it's an absolute requirement.

SAFETY

On these islands, safety is not a major concern, but take the usual precautions you would at any unfamiliar destination.

TAXES

The departure tax is US$22, payable in cash only. There's no sales tax on either St. Kitts or Nevis. Hotels collect a 9% government tax (8% on Nevis).

TELEPHONES

Phone cards, which you can buy in denominations of $5, $10, and $20, are handy for making local phone calls, calling other islands, and accessing U.S. direct lines. Many private lines and hotels charge access rates if you use your AT&T, Sprint, or MCI calling card; there's no regularity, so phoning can be frustrating. Pay phones, usually found in major town squares, take EC coins or phone cards. Port Zante has banks of "international" phones that accept credit and, erratically, calling cards. Tri-band GSM phones rentals are available via Cable & Wireless in both St. Kitts and Nevis. Check with the respective tourism offices for alternative providers. Costs are high but not prohibitive, especially if you are going to be on the islands for a week or more.

To make a local call, dial the seven-digit number. To call St. Kitts and Nevis from the United States, dial the area code 869, then access code 465, 466, 468, or 469 and the local four-digit number.

20

Cable & Wireless ⊠ Fort St., Basseterre, St. Kitts ☎ 869/465-1000 ⊕ www.candw.kn ⊠ Hunkins Plaza, Main St., Charlestown, Nevis ☎ 869/469-5000.

TIPPING

Hotels add up to a 12% service charge to your bill. Restaurants occasionally do the same; ask just in case if it isn't printed on the menu; a 15% tip is appropriate when it isn't included. Taxi drivers typically receive a 10% tip, porters and bellhops $1 per bag; if you feel the service was exemplary, leave $3 to $4 per night for the housekeeping staff.

TOUR OPTIONS

The taxi driver who picks you up will probably offer to act as your guide to the island. Each driver is knowledgeable and does a three-hour tour of Nevis for $50 or a four-hour tour of St. Kitts for $60. He can also make a lunch reservation at one of the plantation restaurants, and you can incorporate this into your tour.

On St. Kitts, Kantours offers comprehensive general island tours, as well as a variety of specialty excursions. The friendly guides at Tropical Tours can run you around St. Kitts ($20 per person), arrange kayaking and snorkeling, and take you to the volcano or rain forest for $52 per person and up.

On Nevis, Fitzroy "Teach" Williams is recommended: he's the former president of the taxi association—even older cabbies call him "the Dean." Kantours arranges half- and full-day tours of the island. TC, a Yorkshire lass who used to drive a double-decker bus in England and has been married to a Nevisian for over a decade, offers entertaining explorations via TC's Island Tours.

Fitzroy "Teach" Williams ☎ 869/469-1140 **Kantours** ☎ 869/465-2098 in St. Kitts, 869/469-0136 in Nevis ⊕ www.kantours.com **TC's Island Tours** ☎ 869/469-2911 **Tropical Tours** ☎ 869/465-4167 ⊕ www.tropicalstkitts-nevis.com.

VISITOR INFORMATION

Before You Leave **Nevis Tourism Authority** ⊠ Elm House, Park La., Lower, Froyle, Alton, Hampshire GU34 4LT, U.K. ☎ 01420/520810 ⊕ www.nevisisland.com. **St. Kitts Tourism Authority** ⊠ 414 E. 75th St., New York, NY 10021 ☎ 212/535-1234, 800/582-6208, 866/556-3847 for Nevis alone ⊕ www.stkittstourism.kn ⊠ 133 Richmond St., Suite 311, Toronto, Ontario M5H 2L3, Canada ☎ 416/368-6707 or 888/395-4887 ⊠ 10 Kensington Ct., London W8 5DL, U.K. ☎ 0171/376-0881.

In St. Kitts & Nevis **Nevis Tourism Authority** ⊠ Main St., Charlestown, Nevis ☎ 869/469-7550 or 869/469-1042 ⊕ www.nevisland.com. **St. Kitts Tourism Authority** ⊠ Pelican Mall, Bay Rd., Box 132, Basseterre, St. Kitts ☎ 869/465-2620 or 869/465-4040 ⊕ www.stkittstourism.kn. **St. Kitts-Nevis Hotel Association** ⊠ Liverpool Row, Box 438, Basseterre, St. Kitts ☎ 869/465-5304.

WEDDINGS

St. Kitts and Nevis are both popular wedding locales, and it's relatively easy and fast to obtain a license. Both bride and groom must be in the country for at least two full working days (weekdays) before the ceremony, and the cost of a license is $80 (the license fee is reduced to $20 if the parties have been on the island for at least 15 days). You must present a valid passport or birth certificate; if divorced, you must have a decree absolute plus a notarized translation if the document is not in English; if you're widowed, you must have a copy of the death certificate of the deceased spouse. There will be a charge for a civil service from the notary public and the marriage officer, who is the local magistrate. Your hotel will help you make the arrangements; most have wedding coordinators. Couples have often tied the knot on the picturesque 18th-hole lawn overlooking the sea on the Four Seasons golf course, at the various plantation inns, and on the beaches throughout the islands.

St. Lucia

The Pitons, viewed from Soufrière

WORD OF MOUTH

"We really enjoyed the Jump Up, the local Friday night party. Fun, a lot of street vendors with good local food. . . . Dress casually, as the locals do."

—Kate

"Take a day to go up to Pigeon Point. This area offers some great hiking and some historical sites as well as a nice beach that you can swim and snorkel at."

—Schultz

www.fodors.com/forums

WELCOME TO ST. LUCIA

THE CARIBBEAN'S TWIN PEAKS

St. Lucia, 27 mi (43.5 km) by 14 mi (22.5 km) is a volcanic island covered to a large extent by a lush rain forest, which is protected as a national park. The small island has produced two Nobel Prize-winners, economist Sir Arthur Lewis and poet Sir Derek Walcott. The most notable geological features are the twin Pitons, some 2,600 feet high.

Soufrière, founded as a French settlement in 1746, was the first colonial capital of St. Lucia. It remains an important agricultural center of the island.

At 2,619 feet, Petit Piton is actually taller than Gros Piton, which is 2,461 feet. However "Gros" is broader at its base; hence, the name.

KEY

⌐	Beaches
⚓	Cruise Ship Terminal
◩	Dive Sites
1	Exploring Sights
⛴	Ferry
1️⃣	Hotels & Restaurants
🌴	Rain Forest

Explorers, pirates, soldiers, sugar planters, and coal miners have made their mark on this lovely landfall, and the lush tropical peaks known as the Pitons (Gros and Petit) have witnessed them all. Today's visitors come to snorkel and scuba dive in the calm cobalt-blue waters, to sun themselves on the scores of multihued beaches, or to go for a sail off tiny Pigeon Island, which juts off St. Lucia's northwest coast.

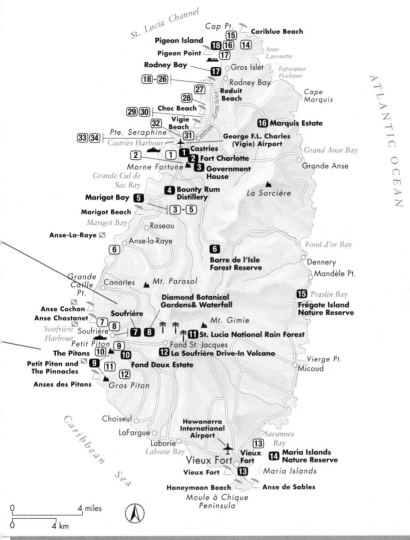

TOP 4 REASONS TO VISIT ST. LUCIA

1 Magnificent, lush scenery, particularly in the south and around Soufrière, makes St. Lucia one of the most beautiful Caribbean islands.

2 A popular honeymoon spot, St. Lucia is filled with romantic retreats.

3 Luxurious options include a pampering all-inclusive spa resort, a luxury dive resort, and a picturesque resort between the Pitons.

4 The St. Lucia Jazz Festival draws performers—and listeners—from all over the world.

ST. LUCIA PLANNER

Getting to St. Lucia

Getting to St. Lucia is the easy part. A fair number of regularly scheduled flights arrive daily from the U.S., Canada, and the U.K. at Hewanorra Airport (UVF), on the island's southern tip; however, you might have to change planes in San Juan, Barbados, or Montego Bay. Air Jamaica reinstated its nonstop flight from New York–JFK in 2006. A few regional Caribbean airlines—as well as American Eagle—fly island-hoppers into the George F.L. Charles Airport (SLU) in Castries, which is much closer to the island's largest concentration of hotels and resorts. Those flying into Hewanorra must make the long—up to 90-minute—trip to the north; happily, the trip to Soufrièr now takes only 30 minutes.

Hassle Factor: Medium to Medium-High, because of the long drive from the airport.

Activities

The island's **beaches** are decent, but you won't find any long stretches of fine white sand; Reduit Beach, in the north, is considered the island's best. St. Lucia has excellent **diving** along its southwest coast. **Deep-sea fishing** is also good. A **day sail** is one of the best ways to see a good bit of the island and a good way to travel from Castries to Soufrière, or vice versa. However, St. Lucia's crown jewel is its well-preserved rain forest, which can best be explored on a guided **hike**. **Climbing** one of the Pitons is a rewarding—if exhausting—experience.

On the Ground

If you land at George F.L. Charles Airport (also referred to as Vigie Airport), in Castries, it's a short drive to resorts in the north, about 30 minutes to Marigot, but more than an hour to Soufrière. Everyone landing at Hewanorra, faces a long—though scenic—drive north. Some resorts include airport transfers in their rates. Taxis are always available at the airports. If you take one, be sure to agree on the fare (and in which currency it's being quoted) before you get in; it's never a cheap trip. Between Hewanorra and Soufrière expect to pay $55 to $60 each way per taxi (not per person); between Hewanorra and the resorts near Castries, $70 to $75; between George F.L. Charles (Vigie) Airport and nearby resorts, $15 to $20; between Vigie and Soufrière, $70 to $75. A helicopter transfer from Hewanorra is an attractive option, but at $100+ per person, not one many people can afford.

Renting a Car

Driving yourself is a fine idea if you want to do some exploring and try lots of restaurants during your stay; a car is more of a necessity if you are staying at a small inn or hotel away from the beach. If you're staying at an all-inclusive beach resort and plan limited excursions off the property, taxis would be a better bet. The drive from Castries to Soufrière is magnificent, but the winding roads can be exhausting for the uninitiated; local drivers are accustomed to the trek.

Where to Stay

St. Lucia's lodgings are nearly all concentrated in three locations along the calm Caribbean coast. They're in the greater Castries area between Marigot Bay, a few miles south of the city, and Choc Bay in the north; in and around Rodney Bay and north to Cap Estate; and around Soufrière on the southwest coast near the Pitons. There's only one resort in Vieux Fort, near Hewanorra. Resorts and small inns are tucked into lush surroundings on secluded coves, unspoiled beaches, or forested hillsides. The advantage of being in the north is easier access to a wider range of restaurants; in the south you are limited to your resort's offerings and a few others, mostly in Soufrière.

TYPES OF LODGING

Beach Resorts: Most people choose to stay in one of St. Lucia's many beach resorts, the majority of which are upscale and fairly pricey. Several are all-inclusive, including three Sandals resorts.

Small Inns: If you are looking for something more intimate and often less expensive, a locally owned small inn or hotel is a good option if you don't mind not being directly on the beach.

Villas: Private apartments and luxury villas are a good choice for families. Virtually all these are in the north, concentrated in and around Castries, near Cap Estate, and in Marigot Bay.

Hotel & Restaurant Costs

Assume that hotels operate on the European Plan (**EP**—with no meals) unless we specify that they use either the Continental Plan (**CP**—with a Continental breakfast), Breakfast Plan (**BP**—with full breakfast), or the Modified American Plan (**MAP**—with breakfast and dinner). Other hotels may offer the Full American Plan (**FAP**—including all meals but no drinks) or may be All-Inclusive (**AI**—with all meals, drinks, and most activities).

WHAT IT COSTS in Dollars					
	$$$$	**$$$**	**$$**	**$**	**¢**
Restaurants	over $30	$20–$30	$12–$20	$8–$12	under $8
Hotels*	over $350	$250–$350	$150–$250	$80–$150	under $80
Hotels**	over $450	$350–$450	$250–$350	$125–$250	under $125

*EP, BP, CP   **AI, FAP, MAP
Restaurant prices are for a main course at dinner and do not include 8% tax or customary 10% service charge. Hotel prices are per night for a double room in high season, excluding 8% tax and meal plans (except at all-inclusives).

When to Go 21

The high season runs from mid-December through mid-April; outside of this period, hotel rates can be significantly cheaper.

The **St. Lucia Jazz Festival** in early May is the year's big event, and during that week, you may have trouble finding a hotel room at any price.

In March, the **St. Lucia Golf Open** is an amateur tournament at the St. Lucia Golf & Country Club in Cap Estate.

St. Lucia's summer **Carnival** is held in Castries each July.

The **St. Lucia Billfishing Tournament** is in late September or early October, attracting anglers from far and wide.

October is **Creole Heritage Month**, which culminates in Jounen Kweyol Etenasyonnal (International Creole Day) on the last Sunday of the month.

In late November or early December, the finish of the **Atlantic Rally for Cruisers,** the world's largest ocean-crossing race, is marked by a week of festivities in Rodney Bay.

By Jane E.
Zarem

ALL EYES FOCUS ON ST. LUCIA FOR 10 DAYS EACH MAY, when the St. Lucia Jazz Festival welcomes renowned international musicians who perform for enthusiastic fans at Pigeon Island National Park and other island venues. St. Lucians themselves love jazz—and, of course, the beat of Caribbean music resonates through their very souls. The irony is that if you randomly ask 10 St. Lucians to name their favorite kind of music, most would say "country." One possible explanation is that many young St. Lucian men take short-term jobs overseas, cutting sugarcane in Florida and working on farms elsewhere in the South, where they inevitably hear country music. And while the work experience isn't something most remember fondly, the music apparently is.

The pirate François Le Clerc, nicknamed Jambe de Bois (Wooden Leg) for obvious reasons, was the first European "settler" in St. Lucia (pronounced *loo*-sha). In the late 16th century, Le Clerc holed up on Pigeon Island, just off the island's northernmost point, and used it as a staging ground for attacking passing ships. Now Pigeon Island is a national park, a playground for locals and visitors alike, and the most popular performance venue for the annual St. Lucia Jazz Festival. Several years ago, Pigeon Island was attached to the mainland by a man-made causeway, and sprawled along that causeway now is one of the largest resorts in St. Lucia—with plans on the drawing board for another one.

St. Lucia has evolved over the years into one of the most popular destinations in the Caribbean—particularly for honeymooners and other romantics, who are enticed by the island's natural beauty, its many splendid resorts and friendly inns, and its welcoming atmosphere. And the evolution continues. Renewed emphasis from both the public and private sectors is being placed on enhancing the island's tourism product and supporting new and renewed lodgings, activities, and attractions. That's great news for vacationers, who already appear delighted with St. Lucia.

Located between Martinique and St. Vincent, and 100 mi (160 km) due west of Barbados, the 27-mi by 14-mi (43½-km by 22½-km) island of St. Lucia occupies a prime position in the Caribbean. Its striking natural beauty easily earns it the moniker "Helen of the West Indies." The capital city of Castries and nearby villages in the northwest are home to 40% of the population and, along with Rodney Bay farther north and Marigot Bay just south of the capital, are the general destination of many vacationers. The south, on the other hand, is dominated by dense rain forest, jungle-covered mountains, and vast banana plantations. A torturously winding road follows most of the coastline, bisecting small villages, cutting through mountains and thick forests, and passing by fertile valleys. On the southwest coast, Petit Piton and Gros Piton, the island's unusual twin peaks, which are familiar navigational landmarks for sailors and aviators alike, rise out of the sea to more than 2,600 feet. Divers are attracted to the reefs found just north of Soufrière, the picturesque capital city during French colonial times. Most of the natural tourist attractions are, in fact, in this area. "If you haven't been to Soufrière," St. Lucians will tell you, "you haven't been to St. Lucia."

Embracing Kwéyòl

ENGLISH IS ST. LUCIA'S OFFICIAL language, but most St. Lucians can speak and often use Kwéyòl—a French-based Creole language—for informal conversations between and among themselves. Primarily a spoken language, Kwéyòl in its written version doesn't look at all like French; pronounce the words phonetically, though—*entenasyonnal* (international), for example, or the word *Kwéyòl* (Creole) itself—and you indeed sound as if you're speaking French.

Pretty much the same version of the creole language, or patois, is spoken in the nearby island of Dominica. Otherwise, the St. Lucian Kwéyòl is quite different from that spoken in other Caribbean islands with a French and African heritage, such as Haiti, Guadeloupe, and Martinique—or elsewhere, such as Louisiana, Mauritius, and Madagascar.

Interestingly, the Kwéyòl spoken in St. Lucia and Dominica is mostly unintelligible to people from those other locations—and vice versa.

St. Lucia embraces its creole heritage by devoting the month of October each year to celebrations that preserve and promote creole culture, language, and traditions. In selected communities throughout the island, events and performances highlight creole music, food, dance, theater, native costumes, church services, traditional games, folklore, native medicine—a little bit of everything, or "tout bagay" as you say in Kwéyòl!

Creole Heritage Month culminates at the end of October with all-day events and activities on Jounen Kwéyòl Entenasyonnal, or International Creole Day, which is recognized by all countries that speak a version of the creole language.

Like most of its neighbors, St. Lucia was first inhabited by the Arawaks and then the Carib Indians. British settlers attempted to colonize the island twice in the early 1600s, but it wasn't until 1651, after the French West India Company secured the island from the Caribs, that Europeans gained a foothold. For 150 years, battles for possession of the island were frequent between the French and the British, with a dizzying 14 changes in power before the British finally took possession in 1814. The Europeans established sugar plantations, using slaves from West Africa to work the fields. By 1838, when the slaves were emancipated, more than 90% of the population was of African descent—also the approximate proportion of today's 170,000 St. Lucians. Indentured East Indian laborers were brought over in 1882 to help bail out the sugar industry, which collapsed when slavery was abolished and all but died in the 1960s, when bananas became the major crop.

On February 22, 1979, St. Lucia became an independent state within the British Commonwealth of Nations, with a resident governor-general appointed by the queen. Still, the island appears to have retained more relics of French influence—notably the island patois (spoken in addition to English), cuisine, village names, and surnames—than of the British. Most likely, that's because the British contribution primarily involved the English language, the educational and legal systems, and the political structure, while the French culture historically had more impact on the arts—music, dance, and all that jazz!

Where to Stay

Luxury villa communities are an important part of the accommodations mix on St. Lucia. Most villas are privately owned, but nonowners may rent a unit from the management company for a family vacation or short-term stay. There are also a couple of notable villa resorts under construction at this writing. For rentals of private, individually owned villas, contact **Tropical Villas** (🗇 Box 189, Castries ☎ 758/452–8240 🖶 758/450–8089 ⊕ www.tropicalvillas.net). **Plantation Beach Resort** (✉ Cas En Bas ☎ 758/450–8199 ⊕ www.plantationbeach.com), which was expected to open in spring 2006, has 74 luxurious, individually designed and decorated villas and town houses situated on 9 idyllic acres wedged between a quiet ocean beach and the St. Lucia Country Club. Guests also enjoy a community pool and may patronize the spa, restaurants, bars, and shops.

Discovery at Marigot Bay (✉ Marigot Bay ☎ 758/458–0790 ⊕ www.marigotbay.com), which will be managed by Sonesta, was expected to open in May 2006, including both a marina village and a luxury spa hotel, with 124 privately owned apartments that blend into the tropical hillside rising up from lovely Marigot Bay. Apartments can be divided into a range of spacious hotel rooms or full suites to accommodate nonowner guests. Moorings Yacht Charter Company operates from Discovery's marina.

A group of locally owned and operated small hotels, comfortable guest houses, and self-catering apartments market themselves through the St. Lucia Tourist Board as **INNtimate St. Lucia** (☎ 758/452–4094 ⊕ www.inntimatestlucia.org). Accommodations, ranging in size from 3 to 71 rooms, have attractively reasonable room rates and are a delightful alternative to the large resorts.

Greater Castries

$$$$ 🏨 **Rendezvous.** Romance is alive and well at this easygoing, friendly, all-inclusive resort (for male-female couples only), which stretches along the dreamy white sand of Malabar Beach opposite the George F. L. Charles Airport runway. The occasional distraction of prop aircraft taking off and landing is completely overshadowed by the beautiful gardens on what was once a coconut plantation and by the convenient access to town. Accommodations are in cheerful gingerbread cottages, elegant oceanfront rooms with sunset-facing terraces (some with hammocks), or cozy poolside suites. Lounge on the beach or participate in a host of activities and sports—your choice and all-included. Buffet-style meals are served at the beachfront terrace restaurant, with fine dining by reservation at the Trysting Place. ✉ *Malabar Beach, Vigie* 🗇 *Box 190, Castries* ☎*758/457–7900* 🖶*758/452–7419* ⊕*www.theromanticholiday. com* ⇨ *81 rooms, 11 suites, 8 cottages* ♿ *2 restaurants, fans, 2 tennis courts, 2 pools, health club, massage, beach, dive shop, boating, water-skiing, bicycles, archery, volleyball, 2 bars, piano bar, shops, complimen-*

tary weddings, concierge, Internet room, airport shuttle; no room TVs, no kids ⊟ *AE, D, MC, V* ⫯⊙⫯ *AI.*

� **$$$$** ▣ **Almond Morgan Bay Beach Resort.** New owner Almond Resorts completely refurbished this venerable property before reopening it in late 2005 as an all-inclusive resort geared to singles, couples, and families alike. Elegant yet informal, Almond Morgan Bay offers quiet seclusion on 22 acres surrounding a stretch of white-sand beach on a pretty cove or an action-packed vacation with more free sports and activities than you'll probably be able to fit into your holiday. Rooms, each with a private balcony or terrace, are in several buildings set among tropical gardens or facing the beachfront. Four restaurants, four swimming pools (two designated for adults only), and all manner of activities are available day and night—even simply relaxing under a palm tree with a frosty drink. A brand-new spa and fitness center is expected at this writing to open in 2007, along with 100 additional guest rooms. ⊠ *Choc Bay, Gros Islet* ⌂ *Box 2167, Castries* ☎ *758/450–2511* 🖷 *758/450–1050* ⊕ *www. almondresorts.com* ⇗ *250 rooms* �ⓓ *4 restaurants, fans, in-room safes, cable TV, golf privileges, 4 tennis courts, 4 pools, health club, spa, beach, snorkeling, windsurfing, boating, waterskiing, 4 bars, shops, babysitting, children's programs (ages newborn–16), dry cleaning, laundry service, concierge, Internet room, business services, meeting rooms* ⊟ *AE, D, MC, V* ⫯⊙⫯ *AI.*

★ **$$$$** ▣ **Sandals Regency St. Lucia Golf Resort & Spa.** One of three Sandals resorts on St. Lucia, this is the second-largest and distinguishes itself with its own 9-hole golf course. Like the others, it's for couples only and is all-inclusive. The resort covers 200 acres on a hillside overlooking the sea on the southern shore of Castries Bay. Guest rooms are lavishly decorated with rich mahogany furniture and king-size four-poster beds. Many rooms have private plunge pools. The main pool, with its waterfall and bridges, and a long crescent beach are focal points for socializing and enjoying water sports. Massages (single or duet), scrubs, and wraps are available at the full-service spa (for an additional charge). Six restaurants serve Asian, Continental, French, Mediterranean, Southwestern, or Caribbean cuisine. An hourly shuttle connects all three Sandals properties. ⊠ *La Toc Rd., Box 399, Castries* ☎ *758/452–3081* 🖷 *758/ 453–7089* ⊕ *www.sandals.com* ⇗ *212 rooms, 116 suites* ⓓ *6 restaurants, room service, in-room safes, cable TV, 9-hole golf course, 5 tennis courts, 3 pools, gym, hair salon, 2 hot tubs, sauna, spa, beach, dive shop, snorkeling, windsurfing, boating, waterskiing, basketball, billiards, boccie, croquet, horseshoes, Ping-Pong, shuffleboard, volleyball, 9 bars, nightclub, recreation room, shops, complimentary weddings, laundry service, concierge floor, Internet room, business services, meeting rooms, airport shuttle; no kids* ⊟ *AE, D, DC, MC, V* ⫯⊙⫯ *AI.*

$ ▣ **Auberge Seraphine.** This is a good choice for vacationers who don't require a beachfront location or the breadth of activities found at a resort. Accommodations are spacious, cheerful, and bright. All but six rooms have a water view, and Room 307 has an amazing view from its balcony: what look like huge snow-white flowers are really cattle egrets nesting in the almond tree right outside the window; beautiful flowers bloom twice monthly in the lily pond down below. A broad, tiled sun-

Fodor's Choice
★

deck, the center of activity, surrounds a small pool. Reserve ahead, as business travelers appreciate the Auberge's convenience to downtown Castries, the airport, and great restaurants—including the inn's own excellent restaurant, which has fine Caribbean, French, and Continental cuisine in addition to a well-stocked wine cellar. ⊠ *Vigie Cove, Box 390, Castries* ☎ *758/453–2073* 🖷 *758/451–7001* ⊕ *www.aubergeseraphine. com* ⤴ *28 rooms* ♻ *Restaurant, some fans, refrigerators, cable TV, in-room data ports, pool, bar, shop, Internet room, meeting room* ⊟ *AE, MC, V* ⦿ *EP.*

Rodney Bay & the North

$$$$
Fodor'sChoice
★
⊞ **The Body Holiday at LeSPORT.** LeSPORT is a unique resort for adults seeking to refresh body, mind, and spirit in luxurious surroundings. Even before your arrival, you can customize your own "body holiday" on-line—from robe size to tee time. Indulge in aromatherapy, a dozen different massages, wraps, yoga, personal trainer services, and more at the splendid Oasis spa; daily treatments are included in the all-inclusive rates. Otherwise, enjoy the beach, scuba diving, golf, and other sports—with free instruction, if needed. The concept is to combine an active beach vacation with revitalization for both body and mind. Rooms have marble floors and king-size four-poster or twin beds. The food is excellent at Cariblue (the main dining room), the casual buffet restaurant, the deli, or the top-of-the-line Tao. Special rates are offered for single guests. ⊠ *Cariblue Beach, Cap Estate* ⅅ *Box 437, Castries* ☎ *758/450–8551* 🖷 *758/450–0368* ⊕ *www.thebodyholiday.com* ⤴ *152 rooms, 2 suites* ♻ *3 restaurants, snack bar, refrigerators, golf privileges, putting green, 2 tennis courts, 3 pools, health club, hair salon, spa, beach, dive shop, snorkeling, windsurfing, boating, waterskiing, archery, croquet, hiking, Ping-Pong, volleyball, 2 bars, piano bar, shops, concierge, Internet room, airport shuttle; no room TVs, no kids under 16* ⊟ *AE, DC, MC, V* ⦿ *AI.*

$$$$
⊞ **Royal St. Lucian.** This truly classy, all-suite resort on Reduit Beach—St. Lucia's best beach—caters to your every whim. The stunning reception area has a vaulted atrium, marble walls, a fountain, and a sweeping grand staircase. The free-form pool has Japanese-style bridges, a waterfall, and a swim-up bar. Sumptuous guest suites all have sitting areas, luxurious bathrooms, large patios or balconies, and soothing color schemes. Eight beachfront suites are huge, with special amenities such as a widescreen TV, DVD, and stereo equipment. Massages, hydrotherapy, and other treatments can be arranged at the Royal Spa. Dine at the elegant Chic!, the sea-view L'Epicure, or two casual restaurants. Alternatively, you're within walking distance of a dozen or so Rodney Bay restaurants, nightclubs, and shopping areas. Tennis, water-sports facilities, and the children's club are shared with the adjacent Rex St. Lucian Hotel. ⊠ *Reduit Beach, Rodney Bay* ⅅ *Box 977, Castries* ☎ *758/452–9999* 🖷 *758/452–9639* ⊕ *www.rexcaribbean.com* ⤴ *96 suites* ♻ *3 restaurants, room service, in-room safes, minibars, cable TV, golf privileges, 2 tennis courts, pool, health club, spa, beach, dive shop, snorkeling, windsurfing, boating, waterskiing, fishing, 2 bars, shops, babysitting, children's programs (ages 4–12), laundry service, concierge, Internet room, business services, meeting rooms* ⊟*AE, DC, MC, V* ⦿*EP.*

$$$$ Sandals Grande St. Lucian Spa & Beach Resort. Grand, indeed! And busy,
Fodor'sChoice busy, busy. Couples love this place, the biggest and splashiest of the three
★ Sandals resorts on St. Lucia, particularly young honeymooners and
those getting married here. Several weddings take place each day, in fact.
Perched on the narrow Pigeon Island Causeway at St. Lucia's northern
tip, Sandals Grande offers panoramic views of Rodney Bay on one side
and the Atlantic on the other. Luxurious rooms, decorated with colorful fabrics and mahogany furniture, all have king-size beds; 24 lagoon-
side rooms have swim-up verandas. With a plethora of land and water
sports, a European-style full-service spa, five excellent restaurants,
nightly entertainment, and romance in the air, there's never a dull moment. A complimentary shuttle connects all three Sandals properties for
additional fun with full exchange privileges. ✉ *Pigeon Island Causeway, Box 2247, Gros Islet* ☎ *758/455–2000* 📠 *758/455–2001* ⊕ *www.
sandals.com* 🛏 *271 rooms, 11 suites* ⛄ *5 restaurants, room service, fans,
in-room safes, cable TV, in-room data ports, golf privileges, 2 tennis courts,
5 pools, health club, hair salon, spa, beach, dive shop, snorkeling, windsurfing, boating, basketball, billiards, croquet, horseshoes, Ping-Pong,
shuffleboard, volleyball, 4 bars, nightclub, recreation room, shops,
complimentary weddings, dry cleaning, laundry service, concierge floor,
Internet room, business services, meeting rooms, airport shuttle, car rental;
no kids* ⊟ *AE, D, DC, MC, V* ¶◎¶ *AI.*

✿ **$$$–$$$$** Windjammer Landing Villa Beach Resort. Windjammer's Mediterranean-
style villas, connected by brick paths, climb the sun-kissed hillside on
one of St. Lucia's prettiest bays. As perfect for families as for a roman-
tic getaway, the resort offers lots to do yet plenty of privacy. Windjam-
mer's stylishly decorated villas can easily be closed off or opened up to
become one-, two-, three-, or four-bedroom villa suites. Some have pri-
vate plunge pools. The resort's reception area opens onto shops, restau-
rants, and two pools. Eat excellently prepared cuisine in the restaurants,
make your own meals, or have dinner prepared and served in your villa.
Shuttles whoosh you between villa and activity areas—including two
hillside pools connected by a waterfall. ✉ *Labrelotte Bay* 🕭 *Box 1504,
Castries* ☎ *758/452–0913* 📠 *758/452–9454* ⊕ *www.windjammer-
landing.com* 🛏 *219 rooms* ⛄ *5 restaurants, grocery, room service,
fans, in-room safes, some kitchens, cable TV, 2 tennis courts, 4 pools,
gym, hair salon, spa, beach, dive shop, snorkeling, windsurfing, boat-
ing, waterskiing, 3 bars, shops, babysitting, children's programs (ages
4–12), laundry service, concierge, car rental* ⊟ *AE, MC, V* ¶◎¶ *EP.*

✿ **$$–$$$** Club St. Lucia by Splash. This sprawling family resort—especially
popular among British families with young children—has a village con-
cept. Rooms and suites are arranged in color-coordinated buildings on
the hillside, and each village has its own concierge, or "mayor." Chil-
dren's activities are grouped by age, starting at six months. The Jump
Club for teenagers has an inline skating track and an e-mail system for
keeping in touch with parents. Live entertainment is scheduled nightly.
In addition to on-site dining and all-day snacks at poolside food carts,
which are included in basic rates, resort guests receive a discount at the
Great House restaurant. You also may enjoy free use of the adjacent St.
Lucia Racquet Club and privileges at a nearby golf course. ✉ *Cap Es-
tate* 🕭 *Box 915, Gros Islet* ☎ *758/450–0551* 📠 *758/450–0281* ⊕ *www.*

splashresorts.com ☞ *297 rooms, 72 suites* ⚐ *5 restaurants, pizzeria, cable TV, golf privileges, 9 tennis courts, 5 pools, gym, health club, hair salon, hot tub, spa, beach, snorkeling, windsurfing, boating, waterskiing, 5 bars, dance club, nightclub, shops, babysitting, children's programs (ages 6 months–17 yrs), laundry service, concierge, airport shuttle, car rental, travel services* ▤ *AE, D, DC, MC, V* ❑ *AI.*

★ **$–$$** ▦ **Coco Palm.** St. Lucia native Allen Chastanet opened this stylish boutique hotel in Rodney Bay Village in 2005, adjacent to his Coco Kreole bed-and-breakfast inn. Guests check in and out in the comfort of their rooms, and personal hosts attend to any need or request. Guest rooms—including six swim-up rooms that are adjacent to the pool—and a dozen spacious suites are beautifully decorated in French Caribbean plantation style, with rich mahogany furniture and elegant upholstered pieces; yet every modern convenience is also at hand. Cordless phones, CD and DVD players, free Wi-Fi and Internet access, flat-screen TVs (in suites), and ultramodern baths with walk-in showers and claw-foot tubs (in suites) are amenities you'd expect at much pricier resorts. Coco Palm combines a high-end atmosphere and extremely affordable rates, making it one of St. Lucia's best deals. The excellent Ti Bananne restaurant and bar overlook the pool and bandstand, and all the action of Rodney Bay Village and beautiful Reduit Beach are within walking distance. ⊠ *Reduit Beach Ave., Rodney Bay* ☎ *758/456–2800* 🖷 *758/452–0774* ⊕ *www.coco-resorts.com* ☞ *60 rooms, 12 suites* ⚐ *Restaurant, fans, in-room safes, refrigerators, cable TV, in-room VCRs, Wi-Fi, pool, bar, Internet room* ▤ *AE, D, MC, V* ❑ *EP.*

$ ▦ **Bay Gardens Hotel.** Independent travelers and regional businesspeople swear by this cheerful, well-run boutique hotel at Rodney Bay Village. Modern, colorful, and surrounded by pretty flower gardens, the hotel is a short walk to beautiful Reduit Beach (shuttle transportation is also provided), several popular restaurants, and shops. Some rooms surround the serpentine pool and Jacuzzi and are close to the restaurant and lobby; more secluded rooms near the back of the property have easy access to a second pool that's smaller and quieter. Spices restaurant offers a fairly extensive menu, along with lobster and shrimp specials, a weekly barbecue, and a Caribbean buffet night. Next door is Bay Gardens Inn, an affiliated hotel. ⊠ *Rodney Bay* ✉ *Box 1892, Castries* ☎ *758/452–8060* 🖷 *758/452–8059* ⊕ *www.baygardenshotel.com* ☞ *59 rooms, 12 suites* ⚐ *Restaurant, room service, fans, in-room safes, some kitchenettes, minibars, refrigerators, cable TV, in-room data ports, 2 pools, wading pool, hot tub, Ping-Pong, bar, babysitting, laundry service, Internet room, business services, meeting rooms, car rental* ▤ *AE, D, MC, V* ❑ *BP.*

Soufrière & the Mid-Coast

$$$$ ▦ **Anse Chastanet Beach Hotel.** Anse Chastanet is magical, if you don't
Fodor'sChoice mind climbing the 100 steps between the beach and reception, followed
★ by another steep climb to most rooms. Spectacular rooms and suites, some with entire walls open to stunning vistas, peek through the thick rain forest that cascades down to the sea. Deluxe hillside rooms have a balcony, tile floors, madras fabrics, handmade wooden furniture, and impressive artwork. Octagonal gazebos and beachfront cottages have similar interiors but slightly less drama. The Jade Mountain Club's two

dozen techno-free Infinity Suites—with sweeping spaces, sophisticated styling, private plunge pools, and open fourth walls overlooking the sea—operate as a resort within a resort, with a separate reception area, concierge, and restaurant. Diving, jungle biking through the estate's 600 acres, and ocean kayaking are premier activities here when you're not luxuriating in your room with a view or rejuvenating at the Kai Belte Spa. ⊠ *Anse Chastanet* ☜ *Box 7000, Soufrière* ☎ *758/459–7000* ☏ *758/459–7700* ⊕ *www.ansechastanet.com* ➥ *49 rooms, 24 suites* ⬧ *2 restaurants, room service, fans, in-room safes, refrigerators, tennis court, fitness classes, spa, 2 beaches, dive shop, snorkeling, windsurfing, boating, bicycles, mountain bikes, hiking, 2 bars, library, shops, babysitting, laundry service, Internet room, meeting room, airport shuttle, car rental; no a/c, no room phones, no room TVs, no kids under 6* ▭ *AE, D, DC, MC, V* ⑩ *MAP.*

★ **$$$$** 🖼 **Jalousie Plantation & Spa.** In the most visually appealing location in St. Lucia, this resort flows down a steep hillside smack between the Pitons, on the remains of an 18th-century sugar plantation 2 mi (3 km) south of Soufrière. Sugar Mill rooms are large and close to the beach. Villas have elegant furnishings, huge bathrooms, and plunge pools; villa suites also have sitting rooms. Shuttles around the property save a climb up and down the hill. Meals range from fine dining to a beach buffet. The spa offers outdoor massage, aromatherapy, and beauty treatments; there are also fitness classes and weight-training sessions. The views here are the island's most dramatic. ⊠ *Anse des Pitons* ☜ *Box 251, Soufrière* ☎ *800/544–2883 or 758/459–7666* ☏ *758/459–7667* ⊕ *www. jalousieplantation.com* ➥ *12 rooms, 65 villas, 35 villa suites* ⬧ *4 restaurants, room service, fans, in-room safes, minibars, cable TV, in-room VCRs, in-room data ports, 3-hole golf course, putting green, 4 tennis courts, pool, health club, hair salon, spa, beach, dive shop, dock, snorkeling, windsurfing, boating, marina, waterskiing, fishing, basketball, billiards, hiking, racquetball, squash, 4 bars, nightclub, shops, babysitting, children's programs (ages 5–12), Internet room, business services, meeting rooms, airport shuttle, car rental, helipad, no-smoking rooms* ▭ *AE, D, DC, MC, V* ⑩ *EP.*

$$$$ 🖼 **Ladera.** One of the most sophisticated small inns in the Caribbean, **Fodor'sChoice** the elegantly rustic Ladera is perched 1,000 feet above the sea, high in ★ the rain forest between the Pitons. Each unique suite or villa is furnished with colonial antiques and local crafts and has an open wall with a dazzling view overlooking the private plunge pool—some with a waterfall. Cooling breezes really do preclude the need for air-conditioning. The Ti Kai Posé Spa (Creole for "Little House of Rest") offers relaxing and therapeutic treatments and beauty services. Dasheene, the open-air restaurant, has the most stunning view of the Pitons—fabulous by day and stupendous at sunset. The inn provides shuttle service to Soufrière and nearby beaches and will arrange diving and other activities. Although children are allowed, the resort is not suitable for very young children. ⊠ *2 mi (3 km) south of Soufrière* ☜ *Box 225, Soufrière* ☎ *758/459– 7323, 800/223–9868, or 800/738–4752* ☏ *758/459–5156* ⊕ *www. ladera-stlucia.com* ➥ *18 suites, 6 villas* ⬧ *Restaurant, refrigerators, pool, 2 bars, library, shops, airport shuttle; no a/c, no room TVs* ▭ *AE, D, MC, V* ⑩ *EP.*

★ **$$–$$$$** ⌑ **Ti Kaye Village.** Ti Kaye is about halfway between Castries and Soufrière and down a mile-long dirt road off the main highway. Once you're there, however, you recognize the specialness of this aerie overlooking Anse Cochon. Gingerbread-style cottages are surrounded by lush greenery and furnished with handcrafted furniture, including four-poster beds with gauzy canopies. Each room has a private garden shower, a large balcony with double hammock, and wooden louvers in doors and windows to catch every breeze; some have private plunge pools. Dine with a view at Kai Manje, socialize at the friendly bar, and cool off in the pool. Or you can maneuver the 166-step wooden stairway down the cliff to the beach—which is one of the best snorkeling sites in St. Lucia. ✉ *Anse Cochon, Box GM669, Castries* ☎ *758/456–8101* 🖷 *758/ 456–8105* ∰ *www.tikaye.com* ☞ *33 rooms* ⌕ *Restaurant, snack bar, fans, in-room safes, refrigerators, pool, gym, massage, beach, snorkeling, boating, 2 bars, shop, laundry service; no room TVs, no kids under 12* ⊟ *AE, D, DC, MC, V* ¶◯¶ *BP.*

$$–$$$ ⌑ **Stonefield Estate Villa Resort.** Guests are warmly welcomed by the Brown family at this former cocoa plantation at the base of Petit Piton. One 18th-century plantation house and several gingerbread-style cottage villas dot this property. All accommodations have oversized, handcrafted furniture (built by the senior Mr. Brown) and one or two bathrooms—some villas also have outdoor garden showers and plunge pools. Living-dining rooms open onto verandas with double hammocks and panoramic views, perfectly romantic at sunset. A nature trail leads to ancient petroglyphs and palm-lined Malgretoute Beach. A complimentary shuttle goes to Soufrière or to Jalousie Beach for snorkeling and scuba diving. ✉ *1 mi (2 km) south of Soufrière* ✇ *Box 228, Soufrière* ☎ *758/459–5648 or 758/459–7037* 🖷 *758/459–5550* ∰ *www. stonefieldvillas.com* ☞ *16 1- to 3-bedroom villas* ⌕ *Restaurant, fans, in-room safes, kitchens, refrigerators, some in-room VCRs, pool, massage, beach, snorkeling, hiking, bar, library, babysitting, laundry service, Internet room, car rental; no a/c, no phones in some rooms, no TV in some rooms* ⊟ *AE, D, MC, V* ¶◯¶ *EP.*

$–$$ ⌑ **Hummingbird Beach Resort.** Unpretentious and welcoming, rooms in this delightful little inn on Soufrière Harbour are in small seaside cabins—most of which have views of the Pitons. Rooms are simply furnished—a primitive motif emphasized by African wood sculptures. Four rooms have mahogany four-poster beds hung with sheer mosquito netting. Most rooms have modern baths; two rooms and a suite share a bath. The two-bedroom country cottage—with a sitting room, kitchenette, and spectacular Piton view—is suitable for a family or two couples vacationing together. The Hummingbird's Lifeline Restaurant is a favorite lunch stop for locals and visitors touring Soufrière. ✉ *Anse Chastanet Rd., Box 280, Soufrière* ☎ *758/459–7232 or 800/223–9815* 🖷 *758/459–7033* ∰ *www.nvo.com/pitonresort* ☞ *9 rooms (7 with bath), 1 suite, 1 cottage* ⌕ *Restaurant, pool, beach, bar, shops; no a/c in some rooms, no room TVs* ⊟ *D, MC, V* ¶◯¶ *EP.*

Vieux Fort

⟳ **$$$** ⌑ **Coconut Bay.** The only resort in Vieux Fort, Coconut Bay is a sprawling seaside retreat on 85 beachfront acres just minutes St. Lucia's

CLOSE UP

Small Inns in St. Lucia

21

CHOOSE ONE OF THESE seven smaller properties if you're looking for something more intimate than the typical beach resort.

GREATER CASTRIES

$$$$ Sandals Halcyon St. Lucia (✉ Choc Bay, Castries ☎ 758/453-0222 or 800/223-6510 ⊕ www.sandals.com). While 170 rooms is usually not considered "small," this is the smallest—and, therefore, the most intimate—of the three Sandals resorts on St. Lucia. Like the others, it's beachfront, all-inclusive, couples only and loaded with amenities and activities. Just 10 minutes north of downtown Castries, it's also convenient to public transportation.

$ Villa Beach Cottages (✉ Choc Bay, Castries ☎ 758/450-2884 ⊕ www.villabeachcottages.com). Tidy housekeeping cottages with gingerbread-laden facades line the beach at this family establishment—a favorite of Nobel Laureate Sir Derek Walcott. Units are cozy and fairly close together, but each has a balcony facing the water, guaranteeing glorious sunset viewing every evening.

MARIGOT BAY

$ Inn on the Bay (✉ Marigot Bay ☎ 758/451-4260 ⊕ www.saint-lucia.com). With just five rooms, this inn treats you as a personal guest (adults only) of owners Normand Viau and Louise Boucher, who prepare your breakfast. Cool sea breezes obviate the need for air-conditioning. The stunning views of Marigot Bay are absolutely enchanting from the balcony outside your room and from the pool deck—you won't miss the absence of televisions here.

RODNEY BAY VILLAGE

$ Caribbean Jewel Beach Resort (✉ Rodney Bay, Gros Islet ☎ 758/452-9199 ⊕ www.caribbeanjewelresort.com). Truly a bargain, the 30 rooms here are huge, modern, and comfortable and have full kitchens—and from every room, the view overlooking Rodney Bay is incredible. Hang around three pools, dine at the restaurant, or walk down the hillside to Reduit Beach and all the action at Rodney Bay.

$ Coco Kreole (✉ Rodney Bay ☎ 758/452-0712 ⊕ www.cocokreole.com). With an ambience more reminiscent of the home of a good friend than of a hotel, this 20-room treasure in the center of the action at Rodney Bay Village—and sister to Coco Palm Hotel, just behind—is stylish, inexpensive, full of amenities, and close to restaurants, nightspots, and beautiful Reduit Beach.

$ Ginger Lily (✉ Rodney Bay ☎ 758/458-0300 ⊕ www.thegingerlilyhotel.com). A small, modern enclave of 11 rooms, with its own restaurant and a swimming pool, the Ginger Lily is across the street from Reduit Beach and smack in the middle of Rodney Bay Village. It's so comfortable, so well located, and is such a good deal that wedding parties or family reunions sometimes book the entire hotel.

$ Harmony Suites (✉ Rodney Bay ☎ 758/452-8756 ⊕ www.harmonysuites.com). Harmony Suites guests (adults only) are scuba divers, boaters, or people who just like being close to Rodney Bay Marina. Of the 30 large suites cloistered around the swimming pool, the 8 waterfront suites, at a whopping 700 square feet each, are the largest. Reduit Beach is across the road.

Hewanorra International Airport. The ocean views are beautiful, and the beach has lovely white sand; but the resort faces the Atlantic Ocean, so swimming in the sea is not advised. Instead, you'll find three swimming pools and a water-park attraction, with a lazy river, waterslides, and a swim-up bar. The Fregate Island and Maria Islands are just offshore, and St. Lucia's Pitons and other natural attractions in Soufrière are just 30 minutes by car. Otherwise, you'll have to be content with the activities in and around the resort—three restaurants, a full-service spa, and plenty of space to relax and socialize. ⊠ *Box 246, Vieux Fort* ☎ *758/459–6000* 🖷 *758/456–9900* ⊕ *www.coconutbayresortandspa. com* ➫ *254 rooms* ⚄ *4 restaurants, fans, in-room safes, cable TV, 4 tennis courts, 3 pools, outdoor hot tub, health club, hair salon, spa, beach, basketball, volleyball, 4 bars, shops, baby-sitting, children's program (ages 3-12), playground* ▤ *AE, MC, V* ⑩ *AI.*

Where to Eat

Mangoes, plantains, breadfruit, avocados, limes, pumpkins, cucumbers, papaya, yams, christophenes (also called chayote), and coconuts are among the fresh local produce that graces St. Lucian menus. The French influence is strong, and most chefs cook with a creole flair. Resort buffets and restaurant fare run the gamut, from steaks and chops to pasta and pizza. Every menu lists fresh fish along with the ever-popular lobster. Caribbean standards include callaloo, stuffed crab back, pepper-pot stew, curried chicken or goat, and *lambi* (conch). The national dish of salt fish and green fig—a stew of dried, salted codfish and boiled green banana—is, let's say, an acquired taste. Soups and stews are traditionally prepared in a coal pot, a rustic clay casserole on a matching clay stand that holds the hot coals. Chicken and pork dishes and barbecues are also popular here. As they do throughout the Caribbean, local vendors who set up barbecues along the roadside, at street fairs, and at Friday-night "jump-ups" do a land-office business selling grilled fish or chicken legs, bakes (fried biscuits), and beer—you can get a full meal for about $5. Most other meats are imported—beef from Argentina and Iowa, lamb from New Zealand. Piton is the local brew, Bounty the local rum.

With so many popular all-inclusive resorts, guests take most meals at hotel restaurants—which are generally quite good and, in some cases, exceptional. It's fun when vacationing, however, to try some of the local restaurants, as well—for lunch when sightseeing or for a special night out.

What to Wear

Dress on St. Lucia is casual but conservative. Shorts are usually fine during the day, but bathing suits and immodest clothing are frowned upon anywhere but at the beach. In the evening the mood is casually elegant, but even the fanciest places generally expect only a collared shirt and long pants for men and a sundress or slacks for women.

Greater Castries

CARIBBEAN ✕ **J. J.'s Paradise.** The view overlooking pretty Marigot Bay is enchant-
$$–$$$ ing, and the local fare is among the best on the island. Superbly grilled fish with fresh vegetables gets top honors, but you might also enjoy shell-

fish (lobster, prawns, or lambi), grilled T-bone steak, chicken (roasted, grilled, curried, or creole), pork chops, a vegetarian platter, or something truly exotic such as curried octopus. The welcome is friendly; the atmosphere, casual. Wednesday is Creole Crab Night, when owner-chef Gerard (J. J.) Felix prepares an enormous selection of local seafood, and diners are serenaded by a local band. ⊠ *Marigot Bay Rd., Marigot* ☏ *758/451–4076* ▭ *D, MC, V.*

CONTEMPORARY
$$$–$$$$
Fodor'sChoice
★

✕ **Rainforest Hideaway.** British chef Jim Verity, whose parents are behind the new Discovery at Marigot Bay resort project, masters and beautifully presents fusion fare at this romantic fine-dining hideaway on the north shore of Marigot Bay. It's definitely worth the 20-minute-or-so drive from Castries. A little ferry whisks you to the alfresco restaurant, perched on a dock, where you're greeted with complimentary champagne. Choose fresh-caught fish, succulent steak or chops, or tenderly prepared shellfish for your dinner, and you'll be blown away by the rich sauces, exotic vegetables, and excellent wines—not to mention the blanket of stars in the sky overhead and the live jazz several times a week. Crisp salads, burgers, pasta dishes, and baguette sandwiches are treats at lunchtime in this picturesque setting. ⊠ *Marigot Bay* ☏ *758/286–0511* ⌲ *Reservations essential* ▭ *AE, D, MC, V* ☉ *Closed Tues.*

ECLECTIC
$$

✕ **Green Parrot.** The best reason to dine here, atop Morne Fortune, is the romantic view overlooking the twinkling lights of Castries Harbor. The food is good, too. Acclaimed chef Harry Edwards prepares a menu of West Indian, creole, and international dishes—and you can count on a good steak. There's also lively entertainment—a floor show with a belly dancer on Wednesday night and limbo dancing on Saturday. On Monday night, tradition stands that if a lady wears a flower in her hair and is accompanied by a "well-dressed" gentleman, she might receive a free dinner. ⊠ *Morne Fortune, Castries* ☏ *758/452–3399* ⌲ *Reservations essential* ⍟ *Jacket required* ▭ *AE, D, MC, V.*

FRENCH
★ $$

✕ **The Coal Pot.** Popular since the early 1960s, this tiny (only 10 tables) waterfront restaurant overlooking pretty Vigie Cove is managed by Michelle Elliott, noted artist and daughter of the original owner, and her French husband, chef Xavier. For a light lunch opt for Greek or shrimp salad, or broiled fresh fish with creole sauce. Dinner might start with divine lobster bisque, followed by fresh seafood accompanied by one (or more) of the chef's fabulous sauces—ginger, coconut-curry, lemon–garlic butter, or wild mushroom. Hearty eaters may prefer duck, lamb, beef, or chicken laced with peppercorns, red wine, and onion or Roquefort sauce. ⊠ *Vigie Marina, Castries* ☏ *758/452–5566* ⌲ *Reservations essential* ▭ *AE, D, MC, V* ☉ *Closed Sun. No lunch Sat.*

★ $$

✕ **Jacques Waterside Dining.** Chef-owner Jacky Rioux creates magical dishes in his open-air garden restaurant (known for years as Froggie Jack's) overlooking Vigie Cove. The cooking style is decidedly French, as is Rioux, but fresh produce and local spices create a fusion cuisine that's memorable at lunch or dinner. You might start with a bowl of creamy tomato-basil or pumpkin soup, a grilled portobello mushroom, or octopus and conch in curried coconut sauce. Main courses include fresh seafood, such as oven-baked kingfish with a white wine and sweet pepper sauce, or breast of chicken stuffed with smoked salmon in a citrus butter sauce. The wine list is also impressive. ⊠ *Vigie Marina, Castries* ☎ *758/458–1900* ⌕ *Reservations essential* ⊟ *AE, MC, V* ⊗ *Closed Sun.*

Rodney Bay & the North

ECLECTIC ✕ **The Lime.** A casual bistro with lime-green gingham curtains, straw hats
¢–$$ decorating the ceiling, and hanging plants, the Lime specializes in local dishes such as spicy jerk chicken or pork and breadfruit salad—as well as char-grilled steak and fresh-caught fish. The meals are well prepared, the portions are plentiful, and the prices are reasonable, which is perhaps why you often see St. Lucians and visitors alike "liming" (an island term that means something akin to hanging around and relaxing) all day and most of the night at this popular restaurant. The Late Lime, a club where the crowd gathers as night turns to morning, is next door. ⊠ *Rodney Bay* ☎ *758/452–0761* ⊟ *D, MC, V* ⊗ *Closed Tues.*

FRENCH ✕ **Great House.** Elegant, gracious, and romantic, the Great House was
★ $$$ reconstructed on the foundation of the original Cap Estate plantation house. The grandeur of those early days has been revived as well. The waitstaff wear traditional St. Lucian costumes. The chef adds a piquant creole touch to traditional French cuisine—with excellent results. The menu, which changes nightly, might include pumpkin-and-potato soup, local crab back with lime vinaigrette, sautéed Antillean shrimp in a creole sauce, and broiled sirloin with thyme butter and sweet-potato chips. Cocktails at the open-air bar are especially enjoyable at sunset. The Derek Walcott Theatre is next door. ⊠ *Cap Estate* ☎ *758/450–0450 or 758/450–0211* ⌕ *Reservations essential* ⊟ *AE, D, DC, MC, V* ⊗ *No lunch.*

ITALIAN ✕ **Key Largo.** Gourmet pizzas baked in a wood-fire oven and a long list
¢–$ of pasta dishes are the specialties at this casual eatery near Rodney Bay's many hotels. You're welcome to stop in for an espresso or cappuccino, but the popular Pizza Key Largo—topped with shrimp, artichokes, and what seems like a few pounds of mozzarella—is tough to pass up. Kids love Key Largo, too. ⊠ *Rodney Heights* ☎ *758/452–0282* ⊟ *MC, V.*

PAN-ASIAN ✕ **Tao.** For exquisite dining, this small restaurant at the Body Holiday
★ $$$ at LeSPORT welcomes nonguests. Perched on a second-floor balcony at the edge of Cariblue Beach, you're guaranteed a pleasant breeze and a starry sky while you enjoy fusion cuisine—a marriage of Asian tastes and a Caribbean touch. Choose from appetizers such as seafood dumplings, sashimi salad, or miso eggplant timbale, followed by tender slices of pork loin teriyaki, twice-cooked duck, wok-seared calves' liver, or tandoori chicken—the results are mouthwatering. Fine wines accompany the meal, desserts are extravagant, and service is superb. Seating is limited; hotel guests have priority. ⊠ *The Body Holiday at LeSPORT, Cap Estate* ☎ *758/450–8551* ⌕ *Reservations essential* ⊟ *AE, DC, MC, V* ⊗ *No lunch.*

Soufrière

CARIBBEAN ✕ **Lifeline Restaurant at The Hummingbird.** Cajou, the chef at this cheer-
$–$$ ful restaurant-bar in the Hummingbird Beach Resort, specializes in French creole cuisine, starting with fresh seafood or chicken seasoned

with local herbs and accompanied by a medley of vegetables just picked from the Hummingbird's garden. Sandwiches and salads are also available. If you stop for lunch, be sure to visit the batik studio and art gallery of proprietor Joan Alexander and her son, adjacent to the dining room. ⊠ *Hummingbird Beach Resort, Anse Chastanet Rd., Soufrière* ☎ *758/459–7232* ⊟ *AE, D, MC, V.*

$–$$ ✕ **The Still.** If you're visiting Diamond Waterfall, this is a popular lunch spot. The two dining rooms of the Still Plantation seat up to 400 people, so it's a popular stop for tour groups and cruise passengers. The emphasis is on local cuisine using vegetables such as christophenes, breadfruits, yams, and callaloo along with grilled fish or chicken, but there are also pork and beef dishes. All fruits and vegetables used in the restaurant are organically grown on the estate. ⊠ *The Still Plantation, Sir Arthur Lewis St., Soufrière* ☎ *758/459–7261* ⊟ *MC, V.*

CONTEMPORARY ✕ **Dasheene Restaurant & Bar.** The terrace restaurant at Ladera Resort
★ **$$$** has breathtakingly close-up views of the Pitons and the sea between them, especially at sunset. Casual by day and magical at night, the restaurant offers a creative menu best described as nouvelle Caribbean. Appetizers may include island crab salad or silky pumpkin soup with ginger. Typical entrées are grilled barracuda or kingfish with jerk- or herb-flavored butter, shrimp Dasheene (panfried with local herbs), seared duck breast with passion-fruit jus, or baron fillet of beef with sweet potato and green-banana mash. Light dishes, salads, and sandwiches are served at lunchtime. ⊠ *Ladera Resort, 2 mi (3 km) south of Soufrière* ☎ *758/459–7323* ⊟ *AE, D, DC, MC, V.*

Beaches

Beaches are all public, but many of those north of Castries are flanked by hotels. A few secluded stretches of beach on the west coast south of Marigot Bay are accessible primarily by boat and are a popular stop on catamaran or powerboat sightseeing trips. Don't swim along the windward (east) coast, as the Atlantic Ocean is too rough—but the views are spectacular.

Anse Chastanet. In front of the resort of the same name, just north of the city of Soufrière, this palm-studded dark-sand beach has a backdrop of green hills, brightly painted fishing skiffs bobbing at anchor, and the island's best reefs for snorkeling and diving. The resort's gazebos are nestled among the palms; its dive shop, restaurant, and bar are on the beach and open to the public. ⊠ *1 mi (1½ km) north of Soufrière.*

Anse Cochon. This remote black-sand beach is reached only by boat or via Ti Kaye Village's mile-long access road. The waters here and adjacent reef are superb for swimming, diving, and snorkeling. Moorings are free, and boaters can enjoy lunch or dinner at Ti Kaye—if you're willing to climb the 166 steps up the hillside. ⊠ *3 mi (5 km) south of Marigot Bay.*

Anse des Pitons. Between the Pitons on Jalousie Bay, the white sand on this crescent beach was imported and spread over the natural black sand. Accessible from the resort or by boat, the beach offers good snorkeling, diving, and breathtaking scenery. ⊠ *Jalousie Bay, 1 mi. south of Soufrière.*

Marigot Beach. Calm waters rippled only by passing yachts lap a sliver of sand studded with palm trees on the north side of Marigot Bay. The beach is accessible by a ferry that operates continually from one side of the bay to the other, and you can find refreshments at adjacent restaurants. ⊠ *Marigot Bay.*

Pigeon Point. At this small beach within Pigeon Island National Historic Park, on the northwestern tip of St. Lucia, a restaurant serves snacks and drinks, but this is also a perfect spot for picnicking. ⊠ *Pigeon Island.*

★ **Reduit Beach.** This long stretch of golden sand frames Rodney Bay and is within walking distance of many small hotels and restaurants in Rodney Bay Village. The Rex St. Lucian Hotel, which faces the beach, has a water-sports center. Many feel that Reduit (pronounced red-*wee*) is the island's finest beach. ⊠ *Rodney Bay.*

Vigie Beach. This 2-mi (3-km) strand runs parallel to the George F. L. Charles Airport runway, in Castries, and continues on to become Malabar Beach, the beachfront for the Rendezvous resort. ⊠ *Castries, next to the airport.*

Sports & the Outdoors

BIKING   Although the terrain is pretty rugged, two tour operators have put together fascinating bicycle and combination bicycle-hiking tours that appeal to novice riders as well as those who enjoy a good workout. Prices
★ range from $60 to $100 per person. **Bike St. Lucia** (⊠ Anse Chastanet, Soufrière ☎ 758/451–2453 ⊕ www.bikestlucia.com) takes small groups of bikers on Jungle Biking™ tours along trails that meander through the remnants of an 18th-century plantation near Soufrière. Stops are made to explore the French colonial ruins, study the beautiful tropical plants and fruit trees, enjoy a picnic lunch, and take a dip in a river swimming hole or a swim at the beach. If you're staying in the north, you can get a tour that includes transportation to the Soufrière area. **Island Bike Hikes** (⊠ Castries ☎ 758/458–0908 ⊕ www.cyclestlucia.com) is suitable for all fitness levels. Jeep or bus transportation is provided across the central mountains to Dennery, on the east coast. After a 3-mi ride through the countryside, bikes are exchanged for shoe leather. The short hike into the rain forest ends with a picnic and a refreshing swim next to a sparkling waterfall—then the return leg to Dennery. All gear is supplied.

BOATING &   Rodney Bay and Marigot Bay are centers for bareboat and crewed
SAILING   yacht charters. Their marinas offer safe anchorage, shower facilities, restaurants, groceries, and maintenance for yachts sailing the waters of the eastern Caribbean. Charter prices range from $1,600 to $7,300 per week, depending on the season and the vessel, plus $200 per day if you want a skipper and cook. **Destination St. Lucia (DSL) Ltd.** (⊠ Rodney Bay Marina, Gros Islet ☎ 758/452–8531 ⊕ www.dsl-yachting.com) offers bareboat yacht charters; vessels range in length from 38 feet to 51 feet. The **Moorings Yacht Charters** (⊠ Marigot Bay ☎ 758/451–4357 or 800/535–7289 ⊕ www.moorings.com) rents bareboat and crewed yachts ranging from Beneteau 39s to Morgan 60s.

CAMPING   **Bay of Freedom Camp Site** (☎ 758/452–5005 or 758/454–5014), St. Lucia's only campsite, is 133 acres of sloping terrain at Anse La Liberté (French for "Bay of Freedom"), on the west coast near the village of Canaries—accessible by boat or by car (a 45-minute drive south from Castries or 15 minutes north from Soufrière). Rough campsites and platforms for tents are available, along with communal toilets and showers, a cooking center, a small secluded beach, and 4 mi of hiking trails. Camping fees are inexpensive, and reservations are required. The facility is on one of the many sites where former slaves celebrated their emancipation in 1834; it's administered by the St. Lucia National Trust.

CRICKET   International and test-series cricket is played at the Beausejour Cricket Ground in Gros Islet and at the impressive National Stadium in Vieux Fort. Contact the tourist board for details on schedules and tickets.

DIVING &   **Anse Chastanet,** near the Pitons on the southwest coast, is the best beach-
SNORKELING   entry dive site. The underwater reef drops from 20 feet to nearly 140
★   feet in a stunning coral wall. A 165-foot freighter, **Lesleen M,** was deliberately sunk in 60 feet of water near **Anse Cochon** to create an artificial reef; divers can explore the ship in its entirety and view huge gorgonians, black coral trees, gigantic barrel sponges, lace corals, schooling fish, angelfish, sea horses, spotted eels, stingrays, nurse sharks, and sea turtles. **Anse-La-Raye,** midway up the west coast, is one of St. Lucia's finest wall and drift dives and a great place for snorkeling. At the base of **Petit Piton,** a spectacular wall drops to 200 feet. You can view an impressive collection of huge barrel sponges and black coral trees; strong currents ensure good visibility. At the **Pinnacles,** four coral-encrusted stone piers rise to within 10 feet of the surface.

Depending on the season and the particular trip, prices range from about $40 to $60 for a one-tank dive, $175 to $260 for a six-dive package over three days, and $265 to $450 for a 10-dive package over five days. Dive shops provide instruction for all levels (beginner, intermediate, and advanced). For beginners, a resort course (pool training), followed by one open-water dive, runs from $65 to $90. Snorkelers are generally welcome on dive trips and usually pay $25 to $50, which includes equipment and sometimes lunch and transportation.

Buddies (✉ Rodney Bay Marina, Rodney Bay ☎ 758/452–8406) offers wall, wreck, reef, and deep dives; resort courses and open-water certification with advanced and specialty courses are taught by PADI-certified instructors. **Dive Fair Helen** (✉ Vigie Marina, Castries ☎ 758/451–7716, 888/855–2206 in U.S. and Canada ⊕ www.divefairhelen.com) is a PADI center that offers half- and full-day excursions to wreck, wall, and marine reserve areas, as well as night dives. **Scuba St. Lucia** (✉ Anse Chastanet, Soufrière ☎ 758/459–7755 ⊕ www.scubastlucia.com) is a PADI five-star training facility. Daily beach and boat dives and resort and certification courses are offered; underwater photography and snorkeling equipment are available. Day trips from the north of the island include round-trip speedboat transportation.

FISHING   Among the deep-sea creatures you can find in St. Lucia's waters are dolphin (also called dorado or mahimahi), barracuda, mackerel, wahoo, kingfish, sailfish, and white and blue marlin. Sportfishing is generally done on a catch-and-release basis, but the captain may permit you to take a fish back to your hotel to be prepared for your dinner. Neither spearfishing nor collecting live fish in coastal waters is permitted. Half- and full-day deep-sea fishing excursions can be arranged at either Vigie Cove or Rodney Bay Marina. A half-day of fishing on a scheduled trip runs about $80 per person. Beginners are welcome. **Captain Mike's** (✉ Vigie Cove ☎ 758/452–1216 or 758/452–7044 ⊕ www.captmikes.com) has a fleet of Bertram power boats (31- to 38-feet) that accommodate as many as eight passengers; tackle and cold drinks are supplied. **Mako Watersports** (✉ Rodney Bay Marina, Rodney Bay ☎ 758/452–0412) takes fishing enthusiasts out on the well-equipped six-passenger *Annie Baby*.

GOLF **St. Lucia Golf & Country Club** (✉ Cap Estate ☎ 758/452–8523 ⊕ www.stluciagolf.com), the island's only public course, is at the island's northern tip and offers panoramic views of both the Atlantic and Caribbean. It's an 18-hole championship course (6,829 yards, par 71). The clubhouse has a bar and a pro shop where you can rent clubs and shoes and arrange lessons. Greens fees are $70 for 9 holes or $95 for 18 holes; carts are required and included; club and shoe rentals are available. Reservations are essential. Complimentary transportation from your hotel or cruise ship is provided for parties of three or more people. The St. Lucia Golf Open, a two-day tournament held in March, is open to amateurs; it's a handicap event, and prizes are awarded.

HIKING The island is laced with trails, but you shouldn't attempt the more challenging ones on your own. Seasoned hikers may aspire to climb the Pitons, the two volcanic cones rising 2,460 feet and 2,619 feet, respectively, from the ocean floor just south of Soufrière. Hiking is recommended only on Gros Piton, which offers a steep but safe trail to the top. Tourists are permitted to hike Petit Piton, but the second half of the hike requires a good deal of rock climbing, and you'll need to provide your own safety equipment. Hiking the Pitons requires the permission of the St. Lucia Forest & Lands Department and a knowledgeable guide from the **Pitons Tour Guide Association** (☎ 758/459–9748). The **St. Lucia Forest & Lands Department** (☎ 758/450–2231 or 758/450–2078) manages trails throughout the rain forest and provides guides who explain the plants and trees you'll encounter and keep you on the right track for a small fee. The **St. Lucia National Trust** (☎ 758/452–5005 ⊕ www.slunatrust.org) maintains two trails: one is at Anse La Liberté, near Canaries on the Caribbean coast; the other is on the Atlantic coast, from Mandélé Point to the Frégate Islands Nature Reserve. Full-day excursions with lunch cost about $50 to $85 per person and can be arranged through hotels or tour operators.

HORSEBACK RIDING Creole horses, a breed indigenous to South America and popular on the island, are fairly small, fast, sturdy, and even-tempered animals suitable for beginners. Established stables can accommodate all skill levels and offer countryside trail rides, beach rides with picnic lunches, plantation tours, carriage rides, and lengthy treks. Prices run about $40 for one hour, $50 for two hours, and $70 for a three-hour beach ride and barbecue. Transportation is usually provided between the stables and nearby hotels. Local people sometimes appear on beaches with their steeds and offer 30-minute rides for $10; ride at your own risk.

Country Saddles (⊠ Marquis Estate, Babonneau ☎ 758/450–5467 or 758/450–0197), 45 minutes east of Castries, guides beginners and advanced riders through banana plantations, forest trails, and along the Atlantic coast. **International Riding Stables** (⊠ Beauséjour Estate, Gros Islet ☎ 758/452–8139 or 758/450–8665) offers English- and western-style riding. The beach-picnic ride includes time for a swim—with or without your horse. **Trim's National Riding Stable** (⊠ Cas-en-Bas, Gros Islet ☎ 758/452–8273 or 758/450–9971), the island's oldest riding stable, offers four sessions per day, plus beach tours, trail rides, and carriage tours to Pigeon Island.

SEA EXCURSIONS A day sail or sea cruise to Soufrière and the Pitons is a wonderful way to see St. Lucia and, perhaps, the perfect way to get to the island's distinctive natural sites. Prices for a full-day sailing excursion to Soufrière run about $75 to $90 per person and include a land tour to the Sulphur Springs and the Botanical Gardens, lunch, a stop for swimming and snorkeling, and a visit to pretty Marigot Bay. Two-hour sunset cruises along the northwest coast cost about $45 per person. Most boats leave from ℭ either Vigie Cove in Castries or Rodney Bay. The 140-foot tall ship **Brig Unicorn** (⊠ Vigie Cove, Castries ☎ 758/452–8644), used in the filming of the TV miniseries *Roots* and more recently the movie *Pirates of the Caribbean*—is a 140-foot replica of a 19th-century sailing ship. Day trips along the coast are fun for the whole family. Several nights each week a sunset cruise, with drinks and a live steel band, sails to Pigeon Point and back. Customized pleasure trips and snorkeling charters can be arranged for small groups (four to six people) through **Captain Mike's** (⊠ Vigie Cove, Castries ☎ 758/452–0216 or 758/452–7044 ⊕ www.captmikes.com). On **Endless Summer** (⊠ Rodney Bay Marina, Rodney Bay ☎ 758/450–8651), a 56-foot "party" catamaran, you can take a day trip to Soufrière or a half-day swimming and snorkeling trip. For romantics, there's a weekly sunset cruise, with dinner and entertainment. **Surf Queen** (⊠ Vigie Cove, Castries ☎ 758/452–8232), a trimaran, runs a fast, sleek sail and has a special tour for German-speaking passengers.

L'Express des Iles (⊠ La Place Carenage, Castries ☎ 758/452–2211) offers an interesting day trip to the French island of Martinique. A hydrofoil departs daily for the 20-mi voyage. As you approach Martinique, be sure to position yourself to be among the first to disembark. There's usually only one immigration-customs agent on duty, and it can take an hour to clear if you're at the end of the line. From Pigeon Island, north of Rodney Bay, you can take a more intimate cruise to the Pitons aboard the 57-foot luxury cruiser **MV Vigie** (⊠ Pigeon Island ☎ 758/452–8232). For a boat trip to Pigeon Island, the **Rodney Bay Ferry** (⊠ Rodney Bay Marina, Rodney Bay ☎ 758/452–8816) departs the ferry slip adjacent to the Lime restaurant twice daily for $50 round-trip, which includes the entrance fee to Pigeon Island and lunch; snorkel equipment can be rented for $12.

SIGHTSEEING Taxi drivers are well informed and can give you a full tour—and often TOURS an excellent one, thanks to government-sponsored training programs. From the Castries area, full-day island tours cost $140 for up to four people; sightseeing trips to Soufrière, $120. If you plan your own day, expect to pay the driver $20 per hour plus tip.

★ **Jungle Tours** (⊠ Cas en Bas, Gros Islet ☎ 758/450–0434) specializes in rain-forest hiking tours for all levels of ability. You're required only to bring hiking shoes or sneakers and have a willingness to get wet and have fun. Prices range from $80 to $90 and include lunch, fees, and transportation via open Land Rover truck. **St. Lucia Helicopters** (⊠ Pointe Seraphine, Castries ☎ 758/453–6950 🖷 758/452–1553 ⊕ www. stluciahelicopters.com) offers a bird's-eye view of the island. A 10-minute North Island tour ($55 per person) leaves from Pointe Seraphine, in Castries, continues up the west coast to Pigeon Island, then flies along the rugged Atlantic coastline before returning inland over Castries. The 20-minute South Island tour ($85 per person) starts at Pointe Seraphine and follows the western coastline, circling picturesque Marigot Bay, Soufrière, and the majestic Pitons before returning inland over the volcanic hot springs and tropical rain forest. A complete island tour combines the two and lasts 30 minutes ($130 per person). **St. Lucia Heritage Tours** (⊠ Pointe Seraphine, Castries ☎ 758/451–6058 ⊕ www. heritagetoursstlucia.com) has put together an "authentic St. Lucia experience," specializing in the local culture and traditions. Groups are small, and some of the off-the-beaten-track sites visited are a 19th-century plantation house surrounded by nature trails, a 20-foot waterfall hidden away on private property, and a living museum presenting creole practices and traditions. Plan on paying $65 per person for a full-day tour. **Sunlink Tours** (⊠ Reduit Beach Ave., Rodney Bay ☎ 758/452–8232 or 800/786–5465 ⊕ www.sunlinktours.com) offers dozens of land, sea, and combination sightseeing tours, as well as shopping tours, plantation, and rain-forest adventures via Jeep safari, deep-sea fishing excursions, and day trips to other islands. Prices range from $20 for a half-day shopping tour to $120 for a full-day land-and-sea Jeep safari to Soufrière.

TENNIS & SQUASH People staying at small inns without tennis courts or those who wish to play squash can access a few private facilities for a fee. The **St. Lucia Racquet Club** (⊠ Club St. Lucia, Cap Estate ☎ 758/450–0106) is the best private tennis facility on the island. The site of the St. Lucia Open each December, it has seven lighted tennis courts, a pro shop, a restaurant-bar, and a squash court. The club charges $10 per person per hour for use of the facilities; reservations are required.

Shopping

The island's best-known products are artwork and wood carvings; clothing and household articles made from batik and silk-screen fabrics, designed and printed in island workshops; and clay pottery. You can also take home straw hats and baskets and locally grown cocoa, coffee, and spices.

Areas & Malls

Along the harbor in Castries you can see the rambling structures with bright-orange roofs that house several markets, which are open from 6 AM to 5 PM Monday through Saturday. Saturday morning is the busiest and most colorful time to shop. For more than a century, farmers' wives have gathered at the **Castries Market** to sell produce—which, alas, you can't import to the United States. But you can bring back spices (such as cocoa, turmeric, cloves, bay leaves, ginger, peppercorns, cinnamon sticks, nutmeg, mace, and vanilla essence), as well as bottled hot pepper sauces—all of which cost a fraction of what you'd pay back home. The **Craft Market,** adjacent to the produce market, has aisles and aisles of baskets and other handmade straw work, rustic brooms made from palm fronds, wood carvings and leather work, clay pottery, and souvenirs—all at affordable prices. The **Vendor's Arcade,** across the street from the Craft Market, is a maze of stalls and booths where you can find handicrafts among the T-shirts and costume jewelry.

Gablewoods Mall, on the Gros Islet Highway in Choc Bay, a couple of miles north of downtown Castries, has about 35 shops that sell groceries, wines and spirits, jewelry, clothing, crafts, books and overseas newspapers, music, souvenirs, household goods, and snacks. At the grocery or liquor store at Gablewoods, you might pick up a bottle of Bounty Rum, the local firewater made at a distillery in Roseau, just south of Castries. Along with 54 boutiques, restaurants, and other businesses that sell services and supplies, a large supermarket is the focal point of each **J. Q.'s Shopping Mall**; one is at Rodney Bay and another at Vieux Fort.

The duty-free shopping areas are at **Pointe Seraphine,** an attractive Spanish-motif complex on Castries Harbour with more than 20 shops, and **La Place Carenage,** an inviting, three-story complex on the opposite side of the harbor. You can also find duty-free items in a few small shops at the arcade at the Rex St. Lucian hotel in Rodney Bay and, of course, in the departure lounge at Hewanorra International Airport. You must present your passport and airline ticket to purchase items at the duty-free price.

Specialty Items

ART **Artsibit Gallery** (⌧ Brazil and Mongiraud Sts., Castries ☎ 758/452–7865) exhibits and sells moderately priced pieces by St. Lucian painters and sculptors. **Caribbean Art Gallery** (⌧ Rodney Bay Yacht Marina, Rodney Bay ☎ 758/452–8071) sells original artwork by local artists, along with antique maps and prints and hand-painted silk. World-renowned St. Lucian artist **Llewellyn Xavier** (⌧ Cap Estate ☎ 758/450–9155) creates modern art, ranging from vigorous oil abstracts that take up half a wall to small objects made from beaten silver and gold. Much of his work has an environmental theme, created from recycled materials. Xavier's work is on permanent exhibit at major museums in New York and Washington, D.C. Call to arrange a visit. **Modern Art Gallery** (⌧ Gros Islet Hwy., Bois d'Orange ☎ 758/452–9079) is a home studio, open by appointment only, where you can buy contemporary and avant-garde Caribbean art. **Snooty Agouti** (⌧ Rodney Bay ☎ 758/452–0321) sells original Caribbean artwork, wood carvings, prints, and maps; it's adjacent to the bar and restaurant of the same name.

BOOKS & **Sunshine Bookshop** (⌧ Gablewoods Mall, Castries ☎ 758/452–3222) MAGAZINES has novels and titles of regional interest, including books by Caribbean authors—among them the works of the St. Lucian Nobel laureate, poet Derek Walcott. You can also find current newspapers and magazines. **Valmont Books** (⌧ Corner of Jeremie and Laborie Sts., Castries

☎ 758/452–3817) has West Indian literature and picture books, as well as stationery.

CLOTHES & TEXTILES ★ **Bagshaw Studios** (✉ La Toc Rd., La Toc Bay, Castries ☎ 758/452–2139 or 758/451–9249) sells clothing and table linens in colorful tropical patterns using Stanley Bagshaw's original designs. The fabrics are silk-screened by hand in the adjacent workroom. You can also find Bagshaw boutiques at Pointe Seraphine, La Place Carenage, and Rodney Bay, and a selection of items in gift shops at Hewanorra Airport. Visit the workshop to see how designs are turned into colorful silk-screen fabrics, which are then fashioned into clothing and household articles. It's open weekdays from 8:30 to 5, Saturday 8:30 to 4, and Sunday 10 to 1. Weekend hours may be extended if a cruise ship is in port. **Batik Studio** (✉ Hummingbird Beach Resort, on the bayfront, north of wharf, Soufrière ☎ 758/459–7232) has superb batik sarongs, scarves, and wall panels designed and created on-site by Joan Alexander and her son David. At **Caribelle Batik** (✉ La Toc Rd., Morne Fortune, Castries ☎ 758/452–3785), craftspeople demonstrate the art of batik and silk-screen printing. Meanwhile, seamstresses create clothing and wall hangings, which you can purchase in the shop. The studio is in an old Victorian mansion, high atop the Morne overlooking Castries. There's a terrace where you can have a cool drink, and there's a garden full of tropical orchids and lilies. Caribelle Batik creations are featured in many gift shops throughout St. Lucia. **Sea Island Cotton Shop** (✉ Bridge St., Castries ☎ 758/452–3674 ✉ Gablewoods Mall, Choc Bay ☎ 758/451–6946 ✉ J. Q.'s Shopping Mall, Rodney Bay ☎ 758/458–4220) sells quality T-shirts, Caribelle Batik clothing and other resort wear, and colorful souvenirs.

GIFTS & SOUVENIRS **Caribbean Perfumes** (✉ Vigie Marina, Castries ☎ 758/453–7249) blends a half-dozen lovely scents for women and two aftershaves for men from exotic flowers, fruits, tropical woods, and spices. Fragrances are all made in St. Lucia, reasonably priced, and available at the perfumery (adjacent to Jacques Waterside Dining Restaurant) and at many hotel gift shops. **Noah's Arkade** (✉ Jeremie St., Castries ☎ 758/452–2523 ✉ Pointe Seraphine, Castries ☎ 758/452–7488) has hammocks, wood carvings, straw mats, T-shirts, books, and other regional goods.

HANDICRAFTS On the southwest coast, halfway between Soufrière and Vieux Fort, you can find locally made clay and straw pieces at the **Choiseul Arts & Crafts Centre** (✉ La Fargue ☎ 758/454–3226). Many of St. Lucia's artisans come from this area. **Eudovic Art Studio** (✉ Morne Fortune, Castries ☎ 758/452–2747) is a workshop and studio where you can buy trays, masks, and figures sculpted from local mahogany, red cedar, and eucalyptus wood.

Nightlife & the Arts

The Arts

FodorśChoice ★ In early May the weeklong **St. Lucia Jazz Festival** (⊕ stluciajazz.org) is one of the premier events of its kind in the Caribbean. International jazz greats perform at outdoor venues on Pigeon Island and at various hotels, restaurants, and nightspots throughout the island; free concerts are also held at Derek Walcott Square in downtown Castries.

THEATER   The small, open-air **Derek Walcott Center Theatre** (⊠ Cap Estate ☎ 758/
450–0551, 758/450–0450 for Great House), next to the Great House
restaurant in Cap Estate, seats 200 people for monthly productions
of music, dance, and drama, as well as Sunday brunch programs. The
Trinidad Theatre Workshop also presents an annual performance
here. For schedule and ticket information, contact the **Great House**
restaurant.

Nightlife

Most resort hotels have entertainment—island music, calypso singers,
and steel bands, as well as disco, karaoke, and talent shows—every night
in high season and a couple of nights per week in the off-season. Otherwise, Rodney Bay is the best bet for nightlife. The many restaurants
and bars there attract a crowd nearly every night.

BARS   The **Captain's Cellar** (⊠ Pigeon Island, Rodney Bay ☎ 758/450–0253)
is a cozy Old English pub with live jazz on weekends. **Shamrocks Pub**
(⊠ Rodney Bay ☎ 758/452–8725) is an Irish-style pub with pool tables and darts, lots of beer, and music.

DANCE CLUBS   Most dance clubs with live bands have a cover charge of $6 to $8
(EC$15 to EC$20), and the music usually starts at 11 PM. **Doolittle's**
(⊠ Marigot Bay ☎ 758/451–4974) has live bands and dance music—
calypso, soul, salsa, steel-band, reggae, and limbo—that changes nightly.
At **Indies** (⊠ Rodney Bay ☎ 758/452–0727) you can dance to the hottest
rhythms Wednesday, Friday, and Saturday; dress is casual though smart—
no hats or sandals, no shorts or sleeveless shirts for men. There's shuttle bus service to and from most major hotels. The **Late Lime** (⊠ Reduit
Beach, Rodney Bay ☎ 758/452–0761) is a particular favorite of St. Lucians; it's air-conditioned and intimate, with live music, a DJ, or karaoke
every night but Tuesday.

THEME NIGHTS   For a taste of St. Lucian village life, head south from Castries to the **Anse
La Raye "Fish Feast"** on a Friday night. Beginning at 6:30 PM, streets in
this tiny fishing village are closed to vehicles and the residents prepare
what they know best: fish cakes for about 40¢ each, fried or stewed fish
for $3 a portion, even a whole lobster for $10 to $15, depending on
size. Walk around, eat, chat with the local people, and listen to live music
in the village square until the wee hours of the morning.

A Friday-night ritual for locals and visitors alike is to head for the **Gros
Islet Jump-Up,** the island's largest street party. Huge speakers are set
up on the village's main street and blast out Caribbean music all night
long. Sometimes there are live bands. When you take a break from
dancing, you can buy barbecued fish or chicken, rotis, beer, and soda
from villagers who set up cookers right along the roadside. It's the ultimate "lime" experience.

The **Green Parrot** (⊠ Morne Fortune, Castries ☎ 758/452–3399) is in
a class all by itself. On Wednesday and Saturday, chef Harry Edwards
hosts the floor show—singing, dancing, and shimmying under the limbo
pole himself. Dress semiformally for these evenings of frolic.

Exploring St. Lucia

One main route circles all of St. Lucia, except for a small area in the extreme northeast. The road snakes along the coast, cuts across mountains, makes hairpin turns and sheer drops, and reaches dizzying heights. It would take at least four hours to drive the whole loop. Even at a leisurely pace with frequent sightseeing stops, the curvy roads make it a tiring drive in a single outing.

The West Coast Road between Castries and Soufrière (a 1½- to 2-hour journey) has steep hills and sharp turns, but it's well marked and incredibly scenic. South of Castries, the road tunnels through Morne Fortune, skirts the island's largest banana plantation (more than 127 varieties of bananas, called "figs" in this part of the Caribbean, are grown on the island), and passes through tiny fishing villages. Just north of Soufrière is the island's fruit basket, where most of the mangoes, breadfruit, tomatoes, limes, and oranges are grown. In the mountainous region that forms a backdrop for Soufrière, you will notice 3,118-foot Mount Gimie (pronounced Jimmy), St. Lucia's highest peak. As you approach Soufrière, you'll also have spectacular views of the Pitons.

The landscape changes dramatically between the Pitons and Vieux Fort on the island's southeastern tip. Along the South Coast Road, the terrain starts as steep mountainside with dense vegetation, progresses to undulating hills, and finally becomes rather flat and comparatively arid. Anyone arriving at Hewanorra International Airport and staying at a resort near Soufrière will travel along this route, a journey of about 30 minutes.

From Vieux Fort north to Castries, a 1¼-hour drive, the East Coast Road twists through Micoud, Dennery, and other coastal villages. It then winds up, down, and around mountains, crosses Barre de l'Isle Ridge, and slices through the rain forest. The scenery is breathtaking. The Atlantic Ocean pounds against rocky cliffs, and acres and acres of bananas and coconut palms cover the hillsides. If you arrive at Hewanorra and stay at a resort near Castries, you'll travel along the East Coast Road.

Numbers in the margin correspond to points of interest on the St. Lucia map.

Castries & the North

Castries, the capital, and the area north of it are the island's most developed areas. The roads are straight, mostly flat, and easy to navigate. The beaches are some of the island's best. Rodney Bay Marina and most of the resorts, restaurants, and nightspots are in this area. Pigeon Island, one of the important historical sites, is at the island's northwestern tip.

WHAT TO SEE
6

Barre de l'Isle Forest Reserve. St. Lucia is divided into eastern and western halves by Barre de l'Isle Ridge. A mile-long (1½-km-long) trail cuts through the reserve, and four lookout points provide panoramic views. Visible in the distance are Mount Gimie, immense green valleys, both the Caribbean Sea and the Atlantic Ocean, and coastal communities. The reserve is about a half-hour drive from Castries; it takes about an hour to walk the trail and another hour to climb Mount La Combe Ridge.

Permission from the St. Lucia Forest & Lands Department is required to access the trail in Barre de l'Isle; a naturalist or forest officer guide will accompany you. ⊠ *Trailhead on East Coast Rd., near Ravine Poisson, midway between Castries and Dennery* ☎ *758/450–2231 or 758/450–2078* 🖙 *$10 for guide services* ⊘ *Daily by appointment only.*

❹ Bounty Rum Distillery. St. Lucia Distillers, which produces the island's own Bounty Rum, offers 90-minute "Rhythm and Rum" tours of its distillery, including information on the history of sugar, the background of rum, a detailed description of the distillation process, colorful displays of local architecture, a glimpse at a typical rum shop, Caribbean music, and, of course, a chance to sample the company's rums and liqueurs. The distillery is at the Roseau Sugar Factory in the Roseau Valley, on the island's largest banana plantation, a few miles south of Castries and not far from Marigot. Reservations for the tour are essential. ⊠ *Roseau Sugar Factory, West Coast Rd., Roseau* ☎ *758/451–4258* 🖙 *$5* ⊘ *Weekdays 9–3.*

🐾 ❶ Castries. The capital, a busy commercial city of about 65,000 people, wraps around a sheltered bay. Morne Fortune rises sharply to the south of town, creating a dramatic green backdrop. The charm of Castries lies almost entirely in its liveliness, since most of the colonial buildings were destroyed by four fires that occurred between 1796 and 1948. Freighters (exporting bananas, coconut, cocoa, mace, nutmeg, and citrus fruits) and cruise ships come and go daily, making Castries Harbour one of the Caribbean's busiest ports. **Pointe Seraphine** is a duty-free shopping complex on the north side of the harbor, about a 20-minute walk or 2-minute cab ride from the city center; a launch ferries passengers across the harbor when ships are in port. Pointe Seraphine's attractive Spanish-style architecture houses more than 20 upscale duty-free shops, a tourist information kiosk, a taxi stand, and car-rental agencies. **Derek Walcott Square** is a green oasis bordered by Brazil, Laborie, Micoud, and Bourbon streets. Formerly Columbus Square, it was renamed to honor the hometown poet who won the 1992 Nobel prize for literature—one of two Nobel laureates from St. Lucia (the late Sir W. Arthur Lewis won the 1979 Nobel prize in economics). Some of the 19th-century buildings that have survived fire, wind, and rain can be seen on Brazil Street, the square's southern border. On the Laborie Street side, there's a huge, 400-year-old *samaan* tree with leafy branches that shade a good portion of the square. Directly across Laborie Street from Derek Walcott Square is the Roman Catholic **Cathedral of the Immaculate Conception,** which was built in 1897. Though it's rather somber on the outside, its interior walls are decorated with colorful murals reworked by St. Lucian artist Dunstan St. Omer in 1985, just prior to Pope John Paul II's visit. This church has an active parish and is open daily for both public viewing and religious services. At the corner of Jeremie and Peynier streets, spreading beyond its brilliant orange roof, is the **Castries Market.** Full of excitement and bustle, the market is open every day except Sunday. It's liveliest on Saturday morning, when farmers bring their fresh produce and spices to town, as they have for more than a century. Next door to the produce market is the **Craft Market,** where you can buy pottery, wood carvings, and handwoven straw articles. Across Peynier

Street from the Craft Market, at the **Vendor's Arcade,** there are still more handicrafts and souvenirs.

② Fort Charlotte. Begun in 1764 by the French as the Citadelle du Morne Fortune, Fort Charlotte was completed after 20 years of battling and changing hands. Its old barracks and batteries are now government buildings and local educational facilities, but you can drive around and look at the remains, including redoubts, a guardroom, stables, and cells. You can also walk up to the Inniskilling Monument, a tribute to the 1796 battle in which the 27th Foot Royal Inniskilling Fusiliers wrested the Morne from the French. At the military cemetery, which was first used in 1782, faint inscriptions on the tombstones tell the tales of French and English soldiers who died here. Six former governors of the island are buried here as well. From this point atop Morne Fortune you can view Martinique to the north and the twin peaks of the Pitons to the south.

③ Government House. The official residence of the governor-general of St. Lucia, one of the island's few remaining examples of Victorian architecture is perched high above Castries, halfway up Morne Fortune—the "Hill of Good Fortune"—which forms a backdrop for the capital city. Morne Fortune has also overlooked more than its share of *bad* luck over the years, including devastating hurricanes and four fires that leveled Castries. Within Government House itself is the **Le Pavillon Royal Museum,** which houses important historical photographs and documents, artifacts, crockery, silverware, medals, and awards; original architectural drawings of Government House are displayed on the walls. However, you must make an appointment to visit. ✉ *Morne Fortune, Castries* ☎ *758/452–2481* ⊕ *www.stluciagovernmenthouse.com* ✑ *Free* ☉ *Tues. and Thurs. 10–noon and 2–4, by appointment only.*

★ ⑤ Marigot Bay. This is one of the prettiest natural harbors in the Caribbean. In 1778 British admiral Samuel Barrington sailed into this secluded bay-within-a-bay and covered his ships with palm fronds to hide them from the French. Today this picturesque community—where parts of the original movie *Doctor Doolittle* were filmed in the late 1960s—is a favorite anchorage. A 24-hour ferry connects the bay's two shores. Marigot Bay is undergoing a radical, yet environmentally friendly, transformation. **Discovery at Marigot Bay,** a luxury resort and marina village to be managed by Sonesta with restaurants, bars, shopping, and other activities, is revitalizing the area. One restaurant and the marina were in operation at this writing; the hotel complex was expected to be completed by early 2006.

⑯ Marquis Estate. If you want a close-up view of a working plantation and are willing to get a little wet and muddy in the process, you can tour the island's largest one. The 600-acre Marquis Estate, situated on the northern Atlantic coast, began as a sugar plantation. Now it produces bananas and copra (dried coconut processed for oil) for export, as well as a number of other tropical fruits and vegetables for local consumption. St. Lucia Representative Services Ltd. conducts the tour and will pick you up at your hotel in an air-conditioned bus. You can see the estate by bus or on horseback; a river ride to the coast and lunch at the plantation house are both included. Self-drive tours and private taxi tours aren't permitted. Wear casual clothes. ⊠ *Marquis Bay* ☎ *758/ 452–3762.*

★ ☕ ⓲ **Pigeon Island.** Jutting out from the northwest coast, Pigeon Island is connected to the mainland by a causeway. Tales are told of the pirate Jambe de Bois (Wooden Leg), who once hid out on this 44-acre hilltop islet— a strategic point during the struggles for control of St. Lucia. Now it's a national landmark and a venue for concerts, festivals, and family gatherings. There are two small beaches with calm waters for swimming and snorkeling, a restaurant, and picnic areas. Scattered around the grounds are ruins of barracks, batteries, and garrisons that date from 18th-century French and English battles. In the Museum and Interpretative Centre, housed in the restored British officers' mess, a multimedia display explains the island's ecological and historical significance. ⊠ *Pigeon Island, St. Lucia National Trust, Rodney Bay* ☎ *758/452– 5005* ⊕ *www.slunatrust.or* 🗐 *$4* ⊙ *Daily 9–5.*

⓱ **Rodney Bay.** About 15 minutes north of Castries, the natural bay and an 80-acre man-made lagoon—surrounded by hotels and many popular restaurants—are named for British admiral George Rodney, who sailed the English Navy out of Gros Islet Bay in 1780 to attack and ultimately decimate the French fleet. Rodney Bay Marina is one of the Caribbean's premier yachting centers and the destination of the Atlantic Rally for Cruisers (transatlantic yacht crossing) each December. Yacht charters and sightseeing day trips can be arranged at the marina. The Rodney Bay Ferry makes hourly crossings between the marina and the shopping complex, as well as daily excursions to Pigeon Island.

Soufrière & the South

The southwest coast is the destination of most sightseeing trips. This is where you can view the landmark Pitons and explore the French-colonial town of Soufrière, with its drive-in volcano, botanical gardens, working plantations, and countless other examples of the natural beauty for which St. Lucia is deservedly famous.

WHAT TO SEE **Diamond Botanical Gardens & Waterfall.** These splendid gardens are part
★ ☕ ❽ of Soufrière Estate, a 2,000-acre land grant made in 1713 by Louis XIV to three Devaux brothers from Normandy in recognition of their services to France. The estate is still owned by their descendants; the gardens are maintained by Joan Du Bouley Devaux. Bushes and shrubs bursting with brilliant flowers grow beneath towering trees and line pathways that lead to a natural gorge. Water bubbling to the surface from underground sulfur springs streams downhill in rivulets to become Diamond Waterfall, deep within the botanical gardens. Through the centuries, the rocks over which the cascade spills have become encrusted with minerals and tinted yellow, green, and purple. Adjacent to the falls, curative mineral baths are fed by the underground springs. For a small fee you can slip into your swimsuit and bathe for 30 minutes in one of the outside pools; a private bath costs slightly more. King Louis XVI of France provided funds in 1784 for the construction of a building with a dozen large stone baths to fortify his troops against the St. Lucian climate. It's claimed that Joséphine Bonaparte bathed here as a young girl while visiting her father's plantation nearby. During the Brigand's War,

just after the French Revolution, the bathhouse was destroyed. In 1930 the site was excavated by André Du Boulay, and two of the original stone baths were restored for his use. The outside baths were added later. ⊠ *Soufrière Estate, Soufrière* ☎ *758/452–4759 or 758/454–7565* ⌑ *$2.75, outside bath $2.50, private bath $3.75* ☉ *Mon.–Sat. 10–5, Sun. 10–3.*

⑩ Fond Doux Estate. One of the earliest French estates established by land grant (1745 and 1763), 135 hilly acres of this old plantation still produce cocoa, citrus, bananas, coconut, and vegetables; the restored 1864 plantation house is still in use as well. A 30-minute walking tour begins at the cocoa fermentary, where you can see the drying process under way. You then follow a trail through the lush cultivated area, where a guide points out the various fruit- or spice-bearing trees and tropical flowers. Additional trails lead to old military ruins, a religious shrine, and another vantage point for the spectacular Pitons. Cool drinks and a creole buffet lunch are available at the restaurant. Souvenirs, including just-made chocolate balls, are sold at the boutique. ⊠ *Chateaubelair, Soufrière* ☎ *758/459–7545* ⊕ *www.fonddouxestate.com* ⌑ *$6, buffet lunch $14* ☉ *Daily 9–4.*

⑮ Frégate Island Nature Reserve. A mile-long (1½-km) trail encircles the nature reserve, which you reach from the East Coast Road near the fishing village of Praslin. In this area, boat builders still fashion traditional fishing canoes, called *gommiers* after the trees from which the hulls are made. The ancient design was used by the original Amerindian people who populated the Caribbean. A natural promontory at Praslin provides a lookout from which you can view the two small islets Frégate Major and Frégate Minor and—with luck—the frigate birds that nest here from May to July. The only way to visit is on a guided tour, which includes a ride in a gommier to Frégate Minor for a picnic lunch and a swim; all trips are by reservation only and require a minimum of two people. Arrange visits through your hotel, a tour operator, or the St. Lucia National Trust; many tours include round-trip transportation from your hotel as well as the tour cost. ⊠ *Praslin* ☎ *758/452–5005, 758/453–7656, 758/454–5014 for tour reservations* ⊕ *www.slunatrust.org* ⌑ *$18* ☉ *Daily by appointment.*

⑭ Maria Islands Nature Reserve. Two tiny islands in the Atlantic Ocean, off St. Lucia's southeast coast, compose the reserve, which has its own interpretive center. The 25-acre Maria Major and the 4-acre Maria Minor, its little sister, are inhabited by two rare species of reptiles (the colorful Maria Island ground lizard and the harmless grass snake) that share their home with frigate birds, terns, doves, and other wildlife. There's a small beach for swimming and snorkeling, as well as an undisturbed forest, a vertical cliff covered with cacti, and a coral reef for snorkeling or diving. Tours, including the boat trip to the islands, are offered by the St. Lucia National Trust by appointment only; you should bring your own picnic lunch, because there are no facilities. ⊠ *St. Lucia National Trust Regional Office, Vieux Fort* ☎ *758/452–5005, 758/453–7656, 758/454–5014 for tour reservations* ⊕ *www.slunatrust.org* ⌑ *$35* ☉ *Aug.–mid-May, Wed.–Sun. 9:30–5, by appointment only.*

9 **The Pitons.** These two unusual mountains, which rise precipitously from the cobalt blue Caribbean Sea just south of Soufrière, have become the symbol of St. Lucia. Covered with thick tropical vegetation, the massive outcroppings were formed by lava from a volcanic eruption 30 to 40 million years ago. They are not identical twins since—confusingly—2,619-foot Petit Piton is taller than 2,461-foot Gros Piton, though Gros Piton is, as the word translates, broader. Gros Piton is currently the only one you are allowed to climb, though the trail up even this shorter Piton is one very tough trek and requires the permission of the Forest & Lands Department and a knowledgeable guide. ☎ *758/450–2231, 758/450–2078 for St. Lucia Forest & Lands Department, 758/459–9748 for Pitons Tour Guide Association* ✉ *Guide services $45* ☉ *Daily by appointment only.*

FodorsChoice ★

11 **St. Lucia National Rain Forest.** Dense tropical rain forest stretches from one side of the island to the other, sprawling over 19,000 acres of mountains and valleys. It's home to a multitude of exotic flowers and plants, as well as rare birds—including the brightly feathered Jacquot parrot. The Edmund Forest Reserve, on the island's western side, is most easily accessible from just east of Soufrière, on the road to Fond St. Jacques. A trek through the lush landscape, with spectacular views of mountains, valleys, and the sea beyond, can take three or more hours. It takes an hour or so just to reach the reserve by car from the north end of the island. You need plenty of stamina and sturdy hiking shoes. Permission from the Forest & Lands Department is required to access reserve trails, and the department requires that a naturalist or forest officer guide you because the vegetation is so dense, so it's an absolute necessity that you make a reservation. ✉ *East of Fond St. Jacques* ☎ *758/450–2231, 758/450–2078 for Forest & Lands Department* ✉ *Guide $10; guided tours that include round-trip transportation from your hotel $55–$85* ☉ *Daily by appointment only.*

7 **Soufrière.** The oldest town in St. Lucia and the former French-colonial capital, Soufrière was founded by the French in 1746 and named for its proximity to the volcano. The wharf is the center of activity in this sleepy town (which currently has a population of about 9,000), particularly when a cruise ship is moored in pretty Soufrière Bay. French-colonial influences can be noticed in the architecture of the wooden buildings, with second-story verandas and gingerbread trim that surround the market square. The market building itself is decorated with colorful murals. The **Soufrière Tourist Information Centre** (✉ Bay St., Soufrière ☎ 758/459–7200) provides information about area attractions. Note that outside some of the popular attractions in and around Soufrière, souvenir vendors can be persistent. Be polite but firm if you're not interested in their wares.

★ ☺ **12** **La Soufrière Drive-In Volcano.** As you approach, your nose will pick up the strong scent of the sulfur springs—more than 20 belching pools of muddy water, multicolor sulfur deposits, and other assorted minerals baking and steaming on the surface. Actually, you don't drive in. You drive up within a few hundred feet of the gurgling, steaming mass, then walk behind your guide—whose service is included in the admission price—around a fault in the substratum rock. It's a fascinating, educational half hour, though it can also be pretty stinky on a hot day. ⊠ *Bay St., Soufrière* ☎ *758/459–5500* 🍴 *$1.25* ⏱ *Daily 9–5.*

⓭ Vieux Fort. St. Lucia's second-largest port is where you'll find Hewanorra International Airport. From the Moule à Chique Peninsula, the island's southernmost tip, you can see all of St. Lucia to the north and the island of St. Vincent 21 mi (34 km) south. This is where the waters of the clear Caribbean Sea blend with those of the deeper blue Atlantic Ocean.

ST. LUCIA ESSENTIALS

To research prices, get advice from other travelers, and book travel arrangements, visit www.fodors.com.

Transportation

BY AIR

Air Canada has direct weekend service to Hewanorra from Toronto and Montréal. Air Jamaica flies daily to Hewanorra from New York nonstop but also via Montego Bay or Barbados and from London via Barbados. American Airlines flies direct between Miami and Hewanorra; American Airlines flies connecting service from New York and other major U.S. cities to San Juan and via American Eagle to George F. L. Charles Airport in Castries. British Airways has direct service to Hewanorra from London via Barbados. BWIA has direct service to George F. L. Charles, via either Barbados or Trinidad, from Miami, New York, Washington, D.C., and London. US Airways flies twice weekly between Philadelphia and Hewanorra. Virgin Atlantic flies nonstop to Hewanorra from London. From other parts of the world, connections must be made through U.S. cities, San Juan, Toronto, or London.

Air Caraïbes, Caribbean Star, and LIAT fly into George F. L. Charles Airport from various neighboring islands. HelenAir flies charter service between Barbados and George F. L. Charles Airport.

🛈 Airline Information **Air Canada** ☎ 758/452-3051 or 758/452-2550. **Air Caraïbes** ☎ 758/452-2463 or 758/453-6660. **Air Jamaica** ☎758/453-6611. **American Airlines/American Eagle** ☎ 758/452-677. **British Airways** ☎ 758/452-3951. **BWIA**

☎ 758/452-3778, 758/451-7700, or 758/454-5075. **Caribbean Star** ☎758/452-5898. **HelenAir** ☎758/453-2777. **LIAT** ☎ 758/452-3051 or 758/452-2348. **US Airways** ☎ 758/454-8186. **Virgin Atlantic** ☎ 758/454-3610.

AIRPORTS & TRANSFERS: Many large resorts—particularly the all-inclusive ones—provide round-trip airport transfers. That's a significant amenity if you're landing at Hewanorra, as the one-way taxi fare for the 60- to 90-minute ride (depending on whether you're headed to Soufrière or Castries) is expensive—$55 to $75 for up to four passengers. Taxis are always available at the airports.

🛈 Airport Information **George F. L. Charles Airport** ☎ 758/452-1156. **Hewanorra International Airport** ☎ 758/454-6355. **St. Lucia Helicopters** ⊠ Pointe Seraphine, Castries ☎ 758/453-6950 🖨 758/452-1553 ⊕ www.stluciahelicopters.com.

BY BOAT & FERRY

Cruise ships from major lines call at Castries and Soufrière. At Port Castries, ships tie up at berths right in town and are convenient to duty-free shops, the market, and transportation for sightseeing excursions. When cruise ships are in port, a water taxi shuttles back and forth between Pointe Seraphine on the north side of the harbor and Place Carenage on the south side of the harbor for $1 per person each way. In Soufrière, ships anchor offshore, and passengers are transferred ashore by tenders.

For visitors arriving at Rodney Bay on their own or chartered yachts, a ferry travels between the marina and the shopping complex daily on the hour, from 9 to 4, for $4 per person round-trip.

🚢 **Rodney Bay Ferry** ☎ 758/452-8816.

BY BUS

Privately owned and operated minivans constitute St. Lucia's bus system, an inexpensive and efficient means of transportation used primarily by local people. Minivan routes cover the entire island and run from early morning until approximately 10 PM. You may find this method of getting around most useful for short distances, between Castries and the Rodney Bay area, for example; longer hauls can be uncomfortable. The fare between Castries and Gablewoods Mall is EC$1; Castries and Rodney Bay, EC$1.50; Castries and Vieux Fort (a trip that takes more than two hours), EC$7. Minivans follow designated routes (signs are displayed on the front window); ask at your hotel for the appropriate route number for your destination. Wait at a marked bus stop or hail a passing minivan from the roadside. In Castries, buses depart from the corner of Micoud and Bridge streets, behind the markets.

Each minivan has a driver and usually a conductor, a young man whose job it is to collect fares, open the door, and generally take charge of the passenger area. If you're sure of where you're going, simply knock twice on the metal window frame to signal that you want to get off at the next stop. Otherwise, just let the conductor or driver know where you're going, and he'll stop at the appropriate place.

BY CAR

To rent a car you must be at least 25 years old and provide a valid driver's license and a credit card. If you don't have an international driver's license, you must buy a temporary St. Lucian driving permit at car-rental firms, the immigration office at either airport, or the Gros Islet police station. The permit costs $20 (EC$54) and is valid for three months. Car-rental rates are usually quoted in U.S. dollars and range from $45 to $80 per day or $250 to $425 per week, depending on the car. Car-rental agencies generally include free pickup at your hotel and unlimited mileage.

St. Lucia has about 500 mi (800 km) of roads, but only about half (281 mi [450 km]) are paved. All towns and villages are connected to major routes. The highways on both coasts are winding and mountainous—particularly on parts of the West Coast Road. Driving in St. Lucia is on the left, British style. Observe speed limits, particularly the 30-mph (50-kph) limit within Castries. Respect no-parking zones; police issue tickets, and penalties start at about $15 (EC$40). Wear your seat belts. Gasoline is expensive.

🚗 **Avis** ✉ Vide Bouteille, Castries ☎ 758/452-2700 ✉ Rodney Bay ☎ 758/452-0782 ✉ Vieux Fort ☎ 758/454-6325 ✉ Vigie ☎ 758/452-2046. **Budget** ✉ Castries ☎ 758/452-0233 ✉ Vieux Fort ☎ 758/454-5311. **Cool Breeze Jeep/Car Rental** ✉ Soufrière ☎ 758/459-7729 ⊕ www.coolbreezecarrental.com. **Courtesy Car Rental** ✉ Bois d'Orange, Gros Islet ☎ 758/452-8140 ⊕ www.courtesycarrentals.com. **Hertz** ✉ Castries ☎ 758/452-0679 ✉ Vieux Fort ☎ 758/454-9636 ✉ Vigie ☎ 758/451-7351.

BY TAXI

Taxis are always available at the airports, the harbor, and in front of major hotels. They're unmetered, although nearly all drivers belong to a taxi cooperative and adhere to standard fares. Sample fares for up to four passengers are as follows: Castries to Rodney Bay, $16; Rodney Bay to Cap Estate, $10; Castries to Cap Estate, $20; Castries to Marigot Bay, $24; Castries to Soufrière, $70. Always ask the driver to quote the price *before* you get in, and be sure that you both understand whether it's in EC or U.S. dollars. Drivers are knowledgeable and courteous.

Contacts & Resources

BANKS & EXCHANGE SERVICES

The official currency is the Eastern Caribbean dollar (EC$). It's linked to the U.S. dollar at EC$2.67, but stores and hotels often exchange at EC$2.50 or EC$2.60. U.S. currency is readily accepted, but you'll probably get change in EC dollars. Major credit cards and traveler's checks are widely accepted. ATMs are available 24 hours a day at bank branches, transportation centers, and shopping malls, where you can use major credit cards to obtain cash (in local currency only). Major banks on the island include the Bank of Nova Scotia, FirstCaribbean International Bank, National Commercial Bank of St. Lucia, and the Royal Bank of Canada.

Prices quoted in this chapter are in U.S. dollars unless otherwise indicated.

Bank of Nova Scotia ✉ William Peter Blvd., Castries ☎ 758/452-2100 ✉ Rodney Bay ☎ 758/452-8805 ✉ Vieux Fort ☎ 758/454-6314. **FirstCaribbean International Bank** ✉ Bridge St., Castries ☎ 758/456-2100 ✉ Rodney Bay Marina, Rodney Bay ☎ 758/452-9384 ✉ Hewanorra Airport, Vieux Fort ☎ 758/454-6255 ✉ Soufrière ☎ 758/459-7255. **National Commercial Bank of St. Lucia** ✉ Bridge St., Castries ☎ 758/456-6000 ✉ Pointe Seraphine, Castries ☎ 758/452-4787 ✉ Hewanorra Airport ☎ 758/454-7780 ✉ Gros Islet ☎ 758/450-9851 ✉ Soufrière ☎ 758/459-7450. **Royal Bank of Canada** ✉ William Peter Blvd., Castries ☎ 758/452-2245 ✉ Rodney Bay Marina, Rodney Bay ☎ 758/452-9921.

BUSINESS HOURS

Banks are open Monday through Thursday from 8 to 3, Friday 8 to 5; a few branches in Rodney Bay are also open Saturday from 9 to noon. Post offices are open weekdays from 8:30 to 4:30. Most stores are open weekdays from 8:30 to 12:30 and 1:30 to 4:30, Saturday from 8 to 12:30; Gablewoods Mall shops are open Monday through Saturday from 9 to 7; J. Q.'s Shopping Mall shops are open from 9 to 8; Pointe Seraphine shops are open weekdays from 9 to 5, Saturday 9 to 2. Some hotel gift shops may be open on Sunday.

ELECTRICITY

The electric current on St. Lucia is 220 volts, 50 cycles, with a European-style square three-pin plug. A few large hotels have 110-volt outlets appropriate for most electric razors. To use most North American appliances, however, you'll need a transformer to convert voltage and a plug adapter; dual-voltage computers or appliances will still need a plug adapter. Hotels will sometimes lend you one for use during your stay.

EMBASSIES & CONSULATES

United Kingdom **British High Commission** ✉ N. I. S. Bldg., Waterfront, 2nd fl., Castries ☎ 758/452-2482.

EMERGENCIES

Victoria Hospital is St. Lucia's main hospital, on the southwest side of Castries harbor heading toward La Toc. Regional medical facilities are at Dennery Hospital, on the island's east coast; St. Jude's Hospital, near Hewanorra International Airport; and Soufrière Hospital, in the southwest.

Ambulance & Fire **Ambulance and fire emergencies** ☎ 911.

Hospitals **Dennery Hospital** ✉ Main Rd., Dennery ☎ 758/453-3310. **St. Jude's Hospital** ✉ Airport Rd., Vieux Fort ☎ 758/454-6041. **Soufrière Hospital** ✉ W. Quinlan St., Soufrière ☎ 758/459-7258. **Victoria Hospital** ✉ Hospital Rd., Castries ☎ 758/452-2421.

Pharmacies **M & C Drugstore** ✉ Bridge St., Castries ☎ 758/452-2811 ✉ J. Q.'s Shopping Mall, Rodney Bay ☎ 758/458-0178 ✉ Gablewoods Mall, Gros Islet Hwy., Choc Bay ☎ 758/451-7808 ✉ New Dock Rd., Vieux Fort ☎ 758/454-3760. **Williams Pharmacy** ✉ Bridge St., Castries ☎ 758/452-2797. Police **Dial 999. Marine police** ☎ 758/453-0770 or 758/452-2595. **Sea-Air Rescue** ☎ 758/452-2894, 758/452-1182, or 758/453-6664.

HEALTH

Tap water is perfectly safe to drink throughout the island, but you should be sure that fruit is peeled or washed thoroughly before eating it. Insects can be a real bother during the wet season (July–November), particularly in the rain forest; bring along repellent to ward off mosquitoes and sand flies.

HOLIDAYS

Public holidays are New Year's Day (Jan. 1), Independence Day (Feb. 22), Good Friday, Easter Monday, Labour Day (May 1), Whitmonday (7th Mon. after Easter), Corpus Christi (8th Thurs. after Easter), Emancipation Day (1st Mon. in Aug.), Carnival (3rd Mon. and Tues. in July), Thanksgiving Day (Oct. 25), National Day (Dec. 13), Christmas, and Boxing Day (Dec. 26).

LANGUAGE

English is the official language of St. Lucia and is spoken everywhere, but you can often hear local people speaking a French-creole patois (Kwéyòl) among themselves. If you're interested in learning some patois words and phrases, pick up a copy of *A Visitor's Guide to St. Lucia Patois,* a small paperback book sold in local bookstores for $4.

As in many of the Caribbean islands, to "lime" is to hang out and a "jump-up" is a big party with lots of dance music (often in the street, as in the village of Gros Islet every Friday night). Don't be surprised if people in St. Lucia call you "darling" instead of "ma'am" or "sir"—they're being friendly, not forward.

INTERNET, MAIL & SHIPPING

Many hotels and resorts in St. Lucia offer free or inexpensive Internet access to their guests. Internet cafés can be found in and around Rodney Bay Marina. Cable Wireless maintains a public Internet kiosk at Point Seraphine, in Castries, that accepts major credits or cash.

The General Post Office is on Bridge Street in Castries and is open weekdays from 8:30 to 4:30; all towns and villages have branches. Postage for airmail letters to the United States, Canada, and United Kingdom is EC95¢ per ½ ounce; postcards are EC65¢. Airmail letters to Australia and New Zealand cost EC$1.35; postcards, EC70¢. Airmail can take two or three weeks to be delivered—even longer to Australia and New Zealand.

🖩 **Cyber Connections** ⊠ Rodney Bay Marina, Gros Islet 🕾 758/450–9309. **Destination St. Lucia (DSL) Ltd.** ⊠ Rodney Bay Marina, Gros Islet 🕾 758/452–8531. **Snooty Agouti** ⊠ Rodney Bay, Gros Islet 🕾 758/452–0321.

PASSPORT REQUIREMENTS

U.S., Canadian, and British citizens whose stay does not exceed six months must have a valid passport or prove citizenship with a birth certificate (with a raised seal) and a government-issued photo ID. Visitors from other countries must present a valid passport. Everyone must have a return or ongoing ticket. We strongly urge all travelers going to the Caribbean to carry a valid passport; even if it's not an absolute requirement, you will always pass through Immigration with much more ease. Beginning January 1, 2008, U.S. citizens will need a valid passport to reenter the United States.

SAFETY

Although crime isn't a significant problem, take the same precautions you would at home—lock your door, secure your valuables, and don't carry too much money or flaunt expensive jewelry on the street.

TAXES & SERVICE CHARGES

The departure tax is $21 (EC$54), payable in cash only (either Eastern Caribbean or U.S. dollars). A government tax of 8% is added to all hotel and restaurant bills. There's no sales tax on goods purchased in shops. Most restaurants add a service charge of 10% to restaurant bills in lieu of tipping.

TELEPHONES

The area code for St. Lucia is 758. You can make direct-dial overseas and interisland calls from St. Lucia, and the connections are excellent. You can charge an overseas call to a major credit card with no surcharge. From public phones and many hotels, you can dial AT&T or MCI Worldcom and charge the call to your calling card to avoid expensive rates or hotel surcharges. Phone cards can be purchased at many retail outlets and used from any touch-tone telephone (including pay phones) in St. Lucia. You can dial local calls throughout St. Lucia directly from your hotel room by connecting to an outside line and dialing the seven-digit number. Some hotels charge a small fee (usually about EC50¢) for local calls. Pay phones accept EC25¢ and EC$1 coins. Phone cards can be used for local calls, as well as for international calls.

Your cell phone may work, but roaming charges may be prohibitively expensive. Cell phones can be rented from Cable & Wireless offices in Castries, Gablewoods Mall, Rodney Bay Marina, and Vieux Fort; or you can purchase a local SIM card at Cingular or Digitech offices in those same areas.

☎ **AT&T** ☎ 800/872-2881. **Cable & Wireless** ☎ 758/453-9922. **Credit Card Charge Call** ☎ 811. **MCI Worldcom** ☎ 800/888-8000.

TIPPING

Most restaurants add a 10% service charge to your bill in lieu of a tip; if one has not been added, a 10% to 15% tip is appropriate for good service. Tip porters and bellhops $1 per bag, although many of the all-inclusive resorts have a no-tipping policy. Taxi drivers also appreciate a 10% to 15% tip.

VISITOR INFORMATION

☎ Before You Leave **St. Lucia Tourist Board** ⊕ www.stlucia.org ⊠ 800 2nd Ave., 9th fl., New York, NY 10017 ☎ 212/867-2950 or 800/456-3984 ⎙ 212/867-2795 ⊠ 8 King St. E, Suite 700, Toronto, Ontario, Canada M5C 1B5 ☎ 416/362-4242 ⎙ 416/362-7832 ⊠ 1 Collingham Gardens, London, U.K. SW5 0HW ☎ 0870/900-7697.

☎ In St. Lucia **St. Lucia Tourist Board** ⊠ Sureline Bldg., Vide Bouteille, Box 221, Castries ☎ 758/452-4094 or 758/452-5968 ⎙ 758/453-1121 ⊠ Jeremie St., Castries ☎ 758/452-2479 ⊠ Pointe Seraphine, Castries ☎ 758/452-7577 ⊠ Bay St., Soufrière ☎ 758/459-7419 ⊠ George F. L. Charles Airport, Vigie, Castries ☎ 758/452-2596 ⊠ Hewanorra International Airport, Vieux Fort ☎ 758/454-6644.

WEDDINGS

St. Lucia may be *the* most popular island in all of the Caribbean for weddings and honeymoons. Nearly all St. Lucia's resort hotels and most of the small inns offer attractive wedding–honeymoon packages, as well as coordinators to handle the legalities and plan a memorable event. Sandals properties offer complimentary weddings to couples booking a minimum-stay honeymoon. Rendezvous, another couples-only resort, is also a popular wedding venue. Perhaps the most striking setting, though, is smack between the Pitons at either Ladera or the Jalousie Plantation.

To marry in St. Lucia, you must both be resident on the island for at least three days before the wedding ceremony. After two days, a local solicitor can apply for a license on your behalf. You must present valid passports, birth certificates, a decree absolute if either party is divorced, an appropriate death certificate if either party is widowed, and a notarized parental consent if either party is under the age of 18. License and registration fees total approximately $200. Most resorts have wedding coordinators who will help you put together the correct paperwork.

St. Maarten/
St. Martin

Beach, Ilet Pinel, Sint Maarten

WORD OF MOUTH

"A lot of St. Maarten is Americanized, touristy, and overbuilt . . . but there are still some very nice areas and it does have . . . excellent beaches, great and numerous restaurants, casinos, shopping, etc."

—RAB

"We were quite charmed by the culture on the French side, and the food is some of the best I have had anywhere. . . . Many beaches on the west side (Baie Rouge etc.) were rough but relatively deserted."

—katethetraveler

www.fodors.com/forums

WELCOME TO ST. MAARTEN & ST. MARTIN

TO ANGUILLA ↗

If you're on the island during the full moon, head out to Kali's Beach Bar, on lovely Baie de Friar, for the Full Moon Party, an island institution.

KEY
- ↗ Beaches
- ⛴ Cruise Ship Terminal
- ◣ Dive Sites
- ❶ Exploring Sights
- ⛴ Ferry
- ① Hotels & Restaurants

Map labels: Bel..., Baie de Grand Case, Grand Case, Baie de Friar, Aeropor l'Espéra..., Pt. Arago, Colombier, Baie de la Potence, 32–36, ❶❶ Le Fort Louis, ❶⓪ Marigot, Pte. du Bluff, Pte. des Pierres à Chaux, Baie Nettlé, Baie de Marigot, ◆ Musée de Saint-Martin, Pt. du Plum, Baie Rouge, Terres Basses, 40, 39, Sandy Ground, 37 38, Dutch Cul-de-Sac, Baie Longue, Simpson Bay Lagoon, Cupecoy Beach, 41 42, Juliana International Airport, Mullet Bay, 43, 46–48, Sentry Hill, ST. MAARTEN, Maho Bay, 44 45, Simpson Bay, 49, Koolbaai, Annie ◣, Cole Bay, Great Bay, 50, Little Bay, 51

TWO NATIONS, ONE ISLAND

St. Maarten/St. Martin is home to approximately 77,000 people from some 70 different countries, but governance of the 37-square-mi (96-square-km) island is split between France and the Netherlands. It's the smallest island in the world divided between two ruling powers. The Dutch capital is Phillipsburg; the French capital is Marigot.

Power shoppers will be drawn to Phillipsburg's recently revitalized Front Street, much of which has been turned into a pedestrian mall.

St. Maarten/St. Martin, a half-Dutch, half-French island, is a place where gastronomy flourishes, where most resorts are large rather than small, where casinos draw gamblers, where sporting opportunities are plentiful, and where the sunning, as on the south end of Orient Beach, is *au naturel*.

TO ST. BARTHÉLEMY →

Creole Rock

Pt. des Froussards

Anse Marcel

Red Rock

Grandes Cayes

Ile → Tintamarre

Ilet Pinel

French Cul de Sac **7**

Plantation Mont Vernon **8** **17** - **21**

Baie Orientale

Green Key

Pic du Paradis **6**

16

Butterfly Farm **5**

Orléans **4**

Galion Beach

Etang aux Poissons

Baie de L. Embouchure

ST. MARTIN

Boven Prinsen

Babit Pt.

Beneden Prinsen

St. Maarten Park **2**

14 **15** Dawn Beach

Mt. Flagstaf

1 - **12**

Sucker Garden Rd.

Guana Bay Point **3**

1 Philipsburg

Geneve Bay

Pelican Key

13

Salt Pond

ATLANTIC OCEAN

Pt. Blanche

Proselyte Reef

0 ___ 2 miles
0 ___ 2 km

TOP 4 REASONS TO VISIT ST. MAARTEN & ST. MARTIN

1 Grand Case is the island's gastronomic capital, but good food seeps from almost every island pore.

2 Phillipsburg is one of the best shopping spots in the Caribbean; with fewer bargains, Marigot is still chock-full of interesting stores.

3 Thirty-seven picture-perfect beaches are spread out all over the island.

4 The wide range of water sports—from sailing to waterskiing, from snorkeling to deep-sea fishing—will meet almost any need.

ST. MAARTEN/ST. MARTIN PLANNER

Getting to St. Maarten/St. Martin

You'll find many nonstop flights to St. Maarten from North America, France, and the Netherlands. Some U.S. airlines provide connecting service in San Juan. St. Maarten is also a hub for smaller, regional airlines, so it's often easier to make the hop to Anguilla, St. Barths, Saba, or St. Eustatius by making a connection here.

St. Maarten/St. Martin has two airports. Aeroport de L'Espérance (SFG), on the French side, is small and handles only island hoppers. Larger jets from North America and Europe fly into Princess Juliana International Airport (SXM), on the Dutch side.

Hassle Factor: Low to Medium

On the Ground

The majority of visitors to St. Maarten rent a car, but taxi service is available at the airport if you don't want to drive yourself, with fixed fares to all hotels on the island. Although the island is small, it's still a long drive to many hotels on the French side, so these taxi fares aren't cheap.

Renting a Car

The best and most economical way to get around St. Maarten is by car. You can book a car at Juliana International Airport, where all major rental companies have booths. There are both major car-rental chains as well as reputable local companies. Rates are among the best in the Caribbean. The only downside is that traffic can be very heavy, particularly around Marigot, where parking is especially difficult during the day.

Activities

The island's **beaches** are always a highlight, but few hotels are built on the very best beaches. Baie Orientale, the island's longest and most beautiful stretch of sand, is also the most developed, but even here few of the hotels are directly on the beachfront. You'll likely want to drive around to explore some of the more out-of-the-way spots. When you're not sunning and swimming, there are many activities to keep you going. **Sailing and snorkeling** trips are often the highlight of an island visit. **Fishing** is good in the waters around St. Maarten, but the **diving** is not the best, though there are some good sites. Baie Orientale is a center for all manner of **water sports,** and you'll see any number of people driving jet skis, parasailing, and water skiing from the shore. Perhaps one of the best activities on the island is eating. St. Martin's **restaurants,** particularly in Grand Case, which has long been known for its restaurant row, are some of the Caribbean's finest. At night, the **casinos** beckon. But don't expect Las Vegas-style gambling palaces; these casinos are much more modest in scale.

Where to Stay

The island, though small, is well-developed—some say over-developed—and offers a wide range of different kinds of lodging. If you want to stay in a larger resort or time-share, concentrate your accommodations search on the Dutch side; the French side has more intimate properties. Just keep in mind that many of the island's best restaurants are in Grand Case, which is a long drive from most Dutch-side hotels. Also remember that at French-side hotels you must pay in euros, so keep that in mind when you budget.

TYPES OF LODGINGS

Resorts & Time-shares:	Villas & Condos:	Small Inns:
Resorts & Time-shares: The island's large resorts are often good, but none can be considered truly great. Many have a large time-share component, so beware the hard sell, especially if someone in Phillipsburg offers you a "free" booze cruise in return for just a few minutes of your time.	**Villas & Condos:** Both sides of the island have a wide variety of villas and condos for every conceivable budget. If you look around, it's inevitable that you will find something that meets your needs. Several resort-style condo complexes offer a good alternative to a traditional hotel stay for families and groups.	**Small Inns:** Small guests houses and inns can be found on both sides of the island. Some of the best places on the island are actually the smallest and most unassuming. They are also booked solidly year-round, so plan ahead.

Hotel & Restaurant Costs

Assume that hotels operate on the European Plan (**EP**—with no meals) unless we specify that they use either the Continental Plan (**CP**—with a Continental breakfast), Breakfast Plan (**BP**—with full breakfast), or the Modified American Plan (**MAP**—with breakfast and dinner). Other hotels may offer the Full American Plan (**FAP**—including all meals but no drinks) or may be All-Inclusive (**AI**—with all meals, drinks, and most activities).

WHAT IT COSTS in Dollars

	$$$$	$$$	$$	$	¢
Restaurants	over $30	$20–$30	$12–$20	$8–$12	under $8
Hotels	over $350	$250–$350	$150–$250	$80–$150	under $80

Restaurant prices are for a main course at dinner, excluding tip. Hotel prices are for two people in a double room in high season excluding 5% tax, 10%–15% service charge, and meal plans.

When to Go

The high season begins in December and runs through the middle of April. During the off-season, hotel rooms can be had for as little as half the high-season rates.

The French side's **Carnival** is a pre-Lenten bash of costume parades, music competitions, and feasts. Carnival takes place after Easter on the Dutch side—last two weeks of April—with a parade and music competition. On the French side, parades, ceremonies and celebration commemorate **Bastille Day** on July 14 and there is more revelry later in the month on **Grand Case Day**. The Dutch side hosts the **Heineken Regatta** in early March, with as many as 300 sailboats competing from around the world. (For the experience of a lifetime, you can sometimes purchase a working berth aboard a regatta vessel.)

22

Updated by
Roberta
Sotonoff

THE MAJORITY OF THE YACHT CREW doesn't know the difference between a gaff and a gallow, but that isn't a deterrent for this race. Off they go aboard Dennis Connor's America's Cup winner *Stars and Stripes.* The wind howls through the sails, and Captain Morgan (not the pirate but a sailor from Jamaica) shouts, "Get ready to tack. We can take the lead." The trimmers, grinders, and winchers man their stations. The boat gets within hearing range of its rival, another America's Cup contender, *Canada II,* and friendly barbs are exchanged.

The St. Maarten 12-Metre Challenge is a singular experience. Then again, the island of St. Maarten/St. Martin is also quite unique. Where else can you find a 37-square-mi (96-square-km) island that is governed by two nations—the Netherlands and France—with residents from 70 different countries who speak who knows how many languages? Happily for Americans, who make up the majority of visitors, English works in both nations. Dutch St. Maarten will feel particularly comfortable for Americans, and you're as likely to run into an American expat there as anyone else, on the beach or not. But once you pass the meandering, unmarked border into the French side, you can find more pronounced differences. You'll be hard-pressed to find a washcloth unless your lodgings are very upscale, and it's almost necessary to be an engineer to bypass the safety mechanisms in the electrical outlets. And another thing: though U.S. dollars are happily accepted, be ready for wallet shock, because everything is priced in euros.

Almost 4,000 years ago, it was salt and not tourism that drove the little island's economy. Arawak Indians, the island's first known inhabitants, prospered until the warring Caribs invaded, adding the peaceful Arawaks to their list of conquests. Columbus spotted the isle in 1493, but it wasn't populated by Europeans until the 17th century, when it was claimed by the Dutch, French, and Spanish. The Dutch and French finally joined forces to claim the island in 1644, and the Treaty of Concordia partitioned the territory in 1648.

Both sides of the island offer a little European culture along with a lot of laid-back Caribbean ambience. Water sports abound—diving, snorkeling, scuba, sailing, windsurfing, and in late February the Heineken Regatta, with as many as 300 sailboats competing from around the world. (For the experience of a lifetime, some visitors purchase a working berth aboard a regatta vessel.)

With soft trade winds cooling the subtropical climate, it's easy to while away the day on one of the 37 beaches, or shop Philipsburg's newly remodeled Front Street or the *rues* (streets) of the very French town of Marigot. While luck is an important commodity at St. Maarten's 13 casinos, chance plays no part in finding a good meal at the excellent eateries or after-dark fun in the subtle to sizzling nightlife. Still, the isle's biggest assets are its friendly residents.

Although the island has been heavily developed—especially on the Dutch side—roads could still use work. When cruise ships are in port (and there can be as many as seven at once), shopping areas get crowded and traffic moves at a snail's pace. Still, these are minor inconveniences

Concordia

CLOSE UP

THE SMALLEST ISLAND in the world to be shared between two different countries, St. Maarten has existed peacefully in its subdivided state for more than 350 years. The Treaty of Concordia, which subdivided the island, was signed in 1648 and was really inspired by the two resident colonies of French and Dutch settlers (not to mention their respective governments) joining forces to repel a common enemy, the Spanish, in 1644. Although the French were promised the side of the island facing Anguilla and the Dutch the south side of the island, the boundary itself wasn't firmly established until 1817 and then after several disputes (16 of them, to be exact).

Visitors to the island will likely not even notice that they have passed from the Dutch to the French side unless they notice the rather distinctive concrete electrical poles. In 2003, the population of French St-Martin voted to secede from Guadeloupe, the administrative capital of the French West Indies, but this hadn't happened at this writing.

22

compared to the feel of the sand between your toes or the breeze through your hair, gourmet food sating your appetite, or the ability to crisscross between two nations on one island.

Where to Stay

Scattered up and down the beaches—particularly Simpson Bay and Maho Bay in St. Maarten and Baies Orientale and Nettle in St. Martin—and within the city limits of both Philipsburg and Marigot are a multitude of accommodations. They offer a variety of prices and tastes. Lodgings range from megaresorts like the Sonesta Maho Beach to condos and small inns. On the Dutch side many hotels cater to groups, and although that's also true to some extent on the French side, you can find a larger collection of intimate accommodations there. Time-shares have become extremely popular options on the island, even though most accommodations are available to the general public. Keep in mind that off-season rates (April through the beginning of December) can be as little as half the high-season rates.

Hotels

DUTCH SIDE

$$$–$$$$

Princess Heights. Sitting on a hill 900 feet above Oyster Bay, this property's spacious suites offer plenty of privacy. Each tastefully decorated apartment has one or two separate bedrooms, a kitchen (whose side-by-side refrigerator comes stocked with complimentary drinks), marble bathrooms with whirlpool tubs, and a white-balustrade balcony with a smashing view of St. Barths. You also get daily maid service. The only downside is the numerous steps, which make it unsuitable for the physically challenged, and the location, which makes a rental car a necessity. It's 4 mi (6 km) from Philipsburg. At this writing, 18 larger suites were under construction and were expected to open sometime in late

2006. ⊠ *156 Oyster Pond Rd., Oyster Pond* 🕾 *599/543–6906 or 800/ 441–7227* 🖷 *599/543–6007* ⊕ *www.princessheights.com* ↩ *15 suites* ᇰ *Fans, in-room safes, kitchens, minibars, cable TV, pool, gym, massage, beach, babysitting, dry cleaning, laundry service, concierge, car rental* ⊟ *AE, MC, V* ⏍ *EP.*

🕲 **$$–$$$** 🖼 **Divi Little Bay Beach Resort.** Popular with tour groups looking more for price than poshness, this resort offers handsome sea views from the balconies of simple and comfortable rooms. At best, service is mediocre. On the other hand, the property borders a lovely, not very crowded beach that juts out into Little Bay, and there are certainly enough activities to keep you busy. It's also a quick trip into the heart of Philipsburg. ⊠ *Little Bay Rd., Box 961, Philipsburg* 🕾 *599/542–2333 or 800/367–3484* 🖷 *599/542–4336* ⊕ *www.diviresorts.com* ↩ *235 rooms* ᇰ *3 restaurants, grocery, some kitchenettes, some refrigerators, cable TV, some in-room VCRs, tennis court, 3 pools, gym, hair salon, spa, beach, dive shop, snorkeling, boating, 3 bars, shops, children's programs (ages 3–12), laundry facilities, laundry service, car rental* ⊟ *AE, D, DC, MC, V* ⏍ *EP.*

$$–$$$$ 🖼 **Oyster Bay Beach Resort.** Jutting out into Oyster Bay, this out-of-the-way apartment resort on the shores of Dawn Beach was renovated in 2004. Rooms are spacious and tastefully decorated with bright colors, and all have balconies that feature a fine view of St. Barths or the marina in Oyster Bay. The open-air lobby is as attractive as the free-form infinity pool. Besides the Jade Restaurant, there's Beau Beau's, which features island dishes and dancing waitresses, the Beaubettes. You definitely need a car if you stay here. Note that there's a $5 per day charge for air-conditioning in the studios. ⊠ *10 Emerald Merit Rd., Oyster Pond* ⊕ *Box 239, Philipsburg* 🕾 *599/543–6040 or 866/978–0212* 🖷 *599/ 543–6695* ⊕ *www.oysterbaybeachresort.com* ↩ *178 condos* ᇰ *2 restaurants, grocery, in-room safes, kitchenettes, cable TV, some in-room VCRs, pool, gym, hot tub, massage, beach, bicycles, bar, shops, laundry facilities, car rental* ⊟ *AE, D, MC, V* ⏍ *EP.*

$$–$$$$ 🖼 **Sonesta Maho Beach Resort & Casino.** Las Vegas glitz and hoopla rule in the island's largest hotel on beautiful Maho Beach. Whatever your pleasure—sunning or swimming, sailing or shopping, dancing to dawn, or being pampered in the full-service spa—the island's largest resort also has the widest range of activities. Rooms have balconies with sea or garden views. Not only is its lobby the biggest in the Caribbean, but the resort has a casino, a Las Vegas–style theater, five clubs, three restaurants, and 40 shops. Seven other restaurants and an outlet mall surround the resort complex; there's no reason to stray farther. ⊠ *Airport Rd., Box 834, Maho Bay* 🕾 *599/545–2115, 800/223–0757, or 800/766–3782* 🖷 *599/545– 3180* ⊕ *www.sonesta.com* ↩ *600 rooms* ᇰ *3 restaurants, in-room safes, cable TV, in-room data ports, 4 tennis courts, 2 pools, health club, spa, beach, 3 bars, casino, dance club, shops, babysitting, business services, meeting rooms, car rental* ⊟ *AE, D, DC, MC, V* ⏍ *EP.*

$$–$$$ 🖼 **The Inn at Cupecoy.** Overlooking Cupecoy Beach, which is just down the road, this cozy little inn oozes comfort and luxury. Rooms are furnished with zebra-skin rugs, antique chaise lounges, and four-poster king-size beds adorned with high-end linens. Large bathrooms have marble vanities and travertine sinks. The complimentary Continental breakfast is served poolside. The Market at Cupecoy supplies gourmet foods, baked goods, cheese, and wine, while the Citrus restaurant specializes in French cuisine. The entire inn can also be rented out as a five-bedroom villa. ✉ *130 Lowlands, Cupecoy* ☎ *599/545–4333* 🖷 *599/545–4333* ⊕ *www. theinnatcupecoy.com* 🛏 *5 rooms* ⚒ *Restaurant, grocery, cable TV, in-room DVD, pool, concierge, airport shuttle* ▭ *AE, D, MC, V* ⏀ *CP* ⊘ *Closed Aug. 20–Oct. 20.*

★ **$$–$$$** ⬚ **La Vista.** Hibiscus and bougainvillea line brick walkways that connect the 32 wood-frame, Caribbean-style bungalows and beachfront suites of this intimate and friendly family-owned resort perched at the foot of Pelican Key. Rooms are somewhat sparse with a small bathroom but include a balcony that faces an awesome view of the sea. The beach is rocky but good for snorkeling. ✉ *Billy Folly Rd. 53, Pelican Key, Box 2086, Simpson Bay* ☎ *599/544–3005 or 599/544–2650/2652* 🖷 *599/ 544–3010* ⊕ *www.lavistaresort.com* 🛏 *18 rooms, 32 suites* ⚒ *Restaurant, fans, in-room safes, some kitchens, some kitchenettes, cable TV, 2 pools, beach, shop, laundry facilities* ▭ *AE, D, MC, V* ⏀ *EP.*

⏀ **$–$$$** ⬚ **Great Bay Beach Resort & Casino.** Location, location, location. Away from the docks that are usually crawling with cruise ships but only a 10-minute walk to downtown Philipsburg and a 15-minute ride from the airport, this resort is especially well positioned. It reopened in early 2005 after a total, $10 million renovation with a circular marble lobby that faces Great Bay and overlooks the cruise-ship pier on one side and mountains on the other. Caribbean-accented guest rooms are spacious but generic and include wood furniture plus new bathrooms with granite vanities. Sound insulation seems to be almost nonexistent, so your neighbors' conversation as well as their comings and goings often reverberate in your room. The hotel caters to tour groups and offers an all-inclusive plan. Its big plus is the white-sand beach, which is not overcrowded. ✉ *1911 Little Bay Rd., Great Bay* ⏀ *Box 91, Philipsburg* ☎ *599/542–2446 or 800/223–0757* 🖷 *599/542–3859* ⊕ *www. greatbaybeachresort.com* 🛏 *210 rooms, 22 studios, 30 suites* ⚒ *3 restaurants, in-room safes, some in-room hot tubs, cable TV, tennis court, 2 pools, gym, hair salon, hot tub, beach, snorkeling, boating, shuffleboard, 4 bars, casino, nightclub, shops, children's programs (ages 4–12), car rental* ▭ *AE, D, DC, MC, V* ⏀ *EP.*

$–$$ ⬚ **The Horny Toad.** This lovely guesthouse is widely considered the best
Fodor's Choice on the Dutch side. Its virtues are many: the stupendous view from the
★ beach out to Simpson Bay, the clean comfort of the rooms, each of which is individually decorated. But the one thing that keeps patrons coming back year after year is the friendly hospitality of owner Betty Vaughn (ask her how the inn got its name). She treats her guests like long-lost relatives and is so welcoming that you simply can't resist her charms. Book early, because the Toad fills up fast. All rooms but one have air-conditioning. ✉ *2 Vlaun Dr., Simpson Bay* ☎ *599/545–4323 or 800/ 417–9361* 🖷 *599/545–3316* ⊕ *www.thehornytoadguesthouse.com* 🛏 *8 rooms* ⚒ *Fans, kitchens, beach, laundry service; no a/c in some rooms, no room TVs, no kids under 7* ▭ *AE, D, MC, V* ⏀ *EP.*

★ **¢–$$$** ⬚ **Mary's Boon Beach Plantation.** On a lovely stretch of Simpson Bay, the small, inviting guesthouse with a shaded courtyard now has 32 rooms.

Pilot Mary Pomeroy chose this site because of its proximity to the airport. Seek out someone to tell you about her life and her mysterious disappearance. Indonesian-style furniture decorates the lobby as well as the rooms, which also have cathedral ceilings, Queen Anne four-poster king-size beds, and verandas. You'll find an honor bar and a well-known restaurant with a menu that has not changed since the mid-1970s. Because of its location, it can get a bit noisy at times. ☒ *117 Simpson Bay Rd., Simpson Bay* ☎ *599/545–7000* 🖷 *599/545–3403* ⊕ *www. marysboon.com* 🖘 *32 rooms* ⚒ *Restaurant, fans, some kitchens, some kitchenettes, cable TV, in-room data ports, pool, beach, 2 bars, Internet room* ☰ *AE, D, MC, V* ⎮○⎮ *EP.*

$–$$ 🏨 **Holland House Beach Hotel.** An ideal location for shopaholics and sun worshippers, this hotel faces directly onto the new Front Street pedestrian mall; to the rear is a lovely stretch of Great Bay Beach. The open lobby provides easy access from street to beach and has free Internet access. Rooms are basic but comfortable and have balconies and kitchenettes; reasonably priced meals are found at the open-air seaside restaurant. ☒ *43 Front St., Box 393, Philipsburg* ☎ *599/542–2572 or 800/ 212–9815* 🖷 *599/542–4673* ⊕ *www.hhbh.com* 🖘 *48 rooms, 6 suites* ⚒ *Restaurant, some in-room faxes, in-room safes, some kitchenettes, refrigerators, cable TV, beach, lounge, Internet room, meeting room* ☰ *AE, D, DC, MC, V* ⎮○⎮ *EP.*

★ **$–$$** 🏨 **Pasanggrahan Royal Inn.** Guests are treated like friends rather than customers at this cozy inn—the oldest hotel on the island. In 1905, it was built as the governor's house. The walls of the entranceway are lined with pictures of Dutch royalty. Specialty rooms have carved furniture, four-poster beds with mosquito netting, and private balconies, while standard rooms have more of an island look, with plantation-style furniture, mosquito netting and shared balconies. The hotel's restaurant serves excellent meals for a reasonable price; the view looking out over the beach on Great Bay isn't bad, either. And, in case you are wondering, *pasanggrahan* means guesthouse in Indonesian. ☒ *15 Front St., Box 151, Philipsburg* ☎ *599/542–3588 or 599/542–2743* 🖷 *599/542–2885* ⊕ *www.pasanhotel.com* 🖘 *31 rooms* ⚒ *Restaurant, in-room safes, refrigerators, cable TV, beach, bar* ☰ *AE, D, MC, V* ⎮○⎮ *EP.*

$ 🏨 **Delfina Hotel.** If you don't need to be directly on the beach, this small, gay-owned gingerbread-style hotel about a half mile from Cupecoy Beach is a good choice. Comfortable, white-tiled rooms are nicely decorated, each with pictures of a famous film icon. Rooms surround a small pool and a tropical garden. An inviting, second-floor space is the site for happy hour and the complimentary Continental breakfast. Close to the airport and Simpson Bay, the hotel is about 15 minutes from Marigot. Friendly owners Boris and Michael will give you advice on what to do and where to eat. Nice anytime, it's a particularly good deal in low season. ☒ *Tigris Rd. 14–16, Côte d'Azur, Cupecoy* ☎🖷 *599/545–3300* ⊕ *www.delfinahotel.com* 🖘 *12 rooms* ⚒ *Fans, in-room safes, refrigerators, cable TV, pool, gym, outdoor hot tub* ☰ *AE, MC, V* ⎮○⎮ *CP.*

FRENCH SIDE Unless otherwise specified, breakfast is included with the room rate.

22

★ **$$$$**   ⌂ **Green Cay Village.** Surrounded by 5 acres of lush greenery high above Orient Bay, these villas are a perfect place for small groups or families who are looking for privacy and quiet. Each villa has its own pool, and both interiors and exteriors have a West Indian creole flair. The villas are quite spacious—the largest is 4,500 square feet with three bedrooms, two baths, living room (only four have air-conditioning), and a large deck, full kitchen, and dining patio. If you rent just the cheaper "studio" portion, you can still get a kitchenette and a large bedroom with a seating area. The beach and restaurants are a short walk away. ⌧ *Parc de la Baie Orientale, Box 3006, Baie Orientale 97063* ☎ *590/ 87–38–63, 888/843–4760, or 866/592–4213* 🖷 *590/87–39–27* ⊕ *www. greencayvillage.com* ➫ *16 villas* ⚹ *Kitchens, cable TV, in-room VCRs, tennis court, 16 pools, babysitting, laundry service, airport shuttle* ⊟ *AE, MC, V* ¶⊙¶ *CP.*

$$$$ ⌂ **La Samanna.** A dazzling stretch of white-sand beach borders 55 luscious acres of this ultrachic resort on St. Martin's French side. Rooms

Fodor's Choice
★

are smartly designed with tiled floors, mahogany and teak imports, as well as DVD players and pop-up TVs. A few of the suites have private sundecks on their roofs. Expect impeccable service and privacy (for $200 per day you can even rent a curtained beach cabana equipped with TV). The hotel offers a wide array of activities, including one-on-one Pilates and yoga at the newly remodeled workout facility. At the Elysées Spa, Mediterranean decor is surrounded by a lush private garden and waterfall. Many treatment rooms include a private outdoor shower. In the main dining room, cuisine combines Asian, French, and creole influences. Each course can be paired with a selection of more than 450 different wines from the hotel's cellar. For cocktails, there's an authentic Moroccan bar. ⌧ *Baie Longue* ⌕ *Box 4007, Marigot 97064* ☎ *590/87–64–00 or 800/854–2252* 🖷 *590/87–87–86* ⊕ *www.lasamanna.orient-express. com* ➫ *27 rooms, 54 suites* ⚹ *2 restaurants, fans, in-room safes, some kitchens, cable TV, in-room VCRs, 3 tennis courts, pool, health club, spa, beach, windsurfing, waterskiing, bar, shops* ⊟ *AE, MC, V* ⊗ *Closed Sept. and Oct.* ¶⊙¶ *BP.*

$$–$$$$ ⌂ **Alamanda Resort.** Esmeralda's sister hotel sits directly on the white-sand beach of Orient Bay. Funky painted doors decorated with cutout boats, fish, and other oceany things lead to roomy, comfortable, colonial-style suites with terraces that overlook the pool, beach, or the ocean. Two-level rooms have sundecks. Alamanda Café is surrounded by a fragrant tropical garden; the Kakao Beach restaurant is seaside. A hotel card gives you access to activities and beach restaurants at any resort in the area. The friendly staff at the 24-hour activity desk will be happy to arrange island activities. ⌧ *Baie Orientale* ⌕ *BP 5166, Grand Case* ☎ *590/52–87–40 or 800/622–7836* 🖷 *590/52–87–41* ⊕ *www.alamanda-resort.com* ➫ *42 rooms* ⚹ *2 restaurants, room service, fans, in-room safes, kitchenettes, cable TV, 2 tennis courts, pool, gym, windsurfing, jet skiing, parasailing, dry cleaning, laundry service, Internet room, meeting rooms, car rental* ⊟ *AE, MC, V* ¶⊙¶ *BP.*

$$–$$$$ ⌂ **Esmeralda Resort.** The short path from Orient Bay is just long enough to whisk you away from the crowds. Seventeen of the 18 upscale villas, which can be configured into separate rooms, have their own private pool. Caribbean-style rooms all have private terraces and fully equipped kitchenettes. A 24-hour activities desk can arrange snorkeling, car rental, tennis, and babysitting. The resort has two restaurants—Astrolabe for fine dining and Coco Beach for anything from Caribbean and tapas to sushi and burgers. To make your beach life easier, you receive a hotel card for activities and beach restaurants, good at any resort in the area. ⌂ *Box 5141, Baie Orientale 97071* ☎ *590/87–36–36 or 800/622–7836* 🖷 *590/87–35–18* ⊕ *www.esmeralda-resort.com* ⇆ *65 rooms in 18 villas* ♨ *2 restaurants, room service, fans, in-room safes, some kitchens, some kitchenettes, cable TV, 2 tennis courts, 17 pools, massage, beach, snorkeling, windsurfing, parasailing, waterskiing, shops, babysitting, laundry service, Internet room, business services* ⊟ *AE, MC, V* ⊠ *EP.*

★ **$$–$$$$** ▦ **Grand Case Beach Club.** A welcome bottle of wine at check-in is a nice touch. Then again, there are many nice things about this beachfront condo property, including a very friendly staff and the spectacular views of neighboring Anguilla. Fully equipped kitchens have a good-size refrigerator plus granite counters; CD players are standard in every apartment. Although room service is available from the Sunset Café, the fabulous restaurants of Grand Case are within walking distance. ⌂ *21 rue de Petit Plage, at north end of blvd. de Grand Case, Box 339, Grand Case 97150* ☎ *590/ 87–51–87 or 800344–3016* 🖷 *590/87–59–93* ⊕ *www. grandcasebeachclub.com* ⇆ *72 condos* ♨ *Restaurant, in-room safes, kitchens, cable TV, in-room DVD, tennis court, beach, snorkeling, waterskiing, bar, shops, laundry facilities, laundry service, Internet room, car rental* ⊟ *AE, MC, V* ⊠ *CP.*

$$–$$$$ ▦ **Hotel Beach Plaza.** What is most appealing about this hotel is its location right on Baie de Marigot and a 10-minute walk from the heart of Marigot itself, making it attractive to both business travelers and vacationers. Terraced rooms are simple but adequate—opt for the seaside view. The three-story atrium lobby is airy and quite attractive. The harbor side has a restaurant and freshwater pool with a poolside bar. Because of the small beach and general lack of amenities, it's not recommended for families with children or for an extended stay. ⌂ *Baie de Marigot, 97150* ☎ *590/87–87–00* 🖷 *590/87–18–87* ⊕ *www. hotelbeachplazasxm.com* ⇆ *144 rooms* ♨ *Restaurant, room service, in-room safes, minibars, cable TV, Wi-Fi, pool, dive shop* ⊠ *BP.*

★ **$$–$$$$** ▦ **Hôtel L'Esplanade Caraïbes.** Guests often return to this popular hilltop, Mediterranean-style hotel for its quiet elegance and excellent service. When you arrive, you'll find your suite stocked with a welcome basket containing a baguette, cookies, and other goodies. All the suites have beamed ceilings, teak furniture, and smashing views of the bay and the village of Grand Case from the patio; some have a loft bedroom. Two curved stone staircases lead to the gardens and pool. A path down the hillside leads to the fabulous restaurants of Grand Case and the beach. ⌂ *Box 5007, Grand Case 97150* ☎ *590/87–06–55 or 866/596–8365* 🖷 *590/87–29–15* ⊕ *www.lesplanade.com* ⇆ *24 units* ♨ *In-room safes, kitchens, cable TV, 2 pools, wading pool, laundry service, car rental* ⊟ *AE, MC, V* ⊠ *EP.*

$$$–$$$$ ▦ **Le Domaine de Lonvilliers.** The former L'Habitation de Lonvilliers has been remodeled and reopened with a new name. One end of its charming, open-air lobby leads to a tropical garden with a covered path that meets the sea. All of the lattice-trimmed, gingerbread-style balconies of the spacious, creole-style rooms face the garden. Accented in yellow and turquoise, each room has a rounded bathtub alongside a window, a flat-screen TV, coffeemaker, and an in-room safe that can accommodate a laptop. The attractive pool area contains a waterfall, gazebo, and Jacuzzi. Continental and fusion cuisines are the specialties at La Veranda Restaurant. To reach the hotel, bear north at French Cul de Sac. ⊠ *Anse Marcel 97150* ☎ *590/52–34–52* 🖨 *590/29–10–81* ⊕ *www.ledomainestmartin.com* ⤵ *120 rooms, 18 suites* ♿ *Restaurant, room service, fans, minibars, some kitchens, in-room safes, cable TV, hair salon, hot tub, massage, pool, wading pool, beach, bar, laundry service, Internet room, airport shuttle, car rental* ▭ *AE, DC, MC, V* �backslash◯ *BP.*

$$–$$$$ 🏨 **Le Petit Hotel.** Surrounded by some of the best restaurants in the Caribbean, this tiny hotel right on the beach in downtown Grand Case oozes charm. A Mediterranean staircase leads to its eight spacious rooms, as well as a studio and a one-bedroom suite. Each room is simple but plush, with a duvet on the bed, kitchenette, flat-screen TV and DVD player, kitchenette, CD player, and even a terrace. Trays and baskets are provided at the self-serve "buffet" breakfast of croissants, coffee, and freshly squeezed juices in the lobby; you can then carry these yummies back to your room. Because the hotel itself has no pool, you're invited to use the pool and beach at the sister hotel, Hôtel L'Esplanade Caraïbes. ⊠ *248 blvd. de Grand Case, Grand Case 97150* ☎ *590/29–09–65* 🖨 *590/87–09–19* ⊕ *www.lepetithotel.com* ⤵ *8 rooms, 1 studio, 1 suite* ♿ *Fans, in-room safes, kitchenettes, cable TV, beach* ▭ *AE, MC, V* ⱺ◯ *CP.*

☾ **$$–$$$** 🏨 **Le Flamboyant.** The creole-style architecture of the indoor-outdoor lobby is quite inviting at this fairly reasonably priced hotel. Rooms are comfortably furnished with creole-style, carved wood and rattan pieces; each room also has a terrace that faces either the garden or the lagoon and is equipped with an outdoor kitchenette. A nightly shuttle to the casinos on the Dutch side is a plus, as are opportunities for a variety of recreational activities, including playing tennis on a lighted tennis court, kayaking and snorkeling in Baie Nettlé, and even enjoying water aerobics. ⊠ *Rte. des Terres Basses, Baie Nettlé* ☎ *590/87–60–00* 🖨 *590/87–60–57* ⊕ *www.hmc-hotels.com* ⤵ *198 junior suites, 62 suites, 11 duplex suites* ♿ *Restaurant, bar, kitchenettes, in-room safes, cable TV, 2 pools, gym, hot tub, beach, meeting rooms* ▭ *AE, DC, MC, V* ☾ *Closed early Sept.–mid-Oct.*

★ **$–$$$** 🏨 **Hotel La Plantation.** Perched high above Orient Bay, this charming, colonial-style hotel is a delight. French doors open to a wraparound veranda that reveals a lovely view of Orient Bay and where sometimes a resident cat can be found napping. Each large villa is composed of a suite and two studios, each of which can be rented separately. Suites and studios are accented with yellow, green, and stenciled wall decorations. All have mosquito nets over their king-size beds, CD players, and a fair-size bathroom with a large shower and two sinks. Alongside the pool is the cozy Café Plantation, where Monday's Lobster Night is a deliciously good deal. The beach is about a 10- to 15-minute walk. ⊠ *C5*

Parc de La Baie Orientale 97150 St. Martin ☎ *590/29–58–00* 🖶 *590/ 29–58–08* ⊕ *www.la-plantation.com* ⊲ᵓ *17 suites, 34 studios* ⚱ *Restaurant, fans, in-room safes, some kitchenettes, cable TV, 2 tennis courts, pool, gym, shop, babysitting, car rental* ▤ *AE, MC, V* ⊺◉⊺ *BP.*

Villas

Both sides of the island have villas of different sizes and for different budgets. **Carimo** (✉ Rue du Général de Gaulle, Box 220, Marigot 97150 ☎ 590/87–57–58 or 866/978–5297 ⊕ www.carimo.com) rents villas in the tony Terres Basses area as well as Simpson Bay and Baie Longue. **French Caribbean International** (✉ 5662 Calle Real, No. 333, Santa Barbara, CA 93117-2317 ☎ 805/967–9850 or 800/322–2223 ⊕ www. frenchcaribbean.com) offers island condos and villas on the French side of the island. **Island Hideaways** (𝄐 3843 Highland Oaks Dr., Fairfax, VA 22033 ☎ 800/832–2302 or 703/378–7840 ⊕ www.islandhideaways. com) represents several rental properties. In business since the 1970s, it's the oldest villa-rental company on the island. **Jennifer's Vacation Villas** (✉ Simpson Bay Yacht Club, St. Maarten ⊕ www. jennifersvacationvillas.com) rents villas on both sides of the island. **Villas of Distinction** (𝄐 951 Transport Way, Petaluma, CA 94904 ☎ 800/ 289–0900 ⊕ www.villasofdistinction.com) is one of the oldest villa rental companies serving the island. **WIMCO** (𝄐 Box 1461, Newport, RI 02840 ☎ 401/849–8012 or 800/932–3222 ⊕ www.wimco.com) has more hotel, villa, apartment, and condo listings in the Caribbean than just about anyone else.

Where to Eat

Although most people come to St. Maarten/St. Martin for fun and sun, they leave craving the cuisine, and that's not surprising. Every day, delicacies are flown here from all over the world. Of course, you'll be able to find fine French cuisine, but foods from around the globe—Argentine, Asian, Italian, Tex-Mex, Vietnamese, American, Bavarian, and of course creole and Caribbean—make their way to the kitchens of the island's restaurants. Dining in St. Maarten is not cheap, but the price usually reflects the high quality of the culinary creations.

During the high season, it's essential to **make reservations,** and making them a month in advance is advisable for some of the best places. Often restaurants include a 15% service charge, so go over your bill before tipping. However, you can't always leave tips on your credit card, so carry cash, too. A taxi is probably the easiest solution to the parking problem in the main restaurant areas, particularly in Grand Case and Philipsburg but during the high season also in Marigot. Marigot has free parking near the waterfront and throughout the town; Grand Case has two lots—each costs $4—at each end of the main boulevard, but they are always crowded.

What to Wear

Appropriate dining attire on this island ranges from swimsuits to sport jackets. For men, a jacket and khakis or jeans will take you anywhere; for women, dressy pants, a skirt, or even fancy shorts are usually acceptable. Jeans are fine in the less formal eateries. In the listings below dress is casual (and chic) unless otherwise noted, but ask when making reservations if you're unsure.

Dutch Side

ASIAN
$$–$$$

✕ **Wajang Doll.** Indonesian dishes are served here in a small, simple setting next to the water. *Nasi goreng* (fried rice) and red snapper in a sweet soy glaze are standouts, as is rijsttafel, a traditional Indonesian meal of rice accompanied by 15 to 20 small dishes. (The restaurant's name comes from the *wajang* doll, which is used in Indonesian shadow plays, a traditional art form.) ⊠ *Royal Village Unit 5, Welfare Rd. 58, Cole Bay* ☎ *599/544–2255* ⊟ *AE, MC, V* ⊙ *No lunch.*

CAFÉ
¢–$

✕ **Au Petit Café Français.** Under new ownership since late 2005, this quaint little bistro with indoor-outdoor seating offers tarts, fresh crêpes, hearty salads, pizza, and hot or cold sandwiches on fresh bread. A little, out-of-the-way café—just off Back Street in Philipsburg—this spot is still worth the visit for a quick, inexpensive snack or for a freshly ground cup of coffee. Watching employees make the crêpes is half the fun; eating them is the other half. It opens at 11 AM. ⊠ *120 Old St., Philipsburg* ☎ *No phone* ⊙ *Closed Sun. No dinner* ⊟ *No credit cards.*

CARIBBEAN
$–$$

✕ **Turtle Pier Bar & Restaurant.** The open-air setting, sea breezes, wood-plank floors, and huge lobster tank leave no doubt that you're sitting on a pier in the Caribbean. Unfortunately, the atmosphere outweighs the food, though both coconut shrimp and lobster that you can choose yourself are decent specialties. Open seven days a week for breakfast, lunch, and dinner, Turtle Pier has a notable lobster night, all-you-can-eat Sunday rib dinners, dinner-cruise specials, and live music several nights a week. ⊠ *114 Airport Rd., Simpson Bay* ☎ *599/545–2562* ⊟ *AE, D, MC, V.*

CONTINENTAL
$–$$$

✕ **Chesterfield's.** On the Great Bay waterfront, a five-minute walk from the ship pier in Philipsburg, nautically themed "Chesty's" serves breakfast, lunch, and dinner at reasonable prices. The main fare is steak and seafood, though the dinner menu includes Duck Chesterfield (roast duckling with fresh pineapple-and-banana sauce) and several different shrimp dishes. The Mermaid Bar is popular with yachties, locals, and tourists alike. There's ample parking. ⊠ *Great Bay Marina, Philipsburg* ☎ *599/542–3484* ⊟ *MC, V.*

ECLECTIC
★ $$$–$$$$

✕ **Saratoga.** Since the late 1980s Saratoga has built a loyal following of return patrons. The handsome mahogany-paneled dining room in the yacht club's stucco and red-tile building overlooks the Simpson Bay Marina. The menu changes daily, but you can never go wrong with one of the fresh fish dishes; several Caribbean and creole dishes are always on the menu and also uniformly good. You might start with a spicy ceviche of snapper with mango and tortilla chips, then segue into grilled grouper fillet or a cured pork tenderloin. The wine list includes 150 different wines, including 12 choices by the glass. ⊠ *Simpson Bay Yacht Club, Airport Blvd., Simpson Bay* ☎ *599/544–2421* 🖶 *599/544–2423* ⚱ *Reservations essential* ⊟ *AE, D, MC, V* ⊙ *Closed Sun. Closed Aug. and Sept. No lunch.*

22

$–$$$ ✕ **Oualichi Beach Bar & Restaurant.** One of the newer kids in town, this fun, nautical-themed eatery serves up mostly pizza and burgers. You can sit outside or inside, where the glass-covered bar is lined with sand, shells, and other beachy things. This is a popular hangout, and everyone on the island seems to love the Oualichi pizza. ✉ *Great Bay Beach Boardwalk, Philipsburg* ☎ *599/543–4316* ☰ *AE, D, MC, V* ☻ *No dinner Sun.*

$–$$$ ✕ **The Green House.** This open-air harborfront restaurant in Philipsburg balances a relaxed atmosphere, reasonable prices, and quality food with a just-right, flavorful bite. All the beef served is black Angus, and some people say the burgers and steaks are the best on the island. If you're seeking something spicy, try the black-bean soup or Jamaica jerked chicken wrap. Monday and Tuesday happy-hour specials, not to mention Friday-night lobster specials, are widely popular. The restaurant is between Bobby's Marina and the start of Front Street at the marina on Great Bay. ✉ *Bobby's Marina, Knaalsteeg, Philipsburg* ☎ *599/542–2941* ☰ *AE, D, MC, V.*

$$ ✕ **Taloula Mango's.** Ribs are the specialty at this casual beachfront restaurant, but the jerk chicken and thin-crust pizza are not to be ignored. Sandwiches, seafood, beef, pasta, and vegetarian entrees also grace the menu. On Sunday evenings, Taloula's has live jazz; each Friday there is a band on the nearby boardwalk. In case you are wondering, the restaurant got its name from the owner's lab puppy. ✉ *Sint Rose Shopping Mall, off Front St. on the beach boardwalk, Philipsburg* ☎ *599/542–1642* ☰ *AE, D, MC, V.*

$ ✕ **Kangaroo Court Café.** This little restaurant is renowned for its great coffee, but the gourmet burgers, pizza, salads, fruit frappés, and one of the island's largest selection of wines by the glass are not too shabby either. The funky patio area in the former childhood home of owner Norman Wathey is the best place to enjoy your repast. Ruins from an old salt storage area, a small waterfall, and a huge ficus tree are the main decor. Almond trees shade it so well that nets are installed to keep nuts and leaves from hitting diners. ✉ *6 Henrick St., Philipsburg* ☎ *599/542–7557 or 599/542–1644* 🖷 *599/542–5378* ☰ *AE, D, MC, V,* ☻ *No dinner.*

FRENCH ✕ **Antoine.** You'd be hard-pressed to find a more enjoyable evening in ★ **$$–$$$$** Philipsburg. Owner Jean Pierre Pomarico's warmth shines through as he greets guests and ushers them into the comfy seaside restaurant. Low-key, blue-accented decor, white bamboo chairs, water-colors lining the walls and candles—along with the sound of the nearby surf—create a very relaxing atmosphere. But you came for the food. Well, the pastas, seafood, and meat entrées are delicious. House specialties are lobster bisque and/or lobster thermidor (a succulent tail oozing with cream and Swiss cheese) and are fabulous. There's valet parking. A $29 prix-fixe menu is a bargain. ✉ *119 Front St., Philipsburg* ☎ *599/542–2964* ⌘ *Reservations essential* ☰ *AE, D, MC, V.*

$$–$$$$ ✕ **L'Escargot.** A wraparound veranda, bunches of grapes hanging from a chandelier, and Toulouse Lautrec–style murals liven up this cheery, colorful cottage, one of St. Maarten's friendliest and most venerable restaurants. Of course, snails are the specialty, but if you're not sure how you like them prepared, ask owners Jöel and Sonya for an escargot sampler appetizer. Or try one of the many lobster, shrimp, duck, or melt-in-your-mouth steak dishes. There's also a Friday-night dinner show in the tradition of *La Cage aux Folles*. ⊠ *84 Front St., Philipsburg* ☎ *599/542–2483* ⊟ *AE, MC, V.*

INDIAN
$$

✕ **Shiv Sagar.** The colors of India—notably yellow and green—as well as Hindu pictures decorate the walls of this large, second-floor restaurant in Philipsburg. The menu emphasizes Kashmiri and Mughal specialties, including marvelous tandooris (especially the boneless chicken) and curries, but try one of the less familiar dishes such as *madrasi machi* (red snapper with hot spices) or curry coconut shrimp. ⊠ *20 Front St., opposite First Caribbean International Bank, Philipsburg* ☎ *599/542–2299* ⊟ *AE, D, DC, MC, V* ⊗ *Closed Sun.*

STEAK
★ $$–$$$$

✕ **Los Gauchos Argentine Grill.** You don't expect to find first-quality Argentine meat on an island where foodies seek out French cuisine and seafood, but here it is. The restaurant, decorated with cow-print chairs, has some of the best beef in town. Specialties are juicy, free-range steaks, complemented with a good helping of potatoes and salad. Non-red-meat-eaters will find chicken, fish, and even vegetarian selections on the menu. Vinos from Argentina are featured on the wine list. ⊠ *Pelican Resort Club Marina, Philipsburg* ☎ *599/542–4084* ⊟ *D, MC, V.*

VEGETARIAN
¢–$

✕ **Top Carrot.** This vegetarian café and juice bar serves sandwiches, salads, and homemade pastries for breakfast and lunch, until closing time at 3 PM. The offerings are both delicious and healthy, including a pastry stuffed with pesto, avocado, red pepper, and feta cheese or a cauliflower, spinach, and tomato quiche. Other health-food specialties include homemade granola and yogurt. Adjacent to the restaurant is a small gift shop with Asian-inspired items plus books on eating healthily. ⊠ *Airport Rd., near Simpson Bay Yacht Club, Simpson Bay* ☎ *599/544–3381* ⊟ *No credit cards.*

French Side

CARIBBEAN
$$–$$$

✕ **Claude Mini-Club.** This brightly decorated upstairs restaurant, with a sweeping view of Marigot Harbor, has served traditional creole and French cuisine since 1969. The chairs and madras tablecloths are a mélange of sun yellow and orange. The whole place is built (tree-house-style) around the trunks of coconut trees. It's the place to be on Wednesday and Saturday nights, when the dinner buffet (40€) includes conch or onion soup, baked ham, blackened goose meat, lobster, roast beef, and all the trimmings. Fresh snapper is one of the specialties on the à la carte menu. There's live music nightly. ⊠ *Front de Mer, Marigot* ☎ *590/87–50–69* ⊟ *AE, MC, V* ⊗ *No lunch Sun.*

$

✕ **Enoch's Place.** Enoch's cooking draws crowds of locals and visitors each day to the blue-and-white-striped awning on a corner of the Marigot Market. Local specialties include garlic and creole shrimp, rice and beans (like your St. Martin mother used to make), and fresh lobster. For breakfast, try cod in fried johnnycakes. Enoch's Place is one of about a dozen mini-restaurants—all worth visiting—in this unusual open-air building on the waterfront. ⊠ *Marigot Market, Front de Mer, Marigot* ☎ *590/29–29–88* ⊟ *No credit cards* ⊗ *Closed Sun. No dinner.*

22

★ $$ ✕ **Paradise View.** This is one place you don't want to miss if you are near Orient Beach. It's hard to figure what's best—the killer view that sweeps over Orient Beach, the coast, Pinel Island, and St. Barths or the tales that owner Claudette Davis weaves from her aerie perch. This friendly lady serves tasty burgers and sandwiches, as well as more substantial fare like ribs, steak, seafood, and some creole specialties. There's always a $10 lunch special, a $15 dinner special, and an abundance of 'ti punch and mango madness. ✉ *Hope Hill, Baie Orientale* ☎ *590/29–45–37* ▭ *AE, MC, V* ☯ *Closed Mon.*

CONTEMPORARY ✕ **Le Tastevin.** Filled with flowers, plants, and coconut trees and deco-
$$$ rated in blue and white, this chic Grand Case enclave looks out on the bay. Owner Daniel Passeri, a native of Burgundy, also founded the homey L'Auberge Gourmande across the street. The menu changes frequently, but you might find ambitious offerings like foie gras with figs, crab tartare with tomato, or beef with sauterne sauce; you'll always find fresh fish and seafood. Two prix-fixe menus can help control costs. ✉ *86 blvd. de Grand Case, Grand Case* ☎ *590/87–55–45* ☯ *Closed Sun. Sept.–Oct.* ⌲ *Reservations essential* ▭ *AE, MC, V.*

ECLECTIC ✕ **Le Pressoir.** Combine excellent food, a good selection of French
★ $$$–$$$$ wine, a setting in a charming 1871 West Indian house, and a bill that won't break the bank, and you have a great restaurant. French and creole cuisine reign, especially fresh local fish. Try the sea scallops and shrimp with saffron sauce, one of the succulent duck or beef entrées, or the house seafood specialty (a first course of shrimp, scallops, and mussels and a second with four types of grilled fish). End your meal with warm chocolate cake served with delicious ice cream. ✉ *30 blvd. de Grand Case, Grand Case* ☎ *590/87–76–62* ▭ *AE, MC, V* ☯ *Closed Sun. No lunch.*

$$$ ✕ **Le Rainbow.** You might be tempted to drift out with the sea breeze
Fodor'sChoice while sitting at one of the beachside tables and watching the waves. That
★ would be a big mistake. The cuisine in this comfortable bistro includes mouthwatering shrimp and scallop *duo de gambas* with an island-style chutney. The attentive staff and friendly owners make the place even more inviting. There's a pipe-and-cigar bar upstairs. ✉ *176 blvd. de Grand Case, Grand Case* ☎ *590/87–55–80* ▭ *AE, MC, V* ☯ *Closed Sun.*

★ $–$$$ ✕ **La Main à La Pâte.** A great place to people-watch, this Marina Royale restaurant offers a world-ranging menu with everything from pizza to fish to pasta, plus daily specials to please most palates. It combines impeccable service (all waitstaff speak at least two languages) with exceptional food, making it one of the outstanding, must-try restaurants on St. Martin. A highlight is the lobster-tail salad, which is a light combination of firm lobster meat. La Palette Caraïbes, which includes three different fish, includes the tastiest tuna steak on the island. Be sure to ask about passion pie with mango ice cream for dessert. ✉ *Marina Royale on waterfront, Marigot* ☎ *590/87–71–19* ▭ *D, MC, V.*

$–$$ ✕ **La Belle Epoque.** A favorite among locals, this sometimes frenzied little bistro is on the marina. Whether you stop for a drink or a meal, you'll soon discover that it's a prime venue for boat- and people-watching. The staff are friendly and the menu varied—pizza, pasta, fresh salads, lobster, and daily specials of seafood and fish. ⊠ *Marina Royale, Marigot* ☎ *590/87–87–70* ⊟ *AE, MC, V.*

$$–$$$ ✗ **Waikiki Beach.** Thatched roofs cover the booths at this happening beach bar and restaurant on beautiful Baie Orientale. The food runs the gamut from marinated tofu with shiitake mushrooms and seaweed to local Caribbean fare and seafood. Service is friendly, and the food is delicious. You can also book a variety of water sports at the restaurant. ⊠ *5 Baie Orientale* ☎ *590/87–43–19* ⊘ *No dinner* ⊟ *MC, V.*

FRENCH ✗ **Le Santal.** One of the island's nicest restaurants is out of the way (turn **$$$$** left immediately before the bridge heading into Marigot from Sandy Ground), and the neighborhood is a bit scruffy, but the interior is transformed by soft lighting, mirrors, china, and crystal. Specialties by chef Marc Daniel, who trained at Paris's Lasserre restaurant, include roasted lobster with shallots and tomatoes, foie gras sautéed in cassis, and lacquered duck. Reserve one of the five cherished waterside tables. ⊠ *40 rue Lady Fish, Sandy Ground* ☎ *590/87–53–48* ⌖ *Reservations essential* ⊟ *AE, MC, V.*

★ **$$$–$$$$** ✗ **Mario's Bistro.** This romantic eatery earns raves for its fine service and high-quality cuisine. Didier Gonnon and Martyne Tardif are out front, while chef Mario Tardif is in the kitchen creating dishes such as sautéed sea scallops with white truffle oil or some sort of poultry dish like honey-garlic glazed, roasted crispy duck. The open-air country French–style restaurant is on the canal just after you cross the bridge from Sandy Ground, and if you didn't know better you might think you were in Venice. ⊠ *At the Sandy Ground Bridge, Sandy Ground* ☎ *590/87–06–36* ⌖ *Reservations essential* ⊟ *MC, V* ⊘ *Closed Sun. and mid-June–Aug. No lunch.*

★ **$$–$$$$** ✗ **Bistrot Nu.** It's hard to top the simple, unadorned fare and reasonable prices you can find at this intimate restaurant tucked in a Marigot alley. Traditional brasserie-style food—coq au vin, fish soup, snails—is served in a friendly, intimate dining room. The prix-fixe menu is a very good value. The place is enormously popular, and the tables are routinely packed until it closes at midnight. It can be difficult to park here, so take your chances at finding a spot on the street—or try a taxi. ⊠ *Rue de Hollande, Marigot* ☎ *590/87–97–09* ⊟ *MC, V* ⌖ *Reservations essential* ⊘ *Closed weekends. No lunch.*

$$$ ✗ **L'Auberge Gourmande.** Decorated arches frame the elegant and charming dining room in this 120-year-old French Antillean house where chef Didier Rochat delights his guests with appetizers like garlic escargost and coquilles St. Jacques with scallops and shrimp. Rack of lamb and a filet mignon are both excellent main-course choices, but be aware that although his offerings are pleasing to the palate, they wreck the waistline. The restaurant also has a good selection of wines. As is the common problem in Grand Case, parking can be a challenge. ⊠ *89 blvd. de Grand Case, Grand Case* ☎ *590/87–73–37* ⊟ *MC, V* ⊘ *No lunch.*

★ **$$–$$$** ✗ **Tropicana.** This bustling but friendly bistro at the Marina Royale attracts shoppers, tourists, and locals who enjoy both the food and the vibrant ambience. Lunch salads, such as the salad niçoise with medallions of crusted goat cheese, are massive and tasty; dinner choices, which include traditional bistro favorites, are also wonderful. The presentations make the food even better. Desserts are especially good, and you will never be disappointed with old standbys like the crème brûlée. You can dine outside or inside along the yacht-filled waterfront. ⊠ *Marina Royale, Marigot* ☎ 590/87–79–07 ▭ D, MC, V.

Beaches

Warm surf and a gentle breeze can be found at the island's 37 beaches, and every one of them is open to the public. What could be better? Each of the beaches is unique: some bustling and some bare, some refined and some rocky, some good for snorkeling and some good for sunning. Whatever you fancy in the beach landscape department, you can find it here, including nude at Baie Orientale's south end. If you plan on keeping your valuables, it's a good idea to leave them at the hotel.

Dutch Side

Cupecoy Beach. This picturesque area of sandstone cliffs, white sand, and shoreline caves is actually a series of beaches that come and go according to the whims of the sea. Though the surf can be rough, it's popular with gay locals and visitors. It's very close to the Dutch-French border. ⊠ *Cupecoy, between Baie Longue and Mullet Bay.*

★ **Dawn Beach–Oyster Pond.** If you're an early riser, Dawn Beach is the place to be at sunrise. On the Atlantic side of Oyster Pond, just south of the French border, this is a first-class beach for sunning and snorkeling. It's not usually crowded, and there are several restaurants nearby. To find it, follow the signs for either Mr. Busby's or Scavenger's restaurant. ⊠ *South of Oyster Pond.*

Great Bay. This beach is probably the easiest to find. Recently widened, the bustling, white sand curves around Philipsburg and is just behind Front Street, shopping, and eateries. Because of the cruise ships and the salt pond, it's not the best for swimming, but if you must, do it west of Captain Hodge pier. ⊠ *Philipsburg.*

Little Bay. Popular with snorkelers and divers as well as kayakers and motorized water-sports enthusiasts, Little Bay isn't as crowded as some beaches, but the sand is somewhat gravelly. What it does have are panoramic views of St. Eustatius, Philipsburg, the cruise-ship terminal, Saba, and St. Kitts. The beach is west of Fort Amsterdam and accessible via the Divi Little Bay Resort. ⊠ *Little Bay Rd.*

Mullet Bay Beach. Many believe that this mile-long, powdery white-sand beach near the medical school is the island's best. Swimmers like it because the water is usually calm. When the swell is up, the surfers hit the beach. It's also the place to listen for the "whispering pebbles" as the waves wash up. ⊠ *Mullet Bay, south of Cupecoy.*

Simpson Bay Beach. This secluded, half-moon stretch of white-sand beach on the island's Caribbean side is a hidden gem. It's mostly surrounded by private residences, so there are no big resorts, jet skiers, food concessions, or crowds. It's just you, the sand, and the water. Southeast of the airport, follow the signs to Mary's Boon and the Horny Toad guesthouses. ⊠ *Simpson Bay.*

French Side

★ **Baie de Friars.** If it's solitude you want, this is the place. Popular with locals, Europeans, and shellers, this white stretch of sand has a couple of simple good-food restaurants, calm waters, and a lovely view of Anguilla. To get to the beach take National Road 7 from Marigot, go toward Grand Case to the Morne Valois hill, and turn left on the dead-end road; it's signposted. From Baie de Friars, you can climb the hill and walk on a trail about ¼ mi (½ km) through an abandoned resort to reach secluded Happy Bay. ⊠ *Baie de Friar.*

Baie de Grand Case. A stripe of a beach, its sandy shoreline borders the fishing community of Grand Case Village. The sea is calm, water sports are available, and if the sun becomes too much, you can stop sunning and have a bite to eat at one of the *lolos* (barbecue huts that serve inexpensive local fare) or explore the charming little hamlet with its gingerbread-style architecture and its renowned restaurants. ⊠ *Grand Case.*

Baie Longue. Though it extends over the French Lowlands, from the cliff at La Samanna to La Pointe des Canniers, the island's longest beach has no facilities or vendors. It's the perfect place for a romantic walk. To get there, take National Road 7 south of Marigot. The entrance marked LA SAMANNA is the first entrance to the beach. ⊠ *Baie Longue.*

Fodor'sChoice
★
Baie Orientale. Many consider this the island's most beautiful beach, but its satiny white sand, underwater marine reserve, variety of water sports, beach bars, and hotels also make it the most crowded. The conservative north end is more family-oriented while the liberal south end is clothing-optional and eventually becomes a full-scale nude beach. To get to Baie Orientale from Marigot, take National Road 7 past Grand Case, past the Aéroport de L'Espérance toward the Atlantic side of the island. ⊠ *Baie Orientale.*

Baie Rouge. The sheltered Baie Rouge, in the French Lowlands, got its name from the lightly tinted, soft sand that borders the shoreline and is thought to have the best snorkeling beaches on the island. It's possible to swim the crystal waters along the point and explore a swim-through cave. The beach is fairly popular with the area's gay men. Baie Rouge is five minutes from Marigot, right off the main western road, Route 7, at the Nettlé Bay turnoff. ⊠ *Baie Rouge.*

Ilet Pinel. A protected nature reserve, this kid-friendly island is a five-minute ferry ride from French Cul de Sac ($5 per person round-trip). The water is clear and shallow, and the shore is sheltered. If you like snorkeling, don your gear and swim along both sides of the coasts of this pencil-shape speck in the ocean. Food is available at the isle's two restaurants. ⊠ *Ilet Pinel.*

Sports & the Outdoors

BOATING &
SAILING
The island is surrounded by water, so why not get out and enjoy it? The water and winds are perfect for skimming the surf. It'll cost you around $1,000 per day to rent a 28- to 40-foot power boat, considerably less for smaller boats or small sailboats.

Lagoon Sailboat Rental (⊠ Airport Rd., near Uncle Harry's, Simpson Bay ☎ 599/557–0714 ⊕ www.lagoonsailboatrental.com) has 20-foot day sailers for rent within Simpson Bay Lagoon for $150 per day, with a half-day for $110. Either explore on your own or rent a skipper to navigate the calm, sheltered waters from around Simpson Bay Yacht Club and miles of coastline on both the French and Dutch sides of the islands.

The **Moorings** (✉ Captain Oliver's Marina, Oyster Pond ☎ 590/87–32–54 or 888/952–8420 ⊕ www.moorings.com) has a fleet of Beneteau yachts as well as bareboat and crewed catamarans for those who opt for a sailing vacation.

Random Wind (☎ 599/544–5148 or 599/557–5742 ⊕ www.randomwind. com) offers half- and full-day sailing and snorkeling trips on a 54-foot clipper. Prices depend on size of the group and whether or not lunch is served, but the Paradise Daysail on the costs $85 per person. Departures are on the Dutch side, from Ric's Place at Simpson Bay.

★ Sailing experience is not necessary for the **St. Maarten 12-Metre Challenge** (✉ Bobby's Marina, Philipsburg ☎ 599/542–0045 or 800/786–2278 ⊕ www.12metre.com), one of the island's most popular activities. Participants compete on 68-foot racing yachts, including Dennis Connor's *Stars and Stripes* (the actual boat that won the America's Cup in 1987) and the *Canada II*. Anyone can help the crew grind winches, trim sails, and punch the stopwatch, or you can just sit back and watch everyone else work. The St. Maarten Challenge imitates an abbreviated America's Cup route, and the cost to participate in the two-plus hour race is $75. The thrill of it is priceless, but book your trip in advance; this is the most popular shore excursion offered by cruise ships in the Caribbean.

FISHING   You can angle for yellowtail snapper, grouper, marlin, tuna, and wahoo on deep-sea excursions. Costs (for four people) range from $425 for a half-day to $750 for a full day. Prices usually include bait and tackle, instruction for novices, and refreshments. Ask about licensing and insurance. **Big Sailfish Too** (✉ Anse Marcel ☎ 690/27–40–90) is your best bet on the French side of the island. **Lee's Deepsea Fishing** (✉ 84 Welfare Rd., Simpson Bay ☎ 599/544–4233 or 599/544–4234 ⊕ www. leesfish.com) organizes excursions, and when you return, Lee's Roadside Grill will cook your tuna, wahoo, or whatever else you catch and keep. **Rudy's Deep Sea Fishing** (✉ 14 Airport Rd., Simpson Bay ☎ 599/ 545–2177 ⊕ www.rudysdeepseafishing.com) has been around for years and is one of the more experienced sport-angling outfits.

GOLF   St. Maarten is not a golf destination. Although **Mullet Bay Golf Course** (✉ Airport Rd., north of the airport ☎ 599/545–2801), on the Dutch side, is an 18-hole course, it's the island's *only* one. Though lately it has been better tended, it is still not in the best of shape and many feel not worth the cost.

HORSEBACK   Island stables offer riding packages—from novice to expert—for $25
RIDING   to $40 (€40 to €60) per hour for a beach ride. Ask about full-moon and sunset rides. You can arrange rides directly or through most hotels. **Bayside Riding Club** (✉ Galion Beach Rd., Baie Orientale ☎ 590/ 87–36–64 ⊕ www.baysideridingclub.com), on the French side, is a long-established outfit that can accommodate experienced and novice riders. On the Dutch side contact **Lucky Stables** (✉ Traybay Drive 2, Cay Bay ☎ 599/544–5255 ⊕ www.luckystable.com), which offers mountain- and beach-trail rides, including a romantic champagne night ride. Rides start at $45.

22

KAYAKING Kayaking is becoming very popular and is almost always offered at the many water-sports operations on both the Dutch and the French sides. Rental starts at about $15 per hour. On the Dutch side, **Little Bay Watersports & Dive Center** (☎ 599/542–2333) rents kayaks. On the Dutch side, **TriSport** (✉ Airport Road 14B, Simpson Bay ☎ 599/545–4384 ⊕ www.trisportsxm.com) does organized lagoon paddles and snorkeling tours by kayak.

On the French side kayaks are available at **Kayak Tour** (✉ French Cul de Sac ☎ 599/557–0112 or 690/47–76–72).

PARASAILING On the French side, **Kontiki Watersports** (✉ Northern beach entrance, Baie Orientale ☎ 590/87–46–89 ⊕ www.sxm-game.com) offers parasailing for $40 per half-hour to $70 per hour on Baie Orientale, giving you aerial views of Green Key, Tintamarre, Ilet Pinel, and St. Barths. Fees are $50 for single fly and $90 for double fly. You can also rent Jet Skis for $45 for a half-hour and $80 for an hour. On the Dutch side, **Westport Water Sports** (✉ Simpson Bay ☎ 599/544–2557), at Kim Sha Beach, has Jet Skis for rent and offers parasailing excursions.

SCUBA DIVING The water temperature here is rarely below 70°F (21°C). Sometimes visibility is excellent, averaging about 100 feet to 120 feet. Other times, it is not. The island has more than 40 good dive sites, from wrecks to rocky labyrinths. Beginners and night divers will appreciate the tugboat *Annie,* which lies in 25 feet to 30 feet of water in Simpson Bay. Off the north coast, in the protected and mostly current-free Grand Case Bay, is **Creole Rock.** The water here ranges in depth from 10 feet to 25 feet, and visibility is excellent. Other sites off the north coast include **Ilet Pinel,** for its good shallow diving; **Green Key,** with its vibrant barrier reef; and **Tintamarre** (Flat Island), for its sheltered coves and geologic faults. Right outside of Philipsburg, 55 feet under the water, is the HMS *Proselyte,* once explored by Jacques Cousteau. Although it sank in 1801, the boat's cannons and coral-encrusted anchors are still visible. On average, one-tank dives start at $55; two-tank dives start at $85. Certification courses start at $390.

On the Dutch side, **Dive Safaris** (✉ Bobby's Marina, Yrausquin Blvd., Philipsburg ☎ 599/544–9001 ⊕ www.thescubashop.net) is a full-service outfit for divers. SSI- (Scuba Schools International) and PADI-certified dive centers include **Ocean Explorers Dive Shop** (✉ 113 Welfare Rd., Simpson Bay ☎ 599/544–5252 ⊕ www.stmaartendiving.com).

On the French side, **Blue Ocean** (✉ Sandy Ground Rd., Baie Nettlé ☎ 590/87–89–73) is a PADI-certified dive center. **Octoplus** (✉ Blvd. de Grand Case, Grand Case ☎ 590/87–20–62) is a complete PADI-certified dive center. **O2 Limits** (✉ Blvd. de Grand Case, Grand Case ☎ 690/50–04–00), in the Grand Case Beach Club, is PADI-certified.

SNORKELING Some of the best snorkeling on the Dutch side can be found around the rocks below Fort Amsterdam off Little Bay Beach, in the west end of Maho Bay, off Pelican Key, and around the reefs off Oyster Pond Beach. On the French side, the area around Orient Bay—including Caye Verte (Green Key), Ilet Pinel, and Flat Island—is especially lovely and is officially classified and protected as a regional underwater nature reserve. Sea creatures also congregate around Creole Rock at the point of Grand Case Bay. The average cost of an afternoon snorkeling trip is about $35 per person. **Aqua Mania** (⊠ Pelican Marina, Simpson Bay ☎ 590/544–2640 ⊕ www.stmaarten-activities.com) is a multitasking water-sports outfitter offering snorkeling and diving trips, motorized and nonmotorized equipment and cruises. **Blue Ocean** (⊠ Sandy Ground Rd., Baie Nettlé ☎ 590/87–89–73) offers snorkeling trips. **Eagle Tours** (⊠ Bobby's Marina, Philipsburg ☎ 599/542–3323 ⊕ www.sailingsxm.com) combines sailing, snorkeling, and lunch aboard a 76-foot catamaran. Arrange equipment rentals and snorkeling trips through **Kontiki Watersports** (⊠ Northern beach entrance, Baie Orientale ☎ 590/87–46–89 ⊕ www.sxm-game.com).

SEA EXCURSIONS The 50-foot catamaran *Bluebeard II* (⊠ Simpson Bay ☎ 599/545–2898) sails around Anguilla's south and northwest coasts to Prickly Pear Cay, where there are excellent coral reefs for snorkeling and powdery white sands for sunning. The cost is $75 (plus $9 tax) per person. For low-impact sunset and dinner cruises, contact skipper Neil of the catamaran *Celine* (⊠ Simpson Bay ☎ 599/545–3961 ⊕ www.sailstmaarten.com), which is moored behind Turtle Pier Bar & Restaurant. The sleek 76-foot catamaran *Golden Eagle* (☎ 599/542–3323) takes day sailors to outlying islets and reefs for snorkeling and partying. You can take day cruises to Prickly Pear Cay, off Anguilla, aboard the *Lambada,* sunset and dinner cruises on the 65-foot sail catamaran *Tango* with **Little Bay Watersports & Dive Center** (☎ 599/552–7749 Ext. 3160).

A cross between a submarine and a glass-bottom boat, the 34-passenger *Seaworld Explorer* (⊠ Blvd. de Grand Case, Grand Case ☎ 599/542–4078 ⊕ www.atlantisadventures.com), a semi-submarine, crawls along the water's surface from Grand Case to Creole Rock; while submerged in a lower chamber, passengers view marine life and coral through large windows. Divers jump off the boat and feed the fish and eels.

WATERSKIING Expect to pay $50 per half-hour for waterskiing, $40 to $45 per half-hour for jet-skiing. On the Dutch side, rent waterskiing and jet-skiing equipment through **Aqua Mania Watersports** (⊠ Pelican Marina, Simpson Bay ☎ 599/544–2640 ⊕ www.stmaarten-activities.com), a full-service water-sports activity center. On the French side, **Kontiki Watersports** (⊠ Northern beach entrance, Baie Orientale ☎ 590/87–46–89 ⊕ www.sxm-game.com) rents windsurfing boards, takes water-skiers out, and provides instruction.

WINDSURFING The best windsurfing is on Galion Bay on the French side. From November to May, trade winds can average 15 knots. **Club Nathalie Simon** (⊠ Northern beach entrance, Baie Orientale ☎ 590/29–41–57 ⊕ www.wind-adventures.com) offers rentals and lessons in both windsurfing and kite surfing. One-hour lessons are about €40. **Windy Reef** (⊠ Galion Beach, past Butterfly Farm ☎ 690/52–58–18) has provided windsurfing lessons and rentals since 1991.

Shopping

It's true that the island sparkles with its myriad outdoor activities—diving, snorkeling, sailing, swimming, and sunning—but shopaholics are drawn to sparkle within the jewelry stores. The huge array of such stores is almost unrivaled in the Caribbean. In addition, duty-free shops offer substantial savings—about 15% to 30% below U.S. and Canadian prices—on cameras, watches, liquor, cigars, and designer clothing. It's no wonder that each year 500 cruise ships make Philipsburg a port of call. On both sides of the island, be alert for idlers. They can snatch unwatched purses.

Prices are in dollars on the Dutch side, in euros on the French side. As for bargains, there are more to be had on the Dutch side.

Areas

Philipsburg's **Front Street** has reinvented itself. Now it's mall-like, with redbrick walk and streets, palm trees lining the sleek boutiques, jewelry stores, souvenir shops, outdoor restaurants, and the old reliables—including McDonald's and Burger King. Here and there a school or a church appears to remind visitors there's more to the island than shopping. Back Street is where you'll find the **Philipsburg Market Place,** an open-air market where you can haggle for bargains on items such as handicrafts, souvenirs, and cover-ups. **Old Street,** near the end of Front Street, has stores, boutiques, and open-air cafés offering French crêpes, rich chocolates, and island mementos. You can find an outlet mall amid the more upscale shops at the **Maho** shopping plaza. The **Plaza del Lago** at the Simpson Bay Yacht Club complex has an excellent choice of restaurants as well as shops.

On the French side, wrought-iron balconies, colorful awnings, and gingerbread trim decorate Marigot's smart shops, tiny boutiques, and bistros in the **Marina Royale** complex and on the main streets, **rue de la Liberté** and **rue de la République.** Also in Marigot is the pricey **West Indies Mall** and the **Plaza Caraïbes,** which houses designer shops like Hermès and Ralph Lauren.

Specialty Stores

ART GALLERIES **Dona Bryhiel Art Gallery** (⌗ Oyster Pond ☎ 590/87–43–93), on the French side before the turnoff to Captain Oliver's Marina, deals mostly in modern figurative paintings by the owner, who will delight you with stories of her life and the paintings, which are steeped in romantic French and Caribbean traditions. **Galerie Lynn** (⌗ 83 blvd. de Grand Case, Grand Case ☎ 590/87–77–24) sells stunning paintings and sculptures created by the multitalented Lynn family, originally from New York. **Gingerbread Galerie** (⌗ Marina Royale, Marigot ☎ 590/87–73–21) specializes in Haitian art. **Greenwith Galleries** (⌗ 33 Front St., Philipsburg ☎ 599/542–3842) has a broad selection of Caribbean artists. **Minguet Art Gallery** (⌗ Rambaud Hill ☎ 590/87–76–06), between Marigot and Grand Case, is managed by the daughter of the late artist Alexandre Minguet. The gallery carries original paintings, lithographs, posters, and postcards depicting island flora and landscapes by Minguet, as well as original works by Robert Dago and Loic BarBotin. **Roland Richardson Gallery** (✉ 6 rue de la République, Marigot ☎ 590/87–32–24) sells oil and watercolor paintings by well-known local artist Roland Richardson. The gallery, with a garden studio in the rear, is worth visiting even if you don't intend to buy a painting, and you may meet the artist himself or his stepmother.

DUTY-FREE GOODS
Carat (✉ 16 rue de la République, Marigot ☎ 590/87–73–40 ✉ 73 Front St., Philipsburg ☎ 599/542–2180) sells china and jewelry. **Lipstick** (✉ Plaza Caraïbes, rue du Kennedy, Marigot ☎ 590/87–73–24 ✉ 31 Front St., Philipsburg ☎ 599/542–6051) has an enormous selection of perfume and cosmetics. **Little Europe** (✉ 80 Front St., Philipsburg ☎ 599/542–4371 ✉ 1 rue du Général de Gaulle, Marigot ☎ 590/87–92–64) sells fine jewelry, crystal, and china. **Little Switzerland** (✉ 6 rue de la Liberté, Marigot ☎ 590/87–09–02 or 800–524–2010 ✉ 52 Front St., Philipsburg ☎ 599/542–3530) purveys watches, fine crystal, and china, as well as perfume and jewelry. **Manek's** (✉ Rue de la République, Marigot ☎ 590/87–54–91) sells, on two floors, luggage, perfume, jewelry, Cuban cigars, duty-free liquors, and tobacco products. **Oro Diamante** (✉ 62-B Front St., Philipsburg ☎ 599/543–0343) carries loose diamonds, jewelry, watches, perfume, and cosmetics.

HANDICRAFTS
The **Guavaberry Emporium** (✉ 8–10 Front St., Philipsburg ☎ 599/542–2965) is the small factory where the island's own guavaberry liqueur is made by the Sint Maarten Guavaberry Company; on sale are myriad versions of the liqueur (including one made with jalapeño peppers) as well as bottled hot sauces. Check out the hand-painted liqueur bottles and the free samples. **Shipwreck Shop** (✉ 42 Front St., Philipsburg ☎ 599/542–2962 ✉ Marina Royale, Marigot ☎ 590/87–27–37) stocks Caribelle batiks, hammocks, handmade jewelry, the local guavaberry liqueur, and herbs and spices.

Nightlife

★ St. Maarten has lots of evening and late-night action. To find out what's doing on the island, pick up *St. Maarten Nights, St. Maarten Quick Pick Guide,* or *St. Maarten Events,* all of which are distributed free in the tourist office and hotels. The glossy *Discover St. Martin/St. Maarten* magazine, also free, has articles on island history and on the newest shops, discos, and restaurants. Or buy a copy of Thursday's *Daily Herald* newspaper, which lists all the week's entertainment.

BARS
Axum Café (☎ No phone), a bar and 1960s-style coffee shop on Front Street on the Dutch side, offers cultural activities as well as live jazz and reggae. It's open daily, 11:30 AM until the wee hours. The open-air **Bliss** (✉ Caravanserai Resort, Simpson Bay ☎ 599/545–3996) not only has techno music but also a restaurant and pool. **Bamboo Bernies** (✉ Caravanserai Resort, 2 Beacon Rd., Simpson Bay ☎ 599/545–3622), is an indoor-outdoor tiki bar that features a different theme every night. **Cheri's Café** (✉ Airport Rd., Simpson Bay ☎ 599/545–3361), across from Maho Beach Resort & Casino, features Sweet Chocolate, the lively band that will get your toes tapping and your tush twisting. Starting at

22

8 each night, the piano player at **Soprano's Piano Bar** (⊠ Sonesta Maho Beach Resort, Maho Beach ☎ 599/522–5725) takes audience requests for oldies, romantic music, or smooth jazz. **Sunset Beach Bar** (⊠ Beacon Hill ☎ 599/545–3998), at the south end of the airport runway, has live music Wednesday through Sunday and a relaxed, anything-goes atmosphere. Enjoy a beer and watch planes take off and land directly over your head.

CASINOS   The island's casinos—all 13 of them—are found only on the Dutch side. All have craps, blackjack, roulette, and slot machines. You must be 18 years or older to gamble. Dress is casual (but excludes bathing suits or skimpy beachwear). Most are found in hotels, but there are also some independents.

Atlantis World Casino (⊠ Rhine Rd. 106, Cupecoy ☎ 599/545–4601) has seven restaurants and never closes. **Beach Plaza Casino** (⊠ Front Street Philipsburg ☎ (599) 543-2031) is in the heart of the shopping area. There are free drinks for players at **Coliseum Casino** (⊠ Front St., Philipsburg) The 24-hour **Casino Royale** (⊠ Maho Beach Resort & Casino, Maho Bay ☎ 599/545–2115) is in bustling Maho, near restaurants and nightlife, and offers valet parking. There are 250 slot machines at the **Diamond Casino** (⊠ 1 Front St., Philipsburg ☎ 599/543–2583). The **Dolphin Casino** (⊠ Caravanserai Resort, Simpson Bay ☎ 599/545–4601) is near the airport. **Golden Casino** (⊠ Great Bay Beach Hotel, Little Bay Rd., Great Bay ☎ 599/542–2446) is on the road that leads into the west side of Philipsburg. **Hollywood Casino** (⊠ Pelican Resort, Pelican Key, Simpson Bay ☎ 599/544–4463) has an upbeat, celebrity theme and a nice late-night buffet. **Jump-Up Casino** (⊠ 1 Emmaplein, Philipsburg) is near the cruise-ship pier and right off Front Street. **Lightning Casino** (⊠ Airport Rd., Cole Bay ☎ 599/544–3290) is easily recognized by its gaudy flashing sign. **Paradise Plaza Casino** (⊠ Airport Rd., Simpson Bay ☎ 599/543–2721) also offers Sportsbook. **Rouge et Noir Casino** (⊠ Front St., Philipsburg ☎ 599/542–2952) is small but busy, catering mostly to cruise-ship passengers. **Tropicana Casino** (⊠ Welfare Rd., Cole Bay ☎ 599/ 544–5654) offers entertainment and free drinks to players.

DANCE CLUBS   **Greenhouse** (⊠ Front St., Philipsburg ☎ 599/542–2941) plays soca, merengue, zouk, and salsa, and has a two-for-one happy hour that lasts all night Tuesday. **Q-Club** (⊠ Sonesta Maho Beach Resort, Maho Bay ☎ 599/545–2632) is a popular disco at the Casino Royale with music for everyone.

Exploring St. Maarten/St. Martin

The best way to explore St. Maarten/St. Martin is by car. Though often congested, especially around Philipsburg and Marigot, the roads are fairly good, though narrow and winding, with some planned speed bumps, unplanned potholes, and an occasional wandering goat herd. Few roads are marked with their names, but destination signs are good. Besides, the island is so small that it's hard to get really lost.

A scenic "loop" around the island can take just half a day, including plenty of stops. If you head up the east shoreline from Philipsburg, follow the signs to Dawn Beach and Oyster Pond. The road winds past soaring hills, turquoise waters, quaint West Indian houses, and wonderful views of St. Barths. As you cross over to the French side, the road leads to Grand Case, Marigot, and Sandy Ground. From Marigot, the flat island of Anguilla is visible. Completing the loop brings you past Cupecoy Beach, through Maho and Simpson Bay, where Saba looms in the horizon, and back over the mountain road into Philipsburg.

Numbers in the margin correspond to points of interest on the St. Maarten/St. Martin map.

❺ Butterfly Farm. Visitors enter a serene, tropical environment when they walk through the terrariumlike Butterfly Sphere amid dozens of colorful butterfly varieties at the farm. At any given time, some 40 species of butterflies, numbering as many as 600, flutter inside the garden under a tented net. Butterfly art and memorabilia are for sale in the gift shop. In case you want to come back, your ticket, which includes a guided tour, is good for your entire stay. ✉ *Rte. de Le Galion, Quartier d'Orléans* ☎ *590/87–31–21* ⊕ *www.thebutterflyfarm.com* 💲 *$12* ⊙ *Daily 9–3.*

❼ French Cul de Sac. North of Orient Bay Beach, the French-colonial mansion of St. Martin's mayor is nestled in the hills. Little red-roof houses look like open umbrellas tumbling down the green hillside. The area is peaceful and good for hiking. There's construction, however, as the surroundings are slowly being developed. From the beach here, shuttle boats make the five-minute trip to **Ilet Pinel,** an uninhabited island that's fine for picnicking, sunning, and swimming.

❾ Grand Case. The island's most picturesque town is set in the heart of the French side on a beach at the foot of green hills and pastures. Though it has only a 1-mi-long (1½-km-long) main street, it's known as the restaurant capital of the Caribbean. More than 27 restaurants serve French, Italian, Indonesian, and Vietnamese fare here. The budget-minded love the half-dozen *lolos*—kiosks at the far end of town that sell savory barbecue and seafood. Grand Case Beach Club is at the end of this road and has two beaches where you can take a dip.

❸ Guana Bay Point. On the rugged, windswept east coast about 10 minutes north of Philipsburg, Guana Bay Point offers isolated, untended beaches and a spectacular view of St. Barths. However, because of the undercurrent, this should be more of a turf than a surf destination.

★ ⓫ Le Fort Louis. Though not much remains of the structure itself, the fort, completed by the French in 1789, commands a sweeping view of Marigot, its harbor, and the English island of Anguilla, which alone makes it worth the climb. There are few signs to show the way, so the best way to find the fort is to go to Marigot and look up. ✉ *Marigot.*

❿ Marigot. This town has a southern European flavor, especially its beautiful harborfront, with shopping stalls, open-air cafés, and fresh-food vendors. It's well worth a few hours to explore if you're a shopper, a gourmand, or just a Francophile. Marina Royale is the shopping complex at the port, but rue de la République and rue de la Liberté, which border the bay, are also filled with duty-free shops, boutiques, and bistros. The West Indies Mall offers a deluxe shopping experience. There's less bustle here than in Philipsburg, and the open-air cafés are tempting places to sit and people-watch. Marigot doesn't die at night, so you might wish to stay here into the evening—particularly on Wednesday, when the market opens its art, crafts, and souvenir stalls, and on Thursday, when the shops of Marina Royale remain open until 10 and shoppers enjoy live music. From the harborfront you can catch the ferry for Anguilla or St. Barths. Overlooking the town is Le Fort Louis, from which you get a breathtaking, panoramic view of Marigot and the surrounding area. Every Wednesday and Saturday at the foot of Le Fort Louis, there's an open-air food market where fresh fish, produce, fruits, and spices are sold and crowds sample the goods. Parking can be a real challenge during the business day and even at night during the high season.

❹ Orléans. North of Oyster Pond and the Étang aux Poissons (Fish Lake) is the island's oldest settlement, also known as the French Quarter. You can find classic, vibrantly painted West Indian–style homes with elaborate gingerbread fretwork.

❶ Philipsburg. The capital of Dutch St. Maarten stretches about a mile (1½ km) along an isthmus between Great Bay and the Salt Pond and has five parallel streets. Most of the village's dozens of shops and restaurants are on Front Street, narrow and cobblestoned, closest to Great Bay. It's generally congested when cruise ships are in port, because of its many duty-free shops and several casinos. Little lanes called *steegjes* connect Front Street with Back Street, which has fewer shops and considerably less congestion.

Wathey Square (pronounced watty) is in the heart of the village. Directly across from the square are the town hall and the courthouse, in the striking white building with the cupola. The structure was built in 1793 and has served as the commander's home, a fire station, a jail, and a post office. The streets surrounding the square are lined with hotels, duty-free shops, fine restaurants, and cafés. The **Captain Hodge Pier,** just off the square, is a good spot to view Great Bay and the beach that stretches alongside. The **Sint Maarten Museum** hosts rotating cultural exhibits and a permanent historical display called Forts of St. Maarten–St. Martin. The artifacts range from Arawak pottery shards to objects salvaged from the wreck of the HMS *Proselyte*. ⊠ *7 Front St., Philipsburg* ☎ *599/542–4917* ⊡ *Free* ☉ *Weekdays 10–4, Sat. 10–2.*

❻ Pic du Paradis. From Friar's Bay Beach, a bumpy, tree-canopied road leads inland to this peak. At 1,492 feet, it's the island's highest point. There are two observation areas. From them, the tropical forest unfolds below and the vistas are breathtaking. The road is quite isolated, so it's best to travel in groups. It's also quite steep and not in particularly good shape, becoming a single lane as you near the summit; if you don't have a four-wheel-drive vehicle, you will not make it. Parking at the top is iffy, and it's best if you turn around before you park. It may not be so easy later.

★ Near the bottom of Pic du Paradis is **Loterie Farm,** a peaceful 150-acre private nature preserve opened to the public in 1999 by American expat B. J. Welch. Designed to preserve island habitats, Loterie Farm offers a rare glimpse of Caribbean forest and mountain land. Welch has renovated an old farmhouse and welcomes visitors for horseback riding, hiking, mountain biking, ecotours, or less strenuous activities, such as meditation and yoga. Raves accompany lunch and dinner fare at the Hidden Forest Café since chef Julie Purkis took over the kitchen. The restaurant is open Tuesday through Sunday. The Loterie Farm's newest attraction, the **Fly Zone**, allows Tarzan wannabes to soar over the forest canopy via a series of ropes, cables, and suspended bridges. ⊠ *Rte. de Pic du Paradis* ☎ *590/87–86–16 or 590/57–28–55* ⊕ *www.loteriefarm. com* 🔳 *$5, 1½-hr tour $25, 4-hr tour $45* ⊙ *Daily sunrise–sunset.*

❽ Plantation Mont Vernon. Wander past indigenous flora, a renovated 1786 cotton plantation, and an old-fashioned rum distillery at a unique, outdoor history and eco-museum. Along the rambling paths of this former wooded estate, bilingual signs give detailed explanations of the island's agricultural history when its economy was dependant on salt, rum, coffee, sugar, and indigo. There is a complimentary coffee bar along the way and a delightful gift shop at the entrance. ⊠ *Rte. d'Orient-Baie* ☎ *590/29–50–62* 🔳 *€12* ⊙ *Daily 9–5.*

⏲ ❷ St. Maarten Park. This delightful little enclave houses animals and plants indigenous to the Caribbean and South America, including many birds that were inherited from a former aviary. There's also a bat cave filled with fruit bats. The zoo's lone male collared peccary now has a female to keep him company. A family of cotton-topped tamarins also have taken residence at the zoo. All the animals live among more than 100 different plant species. The Monkey Bar is the zoo's charming souvenir shop and sells Caribbean and zoo mementos. This is a perfect place to take the kids when they need a break from the sand and sea. ⊠ *Madame Estate, Arch Rd., Philipsburg* ☎ *599/543–2030* ⊕ *www.stmaartenpark.com* 🔳 *$10* ⊙ *Mid-Dec.–mid-Apr., daily 9–5; mid-Apr.–mid-Dec., daily 9:30–6.*

ST. MAARTEN/ST. MARTIN ESSENTIALS

To research prices, get advice from other travelers, and book travel arrangements, visit www.fodors.com.

Transportation

BY AIR

From the United States, American, Delta, Continental, and US Airways offer nonstop and connecting service; most of these flights are nonstops from the U.S. mainland, though American sometimes requires a connection in San Juan. Air Caraïbes, BWIA, Caribbean Sun, LIAT, and Winair offer service from various islands in the Caribbean. KLM and Air France offer service from Europe.

🔳 Air Caraïbes ☎ 599/545–4212 ⊕ www. aircaraibes.com. Air France ☎ 599/545–4212. American Airlines ☎599/545–2040. BWIA ☎599/545–4646. Continental Airlines ☎599/545–3444. Delta Airlines ☎ 599/545–4344, Ext. 0. KLM ☎ 599/545–4747 or 599/545–4344, Ext. 0. LIAT ☎599/545–5428. US Airways ☎599/545–4344. Windward Islands Airways ☎ 599/545–2568.

AIRPORTS: Aéroport de L'Espérance, on the French side, is small and handles only island hoppers. Jumbo jets fly into Princess Juliana International Airport, on the Dutch side. Its new terminal opened in mid-2006 🔳Aéroport de L'Espérance ⊠Grand Case ☎590/87–53–03 and 590/87–78–54. Princess Juliana International Airport ☎ 599/545-4211 for information, 599/545-599/545-4224.

BY BIKE & MOPED

Though traffic can be heavy, road speeds are generally slow, so a moped can be a good way to get around. Parking is easy, filling the tank with gas is affordable, and you've got that sea breeze in your hair. Scooters rent for as low as €25 per day and motorbikes for €37 a day at Eugene Moto, on the French side. At Go Scoot the bikes are in good repair and the counter clerks are helpful. If you're in the mood for a more substantial bike, contact the Harley-Davidson dealer, on the Dutch side, where you can rent a big hog for $150 a day or $900 per week.

🖪 **Eugene Moto** ⊠ Sandy Ground Rd., Sandy Ground ☎ 590/87-13-97. **Go Scoot** ⊠ 20 Airport Rd., Simpson Bay ☎ 599/544-3233. **Harley-Davidson** ⊠ Cole Bay ☎ 599/544-2704 ⊕ www.h-dstmartin.com.

BY BOAT & FERRY

The *Voyager II* offers daily service from Marigot to St. Barths Tuesday through Saturday. The cost for the 75-minute ride is €52 if the return is the same day or €65 if it's on different days. The price includes an open bar, snacks, and port fees; children under 12 travel for about half-price. It takes about 30 to 40 minutes to get to St. Barths on the new *Rapid Explorer,* a high-speed catamaran, which departs from the Chesterfield Marina (€89 round-trip). High-speed passenger ferries *Edge I* and *Edge II* motor from Simpson Bay's Pelican Marina to Saba on Wednesday, Friday, and Sunday in just an hour ($65 round-trip) and to St. Barths on Wednesday, Thursday, and Saturday in 45 minutes ($50 round-trip, plus $7 port fee). The trips depart at 9 and return by 5 the same day. The Link ferries make the 20-minute trip between the Marigot piers, on the Marigot waterfront, and Blowing Point, on Anguilla, departing and returning every half-hour from 8 AM until 7 PM daily. The fare is $10 one-way plus $3 departure tax, or $26 round-trip.

🖪 *Edge II* ☎ 599/544-2640 **Link Ferries** ☎ 264/497-2231 or 264/497-3290 ⊕ www.link.ai. *Rapid Explorer* ☎ 590/27-60-33 ⊕ www.sbhonline.com/Rapid_Explorer.htm. *Voyager II* ☎ 590/87-10-68 ⊕ www.voyager-st-barths.com.

BY CAR

Most people rent a car so they can more easily reach both islands and interesting beaches. Rates, in general, are low for the Caribbean—between $40 and $70 a day with unlimited mileage for a subcompact car. You can rent a car on the French side, but this rarely makes sense for Americans because of the unfavorable exchange rates for the euro.

Most roads are paved and in generally good condition. However, they can be narrow and often crowded, especially when the cruise ships are in port. Be alert for potholes and speed bumps, as well as the island tradition of stopping in the middle of the road to chat with a friend or let someone into traffic. Few roads are identified by name, so use a map and follow destination signs. International symbols are used.

🖪 **Avis** ☎ 599/545-2847 or 590/87-50-60. **Budget** ☎ 599/545-4030 or 590/87-38-22. **Dollar** ☎ 599/545-3281. **Hertz** ☎ 599/545-4541 or 590/87-38-00. **Unity Car Rental** ☎ 599/557-6760, 800/836-4529 in U.S.

BY TAXI

The government regulates taxi rates. You can hail cabs on the street or call the Dutch taxi dispatch on the Dutch side. On the French side of the island, the minimum rate for a taxi is $4, $2 for each additional passenger. Contact the French taxi dispatch for pickups. There's a taxi service at the Marigot port near the tourist information bureau. Fixed fares apply from Juliana International Airport and the Marigot ferry to the various hotels around the island. Fares are 25% higher between 10 PM and midnight, 50% higher between midnight and 6 AM.

🖪 **Dutch taxi dispatch** ☎ 147. **French taxi dispatch** ☎ 590/87-56-54.

Contacts & Resources

BANKS & EXCHANGE SERVICES

It's generally not necessary to change your money in St. Maarten/St. Martin. All banks now have ATMs that accept international cards. On the Dutch side, try RBTT or Windward Islands Bank, both of which have several branches on the island. On the French side, try Banque des Antilles Françaises or Banque Française Commerciale, but they will issue only euros. MasterCard, Visa, and American Express are accepted all over the island, Diners Club and Discover on occasion.

Legal tender on the Dutch side is the Netherlands Antilles florin (guilder), written NAf; on the French side, it's the euro (€). The exchange rates fluctuate, but at this writing they were about NAf 1.78 to US$1 and about €1 to US$1.17. On the Dutch side, prices are usually given in both NAf and U.S. dollars, which are accepted all over the island. Legal tender on the French side is the euro, but in practice most places will accept dollars readily and will often give a favorable exchange rate.

Prices quoted in this chapter are in U.S. dollars unless otherwise noted.

🚩 **Banque des Antilles Françaises** ⊠ Rue de la République, Marigot 🕾 590/29-13-30. **Banque Française Commerciale** ⊠ Rue de Hollande, Marigot 🕾 590/87-53-80.**Credit Mutuel** ⊠ Rue de la République, Marigot 🕾 590/29-54-90. **RBTT** ⊠ Emnaplein, Philipsburg 🕾 599/542-3344 ⊠ Union Rd., Cole Bay 🕾 599/544-3078. **Windward Islands Bank** ⊠ Cannegieter St., Philipsburg 🕾 599/542-2313.

BUSINESS HOURS

Banks on the Dutch side are open Monday through Thursday from 8:30 to 3:30 and Friday from 8:30 to 4:40. The Windward Islands Bank at Le Grand Marché is open on Saturday from 9 to noon. French banks are open weekdays from 8:30 to 12:30 and 2:30 to 4; they are usually closed on Wednesday afternoons and afternoons preceding holidays. Dutch-side post offices are open weekdays from 7:30 to 5. On the

French side, post offices are open weekdays from 7:30 to 4:45 and Saturday from 7:30 to 11:30. Shops on the Dutch side are generally open Monday through Saturday from 9 to noon and 2 to 6; on the French side, Monday through Saturday from 9 to 1 and 3 to 7. In Grand Case and around the Sonesta Maho Beach, the shops generally stay open until 11 to cater to the dinner crowd. Increasingly, however, shops on both sides remain open during lunch. Some of the larger shops are open on Sunday and holidays when cruise ships are in port.

ELECTRICITY

Generally, the Dutch side operates on 110 volts AC (60-cycle) and has outlets that accept flat-prong plugs—the same as in North America. The French side operates on 220 volts AC (60-cycle), with round-prong plugs; you need an adapter and sometimes a converter for North American appliances. The French outlets have a safety mechanism—equal pressure must be applied to both prongs of the plug to connect to the socket.

EMERGENCIES

🚩 Emergency Services **Dutch-side emergencies** 🕾 911. **Ambulance or fire emergencies Dutch side** 🕾 120 or 599/522-6001. **Ambulance French side** 🕾 590/87-50-08 or 590/87-72-00. **Police emergencies Dutch side** 🕾 108 or 599/542-2222. **Police emergencies French side** 🕾 17 or 590/87-50-04.

🚩 Hospitals **Hôpital de Marigot** ⊠ Rue de l'Hôpital, Concordia 🕾 590/87-87-67. **St. Maarten Medical Center** ⊠ Cay Hill 🕾 599/543-1111.

🚩 Pharmacies **Central Drug Store** ⊠ Camille Richardson St., Philipsburg 🕾 599/542-5576. **Simpson Bay Pharmacy** ⊠ Plaza del Lago, Simpson Bay 🕾 599/544-3653. **Pharmacie du Port** ⊠ Rue de la Liberté, Marigot 🕾 590/87-50-79.

HOLIDAYS

Both sides of the island celebrate specific holidays related to their government and culture, and some, such as New Year's, the Easter holidays (Mar. or Apr.), Labor Day (May 1), Christmas, and Boxing Day (Dec. 26) are celebrated together.

Other French-side holidays are Ascension Day (Aug. 15), Bastille Day (July 14), Schoelcher Day (July 21), All Saints' Day (Nov. 1), and the Feast of St. Martin (Nov. 11). Other Dutch-side holidays are Antillean Day (Oct. 21) and St. Maarten Day (Nov. 11; this coincides with Feast of St. Martin on the French side). On many holidays, government offices, shops, and even gas stations may be closed.

LANGUAGE

Dutch is the official language of St. Maarten, and French is the official language of St. Martin, but almost everyone speaks English. If you hear a language you can't quite place, it may be Papiamento—a mix of Spanish, Portuguese, Dutch, French, and English—spoken throughout the Netherlands Antilles.

INTERNET, MAIL & SHIPPING

Many hotels offer Internet service—some complimentary and some for a fee. There are cybercafés scattered throughout the island.

The main Dutch-side post office is on Walter Nisbeth Road in Philipsburg. There's a branch at Simpson Bay on Airport Road. The main post office on the French side is in Marigot, on rue de la Liberté. Letters from the Dutch side to North America and Europe cost NAf 2.85; postcards to all destinations are NAf 1.45. From the French side, letters up to 20 grams and postcards are €.58 to North America. When writing to Dutch St. Maarten, call it "Sint Maarten" and make sure to add "Netherlands Antilles" to the address. When writing to the French side, the proper spelling is "St. Martin," and you add "French West Indies" to the address. Postal codes are used only on the French side.

🛈 **Cyber Link** ✉ 53 Front St., Phillipsburg. **Internet Corner** ✉ 105 rue de Hollande, Marigot. **Coconets** ✉ 29 Hope Estate, Grand Case.

PASSPORT REQUIREMENTS

At this writing, a valid passport was expected to become a requirement for all U.S. citizens traveling to St. Maarten starting on January 1, 2007.

SAFETY

Petty crime can be a problem on both sides of the island. Always lock your valuables and travel documents in your room safe or your hotel's front desk safe. When sightseeing in a rental car, keep valuables locked in the trunk or car, or better yet, don't leave anything in the car. Never leave your things unattended at the beach. Despite the romantic imagery of the Caribbean, it's not good policy to take long walks along the beach at night.

TAXES

Departure tax from Juliana Airport is $15 to destinations within the Netherlands Antilles and $30 to all other destinations. This tax is included in the cost of many airline tickets, so it's best to check with your airline. If it's not included, the tariff must be paid in cash (dollars, euros, or NAf) at a booth before you get on your plane. If you arrive on the island by plane and depart within 24 hours, you'll be considered "in transit" and will not be required to pay the departure tax. It will cost you €3 (usually included in the ticket price) to depart by plane from L'Espérance Airport and $4 by ferry to Anguilla from Marigot's pier. Hotels on the Dutch side add a 15% service charge to the bill as well as a 5% government tax, for a total of 20%. Hotels on the French side add 10% to 15% for service and a *taxe de séjour*; the amount of this visitor tax differs from hotel to hotel and can be as high as 5%.

TELEPHONES

Calling from one side of the island to another is an international call. To phone from the Dutch side to the French, you first must dial 00–590–590 for local numbers, or 00–590–690 for cell phones, then the six-digit local number. To call from the French side to the Dutch, dial 00–599, then the seven-digit local number. Because of this, many businesses will have numbers on each side for their customers.

To call a local number on the French side, dial 0590 plus the six-digit number. On the Dutch side, just dial the seven-digit number with no prefix.

To call the Dutch side from the U.S., dial 011–599/54 plus the local number; for the French side, 011–590–590 plus the six-digit local number. At the Landsradio in Philipsburg, there are facilities for overseas calls and a USADirect phone, where you're directly in touch with an operator who will accept collect or credit-card calls. To call direct with an AT&T credit card or operator, dial 001–800/872–2881. On the French side, AT&T can be accessed by calling 080–099–00–11. If you need to use public phones, go to the special desk at Marigot's post office and buy a *télécarte*. There's a public phone at the tourist office in Marigot where you can make credit-card calls: the operator takes your card number (any major card) and assigns you a PIN (Personal Identification Number), which you then use to charge calls to your card.

TIPPING

Often without consistency, service charges of 10% to 15% may be added to hotel and restaurant bills. Especially in restaurants, be sure to ask if a tip is included; that way, you're not either double tipping or short-changing the staff. Taxi drivers, porters, chambermaids, and restaurant waitstaff depend on tips. The guideline is 10% to 15% for waitstaff and cabbies, $1 per bag for porters, and $1 to $5 per night for chambermaids.

TOUR OPTIONS

A 2½-hour taxi tour of the island costs $50 for one or two people, $18 for each additional person. Your hotel or the tourist office can arrange it for you. Elle Si Belle offers island tours by van or bus for $15.

🚹 **Elle Si Belle** ✉ Airport Blvd., Simpson Bay ☎ 599/545-2271.

VISITOR INFORMATION

🚹 Before You Leave **St. Maarten Tourist Office** ⊕ www.st-maarten.com ✉ 675 3rd Ave., Suite 1806, New York, NY 10017 ☎ 800/786-2278 or 212/953-2084. **St. Martin Office of Tourism** ✉ 675 3rd Ave., Suite 1807, New York, NY 10017 ☎ 877/956-1234 or 212/475-8970 🖷 212/260-8481 ⊕ www.st-martin.org.

🚹 In St. Maarten/St. Martin **Dutch-side Tourist Information Bureau** ✉ Cyrus Wathey Sq., Philipsburg ☎ 599/542-2337. **Dutch-side tourist bureau administrative office** ✉ 33 W. G. Buncamper Rd., in Vineyard Park Bldg., Philipsburg ☎ 599/542-2337. **French-side Tourist Information Office** ✉ Rte. de Sandy Ground, near Marina Port-Royale, Marigot ☎ 590/87-57-21 or 590/87-57-23.

WEDDINGS

Marriages on St. Maarten follow the same rules as on the other Netherlands Antilles islands; getting married on the French side really isn't feasible because of stringent residency requirements, identical to those in France. Couples must be at least 18 years old and submit their documents at least 14 days prior to the wedding date. The application requires notarized original documents to be submitted to the registrar, including birth certificates, passports (for non-Dutch persons), divorce decrees from previous marriages, death certificates of deceased spouses, and passports for six witnesses if the ceremony is to take place outside of the Marriage Hall. The documents must be submitted in Dutch or English—or else they must be translated into Dutch. The cost for this process is $275.55. Some of the larger resorts have wedding coordinators who can help to prepare the paperwork for a wedding. Wedding planners' fees average between $900 and $1,200. Any questions should be directed to the chief registrar.

🚹 **Chief Registrar** ✉ Census Office, Soualiga Rd., Philipsburg ☎ 599/542-5647 🖷 599/542-4267.

St. Vincent & the Grenadines

Tobago Cays, the Grenadines

WORD OF MOUTH

"If spectacular scenery is your thing, then consider a land tour through the Mesopotamia Valley up to Montreal Gardens [on St. Vincent]—a beautiful horticultural experience. . . . Canouan has beautiful beaches—you won't be disappointed in them. But if you are looking for nightlife and shopping, this is not the place."

—curiousx

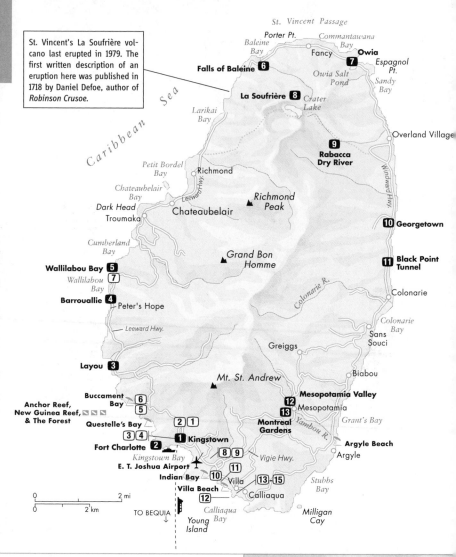

St. Vincent's La Soufrière volcano last erupted in 1979. The first written description of an eruption here was published in 1718 by Daniel Defoe, author of *Robinson Crusoe*.

St. Vincent Passage

Porter Pt.

Baleine Bay

Commantawana Bay

Fancy

Owia 7

Espagnol Pt.

Falls of Baleine 6

Owia Salt Pond

Sandy Bay

La Soufrière 8

Crater Lake

Larikai Bay

Petit Bordel Bay

Richmond

Overland Village

Rabacca Dry River 9

Caribbean Sea

Chateaubelair Bay

Dark Head

Troumaka

Leeward Hwy.

Chateaubelair

Richmond Peak

Windward Hwy.

Georgetown 10

Cumberland Bay

Grand Bon Homme

Black Point Tunnel 11

Wallilabou Bay 5

Wallilabou Bay 7

Colonarie

Colonarie R.

Barrouallie 4

Peter's Hope

Colonarie Bay

Leeward Hwy.

Greiggs

Sans Souci

Layou 3

Mt. St. Andrew

Biabou

Buccament Bay 6 5

Anchor Reef, New Guinea Reef, & The Forest

Mesopotamia Valley 12

Mesopotamia 13

Grant's Bay

Montreal Gardens 13

Yambou R.

Questelle's Bay 2 1

3 4

Fort Charlotte 1 **Kingstown**

2

Argyle Beach

Argyle

8 9

Vigie Hwy.

Kingstown Bay

E. T. Joshua Airport 11

Indian Bay 10 Villa

13 15

Stubbs Bay

Villa Beach 12

Calliaqua

Milligan Cay

TO BEQUIA

Calliaqua Bay

Young Island

0   2 mi
0   2 km

There are 32 perfectly endowed Grenadine islands and cays in this archipelago that provide some of the Caribbean's best anchorages. On land a sense of privilege prevails. Wildlife trusts protect rare species of flora and fauna, and villa walls ensure privacy for the islands' rich and famous human visitors.

WELCOME TO ST. VINCENT & THE GRENADINES

A STRING OF PEARLS

St. Vincent, which is 18 mi (29 km) long and 11 mi (18 km) wide, is the northernmost and largest of the chain of 32 islands that make up the Grenadines, which extend in a string 45 mi southwest toward Grenada. What they all have in common is a get-away-from-it-all atmosphere and a virtual lack of large-scale development.

Inhabitants of Bequia, the largest of the Grenadines islands, have long been known for their boatbuilding skills; now, they are equally known for model boats.

Though they are uninhabited by people, the Tobago Cays and surrounding Horseshoe Reef are rich with underwater marine life, placing them among the best snorkeling sites in the world.

KEY

- Beaches
- Cruise Ship Terminal
- Dive Sites
- **1** Exploring Sights
- Ferry
- ① Hotels & Restaurants

TOP 4 REASONS TO VISIT ST. VINCENT & THE GRENADINES

1. St. Vincent, with hiking trails, botanical gardens, waterfalls, and dive sites, is a good destination for eco-tourism.

2. Since there are few large resorts, you'll find peace and quiet but no crowds throughout St. Vincent and the Grenadines.

3. Island-hopping sailing charters are a perfect way to visit the many beautiful Grenadines.

4. Grenadine beaches, which are brilliant white and powdery soft, are the main draw.

ST. VINCENT & GRENADINES PLANNER

Getting to St. Vincent & the Grenadines

You will have to connect in one of six Caribbean islands (Barbados, Grenada, Martinique, St. Lucia, Puerto Rico, or Trinidad) to reach either St. Vincent or one of its smaller sister islands. Some of the smaller Grenadines actually require more than one flight (or at least more than one stop), then perhaps even a ferry. Unless you're on a private jet, it's an exhausting and time-consuming trip (it's also fairly expensive), yet people still make the effort to reach some of the most wonderful, unspoiled islands left in the Caribbean. Once you've landed on St. Vincent (SVD), it's also possible to hop to several different islands for a day or longer on one of the many inter-island ferry routes.

Hassle Factor: High, but worth it.

On the Ground

St. Vincent's E.T. Joshua Airport is in Arnos Vale, about halfway between Kingstown and Villa Beach. It's a small but busy airport, and it only accommodates turboprop aircraft. In the Grenadines, Bequia and Canouan have small, modern airports. Mustique and Union islands each have an airstrip with frequent regional service.

Taxis and buses are readily available at the airport on St. Vincent. The taxi fare to hotels in either Kingstown or the Villa Beach area is $10 (EC$25). Taxi service is available from the airports on Bequia, Mustique, Canouan, and Union islands.

Renting a Car

You can rent a car on either St. Vincent or Bequia, but rates are fairly expensive, and you must also purchase a temporary driving permit on top of that. If you rent a car, though, you'll have more flexibility to go out to dinner and explore the island at your leisure. Many people will be happy to hire a driver for the day or to take a scheduled tour, but the island scenery is dramatically beautiful, so having the freedom to explore at your own pace may be worth the high price. A scooter or moped is a less expensive possibility.

Activities

Beautiful **beaches** and excellent waters for **sailing** can be found throughout the Grenadines (though the beaches on St. Vincent itself are more volcanic and less than excellent). You come to these islands to really get away from it all and just **relax**, but don't miss the opportunity to do some easy island-hopping. The reef system surrounding the uninhabited Tobago Cays offers some of the best **snorkeling** in the world. Around St. Vincent itself, the waters are rich with marine life, offering **divers** abundant places to explore. On land, you can **hike** through St. Vincent's verdant forests or **climb** its volcano, La Soufrière. But if you are staying at one of the excellent, luxurious resorts on an isolated Grenadine island, you may be tempted to lie back, immerse yourself in the moment, and do little more than to raise your flag for another rum punch.

Where to Stay

Mass tourism hasn't come to St. Vincent & the Grenadines, and the relative isolation of the individual islands means that it probably never will. St. Vincent has only one full-scale resort, and even that has only 30 cottages. Expect simple places and friendly service. If you want luxury and privacy, look to one of the exclusive resorts in the Grenadines, where both can be found in great abundance; you'll probably also be able to hobnob with bigwigs, celebrities, and royals seeking privacy and comfort on an isolated island resort. If you have the time, it's also possible to island-hop on one of the many inter-island ferries, staying on several islands in simple guest houses to maximize both your budget and experiences.

TYPES OF LODGING

Luxury Resorts: Scattered throughout the Grenadines are several fine, luxury resorts that offer a Robinson Crusoe experience without the need to sacrifice the important comforts. Formalities tend to be few; you will pay handsomely for service, comfort, and privacy.

Simple Resorts and Guest Houses: The majority of places in St. Vincent are simple, friendly, and relatively inexpensive. There are a lot of simple guest houses throughout the islands.

Villas: Luxurious villas make up the majority of accommodations on Mustique, and they offer every amenity you can imagine.

Hotel & Restaurant Costs

Assume that hotels operate on the European Plan (**EP**—with no meals) unless we specify that they use either the Continental Plan (**CP**—with a Continental breakfast), Breakfast Plan (**BP**—with full breakfast), or the Modified American Plan (**MAP**—with breakfast and dinner). Other hotels may offer the Full American Plan (**FAP**—including all meals but no drinks) or may be All-Inclusive (**AI**—with all meals, drinks, and most activities).

WHAT IT COSTS in Dollars

	$$$$	$$$	$$	$	¢
Restaurants	over $30	$20–$30	$12–$20	$8–$12	under $8
Hotels*	over $350	$250–$350	$150–$250	$80–$150	under $80
Hotels**	over $450	$350–$450	$250–$350	$125–$250	under $125

*EP, BP, CP   **AI, FAP, MAP
Restaurant prices are for a main course at dinner. Hotel prices are for a double room in high season, excluding 7.7% tax, 10%–15% service charge, and meal plans (except at all-inclusives).

When to Go

High season runs roughly from mid-December through mid-April, then rates are usually reduced by at least 40%, except at inexpensive guest houses, where there is less variation in the rates. Seasonal discounts vary dramatically by resort and by island, with some of the luxury resorts offering better deals periodically throughout the year, though the most luxurious resorts are always expensive.

The **St. Vincent Blues Fest** is held on the last weekend in January. The **National Music Festival** is held in April. **Vincy Mas**, the St. Vincent Carnival celebration, is the island's biggest cultural festival, beginning in June and culminating at the end of July in a huge street party.

Bequia has its own **Bequia Blues Festival** in early February. An **Easter Regatta** brings everyone out to watch boat races. The **Bequia Carnival** is a summer celebration in late June.

Canouan has a regatta in late May. The **Easterval Regatta** on Union island is on Easter weekend. The **Mustique Blues Festival** is in early February.

23

Updated by
Jane E. Zarem

"I KNOW YOU!" That remark was aimed at me as I walked past the taxi stand on Kingstown's Bay Street. Sure enough—when I looked back over my shoulder, I noticed one of the drivers looking at me and smiling. He had, in fact, driven me around the island when I visited St. Vincent the year before. People in St. Vincent and the Grenadines actually have an amusing saying about island living: "You know half the people; the other half knows you!" I think that might be true.

A string of 32 islands and cays compose the single nation of St. Vincent and the Grenadines. SVG, as it's often abbreviated, is in the Windward Islands chain in the southern Caribbean. Mountainous St. Vincent, only 18 mi (29 km) by 11 mi (18 km) and just 13° north of the equator, is the largest and northernmost of the group; the Grenadines extend southwest in a 45-mi (73-km) arc toward Grenada.

St. Vincent is one of the least "touristy" islands in the Caribbean. That has little to do with it being welcoming or attractive or interesting. In fact, St. Vincent and its people reveal all of those qualities. The Vincentians are friendly, the island is beautiful, and getting around is fairly easy. St. Vincent is simply an unpretentious and relatively quiet island, where fishermen are up at the crack of dawn to drop their nets into the sea, working people go about their day-to-day business in town, and farmers spend back-breaking days working their crops in the countryside.

Most visitors to St. Vincent, it seems, are regional businesspeople, Vincentians who live overseas and travel home to visit family, and vacationers en route to the Grenadines. Hotels and inns are rather small, locally owned and operated, and definitely not glitzy. The only "resort" is on a separate island, 600 feet from the mainland. Restaurants serve mainly local food—grilled fish, stewed or curried chicken, rice, and root vegetables. And the beaches are either tiny crescents of black sand on remote leeward bays or sweeping expanses of the same black sand pounded by Atlantic surf.

St. Vincent's major export is bananas, and these plants, along with coconut palms and breadfruit trees, crowd more of the island than the 110,000 inhabitants (another 8,800 live on the Grenadines). This has obvious charm for nature lovers. Actually, more and more independent travelers interested in active, ecofriendly vacations are discovering St. Vincent's natural beauty, its active sports opportunities on land and sea, and the richness of its history. They spend their days walking or hiking St. Vincent's well-defined jungle trails, catching a glimpse of the rare St. Vincent parrot in the Vermont Valley, exploring exotic flora in the Botanical Gardens and Montreal Gardens, delving into history at Fort Charlotte, trekking to the spectacular Trinity Falls or the Falls of Baleine, and climbing the active volcano La Soufrière, which last erupted in 1979. Beneath the surface, snorkeling and scuba landscapes are similarly intriguing.

With all that said about down-to-earth, yet still-captivating St. Vincent, the islands of the Grenadines are quite the opposite and will dazzle you with their amazing inns and resorts, fine white-sand beaches, excellent sailing waters, and get-away-from-it-all atmosphere.

Bequia, the largest of the Grenadines, is just south of St. Vincent and a pleasant hour's voyage by ferry—an easy day trip. But Bequia has a large complement of inns, hotels, restaurants, shops, and activities and, therefore, is a popular vacation destination in its own right. Its Admiralty Bay is one of the prettiest anchorages in the Caribbean. With superb views, snorkeling, hiking, and swimming, the island has much to offer the international mix of backpackers and luxury-yacht owners who frequent its shores.

23

South of Bequia, on the exclusive, private island of Mustique, elaborate villas are tucked into lush hillsides. Mustique does not encourage wholesale tourism, least of all to those hoping for a glimpse of the rich and famous who own or rent villas here. The appeal of Mustique is its seclusion. Nevertheless, Basil's Bar on Brittania Bay and many of the island's lovely beaches are favorite stopovers of the yachting set.

Boot-shape Canouan, just over 5 square mi (11 square km) in area, has been reborn. Still mostly quiet and unspoiled, with only 1,200 or so residents who traditionally earn their living by farming or fishing, Canouan now has paved roads, a clinic, a new fisheries complex, and daily flights from Puerto Rico and Barbados bringing well-heeled guests to Raffles Resort Canouan Island. The posh, full-service resort takes up the entire northern third of the island, boasts one of the Caribbean's most challenging and most scenic golf courses and a European-style casino (both of which are Trump enterprises), and has an incredibly inviting spa.

Tiny Mayreau, next in the chain and with an area of only 1½ square mi (4 square km) the tiniest inhabited Grenadine, has fewer than 200 residents—but one of the area's most beautiful beaches. At Saltwhistle Cay, at the narrow northern tip of the island, the Caribbean Sea is often mirror calm, and, just yards away, the rolling Atlantic surf washes the opposite shore. Otherwise, Mayreau has a single unnamed village, one road, rain-caught drinking water, and a couple of inns—but no airport, no bank, and no problems!

Union Island, with its dramatic landscape punctuated by Mount Parnassus, is the transportation center of the southern Grenadines. Its small but busy airport serves landlubbers, while its yacht harbor and dive operators serve sailors and scuba divers. Clifton, the main town, has shops, restaurants, and a few guesthouses. Union Island is particularly popular among French vacationers, who like to charter a sailing yacht and dine (or stay) at Bigsands Hotel, on the beach not far from town.

Meanwhile, it took decades to turn the 100-acre, mosquito-infested mangrove swamp called Prune Island into the private resort now known as Palm Island. Today, vacationers who can afford it lounge on the island's five palm-fringed white-sand beaches.

Petit St. Vincent is another private island, reclaimed from the overgrowth by owner-manager Hazen K. Richardson II. The luxury resort's cobblestone cottages are so private that, if you wish, you could spend your vacation completely undisturbed.

And finally, the Tobago Cays, five uninhabited islands south of Canouan and east of Mayreau, draw snorkelers and divers who are mesmerized by the marine life here and boaters who are equally impressed with the sheer beauty of the area. Surrounded by a shallow reef, the tiny islands have rustling palm trees, pristine beaches, the clearest water in varying shades of brilliant blue—and plenty of resident fish.

One important thing to keep in mind when considering a vacation trip to St. Vincent and the Grenadines is that the various islands are fairly close together. Whether you travel by boat or by plane, traveling between or among them is not difficult. In fact, St. Vincent and each of the Grenadines are all quite unique. Once there, you'll definitely want to sample more than one.

ST. VINCENT

Where to Stay

With a few exceptions, tourist accommodations and facilities on St. Vincent are in either Kingstown or the Villa Beach area. Most hotel rates are EP (i.e., they include no meals), with MAP (breakfast and dinner included) available as an option; at resorts in the Grenadines, FAP (all meals) or all-inclusive (meals and drinks) plans are common. All guest rooms have air-conditioning, TV, and phone, unless stated otherwise.

★ $$$–$$$$ ☐ **Young Island Resort.** St. Vincent's only real resort is 200 yards offshore (a five-minute ride from Villa Beach by hotel launch) on its own 35-acre island. Airy hillside cottages are decorated in ecru, ocher, and green, with bamboo and rattan furniture. Walls of stone and glass have louvered windows surrounding the sitting areas. Each room has a terrace, and bathrooms have garden showers. All cottages have water views despite being hidden in lush tropical vegetation. Two beachfront and two hillside cottages have private plunge pools. Enjoy fine dining in the terrace dining room or in a private thatched-roof gazebo. Sailaway packages include two nights touring the Grenadines on a 44-foot sailing yacht. ⌂ Box 211, Young Island 🕿 784/458–4826 🖷 784/457–4567 ⊕ www. youngisland.com ⇌ 29 cottages ⟨ Restaurant, room service, fans, in-room safes, refrigerators, tennis court, pool, massage, beach, dock, snorkeling, windsurfing, boating, 2 bars, babysitting, laundry service, meeting room, airport shuttle, car rental; no a/c, no room phones, no room TVs ⊟ AE, D, MC, V ⍵⊙⍵ EP.

$$$ ☐ **Petit Byahaut.** Soft-adventure aficionados love this 50-acre eco-retreat, whose bayfront was one of the locations for the *Pirates of the Caribbean* film and is accessible only by a 10-minute boat ride from Buccament Bay (complimentary airport transfers and water taxi for guests). Accommodations are in large, open-style cabins, complete with wood floors, private decks, queen-size beds, hammocks, batik artwork, solar-powered lighting, and bathrooms with alfresco, solar-heated rainwater showers. Three meals daily, including candlelight dinners, are served in the bayfront dining room. The menu is limited to a couple of choices and always one that's vegetarian. Although well-behaved children are allowed, the rugged terrain and peaceful atmosphere are clearly oriented

23

toward adults. Once you've settled in, you'll find a selection of kayaks, endless nature trails, breezy sitting areas, and countless opportunities for bird-watching, along with free use of the scuba and snorkeling equipment and a private black-sand beach. If you tire of the seclusion, excursions are easily arranged. Weekly rates are available. ⊠ *Petit Bya-haut Bay* 📠 *784/457–7008* ⊕ *www.petitbyahaut.com* ↪ *4 cabins* ⚘ *Restaurant, fans, beach, snorkeling, boating, hiking, bar, library, shop, airport shuttle; no a/c, no room phones, no room TVs* ▭ *D, MC, V* ⊗ *Closed Aug.–Oct.* ↪ *3-night minimum* ⦿ *FAP.*

★ **$$** 🏨 **Grand View Beach Hotel.** This 19th-century greathouse perched just above Indian Bay has extensive facilities and intimate charm—all set on 8 acres that beckon you to explore. Rooms are attractive but not fussy, with plain white walls and hardwood floors, and most offer sweeping vistas of the Grenadines. Luxury rooms have broad terraces with ocean views; two honeymoon suites have king-size beds and whirlpool tubs. Enjoy West Indian and Continental-style cuisine at Wilkie's restaurant or casual dining at the Grand View Grill. Sailboats, Windsurfers, and snorkeling equipment are complimentary, but you have to hike down a rather steep hill to the beach. ⊠ *Villa Point* 📠 *784/458–4811* 📠 *784/ 457–4174* ⊕ *www.grandviewhotel.com* ↪ *17 rooms, 2 suites* ⚘ *2 restaurants, room service, fans, in-room safes, cable TV, tennis court, pool, health club, beach, snorkeling, windsurfing, boating, squash, 3 bars, library, babysitting, laundry service, meeting room* ▭ *AE, MC, V* ⦿ *EP.*

$$ 🏨 **Sunset Shores Beach Hotel.** Down a long, steep driveway off the main road, this lemon-yellow low-rise hotel surrounds a small pool and a gigantic and prolific mango tree (help yourself from January through July). It also faces a lovely curve of Indian Bay beachfront. All rooms are large, with patios or balconies. Opt for a room with a water view; otherwise, you'll have to amble over to the poolside bar to get a glimpse of the gorgeous sunsets. The restaurant is good, with a small but varied menu featuring fresh local fish and lobster (in season); service is friendly and efficient. ⌂ *Box 849, Villa Beach* 📠 *784/458–4411* 📠 *784/457–4800* ⊕ *www.sunsetshores.com* ↪ *32 rooms* ⚘ *Restaurant, room service, cable TV, pool, beach, snorkeling, boating, Ping-Pong, 2 bars, babysitting, laundry service, meeting room* ▭ *AE, D, MC, V* ⦿ *EP.*

$–$$ 🏨 **Mariners Hotel.** This friendly, small hotel faces the Villa Beach waterfront, just across from Young Island. Rooms are large, and each has a balcony or terrace facing the water or overlooking the small pool. The French Verandah serves breakfast and lunch with a picturesque view and dinner by candlelight. Other restaurants are nearby, along the seafront, or you can catch the Young Island ferry, which will take you to the resort just across the channel. Although the hotel doesn't have a good beach, Mariners guests may use the Young Island beach. The hotel can arrange scuba diving, sport fishing, boat charters, and other activities. ⌂ *Box 859, Villa Beach* 📠 *784/457–4000* 📠 *784/457–4333* ⊕ *www. marinershotel.com* ↪ *20 rooms* ⚘ *Restaurant, fans, in-room safes, cable TV, pool, beach, dock, 2 bars, Internet room, business services* ▭ *AE, D, MC, V* ⦿ *EP.*

$ 🏨 **Beachcombers Hotel.** This small, family-owned beachfront hotel and spa is modest but delightful. Half the guest rooms face the sea; the others overlook the Mango Tree Lounge or the garden's frenzy of flowers. Bathrooms have showers only—an insignificant privation when the welcome here is so warm and the rates so low. Best of all, an on-site spa offers aromatherapy, facials, sauna, steam baths, and fitness classes. On weekend evenings you can usually find a live band and dancing on the sundeck adjacent to the restaurant and bar. *Box 126, Villa Beach* 784/458–4283 784/458–4385 *www.beachcombershotel.com* 18 rooms, 2 suites, 1 apartment *Restaurant, room service, fans, kitchenettes, refrigerators, cable TV, pool, fitness classes, spa, Turkish bath, beach, bar, library, babysitting, laundry service, Internet room, meeting room AE, D, MC, V CP.*

$ **The Lagoon Marina & Hotel.** This hotel overlooking sheltered Blue Lagoon Bay may well be the island's busiest. Thanks to its marina, there are usually seafaring types liming (hanging out) at the terrace bar and plenty of yacht traffic to watch from one of two couches on your big balcony. Sliding patio doors lead onto these perches from the wood-ceilinged, carpeted rooms. Basic wooden furniture, twin beds, dim lighting, tiled bathrooms, and ceiling fans provide an adequate level of comfort, but don't expect luxury. Sloping garden grounds contain a secluded two-level pool, a strip of beach, and a pretty terrace restaurant. *Blue Lagoon, Box 133, Ratho Mill* 784/458–4308 784/457–4308 *www.lagoonmarina.com* 19 rooms, 2 apartments *Restaurant, grocery, room service, fans, kitchenettes, cable TV, 2 pools, beach, dock, snorkeling, windsurfing, boating, marina, bar, shop, babysitting, laundry service, Internet room, meeting room AE, V EP.*

$ **Roy's Inn.** Wedged into a residential hillside neighborhood five minutes by taxi from downtown Kingstown and the Botanical Garden, Leroy Lewis's stylish inn was rebuilt on the site of the island's oldest guesthouse (1781) and the home of its first French governor. The inn is especially favored by regional business travelers and perfect for vacationers who want a friendly, attractive atmosphere but don't require planned activities or resort features; there are, however, a pool, a gym, and broad verandas with sweeping views of the harbor. Three meals daily, with a choice of two entrées at dinner, are served in the air-conditioned restaurant and on the open-air dining terrace. Guest rooms are large, attractively decorated, and comfortable, and the service is friendly, efficient, and low-key. *Box 2500, Kingstown* 784/456–2100 784/456–2233 *www.roysinnsvg.com* 19 rooms, 3 suites *Restaurant, room service, fans, in-room safes, cable TV, pool, gym, hair salon, massage, sauna, 2 bars, laundry service, Internet room, meeting rooms, airport shuttle AE, MC, V EP.*

$ **Villa Lodge Hotel.** The venerable Villa Lodge has been welcoming guests since 1961, when a private hillside home was first transformed into a family-operated bed-and-breakfast inn. Additions and renovations over the years turned the inn into a small hotel, but the home-like atmosphere and friendly, personalized service remain. Hotel rooms with king-size beds and small balconies are comfortably yet fairly simply furnished. The eight Breezeville Apartments, which have full kitchens, are better for longer stays. The Patio Restaurant, which attracts local diners as well as hotel guests, offers international cuisine. Indian Bay beach is 100 yards from the hotel. *Box 1191, Indian Bay* 784/458–4641 784/457–

4468 ⊕ *www.villalodge.com* ⤴ *10 rooms, 8 apartments* ⌂ *2 restaurants, fans, in-room safes, refrigerators, cable TV, pool, beach, 2 bars, Internet room* ⊟ *AE, MC, V* ⦿ *EP.*

¢–$ ▣ **The New Montrose Hotel.** Despite the lack of a beach, pool, or activities, this is a fine choice for a comfortable and convenient place to rest your head. Painted a delightful lemon-yellow, the rambling hotel is on the northern outskirts of Kingstown. All suites are modern, with fully equipped kitchenettes, table and chairs, and two queen-size beds. The restaurant serves a limited menu of West Indian cuisine, but the food is good, and service is pleasant. This is a quiet, residential part of Kingstown, yet it's just a few minutes' drive from downtown, the beach, the airport, and the Botanical Gardens. Long-term rates are available. ⊠ *New Montrose, Box 215, Kingstown* ☎ *784/457–0172* 🖨 *784/457–0213* ⊕ *www. newmontrosehotel.com* ⤴ *25 suites* ⌂ *Restaurant, room service, fans, kitchenettes, refrigerators, cable TV, bar, Internet room, business services* ⊟ *AE, D, MC, V* ⦿ *EP.*

¢ ▣ **Cobblestone Inn.** On the waterfront in "the city," as Vincentians call Kingstown, this small hotel occupies a stone structure formerly used as a warehouse for sugar and arrowroot. Converted to a hotel in 1970, the building has original (1814) Georgian architecture, a sunny interior courtyard, and winding cobblestone walkways and arches. Rooms are tiny, but each has stone walls, rattan furniture, and a private bath. Room No. 5, at the front, is lighter and bigger than most of the others—but noisier, too. A rooftop bar-restaurant serves breakfast and light lunches. The popular Basil's Bar and Restaurant is at ground level. ⊠ *Upper Bay St., Box 867, Kingstown* ☎ *784/456–1937* 🖨 *784/456– 1938* ⊕ *www.thecobblestoneinn.com* ⤴ *19 rooms* ⌂ *Restaurant, cable TV, bar, shops, babysitting, laundry service, Internet room, business services, meeting room* ⊟ *AE, D, MC, V* ⦿ *EP.*

Where to Eat

Nearly all restaurants in St. Vincent specialize in local West Indian cuisine, although you can find chefs with broad culinary experience at a few hotel restaurants. Local dishes to try include *callaloo* (similar to spinach) soup, curried goat or chicken, *rotis* (turnovers filled with curried meat or vegetables), seasonal seafood (lobster, kingfish, snapper, and mahimahi), local vegetables (avocados, breadfruit, squashlike christophene, and pumpkin) and "provisions" (roots such as yams and dasheen), and tropical fruit (from mangoes and soursop to pineapples and papaya). Fried or baked chicken is available everywhere, often accompanied by "rice 'n' peas" or *pelau* (seasoned rice). The local beer, Hairoun, is brewed according to a German recipe at Campden Park, just north of Kingstown. Sunset is the local rum.

What to Wear

Restaurants are casual. You may want to dress up a little—long pants and collared shirts for gents, summer dresses or dress pants for the ladies— for an evening out at a pricey restaurant, but none of the places listed below require gentlemen to wear a jacket or tie. Beachwear, however, is never appropriate.

CARIBBEAN
$$–$$$

✕ **Buccama On the Bay.** You'll find Buccama down a mile-long dirt road off the leeward highway in a quaint, Caribbean-style building surrounded by farmland and Carib petroglyphs and facing a black-sand beach. Twenty minutes north of Kingstown, it's a perfect spot for a special dinner or a relaxing lunch when you're touring the leeward coast. Local food is the specialty, particularly seafood. Try conch chowder, grilled lobster or lobster salad, chicken breast stuffed with feta cheese and herbs, or grilled mahimahi. Steel-pan, calypso, or jazz music often accompanies dinner. Changing facilities are available for beachgoers. ⊠ *Leeward Hwy., Buccament Bay* ☎ *784/456–7855* ▭ *AE, D, MC, V.*

$–$$

✕ **Basil's Bar & Restaurant.** It's not just the air-conditioning that makes this restaurant cool. Downstairs at the Cobblestone Inn is owned by Basil Charles, whose Basil's Beach Bar on Mustique is a hangout for the vacationing rich and famous. This is the Kingstown power-lunch venue. Local businesspeople gather for the daily buffet or a full menu of salads, sandwiches, barbecued chicken, or fresh seafood platters. Dinner entrées of pasta, local seafood, and chicken (try it poached in fresh ginger and coconut milk) are served at candlelit tables. There's a Chinese buffet on Friday, and takeout is available that night only. ⊠ *Cobblestone Inn, Upper Bay St., Kingstown* ☎ *784/457–2713* ▭ *AE, MC, V.*

¢–$$

✕ **Vee Jay's Rooftop Diner & Pub.** This eatery opposite the Cobblestone Inn offers downtown Kingstown's best harbor view from beneath a green corrugated-plastic roof. Among the "authentic Vincy cuisine" specials chalked on the blackboard are mutton or fish stew, chicken or vegetable rotis, curried goat, souse, and *buljol* (sautéed codfish, breadfruit, and vegetables). Not-so-Vincy sandwiches, fish-and-chips, and burgers can be authentically washed down with *mauby,* a bittersweet drink made from tree bark; linseed, peanut, passion-fruit, or sorrel punch; local Hairoun beer; or cocktails. Lunch is buffet style. ⊠ *Upper Bay St., Kingstown* ☎ *784/457–2845* ⌢ *Reservations essential* ▭ *AE, D, MC, V* ⊘ *Closed Sun.*

¢–$

✕ **Wallilabou Anchorage.** Halfway up the Caribbean coast of St. Vincent, this is a favorite luncheon stop for folks sailing the Grenadines, for daytrippers returning from a visit to the Falls of Baleine, and for landlubbers touring the leeward coast. The picturesque view of the bay is enhanced by the period stage sets left behind by the *Pirates of the Caribbean* filmmakers. Open all day (from 8 AM), the bar-and-restaurant serves snacks, sandwiches, tempting West Indian dishes, and lobster in season. Ice, telephones, business services, and shower facilities are available to boaters. ⊠ *Leeward Hwy., Wallilabou Bay* ☎ *784/458–7270* ▭ *AE, MC, V.*

CONTINENTAL
★ $$$

✕ **Young Island Resort Restaurant.** Take the ferry (a two-minute ride from Villa Beach) to Young Island for a delightful lunch or a very special, romantic evening. Stone paths lead to candlelit tables, some in breezy, thatchroof huts. Tiny waves lap against the shore. Five-course, prix-fixe dinners of grilled seafood, roast pork, beef tenderloin, and sautéed chicken are accompanied by local vegetables; a board of freshly made breads is offered for your selection. Two or three choices are offered for each course. Lunch is à la carte—soups, salads, grilled meats, or fish—

and served on the beachfront terrace. ⊠ *Young Island* ☎ 784/458–4826 ⚓ *Reservations essential* ⊟ *AE, D, MC, V.*

ECLECTIC ✗ **Lime Restaurant & Pub.** Named for the *pursuit* of liming (relaxing), this
$$–$$$ sprawling waterfront restaurant also has mostly green decor. An exten-
sive all-day menu caters to beachgoers and boaters who drop by for a
roti and a bottle of Hairoun—or burgers, curries, sandwiches, gourmet
pizzas, pastas, soups, and salads. Dinner choices include fresh seafood,
volcano chicken (with a creole sauce that's as spicy as lava is hot), curried goat, and pepper steak. Casual and congenial by day, it's candlelighted and romantic at night—enhanced by the twinkling lights of
anchored boats and the soft sound of waves quietly breaking against
the seawall. ⊠ *Young Island Channel, Villa Harbour* ☎ 784/458–4227
⊟ *AE, D, DC, MC, V.*

FRENCH ✗ **The French Verandah.** Dining by candlelight on the waterfront terrace
$$–$$$ of Mariners Hotel means exquisite French cuisine with Caribbean flair—
Fodor'sChoice and, arguably, the best dining experience on St. Vincent. Start with a
★ rich soup—traditional French onion, fish with aïoli, or callaloo and
conch—or escargots, stuffed crab back, or conch salad. Main courses
include fresh fish and shellfish grilled with fresh herbs, garlic butter and
lime, or creole sauce. Landlubbers may prefer boeuf bourguignon,
suprême de poulet (stuffed chicken breast), or beef tenderloin with béar-
naise, Roquefort, or mushroom sauce. For dessert—the "mi-cuit," a warm
chocolate delicacy with vanilla ice cream, is to die for. Lighter, equally
delicious fare is served at lunch. ⊠ *Mariners Hotel, Villa Beach* ☎ 784/
453–1111 ⊟ *AE, MC, V.*

Beaches

St. Vincent's origin is volcanic, so the sand on its beaches ranges in color
from golden brown to black. Young Island has the only truly white-sand
beach, but since the island is private, you must be a guest at the Young
Island Resort (or the Mariners Hotel, whose guests have beach privileges) in order to use it. Otherwise, all beaches are public. Villa Beach,
on the mainland opposite Young Island, is really more of a waterfront
area than a beach. The strip of sand is so narrow it's sometimes nonexistent; nevertheless, boats bob at anchor in the channel, and dive shops,
inns, and restaurants line the shore, making this an interesting place to
be. On the windward coast, dramatic swaths of broad black sand are
strewn with huge black boulders, but the water is rough and unpredictable.
Swimming is recommended only in the lagoons, rivers, and bays along
the leeward coast.

Argyle. Though this spectacular black-sand beach on St. Vincent's southeast (windward) coast is not safe for swimming, you'll love to watch
the surf crashing here.

Buccament Bay. Good for swimming, this tiny black-sand beach is 20 minutes north of Kingstown.

Indian Bay. South of Kingstown and just north of Villa Beach, Indian Bay
Beach has golden sand but is slightly rocky—a good place for snorkeling.

Questelle's Bay. This beach (pronounced keet-*ells*), north of Kingstown
and next to Campden Park, has a black-sand beach.

Sports & the Outdoors

BICYCLING   Bicycles can be rented for about $15 per day, but roads are not particularly conducive to leisurely cycling. Serious bicyclists, however, will enjoy a day of mountain biking in wilderness areas. **Sailor's Wilderness Tours** (✉ Middle St., Kingstown ☎ 784/457–1712, 784/457–9207 after hours ⊕ www.sailortours.com) takes individuals or groups on half-day bike tours for $35 per person (which includes bike rental).

BOATING &   From St. Vincent you can charter a monohull or catamaran (bareboat
FISHING   or complete with captain, crew, and cook) to weave you through the
Fodor$Choice   Grenadines for a day or a week of sailing—or a full-day fishing trip.
★   One of the most spectacular cruising areas in the world, particularly for sailing, the Grenadines are close enough to allow landfall at a different island nearly every day, yet far enough apart, in some cases, to experience true blue-water sailing. Bequia and Union Island have excellent yacht services and waterfront activity. Mustique is a dream destination, as is Mayreau. Visitors on yachts are welcome to dine at the private Palm Island and Petit St. Vincent resorts. Canouan has come alive in the past year or so, and the Tobago Cays are a don't-miss destination for snorkeling and diving. Boats of all sizes and degrees of luxury are available. Charter rates run about $250 per day and up for sailing yachts, $120 per person for a fishing trip. **Barefoot Yacht Charters** (✉ Blue Lagoon, Ratho Mill ☎ 784/456–9526 🖷 785/456–9238 ⊕ www.barefootyachts. com) has a fleet of catamarans and monohulls in the 32- to 50-foot range. **Crystal Blue Charters** (✉ Indian Bay ☎ 784/457–4532 🖷 784/456–2232) offers sportfishing charters on a 34-foot pirogue for amateur and serious fishermen. **Sunsail St. Vincent** (✉ Blue Lagoon, Ratho Mill ☎ 784/458–4308 ⊕ www.sunsail.com) charters bareboat and crewed yachts ranging from 30 feet to 50 feet.

DIVING &   Novices and advanced divers alike will be impressed by the marine life
SNORKELING   in the waters around St. Vincent—brilliant sponges, huge deepwater coral
★   trees, and shallow reefs teeming with colorful fish. Many sites in the Grenadines are still virtually unexplored.

Most dive shops offer three-hour beginner "resort" courses, full certification courses, and excursions to reefs, walls, and wrecks throughout the Grenadines. A single-tank dive costs about $50; a two-tank, $95; a 10-dive package, $400. All prices include equipment. It can't be emphasized enough, however, that the coral reef is extremely fragile, and you must only look and never touch.

St. Vincent is ringed by one long, almost continuous reef. The best dive spots are in the small bays along the coast between Kingstown and Layou; many are within 20 yards of shore and only 20 to 30 feet down. **Anchor Reef** has excellent visibility for viewing a deep-black coral garden, schools of squid, sea horses, and maybe a small octopus. The **Forest**, a shallow dive, is still dramatic, with soft corals in pastel colors and schools of small fish. **New Guinea Reef** slopes to 90 feet and can't be matched for its quantity of corals and sponges. The pristine waters surrounding the **Tobago Cays,** in the Southern Grenadines, will give you a world-class diving experience.

Dive Fantasea (✉ Villa Beach ☎ 784/457–5560 or 784/457–5577) offers dive and snorkeling trips to the St. Vincent coast and the Tobago Cays. **Dive St. Vincent** (✉ Young Island Dock, Villa Beach ☎ 784/457–4714 or 784/547–4928 ⊕ www.divestvincent.com) is where NAUI- and PADI-certified instructor Bill Tewes and his staff offer beginner and certification courses and dive trips to the St. Vincent coast and the southern Grenadines.

HIKING   St. Vincent offers hikers and trekkers a choice of experiences: easy, picturesque walks near Kingstown; moderately difficult nature trails in the central valleys; and exhilarating climbs through a rain forest to the rim of an active volcano. Bring a hat, long pants, and insect repellent if you plan to hike in the bush.

Fodor'sChoice   **La Soufrière,** the queen of climbs, is St. Vincent's active volcano (which ★   last erupted, appropriately enough, on Friday, April 13, 1979). Approachable from either the windward or leeward coast, this is *not* a casual excursion for inexperienced walkers—the massive mountain covers nearly the entire northern third of the island. Climbs are all-day excursions. You'll need stamina and sturdy shoes to reach the top and peep into the mile-wide (1½-km-wide) crater at just over 4,000 feet. Be sure to check the weather before you leave; hikers have been sorely disappointed to find a cloud-obscured view at the summit. A guide ($25 to $30) can be arranged through your hotel, the Ministry of Tourism & Culture, or tour operators. The eastern approach is more popular. In a four-wheel-drive vehicle you pass through Rabacca Dry River, north of Georgetown, and the Bamboo Forest; then it's a two-hour, 3½-mi (5½-km) hike to the summit. If you are approaching from the west, near Châteaubelair, the climb is longer—10 to 12 mi (6 to 7 km)—and rougher, but even more scenic. If you hike up one side and down the other, arrangements must be made in advance to pick you up at the end.

Trinity Falls, in the north, requires a trip by a four-wheel-drive vehicle from Richmond to the interior, then a steep two-hour climb to a crystal-clear river and three waterfalls, one of which forms a whirlpool where you can take a refreshing swim.

Vermont Nature Trails are two hiking trails that start near the top of the Buccament Valley, 5 mi (8 km) north of Kingstown. A network of 1½-mi (2½-km) loops passes through bamboo, evergreen forest, and rain forest. In the late afternoon you may be lucky enough to see the rare St. Vincent parrot, *Amazona guildingii.*

SIGHTSEEING   Several operators on St. Vincent offer sightseeing tours on land or by TOURS   sea. Per-person prices range from $20 for a two-hour tour to the Botanical Gardens to $140 for a day sail to the Grenadines. A full-day tour around Kingstown and either the leeward or windward coast, including lunch, will cost about $50 per person. You can arrange informal land tours through taxi drivers, who double as knowledgeable guides. Expect to pay $25 per hour for up to four people.

Fantasea Tours (✉ Villa Beach, St. Vincent ☎ 784/457–5555 ⊕ www.fantaseatours.com) will take you on a 38-foot power cruiser to the Falls of Baleine, Bequia, and Mustique, or to the Tobago Cays for snorkeling. For bird-watchers, hikers, and ecotourists, **HazECO Tours** (⊠ Kingstown, St. Vincent ☎ 784/457–8634 ⊕ www.hazecotours.com) offers wilderness tours, bird-watching expeditions, and hikes to explore the natural beauty and see historic sites throughout St. Vincent. **Sailor's Wilderness Tours** (⊠ Middle St., Kingstown, St. Vincent ☎ 784/ 457–1712 ⊕ www.sailortours.com) runs the gamut, from a comfortable sightseeing drive (by day or by moonlight) to mountain biking on remote trails to a strenuous hike up the La Soufrière volcano. **Sam Taxi Tours** (⊠ Cane Garden, St. Vincent ☎ 784/456–4338, 784/458–3686 in Bequia) offers half- and full-day tours of St. Vincent, as well as hiking tours to La Soufrière and scenic walks along the Vermont Nature Trails. Sam's also operates on Bequia, where a sightseeing tour includes snorkeling at Friendship Bay.

Shopping

The 12 blocks that hug the waterfront in **downtown Kingstown** compose St. Vincent's main shopping district. Among the shops that sell goods to fulfill household needs are a few that sell local crafts, gifts, and souvenirs. Bargaining is neither expected nor appreciated. The **Cruise Ship Complex,** on the waterfront in Kingstown, has a collection of a dozen or so boutiques, shops, and restaurants that cater primarily to cruise-ship passengers but welcome all shoppers.

The best souvenirs of St. Vincent are intricately woven straw items, such as handbags, hats, slippers, baskets, and grass mats that range in size from place mats to room-size floor mats. If you're inclined to bring home a floor mat, pack a few heavy-duty plastic bags and some twine. The mats aren't heavy and roll and fold rather neatly; wrapped securely, they can be checked as luggage for the flight home. Otherwise, local artwork and carvings are available in galleries, from street vendors, and in shops at the Cruise Ship Complex.

ANTIQUES & FURNITURE **At Basil's** (⊠ Villa Beach ☎ 784/456–2602) is St. Vincent's only antiques and furniture store. Specializing in 200-year-old Asian pieces and the latest creations from Bali, India, and Africa, Basil's collection appeals to fine-furniture collectors as well as those seeking interesting, affordable objets d'art for either home or garden. Even if you're just looking, you might be smitten by the French wines, chocolates, and cheeses.

DUTY-FREE GOODS **At Gonsalves Duty-Free Liquor** (⊠ Airport Departure Lounge, Arnos Vale ☎ 784/456–4781), spirits and liqueurs are available at discounts of up to 40%. **Voyager** (R. C. Enterprises Ltd. ⊠ Halifax St., Kingstown ☎ 784/456–1686), one of the few duty-free shops in St. Vincent, has a small selection of cameras, electronics, watches, china, and jewelry.

HANDICRAFTS At **FranPaul's Selections** (⊠ 2nd fl., Bonadie's Plaza, Bay St., Kingstown ☎ 784/456–2662), Francelia St. John fashions dresses, pants, and shirts from colorful fabrics she selects in Trinidad. The emphasis is on African, Afro-Caribbean, and casual wear. **Nzimbu Browne** (⊠ Bay St., in front of Cobblestone Inn, Kingstown ☎ 784/457–1677) creates original art from dried banana leaves, carefully selecting and snipping bits and arranging them on pieces of wood to depict local scenes. He often sets up shop on Bay Street, near the Cobblestone Inn. **St. Vincent Craftsmen's Centre** (⌧ Frenches St., Kingstown ☎ 784/457–2516), three blocks from the wharf, sells locally made grass floor mats, place mats, and other straw articles, as well as batik cloth, handmade West Indian dolls, hand-painted calabashes, and framed artwork. The large grass mats can be rolled and folded for easy transport home. No credit cards are accepted.

Nightlife

On St. Vincent, **Vincy Mas,** St. Vincent's Carnival, is the biggest cultural festival of the year, with street parades, costumes, calypso, steel bands, food and drink, and the crowning of Miss Carnival and the Soca Monarch. Vincy Mas begins in late June, builds in intensity through the first two weeks in July, and culminates in a calypso competition on the final Sunday (Dimanche Gras), a huge street party (Jouvert) on the final Monday, and a Parade of Bands on the final Tuesday.

Nightlife here consists mostly of once-a-week (in season) hotel barbecue buffets with local music and jump-ups, so called because the lively steel-band and calypso music makes listeners jump up and dance. At nightspots in Kingstown and at Villa Beach, you can join Vincentians for late-night dancing to live or recorded reggae, hip-hop, and soca music.

DANCE & MUSIC CLUBS Dance clubs generally charge a cover of $4 (EC$10), slightly more for headliners. The **Attic Sports Bar** (⌧ 1 Melville St., Kingstown ☎ 784/457–2558) is above the KFC; you'll hear international jazz and blues on Thursday night; weekend parties begin at 10 PM. **Club Emotions** (⌧ Grenville St., Kingstown ☎ 784/457–2691) has disco music and live bands nightly and attracts a local crowd of mostly young people. **Iguana** (⌧ Villa Beach ☎ 784/457–5557) is a lively scene, with party night on Friday.

THEME NIGHTS **Calliaqua Culture Pot** (⌧ Main Rd., Calliaqua ☎ No phone) (pronounced cal-uh-*quah*) is a community street party held every Friday evening at 8 PM. Join the crowd for barbecue, beer, dancing to local music, arts and crafts, and cultural performances. On Wednesday and Friday evenings at **Vee Jay's Rooftop Diner & Pub** (⌧ Bay St., Kingstown ☎ 784/457–2845), karaoke accompanies dinner, drinks, and the open-air harbor view.

Exploring St. Vincent

Kingstown's shopping and business district, historic churches and cathedrals, and other points of interest can easily be seen in a half-day, with another half-day for the Botanical Gardens. The coastal roads of St. Vincent offer spectacular panoramas and scenes of island life. The Leeward Highway follows the scenic Caribbean coastline; the Windward Highway follows the more dramatic Atlantic coast. A drive along the windward coast or a boat trip to the Falls of Baleine requires a full day. Exploring La Soufrière or the Vermont Trails is also a major undertaking, requiring a very early start and a full day's strenuous hiking.

St. Vincent's Complex History

HISTORIANS BELIEVE that the Ciboney were the first to journey from South America to St. Vincent, which they called Hairoun (Land of the Blessed). The Ciboney ultimately moved on to Cuba and Haiti, leaving St. Vincent to the agrarian Arawak tribes that journeyed north from coastal South America. Not long before Columbus sailed by in 1492, the Arawaks succumbed to the powerful Caribs, who had also paddled north from South America, conquering one island after another en route.

St. Vincent's mountains and forests, however, thwarted European settlement. As colonization advanced elsewhere in the Caribbean, many Caribs fled to St. Vincent. In 1626 the French established a colony, but their success was short-lived; England took over a year later. As "possession" of the island seesawed between France and England, the Caribs continued to make complete European colonization impossible. Ironically, a rift in the Carib community itself enabled the Europeans to gain a foothold.

In 1675 African slaves who had survived a Dutch shipwreck were welcomed into the Carib community. Over time the Carib nation became, for all intents and purposes, two nations—one composed of the original Yellow Caribs, the other of the so-called Black Caribs. Relations between the two groups were often strained. In 1719 tensions rose so high that the Yellow Caribs united with the colonial French against the Black Caribs in what is called the First Carib War. The Black Caribs ultimately retreated to the hills, but they continued to resist the Europeans.

The French established plantations, importing African slaves to work the fertile land. In 1763 the British claimed the island yet again, and a wave of Scottish slave masters arrived with indentured servants from India and Portugal. Communities of direct descendants of the Scots still live near St. Vincent's Dorsetshire Hill and on Bequia.

Meanwhile, the determined French backed the Black Caribs, their previous foe, against the British in 1795's Second Carib War (also known as the Brigands War), during which British plantations were ravaged and burned on the island's windward coast. Black Carib chief Chatoyer managed to push the British troops down the leeward coast to Kingstown. Subsequently, on Dorsetshire Hill high above the town, Chatoyer lost a duel with a British officer. The 5,000 surviving Black Caribs were rounded up and shipped off to Honduras and present-day Belize, where their descendants (the Garifuna people) remain to this day. The few remaining Yellow Caribs retreated to the remote northern tip of St. Vincent, near Sandy Bay, where many of their descendants now live. A monument to Chatoyer has been erected on Dorsetshire Hill, where there's a magnificent westward view over Kingstown and the Caribbean.

The issue of "possession" of St. Vincent has long since been resolved; the nation has been fully independent since 1979 (but still a part of the British Commonwealth). The various ethnic groups have mixed considerably over the years, creating a unique heritage simply described today as "Vincentian."

Numbers in the margin correspond to points of interest on the St. Vincent map.

❹ Barrouallie. This was once an important whaling village; now, however, the fishermen of Barrouallie (pronounced *bar*-relly) earn their livelihoods trawling for blackfish, which are actually small pilot whales. The one-hour drive north from Kingstown, on the Leeward Highway, takes you along ridges that drop to the sea, through small villages and lush valleys, and beside picturesque bays with black-sand beaches and safe bathing.

⓫ Black Point Tunnel. In 1815, under the supervision of British colonel Thomas Browne, Carib and African slaves drilled this 300-foot tunnel through solid volcanic rock to facilitate the transportation of sugar from estates in the north to the port in Kingstown. The tunnel, an engineering marvel for the times, links Grand Sable with Byrea Bay, just north of Colonarie (pronounced con-a-*ree*).

★ ❻ Falls of Baleine. The falls are impossible to reach by car, so book an escorted, all-day boat trip from Villa Beach or the Lagoon Marina. The boat ride along the coast offers scenic island views. When you arrive, you have to wade through shallow water to get to the beach. Then local guides help you make the easy five-minute trek to the 60-foot falls and the rock-enclosed freshwater pool the falls create—plan to take a dip.

★ ☺ ❷ Fort Charlotte. Started by the French in 1786 and completed by the British in 1806, the fort was named for King George III's wife. It sits on Berkshire Hill, a dramatic promontory 636 feet above sea level, with a stunning view of Kingstown and the Grenadines. Interestingly, cannons face inward—the fear of attack by native peoples was far greater than any threat approaching from the sea, though, truth be told, the fort saw no action. Nowadays the fort serves as a signal station for ships; its ancient cells house paintings by Lindsay Prescott depicting early island history.

❿ Georgetown. St. Vincent's second-largest city (and former capital), halfway up the island's east coast, is surrounded by acres and acres of coconut groves. This is also the site of the now defunct Mount Bentinck sugar factory. A small, quiet town—with a few streets, small shops, a restaurant or two, and modest homes—it's completely unaffected by tourism. It's also a convenient place to stop for a cool drink or snack or other essential shopping while traveling along the windward coast.

❶ Kingstown. The capital city of St. Vincent and the Grenadines is on the island's southwestern coast. The town of 13,500 residents wraps around Kingstown Bay; a ring of green hills and ridges, studded with homes, forms a backdrop for the city. This is very much a working city, with a busy harbor and few concessions to tourists. Kingstown Harbour is the only deepwater port on the island.

A few gift shops can be found on and around **Bay Street,** near the harbor. Upper Bay Street, which stretches along the bayfront, bustles with daytime activity—workers going about their business and housewives doing their shopping. Many of Kingstown's downtown buildings are built of stone or brick brought to the island in the holds of 18th-century ships as ballast (and replaced with sugar and spices for the return trip to Europe). The Georgian-style stone arches and second-floor overhangs on former warehouses create shelter from midday sun and the brief, cooling showers common to the tropics.

Grenadines Wharf, at the south end of Bay Street, is busy with schooners loading supplies and ferries loading people bound for the Grenadines. The **Cruise Ship Complex,** south of the commercial wharf, has a mall with a dozen or more shops, plus restaurants, a post office, communications facilities, and a taxi-minibus stand.

An almost infinite selection of produce fills the **Kingstown Produce Market,** a three-story building that takes up a whole city block on Upper Bay, Hillsboro, and Bedford streets in the center of town. It's noisy, colorful, and open Monday through Saturday—but the busiest times (and the best times to go) are Friday and Saturday mornings. In the courtyard, vendors sell local arts and crafts. On the upper floors, merchants sell clothing, household items, gifts, and other products.

Little Tokyo, so called because funding for the project was a gift from Japan, is a waterfront shopping area with a bustling indoor fish market and dozens of stalls where you can buy inexpensive homemade meals, drinks, ice cream, bread and cookies, clothing, and trinkets, and even get a haircut.

St. George's Cathedral, on Grenville Street, is a pristine, creamy yellow Anglican church built in 1820. The dignified Georgian architecture includes simple wooden pews, an ornate chandelier, and beautiful stained-glass windows; one was a gift from Queen Victoria, who actually commissioned it for London's St. Paul's Cathedral in honor of her first grandson. When the artist created an angel with a red robe, she was horrified and sent it abroad. The markers in the cathedral's graveyard recount the history of the island. Across the street is **St. Mary's Cathedral of the Assumption** (Roman Catholic), built in stages beginning in 1823. The strangely appealing design is a blend of Moorish, Georgian, and Romanesque styles applied to black brick. Nearby, freed slaves built the **Kingstown Methodist Church** in 1841. The exterior is brick, simply decorated with quoins (solid blocks that form the corners), and the roof is held together by metal straps, bolts, and wooden pins. **Scots Kirk** (1839–80) was built by and for Scottish settlers but became a Seventh-Day Adventist church in 1952.

★ ☺ A few minutes north of downtown by taxi is St. Vincent's famous **Botanical Garden.** Founded in 1765, it's the oldest botanical garden in the western hemisphere. Captain Bligh—of *Bounty* fame—brought the first breadfruit tree to this island for landowners to propagate. The prolific bounty of the breadfruit tree was used to feed the slaves. You can see a direct descendant of this original tree among the specimen mahogany, rubber, teak, and other tropical trees and shrubs in the 20 acres of gardens. Two dozen rare St. Vincent parrots live in the small aviary. Guides explain all the medicinal and ornamental trees and shrubs; they also appreciate a tip at the end of the tour. ✉ *Off Leeward Hwy., Montrose* ☎ *784/457–1003* 🔗 *$3* ☾ *Daily 6–6.*

❽ **La Soufrière.** The volcano, which last erupted in 1979, is 4,000 feet high and so huge in area that it covers virtually the entire northern third of the island. The eastern trail to the rim of the crater, a two-hour ascent, begins at Rabacca Dry River.

❸ **Layou.** Just beyond this small fishing village, about 45 minutes north of Kingstown, are petroglyphs (rock carvings) left by pre-Columbian inhabitants in the 8th century. Arrange a visit through the Ministry of Tourism & Culture. For $2, Victor Hendrickson, who owns the land, or his wife will escort you to the site.

⓬ **Mesopotamia Valley.** The rugged, ocean-lashed scenery along St. Vincent's windward coast is the perfect counterpoint to the lush, calm west coast. The fertile Mesopotamia Valley (nicknamed Mespo) offers a panoramic view of dense rain forests, streams, and endless banana and coconut plantations. Breadfruit, sweet corn, peanuts, and arrowroot also grow in the rich soil here. The valley is surrounded by mountain ridges, including 3,181-foot Grand Bonhomme Mountain, and overlooks the Caribbean.

★ ⓭ **Montreal Gardens.** Welsh-born landscape designer Timothy Vaughn renovated 7½ acres of neglected commercial flower beds and a falling-down plantation house into a stunning yet informal garden spot. Anthurium, ginger lilies, birds of paradise, and other tropical flowers are planted in raised beds; tree ferns create a canopy of shade along the walkways. The gardens are in the shadow of majestic Grand Bonhomme mountain, deep in the Mesopotamia Valley, about 12 mi from Kingstown. ✉ *Montreal St., Mesopotamia* ☎ *784/458–1198* 🎫 *$3* ⏲ *Dec.–Aug., weekdays 9–4.*

❼ **Owia.** The Carib village of Owia, on the island's far northeast coast about two hours from Kingstown, is the home of many descendants of the Carib people of St. Vincent. It's also the home of the **Owia Arrowroot Processing Factory.** Used for generations to thicken sauces and flavor cookies, arrowroot is now used as a finish for computer paper. St. Vincent produces 90% of the world's supply of arrowroot. Close to the village is the **Owia Salt Pond,** created by the pounding surf of the Atlantic Ocean, which flowed over a barrier reef of lava rocks and ridges. Have a picnic and take a swim before the long, scenic return trip to Kingstown.

❾ **Rabacca Dry River.** This rocky gulch just beyond the village of Georgetown was carved from the earth by the lava flow from the 1902 eruption of nearby **La Soufrière.** When it rains on La Soufrière, the river is no longer dry—and you can be stranded on one side or the other for an hour or two or, in rare cases, longer.

❺ **Wallilabou Bay.** *The Pirates of the Caribbean* left its mark at Wallilabou (pronounced wally-la-*boo*), a location used for filming the recent movies. Many of the buildings and docks built as stage sets remain, giving the pretty bay an intriguingly historic appearance. You can sunbathe, swim, picnic, or buy your lunch at Wallilabou Anchorage. This is a favorite stop for day-trippers returning from the Falls of Baleine and boaters anchoring for the evening. Nearby there's a river with a small waterfall where you can take a freshwater plunge.

THE GRENADINES

The Grenadine Islands are known for great sailing, excellent scuba diving and snorkeling, magnificent beaches, and unlimited chances to relax with a picnic, watch the sailboats, and wait for the sun to set. Each island has a different appeal. Whether you prefer peace and quiet, nonstop activity, or informal socializing—as long as you're not looking for wild nightlife—one or another of the Grenadines will offer the perfect atmosphere for you.

Bequia

Bequia (pronounced *beck*-way) is the Carib word for "island of the cloud." Hilly and green, with several gold-sand beaches, Bequia is 9 mi (14½ km) south of St. Vincent's southwestern shore; with a population of 5,000, it's the largest of the Grenadines.

Although boatbuilding, whaling, and fishing have been the predominant industries here for generations, sailing and Bequia have now become almost synonymous. Bequia's picturesque Admiralty Bay is a favored anchorage for private and chartered yachts. Lodgings range from comfortable resorts and villas to cozy West Indian–style inns. Bequia's airport and regular, frequent ferry service from St. Vincent make this a favorite destination for day-trippers as well. The ferry docks in Port Elizabeth, a tiny town with waterfront bars, restaurants, and shops where you can buy handmade souvenirs, including the exquisitely detailed model sailboats for which Bequia is famous.

The Easter Regatta is held during the four-day Easter weekend; revelers gather to watch boat races and celebrate Bequia's seafaring traditions with food, music, dancing, and competitive games.

Where to Stay

For approximate costs, *see* the lodging price chart *in* St. Vincent.

$$$ ☷ **Bequia Beachfront Villas.** Perfectly located on Friendship Bay Beach, this is an excellent alternative to a hotel for a couple, a group, or a family. The three villas, which range in size from one to four bedrooms, have enormous living spaces with high ceilings and large porches with panoramic beachfront views, and are luxuriously decorated with attractive, comfortable furniture and extensive artwork. You'll feel like a guest in someone's private and very lovely beach house. Kitchens have full-size, modern appliances as well as every tool, dish, and utensil that you could possibly need. The living rooms have plenty of comfortable seating, large areas for dining, and shelves full of books, games, and magazines. You'll need to rent a car to get around the island and do errands, as the property is fairly isolated. ⊠ *Friendship Bay* ☎ *784-457–3423* 🖷 *784/456–3909* ⊕ *www.bequiabeachfrontvillas.com* 🛏 *3 villas* ⚴ *Fans, kitchens, cable TV, beach* ⊟ *AE, MC, V* ⦿ *EP.*

♻ $$ ☷ **Friendship Bay Beach Resort.** Lars and Magrit Abrahamsson left their busy lives in Sweden back in the mid-1990s and became hoteliers on Bequia. Their sprawling hillside complex hugs a mile-long (1½-km-long) arc of white-sand beach on Friendship Bay. Accommodations are in the main building, where rooms are small but have a sweeping view of the sea, and in a group of air-conditioned coral-stone cottages that dot the spacious landscaped grounds; each has a terrace with an ocean panorama and colorful furnishings that combine African and Carib Indian themes. The open-air Moskito Beach Bar & Restaurant serves seafood and creole cuisine. On Saturday night there's a barbecue and jump-up, and the rope-swing seats at the bar will keep you upright even after a potent rum punch. Breakfast and special dinners are served in the main restaurant, A Touch of Class. ✑ *Box 9, Friendship Bay* ☎ *784/458–3222* 🖷 *784/458–3840* ⊕ *www.friendshipbayhotel.com* ➬ *27 rooms, 1 suite* ⌂ *2 restaurants, room service, fans, tennis court, beach, dock, snorkeling, windsurfing, boating, waterskiing, volleyball, 2 bars, shops, babysitting, laundry service, meeting room; no a/c in some rooms, no room phones, no room TVs* ⊟ *AE, D, MC, V* ⭐⭐ *BP.*

★ ⌖ $$ 🖾 **Gingerbread Hotel.** Easily identified by its decorative fretwork, the Gingerbread faces the busy Admiralty Bay waterfront. The breezy Bequia suites—suitable for three—are large, modern, and stylishly decorated, with bedroom alcoves, adjoining salons, and full kitchens. Downstairs rooms have twin beds and large bayfront porches; upper rooms have king-size four-poster beds and verandas with harbor views. Decorated and furnished in a sophisticated tropical style, rooms have Italian tile floors, blue-and-white geometric-print bed quilts, sheer mosquito netting gathered over beds, and natural wood and rattan furniture throughout. Bathrooms are large and modern. Gingerbread restaurant serves full meals; for snacks head to the waterfront café. ⊠ *Admiralty Bay, Box 191, Port Elizabeth* ☎ *784/458–3800* 🖷 *784/458–3907* ⊕ *www. gingerbreadhotel.com* ➬ *9 suites* ⌂ *Restaurant, café, ice cream parlor, fans, in-room safes, kitchens, tennis court, beach, dive shop, snorkeling, boating, bar, babysitting, travel services; no a/c, no room TVs* ⊟ *MC, V* ⭐⭐ *EP.*

$–$$ 🖾 **The Old Fort Country Inn.** This stone greathouse of a former sugar estate is now an intimate inn reminiscent of something you might see in Provence or perhaps Burgundy. It's perched high on a cliff and cooled by trade winds, in a spot both remote and stunning. Each guest room has thick stone walls and windows that overlook a panoramic Grenadine vista. Because the nearest beach, aptly called Ravine, is nearly 450 feet down a rather steep path and the water is too rough for swimming, the inn is a good choice for romantics and getaway purists who are content with a pool. The Old Fort restaurant is well worth the 10-minute trek from town by car or taxi. ⊠ *Mount Pleasant* ☎ *784/458–3440* 🖷 *784/457–3340* ⊕ *www.oldfortbequia.com* ➬ *5 rooms* ⌂ *Restaurant, room service, pool, hiking, bar, babysitting, laundry service, airport shuttle; no a/c, no room TVs* ⊟ *MC, V* ⭐⭐ *EP.*

$–$$ 🖾 **Spring on Bequia.** This small hotel, named for its magnificent view over Spring Bay and operated by the same family since 1979, is about 1 mi (1½ km) north of Port Elizabeth and located on the grounds of a 28-acre working plantation that dates back to the late 18th century. Two spacious guest rooms with balconies are in a hand-cut stone-and-wood building called Fort, highest on the hill, with beautiful views of countless coconut palms and the sea. Four large units in Gull, halfway up the

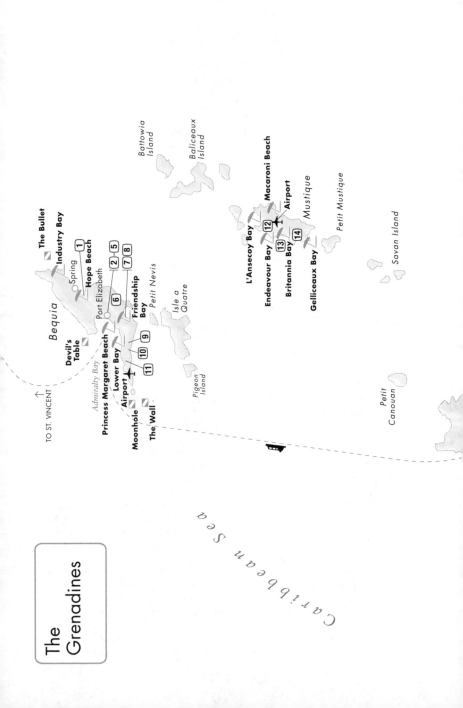

The Grenadines

TO ST. VINCENT

Bequia

Devil's Table

Admiralty Bay

Princess Margaret Beach

Lower Bay

Airport

Moonhole

The Wall

Pigeon Island

Spring

Hope Beach

Port Elizabeth

Friendship Bay

Petit Nevis

Isle a Quatre

The Bullet

Industry Bay

Battowia Island

Baliceaux Island

L'Ansecoy Bay

Endeavour Bay

Britannia Bay

Gelliceaux Bay

Macaroni Beach

Airport

Mustique

Petit Mustique

Savan Island

Petit Canouan

Caribbean Sea

ATLANTIC OCEAN

KEY

Beaches
Dive Sites
Ferry
1 Hotels & Restaurants

0   4 miles
0   6 km

Canouan

Grand Bay

Airport

Bay

Friendship Bay

Glossy Bay
Gibraltar

North Mayreau Channel

Tobago Cays

Saltwhistle Bay Beach

Mayreau

Saline Bay Beach

Union Island

Big Sand

Chatham Bay

Clifton   Airport

Martinique Channel

Palm Island

Petit St. Vincent

Petit Martinique

TO CARRIACOU →

Carriacou

Sail Rock

Hotels

Bequia Beachfront Villas	8
Bigsand Hotel	20
Casa del Mar	17
Cotton House	12
Dennis's Hideaway	19
Firefly	14
Frangipani Hotel	2
Friendship Bay Beach Resort	7
Gingerbread Hotel	3
The Old Fort Country Inn	6
Palm Island Resort	22
Petit St. Vincent Resort	23
Raffles Resort Canouan Island	15
Saltwhistle Bay Club	18
Spring on Bequia	1
Tamarind Beach Hotel & Yacht Club	16

Restaurants

De Reef	11
Frangipani	2
Gingerbread	3
Great Room	12
Lambi's	21
Mac's Pizzeria	4
Old Fort	6
L'Auberge des Grenadines	5
Basil's Bar	13
Bigsand Restaurant & Beach Bar	20
Coco's Place	9
Dawn's Creole Garden	10

hill, have similar full or partial ocean views. Three more rooms are convenient to the pool, garden, open-air bar, and restaurant. Strolling down to the beach—a 10-minute walk—you'll pass the ruins of a sugar mill, now a potter's studio. ☒ *Spring Bay* ☎ *784/458–3414* 🖷 *784/457–3305* ⊕ *www.springonbequia.com* ☒ *U.S. agent: Spring on Bequia, Box 19251, Minneapolis, MN 55419* ☎ *612/823–1202* ⇆ *9 rooms* ⚱ *Restaurant, some fans, some refrigerators, tennis court, pool, beach, snorkeling, hiking, bar; no a/c, no room TVs* ☺ *Closed mid-June–Oct.* ▱ *AE, D, MC, V* ⦿ *EP.*

¢–$$ 🏨 **Frangipani Hotel.** The venerable Frangipani, owned by former prime minister of St. Vincent and the Grenadines James Mitchell and managed by his daughter, is also known for its friendly waterfront bar and excellent restaurant. Five simple, inexpensive rooms in the original shingle-sided sea captain's home have painted-wood walls and floors, grass rugs, and plain furniture and share a cold-water bath at the end of the hall. Luxurious garden and deluxe hillside units, built of local stone and hardwoods, rise on a gentle slope filled with fragrant frangipani trees; these rooms have tile floors, louvered windows and doors, canopy beds, spacious private baths, and verandas with spectacular sunset views of the harbor. ☒ *Admiralty Bay, Box 1, Port Elizabeth* ☎ *784/458–3255* 🖷 *784/458–3824* ⊕ *www.frangipanibequia.com* ⇆ *15 rooms, 10 with bath* ⚱ *Restaurant, room service, some fans, some refrigerators, tennis court, beach, dive shop, snorkeling, boating, bar, shops, babysitting, laundry service; no a/c, no room TVs* ▱ *D, MC, V* ⦿ *EP.*

Where to Eat

Dining on Bequia ranges from casual local-style meals to more elaborate cuisine, and the food and service are both consistently good. Barbecues at Bequia's hotels mean spicy West Indian seafood, chicken, or beef, plus a buffet of side salads, vegetable dishes, and sweet desserts.

CARIBBEAN   ✕ **Frangipani.** Just before sunset, yachties come ashore to what is arguably ★ $$–$$$ the most popular gathering spot in Bequia—the Frangipani Hotel's waterfront bar. After a drink and a chat, the mood turns romantic, with candlelight and excellent Caribbean cuisine in the open-air dining room. The à la carte menu emphasizes seafood and local dishes. On Monday nights in high season, a local string band plays catchy tunes on both usual (mandolin, guitar) and unusual instruments (bamboo, bottles, gourds); on Friday nights, folksingers entertain. The Thursday Frangi barbecue buffet (about $30) is accompanied by steel-band music and a jump-up. ☒ *Frangipani Hotel, Belmont Walkway, Admiralty Bay, Port Elizabeth* ☎ *784/458–3255* ⚱ *Reservations essential* ▱ *MC, V.*

$$–$$$ ✕ **Old Fort.** The food here is good enough to attract nonguests to the romantic atmosphere of this 1700s-era estate house with one of the best views—and coolest breezes—on the island. At lunch, feast on pumpkin or callaloo soup, crêpes, sandwiches, salads, or pasta. At dinner the French creole cuisine focuses on entrées such as spring lamb, tuna steak, lobster, or char-grilled whole snapper, accompanied by fresh, homemade bread and curried pigeon peas. ☒ *Old Fort Country Inn, Mount Pleasant* ☎ *784/458–3440* ⚱ *Reservations essential* ▱ *MC, V.*

$$–$$$ ✕ **Dawn's Creole Garden.** It's worth the walk uphill to the Creole Garden Hotel for the delicious West Indian food and the view. Lunch op-

tions include sandwiches, rotis, fresh mutton, "goat water" (a savory soup with bits of goat meat and root vegetables), fresh fish, and conch. At dinner, the five-course creole seafood, lobster, or vegetarian specials include the christophene (chayote) and breadfruit accompaniments for which Dawn's is known. Barbecue is always available on request. The dinner menu changes daily. There's live guitar music most Saturday nights and a barbecue lunch, with live music, right on the beach on Sunday. ⊠ *Creole Garden Hotel, Lower Bay* ☎ *784/458–3154* ⌕ *Reservations essential* ▭ *AE, MC, V.*

$–$$$ ✕ **Coco's Place.** Ask a local Bequian for his or her favorite restaurant, and Coco's Place will undoubtedly be the answer. Perched on the hillside at the end of Lower Bay, the stunning view of Admiralty Bay is surpassed only by the friendly atmosphere created by Coco Simmons and the fresh grilled or creole-style fish, conch, and lobster emanating from her kitchen. You can also order steak. On Tuesday and Friday nights, lobster specials and live music rule. ⊠ *Lower Bay* ☎ *784/458–3463* ▭ *MC, V.*

¢–$ ✕ **De Reef.** This café-restaurant on Lower Bay is the primary feeding station for long, lazy beach days. When the café closes at dusk, the restaurant takes over—if you've made reservations, that is. For breakfast (from 7) or light lunch, the café bakes its own breads, croissants, coconut cake, and cookies—and blends fresh juices to accompany them. For a full lunch or dinner, conch, lobster, whelk, and shrimp are treated the West Indian way, and the mutton curry is famous. Every other Saturday in season there's a seafood buffet dinner accompanied by live music; on Sunday afternoons there's a music jam. ⊠ *Lower Bay* ☎ *784/458–3958* ⌕ *Reservations essential* ▭ *No credit cards.*

ECLECTIC ✕ **Gingerbread.** The airy dining-room veranda at the Gingerbread Hotel
☺ **$$–$$$** offers a panoramic view of Admiralty Bay and the waterfront activity. The lunch crowd can enjoy barbecued beef kebabs or chicken with fried potatoes or onions, grilled fish, homemade soups, salads, and sandwiches. In the evening, steaks, seafood, and curries are specialties of the house. Save room for warm, fresh gingerbread—served here with lemon sauce. In season, dinner is often accompanied by live music. ⊠ *Gingerbread Hotel, Belmont Walkway, Admiralty Bay, Port Elizabeth* ☎ *784/458–3800* ⌕ *Reservations essential* ▭ *AE, D, MC, V.*

FRENCH ✕ **L'Auberge des Grenadines.** Owned by the French-born Jacques Thevenot
$$–$$$ and his Vincentian wife, Eileen, this quaint restaurant and guesthouse on the waterfront facing Admiralty Bay is convenient for the yachting crowd, day-trippers, and anyone staying a while. The extensive menu marries French and West Indian cuisines: fresh seafood and local vegetables prepared with a French twist. Lobster is a specialty; select your own from the lobster pool to be prepared to taste. Light salads and sandwiches are available at lunch. Delicious baguettes and delicate pastries round out any meal. ⊠ *Belmont Walkway, Admiralty Bay, Port Elizabeth* ☎ *784/458–3201* ⌕ *Reservations essential* ▭ *AE, MC, V.*

PIZZA ✕ **Mac's Pizzeria.** Overheard at the dock in Mustique: "We're sailing over
☺ **$–$$** to Bequia for pizza." The two-hour sunset sail to Admiralty Bay is

worth the trip to Mac's, which has been serving pizza in Bequia since 1980. Choose from 17 mouthwatering toppings (including lobster), or select homemade quiche, conch fritters, pita sandwiches, lasagna, or soups and salads. Mac's home-baked cookies, muffins, and banana bread (by the slice or the loaf) are great for dessert or a snack. Or top off your meal with a scoop or two of Maranne's homemade ice cream in tropical flavors. The outdoor terrace offers fuchsia bougainvillea and water views. ⊠ *Belmont Walkway, Admiralty Bay, Port Elizabeth* ☎ *784/458–3474* ⌕ *Reservations essential* ☰ *AE, D, MC, V.*

Beaches

Bequia has clean, uncrowded white-sand beaches. Some are a healthy trek or water taxi ride from the jetty at Port Elizabeth; others require land transportation.

Friendship Bay. This horseshoe-shape, protected beach on Bequia's mid-south coast can be reached by land taxi. It's a great beach for swimming, snorkeling, and windsurfing; you can rent any equipment you need at Friendship Bay Resort and also grab a bite to eat or a cool drink at the hotel's Moskito Bar & Restaurant.

Hope Bay. Getting to this beach facing Bequia's Atlantic side involves a long taxi ride (about $7.50) and a mile-long (1½-km-long) walk downhill on a semi-paved path. Your reward is a magnificent crescent of white sand, total seclusion, and—if you prefer—nude bathing. Be sure to ask your taxi driver to return at a prearranged time. Bring your own lunch and drinks; there are no facilities. Even though the surf is fairly shallow, swimming may be dangerous because of the undertow.

Industry Bay. This nearly secluded beach is fringed with towering palms on the northeast (windward) side of the island; getting here requires transportation from Port Elizabeth. This is a good beach for snorkelers, but there could be a strong undertow. Bring a picnic; the nearest facilities are at Spring on Bequia resort, a 10- to 15-minute walk from the beach.

★ **Lower Bay.** This broad, palm-fringed beach south of Port Elizabeth and Princess Margaret Beach is reachable by land or water taxi or a healthy hike. It's an excellent beach for swimming and snorkeling. There are restaurants here, as well as facilities to rent water-sports equipment.

Princess Margaret Beach. Quiet and wide, with a natural stone arch at one end, the beach is a half-hour hike over rocky bluffs from Port Elizabeth's Belmont Walkway—or you can take a water or land taxi. Though it has no facilities, it's a popular spot for swimming, snorkeling, or snoozing under the palm and sea-grape trees.

Sports & the Outdoors

BOATING & With regular trade winds, visibility for 30 mi (48 km), and generally
SAILING calm seas, Bequia is a center for some of the best blue-water sailing you
★ can find anywhere in the world, with all kinds of options: day sails or weekly charters, bareboat or fully crewed, monohulls or catamarans—whatever your pleasure. Prices for day trips run $50 to $75 per person, depending on the destination.

Friendship Rose (⊠ Port Elizabeth ☎ 784/458–3373), an 80-foot schooner that spent its first 25 years as a mail boat, was subsequently refitted to take passengers on day trips from Bequia to Mustique and the Tobago Cays. The 65-foot catamaran **Passion** (⊠ Belmont ☎ 784/458–3884), custom-built for day sailing, offers all-inclusive daylong snorkeling and/or sportfishing trips from Bequia to Mustique, the Tobago Cays, and St. Vincent's Falls of Baleine. It's also available for private charter. The Frangipani Hotel owns the **S. Y. Pelangi** (⊠ Port Elizabeth ☎ 784/458–3255 ⊕ www.frangipanibequia.com), a 44-foot CSY cutter, for day sails or longer charters; four people can be accommodated comfortably, and the cost is $200 per day.

DIVING &
SNORKELING

About 35 dive sites around Bequia and nearby islands are accessible within 15 minutes by boat. The leeward side of the 7-mi (11-km) reef that fringes Bequia has been designated a marine park. The **Bullet,** off Bequia's northeast point, has limited access because of rough seas but is a good spot for spotting rays, barracuda, and the occasional nurse shark. **Devil's Table** is a shallow dive at the northern end of Admiralty Bay that's rich in fish and coral and has a sailboat wreck nearby at 90 feet. **Moonhole** is shallow enough in places for snorkelers to enjoy. The **Wall** is a 90-foot drop, off West Cay. Expect to pay dive operators $50 for a one-tank and $85 for a two-tank dive, including equipment. Dive boats welcome snorkelers for about $10 per person, but for the best snorkeling in Bequia, take a water taxi to the bay at Moonhole and arrange a pickup time.

Bequia Dive Adventures (⊠ Belmont Walkway, Admiralty Bay, Port Elizabeth ☎ 784/458–3826 ⊕ www.bequiadiveadventures.com) offers PADI instruction courses and takes small groups on three dives daily; harbor pickup and return is included for customers staying on yachts. **Dive Bequia** (⊠ Belmont Walkway, Admiralty Bay, Port Elizabeth ☎ 784/458–3504 ⊕ www.dive-bequia.com), at the Gingerbread Hotel, offers dive and snorkel tours, night dives, and full equipment rental. Resort and certification courses are available.

Shopping

Bequia's shops are mostly on Front Street and Belmont Walkway, its waterfront extension, just steps from the jetty where the ferry arrives in Port Elizabeth. North of the jetty there's an open-air market, and farther along the road are the model-boat builders' shops. Opposite the jetty, at Bayshore Mall, shops sell ice cream, baked goods, stationery, gifts, and clothing; there's also a grocery, liquor store, pharmacy, travel agent, and bank. On Belmont Walkway, south of the jetty, shops and studios showcase gifts and handmade articles. Shops are open weekdays from 8 to 5, Saturday 8 to noon.

Long renowned for their boatbuilding skills, Bequians have translated that craftsmanship to model-boat building. In their workshops in Port Elizabeth you can watch as hair-thin lines are attached to delicate sails or individual strips of wood are glued together for decking. Other Bequian artisans create scrimshaw, carve wood, crochet, or work with fabric—designing or hand-painting it first, then creating clothing and gift items for sale.

23

At **Banana Patch Studio** (✉ Paget Farm ☎ 784/458–3865), you can view and purchase paintings and scrimshaw work by artist Sam McDowell and shell crafts and "sailors' valentines" by his wife, Donna. Sailors' valentines are framed compositions of tiny shells, often with a flower or heart motif and a sentimental message, which 19th-century sailors on long voyages passing through the Caribbean would traditionally commission from local artisans and bring home to their sweethearts. The studio is open by appointment only. **Bequia Bookshop** (✉ Belmont Walkway, Port Elizabeth ☎ 784/458–3905) has Caribbean literature, plus cruising guides and charts, Caribbean flags, beach novels, souvenir maps, and exquisite scrimshaw and whalebone pen knives hand-carved by Bequian scrimshander Sam McDowell. You can visit the studio of French artist **Claude Victorine** (✉ Lower Bay ☎ 784/458–3150) and admire her delicate hand-painted silk wall hangings and scarves. Large wall hangings cost $100, scarves $50. Her studio is open from noon to 7 PM; it's closed Friday. **Local Color** (✉ Belmont Walkway, Port Elizabeth ☎ 784/458–3202), above the Porthole restaurant—near the jetty—has an excellent and unusual selection of handmade jewelry, wood carvings,

★ scrimshaw, and resort clothing. **Mauvin's Model Boat Shop** (✉ Front St., Port Elizabeth ☎ 784/458–3344) is where you can purchase the handmade model boats for which Bequia is known. You can even special-order a replica of your own yacht. They're incredibly detailed and quite expensive—from a few hundred to several thousand dollars. The simplest models take about a week to make. **Noah's Arkade** (✉ Frangipani Hotel, Belmont Walkway, Port Elizabeth ☎ 784/458–3424) sells gifts, souvenirs, and contemporary arts and crafts from all over the Caribbean.

★ **Sargeant Brothers Model Boat Shop** (✉ Front St., Port Elizabeth ☎ 758/458–3344) sells handmade model boats and will build special requests on commission. Housed in the ruins of an old sugar mill, **Spring Pottery & Studios** (✉ Spring ☎ 784/457–3757) is the working pottery of Mike Goddard and Maggie Overal, with gallery exhibits of ceramics, paintings, and crafts—their own and those of other local artists. All works are for sale. **Withfield Sails** (✉ Front St., Port Elizabeth ☎ 758/457–3638) repairs and makes sails for real sailboats, but proprietor Withfield M. Laidlow also displays and sells his handmade model boats.

Exploring Bequia

To see the views, villages, beaches, and boatbuilding sites around Bequia, hire a taxi at the jetty in Port Elizabeth. Several usually line up under the almond trees to meet each ferry from St. Vincent. The driver will show you the sights in a couple of hours, point out a place for lunch, and drop you (if you wish) at a beach for swimming and snorkeling and pick you up later on. Negotiate the fare in advance, but expect to pay about $15 per hour for the tour.

Water taxis are available for transportation between the jetty in Port Elizabeth and the beaches. The cost is only a couple of dollars per person each way, but keep in mind that most of these operators are not insured: ride at your own risk.

Admiralty Bay. This huge sheltered bay on the leeward side of Bequia is a favorite anchorage of yachters. Throughout the year it's filled with boats; in season they're moored cheek by jowl. It's the perfect spot for watching the sun dip over the horizon each evening—either from your boat or from the terrace bar of one of Port Elizabeth's bayfront hotels.

Hamilton Battery. Just north of Port Elizabeth, high above Admiralty Bay, the 18th-century battery was built to protect the harbor from marauders. Today it's a place to enjoy a magnificent view.

★ **Moonhole.** In 1961 American ad executive Tom Johnston and his wife, Gladys, moved to Bequia, purchased this rocky peninsula with a natural moon hole (through which the moon shines during the vernal and autumnal equinoxes), and designed a Flintstone-like stone home overlooking the sea. Over the next 20 years 18 more houses evolved, which are now individually owned as vacation homes. (One of them can be rented for about $1,200 per week.) Moonhole's unique architectural style was determined by the contour of the land, rocks, and trees. Walls and furniture were constructed of local stone, exotic wood, even whalebone, causing the multilevel "houses" to disappear naturally into the hillside. Johnston's son, Jim, and his wife, Sheena, now live at Moonhole and offer tours of their unusual "live-in sculptures" once a week. ⬠ *Box 30, Moonhole* ☎ *784/4587–3068* ⊕ *www.begos.com/bequiamoonhole* ⬛ *$15* ⊙ *Tues., by appointment only.*

Mount Pleasant. Bequia's highest point (an elevation of 881 feet) is a reasonable goal for a hiking trek. Alternatively, it's a pleasant drive. The reward is a stunning view of the island and surrounding Grenadines.

★ ☺ **Oldhegg Turtle Sanctuary.** In the far northeast of the island, Orton "Brother" King, a retired skin-diving fisherman, tends to endangered hawksbill turtles. He'll be glad to show you around and tell you how his project is increasing the turtle population in Bequia. ⬠ *Park Beach, Industry* ☎ *784/458–3245* ⬛ *$5 donation requested* ⊙ *By appointment only.*

★ **Port Elizabeth.** Bequia's capital is on the northeast side of Admiralty Bay. The ferry from St. Vincent docks at the jetty, in the center of the tiny town, which is only a few blocks long and a couple of blocks deep. Walk north along Front Street, which faces the water, to the open-air market, where you can buy local fruits and vegetables and some handicrafts; farther along, you can find the model-boat builders' workshops for which Bequia is renowned. Walk south along Belmont Walkway, which meanders along the bay front past shops, cafés, restaurants, bars, and hotels.

Canouan

Halfway down the Grenadines chain, this tiny boot-shape island—just 3½ mi (5½ km) long and 1¼ mi (2 km) wide—has only about 1,165 residents. But don't let its slow pace and quiet ways fool you. Canouan (pronounced *can*-no-wan), which is the Carib word for "turtle," has an airstrip—with night-landing facilities and regularly scheduled flights from St. Vincent, Barbados, and Puerto Rico—and boasts one of the region's largest and most exquisite resorts. It also claims five of the most pristine white-sand beaches in the Caribbean.

Where to Stay

☺ $$$$ ⊞ **Raffles Resort Canouan Island.** Guest accommodations at the region's
Fodor'sChoice premier resort are in 60 villas sprinkled around 300 acres of the 1,200-
★ acre resort in an amphitheater setting. Rooms and suites—designated
orchestra or mezzanine level, depending on location—are spectacular
in terms of size, decor, amenities, and view. Each room is assigned its
own golf cart for getting around the property. Center stage is an 18th-
century Anglican stone church (popular for resort weddings), along
with the Galleria Complex—reception, two restaurants and lounges, boutiques, modern health club (with a boxing ring!), hair salon, meeting
rooms, and golf pro shop. And as a backdrop, pick the beach, the sea,
the mountains, or the Trump International Golf Club, an 18-hole, Jim
Fazio–designed championship course touted as one of the best in the
Caribbean. Certainly, the view of the Grenadines from the 13th hole is
something to write home about—as is the beachfront Amrita Spa. Several private treatment rooms are perched on the breezy hillside and accessed by funicular; two others are in palapas, built on stilts in the sea
and accessed by boat. Looking for more action? Head for the Trump
Club Privé, high on the mountainside, which houses a European-style
casino, French restaurant, and ballroom for private functions. ⊠ *Carenage Bay* ☎ *784/458–8000* 🖶 *784/458–8885* ⊕ *www.raffles-
canouanisland.com* ⇴ *40 rooms, 116 suites* ☺ *4 restaurants, fans,
in-room safes, some kitchenettes, minibars, cable TV, in-room data
ports, 18-hole golf course, 4 tennis courts, pro shop, pool, health club,
hair salon, spa, 3 beaches, dock, snorkeling, windsurfing, boating,
mountain bikes, basketball, hiking, volleyball, 4 bars, casino, shops,
babysitting, children's programs (ages 4–14), playground, laundry service, concierge, Internet room, meeting rooms, airport shuttle, car rental,
travel services* ▭ *AE, D, DC, MC, V* ⦿*EP.*

$$$–$$$$ ⊞ **Tamarind Beach Hotel & Yacht Club.** Thatched roofs are a trademark
of this Italian-owned beachfront hotel. Accommodations are in three
buildings facing reef-protected Grand Bay Beach. Louvered wooden doors
in each guest room open onto a spacious veranda and a beautiful
Caribbean vista, while ceiling fans keep you cool. The alfresco Palapa
Restaurant serves Caribbean specialties, grilled meat or fish, pizzas, and
pasta prepared by a European chef. Barbecues and themed dinners ro-
tate throughout the week, and live Caribbean music is featured fairly
regularly at the Pirate Cove bar. A 55-foot catamaran is available for
day sails to the Tobago Cays. ⊠ *Charlestown* ☎ *784/458–8044* 🖶 *784/
458–8851* ⊕ *www.tamarindbeachhotel.com* ⇴ *45 rooms* ☺ *2 restau-
rants, fans, in-room safes, minibars, beach, dive shop, snorkeling, wind-
surfing, boating, marina, fishing, bicycles, 2 bars, shops, babysitting,
laundry service, meeting room, airport shuttle, car rental, travel serv-
ices; no a/c in some rooms, no TV in some rooms* ▭ *AE, MC, V* ⦿*CP.*

$$–$$$$ ⊞ **Casa del Mar.** Canouan native Adonal Foyle, a reserve center for the
NBA's Golden State Warriors, opened this two-story, Mediterranean-style
villa in 2002. This is a great place for families or small groups of up to
12 people who want a comfortable, relaxing, do-your-own-thing villa
experience. On each floor, guest quarters surround a spacious living
room with an entertainment center and video library, along with a fully
equipped modern kitchen and laundry facilities. Once or twice a week,

a barbecue and cash bar is set up on the outdoor patio. The beach is nearby. Weekly and group rates are available. ⊠ *Windward Bay* ☏ *784/482–0639* ⊕ *www.adonalfoyle.com/afe.shtml* ⟟ *3 rooms, 2 suites* ⚬ *Kitchens, cable TV, laundry facilities; no smoking* ⊟ *AE, MC, V* ⧖ *EP.*

Beaches

Godahl Beach. This lovely stretch of white-sand beach is at the south end of Carenage Bay and surrounded by the Raffles property, including the resort's beach bar and restaurant and its spa.

Grand Bay. In the center of the island on the leeward side is the main beach and the site of Charlestown, the largest settlement, where ferries dock; it's also called Charlestown Bay.

Mahault Bay. This lovely but remote expanse of beach (pronounced *ma-ho*) is at the northern tip of the island, surrounded by Mount Royal and accessible through the Raffles property or by sea.

South Glossy Bay. This and other Glossy Bay beaches along the southwest (windward) coast of Canouan are absolutely spectacular. South Glossy Bay is within walking distance of the airport, and the French restaurant at Canouan Beach Hotel is convenient for lunch.

Sports & the Outdoors

BOATING The Grenadines offer sailors some of the most superb cruising waters in the world. Canouan is at the mid-point of the Grenadines, an easy sail north to Bequia and Mustique or south to Mayreau, the Tobago Cays, and beyond. The **Moorings** (⊠ Charlestown Bay ☏ 784/482–0653 🖷 784/482–0654 ⊕ www.moorings.com) operates next to Tamarind Beach Hotel & Yacht Club. It offers bareboat and crewed yacht charters of monohulls and catamarans ranging in size from 38 to 52 feet. Also available are one-way charters between Canouan and the Moorings operation in St. Lucia.

DIVING & The mile-long (1½-km-long) reef and waters surrounding Canouan offer
SNORKELING excellent snorkeling as well as spectacular sites for both novice and experienced divers. **Gibraltar,** a giant stone almost 30 feet down, is a popular site; plenty of colorful fish and corals are visible. The crystalline waters surrounding the **Tobago Cays** offer marvelous diving and snorkeling.

Blue Wave Dive Centre (⊠ Tamarind Beach Hotel, Charlestown ☏ 784/458–8044 🖷 784/458–8851), a full-service dive facility, offers resort and certification courses and dive and snorkel trips to the Tobago Cays, Mayreau, and Palm Island. **Glossy Dive Club** (⊠ Canouan Beach Hotel, South Glossy Bay ☏ 784/458–8888 🖷 784/458–8875) is a full-service PADI facility offering dive and snorkel trips to the Tobago Cays and other nearby sites.

GOLF The only 18-hole, championship golf course in St. Vincent & the Grenadines is also one of the best in the Caribbean. Located on the Raffles Resort property, it's operated by Trump Enterprises.

FodorśChoice **Trump International Golf Club** (⊠ Raffles Resort, Carenage Bay ☏ 784/
★ 458–8000 🖷 784/458–8885) is an 18-hole, par-72 championship course spread over 60 acres that offers unparalleled views. The first 9 holes of the Jim Fazio–designed course, along with holes 10 and 18, are in a pretty green plain that stretches down to the sea. The rest have been carved

into the mountainside, affording spectacular views of Canouan Island, the resort itself, and the surrounding Grenadines. The 13th hole offers a wraparound view; it's also the most challenging, as its unforgiving green is at the edge of a cliff. Greens fees are $175 for resort guests, $200 for nonguests. Golf instruction, carts, and rental clubs are available, and a pro shop and lounge are in the resort.

Mayreau

Privately owned Mayreau (pronounced *my*-row) is minuscule—just 1½ square mi (4 square km). Only 254 residents live in the hilltop village, and there are no proper roads. Guests at the resort on Saltwhistle Bay enjoy the natural surroundings in one of the prettiest locations in the Grenadines—one of the few spots where the calm Caribbean is separated from the Atlantic surf by only a narrow strip of beach. It's a favorite stop for boaters, as well. Except for water sports and hiking, there's not much to do—but everyone prefers it that way. For a day's excursion, you can hike up Mayreau's only hill (wear sturdy shoes) to a stunning view of the Tobago Cays. Then stop for a drink at Dennis's Hideaway and enjoy a swim at Saline Bay Beach, where you may be joined by a few boatloads of cruise-ship passengers. This pretty little island is a favorite stop for small ships that ply the waters of the Grenadines and anchor just offshore for the day. The only access to Mayreau is by boat (ferry, private, or hired), which you can arrange at Union Island.

Where to Stay

For approximate costs, *see* the lodging price chart *in* St. Vincent.

$$$–$$$$ ✕▢ **Saltwhistle Bay Club.** This resort is so cleverly hidden within 22 acres of lush foliage that sailors need binoculars to be sure it's there at all. Gorgeous Saltwhistle Bay is a half-moon of crystal-clear water rimmed by almost a mile of sparkling sandy white beach. Each roomy cottage is decked out with wooden shutters, ceiling fans, and a circular stone shower. You can dry your hair on the breezy second-story veranda atop each bungalow. At the restaurant, individual dining cabanas with stone tables are protected from sun and the occasional raindrop by thatched roofs. You can relish turtle steak, duckling, lobster, and à la carte lunches. Guests are picked up by hotel launch at Union Airport. ✉ *Saltwhistle Bay* ☎ 784/458–8444 📠 784/458–8944 ⊕ *www.saltwhistlebay. com* 🛏 *10 cottages* ⚙ *Restaurant, fans, beach, dive shop, snorkeling, windsurfing, boating, Ping-Pong, volleyball, bar, babysitting; no a/c, no room TVs* ▭ *AE, MC, V* ⱺ *MAP* ⊙ *Closed Sept. and Oct.*

¢ ✕▢ **Dennis's Hideaway.** The rooms in this guesthouse, about a three-minute walk from the beach, are clean but very simple: a bed, a nightstand, a chair, a private bath, and a place to hang some clothes. Each has a private balcony, with a perfect view of the sun as it sets over Saline Bay. Dennis (who plays guitar two nights a week) is a charmer, the seafood (lobster, shrimp, fried squid, sautéed octopus, conch, or kingfish) at the restaurant is great, the drinks are strong, and the view is heavenly. Landlubbers can enjoy rack of lamb, barbecued spareribs or chicken, grilled lamb or pork chops. ✉ *Saline Bay* 784/458–8594 ⊕ www.

dennis-hideaway.com ⬭ 5 rooms ⟡ Restaurant, boating, bar; no a/c, no room phones, no room TVs ▭ No credit cards ⟡ BP.

Beaches

Saline Bay Beach. This beautiful 1-mi (1½-km) curve on the southwest coast has no facilities, but you can walk up the hill to Dennis's Hideaway for lunch or drinks. The dock here is where the ferry from St. Vincent ties up, and small cruise ships and windjammers occasionally anchor offshore to give passengers a beach break.

★ **Saltwhistle Bay Beach.** This beach at the northwestern end of the island takes top honors—it's an exquisite crescent of powdery white sand, shaded by perfectly spaced palms, sea grapes, and flowering bushes. It's also a popular anchorage for the yachting crowd, who stop for a swim and lunch or dinner at the beachfront Saltwhistle Bay Resort.

Sports & the Outdoors

BOATING & FISHING
Yacht charters, drift fishing trips, and day sails on the 44-foot sailing yacht *Georgia* can be arranged at **Dennis's Hideaway** (✉ Saline Bay ☎ 784/458–8594 ⊕ www.dennis-hideaway.com). Expect to pay $40 per person for drift fishing for 1½ hours and $75–$100 per person (depending on the number of passengers) for a full day of sailing, swimming, and snorkeling—lunch included.

Mustique

This upscale hideaway, 18 mi (29 km) southeast of St. Vincent, is only 3 mi (5 km) by 1½ mi (2 km) at its widest point. The island is hilly and has several green valleys, each with a sparkling white-sand beach facing an aquamarine sea. The permanent population is about 300.

Britain's late Princess Margaret put this small, private island on the map after owner Colin Tennant (Lord Glenconner) presented her with a 10-acre plot of land as a wedding gift in 1960 (Tennant had purchased the entire 1,400-acre island in 1958 for $67,500). The Mustique Company—which Tennant formed in 1968 to develop the copra, sea-island cotton, and sugarcane estate into the glamorous hideaway it has become—now manages the privately owned villas, provides housing for all island employees, and operates Mustique Villa Rentals. Arrangements must be made about a year in advance to rent one of the luxury villas that now pepper the northern half of the island.

Sooner or later, stargazers see the resident glitterati at Basil's Bar, the island's social center. Proprietor Basil Charles also runs a boutique crammed with clothes and accessories specially commissioned from Bali. A pair of cotton-candy-colored, gingerbread-style buildings, the centerpiece of the tiny village, houses a gift shop and clothing boutique. There's a delicatessen-grocery to stock yachts and supply residents with fresh Brie and Moët; an antiques shop is filled with fabulous objets d'art to decorate those extraordinary villas—or to bring home.

The Mustique Blues Festival, held during the first two weeks of February, features artists from North America, Europe, and the Caribbean; shows occur nightly at Basil's Bar. The festival has quite a draw.

Where to Stay

For approximate costs, *see* the lodging price chart *in* St. Vincent.

$$$$
FodorśChoice
★
🏨 **Cotton House.** Mustique's grand hotel, the main building of which was once an 18th-century cotton warehouse, has oceanfront rooms and suites with private walkways leading to the beach, a quartet of elegant ocean-view suites, and three poolside cottages with sunken baths, king-size beds with gauzy netting, and terraces affording stunning views. All have dressing areas, French doors and windows, desks, bathrooms with marble fittings, your choice of 11 kinds of pillows, TVs and VCRs by request only, and perfect peace. The beachfront spa offers body treatments and has a fitness center on the ground floor. Enjoy exquisite dining in the Great Room and casual lunches either poolside or at the Beach Terrace. ⌖ *Box 349, Endeavour Bay* ☎ *784/456–4777* 📠 *784/456–5887* ⊕ *www. cottonhouse.net* ⇌ *12 rooms, 5 suites, 3 cottages* ⚘ *3 restaurants, fans, in-room safes, minibars, cable TV (on request), in-room data ports, 2 tennis courts, pool, gym, spa, 2 beaches, dive shop, snorkeling, wind-surfing, boating, horseback riding, 3 bars, library, shops, babysitting, concierge, Internet room, meeting room, airport shuttle; no room phones, no room TVs* ⊟ *AE, D, MC, V* ⊗ *Closed Sept. and Oct.* ❠ *BP.*

$$$$
🏨 **Firefly.** Tiny and charming, this exclusive, reclusive three-story aerie is wedged into dense tropical foliage on a hillside above Britannia Bay. Each room is unique: one has a private deck with hot tub; another, a plunge pool; yet another, an open-air shower. The inn's two pools are connected by a waterfall, and the beach is just down the (rather steep) garden path. Firefly restaurant serves Caribbean cuisine, gourmet pizza, and pasta dishes. A small motorized buggy is included in the room rate. ⌖ *Box 349, Britannia Bay* ☎ *784/456–3414* 📠 *784/456–3514* ⊕ *www. fireflymustique.com* ⇌ *4 rooms* ⚘ *Restaurant, room service, fans, minibars, 2 pools, beach, snorkeling, bar, piano, airport shuttle; no a/c in some rooms, no room phones, no room TVs, no kids under 12* ⊟ *AE, MC, V* ❠ *FAP.*

☺ **$$$$**
🏨 **Mustique Villas.** Villa rentals are arranged solely through Mustique Villa Rentals, even though the villas are privately owned. Villas have two to nine bedrooms, and rentals include a full staff (with a cook), laundry service, and a vehicle or two. Houses range from "rustic" (albeit with en suite bathrooms for every bedroom, phones, pools, cable TVs, VCRs, CD players, and faxes) to extravagant, expansive, faux-Palladian follies with resident butler. All are designer-elegant and immaculately maintained. Weekly rentals run from $3,000 for a two-bedroom villa in the off-season to $40,000 for a palatial eight-bedroom villa in winter. ✉ *The Mustique Co., Ltd., Box 349, St. Vincent* ☎ *784/458–4621* 📠 *784/456–4565* ⊕ *www.mustique-island.com* ⇌ *58 villas* ⊟ *AE, D, DC, MC, V* ❠ *EP.*

Where to Eat

For approximate costs, *see* the dining price chart *in* St. Vincent.

★ **$$$–$$$$**
✕ **Basil's Bar.** Basil's is *the* place to be—and only partly because it is the *only* place to be in Mustique aside from the two hotel restaurants. This rustic eatery is simply a wood deck perched on bamboo stilts over the waves; there's a thatched roof, a congenial bar, and a dance floor

that's open to the stars—in every sense. You never know what celebrity may show up at the next table. The food is simple and good—mostly seafood, homemade ice cream, burgers, and salads, great French toast, the usual cocktails, and unusual wines. Wednesday is barbecue and party night. ⊠ *Britannia Bay* ☎ *784/458–4621* ⚑ *Reservations essential* ▭ *AE, D, MC, V.*

★ $$$–$$$$ ✕ **Great Room.** Expect a memorable experience at the Cotton House's fine restaurant. Executive chef Matt Coates, a New Zealander with broad experience in Australia and Asia, creates simple, fresh dishes by adding Caribbean touches to traditional international cuisines. Appetizers of shredded duck and mango salad or kingfish sashimi are every bit as tempting as the entrées, which include grilled barracuda with lemongrass, lobster tail on a spicy corn fritter, or panfried pork loin with garlic crushed potatoes. Vegetarian and pasta dishes are always available. Homemade ice cream or sorbet may be enough for dessert, if you can blink when just-made pastries are offered. ⊠ *Endeavour Bay* ☎ *784/456–4777* ⚑ *Reservations essential* ▭ *AE, D, MC, V.*

Beaches

Britannia Bay. This beach on the west coast is right next to the Brittania Bay jetty, and Basil's Bar is convenient for lunch.

Endeavour Bay. This is the main beach used by guests of the Cotton House. Swimming and snorkeling are ideal, and a dive shop and water-sports equipment rental are available on-site. The resort's Beach House restaurant and bar are convenient for lunch or snacks.

Gelliceaux Bay. One of 10 marine conservation areas designated by St. Vincent and the Grenadines, this beach on the southwest coast is a perfect spot for snorkeling.

L'Ansecoy Bay. At the island's very northern tip, this broad crescent of white sand fringes brilliant turquoise water. Just offshore, the French liner *Antilles* went aground in 1971.

Fodor'sChoice **Macaroni Beach.** Macaroni is Mustique's most famous stretch of fine white
★ sand—offering swimming (no lifeguards) in moderate surf that's several shades of blue, along with a few palm huts and picnic tables in a shady grove of trees.

Sports & the Outdoors

Water-sports facilities are available at the Cotton House, and most villas have equipment of various sorts. Four floodlighted tennis courts are near the airport for those whose villa lacks its own; there's a cricket field for the Brits (matches on Sunday afternoon), and motorbikes or "mules" (beach buggies) to ride around the bumpy roads rent for $65–$85 per day.

DIVING & Mustique is surrounded by coral reefs. **Mustique Watersports** (⊠ Cotton
SNORKELING House, Endeavour Bay ☎ 784/456–3486 🖷 784/456–4565) offers
↻ PADI instruction and certification and has a 28-foot, fully equipped dive boat. Rates are $55 for an introductory course, $65 for a one-tank dive, and $299 for a five-dive package. A special "bubble maker" introduction-to-diving course for children ages 8–11 costs $40. Snorkelers can rent a mask and fins for $7 per hour or $20 per day; snorkeling trips are $35 per person, with a two-person minimum.

HORSEBACK
RIDING
🐎

Mustique is the only island in the Grenadines where you can find a fine thoroughbred horse or pony to ride. Daily excursions leave from the **Mustique Equestrian Centre** (☎ 784/488–8000 ⊕ www.mustique-island.com), which is one block from the airport. Rates are $65 per hour for an island trek and $60 per hour for lessons. All rides are accompanied, and children over five years are allowed to ride.

Palm Island

A private speck of land only 135 acres in area, exquisite Palm Island used to be an uninhabited, swampy, mosquito-infested spot called Prune Island. One intrepid family put heart and soul—as well as muscle and brawn—into taking the wrinkles out of the prune and rechristened it Palm Island. The family cleaned up the five surrounding beaches, built bungalows, planted palm trees, and irrigated the swamp with seawater to kill the mosquitoes. The rustic getaway existed for 25 years before Palm Island's current owners, Elite Island Resorts, dolled up the property, and now it's one of the finest resorts in the Caribbean. Other than the resort, the island has only a handful of private villas. Access is via Union Island, 1 mi (1½ km) to the west and a 10-minute ride in the resort's launch.

Where to Stay

For approximate costs, *see* the lodging price chart *in* St. Vincent.

$$$$
Fodor'sChoice
★

⊞ **Palm Island Resort.** Perfect for a honeymoon, rendezvous, or luxurious escape, this palm-studded resort offers five dazzling white-sand beaches, a calm aquamarine sea for swimming and enjoying water sports, nature trails for quiet walks, a pool with waterfall, sophisticated dining, impeccable service, and exquisite accommodations. Picture-perfect Casuarina Beach runs the entire length of the western side of the island. Choose a beachfront room with stone bathroom, a palm-view room or plantation suite, or an Island Loft—a remote tree house on stilts. All have wicker and bamboo furniture, rich fabrics, wooden louvers on three walls to catch every breeze, and original artwork. The Royal Palm dining room, for guests only, offers a varied menu; the Sunset Grill & Bar near the dock serves seafood, light fare, and drinks and is open to the public. ⊠ *Palm Island* ☎ *784/458–8824* 🖷 *784/458–8804* ⊕ *www. eliteislandresorts.com* 🛏 *28 rooms, 4 suites, 5 cottages* ⚒ *Restaurant, dining room, room service, fans, in-room safes, refrigerator, 5-hole golf course, tennis court, pool, gym, massage, 5 beaches, dock, snorkeling, windsurfing, boating, bicycles, croquet, hiking, Ping-Pong, 2 bars, library, recreation room, shop, Internet room, airport shuttle; no room TVs* ⊟ *AE, D, DC, MC, V* ⍩ *AI.*

Petit St. Vincent

The southernmost of St. Vincent's Grenadines, tiny (113 acres), private Petit St. Vincent, pronounced "Petty" St. Vincent and affectionately called PSV, is ringed with white-sand beaches and covered with tropical foliage. The resort was created in 1968 by Haze Richardson, who remains the current proprietor; several current staff members have worked with him from the beginning. To get here you fly from Barbados to Union Island, where the resort's motor launch meets you for the 30-minute voyage.

Where to Stay

For approximate costs, *see* the lodging price chart *in* St. Vincent.

★ **$$$$** ▦ **Petit St. Vincent Resort.** No phones, no TVs, no outside interferences, and no planned activities can all be particularly appealing when you can indulge your shipwreck fantasies without foregoing luxury. Each secluded cobblestone cottage has a large bedroom, separate sitting room with sliding glass walls facing the ocean, a patio, and beach access. Bathrooms have cobblestone showers. A system of signal flags conveys your whims to the staff, so you can avoid human encounters entirely if you wish. Hoist your red flag and nobody *dreams* of approaching; hoist the yellow and you can promptly receive whatever you desire—or just a lift to the dining room. Relax, read, swim, and get away from it all in rustic elegance. Or sail away on a Hobie Cat, Sunfish, Windsurfer, or glass-bottom kayak. Fishing trips and day sails are available from the dock, as well. Although the resort doesn't have a strict policy regarding children, the atmosphere here is not exactly kid-friendly. ⊠ *Petit St. Vincent* ☎ *784/458–8801* 🖷 *784/458–8428* ⊕ *www.psvresort.com* ⊠ *U.S. agent: PSV, Box 841338, Pembroke Pines, FL 33084* ☎ *954/963–7401 or 800/654–9326* 🖷 *784/458–8428* ⟿ *22 cottages* ⌂ *Restaurant, room service, fans, tennis court, massage, beach, dock, snorkeling, windsurfing, boating, fishing, hiking, bar, shop, airport shuttle; no a/c, no room phones, no room TVs* ▭ *AE, MC, V* �᐀ *FAP* ⊘ *Closed Sept. and Oct.*

Tobago Cays

Fodor'sChoice
★ A trip to this small group of uninhabited islands, just east of Mayreau in the southern Grenadines and recently declared a wildlife reserve by the St. Vincent & the Grenadines government, will allow you to experience some of the best snorkeling in the world. Horseshoe Reef surrounds five uninhabited islets, each with tiny palm-lined, white-sand beaches. The brilliantly colored water (alternating shades of azure and turquoise) is studded with sponges and coral formations and populated by countless colorful fish. All the major dive operators go here, whether they are based in St. Vincent or anywhere in the Grenadines. Whether you are diving, snorkeling, or simply enjoying the boat ride, a visit to the Tobago Cays is a truly unforgettable experience.

Union Island

The jagged peak of the Pinnacle soars 995 feet in the air, distinguishing Union Island from its neighbors. Union is a popular anchorage for French vacationers sailing the Grenadines and a crossroads for others heading to surrounding islands (Palm, Mayreau, and Petit St. Vincent) just minutes away by speedboat. Clifton, the main town, is small and commercial, with a bustling harbor, a few simple beachfront inns and restaurants, businesses that cater to yachts, and the regional airstrip—perhaps the busiest in the Grenadines. Taxis and minibuses are available.

The Easterval Regatta occurs during the Easter weekend with festivities that include boat races, sports and games, a calypso competition, a beauty pageant, and a cultural show featuring the Big Drum Dance (derived from French and African traditions). Union is one of the few islands (along with Grenada's Carriacou) that perpetuate this festive dance.

Where to Stay

For approximate costs, *see* the lodging price chart *in* St. Vincent.

☺ **$** ⊞ **Bigsand Hotel.** Five minutes north of Clifton, Bigsand's small grouping of bright-white, two-story buildings lies just steps from the sea at picturesque Big Sand Beach. Each suite has a large bedroom, an enormous living room furnished with leather couches, a large bathroom (shower only), and a kitchenette. Living rooms open to private beachfront porches. Only bedrooms are air-conditioned, but cooling breezes constantly sweep through each suite. Windsurfers, surfboards, kayaks, and snorkeling equipment are complimentary. This is a perfect spot to relax and soak up the Caribbean sun, but you can easily walk to town if you wish. ⊠ *Richmond Bay* ☎ *784/485–8447* 🖷 *784/485–7447* ⊕ *www.bigsandhotel.com* ⇆ *10 suites* ⚲ *Restaurant, fans, in-room safes, kitchens, cable TV, beach, snorkeling, windsurfing, boating, bicycles, Ping-Pong, bar, airport shuttle* 🖃 *AE, MC, V* ⏏⊙⏏ *EP.*

Where to Eat

For approximate costs, *see* the dining price chart *in* St. Vincent.

BELGIAN   ✕ **Bigsand Restaurant & Beach Bar.** Although the seafood and produce
$$ are definitely local, diners note a distinctly European finesse in the preparation and presentation at Bigsand, which is owned and operated by a Belgian expat. Local folks, island visitors, and hotel guests can enjoy breakfast, lunch, or dinner alfresco. Onion soup, mixed salad, pasta, and sandwiches on homemade bread or panini are great at lunch. Plus, you can enjoy an imported Belgian beer as you watch pelicans dive for their own lunch just offshore. At dinner, the lobster is incredible—or choose perfectly prepared beef tenderloin with bèarnaise, mushroom, or herbed sauce and a good French wine. ⊠ *Richmond Bay* ☎ *784/485– 8447* 🖃 *AE, MC, V.*

CARIBBEAN   ✕ **Lambi's.** During high season (November to May), Lambi's, which over-
¢–$ looks the waterfront in Clifton, offers a daily buffet for each meal. The dinner buffet includes some 50 dishes, including the specialty, delicious conch creole. In the low season (June to October), dining is à la carte, and you can choose from a menu of fish, chicken, conch, pork, lobster, shrimp, and beef dishes. Lambi is creole patois for "conch," and the restaurant's walls are even constructed from conch shells. Yachts and dinghies can tie up at the wharf, and there's steel-band music and limbo dancing every night in season. ⊠ *Clifton* ☎ *784/458–8549* 🖃 *No credit cards.*

Beaches

Big Sand. Union has relatively few good beaches, but this one at Richmond Bay on the north shore, a five-minute drive from Clifton, is a pretty crescent of powdery white sand, protected by reefs and with lovely views of Mayreau and the Tobago Cays.

Chatham Bay. The desolate but lovely golden-sand beach at Chatham Bay offers good swimming.

Sports & the Outdoors

BOATING &
SAILING

Union is a major base for yacht charters and sailing trips. From a dock 500 yards from the Union Island airstrip, you can arrange a day sail throughout the lower Grenadines: Palm Island, Mayreau, the Tobago Cays, Petit St. Vincent, and Carriacou. A full day of snorkeling, fishing, and/or swimming costs about $200 per person for two people or $120 per person for four or more—lunch and drinks included. At **Anchorage Yacht Club** (⊠ Clifton ☎ 784/458–8221) you can arrange crewed yacht or sailboat charters for a day sail or longer treks around the Grenadines. The marina is also a good place to stock up on fresh-baked bread and croissants, ice, water, food, and other boat supplies. **Captain Yannis** (⊠ Clifton ☎ 784/458–8513) has a charter fleet of three 60-foot catamarans and one 60-foot trimaran. Snorkeling gear, drinks, and a buffet lunch are included in a day sail.

DIVING &
SNORKELING

Grenadines Dive (⊠ Sunny Grenadines Hotel, Clifton ☎ 784/458–8138 ⊕ www.grenadinesdive.com), run by NAUI-certified instructor Glenroy Adams, offers Tobago Cays snorkeling trips and wreck dives at the *Purina,* a sunken World War I English gunboat. A single-tank dive costs $60; multidive packages are discounted. Beginners can take a four-hour resort course, which includes a shallow dive, for $85. Certified divers can rent equipment by the day or week.

ST. VINCENT & THE GRENADINES ESSENTIALS

To research prices, get advice from other travelers, and book travel arrangements, visit www.fodors.com.

Transportation

BY AIR

Travelers from North America and Europe arrive at airports in St. Vincent and the Grenadines via connecting service to major airlines that serve six gateways: Barbados, Grenada, Martinique, St. Lucia, Puerto Rico, and Trinidad. Connections are via American Eagle, Caribbean Star, LIAT, and Grenadines Airways.

American Eagle flies nonstop between either San Juan or Barbados and Canouan. Caribbean Star flies to St. Vincent from St. Lucia or Grenada. LIAT connects St. Vincent, Bequia, and Union with Grenada and St. Lucia. Grenadines Airways, an alliance of Mustique Airways, SVG Air, and TIA, operates shared-charter service linking Barbados with the four airports in

the Grenadines and inter-Grenadine scheduled flights between St. Vincent and the Grenadines.

From other parts of the world, connections must be made through major U.S. cities, Toronto, London, or one of the Caribbean hubs, such as San Juan or Barbados.

✈ Airlines **American Eagle** ☎ 784/456–5555 ⊕ www.aa.com. **Caribbean Star** ☎ 784/456–5800 ⊕ www.flycaribbeanstar.com. **LIAT** ☎ 784/458–4841 in St. Vincent, 784/457–1821 in Bequia, 784/458–8230 in Union. **Grenadine Airways** ☎ 246/418–1654 for shared-charter flights, 784/456–6793 for inter-Grenadine flights ⊕ www.grenadineairways.com.

AIRPORTS & TRANSFERS: Taxis—usually pickup trucks, with their beds fitted with seats and an awning—are readily available at the airport in Bequia to take you to Port Elizabeth, to the various hotels, or for a day of sightseeing. On Canouan, the resorts generally provide airport transfers, although taxis are available. On Mustique, either transfers are provided or taxis are available. On Union Island, Clifton, the main town, is a short walk from the airport; taxis, of course, are also available.

🛪 Airports **Canouan Airport** ✉ Canouan ☎ 784/458-8049. **E. T. Joshua Airport** ✉ Arnos Vale, St. Vincent ☎ 784/458-4011. **James F. Mitchell Airport** ✉ Bequia ☎ 784/458-3948. **Mustique Airport** ✉ Mustique ☎ 784/458-4621. **Union Airport** ✉ Union ☎ 784/458-8750.

BY BOAT & FERRY

St. Vincent's port accomomdates large passenger ships. Cruise ships that call at Port Elizabeth on Bequia, at Mayreau, and elsewhere in the Grenadines anchor offshore and tender passengers to beaches or waterfront jetties.

In St. Vincent, interisland ferries dock at the wharf adjacent to the Cruise Ship Terminal in Kingstown; in Bequia, ferries dock at the jetty in Port Elizabeth. The one-way trip between St. Vincent and Bequia takes 60 minutes and costs $6 (EC$15) each way or $10 (EC$25) round-trip.

Two companies offer frequent ferry services between Bequia and St. Vincent. Admiralty Transport and Bequia Express each operate two ferries that make several round-trips daily, Monday through Saturday, beginning at 6:30 AM in Bequia and 8 AM in St. Vincent; the latest departure each day is at 5 PM from Bequia and 7 PM from St. Vincent. On Sunday and public holidays, each company operates two round-trips, one in the morning and one in the evening.

The interisland ferry, MV *Barracuda,* which is also known as "the mail boat," operates twice weekly. It leaves St. Vincent on Monday and Thursday mornings, stopping in Canouan, Mayreau, and Union Island. It makes the return trip Tuesday and Friday. On Saturday it does the round-trip from St. Vincent to each island and returns in a day. Including stopover time, the trip from St. Vincent takes 2¾ hours (sometimes via Bequia) to Canouan ($8), 4½ hours to Mayreau ($10), and 5½ hours to Union Island ($12).

🚢 **Admiralty Transport** 🚢🚢 784/458-3348. **MV Barracuda** ☎ 784/456-5180. **MV Bequia Express** ☎ 784/458-3472.

BY BUS

Public buses on St. Vincent are privately owned, brightly painted minivans with colorful names like *Confidence, Fully Loaded, Irie,* and *Who to Blame.* Bus fares range from EC$1 to EC$6 (40¢ to $2.25) on St. Vincent; the 10-minute ride from Kingstown to Villa Beach, for example, costs EC$1.50 (60¢). Buses operate from early morning until about midnight. Routes are indicated on a sign on the windshield, and the bus will stop on demand. Just wave from the road or point your finger to the ground as a bus approaches, and the driver will stop. When you want to get out, signal by knocking twice on a window. A conductor rides along to open the door and collect fares; it's helpful to have the correct change in EC coins. In Kingstown the central departure point is the bus terminal at the New Kingstown Fish Market. Buses serve the entire island, although trips to remote villages are infrequent.

BY CAR

Car rental is available only on St. Vincent and Bequia. Renting a car on St. Vincent is a good idea if you would like to explore the leeward or windward coast on your own. Either drive is interesting and picturesque, the roads easy to navigate, and the sights easy to find. If you're planning an extended stay on St. Vincent and expect to travel frequently between Kingstown and, say, the Villa Beach area, a rental car might be useful—although not necessary, as both taxis and buses are inexpensive, and readily available. On Bequia, a rental car will be handy if you're staying for several days in a remote location—that is, anywhere beyond Port Elizabeth. For brief stays, taxis offer prompt service and will even drop you at the beach and pick you up later, if you wish.

Rental cars in St. Vincent and Bequia cost about $55 per day or $300 a week, with some free miles. Unless you already have an international driver's license, you'll need to buy a temporary local permit for EC$50 (US$20), valid for six months. To get one, present your valid driver's license at the police station on Bay Street or the Licensing Authority on Halifax Street, both in Kingstown, St. Vincent, or the Revenue Office in Port Elizabeth, Bequia.

Avis is the one international agency represented on St. Vincent. Local firms are reliable and offer comparable rates, including some four-wheel-drive vehicles. If you'd prefer "the slow lane," two-seater scooters or mopeds can be rented for $30 per day or $180 per week from Speedway Bike & Scooter Rental.

In Bequia, you can rent a four-wheel-drive vehicle from B&G Jeep Rental, a car from Phil's Car Rental, or a Mini-Moke fun car from Mokes for Rent.

About 360 mi (580 km) of paved roads wind around St. Vincent's perimeter, except for a section in the far north with no road at all, precluding a circle tour of the island. A few roads jut into the interior a few miles, and only one east–west road (through the Mesopotamia Valley) bisects the island. It's virtually impossible to get lost; but if you do make a wrong turn, local folks are friendly and will be happy to point you in the right direction. Roads are narrow in the country, often not wide enough for two cars to pass, and people (including schoolchildren), dogs, goats, and chickens often share the roadway with cars, minibuses, and trucks. Outside populated areas, roads can be bumpy and potholed; be sure your rental car has proper tire-changing equipment and a spare in the trunk. Drive on the left, and toot your horn before you enter blind curves out in the countryside, where you'll encounter plenty of steep hills and hairpin turns. Gasoline costs about $4 per gallon.

LOCAL CAR RENTAL COMPANIES: 🇫 St. Vincent Avis ⊠ Airport, Arnos Vale, St. Vincent ☎784/456-2929. Ben's Auto Rental ⊠ Arnos Vale, St. Vin-

cent ☎784/456-2907. David's Auto Clinic ⊠ Sion Hill, St. Vincent ☎784/456-4026. Speedway Bike & Scooter Rental ⊠ Arnos Vale, St. Vincent ☎784/456-4894. Star Garage ⊠ Grenville St., Kingstown, St. Vincent ☎784/456-1743.
🇫 Bequia B&G Jeep Rental ⊠ Port Elizabeth, Bequia ☎784/458-3760. Mokes for Rent ⊠ Port Elizabeth, Bequia ☎784/457-3238. Phil's Car Rental ⊠ Port Elizabeth, Bequia ☎784/458-3304.

BY TAXI

Fares are set by the government, but taxis are not metered. Therefore, it's smart to settle on the price before entering the taxi—and be sure you know what currency is being quoted. On St. Vincent, the one-way fare between Kingstown and Villa is about $10 (EC$25).

On some islands, most notably Bequia, water taxis can take you between Port Elizabeth and the beaches for a couple of dollars each way. Keep in mind that these taxi operators aren't regulated or insured, so travel at your own risk.

Contacts & Resources

BANKS & EXCHANGE SERVICES

Branches of several regional and international banks are in Kingstown, with other branches elsewhere on St. Vincent & and in the Grenadines. ATMs are at banks in Kingstown and at their branches.

Large U.S. bills may be difficult to change in small shops. U.S. coins are not accepted anywhere. Although U.S. dollars are accepted nearly everywhere, you'll receive change in Eastern Caribbean currency (EC$), which is the official currency and preferred. The exchange rate is fixed at EC$2.67 to US$1. Price quotes in shops are often given in both currencies. Prices quoted in this chapter are in U.S. dollars unless otherwise noted. Major credit cards—including American Express, Diners Club, Discover, MasterCard, and Visa—and traveler's checks are accepted by hotels, car-rental agencies, and some shops and restaurants.

St. Vincent **Bank of Nova Scotia** ⊠ Halifax St., Kingstown ☎ 784/457-1601. **First Caribbean International Bank** ⊠ Halifax St., Kingstown ☎ 784/456-1706. **National Commercial Bank of St. Vincent** ⊠ Bedford St., Kingstown ☎ 784/457-1844 ⊠ E. T. Joshua Airport, Arnos Vale, Kingstown ☎ 784/458-4943.

The Grenadines **National Commercial Bank of St. Vincent** ⊠ Port Elizabeth, Bequia ☎ 784/458-3700 ⊠ Charlestown, Canouan ☎ 784/458-8595 ⊠ Clifton, Union ☎ 784/458-8347.

BUSINESS HOURS

Banks are open Monday through Thursday from 8 to 1 or 3, Friday until 3 or 5. The bank at the airport is open Monday through Saturday from 7 to 5. Bank branches on Bequia, Canouan, and Union are open Monday through Thursday from 8 to 1 and Friday 8 to 5. The General Post Office, on Halifax Street in Kingstown, is open daily from 8:30 to 3, Saturday from 8:30 to 11:30. Shops and businesses in Kingstown are open weekdays from 8 to 4; some close for lunch from noon to 1. Saturday hours are from 8 to noon. Shops are closed on Sunday, but supermarkets in Kingstown and Arnos Vale are open Sunday mornings.

ELECTRICITY

Electricity is generally 220–240 volts, 50 cycles. Some resorts, such as Petit St. Vincent, have 110 volts, 60 cycles (U.S. standard); most have 110-volt shaver outlets. Dual-voltage computers or small appliances will still require a plug adapter (three rectangular pins). Some hotels will lend transformers and/or plug adapters.

EMBASSIES

United Kingdom **British High Commission** ⊠ Grenville St., Box 132, Kingstown, St. Vincent ☎ 784/457-1701 or 784/458-4381.

EMERGENCIES

ST. VINCENT: Ambulance & Fire **Ambulance and fire emergencies** ☎ 911.
Coast Guard **Coast Guard emergencies** ☎ 911. **Coast Guard nonemergencies** ☎ 784/457-4578.
Hospitals **Milton Cato Memorial Hospital** ⊠ Kingstown ☎ 784/456-1185.

Pharmacies **Medcare** ⊠ Arnos Vale, St. Vincent ☎ 784/457-0212. **People's Pharmacy** ⊠ Bedford St., Kingstown ☎ 784/456-1170. **Victoria Pharmacy** ⊠ Bentick Sq., Kingstown ☎ 784/451-2668.
Police **Police emergencies** ☎ 911. **Police non-emergencies** ☎ 784/457-1211.

THE GRENADINES: Ambulance & Fire **Ambulance and fire** ☎ 911.
Hospitals **Bequia Casualty Hospital** ⊠ Port Elizabeth, Bequia ☎ 784/458-3294. **Canouan Clinic** ⊠ Charlestown, Canouan ☎ 784/458-8305. **Mustique Company Island Clinic** ⊠ Adjacent to Mustique Airport, Mustique ☎ 784/458-4621 Ext. 353. **Union Island Health Centre** ⊠ Clifton, Union ☎ 784/458-8339.
Pharmacies **Imperial Pharmacy** ⊠ Off Back St., Port Elizabeth, Bequia ☎ 784/458-3373.
Police **Police emergencies** ☎ 911.

HEALTH

Water from the tap in your hotel is safe to drink, but bottled water is always available. Fresh fruits and vegetables from the market are safe to eat, but (as at home) you should wash them first. Cooked food purchased at the market, in small shops, or at village snackettes is wholesome and safe to enjoy.

HOLIDAYS

Holidays include New Year's Day (Jan. 1), National Heroes Day (Mar. 14), Good Friday, Easter Monday, Labour Day (May 1), Whitmonday (7th Mon. after Easter), Carnival Monday (2nd Mon. in July), Carnival Tuesday (2nd Tues. in July), Emancipation Day (Aug. 1), Independence Day (Oct. 27), Christmas, and Boxing Day (Dec. 26).

INTERNET, MAIL & SHIPPING

On St. Vincent, the E@gles Internet Cafe offers high-speed computers and broadband Internet access for as little as $2 per hour. On Bequia, the Surf 'n' Send Internet Cafe, the Sunset Internet Cafe, and the Lenroc Internet Cafe are all in Port Elizabeth.

The General Post Office is on Halifax Street in Kingstown, St. Vincent. Most villages on St. Vincent have branch offices. Bequia's post office is in Port Elizabeth, across from the jetty. Airmail postcards cost EC.60 to the United States, Canada, the United Kingdom, Australia, and New Zealand; airmail letters cost EC.90 per ounce to the United States and Canada, EC$1.10 to the United Kingdom, Australia, and New Zealand. When you are writing to a location in the Grenadines, the address on the envelope should always indicate the specific island name followed by "St. Vincent and the Grenadines, West Indies."

E@gles Internet Cafe ⊠ Halifax St., opposite the General Post Office, Kingstown, St. Vincent. **Lenroc Internet Cafe** ⊠ Back St., Port Elizabeth, Bequia. **Sunset Internet Cafe** ⊠ Front St., Port Elizabeth, Bequia **Surf 'n' Send Internet Cafe** ⊠ Belmont Walkway, Port Elizabeth, Bequia.

LANGUAGE

English is the official language of St. Vincent and the Grenadines. Although there's certainly a Caribbean lilt, you won't hear the creole patois common on other islands that have a historical French background. One term to listen for is "jump-up," in which case you can expect a party with music and dancing. And if you're going to "lime" at the next "gap," you'll be relaxing—perhaps with a cool drink in hand—down the road. Women travelers find it particularly charming to be referred to as "milady."

PASSPORTS & VISAS

Citizens of the United States, Canada, and the United Kingdom need only a passport or birth certificate and government-issued identification card, along with an ongoing or return ticket, in order to enter St. Vincent and the Grenadines. A passport will be required to reenter the U.S. beginning January 1, 2007.

SAFETY

There's relatively little crime here, but don't tempt fate by leaving your valuables lying around or your room or your rental car unlocked. Also, be alert and mindful of your belongings around the wharf areas in Kingstown, which can be congested when

passengers are disembarking from ferries or cruise ships.

TAXES & SERVICE CHARGES

The departure tax from St. Vincent and the Grenadines is $15 (EC$40), payable in cash in either U.S. or EC currency; children under 12 are exempt. A government tax of 7% is added to hotel bills, and a 10% service charge is included on hotel bills and often on restaurant bills.

TELEPHONES

Pay phones are readily available and best operated with the prepaid phone cards that are sold at many stores and can be used on many Caribbean islands. Most cell phones can roam in St. Vincent and the Grenadines—for outgoing calls only—but you may be shocked by the charges, which can be exorbitant, when you get the bill. The area code for St. Vincent and the Grenadines is 784.

Local calls are free from private phones and most hotels. Prepaid phone cards, which can be used in special card phones throughout St. Vincent and other Caribbean islands, are sold at shops, transportation centers, and other convenient outlets. (The phone cards can be used for local or international calls.)

INTERNATIONAL CALLS: **International Operator** ☎ 115. **Operator-Assisted Credit Card Calls** ☎ 117.

TIPPING

If a 10% service charge has not been added to your restaurant tab, a gratuity at that rate is appropriate. Otherwise, tipping is expected only for special service. For bellmen and porters, $1 per bag is appropriate; for room maids, $2 per day.

VISITOR INFORMATION

Before You Leave **St. Vincent & the Grenadines Tourist Office** ⊕ www.svgtourism.com ⊠ 801 2nd Ave., 21st fl., New York, NY 10017 ☎ 212/687-4981 or 800/729-1726 ⊠ 333 Wilson Ave., Suite 601, Toronto, Ontario M3H 1T2, Canada ☎ 416/633-3100 ⊠ 10 Kensington Ct., London W8 5DL, U.K. ☎ 0207/937-6570. **St. Vincent Hotels & Tourism Association** ⊕ www.svghotels.com.

🔢 In St. Vincent & the Grenadines **St. Vincent & the Grenadines Ministry of Tourism & Culture** ✉ Cruise Ship Terminal, Harbour Quay, Kingstown, St. Vincent ☎ 784/457-1502 🖷 784/451-2425. **Tourist information desks** ✉ E. T. Joshua Airport, Arnos Vale, St. Vincent ☎ 784/458-4685 ✉ Union Airport, Clifton, Union ☎ 784/458-8350. **Bequia Tourism Association** ⊕ www.bequiatourism.com ✉ Main Jetty, Box 146BQ, Port Elizabeth, Bequia ☎ 784/458-3286 🖷 784/458-3964.

WEDDINGS

Young Island, Palm Island, Petit St. Vincent, a villa on Mustique, a hilltop on Bequia, a 19th-century church on Canouan, the beach on Mayreau—all are lovely settings for a Caribbean wedding.

Visitors wishing to marry in St. Vincent and the Grenadines must be resident in the country for a minimum of three days before a marriage ceremony can take place. A marriage license must be obtained from the Registrar's Office, Granby Street, Kingstown, St. Vincent, on weekdays between 8:30 and 3, excluding the lunch hour. Processing usually takes no more than three hours. You'll need to bring your valid passports, recent birth certificates (issued within the past six months), divorce decrees if you've been divorced, and an appropriate death certificate if either party is widowed. The license fee is $185 (EC$500) plus $7.50 (EC$15 and EC$5) for two required stamps. An official marriage officer, priest, or minister registered in St. Vincent and the Grenadines must officiate at the ceremony, and two witnesses must be present.

Trinidad & Tobago

Carnival in Trinidad

WORD OF MOUTH

"Around January in Trinidad the steel bands will be practicing in their pan yards for Panarama. . . . Even if you don't like pan, you can't help but get caught up in the excitement of the music."

—mike

"Of course you know what to expect in birding—it's one of THE places in the world for this. The Scarlet Ibis flying in at dusk are so beautiful."

—l.martin

www.fodors.com/forums

WELCOME TO TRINIDAD & TOBAGO

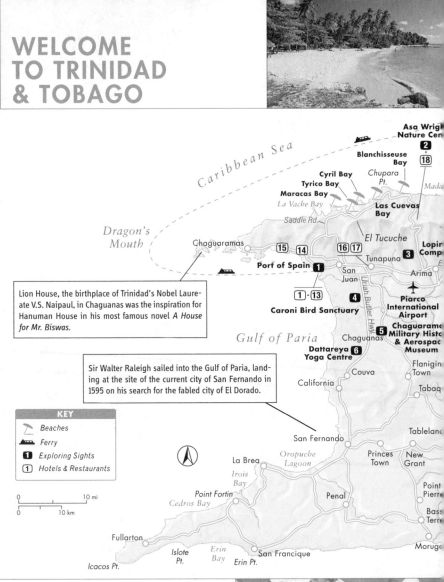

Caribbean Sea

Asa Wright Nature Cen 2

Blanchisseuse Bay 18

Chupara Pt.

Mada

Cyril Bay
Tyrico Bay
Maracas Bay
La Vache Bay
Saddle Rd.

Las Cuevas Bay

Dragon's Mouth

Chaguaramas

15 14

16 17

El Tucuche

Tunapuna

Lopir Comp 3

Arima

Port of Spain 1

San Juan

1 · 13

4

Caroni Bird Sanctuary

Gulf of Paria

Chaguanas

Piarco International Airport

Chaguarama Military Histo & Aerospac Museum 5

Dattareya Yoga Centre 6

Couva

California

Flanigin Town

Tabaq

Lion House, the birthplace of Trinidad's Nobel Laureate V.S. Naipaul, in Chaguanas was the inspiration for Hanuman House in his most famous novel *A House for Mr. Biswas*.

Sir Walter Raleigh sailed into the Gulf of Paria, landing at the site of the current city of San Fernando in 1595 on his search for the fabled city of El Dorado.

San Fernando

Oropuche Lagoon

Princes Town

New Grant

Tableland

Point Pierre

KEY
- ⌐ Beaches
- ⛴ Ferry
- 1 Exploring Sights
- 1 Hotels & Restaurants

0 _____ 10 mi
0 _____ 10 km

La Brea

Irois Bay

Point Fortin

Cedros Bay

Penal

Bass Terre

Moruge

Fullarton

Islote Pt.

Erin Bay

San Francique

Erin Pt.

Icacos Pt.

The most southerly of the Caribbean islands, Trinidad is also the most colorful. Islanders trace their roots to India, China, and Madeira; and they speak English, Spanish, and French Patois. On much quieter Tobago the most exciting event is often the palm trees swaying high above a gentle arc of a beach.

BUSINESS AND PLEASURE

The two-island republic is the southernmost link in the Antillean island chain, some 9 mi (14½) km off the coast of Venezuela, but Tobago's Main Ridge and Trinidad's Northern Range are believed to represent the farthest reaches of the Andes Mountains. Trinidad is a large petroleum and natural-gas producer. Tiny Tobago is known more for its quiet atmosphere and gorgeous, wild beaches.

24

TRINIDAD & TOBAGO

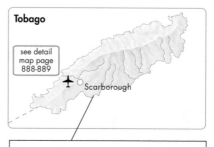

Tobago

see detail map page 888-889

Scarborough

Bacolet Beach was the location where the Disney movie The *Swiss Family Robinson* was filmed. It was also used for many scenes in John Huston's Heaven Knows, Mr. Allison.

Hotels .... ▼	Restaurants .... ▼
Asa Wright Nature Centre Lodge **18**	A La Bastille **13**
Coblentz Inn **6**	Apsara **10**
Courtyard by Marriott **14**	Battimamzelle **6**
	Il Colosseo **3**
Crewes Inn **15**	La Boucan **1**
Crowne Plaza **7**	Mélange **12**
Hilton Trinidad **1**	Solimar **4**
Kapok Hotel **2**	Tamnak Thai **9**
La Grande Almandier **19**	Tiki Village **2**
	Veni Mangé **5**
Monique's **8**	The Verandah **11**
Pax Guest House **16**	Wings Restaurant **17**

Map labels

Grande Rivière
Matelot
Toco
Salibea Bay
Galera Pt.
7 Point Galera Lighthouse
Sans Souci
Mt. Oropuche
Redhead
19
Cerro del Aripo
Balandra Bay
Matura
Saline Bay
lain Rd.
Valencia
urchill-osevelt ry.
Sangre Grande
Matura Bay
Manzanilla Beach
ATLANTIC OCEAN
Cocos Bay
Guataro Pt.
Rio Claro
Pierreville
Mayaro Bay
Guayaguayare
Galeota Pt.
Guayaguayare Bay

) TOBAGO

TOP 4 REASONS TO VISIT TRINIDAD & TOBAGO

1 Trinidad's Carnival is the Caribbean's biggest and best party, but nightlife is hopping the rest of the year, too.

2 Both Trinidad and Tobago are major bird watching destinations; Trinidad itself has more resident species than any other Caribbean island.

3 A melding of many cultures means lively festivals year-round and excel lent multicultural cuisine.

4 The steel pan was invented in Trinidad, and excellent bands play all over the island.

TRINIDAD & TOBAGO PLANNER

Getting to Trinidad & Tobago

You can fly nonstop to Trinidad from several U.S. cities and from Toronto, but not directly to Tobago. Most people hop over to Tobago on a small plane from Trinidad. If you are coming from the U.K., there are nonstops to both Trinidad and Tobago.

Trinidad's Piarco International Airport (POS), about 30 minutes east of Port of Spain (take Golden Grove Road north to Arouca and then follow Eastern Main Road west for about 10 mi [16 km] to Port of Spain), is a thoroughly modern facility complete with 16 air bridges. Tobago's small Crown Point Airport (TAB) is the gateway to the island.

Hassle Factor: Medium to High

On the Ground

Few hotels provide shuttle service, but you can always ask when you make your reservations. If you've booked a package, sometimes transfers are included. In Trinidad, taxis are readily available at Piarco Airport; the fare to Port of Spain is set at $30 ($45 after 10 PM) and $25 to the Hilton. In Tobago the fare from Crown Point Airport to Scarborough or Grafton Beach is about $50.

Renting a Car

Don't rent a car if you're staying in Port of Spain, but if you're planning to tour Trinidad, you'll need some wheels, as you will if you end up staying out on the island. In Tobago you're better off renting a four-wheel-drive vehicle than relying on expensive taxi service. Be cautious driving on either island, as the country has very lax and seldom enforced drinking and driving laws.

Activities

Trinidad has some good **beaches**—the best being Maracas Bay—but none is as picture-perfect as those on Tobago. Though they don't have the manicured, country-club elegance you will find on many islands, the beaches on Tobago feel wilder and hark back to a time when towering hotels didn't line every picturesque Caribbean crescent. **Bird-watching** is one of the highlights of a trip to either Trinidad or Tobago; both islands have reserves where you'll see a wide variety of species. **Diving** is good off the shores of Tobago, particularly around Arnos Vale Reef, off the island's west coast. **Golfers** will do better on Tobago, which has one excellent course and two other good ones. **Nightlife** is much better in Port of Spain, with live music being a particular highlight, but Tobago as a whole is much quieter after dark.

Where to Stay

Trinidad isn't a top tourist destination, so resorts are few and far between, and many are a long drive from Port of Spain and the airport. However, a few eco-conscious options are worth the hassle, particularly if you are a bird-watcher. Tobago has a wide array of lodging options, and it's a much smaller island with better beaches, so your choice of resort is more driven by the amenities you want and your budget—rather than the resort's location.

TYPES OF LODGINGS

Hotels: Though they have nice pools and other resort-type amenities, Trinidad's hotels are geared more for business travelers. Options for beach-goers are more limited and farther removed from Port of Spain.

Beach Resorts: Tobago has a nice mix of mid-sized resorts, including several offering a fair degree of luxury, but there are also many choices for budget-oriented tourists, as is the case in Trinidad, where fewer tourists mean better value at the small beach resorts that cater primarily to locals. Few hotels on either island offer anything but room-only rates, though there is now one all-inclusive resort on Tobago.

Eco-Resorts: Nature-lovers, particularly bird-watchers, have an especially good option in Trinidad in the Asa Wright Nature Centre Lodge. Several of Tobago's small resorts are particularly eco-conscious.

When to Go

Trinidad is more of a business destination than a magnet for tourists, so hotel rates (particularly in Port of Spain) are much more stable year-round; nevertheless, you can usually get a price break during the traditional Caribbean low season (from May to December). However, Carnival (in January or February) brings the highest rates. Tobago is much more of a tourist destination, but busy periods on Tobago—since it is still more popular with Europeans than Americans—can sometimes differ from the typical vacation periods in the U.S.

Trinidad's **Carnival** is the biggest and best celebration in the Caribbean. The **Tobago Heritage Festival** is usually held in late July. **Divali**, held in October or November and called the festival of lights, is one of the more popular Hindu festivals in Trinidad.

Hotel & Restaurant Costs

Assume that hotels operate on the European Plan (**EP**—with no meals) unless we specify that they use either the Continental Plan (**CP**—with a Continental breakfast), Breakfast Plan (**BP**—with full breakfast), or the Modified American Plan (**MAP**—with breakfast and dinner). Other hotels may offer the Full American Plan (**FAP**—including all meals but no drinks) or may be All-Inclusive (**AI**—with all meals, drinks, and most activities).

WHAT IT COSTS in Dollars					
	$$$$	**$$$**	**$$**	**$**	**¢**
Restaurants	over $30	$20–$30	$12–$20	$8–$12	under $8
Hotels*	over $350	$250–$350	$150–$250	$80–$150	under $80
Hotels**	over $450	$350–$450	$250–$350	$125–$250	under $125

*EP, BP, CP **AI, FAP, MAP

Restaurant prices are for a main course excluding 10% service charge. Hotel prices are for two people in a double room in high season excluding 10% tax, customary 10%–15% service charge, and meal plans (except at all-inclusives).

24

By Vernon
O'Reilly-
Ramesar

SENSORY OVERLOAD IS INSUFFICIENT to describe the Queen's Park Savannah on Carnival Tuesday. Thousands of costumed masqueraders in dozens of bands form pulsing sections of color on the dusty path leading to the judging stage, the line snaking back as far as the eye can see. The driving sound of steel bands fills the air and barely competes with the throb of massive music trucks blaring soca. The faces in the waiting throng reflect every imaginable ethnic background. Since the wee hours, they have slogged through packed streets to reach this point. Once off the stage—champions or not—they will continue their musical march until their feet can take no more. On an island built on trade, where the roads are usually packed with honking cars, today the traffic lights are off as Trinis ecstatically celebrate life with a multicultural human traffic jam.

The birthplace of the steel pan (the national instrument), limbo, calypso, and soca (a harder-edged version of calypso), these lush islands can also lay claim to being the economic powerhouse of the Caribbean. Vast oil and gas reserves have led to a high standard of living and a great sense of optimism about the future, where tourism is not the mainstay of the economy. Indeed, the word *tourist* is seldom mentioned here; the preference is for the much friendlier *visitor*. T&T, as the dual-island nation is commonly called—is the southernmost link in the Antillean island chain, lying some 7 mi (11 km) off the coast of Venezuela and safely outside the path of most Caribbean hurricanes. Geologically, though, the islands are actually extensions of the South American mainland. Trinidad's Northern Range is thought to be part of the Andes (and was connected to the mainland as recently as the last Ice Age). This geological history helps explain why the range of flora and fauna is much greater than on other Caribbean Islands. And though connected politically and geologically, Trinidad and Tobago offer dramatically different cultural experiences.

Trinidad's capital city, Port of Spain, is home to some 300,000 of the island's 1.3 million inhabitants. In fact, the capital merges seamlessly with other towns and residential areas to form a dense population belt that runs from Westmoorings in the west to Arima in the east. Downtown Port of Spain is a bustling commercial center complete with high-rise office buildings and seemingly perpetual traffic. Happily, the northern mountain range rises just behind the city and helps to take much of the edge off the urban clamor.

Much of the charm of Trinidad lies in the ethnic mix of the population. The majority of the population is of either African or East Indian background—the descendants of African slaves brought here during the island's relatively short slave history of some 80 years, and indentured East Indian laborers, who came to work the plantations in the 19th century. The island is always buzzing with a variety of celebrations and arts performances that can range from African drumming to classical Indian dance. The national cuisine has also absorbed the best of both cultures. Although these two groups compose more than 80% of the population, other groups such as the French, Spanish, Chinese, and even Lebanese have left their mark.

The Steel Pan

THE SOUND OF A STEEL BAND

playing poolside has become emblematic of the Caribbean. What you may not know is that the fascinating instrument has an interesting and humble history that began in Trinidad.

In 1883 the British government banned the playing of drums on the island, fearful that they were being used to carry secret messages. Enterprising Afro-Trinidadians immediately found other means of creating music. Some turned to cut bamboo poles beaten rhythmically on the ground; these were called Tamboo Bamboo bands, and they soon became a major musical force on the island. With the coming of industry, new materials such as hub caps and biscuit tins were added as "instruments" in the bands. These metal additions were collectively known as "pan." Later, after the Americans established military bases on the islands during World War II, empty oil drums became available and were quickly put to musical use.

At some point it was discovered that these drums could be cut down,

heated in a fire, and beaten into a finely tuned instrument. The steel pan as we know it was thus born. Soon there were entire musical bands playing nothing but steel pans. For years the music gestated in the poorer districts of Port of Spain and was seen as being suitable only for the lower classes of society, a reputation not helped by the fact that the loyal followers of early steel bands sometimes clashed violently with their rivals. Eventually, the magical sound of the "pan" and its amazing ability to adapt to any type of music won it widespread acceptance.

Today the government recognizes the steel pan as the official musical instrument of Trinidad and Tobago. It's played year-round at official functions and social gatherings, but the true time for the steel pan is Carnival. In the annual Panorama festival, dozens of steel bands from around the country compete for the "Band of the Year" title. Some have fewer than a dozen steel pans, while others number in the hundreds. The performance of the larger bands creates a thunderous wall-of-sound effect.

24

Many of the art forms that are considered synonymous with the Caribbean were created on this relatively small island. Calypso was born here, as were soca, limbo and the steel pan (steel drum). The island can also claim two winners of the Nobel prize in literature—V. S. Naipaul (2001), who was born in Trinidad and wrote several of his earlier books about the island, and Derek Walcott (1992), a St. Lucian who moved to Trinidad in 1953. Many tourists make a pilgrimage simply to trace the places mentioned in Naipaul's magnum opus, *A House for Mr. Biswas*.

Physically, the island offers an exact parallel to the rain forests of South America, which allows for interesting—and sometimes challenging—ecological adventures. Beach lovers accustomed to the electric blue water and dazzling white sand of coral islands may be disappointed by the beaches on Trinidad. The best beaches are on the north coast, with peach sand, clean blue-green water, and the forest-covered Northern Range as a backdrop. Beaches are almost completely free of hotel development.

Tobago is 23 mi (37 km) northeast of Trinidad. The population here is much less ethnically diverse than that of Trinidad, with the majority being of African descent. Tobagonians have their own dialect and distinct culture. Tourism is much more a part of the island's economy, and you can find excellent resorts and facilities. Tobago also has excellent white-sand beaches.

The two islands have very different histories. Sadly, the Amerindian populations of both islands were virtually wiped out by the arrival of Europeans. After Columbus landed in Trinidad in 1498, the island came under Spanish rule. In an attempt to build the population and provide greater numbers to fend off a potential British conquest, the government at the time encouraged French Catholics from nearby islands to settle in Trinidad. This migration can be seen in the large number of French place names scattered around the island. Despite this effort, the British conquered the island in 1797.

Tobago had a much more turbulent history. Named after the tobacco that was used by the native Amerindian population, it was settled by the British in 1508. The island was to change hands a total of 22 times before eventually returning to Britain in 1814.

The two islands were merged into one crown colony in 1888, with Tobago being made a ward of Trinidad. Independence was achieved in 1962 under the leadership of Dr. Eric Williams, who became the first prime minister. The islands became an independent republic in 1976 with a bicameral Parliament and an appointed president.

TRINIDAD

Where to Stay

Because Trinidad is primarily a business destination, most accommodations are in or near Port of Spain. Standards are generally good, though not lavish by any means. Port of Spain has a small downtown core—with a main shopping area along Frederick Street—and is surrounded by inner and outer suburbs. The inner areas include Belmont, Woodbrook, Newtown, St. Clair, St. Ann's, St. James, and Cascade. The nearest beach to most hotels is Maracas Bay, which is a half-hour drive over the mountains. Carnival visitors should book many months in advance and be prepared to pay top dollar for even the most modest hotel.

★ $$–$$$　　🖼 **Hilton Trinidad & Conference Centre.** The Hilton is the most upscale hotel on the island. On the side of a hill overlooking the Queen's Park Savannah, it offers beautiful landscaping and breathtaking views of Port of Spain and the Gulf of Paria. Its unique construction means that the lobby is at the top of the hill and guests take an elevator *down* to the rooms. Although rates are high by island standards, you're paying for the comfort of knowing that everything here will be standard Hilton issue. Spa, golf, and wedding packages are available for vacationers. The hotel underwent a $32 million upgrade to all rooms and facilities in 2005. ⊠ *Lady Young Rd., Box 442, Port of Spain* ☎ *868/624–3211, 800/445–8667 in U.S.* 🖷 *868/624–4485* ⊕ *www.hiltoncaribbean.com* 🛏 *380 rooms, 27 suites* ⚴ *2 restaurants, room service, in-room safes, minibars, 2 tennis courts, pool, wading pool, gym, 3 bars, shops, babysitting, dry cleaning, laundry service, business services, meeting rooms, car rental, travel services, no-smoking rooms* ☰ *AE, DC, MC, V* ⊚ *EP.*

$$$ 🏨 **Asa Wright Nature Centre Lodge.** Those seeking to really get away from it all will find this mountain retreat the perfect choice, but the average traveler may find the isolation a bit much. A hotel designed for serious bird-watchers, it's surrounded by 200 acres of wilderness and by streams, waterfalls, and natural pools an hour's drive from the nearest beach or town. From a veranda overlooking the Arima Valley, you can sip a cup of tea (or delicious home-grown coffee) while hummingbirds dart around your head. Rooms in outlying bungalows are simple but adequate; those in the main house are a bit grander and furnished with period furniture but can be noisy. Meals are taken communally in the large dining room, which allows guests to exchange bird stories over good basic food. Well-behaved kids over 12 are welcome, but the lack of TV might prove too much for young minds to bear. ⌖ *Box 4710, Arima Valley* ☎ *868/667–4655 or 800/426–7781* 🖷 *868/667–4540* ⊕ *www.asawright. org* 🛏 *24 rooms, 1 bungalow* ⚴ *Dining room, fans, pond, hiking, shops; no a/c, no room TVs, no kids under 12* ☰ *MC, V* ⊚ *FAP.*

★ $$ 🏨 **Courtyard by Marriott.** This is the newest large hotel in the capital and offers excellent facilities and a great location. Guests can take advantage of a variety of restaurants, shops, and entertainment possibilities available next door at the ultramodern Movietowne complex. Rooms are spacious and feature lovely high-backed wooden headboards on the beds. This hotel caters mainly to business travelers and offers a range of free services, including high-speed Internet in rooms as well as free Wi-Fi, and printing and local faxing at the business center. ⊠ *Invader's Bay, Audrey Jeffer's Hwy., Port of Spain* ☎ *868/627–5555* 🖷 *868/627–6317* ⊕ *www.marriott.com* 🛏 *116 rooms, 3 suites* ⚴ *Restaurant, room service, refrigerators, in-room safes, cable TV, in-room broadband, Wi-Fi, pool, gym, bar, shops, dry cleaning, laundry facilities, laundry service, business services, meeting rooms, travel services, car rental, no-smoking rooms* ☰ *AE, D, MC, V* ⊚ *EP.*

$$ 🏨 **Crowne Plaza Trinidad.** Proximity to the port and Independence Square is both the draw and the drawback here. From any upper-floor room you have a lovely pastel panorama of the Old Town and of ships idling in the Gulf of Paria, and you're within walking distance of the downtown sights and shops. But with proximity to the action come traffic and noise. Although rooms are adequate, they are not luxurious by any means. A revolving rooftop restaurant called 360 offers a striking view of the city and has a superb Sunday brunch. ⊠ *Wrightson Rd., Box 1017, Port of Spain* ☎ *868/625–3361 or 800/227–6963* 🖷 *868/625–4166* ⊕ *www.ichotelsgroup.com* 🛏 *233 rooms, 5 suites* ⚴ *2 restaurants, room service, in-room safes, cable TV, in-room broadband, Wi-Fi, pool, gym, 3 bars, shops, babysitting, laundry service, concierge, business services, meeting rooms, car rental, no-smoking rooms* ☰ *AE, MC, V* ⊚ *BP.*

$$ 🏨 **Kapok Hotel.** This hotel in a good neighborhood just off Queen's Park Savannah is the best all-around value if you want to stay in the city; it offers a high level of comfort and service. Although it does not have the myriad amenities of the nearby Hilton, many people prefer the more intimate feel of the Kapok. Rooms vary greatly in size, with the Savannah-facing rooms being generally much larger. The hotel's restaurant, Tiki Village, offers some of the most reliably good food on the island and is popular with locals. Bois Cano, the alfresco bistro and wine bar, is lovely and relaxed and has live jazz on Thursday evenings, not to mention afternoon tea. The Ellerslie Plaza mall is a three-minute walk from the front door. ⊠ *16–18 Cotton Hill, St. Clair, Port of Spain* ☎ *868/622–5765 or 800/344–1212* 🖷 *868/622–9677* ⊕ *www.kapokhotel.com* ⤳ *73 rooms, 12 suites, 9 studios* ⌂ *2 restaurants, room service, in-room safes, some kitchenettes, cable TV, in-room broadband, pool, gym, hair salon, shops, dry cleaning, laundry facilities, laundry service, business services, meeting rooms, no-smoking rooms* ▭ *AE, MC, V* � ⁄○⁄ *EP.*

$ 🏨 **Coblentz Inn.** This small boutique hotel is bursting at the seams with charm. Just a short drive from downtown in the quiet suburb of Cascade, the hotel offers peace, quiet, and style at a relatively affordable price. Each room is done in a different whimsical theme; the Rumshop Room, for example, comes complete with full bottles of rum and playing cards on the coffee table. Amazingly, for the price, all rooms offer a complimentary fully stocked minibar. The one suite on offer is really just a very large room. The convenience of having Batimamzelle, one of the island's best restaurants, in the same complex is handy. ⊠ *44 Coblentz Ave., Cascade* ☎ *868/621–0541* 🖷 *868/624–7566* ⊕ *www.coblentzinn.com* ⤳ *16 rooms* ⌂ *Restaurant, room service, minibars, Wi-Fi, hot tub, massage, dry cleaning, laundry service, business services; no smoking* ▭ *AE, MC, V* ⁄○⁄ *BP.*

$ 🏨 **Crews Inn Hotel & Yachting Centre.** On Trinidad's western peninsula, this hotel is about 20 minutes from downtown but smack in the middle of the island's most popular nightlife area. The hotel complex caters to the yachting crowd with a huge marina and a wide range of shops. The Lighthouse Restaurant is popular with locals and has a large and lively bar. Rooms are well appointed, with views of the marina and pool. The nearest beach is a 10-minute drive but isn't particularly good. ⊠ *Point Gourde, Chaguaramas* ☎ *868/634–4384* 🖷 *868/634–4175* ⊕ *www.crewsinn.com* ⤳ *42 rooms, 4 suites* ⌂ *Restaurant, grocery, room service, kitchenettes, some microwaves, in-room VCRs, Wi-Fi, golf privileges, pool, gym, massage, dock, marina, fishing, 2 bars, wine shop, shops, babysitting, dry cleaning, laundry facilities, laundry service, business services, meeting rooms, car rental, travel services, no-smoking rooms* ▭ *AE, MC, V* ⁄○⁄ *EP.*

★ ¢ 🏨 **Pax Guest House.** Built in 1932 on the grounds of a hilltop monastery, this charming, antiques-furnished guesthouse is ideal for budget travelers seeking a chance to observe nature up close. The 800-foot elevation provides excellent views of the plains to the south as well as the 600-odd acres of monastery grounds to the north. Owners Gerard Ramsawak and Oda van der Haijden are gracious and chatty and will fill you in on the history of the house and the furniture they have collected from around the world over breakfast or dinner, both of which are included. Afternoon tea in the courtyard is cheap and popular with older locals. ⊠ *Mt. St. Benedict, Tunapuna* ☎ *868/662–4084* ⊕ *www. paxguesthouse.com* ↝ *18 rooms* ⌂ *Dining room, fans, Wi-Fi, tennis court, boccie, laundry service; no a/c in some rooms, no room phones, no TV in some rooms, no smoking* ▭ *MC, V* ⦿ *MAP.*

★ ¢ ▦ **Le Grande Almandier.** This low-priced hotel is on Trinidad's remote and beautiful northeast coast. The area is a popular weekend escape for locals who go to experience the lush rain-forest backdrop and expansive beach. Rooms here are cozy, and each is decorated in a different theme. Some rooms are air-conditioned (a rarity for a hotel on this part of the island), but cool ocean breezes are usually quite adequate. The restaurant here serves extraordinary creole dishes featuring seafood caught just off the premises. The nearest shopping or nightlife is a two-hour drive away, so this is strictly a place for those seeking peace, quiet, and good food. ⊠ *2 Hosang St., Grande Riviere* ☎ *868/670–1013* ⊟ *868/670–2294* ⊕ *www.legrandealmandier.com* ↝ *10 rooms* ⌂ *Restaurant, room service, fans, bar, babysitting, laundry service; no a/c in some rooms* ▭ *MC, V* ⦿ *EP.*

¢ ▦ **Monique's.** Spacious rooms and proximity to Port of Spain ensure the popularity of this guest house, which consists of two separate buildings. Rooms in "Monique's on the Hill" have kitchenettes and sizable balconies, but getting to these rooms is a bit of a trek. The staff are justifiably famous for their friendliness. ⊠ *114–116 Saddle Rd., Maraval, Port of Spain* ☎ *868/628–3334 or 868/628–2351* ⊟ *868/622–3232* ⊕ *www.moniquestrinidad.com* ↝ *20 rooms* ⌂ *Dining room, some kitchenettes, cable TV, in-room data ports, bar, babysitting, laundry service, airport shuttle, travel services* ▭ *AE, DC, MC, V* ⦿ *CP.*

Where to Eat

The food on T&T is a delight to the senses and has a distinctively creole touch, though everyone has a different idea about what creole seasoning is (just ask around, and you'll see). Bountiful herbs and spices include bay leaf, *chadon beni* (similar in taste to cilantro), nutmeg, turmeric, and different varieties of peppers. The cooking also involves a lot of brown sugar, rum, plantain, and local fish and meat. If there's fresh juice on the menu, be sure to try it. You can taste Asian, Indian, African, French, and Spanish influences, among others, often in a single meal. Indian-inspired food is a favorite: *rotis* (ample sandwiches of soft dough with a filling, similar to a burrito) are served as a fast food; a mélange of curried meat or fish and vegetables frequently makes an appearance, as do *vindaloos* (spicy meat, vegetable, and seafood dishes). *Pelau* (chicken stewed in coconut milk with peas and rice), a Spanish-influenced dish, is another local favorite. Crab lovers will find large blue-backs curried, peppered, or in callaloo (Trinidad's national dish), a stew made with green dasheen leaves, okra, and coconut milk. Shark-and-bake (lightly seasoned, fried shark meat) is the sandwich of choice at the beach.

What to Wear

Restaurants are informal: you won't find any jacket-and-tie requirements. Beachwear, however, is too casual for most places. A nice pair of shorts is appropriate for lunch; for dinner you'll probably feel most comfortable in a pair of slacks or a casual sundress.

ASIAN ★ $$–$$$ ╳ **Tiki Village.** Port of Spainers in the know flock to the eighth floor of the Kapok Hotel, where the views of the city day and night are simply spectacular and the food always dependable. The dining room is lined with teak, and the menu includes the best of Polynesian and Asian fare. The Sunday dim sum—with tasting-size portions of dishes such as pepper squid and tofu-stuffed fish—is very popular. ⊠ *Kapok Hotel, 16–18 Cotton Hill, St. Clair, Port of Spain* ☎ *868/622–5765* ⌣ *Reservations essential* ▭ *AE, MC, V* ⊘ *No lunch Sat.*

$–$$$ ╳ **Tamnak Thai.** In a beautifully renovated colonial house on Queen's Park Savannah, you can find the best Thai cuisine on Trinidad. On the patio you're surrounded by flowing water and lush foliage; the elegant dining room is a more intimate (and cooler) experience. You might well start with the Thai seafood chowder with local root vegetables and move on to mussels stuffed with shrimp and simmered in coconut milk and herbs. Alfresco diners should use insect repellent, as the mosquitoes seem more ravenous than most of the diners. Valet parking is an unusual but welcome touch. ⊠ *13 Queen's Park E, Belmont, Port of Spain* ☎ *868/ 625–0647* ⊞ *868/623–7510* ▭ *AE, MC, V.*

CARIBBEAN ★ $$–$$$ ╳ **The Verandah.** Owner and hostess Phyllis Vieira has been hosting diners for 20 years and prides herself on her "free-style Caribbean" menu, which is one of the best-kept secrets on the island. But the reasonable prices and consistently excellent cuisine make this a secret we can no longer keep. The open veranda, interior, and courtyard of this beautiful gingerbread-style colonial house provide a suitable setting for the menu, which changes weekly and is brought to you on a blackboard by the attentive, white-garbed staff. ⊠ *10 Rust St., St. Clair, Port of Spain* ☎ *868/622–6287* ⌣ *Reservations essential* ▭ *No credit cards* ⊘ *Closed Sun. No dinner Mon, Tues., Wed., or Fri.*

☺ $–$$ Fodors Choice ★ ╳ **Veni Mangé.** The best lunches in town are served upstairs in this traditional West Indian house. Credit Allyson Hennessy—a Cordon Bleu–trained chef and local television celebrity—and her friendly, flamboyant sister and partner, Rosemary (Roses) Hezekiah. Despite Allyson's training, home cooking is the order of the day here. The creative creole menu changes regularly, but there's always an unusual and delicious vegetarian entrée. Veni's version of Trinidad's national dish, callaloo, is considered one of the best on the island. The *chip chip* (a small local clam) cocktail is deliciously piquant and is a restaurant rarity. Those with hearty appetites can try the oxtail and dumpling stew. ⊠ *67A Ariapita Ave., Woodbrook, Port of Spain* ☎ *868/624–4597* ⌣ *Reservations essential* ▭ *AE, MC, V* ⊘ *Closed weekends. No dinner Mon., Tues., or Thurs.*

ECLECTIC $$$–$$$$ ╳ **Battimamzelle.** When skilled chef Khalid Mohammed decided to open his own restaurant, he named it using the local name for a dragonfly and painted it in colors to match. The decor of this lovely little establishment—tucked away in a small inn—is truly vibrant, but steer clear if you don't like bright yellow walls. Happily, the food presentations are just as attention-grabbing. Be sure to try the pomegranate-glazed duck breast. The tamarind-glazed pork chop is also an excellent dinner bet and one of the lowest-priced items on the menu. The dinner menu may be a bit pricey for those on a budget, but the lunch menu offers a three-course meal for $26. ⊠ *Coblentz Inn, 44 Coblentz Ave., Cascade, Port of Spain* ☎ *868/621–0541* ◢ *Reservations essential* ▭ *AE, MC, V* ⊘ *Closed Sun.*

$$–$$$$ ✕ **La Boucan.** Trinidadian Geoffrey Holder painted the large mural of a social idyll in Queen's Park Savannah that dominates one wall of the Hilton's main restaurant. A more leisurely Trinidad is also reflected in the old-fashioned charm of silver service, uniformed waiters, soft lighting, and pink tablecloths. The menu is international, including steaks, seafood grills, and other simple preparations, but you can also find such local specialties as callaloo soup, shrimp creole, and West Indian chicken curry. ⊠ *Hilton Trinidad & Conference Centre, Lady Young Rd., Port of Spain* ☎ *868/624–3211* ▭ *AE, DC, MC, V.*

$$–$$$ ✕ **Mélange.** Some of the finest and most imaginative food on the island is to be found at this elegant establishment on restaurant row. Chef and owner Moses Ruben uses his years of experience as head chef at the Hilton to create delightfully balanced meals. His imaginative curried crab and dumplings appetizer, which consists of delicately curried crab meat served on a shell full of miniature dumplings, is an exceptional treat. ⊠ *40 Ariapita Ave., Woodbrook, Port of Spain* ☎ *868/628–8687* ▭ *AE, MC, V* ⊘ *Closed Sun. No lunch Sat., no dinner Mon.*

$$–$$$$ ✕ **Solimar.** In a series of dimly lighted, plant-filled dining areas, chef Joe Brown offers a menu that travels the world in one meal: there's always a choice of a European, Asian, or North American main course. You may also find a prix-fixe menu that includes accompanying wines. Caesar salad fans can rejoice, as the classical caesar on the menu is easily the best on the island. Bartender Roger mixes a mean cocktail, so be sure to ask him for one of his specials. The restaurant's humidor offers a fine cigar selection. Solimar is popular with expats and is known for being a relaxed and informal spot. Valet parking is available. ⊠ *6 Nook Ave., St. Ann's, Port of Spain* ☎ *868/624–6267* ▭ *AE, MC, V* ⊘ *Closed Sun. No lunch Fri.*

FRENCH ✕ **A La Bastille.** Frenchman Gerard Mouille has managed to create an
★ **$$–$$$** authentic French brasserie in the heart of Port of Spain. Homemade bread is made daily, and the menu features many items that are imported straight from Brittany. Tribute is also paid to island ingredients, so you can start your meal with local escargots and end it with delicious mango ice cream. Add a selection of hundreds of wines and you have a memorable dining option. The crêpe special on Saturday from 10 to 3 draws an appreciative crowd. ⊠ *84A Ariapita Ave., Woodbrook, Port of Spain* ☎ *868/622–1789* ▭ *AE, MC, V* ⊘ *Closed Sun.*

INDIAN ✕ **Apsara.** This upscale Indian eatery is one of the few in Trinidad that
$$–$$$$ feature genuine Indian cuisine and not the local (though equally tasty) version. The name means "celestial dancer," and the food here is indeed heavenly. The inviting terra-cotta interior is decorated with hand-painted

interpretations of Moghul art. Choosing dishes from the comprehensive menu is a bit daunting, so don't be afraid to ask for help. The *Husseini boti kebab* (lamb marinated in poppy seeds and masala) is an excellent choice. The restaurant is in the same building as the equally popular Tamnak Thai. ⊠ *13 Queen's Park E, Belmont, Port of Spain* ☎ *868/627–7364 or 868/623–7659* ⊟ *AE, MC, V* ☉ *Closed Sun.*

¢ ✕ **Wings Restaurant & Bar.** Rum shops and good food are an intrinsic part of Trinidad life, and both are combined in this colorful eatery, which is open only from 10 to 6. Regulars from the nearby university and industrial park flock here at lunchtime to enjoy a wide selection of local Indian food. It can get a bit loud, but at least fans keep the heat in control—just barely. To get here, turn off the Churchill Roosevelt Highway at the FedEx building (north side of the highway) in Tunapuna, and take the first left. ⊠ *16 Mohammed Terr., Tunapuna* ☎ *868/645–6607* ⊟ *No credit cards* ☉ *Closed Sun. No dinner.*

ITALIAN   ✕ **Il Colosseo.** Calabrian chef Angelo Cofone married a Trinidadian and
$$–$$$$ soon found himself co-owning the island's best Italian restaurant, popular with locals and visiting businesspeople alike. The innovative Italian menu changes regularly, and there is always a daily special. If it's offered, try the calamari done Mediterranean style. The prix-fixe lunch for $16 is a steal and a good way to test the menu. ⊠ *16 Rust St., St. Clair, Port of Spain* ☎ *868/622–8418* ⊟ *AE, MC, V* ☉ *Closed Sun. No lunch Sat.*

Beaches

Trinidad has some good beaches for swimming and sunning, though none as picture-perfect as those in Tobago. North-coast beaches are the closest to Port of Spain and have peach-colored sand, palm trees galore, and excellent water for swimming. The northeast involves a longer drive but offers rugged scenery en route, as well as rougher water and coarser sand. The entire east coast of the island is basically one unbroken beach. Miles of coconut trees line this coast, where finding a secluded spot is never a problem. Unfortunately, the water here tends to be muddy and the undertows dangerous. Although popular with some locals, the beaches of the western peninsula (such as Maqueripe) are not particularly attractive, and the water in this area is often polluted by sewage.

Balandra Bay. On the northeast coast, the beach—popular with locals on weekends—is sheltered by a rocky outcropping and is a favorite of bodysurfers. Much of this beach is suitable for swimming. The noise level on weekends can be a problem for those seeking solace. Take the Toco Main Road from the Valencia Road, and turn off at the signs indicating Balandra (just after Salybia). ⊠ *Off Valencia Rd. near Salybia.*
Blanchisseuse Bay. On North Coast Road you can find this narrow, palm-fringed beach. Facilities are nonexistent, but it's an ideal spot for a romantic picnic. A lagoon and river at the east end of the beach allow you to swim in fresh water, but beware of floating logs in the river, as they sometimes contain mites that can cause a body rash (called *bete rouge* locally). You can haggle with local fishermen to take you out in their boats to explore the coast. This beach is about 14 mi (23 km) after Maracas; just keep driving along the road until you pass the Arima turnoff.

The coastal and rain-forest views here are spectacular. ⊠ *North Coast Rd., just beyond Arima turnoff.*

Grande Riviere. On Trinidad's rugged northeast coast, Grande Riviere is well worth the drive. Swimming is good, and there are several guesthouses nearby for refreshments, but the main attractions here are turtles. Every year up to 500 giant leatherback turtles come onto the beach to lay their eggs. If you're here at night, run your hand through the black sand to make it glow—a phenomenon caused by plankton. ⊠ *Toco Main Rd., at end of Rd.*

Las Cuevas Bay. This narrow, picturesque strip on North Coast Road is named for the series of partially submerged and explorable caves that ring the beach. A food stand offers tasty snacks, and vendors hawk fresh fruit across the road. You can also buy fresh fish and lobster from the fishing depot near the beach. You have to park your car in the small car park and walk down a few steps to get to the beach, so be sure to take everything from the car (which is out of sight once you are on the beach). There are basic changing and toilet facilities. It's less crowded here than at nearby Maracas Bay and seemingly serene, although, as at Maracas, the current can be treacherous. ⊠ *North Coast Rd., 7 mi (11 km) east of Maracas Bay.*

Manzanilla Beach. You can find picnic facilities and a pretty view of the Atlantic here, though the water is occasionally muddied by Venezuela's Orinoco River. The Cocal Road running the length of this beautiful beach is lined with stately palms, whose fronds vault like the arches at Chartres. This is where many well-heeled Trinis have vacation homes. The Nariva River, which enters the sea just south of this beach and the surrounding Nariva Swamp, is home to the protected manatee and many other rare species, including the much-maligned anaconda. To get to this beach take the Mayaro turnoff at the town of Sangre Grande. Manzanilla is where this road first meets the coast. ⊠ *Southeast of Sangre Grande.*

★ **Maracas Bay.** This long stretch of sand has a cove and a fishing village at one end. It's *the* local favorite, so it can get crowded on weekends. Lifeguards will guide you away from strong currents. Parking sites are ample, and there are snack bars and restrooms. Try a shark-and-bake ($2, to which you can add any of dozens of toppings, such as tamarind sauce and coleslaw) at one of the beach huts or in the nearby car park (Richard's is by far the most popular). Take the North Coast Road from Maraval (it intersects with Long Circular Road right next to KFC Maraval) over the Northern Range; the beach is about 7 mi from Maraval. ⊠ *North Coast Rd.*

Salibea Bay (Salybia Bay). Past Galera Point, which juts toward Tobago, this gentle beach has shallows and plenty of shade—perfect for swimming. Snack vendors abound in the vicinity. Like many of the beaches on the northeast coast, this one is packed with people and music trucks blaring soca and reggae on weekends. It's off the Toco Main Road, just after the town of Toco. ⊠ *Off Toco Main Rd., east of Toco.*

Sports & the Outdoors

BIRD-WATCHING Trinidad and Tobago are among the top 10 spots in the world in terms
★ of the number of species of birds per square mile—more than 430, many

living within pristine rain forests, lowlands and savannahs, and fresh- and saltwater swamps. If you're lucky, you might spot the collared tro- gon, Trinidad piping guan (known locally as the common pawi), or rare white-tailed Sabrewing hummingbird. Restaurants often hang feeders outside on their porches, as much to keep the birds away from your food as to provide a chance to see them. Both the Asa Wright Nature Cen- tre and Caroni Bird Sanctuary are major bird-watching destinations (*see* ⇨ Exploring Trinidad, *below*).

The **Point-a-Pierre Wildfowl Trust** (⊠ Petrotrin Complex, Point-a-Pierre ☎ 868/658–4200 Ext. 2512) is a haven for rare bird species on 26 acres within the unlikely confines of a petrochemical complex; you must call in advance for a reservation. **Winston Nanan** (☎ 868/645–1305) is a self- taught ornithologist who knows the local fauna as well as his own chil- dren. He will arrange personal tours in his own car anywhere on the island. His business is based at the Caroni Bird Sanctuary, but his ex- pertise makes a trip with him to the Northern Range or the northeast a must for any true bird-watcher. It won't be cheap, but the personal attention and his willingness to try to find rare species are well worth the expense.

FISHING   The islands off the northwest coast of Trinidad have excellent waters for deep-sea fishing; you may find wahoo, king fish, and marlin, to name a few. The ocean here was a favorite angling spot of Franklin D. Roo- sevelt. Through **Bayshore Charters** (⊠ 29 Sunset Dr., Bayshore, Westmoor- ings ☎ 868/637–8711) you can fish for an afternoon or hire a boat for a weekend; the *Melissa Ann* is fully equipped for comfortable cruising, sleeps six, and has an air-conditioned cabin, refrigerator, cooking facil- ities, and, of course, fishing equipment. Capt. Sa Gomes is one of the most experienced charter captains on the islands. Members of the **Trinidad & Tobago Yacht Club** (⊠ Western Main Rd., Bayshore, Westmoor- ings ☎ 868/637–4260) may be willing to arrange a fishing trip for you.

GOLF   The best course in Trinidad is the 18-hole course at **St. Andrew's Golf Club** (⊠ Moka, Saddle Rd., Maraval, Port of Spain ☎ 868/629–2314), just outside Port of Spain. Greens fees are approximately $35 for 18 holes. The most convenient tee times are available on weekdays.

Shopping

Good buys in Trinidad include Angostura bitters, Old Oak or Vat 19 rum, and leather goods, all widely available throughout the country. Thanks in large part to Carnival costumery, there's no shortage of fab- ric shops. The best bargains for Asian and East Indian silks and cottons can be found in downtown Port of Spain, on Frederick Street and around Independence Square. Recordings of local calypsonians and steel-pan performances as well as *chutney* (a local East Indian music) are available throughout the islands and make great gifts.

Areas & Malls

Downtown Port of Spain, specifically **Frederick, Queen,** and **Henry streets,** is full of fabrics and shoes. **Ellerslie Plaza** is an attractive outdoor mall well worth a browse. **Excellent City Centre** is set in an old-style oasis under the lantern roofs of three of downtown's oldest commercial buildings. Look for cleverly designed keepsakes, trendy cotton garments, and original artwork. The upstairs food court overlooks bustling Frederick Street. **Long Circular Mall** has upscale boutiques that are great for window-shopping. The **Falls at West Mall,** just west of Port of Spain, is a dazzling temple to upscale shopping that could easily hold its own anywhere in the world. The **Market at the Normandie Hotel** is a small collection of shops that specialize in indigenous fashions, crafts, jewelry, basketwork, and ceramics. You can also have afternoon tea in the elegant little café.

Specialty Items

CLOTHING   A fine designer shop, **Meiling** (✉ Kapok Hotel, Maraval, Port of Spain ☎ 868/627–6975), sells classically detailed Caribbean resort clothing. **Radical** (✉ The Falls at West Mall, Western Main Rd., Westmoorings ☎ 868/632–5800 ✉ Long Circular Mall, Long Circular Rd., St. James, Port of Spain ☎ 868/628–5693 ✉ Excellent City Centre, Independence Square, Port of Spain ☎ 868/627–6110), which carries T-shirts and original men's and women's clothing, is something like the Gap of the Caribbean.

DUTY-FREE   Duty-free goods are available only at the airport upon departure or ar-
GOODS   rival. **De Lima's** (✉ Piarco International Airport, Piarco ☎ 868/669–4738) sells traditional duty-free luxury goods. **Stecher's** (✉ Piarco International Airport, Piarco ☎ 868/669–4793) is a familiar name for those seeking to avoid taxes on fine perfumes, china, crystal, handcrafted pieces, and jewelry. **T-Wee Liquor Store** (✉ Piarco International Airport, Piarco ☎ 868/669–4748) offers deals on alcohol that you probably won't find in many other places around the world.

HANDICRAFTS   The tourism office can provide a list of local artisans who specialize in everything from straw and cane work to miniature steel pans. For painted plates, ceramics, aromatic candles, wind chimes, and carved wood pieces and instruments, check out **Cockey** (✉ Long Circular Mall, Long
★   Circular Rd., St. James, Port of Spain ☎ 868/628–6546). The **101 Art Gallery** (✉ Art Society of Trinidad and Tobago Bldg., At Jamaica Blvd. and St. Vincent Ave., Federation Park, Port of Spain ☎ 868/628–4081) is Trinidad's foremost gallery, showcasing local artists such as Jackie Hinkson (figurative watercolors); Peter Sheppard (stylized realist local landscapes in acrylic); and Sundiata (semi-abstract watercolors). Openings are usually held Tuesday evenings; the gallery is closed Sunday and Monday. **Poui Boutique** (✉ Ellerslie Plaza, Long Circular Rd., Maraval, Port of Spain ☎ 868/622–5597) has stylish handmade batik articles, Ajoupa ware (an attractive, local terra-cotta pottery), and many other gift items. The miniature ceramic houses and local scenes are astoundingly realistic, and are all handcrafted by owners Rory and Bunty O'Connor.

JEWELRY   The design duo of Barbara Jardine and Rachel Ross creates the Alchemy jewelry line. Their handmade works of art with sterling silver, 18K gold, and precious and semiprecious stones are for sale at **Precious Little** (✉ The Falls at West Mall, Western Main Rd., Westmoorings ☎ 868/632–1077).

MUSIC   **Just CDs and Accessories** (✉ Long Circular Mall, Long Circular Rd., St. James, Port of Spain ☎ 868/622–7516) has a good selection of popular local musicians as well as other music genres. **Rhyner's Record Shop** (✉ 54 Prince St., Downtown, Port of Spain 📞 868/625–2476 ✉ Piarco International Airport, Piarco 📞 868/669–3064) has a decent (and duty-free) selection of calypso and soca music.

Nightlife & the Arts

Nightlife

There's no lack of nightlife in Port of Spain, and spontaneity plays a big role—around Carnival time look for the handwritten signs announcing the PANYARD, where the next informal gathering of steel-drum bands is going to be. Gay and lesbian travelers can take advantage of an increasingly lively gay scene in Trinidad, with parties drawing upwards of 200 people on most weekends.

Two of the island's top nightspots are on a former American army base in Chaguaramas. The **Anchorage** (✉ Point Gourde Rd., Chaguaramas 📞 868/634–4334) is a good spot for early-evening cocktails and snacks. ★ **Pier 1** (✉ Western Main Rd., Chaguaramas 📞 868/634–4426) is *the* place for lively late-night action. You can dance through the night on a large wooden deck jutting into the ocean with gentle sea breezes to cool you down. It's about 20 minutes west of Port of Spain, so get a party together from your hotel and hire a cab. It opens at 9 PM Wednesday through Sunday. For the serious partyers, Pier 1 offers a "party boat" that leaves on Friday, Saturday, and Sunday night for a floating party for $10.

★ At **Club Coconuts** (✉ Cascadia Hotel, St. Ann's, Port of Spain 📞 868/623–6887) you can dance until the wee hours with a fun crowd. **51° Lounge** (✉ 51 Cipriani Blvd., Woodbrook, Port of Spain 📞 868/627–0051) is where the smart set hangs out. There's entertainment on most nights, and though admission is often free, it's advisable to call to confirm. Don't even think about showing up in shorts, as there's a strict "elegant casual" dress code and an age limit of 25 years and older. **Mas Camp Pub** (✉ Ariapata Ave. and French St., Woodbrook, Port of Spain 📞 868/627–4042) is Port of Spain's most dependable nightspot. Along with a bar and a large stage where a DJ or live band reigns, the kitchen dishes up hearty, reasonably priced creole lunches, and if one of the live bands strikes your fancy, chances are you can also buy a tape here. **More Vino** (✉ 23 O'Connor St., Woodbrook, Port of Spain 📞 868/622–8466) attracts a crowd of young professionals who come to network while sipping one of the more than 100 varieties of wine. While most people choose to sit outside during the evening, there is also seating available in the air-conditioned interior. Inside, you will also find an astonishing number of bottles on display for consumption on the premises or to take away. Cheeses and other items for nibbling are available but no proper meals. **Sky Bar & Lounge** (✉ 46 Ariapita Ave., Woodbrook, Port of Spain) is the new kid on the scene and pulls a lively crowd from Wednesday to Saturday. The rooftop setting is free of walls and offers dazzling views of Port of Spain harbor. There are occasional live performances and always a large crowd on weekends. There is a nominal admission price of $4 on Fridays, when the bar is packed with a mostly gay crowd after 10 PM. **Trotters** (✉ Maraval and Sweet Briar Rd., St. Clair, Port of Spain 📞 868/627–8768) is a sports bar in a two-story atrium. You can find an abundance of TV monitors as well as more than 30 varieties of beer from around the globe. It's incredibly popular on weekends despite the pricey drinks.

Babylon Boys (☏ 868/672–2000) is one of the main party organizers on the island and serves as a clearinghouse for gay events in general. Although these parties are aimed at a gay crowd, they have become increasingly popular with a broader audience, since the crowd and music are usually top-notch.

The Arts

Trinidad always seems to be anticipating, celebrating, or recovering from a festival. Visitors are welcome at these events, which are a great way to explore the island's rich cultural traditions.

CARNIVAL
Fodor'sChoice
★

Trinidad's version of the pre-Lenten bacchanal is reputedly the oldest in the western hemisphere; there are festivities all over the country, but the most lavish are in Port of Spain. Trinidad's Carnival has the warmth and character of a massive family reunion and is billed by locals (not unreasonably) as "The Greatest Show on Earth."

The season begins right after Christmas, and the parties, called fêtes, don't stop until Ash Wednesday. Listen to a radio station for five minutes, and you can find out where the action is. The Carnival event itself officially lasts only two days, from *J'ouvert* (2 AM) on Monday to midnight the following day, Carnival Tuesday. It's best to arrive in Trinidad a week or two early to enjoy the preliminary events. (Hotels fill up quickly, so be sure to make reservations months in advance, and be prepared to pay premium prices for a minimum five-night stay. Even private homes have been known to rent bedrooms for as much as $225 per night.) If you visit during Carnival, try to get tickets to one of the all-inclusive parties where thousands of people eat and drink to the sound of soca music all night long. The biggest Carnival party in Trinidad is **UWI Fête,** which raises money for the university and attracts several thousand people. A ticket will cost you about $70 but includes all drinks and food.

Carnival is about extravagant costumes. Colorfully attired *mas* (troupes), whose membership sometimes numbers in the thousands, march to the beat set by massive music trucks and steel bands. You can visit the various mas "camps" around Port of Spain, where these elaborate getups are put together—the addresses are listed in the newspapers—and perhaps join one that strikes your fancy. Fees run anywhere from $35 to $400; you get to keep the costume. As a rule you will find that different bands attract different sorts of participants. **Harts** tends to attract a younger crowd, **Poison** a more raucous bunch, and **Brian MacFarlane's The Art Factory** a more artistic assortment of people. You can also buy your costume online at the tourist board's Web site, which has links to all the major camps. Children can parade in a kiddie carnival that takes place on the Saturday morning before the official events.

Carnival is also a showcase for performers of calypso, which mixes dance rhythms with social commentary—sung by characters with such evocative names as Shadow, the Mighty Sparrow, and Black Stalin—and soca, which fuses calypso with a driving dance beat. As Carnival approaches, many of these singers perform nightly in calypso tents around the city. Many hotels also have special concerts by popular local musicians. You can also visit the city's "panyards," where steel orchestras such as the Renegades, Desperadoes, Neal and Massy All-Stars, Invaders, and Phase II rehearse their musical arrangements (most can also be heard during the winter season).

For several nights before Carnival, costume makers display their work, and the steel bands and calypso singers perform in competitions at Queen's Park Savannah. Here the Calypso Monarch is crowned on the Sunday night before Carnival (Dimanche Gras). The city starts to fill with metal-frame carts carrying steel bands, trucks hauling sound systems, and revelers squeezing into the narrow streets. At midnight on Carnival Tuesday, Port of Spain's exhausted merrymakers go to bed. The next day feet are sore, but spirits have been refreshed. Lent (and theoretical sobriety) takes over for a while.

MUSIC Trinidadian culture doesn't end with music, but it definitely begins with it. Although both calypso and steel bands are at their best during Carnival, steel bands play at clubs, dances, and fêtes throughout the year. At Christmastime the music of the moment is a Venezuelan-derived folk music called *parang,* sung in Spanish to the strains of a stringed instrument called a *quattro.* The Lopinot Complex in Arouca is a parang center. If you can stomach the steep uphill drive, Paramin, near Port of Spain (take Maracas Road and turn on Paramin Road), is another spectacular place to hear this music.

Exploring Trinidad

The intensely urban atmosphere of Port of Spain belies the tropical beauty of the countryside surrounding it. You'll need a car and three to eight hours to see all there is to see. Begin by circling the Queen's Park Savannah to Saddle Road, in the residential district of Maraval. After a few miles the road begins to narrow and curve sharply as it climbs into the Northern Range and its undulating hills of dense foliage. Stop at the lookout on North Coast Road; a camera is a must-have here. You pass a series of lovely beaches, starting with Maracas. From the town of Blanchisseuse there's a winding route to the Asa Wright Nature Centre that takes you through canyons of towering palms, mossy grottoes, and imposing bamboo. In this rain forest keep an eye out for vultures, parakeets, hummingbirds, toucans, and, if you're lucky, maybe red-bellied, yellow-and-blue macaws. Trinidad also has more than 600 native species of butterflies and well over 1,000 varieties of orchids.

Numbers in the margin correspond to points of interest on the Trinidad map.

❷ Asa Wright Nature Centre. Nearly 200 acres here are covered with plants, Fodor'sChoice trees, and multihued flowers, and the surrounding acreage is atwitter
★ with more than 200 species of birds, from the gorgeous blue-crowned motmot to the rare (and protected) nocturnal oilbird. If you stay at the center's inn for two nights or more, take one of the guided hikes (in-

cluded in your room price if you are staying here) to the oilbirds' breeding grounds in Dunston Cave (reservations for hikes are essential). Those who don't want to hike can relax on the inn's veranda and watch birds swoop about the porch feeders—an armchair bird-watcher's delight. You are also more than likely to see a variety of other animal species, including agoutis and alarmingly large golden tegu lizards. This stunning plantation house looks out onto the lush, untouched Arima Valley. Even if you're not staying over, book ahead for lunch (TT$75), offered Monday through Saturday, or for the noontime Sunday buffet (TT$100). The center is an hour outside Blanchisseuse; take a right at the fork in the road (signposted to Arima) and drive another hour (the sign for the center is at milepost 7¾) on Blanchisseuse Road; turn right there. ⬠ *Box 4710, Arima Valley* ☎ *868/667–4655* ⊕ *www.asawright.org* ✉ *$10* ⊙ *Daily 9–5. Guided tours at 10:30 and 1:30.*

24

⟲ ➍ **Caroni Bird Sanctuary.** This large swamp with mazelike waterways is bordered by mangrove trees, some plumed with huge termite nests. If you're lucky, you may see lazy caimans idling in the water and large snakes hanging from branches on the banks taking in the sun. In the middle of the sanctuary are several islets that are home to Trinidad's national bird, the scarlet ibis. Just before sunset the ibis arrive by the thousands, their richly colored feathers brilliant in the gathering dusk, and as more flocks alight they turn the mangrove foliage a brilliant scarlet. Bring a sweater and insect repellent. The sanctuary's only official tour operator is Winston Nanan (*see* ⇨ Bird-Watching *in* Sports & the Outdoors). ✣ *½ hr from Port of Spain; take Churchill Roosevelt Hwy. east to Uriah Butler south; turn right and in about 2 min, after passing Caroni River Bridge, follow sign for sanctuary* ✉ *Free* ⊙ *Daily dawn–dusk.*

⟲ ➏ **Dattatreya Yoga Centre.** This impressive temple site was constructed fairly recently using artisans brought in from India. It is well worth a visit to admire the intricate architectural details of the main temple, learn about Trinidad Hinduism, and marvel at the towering 85-foot statue of the god Hanuman. Krishna Ramsaran, the compound manager, is extremely helpful and proud to explain the history of the center and the significance of the various *murtis* (sacred statues). Kids are welcome, so this makes for a pleasant and educational family outing (kids seem especially interested in the giant elephant statues that guard the temple doors). This is a religious site, so appropriate clothing is required (no shorts), and shoes must be left outside the temple door. It is fine to take pictures of the statue and the temple exterior and grounds, but permission is required to take pictures inside, as it is an active place of worship. The temple is half an hour from Port of Spain; take Churchill Roosevelt Highway east to Uriah Butler south; turn right until the Chase Village flyover; follow the signs south to Waterloo; then follow signs to the temple. ✉ *Datta Dr. at Orangefield Rd., Carapichaima* ☎ *868/ 673–5328* ✉ *Free* ⊙ *Daily dawn–dusk, services daily.*

➌ **Lopinot Complex.** It's said that the ghost of the French count Charles Joseph de Lopinot prowls his former home on stormy nights. Lopinot came to Trinidad in 1800 and chose this magnificent site to plant cocoa. His restored estate house has been turned into a museum—a guide is avail-

CLOSE UP

East Indians in Trinidad

WITH THE ABOLITION OF slavery in the British colonies in 1838, many plantation economies like Trinidad were left looking for alternative sources of cheap labor. Trinidad tried to draw Europeans, but the heat made them ineffective. Attention finally turned to the Indian subcontinent, and in 1845 the first ship of Indian laborers arrived in Trinidad. These workers were hired indentured and came mainly from the poorer parts of Uttar Pradesh. They undertook the three-month journey to the New World with the understanding that after their five-year work stint was over, they could reindenture themselves or return to India. The system stayed in place until 1917.

The Indians proved effective on the sugarcane and cocoa plantations, helping them return to prosperity. In an effort to discourage the Indians from returning home, the colony eventually offered a land grant as an incentive for those who chose to stay. Many took up the offer and stayed to make new lives in their adopted homeland. Their descendants still maintain many traditions and, to some extent, language. East Indian culture is a vibrant component of T&T's national culture, and you can find Indian festivals and music sharing center stage at all national events. East Indians actually compose about half the island's population and are an integral part of Trinidad and Tobago society.

able from 10 to 6—and a center for parang, the Venezuelan-derived folk music. Although worthwhile for those interested in the finer points of Trinidad history, this may not be worth the long drive to most visitors. ⊹ *Take Eastern Main Rd. from Port of Spain to Arouca; look for sign that points north* 🕾 *No phone* 🎫 *Free* ⊘ *Daily 6–6.*

🕒 **❼ Point Galera Lighthouse.** An essential stop when touring the northeast, this lighthouse was constructed in 1897 on a stunning cliff and is still actively used to warn ships about the rough waters below, the point where the Atlantic Ocean and Caribbean Sea meet. You can walk out onto a nearby rocky outcropping that marks Trinidad's easternmost point. On most days Tobago is clearly visible from here. A local legend (unprovable) tells that a group of Arawaks jumped off this point to their deaths rather than be captured by the Spanish. You'll pass several beautiful beaches on the drive from Toco to the lighthouse. The journey from Port of Spain takes about two hours; take Churchill Roosevelt Highway east to Valencia Road; follow the road east to Toco Main Road sign; take this road all the way to Toco; from the Toco intersection, follow the sign to Point Galera. ⊠ *Galera Rd., 3 mi from the triangular Toco intersection* 🎫 *Free* ⊘ *Daily dawn–dusk.*

NEED A BREAK? On the long drive to Point Galera, be sure to stop at **Kay's Pot** (⊠ Toco Main Rd., Rampanalgas 🕾 No phone) for a great meal en route. Many consider it worth the drive all by itself. In a corner of the front parking lot of Arthur's Grocery & Bar, Kay serves an incredible array of local food such as *souse* (pickled pigs' feet) in a lime-and-cucumber sauce, curried crab, and her signature dish, curried crayfish freshly caught in the pristine mountain streams nearby. The informal atmosphere, low prices, and music pouring out of the bar make for a fun and unusual dining experience.

➊ Port of Spain. Most organized tours begin at the port. If you're planning to explore on foot, which will take two to four hours, start early in the day; by midday the port area can be as hot and packed as Calcutta. It's best to end your tour on a bench in the Queen's Park Savannah, sipping a cool coconut water bought from one of the vendors operating out of flatbed trucks. For about 35¢ he'll lop the top off a green coconut with a deft swing of the machete and, when you've finished drinking, lop again, making a bowl and spoon of coconut shell for you to eat the young pulp. As in most cities, take extra care at night; women should not walk alone.

The town's main dock, **King's Wharf,** entertains a steady parade of cruise and cargo ships, a reminder that the city started from this strategic harbor. When hurricanes threaten other islands, it's not unusual to see as many as five large cruise ships taking advantage of the safety of the harbor. It's on Wrightson Road, the main street along the water on the southwest side of town.

Across Wrightson Road and a few minutes' walk from the south side of King's Wharf, the busy **Independence Square** has been the focus of the downtown area's major gentrification. Flanked by government buildings and the familiar twin towers of the Financial Complex (they adorn all T&T dollar bills), the square (really a long rectangle) is a lovely park with trees, flagstone walkways, chess tables, and the Brian Lara Promenade (named after Trinidad's world-famous cricketer). On its south side the cruise-ship complex, full of duty-free shops, forms an enclave of international anonymity with the Crowne Plaza Trinidad. On the eastern end of the square is the Cathedral of the Immaculate Conception; it was by the sea when it was built in 1832, but subsequent landfill around the port gave it an inland location. The imposing Roman Catholic structure is made of blue limestone from nearby Laventille.

Frederick Street, Port of Spain's main shopping drag, starting north from the midpoint of Independence Square, is a market street of scents and sounds—perfumed oils sold by sidewalk vendors and music tapes being played from vending carts—and crowded shops.

At Prince and Frederick streets, **Woodford Square** has served as the site of political meetings, speeches, public protests, and occasional violence. It's dominated by the magnificent Red House, a Renaissance-style building that takes up an entire city block. Trinidad's House of Parliament takes its name from a paint job done in anticipation of Queen Victoria's Diamond Jubilee in 1897. The original Red House was burned to the ground in a 1903 riot, and the present structure was built four years later. The chambers are open to the public.

The view of the south side of the square is framed by the Gothic spires of Trinity, the city's Anglican cathedral, consecrated in 1823; its mahogany-beam roof is modeled after that of Westminster Hall in London. On the north are the impressive Public Library, the Hall of Justice, and City Hall.

If the downtown port area is the pulse of Port of Spain, the great green expanse of **Queen's Park Savannah,** roughly bounded by Maraval Road, Queen's Park West, Charlotte Street, and Saddle Road, is the city's soul. You can walk straight north on Frederick Street and get there within 20 minutes. Its 2-mi (3-km) circumference is a popular jogger's track. The grandstand on the southern end is a popular venue for Calypso and cultural shows. The northern end of the Savannah is devoted to plants. A rock garden, known as the the Hollows, and a fishpond add to the rusticity. In the middle of the Savannah you will find a small graveyard where members of the Peschier family—who originally owned the land—are buried.

A series of astonishing buildings constructed in several 19th-century styles—known collectively as the **Magnificent Seven**—flanks the western side of the Savannah. Notable are Killarney, patterned (loosely) after Balmoral Castle in Scotland, with an Italian-marble gallery surrounding the ground floor; Whitehall, constructed in the style of a Venetian palace by a cacao-plantation magnate and currently the office of the prime minister; Roomor (named for the Roodal and Morgan families—it's still occupied by the Morgans), a flamboyantly baroque colonial house with a preponderance of towers, pinnacles, and wrought-iron trim that suggests an elaborate French pastry; and the Queen's Royal College, in German Renaissance style, with a prominent tower clock that chimes on the hour. Sadly, several of these fine buildings have fallen into advanced decay.

Head over to the southeast corner of the Savannah to see the **National Museum & Art Gallery,** especially its Carnival exhibitions, the Amerindian collection and historical re-creations, and the fine 19th-century paintings of Trinidadian artist Cazabon. ☒ *117 Upper Frederick St., Port of Spain* ☏ *868/623–5941* ☒ *Free* ☽ *Tues.–Sat. 10–6.*

The cultivated expanse of parkland north of the Savannah is the site of the president's and prime minister's official residences and also the **Emperor Valley Zoo and the Botanical Gardens.** A meticulous lattice of walkways and local flora, the parkland was first laid out in 1820 for Governor Ralph Woodford. In the midst of the serene wonderland is the 8-acre zoo, which exhibits mostly birds and animals of the region—from the brilliantly plumed scarlet ibis to slithering anacondas and pythons; you can also see (and hear) the wild parrots that breed in the surrounding foliage. The zoo draws a quarter of a million visitors a year. The admission prices are a steal, and tours are free during opening hours. ☒ *Botanical Gardens, Port of Spain* ☏ *868/622–3530 or 868/622–5343* ☒ *Zoo TT$4, gardens free* ☽ *Daily 9:30–5:30.*

⑤ Chaguaramas Military History & Aerospace Museum. On the former U.S. military base, this is a must-see for history buffs. The exhibits are in a large hangarlike shed without air-conditioning, so dress appropriately. Exhibits cover everything from Amerindian history to the Cold War, but the emphasis is on the two World Wars. There's a decidedly charming and homemade feel to the place; in fact, most exhibits were made by the curator and founder, Commander Gaylord Kelshall of the T&T Coast Guard. The museum is set a bit off the main road but is easily spotted by the turquoise BWIA L1011 jet parked out front (it's part of the permanent collection). ⊠ *Western Main Rd., Chaguaramas* ☎ *868/634–4391* ▱ *$20TT* ☉ *Mon.–Sat. 9–5.*

TOBAGO

Where to Stay

Tobago is much more of a tourist destination than Trinidad, and this is reflected in the range of accommodations. Those seeking luxury can find a number of upscale resorts and villas, while the budget-minded can take advantage of several smaller and more intimate establishments.

For approximate costs, *see* the dining and lodging price chart on the Trinidad and Tobago Planner at the beginning of this chapter.

$$$ 🏨 **Le Grand Courlan Resort & Spa.** This hotel is more upscale than its sister property, the Grafton Beach Resort, located next door. Rooms have large balconies, and the beach is one of the best on the island. The all-inclusive price includes basic water sports; one spa treatment per day is included, but because of the volume of requests, they sometimes feel rushed. Food is occasionally not great, and service can be a bit slow and impersonal; in truth, both the Coco Reef Resort and the Hilton Tobago offer nicer rooms and better spa treatments and meals for roughly the same price, albeit with à la carte pricing. ⊠ *Shirvan Rd., Black Rock* ☎ *868/639–9667, 800/468–3750, 800/424–5500 in Canada* 🖷 *868/639–9292* ⊕ *www.legrandcourlan-resort.com* ⇥ *80 rooms, 3 suites* ♿ *3 restaurants, in-room safes, cable TV, 2 tennis courts, pool, health club, billiards, hair salon, hot tub, spa, beach, dive shop, windsurfing, 3 bars, shops, laundry service, car rental, travel services; no kids under 16* ⊟ *AE, MC, V* ⦿ *AI.*

$$$$ 🏨 **Plantation Beach Villas.** If you're looking for luxury living in a well-appointed Caribbean villa, you should be blissfully happy here. Each of the six pink three-bedroom villas is prettily done in colonial style, complete with fretwork; an enormous front porch can hold up to six people comfortably. Daily maid service is included in the price. The grounds feature lush landscaping, and the communal pool and bar area is a lively meeting place for villa guests. This property makes an excellent alternative to a regular hotel for larger families, and considering that the entire villa costs the same as a luxury hotel room, it's a huge bargain as well. ⊠ *Stone Haven Bay Rd., Black Rock* ⦿ *Box 434, Scarborough* 🖷 *868/639–9377* ⊕ *www.plantationbeachvillas.com* ⇥ *6 3-bedroom villas* ♿ *Snack bar, in-room safes, kitchens, cable TV, pool, beach, bar, shop, babysitting, laundry facilities, laundry service, business services* ⊟ *AE, MC, V* ⦿ *EP.*

$$$$ 🏨 **The Villas at Stonehaven.** Perched on a hillside overlooking the ocean, this villa complex sets the standard for luxury self-catering accommodations on Tobago. There are 14 French colonial–style villas in the complex, spaced well enough to allow for maximum privacy. Each

Tobago

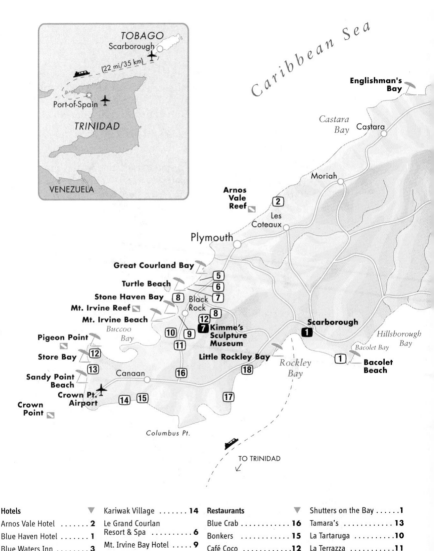

Caribbean Sea

St. Giles
Island

North Pt.

Lovers Beach

The
Sisters

Man O'War Bay

Charlotteville

Bird of Paradise
Island

Bloody Bay

Flagstaff Hill

Parlatuvier

Speyside

Little
Tobago

Parlatuvier

Pigeon
Peak

Delaford

King's Bay

Roxborough

Carapuse
Bay

Ft. King George

ATLANTIC OCEAN

0   4 mi

0   4 km

KEY
Beaches
Dive Sites
Ferry
Exploring Sights
Hotels & Restaurants
Trail

three-bedroom villa has an infinity pool and spectacular views. Individually owned units are all different. A 200-acre bird sanctuary is next door for those who might want a little nature jaunt. Housekeeping is provided, and cooks are available for those who don't wish to make use of the impressive kitchens. The only minor disadvantage here is that the beach is a trek down the hill. Villas are priced for four or six people sharing. ⊠ *Bon Accord, Grafton Estate, Shirvan Rd., Box 1079, Black Rock* ☎ *868/639–9887* 🖷 *868/639–0102* ⊕ *www.stonehavenvillas. com* ↩ *14 villas* ᗱ *Restaurant, in-room safes, kitchens, cable TV, in-room data ports, pool, bar, babysitting, laundry facilities, meeting rooms, airport shuttle;* ▭ *AE, MC, V* ⦿*I EP.*

★   🏨 **Coco Reef Resort.** This expansive enclave is just a short distance from
🕊 **$$$–$$$$**   the airport but somehow seems miles away. Pink buildings sprawl along a perfect stretch of coast. Just in front of the hotel is the only private (though man-made) beach on the island. The resort has all the usual amenities, including a highly regarded spa. The hotel restaurants are among the best in Tobago, and there's always an animated crowd around the pool bar. Store Bay is quite literally next door and Pigeon Point a short walk away. You can't beat the ocean-view villa for its glitz factor, including gold-plated bathroom fittings, a TV the size of a small car, and a private sun deck. Arrive in style by booking the hotel's Rolls (originally owned by Errol Flynn) for the two-minute trip from the airport ($10 per person). ⊠ *Coconut Bay, Box 434, Crown Point* ☎ *868/639–8571 or 800/ 221–1294* 🖷 *868/639–8574 or 305/639–2717* ⊕ *www.cocoreef.com* ↩ *135 rooms, 35 suites, 11 villas* ᗱ *2 restaurants, room service, refrigerators, cable TV, 2 tennis courts, pool, gym, hair salon, spa, beach, dive shop, snorkeling, windsurfing, 2 bars, shops, babysitting, business services, meeting rooms, car rental, travel services* ▭*AE, D, DC, MC, V* ⦿*I BP.*

$$–$$$$ 🏨 **Blue Haven Hotel.** Justifiably celebrated, this 1940s-era hotel overlooks
Fodor'sChoice   a spectacular secluded beach on Bacolet Bay just outside Scarborough
★   and has been fully restored and updated to luxury status. Though long neglected, it has been brought back to life by Austrian Karl Pilstl and his wife. The lobby is a study in 1940s perfection and appears now as it must have when Rita Hayworth came through. Rooms have teak floors and glass-partitioned bathrooms (with curtains for private moments); four-poster beds and lavish beddings are standard. Rooms in a new wing have sunken sitting areas. Most activity takes place at the No Problem beach bar, where a barbecue always seems to be in progress. The hotel is surrounded by water on three sides, so every room has a spectacular ocean view. The hotel's restaurant, **Shutters on the Bay,** offers splendid food and an unbeatable atmosphere. Meal plans are available. ⊠ *Bacolet Bay, Scarborough* ☎☎ *868/660–7400* ⊕ *www.bluehavenhotel.com* ↩ *43 rooms, 8 suites, 1 villa* ᗱ *Restaurant, fans, cable TV, in-room data ports, tennis court, pool, gym, spa, beach, Ping-Pong, 2 bars, babysitting, laundry facilities, laundry service, business services, meeting room* ▭ *AE, DC, MC, V* ⦿*I EP.*

$$–$$$ 🏨 **Mt. Irvine Bay Hotel.** Before the Hilton Tobago, the Mt. Irvine was the premier golf hotel on the island, though it's now been eclipsed. Rooms are spacious and perfectly adequate, though not as fancy as those in some other similarly priced hotels on the island. Although the hotel lacks some of the fancier amenities, there's still something magical about its air of 1970s grandeur, which cannot be found at any of the flashy new resorts. A lovely beach, where drinks are served and towels dispensed, sits right across the road. The hotel's restaurants are best avoided, though, since the service is generally slow and the food insipid. ⊠ *Shirvan Rd., Box 222, Mt. Irvine* ☎ *868/639–8871* 🖷 *868/639–8800* ⊕ *www.mtirvine. com* ➯ *105 rooms, 6 suites, 46 cottages ⚷ 3 restaurants, cable TV, in-room safes, 18-hole golf course, 2 tennis courts, pool, hair salon, sauna, beach, snorkeling, windsurfing, waterskiing, fishing, 4 bars, meeting rooms, no-smoking rooms* ⊟ *AE, MC, V* ⧖ *EP.*

24

$$ 🏨 **Arnos Vale Hotel.** On 450 hillside acres, this hillside hotel is the perfect retreat for nature lovers and lovers in general. Princess Margaret spent her honeymoon here, and it's easy to see why—the world seems very far away. Rooms are little white cottages set into the hillside, so privacy isn't hard to find. A winding path takes guests down to a picture-perfect beach, pool, and bar. Some of the best snorkeling on the island can be done off the hotel's beach. The hilltop restaurant—furnished with antiques, iron-lattice tables, and a chandelier—has a magnificent patio with sweeping sea views. ⊠ *Arnos Vale and Franklin Rds., Box 208, Scarborough* ☎ *868/639–2881* 🖷 *868/639–4629* ⊕ *www.arnosvalehotel. com* ➯ *29 rooms, 3 suites ⚷ Restaurant, some refrigerators, tennis court, pool, beach, snorkeling, dive shop, 2 bars, shops; no room TVs* ⊟ *AE, DC, MC, V* ⧖ *EP.*

★ $$ 🏨 **Blue Waters Inn.** A tropical rain forest creeps up behind this sprawling ecofriendly hotel, which sits on a sheltered turquoise Batteaux Bay with a white-sand beach just east of Speyside. A 90-minute drive from Scarborough, the hotel makes every effort to make guests feel at home. One- and two-bedroom apartments are directly on the beach, and kitchens can be stocked with food for your arrival. The resort caters primarily to divers and bird-watchers, but it's also a fine place from which to explore Tobago's north coast. The restaurant serves the freshest of fish, and barbecue dinners are cooked up on the beach patio. ⊠ *Bateaux Bay, Speyside* ☎ *868/660–4077 or 800/742–4276* 🖷 *868/660–5195* ⊕ *www.bluewatersinn.com* ➯ *31 rooms, 3 suites, 4 bungalows ⚷ Restaurant, some kitchens, tennis court, beach, dive shop, snorkeling, dive shop, boating, bar, library, recreation room, shop, babysitting, Internet room, meeting rooms, car rental; no room TVs* ⊟ *AE, MC, V* ⧖ *EP.*

☝ $$ 🏨 **Grafton Beach Resort.** The first all-inclusive hotel in Tobago remains a very popular choice for young couples. This is not a luxury hotel, and the restaurants are mediocre; however, it is not a bad value for those looking for the basics. Although the hotel is on one of the nicer beaches in Tobago, it is a public beach and peddlers may sometimes be a problem. Guests here can also use the spa facilities at the tonier Le Grand Courlan for a fee. ⊠ *Shirvan Rd., Black Rock* ☎ *868/639–0191* 🖷 *868/ 639–0030* ⊕ *www.grafton-resort.com* ➯ *102 rooms, 4 suites ⚷ 3 restaurants, in-room safes, refrigerators, cable TV, pool, beach, dive shop, snorkeling, windsurfing, boating, squash, 3 bars, shops, business services, meeting rooms* ⊟ *AE, MC, V* ⧖ *AI.*

$$ 🏨 **Hilton Tobago Golf & Spa Resort.** The scale and setting of this sprawling plantation-style resort are impressive, but the location is also its biggest drawback. On the Windward coast, the beach is minuscule, requiring a complimentary shuttle to the much better Pigeon Point Beach, and the omnipresent sea spray makes all tiled surfaces slippery. The two-story buildings seem to rise magically from the landscape at the end of a gorgeous 18-hole golf course, and the massive atrium lobby, which is filled with local art, has floor-to-ceiling sea views. All rooms are oceanfront, though the trade-off is a very long walk for guests at each end. All rooms have either a balcony or charming patio. ⌂ *Box 633, Scarborough* 🖀 *868/ 660–8500* 🖷 *868/660–8503* ⊕ *www.hiltoncaribbean.com* ⤵ *178 rooms, 22 suites* ⚬ *2 restaurants, in-room safes, minibars, cable TV, Wi-Fi, 18-hole golf course, 2 tennis courts, 3 pools, gym, hair salon, sauna, dive shop, snorkeling, windsurfing, waterskiing, fishing, 3 bars, shops, dry cleaning, laundry service, business services, meeting rooms, no-smoking rooms* ⊟ *AE, MC, V* ⦿ *EP.*

★ $ 🖭 **Kariwak Village.** Alan and Cynthia Cloves have created an intimate, tranquil oasis for their loyal guests who return year after year to this holistic retreat. Even the cabanas have been designed with pitched roofs to help "maximize your energy potential." Hearty souls who wish to atone for an excess of nightly rum punches can indulge in daily morning yoga. The bar and restaurant are in a bamboo pavilion and welcome local entertainers on weekends. Choose a garden room for a more peaceful stay; those near the pool can be noisy. The complex is near the airport, Store Bay, and Pigeon Point but is not on the beach. ⌂ *Box 27, Crown Point* 🖀 *868/639–8442* 🖷 *868/639–8441* ⊕ *www.kariwak. com* ⤵ *24 rooms* ⚬ *Restaurant, pool, fitness classes, outdoor hot tub, massage, bar; no room TVs* ⊟ *AE, MC, V* ⦿ *EP.*

$ 🖭 **Toucan Inn.** This budget hotel near the airport offers simple, clean rooms and a lively social scene. The hotel's restaurant, Bonkers, is a popular hangout for locals and visitors, so entertainment is never far away. Rooms are furnished with locally made teak furniture and comfy beds. Guests staying for a week or more get breakfast included in the rate. The hotel has a small pool, but the beach is a fairly long trek down the road. ⊠ *Store Bay Local Rd., Crown Point* 🖀 *868/639–7173* 🖷 *868/ 639–8933* ⊕ *www.toucan-inn.com* ⤵ *20 rooms* ⚬ *Restaurant, pool, bar* ⊟ *AE, MC, V* ⦿ *EP.*

Where to Eat

Curried crab and dumplings is Tobago's Sunday-dinner favorite. Oil-down—a local dish—tastes better than it sounds: it's a gently seasoned mixture of boiled breadfruit and salt beef or pork flavored with coconut milk. Mango ice cream or a sweet-and-sour tamarind ball makes a tasty finish. You may want to take home some hot-pepper sauce or chutney to a spice-loving friend or relative.

For approximate costs, *see* the dining and lodging price chart at the beginning of this chapter.

CAFÉS   ✕ **Shore Things Café & Craft.** With a dramatic setting over the ocean on
¢   the Milford Road between Crown Point and Scarborough, this is a good spot to stop for a lunch or coffee break. Survey the view from the deck tables while enjoying a variety of freshly prepared juices (the

tamarind is particularly refreshing) and nibbling on excellent sandwiches. The whole-wheat pizza here may well be the best on the island. While waiting for your meal, you can shop for local crafts in the lovely and comprehensive gift shop. ⊠ *25 Old Milford Rd., Lambeau* ☎ *868/ 635–1072* ═ *MC, V* ⊘ *Closed Sun. No dinner.*

CARIBBEAN ✕ **Kariwak Village Restaurant.** Recorded steel-band music plays gently
★ **$$–$$$** in the background at this romantic, candlelit spot in the Kariwak Village complex. In a bamboo pavilion that resembles an Amerindian round hut, Cynthia Clovis orchestrates a very original menu. Whatever the dish, it will be full of herbs and vegetables picked from her organic garden. Be sure to try the delicious homemade ice cream. Friday and Saturday buffets, with live jazz or calypso, are a Tobagonian highlight. ⊠ *Crown Point* ☎ *868/639–8442* ═ *AE, MC, V.*

★ **$** ✕ **Blue Crab Restaurant.** The Sardinha family have been serving the best local lunches at their home for more than 20 years. The ebullient Alison entertains and hugs diners while her husband, Ken, does the cooking. The food is hearty and usually well seasoned in the creole style. The only bad news here is that the restaurant is rarely open for dinner; the good news is that you may not have room for dinner after lunch. ⊠ *Corner of Robinson and Main Sts., Scarborough* ☎ *868/639–2737* ═ *AE, MC, V* ⊘ *Closed weekends. No dinner.*

CONTEMPORARY ✕ **Tamara's.** At the elegant Coco Reef Resort you can dine on contem-
$$$ porary cuisine with an island twist. The peach walls and whitewashed wooden ceiling make the resort's restaurant feel airy and light, and island breezes waft through the palm-lined terrace. The prix-fixe menu changes seasonally, but the fish dishes are sure to please. A full tropical buffet breakfast is served daily; dinner is served nightly. ⊠ *Coco Reef Resort, Crown Point, Scarborough* ☎ *868/639–8571* ═ *AE, MC, V* ⊘ *No lunch.*

★ **$$–$$$** ✕ **Shutters on the Bay.** In the stylish Blue Haven Hotel, this restaurant is sure to please even the most discerning diners. The warm-yellow dining area is on the second floor of a colonial-style building and is surrounded by white push-out shutters that afford a magical view of Bacolet Bay. The menu features a variety of dishes all with a contemporary Caribbean twist. If crayfish is on the menu, get it, as it's a sure pleaser. ⊠ *Blue Haven Hotel, Bacolet Bay, Scarborough* ☎ *868/660–7500* ⌂ *Reservations essential* ═ *AE, MC, V.*

ECLECTIC ✕ **Bonkers.** Despite the rather odd name, this restaurant at the Toucan
$–$$$ Inn is atmospheric and excellent. Designed by expat British co-owner Chris James, the architecture is a blend of Kenyan and Caribbean styles, executed entirely in local teak and open on all sides. The menu is huge; Chris claims it pains him to remove any items, so he just keeps adding more. You can savor your lobster Rockefeller while enjoying the nightly entertainment. Open for breakfast and lunch seven days a week, this is the busiest eatery on the island. ⊠ *Toucan Inn, Store Bay Local Rd., Crown Point* ☎ *868/639–7173* ▤ *868/639–8933* ═ *AE, MC, V.*

$–$$ ✕ **Café Coco.** This smart eatery—though it seats 200—is broken into multiple levels, so there's still a sense of intimacy. Statuary is strewn about with carefree abandon, and the sound of flowing water permeates the room. Very reasonably priced by Tobago standards, the main courses range from Cuban stewed beef to shrimp tempura. The zingy *pimento Mexicano,* mozzarella-stuffed jalapeños and shrimp on a bed of greens, is a great appetizer. The restaurant is seldom full, so getting a table is usually not a problem. ⊠ *TTEC Substation Rd., off Crown Point Rd., Crown Point* ☎ *868/639–0996* ▤ *AE, MC, V.*

ITALIAN **✕ La Tartaruga.** Milanese owner Gabriele de Gaetano has created one of
$–$$$ the island's most delightful dining experiences. Sitting on the large patio surrounded by lush foliage with Gabriele rushing from table to table chatting in Italian-laced English is all the entertainment you'll need. An impressive cellar is stocked solely with Italian wines. ⊠ *Buccoo Rd., Buccoo* ☎ *868/639–0940* ⚏ *Reservations essential* ▤ *AE, MC, V* ☉ *Closed Sun.*

★ **$–$$$** **✕ La Terrazza.** This romantic Italian restaurant is garnering rave reviews and has forced La Tartaruga, the previous gold standard for Italian food on the island, to drop prices drastically in order to compete. Keisha and Stefano Monti, the husband-and-wife owners, handle every aspect of the restaurant from the cooking to the serving. The menu is light, imaginative, and eminently affordable. The salmon tartare appetizer is heavenly. Stefano, an avid wine collector, stocks the excellent cellar; Keisha insists that anything he collects be offered for sale—good news for diners. Choose to sit under fans in the main house or outdoors on the torchlit deck. ⊠ *196 Shirvan Rd., Buccoo* ☎ *868/639–8242* ⚏ *Reservations essential* ▤ *MC, V* ☉ *Closed Mon.*

Beaches

You won't find manicured country-club sand here. But those who enjoy feeling as though they've landed on a desert island will relish the untouched quality of these shores.

Bacolet Beach. This dark-sand beach was the setting for the films *Swiss Family Robinson* and *Heaven Knows, Mr. Allison.* Though used by the Blue Haven Hotel, like all local beaches it's open to the public. If you are not a guest at the hotel, access to the beach is down a track next door to the hotel. The bathroom and changing facilities on the beach are for hotel guests only. ⊠ *Windward Rd., east of Scarborough.*

★ **Englishman's Bay.** This charming, mile-long, somewhat wild beach is usually completely deserted. Keep in mind that the price paid for solitude is a lack of facilities. ⊠ *North Side Rd., east of Castara Bay.*

Great Courland Bay. Near Fort Bennett, the bay has clear, tranquil waters. Along the sandy beach—one of Tobago's longest—you can find several glitzy hotels. A marina attracts the yachting crowd. ⊠ *Leeward Rd., northeast of Black Rock, Courland.*

King's Bay. Surrounded by steep green hills, this is the most visually satisfying of the swimming sites off the road from Scarborough to Speyside—the bay hooks around so severely you can feel like you're in a lake. The crescent-shaped beach is easy to find because it's marked by a sign about halfway between the two towns. Just before you reach the bay, there's a bridge with an unmarked turnoff that leads to a gravel parking lot; beyond that, a landscaped path leads to a waterfall with a rocky pool. You may meet locals who can offer to guide you to the top of the falls; however, you may find the climb not worth the effort. ⊠ *Delaford.*

Lovers Beach. So called because of its pink sand and its seclusion—you have to hire a local to bring you here by boat—it's an isolated and quiet retreat. Ask one of the fishermen in Charlotteville to arrange a ride for you, but be sure to haggle. It should cost you no more than $20 a person for a return ride (considerably less sometimes). ⊠ *North coast, reachable only by boat from Charlotteville.*

Mt. Irvine Beach. Across the street from the Mt. Irvine Bay Hotel is this unremarkable beach, but it has great surfing in July and August; the snorkeling is excellent, too. It's also ideal for windsurfing in January and April. There are picnic tables surrounded by painted concrete pagodas and a snack bar. ⊠ *Shirvan Rd., Mt. Irvine.*

Parlatuvier. On the north side of the island, the beach is best approached via the road from Roxborough. It's a classic Caribbean crescent, a scene peopled by villagers and fishermen. ⊠ *Parlatuvier.*

Pigeon Point Beach. This stunning locale is often displayed on Tobago travel brochures. Although the beach is public, it abuts part of what was once a large coconut estate, and you must pay a token admission (about TT$18) to enter the grounds and use the facilities. ⊠ *Pigeon Point.*

Sandy Point Beach. Situated at the end of the Crown Point Airport runway, this beach is abutted by several hotels, so you won't lack for amenities around here. The beach is accessible by walking around the airport fence to the hotel area. ⊠ *At Crown Point Airport.*

Stone Haven Bay. A gorgeous stretch of sand is across the street from the Grafton Beach Resort. ⊠ *Shirvan Rd., Black Rock.*

Store Bay. The beach, where boats depart for Buccoo Reef, is little more than a small sandy cove between two rocky breakwaters, but the food stands here are divine: several huts licensed by the tourist board to local ladies who sell roti, pelau, and the world's messiest dish—crab and dumplings. Near the airport, just walk around the Crown Point Hotel to the beach entrance. ⊠ *Crown Point.*

Turtle Beach. Named for the leatherback turtles that lay their eggs here at night between February and June, it's on Great Courland Bay. (If you're very quiet, you can watch; the turtles don't seem to mind.) It's 8 mi from the airport between Black Rock and Plymouth. ⊠ *Southern end of Great Courland Bay, between Black Rock and Plymouth.*

Sports & the Outdoors

BIRD-WATCHING ★ Some 200 varieties of birds have been documented on Tobago: look for the yellow oriole, scarlet ibis, and the comical motmot—the male of the species clears sticks and stones from an area and then does a dance complete with snapping sounds to attract a mate. The flora is as vivid as the birds. Purple-and-yellow *poui* trees and spectacular orange immortelles splash color over the countryside, and something is blooming virtually every season. Naturalist and ornithologist David Rooks operates **Rooks Nature Tours** (⊠ 462 Moses Hill, Lambeau ☎ 868/756–8594 ⊕ www. rookstobago.com), offering bird-watching walks inland and trips to offshore bird colonies. He's generally considered to be the best guide on the island. Pat Turpin and Renson Jack at **Pioneer Journeys** (☎ 868/660–4327 or 868/660–5175) can give you information about their bird-watching tours of Bloody Bay rain forest and Louis d'Or River valley wetlands.

BOAT TOURS Tobago offers many wonderful spots for snorkeling. Although the reefs around Speyside in the northeast are becoming better known, **Buccoo Reef,** off the island's southwest coast, is still the most popular—perhaps too popular. Over the years the reef has been damaged by the ceaseless boat traffic and by the thoughtless visiting divers who take pieces of coral as souvenirs. Still, it's worth experiencing, particularly if you have children. Daily 2½-hour tours by glass-bottom boats let you snorkel at the reef, swim in a lagoon, and gaze at Coral Gardens—where fish and coral are as yet untouched. Most dive companies in the Black Rock area also arrange snorkeling tours. There's also good snorkeling near the **Arnos Vale Hotel** and the **Mt. Irvine Bay Hotel.**

Hew's Glass Bottom Boat Tours (✉ Pigeon Point ☎ 868/639–9058) are perfect excursions for those who neither snorkel nor dive. Boats leave daily at 11:30 AM. **Kalina Kats** (✉ Scarborough ☎ 868/639–6306) has a 50-foot catamaran on which you can sail around the Tobago coastline with stops for snorkeling and exploring the rain forest. The romantic sunset cruise with cocktails is a great way to end the day.

DIVING An abundance of fish and coral thrives on the nutrients of Venezuela's Orinoco River, which are brought to Tobago by the Guyana current. Off the west coast is **Arnos Vale Reef,** with a depth of 40 feet and several reefs that run parallel to the shore. Here you can spot French and queen angelfish, moray eels, southern stingrays, and even the Atlantic torpedo ray. Much of the diving is drift diving in the mostly gentle current. **Crown Point,** on the island's southwest tip, is a good place for exploring the Shallows—a plateau at 50 to 100 feet that's favored by turtles, dolphins, angelfish, and nurse sharks. Just north of Crown Point on the southwest coast, **Pigeon Point** is a good spot to submerge. North of Pigeon Point, long, sandy beaches line the calm western coast; it has a gradual offshore slope and the popular **Mt. Irvine Wall,** which goes down to about 60 feet.

A short trip from Charlotteville, off the northeast tip of the island, is **St. Giles Island.** Here are natural rock bridges—London Bridge, Marble Island, and Fishbowl—and underwater cliffs. The **waters off Speyside** on the east coast draw scuba-diving aficionados for the many manta rays in the area. Exciting sites in this area include Batteaux Reef, Angel Reef, Bookends, Blackjack Hole, and Japanese Gardens—one of the loveliest reefs, with depths of 20 to 85 feet and lots of sponges.

Tobago is considered a prime diving destination, as the clear waters provide maximum visibility. Every species of hard coral and most soft corals can be found in the waters around the island. Tobago is also home to the largest-known brain coral. Generally, the best diving is around the Speyside area. Many hotels and guesthouses in this area cater to the diving crowd with minimalist accommodations and easy access to the water. You can usually get the best deals with these "dive and stay" packages. **Tobago Dive Experience** (✉ Manta Lodge, Speyside ☎ 868/639–7034 ⊕ www.tobagodiveexperience.com) offers the most comprehensive range of courses, including PADI, NAUI, and BSAC. Prices are very competitive, and class sizes are kept small to ensure that all divers get the attention they need. This is also the only dive operation to have locations in both the north and south areas of the island. **AquaMarine Dive Ltd.** (⌧ Blue Waters Inn, Batteaux Bay, Speyside ☎ 868/639–4416 ⊕ www.aquamarinedive.com) is on the northeast coast at the Blue Waters Inn and offers a friendly and laid-back approach, which makes it popular with casual divers.

FISHING **Dillon's Deep Sea Charters** (⌧ Crown Point ☎ 868/639–8763) is excellent for full- and half-day trips for kingfish, barracuda, wahoo, mahimahi, blue marlin, and others. Trips start at $165 for four hours, including equipment. With **Hard Play Fishing Charters** (⌧ 13 The Evergreen, Old Grange, Mt. Irvine Bay ☎ 868/639–7108 ⊕ www.hardplay.net), colorful skipper Gerard "Frothy" De Silva helps you bag your own marlin. The cost is $350 for four hours on the 42-foot *Hard Play* or $200 on the 31-foot *Hard Play Lite*.

24

GOLF The 18-hole, par-72 course at the **Mt. Irvine Golf Club** (⌧ Mt. Irvine Bay
★ Hotel, Shirvan Rd., Mt. Irvine ☎ 868/639–8871) has been ranked among the top courses in the Caribbean and among the top 100 in the world, but course maintenance has suffered over the years. Greens fees are $30 for 9 holes, $48 for 18 holes. The 18-hole, PGA-designed cham-
Fodor'sChoice pionship par-72 course at **Tobago Plantations Golf & Country Club** (⌧ Low-
★ lands ☎ 868/631–0875) is set amid rolling greens and mangroves. It offers some amazing views of the ocean as a bonus. Greens fees are $82 for one round, $142 for two rounds (these rates include a golf cart and taxes). This is the newer of the two main courses on the island and is by far the most popular. The course is well maintained and contains areas of mangrove and forest that are home to many bird species.

HIKING Eco-consciousness is strong on Tobago, where the rain forests of the Main Ridge were set aside for protection in 1764, creating the first such preserve in the western hemisphere. Natural areas include Little Tobago and St. Giles islands, both major seabird sanctuaries. In addition, the endangered leatherback turtles maintain breeding grounds on some of Tobago's leeward beaches.

Harris Jungle Tours (⌧ Golden Grove Rd., Canaan ☎ 868/639–0513 ⊕ www.harris-jungle-tours.com) is run by the knowledgeable Harris McDonald and offers a variety of tours ranging from strenuous to laid-back. The more adventurous might want to try the rain-forest-at-night tour, which promises the possibility of encounters with some of Tobago's folklore characters, including La Diablesse (a beautifully dressed she-devil with a cloven hoof). **Yes Tourism** (⌧ Pigeon Point Rd., Crown Point ☎ 868/ 631–0287 ⊕ www.yes-tourism.com) offers a comprehensive range of tours for individuals and groups. The Rain Forest tour is an excellent guided hike. Sightseeing tours around Tobago as well as to Trinidad and the Grenadines are also possible.

Shopping

The souvenir-bound will do better in Trinidad than in Tobago, but determined shoppers should manage to find a few things to take home.

Scarborough has the largest collection of shops, and Burnett Street, which climbs sharply from the port to St. James Park, is a good place to browse.

FOODSTUFFS **Forro's Homemade Delicacies** (⊠ The Andrew's Rectory, Bacolet St., opposite fire station, Scarborough ☎ 868/639–2485) sells its own fine line of homemade tamarind chutney, lemon and lime marmalade, hot sauce, and guava and golden-apple jelly. Eileen Forrester, wife of the Anglican archdeacon of Trinidad and Tobago, supervises a kitchen full of good cooks who boil and bottle the condiments and pack them in little straw baskets—or even in bamboo. Most jars are small, easy to carry, and inexpensive.

HANDICRAFTS **Cotton House** (⊠ Bacolet St., Scarborough ☎ 868/639–2727) is a good bet for jewelry and imaginative batik work. Paula Young runs her shop like an art school. You can visit the upstairs studio; if it's not too busy, you can even make a batik square at no charge. **Shore Things Café & Crafts** (⊠ 25 Old Milford Rd., Lambeau ☎ 868/635–1072) has a wide variety of souvenir items ranging from masks to music (and everything in between). **Souvenir and Gift Shop** (⊠ Port Mall, Wrightson Rd., Scarborough ☎ 868/639–5632) stocks straw baskets and other crafts.

Nightlife

Tobago is not the liveliest island after dark, but there's usually some form of nightlife to be found. Whatever you do the rest of the week, don't miss the huge impromptu party, affectionately dubbed Sunday School, that gears up after midnight on all the street corners of Buccoo and breaks up around dawn. Pick your band, hang out for a while, then move on. In downtown Scarborough on weekend nights you can also find competing sound systems blaring at informal parties that welcome extra guests. In addition, "blockos" (spontaneous block parties) spring up all over the island; look for the hand-painted signs. Tobago also has harvest parties on Sunday throughout the year, when a particular village extends its hospitality and opens its doors to visitors.

Bonkers (⊠ Toucan Inn, Store Bay Local Rd., Crown Point ☎ 868/639–7173) is lively on most evenings, with live entertainment every night
★ except Sunday. **Diver's Den Bar & Grill** (⊠ Mt. Pleasant Rd. and Robert St., Crown Point ☎ 868/639–8533), near the gas station, is the only island hangout that consistently stays open really late. **Grafton Beach Resort** (⊠ Shirvan Rd., Black Rock ☎ 868/639–0191) has some kind of organized cabaret-style event every night. Even if you hate that touristy stuff, check out Les Couteaux Cultural Group, which does a high-octane dance version of Tobagonian history. **Kariwak Village** (⊠ Crown Point ☎ 868/639–8442) has hip hotel entertainment and is frequented as much by locals as visitors on Friday and Saturday nights—one of the better local jazz-calypso bands almost always plays.

Exploring Tobago

A driving tour of Tobago, from Scarborough to Charlotteville and back, can be done in about four hours, but you'd never want to undertake this spectacular, and very hilly, ride in that time. The switchbacks can make you wish you had motion-sickness pills (take some along if you're prone). Plan to spend at least one night at the Speyside end of the island, and give yourself a chance to enjoy this largely untouched country and seaside at leisure.

Numbers in the margin correspond to points of interest on the Tobago map.

5 **Charlotteville.** This delightful fishing village in the northeast is enfolded in a series of steep hills. Fishermen here announce the day's catch by sounding their conch shells. A view of Man O' War Bay with Pigeon Peak (Tobago's highest mountain) behind it at sunset is an exquisite treat.

NEED A BREAK?

If you're exploring the windward coast, the funky, inexpensive **First Historical Café/Bar** (⊠ Mile Marker 8, Windward Main Rd. ☎ 868/660–2233), which is owned by the Washington family, is near Studley Park en route to Charlotte. It's got a thatch roof and a crushed-rock-and-coral floor, and you can eat overlooking the sea on the back porch. The food is simple, featuring such island delights as fruit plates, coconut bread, and fish sandwiches.

4 **Flagstaff Hill.** One of the highest points on the island sits at the northern tip of Tobago. Surrounded by ocean on three sides and with a view of other hills, Charlotteville, and St. Giles Island, this was the site of an American military lookout and radio tower during World War II. It's an ideal spot for a sunset picnic. The turnoff to the hill is at the major bend on the road from Speyside to Charlotteville. It's largely unpaved, so the going may be a bit rough.

2 **Fort King George.** On Mt. St. George, a short drive up the hill from Scarborough, Tobago's best-preserved historic monument clings to a cliff high above the ocean. Fort King George was built in the 1770s and operated until 1854. It's hard to imagine that this lovely, tranquil spot commanding sweeping views of the bay and landscaped with lush tropical foliage was ever the site of any military action, but the prison, officers' mess, and several stabilized cannons attest otherwise. Just to the left of the tall wooden figures dancing a traditional Tobagonian jig is the former barrack guardhouse, now housing the small **Tobago Museum.** Exhibits include weapons and other pre-Colombian artifacts found in the area; the fertility figures are especially interesting. Upstairs are maps and photographs of Tobago's past. Be sure to check out the gift display cases for the perversely fascinating jewelry made from embalmed and painted lizards and sea creatures; you might find it hard to resist a pair of bright-yellow shrimp earrings. The **Fine Arts Centre** at the foot of the Fort King George complex shows the work of local artists. ⊠ *84 Fort St., Scarborough* ☎ *868/639–3970* ✉ *Fort free, museum TT$2* ⏱ *Weekdays 9–5.*

★ **7** **Kimme's Sculpture Museum.** The diminutive and eccentric German-born sculptress Luise Kimme fell in love with the form of Tobagonians and has devoted her life to capturing them in her sculptures. Her pieces can exceed 12 feet in height and are often wonderfully whimsical. Much of her work is done in wood (none of it local), but there are many bronze pieces as well. The museum itself is a turreted structure with a commanding view of the countryside. Most locals refer to it as "The Castle." There are numerous signs in Mt. Irvine directing visitors to the museum. ⊠ *Mt. Irvine* ☎ *868/639–0257* ⊕ *www.luisekimme.com* 🖾 *TT$3.50* ⊙ *Sun. 10 AM–2 PM or by appointment.*

❻ St. Giles Island. The underwater cliffs and canyons here off the northeastern tip of Tobago draw divers to this spot where the Atlantic meets the Caribbean. ✛ *Take Windward Rd. inland across mountains from Speyside.*

❶ Scarborough. Around Rockley Bay on the island's leeward hilly side, this town is both the capital of Tobago and a popular cruise-ship port, but it conveys the feeling that not much has changed since the area was settled two centuries ago. It may not be one of the delightful pastel-color cities of the Caribbean, but Scarborough does have its charms, including several interesting little shops. Whatever you do, be sure to check out the busy Scarborough Market, an indoor and outdoor affair featuring everything from fresh vegetables to live chickens and clothing. Note the red-and-yellow Methodist church on the hill, one of Tobago's oldest churches.

⌐ NEED A BREAK?   **Ciao Café** (⊠ 20 Burnett St., Scarborough ☎ 868/639-3001) is an essential stop on any visit to the capital and offers a selection of more than 20 flavors of gelato, as well as the usual complement of coffees. You can also get pizza slices and sandwiches if you're looking for a quick snack. There's seating in the air-conditioned interior and a lovely outdoor perch from which to absorb the downtown action sheltered from the blazing sun. Stronger cocktails are also available.

❸ Speyside. At the far reach of Tobago's windward coast, this small fishing village has a few lodgings and restaurants. Divers are drawn to the unspoiled reefs in the area and to the strong possibility of spotting giant manta rays. The approach to Speyside from the south affords one of the most spectacular vistas of the island. Glass-bottom boats operate between Speyside and **Little Tobago Island,** one of the most important seabird sanctuaries in the Caribbean.

TRINIDAD & TOBAGO ESSENTIALS

To research prices, get advice from other travelers, and book travel arrangements, visit www.fodors.com.

Transportation

BY AIR

There are nonstop flights to Trinidad from New York, Miami, and Washington, D.C. There are nonstop flights from London to Tobago but none from the United States. More likely, you will have to hop over to Tobago from Trinidad on Caribbean Star or Tobago Express.

🔃 Airline Information **Aeropostal** ☎ 868/623-4174. **Air Canada** ☎ 868/664-4065. **American Airlines** ☎ 868/664-4661. **British Airways** ☎ 800/744-2997. **BWIA West Indies Airways** ☎ 868/625-1010 or 868/669-3000. **Caribbean Star** ☎ 800/744-7827. **Continental Airlines** ☎ 800/461-2744. **LIAT** ☎ 868/627-2942 or 868/623-1838. **Tobago Express** ☎ 868/625-1010 or 868/669-3000.

AIRPORTS & TRANSFERS: Authorized airport taxis can be arranged just outside the baggage claim areas of the airports on both Trinidad and Tobago. (You will certainly be assailed by shouts of "Taxi?" by the nonauthorized drivers as you exit the baggage area.) The trip from the airport into Port of Spain costs about $30 during the day and $45 at night using the authorized taxis. In Tobago, the cost will vary greatly depending on the location of your hotel; a board in the baggage claim area claims to give accurate rates to all the major hotels. Generally, hotels in the Crown Point area should cost about $25 (a bit of a rip-off, as most hotels in that area are within walking distance) while hotels in Scarborough and Grafton Beach will cost approximately $50.

A service available in Trinidad, called 628–TAXI, will take you from the airport to any point on the island. The cost to get to hotels in Port of Spain is about $16 each way, but you will have to call from the airport or your hotel to arrange the pickup.

📑 **Airport Information Crown Point Airport** ☎ 868/639–0509. **Piarco International Airport** ☎ 868/669–4101 ⊕ www.tntairports.com.

BY BOAT & FERRY

The Port Authority maintains ferry service every day between Trinidad and Tobago, although flying is preferable because the seas can be very rough. The trip can be made by either a conventional or high-speed CAT ferry. The ferries leave once a day (from St. Vincent Street Jetty in Port of Spain and from the cruise-ship complex in Scarborough); the trip on the conventional ferry takes about 5 hours and the high-speed CAT takes 2½ hours. The round-trip fare is TT$100. The conventional ferry runs TT$75 (round-trip).

📑 **Port Authority of Trinidad & Tobago** ☎ 868/ 625–2901 in Port of Spain, 868/639–2181 in Scarborough ⊕ www.patnt.com.

BY CAR

Trinidad has excellent roads throughout the island. Be careful when driving during the rainy season, as roads often flood.

Never drive into downtown Port of Spain during afternoon rush hour (generally from 3 to 6:30), when traffic is at its heaviest. In Tobago, many roads, particularly in the interior or on the coast near Speyside and Charlotteville, are bumpy, pitted, winding, and/or steep (though the main highways are smooth and fast). On either island, driving is on the left, in the British style, so remember to look to your right when pulling out into traffic. Also be aware that Tobago has very few gas stations—the main ones are in Crown Point and Scarborough.

📑 Trinidad Car Rentals **Auto Rentals** ⊠ Piarco International Airport, Piarco, Trinidad ☎ 868/669–2277. **Kalloo's Auto Rentals** ⊠ Piarco International Airport, Piarco, Trinidad ☎ 868/669–5673 ⊕ www.kalloos.com. **Southern Sales Car Rentals** ⊠ Piarco International Airport, Piarco, Trinidad ☎ 868/669–2424, 269 from courtesy phone in airport baggage area. **Thrifty** ⊠ Piarco International Airport, Piarco, Trinidad ☎ 868/669–0602.

📑 Tobago Car Rentals **Baird's Rentals** ⊠ Crown Point Airport, Crown Point, Tobago ☎ 868/639–7054. **Rattan's Car Rentals** ⊠ Crown Point Airport, Crown Point, Tobago ☎ 868/639–8271. **Rollock's Car Rentals** ⊠ Crown Point Airport, Crown Point, Tobago ☎ 868/639–0328. **Singh's Auto Rentals** ⊠ Grafton Beach Resort, Shirvan Rd., Black Rock, Tobago ☎ 868/639–0191 Ext. 53. **Thrifty** ⊠ Rex Turtle Beach Hotel, Courland Bay, Black Rock, Tobago ☎ 868/639–8507.

BY TAXI

Taxis in Trinidad and Tobago are easily identified by their license plates, which begin with the letter *H*. Passenger vans, called Maxi Taxis, pick up and drop off passengers as they travel (rather like a bus) and are color-coded according to which of the six areas they cover. Rates are generally less than $1 per trip. (Yellow is for Port of Spain, red for eastern Trinidad, green for south Trinidad, and black for Princes Town. Brown operates from San Fernando to the southeast—Erin, Penal, Point Fortin. The only color for Tobago is blue.) They're easy to hail day or night along most of the main roads near Port of Spain. For longer trips you need to hire a private taxi. Cabs aren't metered, and hotel taxis can be expensive. A taxi service available in Trinidad, called 628–TAXI, will take you to the beach for $15 and around town for $8. 🖪 **628-TAXI** ☎ 868/628-8294.

Contacts & Resources

BANKS & EXCHANGE SERVICES

At this writing, the exchange rate for the Trinidadian dollar (TT$) was about TT$6.20 to US$1. Most businesses on the island will accept U.S. currency if you're in a pinch. Credit cards and ATM cards are almost universally accepted for payment by businesses, hotels, and restaurants. Cash is necessary only in the smallest neighborhood convenience shops and roadside stalls. Trinidad has ATMs in all but the most remote areas. in Tobago there are only a few in Scarborough and at the airport in Crown Point. Be aware that there are far fewer bank branches in Tobago than in Trinidad.

BUSINESS HOURS

Banks are open Monday through Thursday 8 to 3, Friday 8 to noon and 3 to 5. Banks in malls often stay open until 7 PM. Post offices are open 8 to noon and 1 to 4:30 on weekdays. Most shops are open weekdays 8 to 4:30, Saturday 8 to noon; malls stay open later during the week, often until at least 6 or 7 PM, and operate all day Saturday.

ELECTRICITY

Electric current is usually 110 volts/60 cycles, but some establishments provide 220-volt outlets.

EMBASSIES

🖪 Canada **Canadian High Commission** ✉ 3-3A Sweet Briar Rd., St. Clair, Port of Spain, Trinidad ☎ 868/622-6232.
🖪 United Kingdom **British High Commission** ✉ 19 St. Clair Ave., St. Clair, Port of Spain, Trinidad ☎ 868/622-2748.
🖪 United States **U.S. Embassy** ✉ 15 Queen's Park W, Port of Spain, Trinidad ☎ 868/622-6371.

EMERGENCIES

🖪 Emergency Services **Ambulance and fire** ☎ 990. **Police** ☎ 999.
🖪 Hospitals **Port of Spain General Hospital** ✉ 169 Charlotte St., Port of Spain, Trinidad ☎ 868/623-2951. **St. Clair Medical Centre** ✉ 18 Elizabeth St., St. Clair, Port of Spain, Trinidad ☎ 868/628-1451 is a private health-care provider in Port of Spain that is highly recommended. **Scarborough Hospital** ✉ Fort St., Scarborough, Tobago ☎ 868/639-2551.
🖪 Pharmacies **Bhaggan's** ✉ Charlotte and Oxford Sts., Port of Spain, Trinidad ☎ 868/627-4657. **Kappa Drugs** ✉ Roxy Round-a-bout, St. James, Port of Spain, Trinidad ☎ 868/622-2728. **Scarborough Drugs** ✉ Carrington St. and Wilson Rd., Scarborough, Tobago ☎ 868/639-4161.

HOLIDAYS

Public holidays are New Year's Day, Good Friday, Easter Monday, Spiritual Baptist Liberation Day (Mar. 30), Indian Arrival Day (May 30), Corpus Christi (June 10), Labour Day (June 19), Emancipation Day (Aug. 1), Independence Day (Aug. 31), Republic Day (Sept. 24), Divali (date is announced by the government a few months before, but it's usually in October or November), Eid (a Muslim festival whose actual date varies), Christmas, and Boxing Day (Dec. 26). Carnival Monday and Tuesday are not official holidays, but don't expect anything to be open.

INTERNET, MAIL & SHIPPING

The local phone company offers a handy dial-up service on both islands called 619–EASY. Simply connect your laptop to the phone line and dial 619-EASY using the word EASY as your username. The charge is 12¢ a minute. Because of crime concerns in Trinidad, it is inadvisable to use Internet cafés in downtown Port of Spain or in areas along the east–west corridor. Almost every hotel offers Internet service, and newer ones (such as the Marriott) offer wireless high-speed access. In Trinidad, most hotels allow nonguests to use their Internet services for a fee.

In Tobago, the best Internet café in the Scarborough area is J-Puter Tech, which offers access for about $4 an hour. In Crown Point, the most fun choice is the Original House of Pancakes Ltd., which happily combines Internet access and pancakes. The Internet is $5 an hour, but the pancakes are an additional cost.

Postage to the United States and Canada is TT$3.45 for first-class letters and TT$2.25 for postcards; prices are slightly higher for other destinations. The main post offices are on Wrightson Road (opposite the Crowne Plaza) in Port of Spain and in the N. I. B. Mall on Wilson Street (near the docks) in Scarborough. There are no zip codes on the islands. To write to an establishment here, you simply need its address, town, and "Trinidad and Tobago, West Indies."

🖪 Internet Cafés **Computer Planet Ltd.** ✉ Corner of Ariapita Ave. and Luis St., Port of Spain, Trinidad ☎ 868/622-6888. **J-Puter Tech** ✉ 20 Burnett St., Scarborough, Tobago ☎ 868/639-3393. **Jus Click** ✉ Royal Palm Plaza, 7 Saddle Rd., Maraval, Trinidad ☎ 868/628-2316. **The Original House of Pancakes Ltd.** ✉ Milford Rd. and John Gorman Trace, Crown Point, Tobago ☎ 868/39-9866.

PASSPORTS REQUIREMENTS

Everyone coming into Trinidad & Tobago must have a valid passport.

SAFETY

Travelers should exercise reasonable caution in Trinidad, especially in the highly populated east–west corridor and downtown Port of Spain, where walking on the streets at night is not recommended unless you're with a group. A surge in crime on Charlotte Street in Port of Spain suggests that it's best to avoid this street altogether. As a general rule, Tobago is safer than its larger sister island, though this should not lure you into a false sense of security. Petty theft occurs on both islands, so don't leave cash in bags that you check at the airport, and use hotel safes for valuables.

TAXES

Departure tax, payable in cash at the airport, is TT$100. All hotels add a 10%

government tax. Prices for almost all goods and services include a 15% V.A.T.

TELEPHONES

The area code for both islands is 868 ("TNT" if you forget). This is also the country code if you're calling to Trinidad and Tobago from another country. From the United States, just dial "1" plus the area code and number.

To make a local call to any point in the country simply dial the seven-digit local number. Most hotels and guesthouses will allow you to dial a direct international call. To dial a number in North America or the Caribbean simply dial "1" and the U.S. or Canadian area code before the number you're calling, but be warned that most hotels add a hefty surcharge for overseas calls. Calls to Europe and elsewhere can be made by checking for the appropriate direct-dial codes in the telephone directory. To make an international call from a pay phone you must first purchase a "companion" card, which is readily available from most convenience shops—then simply follow the instructions on the card. Cards are available in various denominations.

Cell phones here are GSM at a frequency of 1800 Mhz, but your cell-phone company must have a roaming agreement with Trinidad Telephone & Telegraph Service (TSTT) in order for your phone to work here. You can also purchase a SIM card to make local calling cheaper in Trinidad, but you'll be assigned a new phone number.

🖪 TSTT ⊕ www.tstt.net.tt.

TIPPING

Almost all hotels will add a 10% to 15% service charge to your bill. Most restaurants include a 10% service charge, which is considered standard on these islands. If it isn't on the bill, tip according to service: 10% to 15% is fine. Cabbies expect a token tip of around 10%. At drinking establishments tipping is optional, and the staff at smaller bars may tell you on your way out that you forgot your change.

TOUR OPTIONS

Although any taxi driver in Trinidad or Tobago can take visitors to the major attractions, using a tour company allows for a more leisurely and educational adventure. Tour operators are also more mindful of the sensitivities of tourists and are much less likely to subject passengers to breakneck speeds and "creative" driving.

In Trindad, Caribbean Discovery Tours is operated by Stephen Broadbridge. His tours are completely personalized and can include both on- and offshore activities. Tours can range from the strenuous to the leisurely, with prices based on the duration of the expedition and the number of participants. Kalloo's offers tours ranging from a fascinating three-hour tour of Port of Spain to an overnight turtle-watching tour. Sensational Tours & Transport comes highly recommended and is your best choice for island tours. Owner Gerald Nicholas worked for the tourist board for many years and knows the island intimately. He is a complete delight to be with, and his tour prices are the lowest on the island by far.

In Tobago, Frank's Glass Bottom Boat & Birdwatching Tours offers glass-bottom-boat and snorkeling tours of the shores of Speyside; Frank also conducts guided tours of the rain forest and Little Tobago. As a native of Speyside, he's extremely knowledgeable about the island's flora, fauna, and folklore. Tobago Travel is the island's most experienced tour operator, offering a wide variety of services and tours.

🚩 In Trinidad **Caribbean Discovery Tours Ltd.** ✉ 9B Fondes Amandes, St. Ann's, Port of Spain ☎ 868/624-7281 or 868/620-1989 🖨 868/624-8596 ⊕ www.caribbeandiscoverytours.com **Kalloo's** ✉ Piarco International Airport, Piarco ☎ 868/669-5673 or 868/622-9073 ⊕ www.kalloos.com

Sensational Tours &Transport ✉ 47 Reservoir Rd., La Pastora, Santa Cruz ☎ 868/676-2937 or 868/6687-7832 🖨 868/676-3008 ⊕ www.sensationaltours.ne.

🚩 In Tobago **Frank's Glass Bottom Boat & Birdwatching Tours** ✉ Speyside ☎☎ 868/660-5438 **Tobago Travel** ✉ Scarborough ☎ 868/639-8778

VISITOR INFORMATION

🚩 Before You Leave **Tourism Hotline** ☎ 888/595-4868. **Trinidad and Tobago Tourism Office** ✉ 331 Almeria Ave., Coral Gables, FL 33134 ☎ 800/748-4224 ⊕ www.visitTNT.com ✉ Mitre House, 66 Abbey Rd., Bush Park Hill, Enfield, Middlesex, UK. EN1 2RQ ☎ 208/350-1000 ✉ Taurus House, 512 Duplex Ave., Toronto, Ontario, Canada M4R 2E3 ☎ 416/535-5617 or 416/485-8724.

🚩 In Trinidad **TDC** ✉ 63 Tragarete Rd., Port of Spain, Trinidad ☎ 868/623-1425 🖨 868/638-3560 ✉ Piarco International Airport, Piarco, Trinidad ☎ 868/669-5196.

🚩 In Tobago **Tobago Division of Tourism** ✉ N. I. B. Mall, Level 3, Scarborough, Tobago ☎ 868/639-2125 ✉ Crown Point Airport, Crown Point, Tobago ☎ 868/639-0509.

WEDDINGS

Getting married in Trinidad and Tobago is still not as easy as on some other islands, but idyllic Tobago is still fairly popular as a wedding spot. Both parties must prove that they have been in the country for three days (calculated from the day after arrival). A passport, airline ticket, and proof of divorce (if you've been married before) are all required, as is a $55 license fee. Further information can be obtained from the Registrar General's office. The Coco Reef Resort in Tobago specializes in beach weddings.

🚩 **Coco Reef Resort** ✉ Coconut Bay, Box 434, Crown Point, Tobago ☎ 868/639-8571 or 800/221-1294 ⊕ www.cocoreef.com. **Registrar General** ✉ Jerningham St., Scarborough, Tobago ☎ 868/639-3210 ✉ 72-74 South Quay, Port of Spain, Trinidad ☎ 868/624-1660.

Turks & Caicos

Leeward Marina, Providenciales

WORD OF MOUTH

"We actually did less than we intended. We blamed it on the high beach gravity around there. Once you got on the beach relaxing, it was so hard to get up the gumption to do anything. We're really looking forward to returning."

—Ken_in_Mass

WELCOME TO THE TURKS & CAICOS ISLANDS

TO BAHAMAS

Caicos Passage

Three Mary's Cays
24
25 26

Parrot Cay

Fort George Cay
Spanish Point

Football Fields
Pine Cay
Highas Cay

Northwest Point
Little Water Cay
North
Juniper
Platico

23
Caicos
Hole
Point

Providenciales
27

Grace Bay
Caicos Conch
4 North Caicos

Cheshire Hall 2
1 Farm

Middle Caico.

Sapodilla Hill 3
Juba Point
5 Middle

Southwest
Caicos

Bluff
see
Ocean

West
Providenciales
Vine Point Hole
Toll Craw

Caicos
map on pages
Point

912-913

Southwest Reef
1 - 22
C A I C O S
I S L
A

Molasses Reef

The largest but least developed of the islands is Middle Caicos. It's 48 square mi (124
square km) but has only 300 residents and
an extensive system of limestone caves.

CAICOS

0   14 miles

0   21 km

CAICOS

BANK

Little Ambergris Ca

KEY
Dive Sites
1 Exploring Sights
1 Hotels & Restaurants

SEAL CAY

White Cay

Only 8 of these 40 islands between the Bahamas and Haiti are inhabited. Divers and
snorkelers can explore one of the world's
longest coral reefs. Land-based pursuits
don't get much more taxing than teeing off at
Provo's Provo Golf Club, or sunset-watching
from the seaside terrace of a laid-back
resort.

GEOGRAPHICAL INFO

Though Providenciales is a major offshore banking center, sea creatures far outnumber humans in this archipelago of 40 islands, where the total population is a mere 25,000. From developed Provo to sleepy Grand Turk to sleepier South Caicos, the islands offer miles of undeveloped beaches, crystal-clear water, and laid-back luxury resorts.

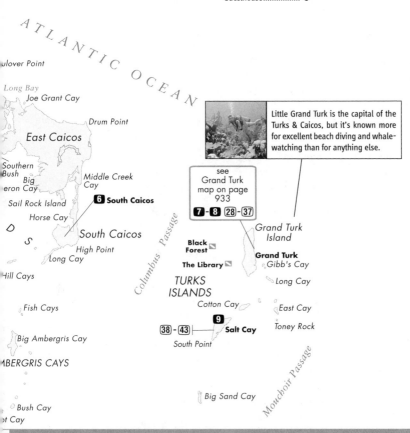

Little Grand Turk is the capital of the Turks & Caicos, but it's known more for excellent beach diving and whale-watching than for anything else.

ATLANTIC OCEAN

ulover Point

Long Bay
Joe Grant Cay

Drum Point

East Caicos

Southern
Bush
Big
eron Cay *Middle Creek Cay*

Sail Rock Island

Horse Cay

6 South Caicos

D *S*

South Caicos

High Point
long Cay

Hill Cays

Fish Cays

Big Ambergris Cay

MBERGRIS CAYS

Bush Cay
t Cay

see
Grand Turk
map on page
933
7-**8** **28**-**37**

*Grand Turk
Island*

**Black
Forest**

The Library

Grand Turk
Gibb's Cay

Long Cay

*TURKS
ISLANDS*

Cotton Cay

9

38-**43**   **Salt Cay**

South Point

East Cay

Toney Rock

Columbus Passage

Mouchoir Passage

Big Sand Cay

25

TURKS & CAICOS ISLANDS

TOP 4 REASONS TO VISIT THE TURKS & CAICOS ISLANDS

❶ Even on well-developed Provo, there are still miles of deserted beaches without any footprints or beach umbrellas in sight.

❷ The third-largest coral reef system in the world is among the world's top dive sites.

❸ Island-hopping beyond the beaten path will give you a feel of the past in the present.

❹ Destination spas, penthouse suites, and exclusive villas and resorts make celebrity spotting a popular sport.

TURKS & CAICOS PLANNER

Getting to the Turks & Caicos

Several major airlines fly nonstop to Providenciales from the U.S., London, and Toronto; there are also connecting flights through Montego Bay and San Juan. Club Med has nonstop charter service from the northeast during the high season. If you are going to one of the smaller islands, you'll usually need to make a connection in Provo.

All international flights arrive at Providenciales International Airport (PLS). There are smaller airports on Grand Turk (GDT), North Caicos NCS), Middle Caicos (MDS), South Caicos (XSC), and Salt Cay (SLX). All have paved runways in good condition. Providenciales International Airport has modern, secure arrival and check-in services.

Hassle Factor: Low to Medium-High

Activities

The vast majority of people come to the Turks & Caicos to relax and enjoy the clear, turquoise water and luxurious **hotels**. The smaller islands provide a more relaxed environment and are substantially less developed. Provo has excellent **beaches**, particularly the long, soft beach along Grace Bay, where most of the island's hotel development has taken place. Some of the smaller, more isolated islands in the chain have even better beaches. Reefs are plentiful and are often close to shore, making **snorkeling** excellent. The reef and wall **diving** are among the best in the Caribbean. The same reefs that draw colorful tropical fish draw big-game fish, so deep-sea **fishing** is also very good. If you are a **golfer**, Provo has one of the Caribbean's finest courses.

On the Ground

You can find taxis at the airports, and most resorts provide pickup service as well. A trip between Provo's airport and most major hotels runs about $15. On Grand Turk a trip from the new airport to Cockburn Town is about $8; it's $8 to $15 to hotels outside town on Grand Turk. Transfers can cost more on the smaller islands, where gas is much more expensive.

Renting a Car

If you are staying on Provo, you may find it useful to have a car since the island is so large and the resorts so far-flung, if only for a few days of exploring or to get away from your hotel for dinner. A bus service, the Gecko Shuttle, was introduced in 2005, and many people may find that sufficient for their needs. On Grand Turk, you can rent a car, but you probably won't need to.

Car- and jeep-rental rates average $35 to $80 per day on Provo, plus a $15 surcharge per rental as a government tax. Reserve well ahead of time during the peak winter season. Most agencies offer free mileage and airport pickup service. Several agencies—both locally owned and larger chains—operate on Provo, but Ed Ricos Car Rental is the only player on Grand Turk.

Where to Stay

Providenciales in particular is a fairly upscale destination, and there are few moderately-priced options, but gorgeous beaches and decent restaurants make it the major draw for tourists. Since virtually all the island's development is on Grace Bay, only the budget-minded are likely to stay elsewhere, though some villas are scattered around the island. You'll find a few upscale proper-ties on the outer islands—including the famous Parrot Cay—but the majority of places are smaller inns. What you give up in luxury, however, you gain back tenfold in island charm. Many of the smaller islands are fairly isolated, and that's arguably what makes them so attractive in the first place, making your trip more of a redeeming journey than a hassle.

TYPES OF LODGINGS

Resorts: Most of the resorts on Provo are upscale; many are condo-style, so at least you will have a well-furnished kitchen for breakfast and a few quick lunches. There are two all-inclusive resorts on Provo. A handful of other luxury resorts are on the smaller islands.

Small Inns: Aside from the exclusive, luxury resorts, most of the places on the outlying islands are smaller, modest inns with relatively few amenities. Some are devoted to diving.

Villas & Condos: Villas and condos are plentiful, particularly on Provo and usually represent a good value for families. However, you need to plan a few months in advance to get one of the better choices, less if you want to stay in a more devel-oped condo complex.

When to Go

High season in Turks and Caicos runs roughly from January through March, with the usual extra-high rates during the Christmas and New Year's holiday period. Several hotels on Provo offer shoulder-season rates in April and May. During the off-season, rates are reduced substantially, as much as 40%.

There aren't really any major festivals or events to draw travelers. The main draw in the islands is consistently good weather (except for the occasional tropical storm).

25

Hotel & Restaurant Costs

Assume that hotels operate on the European Plan (**EP**—with no meals) unless we specify that they use either the Continental Plan (**CP**—with a Continental breakfast), Breakfast Plan (**BP**—with full breakfast), or the Modified American Plan (**MAP**—with breakfast and dinner). Other hotels may offer the Full American Plan (**FAP**—including all meals but no drinks) or may be All-Inclusive (**AI**—with all meals, drinks, and most activities).

WHAT IT COSTS in Dollars

	$$$$	$$$	$$	$	¢
Restaurants	over $30	$20–$30	$12–$20	$8–$12	under $8
Hotels*	over $350	$250–$350	$150–$250	$80–$150	under $80
Hotels**	over $450	$350–$450	$250–$350	$125–$250	under $125

*EP, BP, CP   **AI, FAP, MAP
Restaurant prices are for a main course excluding 10% tax and tip. Hotel prices are for two people in a double room in high season, excluding 10% tax, 10%–15% service charge, and meal plans (except at all-inclusives).

Updated by
Jackie Mulligan

LINDSAY—OR, AS HE LIKES TO BE KNOWN, "ZEUS"—has a rusty saw balanced precariously against his upper thigh. His eyes are understandably focused on it. He strums an old screwdriver against its teeth, bending the saw in perfect rhythm and harmony with the drummers and guitar player of his Turks Island ripsaw band. This performance, a common sight for the friendly local crowd, leaves a lasting impression on me. I file the picture beside the indelible images of the turquoise blue patchwork of water and white-sand beaches and decide to stay right here. Right here in these tiny islands, where everybody knows your name and everyone has a story to tell.

A much-disputed legend has it that Columbus first discovered these islands in 1492. Despite being on the map for longer than most other island groups, the Turks and Caicos Islands (pronounced *kay*-kos) still remain part of the less-discovered Caribbean. More than 40 islands—only 8 inhabited—make up this self-governing British overseas territory that lies just 575 mi (862 km) southeast of Miami on the third-largest coral reef system in the world.

While ivory-white, soft sandy beaches and breathtaking turquoise waters are shared among all the islands, the landscapes are a series of contrasts; from the dry, arid bush and scrub on the flat, coral islands of Grand Turk, Salt Cay, South Caicos, and Providenciales to the greener, foliage-rich undulating landscapes of Middle Caicos, North Caicos, Parrot Cay, and Pine Cay.

The political and historical capital island of the country is Grand Turk, but most of the tourism development, which consists primarily of boutique hotels and condo resorts, has occurred in Providenciales, thanks to the 12-mi (18-km) stretch of ivory sand that is Grace Bay. Once home to a population of around 500 people plus a few donkey carts, Provo has become a hub of activity, resorts, spas, restaurants, and water sports with a population of around 18,000. It's the temporary home for the majority of visitors who come to the Turks and Caicos.

Despite the fact that most visitors land and stay in Provo, the Turks & Caicos National Museum—predictably a stickler for tradition—is in Grand Turk. The museum tells the history of the islands that have all, at one time or another, been claimed by the French, Spanish, and British as well as many pirates, long before the predominately North American visitors discovered its shores.

Marks of the country's colonial past can be found in the wooden and stone, Bermudian-style clapboard houses—often wrapped in deep-red bougainvillea—that line the streets on the quiet islands of Grand Turk, Salt Cay, and South Caicos. Donkeys roam free in and around the salt ponds, which are a legacy from a time when residents of these island communities worked hard as both slaves and then laborers to rake salt (then known as "white gold") bound for the United States and Canada. In Salt Cay the remains of wooden windmills are now home to large Osprey nests. In Grand Turk and South Caicos, the crystal-edge tidal ponds are regularly visited by flocks of rose pink flamingos hungry for the shrimp to be found in the shallow, briny waters.

Sea Island Cotton, believed to be the highest quality, was produced on the Loyalist plantations in the Caicos Islands from the 1700s. The native cotton plants can still be seen dotted among the stone remains of former plantation houses in the more fertile soils of Middle Caicos and North Caicos. Here communities in tiny settlements have retained age-old skills using fanner grasses, silver palms, and sisal to create exceptional straw baskets, bags, mats, and hats.

In all, only 25,000 people live in the Turks and Caicos Islands; more than half are Belongers, the term for the native population, mainly descended from African and Bermudian slaves who settled here beginning in the 1600s. The majority of residents work in tourism, fishing, and off-shore finance, as the country is a haven for the overtaxed. Indeed for residents and visitors, life in "TCI" is anything but taxing. But while most visitors come to do nothing—a specialty in the islands—this does not mean there's nothing to do.

25

THE CAICOS

Providenciales

Passengers typically become oddly silent when their plane starts its descent, mesmerized by the shallow, crystal clear turquoise waters of Chalk Sound National Park. This island, nicknamed Provo, was once called Blue Hills after the name of its first settlement. Just south of the airport and downtown area, Blue Hills still remains the closest thing you can get to a more typical Caicos Island settlement on this, the most developed of the island chain. Most of the modern resorts, exquisite spas, water-sports operators, shops, business plazas, restaurants, bars, cafés, and the championship golf course are on or close by the 12-mi stretch of Grace Bay beach. In spite of the ever increasing number of taller and grander condominium resorts—either completed or under construction—it's still possible to find deserted stretches on this priceless, ivory white shoreline. For guaranteed seclusion, hire a car and go explore the southern shores and western tip of the island, or set sail for a private island getaway on one of the many deserted cays nearby.

While you may be kept quite content enjoying the beachscape and top-notch amenities of Provo itself, it's also a great starting point for island-hopping tours by sea or by air as well as fishing and diving trips. Resurfaced roads and a regular bus service—the Gecko Shuttle—should help you get around and make the most of the main tourism and sightseeing spots.

Where to Stay

For approximate costs, *see* the dining and lodging price chart on the Turks & Caicos Planner, at the beginning of this chapter.

VILLA RENTALS A popular option on Provo is renting a self-catering villa or private home. For the best villa selection, plan to make your reservations three to six months in advance.

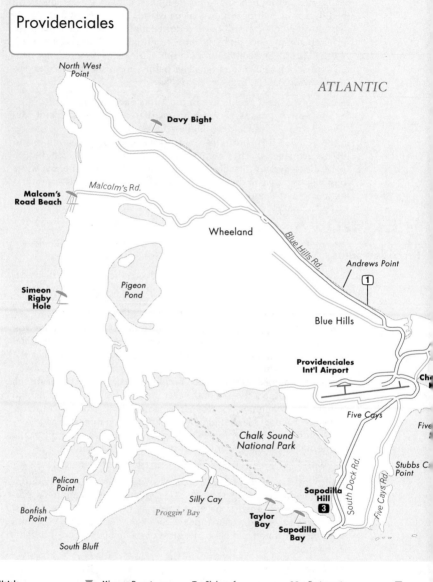

Providenciales

North West Point

ATLANTIC

Davy Bight

Malcolm's Rd.

Malcom's
Road Beach

Wheeland

Blue Hills Rd.

Andrews Point

1

Simeon
Rigby
Hole

Pigeon
Pond

Blue Hills

Providenciales
Int'l Airport

Ch

Five Cays

Five

Chalk Sound
National Park

Stubbs C
Point

Pelican
Point

South Dock Rd.

Silly Cay

Five Cays Rd.

Bonfish
Point

Proggin' Bay

Sapodilla
Hill
3

Taylor
Bay

Sapodilla
Bay

South Bluff

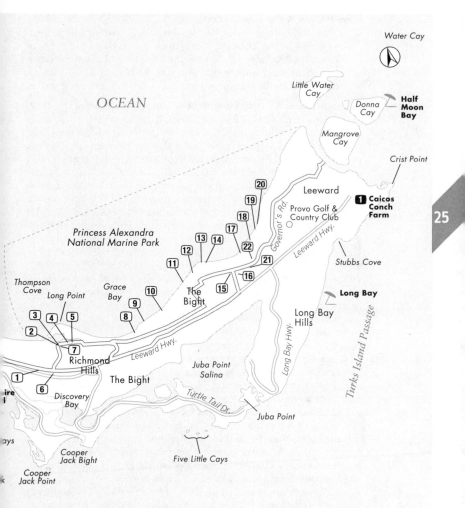

25

Caicos Café **21**
Coyaba Restaurant **9**
Gecko Grille **20**
Grace's Cottage **13**
Hey Jose's Caribbean
Cantina **1**

Magnolia Wine Bar
& Restaurant **2**
Simba **8**

Elliot Holdings & Management Company (⊕ Box 235 ☎ 649/946–5355 ⊕ www.elliotholdings.com) offers a wide selection of modest to magnificent villas in the Leeward, Grace Bay, and Turtle Cove areas of Providenciales. **T. C. Safari** (⊕ Box 64 ☎ 649/941–5043 ⊕ www.tcsafari. tc) has exclusive oceanfront properties in the beautiful and tranquil Sapodilla Bay–Chalk Sound neighborhood on Provo's southwest shores.

HOTELS & RESORTS
★ ☾ $$$$

Beaches Turks & Caicos Resort & Spa. The largest resort in the Turks and Caicos Islands can satisfy families as eager to spend time apart as together. Younger children and teenagers will appreciate a children's park, complete with video-game center, water slides, a swim-up soda bar, and even a teen disco. Parents may prefer the extensive spa, pretty beach, and complimentary scuba diving. Rooms, suites, and cottage villas are decorated in standard tropical themes, but the resort's major draw is found outside the rooms, where there are numerous activities and a choice of dining options, from a 1950s-style diner to a Japanese restaurant. This is one of the company's top resorts, with a generally helpful staff and excellent amenities. Butler service is included for the presidential and penthouse suites. ☒ *Lower Bight Rd., Grace Bay* ☎ *649/946–8000 or 800/726–3257* ☒ *649/946–8001* ⊕ *www.beaches.com* ☞ *359 rooms, 103 suites* ☾ *9 restaurants, in-room safes, cable TV with movies, miniature golf, 4 tennis courts, 5 pools, health club, hair salon, 3 hot tubs, spa, beach, dive shop, snorkeling, windsurfing, boating, parasailing, fishing, bicycles, 12 bars, nightclub, recreation room, theater, video game room, shops, babysitting, children's programs (ages newborn–12), concierge, meeting rooms, car rental* ▭ *AE, MC, V* ☒ *All-inclusive.*

★ ☾ $$$$

Grace Bay Club & Villas at Grace Bay Club. This small and stylish resort retains a loyal following because of its helpful, attentive staff and aura of unpretentious elegance. The architecture is reminiscent of Florence, with terra-cotta rooftops and a shaded courtyard, complete with fountain. Suites, all with sweeping sea views, have earthy tiles, luxurious white Egyptian cotton–covered beds, and Elemis toiletries. The ground-floor suites, fronted by large arched patios and lush azaleas, have a palatial feel and turquoise water views. New, ultraluxurious villas offer families a Grace Bay experience with large pool, a bar and grill, and an impressive range of children's activities, bouncy castle in Kids Town as well as kayaking trips and all sorts of "edutainment" to keep even teenagers well occupied. There are also cookies, of course. Anacaona remains one of the island's best restaurants; cocktails and tapas are offered in the Lounge, a Provo hot spot that gently cascades down to the beach. ⊕ *Box 128, Grace Bay* ☎ *649/946–5050 or 800/946–5757* ☒ *649/946– 5758* ⊕ *www.gracebayclub.com* ☞ *21 suites* ☾ *Restaurant, room service, in-room safes, kitchens, cable TV with movies, in-room VCRs, in-room broadband, Wi-Fi, golf privileges, 2 tennis courts, 2 pools, hot tub, spa, beach, snorkeling, windsurfing, boating, parasailing, bicycles, bar, shop, babysitting, laundry facilities, laundry service, concierge, Internet room, business services, meeting rooms* ▭ *AE, D, MC, V* ☒ *CP.*

$$$$

Le Vele Resort. The Armani family (not those Armanis, but with a similar savoir faire) have created a well-run, family-friendly condominium resort, though prices are steep given the lack of many resort-style amenities. Design, inside and out, is sleek and modern, with interiors that fuse

From Salt Glows to Thalassotherapy

A TURKS ISLAND SALT GLOW, where the island's sea salt is mixed with gentle oils to exfoliate, smooth, and moisturize the skin, is just one of the treatments you can enjoy in one of the island spas. Being pampered spa-style has become as much a part of a Turks and Caicos vacation as sunning on the beach. Marine-based ingredients fit well with the Grace Bay backdrop at the Thalasso Spa at **Point Grace,** where massages take place in two simple, bleached-white cottages standing on the dune line, which means you have a spectacular view of the sea-blue hues if you manage to keep your eyes open. The spa at **Reef Residences at Grace Bay** offers similarly sweeping vistas at its two-story treatment center specializing in Ayurveda treatments. In this spa, guests are treated head to toe and through dietary recommendations

and menu items to suit their body types. But the widest choice of Asian-inspired treatments (and the most unforgettable scenery) can be found at the 6,000-square-foot Como Shambhala Spa at the **Parrot Cay Resort,** which has outdoor whirlpools and a central beechwood lounge overlooking the shallow turquoise waters and mangroves. Provo also has a noteworthy day spa that's not in one of the Grace Bay resorts. Manager Terri Tapper of **Spa Tropique** (⊠ Ports of Call, Grace Bay Rd. ☎ 649/941–5720 ⊕ www.spatropique.com) blends Swedish, therapeutic, and reflexology massage techniques using oils made from natural plants and products produced locally and within the Caribbean region. The Turks Island Salt Glow has become one of her most popular treatments.

natural fibers with contemporary furnishings, cutting-edge appliances, and plenty of space. If you're a fan of top-notch Italian modern design, book eastside Suite 102. The glass-fronted show-room-style reception overlooks the infinity pool. Though the resort lacks any dining options, the staff will transport you to the restaurant of your choice. Local islander and manager Beverly Williams is helpful and informative. ⌂ *Box 240, Grace Bay* ☎ *649/941–8800* 🖶 *649/941–8001* ⊕ *www.levele.tc* ⬠ *18 suites* ⚭ *In-room safes, in-room hot tubs, kitchens, cable TV, in-room VCRs, in-room data ports, Wi-Fi, pool, gym, beach, snorkeling, boating, laundry facilities, concierge, Internet room* ▤ *AE, D, MC, V* Ⓞ *EP.*

$$$$ 🖼 **Point Grace.** Provo's answer to Parrot Cay has attracted such celebrities as Donatella Versace. Asian-influenced rooftop domes blend with Romanesque stone pillars and wide stairways in this plush resort, which offers spacious beachfront suites and romantic cottages surrounding the centerpiece: a turquoise infinity pool with perfect views of the beach. Antique furnishings, four-poster beds, and art reproductions give a classic style to the rooms. The second-story cottage suites are especially romantic. Bleached-wood cottages, on the sand dune, house a thalassotherapy spa presided over by elegant French spa manager Edmonde Sidibé. Other highlights include the restaurants, particularly the beautiful Grace's Cottage. Honeymooners can arrange a transfer in an authentic London taxi. ⌂ *Box 700, Grace Bay* ☎ *888/924–7223 or*

649/946–5096 🖨 *970/513–0657 or 649/946–5097* ⊕ *www.pointgrace. com* 🛏 *23 suites, 9 cottage suites, 2 villas* 🍴 *2 restaurants, room service, in-room fax, in-room safes, some in-room hot tubs, kitchens, kitchenettes, microwaves, cable TV with movies, in-room VCRs, pool, spa, beach, snorkeling, windsurfing, boating, parasailing, fishing, bicycles, 2 bars, library, babysitting, laundry service, concierge, Internet room, business services, car rental, no-smoking rooms* ▭ *AE, D, MC, V* ⊘ *Closed Sept.* ¶⊙¶ *CP.*

$$$$ 🏨 **Turks & Caicos Club.** On the quieter, western end of Grace Bay, this intimate all-suite hotel is one of a handful with a gated entrance. The buildings are in a colonial style with lovely gingerbread trim. Though the resort aims for an aura of exclusivity, the staff is warm and friendly. Safari-theme suites, complete with raised four-poster beds and spacious balconies, are a definite plus to this quiet retreat, which gets less bustle than either Grace Bay Club or Point Grace, its main competitors. ⊠ *West Grace Bay Beach, Box 687, West Grace Bay* 🕾 *888/482–2582 or 649/ 946–5800* 🖨 *649/946–5858* ⊕ *www.turksandcaicosclub.com* 🛏 *21 suites* 🍴 *Restaurant, room service, fans, in-room safes, kitchens, cable TV, in-room VCRs, in-room data ports, Wi-Fi, pool, gym, beach, snorkeling, windsurfing, kayaks, bicycles, bar, laundry facilities* ▭ *AE, MC, V* ⊘ *Closed Sept.* ¶⊙¶ *CP.*

$$$–$$$$ 🏨 **Club Med Turkoise.** Guests still fly in from the United States, Europe, and Canada to enjoy the scuba diving, windsurfing, and waterskiing on the turquoise waters at the doorsteps of the area's first major resort. Rooms in the village are basic and set in small, colorful bungalows (ask for a renovated room to avoid disappointment). In contrast to the otherwise tranquil Grace Bay resorts, this energetic property has a vibrant party atmosphere, nightly entertainment, and even a flying trapeze, catering primarily to fun-loving singles and couples. ⊠ *Grace Bay* 🕾 *649/946– 5500 or 888/932–2582* 🖨 *649/946–5497* ⊕ *www.clubmed.com* 🛏 *293 rooms* 🍴 *2 restaurants, cable TV with movies, 8 tennis courts, pool, health club, hot tub, massage, beach, dive shop, snorkeling, windsurfing, boating, fishing, bicycles, billiards, soccer, volleyball, 3 bars, dance club, theater, shops, laundry service; no kids* ▭ *AE, D, MC, V* ¶⊙¶ *All-inclusive.*

★ $$$–$$$$ 🏨 **Reef Residences at Grace Bay.** André Niederhauser has brought his own Caribbean flair to this intimate beachfront hotel, which was refurbished and expanded in 2006. The staff is friendly, and Niederhauser is especially attentive. Turtle sightings, thanks to a location opposite one of the island's most popular snorkeling spots, are just one of the highlights. All but the cheapest rooms have sweeping views of the much less-developed western end of Grace Bay; the suites in particular are breathtaking. The resort's location, the exquisite two-story Ayurveda Spa, and romantic on-beach dining experiences at the Tide Affair make this a romantic and gastronomic delight. ⊠ *Penn's Rd., Box 281, The Bight* 🕾 *649/941–3713 or 800/950–2862* 🖨 *649/941–5171* ⊕ *www. cunadevida.com* 🛏 *54 suites* 🍴 *2 restaurants, room service, in-room safes, kitchens, cable TV with movies, in-room VCRs, in-room data ports, Wi-Fi, 3 pools, hair salon, spa, beach, dive shop, snorkeling, boating, fishing, boccie, 2 bars, laundry facilities, concierge, Internet room, car rental* ▭ *AE, MC, V* ¶⊙¶ *CP.*

★ ☼ **$$–$$$$**   ▦ **Ocean Club Resorts.** Enormous locally painted pictures of hibiscus make a striking first impression as you enter the reception area at one of the island's most well-established condominium resorts. Regular shuttles run along the ½-mi (1-km) stretch of Grace Bay Beach between two artfully landscaped properties, Ocean Club and Ocean Club West. Both resorts claim some of Provo's best amenities. Ocean Club has the advantage of a quieter location away from most of the development and is just a short walk from Provo Golf & Country Club. Ocean Club West has a larger pool with a swim-up bar. Management and service are superb, as are the special value packages offered throughout most of the year. Plenty of beach and pool toys make Ocean Club a good family option. ⬡ *Box 240, Grace Bay* ☎ *649/946–5880 or 800/457–8787* 🖷 *649/946–5845* ⬡ *www.oceanclubresorts.com* ↩ *174 suites, 86 at Ocean Club, 88 at Ocean Club West* ⅊ *2 restaurants, in-room safes, some kitchens, some kitchenettes, cable TV with games and movies, in-room VCRs, in-room data ports, Wi-Fi, golf privileges, tennis court, 2 pools, gym, spa, beach, dive shop, snorkeling, boating, 2 bars, shops, laundry facilities, concierge, Internet room, meeting room, car rental* ▭ *AE, D, MC, V* ⌶⦿⌶ *EP.*

25

★ **$$–$$$$**   ▦ **Royal West Indies Resort.** With a contemporary take on colonial architecture and the outdoors feel of a botanical garden, this unpretentious resort has plenty of garden-view and beachfront studios and suites for moderate self-catering budgets. Room 135 on the western corner has the most dramatic ocean views. Right on Grace Bay Beach, the property has a small restaurant and bar for poolside cocktails and dining. Ask at the reception desk for help and advice on where to go explore. Special packages and free-night offers are available during the low season. ⬡ *Box 482, Grace Bay* ☎ *649/946–5004 or 800/332–4203* 🖷 *649/946–5008* ⬡ *www.royalwestindies.com* ↩ *99 suites* ⅊ *Restaurant, fans, in-room safes, kitchenettes, cable TV with movies, in-room VCRs, in-room data ports, in-room broadband, 2 pools, hot tub, massage, beach, snorkeling, boating, bicycles, bar, babysitting, laundry facilities, laundry service, concierge, car rental, no-smoking rooms* ▭ *AE, MC, V* ⌶⦿⌶ *EP.*

☼ **$$–$$$$**   ▦ **The Sands at Grace Bay.** Spacious gardens and two pools are surrounded by six rather impersonal three-story buildings at this otherwise well-appointed resort. Guests can expect friendly and helpful staff and excellent amenities, including a spa, good-size fitness room, and a beachside cabana restaurant called Hemingway's. Sparkling ocean views from huge screened patios and floor-to-ceiling windows are best in the oceanfront suites in blocks 3 and 4, which are also closest to the beach, restaurant, and pool. There are good discount packages in the off-season. ⬡ *Box 681, Grace Bay* ☎ *649/941–5199 or 877/777–2637* 🖷 *649/946–5198* ⬡ *www.thesandsresort.com* ↩ *118 suites* ⅊ *Restaurant, in-room safes, some kitchens, some kitchenettes, cable TV with movies, in-room data ports, tennis court, 2 pools, gym, hot tub, spa, beach, snorkeling, boating, bicycles, bar, shops, babysitting, laundry facilities, laundry service, concierge, Internet room, car rental, some pets allowed, no-smoking rooms* ▭ *AE, MC, V* ⌶⦿⌶ *EP.*

$$ ▦ **Comfort Suites.** This franchise hotel provides satisfactory accommodations for budget travelers thanks to good service, brightly colored and neat rooms, and a convenient location near restaurants and bars, a dive shop, a day spa, and an Internet café at Ports of Call. Rooms, though basic, are comfortable and are set around an attractively landscaped pool, which makes up for the fact that the property is across the street from the beach. A basic Continental breakfast buffet is included in the price. The bar manager, a North Caicos native named Watson, is more than happy to share his insights about the local culture. The bar attracts government officials on business trips, so it is a useful base for those seeking insights into island living. ⌂ *Box 590, Grace Bay* ☎ *649/946–8888 or 888/678–3483* ⌨ *649/946–5444* ⊕ *www.comfortsuitestci.com* ⟳ *100 suites* ⌂ *Fans, in-room safes, refrigerators, cable TV with movies, in-room data ports, pool, bar, shops, travel services* ▭ *AE, D, MC, V* ¶⊙¶ *CP.*

$–$$ ⊞ **Caribbean Paradise Inn.** Not far from Grace Bay Beach—but tucked away inland about a 10-minute walk from the beach—this two-story B&B has terra-cotta walls and cobalt blue trimmings. If you get to know manager Jean-Luc Bohic, you can sometimes persuade him to prepare a barbecue. Indeed, the Parisian's passion for cooking means that as well as a delicious Continental breakfast, you might be able to join him for lunch and dinner, too. Rooms are smaller than the usual Provo fare and are simply decorated with balconies overlooking the palm-fringed pool. ⌂ *Box 673, Grace Bay* ☎ *649/946–5020* ⌨ *649/946–5020* ⊕ *www. paradise.tc* ⟳ *16 rooms* ⌂ *Fans, in-room safes, some kitchenettes, cable TV, pool, bar, Internet room, no-smoking rooms* ▭ *AE, MC, V* ¶⊙¶ *CP.*

$–$$ ⊞ **Sibonné.** Dwarfed by most of the nearby resorts, the smallest hotel on Grace Bay beach has snug (by Provo's spacious standards) but pleasant rooms with Bermuda-style balconies and a completely circular but tiny pool. Of course, the pool is hardly used because the property is right on the beach. Rooms on the second floor have airy, vaulted ceilings; downstairs rooms have views of and access to the attractively planted courtyard garden, replete with palms, yellow elder, and exotic birdlife. The popular beachfront Bay Bistro serves breakfast, lunch, and dinner. Book early to get one of the two simple value rooms or the beachfront apartment, complete with four-poster bed, which is four steps from the beach; all three are usually reserved months in advance. ⌂ *Box 144, Grace Bay* ☎ *649/946–5547 or 800/528–1905* ⌨ *649/946–5770* ⊕ *www. sibonne.com* ⟳ *29 rooms, 1 apartment* ⌂ *Restaurant, in-room safes, cable TV, in-room data ports, pool, beach, snorkeling, boating, bicycles, bar, laundry service* ▭ *AE, MC, V* ¶⊙¶ *CP.*

$ ⊞ **Miramar Resort.** This ridge-top property, on one of the few hills in Provo, overlooks Turtle Cove Marina and provides a different point of view from the beachfront accommodations. Pretty but basic marina-facing and poolside rooms and cottages—which seem to be precariously balanced on the hillside—are a great value. The Magnolia Wine Bar & Restaurant has one of the best sunset views on the island. Free transfers to Grace Bay are available to guests, or it's a 15- to 20-minute walk to the closest beach. ⊠ *Turtle Cove Marina, Box 131, Turtle Cove* ☎ *649/946–4240* ⌨ *649/946–4704* ⊕ *www.miramarresort.tc* ⟳ *19 rooms, 4 suites* ⌂ *Restaurant, refrigerators, cable TV, in-room data ports, tennis court, pool, marina, fishing, bar* ▭ *AE, MC, V* ¶⊙¶ *EP.*

$ ⊞ **Turtle Cove Inn.** This pleasant two-story inn offers affordable and comfortable lodging in Turtle Cove Marina. All rooms have either a private balcony or patio overlooking the lush tropical gardens and pool or the marina. Besides the dockside Aqua Bar & Terrace, there's also a souvenir shop and liquor store. The inn is ideally situated for divers looking to roll from their beds into the ocean. ☒ *Turtle Cove Marina, Box 131, Turtle Cove* ☎ *649/946–4203 or 800/887–0477* 🖨 *649/946–4141* ⊕ *www. turtlecoveinn.com* ⇆ *28 rooms, 2 suites* ◇ *Restaurant, in-room safes, refrigerators, cable TV with movies, pool, marina, fishing, bicycles, bar, shops, car rental, no-smoking rooms* ▭ *AE, D, MC, V* ⍾ *EP.*

Where to Eat

There are more than 50 restaurants on Provo, from casual to elegant, with cuisine from Asian to Tex-Mex (and everything in between). You can spot the islands' own Caribbean influence no matter where you go, exhibited in fresh seafood specials, colorful presentations, and a tangy dose of spice.

For approximate costs, *see* the dining and lodging price chart on the Turks & Caicos Planner, at the beginning of this chapter.

25

CARIBBEAN ✕ **Simba.** Fish-bowl-size glassware is all part of the charm at this larger-
$$–$$$ than-life, safari-theme poolside restaurant at the quieter end of Grace Bay. For the price, presentation of the Caribbean-inspired dishes with fruity twists like the grouper with curry and mango sauce is above expectations. ☒ *Turks & Caicos Club, West Grace Bay* ☎ *649/946– 5888* ◇ *Reservations essential* ▭ *D, MC, V* ⍾ *No dinner Wed.*

DELI ✕ **Angela's Top o' the Cove New York Style Delicatessen.** Order deli sand-
¢–$ wiches, salads, and enticingly rich desserts and freshly baked pastries at this island institution on Leeward Highway, just south of Turtle Cove. From the deli case you can buy the fixings for a picnic; the shelves are stocked with an eclectic selection of fancy foodstuffs, as well as beer and wine. It's open at 6:30 AM for a busy trade in coffees, cappuccinos, and frappaccinos. ☒ *Leeward Hwy., Turtle Cove* ☎☎ *649/946–4694* ▭ *No credit cards* ⍾ *No dinner.*

ECLECTIC ✕ **Coyaba Restaurant.** Hidden behind the former Coral Gardens, this posh
★ **$$$$** eatery serves nostalgic favorites with tempting twists in conversation-piece crockery and in a palm-fringed setting. Chef Paul Newman uses his culinary expertise for the daily-changing main courses, which include exquisitely presented dishes such as crispy whole yellow snapper fried in Thai spices. To minimize any possible pretension, he keeps the resident expat crowd happy with traditional favorites like lemon meringue pie, albeit with his own tropical twist. The service is seamless. ☒ *Coral Gardens Resort, Penn's Rd., The Bight* ☎ *649/946–5186* ◇ *Reservations essential* ▭ *AE, MC, V* ⍾ *Closed Tues. No lunch.*

$$$$ ✕ **Grace's Cottage.** At one of the prettiest dining settings on Provo, tables are artfully set under wrought-iron cottage-style gazebos and around the wraparound verandah, which skirts the gingerbread-covered main building. In addition to such tangy and exciting entrées as the panfried red snapper served with roasted pepper sauce or the melt-in-your-mouth grilled beef tenderloin served with truffle-scented mashed potatoes, the soufflés are well worth the 15-minute wait and the top-tier price tag.

✉ *Point Grace, Grace Bay* ☎ *649/946–5096* ⌂ *Reservations essential* 🚭 *D, MC, V* ☉ *No lunch.*

★ **$$$–$$$$**   ✗ **Anacaona.** At the Grace Bay Club, this palapa-shaded restaurant has become a favorite of the country's chief minister. In spite of this, the restaurant continues to offer a memorable dining experience minus the tie, the air-conditioning, and the attitude. Start with a bottle of fine wine; then enjoy the light and healthy Mediterranean-influenced cuisine. The kitchen utilizes the island's bountiful seafood and fresh produce. Oil lamps on the tables, gently revolving ceiling fans, and the murmur of the trade winds add to the Eden-like environment. The entrancing ocean view and the careful service make it an ideal choice when you want to be pampered. ✉ *Grace Bay Club, Grace Bay* ☎ *649/946–5050* ⌂ *Reservations essential* 🚭 *AE, D, MC, V* ☞ *No kids under 12.*

☼ **$$–$$$$**   ✗ **Gecko Grille.** You can eat indoors surrounded by giant, painted banana-leaf murals of camouflaged geckoes or out on the garden patio, where the trees are interwoven with tiny twinkling lights. Creative "Floribbean" fare combines native specialties with exotic fruits and zesty island spices and includes Black Angus steaks grilled to perfection. Pecan-encrusted grouper is a long-time menu favorite. ✉ *Ocean Club, Grace Bay* ☎ *649/946–5885* 🚭 *AE, D, MC, V* ☉ *Closed Mon. and Tues.*

$$$ ✗ **Caicos Café.** There's a pervasive air of celebration on the tree-shaded terrace of this popular eatery. Choose from grilled seafood, steak, lamb, or chicken served hot off the outdoor barbecue. Owner-chef Pierrik Marziou adds a French accent to his appetizers, salads, and homemade desserts, along with an outstanding collection of fine French wines. ✉ *Grace Bay* ☎ *649/946–5278* 🚭 *AE, D, MC, V* ☉ *No lunch.*

★ **$$$**   ✗ **Magnolia Wine Bar & Restaurant.** Restaurateurs since the early 1990s, hands-on owners Gianni and Tracey Caporuscio make success seem simple. Expect well-prepared, uncomplicated choices that range from European to Asian to Caribbean. The atmosphere is romantic, the presentations attractive, and the service careful. It's easy to see why the Caporuscios have a loyal following. The adjoining wine bar includes a hand-picked list of specialty wines, which can be ordered by the glass. ✉ *Miramar Resort, Turtle Cove* ☎ *649/941–5108* 🚭 *AE, D, MC, V* ☉ *Closed Mon. No lunch.*

$–$$ ✗ **Barefoot Café.** This lively indoor-outdoor café is always bustling, drawing residents and tourists with hearty, affordable fare that includes farm-raised conch. Fresh-roasted gourmet coffee, homemade muffins and pastries, and breakfast sandwiches start the day. Huge burgers, grinders, and savory pizzas are popular lunchtime options, along with fresh fruit smoothies and ice cream. Dinner fare always includes fresh island seafood—the barefoot seafood platter is a must for fish fanatics. Look for value-priced evening specials, such as the popular $15 Caribbean Tuesday dinner. Centrally located on the lower level of Ports of Call shopping plaza, it's also a great place to people-watch. ✉ *Ports of Call, Grace Bay* ☎ *649/946–5282* 🚭 *AE, MC, V.*

ITALIAN   ✗ **Baci Ristorante.** Aromas redolent of the Mediterranean waft from the
$$–$$$ open kitchen as you enter this intimate eatery east of Turtle Cove. Outdoor seating is on a romantic canal-front patio. The menu offers a small but varied selection of Italian dishes. Veal is prominent on the menu, but

main courses also include pasta, chicken, fish, and brick-oven pizzas. House wines are personally selected by the owners and complement the tasteful wine list. Try the tiramisu for dessert with a flavored coffee drink. ⊠ *Harbour Town, Turtle Cove* ☏ 649/941–3044 ▭ *AE, MC, V.*

SEAFOOD ⨉ **Aqua Bar & Terrace.** This popular restaurant on the grounds of the Turtle Cove Inn has an inviting waterfront dining deck. Specializing in locally caught seafood and farm-raised conch, the menu includes longtime favorites like wahoo sushi, pecan-encrusted conch fillets, and grilled fish served with flavorful sauces. A selection of more casual entrées, including salads and burgers, appeals to the budget-conscious. There are plenty of child-friendly menu options. ⊠ *Turtle Cove Inn, Turtle Cove Marina, Turtle Cove* ☏ 649/946–4763 ▭ *AE, MC, V.*

$-$$ ⨉ **Banana Boat.** Buoys and other sea relics deck the walls of this lively restaurant-bar on the wharf. Grilled grouper, lobster salad sandwiches, conch fritters, and conch salad are among the options. Tropical drinks include the rum-filled Banana Breeze—a house specialty. ⊠ *Turtle Cove Marina, Turtle Cove* ☏ 649/941–5706 ▭ *AE, D, MC, V.*

TEX-MEX ⨉ **Hey Jose's Caribbean Cantina.** Frequented by locals, this restaurant south $-$$$ of Turtle Cove claims to serve the island's best margaritas. Customers also return for the tasty Tex-Mex treats: tacos, tostadas, nachos, burritos, fajitas, and special-recipe hot chicken wings. Thick, hearty pizzas are another favorite—especially the Kitchen Sink, with a little bit of everything thrown in. ⊠ *Leeward Hwy., Central Square* ☏ 649/946–4812 ▭ *D, MC, V* ☉ *Closed Sun.*

Beaches

The best of the many secluded beaches and pristine sands around Provo can be found at **Sapodilla Bay** (⊠ North of South Dock, at end of South Dock Rd.), a peaceful ¼-mi (½-km) cove protected by Sapodilla Hill, where calm waves lap against the soft sand, and yachts and small boats move with the gentle tide. **Half Moon Bay** (⊠ 15 minutes from Leeward Marina, between Pine Cay and Water Cay, accessible only by boat) is a natural ribbon of sand linking two uninhabited cays; it's only inches above the sparkling turquoise waters and only a short boat ride away from Provo. **Grace Bay** (⊠ Grace Bay, on north shore), a 12-mi (18-km) sweeping stretch of ivory-white, powder-soft sand on Provo's north coast is simply breathtaking and home to migrating starfish as well as shallow snorkeling trails. The majority of Provo's beachfront resorts are along this shore.

Sports & the Outdoors

BICYCLING Provo has a few steep grades to conquer, but they're short. Unfortunately, traffic on Leeward Highway makes pedaling here a less than relaxing experience, so it's best to stick to the main Grace Bay and Lower Bight roads. Most hotels have bikes available. **Provo Fun Cycles** (⊠ Ports of Call, Providenciales ☏ 649/946–5868 ⊕ www.provo.net/provofuncycles) rents double-seater scooters and bicycles (as well as jeeps, vans, cars, and SUVs). Rates are $16 per day for bicycles and $32 to $44 per day for scooters. You can rent mountain bikes at **Scooter Bob's** (⊠ Turtle Cove Marina, Turtle Cove ☏ 649/946–4684) for $15 a day.

25

BOATING & SAILING

Provo's calm, reef-protected seas combine with constant easterly trade winds for excellent sailing conditions. Several multihull vessels offer charters with snorkeling stops, food and beverage service, and sunset vistas. Prices range from $39 for group trips to $600 or more for private charters. **Sail Provo** (☎ 649/946–4783 ⊕ www.sailprovo.com) runs 52-foot and 48-foot catamarans on scheduled half-day, full-day, sunset, and kid-friendly glow-worm cruises, where underwater creatures light up the sea's surface for several days after each full moon. The *Atabeyra,* run by **Sun Charters** (☎ 649/941–5363 ⊕ www.suncharters.tc), is a retired rum runner and the choice of residents for special events.

For sightseeing below the waves, try the semisubmarine operated by **Caicos Tours** (✉ Turtle Cove Marina, Turtle Cove ☎ 649/231–0006 ⊕ www.caicostours.com). You can stay dry within the small, lower observatory as it glides along on a one-hour tour of the reef, with large viewing windows on either side. The trip costs $39.

DIVING & SNORKELING

Fodor's Choice
★

The island's many shallow reefs offer excellent and exciting snorkeling relatively close to shore. Try **Smith's Reef,** over Bridge Road east of Turtle Cove.

Scuba diving in the crystalline waters surrounding the islands ranks among the best in the Caribbean. The reef and wall drop-offs thrive with bright, unbroken coral formations and lavish numbers of fish and marine life. Mimicking the idyllic climate, waters are warm all year, averaging 76°F to 78°F in winter and 82°F to 84°F in summer. With minimal rainfall and soil runoff, visibility is usually good and frequently superb, ranging from 60 feet to more than 150 feet. An extensive system of marine national parks and boat moorings, combined with an eco-conscious mindset among dive operators, contributes to an uncommonly pristine underwater environment.

Dive operators in Provo regularly visit sites at **Grace Bay** and **Pine Cay** for spur-and-groove coral formations and bustling reef diving. They make the longer journey to the dramatic walls at **North West Point** and **West Caicos** depending on weather conditions. Instruction from the major diving agencies is available for all levels and certifications, even technical diving. An average one-tank dive costs $45; a two-tank dive, $90. There are also two live-aboard dive boats available for charter working out of Provo.

Provo Turtle Divers (✉ Turtle Cove Marina, Turtle Cove ☎ 649/946–4232 or 800/833–1341 ⊕ www.provoturtledivers.com), which also operates satellite locations at the Ocean Club and Ocean Club West, has been on Provo since the 1970s. The staff is friendly, knowledgeable, and unpretentious. With a certified marine biologist on staff, **Big Blue Unlimited** (✉ Leeward Marina, Leeward ☎ 649/946–5034 ⊕ www.bigblue.tc) specializes in eco-friendly diving adventures, including special trips for kids involving kayaking through the mangroves or walking along nature trails. It also offers Nitrox and Trimix. **Caicos Adventures** (✉ La Petite Pl., Grace Bay ☎ 649/941–3346 ⊕ www.tcidiving.com), run by friendly Frenchman Fifi Kuntz, offers daily trips to West Caicos, French Cay, and Molasses Reef. **Dive Provo** (✉ Ports of Call, Grace Bay ☎ 649/

Diving the Turks & Caicos Islands

CLOSE UP

SCUBA DIVING WAS THE original water sport to draw visitors to the Turks and Caicos Islands in the 1970s. Aficionados are still drawn by the abundant marine life, including humpback whales in winter, sparkling clean waters, warm and calm seas, and the coral walls and reefs around the islands. Diving in the Turks and Caicos—especially off Grand Turk, South Caicos, and Salt Cay—is still considered among the best in the world.

Off Providenciales, dive sites are along the north shore's barrier reef. Most sites can be reached in anywhere from 10 minutes to 1½ hours. Dive sites feature spur-and-groove coral formations atop a coral-covered slope. Popular stops like **Aquarium, Pinnacles,** and **Grouper Hole** have large schools of fish,

turtles, nurse sharks, and gray reef sharks. From the south side dive boats go to **French Cay, West Caicos, South West Reef,** and **Northwest Point.** Known for typically calm conditions and clear water, the West Caicos Marine National Park is a favorite stop. The area has dramatic walls and marine life, including sharks, eagle rays, and octopus, with large stands of pillar coral and huge barrel sponges.

Off Grand Turk, the 7,000-foot coral wall **drop-off** is actually within swimming distance of the beach. Buoyed sites along the wall have swim-through tunnels, cascading sand chutes, imposing coral pinnacles, dizzying vertical drops, and undercuts where the wall goes beyond the vertical and fades beneath the reef.

25

946–5040 or 800/234–7768 ⊕ www.diveprovo.com) is a PADI five-star operation that runs daily one- and two-tank dives to popular Grace Bay sites. The **Turks and Caicos Aggressor II** (☎ 800/348–2628 ⊕ www. turksandcaicosaggressor.com), a live-aboard dive boat, plies the islands' pristine sites with weekly charters from Turtle Cove Marina.

FISHING The island's fertile waters are great for angling—anything from bottom- and reef-fishing (most likely to produce plenty of bites and a large catch) to bonefishing and deep-sea fishing (among the finest in the Caribbean). Each July the Caicos Classic Catch & Release Tournament attracts anglers from across the islands and the United States who compete to catch the biggest Atlantic blue marlin, tuna, or wahoo. For any fishing activity, you are required to purchase a $15 visitor's fishing license; operators generally furnish all equipment, drinks, and snacks. Prices range from $100 to $375, depending on the length of trip and size of boat. For deep-sea fishing trips in search of marlin, sailfish, wahoo, tuna, barracuda, and shark, look up **Gwendolyn Fishing Charters** (✉ Turtle Cove Marina, Turtle Cove ☎ 649/946–5321 ⊕ www.fishingtci.com). You can rent a boat with a captain for a half- or full-day of bottom- or bone-fishing through **J&B Tours** (✉ Leeward Marina, Leeward ☎ 649/946–5047 ⊕ www.jbtours.com). Capt. Arthur Dean at **Silver Deep** (✉ Leeward Marina, Leeward ☎ 649/946–5612 ⊕ www.silverdeep.com) is said to be among the Caribbean's finest bonefishing guides.

GOLF The par-72, 18-hole championship course at **Provo Golf & Country Club**
Fodor'sChoice (⊠ Governor's Rd., Grace Bay ☎ 649/946–5991) is a combination of
★ lush greens and fairways, rugged limestone outcroppings, and freshwater lakes and is ranked among the Caribbean's top courses. Fees are $130
for 18 holes with shared cart. Premium golf clubs are available.

HORSEBACK Provo's long beaches and secluded lanes are ideal for trail rides on
RIDING horseback. **Provo Ponies** (☎ 649/946–5252 ⊕ www.provo.net/
provoponies) offers morning and afternoon rides for all levels of experience. A 45-minute ride costs $45; an 80-minute ride is $65.

PARASAILING A 15-minute parasailing flight over Grace Bay is available for $70 (sin-
gle) or $120 (tandem) from **Captain Marvin's Watersports** (☎ 649/231–
0643 ⊕ www.captainmarvinsparasail.com), who will pick you up at
your hotel for your flight. The views as you soar over the bite-shape
Grace Bay area, with spectacular views of the barrier reef, are truly
unforgettable.

TENNIS You can rent equipment at **Provo Golf & Country Club** (⊠ Grace Bay ☎ 649/
946–5991 ⊕ www.provogolf.com) and play on the two lighted courts,
which are among the island's best courts.

WINDSURFING Windsurfers find the calm, turquoise water of Grace Bay ideal. **Windsurfing Provo** (⊠ Ocean Club, Grace Bay ☎ 649/946–5649 ⊠ Ocean
Club West, Grace Bay ☎ 649/231–1687 ⊕ www.windsurfingprovo.tc)
rents kayaks, motorboats, Windsurfers, and Hobie Cats and offers
windsurfing instruction.

Shopping

There are several main shopping areas in Provo: Market Place and Central Square are on Leeward Highway about ½ mi to 1 mi (1 to 1½ km)
east of downtown; Grace Bay has the new Saltmills complex and La Petite Place retail plaza as well as the original Ports of Call shopping village. Two newly constructed markets on the beach near the Ocean Club
and the Beaches Resort allow for barefooted shopping. Hand-woven straw
baskets and hats, polished conch-shell crafts, paintings, wood carvings,
model sailboats, handmade dolls, and metalwork are crafts native to the
islands and nearby Haiti. The natural surroundings have inspired local
and international artists to paint, sculpt, print, craft, and photograph;
most of their creations are on sale in Providenciales.

★ **Anna's Art Gallery & Studio** (⊠ The Saltmills, Grace Bay ☎ 449/231–3293)
sells original artworks, silk-screen paintings, sculptures, and handmade
sea-glass jewelry. **ArtProvo** (⊠ Ocean Club Plaza, Grace Bay ☎ 649/941–
4545) is the island's largest gallery of designer wall art; also shown are
native crafts, jewelry, hand-blown glass, candles, and other gift items.
★ **Bamboo Gallery** (⊠ Leeward Hwy., The Market Place ☎ 649/946–4748)
sells Caribbean art, from vivid Haitian paintings to wood carvings and
local metal sculptures, with the added benefit that artists are usually on-
hand to describe their works. **Caicos Wear Boutique** (⊠ La Petite Pl., Grace
Bay Rd., Grace Bay ☎ 649/941–3346) is filled with casual resort wear,
including Caribbean-print shirts, swimsuits from Brazil, sandals, beach
jewelry, and gifts. **Greensleeves** (⊠ Central Sq., Leeward

Hwy., Turtle Cove 🏬 649/946–4147) offers paintings and pottery by local artists, baskets, jewelry, and sisal mats and bags. **Marilyn's Craft** (✉ Ports of Call, Grace Bay 🕾 No phone) sells handmade dolls, rag rugs, and wood carvings, plus tropical clothing and knickknacks. **Royal Jewels** (✉ Providenciales International Airport 🕾 649/941–4513 ✉ Arch Plaza 🕾 649/946–4699 ✉ Beaches Turks & Caicos Resort & Spa, Grace Bay 🕾 649/946–8285 ✉ Club Med Turkoise, Grace Bay 🕾 649/946–5602) sells gold and other jewelry, designer watches, perfumes, fine leather goods and cameras—all duty-free—at several outlets. Termed "the best little water-sports shop in Provo," **Seatopia** (✉ Ports of Call, Grace Bay 🕾 649/941–3355) sells reasonably priced scuba and snorkeling equipment, swimwear, beachwear, sandals, hats, and related water gear and swim toys. The **Tourist Shoppe** (✉ Central Sq., Leeward Hwy., Turtle Cove 🕾 649/946–4627) has a large selection of souvenirs, including CDs, cards and postcards, beach toys, and sunglasses. If you need to supplement your beach-reading stock or are looking for island-specific materials, ★ ☾ visit the **Unicorn Bookstore** (✉ In front of Graceway IGA Mall, Leeward Hwy., Grace Bay 🕾 649/941–5458) for a wide assortment of books and magazines, lots of information and guides about the Turks and Caicos Islands and the Caribbean, and a large children's section with crafts, games, and art supplies.

For a large selection of duty-free liquor, visit **Discount Liquors** (✉ Leeward Hwy., east of Suzie Turn Rd. 🕾 649/946–4536). Including a large fresh-produce section, bakery, gourmet deli, and extensive meat counter, **Graceway IGA Supermarket** (✉ Leeward Hwy., Grace Bay 🕾 649/941–5000), Provo's largest, is likely to have what you're looking for. Be prepared for sticker shock, as prices are much higher than you would expect at home. Besides having a licensed pharmacist on duty, **Lockland Trading Co.** (✉ Neptune Plaza, Grace Bay 🕾 649/946–8242)Stay sells flavored coffees, snacks, ice cream, and a selection of souvenirs.

Nightlife

Residents and tourists alike flock to the **BET Soundstage & Gaming Lounge** (✉ Leeward Hwy., Grace Bay 🕾 649/941–4318) for video lottery games, live music, and other entertainment, a casino, and a late-night disco almost every night. **Bonnie's** (✉ Lower Bight Rd., Grace Bay 🕾 649/941–8452) is a favorite local spot for sports events, movie nights, and endless happy hour specials. On Friday nights you can find a local band and lively crowd at **Calico Jack's Restaurant & Bar** (✉ Ports of Call, Grace Bay 🕾 649/946–5129). A popular gathering spot for locals to shoot pool, play darts, slam dominoes, and catch up on gossip is **Club Sodax Sports Bar** (✉ Leeward Hwy., Grace Bay 🕾 649/941–4540). You won't go hungry with snacks such as conch and fish fingers, jerk pork, and typical native dishes.

Exploring Providenciales

Numbers in the margin correspond to points of interest on the Turks & Caicos Islands map.

☾ ❶ **Caicos Conch Farm.** On the northeast tip of Provo, this is a major mariculture operation where mollusks are farmed commercially (more than

3 million conch are here). Guided tours are available; call to confirm times. The small gift shop sells conch-related souvenirs, and the world's only pet conchs, Sally and Jerry, seem more than happy to come out of their shells. ⊠ *Leeward-Going-Through, Leeward* ☎ *649/946–5330* ⬛ *$6* ☉ *Mon.–Sat. 9–4.*

② **Cheshire Hall.** Standing eerily just west of downtown Provo are the remains of a circa-1700 cotton plantation owned by Loyalist Thomas Stubbs. A trail weaves through the ruins, where interpretive signs tell the story of the island's doomed cotton industry. A variety of local plants are also identified. To visit, you must arrange for a tour through the Turks & Caicos National Trust. The lack of context can be disappointing for history buffs; a visit to North Caicos Wades Green Plantation or the Turks & Caicos National Museum could well prove a better fit. ⊠ *Near downtown Providenciales* ☎ *649/941–5710 for National Trust* ⊕ *www.turksandcaicos.tc/nationaltrust* ⬛ *$5* ☉ *Daily by appointment.*

☾ ③ **Sapodilla Hill.** On this cliff overlooking the secluded Sapodilla Bay, you can discover rocks carved with the names of shipwrecked sailors and dignitaries from TCI maritime and colonial past. The less adventurous can see molds of the carvings at Provo's International Airport. ⊠ *Off South Dock Rd., west of South Dock.*

Little Water Cay

★ ☾ This small, uninhabited cay is a protected area under the Turks & Caicos National Trust. On these 150 acres are two trails, small lakes, red mangroves, and an abundance of native plants. Boardwalks protect the ground, and interpretive signs explain the habitat. The cay is home to about 2,000 rare, endangered rock iguanas. Experts say the iguanas are shy, but these creatures actually seem rather curious. They waddle right up to you, as if posing for a picture. Several water-sports operators from Provo and North Caicos include a stop on the island as a part of their snorkel or sailing excursions. There's a $5 fee for a permit to visit the cay, and the proceeds go toward conservation in the islands.

Parrot Cay

Once said to be a hideout for pirate Calico Jack Rackham and his lady cohorts Mary Reid and Anne Bonny, the 1,000-acre cay, between Fort George Cay and North Caicos, is now the site of an ultraexclusive hideaway resort.

For approximate costs, *see* the dining and lodging price chart on the Turks & Caicos Planner, at the beginning of this chapter.

★ **$$$$** ⬛ **Parrot Cay Resort.** This private paradise—a favorite for celebrities and aspiring ones—comes with all the trimmings you'd expect for the substantial price. Elaborate oceanfront villas border the island, and their wooden, Far Eastern feel contrasts with the rather bland hillside terracotta and stucco building that houses the spacious suites. Suite and villa interiors are a minimalist and sumptuous mix of cool-white interiors, Indonesian furnishings, and four-poster beds. The villas are the ultimate indulgence, with heated lap-edge pools, hot tubs, and butler service. The resort's main pool is surrounded by a round, thatched bar and the Asian-inspired Lotus restaurant. The giant Como Shambhala Spa takes destination spas to a whole new level with Indonesian and Balinese therapists. If you have traveled far, Shambhala's own jetlag tea will put the zing back in your ying. If you wish to splash out in Parrot style without remortgaging your home, look out for special three- to five-night packages in the off-season. ⊠ *Parrot Cay* ⌂ *Box 164, Providenciales* ☎ *649/946–7788* 🖶 *649/946–7789* ⊕ *www.parrotcay.como.bz* ⇨ *42 rooms, 4 suites, 14 villas* ♿ *2 restaurants, room service, in-room safes, some kitchens, some kitchenettes, minibars, cable TV with movies, in-room VCRs, in-room data ports, Wi-Fi, 2 tennis courts, pool, health club, hot tub, Japanese baths, sauna, spa, Turkish bath, beach, snorkeling, windsurfing, boating, waterskiing, fishing, 2 bars, library, babysitting, laundry service, Internet room, airport shuttle* 🖃 *AE, MC, V* ⭗ *BP.*

25

Pine Cay

Pine Cay's 2½-mi-long (4-km-long) beach is among the most beautiful in the archipelago. The 800-acre private island is home to a secluded resort and around 37 private residences.

For approximate costs, *see* the dining and lodging price chart on the Turks & Caicos Planner, at the beginning of this chapter.

$$$$
Fodor'sChoice
★

🏠 **Meridian Club.** You might feel unplugged when you step onto Pine Cay, since there are no televisions, telephones, or traffic to be found on the tiny private island. The charm of this resort, which was built in the 1970s, is that it never changes, and unlike Parrot Cay, it prides itself on simplicity rather than celebrity. The simple beachfront cottages, most of the staff, and what is perhaps the world's smallest airport (in truth, a gazebo) have all stayed pretty much the same for years. The 2½-mi (4-km)stretch of beach is deserted, and instead of roads you can find nature trails and sun-dappled paths that crisscross the island, which can be explored by bike or on foot. Rates are fully inclusive and even include the flight from Provo. Cuisine is excellent, with fresh seafood and delicious cakes and tarts served at lunch, dinner, and afternoon tea. Far from being an ivory tower experience, the club enables you to become a part of a small community. Guests are mostly overstressed executives, mature couples, and honeymooners; a large percentage of guests are repeats. Families are welcomed in June. ⊠ *Pine Cay* ☎ *866/746–3229 or 770/500–1134* 🖶 *649/941–7010, 203/602–2265 in the U.S.* ⊕ *www. meridianclub.com* ⇨ *12 rooms, 7 cottages* ♿ *Restaurant, fans, tennis court, pool, beach, snorkeling, windsurfing, boating, fishing, bicycles, hiking, bar, library, laundry service, Internet room, airstrip; no a/c, no room phones, no room TVs, no kids under 12* 🖃 *No credit cards* ⭗ *AI* ⊗ *Closed Aug.–Oct.*

North Caicos

❹ Thanks to abundant rainfall, this 41-square-mi (106-square-km) island is the lushest of the Turks and Caicos. Bird lovers can see a large flock

Coming Attractions

THE BUZZ ABOUT TURKS AND CAICOS has increased steadily over the last five years, a fact that hasn't the ears of developers. Grace Bay, a 12-mi (19-km) stretch of ivory sand on Providenciales, is still a favored location for new properties. At the time of writing, several new resorts had almost been completed on Grace Bay, including the breathtaking **Somerset,** a luxurious retreat owned by the Sheikh of Qatar, and **Seven Stars,** a seven-story condominium resort that will be taking the destination to new heights, quite literally. Given the volume of construction, it is worth asking your hotel about nearby construction projects to avoid the noise, dust, and obstructed views that can sometimes result. Investors are looking beyond this golden north-shore strip. An

Aman resort is planned for Provo's North West Point, for example.

West Caicos, the most westerly cay—closest to one of the best dive sites around Turks and Caicos—will be home to **Molasses Reef,** a resort owned by Ritz-Carlton. On North Caicos, the handful of small guesthouses will be joined by **St. Charles,** a five-story condominium resort on Horse Stable Beach, and the three-story **Royal Reef Resort at Sandy Point.** Even South Caicos, the islands' sleepy fishing capital, has three new hotels under construction; the **South Caicos Lodge** and the **Old Commissioner's House** are under renovation at this writing. All of this adds up to more choice for vacationers wanting to explore and be pampered in the very near future.

of flamingos here, anglers can find shallow creeks full of bonefish, and history buffs can visit the ruins of a Loyalist plantation. Although there's no traffic, almost all the roads are paved, so bicycling is an excellent way to sightsee. The island is predicted to become one of the next tourism hot spots, and foundations have been laid for condo resorts on Horse Stable beach and Sandy Point. Even though it's a quiet place, you can find some small eateries around the airport and in Whitby, giving you a chance to try local and seafood specialties, sometimes served with homegrown okra or corn.

Where to Stay

For approximate costs, *see* the dining and lodging price chart on the Turks & Caicos Planner, at the beginning of this chapter.

$$ **Pelican Beach Hotel.** North Caicos islanders Susan and Clifford Gardiner built this small palmetto-fringed hotel in the 1980s on the quiet, mostly deserted Whitby Beach. The couple's friendliness and insights into island life, not to mention Susan's home-baked bread and island dishes (Cliff's favorite is her cracked conch and island lobster), are the best features. Over the years upkeep of the property has been somewhat inconsistent, but rooms are nevertheless comfortable. Best, the line of cottage-style rooms 1 through 6 is exactly 5 steps from the windswept beach. ⊠ *Whitby* ☎ *649/946–7112* 🖶 *649/946–7139* ⊕ *www.pelicanbeach.tc* ➦ *14 rooms, 2 suites* ⌂ *Restaurant, beach, snorkeling,*

fishing, bar; no room phones, no room TVs ☰ *MC, V* ⊘ *Closed Aug. 15–Sept. 15* ⦿| *MAP.*

$–$$ ⊡ **Ocean Beach Hotel & Condominiums.** On Whitby Beach, this horse-shoe-shape two-story, solar-paneled resort offers ocean views, comfortable and neatly furnished apartments, and a freshwater pool at quite reasonable rates. The Silver Palm restaurant is a welcome addition to the on-site amenities, which also include a dive and water-sports operation called Beach Cruiser. Unit 5 has the best views over the beach—especially for honeymooners, who automatically receive a 10% discount. You pay extra for air-conditioning, however. ⊠ *Whitby* ☏ *649/946–7113, 800/710–5204, 905/690–3817 in Canada* 🖷 *649/946–7386* ⊕ *www.turksandcaicos.tc/oceanbeach* ⇆ *10 suites* ⚲ *Restaurant, fans, some kitchenettes, pool, beach, dive shop, snorkeling, boating, fishing, bicycles, bar, car rental; no room TVs* ☰ *AE, D, MC, V* ⊘ *Closed June 15–Oct. 15* ⦿| *EP.*

Beaches

The beaches of North Caicos are superb for shallow snorkeling and sunset strolls, and the waters offshore have excellent scuba diving. Horse Stable Beach is the main beach for annual events and beach parties. Whitby Beach usually has a gentle tide, and its thin strip of sand is bordered by palmetto plants and taller trees.

Exploring North Caicos

Flamingo Pond. This is a regular nesting place for the beautiful pink birds. They tend to wander out in the middle of the pond, so bring binoculars.

Kew. This settlement has a small post office, a school, a church, and ruins of old plantations—all set among lush tropical trees bearing limes, papayas, and custard apples. Visiting Kew will give you a better understanding of the daily life of many islanders.

☾ **Wades Green.** Visitors can view well-preserved ruins of the greathouse, overseer's house, and surrounding walls of one of the most successful plantations of the Loyalist era. A lookout tower provides views for miles. Contact the National Trust for tour details. ⊠ *Kew* ☏ *649/941–5710 for National Trust* ⊡ *$5* ⊘ *Daily, by appointment only.*

Middle Caicos

❺ At 48 square mi (124 square km) and with fewer than 300 residents, this is the largest and least developed of the inhabited islands in the Turks and Caicos chain. A limestone ridge runs to about 125 feet above sea level, creating dramatic cliffs on the north shore and a cave system farther inland. Middle Caicos has rambling trails along the coast; the **Crossing Place Trail,** maintained by the National Trust, follows the path used by the early settlers to go between the islands. Inland are quiet settlements with friendly residents.

Where to Stay

For approximate costs, *see* the dining and lodging price chart on the Turks & Caicos Planner, at the beginning of this chapter.

25

$$ 🏨 **Blue Horizon Resort.** At this resort, undulating cliffs skirt one of the most dramatic beaches in the Turks and Caicos. Blue-tin roofs mark the small self-contained open-plan cottages. Screened-in porches and careful positioning ensure that all of the cottages have unobstructed views along the cliffs and out to sea. Owners Mike and Nikki Witt can purchase your groceries before you get there, as resources and amenities on the island are minimal. But the lack of amenities and development is actually what makes this spot so special. Tropical Cottage has large, attractive murals; Dragon View cottage has spectacular views of Dragon Cay and is closest to the Crossing Place trail that winds along the clifftops. ⊠ *Mudjin Harbor, Conch Bar* ☎ *649/946–6141* 🖨 *649/946–6139* ⊕ *www.bhresort.com* 🛌 *5 cottages, 2 villas* ♤ *Fans, some kitchens, some kitchenettes, cable TV with movies, beach, snorkeling, fishing, bicycles, hiking, laundry service; no a/c in some rooms, no phones in some rooms, no TV in some rooms* 🖃 *AE, MC, V* ⦿ *EP.*

Exploring Middle Caicos

☘ **Conch Bar Caves.** These limestone caves have eerie underground lakes and milky-white stalactites and stalagmites. Archaeologists have discovered Lucayan Indian artifacts in the caves and the surrounding area. The caves are inhabited by some harmless bats. If you visit, don't worry—they don't bother visitors. It's best to get a guide. If you tour the caves, be sure to wear sturdy shoes, not sandals.

CAVE TOURS   Taxi driver and fisherman **Cardinal Arthur** (☎ 649/946–6107) can give you a good cave tour. Local cave specialist and taxi driver **Ernest Forbes** (☎ 649/946–6140) is also happy to oblige with a cave tour and may even arrange a fixed-fee lunch at his house afterward if you ask nicely.

South Caicos

❻ This 8½-square-mi (21-square-km) island was once an important salt producer; today it's the heart of the fishing industry. Nature prevails, with long, white beaches, jagged bluffs, quiet backwater bays, and salt flats. Diving and snorkeling on the pristine wall and reefs are a treat enjoyed by only a few.

Beaches

The beaches at **Belle Sound** on South Caicos will take your breath away, with lagoonlike waters. On the opposite side of the ridge from Belle Sound, **Long Bay** is an endless stretch of beach, but it can be susceptible to rough surf; however, on calmer days this stretch makes you feel you're on a deserted island. Due south of South Caicos is **Big Ambergris Cay**, an uninhabited cay about 14 mi (23 km) beyond the Fish Cays, with a magnificent beach at Long Bay. To the north of South Caicos, uninhabited **East Caicos** has a beautiful 17-mi (27-km) beach on its north coast. The island was once a cattle range and the site of a major sisal-growing industry. Both places are accessible only by boat.

Exploring South Caicos

At the northern end of the island are fine white-sand beaches; the south coast is great for scuba diving along the drop-off; and there's excellent

All in the Family

BELONGERS, from the taxi driver meeting you to the chef feeding you, are often connected. "Oh, him?" you will hear. "He my cousin!" As development has been mercifully slow, such family connections, as well as crafts, bush medicine, ripsaw music, storytelling, and even recipes, have remained constant. But where do such traditions come from? Recently, researchers came closer to finding out. Many Belongers had claimed that their great-great-grandparents had told them their forebears had come directly from Africa. For decades their stories were ignored. Indeed, most experts believed that Belongers were descendants of mostly second-generation Bermudian and Caribbean slaves.

In 2005, museum researchers continued their search for a lost slave ship called *Trouvadore*. The ship, which wrecked off East Caicos in 1841, carried a cargo of 193 Africans, captured to be sold into slavery, almost all of whom miraculously survived the wreck. As slavery had been abolished in this British territory at the time, all the Africans were found and freed in the Turks and Caicos Islands. Since there were only a few thousand inhabitants in the islands at the time, these first-generation African survivors were a measurable minority (about 7% of the population then). Researchers have concluded that all the existing Belongers may be linked by blood or marriage to this one incident.

During one expedition, divers found a wrecked ship of the right time period. If these remains are *Trouvadore*, the Belongers may finally have a physical link to their past, to go with their more intangible cultural traditions. So while you're in the islands, look closely at the intricately woven baskets, listen carefully to the African rhythms in the ripsaw music, and savor the stories you hear. They may very well be the legacy of *Trouvadore* speaking to you from the past. For more information, check out ⊕ www. slaveshiptrouvadore.com.

25

---

snorkeling off the windward (east) coast, where large stands of elkhorn and staghorn coral shelter several varieties of small tropical fish. Spiny lobster and queen conch are found in the shallow Caicos Bank to the west and are harvested for export by local processing plants. The bone-fishing here is some of the best in the West Indies. **Beyond the Blue** (✉ Cockburn Harbour ☎ 649/231–1703 ⊕ www.beyondtheblue.com) offers bonefishing charters on a specialized airboat, which can operate in less than a foot of water. Lodging packages are available

Boiling Hole. Abandoned salinas make up the center of this island—the largest, across from the downtown ballpark, receives its water directly from an underground source connected to the ocean through this boiling hole.

Cockburn Harbour. The best natural harbor in the Caicos chain hosts the South Caicos Regatta, held each year in May.

THE TURKS

Grand Turk

Just 7 mi (11 km) long and a little over 1 mi (2½ km) wide, this island, the capital and seat of the Turks and Caicos government, has been a longtime favorite destination for divers eager to explore the 7,000-foot-deep pristine coral walls that drop down only 300 yards out to sea. On shore, the tiny, quiet island is home to white-sand beaches, the National Museum, and a small population of wild horses and donkeys, which leisurely meander past the white-walled courtyards, pretty churches, and bougainvillea-covered colonial inns on their daily commute into town. A new cruise-ship dock that opened at the southern end of the island in 2006 is set to bring around 300,000 visitors per year. In spite of the dramatic changes this could make to this peaceful tourist spot, the dock is likely to be self-contained and is about 3 mi (5 km) from the tranquil, small hotels of Cockburn Town, Pillory Beach, and the Ridge and far from most of the western-shore dive sites. However, some development will alter and in some cases open up a few new historic sites, including Grans Turk's Old Prison, Gun Hill, and the Lighthouse.

Where to Stay

Accommodations include original Bermudian inns, more modern but small beachfront hotels, and very basic to well-equipped self-catering suites and apartments. Almost all hotels offer dive packages, which are an excellent value.

$$ 🏨 **The Arches of Grand Turk.** Upstairs and downstairs, east- and west-facing balconies from these four ridgetop town houses ensure nicely framed views of both sunrise and sunset. Canadian husband-and-wife team Wally and Cecile Wennick left Florida in the 1990s after more than a decade in the hospitality industry to create this hillside home away from home, less than a five-minute walk from the deserted east beach. The well-equipped town houses are peppered with Cecille's handicrafts, including painted glass bottles, embroidery, and wall hangings that combine to give the airy houses a homespun feel. Weekly housekeeping is included in the rate, but daily maid service costs extra. ⊠ *Lighthouse Rd., Box 226* 🏠 *649/946–2941* ⊕ *www.grandturkarches.com* 🔗 *4 town houses* ⚲ *BBQs, fans, kitchens, cable TV with movies, pool, bicycles, laundry service* ⊟ *D, MC, V* 🍽 *EP.*

$$ 🏨 **Bohio Dive Resort & Spa.** Formerly the Pillory Beach Resort, this resort sits on an otherwise deserted stretch of beach. It's a dream come true for British couple Kelly Shanahan and Nick Gillings, who have created their own retreat on Grand Turk after years of visiting the tiny island. The resort's restaurant is the best on the island. You can relax with yoga sessions or party with the locals at the Sunday sail and kayak races or Thursday night's "pit party" with roasted meats and music. ⊠ *Pillory Beach* ☎ *649/946–2135* 🖨 *649/946–2135* ⊕ *www.bohioresort.com* 🔗 *12 rooms, 4 suites* ⚲ *Restaurant, some kitchenettes, cable TV, pool, spa, beach, dive shop, snorkeling, 2 bars, Internet room* ⊟ *AE, MC, V* 🍽 *EP.*

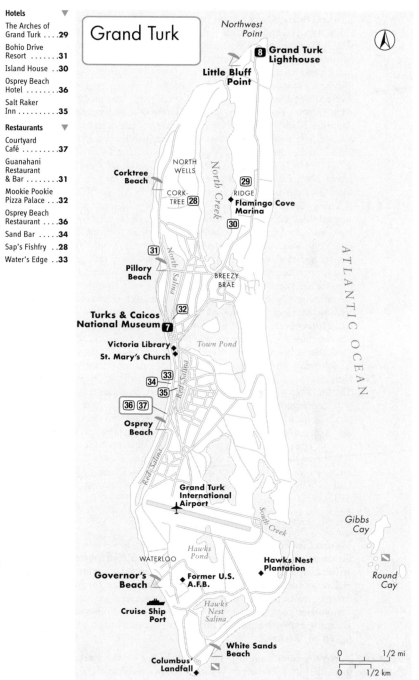

Grand Turk

Northwest
Point

8 **Grand Turk
Lighthouse**

**Little Bluff
Point**

NORTH
WELLS

**Corktree
Beach**

29

RIDGE

**♦ Flamingo Cove
Marina**

CORK-
TREE **28**

North Creek

30

31

North Salina

**Pillory
Beach**

BREEZY
BRAE

**Turks & Caicos
National Museum** **7**

32

Victoria Library ♦
St. Mary's Church ♦

Town Pond

34 **33**

35

36 **37**

**Osprey
Beach**

Red Salina

**Grand Turk
International
✈ Airport**

South Creek

*Gibbs
Cay*

A T L A N T I C   O C E A N

25

*Hawks
Pond*

WATERLOO

**Hawks Nest
Plantation**

*Round
Cay*

**Governor's
Beach**

**♦ Former U.S.
A.F.B.**

**Cruise Ship
Port**

*Hawks
Nest
Salina*

**White Sands
Beach**

**Columbus'
Landfall ♦**

0 ———— 1/2 mi

0 ———— 1/2 km

☾ **$$** ⌂ **Island House.** Owner Colin Brooker gives his guests a personal intro-duction to the capital island, thanks to his family's long history here. His years of business travel experience have gone into the comfortable, peace-ful suites that overlook North Creek. Balcony barbecues, shaded ham-mocks, and flatscreen TVs are served against a backdrop of splendid island and ocean views. Suites 3 and 7 command the best sunset views. Gradu-ated terraces descend the hillside to a small pool surrounded by pink-and-white climbing bougainvillea, creating the feel of a Mediterranean hideaway. An array of inflatable toys keeps kids happy. The deserted east beach is a 12-minute walk away. If you stay more than three nights, a car is in-cluded in the rental price. ✉ *Lighthouse Rd., Box 36* ☎ *649/946–1519* 📠 *649/946–2646* ⊕ *www.islandhouse-tci.com* 📑 *8 suites* ⌕ *BBQs, kitchenettes, cable TV with movies, pool, dock, fishing, bicycles, laundry facilities, Internet room, some pets allowed* ⊟ *AE, D, MC, V* ⊧⦶ *EP.*

$–$$ ⌂ **Osprey Beach Hotel.** Grand Turk veteran hotelier Jenny Smith has trans-formed this two-story oceanfront hotel with her artistic touches. Palms, frangipani, and deep green azaleas frame it like a painting. Inside, evoca-tive island watercolors, painted by her longtime friend, Nashville artist Tupper Saussay, thread through the property. Vaulted ceilings and Indone-sian four-poster beds are the highlight of upstairs suites 51, 52, and 53. Downstairs you can enjoy beach access through your own garden. On the opposite side of Duke Street, 13 new suites were slated to open in 2006. ✉ *Duke St., Cockburn Town* ☎ *649/946–2666* 📠 *649/946–2817* ⊕ *www. ospreybeachhotel.com* 📑 *11 rooms, 16 suites* ⌕ *Restaurant, some kitch-enettes, cable TV with movies, golf privileges, pool, beach, snorkeling, bar, some pets allowed* ⊟ *AE, MC, V* ⊧⦶ *EP* ⌕ *3-night minimum.*

$ ⌂ **Salt Raker Inn.** A large anchor on the sun-dappled pathway marks the entrance to this 19th-century house, which is now an unpretentious inn. The building was built by a shipwright and has a large, breezy balcony with commanding views over the sea, but its best feature is hidden be-hind the facade: a secret garden of tall tamarind and neme trees, climb-ing vines, hanging plants, potted hibiscus, climbing bougainvillea, and even a pond. The greenery, as well as providing a quiet spot for natural shade, is home to the inn's Secret Garden Restaurant. Rooms A2, B2, and C2 are nicely shaded havens but have no sea views. Upstairs, Rooms G and H share a balcony with unobstructed views of the ocean and Duke Street. ✉ *Duke St., Box 1, Cockburn Town* ☎ *649/946–2260* 📠 *649/946–2263* ⊕ *www.hotelsaltraker.com* 📑 *10 rooms, 3 suites* ⌕ *Restaurant, re-frigerators, cable TV, in-room data ports, bar* ⊟ *D, MC, V* ⊧⦶ *EP.*

Where to Eat

Conch in every shape and form, fresh grouper, and lobster (in season) are the favorite dishes at the laid-back restaurants that line Duke Street in Grand Turk and Balfour Town in Salt Cay. Away from these more touristy areas, smaller and less-expensive eateries serve chicken and ribs, curried goat, peas and rice, and other native island specialties. Prices are more expensive than in the United States, as most of the produce has to be imported.

AMERICAN ✗ **Water's Edge.** Seamus, the British owner of this lively, well-estab-

☾ **$$–$$$** lished bar and restaurant, is locally known as Shameless, owing to the

potent concoctions he creates and pours. Arrive early to secure a table on the deck for spectacular views of the sunset and the legendary green flash. The eclectic menu includes seafood and chicken quesadillas, conch salads, and burgers. There's live music on weekends and special internationally themed evenings once a week, so check the board for details. Service can be slow, so order before you're too hungry. ⊠ *Duke St., Cockburn Town* ☎ *649/946–1680* ⊟ *MC, V.*

$–$$ ✕ **Sand Bar.** Run by two Canadian sisters, this popular beachside bar is a good value, though the menu is limited to fish-and-chips, quesadillas, and similarly basic bar fare. The tented wooden terrace jutting out on to the beach provides shade during the day, making it an ideal lunch spot. The service is friendly, and the local crowd often spills into the street. ⊠ *Duke St., Cockburn Town* ⊟ *MC, V.*

¢–$ ✕ **Courtyard Café.** A great spot for people-watching, this spot offers omelets, wraps, and giant subs, as well as cakes for those with sweeter tastes. Daily specials range from lasagna and quiche to island-style beef patties. ⊠ *Duke St., Cockburn Town* ☎ *649/946–1453* ⊟ *AE, MC, V.*

CARIBBEAN ✕ **Osprey Beach Restaurant.** At the top of Duke Street, this has become
★ **$$–$$$** the place to be on Sunday and Wednesday nights, when a sizzling barbecue of ribs, chicken, and lobster combines with live "rake-and-scrape" music from a local group called High Tide to draw an appreciative crowd. Arrive before 8 PM to secure beachside tables and an unrestricted view of the band. The rest of the week, enjoy more elegant and eclectic fare accompanied by an increasingly impressive wine list. ⊠ *Duke St., Cockburn Town* ☎ *649/946–2666* ⊟ *MC, V.*

¢–$ ✕ **Mookie Pookie Pizza Palace.** Local husband-and-wife team "Mookie" and "Pookie" have created a wonderful backstreet parlor that has gained well-deserved popularity over the years as much more than a pizza place. At lunchtime, the tiny eatery is packed with locals ordering specials like steamed beef, curried chicken, and curried goat. You can also get burgers and omelets, but stick to the specials if you want fast service, and dine in if you want to get a true taste of island living. By night, the place becomes Grand Turk's one and only pizza take-out and delivery service, so if you're renting a villa or condo, put this spot on speed dial. ⊠ *Hospital Rd.* ☎ *649/946–1538* ⊟ *No credit cards* ☉ *Closed Sun.*

ECLECTIC ✕ **Guanahani Restaurant & Bar.** Off the town's main drag, this restau-
★ **$$–$$$** rant sits on a stunning but quiet stretch of beach. The food goes beyond the usual Grand Turk fare, thanks to the talents of Canadian-born chef Zev Beck, who takes care of the evening meals. His pecan-encrusted mahimahi and crispy sushi rolls are to die for. For lunch, Middle Caicos native Miss Leotha makes juicy jerk chicken to keep the crowd happy. The menu changes daily. ⊠ *Bohio Dive Resort & Spa, Pillory Beach* ☎ *649/946–2135* ⊟ *MC, V.*

SEAFOOD ✕ **Sap's Fishfry.** Down a lesser-known road that runs to the west of North
$–$$$ Creek lies an even lesser-known restaurant. If you survive the potholed road trip, you will undoubtedly feel you deserve a taste of the freshly caught grouper, conch, and lobster specialties served at this small hideaway on the water. This is a favorite (if slightly scandalous) spot, where

local married men like to bring their "sweethearts." The prices and food are certainly good enough to make it the best choice for a cheap date. ⊠ *North Creek* ☎ *649/242–1723* ▭ *No credit cards* ⊘ *No lunch.*

Beaches

Grand Turk is spoiled for choices when it comes to beach options: Sunset strolls along miles of deserted beaches, picnics in secluded coves, beach-combing on the coralline sands, snorkeling around shallow coral heads

★ close to shore, and admiring the impossibly turquoise-blue waters. **Governor's Beach,** a secluded crescent of powder-soft sand and shallow, calm turquoise waters that fronts the official British Governor's residence, called Waterloo, is framed by tall casuarina trees that provide plenty of natural shade. For more of a beachcombing experience, **Little Bluff Point Beach,** just west of the Grand Turk Lighthouse, is a low, limestone cliff-edged, shell-covered beach that looks out onto shallow waters, mangroves, and often flamingos, especially in spring and summer.

Sports & the Outdoors

CYCLING   The island's mostly flat terrain isn't very taxing, and most roads have hard surfaces. Take water with you: there are few places to stop for refreshment. Most hotels have bicycles available, but you can also rent them for $10 to $15 a day from **Oasis Divers** (⊠ Duke St., Cockburn Town ☎☎ 649/946–1128 ⊕ www.oasisdivers.com).

DIVING &   In these waters you can find undersea cathedrals, coral gardens, and count-
SNORKELING   less tunnels, but note that you must carry and present a valid certificate
★ card before you'll be allowed to dive. As its name suggests, the **Black Forest** offers staggering black-coral formations as well as the occasional black-tip shark. In the **Library** you can study fish galore, including large numbers of yellowtail snapper. At the Columbus Passage separating South Caicos from Grand Turk, each side of a 22-mi-wide (35-km-wide) channel drops more than 7,000 feet. From January through March, thousands of Atlantic humpback whales swim through en route to their winter breeding grounds.

Dive outfitters can all be found in Cockburn Town. Two-tank boat dives generally cost $60 to $75. **Blue Water Divers** (⊠ Duke St., Cockburn Town ☎☎ 649/946–2432 ⊕ www.grandturkscuba.com) has been in operation on Grand Turk since 1983 and is the only PADI Gold Palm five-star dive center on the island. Owner Mitch will doubtless put some of your underwater adventures to music in the evenings when he plays at the Osprey Beach Hotel or Salt Raker Inn. **Oasis Divers** (⊠ Duke St., Cockburn Town ☎☎ 649/946–1128 ⊕ www.oasisdivers.com) specializes in complete gear handling and pampering treatment. It also supplies Nitrox and rebreathers. Besides daily dive trips to the Wall, **Sea Eye Diving** (⊠ Duke St., Cockburn Town ☎☎ 649/946–1407 ⊕ www.seaeyediving.com) offers encounters with friendly stingrays on a popular snorkeling trip to nearby Gibbs Cay.

Nightlife

On weekends and holidays the younger crowd heads over to the **Nookie Hill Club** (⊠ Nookie Hill ☎ No phone) for late-night drinking and dancing. Every Wednesday and Sunday, there's lively "rake-and-scrape" music at the **Osprey Beach Hotel** (⊠ Duke St., Cockburn Town ☎ 649/946–2666). On Friday, "rake-and-scrape" bands play at the **Salt Raker Inn** (⊠ Duke St., Cockburn Town ☎ 649/946–2260). A fun crowd gathers most nights and for live music each Saturday at the **Water's Edge** (⊠ Duke St., Cockburn Town ☎ 649/946–1680).

Exploring Grand Turk

Pristine beaches with vistas of turquoise waters, small local settlements, historic ruins, and native flora and fauna are among the sights on Grand Turk. Fewer than 5,000 people live on this 7½-square-mi (19-square-km) island, and it's hard to get lost, as there aren't many roads.

Cockburn Town. The buildings in the colony's capital and seat of government reflect a 19th-century Bermudian style. Narrow streets are lined with low stone walls and old street lamps, which are now powered by electricity. The once-vital salinas have been restored, and covered benches along the sluices offer shady spots for observing wading birds, including flamingos that frequent the shallows. Be sure to pick up a copy of the Tourist Board's Heritage Walk guide to discover Grand Turk's rich architecture.

25

☺ ❼ In one of the oldest stone buildings on the islands, the **Turks & Caicos National Museum** houses the Molasses Reef wreck, the earliest shipwreck—dating to the early 1500s—discovered in the Americas. The natural-history exhibits include artifacts left by Taíno, African, North American, Bermudian, French, and Latin American settlers. The museum has a 3-D coral reef exhibit, a walk-in Lucayan cave with wooden artifacts, and a gallery dedicated to Grand Turk's little-known involvement in the Space Race. An interactive children's gallery keeps knee-high visitors even more "edutained." ⊠ *Duke St., Cockburn Town* ☎ *649/946–2160* ⊕ *www.tcmuseum.org* 🏷 *$5* ⊙ *Mon., Tues., Thurs., and Fri. 9–4, Wed. 9–5, Sat. 9–1.*

❽ **Grand Turk Lighthouse.** More than 150 years old, the lighthouse, built in the United Kingdom and transported piece by piece to the island, used to protect ships in danger of wrecking on the northern reefs. Use this panoramic landmark as a starting point for a breezy clifftop walk by following the donkey trails to the deserted eastern beach. ⊠ *Lighthouse Rd., North Ridge.*

Salt Cay

❾ Fewer than 100 people live on this 2½-square-mi (6-square-km) dot of land, maintaining an unassuming lifestyle against a backdrop of quaint stucco cottages, stone ruins, and weathered wooden windmills standing sentry in the abandoned salinas. The beautifully preserved island is bordered by picturesque beaches, where weathered green and blue sea glass and pretty shells often wash ashore. Beneath the waves, 10 dive sites are minutes from shore.

Where to Stay

For approximate costs, *see* the dining and lodging price chart on the Turks & Caicos Planner, at the beginning of this chapter.

$$$$ ⊡ **Windmills Plantation.** Arched balconies frame the perfect north-shore
Fodor'sChoice beach views in this outstanding small luxury hotel, which is presided
★ over by former Meridian Club managers Jim and Sharon Shafer. Wooden
decking winds through an eclectic plantation-inspired arrangement of
colorful buildings that hide a delightful mix of atmospheric, romantic
hideaways complete with dark wooden beams, four-poster beds, and original art. Jim, clearly a frustrated pirate, serves possibly the country's best
piña coladas from his cozy bar. Sharon, a natural and gracious hostess,
oversees her own boutique, a quiet library, and—most important—
scrumptious meals with desserts like blueberry crème brûlée and out-
standingly decadent breakfast pancakes that are to die for. Rates include
full board. ⊠ *North Beach Rd.* ☎ *649/946–6962 or 203/602–2265*
🖷 *649/946–6930* ⊕ *www.windmillsplantation.com* 🛏 *4 rooms, 4
suites* ♿ *Restaurant, pool, beach, snorkeling, fishing, hiking, horseback riding, bar, library; no a/c, no room phones, no room TVs, no kids,
no smoking* ⊟ *AE, MC, V* ⍟ *FAP.*

$–$$ ⊡ **Pirate's Hideaway & Blackbeard's Quarters.** Owner Candy Herwin—
true to her self-proclaimed pirate status—has smuggled artistic treasures across the ocean and even created her own masterpieces to deck
out this lair. Quirkily decorated rooms show her original style and sense
of humor. The African and Crow's Nest suites have private baths; Blackbeard's Quarters is a four-bedroom house with rooms that can be rented
separately but share a living room and kitchen (one room has an en-
suite bath; the others share a single bath). On a good day, Candy will
cook, but only if you entertain her and other guests—whether by
reading a sonnet or singing a song. If you love eclectic and artistically
inspiring surroundings and want to meet a true pirate queen, this
could well be your perfect hideaway. ⊠ *Victoria St., South District*
☎ *649/946–6909* 🖷 *649/946–6909* ⊕ *www.saltcay.tc* 🛏 *2 rooms,
1 4-bedroom house* ♿ *Some kitchens, beach, snorkeling, fishing, bicycles; no a/c in some rooms, no room phones, no room TVs* ⊟ *MC,
V* ⍟ *EP.*

$–$$ ⊡ **Sunset Reef.** A blue whale on the rooftop denotes this Victoria Street
property, which has two very basic villas with excellent ocean views and
a whale-watching balcony ideal for communal dining. You must pay extra
to use the air-conditioning. ⊠ *Victoria St., Balfour Town* ☎ *649/941–
7753* 🖷 *649/941–7753* ⊕ *www.sunsetreef.com* 🛏 *1 1-bedroom villa,
1 2-bedroom villa* ♿ *Fans, in-room fax, in-room safe, kitchens, in-
room VCRs, beach, snorkeling, fishing, laundry facilities, some pets allowed; no room phones* ⊟ *MC, V* ⍟ *EP.*

$–$$ ⊡ **Tradewinds Guest Suites.** Yards away from Dean's Dock, a grove of
whispering casuarina trees surrounds these five single-story, basic
apartments, which offer a moderate-budget option on Salt Cay with the
possibility of all-inclusive and dive packages. Screened porches, hammocks overlooking the comings and goings of the small dock, and the
friendly staff are the best features. You must pay extra to use the air-
conditioning. ⊠ *Victoria St., Balfour Town* ☎ *649/946–6906* 🖷 *649/
946–6940* ⊕ *www.tradewinds.tc* 🛏 *5 suites* ♿ *Some kitchens, some
kitchenettes, beach, snorkeling, fishing, bicycles; no room phones, no
room TVs* ⊟ *MC, V* ⍟ *EP.*

Where to Eat

$–$$ ✕ **Island Thyme Bistro.** Owner Porter Williams serves potent alcoholic creations like "The Wolf" and other creatures, as well as fairly sophisticated local and international cuisine. Look for steamed, freshly caught snapper served in a pepper wine sauce with peas and rice or spicy-hot chicken curry served with a tangy range of chutneys. The airy, trellis-covered spot overlooks the Salinas. ⊠ *North District* ☎ *649/946–6977* ▭ *MC, V* ⊘ *Closed Wed.*

$–$$ ✕ **Pat's Place.** Born and bred on the island, Pat Simmons can give you a lesson in the medicinal qualities of her garden plants and periwinkle flowers as well as excellent native cuisine for a down-home price in her typical Salt Cay home. Try conch fritters for lunch and her steamed grouper with okra rice for dinner. Be sure to call ahead, as she cooks only when there's someone to cook for. ⊠ *South District* ☎ *649/946–6919* ⚐ *Reservations essential* ▭ *No credit cards.*

Beaches

★ The north coast of **Salt Cay** has superb beaches, with tiny, pretty shells and weathered sea glass. Accessible by boat with the on-island tour operators, **Big Sand Cay,** 7 mi (11 km) south of Salt Cay, is tiny and totally uninhabited, but it's also known for its long, unspoiled stretches of open sand.

Sports & the Outdoors

DIVING & SNORKELING Scuba divers can explore the wreck of the **Endymion,** a 140-foot wooden-hull British warship that sank in 1790. It's off the southern point of Salt Cay. **Salt Cay Divers** (⊠ Balfour Town ☎ 649/946–6906 ⊕ www.saltcaydivers.tc) conducts daily trips and rents all the necessary equipment. It costs around $80 for a two-tank dive.

WHALE-WATCHING During the winter months (January through April), Salt Cay is a center for whale-watching, when some 2,500 humpback whales pass close to shore. Whale-watching trips can most easily be organized through your inn or guesthouse.

Exploring Salt Cay

Salt sheds and salinas are silent reminders of the days when the island was a leading producer of salt. Now the salt ponds attract abundant birdlife. Island tours are often conducted by motorized golf cart. From January through April, humpback whales pass by on the way to their winter breeding grounds.

Balfour Town. What little development there is on Salt Cay is found here. It's home to several small hotels and a few cozy stores, as well as the main dock and the Green Flash Gazebo, where locals hang out with tourists to watch the sunset and sink a beer.

The grand stone **White House,** which once belonged to a wealthy salt merchant, is testimony to the heyday of Salt Cay's eponymous industry. Still privately owned by the descendants of the original family, it's sometimes opened up for tours. It's worth asking your guesthouse or hotel owner—or any local passer-by—if Salt Cay Islander "Uncle Lionel" is on-island, as he may give you a personal tour to see the still-

25

intact, original furnishings, books, and medicine cabinet that date back to the early 1800s. ⊠ *Victoria St.*

TURKS & CAICOS ESSENTIALS

To research prices, get advice from other travelers, and book travel arrangements, visit www.fodors.com.

Transportation

BY AIR

The main gateways into the regions are Providenciales International Airport and Grand Turk International Airport. For private planes, Provo Air Center is a full service FBO (Fixed Base Operator) offering refueling, maintenance, and short-term storage, as well as on-site customs and immigration clearance, a lounge, and concierge services.

Although carriers and schedules can vary according to season, you can find nonstop and connecting flights to Providenciales from several U.S. cities on American, Delta, and USAirways; Air Jamaica provides connecting service on Air Jamaica Express through Montego Bay. During the high season, there are weekly charters from a number of North American cities (Club Med, for example, organizes its own weekly charter from the New York City area). Air Canada flies nonstop from Toronto. British Airways flies from the United Kingdom. There are also flights from the Bahamas and parts of the Caribbean on Bahamasair, Air Turks & Caicos, and Sky King; these airlines also fly to some of the smaller islands in the chain from Provo.

📵 Airline Contacts **Air Canada** ☎ 888/247-2262. **Air Jamaica Express** ☎ 800/523-5585 ⊕ www. airjamaica.com. **Air Turks & Caicos** ☎ 649/946–4181 or 649/941–5481 ⊕ www.airturksandcaicos. com. **American Airlines** ☎ 649/946–4948 or 800/ 433-7300. **Bahamasair** ☎ 649/946–4999 or 800/ 222-4262 ⊕ www.bahamasair.com. **British Airways** ☎ 649/941–3352 or 800/247-9297. **Delta** ☎800/241–1141. **SkyKing** ☎649/941–5464 ⊕www. skyking.tc. **US Airways** ☎ 800/622-1015.
📵 Airport Contacts **Grand Turk International**

Airport ☎ 649/946-2233. **Providenciales International Airport** ☎ 649/941–5670. **Provo Air Center** ☎ 649/946–4181 ⊕ www.provoaircenter.com.

BY BOAT & FERRY

Surprisingly, there's no scheduled boat or ferry service between Provo and the other Turks and Caicos Islands. Instead, islanders tend to catch rides leaving from the marina at Leeward-Going-Through. There's a thrice-weekly ferry from Salt Cay to Grand Turk.

BY CAR

Major reconstruction of Leeward Highway on Providenciales has been completed, and most of the road is now a four-lane divided highway complete with roundabouts. However, the paved two-lane roads through the settlements on Providenciales can be quite rough, although signage is improving. The less-traveled roads in Grand Turk and the family islands are, in general, smooth and paved. Gasoline is expensive, much more so than in the United States.

Driving here is on the left side of the road, British style; when pulling out into traffic, remember to look to your right. Give way to anyone entering a roundabout, as roundabouts are still a relatively new concept in the Turks and Caicos; stop even if you are on what appears to be the primary road. The maximum speed is 40 mph, 20 mph through settlements, and limits, as well as the use of seat belts, are enforced.

Avis and Budget have offices on the islands. You might also try local agencies such as Provo Rent-a-Car, Rent a Buggy, and Tropical Auto Rentals.

📵 **Avis** ☎ 649/946-4705 ⊕ www.Avistci.com. **Budget** ☎ 649/946-4079 ⊕ www.provo.net/ budget. **Provo Rent-a-Car** ☎ 649/946-4404

⊕ www.provo.net/rentacar. **Rent a Buggy** ☎ 649/946-4158 ⊕ www.rentabuggy.tc. **Tropical Auto Rentals** ☎ 649/946-5300 ⊕ www.provo.net/tropicalauto.

BY TAXI

Cabs (actually large vans) in Providenciales are now metered, and rates are regulated by the government at $2 per person per mile traveled. In Provo call the Provo Taxi & Bus Group for more information. In the family islands, cabs may not be metered, so it's usually best to try to negotiate a cost for your trip when you book your taxi. Many resorts and car-rental agencies offer complimentary airport transfers. Ask ahead of time.

🚖 **Provo Taxi & Bus Group** ☎ 649/946-5481.

Contacts & Resources

BANKS & EXCHANGE SERVICES

Prices quoted in this chapter are in U.S. dollars, which is the official currency in the islands. Major credit cards and traveler's checks are accepted at many establishments. The islands' few ATMs are primarily at the banks.

Scotiabank and FirstCaribbean have offices on Provo, with branches on Grand Turk. Many larger hotels can take care of your money requests. Bring small denominations to the less-populated islands.

BUSINESS HOURS

Banks are open Monday through Thursday from 9 to 3, Friday 9 to 5. Post offices are open weekdays from 8 to 4. Shops are generally open weekdays from 8 or 8:30 to 5.

ELECTRICITY

Electricity is fairly stable throughout the islands, and the current is suitable for all U.S. appliances (120/240 volts, 60 Hz).

EMERGENCIES

🚑 Emergency Services **Ambulance & Fire** ☎ 999 or 911. **Police** ☎ 649/946-2499 in Grand Turk, 649/946-7116 in North Caicos, 649/946-4259 in Provo, 649/946-3299 in South Caicos.

🏥 Hospitals **Associated Medical Practices** ⊠ Leeward Hwy., Glass Shack, Providenciales ☎ 649/946-4242. **Grand Turk Hospital** ⊠ Hospital Rd., Grand Turk ☎ 649/946-2040.

💊 Pharmacies **Grand Turk Hospital** ⊠ Grand Turk Hospital, Grand Turk ☎ 649/946-2040. **Grace Bay Medical Center** ⊠ Neptune Plaza, Grace Bay, Providenciales ☎ 649/941-5252.

🤿 Scuba Diving Emergencies **Associated Medical Practices** ⊠ Leeward Hwy., Glass Shack, Providenciales ☎ 649/946-4242.

HOLIDAYS

Public holidays are New Year's Day, Commonwealth Day (2nd Mon. in Mar.), Good Friday, Easter Monday, National Heroes Day (last Mon. in May), Queen's Birthday (3rd Mon. in June), Emancipation Day (1st Mon. in Aug.), National Youth Day (last Mon. in Sept.), Columbus Day (2nd Mon. in Oct.), International Human Rights Day (last Mon. in Oct.), Christmas Day, and Boxing Day (Dec. 26).

INTERNET, MAIL & SHIPPING

The post office is in downtown Provo at the corner of Airport Road. Collectors will be interested in the wide selection of stamps sold by the Philatelic Bureau. It costs 50¢ to send a postcard to the United States, 60¢ to Canada and the United Kingdom, and $1.25 to Australia and New Zealand; letters, per ½ ounce, cost 60¢ to the United States, 80¢ to Canada and the United Kingdom, and $1.40 to Australia and New Zealand. When writing to the Turks and Caicos Islands, be sure to include the specific island and "Turks and Caicos Islands, BWI" (British West Indies). Delivery service is provided by FedEx, with offices in Provo and Grand Turk.

📦 **FedEx** ☎ 649/946-4682 on Provo. **Philatelic Bureau** ☎ 649/946-1534.

MEDIA

The *Turks and Caicos Free Press* and the *Turks and Caicos Weekly News* are English-language newspapers that appeal to those interested in gaining some insight into the local culture. Magazines include

25

the wonderful *Times of the Islands*, the upscale *S3*, and *Baller*. WIV provides local television programming, usually channel 4. Radio Turks and Caicos broadcasts laid-back discussions and sounds from the islands on 97.3FM

PASSPORT REQUIREMENTS

U.S. and Canadian citizens need some proof of citizenship, such as a birth certificate (original or certified copy), plus a photo ID or a current passport. All other travelers, including those from the United Kingdom, Australia, and New Zealand, require a current passport. Everyone must have an ongoing or return ticket. A valid passport will be a requirement to all U.S. citizens traveling to the Turks and Caicos beginning January 1, 2007.

SAFETY

Although crime is not a major concern in the Turks and Caicos Islands, petty theft does occur here, and you're advised to leave your valuables in the hotel safe-deposit box and lock doors in cars and rooms when unattended.

TAXES & SERVICE CHARGES

The departure tax is $35 and is usually built into the cost of your tickets. If not, it's payable only in cash or traveler's checks. Restaurants and hotels add a 10% government tax. Hotels also add 10% to 15% for service.

TELEPHONES

The area code for the Turks and Caicos is 649. Just dial 1 plus the 10-digit number, including area code, from the United States. To make local calls, dial the seven-digit number. To make calls from the Turks and Caicos, dial 0, then 1, the area code, and the number.

All telephone service is provided by Cable & Wireless. Many U.S.–based cell phones work on the islands; use your own or rent one from Cable & Wireless. Internet access is available via hotel-room phone connections or Internet kiosks on Provo and Grand Turk. You can also connect to the World Wide Web from any telephone line by dialing C-O-N-N-E-C-T to call Cable & Wireless and using the user name *easy* and the password *access*. Calls from the islands are expensive, and many hotels add steep surcharges for long-distance. Talk fast.
🆔 **Cable & Wireless** ☎ 649/946–2200, 800/744–7777 for long distance, 649/266–6328 for Internet access, 811 for mobile service ⊕ www.tcimall.tc.

TIPPING

At restaurants, tip 15% if service isn't included in the bill. Taxi drivers also expect a token tip, about 10% of your fare.

TOUR OPTIONS

Whether by taxi, boat, or plane, you should try to venture beyond your resort's grounds and beach. The natural environment is one of the main attractions of the Turks and Caicos, yet few people explore beyond the natural wonder of the beach. Big Blue Unlimited has taken ecotouring to a whole new level with educational eco-tours, including three-hour kayak trips and more land-based guided journeys around the family islands. The Coastal Ecology & Wildlife tour is a kayak adventure through red mangroves to bird habitats, rock iguana hideaways, and natural fish nurseries. The North Caicos Mountain Bike Eco Tour gets you on a bike exploring the island, the plantation ruins, the inland lakes, and a flamingo pond with a stop-off at Susan Butterfield's home for lunch. Package costs range from $85 to $225 per person. J&B Tours offers sea and land tours, including trips to Middle Caicos, the largest of the islands, for a visit to the caves, or to North Caicos to see flamingos and plantation ruins. Nell's Taxi offers taxi tours of the islands, priced between $25 and $30 for the first hour and $25 for each additional hour.

Special day excursions are available from local airline Air Turks & Caicos. Trips include whale-watching in Salt Cay, and if you venture to Middle Caicos and North Caicos, in addition to flights, you get a map, water, a lunch voucher, and a moun-

tain bike to explore for the day. Trips start from $99, which includes round-trip air tickets. Day trips to Grand Turk are available with SkyKing. For around $155, you get a round-trip flight to the capital island, a short tour, admission to the Turks & Caicos National Museum, a stop off for lunch, and time to explore on your own.
🛈 **Air Turks & Caicos** ☎ 649/946–5481 or 649/946–4181 ⊕ www.airturksandcaicos.com. **Big Blue Unlimited** ✉Leeward Marina, Leeward ☎649/946–5034 ⊕www.bigblue.tc. **J&B Tours** ☎649/946–5047 ⊕ www.jbtours.com. **Nell's Taxi** ☎ 649/231–0051. **SkyKing** ☎ 649/941–5464 ⊕ www.skyking.tc.

VISITOR INFORMATION

The tourist offices on Grand Turk and Providenciales are open daily from 9 to 5.
🛈 Before You Leave **Turks & Caicos Islands Tourist Board** ✉ 2715 E. Oakland Park Blvd., No. 101, Fort Lauderdale, FL 33316 ☎ 954/568–6588 or 800/241–0824 ⊕ www.turksandcaicostourism.com.
🛈 In Turks & Caicos Islands **Turks & Caicos Islands Tourist Board** ✉ Front St., Cockburn Town, Grand Turk ☎ 649/946–2321 ✉ Stubbs Diamond Plaza, The Bight, Providenciales ☎ 649/946–4970 ⊕ www.turksandcaicostourism.com.

WEDDINGS

Beautiful oceanfront backdrops, endless starlight nights, and a bevy of romantic accommodations make the islands an ideal wedding destination. The residency requirement is only 24 hours, after which you can apply for a marriage license to the registrar in Grand Turk; the ceremony can take place at any time after the application has been granted, generally within two to three days. You must present a passport, original birth certificate, and proof of current marital status, as well as a letter stating both parties' occupations, ages, addresses, and fathers' full names. No blood tests are required, and the license fee is $50. The ceremony is conducted by a local minister, justice of the peace, or the registrar. The marriage certificate is filed in the islands, although copies can be sent to your home. There are a number of wedding coordinators on-island, and many resorts offer special wedding packages, which include handling all the details.
🛈 **Nila Destinations Wedding Planning** ☎ 649/941–4375 ⊕ www.nilavacations.com.

25

United States
Virgin Islands

Snorkelers, St. Thomas

WORD OF MOUTH

"Magens Bay St. Thomas would be my vote for best and most beautiful beach we've been to."   —Fran

"St. John is where you want to be. We took our whole family last summer and had a wonderful time. Very laid back."

—regansmom

"When on St. Croix, make sure you take a day trip over to Buck Island. . . ."   —Leigh

www.fodors.com/forums

WELCOME TO THE UNITED STATES VIRGIN ISLANDS

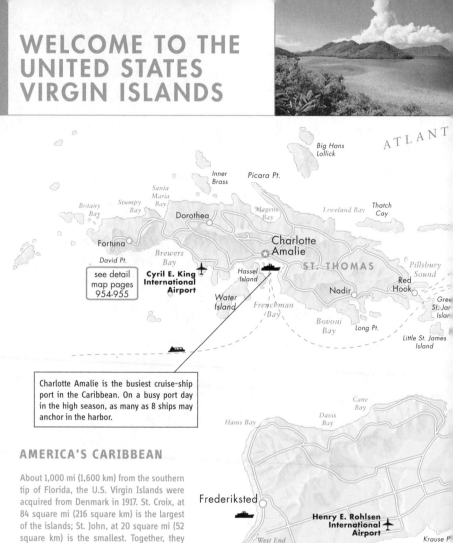

ATLANT

Big Hans
Lollick

Inner
Brass

Picara Pt.

Santa
Maria
Bay

Stumpy
Bay

Botany
Bay

Magens
Bay

Lovelund Bay

Thatch
Cay

Dorothea

Fortuna

Brewers
Bay

David Pt.

see detail
map pages
954-955

Cyril E. King
International
Airport

Hassel
Island

Water
Island

Frenchman
Bay

Charlotte
Amalie

ST. THOMAS

Pillsbury
Sound

Nadir

Red
Hook

Gre
St. Jar
Islan

Bovoni
Bay

Long Pt.

Little St. James
Island

Charlotte Amalie is the busiest cruise-ship
port in the Caribbean. On a busy port day
in the high season, as many as 8 ships may
anchor in the harbor.

Hams Bay

Davis
Bay

Cane
Bay

Frederiksted

Henry E. Rohlsen
International
Airport

Krause P

West End
Salt Pond

Long Pt.
Bay

Long Pt.

Sandy
Pt.

AMERICA'S CARIBBEAN

About 1,000 mi (1,600 km) from the southern
tip of Florida, the U.S. Virgin Islands were
acquired from Denmark in 1917. St. Croix, at
84 square mi (216 square km) is the largest
of the islands; St. John, at 20 square mi (52
square km) is the smallest. Together, they
have a population of around 110,000, half of
whom live on St. Thomas.

A perfect combination of the familiar and the
exotic, the U.S. Virgin Islands are a little bit of
home set in an azure sea. With hundreds of
idyllic coves and splendid beaches, chances
are that on one of the three islands you'll find
your ideal Caribbean vacation spot.

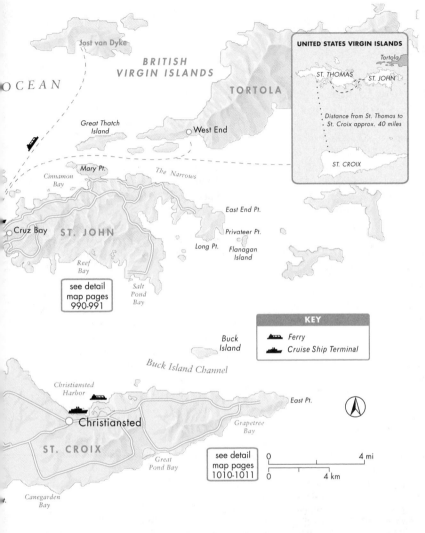

OCEAN

Jost van Dyke

BRITISH VIRGIN ISLANDS

TORTOLA

Great Thatch Island

○West End

Cinnamon Bay

Mary Pt.

The Narrows

○Cruz Bay **ST. JOHN**

East End Pt.

Privateer Pt.

Long Pt. Flanagan Island

Reef Bay

see detail map pages 990-991

Salt Pond Bay

UNITED STATES VIRGIN ISLANDS

Tortola

ST. THOMAS   ST. JOHN

Distance from St. Thomas to St. Croix approx. 40 miles

ST. CROIX

Buck Island

Buck Island Channel

KEY

⛴ Ferry
🚢 Cruise Ship Terminal

Christiansted Harbor

○Christiansted

Grapetree Bay

East Pt.

ST. CROIX

Great Pond Bay

see detail map pages 1010-1011

Canegarden Bay

0   4 mi
0   4 km

26

UNITED STATES VIRGIN ISLANDS

TOP 4 REASONS TO VISIT THE UNITED STATES VIRGIN ISLANDS

❶ St. Thomas is one of the Caribbean's major sailing centers.

❷ Two-thirds of St. John is a national park, which is criss-crossed by excellent hiking trails.

❸ Though Magens Bay on St. Thomas and Trunk Bay on St. John are two of the most perfect beaches you'll ever find, St. Croix's west-end beaches are fetching in their own way.

❹ Shopping on both St. Thomas and St. Croix is stellar.

U.S. VIRGIN ISLANDS PLANNER

Getting to the U.S. Virgin Islands

Most major airlines fly nonstop to St. Thomas (STT) from the U.S. There are also a few nonstops to St. Croix (STX). Otherwise, you may have to connect in San Juan. It's also possible to take a seaplane between St. Thomas and St. Croix. There are no flights to St. John because it has no airport; the only option is a ferry from either Red Hook or Charlotte Amalie in St. Thomas. Both Caneel Bay and the Westin have private ferries.

St. Thomas's Cyril E. King Airport sits at the western end of the island. St. Croix's Henry Rohlsen Airport sits outside Frederiksted; the east end is 45 minutes away. The ferry dock in St. John is right in the heart of Cruz Bay.

Hassle Factor: Low to Medium

Activities

St. Thomas is one of the Caribbean's most important centers for **sailing**. **Beaches** are excellent on both St. Thomas and St. John, good on St. Croix. Of the three, St. Croix is more known for **diving**. Other activities are too varied and numerous to list, particularly on St. Thomas, which is the most developed of the three islands, but you'll find every imaginable kind of water- and land-based activity, **historic sights**, **golf** (except on St. John), **biking**, **horseback riding**, and **hiking**, to mention but a few. Since most of St. John is a national park, the island is in pristine condition and well worth exploring on foot. St. Croix's Buck Island and its surrounding reefs are also a protected part of the national park system.

On the Ground

In St. Thomas, taxi vans are plentiful at the airport. Fees (set by the VI Taxi Commission) are per-person. You'll usually be charged a small fee for each piece luggage. East End resorts are typically a half-hour from the airport. In St. Croix, you'll pay $10 to $20 for a taxi to your hotel. In St. John, safari-style taxi vans meet all the ferries and will drop you at your hotel; as on St. Thomas, the rates are per person.

Renting a Car

If you are renting a villa on any of the three islands, you'll need a car. Otherwise, it's possible to get by with taxis on St. Thomas. You'll probably want a car on St. Croix, if only for a few days, to explore the island; if you are staying near Christiansted and your hotel has a shuttle into Christiansted, you might do without one entirely. In St. John, you will probably need a car to get around and to the beach unless you are staying at Caneel Bay or the Westin.

You need only a valid driver's license and credit card to rent a car; the minimum age for drivers is 18, although many agencies won't rent to anyone under the age of 25. Always make a reservation for a car during the high season.

Where to Stay

St. Thomas is the most developed of the Virgin Islands; choose it if you want extensive shopping opportunities and a multitude of activities and restaurants. The more luxurious resorts tend to be at the east end of the island. St. John is the least developed of the three and has a distinct following; it's the best choice if you want a small-island feel and easy access to great hiking. However, most villas there aren't directly on the beach. St. Croix is a sleeper. With a wide range of accommodations, from simple inns to luxury resorts, including some dive-oriented resorts on the north coast, it's remarkably diverse, but none of the beaches is as breathtaking as those on St. Thomas and St. John.

TYPES OF LODGINGS

Resorts: Whether you are looking for a luxury retreat or a moderately-priced vacation spot, there's going to be something for you in the USVI. St. Thomas has the most options. St. John has only two large resorts, both upscale; others are small, but it has some unique eco-oriented camping options. St. Croix's resorts are more mid-sized. The island also has two gay-oriented resorts.

Small Inns: Particularly on St. Croix, you'll find a wide range of attractive and accommodating small inns; if you can live without being directly on the beach; these friendly, homey places are a good option. St. Thomas also has a few small inns.

Villas: Villas are plentiful on all three islands, but they are especially popular on St. John, where they represent more than half the available lodging. They're always a good bet for families who can do without a busy resort environment.

Hotel & Restaurant Costs

Assume that hotels operate on the European Plan (**EP**—with no meals) unless we specify that they use either the Continental Plan (**CP**—with a Continental breakfast), Breakfast Plan (**BP**—full breakfast), or the Modified American Plan (**MAP**—with breakfast and dinner). Other hotels may offer the Full American Plan (**FAP**—including all meals but no drinks) or may be All-Inclusive (**AI**—with all meals, drinks, and most activities).

WHAT IT COSTS in Dollars					
	$$$$	**$$$**	**$$**	**$**	**¢**
Restaurants	over $30	$20–$30	$12–$20	$8–$12	under $8
Hotels*	over $350	$250–$350	$150–$250	$80–$150	under $80
Hotels**	over $450	$350–$450	$250–$350	$125–$250	under $125

*EP, BP, CP   **AI, FAP, MAP
Restaurant prices are for a main course at dinner excluding tip. Hotel prices are for two people in a double room in high season excluding 8% tax, service and energy charges (which can vary significantly), and meal plans (except for all-inclusives).

When to Go

High season coincides with that on most other Caribbean islands, from December through April or May; before and after that time, rates can drop by as much as 25% to 50%, depending on the resort.

St. Thomas's **International Rolex Regatta** in March is a big draw, as are the big **sport-fishing tournaments**, which usually begin in May and go through the summer. The St. Croix **Half Ironman Triathlon** attracts international-class athletes as well as amateurs every May. In February and March, the **St. Croix Landmarks Society House Tours** give you a chance to peek inside many historic homes that aren't usually open to the public. There aren't too many big events on St. John, but **Carnival** tends to bring many people to all three islands.

26

By Carol M.
Bareuther &
Lynda Lohr

WE PILED INTO THE TAXI VAN, BAGS IN THE BACK, and set off for our hotel on the opposite end of the island. Minutes later, cars slowed as we crept through the heart of town. But this traffic jam came with a view. Ballast-brick-walled 19th-century buildings touted contemporary buys on gold, diamonds, and emeralds, while turquoise seas glittered on the other side. Then our world turned topsy-turvy. Up we drove at a 45-degree angle or steeper, along former donkey trails to the mountain-ridge road that ran down the spine of the island. From this vantage point, the red-roof buildings and harbor below looked like miniatures on a postcard. Back on level ground, we pulled up to a green-painted van parked alongside stands brimming with tropical produce. "Sorry, I didn't have lunch," our driver apologized as he hopped back into his seat while holding a large paper bag. He pulled out a fried-bread oval, took a bite and passed the rest of the bag back to us. "Here, try a johnnycake," he offered. We were still happily munching as we finally pulled into our hotel. In 40 minutes, we had not merely reached where we were going but had a good idea of where we'd come. True, the U.S. flag blows here, but "America's Paradise" is in reality a delightful mix of the foreign and familiar that offers something for everyone to enjoy.

The U.S. Virgin Islands—St. Thomas, St. John, and St. Croix—float in the Greater Antilles between the Atlantic and Caribbean seas and some 1,000 mi (1,600 km) from the southern tip of Florida. History books give credit to Christopher Columbus for "discovering" the New World. In reality, the Virgin Islands, like the rest of the isles in the Caribbean chain, were populated as long ago as 2000 BC by nomadic waves of seagoing settlers as they migrated north from South America and eastward from Central America and the Yucatán Peninsula.

Columbus met the descendants of these original inhabitants during his second voyage to the New World, in 1493. He anchored in Salt River, a natural bay west of what is now Christiansted, St. Croix, and sent his men ashore in search of fresh water. Hostile arrows rather than welcoming embraces made for a quick retreat. In haste, Columbus named the island Santa Cruz (Holy Cross) and sailed north. He eventually claimed St. John, St. Thomas, and what are now the British Virgin Islands for Spain and at the same time named this shapely silhouette of 60-some islands Las Once Mil Virgenes, for the 11,000 legendary virgin followers of St. Ursula. Columbus believed the islands barren of priceless spices, so he sailed off leaving more than a century's gap in time before the next Europeans arrived.

Pioneers, planters, and pirates from throughout Europe ushered in the era of colonization. Great Britain and the Netherlands claimed St. Croix in 1625. This peaceful coexistence ended abruptly when the Dutch governor killed his English counterpart, thus launching years of battles for possession that would see seven flags fly over this southernmost Virgin isle. Meanwhile, St. Thomas's sheltered harbor proved a magnet for pirates like Blackbeard and Bluebeard. The Danes first colonized the island in 1666, naming their main settlement Taphus for its many beer halls. In 1691 the town received the more respectable name of Charlotte Amalie in honor of Danish king Christian V's wife. It wasn't until

1718 that a small group of Dutch planters raised their country's flag on St. John. As on its sibling Virgins, a plantation economy soon developed.

Plantations depended on slave labor, and the Virgin Islands played a key role in the triangular route that connected the Caribbean, Africa, and Europe in the trade of sugar, rum, and human cargo. By the early 1800s a sharp decline in cane prices due to competing beet sugar and an increasing number of slave revolts motivated Governor General Peter von Scholten to abolish slavery in the Danish colonies on July 3, 1848. This holiday is now celebrated as Emancipation Day.

After emancipation, the island's economy slumped. Islanders owed their existence to subsistence farming and fishing. Meanwhile, during the American Civil War, the Union began negotiations with Denmark for the purchase of the Virgin Islands in order to establish a naval base. However, the sale didn't happen until World War I, when President Theodore Roosevelt paid the Danes $25 million for the three largest islands; an elaborate Transfer Day ceremony was held on the grounds of St. Thomas's Legislature Building on March 31, 1917. A decade later, Virgin Islanders were granted U.S. citizenship. Today the U.S. Virgin Islands is an unincorporated territory, meaning that citizens govern themselves, vote for their own senators and governors, but cannot vote for president or congressional representation.

26

Nowadays, Virgin Islanders hail from more than 60 nations. Descendants of African slaves are the largest segment of the population, so it's not surprising that they also provide the largest percentage of workers and owners of restaurants, resorts, and shops. The Danish influence is still strong in architecture and street names. Americana is everywhere, too, most notably in recognizable fast-food chains, familiar shows on cable TV, and name-brand hotels. Between this diversity and the wealth that tourism brings, Virgin Islanders struggle to preserve their culture. Their rich, spicy West Indian–African heritage comes to full bloom at Carnival time, when celebrating and playing *mas* (with abandon) take precedence over everything else.

About 60,000 people live on 32-square-mi (83-square-km) St. Thomas (about the size of Manhattan); 51,000 on the 84 square mi (216 square km) of pastoral St. Croix; and about 5,000 on 20-square-mi (52-square-km) St. John, two-thirds of which is a national park. The backbone of the islands' economy is tourism, but at their heart is an independent, separate being: a rollicking hodgepodge of West Indian culture with a sense of humor that puts sex and politics in almost every conversation. Lacking a major-league sports team, Virgin Islanders follow the activities and antics of their 15 elected senators with the rabidity of Washingtonians following the Redskins. Loyalty to country and faith in God are the rules in the USVI, not the exceptions. Prayer is a way of life, and ROTC is one of the most popular high-school extracurricular activities.

Although the idyllic images of a tropical isle are definitely here, there's evidence, too, of growing pains. Traffic jams are common, a clandestine drug trade fuels crime, and—particularly on St. Thomas—there are few beaches left that aren't fronted by a high-rise hotel. Virgin Islanders are friendly folks, yet they can be prone to ungracious moments. Saying "Good morning" to the woman behind the jewelry counter, "Good afternoon" to the man who drives your cab, or "Goodnight" as you arrive at a restaurant for dinner will definitely pave the way for more pleasantries. Despite fairly heavy development, wildlife has found refuge here. The brown pelican is on the endangered list worldwide but is a common sight in the USVI. The endangered native boa tree is protected, as is the hawksbill turtle, whose females lumber onto the beaches to lay eggs.

With three islands to choose from, you're likely to find your piece of paradise. Check into a beachfront condo on the east end of St. Thomas; then eat burgers and watch football at a beachfront bar and grill. Or stay at an 18th-century plantation greathouse on St. Croix, dine on everything from local food to Continental cuisine, and go horseback riding at sunrise. Rent a tent or a cottage in the pristine national park on St. John; then take a hike, kayak off the coast, read a book, or just listen to the sounds of the forest. Or dive deep into "island time" and learn the art of limin' (hanging out, Caribbean-style) on all three islands.

ST. THOMAS

By Carol M. Bareuther

If you fly to the 32-square-mi (83-square-km) island of St. Thomas, you land at its western end; if you arrive by cruise ship, you come into one of the world's most beautiful harbors. Either way, one of your first sights is the town of Charlotte Amalie. From the harbor you see an idyllic-looking village that spreads into the lower hills. If you were expecting a quiet hamlet with its inhabitants hanging out under palm trees, you've missed that era by about 300 years. Although other islands in the USVI developed plantation economies, St. Thomas cultivated its harbor, and it became a thriving seaport soon after it was settled by the Danish in the 1600s.

The success of the naturally perfect harbor was enhanced by the fact that the Danes—who ruled St. Thomas with only a couple of short interruptions from 1666 to 1917—avoided involvement in some 100 years' worth of European wars. Denmark was the only European country with colonies in the Caribbean to stay neutral during the War of the Spanish Succession in the early 1700s. Thus, products of the Dutch, English, and French islands—sugar, cotton, and indigo—were traded through Charlotte Amalie, along with the regular shipments of slaves. When the Spanish wars ended, trade fell off, but by the end of the 1700s Europe was at war again, Denmark again remained neutral, and St. Thomas continued to prosper. Even into the 1800s, while the economies of St. Croix and St. John foundered with the market for sugarcane, St. Thomas's economy remained strong. This prosperity led to the development of shipyards, a well-organized banking system, and a large merchant class. In 1845 Charlotte Amalie had 101 large importing houses owned by the English, French, Germans, Haitians, Spaniards, Americans, Sephardim, and Danes.

Charlotte Amalie is still one of the most active cruise-ship ports in the world. On almost any day at least one and sometimes as many as eight cruise ships are tied to the dock or anchored outside the harbor. Gently rocking in the shadows of these giant floating hotels are just about every other kind of vessel imaginable: sleek sailing mono- and multihulls that will take you on a sunset cruise complete with rum punch and a Jimmy Buffett sound track, private megayachts that spirit busy executives away, and barnacle-bottom sloops—with laundry draped over the lifelines— that are home to world-cruising gypsies. Huge container ships pull up in Sub Base, west of the harbor, bringing in everything from breakfast cereals to tires. Anchored right along the waterfront are down-island barges that ply the waters between the Greater Antilles and the Leeward Islands, transporting goods like refrigerators, VCRs, and disposable diapers.

The waterfront road through Charlotte Amalie was once part of the harbor. Before it was filled to build the highway, the beach came right up to the back door of the warehouses that now line the thoroughfare. Two hundred years ago those warehouses contained indigo, tobacco, and cotton. Today the stone buildings house silk, crystal, linens, and leather. Exotic fragrances are still traded—but by island beauty queens in air-conditioned perfume palaces instead of through open market stalls. The pirates of old used St. Thomas as a base from which to raid merchant ships of every nation, though they were particularly fond of the gold- and silver-laden treasure ships heading to Spain. Pirates are still around, but today's versions use St. Thomas as a drop-off for their contraband: illegal immigrants and drugs.

Where to Stay

Of the USVI, St. Thomas has the most rooms and the greatest number and variety of resorts. You can let yourself be pampered at a luxurious resort—albeit at a price of $300 to more than $500 per night, not including meals. If your means are more modest, there are fine hotels (often with rooms that have a kitchen and a living area) in lovely settings throughout the island. There are also guesthouses and inns with great views (if not a beach at your door) and great service at about half the cost of what you'll pay at the beachfront pleasure palaces. Many of these are east and north of Charlotte Amalie or overlooking hills—ideal if you plan to get out and mingle with the locals. There are also inexpensive lodgings (most right in town) that are perfect if you just want a clean room to return to after a day of exploring or beach-bumming. You can learn more about the smaller properties on the island from the **St. Thomas–St. John Hotel & Tourism Association** (see ⇨ Visitor Information *in* U.S. Virgin Islands Essentials).

East-end condominium complexes are popular with families. Although condos are pricey (winter rates average $350 per night for a two-bedroom unit, which usually sleeps six), they have full kitchens, and you can definitely save money by cooking for yourself—especially if you bring some of your own nonperishable foodstuffs. (Virtually everything on St. Thomas is imported, and restaurants and shops pass shipping costs on to you.) Though you may spend some time laboring in the kitchen, many condos ease your burden with daily maid service and on-site

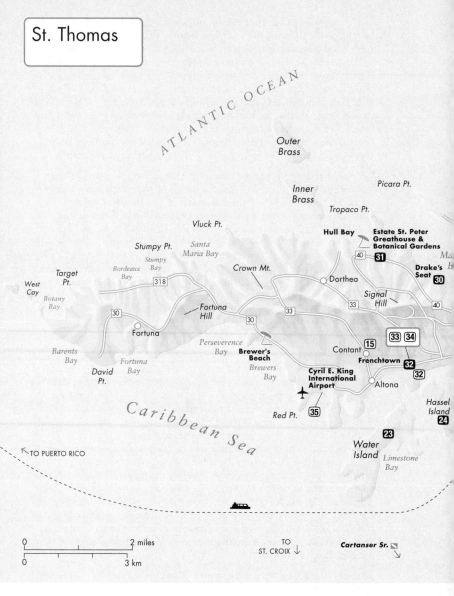

St. Thomas

ATLANTIC OCEAN

Outer Brass

Inner Brass

Picara Pt.

Tropaco Pt.

Vluck Pt.

Hull Bay

Estate St. Peter Greathouse & Botanical Gardens

Stumpy Pt.

Santa Maria Bay

40 **31**

Drake's Seat
30

Stumpy Bay

Bordeaux Bay

Crown Mt.

Dorthea

Signal Hill

40

Target Pt.

318

West Cay

Botany Bay

Fortuna Hill

33

33

33 **34**

30

Fortuna

15

Contant

Frenchtown
32

32

Barents Bay

Perseverence Bay

Brewer's Beach

Brewers Bay

Fortuna Bay

David Pt.

Cyril E. King International Airport

Altona

Hassel Island
24

Red Pt.
35

Caribbean Sea

23

Water Island

Limestone Bay

← TO PUERTO RICO

| 0 | 2 miles |
| 0 | 3 km |

TO ST. CROIX ↓

Cartanser Sr. ↘

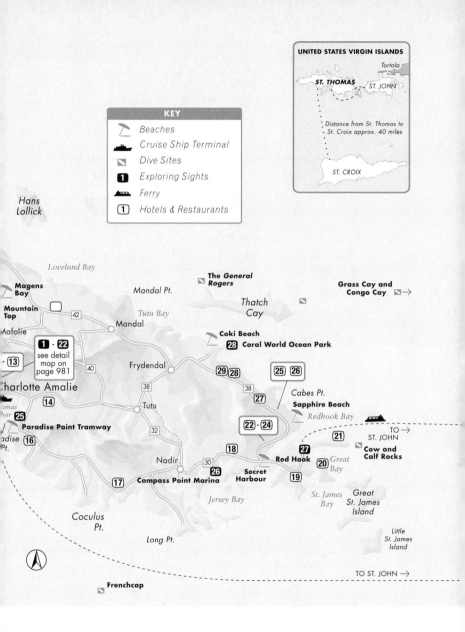

KEY

	Beaches
	Cruise Ship Terminal
	Dive Sites
1	Exploring Sights
	Ferry
(1)	Hotels & Restaurants

UNITED STATES VIRGIN ISLANDS

Tortola

ST. THOMAS   ST. JOHN

Distance from St. Thomas to
St. Croix approx. 40 miles

ST. CROIX

Hans
Lollick

Lovelund Bay

Magens
Bay

Mountain
Top

Mafolie

42

13

Charlotte Amalie

omas
bor **25**

14

Paradise Point Tramway

adise
Pt. **16**

Mandal Pt.

Tutu Bay

Mandal

40

38

Frydendal

Tutu

32

Nadir

17

30

Compass Point Marina

26

1 - **22**
see detail
map on
page 981

**The General
Rogers**

Thatch
Cay

Coki Beach
28 Coral World Ocean Park

29 **28**

38

27

18

Secret
Harbour

Jersey Bay

Coculus
Pt.

Long Pt.

Frenchcap

Grass Cay and
Congo Cay

Cabes Pt.
Sapphire Beach

25 **26**

Redhook Bay

21

TO
ST. JOHN

Cow and
Calf Rocks

27

Red Hook **20** Great
Bay

19

St. James
Bay

Great
St. James
Island

Little
St. James
Island

TO ST. JOHN →

restaurants; a few also have resort amenities, including pools and tennis courts. The east end is convenient to St. John, and it's a hub for the boating crowd, with some good restaurants. The prices below reflect rates in high season, which runs from December 15 to April 15. Rates are 25% to 50% lower the rest of the year.

Hotels

CHARLOTTE AMALIE
Accommodations in town and near town offer the benefits of being close to the airport, shopping, and a number of casual and fine-dining restaurants. The downside is that this is the most crowded and noisy area of the island. Crime can also be a problem. Don't go for a stroll at night in the heart of town. Use common sense and take the same precautions you would in any U.S. city. Those properties located up along the hillsides are less likely to incur crime problems, plus they command a steady breeze from the cool trade winds. This is especially important if you're visiting in summer and early fall.

$$$ ▦ **Best Western Emerald Beach Resort.** You get beachfront ambience at this reasonably priced miniresort tucked beneath the palm trees, but the tradeoff is that it's directly across from a noisy airport runway. You'll definitely want to spend time on the white-sand beach, which can be seen from nearly every room in the four three-story, peach-color buildings. Rooms are acceptable, but the tropical-print bedspreads and rattan furnishings look worn. Stay here if you need the beach on a budget or if you have an early-morning flight. ⊠ *8070 Lindberg Bay, 00802* ☎ *340/777–8800 or 800/233–4936* 🖨 *340/776–3426* ⊕ *www. emeraldbeach.com* ⇨ *90 rooms* ⌂ *Restaurant, refrigerators, cable TV, in-room data ports, tennis courts, pool, gym, beach, boating, volleyball, bar* ⊟ *AE, D, MC, V* ¶◎¶ *CP.*

$$ ▦ **Holiday Inn St. Thomas.** Business travelers, those laying over on the way to the British Virgin Islands, or laid-back vacationers who want the convenience of being able to walk to duty-free shopping, sights, and restaurants stay at this harborfront hotel. But if your ideal Caribbean beach vacation means having the beach at your doorstep, this isn't the place for you, despite the presence of a free beach shuttle. Contemporarily furnished rooms have such amenities as coffeemakers, hair dryers, ironing boards, and irons. An introductory dive lesson with Admiralty Dive Center is complimentary. ⊠ *Waterfront Hwy., Box 640, 00804* ☎ *340/ 774–5200 or 800/524–7389* 🖨 *340/774–1231* ⊕ *www.holidayinn.st-thomas.com* ⇨ *140 rooms, 11 suites* ⌂ *Restaurant, room service, in-room safes, refrigerators, cable TV with movies and video games, in-room data ports, pool, gym, hair salon, dive shop, bar, shops, laundry service, business services, meeting rooms, car rental* ⊟ *AE, D, DC, MC, V* ¶◎¶ *EP.*

$–$$ ▦ **The Green Iguana.** Atop Blackbeard's Hill, this B&B offers the perfect mix of gorgeous harbor views, proximity to town and shopping (five minutes away by foot), and secluded privacy provided by the surrounding flamboyant trees and bushy hibiscus. Accommodations range from a roomy, top-floor junior suite with two queen beds to a balcony room with queen bed and full kitchen. All rooms have air-conditioning, refrigerators, microwave ovens, and coffeemakers. Guests have use of wash-

Fodor'sChoice
★

ers and dryers. There's also a picnic area with a gas barbecue grill. The managing couple live on property and are very helpful in giving restaurant, sightseeing, or beach suggestions. ⊠ *37B Blackbeard's Hill, 00802* ☎ *340/776–7654 or 800/484–8825* 📠 *340/777–4312* ⊕ *www.thegreeniguana.com* 📨 *6 rooms* ♿ *Fans, some kitchens, some kitchenettes, microwaves, refrigerators, cable TV, pool, laundry facilities, no-smoking rooms* ▭ *AE, D, MC, V* ⼌ *EP.*

$–$$ 🖪 **Villa Santana.** Built by exiled general Santa Anna of Mexico, this 1857
Fodor\$Choice landmark provides a panoramic view of the harbor and plenty of West
★ Indian charm, which will make you feel as if you're living in a charming slice of Virgin Islands history with all the modern conveniences. Each of the rooms is unique and lovely. Our two favorites are La Mansion, a former library that is now an elegant villa with a large living area crowned by cathedral ceilings, full kitchen, two baths, and four-poster bed; and El Establo, a three-bedroom house with a full kitchen and laundry facilities that is rented by the week for up to six guests. Modern amenities aren't lacking; you can even sit by the pool with your laptop and indulge in wireless Internet access. ⊠ *2D Denmark Hill, 00802* ☎ *340/776–1311* 📠 *340/776–1311* ⊕ *www.villasantana.com* 📨 *6 rooms* ♿ *Fans, some kitchens, some kitchenettes, Wi-Fi, pool, croquet; no a/c in some rooms, no room phones, no TV in some rooms* ▭ *AE, MC, V* ⼌ *EP.*

¢–$$ 🖪 **Hotel 1829.** Antique charm is readily apparent in this rambling 19th-century merchant's house, from the hand-painted Moroccan tiles to a Tiffany window. Rooms on several levels range from stylish and spacious suites with vaulted ceilings to small and cozy rooms, with prices that range accordingly. The bar is open nightly and attracts locals as well as hotel guests; in the corner, a backgammon table attests to the prowess of the former owner, 1976 world champion Baron Vernon Ball. The second-floor botanical gardens and open-air champagne bar make a romantic spot for sunset viewing. Main Street, with its duty-free shops, is down the hill one block away. ⊠ *Government Hill, Box 1567, 00804* ☎ *340/776–1829 or 800/524–2002* 📠 *340/776–4313* ⊕ *www.hotel1829.com* 📨 *15 rooms* ♿ *Refrigerators, cable TV, pool, bar; no room phones, no kids* ▭ *AE, D, MC, V* ⼌ *CP.*

¢–$ 🖪 **Island View Guesthouse.** Perched 545 feet up the face of Crown Mountain, this small inn has a homey feel; hands-on owners can book tours or simply offer tips about the best sightseeing spots. Rooms range from a suite with a kitchenette that's perfect for families to two simply furnished veranda rooms that share a bath. Although the two veranda rooms and six poolside rooms have no air-conditioning, at this altitude, there's always a breeze, which makes that less of a burden. All rooms have telephones, six have kitchenettes, and laundry facilities are on-site. There's an honor bar for drinks and snacks and a communal verandah where guests congregate for Continental breakfasts and home-cooked dinners. You'll need a car to explore the island. ⊠ *Rte. 332, Box 1903, Estate Contant 00803* ☎ *340/774–4270 or 800/524–2023* 📠 *340/774–6167* ⊕ *www.islandviewstthomas.com* 📨 *16 rooms, 14 with private bath* ♿ *Fans, some kitchenettes, cable TV, pool, hot tub, laundry facilities; no a/c in some rooms* ▭ *AE, MC, V* ⼌ *CP.*

26

EAST END You can find most of the large, luxurious beachfront resorts on St. Thomas's east end. The downside is that these properties are about a 30-minute drive from town and 45-minute drive from the airport (substantially longer during peak hours). On the upside, these properties tend to be self-contained, plus there are a number of good restaurants, shops, and water-sports operators on the east end. Thus, once you've arrived, you don't need to travel far to have many activities and services at your fingertips.

$$$$ **Ritz-Carlton, St. Thomas.** Everything sparkles at the island's most lux-
Fodor'sChoice urious resort, from the marble-floor lobby to the infinity pool, which
★ seems to become one with the turquoise sea. Spacious guest rooms, with mahogany furnishings, high-speed Internet access, private balconies, and marble bathrooms with deep soaking tubs, are in six buildings fanning out from the main building. Six tall, somewhat institutional-looking buildings, composing the Ritz-Carlton Club, are two- and three-bedroom condos on their own adjacent beach. The spa, salon, and fitness center serve adults, both body and soul; the Ritz Kids program packs in a full day of activities for kids, including collecting seashells and feeding live iguanas. A 54-foot catamaran is a must-do for a day or sunset sail. ⊠ *Rte. 317, Box 6900, Estate Great Bay 00802* ☎ *340/775–3333 or 800/241–3333* 🖷 *340/775–4444* ⊕ *www.ritzcarlton.com* ↪ *200 rooms, 81 condos* ♨ *4 restaurants, room service, in-room safes, minibars, cable TV with movies and video games, Wi-Fi, 2 tennis courts, 2 pools, health club, hair salon, spa, beach, windsurfing, boating, 5 bars, shops, babysitting, children's programs (ages 4–12), laundry service, concierge, Internet room, business services, meeting rooms, airport shuttle, no-smoking rooms* ▭ *AE, D, DC, MC, V* ⦿ *EP.*

$$$$ **Wyndham Sugar Bay Resort & Spa.** Though this terra-cotta high-rise
Fodor'sChoice is surrounded by palm trees and lush greenery, rooms and the walkways
★ between them have a bit of an institutional feel. However, the sixth and seventh levels of building D have spectacular ocean views. Deluxe and superior rooms are spacious and comfortable. The beach is small, although the giant pool is replete with waterfalls that make a day of lounging here idyllic; however, it's a long, 99-step hike down here from guest rooms. Health buffs will enjoy the full-service spa and fitness center, as well as an outdoor fitness trail. If you're feeling lucky, head to the Ocean Club, where more than 50 slot machines were added in early 2005. ⊠ *Rte. 38, Box 6500, Estate Smith Bay 00802* ☎ *340/777–7100 or 800/927–7100* 🖷 *340/777–7200* ⊕ *www.wyndham.com* ↪ *300 rooms, 9 suites* ♨ *2 restaurants, snack bar, room service, fans, in-room safes, refrigerators, cable TV, in-room data ports, Wi-Fi, 4 tennis courts, pool, health club, spa, beach, snorkeling, windsurfing, boating, bar, nightclub, shop, babysitting, children's programs (ages 4–12), laundry service, concierge, business services, meeting rooms, car rental* ▭ *AE, D, DC, MC, V* ⦿ *AI.*

$$$–$$$$ **Point Pleasant Resort.** Hilltop suites give you an eagle's-eye view of the east end and the BVI beyond, while those in a building adjacent to the reception area offer incredible sea views. Sea-level junior suites are smaller, but the sounds of lapping waves will lull you to sleep. There's a resort shuttle, but some walking is necessary and hills are steep. The

beach is very small, though some may call it wonderfully private, but three pools give you more swimming and sunning options. The property also has a labyrinth of well-marked nature trails to explore. If you like seafood, don't miss dinner at the Agave Terrace restaurant; Fungi's on the Beach is a casual alternative. ⊠ *6600 Rte. 38, Estate Smith Bay 00802* ☎ *340/775–7200 or 800/524–2300* 🖷 *340/776–5694* ⊕ *www.pointpleasantresort.com* 🛏 *128 suites* ⚲ *2 restaurants, in-room safes, kitchenettes, cable TV, in-room data ports, tennis court, 3 pools, gym, beach, bar, shops, laundry facilities, concierge, Internet room* ▭ *AE, D, DC, MC, V* ⫟ *EP.*

☾ **$$$–$$$$** 🏨 **Sapphire Beach Resort & Marina.** A beautiful half-mile-long white-sand beach is the real ace here. The buildings have a weathered look, which could be construed as rustic, if not for the needed renovations and refurbishments also lacking in the guest rooms. Some bedspreads, upholstery, and curtains are faded, and bathroom fixtures and kitchen appliances could be replaced. The property is nicely landscaped on the seaside; however, on the land-side is a long-awaited, yet-to-be-built convention center, marina office, and shopping complex that is now a big grassy spot occupied by the odd car and piece of construction equipment. The property came under new management in the fall of 2005, a transition that has eliminated many problems with check in, frequency of maid service, and use of water-sports equipment that occurred when two management companies shared responsibility for separate rooms on the property. The kids club program no longer exists. ⊠ *6720 Estate Smith Bay* ☎ *800/524–2090, 340/773–9150, 800/874–7897* 🖷 *340/778–4009* ⊕ *www.antillesresorts.com* 🛏 *171 suites* ⚲ *2 restaurants, snack bar, room service, some kitchenettes, cable TV, 4 tennis courts, pool, health club, beach, snorkeling, windsurfing, boating, jet skiing, marina, parasailing, volleyball, bar, shop, babysitting, playground, laundry facilities, concierge, meeting room, car rental* ▭ *AE, MC, V* ⫟ *EP.*

$$$–$$$$ 🏨 **Secret Harbour Beach Resort & Villas.** There's no bad view from these low-rise studio, one-, and two-bedroom condos, which are either beachfront or perched on a hill overlooking the inviting cove beyond. All units, which have white-tile floors and tropical-print wood and wicker furnishings, are spacious; even the studios are more than 600 square feet and certainly big enough for a family with two children. The pool is small, but the beach is the real focal point here, where calm seas make for excellent swimming; snorkeling is especially good near the small dock to the east of the cove, where coral outcroppings attract a bevy of marine life. Watch spectacular sunsets from your balcony or at the beachfront bar. Kids under 13 stay free, making this a good value for families. ⊠ *Rte. 317, Box 6280, Estate Nazareth 00802-1104* ☎ *340/775–6550 or 800/524–2250* 🖷 *340/775–1501* ⊕ *www.secretharbourvi.com* 🛏 *49 suites, 15 studios* ⚲ *Restaurant, fans, kitchens, cable TV, 3 tennis courts, pool, health club, beach, dive shop, snorkeling, windsurfing, boating, bar, shop* ▭ *AE, MC, V* ⫟ *CP.*

SOUTH SHORE The south shore of St. Thomas connects town to the east end of the island via a beautiful road that rambles along the hillside with frequent peeks between the hills for a view of the ocean and, on a clear day, of

St. Croix some 40 mi (60 km) to the south. The resorts here are on their own beaches. They offer several opportunities for water sports, as well as land-based activities, fine dining, and evening entertainment.

✪ $$$$ ▦ **Marriott Frenchman's Reef & Morning Star Beach Resorts.** Set majestically on a promontory overlooking the east side of Charlotte Amalie's harbor, Frenchman's Reef is the high-rise full-service superhotel while Morning Star is the even more upscale boutique property nestled surfside along the fine white-sand beach. Meals here include lavish buffets for breakfast and dinner. Live entertainment and dancing, scheduled activities for all ages, and a shuttle boat to town that runs on the hour make having fun easy. ✉ *Rte. 315, Box 7100, Estate Bakkeroe 00801* ☎ *340/776–8500 or 800/233–6388* 🖷 *340/715–6193* ⊕ *www. marriottfrenchmansreef.com* ☞ *504 rooms, 27 suites* ♿ *4 restaurants, snack bar, room service, in-room safes, minibars, cable TV with movies, in-room data ports, Wi-Fi, 4 tennis courts, 2 pools, health club, hair salon, spa, beach, boating, volleyball, bar, piano bar, dance club, shops, babysitting, children's programs (ages 4–12), concierge, business services, convention center* ☰ *AE, D, DC, MC, V* �ĭⓞⅠ *EP.*

$$$ ▦ **Bolongo Bay Beach Club.** All the rooms at this small, family-run resort tucked along a 1,000-foot palm-lined beach have balconies with ocean views; down the beach are 12 studio and two-bedroom condos with full kitchens. This place is more homey than resort-fancy, but the friendliness of the longtime staff keeps visitors, including many honeymooners and even some families, coming back. The beach is a bit rocky for swimming, but sails aboard the resort's 53-foot catamaran and excursions arranged by the on-site dive shop are popular. You can opt out of the all-inclusive plan and pay less, but then you'd have to rent a car because the resort is a bit removed from the main parts of the island. The creative Caribbean cuisine at the Beach House, especially the seven-course tasting menu, which is paired with wines, shouldn't be missed. ✉ *Rte. 30, Box 7150, Estate Bolongo 00802* ☎ *340/775–1800 or 800/ 524–4746* 🖷 *340/775–3208* ⊕ *www.bolongobay.com* ☞ *65 rooms, 12 studio and 2-bedroom condos* ♿ *2 restaurants, in-room safes, some kitchenettes, refrigerators, cable TV, 2 tennis courts, pool, beach, dive shop, dock, snorkeling, windsurfing, boating, jet skiing, volleyball, bar, nightclub, shop, babysitting* ☰ *AE, D, DC, MC, V* �ĭⓞⅠ *EP.*

Villas & Condominiums

All the villa and condominium complexes listed here are on the East End of St. Thomas.

✪ $$$$ ▦ **The Anchorage.** A beachfront setting and homey conveniences that include full kitchens and washer-dryer units are what you can find in these two- and three-bedroom suites on Cowpet Bay next to the St. Thomas Yacht Club. The complex has two lighted tennis courts, a freshwater pool, and an informal restaurant. ✉ *Rte. 317, Estate Nazareth* 🖃 *Antilles Resorts, Box 24786, Christiansted, St. Croix 00824-0786* ☎ *800/874–7897* 🖷 *340/778–4009* ⊕ *www.antillesresorts.com* ☞ *11 suites* ♿ *Restaurant, kitchens, cable TV, 2 tennis courts, pool, beach, bar, laundry facilities* ☰ *AE, D, MC, V* ⅠⓞⅠ *EP.*

$$ ▦ **Sapphire Village.** These high-rise condos have the feel of an apartment house more than a luxury resort, so if you're looking for a home away from home, this might be the place. There are full kitchens, so you can avoid pricey restaurant meals. The view from your balcony is the marina and the Atlantic to the north. The beach, a spectacular half mile of white sand, is a five-minute walk down the hill. There's a restaurant on property and two more down the hill at the Sapphire Beach Resort. Additional restaurants, a shopping complex, and ferries to St. John are a mile away in Red Hook, albeit along a busy road. ⊠ *Rte. 38, Sapphire Bay* ⊕ *Antilles Resorts, Box 24786, Christiansted, St. Croix 00824-0786* ☎ *340/779–1540 or 800/874–7897* 🖷 *340/778–4009* ⊕ *www.antillesresorts.com* ↻ *15 condos* ♨ *Restaurant, kitchens, cable TV, 2 tennis courts, 2 pools, beach, dock, snorkeling, windsurfing, boating, jet skiing, marina, parasailing, volleyball, bar, pub, laundry facilities* ▭ *AE, D, MC, V* ⏧ *EP.*

★ **$** ▦ **Caribbean Style.** Couples will enjoy the romantic feel of these private, individually decorated condos. Each has a king-size bed, a reading and video library, and a kitchen stocked with breakfast foods and special requests, such as your favorite ice cream or preferred brand of rum. You can literally toss an ice cube into the sea from the hammock or lounge chairs on the private porches of the two smaller condos, while the two larger condos are only about 20 feet away from the rocky waterfront. Vessup Beach and water sports are a 10-minute walk away. Couples who would like to tie the knot will find that wedding arrangements, including professional photography, are a specialty of the owner. ⊠ *Rte. 317, at Cabrita Point, Estate Vessup Bay* ⊕ *6501 Red Hook Plaza, Suite 201, 00802* ☎ *340/715–1117 or 800/593–1390* ⊕ *www.cstylevi.com/cstyle_new/html* ↻ *4 1-bedroom condos* ♨ *Kitchens, pool, snorkeling, windsurfing, boating; no kids under 15, no smoking* ▭ *AE, MC, V* ⏧ *CP.*

PRIVATE VILLAS You can arrange private villa rentals through various agents that represent luxury residences and usually have both Web sites and brochures that show photos of the properties they represent. Some are suitable for travelers with disabilities, but be sure to ask specific questions regarding your own needs. **Calypso Realty** (⊕ Box 12178, 00801 ☎ 340/774–1620 or 800/747–4858 ⊕ www.calypsorealty.com) specializes in rental properties in St. Thomas. **McLaughlin-Anderson Villas** (⊠ 100 Blackbeard's Hill, Suite 3, 00802 ☎ 340/776–0635 or 800/537–6246 ⊕ www.mclaughlinanderson.com) handles rental villas throughout the U.S. Virgin Islands, British Virgin Islands, and Grenada.

Where to Eat

The beauty of St. Thomas and its sister islands has attracted a cadre of professionally trained chefs who know their way around fresh fish and local fruits. You can dine on everything from terrific cheap local dishes such as goat water (a spicy stew) and fungi (a cornmeal polenta-like side dish) to imports such as hot pastrami sandwiches and raspberries in crème fraîche.

Restaurants are spread all over the island, although fewer are found on the northwest and far west of the island. Most restaurants out of town are easily accessible by taxi and have ample parking. If you dine in Charlotte Amalie, take a taxi. Parking close to restaurants can be difficult to find, and walking around after dark isn't advisable for safety reasons.

If your accommodations have a kitchen and you plan to cook, there's good variety in St. Thomas's mainland-style supermarkets. Just be prepared for grocery prices that are about 20% higher than those in the United States. As for drinking, outside the hotels a beer in a bar will cost between $2 and $3 and a piña colada $5 or more.

What to Wear

Dining on St. Thomas is informal. Few restaurants require a jacket and tie. Still, at dinner in the snazzier places shorts and T-shirts are inappropriate; men would do well to wear slacks and a shirt with buttons. Dress codes on St. Thomas rarely require women to wear skirts, but you can never go wrong with something flowing.

Charlotte Amalie

AMERICAN
⟳ $–$$$

✕ **Greenhouse Bar & Restaurant.** The eight-page menu at this bustling waterfront restaurant offers burgers, salads, sandwiches, and pizza served all day long, along with more upscale entrées like peel-and-eat shrimp, Maine lobster, Alaskan king crab, and certified Black Angus prime rib that are reasonably priced. This is generally a family-friendly place, though the Two-for-Tuesdays happy hour and Friday-night live reggae music that starts thumping at 10 PM draw a lively young-adult crowd. ⊠ *Waterfront Hwy. at Storetvaer Gade* ☎ *340/774–7998* ▭ *AE, D, MC, V.*

⟳ ¢–$

✕ **Jen's Gourmet Cafe & Deli.** This hole-in-the-wall eatery is the closest thing you'll find to a New York–style Jewish deli. Choose the smoked salmon platter for breakfast or hot pastrami on rye at lunch. Homemade desserts like chocolate layer cake, apple strudel, and peaches-and-cream-cheese strudel are yummy. ⊠ *Grand Galleria, 43-46 Norre Gade* ☎ *340/777–4611* ▭ *AE, MC, V* ⊘ *No dinner.*

CARIBBEAN
$$
Fodor's Choice
★

✕ **Cuzzin's Caribbean Restaurant & Bar.** The top picks in this restaurant in a 19th-century livery stage are Virgin Islands staples. For lunch, order tender slivers of conch stewed in a rich onion butter sauce, savory braised oxtail, or curried chicken. At dinner, the island-style mutton served in a thick gravy and seasoned with locally grown herbs offers a tasty treat that's deliciously different. Side dishes include peas and rice, boiled green bananas, fried plantains, and potato stuffing. ⊠ *7 Wimmelskafts Gade, also called Back St.* ☎ *340/777–4711* ▭ *AE, MC, V.*

$–$$
Fodor's Choice
★

✕ **Gladys' Cafe.** Even if the local specialties—conch in butter sauce, saltfish and dumplings, hearty red bean soup—didn't make this a recommended café, it would be worth coming for Gladys's smile. While you're here, pick up a $5 or $10 bottle of her hot sauce. There are mustard-, oil and vinegar-, and tomato-based versions; the last is the hottest. ⊠ *Waterfront, at Royal Dane Mall* ☎ *340/774–6604* ▭ *AE* ⊘ *No dinner.*

ECLECTIC
★ $$$–$$$$

✕ **Banana Tree Grille.** The eagle's-eye view of the Charlotte Amalie harbor from this open-air restaurant is as fantastic as the food. Come before 6 PM and watch the cruise ships depart from the harbor and the sun set over the sea while you have a drink at the bar. Liz Buckalew, who with husband Jerry has been in the island restaurant business since the early 1980s, always greets you with a warm welcome. For starters, try the combination of lobster, shrimp, scallops, and squid marinated in a savory herb vinaigrette. The dark rum, honey, and brown sugar–glazed salmon fillet served with yams is an excellent entrée. ⊠ *Bluebeard's Castle, Bluebeard's Hill* ☎ *340/776–4050* ⚄ *Reservations essential* ⊟ *AE, D, MC, V* ⊘ *Closed Mon. No lunch.*

★ **$$–$$$** ✕ **Randy's Bar & Bistro.** There's no view here—even though you're at the top of a hill—but the somewhat hidden location has helped to keep this one of the island's best dining secrets. This wine shop and deli caters to a local lunch crowd. At night, you forget you're tucked into a nearly windowless building. The tableside bread for starters is a thick, crusty focaccia flavored with nearly 10 different vegetables. Try the brie-stuffed filet mignon or rack of lamb. After-dinner cigars and wine complete the experience. ⊠ *Al Cohen's Plaza, atop Raphune Hill, ½ mi (¾ km) east of Charlotte Amalie* ☎ *340/777–3199* ⊟ *AE, D, MC, V.*

FRENCH ✕ **Hervé Restaurant & Wine Bar.** In the glow of candlelight—at tables im-
★ **$$$–$$$$** peccably dressed with fine linens, silver settings, and fine crystal—you can start off with French-trained Hervé Chassin's crispy conch fritters served with a spicy-sweet mango chutney, then choose from such entrées as black-sesame-crusted tuna with a ginger raspberry sauce or succulent roast duck with a ginger-and-tamarind sauce. The passion-fruit cheesecake is to die for. For lunch, lighter-air fare like quiche, salads, and grilled sandwiches is served in the open-air bistro on the first floor. ⊠ *Government Hill* ☎ *340/777–9703* ⚄ *Reservations essential* ⊟ *AE, MC, V.*

ITALIAN ✕ **Virgilio's.** For the island's best northern Italian cuisine, don't miss
★ **$$$–$$$$** this intimate, elegant hideaway tucked on a quiet side street. Eclectic art covers the two-story brick walls, and the sound of Italian opera sets the stage for a memorable meal. Come here for more than 40 home-made pastas topped with superb sauces—cappellini with fresh tomatoes and garlic or peasant-style spaghetti in a rich tomato sauce with mushrooms and prosciutto. House specialties include osso buco and tiramisu—expertly crafted by chef Ernesto Garrigos, who has prepared these two dishes on the Discovery Channel's "Great Chefs of the World" series. ⊠ *18 Main St.* ☎ *340/776–4920* ⚄ *Reservations essential* ⊟ *AE, MC, V* ⊘ *Closed Sun.*

$–$$ ✕ **Café Amici.** Set within the historic stonework and cascading tropical blossoms of A. H. Riise Alley, this charming open-air eatery has an Italian name but boasts a menu with Caribbean flair. Choose anything from brick oven pizzas to fresh salads, open-faced sandwiches, and unique pasta dishes that are cooked to order. House specialties include tamarind barbecued shrimp salad and pizza topped with house-made sausage and apples. ⊠ *37 Main St.* ☎ *340/776–0444* ⊟ *AE, MC, V* ⊘ *Closed Sun. No dinner.*

SPANISH ✕ **Café Amalia.** Tucked into the alleyway of Palm Passage, this open-air
★ **$$$–$$$$** café owned by Antiguan-born Randolph Maynard and his German wife, Helga, serves authentic Spanish cuisine. Try tapas such as mussels in brandy sauce, escargots with mushrooms and herb butter, or Galician-style octopus and baby eels served in a sizzling garlic sauce. Paella is a

house specialty, as is the caramel flan. ⊠ *Palm Passage, 24 Dronnigens Gade* ☎ *340/714–7373* 🗢 *AE, MC, V.*

East End

AMERICAN
😊 **$$–$$$**

✗ **Blue Moon Café.** Watch the serene scene of sailboats floating at anchor while supping; sunsets are especially spectacular here. Enjoy French toast topped with toasted coconut for breakfast, a grilled mahimahi sandwich with black olive–caper mayonnaise at lunch, or red snapper with pecans, bananas, and a coconut rum sauce for dinner. ⊠ *Secret Harbour Beach Resort, Rte. 32, Red Hook* ☎ *340/779–2080* 🗢 *AE, D, MC, V.*

ECLECTIC
$$–$$$$
Fodor'sChoice
★

✗ **Old Stone Farmhouse.** Dine in the splendor of a beautifully restored plantation house. You might try the three-day mango Asian duck or something from the excellent sushi menu. For a truly memorable meal, forget the menu entirely. Chef Brian Katz will note your table's likes and dislikes, then surprise you with a customized six-course meal. That kind of personalized attention makes dining here a delight. Finish with one of the tropical fruit sorbets. ⊠ *Rte. 42, 1 mi (1½ km) west of entrance to Mahogany Run Golf Course, Estate Lovenlund* ☎ *340/777–6277* ⌕ *Reservations essential* 🗢 *AE, MC, V* 𝄐 *Closed Mon.*

$

✗ **Duffy's Love Shack.** If the floating bubbles don't attract you to this zany eatery, the lime-green shutters, loud rock music, and fun-loving waitstaff surely will. It's billed as the "ultimate tropical drink shack," and the bartenders shake up such exotic concoctions as the Love Shack Volcano—a 50-ounce flaming extravaganza. The menu has a selection of burgers, tacos, burritos, and salads. Try the grilled mahimahi taco salad or jerk Caesar wrap. Wednesday night is usually a theme party complete with giveaways. ⊠ *Rte. 32, Red Hook* ☎ *340/779–2080* 🗢 *No credit cards.*

IRISH
😊 **$$–$$$**

✗ **Molly Molone's.** This open-air eatery has a devout following among locals who live and work on boats docked nearby. Traditional Irish dishes include bangers and mash (sausage and mashed potatoes), as well as fresh fish, oversize deli sandwiches, and rich soups and stews. Beware: the iguanas will beg for table scraps—bring your camera. Upstairs, the same owners run A Whale of a Tale, a pricier seafood eatery that also serves freshly made pasta dishes and fine wines. ⊠ *Rte. 32, at American Yacht Harbor, Bldg. D, Red Hook* ☎ *340/775–1270* 🗢 *MC, V.*

ITALIAN
★ **$$$–$$$$**

✗ **Romanos.** Inside this huge, old stucco house is a delightful surprise: a spare yet elegant restaurant serving superb northern Italian cuisine. Try the pastas, either with a classic sauce or a more unique creation such as cream sauce with mushrooms, prosciutto, pine nuts, and Parmesan. ⊠ *Rte. 388, at Coki Point, Estate Frydendal* ☎ *340/775–0045* ⌕ *Reservations essential* 🗢 *MC, V* 𝄐 *Closed Sun. No lunch.*

SEAFOOD
$$–$$$$

✗ **Agave Terrace.** At this open-air restaurant in the Point Pleasant Resort, fresh fish is the specialty, served as steaks or fillets, and the catch of the day is listed on the blackboard. More than a dozen sauces, including teriyaki-mango and lime-ginger, liven up your entrée. If you get lucky on a sportfishing day charter, the chef will cook your catch if you bring the fish in by 3 PM. Come early and have a drink at the Lookout Lounge, which has breathtaking views of the British Virgins. ⊠ *Point*

Pleasant Resort, Rte. 38, Estate Smith Bay ☎ *340/775–4142* ▤ *AE, MC, V* ⊗ *No lunch.*

$$–$$$ ✕ **Off the Hook.** The fish is so fresh here that you may see it coming in from one of the boats tied up at the dock just steps away. For starters, try the crispy conch fritters with sweet-hot banana-chili chutney. Entrées include a rib-sticking fish stew with scallops, shrimp, mahimahi, mussels, conch, and calamari swimming in a coconut curry broth. Steak, poultry, and pasta lovers will also find something to please at this open-air eatery. There's also a children's menu. ⊠ *Rte. 32, Red Hook* ☎ *340/ 775–6350* ▤ *AE, MC, V* ⊗ *No lunch.*

Frenchtown

AMERICAN ✕ **Tickle's Dockside Pub.** Nautical types as well as the local working
♨ **$–$$** crowd come here for casual fare with homey appeal: chicken-fried steak, meat loaf and mashed potatoes, and baby back ribs. Hearty breakfasts feature eggs and pancakes, while lunch is a full array of burgers, salads, sandwiches, and soups. From November through April, the adjacent marina is full of megayachts that make for some great eye candy while you dine. ⊠ *Crown Bay Marina, Rte. 304, Estate Contant* ☎ *340/ 776–1595* ▤ *AE, D, MC, V.*

CARIBBEAN ✕ **Victor's New Hide-Out.** Although it's a little hard to find—it's up the
$$–$$$ hill between the Nisky shopping center and the airport—this landmark restaurant is worth the search. Local food, including steamed fish, marinated pork chops, and local lobster, is offered in a casual, friendly West Indian spot. While you eat, enjoy live local music. ⊠ *Sub Base* ☎ *340/ 776–9379* ▤ *AE, MC, V.*

ECLECTIC ✕ **Craig & Sally's.** In the heart of Frenchtown, culinary wizard Sally Darash
$$–$$$ creates menus with a passionate international flavor using fresh ingre-
Fodor'sChoice dients and a novel approach that makes for a delightful dining experi-
★ ence at this friendly, casual eatery. Sally's constantly changing menu is never the same, which means your favorite dish may not appear again, but then again there's always something new to tantalize your taste buds. Husband Craig maintains a 300-bottle wine list that's received accolades. ⊠ *22 Honduras at Rue Normandie* ☎ *340/777–9949* ▤ *AE, MC, V* ⊗ *Closed Mon. and Tues. No lunch weekends.*

SEAFOOD ✕ **Hook, Line & Sinker.** Anchored right on the breezy Frenchtown water-
♨ **$$** front, adjacent to the pastel-painted boats of the local fishing fleet, this harbor-view eatery serves quality fish dishes. The almond-crust yellow-tail snapper is a house specialty. Spicy jerk-seasoned swordfish and grilled tuna topped with a yummy mango-rum sauce are also good bets. This is one of the few independent restaurants that serves Sunday brunch. ⊠ *2 Honduras, in Frenchtown Mall* ☎ *340/776–9708* ▤ *AE, MC, V.*

Beaches

All 44 St. Thomas beaches are open to the public, although you can reach some of them only by walking through a resort. Hotel guests frequently have access to lounge chairs and floats that are off-limits to nonguests; for this reason you may feel more comfortable at one of the beaches not

26

associated with a resort, such as Magens Bay (which charges an entrance fee to cover beach maintenance) or Coki. Whichever one you choose, remember to remove your valuables from the car and keep them out of sight when you go swimming.

Brewer's Beach. Watch jets land at the Cyril E. King Airport as you dip into the usually calm seas. Rocks at either end of the shoreline, patches of grass poking randomly through the sand, and shady tamarind trees 30 feet from the water give this beach a wild, natural feel. Civilization is here (one or two mobile food vans park on the nearby road). Buy a fried-chicken leg and johnnycake or burgers, chips, and beverages to munch on at the picnic tables. ⊠ *Rte. 30, west of University of the Virgin Islands.*

Fodor'sChoice **Coki Beach.** Funky beach huts selling local foods like meat pates (fried
★ turnovers with a spicy ground-beef filling), picnic tables topped with
☾ umbrellas sporting beverage logos, and a brigade of hair braiders and taxi men give this beach overlooking picturesque Thatch Cay a Coney Island feel. But this is the best place on the island from which to snorkel and scuba dive. Fish, including grunts, snappers, and wrasses, team in schools like an effervescent cloud you can wave your hand through. Ashore, find conveniences like restrooms, changing facilities, rentals for masks, fins, air tanks, and even fish food. ⊠ *Rte. 388, next to Coral World Marine Park.*

Hull Bay. Watch surfers ride the waves here from December to March, when huge swells roll in from north Atlantic storms. The rest of the year, tranquility prevails. Local fishermen keep their runabouts anchored here. For a small fee, they will take you on a short tour out to Tropaco Point, where you can look across to the uninhabited isle of Hans Lollick. Enjoy hot pizza, barbecue ribs, and a game of darts or pool at the Hull Bay Hideaway bar and restaurant. ⊠ *Rte. 37, at end of road on north side.*

Fodor'sChoice **Magens Bay.** Deeded to the island as a public park, this ½-mi (¾-km)
★ heart-shape stretch of white sand is considered one of the most beauti-
☾ ful in the world. The bottom of the bay here is flat and sandy, so this is a place for sunning and swimming rather than snorkeling. On weekends and holidays the sounds of music from groups partying under the sheds fill the air. There's a bar, snack bar, water-sports-equipment rental kiosk, and beachwear boutique; bathhouses with toilets, changing rooms, and saltwater showers are also here. Sunfish and paddleboats are the most popular rentals. East of the beach is Udder Delight, a one-room shop at St. Thomas Dairies that serves a Virgin Islands tradition—a milk shake with a splash of Cruzan rum. Kids can enjoy virgin versions, which have a touch of soursop, mango, or banana flavoring. If you arrive between 8 AM and 5 PM, you have to pay an entrance fee of $3 per person, $1 per vehicle, and 25¢ per child under age 12. ⊠ *Rte. 35, at end of road on north side of island.*

★ **Morningstar Beach.** Nature and nurture combine at this ¼-mi-long (½-km) beach between Marriott Frenchman's Reef and Morning Star Beach Resorts where amenities range from water-sports rentals to beachside bar service. A concession rents floating mats, snorkeling equipment, sailboards, Sunfish, and Jet Skis. Swimming is excellent; there are good-size rolling waves year-round, but do watch the undertow. If you're feeling lazy, rent a lounge chair with umbrella and order a libation from one of two full-service beach bars. At 7 AM and again at 5 PM, watch the mega cruise ships glide majestically out to sea from the Charlotte Amalie harbor. ⊠ *Rte. 315, 2 mi (3 km) southeast of Charlotte Amalie, past Havensight Mall and cruise-ship dock.*

★ **Sapphire Beach.** A steady breeze makes this beach a boardsailor's Mecca. The swimming is great, as is the snorkeling, especially at the reef near Pettyklip Point. Beach volleyball is big here on the weekends. There's also a restaurant, bar, and water-sports rentals at Sapphire Beach Resort & Marina. ⊠ *Rte. 38, Sapphire Bay.*

Secret Harbour. Placid waters make it an easy job to stroke your way out to a swim platform offshore from the Secret Harbour Beach Resort & Villas. Nearby reefs give snorkelers a natural show. There's a bar and restaurant, as well as a dive shop. ⊠ *Rte. 32, Red Hook.*

★ **Vessup Beach.** This wild, undeveloped beach is lined with sea-grape trees and century plants, and it's close to Red Hook harbor, so you can watch the ferries depart. Calm waters are excellent for swimming. West Indies Windsurfing is here, so you can rent Windsurfers, kayaks, and other water toys. There are no restroom or changing facilities. It's popular with locals on weekends. ⊠ *Off Rte. 322, Vessup Bay.*

Sports & the Outdoors

AIR TOURS **Air Center Helicopters** (⊠ Waterfront, Charlotte Amalie, St. Thomas ☎ 340/775–7335 or 800/619–0013 ⊕ www.aircenterhelicopters.com), on the Charlotte Amalie waterfront (next to Tortola Wharf), offers two tours, both pretty pricey: a 17-minute tour of St. Thomas and St. John priced at $256 (for up to four passengers) per trip, and a 25-minute tour that includes St. Thomas, St. John, and Jost Van Dyke priced at $348 (for up to four passengers) per trip. If you can afford the splurge, it's a nice ride, but in truth, you can see most of the aerial sights from Mountain Top or Paradise Point, and there's no place you can't reach easily by car or boat.

BOATING & SAILING Calm seas, crystal waters, and nearby islands (perfect for picnicking, snorkeling, and exploring) make St. Thomas a favorite jumping-off spot for day- or weeklong sails or powerboat adventures. With more than 100 vessels from which to choose, St. Thomas is the charter-boat center of the U.S. Virgin Islands. You can go through a broker to book a sailing vessel with a crew or contact a charter company directly. Crewed charters start at $1,500 per person per week, while bareboat charters can start at $1,200 per person for a 50- to 55-foot sailboat (not including provisioning), which can comfortably accommodate up to six people. If you want to rent your own boat, hire a captain. Most local captains are excellent tour guides.

Single-day charters are also a possibility. You can hire smaller power boats for the day, including the services of a captain if you wish to have someone take you on a guided snorkel trip around the islands.

Island Yachts (⊠ 6100 Red Hook Quarter, 18B, Red Hook ☎ 340/775–6666 or 800/524–2019 ⊕ www.iyc.vi) offers sail- or powerboats with

26

or without crews. Luxury is the word at **Magic Moments** (✉ American Yacht Harbor, Red Hook ☎ 340/775–5066 ⊕ www.yachtmagicmoments. com), where the crew of a 45-foot Sea Ray offers a pampered island-hopping snorkeling cruise that includes icy-cold eucalyptus-infused washcloths to freshen up and a gourmet wine and lobster lunch. **Stewart Yacht Charters** (✉ 6501 Red Hook Plaza, Suite 20, Red Hook ☎ 340/775–1358 or 800/432–6118 ⊕ www.stewartyachtcharters.com) is run by longtime sailor Ellen Stewart, who is an expert at matching clients with yachts for weeklong crewed charter holidays. Bareboat sail and powerboats, including a selection of stable trawlers, are available at **VIP Yacht Charters** (✉ South off Rte. 32, Estate Frydenhoj ☎ 340/774–9224 or 866/847–9224 ⊕ www.vipyachts.com), at Compass Point Marina.

Awesome Powerboat Rentals (✉ 6100 Red Hook Quarter, Red Hook ☎ 340/775–0860 ⊕ www.powerboatrentalsvi.com), at "P" dock next to the Off the Hook restaurant, offers 22-foot to 26-foot twin-engine catamarans for day charters. Rates range from $185 to $375 for half- or full-day. A captain can be hired, if desired, for $75 to $100 for half- or full-day. **Mangrove Adventures** (✉ Rte. 32, Estate Nadir ☎ 340/779–2155 ⊕ www.viecotours.com) offers inflatable boat rentals for $60 per day to explore and snorkel the east end of St. Thomas. **Nauti Nymph** (✉ 6501 Red Hook Plaza, Suite 201, Red Hook ☎☎ 340/775–5066 ☎ 800/734–7345 ⊕ www.st-thomas.com/nautinymph) has a large selection of 25-foot to 29-foot powerboats for rent. Rates vary from $345 to $540 a day, including snorkel gear, water skis, and outriggers but not including fuel. You can hire a captain for $115 more.

CYCLING **Water Island Adventures** (✉ Water Island ☎ 340/714–2186 or 340/775–
Fodor'sChoice 5770 ⊕ www.waterislandadventures.com) offers a cycling adventure to
★ the USVI's "newest" Virgin. You take a ferry ride from the West Indian Company dock near Havensight Mall to Water Island before jumping on a Cannondale mountain bike for a 90-minute tour over rolling hills on dirt and paved roads. Explore the remains of the Sea Cliff Hotel, the inspiration for Herman Wouk's book *Don't Stop the Carnival,* and take a cooling swim at beautiful Honeymoon Beach. Helmets, water, a guide, juices, and ferry fare are included in the $60 cost.

DIVING & Popular dive sites include such wrecks as the Cartanser Sr., a beautifully
SNORKELING encrusted World War II cargo ship sitting in 35 feet of water, and the General Rogers, a Coast Guard cutter with a gigantic resident barracuda resting at 65 feet. Reef dives offer hidden caves and archways at **Cow and Calf Rocks,** coral-covered pinnacles at **Frenchcap,** and tunnels where you can explore undersea from the Caribbean to the Atlantic at **Thatch Cay, Grass Cay,** and **Congo Cay.** Many resorts and charter yachts offer dive packages. A one-tank dive starts at $60; two-tank dives are $80 or more. Call the USVI Department of Tourism to obtain a free eight-page guide to Virgin Islands dive sites. There are plenty of snorkeling possibilities too.

Admiralty Dive Center (✉ Holiday Inn St. Thomas, Waterfront Hwy., Charlotte Amalie ☎ 340/777–9802 or 888/900–3483 ⊕ www.admiraltydive. com) provides boat dives, rental equipment, and a retail store. Four-tank to 12-tank packages are available if you want to dive over several days. **Aqua Adventures** (⊠ Crown Bay Marina, Rte. 304, Charlotte Amalie ☎ 340/715–0348 ⊕ www.bobusvi.com) offers an alternative to traditional diving in the form of an underwater motor scooter called BOB, or Breathing Observation Bubble. A half-day tour, including snorkel equipment, rum punch, and towels, is $99 per person. **Blue Island Divers** (⊠ Crown Bay Marina, Rte. 304, Estate Contant ☎ 340/774–2001 ⊕ www.blueislanddivers.com) is a full-service dive shop that offers both day and night dives to wrecks and reefs. **Chris Sawyer Diving Center** (☎ 340/775–7320 or 877/929–3483 ⊕ www.sawyerdive.vi) is a PADI five-star outfit that specializes in dives to the 310-foot-long *Rhone,* in the British Virgin Islands. Hotel-dive packages are offered through the Wyndham Sugar Bay Beach Club & Resort. **Coki Beach Dive Club** (⊠ Rte. 388, at Coki Point, Estate Frydendal ☎ 340/775–4220 ⊕ www.cokidive.com) is a PADI Gold Palm outfit run by avid diver Peter Jackson in the fish-filled reefs off Coki Beach. Snorkel and dive tours are available, as are classes from beginner to underwater photography. **Snuba of St. Thomas** (⊠ Rte. 388, at Coki Point, Estate Smith Bay ☎ 340/693–8063 ⊕ www.visnuba.com) offers something for nondivers, a cross between snorkeling and scuba diving: a 20-foot air hose connects you to the surface. The cost is $59. Children must be eight or older to participate. **Underwater Safaris** (⊠ Havensight Mall, Bldg. VI, Rte. 30, Charlotte Amalie ☎ 340/774–1350 ⊕ www.scubadivevi.com) is another PADI five-star center that offers boat dives to the reefs around Buck Island and nearby offshore wrecks.

FISHING ★ Fishing here is synonymous with blue marlin angling—especially from June through October. Four 1,000-pound-plus blues, including three world records, have been caught on the famous North Drop, about 20 mi (32 km) north of St. Thomas. A day charter for marlin with up to six anglers costs $1,300 for the day. If you're not into marlin fishing, try hooking up sailfish in the winter, dolphin (the fish, not the mammal; aka mahimahi) come spring, and wahoo in the fall. Inshore trips for two to four hours range in cost from $200 to $550, respectively. To really find the trip that will best suit you, walk down the docks at either American Yacht Harbor or Sapphire Beach Marina in the late afternoon and chat with the captains and crews.

For marlin, Captain Red Bailey's Abigail III (☎ 340/775–6024 ⊕ www.sportfishvi.com) operates out of the Sapphire Beach Resort & Marina. The **Charter Boat Center** (⊠ 6300 Red Hook Plaza, Red Hook ☎ 340/775–7990 ⊕ www.charterboat.vi) is a major source for sportfishing charters, both marlin and inshore. For inshore trips, **Peanut Gallery Charters** (⊠ Crown Bay Marina, Rte. 304, Estate Contant ☎ 340/775–5274 ⊕ www.fishingstthomas.com) offers trips on its 18-foot *Dauntless* or 28-foot custom sportfishing catamaran. Capt. Eddie Morrison, aboard the 45-foot Viking Marlin Prince (⊠ American Yacht Harbor, Red Hook ☎ 340/693–5929 ⊕ www.marlinprince.com), is one of the most experienced charter operators in St. Thomas and specializes in fly-fishing for blue marlin. Captain Mark Lamborn, who pilots the Prowler (⊠ American Yacht Harbor, Red Hook ☎ 340/779–2515), offers marlin and game-fishing trips year-round.

GOLF The **Mahogany Run Golf Course** (✉ Rte. 42, Estate Lovenlund ☎ 340/
Fodor'sChoice 777–6006 or 800/253–7103 ⊕ www.mahoganyrungolf.com) attracts
★ golfers for its spectacular view of the British Virgin Islands and the challenging 3-hole Devil's Triangle on this Tom and George Fazio–designed
par-70, 18-hole course. Greens and half-cart fees for 18 holes are $130.
There's a fully stocked pro shop, snack bar, and open-air club house.
The course is open daily, and there are frequently informal weekend tournaments. It's the only course on St. Thomas.

PARASAILING The waters are so clear around St. Thomas that the outlines of coral
reefs are visible from high in the sky. Parasailers sit in a harness attached
to a parachute that lifts them off a boat deck until they're sailing up in
the air. Parasailing trips average a 10-minute ride in the sky that costs
$65 per person. Friends who want to ride along pay $15 for the boat
trip. **Caribbean Watersports & Tours** (✉ 6501 Red Hook Plaza, Red Hook
☎ 340/775–9360) makes parasailing pickups from 10 locations around
the island, including many major beachfront resorts. It also rents Jet Skis,
kayaks, and floating battery-power chairs.

SEA EXCURSIONS Landlubbers and seafarers alike will enjoy the wind in their hair and
salt spray in the air while exploring the waters surrounding St. Thomas.
Several businesses can book you on a snorkel-and-sail to a deserted cay
for the day that costs on average $85 to $125 per person; a luxury daylong motor-yacht cruise complete with gourmet lunch for $325 or more
per person; or an excursion over to the British Virgin Islands starting
at $100 per person plus $20 custom's fees.

For a soup-to-nuts choice of sea tours, contact the **Adventure Center**
(✉ Marriott's Frenchman's Reef Hotel, Rte. 315, Estate Bakkeroe
☎ 340/774–2992 or 866/868–7784 ⊕ www.adventurecenters.net). The
Charter Boat Center (✉ 6300 Red Hook Plaza, Red Hook ☎ 340/775–
7990 ⊕ www.charterboat.vi) specializes in day trips to the British Virgin Islands and day- or weeklong sailing charters. The party boat Kon
Tiki (✉ Gregorie Channel East Dock, Frenchtown ☎ 340/775–5055) is
a kick. Put your sophistication aside, climb on this big palm-thatched
raft, and dip into bottomless barrels of rum punch along with a couple
hundred of your soon-to-be closest friends. Dance to the steel-drum band,
sun on the roof (watch out: you'll fry), and join the limbo dancing on
the way home from an afternoon of swimming and beachcombing at
Honeymoon Beach on Water Island. This popular 3½-hour afternoon
excursion costs $32 for adults, $18 for children under 13 (although few
come on this booze cruise). **Limnos Charters** (✉ Compass Point Marina,
Rte. 32, Estate Frydenhoj ☎ 340/775–3203 ⊕ www.limnoscharters.com)
offers one of the most popular British Virgin Islands day trips, complete
with lunch, open bar, and snorkel gear. Jimmy Loveland at **Treasure Isle
Cruises** (✉ Rte. 32, Box 6616, Estate Nadir ☎ 340/775–9500 ⊕ www.
treasureislecruises.com) can set you up with everything from a half-day
sail to a seven-day U.S. and British Virgin Islands trip that combines sailing with accommodations and sightseeing trips onshore.

SEA KAYAKING Fish dart, birds sing, and iguanas lounge on the limbs of dense mangroves deep within a marine sanctuary on St. Thomas's southeast shore.

Learn about the natural history here in a guided kayak-snorkel tour to Patricia Cay or via an inflatable boat tour to Cas Cay for snorkeling and hiking. Both are 2½ hours long. The cost is $60 per person. **Mangrove Adventures** (⊠ Rte. 32, Estate Nadir ☎ 340/779–2155 ⊕ www.viecotours.com) rents its two-person sit-atop ocean kayaks and inflatable boats for self-guided exploring. In addition, many resorts on St. Thomas's eastern end also rent kayaks.

SIGHTSEEING TOURS **Accessible Adventures** (☎ 340/775–2346 ⊕ www.accessvi.com) provides a 2- to 2½-hour island tour aboard a special trolley that's especially suitable for those in wheelchairs. Tours include major sights like Magens Bay and Mountain Top and provide a stop for shopping and refreshments. The cost is $32 per person. **Tropic Tours** (☎ 340/774–1855 or 800/524–4334 ⊕ www.tropictours-virginislands.com) offers half-day shopping and sightseeing tours of St. Thomas by bus six days a week. The cost is $30 per person. The company also has a full-day ferry tour to St. John that includes snorkeling and lunch. The cost is $85 per person. **V. I. Taxi Association St. Thomas City-Island Tour** (☎ 340/774–4550) gives a two-hour $30 tour for two people in an open-air safari bus or enclosed van; aimed at cruise-ship passengers, this tour includes stops at Drake's Seat and Mountain Top. For just a bit more ($35 to $40 for two) you can hire a taxi and ask the driver to take the opposite route to avoid the crowds. But do see Mountain Top: the view is wonderful.

SUBMARINING Dive 90 feet under the sea to one of St. Thomas's most beautiful reefs without getting wet. **Atlantis Adventures** (⊠ Havensight Mall, Bldg. VI, Charlotte Amalie ☎ 340/776–5650 ⊕ www.atlantisadventures.com) has a 46-passenger submarine that takes you to a watery world teeming with brightly colored fish, vibrant sea fans, and an occasional shark. A guide narrates the one-hour underwater journey, while a diver makes a mid-tour appearance for a fish-feeding show. The cost is $89. No children shorter than 36 inches are allowed.

WALKING TOURS The *St. Thomas–St. John Vacation Handbook,* available free at hotels and tourist centers, has an excellent self-guided walking tour of Charlotte Amalie on St. Thomas.

Blackbeard's Castle (☎ 340/776–1234 or 340/776–1829 ⊕ www.blackbeardscastle.com) conducts a 45-minute to one-hour historic walking tour that starts at Blackbeard's Castle, then heads downhill to Villa Notman, Haagensen House, and the 99-steps. The cost is $35 per person and includes a tour of Haagensen House and rum punch.

Cindy Born (☎ 340/714–1672 ⊕ www.st-thomas.com/walktour) conducts a two-hour historical walking tour of Charlotte Amalie at 9:30 each weekday that starts at Emancipation Garden. The tour covers all the in-town sights and can be narrated in Spanish, Danish, German, and Japanese as well as in English. The cost is $20 per person; wear a hat and comfortable walking shoes. The tour is offered again at 12:30, but you must make a reservation.

The **St. Thomas Historical Trust** (☎ 340/774–5541 ⊕ www.stthomashistoricaltrust.org) has published a self-guided tour of the his-

26

toric district; it's available in book and souvenir shops for $1.95. Trust members also conduct a two-hour guided historic walking tour by reservation only. Call for more information and to make a reservation.

WINDSURFING Expect some spills, anticipate the thrills, and try your luck clipping through the seas. Most beachfront resorts rent Windsurfers and offer one-hour lessons for about $45 to $60. One of the island's best-known independent windsurfing companies is **West Indies Windsurfing** (✉ Vessup Beach, No. 9, Estate Nazareth ☎ 340/775–6530). Owner John Phillips is the board buff who introduced the sport of kite boarding to the USVI; it entails using a kite to lift a boardsailor off the water for an airborne ride. A two-hour, land-based kite-boarding lesson costs $90, while a two-hour lesson with on-the-water time is $175. Go-fast WindRider 17 trimarans are the new water toy here. They rent for $75 an hour or $250 a day.

Shopping

FodorsChoice St. Thomas lives up to its billing as a duty-free shopping destination. ★ Even if shopping isn't your idea of how to spend a vacation, you still may want to slip in on a quiet day (check the cruise-ship listings—Monday and Sunday are usually the least crowded) to browse. Among the best buys are liquor, linens, china, crystal (most stores will ship), and jewelry. The amount of jewelry available makes this one of the few items for which comparison shopping is worth the effort. Local crafts include shell jewelry, carved calabash bowls, straw brooms, woven baskets, fragrances, and dolls. Creations by local doll maker Gwendolyn Harley—like her costumed West Indian market woman—have been little goodwill ambassadors, bought by visitors from as far away as Asia. Spice mixes, hot sauces, and tropical jams and jellies are other native products.

On St. Thomas, stores on Main Street in Charlotte Amalie are open weekdays and Saturday 9 to 5. The hours of the shops in the Havensight Mall (next to the cruise-ships dock) are the same, though occasionally some stay open until 9 on Friday, depending on how many cruise ships are at the dock. You may also find some shops open on Sunday if cruise ships are in port. Hotel shops are usually open evenings, as well.

There's no sales tax in the USVI, and you can take advantage of the $1,200 duty-free allowance per family member (remember to save your receipts). Although you can find the occasional salesclerk who will make a deal, bartering isn't the norm.

Areas & Malls

The prime shopping area in **Charlotte Amalie** is between Post Office and Market squares; it consists of two parallel streets that run east–west (Waterfront Highway and Main Street) and the alleyways that connect them. Particularly attractive are the historic **A. H. Riise Alley, Royal Dane Mall, Palm Passage,** and pastel-painted **International Plaza.**

Vendors Plaza, on the waterfront side of Emancipation Gardens in Charlotte Amalie, is a central location for vendors selling handmade ear-

Made in St. Thomas

DATE PALM BROOMS, frangipani-scented perfume, historically clad dolls, sun-scorched hot sauces, aromatic mango candles: these are just a few of the handicrafts made in St. Thomas.

Justin Todman, aka the Broom Man, keeps the dying art of broom-making alive. It's a skill he learned at the age of six from his father. From the fronds of the date palm, Todman delicately cuts, strips, and dries the leaves, a process that can take up to a week. Then he creatively weaves the leaves into distinctively shaped brooms with birch-berry wood for handles. His styles? There are feather brooms, cane brooms, multicolor yarn brooms, tiny brooms to fit into a child's hand, and tall long-handled brooms to reach cobwebs on the ceiling. Some customers buy Todman's brooms—sold at the Native Arts & Crafts Cooperative—not for cleaning but rather for celebrating their nuptials. It's an old African custom for the bride and groom to jump over a horizontally laid broom to start their new life.

Gail Garrison puts the essence of local flowers, fruits, and leaves into perfumes, powders, and body splashes. Her Island Fragrances line includes frangipani-, white-ginger-, and jasmine-scented perfumes; aromatic mango, lime, and coconut body splashes; and bay rum aftershave for men. Garrison compounds, mixes, and bottles the products herself in second-floor offices on Charlotte Amalie's Main Street. You can buy the products in the Tropicana Perfume Shop.

Gwendolyn Harley preserves Virgin Islands culture in the personalities of her hand-sewn, softly sculptured historic dolls for sale at the Native Arts & Crafts Cooperative. There are quadrille dancers clad in long, colorful skirts; French women with their neat peaked bonnets; and farmers sporting hand-woven straw hats. Each one-of-kind design is named using the last three letters of Harley's first name; the dolls have names like Joycelyn, Vitalyn, and Iselyn. From her adoption log, she knows her dolls have traveled as far as Asia.

Cheryl Miller cooks up ingredients like sun-sweetened papayas, fiery Scotch bonnet peppers, and aromatic basil leaves into the jams, jellies, and hot sauces she sells under her Cheryl's Taste of Paradise line. Five of Miller's products—Caribbean Mustango Sauce, Caribbean Sunburn, Mango Momma Jam, Mango Chutney, and Hot Green Pepper Jelly—have won awards at the National Fiery Foods Show in Albuquerque, New Mexico. Miller makes her products in a professional kitchen in the Compass Point Marina and sells them from a storefront there as well as from Cost-U-Less and the Native Arts & Crafts Cooperative.

Jason Budsan traps the tropically enticing aromas of the islands into sumptuously scented candles he sells at his Tillett Gardens workshop and at stores throughout the island such as the Native Arts & Crafts Cooperative. Among the rich scents are Ripe Mango, Night Jasmine, Lime in de Coconut, Frenchie Connection (with vanilla and lavender), and Ripe Pineapple. Some candles, such as the Ripe Mango, are uniquely set in beautiful tonna shells or wrapped in aromatic sea-grape leaves.

26

rings, necklaces, and bracelets; straw baskets and handbags; T-shirts; fabrics; African artifacts; and local fruits. Look for the many brightly colored umbrellas.

West of Charlotte Amalie, the pink-stucco **Nisky Center,** on Harwood Highway about ½ mi (¾ km) east of the airport, is more of a hometown shopping center than a tourist area, but there's a bank, clothing store, record shop, and Radio Shack.

Havensight Mall, next to the cruise-ship dock, may not be as charming as downtown Charlotte Amalie, but it does have more than 60 shops. It also has an excellent bookstore, a bank, a pharmacy, a gourmet grocery, and smaller branches of many downtown stores. The shops at **Port of Sale,** which adjoins the Havensight Mall (its buildings are pink instead of the brown of the Havensight shops), sell discount goods.

East of Charlotte Amalie on Route 38, **Tillett Gardens** is an oasis of artistic endeavor across from the Tutu Park Shopping Mall. The late Jim and Rhoda Tillett converted this old Danish farm into an artists' retreat in 1959. Today you can watch artisans produce silk-screen fabrics, candles, watercolors, jewelry, and other handicrafts. Something special is often happening in the gardens as well: the Classics in the Gardens program is a classical music series presented under the stars, Arts Alive is an annual arts and crafts fair held in November, and the Pistarckle Theater holds its performances here. **Tutu Park Shopping Mall,** across from Tillett Gardens, is the island's one and only enclosed mall. More than 50 stores and a food court are anchored by Kmart and Plaza Extra grocery store. Archaeologists have discovered evidence that Arawak Indians once lived near the grounds.

Red Hook has **American Yacht Harbor,** a waterfront shopping area with a dive shop, a tackle store, clothing and jewelry boutiques, a bar, and a few restaurants.

Don't forget **St. John.** A ferry ride (an hour from Charlotte Amalie or 20 minutes from Red Hook) will take you to the charming shops of **Mongoose Junction** and **Wharfside Village,** which specialize in unusual, often island-made articles.

Specialty Items

ART **Camille Pissarro Art Gallery.** This second-floor gallery, in the birthplace of St. Thomas's famous artist, offers a fine collection of original paintings and prints by local and regional artists. ✉ *14 Main St., Charlotte Amalie* ☎ *340/774–4621.*

The Color of Joy. Find locally made arts and crafts here, including pottery, batik, hand-painted linen and cotton clothing, glass plates and ornaments, and watercolors by owner Corinne Van Rensselaer. There are also original prints by many local artists. ✉ *Rte. 317, about 100 yards west of Ritz-Carlton, Red Hook* ☎ *340/775–4020.*

Gallery St. Thomas. Fine art and collectibles are found in this charming gallery, including paintings, wood sculpture, glass, and jewelry that are from or inspired by the Virgin Islands. ✉ *1 Main St., 2nd fl., Charlotte Amalie* ☎ *340/777–6363.*

Kilnworks Pottery & Caribbean Art Gallery. A 12-foot statue of a green iguana marks the entrance to this pottery paradise. Owner Peggy Seiwert is best known for her lizard collection of ceramic cups, bowls, and platters. There are also pottery pieces by other local artists, as well as paintings and gift items. ⊠ *Rte. 38, across from the Toad & Tart English Pub, Estate Smith Bay* ☎ *340/775–3979.*

Mango Tango. Works by popular local artists—originals, prints, and note cards—are displayed (there's a one-person show at least one weekend a month) and sold here. There's also the island's largest humidor and a brand-name cigar gallery. ⊠ *Al Cohen's Plaza, ½ mi (¾ km) east of Charlotte Amalie* ☎ *340/777–3060.*

BOOKS **Dockside Bookshop.** This place is packed with books for children, travelers, cooks, and historians, as well as a good selection of paperback mysteries, best-sellers, art books, calendars, and prints. It also carries a selection of books written in and about the Caribbean and the Virgin Islands. ⊠ *Havensight Mall, Bldg. VI, Rte. 30, Charlotte Amalie* ☎ *340/774–4937.*

CAMERAS & **Boolchand's.** Brand-name cameras, audio and video equipment, and binoculars are sold here. ⊠ *31 Main St., Charlotte Amalie* ☎ *340/776–0794* ⊠ *Havensight Mall, Bldg. II, Rte. 30, Charlotte Amalie* ☎ *340/776–0302.*
ELECTRONICS

Royal Caribbean. Shop here for cameras, camcorders, stereos, watches, and clocks. ⊠ *23 Main St., Charlotte Amalie* ☎ *340/776–5449* ⊠ *33 Main St., Charlotte Amalie* ☎ *340/776–4110* ⊠ *Havensight Mall, Bldg. I, Rte. 30, Charlotte Amalie* ☎ *340/776–8890.*

CHINA & CRYSTAL **Little Switzerland.** All of this establishment's shops carry crystal from Baccarat, Waterford, and Orrefors; and china from Kosta Boda, Rosenthal, and Wedgwood, among others. There's also an assortment of Swarovski cut-crystal animals, gemstone globes, and many other affordable collectibles. It also does a booming mail-order business; ask for a catalog. ⊠ *5 Dronningens Gade, across from Emancipation Garden, Charlotte Amalie* ☎ *340/776–2010* ⊠ *3B Main St., Charlotte Amalie* ☎ *340/776–2010* ⊠ *Havensight Mall, Bldg. II, Rte. 30, Charlotte Amalie* ☎ *340/776–2198.*

Scandinavian Center. The best of Scandinavia is here, including Royal Copenhagen, Georg Jensen, Kosta Boda, and Orrefors. Owners Soøren and Grace Blak make regular buying trips to northern Europe and are a great source of information on crystal. Online ordering is available if you want to add to your collection once home. ⊠ *Havensight Mall, Bldg. III, Rte. 30, Charlotte Amalie* ☎ *340/776–5030 or 800/524–2063.*

CLOTHING **Fresh Produce.** You won't find lime-green mangoes, peachy-pink guavas, or sunny-yellow bananas in this store. But you will find these fun, casual colors in the Fresh Produce clothing line. This is one of only 16 stores to stock 100% of this California-created, tropical-feel line of apparel for women. Find dresses, shirts, slacks, and skirts in small to plus sizes as well as accessories such as bags and hats. ⊠ *Riise's Alley, Charlotte Amalie* ☎ *340/774–0807.*

Local Color. Men, women, and children will find something to choose from among brand-name wear like Jams World, Fresh Produce, and

26

Urban Safari. There's also St. John artist Sloop Jones's colorful, hand-painted island designs on cool dresses, T-shirts, and sweaters. Find tropically oriented accessories like big-brim straw hats, bold-color bags, and casual jewelry. ⊠ *Royal Dane Mall, at Waterfront, Charlotte Amalie* ☎ *340/774–2280.*

Nicole Miller. The New York designer has created an exclusive motif for the USVI: a map of the islands, a cruise ship, and a tropical sunset. Find this print, and Miller's full line of other designs, on ties, scarves, boxer shorts, sarongs, and dresses. ⊠ *24 Main St., at Palm Passage, Charlotte Amalie* ☎ *340/774–8286.*

Tommy Hilfiger Boutique. Stop by this shop for classic American jeans and sportswear, as well as trendy bags, belts, ties, socks, caps, and wallets. ⊠ *Waterfront Hwy. at Trompeter Gade, Charlotte Amalie* ☎ *340/ 777–1189.*

FOODSTUFFS **Cost-U-Less.** The Caribbean equivalent of Costco and Sam's Club sells everything from soup to nuts, but in giant sizes and case lots. The meat-and-seafood department, however, has smaller, family-size portions. ⊠ *Rte. 38, ¼ mi (½ km) west of Rte. 39 intersection, Estate Donoe* ☎ *340/777–3588.*

Food Center. Fresh produce, meats, and seafood, plus an on-site bakery and deli with hot-and-cold prepared foods, are the draw here, especially for those renting villas, condos, or charter boats in the East End area. ⊠ *Rte. 32, Estate Frydenhoj* ☎ *340/777–8806.*

Fruit Bowl. For fresh fruits and vegetables, this is the best place on the island to go. ⊠ *Wheatley Center, Rtes. 38 and 313 intersection, Charlotte Amalie* ☎ *340/774–8565.*

Gourmet Gallery. Visiting millionaires buy their caviar here. There's also an excellent and reasonably priced wine selection, as well as specialty ingredients for everything from tacos to curries to chow mein. A full-service deli offers imported meats, cheeses, and in-store prepared foods that are perfect for a gourmet picnic. ⊠ *Crown Bay Marina, Rte. 304, Estate Contant* ☎ *340/776–8555* ⊠ *Havensight Mall, Bldg. VI, Rte. 30, Charlotte Amalie* ☎ *340/774–4948.*

Marina Market. You won't find better fresh meat or seafood anywhere on the island. ⊠ *Rte. 32, across from Red Hook ferry, Red Hook* ☎ *340/779–2411.*

Plaza Extra. This large U.S.-style supermarket has everything you need from produce to meat, including fresh seafood, an excellent deli, and a bakery. There's a liquor department, too. ⊠ *Tutu Park Shopping Mall, Rte. 38, Estate Tutu* ☎ *340/775–5646.*

PriceSmart. Everything from electronics to housewares is found in this warehouse-size store. The meat, poultry, and seafood departments are especially popular. A small café in front sells pizzas, hot dogs, and the cheapest bottled water on the island–just 75¢ a pop. ⊠ *Rte. 38, west of Fort Mylner, Estate Tutu* ☎ *340/777–3430.*

Pueblo Supermarket. This Caribbean chain carries stateside brands of most products—but at higher prices because of shipping costs to the islands. ⊠ *Sub Base, ½ mi (¾ km) east of Crown Bay Marina, Estate Contant* ☎ *340/774–4200* ⊠ *Rte. 30, 1 mi (1½ km) north of Havensight Mall, Estate Thomas* ☎ *340/774–2695.*

HANDICRAFTS **Caribbean Marketplace.** This is a great place to buy handicrafts from the Caribbean and elsewhere. Also look for Sunny Caribee spices, soaps, coffee, and teas from Tortola, and coffee from Trinidad. ⊠ *Havensight Mall, Rte. 30, Charlotte Amalie* ☎ *340/776–5400.*

Down Island Traders. These traders deal in hand-painted calabash bowls; finely printed Caribbean note cards; jams, jellies, spices, hot sauces, and herbs; teas made of lemongrass, passion fruit, and mango; coffee from Jamaica; and handicrafts from throughout the Caribbean. ⊠ *Waterfront Hwy. at Post Office Alley, Charlotte Amalie* ☎ *340/776–4641.*

Native Arts & Crafts Cooperative. More than 40 local artists—including schoolchildren, senior citizens, and people with disabilities—create the handcrafted items for sale here: African-style jewelry, quilts, calabash bowls, dolls, carved-wood figures, woven baskets, straw brooms, note cards, and cookbooks. ⊠ *Tolbod Gade, across from Emancipation Garden, Charlotte Amalie* ☎ *340/777–1153.*

JEWELRY **Amsterdam Sauer.** Many fine one-of-a-kind designs are displayed at this jeweler's three locations. The Imperial Topaz Collection at the Main Street store is a stunner. ⊠ *1 Main St., Charlotte Amalie* ☎ *340/774–2222* ⊠ *Havensight Mall, Rte. 30, Charlotte Amalie* ☎ *340/776–3828* ⊠ *Ritz-Carlton, Rte. 317, Estate Great Bay* ☎ *340/779–2308.*

Cardow Jewelry. A chain bar—with gold in several lengths, widths, sizes, and styles—awaits you here, along with diamonds, emeralds, and other precious gems. You're guaranteed 40% to 60% savings off U.S. retail prices or your money will be refunded within 30 days of purchase. ⊠ *33 Main St., Charlotte Amalie* ☎ *340/776–1140* ⊠ *Havensight Mall, Bldg. I, Rte. 30, Charlotte Amalie* ☎ *340/774–0530 or 340/774–5905* ⊠ *Marriott Frenchman's Reef Resort, Rte. 315, Estate Bakkeroe* ☎ *340/774–0434.*

Colombian Emeralds. Well known in the Caribbean, this store offers set and unset emeralds as well as gems of every description. The watch boutique carries upscale brands like Ebel, Tissot, and Jaeger LeCoultre. ⊠ *30 Main St., Charlotte Amalie* ☎ *340/777–5400* ⊠ *Waterfront at A. H. Riise Mall, Charlotte Amalie* ☎ *340/774–1033* ⊠ *Havensight Mall, Bldg. V, Rte. 30, Charlotte Amalie* ☎ *340/774–2442.*

Diamonds International. Choose a diamond, emerald, or tanzanite gem and a mounting, and you can have your dream ring set in an hour. Famous for having the largest inventory of diamonds on the island, this shop welcomes trade-ins, has a U.S. service center, and offers free diamond earrings with every purchase. ⊠ *31 Main St., Charlotte Amalie* ☎ *340/774–3707* ⊠ *3 Drakes Passage, Charlotte Amalie* ☎ *340/775–2010* ⊠ *7AB Drakes Passage, Charlotte Amalie* ☎ *340/774–1516* ⊠ *Havensight Mall, Bldg. II, Rte. 30, Charlotte Amalie* ☎ *340/776–0040* ⊠ *Wyndham Sugar Bay Beach Club & Resort, Rte. 38, Estate Smith Bay* ☎ *340/714–3248.*

H. Stern Jewelers. The World Collection of jewels set in modern, fashionable designs and an exclusive sapphire watch have earned this Brazilian jeweler a stellar name. ⊠ *8 Main St., Charlotte Amalie* ☎ *340/776–1939* ⊠ *Havensight Mall, Bldg. II, Rte. 30, Charlotte Amalie* ☎ *340/776–1223* ⊠ *Marriott Frenchman's Reef Resort, Rte. 315, Estate Bakkeroe* ☎ *340/776–3550.*

26

Jewels. Name-brand jewelry and watches are in abundance here. Designer jewelry lines include David Yurman, Bulgari, Chopard, and Penny Preville. The selection of watches is extensive, with brand names including Jaeger le Coultre, Tag Heuer, Breitling, Movado, and Gucci. ⊠ *Main St., at Riise's Alley, Charlotte Amalie* ☎ *340/777–4222* ⊠ *Waterfront at Hibiscus Alley, Charlotte Amalie* ☎ *340/777–4222* ⊠ *Havensight Mall, Bldg. II, Rte. 30, Charlotte Amalie* ☎ *340/776–8590.*

Rolex Watches at A. H. Riise. As the Virgin Islands' official Rolex retailer, this shop offers one of the largest selections of these fine timepieces in the Caribbean. An After Sales Service Center assures that your Rolex keeps on ticking for your lifetime. ⊠ *37 Main St., at Riise's Alley, Charlotte Amalie* ☎ *340/776–2303* ⊠ *Havensight Mall, Bldg. II, Rte. 30, Charlotte Amalie* ☎ *340/776–4002.*

LEATHER GOODS   **Coach Boutique at Little Switzerland.** Find a full line of fine leather handbags, belts, gloves, and more for women, plus briefcases and wallets for men. Accessories for both sexes include organizers, travel bags, and cellphone cases. ⊠ *5 Main St., Charlotte Amalie* ☎ *340/776–2010.*

Longchamp Boutique. Classic Longchamp brings you authentic French hand-crafted leather goods like handbags, briefcases, wallets, key chains, belts, and luggage. The exclusive line of canvas and leather travel bags is as beautiful as the items are practical. ⊠ *25 Main St., Charlotte Amalie* ☎ *340/777–5240.*

Ⓒ **Zora's.** Fine leather sandals made-to-order are the specialty here. There's also a selection of locally made backpacks, purses, and briefcases in durable, brightly colored canvas. ⊠ *Norre Gade, across from Roosevelt Park, Charlotte Amalie* ☎ *340/774–2559.*

LINENS   **Fabric in Motion.** Fine Italian linens share space with Liberty's of London silky cottons, colorful batiks, cotton prints, ribbons, and accessories at this small shop. ⊠ *Storetvaer Gade, Charlotte Amalie* ☎ *340/774–2006.*

Mr. Tablecloth. The friendly staff here will help you choose from the floor-to-ceiling selection of linens, from Tuscany lace tablecloths to Irish linen pillowcases. The prices will please. ⊠ *6–7 Main St., Charlotte Amalie* ☎ *340/774–4343.*

LIQUOR &   **A. H. Riise Liquors & Tobacco.** This Riise venture offers a large selection
TOBACCO   of tobacco (including imported cigars), as well as cordials, wines, and rare vintage Armagnacs, cognacs, ports, and Madeiras. It also stocks fruits in brandy and barware from England. Enjoy rum samples at the tasting bar. ⊠ *37 Main St., at Riise's Alley, Charlotte Amalie* ☎ *340/776–2303* ⊠ *Havensight Mall, Bldg. I, Rte. 30, Charlotte Amalie* ☎ *340/776–7713.*

Al Cohen's Discount Liquor. The wine selection at this warehouse-style store is extremely large. ⊠ *Rte. 30 across from Havensight Mall, Charlotte Amalie* ☎ *340/774–3690.*

Tobacco Discounters. Find here a full line of discounted brand-&name cigarettes, cigars, and tobacco accessories. ⊠ *Port of $ale Mall, Rte. 30, next to Havensight Mall* ☎ *340/774–2256.*

MUSIC   **Modern Music.** Shop for the latest stateside and Caribbean CD and cas-
Ⓒ   sette releases, plus oldies, classical, and New Age music. ⊠ *Rte. 30, across*

from Havensight Mall, Charlotte Amalie ☎ *340/774–3100* ✉ *Nisky Center, Rte. 30, Charlotte Amalie* ☎ *340/777–8787.*

☺ **Parrot Fish Music.** A stock of standard stateside tapes and CDs, plus a good selection of Caribbean artists, including local groups, can be found here. You can browse through the collection of calypso, soca, steel band, and reggae music online. ✉ *Back St., Charlotte Amalie* ☎ *340/ 776–4514* ⊕ *www.parrotfishmusic.com.*

PERFUME **Tropicana Perfume Shoppe.** Displayed in an 18th-century Danish building is a large selection of fragrances for men and women, including those locally made by Gail Garrison from the essential oils of tropical fruits and flowers like mango and jasmine. ✉ *2 Main St., Charlotte Amalie* ☎ *340/774–0010.*

SUNGLASSES **Davante.** This designer eyewear store carries brands like Cartier, Dunhill, Giorgio Armani, and Christian Dior. ✉ *Riise's Alley, Charlotte Amalie* ☎ *340/714–1220.*

Fashion Eyewear. Take your pick from name-brand eyewear. A real plus here is prescription sunglasses, copied from your present eyewear, ready in a half hour for $99. ✉ *International Plaza, Charlotte Amalie* ☎ *340/ 776–9075.*

TOYS **Quick Pics.** Birds sing, dogs bark, and fish swim in this animated toy land,
☺ which is part of a larger electronics and souvenir store. Adults have as much fun trying out the wares as do kids. ✉ *Havensight Mall, Bldg. IV, Rte. 30, Charlotte Amalie* ☎ *340/774–3500.*

Nightlife & the Arts

On any given night, especially in season, you can find steel-pan orchestras, rock and roll, piano music, jazz, broken-bottle dancing (actual dancing atop broken glass), disco, and karaoke. Pick up a copy of the free, bright yellow *St. Thomas–St. John This Week* magazine when you arrive (it can be found at the airport, in stores, and in hotel lobbies); the back pages list who's playing where. The Friday edition of the *Daily News* carries complete listings for the upcoming weekend.

Nightlife

BARS **Agave Terrace.** Island-style steel-pan bands are a treat that should not be missed. Pan music resonates after dinner here on Tuesday and Thursday. ✉ *Point Pleasant Resort, Rte. 38, Estate Smith Bay* ☎ *340/775–4142.*

Duffy's Love Shack. A live band and dancing under the stars are the big draws for locals and visitors alike. ✉ *Red Hook Plaza, Red Hook* ☎ *340/779–2080.*

Epernay Bistro. This intimate nightspot has small tables for easy chatting, wine and champagne by the glass, and a spacious dance floor. Mix and mingle with island celebrities. The action runs from 4 PM until the wee hours Monday through Saturday. ✉ *Frenchtown Mall, 24-A Honduras, Frenchtown* ☎ *340/774–5348.*

Greenhouse Bar & Restaurant. Once this favorite eatery puts away the salt-and-pepper shakers at 10 PM, it becomes a rock-and-roll club with a DJ or live reggae bands raising the weary to their feet six nights a week. ✉ *Waterfront Hwy. at Storetvaer Gade, Charlotte Amalie* ☎ *340/774–7998.*

26

Iggies Beach Bar. Sing along karaoke-style to the sounds of the surf or the latest hits at this beachside lounge. There are live bands on the weekends, and you can dance inside or kick up your heels under the stars. At the adjacent Beach House restaurant, there's Carnival Night, complete with steel-pan music on Wednesday. ☒ *Bolongo Bay Beach Club & Villas, Rte. 30, Estate Bolongo* ☎ *340/775–1800.*

Ritz-Carlton, St. Thomas. On Monday nights, catch pan music at this resort's bar. ☒ *Rte. 317, Estate Great Bay* ☎ *340/775–3333.*

The Arts

THEATER **Pistarkle Theater.** This air-conditioned theater with more than 100 seats, which is in the Tillett Gardens complex, is host to a dozen or more productions annually, plus a children's summer drama camp. ☒ *Tillett Gardens, Rte. 38, across from Tutu Park Shopping Mall, Estate Tutu* ☎ *340/775–7877.*

Reichhold Center for the Arts. This amphitheater has its more expensive seats covered by a roof. Schedules vary, so check the paper to see what's on when you're in town. Throughout the year there's an entertaining mix of local plays, dance exhibitions, and music of all types. ☒ *Rte. 30, across from Brewers Beach, Estate Lindberg Bay* ☎ *340/693–1559.*

Exploring St. Thomas

St. Thomas is only 13 mi (21 km) long and less than 4 mi (6½ km) wide, but it's extremely hilly, and even an 8- or 10-mi (13- or 16-km) trip could take well over an hour. Don't let that discourage you, though; the mountain ridge that runs east to west through the middle and separates the island's Caribbean and Atlantic sides has spectacular vistas.

Charlotte Amalie

Look beyond the pricey shops, T-shirt vendors, and bustling crowds for a glimpse of the island's history. The city served as the capital of Denmark's outpost in the Caribbean until 1917, an aspect of the island often lost in the glitz of the shopping district.

Emancipation Gardens, right next to the fort, is a good place to start a walking tour. Tackle the hilly part of town first: head north up Government Hill to the historic buildings that house government offices and have incredible views. Several regal churches line the route that runs west back to the town proper and the old-time market. Virtually all the alleyways that intersect Main Street lead to eateries that serve frosty drinks, sandwiches, burgers, and West Indian fare. There are public restrooms in this area, too. Allow an hour for a quick view of the sights.

A note about the street names: In deference to the island's heritage, the streets downtown are labeled by their Danish names. Locals will use both the Danish name and the English name (such as Dronningens Gade and Norre Gade for Main Street), but most people refer to things by their location ("a block toward the Waterfront off Main Street" or "next to the Little Switzerland Shop"). You may find it more useful if you ask for directions by shop names or landmarks.

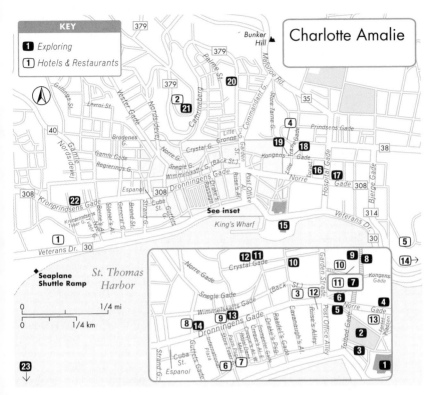

Charlotte Amalie

KEY

1 Exploring

1 Hotels & Restaurants

Numbers in the margin correspond to points of interest on the Charlotte Amalie map.

㉠ All Saints Anglican Church. Built in 1848 from stone quarried on the island, the church has thick, arched window frames lined with the yellow brick that came to the islands as ballast aboard ships. Merchants left the brick on the waterfront when they filled their boats with molasses, sugar, mahogany, and rum for the return voyage. The church was built in celebration of the end of slavery in the USVI. ⊠ *Domini Gade* ☎ *340/774–0217* ⊙ *Mon.–Sat. 9–3.*

㉒ Cathedral of St. Peter & St. Paul. This building was consecrated as a parish church in 1848 and serves as the seat of the territory's Roman Catholic diocese. The ceiling and walls are covered with murals painted in 1899 by two Belgian artists, Father Leo Servais and Brother Ildephonsus. The San Juan–marble altar and side walls were added in the 1960s. ⊠ *Lower Main St.* ☎ *340/774–0201* ⊙ *Mon.–Sat. 8–5.*

㉑ Danish Consulate Building. Built in 1830, this structure once housed the Danish Consulate. Although the Danish Consul General, Soøren Blak, has an office in Charlotte Amalie, it's now in the Scandinavian Center in Havensight Mall. This building is not open to the public. ⊠ *Take stairs north at corner of Bjerge Gade and Crystal Gade to Denmark Hill.*

❿ Dutch Reformed Church. This church has an austere loveliness that's amazing considering all it's been through. Founded in 1744, it's been rebuilt twice following fires and hurricanes. The unembellished cream-color hall gives you a sense of peace—albeit monochromatically. The only other color is the forest green of the shutters and the carpet. Call ahead if you need to visit at a particular time; the doors are sometimes locked. ⊠ *Nye Gade and Crystal Gade* ☎ *340/776–8255* ⊙ *Weekdays 9–5.*

➏ Educators Park. A peaceful place amid the town's hustle and bustle, the park has memorials to three famous Virgin Islanders: educator Edith Williams, J. Antonio Jarvis (a founder of the *Daily News*), and educator and author Rothschild Francis. The last gave many speeches here. ⊠ *Main St., across from post office.*

☾ ➋ **Emancipation Garden.** Built to honor the freeing of slaves in 1848, the garden was the site of a 150th anniversary celebration of emancipation. A bronze bust of a freed slave blowing a symbolic conch shell commemorates this anniversary. The gazebo here is used for official ceremonies. Two other monuments show the island's Danish-American tie—a bust of Denmark's King Christian and a scaled-down model of the U.S. Liberty Bell. ⊠ *Between Tolbod Gade and Fort Christian.*

☾ ⓮ **Enid M. Baa Public Library.** Like so many other structures on the north side of Main Street, this large pink building is a typical 18th-century town house. Merchants built their houses (stores downstairs, living quarters above) across from the brick warehouses on the south side of the street. The library was once the home of merchant and landowner Baron von Bretton. It's the island's first recorded fireproof building, meaning it was built of ballast brick instead of wood. Its interior of high ceilings and cool stone floors is the perfect refuge from the afternoon sun. You can browse through historic papers or just sit in the breeze by an open window reading the paper. ⊠ *Main St.* ☎ *340/774–0630* ⊙ *Weekdays 9–5, Sat. 10–3.*

① Fort Christian. St. Thomas's oldest standing structure, this monument was built between 1672 and 1680 and now has U.S. National Landmark status. The clock tower was added in the 19th century. This remarkable building has, over time, been used as a jail, governor's residence, town hall, courthouse, and church. Fort Christian now houses the **Virgin Islands Museum,** where you can see exhibits on USVI history, natural history, and turn-of-the-20th-century furnishings. Local artists display their works monthly in the gallery. A gift shop sells local crafts, books, and other souvenirs. This is also the site of the Chamber of Commerce's Hospitality Lounge, where there are public restrooms, brochures, and a place where you can stash your luggage for some last-minute shopping on the way to the airport. ⊠ *Waterfront Hwy., east of shopping district* ☎ *340/776–4566.*

④ Frederick Lutheran Church. This historic church has a massive mahogany altar, and its pews—each with its own door—were once rented to families of the congregation. Lutheranism is the state religion of Denmark, and when the territory was without a minister the governor—who had his own elevated pew—filled in. ⊠ *Norre Gade* ☎ *340/776–1315* ⊙ *Mon.–Sat. 9–4.*

⑲ Government House. Built in 1867, this neoclassical white brick-and-wood structure houses the offices for the governor of the Virgin Islands. Inside, the staircases are of native mahogany, as are the plaques hand-lettered in gold with the names of the governors appointed and, since 1970, elected. Brochures detailing the history of the building are available, but you may have to ask for them. ⊠ *Government Hill* ☎ *340/774–0294* ☞ *Free* ⊙ *Weekdays 8–5.*

⑨ Haagensen House. Behind Hotel 1829, this lovingly restored home was built in the early 1800s by Danish entrepreneur Hans Haagensen and is surrounded by an equally impressive cookhouse, outbuildings, and terraced gardens. A lower-level banquet hall now showcases an antique-print and photo gallery. Guided walking tours are available of Haagensen House. The tour begins at the lookout tower at Blackbeard's Castle and continues to the circa-1860s Villa Notman, Haagensen House, and Hotel 1829. The first tour starts at 9:30 AM. ⊠ *Government Hill* ☎ *340/776–1234 or 340/776–1829* ☞ *Tours $20* ⊙ *Oct.–May, daily 9–4; June–Sept., by appointment only.*

㉔ Hassel Island. East of Water Island in Charlotte Amalie harbor, Hassel Island is part of the Virgin Islands National Park, as it has the ruins of a British military garrison (built during a brief British occupation of the USVI during the 1800s) and the remains of a marine railway (where ships were hoisted into dry dock for repairs). There's a small ferry that runs from the Crown Bay Marina to the island; departure times are posted at Tickles Dockside Pub, and the fare is $5 or $10 round-trip.

⑦ Hotel 1829. As its name implies, the hotel was built in 1829, albeit as the private residence of a prominent merchant named Lavalette. The

FodorsChoice ★

26

building's bright, coral-color exterior walls are accented with fancy black wrought iron, and the interior is paneled in dark wood, which makes it feel delightfully cool. From the terrace there's an exquisite view of the harbor framed by brilliant orange bougainvillea. You can combine a visit to this hotel with a walking tour of Haagensen House, Villa Notman, and the lookout tower at Blackbeard's Castle just behind the hotel. ⊠ *Government Hill* ☎ *340/776–1829 or 340/776–1234* ⊕ *www. hotel1829.com* ⏭ *Tour $20* ⊙ *Oct.–May, daily 9–4; June–Sept., by appointment only.*

⓯ Legislature Building. Its pastoral-looking lime-green exterior conceals the vociferous political wrangling of the Virgin Islands Senate inside. Constructed originally by the Danish as a police barracks, the building was later used to billet U.S. Marines, and much later it housed a public school. You're welcome to sit in on sessions in the upstairs chambers. ⊠ *Waterfront Hwy., across from Fort Christian* ☎ *340/774–0880* ⊙ *Daily 8–5.*

⓱ Memorial Moravian Church. Built in 1884, it was named to commemorate the 150th anniversary of the Moravian Church in the Virgin Islands. ⊠ *17 Norre Gade* ☎ *340/776–0066* ⊙ *Weekdays 8–5.*

☾ ❽ 99 Steps. This staircase "street," built by the Danes in the 1700s, leads to the residential area above Charlotte Amalie and Blackbeard's Castle. The castle's tower, built in 1679, was once used by the notorious pirate Edward Teach. If you count the stairs as you go up, you will discover, as have thousands before you, that there are more than 99. ⊠ *Look for steps heading north from Government Hill.*

⓭ Pissarro Building. Housing several shops and an art gallery, this was the birthplace and childhood home of Camille Pissarro, who later moved to France and became an acclaimed Impressionist painter. The art gallery contains three original pages from Pissarro's sketchbook and two pastels by Pissarro's grandson, Claude. ⊠ *Main St., between Raadets Gade and Trompeter Gade.*

☾ ⓰ Roosevelt Park. You can see members of the local legal community head to the nearby court buildings while you rest on a bench in this park— a good spot to people-watch. The small monument on the park's south side is dedicated to USVI war veterans. Kids enjoy the playground made of wood and tires. ⊠ *Norre Gade.*

★ ⓲ Seven Arches Museum. This restored 18th-century home is a striking example of classic Danish–West Indian architecture. There seem to be arches everywhere—seven to be exact—all supporting a "welcoming arms" staircase that leads to the second floor and the flower-framed front doorway. The Danish kitchen is a highlight: it's housed in a separate building off the main house, as were all cooking facilities in the early days (for fire prevention). Inside the house you can see mahogany furnishings and gas lamps. ⊠ *Government Hill, 3 bldgs. east of Government House* ☎ *340/774–9295* ⏭ *$5 suggested donation* ⊙ *Oct.–July, daily 10–4; Aug. and Sept., by appointment only.*

⑪ Synagogue of Beracha Veshalom Vegmiluth Hasidim. The synagogue's Hebrew name translates to the Congregation of Blessing, Peace, and Loving Deeds. The small building's white pillars contrast with rough stone walls, as does the rich mahogany of the pews and altar. The sand on the floor symbolizes the exodus from Egypt. Since the synagogue first opened its doors in 1833 it has held a weekly Sabbath service, making it the oldest synagogue building in continuous use under the American flag and the second-oldest (after the one on Curaçao) in the western hemisphere. Guided tours are available. Brochures detailing the key structures and history are also available. Next door, the Weibel Museum showcases Jewish history on St. Thomas. ⊠ *15 Crystal Gade* ☎ *340/774–4312* ⊕ *new.onepaper.com/synagogue* ⊘ *Weekdays 9–4.*

⑤ U.S. Post Office. While you buy your postcard stamps, contemplate the murals of waterfront scenes by *Saturday Evening Post* artist Stephen Dohanos. His art was commissioned as part of the Works Project Administration (WPA) in the 1930s. ⊠ *Tolbod Gade and Main St.*

⑬ Vendors Plaza. Here merchants sell everything from T-shirts to African attire to leather goods. Look for local art among the ever-changing selections at this busy market. ⊠ *Waterfront, west of Fort Christian* ⊘ *Weekdays 8–6, weekends 9–1.*

㉓ Water Island. This island, once owned by the U.S. Department of the Interior and about ¼ mi (½ km) out in Charlotte Amalie Harbor, was once a peninsula. A channel was cut through so that U.S. submarines could get to their base in a bay just to the west, known as Sub Base. Today, this is the fourth-largest U.S. Virgin Island. A ferry goes between Crown Bay Marina and the island several times daily, at a cost of $5 or $10 round-trip.

⑫ Weibel Museum. In this museum next to the synagogue, 300 years of Jewish history on St. Thomas are showcased. The small gift shop sells a commemorative silver coin celebrating the anniversary of the Hebrew congregation's establishment on the island in 1796. There are also tropically inspired items, like a shell seder plate and menorahs painted to resemble palm trees. ⊠ *15 Crystal Gade* ☎ *340/774–4312* ⊡ *Free* ⊘ *Weekdays 9–4.*

Around the Island

To explore outside Charlotte Amalie, rent a car or hire a taxi. Your rental car should come with a good map; if not, pick up the pocket-size "St. Thomas–St. John Road Map" at a tourist information center. Roads are marked with route numbers, but they're confusing and seem to switch numbers suddenly. Roads are also identified by signs bearing the St. Thomas–St. John Hotel and Tourism Association's mascot, Tommy the Starfish. More than 100 of these color-coded signs line the island's main routes. Orange signs trace the route from the airport to Red Hook, green signs identify the road from town to Magens Bay, Tommy's face on a yellow background points from Mafolie to Crown Bay through the north side, red signs lead from Smith Bay to Four Corners via Skyline Drive, and blue signs mark the route from the cruise-ship dock at Havensight to Red Hook. These color-coded routes are not marked on most visitor maps, however. Allow yourself a day to explore, especially if you want to stop to take pictures or to enjoy a light bite or refreshing swim. Most gas stations are on the island's more populated eastern end, so fill up before heading to the north side. And remember to drive on the left!

Although the eastern end has many major resorts and spectacular beaches, don't be surprised if a cow or a herd of goats crosses your path as you drive through the relatively flat, dry terrain. The north side of the island is more lush and hush—fewer houses and less traffic. Here there are roller-coaster routes (made all the more scary because the roads have no shoulders) and incredible vistas. Leave time in the afternoon for a swim. Pick up some sandwiches from delis in the Red Hook area for a picnic lunch, or enjoy a slice of pizza at Magens Bay. A day in the country will reveal the tropical pleasures that have enticed more than one visitor to become a resident.

Numbers in the margin correspond to points of interest on the St. Thomas map.

㉖ Compass Point Marina. It's fun to park your car and walk around this marina. The boaters—many of whom have sailed here from points around the globe—are easy to engage in conversation. Turn south off Route 32 at the well-marked entrance road just east of Independent Boat Yard. ⊠ *Estate Frydenhoj.*

㉘ Coral World Ocean Park. Coral World has an offshore underwater observatory that houses the Predator Tank, one of the world's largest coral-reef tanks, and an aquarium with more than 20 portholes providing close-ups of Caribbean sea life. Sea Trekkin' lets you tour the reef outside the park at a depth of 15 feet, thanks to specialized high-tech headgear and a continuous air supply that's based on the surface. A guide leads the half-hour tour, and the narration is piped through a specialized microphone inside each trekker's helmet; the minimum age to participate is eight years. Adventure Island, added in early 2006, is St. Thomas's first and only water park. A large catamaran, equipped with two tunnel-like water slides, a water trampoline, water cannon, and other water toys, takes visitors on a fun-filled snorkeling excursion three days a week. The park also has several outdoor pools where you can shake hands with a starfish, pet a baby shark, feed stingrays, and view endangered sea turtles. In addition there's a mangrove lagoon and a nature trail full of lush tropical flora. Daily feedings and talks take place at most every exhibit. ⊠ *Coki Point, north of Rte. 38, Estate Frydendal* ☎ *340/775–1555* ⊕ *www.coralworldvi.com* 🖃 *$18, Adventure Island $45, Sea Trekkin $50* ☉ *Daily 9–5.*

㉚ Drake's Seat. Sir Francis Drake was supposed to have kept watch over his fleet and looked for enemy ships from this vantage point. The panorama is especially breathtaking (and romantic) at dusk, and if you arrive late in the day you can miss the hordes of day-trippers on taxi tours who stop here to take a picture and buy a T-shirt from one of the many vendors. ⊠ *Rte. 40, Estate Zufriedenheit.*

FodorsChoice
★

㉛ Estate St. Peter Greathouse & Botanical Gardens. This unusual spot is perched on a mountainside 1,000 feet above sea level, with views of more than 20 islands and islets. You can wander through a gallery displaying local art, sip a complimentary rum punch while looking out at the view, or follow a nature trail that leads by nearly 200 varieties of trees and plants, including an orchid jungle. ⊠ *Rte. 40, Estate St. Peter* ☎ *340/774–4999* ⊕ *www.greathouse-mountaintop.com* ▨ *$15* ☻ *Mon.–Sat. 9–4:30.*

㉜ Frenchtown. Popular for its several bars and restaurants, Frenchtown is also the home of descendants of immigrants from St. Barthélemy (St. Barths). You can watch them pull up their brightly painted boats and display their equally colorful catch of the day along the waterfront. If you chat with them, you can hear speech patterns slightly different from those of other St. Thomians. Get a feel for the residential district of Frenchtown by walking west to some of the town's winding streets, where tiny wooden houses have been passed down from generation to generation. Next to Joseph Aubain Ballpark, the **French Heritage Museum** (⊠ Intersection of rue de St. Anne and rue de St. Barthélemy ☎ 340/774–2320) houses century-old artifacts such as fishing nets, accordions, tambourines, mahogany furniture, and historic photographs that illustrate the lives of the French descendants during the 18th through 20th centuries. The museum is open Monday through Saturday from 9 AM to 6 PM; admission is free. ⊠ *Turn south off Waterfront Hwy. at post office.*

★ ☺ ㉙ Mountain Top. Stop here for a banana daiquiri and spectacular views from the observation deck more than 1,500 feet above sea level. There are also shops that sell everything from Caribbean art to nautical antiques, ship models, and T-shirts. Kids will like talking to the parrots—and hearing them answer back. ⊠ *Head north off Rte. 33, look for signs* ⊕ *www.greathouse-mountaintop.com.*

★ ☺ ㉕ Paradise Point Tramway. Fly skyward in a gondola to Paradise Point, an overlook with breathtaking views of Charlotte Amalie and the harbor. There are several shops, a bar, restaurant, and a wedding gazebo; kids enjoy the tropical bird show held daily at 10:30 AM and 1:30 PM. A ¼-mi (½-km) hiking trail leads to spectacular views of St. Croix to the south. Wear sturdy shoes; the trail is steep and rocky. ⊠ *Rte. 30, across from Havensight Mall, Charlotte Amalie* ☎ *340/774–9809* ⊕ *www. paradisepointtramway.com* ▨ *$16* ☻ *Thurs.–Tues. 9–5, Wed. 9–9.*

㉗ Red Hook. In this nautical center there are fishing and sailing charter boats, dive shops, and powerboat-rental agencies at the American Yacht Harbor marina. There are also several bars and restaurants, including Molly Molone's, Duffy's Love Shack, and Off the Hook. One grocery store and two delis offer picnic fixings—from sliced meats and cheeses to rotisserie-roasted chickens, prepared salads, and freshly baked breads.

ST. JOHN

By Lynda Lohr   The sun slipped up over the horizon like a great orange ball, streaking the sky with wisps of gold. Watching from my porch overlooking Coral

Bay, I thanked Mother Nature, as I do almost every day, for providing glorious sunrises, colorful rainbows and green hillsides, and the opportunity to enjoy them all. It was a magnificent start to another gorgeous St. John day, an island where nature is the engine that fuels the island's economy and brings more than 800,000 visitors a year.

St. John's heart is Virgin Islands National Park, a treasure that takes up a full two-thirds of St. John's 20 square mi (53 square km). The park helps keep the island's interior in its pristine and undisturbed state, but if you go at midday, you'll probably have to share your stretch of beach with others, particularly at Trunk Bay.

The island is booming, and it can get a tad crowded at the ever-popular Trunk Bay Beach during the busy winter season; parking woes plague the island's main town of Cruz Bay, but you won't find traffic jams or pollution. It's easy to escape from the fray, however: just head off on a hike or go early or late to the beach. The sun won't be as strong, and you may have that perfect crescent of white sand all to yourself.

St. John doesn't have a grand agrarian past like her sister island, St. Croix, but if you're hiking in the dry season, you can probably stumble upon the stone ruins of old plantations. The less adventuresome can visit the repaired ruins at the park's Annaberg Plantation and Caneel Bay resort.

In 1675 Jorgen Iverson claimed the unsettled island for Denmark. By 1733 there were more than 1,000 slaves working more than 100 plantations. In that year the island was hit by a drought, hurricanes, and a plague of insects that destroyed the summer crops. With famine a real threat and the planters keeping them under tight reign, the slaves revolted on November 23, 1733. They captured the fort at Coral Bay, took control of the island, and held on to it for six months. During this period, about 20% of the island's total population was killed, the tragedy affecting both black and white residents in equal percentages. The rebellion was eventually put down with the help of French troops from Martinique. Slavery continued until 1848, when slaves in St. Croix marched on Frederiksted to demand their freedom from the Danish government. This time it was granted. After emancipation, St. John fell into decline, with its inhabitants eking out a living on small farms. Life continued in much the same way until the national park opened in 1956 and tourism became an industry.

Of the three U.S. Virgin Islands, St. John, which has 5,000 residents, has the strongest sense of community, which is primarily rooted in a desire to protect the island's natural beauty. Despite the growth, there are still many pockets of tranquility. Here you can truly escape the pressures of modern life for a day, a week—perhaps, forever.

Where to Stay

St. John doesn't have many beachfront hotels, but that's a small price to pay for all the pristine sand. However, the island's two excellent resorts—Caneel Bay Resort and the Westin St. John Resort & Villas—*are* on the beach. Sandy, white beaches string out along the north

St. John Archaeology

ARCHAEOLOGISTS CONTINUE to unravel St. John's past through excavations at Trunk Bay and Cinnamon Bay, both prime tourist destinations within Virgin Islands National Park.

Work began back in the early 1990s, when the park wanted to build new bathhouses at the popular Trunk Bay. In preparation for that project, the archaeologists began to dig, turning up artifacts and the remains of structures that date to AD 900. The site was once a village occupied by the Taino, a peaceful group that lived in the area for many centuries. A similar but not quite as ancient village was discovered at Cinnamon Bay.

By the time the Tainos got to Cinnamon Bay—they lived in the area from about AD 1000 to 1500—their society had developed to include chiefs, commoners, workers,

and slaves. The location of the national park's busy Cinnamon Bay campground was once a Taino temple that belonged to a king or chief. When archaeologists began digging in 1998, they uncovered several dozen *zemis,* which are small clay gods used in ceremonial activities, as well as beads, pots, and many other artifacts.

Near the end of the Cinnamon Bay dig, archaeologists turned up another less ancient but still surprising discovery. A burned layer indicated that a plantation slave village had also stood near Cinnamon Bay campground; it was torched during the 1733 revolt because its slave inhabitants had been loyal to the planters. Since the 1970s, bones from slaves buried in the area have been uncovered at the water's edge by beach erosion.

26

coast, which is popular with sunbathers and snorkelers and is where you can find the Caneel Bay Resort and Cinnamon and Maho Bay campgrounds. Most villas are in the residential south-shore area, a 15-minute drive from the north-shore beaches. If you head east you come to the laid-back community of Coral Bay, where there are growing numbers of villas and cottages. A stay outside of Coral Bay will be peaceful and quiet.

If you're looking for West Indian village charm, there are a few inns in Cruz Bay. Just know that when bands play at any of the town's bars (some of which stay open until the wee hours), the noise can be a problem. Your choice of accommodations also includes condominiums and cottages near town; two campgrounds, both at the edges of beautiful beaches (bring bug repellent); eco-resorts; and luxurious villas, often with a pool or a hot tub (sometimes both) and a stunning view.

If your lodging comes with a fully equipped kitchen, you'll be happy to know that St. John's handful of grocery stores sell everything from the basics to sun-dried tomatoes and green chilies—though the prices will take your breath away. If you're on a budget, consider bringing some staples (pasta, canned goods, paper products) from home. Hotel rates

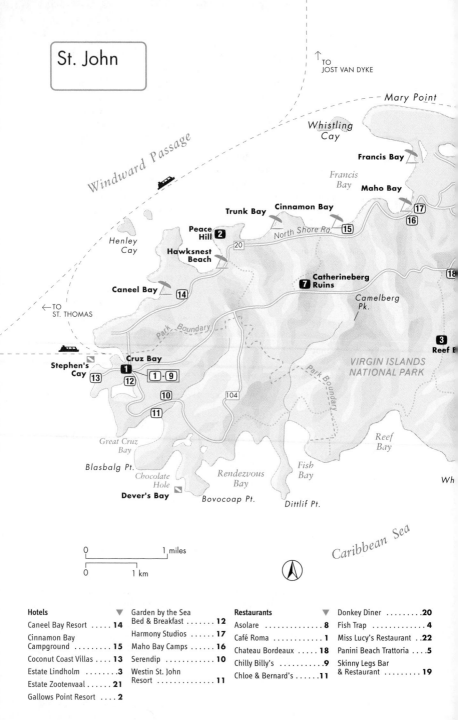

St. John

↑ TO
JOST VAN DYKE

Mary Point

Whistling Cay

Windward Passage

Francis Bay

Francis Bay

Maho Bay

Trunk Bay

Cinnamon Bay

North Shore Rd.

17

16

15

Peace Hill **2**

20

Hawksnest Beach

Henley Cay

Catherineberg Ruins **7**

Camelberg Pk.

18

Caneel Bay **14**

← TO ST. THOMAS

Park Boundary

3
Reef B

VIRGIN ISLANDS
NATIONAL PARK

Stephen's Cay

13 **12**

Cruz Bay **1**

1 – **9**

Park Boundary

10

11

104

Great Cruz Bay

Reef Bay

Blasbalg Pt.

Chocolate Hole

Dever's Bay

Rendezvous Bay

Fish Bay

Bovocoap Pt.

Dittlif Pt.

Wh

Caribbean Sea

0 — 1 miles
0 — 1 km

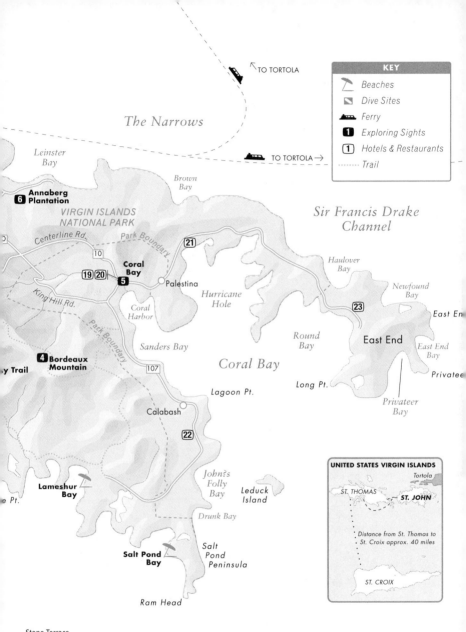

KEY

⤚ Beaches
◩ Dive Sites
🚢 Ferry
1 Exploring Sights
① Hotels & Restaurants
...... Trail

↖ TO TORTOLA

The Narrows

TO TORTOLA →

Leinster Bay

Brown Bay

Sir Francis Drake Channel

6 **Annaberg Plantation**

VIRGIN ISLANDS NATIONAL PARK

Centerline Rd.   Park Boundary

21

Haulover Bay

10

Newfound Bay

19 **20**   **Coral Bay**

5   Palestina

Hurricane Hole

King Hill Rd.

Coral Harbor

23   *East En*

Park Boundary

East End Bay

Sanders Bay   *Round Bay*   **East End**

4 **Bordeaux Mountain**

Coral Bay

y Trail

107   *Long Pt.*   *Privatee*

Lagoon Pt.

Calabash   *Privateer Bay*

22

John's Folly Bay

Leduck Island

Lameshur Bay

e Pt.   *Drunk Bay*

Salt Pond Peninsula

Salt Pond Bay

Ram Head

UNITED STATES VIRGIN ISLANDS

Tortola

ST. THOMAS   **ST. JOHN**

Distance from St. Thomas to St. Croix approx. 40 miles

ST. CROIX

throughout the island, though considered expensive by some, do include endless privacy and access to most water sports.

For approximate costs, *see* the dining and lodging price chart on the U.S. Virgin Islands Planner, at the beginning of this chapter.

Hotels & Inns

$$$$
Fodor'sChoice
★

⊞ Caneel Bay Resort. Well-heeled honeymooners, couples celebrating anniversaries, and extended families all enjoy Caneel Bay Resort's laid-back luxury. If you want to spend your days sunning on any one of its seven gorgeous beaches, taking a kayak out for a paddle, or enjoying lingering dinners at its fine restaurants, you'll find no finer resort on St. John. Your room, which has air-conditioning or can be opened to the breezes, won't come with a TV or even a telephone (though management will loan you a cellular)—all the better to get away from it all. Rooms look as if they're modeled right out of a magazine; if you opt for one of the beachfront rooms, you can get out of bed and stumble a few steps across the sand to the Caribbean. Otherwise, you can look out on the gardens or the tennis courts. Nightlife runs to steel-pan music or an easy-listening combo; if you want lots of action, go elsewhere. ⊠ *Rte. 20, Caneel Bay ⬧ Box 720, Cruz Bay 00830 ☎ 340/776–6111 or 888/767–3966 ☒ 340/693–8280 ⊕ www.caneelbay.com ⇆ 166 rooms ⚐ 4 restaurants, fans, minibars, Wi-Fi, 11 tennis courts, pool, spa, beach, dive shop, dock, snorkeling, windsurfing, boating, billiards, children's programs (ages infant–12), meeting rooms; no room phones, no room TVs ⊟ AE, DC, MC, V ⌾ CP.*

$$$$
⊞ Westin St. John Resort & Villas. Other than Caneel Bay, this is the only big resort on the island. Although it doesn't provide the same casual luxury, it does have a nice beachfront location and enough activities to make you never want to leave. That said, most guests rent a car for at least a couple of days to explore the many lovely beaches and the nearby town of Cruz Bay. The hotel is spread over 47 beachfront acres adjacent to Great Cruz Bay, with lushly planted gardens, a white sandy beach that beckons sunbathers, and nice—but not luxurious—rooms with tropical touches. Those strung out behind the beach put you closest to the water, but even the hillside villas are only a seven-minute stroll to the sand. You can keep very busy here with tennis and water sports, or you can idle the day away at the pool or beach. ⊠ *Rte. 104, Great Cruz Bay ⬧ Box 8310, Cruz Bay 00831 ☎ 340/693–8000 or 800/808–5020 ☒ 340/779–4985 ⊕ www.westinresortstjohn.com ⇆ 282 rooms, 67 villas ⚐ 4 restaurants, in-room safes, minibars, refrigerators, cable TV, in-room broadband, Wi-Fi, 6 tennis courts, pool, gym, outdoor hot tub, massage, beach, dive shop, snorkeling, windsurfing, boating, fishing, shops, children's programs (ages 3–12), meeting rooms, no-smoking rooms ⊟ AE, D, DC, MC, V ⌾ EP.*

$$$
⊞ Estate Lindholm Bed & Breakfast. Built among old stone ruins on a lushly planted hill overlooking Cruz Bay, Estate Lindholm provides a charming setting, with the convenience of being close to Cruz Bay's restaurants, shopping, and nightlife. You'll feel as if you're out of the fray but still near enough to run into town when you want. Rooms are sophisticated, with crisp white spreads accented by teak furniture. Although

you can easily walk to Cruz Bay, the return trip is up a big hill. To get out and about, rent a car. The sunset views from Asolare restaurant, on the property, provide a stunning end to your day. ⌂ *Box 1360, Cruz Bay 00831* ☎ *340/776–6121* 🖷 *800/322–6335* ⊕ *www.estatelindholm. com* ↦ *10 rooms* ♿ *Restaurant, fans, microwaves, refrigerators, cable TV, pool, gym; no smoking* ▭ *AE, D, MC, V* ℗ *CP.*

$$ ▢ **Garden by the Sea Bed & Breakfast.** A stay here will allow you to live like a local in a middle-class residential neighborhood near a bird-filled salt pond. This cozy B&B is also an easy walk from Cruz Bay, which makes it convenient. White spreads and curtains provide pristine counterpoints to the blue-and-green hues that predominate your room. Your hosts serve a delightful breakfast—piña colada French toast is a specialty—on the front deck. It's perfect for folks who enjoy peace and quiet: there are no phones or TVs in the rooms. ⌂ *Enighed* ⌂ *5004A Enighed 87, Cruz Bay 00830* ☎🖷 *340/779–4731* ⊕ *www.gardenbythesea.com* ↦ *3 rooms* ♿ *Fans, no-smoking rooms; no a/c, no room phones, no room TVs* ▭ *No credit cards* ℗ *BP.*

WHERE TO CAMP ⌂ **Cinnamon Bay Campground.** Cinnamon Bay Campground sits in the heart of Virgin Islands National Park, a stellar location right at the beach. Tents and rustic cottages are nestled in the trees that stretch behind the shore, and you have easy access to hiking, water sports, and ranger-led evening programs. The amenities are basic but include propane stoves, cooking equipment, and bed linens; reserve early if you'd like a cottage right behind the beach. Only the screened cottages have electric lights; tenters depend on propane lanterns. If you have your own gear, the tent sites are a steal at $27 per night. Showers and flush toilets, as well as a restaurant and a small store, are a short walk away from the camping area. ♿ *BBQs, flush toilets, drinking water, showers (cold), picnic tables, food service, some electricity, public telephone, general store, ranger station, swimming (ocean)* ↦ *55 tents, 40 cottages, 31 tent sites* ⌂ *Rte. 20, Cinnamon Bay* ⌂ *Box 720, Cruz Bay 00830-0720* ☎ *340/ 776–6330 or 800/539–9998* 🖷 *340/776–6458* ⊕ *www.cinnamonbay. com* ⌂ *Reservations essential* ▭ *AE, MC, V* ☾ *Oct.–Aug.*

⌂ ⌂ **Maho Bay Camps.** Tucked into the greenery along the island's north
Fodor'sChoice shore, Maho Bay Camps is particularly eco-conscious, and it attracts a
★ sociable crowd that likes to explore the undersea world off the campground's beach or attend on-site educational seminars. The "tents" (wooden platforms protected from the elements by canvas and screening) are linked by wooden stairs, ramps, and walkways—all of them elevated—so that you can trek around camp, down to the beach, and to the unheated, coolish public showers without disturbing the terrain. Although the tents have some amenities like real beds and electricity, there are no refrigerators; ice-filled coolers keep your food from spoiling. ♿ *BBQs, Internet room, flush toilets, drinking water, showers (cold), picnic tables, food service, electricity, public telephone, general store, swimming (beach)* ↦ *114 tent cottages* ⌂ *Maho Bay* ⌂ *Box 310, Cruz Bay 00830* ☎ *340/776–6240 or 800/392–9004* 🖷 *340/776–6504* ⊕ *www.maho.org* ⌂ *Reservations essential* ▭ *AE, MC, V.*

26

Condominiums & Cottages

Many of the island's condos are just minutes from the hustle and bustle of Cruz Bay, but you'll find more condos and cottages around the island.

$$$$ ⊡ **Gallows Point Resort.** Gallows Point Resort has an excellent waterfront location just outside Cruz Bay's center. You're a short walk to restaurants and shops, but once you step into your condo, the hustle and bustle are left behind at the door. The upper-level apartments have loft bedrooms and the best views. The harborside villas get better trade winds, but they're a tad noisier. Tropical rooms have wicker furniture, tile floors, and brightly colored spreads in colors that reflect the sea and sky. Zozo's Ristorante, a popular spot for sunset watching, serves northern Italian cuisine above the lobby. ⊠ *Gallows Point, Bay St., Box 58, Cruz Bay 00831* ☎ *340/776–6434 or 800/323–7229* 🖷 *340/776–6520* ⊕ *www.gallowspointresort.com* ⤳ *60 units* ⚘ *Restaurant, fans, kitchens, cable TV, pool, beach, snorkeling* ⊟ *AE, MC, V* ¶◯¶ *EP.*

$$$–$$$$ ⊡ **Coconut Coast Villas.** This small condominium complex with studio, two-, and three-bedroom apartments is a 10-minute walk from Cruz Bay but still insulated from the town's noise in a sleepy suburban neighborhood. You can swim and snorkel at the small beach or relax poolside for some sun. Rooms have a fresh feel; each is a little bit different in decor, with whites, blues, and greens predominating in the color scheme. Colorful artwork by the owner's mother, St. John artist Elaine Estern, graces the walls. ⊠ *Turner Bay* ⌂ *Box 618, Cruz Bay 00831* ☎ *340/693–9100 or 800/858–7989* 🖷 *340/779–4157* ⊕ *www.coconutcoast.com* ⤳ *9 units* ⚘ *Fans, kitchens, cable TV, pool, beach* ⊟ *MC, V* ¶◯¶ *EP.*

$$$–$$$$ ⊡ **Estate Zootenvaal.** The modest cottages may look dated, but you can't beat the peace and quiet. They are certainly out of the way, along the island's East End Road; the small but very private beach across the road is a major plus. Though you will feel that you're getting away from it all, a five-minute drive will bring you to Coral Bay's few restaurants, a handful of shops, and tiny grocery store. ⊠ *Rte. 10, Hurricane Hole, Zootenvaal 00830* ☎ *340/776–6321* ⊕ *www.estatezootenvaal.com* ⤳ *4 units* ⚘ *Fans, kitchens, beach; no a/c, no room phones, no room TVs* ⊟ *No credit cards* ¶◯¶ *EP.*

$$ ⊡ **Harmony Studios.** The condominium-style units sit hillside at Maho Bay, giving you more of the comforts of home—albeit in an ecologically correct environment—than the Maho Bay Camp tents just below. Entryway mats are made of recycled tires, the pristine white walls of recycled newspapers, and your electricity comes from the wind and the sun. Best of all, you share access to interesting evening programs and a nice beach at Maho. Be prepared to hike up and down long flights of steep, wooden stairs. ⊠ *Maho Bay* ⌂ *Box 310, Cruz Bay 00830* ☎ *340/776–6240 or 800/392–9004* 🖷 *340/776–6504* ⊕ *www.maho.org* ⤳ *12 units* ⚘ *Restaurant, fans, kitchens, beach, snorkeling, windsurfing, children's programs (ages 10 and over), Internet room, no-smoking rooms; no a/c, no room phones, no room TVs* ⊟ *AE, MC, V* ¶◯¶ *EP.*

$–$$ ⊡ **Serendip.** We'd pick Serendip for a budget vacation in a residential locale. This complex offers modern apartments on lush grounds with lovely views. Although this is an older property dating from the 1960s, the units don't feel dated. There are colorful spreads, fully equipped kitchens, and bookshelves filled with good vacation reads. You definitely need a car if you stay here, though; it's about 1 mi (1½ km) up a steep hill out of Cruz Bay. ⊠ *Enighed* ✆ *Box 273, Cruz Bay 00831* ☎ *340/776–6646 or 888/800–6445* ⊕ *www.serendipstjohn.com* ↝ *10 apartments* ⚬ *Fans, kitchens, cable TV* ▭ *MC, V* ⍩ *EP.*

Private Condos & Villas

Tucked here and there between Cruz Bay and Coral Bay are about 350 private villas and condos (prices range from $ to $$$$). With pools and/or hot tubs, full kitchens, and living areas, these lodgings provide a fully functional home away from home. They're perfect for couples and extended groups of families or friends. You need a car, since most lodgings are in the hills (very few are at the beach). Villa managers usually pick you up at the dock, arrange for your rental car, and answer questions you have upon arrival as well as during your stay. Prices drop in the summer season, which is generally after April 15, though some companies begin off-season pricing a week or two later, so be sure to ask.

If you want to be close to Cruz Bay's restaurants and boutiques, a villa in the Chocolate Hole and Great Cruz Bay areas will put you just a few minutes away. The Coral Bay area has a growing number of villas, but you'll be about 20 minutes from Cruz Bay. Beaches string out along the North Shore, so you won't be more than 15 minutes away from the water no matter where you stay.

26

Book-It VI (✆ Box 1552, Cruz Bay 00831 ☎ 340/693–8261 or 800/416–1205 🖷 340/693–8480 ⊕ www.bookitvi.com) handles villas all across St. John. **Caribbean Villas & Resorts** (✆ Box 458, Cruz Bay 00831 ☎ 340/776–6152 or 800/338–0987 🖷 340/779–4044 ⊕ www.caribbeanvilla.com) handles condo rentals for Cruz Views and Gallow's Point Resort, as well as for many private villas. **Carefree Get-Aways** (✆ Box 1626, Cruz Bay 00831 ☎ 340/779–4070 or 888/643–6002 🖷 340/774–6000 ⊕ www.carefreegetaways.com) manages vacation villas on the island's southern and western edges. **Catered to Vacation Homes** (⊠ Marketplace Suite 206, 5206 Enighed, Cruz Bay 00830 ☎ 340/776–6641 or 800/424–6641 🖷 340/693–8191 ⊕ www.cateredto.com) has luxury homes, mainly mid-island and on the western edge. **Destination St. John** (✆ Box 8306, Cruz Bay 00831 ☎ 340/779–4647 or 800/562–1901 🖷 340/715–0073 ⊕ www.destinationstjohn.com) manages villas across the island. **Great Caribbean Getaways** (✆ Box 8317, Cruz Bay 00831 ☎ 340/693–8692 or 800/341–2532 🖷 340/693–9112 ⊕ www.greatcaribbeangetaways.com) handles private villas from Cruz Bay to Coral Bay. **Island Getaways** (✆ Box 1504, Cruz Bay 00831 ☎ 340/693–7676 or 888/693–7676 🖷 340/693–8923 ⊕ www.islandgetaways.net) has villas in the Great Cruz Bay–Chocolate Hole area, with a few others scattered around the island.

On-Line Vacations (✆ Box 9901, Emmaus 00830 ☎ 340/776–6036 or 888-842-6632 🖷 340/693–5357) books vacation villas around St. John. **Private Homes for Private Vacations** (⊠ 8D Carolina, Mamey Peak 00830 ☎🖷 340/776–6876 ⊕ www.privatehomesvi.com) has homes across the island. **Seaview Vacation Homes** (✆ Box 644, Cruz Bay 00831 ☎ 340/

776–6805 or 888/625–2963 🖷 340/779–4349 ⊕ www.seaviewhomes. com) handles homes with sea views in the Chocolate Hole, Great Cruz Bay, and Fish Bay areas. **Star Villas** (🖃 Box 599, Cruz Bay 00830 ☎ 340/776–6704 or 888/897–9759 🖷 340/776–6183 ⊕ www.starvillas. com) has cozy villas just outside Cruz Bay. **Vacation Vistas** (🖃 Box 476, Cruz Bay 00831 ☎ 340/776–6462 ⊕ www.vacationvistas.com) manages villas mainly in the Chocolate Hole, Great Cruz Bay, and Rendezvous areas. **Windspree** (✉ 7924 Emmaus, Cruz Bay 00830 ☎ 340/693–5423 or 888/742–0357 🖷 340/693–5623 ⊕ www.windspree.com) handles villas mainly in the Coral Bay area.

Where to Eat

The cuisine on St. John seems to get better every year, with culinary-school-trained chefs vying to see who can come up with the most imaginative dishes. There are restaurants to suit every taste and budget—from the elegant establishments at Caneel Bay Resort (where men may be required to wear a jacket at dinner) to the casual in-town eateries of Cruz Bay. For quick lunches, try the West Indian food stands in Cruz Bay Park and across from the post office. The cooks prepare fried chicken legs, pates (meat- and fish-filled pastries), and callaloo.

Some restaurants close for vacation in September and even October. If you have your heart set on a special place, call ahead to make sure it's open during these months.

For approximate costs, *see* the dining and lodging price chart on the U.S. Virgin Islands Planner, at the beginning of this chapter.

Bordeaux

CONTEMPORARY
★ $$$$

✕ **Chateau Bordeaux.** This rustic restaurant with a to-die-for view of Coral Bay is a bit out of the way but worth the trip. Its interior is made elegant with lace tablecloths, glowing candles, and stylish dinner presentations. Start with a bowl of creamy asparagus soup; then segue into seared sea scallops with sautéed spinach, wild mushrooms, and a potato galette or herb-encrusted rack of lamb with roasted corn and a raspberry sauce. Save room for dessert—the fresh berry cups with Chambord and caramel are wonderful. ✉ *Rte. 10, Bordeaux* ☎ *340/776–6611* ▭ *AE, MC, V* ☽ *No lunch.*

Coral Bay & Environs

AMERICAN
¢–$
Fodor'sChoice
★

✕ **Skinny Legs Bar & Restaurant.** Sailors who live aboard boats anchored just offshore and an eclectic coterie of residents gather for lunch and dinner at this funky spot in the middle of a boatyard-cum-shopping complex. If owner Moe Chabuz is around, take a gander at his gams; you'll see where the restaurant got its name. It's a great place for burgers, fish sandwiches, and whatever sports event is on the satellite TV. ✉ *Rte. 10, Coral Bay* ☎ *340/779–4982* ▭ *AE, D, MC, V.*

CARIBBEAN
★ $$

✕ **Miss Lucy's Restaurant.** Sitting seaside at remote Friis Bay, Miss Lucy's dishes up Caribbean food with a contemporary flair. Dishes like tender conch fritters, a spicy West Indian stew called callaloo, and fried fish make up most of the menu, but you also find a generous pot of seafood, sausage, and chicken paella on the menu. Sunday brunches are legendary, and if you're around on the full moon, stop by for the monthly full-moon party. The handful of small tables near the water are the nicest, but if they're taken or the mosquitoes are bad, the indoor tables do nicely. ⌧ *Rte. 107, Friis Bay* ☎ *340/693–5244* ⊟ *AE, D, MC, V* ⊙ *Closed Mon. No dinner Sun.*

★ ¢–$ ╳ **Vie's Snack Shack.** Stop by Vie's when you're out exploring the island. Although it's just a shack by the side of the road, Vie's serves up some great cooking. The garlic chicken legs are crisp and tasty, and the conch fritters are really something to write home about. Plump and filled with fresh herbs, a plateful will keep you going for the rest of the afternoon. Save room for a wedge of coconut pie, called a tart in this neck of the woods. When you're done eating, a spectacular white-sand beach across the road beckons. ⌧ *Rte. 10, Hansen Bay* ☎ *340/693–5033* ⊟ *No credit cards* ⊙ *Closed Sun. and Mon. No dinner.*

ECLECTIC ╳ **Donkey Diner.** In an odd combination that works well for Coral Bay
$$–$$$ visitors and residents, this tiny spot along the main road through Coral Bay sells yummy breakfasts and tasty pizza. Breakfasts can be as ordinary or as innovative as you like, with the menu running from fried eggs with bacon to blueberry pancakes to scrambled tofu served with home fries. Pizzas are equally eclectic, with toppings that include everything from the usual pepperoni and mushrooms to more exotic corn, raisins, and kalamata olives. ⌧ *Rte. 10, Coral Bay* ☎ *340/693–5240* ⊟ *No credit cards* ⊙ *Closed Mon. and Tues.*

Cruz Bay & Environs

CONTEMPORARY ╳ **Stone Terrace Restaurant.** A delightful harbor view, soft lantern light, and
$$$–$$$$ white-linen tablecloths provide the backdrop for chef Aaron Willis's imaginative cuisine. To standards like rack of lamb, he adds a crisp Dijon mustard–onion crust, a few savory carrot gnocchi, and a Stilton cheese cream sauce and rosemary glaze. He jazzes up the salad course with seared tuna sashimi perched on a spinach salad drizzled with a hoisin vinaigrette. The desserts change daily but are always as intriguing as the other courses. ⌧ *Bay St.* ☎ *340/693–9370* ⊟ *D, MC, V* ⊙ *Closed Mon. No lunch.*

★ $$$–$$$$ ╳ **Tage.** Tage gets rave reviews from locals and visitors alike for its imaginative cuisine. The menu isn't large but changes seasonally; look for dishes like pan-seared yellowfin tuna served with salad of pear, fennel, and arugula drizzled with a champagne truffle vinaigrette. Save room for a dessert such as almond and lemon pound cake topped with a passion fruit–caramel sauce. Although you may be tempted to eat outside, resist the urge—it's much quieter indoors. ⌧ *Rte. 104, across from Julius E. Sprauve School* ☎ *340/715–4270* ⊟ *AE, D, MC, V* ⊙ *Closed Mon. No lunch.*

$$$ ╳ **Chloe & Bernard's.** With a focus on Asian cuisine, Chloe & Bernard's is always delightful. The menu changes regularly, but you might start with a tasty wasabi-potato pancake or a pea sprout salad drizzled with a sweet chili-lemongrass dressing. Dinner might be marinated tuna served with mandarin fried rice and a lobster-mango summer roll. ⌧ *Westin St. John Resort & Villas, Rte. 104* ☎ *340/693–8000* ⊟ *AE, MC, V* ⊙ *No lunch.*

26

ECLECTIC
☺ $$–$$$

✕ **Fish Trap.** The rooms here all open to the breezes and buzz with a mix of locals and visitors. Chef Aaron Willis, who also presides over the kitchen at Stone Terrace, conjures up such tasty appetizers as conch fritters and fish chowder (a creamy combination of snapper, white wine, paprika, and secret spices). You can always find steak and chicken dishes, as well as an interesting pasta of the day. ⊠ *Bay and Strand Sts., next to Our Lady of Mount Carmel Church* ☎ *340/693–9994* ▭ *D, MC, V* ⊗ *Closed Mon. No lunch.*

¢–$

✕ **Chilly Billy's.** Although you might stop by this restaurant at lunchtime for a heartburn-inducing St. John Reuben (with turkey, cheese, sauerkraut, and mustard on rye), this restaurant's claim to fame is breakfast. The stuffed French toast is one step this side of heaven: before it's fried, the bread is soaked in a mixture of eggs and Bailey's. If you're not one for morning sweets, try a savory breakfast burrito stuffed with eggs and jalepeño jack cheese. ⊠ *Lumberyard Shopping Center, Boulon Center Rd.* ☎ *340/693–8708* ▭ *MC, V* ⊗ *No dinner.*

ITALIAN
$$$–$$$$
Fodor'sChoice
★

✕ **Zozo's Ristorante.** Creative takes on old standards coupled with lovely presentation draw the crowds to this restaurant at Gallows Point Resort. Start with crispy fried calamari served with a pesto mayonnaise. The chef dresses up roasted grouper with a pistachio crust and serves it with a warm goat cheese and arugula salad. The grilled veal chop comes with a pancetta and spinach gratin and crisp fried potatoes. The sunset views will take your breath away. ⊠ *Gallows Point Resort, Bay St.* ☎ *340/693–9200* ▭ *AE, MC, V* ⊗ *No lunch.*

☺ $$–$$$

✕ **Café Roma.** This casual second-floor restaurant in the heart of Cruz Bay is *the* place for traditional Italian cuisine: lasagna, spaghetti and meatballs, and chicken piccata. There are also excellent pizzas, but they are for takeout only. Rum-caramel bread pudding is a dessert specialty. The place can get crowded in the winter season, so show up early. ⊠ *Vesta Gade* ☎ *340/776–6524* ▭ *MC, V* ⊗ *No lunch.*

$$–$$$

✕ **Panini Beach Trattoria.** Taking its name from the pressed and grilled sandwiches that are a staple here at lunchtime, this cozy seaside bistro serves delightful northern Italian fare. Lunch includes basics like pizza, soup, and salads; the dinner menu includes everything from freshly made pasta to chicken to seafood dishes cooked with herbs and spices. Save room for dessert, because the chocolate panini is heavenly. The dining room is air-conditioned, but the alfresco beachfront tables are the best spots. ⊠ *Wharfside Village, Strand St.* ☎ *340/693–9119* ▭ *AE, MC, V* ⊗ *No lunch weekends.*

PAN-ASIAN
★ $$$$

✕ **Asolare.** Contemporary Asian cuisine dominates the menu at this elegant open-air eatery in an old St. John house. Come early and relax over drinks while you enjoy the sunset lighting up the harbor. Start with an appetizer such as pork dumplings served with a glass noodle salad; then move on to entrées such as beef fillet served with roasted haystack potatoes and napa cabbage, or seared tuna served with an orange-and-greens salad. If you still have room for dessert, try the chocolate pyramid, a luscious cake with homemade ice cream melting in the middle. ⊠ *Estate Lindholm, Rte. 20 on Caneel Hill* ☎ *340/779–4747* ▭ *AE, MC, V* ⊗ *No lunch.*

Beaches

St. John is blessed with many beaches, and all of them fall into the good, great, and don't-tell-anyone-else-about-this-place categories. Those along the north shore are all within the national park. Some are more developed than others—and many are crowded on weekends, holidays, and in high season—but by and large they're still pristine. Beaches along the south and eastern shores are quiet and isolated.

Cinnamon Bay Beach. This long, sandy beach faces beautiful cays and abuts the national park campground. The facilities are open to the public and include cool showers, toilets, a commissary, and a restaurant. You can rent water-sports equipment here—a good thing, because there's excellent snorkeling off the point to the right; look for the big angelfish and large schools of purple triggerfish. Afternoons on Cinnamon Bay can be windy—a boon for windsurfers but an annoyance for sunbathers—so arrive early to beat the gusts. The Cinnamon Bay hiking trail begins across the road from the beach parking lot; ruins mark the trailhead. There are actually two paths here: a level nature trail (signs along it identify the flora) that loops through the woods and passes an old Danish cemetery, and a steep trail that starts where the road bends past the ruins and heads straight up to Route 10. Restrooms are located on the main path from the commissary to the beach and scattered around the campground. ⊠ *North Shore Rd., Rte. 20, about 4 mi (6 km) east of Cruz Bay.*

Francis Bay Beach. Because there's little shade, this beach gets toasty warm in the afternoon when the sun comes around to the west, but the rest of the day, it's a delightful stretch of white sand. The only facilities are a few picnic tables tucked among the trees and a portable bathroom, but folks come here to watch the birds that live in the swampy area behind the beach. The park offers bird-watching hikes here on Sunday morning; sign up at the Visitor's Center in Cruz Bay. To get here, turn left at the Annaberg intersection. ⊠ *North Shore Rd., Rte. 20, ¼ mi from Annaberg intersection.*

Hawksnest Beach. Sea-grape and waving palm trees line this narrow beach, and there are restrooms, cooking grills, and a covered shed for picnicking. A patchy reef just offshore near the middle of the beach offers snorkeling an easy swim away, but the best underwater views are reserved for ambitious snorkelers who head farther to the east along the bay's fringes. Watch out for boat traffic—a channel guides dinghies to the beach, but the occasional boater strays into the swim area. It's the closest drivable beach to Cruz Bay, so it's often crowded with locals and visitors. ⊠ *North Shore Rd., Rte. 20, about 2 mi (3 km) east of Cruz Bay.*

Lameshur Bay Beach. This sea-grape-fringed beach is toward the end of a very long, partially paved road on the southeast coast. The reward for your long drive is solitude, good snorkeling, and a chance to spy on some pelicans. The beach has a couple of picnic tables, rusting barbecue grills, and a portable restroom. The ruins of the old plantation are a five-minute walk down the road past the beach. The area has good hiking trails, including the trek (more than a mile) up Bordeaux Moun-

26

tain before an easy walk to Yawzi Point. ⊠ *Off Rte. 107, about 1½ mi from Salt Pond.*

Maho Bay Beach. This popular beach is below Maho Bay Camps—a wonderful hillside enclave of tent cabins. The campground offers breakfast and dinner at its Pavillion Restaurant, water-sports equipment rentals at the beach, and restrooms. After a five-minute hike down a long flight of stairs to the beach, snorkelers head off along rocky outcroppings for a look at all manner of colorful fish. Watch for a sea turtle or two to cross your path. Another lovely strip of sand with the same name sits right along the North Shore Road. Turn left at the Annaberg intersection and follow the signs about 1 mi (1½ km) for Maho Bay Camps. ⊠ *Off North Shore Rd., Rte. 20, Maho Bay.*

Salt Pond Bay Beach. If you're adventurous, this rocky beach on the scenic southeastern coast—next to Coral Bay and rugged Drunk Bay—is worth exploring. It's a short hike down a hill from the parking lot, and the only facilities are an outhouse and a few picnic tables scattered about. Tide pools are filled with all sorts of marine creatures, and the snorkeling is good, particularly along the bay's edges. A short walk takes you to a salt pond, where salt crystals collect around the edges. Hike farther uphill past cactus gardens to Ram Head for see-forever views. Leave nothing valuable in your car; reports of thefts are common. ⊠ *Rte. 107, about 3 mi south of Coral Bay.*

Fodor'sChoice ★ **Trunk Bay Beach.** St. John's most-photographed beach is also the preferred spot for beginning snorkelers because of its underwater trail. (Cruiseship passengers interested in snorkeling for a day flock here, so if you're looking for seclusion, arrive early or later in the day.) Crowded or not, this stunning beach is one of the island's most beautiful. There are changing rooms with showers, bathrooms, a snack bar, picnic tables, a gift shop, phones, lockers, and snorkeling-equipment rentals. The parking lot often overflows, but you can park along the road. ⊠ *North Shore Rd., Rte. 20, about 2½ mi east of Cruz Bay.*

Sports & the Outdoors

BOATING & SAILING ★ If you're staying at a hotel or campground, your activities desk will usually be able to help you arrange a sailing excursion aboard a nearby boat. Most day sails leaving Cruz Bay head out along St. John's north coast. Those that depart Coral Bay might drop anchor at some remote cay off the island's east end or even in the nearby British Virgin Islands. Your trip usually includes lunch, beverages, and at least one snorkeling stop. Keep in mind that inclement weather could interfere with your plans, though most boats will still go out if rain isn't too heavy. If you're staying in a villa, or if your hotel or campground doesn't have an affiliated charter sailboat, contact **Connections** (⊠ 1 block up from ferry dock, diagonal to First Bank, Cruz Bay ☎ 340/776–6922 ⊠ Skinny Legs Bar & Restaurant, Coral Bay ☎ 340/779–4994 ⊕ www.connectionsstjohn.com). The very capable staff can find a boat that fits your style and pocketbook. The company also books fishing and scuba trips from both its offices.

For a speedier trip to the cays and remote beaches off St. John, you can rent a power boat from **Ocean Runner** (⊠ On the waterfront, Cruz Bay

☎ 340/693–8809 ⊕ www.oceanrunner.vi). The company rents one- and two-engine boats for around $300 to $400 per day. Gas and oil will run you $75 to $250 a day extra, depending on how far you're going. It's a good idea to have some skill with power boats for this self-drive adventure, but if you don't, you can hire a captain to go along to instruct you.

DIVING & SNORKELING Although just about every beach has nice snorkeling—Trunk Bay, Cinnamon Bay, and Waterlemon Cay at Leinster Bay get the most praise—you need a boat to head out to the more remote snorkeling locations and the best scuba spots. Sign on with any of the island's water-sports operators to get to spots farther from St. John. If you use the one at your hotel, just stroll down to the dock to hop aboard. Their boats will take you to hot spots between St. John and St. Thomas, including the tunnels at **Thatch Cay,** the ledges at **Congo Cay,** and the wreck of the General Rogers. Dive off St. John at **Stephens Cay,** a short boat ride out of Cruz Bay, where fish swim around the reefs as you float downward. At **Devers Bay,** on St. John's south shore, fish dart about in colorful schools. **Carval Rock,** shaped somewhat like an old-time ship, has gorgeous rock formations, coral gardens, and lots of fish. It can be too rough here in the winter, though. Count on paying $70 for a one-tank dive and $90 for a two-tank dive. Rates include equipment and a tour. If you've never dived before, try an introductory course, called a resort course. Or if certification is in your vacation plans, the island's dive shops can help you get your card.

Cruz Bay Watersports (☎ 340/776–6234 ⊕ www.divestjohn.com) has two locations: in Cruz Bay at the Lumberyard Shopping Complex and at the Westin St. John Resort. Owners Marcus and Patty Johnston offer regular reef, wreck, and night dives and USVI and BVI snorkel tours. The company holds both PADI five-star facility and NAUI Dream Resort status. **Low Key Watersports** (☎ 340/693–8999 or 800/835–7718 ⊕ www.divelowkey.com), at Wharfside Village, offers one- and two-tank dives and specialty courses. It's certified as a PADI five-star training facility.

FISHING Well-kept charter boats—approved by the U.S. Coast Guard—head out to the north and south drops or troll along the inshore reefs, depending on the season and what's biting. The captains usually provide bait, drinks, and lunch, but you need to bring your own hat and sunscreen. Fishing charters run between $550 and $700 per half day for the boat. **Capt. Bryon Oliver** (☎ 340/693–8339) takes you out to the north and south drops or closer in to St. John. **Gone Ketchin'** (☎ 340/714–1175 ⊕ www.goneketchin.com), in St. John, arranges trips with old salt Captain Griz.

HIKING Although it's fun to go hiking with a Virgin Islands National Park guide, don't be afraid to head out on your own. To find a hike that suits your ability, stop by the park's visitor center in Cruz Bay and pick up the free trail guide; it details points of interest, dangers, trail lengths, and estimated hiking times. Although the park staff recommends long pants to protect against thorns and insects, most people hike in shorts because it can get very hot. Wear sturdy shoes or hiking boots even if you're hiking to the beach. Don't forget to bring water and insect repellent.

Fodor's Choice
★

The **Virgin Islands National Park** (☎ 340/776–6201 ⊕ www.nps.gov/viis) maintains more than 20 trails on the north and south shores and offers guided hikes along popular routes. A full-day trip to Reef Bay is a must; it's an easy hike through lush and dry forest, past the ruins of an old plantation, and to a sugar factory adjacent to the beach. It can be a bit arduous for young kids, however. Take the public Vitran bus or a taxi to the trailhead, where you can meet a ranger who'll serve as your guide. The park provides a boat ride back to Cruz Bay for $15 to save you the walk back up the mountain. The schedule changes from season to season; call for times and reservations, which are essential.

HORSEBACK RIDING

Clip-clop along the island's byways for a slower-pace tour of St. John. **Carolina Corral** (☎ 340/693–5778) offers horseback trips down scenic roads with owner Dana Barlett. She has a way with horses and calms even the most novice riders. Rates start at $65 for a 1½-hour ride.

SAILING

Even novice sailors can take off in a small sailboat from Cruz Bay Beach with **Sail Safaris** (☎ 340/998–1265 or 866/820-6906 ⊕ www.sailsafaris.net) to one of the small islands off St. John. Guided half-day tours, rentals, and lessons each run $70 per person.

SEA KAYAKING

Poke around crystal bays and explore undersea life from a sea kayak. Rates run about $60 for a full day in a double kayak. Tours start at $50 for a half day. On the Cruz Bay side of the island, **Arawak Expeditions** (☎ 340/693–8312 or 800/238–8687 ⊕ www.arawakexp.com), which operates out of Low Key Watersports in Cruz Bay's Wharfside Village, has professional guides who use traditional and sit-on-top kayaks to ply coastal waters. The company also rents single and double kayaks so you can head independently to nearby islands like Stephen's Cay. Explore Coral Bay Harbor and Hurricane Hole on the eastern end of the island in a sea kayak from **Crabby's Watersports** (✉ Rte. 107, outside Coral Bay ☎ 340/714–2415 ⊕ www.crabbyswatersports.com). If you don't want to paddle into the wind to get out of Coral Bay Harbor, the staff will drop you off in Hurricane Hole so you can paddle downwind back to Coral Bay. Crabby's also rents Sunfish sailboats, dinghies, and fishing tackle.

SIGHTSEEING TOURS

In St. John, taxi drivers provide tours of the island, making stops at various sites, including Trunk Bay and Annaberg Plantation. Prices run around $15 a person. The taxi drivers congregate near the ferry in Cruz Bay. The dispatcher will find you a driver for your tour.

WALKING TOURS

Along with providing trail maps and brochures about Virgin Islands National Park, the park service also gives several guided tours on- and offshore. Some are only offered during particular times of the year, and some require reservations. For more information, contact the **V. I. National Park Visitors Center** (✉ Cruz Bay ☎ 340/776–6201 ⊕ www.nps.gov/viis).

WINDSURFING

Steady breezes and expert instruction make learning to windsurf a snap. Try **Cinnamon Bay Campground** (✉ Rte. 20, Cinnamon Bay ☎ 340/693–5902 or 340/626–4769), where rentals are $30 to $70 per hour. Lessons are available right at the waterfront; just look for the Windsurfers stacked up on the beach. The cost for a one-hour lesson starts at $70. You can also rent kayaks.

Shopping

Areas & Malls

Luxury goods and handicrafts can be found on St. John. Most shops carry a little of this and a bit of that, so it pays to poke around. The Cruz Bay shopping district runs from **Wharfside Village,** just around the corner from the ferry dock, through the streets of town to North Shore Road and **Mongoose Junction,** an inviting shopping center with stonework walls (its name is a holdover from a time when those furry island creatures gathered at a nearby garbage bin); steps connect the two sections of the center, which has unusual, upscale shops. Out on Route 104, stop in at the **Marketplace** to explore its handful of gift and crafts shops. At the island's other end, there are a few stores—selling clothes, jewelry, and artwork—here and there from the village of **Coral Bay** to the small complex at **Shipwreck Landing.**

On St. John, store hours run from 9 or 10 to 5 or 6. Wharfside Village and Mongoose Junction shops in Cruz Bay are often open into the evening.

Specialty Items

ART **Bajo el Sol.** Bajo el Sol sells works by owner Livy Hitchcock plus those from a roster of the island's best artists. Shop for oil and acrylics, jewelry, sculptures, and ceramics. ✉ *Mongoose Junction, North Shore Rd., Cruz Bay* ☎ *340/693–7070.*

Coconut Coast Studios. This waterside shop, a five-minute walk from Cruz Bay, showcases the work of Elaine Estern. She specializes in undersea scenes. ✉ *Frank Bay, Cruz Bay* ☎ *340/776–6944.*

BOOKS **National Park Headquarters.** The headquarters sells several good histories of St. John, including *St. John Back Time,* by Ruth Hull Low and Rafael Lito Valls, and, for linguists, Valls's *What a Pistarckle!*—an explanation of the colloquialisms that make up the local version of English (*pistarckle* is a Dutch Creole word that means "noise" or "din," which pretty much sums up the language here). ✉ *Cruz Bay* ☎ *340/776–6201.*

CLOTHING **Big Planet Adventure Outfitters.** You knew when you arrived that some place on St. John would cater to the outdoor enthusiasts who hike up and down the island's trails. Well, this outdoor-clothing store is where you can find the popular Naot sandals and Reef footware, along with colorful and durable cotton clothing and accessories by Billabong. The store also sells children's clothes. ✉ *Mongoose Junction, North Shore Rd., Cruz Bay* ☎ *340/776–6638.*

Bougainvillea Boutique. If you want to look as if you stepped out of the pages of the resort-wear spread in an upscale travel magazine, try this store. Owner Susan Stair carries *very* chic men's and women's resort wear, straw hats, leather handbags, and fine gifts. ✉ *Mongoose Junction, North Shore Rd., Cruz Bay* ☎ *340/693–7190.*

The Clothing Studio. Several talented artists put their original designs on clothing for all members of the family. This shop carries T-shirts, beach cover-ups, pants, shorts, and even bathing suits with beautiful hand-painted creations. ☒ *Mongoose Junction, North Shore Rd., Cruz Bay* ☎ *340/776–6585.*

Jolly Dog. Stock up on the stuff you forgot to pack at this store. Sarongs in cotton and rayon, beach towels with tropical motifs, and hats and T-shirts sporting the Jolly Dog logo fill the shelves. ☒ *Shipwreck Landing, Rte. 107, Sanders Bay* ☎ *340/693–5333* ☒ *Skinny Legs Shopping Complex, Rte. 10, Coral Bay* ☎ *340/693–5900.*

Sloop Jones. It's worth the trip all the way out to the island's east end to shop for made-on-the-premises clothing, pillows, and fabrics by the yard splashed with tropical bright colors. Fabrics are in cotton, linen, and rayon and are supremely comfortable. ☒ *Off Rte. 10, East End* ☎ *340/779–4001.*

St. John Editions. Shop here for nifty cotton dresses that go from beach to dinner with a change of shoes and accessories. Owner Molly Soper also carries attractive straw hats and inexpensive jewelry. ☒ *North Shore Rd., Cruz Bay* ☎ *340/693–8444.*

FOODSTUFFS If you're renting a villa, condo, or cottage and doing your own cooking, there are several good places to shop for food; just be aware that prices are much higher than those at home.

Love City Mini Mart. This market doesn't look like much, but it's just about the only place to shop in Coral Bay and has a surprising selection of items. ☒ *Off Rte. 107, Coral Bay* ☎ *340/693–5790.*

Starfish Market. The island's largest store usually has the best selection of meat, fish, and produce. ☒ *The Marketplace, Rte. 104, Cruz Bay* ☎ *340/779–4949.*

GIFTS **Bamboula.** Owner Jo Sterling travels the Caribbean and the world to find unusual housewares, art, rugs, bedspreads, accessories, shoes, and men's and women's clothes for this multicultural boutique. ☒ *Mongoose Junction, North Shore Rd., Cruz Bay* ☎ *340/693–8699.*

The Canvas Factory. If you're a true shopper who needs an extra bag to carry home all your treasures, this store offers every kind of tote and carrier imaginable, from simple bags to suitcases with numerous zippered compartments. All are made of canvas, naturally. It also sells great canvas hats. ☒ *Mongoose Junction, North Shore Rd., Cruz Bay* ☎ *340/776–6196.*

Donald Schnell Studio. In addition to pottery, this place sells unusual hand-blown glass, wind chimes, kaleidoscopes, fanciful fountains, and more. Your purchases can be shipped worldwide. ☒ *Mongoose Junction, North Shore Rd., Cruz Bay* ☎ *340/776–6420.*

Every Ting. As its name implies, this store has some of this and a bit of that. Shop for Caribbean music CDs, books, picture frames decorated with shells, and T-shirts with tropical motifs. Residents and visitors also drop by to have a cup of espresso or to use the Internet terminals. ☒ *Bay St., Cruz Bay* ☎ *340/693–5820.*

Fabric Mill. Shop here for women's clothing in tropical brights, as well as place mats, napkins, and batik wraps. Or take home a brilliant-hued bolt from the upholstery-fabric selection. ☒ *Mongoose Junction, North Shore Rd., Cruz Bay* ☎ *340/776–6194.*

Mumbo Jumbo. With what may be the best prices in St. John, this cozy shop carries everything from tropical clothing to stuffed sea creatures to gift items. ⊠ *Skinny Legs Shopping Complex, Rte. 10, Coral Bay* ☎ *340/779–4277.*

Pink Papaya. This store is where you can find the well-known work of longtime Virgin Islands resident M. L. Etre, plus a huge collection of one-of-a-kind gifts, including bright tablecloths, unusual trays, dinnerware, and unique tropical jewelry. ⊠ *Lemon Tree Mall, King St., Cruz Bay* ☎ *340/693–8535.*

Wicker, Wood and Shells. Shop the second floor of this store for lovely sculptures and other objets d'art, all with a tropical theme. The first floor houses the island's best selection of greeting cards, notepaper, and other interesting gifts to tuck in your suitcase for friends back home. ⊠ *Mongoose Junction, North Shore Rd., Cruz Bay* ☎ *340/776–6909.*

JEWELRY **Caravan Gallery.** Owner Radha Speer travels the world to find much of the unusual jewelry she sells here. And the more you look, the more you see—folk art, tribal art, and masks for sale cover the walls and tables, making this a great place to browse. ⊠ *Mongoose Junction, North Shore Rd., Cruz Bay* ☎ *340/779–4566.*

Free Bird Creations. Head here for special handcrafted jewelry—earrings, bracelets, pendants, chains—as well as the good selection of water-resistant watches for your excursions to the beach. ⊠ *Wharfside Village, Strand St., Cruz Bay* ☎ *340/693–8625.*

R&I Patton Goldsmiths. Rudy and Irene Patton design most of the lovely silver and gold jewelry displayed in this shop. The rest comes from various designer friends. Sea fans (those large, lacy plants that sway with the ocean's currents) in filigreed silver, lapis lazuli set in gold, starfish and hibiscus pendants in silver or gold, and gold sand-dollar-shape charms and earrings are choice selections. ⊠ *Mongoose Junction, North Shore Rd., Cruz Bay* ☎ *340/776–6548.*

Verace. Jewelry from such well-known designers as John Bagley and Patrick Murphy fill the shelves. Murphy's stunning silver sailboats with gems for hulls will catch your attention. ⊠ *Wharfside Village, Strand St., Cruz Bay* ☎ *340/693–7599.*

PHOTO **Cruz Bay Photo.** Pick up disposable-film cameras, film, and other photo
DEVELOPING needs, or when your memory card fills up, download your digital photos to a disk or print them out. Shop here also for good-quality sunglasses, a must for your tropical vacation. ⊠ *Wharfside Village, Strand St., Cruz Bay* ☎ *340/779–4313.*

Nightlife

St. John isn't the place to go for glitter and all-night partying. Still, after-hours Cruz Bay can be a lively little town in which to dine, drink, dance, chat, or flirt. Notices posted on the bulletin board outside the Connections telephone center—up the street from the ferry dock in Cruz Bay—or listings in the island's two small newspapers (the *St. John Sun Times* and *Tradewinds*) will keep you apprised of special events, comedy nights, movies, and the like.

After a sunset drink at **Zozo's Ristorante** (✉ Gallows Point Resort, Bay St., Cruz Bay ☎ 340/693–9200), up the hill from Cruz Bay, you can stroll around town (much is clustered around the small waterfront park). Many of the young people from the U.S. mainland who live and work on St. John will be out sipping and socializing, too.

Lizard's Landing (✉ Veste Gade, Cruz Bay ☎ 340/776–6065) is the wild and crazy place. Loud music and drinks like the Sunburned Lizard make this Cruz Bay's hottest late-night spot. There's calypso and reggae on Friday night at **Fred's** (✉ King St., Cruz Bay ☎ 340/776–6363). Young folks like to gather at **Woody's** (✉ Road up from ferry, across from Subway restaurant, Cruz Bay ☎ 340/779–4625), where sidewalk tables provide a close-up view of Cruz Bay's action.

On the far side of the island, landlubbers and old salts listen to music and swap stories at **Skinny Legs Bar & Restaurant** (✉ Rte. 10, Coral Bay ☎ 340/779–4982).

Exploring St. John

St. John is an easy place to explore. One road runs along the north shore, another across the center of the mountains. There are a few roads that branch off here and there, but it's hard to get lost. Pick up a map at the visitor center before you start out, and you'll have no problems. Few residents remember the route numbers, so have your map in hand if you stop to ask for directions. Bring along a swimsuit for stops at some of the most beautiful beaches in the world. You can spend all day or just a couple of hours exploring, but be advised that the roads are narrow and wind up and down steep hills, so don't expect to get anywhere in a hurry. There are lunch spots at Cinnamon Bay and in Coral Bay, or you can do what the locals do—find a secluded spot for a picnic. The grocery stores in Cruz Bay sell Styrofoam coolers just for this purpose.

If you plan to do a lot of touring, renting a car will be cheaper and will give you much more freedom than relying on taxis; on St. John, taxis are shared safari vans, and they are reluctant to go anywhere until they have a full load of passengers. Although you may be tempted by an open-air Suzuki or Jeep, a conventional car can get you just about everywhere on the paved roads, and you'll be able to lock up your valuables. You may be able to share a van or open-air vehicle (called a safari bus) with other passengers on a tour of scenic mountain trails, secret coves, and eerie bush-covered ruins.

Numbers in the margin correspond to points of interest on the St. John map.

★ ❻ **Annaberg Plantation.** In the 18th century, sugar plantations dotted the steep hills of this island. Slaves and free Danes and Dutchmen toiled to harvest the cane that was used to create sugar, molasses, and rum for export. Built in the 1780s, the partially restored plantation at Leinster Bay was once an important sugar mill. Though there are no official visiting hours, the National Park Service has regular tours, and some well-informed taxi drivers will show you around. Occasionally you may see a living-history demonstration—someone making johnnycake or weaving baskets. For information on tours and cultural events, contact the St. John National Park Service Visitors Center. ✉ *Leinster Bay Rd., Annaberg* ☎ *340/776–6201* ⊕ *www.nps.gov/viis* ☽ *Daily sunrise–sunset.*

★ ❹ **Bordeaux Mountain.** St. John's highest peak rises to 1,277 feet. Route 10 passes near enough to the top to offer breathtaking views. Don't stray into the road here—cars whiz by at a good clip along this section. Instead, drive nearly to the end of the dirt road that heads off next to the restaurant and gift shop for spectacular views at Picture Point and the trailhead of the hike downhill to Lameshur. Get a trail map from the park service before you start. ✉ *Rte. 10.*

❼ **Catherineberg Ruins.** At this fine example of an 18th-century sugar and rum factory, there's a storage vault beneath the windmill. Across the road, look for the round mill, which was later used to hold water. In the 1733 slave revolt, Catherineberg served as headquarters for the Amina warriors, a tribe of Africans captured into slavery. ✉ *Rte. 10, Catherineberg.*

❺ **Coral Bay.** This laid-back community at the island's dry, eastern end is named for its shape rather than for its underwater life—the word *coral* comes from *krawl,* Dutch for "corral." It's a small, quiet, neighborhoody settlement—a place to get away from it all. You'll need a four-wheel-drive vehicle if you plan to stay at this end of the island, as some of the rental houses are up unpaved roads that wind around the mountain. If you come just for lunch, a regular car will be fine.

❶ **Cruz Bay.** St. John's main town may be compact (it consists of only several blocks), but it's definitely a hub: the ferries from St. Thomas and the BVI pull in here, and it's where you can get a taxi or rent a car to travel around the island. There are plenty of shops in which to browse, a number of watering holes where you can stop for a breather, many restaurants, and a grassy square with benches where you can sit back and take everything in. Look for the current edition of the handy, amusing "St. John Map" featuring Max the Mongoose. To pick up a useful guide to St. John's hiking trails, see various large maps of the island, and find out about current park service programs, including guided walks and cultural demonstrations, stop by the **V. I. National Park Visitors Center** (✉ Near the baseball field, Cruz Bay ☎ 340/776–6201 ⊕ www.nps. gov/viis). It's open daily from 8 to 4:30.

❷ **Peace Hill.** It's worth stopping at this spot just past the Hawksnest Bay overlook for great views of St. John, St. Thomas, and the BVI. On the flat promontory is an old sugar mill. ✉ *Off Rte. 20, Denis Bay.*

★ ❸ **Reef Bay Trail.** Although this is one of the most interesting hikes on St. John, unless you're a rugged individualist who wants a physical challenge (and that describes a lot of people who stay on St. John), you can probably get the most out of the trip if you join a hike led by a park service ranger, who can identify the trees and plants on the hike down, fill you in on the history of the Reef Bay Plantation, and tell you about the petroglyphs on the rocks at the bottom of the trail. A side trail takes you to the plantation's greathouse, a gutted but mostly intact structure

26

that maintains vestiges of its former beauty. Take the safari bus from the park's visitor center. A boat takes you from the beach at Reef Bay back to the visitor center, saving you the uphill climb. ✉ *Rte. 10, Reef Bay* ☎ *340/776–6201 Ext. 238 reservations* ⊕ *www.nps.gov/viis* 🖃 *Free, safari bus $5, return boat trip to Cruz Bay $15* ☉ *Tours at 10 AM, days change seasonally.*

ST. CROIX

By Lynda Lohr   As my seaplane skimmed St. Croix's north coast on the flight from St. Thomas, the island's agrarian past played out below. Stone windmills left over from the days when sugar ruled stood like sentinels in the fields. As we closed in on Christiansted, the big yellow Fort Christianvaern loomed on the waterfront, and the city's red roofs created a colorful counterpoint to the turquoise harbor. A visit to St. Croix, once a Danish colony, always puts me in touch with my Danish roots (my grandmother was a Poulsen). Indeed, history is so popular in St. Croix that planes are filled with Danish visitors who, like other vacationers, come to sun at the island's powdery beaches, enjoy pampering at the hotels, and dine at interesting restaurants but mainly wish to explore the island's colonial history.

Until 1917 Denmark owned St. Croix and her sister Virgin Islands, an aspect of the island's past that is reflected in street names in the main towns of Christiansted and Frederiksted as well as surnames of many island residents. Those early Danish settlers, as well as those from other European nations, left behind slews of 18th- and 19th-century ruins, all of them worked by slaves brought over on ships from Africa, their descendants, and white indentured servants lured to St. Croix to pay off their debt to society. Some—such as the Christiansted National Historic site, Whim Plantation, the ruins at St. George Village Botanical Garden, the Nature Conservancy's property at Estate Princess, and the ruins at Estate Mount Washington and Judith's Fancy—are open for easy exploration. Others are on private land, but a drive around the island reveals the ruins of 100 plantations here and there on St. Croix's 84 square mi. Their windmills, greathouses, and factories are all that's left of the 224 plantations that once grew sugarcane, tobacco, and other agriculture products at the height of the island's plantation glory.

The downturn began in 1801 when the British occupied the island. Another British occupation in 1807 through 1815, droughts, the demise of the slave trade in 1803, the development of the sugar beet industry in Europe, political upheaval, and a depression sent the island on a downward spiral.

St. Croix never recovered from these blows. The end of slavery in 1848, followed by labor riots, fires, hurricanes, and an earthquake during the last half of the 19th century, brought what was left of the island's economy to its knees. The start of prohibition in 1922 called a halt to the island's rum industry, further crippling the economy. The situation remained dire—so bad that President Herbert Hoover called the territory an "effective poorhouse" during a 1931 visit—until the rise of tourism in the late 1950s and 1960s. With tourism came economic improvements

Turtles on St. Croix

LIKE CREATURES from the earth's prehistoric past, green, leatherback, and hawksbill turtles crawl ashore during the annual April-to-November turtle nesting season to lay their eggs. They return from their life at sea every two to seven years to the beach where they were born. Since turtles can live for up to 100 years, they may return many times to nest in St. Croix.

The leatherbacks like Sandy Point National Wildlife Refuge and other spots on St. Croix's western end, but the hawksbills prefer Buck Island and the East End. Green turtles are also found primarily on the East End.

All are endangered species that face numerous natural and man-made predators. Particularly in the Frederiksted area, dogs and cats prey on the nests and eat the hatchlings.

Occasionally a dog will attack a turtle about to lay its eggs, and cats train their kittens to hunt at turtle nests, creating successive generations of turtle-egg hunters. In addition, turtles have often been hit by fast-moving boats that leave large slices in their shells if they don't kill them outright.

The leatherbacks are the subject of a project by the international group Earthwatch. Each summer, teams arrive at Sandy Point National Wildlife Refuge to ensure that poachers, both natural and human, don't attack the turtles as they crawl up the beach. The teams also relocate nests that are laid in areas prone to erosion. When the eggs hatch, teams stand by to make sure the turtles make it safely to the sea, and scientists tag them so they can monitor their return to St. Croix.

26

---

coupled with an influx of residents from other Caribbean islands and the mainland, but St. Croix depends partly on industries like the huge oil refinery outside Frederiksted to provide employment.

Today, suburban subdivisions fill the fields where sugarcane once waved in the tropical breeze. Condominium complexes line the beaches along the north coast outside Christiansted. Homes that are more elaborate dot the rolling hillsides. Modern strip malls and shopping centers sit along major roads, and it's as easy to find a McDonald's as it is Caribbean fare.

Although St. Croix sits definitely in the 21st century, with only a little effort you can easily step back into the island's past.

Where to Stay

You can find everything from plush resorts to simple beachfront digs in St. Croix. If you sleep in either the Christiansted or Frederiksted area, you'll be closest to shopping, restaurants, and nightlife. Most of the island's other hotels will put you just steps from the beach. St. Croix has several small but special properties that offer personalized service. If you like all the comforts of home, you may prefer to stay in a condominium or villa. Room rates on St. Croix are competitive with those on other islands, and if you travel off-season, you'll find substantially reduced prices. Many properties offer money-saving honeymoon and dive pack-

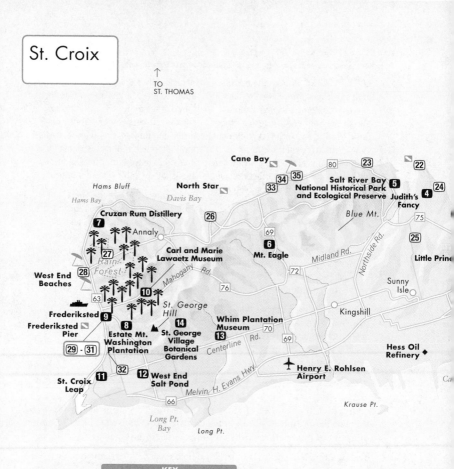

St. Croix

TO
ST. THOMAS

Cane Bay

North Star

Hams Bluff

Davis Bay

Hams Bay

Cruzan Rum Distillery

80 23 22

34 35

33

Salt River Bay
National Historical Park
and Ecological Preserve

Judith's
Fancy

5

4 24

Blue Mt.

75

7

Annaly

26

69

6

Mt. Eagle

25

Midland Rd.

Little Princ

27

Carl and Marie
Lawaetz Museum

72

Northside Rd.

West End
Beaches

28

Rain
Forest

Mahogany Rd.

76

Sunny
Isle

63

10

Kingshill

9

St. George
Hill

14

Whim Plantation
Museum

Hess Oil
Refinery

Frederiksted

Frederiksted
Pier

8

Estate Mt.
Washington
Plantation

St. George
Village
Botanical
Gardens

13

70

69

29 - 31

32

Centerline Rd.

St. Croix
Leap

11

12

West End
Salt Pond

Melvin H. Evans Hwy.

Henry E. Rohlsen
Airport

66

Krause Pt.

Long Pt.
Bay

Long Pt.

KEY	
⚲	Beaches
◺	Dive Sites
⛴	Cruise Ship Terminal
1	Exploring Sights
1	Hotels & Restaurants
🌴	Rain Forest

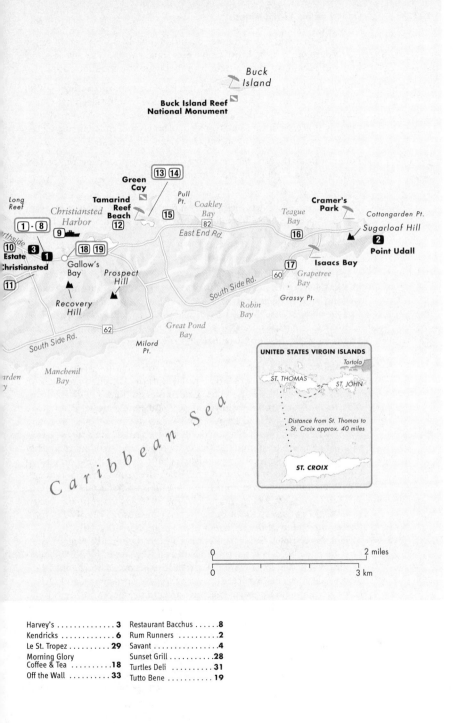

Buck
Island

Buck Island Reef
National Monument

Green
Cay

Tamarind
Reef
Beach

Pull
Pt.

Coakley
Bay

Cramer's
Park

Teague
Bay

Cottongarden Pt.

Long
Reef

Christiansted
Harbor

rthside

Estate

Christiansted

Gallow's
Bay

Prospect
Hill

East End Rd.

Sugarloaf Hill

Point Udall

Isaacs Bay

Grapetree
Bay

Grassy Pt.

Robin
Bay

South Side Rd.

Recovery
Hill

Great Pond
Bay

Milord
Pt.

Manchenil
Bay

South Side Rd.

arden
y

Caribbean Sea

UNITED STATES VIRGIN ISLANDS

Tortola

ST. THOMAS   ST. JOHN

Distance from St. Thomas to
St. Croix approx. 40 miles

ST. CROIX

0   2 miles
0   3 km

ages. Whether you stay in a hotel, a condominium, or a villa, you'll enjoy up-to-date amenities. Most properties have room TVs, but at some bed-and-breakfasts there might be only one in the common room.

Although a stay right in historic Christiansted may mean putting up with a little urban noise, you probably won't have trouble sleeping. Christiansted rolls up the sidewalks fairly early, and air-conditioners drown out any noise. Solitude is guaranteed at hotels and inns outside Christiansted and those on the outskirts of sleepy Frederiksted.

For approximate costs, *see* the dining and lodging price chart on the U.S. Virgin Islands Planner, at the beginning of this chapter.

Hotels

CHRISTIANSTED

$–$$

Hotel Caravelle. Near the harbor, at the waterfront end of a pleasant shopping arcade, the Caravelle's in-town location puts you just steps away from shops and restaurants. Rooms are tasteful and tropical, with white walls and floral-print bedspreads and curtains; most have ocean views. A small pool provides a swimming and sunning option. The ever-popular Rum Runners restaurant sits just off the lobby. Although its location provides city conveniences, use your normal prudence when walking back to the hotel at night. ⊠ *44A Queen Cross St., 00820* 🕾 *340/773–0687 or 800/524–0410* 🖷 *340/778–7004* ⊕ *www.hotelcaravelle. com* ➟ *43 rooms, 1 suite* ♢ *Restaurant, refrigerators, cable TV, in-room broadband, Wi-Fi, pool, bar, Internet room, meeting room* ⊟ *AE, D, DC, MC, V* ⧋ *EP.*

$–$$

Hotel on the Cay. Hop on the free ferry to reach this casual spot on an island in the middle of Christiansted Harbor. Although the location sounds a bit inconvenient, the ferry ride takes no time. The captain zips over to the waterfront whenever he sees someone waiting. Rooms are pleasantly furnished and have harbor views, balconies or patios, and kitchenettes for times when you don't want to eat at the hotel's restaurant. In addition to sunning at the small beach and strolling the lushly planted grounds, you can try windsurfing and other water sports. Keep an eye out for one of the endangered St. Croix ground lizards that call the island home. ⊠ *Protestant Cay, Christiansted 00820-4441* 🕾 *340/773–2035 or 800/524–2035* 🖷 *340/773–7046* ⊕ *www.hotelonthecay. com* ➟ *53 rooms* ♢ *Restaurant, kitchenettes, cable TV, Wi-Fi, pool, beach, snorkeling, Internet room* ⊟ *AE, D, MC, V* ⧋ *CP.*

$–$$

Pink Fancy Hotel. Offering a connection to the island's elegant past, the venerable hotel is listed on the National Register of Historic Places. While the building dates from 1780, it did not become a hotel until 1948. Rooms are furnished with antiques, mahogany furnishings, and Oriental carpets, and lush gardens meander around the fenced-in compound, creating a comfortable base for folks who like to get out and about. Guests gather poolside for breakfast and conversation. Although the hotel shines brightly, its neighborhood is run-down, so take a taxi back after nighttime excursions. Continental breakfast isn't offered for the least expensive rooms. ⊠ *27 Prince St., 00820* 🕾 *340/773–8460 or 800/524–2045* 🖷 *340/773–6448* ⊕ *www.pinkfancy.com* ➟ *12 rooms* ♢ *Fans, kitchenettes, cable TV with movies, in-room data ports, no-smoking rooms* ⊟ *AE, MC, V* ⧋ *CP.*

$ 🏨 **King Christian Hotel.** A stay at the King Christian puts you right in the heart of Christiansted's historic district. Parts of the building date back to the mid-1700s, but numerous additions and refurbishments have brought it up to modern standards. Rooms are a bit on the pedestrian side, but floral spreads and pastel walls brighten things up considerably. We recommend this hotel for its location. You can hop a ferry to nearby Protestant Cay for an afternoon at the beach when you tire of the pool. Out the front door and you're a quick walk to restaurants, shops, and water-sports excursions. ⊠ *57 King St., Box 24467, 00824-0467* ☎ *340/773–6330 or 800/524–2012* 🖷 *340/773–9411* ⊕ *www.kingchristian. com* ⤳ *39 rooms* ⚲ *Fans, some in-room safes, refrigerators, cable TV, pool, dive shop, boating, fishing, meeting room, car rental* ▭ *AE, D, MC, V* �﴾⊙⾙ *EP.*

OUTSIDE
CHRISTIANSTED
$
Fodor's Choice
★

🏨 **Carringtons Inn.** Hands-on owners Claudia and Roger Carrington are the real reason to stay here, and they conjure up delicious breakfasts—rum-soaked French toast is a house specialty—dole out advice, and make you feel right at home. Formerly a private home, the comfy bed-and-breakfast is a 10-minute drive from Christiansted. Each room is different, with a decorating theme that reflects a namesake flower. Wicker furniture, hand-woven carpets, and balconies in some rooms, colorful spreads, and sea or pool views create an inviting atmosphere. The hillside suburban location means you need a rental car if you stay. ⊠ *4001 Estate Hermon Hill, Christiansted 00820* ☎ *340/713–0508 or 877/658–0508* 🖷 *340/719–0841* ⊕ *www.carringtonsinn.com* ⤳ *5 rooms* ⚲ *Fans, some kitchenettes, refrigerators, pool, Internet room; no room TVs, no smoking* ▭ *AE, MC, V* �﴾⊙⾙ *BP.*

26

EAST END
⊙ **$$$–$$$$**

🏨 **The Buccaneer.** Offering a total resort experience just outside of Christiansted, this property has sandy beaches, swimming pools, and extensive sports facilities. A palm-tree-lined main drive leads to the large, pink main building atop a hill; the rest of the resort sprawls over the grounds of a 300-acre former sugar plantation, where shops, restaurants, and guest quarters are scattered about the manicured lawns. Spacious rooms are Mediterranean in style, with tile floors, four-poster beds, massive wardrobes of pale wood, marble baths, and local works of art. Beach-side doubloon rooms are the largest and are steps from the beach, but you can be perfectly comfortable no matter where you stay. All rooms are stocked with hair dryers, irons, and a nice selection of toiletries. ⊠ *Rte. 82, Box 25200, Shoys 00824* ☎ *340/712–2100 or 800/255–3881* 🖷 *340/712–2104* ⊕ *www.thebuccaneer.com* ⤳ *138 rooms* ⚲ *4 restaurants, in-room safes, refrigerators, cable TV, Wi-Fi, 18-hole golf course, 8 tennis courts, 2 pools, gym, spa, beach, snorkeling, hiking, bar, shops, children's programs (ages 4–12), Internet room, meeting rooms, no-smoking rooms* ▭ *AE, D, DC, MC, V* �﴾⊙⾙ *BP.*

$$$–$$$$ 🏨 **Divi Carina Bay Resort.** An oceanfront location puts most rooms at the Divi Carina Bay Resort close to the beach, though villas are across the road, behind the main building. Because it has the island's only casino and regular evening entertainment, it's your best choice if you enjoy non-stop nightlife. The rooms have rattan and wicker furniture, white-tile floors, sapphire-and-teal linens, and accessories that complement the creamy white walls. Although its location way out on the island's East End puts you a long way from anywhere, the hotel provides a fair amount of activities to keep you busy. If you still have some energy left after dancing the night away, you'll need a car for treks outside the hotel. ⊠ *25 Rte. 60, Estate Turner Hole 00820* ☎ *340/773–9700 or 877/773–9700* 🖷 *340/773–6802* ⊕ *www.divicarina.com* ⇗ *146 rooms, 2 suites, 20 villas* ♻ *2 restaurants, snack bar, fans, in-room safes, microwaves, refrigerators, cable TV, in-room data ports, Wi-Fi, 2 tennis courts, pool, gym, outdoor hot tub, beach, dock, snorkeling, billiards, 2 bars, casino, video game room, Internet room* ▭ *AE, D, DC, MC, V* ¶Ⓞ¶ *EP.*

❁ **$$$** 🖽 **Chenay Bay Beach Resort.** The beachfront location and complimentary tennis and water-sports equipment (including kayaks) make this resort a real find, particularly for families with active kids. Recent refurbishment projects have upgraded nearly all the rooms, which have ceramic-tile floors, bright peach or yellow walls, rattan furnishings, and front porches. Gravel paths meander among terraced wood or stucco cottages. Other facilities include a large L-shape pool, a protected beach, a picnic area, and a casual restaurant. There's also a shuttle to grocery stores and shopping areas for a reasonable fee. ⊠ *Rte. 82, Green Cay* 🖃 *Box 24600, Christiansted 00824* ☎ *340/773–2918 or 800/548–4457* 🖷 *340/773–6665* ⊕ *www.chenaybay.com* ⇗ *50 rooms* ♻ *Restaurant, picnic area, kitchenettes, cable TV, in-room data ports, Wi-Fi, 2 tennis courts, pool, outdoor hot tub, beach, snorkeling, boating, volleyball, bar, babysitting, children's programs (ages 4–12)* ▭ *AE, MC, V* ¶Ⓞ¶ *EP.*

$$ 🖽 **Tamarind Reef Hotel.** Spread out along a small, sandy beach, these motel-like buildings offer casual comfort. Independent travelers who want the option to eat in or out will enjoy the rooms with basic kitchenettes. The spacious modern rooms have rattan furniture, tropical-print fabrics, and either a terrace or a deck with views of St. Croix's sister islands to the north. Snorkelers can explore a nearby reef, but shallow water makes serious swimming difficult. There's a snack bar just off the beach, and the Galleon Restaurant is next door at Green Cay Marina. ⊠ *5001 Tamarind Reef, off Rte. 82, Annas Hope 00820* ☎ *340/773–4455 or 800/619–0014* 🖷 *340/773–3989* ⊕ *www.usvi.net/hotel/tamarind* ⇗ *46 rooms* ♻ *Restaurant, refrigerators, cable TV, in-room data ports, pool, snorkeling, meeting rooms, no-smoking rooms* ▭ *AE, DC, MC, V* ¶Ⓞ¶ *CP.*

FREDERIKSTED   🖽 **Sandcastle on the Beach.** Right on a gorgeous stretch of white beach,
$–$$$ this hotel caters primarily to gay men and lesbians, but anyone is welcome. The hotel has a tropical charm that harks back to a simpler time in the Caribbean; proximity to Frederiksted's interesting dining scene is also a plus. Rooms, which have contemporary decor, tile floors, and bright fabrics, come in several sizes and locations. All have kitchens or kitchenettes, and most have sea views. Packages that include a car and bar privileges are a good value. ⊠ *127 Smithfield, Rte. 71, Frederiksted 00840* ☎ *340/772–1205 or 800/524–2018* 🖷 *340/772–1757* ⊕ *www.sandcastleonthebeach.com* ⇗ *8 rooms, 8 suites, 5 villas* ♻ *Restaurant, fans, in-room safes, some kitchens, some kitchenettes, cable TV, in-room VCRs, 2 pools, gym, massage, beach, snorkeling,*

laundry facilities; meeting room, no room phones, no kids ⊟ *AE, D, MC, V* ⫧ *CP.*

NORTH SHORE
$$$
Fodor'sChoice
★

⊡ **Villa Greenleaf.** This spacious B&B is all about the details—four-poster beds with elegant duvets, towels folded just so, hand-stenciled trim on the walls, and gardens tastefully planted. Staying here is like visiting a well-heeled relative who happens to have home in the Caribbean. The house was built in the 1950s but was totally renovated in 2004. Unless you want to spend your days gazing at the lovely view of St. Croix's north shore or relaxing beside the sparkling pool, you'll need a car for trips around the island. ⊠ *Island Center Rd., Montpelier* ✆ *Box 675, Christiansted, 00821* ☎ *340/719–1958 or 888/282–1001* 🖷 *340/772–5425* ⊕ *www.villagreenleaf.com* ⇨ *6 rooms* ⚹ *Fans, Wi-Fi, pool; some refrigerators, no room phones, no room TVs* ⊟ *AE, D, MC, V* ⫧ *BP.*

$$
⊡ **Cane Bay Reef Club.** These modestly sized lodgings sit seaside in the peaceful community of Cane Bay. They're perfect for folks who don't need every amenity but want to be right at the water's edge. All the rooms in the two-story buildings have no-frills kitchenettes, the usual rattan furniture with tropical accents, and balconies or porches that put you almost on the beach. You can rent dive gear nearby to explore St. Croix's famous Cane Bay Wall. ⊠ *Rte. 80, Cane Bay* ✆ *Box 1407, Kingshill 00851* ☎☎ *340/778-2966* 🖷 *800/253–8534* ⊕ *www.canebay. com* ⇨ *9 units* ⚹ *Restaurant, fans, cable TV, kitchenettes, pool, Internet room* ⊟ *AE, D, DC, MC, V* ⫧ *EP.*

$$
⊡ **Carambola Beach Resort.** We like this resort's stellar beachfront setting and peaceful ambience, even though it means overlooking some chipped paint, a cracked tile here and there, and other problems caused by several changes in ownership. Although a total overhaul is promised within the next year or so, it had not yet begun at this writing. Rooms in the 25 two-story red-roof villas are identical except for the view— ocean or garden—and have terra-cotta floors, ceramic lamps, mahogany ceilings and furnishings, and rocking chairs. Each has a patio and a huge bath (shower only). Lushly planted walkways connect the rooms and the hotel's restaurants and pool. ⊠ *Rte. 80, Davis Bay* ✆ *Box 3031, Kingshill 00851* ☎ *340/778–3800 or 888/503–8760* 🖷 *340/778–1682* ⇨ *151 rooms* ⚹ *3 restaurants, fans, in-room safes, cable TV, in-room data ports, 2 tennis courts, pool, gym, beach, dive shop, snorkeling, Internet room, meeting rooms* ⊟ *AE, D, DC, MC, V* ⫧ *EP.*

$$
⊡ **Hibiscus Beach Hotel.** This hotel is right at a lovely beach, which is the best reason to stay here. Rooms, each named for a tropical flower, show obvious wear and tear, but all have roomy balconies and are decorated with brightly colored fabrics. Bathrooms are clean but nondescript—both the shower stalls and the vanity mirrors are on the small side. You'll need a car to get around, as the surrounding neighborhood doesn't encourage walks through its streets. ⊠ *4131 Estate La Grande Princesse, off Rte. 752, La Grande Princesse 00820-4441* ☎ *340/773– 4042 or 800/442–0121* 🖷 *340/773–7668* ⊕ *www.hibiscusbeachresort. com* ⇨ *37 rooms* ⚹ *Restaurant, in-room safes, minibars, microwaves, refrigerators, cable TV, in-room data ports, pool, beach, snorkeling, Internet room* ⊟ *AE, D, MC, V* ⫧ *CP.*

26

$–$$ ⊞ **Inn at Pelican Heights.** If you don't mind renting a car to explore the
FodorsChoice island, a stay at this comfortable B&B will make you feel as if you are
★ leaving the rest of the world far behind. The buildings ramble over the
hillside, providing sea views and a comfortable ambience. Each room is
a bit different, though all have typical tropical decor—brightly colored
spreads and wicker or rattan furniture. Innkeeper Fred Laue conjures up
elaborate breakfasts that might include anything from breakfast lasagna
to pancakes with fruit and sausage. You can walk to the spacious beach
at Pelican Cove in 10 minutes. If you need a dose of civilization, Christiansted is a 15-minute drive away. ⊠ *Off Rte. 751, 4201 Estate St. John,
Christiansted 00820-4491* ☎ *340/713–8022 or 888/445–9458* ▤ *340/
713–8526* ⊕ *www.innatpelicanheights.com* ➹ *6 rooms* ⟳ *Fans, kitchenettes, cable TV, pool, Internet room* ▤ *MC, V* ⑪ *BP.*

$–$$ ⊞ **Villa Margarita.** This quiet retreat is along a tranquil north-shore beach,
about 20 minutes from Christiansted's shops and restaurants. It provides
a particularly good base if you want to admire the dramatic views of the
windswept coast. You'll want to rent a car to explore the island, as the
resort's amenities are limited. Units vary in size but come complete with
kitchenettes, tropical furnishings, private balconies, and those spectacular views. Swimming in front of the hotel is a bit difficult because of shallow water, but sandy beaches are steps away. The snorkeling nearby is is
excellent. ⊠ *Off Rte. 80, Salt River* ⟑ *9024 Salt River, Christiansted 00820*
☎ *340/713–1930 or 866/274–8811* ▤ *340/719–3389* ⊕ *www.
villamargarita.com* ➹ *3 units* ⟳ *Fans, kitchenettes, refrigerators, cable
TV, pool; no room phones, no kids under 17* ▤ *MC, V* ⑪ *EP.*

$–$$ ⊞ **Waves at Cane Bay.** St. Croix's famed Cane Bay Wall is just offshore
from this resort, giving it an enviable location. It's still a good bet for
divers, as the hotel will loan you weights and tanks. Although the hotel's
stretch of beach is rocky, you can sunbathe at a small patch of sand beside the pool, which has been carved from the coral along the shore.
Two peach-and-mint-green buildings house large, balconied rooms decorated with soft pastel prints. Sadly, maintenance has slipped a bit in
recent years. The other drawback is the isolation; you definitely need a
car if you stay here. ⊠ *Rte. 80, Cane Bay* ⟑ *Box 1749, Kingshill
00851* ☎ *340/778–1805 or 800/545–0603* ▤ *340/778–4945* ⊕ *www.
canebaystcroix.com* ➹ *12 rooms* ⟳ *Restaurant, fans, in-room safes, kitchenettes, cable TV, in-room data ports, pool, dive shop, snorkeling, bar,
Internet room; no room phones* ▤ *AE, MC, V* ⑪ *EP.*

Condominiums & Villas

In addition to several condo and villa complexes, you can also rent a
private home—usually for a week or more. Renting a house gives you
the convenience of home as well as top-notch amenities. Many have pools,
hot tubs, and deluxe furnishings. Most companies meet you at the airport, arrange for a rental car, and provide helpful information.

If you want to be close to the island's restaurants and shopping, look for
a villa or condominium in the hills above Christian or on either side of
the town. An East End location gets you out of Christiansted's hustle and
bustle, but you're still only 15 minutes from town. North Shore locations are lovely, with gorgeous sea views and lots of peace and quiet.

Caribbean Property Management (☎ 340/778–8782 or 800/496–7379 ⊕ www.enjoystcroix.com) has villas on the east end. **Rent A Villa** (☎ 800/533–6863 ⊕ www.rentavillavacations.com) specializes in villas on the island's east end. **Vacation St. Croix** (☎ 340/778–0361 or 877/788–0361 ⊕ www.vacationstcroix.com) has villas all around the island.

★ $$$–$$$$ ▦ **Villa Madeleine.** If you like privacy and lovely accommodations, we think you'll like Villa Madeline. The two-story units flow downhill from this condominium resort's centerpiece, a West Indian plantation greathouse. Each villa has a full kitchen and a private pool. The decor evokes the property's natural surroundings: rattan furniture with plush cushions, rocking chairs, and, in some, bamboo four-poster beds. Special touches include pink-marble showers and hand-painted floral wall borders. You definitely need a car for sightseeing and dining out. ⊠ *Off Rte. 82, Teague Bay* 🖈 *52 King St., Christiansted 00820* ☎ *340/773–4850 or 800/237–1959* 🖷 *340/773–8989* ⊕ *www.teaguebayproperties.com* 🖈 *43 villas* ⚬ *Fans, kitchens, cable TV, tennis court, 43 pools* ▭ *AE, MC, V* ⧉ *EP.*

☾ $$–$$$$ ▦ **Sugar Beach.** With all the conveniences of home, Sugar Beach has apartments that are immaculate and breezy. Each has a full kitchen and a large patio or balcony with an ocean view; larger units have washers and dryers. Though the exteriors of these condos are drab beige stucco, the interiors are white with tropical furnishings. The pool occupies the ruins of a 250-year-old sugar mill. A lovely beach is just steps away, and Christiansted's conveniences are an easy 10-minute drive. It's one of a string of condominium complexes near a public housing project, so don't walk in the neighborhood at night. ⊠ *Rte. 752, Estate Golden Rock 00820* ☎ *340/773–5345 or 800/524–2049* 🖷 *340/773–1359* ⊕ *www.sugarbeachstcroix.com* 🖈 *46 apartments* ⚬ *Fans, kitchens, cable TV, 2 tennis courts, pool, beach, Internet room, meeting rooms* ▭ *AE, D, MC, V* ⧉ *EP.*

☾ $$ ▦ **Colony Cove.** In a string of condominium complexes, Colony Cove lets you experience comfortable beachfront living. Units all have two bedrooms, two bathrooms, and washer/dryer combos, making it a good choice for families. They have typical tropical furnishings with most furniture made of rattan and wicker. Floors are tile. The neighorhood isn't the best, so don't plan on strolling too far at night. ⊠ *Rte. 752, Estate Golden Rock 00824* ☎ *340/773–1965 or 800/828–0746* ⊕ *www.antillesresorts.com* 🖈 *62 apartments* ⚬ *Fans, kitchens, cable TV, in-room data ports, Wi-Fi, pool, beach* ▭ *AE, MC, V* ⧉ *EP.*

WHERE TO CAMP △ **Mount Victory Camp.** A remarkable quietude distinguishes this out-
☾ of-the-way spread on 8 acres in the island's rain forest. If you really want to commune with nature, you'll be hard-pressed to find a better way to do it on St. Croix. Hosts Bruce and Mathilde Wilson are on hand to explain the environment. You sleep in screened-in tent-cottages perched on a raised platform and covered by a roof. Each has a rudimentary outdoor kitchen. The shared, spotlessly clean bathhouse is an easy stroll away. The location feels remote, but a lovely sand beach and the Sunset Grill restaurant are a 2-mi (3-km) drive down the hill. In another 10 minutes you're in Frederiksted. ⚬ *BBQs, flush toilets, drinking water, showers, picnic tables, public telephone* 🖈 *5 tents* ⊠ *Creque Dam*

26

Rd., Frederiksted 00841 ☎ *340/772–1651 or 866/772–1651* ⊕ *www.mtvictorycamp.com* ≋ *Reservations essential* ⊟ *No credit cards.*

Where to Eat

Seven flags have flown over St. Croix, and each has left its legacy in the island's cuisine. You can feast on Italian, French, and American dishes; there are even Chinese and Mexican restaurants in Christiansted. Fresh local seafood is plentiful and always good; wahoo, mahimahi, and conch are most popular. Island chefs often add Caribbean twists to familiar dishes. For a true island experience, stop at a local restaurant for goat stew, curried chicken, or fried pork chops. Regardless of where you eat, your meal will be an informal affair. As is the case everywhere in the Caribbean, prices are higher than you'd pay on the mainland. Some restaurants may close for a week or two in September or October, so if you are traveling during these months it's best to call ahead.

For approximate costs, *see* the dining and lodging price chart on the U.S. Virgin Islands Planner, at the beginning of this chapter.

Christiansted

CARIBBEAN
$–$$
✕ **Harvey's.** The dining room is plain, even dowdy, and plastic lace tablecloths constitute the sole attempt at decor—but who cares? The food is delicious. Daily specials, such as mouthwatering goat stew and tender whelks in butter, served with big helpings of rice, fungi, and vegetables, are listed on the blackboard. Genial owner Sarah Harvey takes great pride in her kitchen, bustling out from behind the stove to chat and urge you to eat up. ⊠ *11B Company St.* ☎ *340/773–3433* ⊟ *No credit cards* ⊘ *Closed Sun. No dinner.*

CONTEMPORARY
★ **$$$–$$$$**
✕ **Kendricks.** The chef at this open-air restaurant—a longtime favorite among locals—conjures up creative contemporary cuisine. To start, try the Alaskan king crab cakes with lemon black-pepper aioli or the warm chipotle pepper with garlic and onion soup. Move on to the house specialty: pecan-crusted roast pork loin with ginger mayonnaise. ⊠ *21–32 Company St.* ☎ *340/773–9199* ⊟ *AE, MC, V* ⊘ *Closed Sun. No lunch.*

★ **$$–$$$$**
✕ **Restaurant Bacchus.** On the chic side, this restaurant is as notable for its extensive wine list as it is for its food. The menu changes regularly but often includes favorites like mussels topped with pieces of slab bacon and served in a fennel broth. Entrées include a crispy duck confit with a mango rum sauce, steak swimming in a mushroom sauce, and pasta with Parmesan cheese and truffle oil. For dessert, try the rum-drenched sourdough-bread pudding. ⊠ *Queen Cross St., off King St.* ☎ *340/692–9922* ⊟ *AE, D, DC, MC, V* ⊘ *Closed Mon. No lunch.*

★
🕐 **$$–$$$$**
✕ **Rum Runners.** The view is as stellar as the food at this highly popular local standby. Sitting right on Christiansted Boardwalk, Rum Runners serves everything, including a to-die-for salad of crispy romaine lettuce and tender grilled lobster drizzled with a lemongrass vinaigrette. More hearty fare includes baby back ribs cooked with the restaurant's special spice blend and Guinness stout. ⊠ *Hotel Caravelle, 44A Queen Cross St.* ☎ *340/773–6585* ⊟ *AE, MC, V.*

★ **$$–$$$$** ✕ **Savant.** Savant is one of those small but special spots that locals love. The cuisine is a fusion of Mexican, Thai, and Caribbean—an unusual combination that works surprisingly well. You can find anything from vegetables in a red curry sauce to enchiladas stuffed with chicken to maple-teriyaki pork tenderloin coming out of the kitchen. With 20 tables crammed into the indoor area and small courtyard, this little place can get crowded. Call early for reservations. ✉ *4C Hospital St.* ☎ *340/713–8666* ▭ *AE, DC, MC, V* ⊗ *No lunch.*

ECLECTIC ✕ **Avocado Pitt.** Locals gather at this Christiansted waterfront spot for **$** the breakfast and lunch specials as well as for a bit of gossip. Breakfast runs to stick-to-the-ribs dishes like oatmeal and pancakes. Lunches include such dressed-up basics as the Yard Bird on a Bun, a chicken breast sandwich tarted up with a liberal dose of hot sauce. The yellowfin tuna sandwich is made from fresh fish and gives a new taste to a standard lunchtime favorite. ✉ *King Christian Hotel, 59 Kings Wharf* ☎ *340/773–9843* ▭ *No credit cards* ⊗ *No dinner.*

¢–$ ✕ **Morning Glory Coffee & Tea.** Stop by this cozy spot in a popular shopping center for light fare. Lunch runs to wraps and sandwiches filled with veggies, cheeses, and sliced meats. If you can't decide, try the restaurant's famous chicken salad made with walnuts and grapes. For breakfast, the chef cooks up waffles, beignets, croissants, and eggs cooked any way you like. Smoothies are a house specialty. ✉ *Gallows Bay Market Pl.* ☎ *340/773–6620* ▭ *No credit cards* ⊗ *Closed Sun. No dinner.*

FRENCH ✕ **Café Christine.** A favorite with the professionals who work in down-★ **$–$$** town Christiansted, Café Christine's presentation is as lovely as the food. The small menu changes daily, but look for dishes like a shrimp salad drizzled with a lovely vinaigrette dressing or a vegetarian plate with quiche, salad, and lentils. Desserts are perfection. If the pear pie topped with chocolate is on the menu, don't hesitate. This tiny restaurant has both air-conditioned indoor tables and an outside porch that overlooks historic buildings. ✉ *Apothecary Hall Courtyard, 4 Company St.* ☎ *340/713–1500* ▭ *No credit cards* ⊗ *Closed weekends. No dinner.*

ITALIAN ✕ **Tutto Bene.** Its muraled walls, brightly striped cushions, and painted **$$–$$$$** trompe-l'oeil tables make Tutto Bene look more like a sophisticated Mexican cantina than an Italian cucina. One bite of the food, however, will clear up any confusion. Written on hanging mirrors is the daily menu, which includes such specialties as veal saltimbocca, a scallopine of veal with prosciutto and sage, all topped with mozzarella and parmesan cheeses. Desserts, including a decadent tiramisu, are on the menu as well. ✉ *Hospital St. in Boardwalk shopping center* ☎ *340/773–5229* ⊗ *No lunch* ▭ *AE, MC, V.*

Outside Christiansted

ECLECTIC ✕ **Breezes.** This aptly named restaurant is poolside at Club St. Croix ⌚ **$$–$$$** condominiums. Visitors and locals are drawn by its reasonable prices and good food. This is *the* place on the island to be for Sunday brunch, where the menu includes Caesar salad, burgers, and blackened prime rib with Cajun seasonings and horseradish sauce. For dessert, try the flourless chocolate torte—a wedge of rich chocolate served with a river

26

of chocolate sauce. ⊠ *Club St. Croix, 3220 Golden Rock, off Rte. 752, Golden Rock* ☎ *340/773–7077* ▭ *AE, D, MC, V.*

$$–$$$ ✕ **Elizabeth's.** In a nondescript shopping center, this small place has surprisingly imaginative food. Dinner entrées include a tasty ravioli served with mussels, scallops, and shrimp in a sherry cream sauce and tilapia stuffed with crab. Lunch brings out lots of locals for the generous helping of curried chicken salad and a crab cake wrapped in a flavorful tortilla. The piquant horseradish sauce adds a tasty touch. ⊠ *Princesse Plaza, 3220 Golden Rock, Rte. 75, Estate Princesse* ☎ *340/719–0735* ⊗ *No lunch weekends* ▭ *AE, D, MC, V.*

East End

ECLECTIC ✕ **The Galleon.** This popular dockside restaurant is always busy. Start
$$$–$$$$ with the Caesar salad or perhaps a flaky layered duck napolean. The chef's signature dish is a tender filet mignon topped with fresh local lobster. Pasta lovers should sample the penne with smoked chicken, roasted red peppers, portobello mushrooms, and a smoked garlic cream sauce. Take Route 82 out of Christiansted; then turn left at the sign for Green Cay Marina. ⊠ *Annas Hope* ☎ *340/773–9949* ▭ *MC, V.*

Frederiksted

ECLECTIC ✕ **Blue Moon.** This terrific little bistro, which has a loyal local follow-
$$–$$$ ing, offers a changing menu that draws on Cajun and Caribbean flavors. Try the spicy gumbo with andouille sausage or crab cakes with a spicy aioli as an appetizer; shrimp scampi loaded with garlic and served over pasta as an entrée; and the Almond Joy sundae for dessert. There's live jazz on Fridays. ⊠ *7 Strand St.* ☎ *340/772–2222* ▭ *AE, D, MC, V* ⊗ *Closed Mon.*

☾ **¢–$** ✕ **Turtles Deli.** Eat outside at this tiny spot just as you enter downtown Frederiksted. Lunches are as basic as a corned beef on rye or as imaginative as "The Raven" (turkey breast with bacon, tomato, and melted cheddar cheese on French bread). Also good is "The Beast," named after the grueling hill that challenges bikers in the annual triathlon. It is piled high with hot roast beef, raw onion, and melted Swiss cheese with horseradish and mayonnaise. Early risers stop by for cinnamon buns and espresso. ⊠ *37 Strand St., at Prince Passage* ☎ *340/772–3676* ▭ *No credit cards* ⊗ *Closed Sun. No dinner.*

FRENCH ✕ **Le St. Tropez.** A ceramic-tile bar and soft lighting set the mood at this
$$–$$$$ Mediterranean-style bistro tucked into a courtyard one street from the waterfront. Seated either inside or on the adjoining patio, you can enjoy grilled meats in delicate sauces. The menu changes daily, often taking advantage of local seafood. The fresh basil, tomato, and mozzarella salad is heavenly. ⊠ *227 King St.* ☎ *340/772–3000* ▭ *AE, MC, V* ⊗ *Closed Sun. No lunch Sat.*

Outside Frederiksted

☾ **$$–$$$** ✕ **Sunset Grill.** As you would expect, this alfresco restaurant is a hot spot for sunset watchers, as well as a social hub for locals. The ever-changing menu features fish, fish, and more fish. Try the almond-crusted grouper in a soy-butter sauce or whatever else the chef whipped up that day. Those who aren't fond of fish can pick from dishes like a rib-eye steak for dinner; on the lunch menu is a buffalo burger. Desserts might include fresh blueberries and strawberries in a rum sauce. ⊠ *Rte. 63* ☎ *340/772–5855* ⊟ *MC, V* ☉ *Closed Mon.*

North Shore

ECLECTIC ✕ **Off the Wall.** Divers fresh from a plunge at the north shore's popular
$–$$ Cane Bay Wall gather at this breezy spot on the beach. If you want to sit a spell before you order, a hammock beckons. Burgers, quesadillas, and steak sandwiches make up most of the menu. The potato salad that comes with your sandwich is as good as you'd get at home. You might find blues and jazz Tuesday through Sunday nights. ⊠ *Rte. 80, Cane Bay* ☎ *340/778–4771* ⊟ *AE, MC, V.*

Beaches

★ **Buck Island.** A visit to this island beach, part of Buck Island Reef National Monument, is a must. The beach is beautiful, but its finest treasures are those you can see when you plop off the boat and adjust your mask, snorkel, and fins to swim over colorful coral and darting fish. To get here you have to charter a boat or go on an organized trip. Don't know how to snorkel? No problem—the boat crew will have you outfitted and in the water in no time. Take care not to step on those black-pointed spiny sea urchins or touch the mustard-color fire coral, which can cause a nasty burn. Most charter boat trips start with a snorkel over the lovely reef before a stop at the island's beach. An easy 20-minute hike leads uphill to an overlook for a bird's-eye view of the reef below. Find restrooms at the beach. Buck Island is 5 mi (8 km) north of St. Croix.

Cane Bay. The waters aren't always gentle at this breezy north-shore beach, but there are seldom many people around, and the scuba diving and snorkeling are wondrous. You can see elkhorn and brain corals, and less than 200 yards out is the drop-off called Cane Bay Wall. Cane Bay can be an all-day destination. You can rent kayaks and snorkeling and scuba gear at water-sports shops across the road, and a couple of very casual restaurants beckon when the sun gets too high. The Waves at Cane Bay sits seaside nearby, as do other restaurants, but the beach has no public restrooms. ⊠ *Rte. 80, about 4 mi (6 km) west of Salt River.*

West End Beaches. There are several unnamed beaches along the coast road north of Frederiksted, but it's best if you don't stray too far from civilization. For safety's sake, most vacationers plop down their towel near one of the very casual restaurants spread out along Route 63. The beachfront Sunset Grill makes a nice spot for lunch. The beach at the Rainbow Beach Club, a five-minute drive outside Frederiksted, has a bar, a casual restaurant, water sports, and volleyball. If you want to be close to the cruise-ship pier, just stroll on over to the adjacent sandy beach in front of Fort Frederik. On the way south out of Frederiksted, the stretch near Sandcastle on the Beach hotel is also lovely. ⊠ *Rte. 63, north and south of Frederiksted.*

Sports & the Outdoors

BOAT TOURS   Almost everyone takes a day trip to Buck Island aboard a charter boat. Most leave from the Christiansted waterfront or from Green Cay Ma-

26

rina and stop for a snorkel at the island's eastern end before dropping anchor off a gorgeous sandy beach for a swim, a hike, and lunch. Sailboats can often stop right at the beach; a larger boat might have to anchor offshore a bit farther. A full-day sail runs about $75 with lunch included on most trips. A half-day sail costs about $50. **Big Beard's Adventure Tours** (☎ 340/773–4482 ⊕ www.bigbeards.com) takes you on a catamaran, the *Renegade* or the *Flyer,* from the Christiansted waterfront to Buck Island for snorkeling before dropping anchor at a private beach for a barbecue lunch. **Caribbean Sea Adventures** (☎ 340/773–2628 ⊕ www.caribbeanseadventures.com) departs from the Christiansted waterfront for half- and full-day trips on various boats. The **Teroro Charters** (☎ 340/773–3161 ⊕ www.visitstcroix.com/captainheinz.html) trimaran *Teroro II* leaves Green Cay Marina for full- or half-day sails. Bring your own lunch.

DIVING & SNORKELING At **Buck Island,** a short boat ride from Christiansted or Green Cay Marina, the reef is so nice that it's been named a national monument. You can dive right off the beach at **Cane Bay,** which has a spectacular drop-off called the Cane Bay Wall. Dive operators also do boat trips along the Wall, usually leaving from Salt River or Christiansted. **Frederiksted Pier** is home to a colony of sea horses, creatures seldom seen in the waters off the Virgin Islands. At **Green Cay,** just outside Green Cay Marina in the east end, you can see colorful fish swimming around the reefs and rocks. Two exceptional north-shore sites are **North Star** and **Salt River,** which you can reach only by boat. At Salt River you can float downward through a canyon filled with colorful fish and coral.

The island's dive shops take you out for one- or two-tank dives. Plan to pay about $65 for a one-tank dive and $85 for a two-tank dive, including equipment and an underwater tour. All companies offer certification and introductory courses called resort dives for novices.

Which dive outfit you pick usually depends on where you're staying. Your hotel may have one on-site. If not, others are located close by. If you use the hotel's dive operation, you're just a short stroll away from the dock. Where the dive boat goes on a particular day depends on the weather, but in any case, all St. Croix's dive sites are special. All shops are affiliated with PADI, the Professional Association of Diving Instructors.

If you're staying in Christiansted, **Dive Experience** (✉ 1111 Strand St., Christiansted ☎ 340/773–3307 or 800/235–9047 ⊕ www.divexp.com) has PADI five-star status and runs trips to the north-shore walls and reefs in addition to offering the usual certification and introductory classes. **St. Croix Ultimate Bluewater Adventures** (✉ Queen Cross St., Christiansted ☎ 340/773–5994 or 877/567–1367 ⊕ www.stcroixscuba.com) can take you to your choice of more than 75 sites; it also offers a variety of packages that include hotel stays.

Folks staying in the Judith's Fancy area are closest to **Anchor Dive Center** (✉ Salt River Marina, Rte. 801, Salt River ☎ 340/778–1522 or 800/532–3482 ⊕ www.anchordivestcroix.com). The company also has facilities at the Buccaneer and Carambola Beach Resort. Anchor takes divers to more than 35 sites, including the wall at Salt River Canyon.

Cane Bay Dive Shop (⊠ Rte. 80, Cane Bay ☎ 340/773–9913 or 800/338–3843 ⊕ www.canebayscuba.com) is the place to go if you want to do a beach dive or boat dive along the north shore. The famed Cane Bay Wall is 150 yards from the five-star PADI facility. This company also has shops at Pan Am Pavilion in Christiansted, on Strand Street in Frederiksted, and at the Divi Carina Bay hotel.

In Frederiksted, **Scuba Shack** (⊠ Frederiksted Beach, Rte. 631, Frederiksted ☎ 340/772–3483 or 888/789–3483 ⊕ www.stcroixscubashack.com) takes divers right off the beach near the Changes in Latitude restaurant, on night dives off the Frederiksted Pier, or on boat trips to wrecks and reefs. **Scuba West** (⊠ 330 Strand St., Frederiksted ☎ 340/772–3701 or 800/352–0107 ⊕ www.divescubawest.com) runs trips to reefs and wrecks from its base in Frederiksted but specializes in showing divers the sea horses that live around the Frederiksted Pier.

FISHING Since the early 1980s, some 20 world records—many for blue marlin—have been set in these waters. Sailfish, skipjack, bonito, tuna (allison, blackfin, and yellowfin), and wahoo are abundant. A charter runs about $100 an hour per person, with most boats going out for four-, six-, or eight-hour trips. **Caribbean Sea Adventures** (⊠ 59 Kings Wharf, Christiansted ☎ 340/773–2628 ⊕ www.caribbeanseaadventures.com) will take you out on a 38-foot powerboat called the *Fantasy*.

GOLF St. Croix's courses welcome you with spectacular vistas and well-kept greens. Check with your hotel or the tourist board to determine when major celebrity tournaments will be held. There's often an opportunity to play with the pros. The **Buccaneer** (⊠ Rte. 82, Shoys ☎ 340/712–2144 ⊕ www.thebuccaneer.com) has an 18-hole course that is close to Christiansted and is the centerpiece of the Buccaneer Hotel. Greens fees are $92, not including $18 for a cart rental. The spectacular 18-hole course
★ at **Carambola Golf Club** (⊠ Rte. 80, Davis Bay ☎ 340/778–5638 ⊕ www.golfcarambola.com), in the northwest valley, was designed by Robert Trent Jones, Sr. It sits near Carambola Beach Resort. Greens fees are $79 for 18 holes, which includes the use of a golf cart. The **Reef Golf Course** (⊠ Teague Bay ☎ 340/773–8844), a public course on the island's east end, has 9 holes. Greens fees are $18, and cart rental is $10.

HIKING Although you can set off by yourself on a hike through a rain forest or along a shore, a guide will point out what's important and tell you why. **Ay-Ay Eco Hike & Tours Association** (⌂ Box 2435, Kingshill 00851 ☎ 340/772–4079), run by Ras Lumumba Corriette, takes hikers up hill and down dale in some of St. Croix's most remote places, including the rain forest and Mount Victory. Some hikes include stops at places like the Carl and Marie Lawaetz Museum and old ruins. The cost is $40 to $50 per person for a three- or four-hour hike. There's a three-person minimum. A jeep tour through the rain forest runs $100 per person.

HORSEBACK Well-kept roads and expert guides make horseback riding on St. Croix RIDING pleasurable. At Sprat Hall, just north of Frederiksted, Jill Hurd runs **Paul & Jill's Equestrian Stables** (⊠ Rte. 58, Frederiksted ☎ 340/772–2880 or 340/772–2627 ⊕ pws.prserv.net/paul-and-jills). She will take you clip-clopping through the rain forest, across the pastures, along the beaches, and over the hilltops—explaining the flora, fauna, and ruins on the way. A 1½-hour ride costs $60.

KAYAKING   **Caribbean Adventure Tours** (✉ Columbus Cove Marina, Rte. 80, Salt River ☎ 340/778–1522 ⊕ www.stcroixkayak.com) takes you on trips through Salt River Bay National Historical Park and Ecological Preserve, one of the island's most pristine areas. All tours run $45. **Virgin Kayak Tours** (✉ Rte. 80, Cane Bay ☎ 340/778–0071 ⊕ www. kayakstcroix.com) runs guided kayak trips through the Salt River and also rents kayaks so you can tour around the Cane Bay area by yourself. All tours run $45. Kayak rentals are $15 an hour or $40 for the entire day.

SIGHTSEEING TOURS   **St. Croix Safari Tours** (☎ 340/773–6700 ⊕ www.gotostcroix.com/ safaritours) offers van tours of St. Croix. Tours depart from Christiansted and last about five hours. Costs run from $25 per person plus admission fees to attractions.

WINDSURFING   St. Croix's trade winds make windsurfing a breeze. Most hotels rent Windsurfers and other water-sports equipment to nonguests. **St. Croix Watersports** (✉ Hotel on the Cay, Protestant Cay, Christiansted ☎ 340/773–7060 ⊕ www.stcroixwatersports.com) offers Windsurfer rentals, sales, and rides; parasailing; and water-sports equipment such as kayaks. Renting a Windsurfer runs about $25 an hour.

Shopping

Areas & Malls

Although the shopping on St. Croix isn't as varied or extensive as that on St. Thomas, the island does have several small stores with unusual merchandise. In Christiansted the best shopping areas are the **Pan Am Pavilion** and **Caravelle Arcade,** off Strand Street, and along **King** and **Company streets.** These streets give way to arcades filled with boutiques. **Gallows Bay** has a blossoming shopping area in a quiet neighborhood. St. Croix shop hours are usually Monday through Saturday 9 to 5, but there are some shops in Christiansted open in the evening. Stores are often closed on Sunday.

The best shopping in Frederiksted is along **Strand Street** and in the side streets and alleyways that connect it with **King Street.** Most stores close Sunday except when a cruise ship is in port. One caveat: Frederiksted has a reputation for muggings, so for safety's sake stick to populated areas of Strand and King streets, where there are few—if any—problems.

Specialty Items

ART   **Maria Henle Studio.** Stunning paintings by Maria Henle hang on the walls, but you can also find prints by her father, the late Fritz Henle. He was an acclaimed St. Croix photographer, whose works chronicle St. Croix's recent history. ✉ *55 Company St., Christiansted* ☎ 340/773–7376.

BOOKS   **Undercover Books.** For Caribbean books or the latest good read, try this bookstore across from the post office in the Gallows Bay shopping area. ✉ *5030 Anchor Way, Gallows Bay* ☎ *340/719–1567.*

CLOTHING **Coconut Vine.** Pop into this store at the start of your vacation, and you'll
Fodor'sChoice leave with enough comfy cotton or rayon batik men's and women's clothes
★ to make you look like a local. Although the tropical designs and colors
originated in Indonesia, they're perfect for the Caribbean. ✉ *1111*
Strand St., Christiansted ☎ *340/773–1991.*

From the Gecko. Come here for the hippest clothes on St. Croix, including superb hand-painted sarongs and other items. ✉ *1233 Queen Cross*
St., Christiansted ☎ *340/778–9433.*

Hot Heads. Hats, hats, and more hats perch on top of cotton shifts, comfortable shirts, and other tropical wear at this small store. If you forgot
your bathing suit, this store has a good selection. ✉ *Kings Alley Walk,*
Christiansted ☎ *340/773–7888.*

Pacificotton. Round out your tropical wardrobe with something from this
store. Shifts, tops, and pants in sherbet colors as well as bags and hats
fill the racks. ✉ *1110 Strand St., Christiansted* ☎ *340/773–2125.*

FOODSTUFFS If you've rented a condominium or a villa, you'll appreciate St. Croix's
excellent stateside-style supermarkets. Fresh vegetables, fruits, and meats
arrive frequently. Try the open-air stands strung out along Route 70 for
island produce.

Cost-U-Less. This warehouse-type store across from Sunshine Mall
doesn't charge a membership fee. It's east of Sunny Isle Shopping Center. ✉ *Rte. 70, Sunny Isle* ☎ *340/719–4442.*

Plaza Extra. Shop here for Middle Eastern foods in addition to the usual
grocery-store items. ✉ *United Shopping Plaza, Rte. 70, Sion Farm*
☎ *340/778–6240* ✉ *Rte. 70, Mount Pleasant* ☎ *340/719–1870.*

Pueblo. This stateside-style market has branches all over the island. ✉ *Orange Grove Shopping Center, Rte. 75, Christiansted* ☎ *340/773–0118*
✉ *Villa La Reine Shopping Center, Rte. 75, La Reine* ☎ *340/778–1272.*

Schooner Bay Market. Although it's on the smallish side, Schooner Bay has
good-quality deli items. ✉ *Rte. 82, Mount Welcome* ☎ *340/773–3232.*

GIFTS **Gone Tropical.** Whether you're looking for inexpensive souvenirs of your
trip or a special, singular gift, you can probably find it here. On her travels about the world, Margo Meacham keeps her eye out for special delights for her shop—from tablecloths and napkins in bright Caribbean
colors to carefully crafted wooden birds. ✉ *5 Company St., Christiansted* ☎ *340/773–4696.*

Island Webe. The coffees, jams, and spices—produced on St. Croix and
elsewhere in the Caribbean—will tempt your taste buds. Small *mocko
jumbie* dolls depict an African tradition transported to the islands during slave days (they represent the souls of the ancestors of African
slaves). The fabric dolls wearing Caribbean costumes will delight kids
of all ages. Turn the double dolls upside down to see a white face on
one side and a black one on the other. ✉ *210 Strand St., Frederiksted*
☎ *340/772–2555.*

Many Hands. Pottery in cool and bright colors, paintings of St. Croix
and the Caribbean, prints, and maps—all made by local artists—make
perfect take-home gifts. The owners ship all over the world if your purchase is too cumbersome to carry. ✉ *21 Pan Am Pavilion, Strand St.,*
Christiansted ☎ *340/773–1990.*

26

Mitchell-Larsen Studio. Carefully crafted glass plates, sun-catchers, and more grace the shelves of this interesting store. All made on-site by two St. Croix glassmakers, the pieces are often whimsically adorned with tropical fish, flora, and fauna. ⊠ *58 Company St., Christiansted* ☎ *340/719–1000.*

FodorśChoice **Royal Poinciana.** This attractive shop is filled with island seasonings and
★ hot sauces, West Indian crafts, bath gels, and herbal teas. Shop here for tablecloths and paper goods in tropical brights. ⊠ *1111 Strand St., Christiansted* ☎ *340/773–9892.*

Tesoro. The colors are bold and the merchandise eclectic at this crowded store. Shop for metal sculpture made from retired steel pans, mahogany bowls, and hand-painted place mats in bright tropical colors. ⊠ *36C Strand St., Christiansted* ☎ *340/773–1212.*

Tradewinds Shop. Whatever the wind blew in seems to land here. Glass sailboats glide across the shelves while metal fish sculptures swim nearby. Candles with tropical motifs, note cards, and costume jewelry jostle for space with Naot sandals. ⊠ *53 King St., Christiansted* ☎ *340/719–3918.*

HOUSEWARES **St. Croix Landmarks Museum Store.** If a mahogany armoire or cane-back rocker catches your fancy, the staff will arrange to have it shipped to your mainland home at no charge from its mainland warehouse. Furniture aside, this store has one of the largest selections of local art along with Caribbean-inspired bric-a-brac in all price ranges. ⊠ *6 Company St., Christiansted* ☎ *340/713–8102.*

JEWELRY **Crucian Gold.** This store carries the unique gold creations of St. Croix native Brian Bishop. His trademark piece is the Turk's Head ring (a knot of interwoven gold strands), but the chess sets with Caribbean motifs as the playing pieces are just lovely. ⊠ *59 Kings Wharf, Christiansted* ☎ *340/773–5241.*

Nelthropp and Low. Specializing—of course—in gold jewelry, this store also carries diamonds, emeralds, rubies, and sapphires. Jewelers will create one-of-a-kind pieces to your design. ⊠ *1102 Strand St., Christiansted* ☎ *340/773–0365 or 800/416–9078.*

Gold Worker. In silver and gold, the hand-crafted jewelry at this tiny store will remind you of the Caribbean. Hummingbirds dangle from silver chains, and sand dollars adorn gold necklaces. The sugar mills in silver and gold speak of St. Croix's past. ⊠ *3 Company St., Christiansted* ☎ *340/773–5167.*

Sonya's. Sonya Hough invented the hook bracelet, popular among locals as well as visitors. With hurricanes hitting the island so frequently, she has added an interesting decoration to these bracelets: the swirling symbol used in weather forecasts to indicate these storms. ⊠ *1 Company St., Christiansted* ☎ *340/778–8605.*

LIQUOR & **Baci Duty Free Liquor and Tobacco.** A walk-in humidor with a good selec-
TOBACCO tion of Arturo Fuente, Partagas, and Macanudo cigars is the centerpiece of this store, which also carries sleek Danish-made watches and Lladro figurines. ⊠ *1235 Queen Cross St., Christiansted* ☎ *340/773–5040.*

Kmart. The two branches of this discount department store—a large one in the Sunshine Mall and a smaller one mid-island at Sunny Isle Shopping Center—carry a huge line of discounted, duty-free liquor. ⊠ *Sun-*

shine Mall, Rte. 70, Frederiksted ☎ 340/692–5848 ✉ Sunny Isle Shopping Center, Rte. 70, Sunny Isle ☎ 340/719–9190.

PERFUMES **Violette Boutique.** Perfumes, cosmetics, and skin-care products are the draws here. ✉ *Caravelle Arcade, 38 Strand St., Christiansted ☎ 340/ 773–2148.*

Nightlife & the Arts

The island's nightlife is ever-changing, and its arts scene is eclectic—ranging from Christmastime performances of *The Nutcracker* to any locally organized shows. Folk-art traditions, such as quadrille dancers, are making a comeback. To find out what's happening, pick up the local newspapers—*V. I. Daily News* and *St. Croix Avis*—available at newsstands. Christiansted has a lively and eminently casual club scene near the waterfront. Frederiksted has a couple of restaurants and clubs offering weekend entertainment.

Nightlife

Hotel on the Cay (✉ Protestant Cay, Christiansted ☎ 340/773–2035) has a West Indian buffet on Tuesday nights in the winter season, when you can watch a broken-bottle dancer (a dancer who braves a carpet of shattered glass) and mocko jumbie characters. Although you can gamble at the island's only casino, it's the nightly music that draws big crowds to **Divi Carina Bay Casino** (✉ Rte. 60, Estate Turner Hole ☎ 340/773–9700). The **Moonraker** (✉ 43A Queen Cross St., Christiansted ☎ 340/ 713–8025) attracts a youthful crowd for DJ music on Wednesday through Saturday nights.

Blue Moon (✉ 17 Strand St., Frederiksted ☎ 340/772–2222) a waterfront restaurant, is the place to be for live jazz on Friday from 9 PM to 1 AM. Outside Frederiksted, **Off the Wall** (✉ Rte. 80, Cane Bay ☎ 340/778–4471) has blues or jazz Tuesday through Sunday from 6 PM to 9 PM.

The Arts

Sunset Jazz (✉ Waterfront, Frederiksted ☎ 340/277–0692), has become the hot event in Frederiksted, drawing crowds of both visitors and locals at 6 PM on the third Friday of every month to watch the sun go down and hear good music.

The **Whim Plantation Museum** (✉ Rte. 70, Estate Whim ☎ 340/772–0598), outside of Frederiksted, hosts classical music concerts in winter.

Exploring St. Croix

Though there are things to see and do in St. Croix's two towns, Christiansted and Frederiksted (both named after Danish kings), there are lots of interesting spots in between them and to the east of Christiansted. Just be sure you have a map in hand (pick one up at rental-car agencies, or stop by the tourist office for an excellent one that's free). Many secondary roads remain unmarked; if you get confused, ask for help.

Numbers in the margin correspond to points of interest on the St. Croix map.

26

Christiansted & the East

Christiansted is a historic Danish-style town that always served as St. Croix's commercial center. Your best bet is to see the historic sights in the morning, when it's still cool. This two-hour endeavor won't tax your walking shoes and will leave you with energy to poke around the town's eclectic shops. Break for lunch at an open-air restaurant before spending as much time as you like shopping.

An easy drive (roads are flat and well marked) to St. Croix's eastern end takes you through some choice real estate. Ruins of old sugar estates dot the landscape. You can make the entire loop on the road that circles the island in about an hour, a good way to end the day. If you want to spend a full day exploring, you can find some nice beaches and easy walks with places to stop for lunch.

❶ **Christiansted.** In the 1700s and 1800s this town was a trading center for sugar, rum, and molasses. Today there are law offices, tourist shops, and restaurants, but many of the buildings, which start at the harbor and go up into the gentle hillsides, still date from the 18th century. You can't get lost. All streets lead gently downhill to the water. If you want some friendly advice, stop by the **Visitor Center** (⊠ 53A Company St. ☎ 340/773–0495) weekdays between 8 and 5 for maps and brochures.

FodorsChoice
★

Large, yellow **Fort Christiansvaern** (⊠ Hospital St. ☎ 340/773–1460 ⊕ www.nps.gov/chri) dominates the waterfront. Because it's so easy to spot, it makes a good place to begin a walking tour. In 1749 the Danish built the fort to protect the harbor, but the structure was repeatedly damaged by hurricane-force winds and had to be partially rebuilt in 1771. It's now a national historic site, the best preserved of the few remaining Danish-built forts in the Virgin Islands, and houses the park's visitor center. The $3 admission includes the Steeple Building. Rangers are on hand to answer questions. Hours are weekdays 8 to 4:45 and weekends 9 to 4:45.

Built in 1830 on foundations that date from 1734, the **Danish Customs House** (⊠ King St. ☎ 340/773–1460 ⊕ www.nps.gov/chri), near Fort Christiansvaern, originally served as both a customs house and a post office. In 1926 it became the Christiansted Library, and it's been a national park office since 1972. It's open weekdays from 8 to 5. There's not much to see, other than park staff at work, but the architecture makes it worth a peek inside.

Constructed in 1856, the **Scale House** (⊠ King St. ☎ 340/773–1460 ⊕ www.nps.gov/chri) was once the spot where goods passing through the port were weighed and inspected. Park staffers now sell a good selection of books about St. Croix history and its flora and fauna. The Scale House is open weekdays 8 to 4:30 and weekends 9 to 4:30.

Built by the Danes in 1753, the **Steeple Building** (⊠ Church St. ☎ 340/773–1460) was the first Danish Lutheran church on St. Croix. It's now a national park museum and contains exhibits that document the island's Indian inhabitants. It's worth the short walk to see the building's collection of archaeological artifacts, displays on plantation life, and exhibits on the architectural development of Christiansted, the early history of the church, and Alexander Hamilton, the first secretary of the U.S. Treasury, who grew up in St. Croix. It's open weekdays from 9 to 4:30; the $3 admission includes Fort Christiansvaern.

The **Post Office Building** (✉ Church St.), built in 1749, was once the Danish West India & Guinea Company warehouse. At this writing, it was closed for a major renovation, but it's worth a look from the outside. One of the town's most elegant structures, **Government House** (✉ King St. ☎ 340/773–1404) was built as a home for a Danish merchant in 1747. Today it houses government offices. If you're here weekdays from 8 to 4:30, slip into the peaceful inner courtyard to admire the still pools and gardens. A sweeping staircase leads you to a second-story ballroom, still used for official government functions.

★ **Buck Island Reef National Monument** (✉ Off north shore of St. Croix ☎ 340/773–1460 ⊕ www.nps.gov/buis) has pristine beaches that are just right for sunbathing, but there's also some shade for those who don't want to fry. The snorkeling trail set in the reef allows close-up study of coral formations and tropical fish. After recovering from the spate of hurricanes that started in 1989, the coral now suffers from a disease called bleaching that that leaves the coral white. The reefs are expected to recover, but how long it will take is anyone's guess. There's an easy hiking trail to the island's highest point, where you'll be rewarded for your efforts by spectacular views of the reef and St. John. Charter-boat trips leave daily from the Christiansted waterfront or from Green Cay Marina, about 2 mi (3 km) east of Christiansted. Check with your hotel for recommendations.

❷ **Point Udall.** This rocky promontory, the easternmost point in the United States, is about a half-hour drive from Christiansted. A paved road takes you to an overlook with glorious views. More adventurous folks can hike down to the pristine beach below. On the way back, look for the castle, an enormous mansion that can only be described as a cross between a Moorish mosque and the Taj Mahal. It was built by an extravagant recluse known only as the Contessa. It's sometimes a popular spot for vandals. Residents advise taking your valuables with you and leaving your car unlocked so they won't break into your car to look inside. ✉ Rte. 82, Et Stykkeland.

Between Christiansted & Frederiksted

A drive through the countryside between these two towns will take you past ruins of old plantations, many bearing whimsical names (Morningstar, Solitude, Upper Love) bestowed by early owners. The traffic moves quickly—by island standards—on the main roads, but you can pause and poke around if you head down some side lanes. It's easy to find your way west, but driving from north to south requires good navigation. Don't leave your hotel without a map. Allow an entire day for this trip, so you'll have enough time for a swim at a north-shore beach. Although you can find lots of casual eateries on the main roads, pick up a picnic lunch if you plan to head off the beaten path.

❼ Cruzan Rum Distillery. A tour of the company's factory, established in 1760, culminates in a tasting of its products, all sold here at bargain prices. It's worth a stop to look at the distillery's charming old buildings even if you're not a rum connoisseur. ⊠ *West Airport Rd., Estate Diamond* ☎ *340/692–2280* ⊕ *www.cruzanrum.com* 🖾 *$4* ☉ *Weekdays 9–11:30 and 1–4:15.*

❹ Judith's Fancy. In this upscale neighborhood are the ruins of an old greathouse and tower of the same name, both remnants of a circa-1750 Danish sugar plantation. The "Judith" comes from the first name of a woman buried on the property. From the guard house at the neighborhood entrance, follow Hamilton Drive past some of St. Croix's loveliest homes. At the end of Hamilton Drive the road overlooks Salt River Bay, where Christopher Columbus anchored in 1493. On the way back, make a detour left off Hamilton Drive onto Caribe Road for a close look at the ruins. The million-dollar villas are something to behold, too. ⊠ *Turn north onto Rte. 751, off Rte. 75.*

❸ Little Princess Estate. If the old plantation ruins decaying here and there around St. Croix intrigue you, a visit to this Nature Conservancy project will give you even more of a glimpse into the past. The staff has carved walking paths out of the bush that surrounds what's left of a 19th-century plantation. It's easy to stroll among well-labeled fruit trees and see the ruins of the windmill, the sugar and rum factory, and the laborers' village. This is the perfect place to reflect on St. Croix's agrarian past fueled with labor from African slaves. ⊠ *Off Rte. 75; turn north at Five Corners traffic light* ☎ *340/773–5575* 🖾 *Donations accepted* ☉ *Tues. and Thurs. 3–5.*

❻ Mt. Eagle. At 1,165 feet, this is St. Croix's highest peak. Leaving Cane Bay and passing North Star Beach, follow the coastal road that dips briefly into a forest; then turn left on Route 69. Just after you make the turn, the pavement is marked with the words THE BEAST and a set of giant paw prints. The hill you're about to climb is the famous Beast of the St. Croix Half Ironman Triathlon, an annual event during which participants must bike this intimidating slope. ⊠ *Rte. 69.*

❺ Salt River Bay National Historical Park & Ecological Preserve. This joint national and local park commemorates the area where Christopher Columbus's men skirmished with the Carib Indians in 1493 on his second visit to the New World. The peninsula on the bay's east side is named for the event: Cabo de las Flechas (Cape of the Arrows). Although the park is just in the developing stages, it has several sights with cultural significance. A ball court, used by the Caribs in religious ceremonies, was discovered at the spot where the taxis park. Take a short hike up the dirt road to the ruins of an old earthen fort for great views of Salt River Bay and the surrounding countryside. The area also encompasses a biodiverse coastal estuary with the largest remaining mangrove forest in the region, a submarine canyon, and several endangered species, including the hawksbill turtle and the roseate tern. A visitor center sits just uphill to the west. The water at the beach can be on the rough side, but it's a nice place for sunning. ⊠ *Rte. 75 to Rte. 80, Salt River* ☎ *340/773–1460* ⊕ *www.nps.gov/sari.*

Frederiksted & Environs

St. Croix's second-largest town, Frederiksted, was founded in 1751. A stroll around its historic sights will take you no more than an hour. Allow a little more time if you want to browse in the few small shops. The area just outside town has old plantations, some of which have been preserved as homes or historic structures that are open to the public.

⑩ Carl & Marie Lawaetz Museum. For a trip back in time, tour this circa-1750 farm. Owned by the prominent Lawaetz family since 1896, just after Carl Lawaetz arrived from Denmark, the lovely two-story house is in a valley at La Grange. A Lawaetz family member shows you the four-poster mahogany bed Carl and Marie shared, the china Marie painted, the family portraits, and the fruit trees that fed the family for several generations. Initially a sugar plantation, it was subsequently used to raise cattle and grow produce. ⊠ *Rte. 76, Mahogany Rd., Estate Little La Grange* ☎ *340/772–1539* ⊕ *www.stcroixlandmarks.com* ⊡ *$8* ☉ *Tues., Thurs., and Sat. 10–4.*

⑧ Estate Mount Washington Plantation. Several years ago, while surveying the property, the owners discovered the ruins of a sugar plantation beneath the rain-forest brush. The grounds have since been cleared and opened to the public. You can take a self-guided walking tour of the mill, the rum factory, and other ruins. There's an antiques shop in what were once the stables. ⊠ *Rte. 63, Mount Washington* ☎ *340/772–1026* ☉ *Ruins open daily dawn–dusk.*

⑨ Frederiksted. The town is noted less for its Danish than for its Victorian architecture, which dates from after the slave uprising and the great fire of 1878. One long cruise-ship pier juts into the sparkling sea. It's the perfect place to start a tour of this quaint city. The **Visitor Center** (⊠ 200 Strand St. ☎ 340/772–0357), across from the pier, has brochures from numerous St. Croix businesses. You can stop in weekdays from 8 to 5 to view exhibits on St. Croix. On July 3, 1848, 8,000 slaves marched on the red-brick **Fort Frederik** (⊠ Waterfront ☎ 340/772–2021) to demand their freedom. Danish governor Peter von Scholten, fearing they would burn the town to the ground, stood up in his carriage parked in front of the fort and granted their wish. The fort, completed in 1760, houses a number of interesting historical exhibits as well as an art gallery and a display of police memorabilia. It's within earshot of the visitor center. Admission is $3; it's open weekdays from 8 to 5. **St. Patrick's Roman Catholic Church** (⊠ Prince St.), complete with three turrets, was built in 1843 of coral. Wander inside, and you can see woodwork handcrafted by Frederiksted artisans. The churchyard is filled with 18th-century gravestones. **St. Paul's Anglican Church** (⊠ Prince St.), built circa 1812, is a mix of Georgian and Gothic Revival architecture. The bell tower of exposed sandstone was added later. The simple interior has gleaming woodwork and a tray ceiling (resembling an upside-down platter) popular in Caribbean architecture. Built in 1839, **Apothecary Hall** (⊠ King Cross St.) is a good example of 19th-century architecture; its facade has both Gothic and Greek Revival elements.

26

⓫ St. Croix Leap. This workshop sits in the heart of the rain forest, about a 15-minute drive from Frederiksted. It sells mirrors, tables, bread boards, and mahogany jewelry boxes crafted by local artisans. ⊠ *Rte. 76, Brooks Hill* ☎ *340/772–0421* ⊘ *Weekdays 9–5, Sat. 10–5.*

⓮ St. George Village Botanical Gardens. At this 17-acre estate, lush, fragrant flora grows amid the ruins of a 19th-century sugarcane plantation village. There are miniature versions of each ecosystem on St. Croix, from a semiarid cactus grove to a verdant rain forest. ⊠ *Rte. 70, turn north at sign, St. George* ☎ *340/692–2874* ⊕ *www.sgvbg.org* ⊞ *$6* ⊘ *Daily 9–5.*

⓬ West End Salt Pond. A bird-watcher's delight, this salt pond attracts a large number of winged creatures, including flamingos. ⊠ *Veteran's Shore Dr., Hesselberg.*

★ ☾ ⓭ Whim Plantation Museum. The lovingly restored estate, with a windmill, cook house, and other buildings, will give you a sense of what life was like on St. Croix's sugar plantations in the 1800s. The oval-shape greathouse has high ceilings and antique furniture and utensils. Notice its fresh, airy atmosphere—the waterless stone moat around the greathouse was used not for defense but for gathering cooling air. If you have kids, the grounds are the perfect place for them to stretch their legs, perhaps while you browse in the museum gift shop. It's just outside of Frederiksted. ⊠ *Rte. 70, Estate Whim* ☎ *340/772–0598* ⊕ *www. stcroixlandmarks.com* ⊞ *$8* ⊘ *Mon., Wed., Fri., and Sat. 10–4.*

U.S. VIRGIN ISLANDS ESSENTIALS

To research prices, get advice from other travelers, and book travel arrangements, visit www.fodors.com.

Transportation

BY AIR

One advantage to visiting the USVI is the abundance of nonstop and connecting flights to St. Thomas and St. Croix that can have you at the beach in three to four hours from East Coast airports. Small island-hopper planes and a seaplane connect St. Thomas and St. Croix, and a ferry takes you from St. Thomas to St. John.

American, Continental, Delta, Spirit, United, and US Airways fly to the islands; some flights connect through Puerto Rico. Cape Air and Caribbean Sun fly from San Juan; Cape Air has code-share arrangements with all major airlines, so your luggage can transfer seamlessly. Seaborne

Airlines flies between St. Thomas, St. Croix, and San Juan, Puerto Rico.

🛪 Airlines **American/American Eagle** ☎ 340/776–2560 in St. Thomas, 340/778–2000 in St. Croix. **Cape Air** ☎ 340/774–2204 or 800/352–0714 ⊕ www.flycapeair.com. **Caribbean Sun** ☎ 866–864–6272 ⊕ www.flycsa.com. **Continental** ☎ 800/231–0856. **Delta** ☎ 340/777–4177. **Seaborne** ☎ 340/773–6442 ⊕ www.flyseaborne.com. **Spirit** ☎ 800/772–7117 ⊕ www.spiritairlines.com. **United** ☎ 340/774–9190. **US Airways** ☎ 800/622–1015.

🛪 Airports **Cyril E. King Airport** ⊠ St. Thomas ☎ 340/774–5100 ⊕ www.viport.com. **Henry Rohlsen Airport** ⊠ St. Croix ☎ 340/778–1012 ⊕ www.viport.com.

BY BOAT & FERRY

Ferries are a great way to travel around the islands. There's frequent service between St. Thomas and St. John and their neighbors, the BVI. There's something special about spending a day on St. John and

then joining your fellow passengers—
a mix of tourists, local families, and construction workers on their way home—
for a peaceful sundown ride back to
St. Thomas. Sometimes one of the St. John
ferry services offers a special weekend trip
to Fajardo, Puerto Rico. Such junkets depart from the waterfront in St. Thomas on
a Friday evening and return to the same
locale on Sunday afternoon.

Ferries to Cruz Bay, St. John, leave St.
Thomas from either the Charlotte Amalie
waterfront west of the U.S. Coast Guard
dock or from Red Hook. From Charlotte
Amalie ferries depart at 9, 11, 1, 3, 4, and
5:30. Ferries from Cruz Bay to Charlotte
Amalie leave at 7:15, 9:15, 11:15, 1:15,
2:15, and 3:45. The one-way fare for the
45-minute ride is $8. From Red Hook,
ferries to Cruz Bay leave at 6:30 AM and
7:30 AM. Starting at 8 AM, they leave
hourly until midnight. Returning from
Cruz Bay, ferries leave hourly starting at
6 AM until 11 PM. The 15- to 20-minute
ferry ride is $4.

Car ferries, called barges, run about every
half hour between Red Hook, St. Thomas,
and Cruz Bay, St. John. The ride costs $35
(round-trip). Plan to arrive at least 15 minutes before departure.

Reefer is the name of both of the brightly
colored 26-passenger skiffs that run between the Charlotte Amalie waterfront
and Marriott Frenchman's Reef hotel daily
on the half hour from 8 to 5. It's a good
way to beat the traffic (and is about the
same price as a taxi) to Morning Star
Beach, which adjoins the hotel. And you
get a great view of the harbor as you bob
along in the shadow of the giant cruise
ships anchored in the harbor. The captain
may be persuaded to drop you at Yacht
Haven, but check first. The one-way fare
is $5 per person, and the trip takes about
15 minutes.

There's daily service between either Charlotte Amalie or Red Hook, on St. Thomas,
and West End or Road Town, Tortola, BVI,
by either Smith's Ferry or Native Son, and
to Virgin Gorda, BVI, by Smith's Ferry. The
times and days the ferries run change, so it's
best to call for schedules once you're in the
islands. The fare is $22 one-way or $40
round-trip, and the trip from Charlotte
Amalie takes 45 minutes to an hour to West
End, up to 1½ hours to Road Town; from
Red Hook the trip is only a half hour. The
twice-weekly 2¼-hour trip from Charlotte
Amalie to Virgin Gorda costs $28 one-way
and $50 round-trip. From Red Hook and
Cruz Bay, the boat goes Thursday and Sunday. Prices vary by barge company, but the
most you'll pay is $52 round-trip. Three
days a week (Friday, Saturday, and Sunday)
a ferry operates between Red Hook, Cruz
Bay, and Jost Van Dyke in the BVI; the trip
takes 45 minutes and costs $50 per person
round-trip.

There's also daily service between Cruz
Bay, St. John, and West End, Tortola,
aboard an Inter-Island Boat Service ferry.
The half-hour trip costs $40 round-trip.
You need to present proof of citizenship
upon entering the BVI; a passport is best,
but a birth certificate with a raised seal in
addition to a government-issue photo ID
will suffice.

🚢 **Inter-Island Boat Service** ☎ 340/776-6597.
Native Son ☎ 340/774-8685 ⊕ www.nativesonbvi.
com. *Reefer* ☎ 340/776-8500 Ext. 6814 ⊕ www.
marriottfrenchmansreef.com. **Smith's Ferry** ☎ 340/
775-7292 ⊕ www.smithsferry.com.

BY BUS

On St. Thomas, the island's large buses
make public transportation a very comfortable—though slow—way to get from
east and west to Charlotte Amalie and
back (service to the north is limited). Buses
run about every 30 minutes from stops
that are clearly marked with VITRAN signs.
Fares are $1 between outlying areas and
town and 75¢ in town.

Privately owned taxi vans crisscross St.
Croix regularly, providing reliable service
between Frederiksted and Christiansted
along Route 70. This inexpensive ($1.50

one-way) mode of transportation is favored by locals, and though the many stops on the 20-mi (32-km) drive between the two main towns make the ride slow, it's never dull. Vitran public buses aren't the quickest way to get around the island, but they're comfortable and affordable. The fare is $1 between Christiansted and Frederiksted or to places in between.

Modern Vitran buses on St. John run from the Cruz Bay ferry dock through Coral Bay to the far eastern end of the island at Salt Pond, making numerous stops in between. The fare is $1 to any point.

BY CAR

Even at a sedate speed of 20 mph, driving can be an adventure—for example, you may find yourself slogging behind a slow tourist-packed safari bus at a steep hairpin turn. It's a good idea to give a little beep at blind turns. Note that the general speed limit on these islands is only 25 to 35 mph, which will seem fast enough for you on most roads. If you don't think you'll need to lock up your valuables, a Jeep or open-air Suzuki with four-wheel drive will make it easier to navigate potholed dirt side roads and to get up slick hills when it rains. All the major roads are paved.

Driving is on the left side of the road, British-style (although your steering wheel will be on the left side of the car, American-style). The law requires *everyone* in a car to wear a seat belt: many of the roads are narrow, and the islands are dotted with hills, so there's ample reason to put safety first.

In St. Thomas traffic can get pretty bad, especially in Charlotte Amalie at rush hour (7 to 9 and 4:30 to 6). Cars often line up bumper to bumper along the waterfront. If you need to get from an East End resort to the airport during these times, find the alternate route (starting from the East End, Route 38 to 42 to 40 to 33) that goes up the mountain and then drops you back onto Veterans Highway. If you plan to explore by car, be sure to pick up the latest edition of "Road Map St. Thomas–St. John," which includes the route numbers *and* the names of the roads that are used by locals. It's available anywhere you find maps and guidebooks.

St. Croix, unlike St. Thomas and St. John, where narrow roads wind through hillsides, is relatively flat, and it even has a four-lane highway. The speed limit on the Melvin H. Evans Highway is 55 mph and ranges 35 to 40 mph elsewhere. Roads are often unmarked, so be patient—sometimes getting lost is half the fun.

In St. John, use caution. The terrain is very hilly, the roads winding, and the blind curves numerous. You may suddenly come upon a huge safari bus careening around a corner or a couple of hikers strolling along the side of the road. Major roads are well paved, but once you get off a specific route, dirt roads filled with potholes are common. For such driving, a four-wheel-drive vehicle is your best bet.

Gas is expensive on St. Thomas and St. John; expect to pay considerably more than in the United States. But on St. Croix, where the big HOVENSA refinery is located, the prices are much closer to what you might expect to pay stateside.

ST. THOMAS: Avis, Budget, and Hertz all have counters at Cyril E. King Airport. Dependable Car Rental offers pickups and drop-offs at the airport and to and from major hotels. Cowpet Rent-a-Car is on the east end of the island. Discount has a location at Bluebeard's Castle hotel. Avis is at the Marriott Frenchman's Reef, Havensight Mall (adjacent to the cruise ship dock), and Seaborn Airlines terminal on the Charlotte Amalie waterfront; Budget has branches at the Sapphire Beach Resort & Marina and at the Havensight Mall, adjacent to the main cruise-ship dock.
🚗 **Avis** ☎ 340/774-1468. **Budget** ☎ 340/776-5774. **Cowpet Rent-a-Car** ☎ 340/775-7376. **Dependable Car Rental** ☎ 340/774-2253 or 800/522-3076. **Discount** ☎ 340/776-4858. **Hertz** ☎ 340/774-1879.

ST. CROIX: Atlas is outside Christiansted but provides pickups at hotels. Avis is at Henry Rohlsen Airport and at the seaplane ramp in Christiansted. Budget has branches at the airport and in the King Christian Hotel in Christiansted. Judi of Croix delivers vehicles to your hotel. Midwest is outside Frederiksted but picks up at hotels. Olympic and Thrifty are outside Christiansted but will pick up at hotels.
🚗 **Atlas** ☎ 340/773-2886 or 800/426-6009. **Avis** ☎340/778-9355. **Budget** ☎340/778-9636 ⊕www.budgetstcroix.com. **Judi of Croix** ☎ 340/773-2123 or 877/903-2123 ⊕ www.judiofcroix.com. **Midwest** ☎ 340/772-0438 or 877/772-0438 ⊕ www.midwestautorental.com. **Olympic** ☎340/773-8000 or 888/878-4227 ⊕ www.stcroixcarrentals.com. **Thrifty** ☎ 340/773-7200.

ST. JOHN: Best is just outside Cruz Bay near the public library, off Route 10. Cool Breeze is in Cruz Bay across from the Creek. Delbert Hill Taxi & Jeep Rental Service is in Cruz Bay around the corner from the ferry dock, across from Wharfside Village. Denzil Clyne is across from the Creek. O'Connor Jeep is in Cruz Bay at the Texaco Station. St. John Car Rental is across from Wharfside Village shopping center on Bay Street in Cruz Bay. Spencer's Jeep is across from the Creek in Cruz Bay. Sun & Sand is in Cruz Bay across from the Creek.
🚗 **Best** ☎ 340/693-8177. **Cool Breeze** ☎ 340/776-6588 ⊕ www.coolbreezecarrental.com. **Delbert Hill Taxi & Jeep Rental Service** ☎ 340/776-6637. **Denzil Clyne** ☎ 340/776-6715. **O'Connor Jeep** ☎ 340/776-6343 ⊕ www.oconnorcarrental.com. **St. John Car Rental** ☎340/776-6103 ⊕www.stjohncarrental.com. **Spencer's Jeep** ☎ 340/693-8784 or 888/776-6628. **Sun & Sand Car Rental** ☎ 340/776-6374.

BY TAXI

USVI taxis don't have meters, but you needn't worry about fare gouging if you check a list of standard rates to popular destinations (required by law to be carried by each driver and often posted in hotel and airport lobbies and printed in free tourist periodicals, such as *St. Thomas-St. John This Week* and *St. Croix This Week*)

and settle on the fare before you start out. Fares are per person, not per destination, but drivers taking multiple fares (which often happens, especially from the airport) will charge you a lower rate than if you're in the cab alone.

ST. THOMAS: On St. Thomas, taxi vans line up along Havensight and Crown Bay docks when a cruise ship pulls in. If you booked a shore tour, the operator will lead you to a designated vehicle. Otherwise, there are plenty of air-conditioned vans and open-air safari buses to take you to Charlotte Amalie or the beach. The cab fare from Havensight to Charlotte Amalie is $5 per person if you ride alone or $4 per person if you share a cab; you can, however, make the 1½-mi (2½-km) walk into town in about 30 minutes along the beautiful waterfront. From Crown Bay to town the taxi fare is $4 or $3.50 per person if you share; it's a 1-mi (1½-km) walk, but the route passes along a busy highway, so it's not advisable. Transportation from Havensight to Magens Bay for swimming is $8.50 per person ($6 if you share).

Additionally, taxis of all shapes and sizes are available at various ferry, shopping, resort, and airport areas, and they also respond to phone calls. There are taxi stands in Charlotte Amalie across from Emancipation Garden (in front of Little Switzerland, behind the post office) and along the waterfront. But you probably won't have to look for a stand, as taxis are plentiful and routinely cruise the streets. Walking down Main Street, you'll be asked "Back to ship?" often enough to make you never want to carry another shopping bag.
🚕 **East End Taxi** ☎ 340/775-6974. **Islander Taxi** ☎ 340/774-4077. **VI Taxi Association** ☎ 340/774-4550.

ST. CROIX: Taxis, generally station wagons or minivans, are a phone call away from most hotels and are available in downtown Christiansted, at the Henry E. Rohlsen Airport, and at the Frederiksted pier during cruise-ship arrivals.

26

In Frederiksted all the shops are a short walk away, and you can swim off the beach. Most ship passengers visit Christiansted on a tour; a taxi will cost $24 for one or two people.

🚕 **Antilles Taxi Service** ☎ 340/773-5020. **St. Croix Taxi Association** ☎ 340/778-1088.

ST. JOHN: Taxis meet ferries arriving in Cruz Bay. Most drivers use vans or open-air safari buses. You can find them congregated at the dock and at hotel parking lots. You can also hail them anywhere on the road. You're likely to travel with other tourists en route to their destinations. Paradise Taxi will pick you up if you call, but most of the drivers don't provide that service. If you need one to pick you up at your rental villa, ask the villa manager for suggestions on whom to call or arrange a ride in advance.

Some cruise ships stop at St. John to let passengers disembark for a day. The main town of Cruz Bay is near the area where the ships drop off passengers. If you want to swim, the famous Trunk Bay is a $6 taxi ride per person from town.

🚕 **Paradise Taxi** ☎ 340/714-7913.

Contacts & Resources

BANKS & EXCHANGE SERVICES

The American dollar is used throughout the territory, just as in the neighboring BVI. If you need to exchange foreign currency, you need to go to the main branch of major banks. All major credit cards and traveler's checks are generally accepted. Some places will take Discover, though it's not as widely accepted as Visa, Master-Card, and American Express.

Each of the islands has several banks. On St. Thomas, First Bank has locations in Market Square, Waterfront, Estate Thomas, Port of $ale, Red Hook, and Tutu. There are waterfront locations for Banco Popular, as well as branches in Hibiscus Alley, Sugar Estate, Fort Mylner, Red Hook, and Altona, a mile east of the airport. The Scotia Bank has branches at Havensight Mall, Nisky Center, Tutu Park Mall, and the Waterfront.

St. Croix has branches of Banco Popular in Orange Grove and Sunny Isle shopping centers. V. I. Community Bank is in Orange Grove Shopping Center and in downtown Christiansted. Scotia Bank has branches in Sunny Isle, Frederiksted, Christiansted, and Sunshine Mall.

St. John has two banks. First Bank is one block up from the ferry dock, and Scotia Bank is at the Marketplace on Route 107.

BUSINESS HOURS

Bank hours are generally Monday through Thursday 9 to 3 and Friday 9 to 5; a handful open Saturday (9 to noon). Walk-up windows open at 8:30 on weekdays. Hours may vary slightly from branch to branch and island to island, but they are generally weekdays 7:30 or 8 to 4 or 5:30 and Saturday 7:30 or 8 to noon or 2:30.

On St. Thomas, stores on Main Street in Charlotte Amalie are open weekdays and Saturday 9 to 5. The hours of the shops in the Havensight Mall (next to the cruise-ships dock) are the same, though occasionally some stay open until 9 on Friday, depending on how many cruise ships are at the dock. You may also find some shops open on Sunday if cruise ships are in port. Hotel shops are usually open evenings, as well.

St. Croix shop hours are usually Monday through Saturday 9 to 5, but there are some shops in Christiansted open in the evening.

On St. John, store hours run from 9 or 10 to 5 or 6. Wharfside Village and Mongoose Junction shops in Cruz Bay are often open into the evening.

ELECTRICITY

The USVI use the same current as the U.S. mainland—110 volts. European appliances will require adaptors. Since power fluctuations occasionally occur, bring a heavy-duty surge protector (available at hardware stores) if you plan to use your computer.

EMERGENCIES

Emergency Services Air Ambulance Network ☎ 800/327-1966. **Ambulance and fire emergencies** ☎ 911. **Medical Air Services** ☎ 340/777-8580 or 800/643-9023. **Police emergencies** ☎ 911. **Coast Guard Marine Safety Detachment** ☎ 340/776-3497 in St. Thomas and St. John, 340/772-5557 in St. Croix. **Rescue Coordination Center** ☎ 787/289-2040 in San Juan, PR.

Hospital on St. Thomas Roy L. Schneider Hospital & Community Health Center ⊠ Sugar Estate, 1 mi [1½ km] east of Charlotte Amalie ☎ 340/776-8311.

Hospitals on St. Croix Gov. Juan F. Luis Hospital and Health Center ⊠ 6 Diamond Ruby, north of Sunny Isle Shopping Center on Rte. 79, Christiansted ☎ 340/778-6311. **Ingeborg Nesbitt Clinic** ⊠ 516 Strand St., Frederiksted ☎ 340/772-0260.

Hospital on St. John Myrah Keating Smith Community Health Center ⊠ Rte. 10, about 7 mins east of Cruz Bay, Susannaberg ☎ 340/693-8900.

Pharmacies on St. Thomas Havensight Pharmacy ⊠ Havensight Mall, Charlotte Amalie ☎ 340/776-1235. **Kmart Pharmacy** ⊠ Tutu Park Mall, Tutu ☎ 340/777-3854. **Doctor's Choice Pharmacy** ⊠ Wheatley Shopping Center, across from Roy L. Schneider Hospital, Sugar Estate ☎ 340/777-1400 ⊠ Medical Arts Complex, off Rte. 30, 1½ mi east of Cyril E. King Airport ☎ 340/774-8988.

Pharmacies on St. Croix Kmart Pharmacy ⊠ Sunshine Mall, Cane Estate ☎ 340/692-2622. **People's Drug Store** ⊠ Sunny Isle Shopping Center, Rte. 70, Christiansted ☎ 340/778-5537.

Pharmacy on St. John Chelsea Drug Store ⊠ The Marketplace, Rte. 104, Cruz Bay ☎ 340/776-4888.

Scuba-Diving Emergencies Roy L. Schneider Hospital & Community Health Center ⊠ Sugar Estate, 1 mi [1½ km] east of Charlotte Amalie ☎ 340/776-2686.

HOLIDAYS

Public holidays, in addition to the U.S. federal holidays are: Three Kings Day (Jan. 6); Transfer Day (commemorates Denmark's 1917 sale of the territory to the United States, Mar. 31); Holy Thursday and Good Friday; Emancipation Day (when slavery was abolished in the Danish West Indies in 1848, July 3); Columbus Day and USVI–Puerto Rico Friendship Day (always on Columbus Day weekend); and Liberty Day (honoring David Hamilton Jackson, who secured freedom of the press and assembly from King Christian X of Denmark, Nov. 1).

INTERNET, MAIL & SHIPPING

The main U.S. Post Office on St. Thomas is near the hospital, with branches in Charlotte Amalie, Frenchtown, Havensight, and Tutu Mall; there are post offices at Christiansted, Frederiksted, Gallows Bay, and Sunny Isle on St. Croix and at Cruz Bay on St. John. Postal rates are the same as if you were in the mainland United States, but Express Mail and Priority Mail aren't as quick.

On St. Thomas, FedEx offers overnight service if you get your package to the office before 5 PM. The FedEx office on St. Croix is in Peter's Rest Commercial Center; try to drop off your packages before 5:30 PM. Shipping services on St. Thomas are also available at Fast Shipping & Communications Nisky Mail Center and at Red Hook Mail Services. On St. John, call for Federal Express pickup.

Beans, Bytes & Websites is an Internet café in Charlotte Amalie. East End Secretarial Services offers long-distance dialing, copying, and fax services. At Little Switzerland, there's free Internet access along with an ATM, big-screen TV, telephones, and a bar with cold drinks. Near Havensight Mall, go to Soapy's Station or the Cyber Zone at Port of $ale, where there are 16 computers. Rates for Internet access range from $4 to $6 for 30 minutes to $8 to $12 per hour. On St. Croix, check your e-mail, make phone calls, and buy postage stamps at Strand Street Station Internet Café in Christiansted. Rates run $5 for a half hour of Internet time. On St. John the place to go to check your e-mail, make phone calls, or receive messages is Connections. You'll pay $5 a half hour for Internet service.

Internet Cafes Beans, Bytes & Websites ⊠ Royal Dane Mall, behind Tavern on the Waterfront, Charlotte Amalie, St. Thomas ☎ 340/775-5262 ⊕ www.usvi.net/cybercafe. **Connections** ⊠ Cruz

26

Bay, St. John ☎ 340/776-6922 ✉ Coral Bay, St. John ☎ 340/779-4994 ⊕ www.connectionsstjohn.com. **Cyber Zone** ✉ Port of $ale, Charlotte Amalie, St. Thomas ☎ 340/714-7743. **East End Secretarial Services** ✉ Upstairs at Red Hook Plaza, Red Hook, St. Thomas ☎ 340/775-5262. **Little Switzerland** ✉ 5 Dronnigens Gade, across from Emancipation Garden, Charlotte Amalie, St. Thomas ☎ 340/776-2010. **Soapy's Station** ✉ Havensight Mall, above Budget, Charlotte Amalie, St. Thomas ☎ 340/776-7170. **Strand Street Station** ✉ Pan Am Pavilion, 1102 Strand St., Christiansted, St. Croix ☎ 340/719-6245. 🛒 **Shipping** **Fast Shipping & Communications** ✉ Rte. 30, across from Havensight Mall, Charlotte Amalie, St. Thomas ☎ 340/714-7634. **FedEx** ✉ Cyril E. King Airport, St. Thomas ☎ 340/777-4140 ⊕ www.fedex.com ✉ Peter's Rest Commercial Center, Rte. 708, Peter's Rest, St. Croix ☎ 800/463-3339 ✉ St. John ☎ 800/463-3339. **Nisky Mail Center** ✉ Nisky Center, Rte. 30, Charlotte Amalie, St. Thomas ☎ 340/775-7055. **Red Hook Mail Services** ✉ Red Hook Plaza, Rte. 32, 2nd fl., Red Hook, St. Thomas ☎ 340/779-1890.

PASSPORT REQUIREMENTS

Since the U.S. Virgin Islands are a U.S. territory, you won't pass through immigration on arrival if you are coming on a flight from the U.S. However, you must still prove citizenship when you head back home regardless of where you are going. So long as you are a U.S. citizen, you will not have to carry a valid passport to visit the U.S. Virgin Islands unless you are flying from another country, including all other Caribbean islands except for St. Croix and Puerto Rico.

SAFETY

Vacationers tend to assume that normal precautions aren't necessary in paradise. They are. Though there isn't quite as much crime here as in large U.S. mainland cities, it does exist. To be safe, keep your hotel or vacation villa door locked at all times, stick to well-lighted streets at night, and use the same kind of street sense that you would in any unfamiliar territory. Don't wander the streets of Charlotte Amalie, Christiansted, or Frederiksted alone at night. If you plan to carry things around,

rent a car—not a Jeep—and lock possessions in the trunk. Keep your rental car locked wherever you park. Don't leave cameras, purses, and other valuables lying on the beach while you snorkel for an hour (or even for a minute), whether you're on the deserted beaches of St. John or the more crowded Magens and Coki beaches on St. Thomas. St. Croix has several good but remote beaches outside Frederiksted and on the East End; it's best to visit them with a group rather than on your own.

TAXES

There's no sales tax in the USVI, but there's an 8% hotel-room tax (which may be raised to 10% by 2006); most hotels also add a 10% service charge to the bill. The St. John Accommodations Council members ask that hotel and villa guests voluntarily pay a $1 a day surcharge to help fund school and community projects and other good works. Many hotels add additional energy surcharges and the like, so please ask about any additional charges, but these are not government-imposed taxes.

TELEPHONES

Phone service to and from the Virgin Islands is up-to-date and efficient. Phone cards are used throughout the islands; you can buy them (in several denominations) at many retail shops and convenience stores. They must be used in special card phones, which are also widely available. Dialing a call to or from the USVI is exactly like dialing one in the rest of the U.S. All U.S. calling cards work in the USVI, and most charge domestic long-distance rates. The area code for the USVI is 340.

Cell phones from the U.S. companies Cingular and Sprint work in most locations in the USVI if you have a roaming feature; if you are on St. John's north coast, you may have some difficulties with service, where you may find yourself connected to Boat-Phone, a Tortola service. Phones from other companies may work, but only Cingular and Sprint have offices in the USVI. Many cell phone companies treat calls in the USVI just like any other calls in the U.S., but be sure to ask; this is not always the case.

TIPPING

Many hotels in the USVI add a 10% to 15% service charge to cover the room maid and other staff. However, some hotels may use part of that money to fund their operations, passing on only a portion of it to the staff. Check with your maid or bellhop to determine the hotel's policy. If you discover you need to tip, give bellhops and porters 50¢ to $1 per bag and maids $1 or $2 per day. Special errands or requests of hotel staff always require an additional tip. At restaurants bartenders and waiters expect a 10%–15% tip, but always check your tab to see whether service is included. Taxi drivers in the USVI get a 15% tip.

VISITOR INFORMATION

St. Thomas–St. John Hotel & Tourism Association ☎ 340/774-6835 ⊕ www.sttstjhta.com. USVI Division of Tourism ✉ 78-123 Estate Contant, Charlotte Amalie, St. Thomas 00804 ☎ 340/774-8784 or 800/372-8784 ✉ 53A Company St., Christiansted, St. Croix 00822 ☎ 340/773-0495 ✉ Strand St., Frederiksted, St. Croix 00840 ☎ 340/772-0357 ✉ Henry Samuel St. (next to post office), Cruz Bay, St. John ☎ 340/776-6450 ⊕ www.usvitourism.vi. Virgin Islands National Park ✉ At the Creek, Cruz Bay, St. John 00831 ☎ 340/776-6201 ⊕ www.nps.gov/viis.

WEDDINGS

The Virgin Islands provide a lovely backdrop for a wedding. Many couples opt to exchange vows on a white sandy beach or in a tropical garden. The process is easy but does require advance planning. The U.S. Virgin Islands Department of Tourism publishes a brochure with all the details and relevant contact information; you can also download marriage license applications from the Web site.

You must first apply for a marriage license at the Superior Court; there are offices in St. Thomas (which is also where you apply if you're getting married in St. John) and St. Croix. The fee is $50 for the application and $50 for the license. You have to wait eight days after the clerk receives the application to get married, and licenses must be picked up in person weekdays, though you can apply by mail. To make the process easier, most couples hire a wedding planner. If you plan to get married at a large hotel, most have planners on staff, but if you're staying in a villa, at a small hotel or inn, or are arriving on a cruise ship, you'll have to hire your own. Anne Marie Weddings, a wedding planner on St. John, provides a lovely service.

The wedding planner will help you organize your marriage license application as well as arrange for a location, flowers, music, refreshments, and whatever else you want to make your day special. The wedding planner will also hire a clergyman if you'd like a religious service or a nondenominational officiant if you prefer. Indeed, many wedding planners are licensed by the territory as nondenominational officiants and will preside at your wedding.

Superior Court Offices In St. Croix ⌂ Box 929, Christiansted 00821 ☎ 340/778-9750. In St. Thomas ⌂ Box 70, St. Thomas 00804 ☎ 340/774-6680.

Wedding Planners Anne Marie Weddings ✉ 5000-4A Enighed, St. John 00830 ☎ 340/693-5153 or 888/676-5701 ⊕ www.stjohnweddings.com. Weddings the Island Way ⌂ Box 11694, St. Thomas 00801 ☎ 340/777-6505 or 800/582-4784 ⊕ www.weddingstheislandway.com.

26

HOTELS AT A GLANCE

The following chart lists—in alphabetical order by chapter—all hotels reviewed in this guide, along with a summary of useful information about each hotel.

HOTELS AT A GLANCE

★ HOTEL NAME	Worth Noting	Cost	Rooms	Restaurants	Golf Courses	Tennis Courts	Pools	Health Clubs	Spa	On The Beach	Kids' Programs	Dive Shops	Location
Anguilla													
Allamanda Beach Club	younger crowd	$100–$160	16	2			1						Upper Shoal
Altamer	staffed villas	$38K/week	3	Yes		1	1	hot tub					Shoal West
Anguilla Great House	charming bungalows	$250–$280	27	Yes			1			yes			Rendezvous
Arawak Beach Inn	low-key, intimate	$175–$245	17	Yes			1			yes			Island Hrbr
★ Cap Juluca	Anguilla's best	$780–$980	85	3	range	3	1	yes	yes	yes	3–14		Maundays
Caribella	simple villas	$350	6										Barnes Bay
Carimar Beach Club	full kitchens	$340–$515	24	Yes		2				yes			Meads Bay
Covecastles Villa Resort	high-tech amenities	$895–$1,395	15	Yes		2				yes			Shoal West
★ CuisinArt Resort & Spa	family-friendly	$495–$995	95	3		3	1	yes	yes	yes			Rendezvous
Easy Corner Villas	modest, inexpensive	$160–$240	12										South Hill
Frangipani Beach Club	condo feel	$350–$750	25	Yes		1	1			yes			Meads Bay
★ Kú	chic, all suites	$295–$395	27	Yes			1		yes	yes			Shoal East
★ La Sirena	5 mins. from beach	$260–$330	32	Yes		2	2		mass.			yes	Meads Bay
★ Malliouhana	excellent cuisine	$620–$1,020	53	2		4	3	yes	yes	yes			Meads Bay
★ Paradise Cove	full kitchens	$235–$550	29	Yes		2	2	hot tub					The Cove
★ Rendezvous Bay Hotel	prime location	$130–$295	54	2		2				yes			Rendezvous
★ St. Regis Temenos	glamorous, chic	$30K–$35K	3			3	3	hot tub					Long Bay
Antigua & Barbuda													
★ Admiral's Inn	historic building	$140–$175	15	Yes						yes			English Hrbr
★ The Beach House	serene, secluded	$750	21	Yes					mass.				Barbuda
★ Blue Waters Hotel	swank, understated	$627–$1,025	79	2		1	3	hot tub	yes	yes	5–13		St. John's
★ Carlisle Bay	deluxe gadgetry	$990	88	2		9	1	yes	yes	yes	3–12	yes	St. Mary's
★ Catamaran Hotel	kid-friendly	$130–$165	14	Yes			1			yes			Falmouth
CocoBay	wellness retreat	$340–$400	45	2			1		yes	yes			Valley Ch

★ Curtain Bluff	25k bottle wine cellar	$850–$2,995	68	2	putting	4	1		mass.	yes	4–12	yes	Morris Bay
★ Dickenson Bay Cottages	hillside location	$160–$305	11	1		1	1			yes			Marble Hill
★ Galley Bay	posh AI	$825–$1,000	70	2		1	2		yes	yes		yes	Five Islands
Hawksbill by Rex	four beaches	$400–$450	112	2		1	1		yes	yes			Five Islands
Inn at English Harbour	inconsistent	$216–$434	34	2		2	1			yes			English Hrbr
Jolly Beach Resort	"supersaver" rooms	$280–$470	462	5		4	2	hot tub		yes	2–12	yes	Jolly Hrbr
Jolly Harbour Villas	duplexes, sprawling	$200–$220	150	7		4	3			yes	3–11	yes	Jolly Hrbr
Jumby Bay	imperfect refinement	$1,150–$1,900	51	2	1 x 18	4	1		yes	yes			Long Island
Occidental Grand	not quite grand	$500–$580	180	3	putting	3	2		mass.	yes	4–12		Long Bay
Ocean Inn	great views	$85–$150	14	Yes		4	1			yes			English Hrbr
Rex Blue Heron	only for the beach	$320–$400	64	Yes		2	1		yes	yes		yes	Johnson's
Sandals Antigua	2006 renovation	$600–$1,000	373	7		2	6	hot tub	yes	yes		yes	Dickenson
Siboney Beach Club	affordable suites	$170–$310	12	Yes		1	1			yes			Dickenson
St. James's Club	excellent location	$570–$795	259	4	priv.	7	4	hot tub	yes	yes	2–12	yes	Mamora Bay
Sunsail Club Colonna	sailing school	$240–$320	114	2		1	1		yes	yes	4 m–17	yes	Hodges Bay
Aruba													
Allegro Aruba	party atmosphere	$552–$607	417	3		2	1	hot tub		yes	4–12		Palm Beach
★ Amsterdam Manor	excellent value	$225–$245	72	Yes		2	1			yes			Eagle Beach
★ Aruba Marriott Resort	largest rooms	$469–$559	410	5		2	1	yes	yes	yes		yes	Palm Beach
★ Bucuti Beach Resort	Wi-Fi throughout	$240–$330	148	Yes		2	1			yes			Eagle Beach
Divi Aruba	prime beachfront	$300–$360	203	3	priv.	1	2	hot tub		yes	5–12	yes	Manchebo
Divi Village	all suites with kitchens	$302–$358	250	3	1 x 9	3	3			yes			Oranjestad
Holiday Inn SunSpree	family resort	$76–$192	607	4		6	2		mass.	yes	5–12	yes	Palm Beach
Hotel Riu Aruba Grand	small balconies	$300–$318	171	3		2	1			yes		yes	Palm Beach
★ Hyatt Regency Aruba	extensive kids program	$460–$535	360	5		2	1	yes	yes	yes	3–12	yes	Palm Beach

priv. = golf privileges
mass. = massage only

HOTEL NAME	Worth Noting	Cost	Rooms	Restaurants	Golf Courses	Tennis Courts	Pools	Health Clubs	Spa	On The Beach	Kids' Programs	Dive Shops	Location
Aruba (cont.)													
La Cabana	family-friendly	$324–$346	811	4		5	3	yes	yes		5-12	yes	Eagle Beach
★ Mill Resort & Suites	friendly staff	$197–$225	192	Yes		2	2	sauna	yes				Oranjestad
★ MVC Eagle Beach	bargain for location	$70–$100	19	Yes		1	1			yes			Eagle Beach
★ Radisson Aruba	popular with families	$460–$578	390	4	priv.	2	2	yes	yes	yes	5-12	yes	Palm Beach
★ Renaissance Aruba	private beach island	$339–$449	559	5		1	3	yes	yes	yes	5-12	yes	Oranjestad
Tamarijn Aruba	laid-back, all-inclusive	$340–$360	236	3	priv.	2	2	yes	yes	yes			Punta Brabo
★ Wyndham Aruba	pampering service	$280–$300	562	8		1	1	hot tub	yes	yes		yes	Palm Beach
Barbados													
Accra Beach Hotel	swim-up bar	$191–$240	146	3			1	hot tub		yes			Rockley
Almond Beach Club	small, adults only AI	$560–$660	161	3		1	4	yes	yes	yes			Vauxhall
Almond Beach Village	family AI	$560–$735	396	5	1 x 9	4	10	yes	yes	yes	inf-17		Heywoods
★ Cobblers Cove Hotel	elegant, upscale	$620–$1,000	40	yes	priv.	1	1		yes	yes	2-12		Speightstwn
★ Colony Club Hotel	lagoon pool	$834–$984	96	2		2	4	hot tub		yes			Porters
★ Coral Reef Club	best in Barbados	$535–$620	88	yes	priv.	2	2	hot tub	mass.	yes	2-12	yes	Holetown
★ The Crane	need a car	$205–$370	146	2		4	4			yes			Crane Bay
★ Divi Heritage	best west coast value	$190	22			1		hot tub		yes			Sunset Crest
★ Divi Southwinds	all-suites, full kitchens	$220–$285	133	2	priv.	2	3			yes			Dover
★ Fairmont Royal Pavilion	all sea-view suites	$845	73	2	priv.	2	1	yes		yes		yes	Porters
Grand Barbados	pier suites	$195–$250	133	2			1	sauna	mass.	yes		yes	Aquatic Gap
Hilton Barbados	balconies, great pool	$460–$515	350	3		3	1	yes		yes	3-12	yes	Aquatic Gap
★ Little Arches Hotel	romantic, adults only	$275–$347	10	yes			1			yes			Enterprise
★ Peach & Quiet	great deal	$89–$99	22	yes		1	swater						Inch Marlow
★ Sandy Lane	every extravagance	$1,000–$1,900	113	3	1 x 9	9	1	yes	yes	yes	3-12		Paynes Bay
The Savannah	lagoon pool	$315–$350	98	2	priv.		2	yes	yes	yes			Hastings

Hotel	Description	Price	Rooms		Golf						Children's programs		Location
Tamarind Cove Hotel	something for everyone	$440–$480	105	3	priv.	2	3			yes			Paynes Bay
Treasure Beach	quiet, residential feel	$595–$895	29	yes		2	1			yes			Paynes Bay
Turtle Beach Resort	family resort	$754–$834	161	3	priv.	2	3	hot tub		yes	3–11	yes	Dover
★ Villa Nova	country club feel	$650–$800	28	2	priv.	2	1		yes			yes	Villa Nova
Bonaire													
★ Bellafonte Chateau	intimate, chic	$130–$270	22					hot tub				yes	Belnem
★ Bruce Bowker's Carib Inn	PADI five-star	$99–$119	10				1			yes		yes	Kralendijk
Buddy Dive Resort	diving, apartments	$130–$180	78	2			3			yes	5–15	yes	Kralendijk
★ Captain Don's Habitat	great dive center	$174–$196	53	yes			1			yes		yes	Kralendijk
★ Coco Palm Garden	simple, friendly	$66–$105	22				1						Belnem
Den Laman Condos	location, location	$100–$180	15	yes								yes	Kralendijk
★ Divi Flamingo Resort	diving, casino	$116–$193	129	2			2	hot tub	yes	yes		yes	Kralendijk
Golden Reef Inn	inland apartments	$55–$65	16				1					yes	Hato
★ Harbour Village Bonaire	most luxurious	$350–$554	30	2		4	1	yes	yes	yes		yes	Kralendijk
Plaza Resort Bonaire	nice villas	$170	222	3		4	1		mass.	yes	5–15	yes	Kralendijk
Sand Dollar Condos	condos near shopping	$155	68	yes		2	1			yes	3–17	yes	Kralendijk
Sorobon Beach	all-nude, family-friendly	$245	30	yes					mass.	yes			Sorobon
★ Yachtclub Apartments	best budget resort	$65	13	yes						yes			Kralendijk
British Virgin Islands													
Anegada Reef Hotel	serene, simple	$250–$275	16	yes						yes		yes	Anegada
Biras Creek Resort	upscale, all suites	$840–$1,110	31	2		2	1	yes	yes	yes			Virgin Gorda
★ Bitter End Yacht Club	sailing school on-site	$670–$1,740	87	3			1			yes	6–18	yes	Virgin Gorda
★ Cooper Island	removed, few frills	$195	12	yes						yes		yes	Cooper Island
Fischer's Cove	great location, basic	$125–$200	20	yes						yes		yes	Virgin Gorda
Frenchman's Cay Hotel	just villas	$265	9	yes		1	1			yes			Tortola

priv. = golf privileges
mass. = massage only

★ HOTEL NAME	Worth Noting	Cost	Rooms	Restaurants	Golf Courses	Tennis Courts	Pools	Health Clubs	Spa	On The Beach	Kids' Programs	Dive Shops	Location
British Virgin Islands (cont.)													
Guana Island Resort	private island	$895	15	yes						yes			Guana Island
★ Guavaberry Spring Bay	cottages, villas	$210–$275	36							yes			Virgin Gorda
Hodge's Creek Marina	busy marina	$175	24	yes			1						Tortola
Lambert Beach Resort	excellent beach	$176–$410	67	yes		1	1	yes		yes			Tortola
Leverick Bay	busy marina	$125	18	2		1	1	yes		yes		yes	Virgin Gorda
★ Little Dix Bay	laid-back luxury	$650–$1,900	108	3		7		yes		yes	3–16		Virgin Gorda
Long Bay Beach Resort	Tortola's only full resort	$380–$1,050	90	2		2	1	yes		yes	yes		Tortola
Mango Bay Resort	contemporary duplexes	$132–$435	20							yes			Virgin Gorda
Maria's Hotel by the Sea	budget inn	$160–$200	41	yes									Tortola
Moorings-Mariner Inn	charter boat hot spot	$170–$230	40	yes		1	1				yes		Tortola
Myett's	tiny, near nightlife	$175–$185	3	yes						yes			Tortola
★ Nail Bay Resort	kitchens/kitchenettes	$200–$600	21	yes		1				yes			Virgin Gorda
Nanny Cay Hotel	near marina	$160	38	2		1					yes		Tortola
Neptune's Treasure	basic, guesthouse	$105	9	yes									Anegada
Olde Yard Village	condos, under constr.	$275–$295	26	yes			1			yes			Virgin Gorda
Peter Island Resort	total pampering	$900–$1,230	54	2			1	yes		yes	yes		Peter Island
Pusser's Marina Cay	ferry from Tortola	$195–$450	6	yes						yes			Marina Cay
Saba Rock Resort	on a private island	$150–$550	9	yes						yes			Virgin Gorda
★ Sandcastle	cottages	$225–$275	6	yes						yes			Jost
Sebastian's on the Beach	charming, laid-back	$160–$285	35	yes						yes			Tortola
★ Sugar Mill Hotel	Tortola's best hotel	$325–$355	23	2		1		yes		yes			Tortola
Village Cay	Rd Town location	$150–$190	21	yes			1						Tortola
The Villas of Ft. Recovery	villas, good service	$250–$522	30				1	mass.		yes			Tortola
White Bay Villas	villas, cottages	$125–$585	6							yes			Jost

Cayman Islands

		Price	Rooms									Location
★ Brac Caribbean	condos	$185-$245	42	yes			1		yes		yes	Cayman Brac
★ Brac Reef Beach Resort	good dive program	$350	40	yes		1	1	hot tub	yes		yes	Cayman Brac
Cayman Breakers	condos	$990-$1600/w	18	no			1					Cayman Brac
The Club	newest island condos	$250	7	no			1	hot tub	yes		yes	Little Cayman
Cobalt Coast	good dive program	$256-$495	18	yes			1	hot tub			yes	Gr. Cayman
Conch Club	condos	$350-$450	12	no			1	hot tub			yes	Little Cayman
★ Courtyard by Marriott	good value, good beach	$220-$240	232	2			1		yes		yes	Gr. Cayman
Discovery Point Club	condos and suites	$245-$475	47	no		2	1		yes		yes	Gr. Cayman
Divi Tiara Beach Resort	basic dive resort	$182-$285	71	yes		1	1	hot tub	yes		yes	Cayman Brac
Eldemire's	good value	$96-$212	11	no			1					Gr. Cayman
Grand Cayman Marriott	good value	$249-$309	313	yes			1	hot tub	yes		yes	Gr. Cayman
★ Hyatt Regency	plush, on beach	$575-$2,100	175	2	1 x 9		1	yes	yes	3-12	yes	Gr. Cayman
Lacovia Condominiums	condos, on beach	$360-$470	35	no		1	1	yes	yes		yes	Gr. Cayman
Little Cayman Beach	diving, spa	$350-$440	40	yes		1	1	hot tub			yes	Little Cayman
Paradise Villas	1-bedroom villas	$157	12	no			1				yes	Little Cayman
★ Pirates Point Resort	no a/c in some	$520	10	yes							yes	Little Cayman
★ Reef Resort	time-share, East End	$210-$395	70	yes		1	1	hot tub	yes		yes	Gr. Cayman
Ritz-Carlton	luxury high-rise	$949-$1950	365	5		2		yes	yes		yes	Gr. Cayman
Rocky Shore	local feel	$100-$130	6	no								Gr. Cayman
Sam McCoy's	family-style meals	$250	8	no								Little Cayman
★ Southern Cross Club	diving, fishing	$3,680/week	12	yes			1				yes	Little Cayman
Spanish Bay Reef Resort	all-inclusive	$190-$325	67	yes			1	hot tub				Gr. Cayman
Sunset House	diving	$198-$242	60	yes			1				yes	Gr. Cayman
★ Sunshine Suites Resort	all-suites, kitchens	$225-$270	130	yes			1				yes	Gr. Cayman

priv. = golf privileges
mass. = massage only

★ HOTEL NAME	Worth Noting	Cost	Rooms	Restaurants	Golf Courses	Tennis Courts	Pools	Health Clubs	Spa	On The Beach	Kids' Programs	Dive Shops	Location
Cayman Islands (cont.)													
★ Turtle Nest Inn	affordable apartments	$129–$229	8	no						yes			Gr. Cayman
★ Walton's Mango Manor	friendly B&B	$90–$160	6	no									Cayman Brac
Westin Casuarina Resort & Spa	full resort on beach	$284–$2,050	347	3			1	hot tub		yes		yes	Gr. Cayman
Curaçao													
★ Avila Beach Hotel	pool in 2006	$247–$350	108	2		1	1			yes			Willemstad
Breezes Curaçao	all-inclusive	$369–$449	339	3		2	4	yes	yes	yes	2–16	yes	Willemstad
★ Curaçao Marriott	island's best resort	$285–$370	247	3	priv.	2	1	yes	yes	yes	5–12	yes	Piscadera
Floris Suite Hotel	spacious suites	$210–$285	71	yes	priv.	1	1					yes	Piscadera
Habitat Curaçao	shore diving	$133–$150	76	yes		1	1	yes		yes		yes	Rif St. Marie
★ Hilton Curaçao	2 beautiful beaches	$135–$220	208	2	priv.	2	2	yes	yes	yes	2–12	yes	Piscadera
Holiday Beach Hotel	large casino	$175–$190	201	2		2	1	yes	yes	yes			Otrobanda
★ Hotel Kurá Hulanda	historic area	$240–$340	92	4	priv.	2	2	yes	yes				Otrobanda
Howard Johnson Plaza	in town	$110–$120	50	yes			1						Otrobanda
Lions Dive	good diving, beach	$150–$197	111	yes		1	1	yes	yes	yes		yes	Bapor Kibra
★ Lodge Kurá Hulanda	remote, kitchens	$200–$325	77	3	1		1	hot tub	mass.	yes		yes	Westpunt
Plaza Hotel Curaçao	in town, great views	$115–$145	220	2			1						Punda
Sunset Waters	remote, kids programs	$290–$390	70	yes	1		1	yes		yes	2–16	yes	Santa Marta
Dominica													
Anchorage Hotel	dive lodge	$60–$80	32	yes			1					yes	Castle Com.
★ Beau Rive	elegant, modern	$120	8	no			1						Roseau
Calibishie Lodges	apartments	$80–$90	6	yes			1						Calibishie
Castle Comfort Lodge	best dive lodge	$248	15	yes			1	hot tub				yes	Castle Com.

Hotel	Notes	Price	Rooms	Rest.	Golf	Tennis	Pools	Spa	Spa 2	Extra	Kids	Beach	Location
Cocoa Cottages	rustic but comfortable	$80–$85	6	yes									Trafalgar
★ Crescent Moon Cabins	remote cabins	$85–$115	4	no			1	hot tub					Sylvania
Evergreen Hotel	not dive-oriented	$105–$140	17	yes			1						Castle Com.
Exotica	bird-watching	$109–$140	6	2									Giraudel
Fort Young Hotel	modern hotel	$85–$150	73	3			1	hot tub					Roseau
★ Habitation Chabert	fanciest island resort	$175–$230	5	yes			1	hot tub	yes				Hatton Gdn
Hummingbird Inn	honeymoon retreat	$89	10	yes									Morne Dan.
Itassi Cottages	simple cottages	$60	3	no									Morne Bruce
★ Jungle Bay & Spa	yoga retreat	$139–$159	35	yes			1		yes				Delices
★ Papillote	natural hot springs	$95–$125	7	yes				hot tub					Trafalgar
Picard Beach Cottages	stand-alone cottages	$100–$180	18	no						yes			Pr. Rupert
Roseau Valley Hotel	no TVs in some rooms	$84–$140	10	yes			1						Roseau
Roxy's Mountain Lodge	near Morne Trois Pitons	$64–$109	16	yes									Laudat
Sunset Bay Club	all-inclusive plan	$125–$215	13	yes			1	sauna	yes			yes	Coulibistrie
Tamarind Tree Hotel	friendly, no frills	$97	9	yes			1						Salisbury
3 Rivers Eco Lodge	free-standing cottages	$70	6	yes									N. Foundland
★ Zandoli Inn	amazing views	$145	5	no			1						Stowe
Dominican Republic													
Barceló Capella	estatelike grounds	$190	509	5		2	2	yes	mass.	yes	4–12	yes	Juan Dolio
★ Casa Colonial	all suites, luxurious	$350–$420	50	2	priv.		1	hot tub	yes		1–18		Puerto Plata
★ Casa de Campo	world-class golf	$706–$738	500	9	3 × 18	13	16	yes	mass.	yes		yes	La Romana
★ Club Med Punta Cana	good for families	$250	519	2			3		mass.		2–12	yes	Punta Cana
Gran Ventana	sophisticated style	$240–$350	502	5	priv.	1	2	sauna			4–12		Puerto Plata
Hilton Santo Domingo	best value in S.D.	$99–$155	260	2	priv.		1		yes				Santo Dom.
Hodelpa Caribe Colonial	Friday-night fiesta	$90–$130	54	yes									Santo Dom.

priv. = golf privileges
mass. = massage only

Dominican Republic (cont.)

HOTEL NAME	Worth Noting	Cost	Rooms	Restaurants	Golf Courses	Tennis Courts	Pools	Health Clubs	Spa	On The Beach	Kids' Programs	Dive Shops	Location
Hotel Bahía Las Ballenas	open-air baths	$95–$110	32	yes			1			yes		yes	Las Terrenas
Iberostar Bávaro Resort	3 resorts in 1	$378–$390	598	11		3	1	yes	mass.	yes	4–12	yes	Punta Cana
★ Iberostar Hac. Dominicus	PADI 5-star dive center	$250	498	4		2	3	yes	yes	yes	4–12	yes	Bayahibe
InterContinental	improved in 2006	$109–$145	196	2	priv.	1	1	hot tub	yes	yes			Santo Dom.
Meliá Caribe Tropical	Cocotal Golf Club	$450–$600	1,044	15	3 x 9	8	2	yes	yes	yes	4–11	yes	Punta Cana
★ Natura Cabanas	family-owned, laid-back	$148	10	2			1		yes	yes			Cabarete
Natura Park	eco-sensitive	$220–$290	510	3		3	1	hot tub	yes	yes	4–11		Punta Cana
Ocean Bávaro	active, international	$360	749	7		2	3	hot tub	yes	yes	4–12	yes	Punta Cana
Ocean Blue	suites w/Jacuzzi tubs	$360	708	9	priv.		2	sauna	mass.	yes	4–12	yes	Punta Cana
Orchid Bay Estates	fully-staffed villas	$500–$2,500	7	no		1	7			yes			Cabrera
Palladium Bávaro Grand	family suites for up to 8	$220–$250	1,363	4		2	4	hot tub	yes	yes	3–12	yes	Punta Cana
Paradisus Punta Cana	climbing wall	$660	527	11	priv.	4	1	yes	yes	yes	4–12	yes	Punta Cana
Piergiorgio Palace Hotel	clifftop boutique hotel	$85–$95	54	2			2	hot tub	yes	yes			El Batey
★ PuntaCana Resort & Club	golf villas	$280–$320	300	9	1 x 18	6	4	yes	yes	yes	5–12	yes	Punta Cana
Renaissance Jaragua	large gym	$154	300	3	priv.	4	1	sauna	yes	yes			Santo Dom.
Sea Horse Ranch	luxury villas, horses	$420–$2,500	75	yes		5				yes			Cabarete
★ Secrets Excellence	adults only	$350	558	8	priv.	3	2	hot tub	yes	yes		yes	Punta Cana
Serenity House	secluded, intimate	$350	21	yes			1			yes			Samaná
Sirenis Tropical Suites	excellent beach	$260	816	9		4	4	hot tub		yes	4–12	yes	Punta Cana
★ Sofitel Frances	historic building	$178–$238	19	yes						yes			Santo Dom.
★ Sofitel Nicolas Ovando	boutique luxury	$345–$390	104	yes			1		mass.	yes			Santo Dom.
Sosúa Bay Hotel	panoramic bay views	$320–$340	193	5		2	2	hot tub		yes	4–12	yes	Puerto Plata
Sun Village	luxury suites, spa	$274	300	5	priv.	7	7	yes	yes	yes	4–12	yes	Puerto Plata
Sunscape Casa del Mar	spa, kids club	$180–$250	568	4		4	2	hot tub	yes	yes	4–12	yes	La Romana

★ Sunscape The Beach	excellent value	$360	722	7	priv.	2	2	yes		yes	4-17	yes	Punta Cana
★ Velero Beach Resort	spacious suites	$110–$130	29	yes			1	hot tub		yes		yes	Cabarete
★ Victoria Resort	major reno. in 2005	$200–$300	193	4	priv.	1	2	hot tub		yes	4-12	yes	Puerto Plata
★ Victorian House	clifftop boutique hotel	$350	50	5			2	yes				yes	Puerto Plata
Villa Taína	young & sporty crowd	$75–$105	56	yes			1		mass.			yes	Cabarete
Viva Wyndham Samaná	beach cabanas	$230–$260	218	5			1			yes	4-12	yes	Samaná
Windsurf Resort Hotel	apartments, windsurfing	$107–$125	102	yes			1						Cabarete
Grenada with Carriacou													
Ade's Dream	some shared baths	$32–$54	39	yes			1			yes			Carriacou
Allamanda Beach Resort	AI option w/massage	$125–$155	50	yes		1	1			yes			Grand Anse
★ Bel Air Plantation	cottages	$325–$475	11	yes			1		mass.	yes			St. David
Blue Horizons	affordable suites	$170–$195	32	yes	priv.		1	hot tub					Grand Anse
★ Calabash Hotel	all suites	$385–$615	30	yes	priv.	1	1		yes	yes			Anse Épines
Carriacou Grand View	hillside views	$60–$95	13	yes			1					yes	Carriacou
Coyaba	directly on the beach	$304	80	2	priv.	1	1	hot tub	mass.	yes		yes	Grand Anse
Flamboyant	suites and cottages	$130–$140	60	yes	priv.		1			yes		yes	Grand Anse
Gem Holiday Beach	no-frills apartments	$126–$135	19	yes			1			yes			Morne Rouge
Green Roof Inn	small, family-owned	$65–$120	5	yes			1			yes			Carriacou
Grenada Grand	convention center	$145–$230	240	2	1 x 9	2	2	hot tub	mass.	yes		yes	Grand Anse
Grenadian by Rex	Europeans abound	$155–$185	212	3		2	1			yes			Point Salines
La Sagesse	bird sanctuary	$130–$150	12	yes			1			yes			La Sagesse
★ Laluna	remote, upscale	$610–$880	16	yes			1			yes			Morne Rouge
★ Maca Bana Villas	upscale villas	$360	7	yes			1	hot tub	mass.	yes			St. George
Mariposa Beach Resort	private jetty	$100–$130	46	2			1	hot tub		yes			Morne Rouge
Silver Beach Resort	fishing boat	$60–$80	16	yes		1	1					yes	Carriacou
★ Spice Island	Grenada's best reborn	$725–$850	64	2	priv.	1	1	hot tub	yes	yes		yes	St. George

priv. = golf privileges
mass. = massage only

★ HOTEL NAME	Worth Noting	Cost	Rooms	Restaurants	Golf Courses	Tennis Courts	Pools	Health Clubs	Spa	On The Beach	Kids' Programs	Dive Shops	Location
Grenada with Carriacao (cont.)													
True Blue Bay	on-site marina	$160–$180	31	yes			2			yes		yes	True Blue Bay
Twelve Degrees North	personal housekeeper	$225	8	no		1	1		mass.	yes			Anse Épines
Guadeloupe													
★ Auberge les Petits Saints	small, atmospheric inn	€150	8	no			1						Terre-de-Haut
★ Club Med La Caravelle	family-friendly	€280–€380	329	2	6	1	1			yes	4–17		Ste-Anne
La Cohoba Hôtel	all-suites	€130	100	yes	2	1	1			yes			Marie-Galante
La Créole Beach Hotel	large, sprawling	€130–€180	373	2			1			yes	yes		Gosier
Eden Palm	stylish, sophisticated	€158–€220	63	yes	1	1	1	sauna		yes			Ste-Anne
★ Le Jardin de Malanga	romantic, atmospheric	€228	9	no			1						Trois-Rivières
Le Jardin Tropical	bungalows	€64	6	no			1						Bouillante
★ Habitation Grande Anse	views, family-friendly	€108–€200	45	yes			1						Ziotte
Hôtel Cocoplaya	in town	€91–€114	10	yes			1						Terre-de-Haut
Hôtel La Toubana	views, 2006 renovation	€172–€212	33	yes	1	1	1			yes			Ste-Anne
★ Le Méridien	good service	€419–€633	50	yes	priv.	2	1		mass.	yes			St-François
★ La Métisse	small, caring owners	€140	7	no			1	hot tub					St-François
★ Paradis Saintois	hammocks	€81–€92	9	no			2						Terre-de-Haut
Rayon Vert	small, romantic	€156–€186	22	yes			1						Deshaies
Salako Beach Resort	3 resorts in 1	€112–€150	270	3		2	2	hot tub		yes	6–11	yes	Gosier
★ Sofitel Auberge	weekly folkloric show	€320–€400	213	3			1		mass.	yes			Gosier
Tainos Cottages	Balinese bungalows	€200	7	yes			1			yes			Deshaies
Jamaica													
★ Beaches Boscobel	family-friendly	$670–$730	230	5	priv.	4	4		yes	yes	inf.–17	yes	St. Ann
Breezes Montego Bay	Doctor's Cave Beach	$267–$287	124	3	1	1	1			yes		yes	MoBay
Breezes Runaway Bay	sports-oriented	$335–$355	234	4	1 x 18	4	1	hot tub		yes		yes	Runaway Bay

							swater	hot tub	yes			
The Caves	villas on the Rocks	$665–$1,250	10	yes					yes			Negril
Charela Inn	weekly folkloric show	$166–$221	49	yes		1		yes	yes			Negril
ClubHotel Riu Negril	bargain in Negril	$260–$520	438	4		2	2	yes	yes	4–12	yes	Negril
Coco La Palm	oversized rooms	$145–$195	76	2			1	hot tub	yes			Negril
Country Country	private patios	$160–$180	14	yes					yes			Negril
Couples Negril	romance and relaxation	$579–$683	234	3		4	2	yes	yes		yes	Negril
Couples Ocho Rios	private plunge pools	$535–$573	206	4		5	1	sauna	yes		yes	Tower Isle
Couples Sans Souci	spa treatment included	$590–$900	146	4		2	4	yes	yes		yes	Mammee Bay
★ Couples Swept Away	best sports facilities	$590–$733	134	2	priv.	10	2	yes	yes		yes	Negril
Coyaba Beach Resort	like a country inn	$300–$400	50	3		1	1	hot tub	yes			Little River
FDR Pebbles	personal nanny	$440–$480	96	3		1			yes	nb.–16		Runaway Bay
★ FDR, Franklyn D.	personal nanny	$390–$840	76	4		1	1		yes	nb.–16	yes	Runaway Bay
Goblin Hill Villas	villas	$125–$195	28	no		2	1		yes			Port Antonio
★ Goldeneye	villas	$950–$3,800	5	yes		1	1	mass.	yes			Ocho Rios
Grand Lido Braco	nude rooms & beach	$449–$525	284	5	1 x 9	3	2	yes	yes		yes	Runaway Bay
★ Grand Lido Negril	nude beach	$522–$591	210	6		4	2	yes	yes		yes	Negril
★ Half Moon	villas, dolphin swim	$410–$645	249	7	1 x 18	13	51	sauna	yes		yes	MoBay
★ Hedonism II	party all night, nudity	$449–$466	280	6		6	4	yes	yes		yes	Negril
★ Hedonism III	swim-up rooms, nudity	$449–$466	225	5		2	3	yes	yes		yes	Runaway Bay
Hilton Kingston	business favorite	$150–$190	303	2		2	1	yes	yes		yes	Kingston
Holiday Inn SunSpree	family-friendly	$293–$329	524	4		4	3	mass.	yes			MoBay
Hotel Mocking Bird Hill	B&B feel	$245–$295	10	yes			1		yes	6 m–12	yes	Port Antonio
Jake's	villas	$115–$325	15	2			swater	mass.				Treasure Bch
Jamaica Inn	large verandahs	$500–$780	53	yes		1	1	mass.	yes	yes		Ocho Rios
Jamaica Pegasus	24-hour room service	$131–$160	315	yes	priv.	2	1	yes	yes			Kingston

priv. = golf privileges
mass. = massage only

Jamaica (cont.)

HOTEL NAME	Worth Noting	Cost	Rooms	Restaurants	Golf Courses	Tennis Courts	Pools	Health Clubs	Spa	On The Beach	Kids' Programs	Dive Shops	Location
Negril Gardens	relaxed, small AI	$230–$270	65	yes			1			yes			Negril
Point Village Resort	apartments	$280–$440	165	3		1	1	hot tub	mass.	yes	nb-12		Negril
Ritz-Carlton Rose Hall	high tea	$499–$549	427	4	1 x 18	1	1	yes	yes	yes	5-12	yes	St. James
★ Rockhouse Hotel	hip, stylish villas	$125–$150	34	yes			1						Negril
Rooms Ocho Rios	value choice, room only	$94–$124	93	yes						yes		yes	Ocho Rios
Rose Hall Resort	waterpark	$180–$270	489	5	6	3	3		mass.	yes	4-12	yes	MoBay
★ Round Hill	villas, golf, reno. in 2005	$570–$620	63	yes	5	1	1	yes	yes	yes		yes	MoBay
★ Royal Plantation	beach butler	$450–$700	77	4	priv.	2	1	yes	yes	yes		yes	Ocho Rios
Sandals Grande Ocho Rios	some villas	$580–$740	529	8	priv.	4	96	yes	yes	yes		yes	Ocho Rios
★ Sandals Royal Caribbean	dragon boat to island	$620–$770	190	4		3	4	sauna		yes		yes	MoBay
★ Starfish Trelawny	bargain-priced AI	$227–$247	350	6		4	4	hot tub		yes	6 m-12	yes	Falmouth
★ Strawberry Hill	villas, Aveda spa	$335–$775	12	yes			1	sauna	yes				Irishtown
Sunset at the Palms	Green Globe award	$375–$475	85	2	1	1	1	sauna	yes	yes			Negril
Sunset Beach Resort	waterpark	$280–$340	420	4	4	3	3		yes	yes	2-12		MoBay
Sunset Jamaica Grande	waterfall pool	$350–$410	730	5	2	5	5	sauna	yes	yes	2-12		Ocho Rios
Sunset Resort & Villas	owner-managed	$105–$315	12	yes			1			yes			Treasure Bch
Trident Villas	villas, formal	$220–$340	23	yes	2	1			mass.	yes			Port Antonio
★ Tryall Club	villas, excellent golf	$320–$686	56	yes	1 x 18	9	1		mass.	yes	5-12		Sandy Bay
Martinique													
Amandiers Resort	3 hotels w/shared fac.	€108–€138	299	2	1	3				yes	4-11		Ste-Luce
★ Cap Est	island's ritziest resort	€500–€1,200	50	2	1	1		yes	yes	yes			Le François
La Caravelle	family-run	€64–€98	15	yes									Tartane
Club Med Buccaneer's	complete rebirth	€380–€410	293	3	6	1		yes	yes	yes			Ste-Anne
Le Domaine St. Aubin	hilltop inn	€146	11	yes			1						La Trinité

Name		Cost	Rooms								Location
Engoulevent	personalized service	€120	5	no			1	hot tub			Ft-de-France
Manoir de Beauregard	bungalows	€120–€150	14	yes			1				Ste-Anne
Pierre & Vacances	family-friendly apts.	€150	337	3			1		yes	3-12	Ste-Luce
La Plantation Leyritz	17th-century estate	€115	50	yes	1		1				Basse-Pte
★ Le Plein Soleil	total reno. in 2006	€164–€199	16	yes	1		1				Le François
Sofitel Bakoua	beach access from room	€516–€620	139	3		2	1		yes		Pte du Bout
Squash Hôtel	cheery, bright	€132	105	yes			1				Ft-de-France
La Valmenière	business travelers	€160	120	2			1				Ft-de-France
Montserrat											
Erindell Villa	treat you like family	$65	2	yes			1				Woodlands
★ Gingerbread Hill	secluded, value	$45–$150	4	no							St. Peter's
Grand View B&B	service, good food	$90–$120	6	yes							Baker Hill
Travellers Palm	lush grounds	$45–$65	3	no							Olveston
Tropical Mansion Suites	modern, motel-like	$119–$129	18	yes			1				Sweeney's
★ Vue Pointe Hotel	island's classiest	$100–$120	27	2	2		1			yes	Old Rd. Bay
Puerto Rico											
At Wind Chimes	spacious rooms	$99–$110	22	no			1				San Juan
★ Bravo Beach Hotel	upscale boutique hotel	$175–$245	10	yes			2	yes			Vieques
Caribe Hilton	private man-made beach	$340–$450	646	76	3		1	yes	yes	4-12	San Juan
★ Casa Grande	hammocks, porches	$90–$95	20	yes			1	hot tub	yes		Utuado
Casa Isleña	simple, romantic	$115–$165	9	yes			1	hot tub			Barrio Puntas
Club Seaborne	secluded, good food	$189–$219	12	yes			1				Culebra
★ Copamarina	beauty, family-friendly	$205–$270	106	yes	2		2	hot tub	yes	yes	Guánica
Coral Princess	pool on terrace	$115	26	no			1	hot tub			San Juan
Courtyard Isla Verde	good value	$150–$345	293	3			3	hot tub	yes		San Juan

priv. = golf privileges
mass. = massage only

HOTEL NAME	Worth Noting	Cost	Rooms	Restaurants	Golf Courses	Tennis Courts	Pools	Health Clubs	Spa	On The Beach	Kids' Programs	Dive Shops	Location
Puerto Rico (cont.)													
★ El Conquistador	offshore island beach	$339–$489	922	17	1 x 18	4	8	yes	yes	yes	4-12	yes	Fajardo
★ El Convento	historic convent	$355–$410	68	3			1		yes				San Juan
El Prado Inn	close yet removed	$80–$139	22	no			1	hot tub					San Juan
Embassy Suites Dorado	Dorado Beach	$185	209	2	1 x 18	2	1	hot tub					Dorado
★ Gallery Inn	quirky, relaxed	$175–$270	23	no									San Juan
★ Hacienda Tamarindo	relaxed, casual	$170–$200	16	no			1						Vieques
Hilton Ponce	not a good beach	$180–$260	253	4	3 x 9	4	1	sauna	yes	yes	8-12		La Guancha
★ Horned Dorset Primavera	island's best villas	$590–$850	22	yes			2		mass.	yes			Rincón
Hostería del Mar	apartments	$89–$209	13	yes						yes			San Juan
★ Hotel Meliá	good restaurant	$100–$110	78	yes			1						Ponce
Inn on the Blue Horizon	romantic	$160–$370	10	yes			1	hot tub	mass.	yes			Vieques
Lazy Parrot	balconies with views	$110–$135	11	2			1			yes			Rincón
Lemontree	on-beach apartments	$125–$140	6	no				hot tub	mass.	yes			Rincón
★ Normandie Hotel	reno. art deco gem	$280–$320	175	2			1		yes	yes			San Juan
Numero Uno	small, friendly inn	$135–$185	13	yes			1			yes			San Juan
Paradisus Puerto Rico	all-inclusive	$700–$1,000	505	6	2 x 18	3	1	yes	yes	yes	4-12	yes	Coco Beach
Par. Baños de Coamo	rustic old inn	$85–$90	48	yes			2						Coamo
Par. Hacienda Gripiñas	coffee plantation	$85–$118	19	yes			2						Jayuya
Rincón Beach Resort	secluded, stylish	$220–$265	112	yes			1		yes	yes		yes	Añasco
Rincón Surf & Board	surf school	$70–$90	15	yes			1	hot tub		yes			Barrio Puntas
★ Ritz-Carlton San Juan	luxury, good beach	$469	414	3		2	2	sauna	yes	yes	4-12		San Juan
Sheraton Old San Juan	near cruise ship pier	$165–$255	240	yes			1	hot tub					San Juan
Villa Montaña	villas	$300	56	yes		2	2			yes			Isabela
Villas del Mar Hau	good for big families	$102–$159	40	yes		1	1			yes			Isabela

Hotel	Comments	Rates	Rms.	Rest.	Golf	Tennis	Pool	Hot Tub	mass.	A/C	Kids	priv.	Location
The Water Club	hip boutique hotel	$239–$299	84	yes			1		yes	yes			San Juan
★ Westin Río Mar	sprawling, good golf	$399–$680	659	7	2 x 18	13	2	yes	yes	yes	4–12	yes	Río Grande
Saba													
Cottage Club	cottages	$105–$118	10	no			1						Windward.
Ecolodge Rendez-Vous	very rustic cottages	$85	12	yes									Windward.
El Momo	eco-lodge w/comfort	$40–$90	12	no			1						Booby Hill
Gate House	villa	$135	7	yes			1						Hell's Gate
★ Juliana's Hotel	apartment/cottages	$110–$165	12	yes			1						Windward.
Mountain Spring Villas	villas	$100	3	no			1						Booby Hill
★ Queen's Garden Resort	hot tub suites	$225–$325	12	yes			1	hot tub					Troy Hill
Scout's Place	dive packages	$83–$110	13	yes			1					yes	Windward.
Willard's of Saba	incredible view, upscale	$350–$500	9	yes		1	1	hot tub					Windward.
St. Barthélemy													
Carl Gustaf	private plunge pools	€995–€1,400	14	yes			1	yes					Gustavia
Le Christopher	large infinity pool	€421–€527	43	2			1	yes					Pointe Milou
★ Eden Rock	one of the very best	€615–€2,500	29	2			1						St-Jean
Emeraude Plage	bungalows	€330–€645	28	no						yes			St-Jean
François Plantation	off-season bargains	€400–€470	12	yes			1						Colombier
Hôtel Baie des Anges	casual	€290–€420	10	yes			1			yes			Flamands
★ Hôtel Village St-Jean	cottages/villa	€190–€420	26	yes			1	hot tub					St-Jean
★ Hôtel Isle de France	casually refined	€680–€1,930	33	yes		1	1						Flamands
★ Hôtel Guanahani	full-service resort	€550–€1,440	72	2		2	2				2–12		G. Cul de Sac
Hotel La Banane	chic rooms	€450	9	yes			2						Lorient
★ Les Îlets de la Plage	bungalows	€460–€545	11	no			1			yes			St-Jean
Les Mouettes	bungalows	€135–€190	7	no						yes			Lorient

priv. = golf privileges
mass. = massage only

★ HOTEL NAME	Worth Noting	Cost	Rooms	Restaurants	Golf Courses	Tennis Courts	Pools	Health Clubs	Spa	On The Beach	Kids' Programs	Dive Shops	Location
St. Barthélemy (cont.)													
★ La Paillote	bungalows	€350–€550	5	no			1						G. Cul de Sac
★ Le P'tit Morne	panoramic views	€163–€230	14	no			1						Colombier
★ Le Sereno	total reno. in 2005	€600–€1400	0	yes			1						G. Cul de Sac
St-Barth's Beach Hotel	family-friendly	€275–€300	44	yes			1			yes			G. Cul de Sac
★ Le Toiny	perfection at a price	€1,500–€2500	16	yes			1						Anse à Toiny
Le Tom Beach	plantation-style rooms	€445–€645	12	yes			1			yes			St-Jean
Tropical Hôtel	stylish value	€185–€230	21	no			1						St-Jean
St. Eustatius													
Country Inn	basic, lush garden	$40–$55	6	no									Concordia
Golden Era Hotel	friendly service	$75–$110	20	yes			swater						Oranjestad
King's Well Hotel	eclectic furnishings	$90–$140	12	yes			1	hot tub					Oranjestad
★ The Old Gin House	nicest on island	$135–$275	20	2			1						Oranjestad
Ruby's Inn	new, small & simple	$95	13	no									Oranjestad
St. Kitts & Nevis													
Banyan Tree B&B	cottages, working farm	$125–$175	3	no									Nevis
Bird Rock	amazing views	$100–$125	50	2		1	2			yes	yes		St. Kitts
★ Four Seasons Resort	best golf course	$645–$935	257	4	1 x 18	10	3	yes	yes	yes	2–12	yes	Nevis
Frigate Bay Resort	swim-up bar	$120–$200	64	yes	priv.	1	1						St. Kitts
★ Golden Lemon	tranquil, remote	$325–$495	26	yes			1			yes			St. Kitts
Golden Rock Plantation	family-owned, nature	$220–$285	17	2		1	1						Nevis
★ Hermitage Plantation	historic, friendly	$325–$450	17	yes		1	1						Nevis
★ Hurricane Cove	cliffside cottages	$210–$595	13	no			1						Nevis
★ Inn at Cades Bay	spacious rooms	$195–$250	16	yes			1			yes			Nevis
★ Montpelier Plantation	understated elegance	$460–$535	17	3		1	1						Nevis

Hotel	Description	Price	Rooms	Restaurants	Golf			Hot tub	Spa	Pool	Kids	Gym	Location
★ Mount Nevis Hotel	contemporary amenities	$350–$400	33	2			1	hot tub					Nevis
★ Nisbet Plantation	superior rooms	$475–$645	36	3		1	1	hot tub	mass.	yes			Nevis
Ocean Terrace Inn	business hotel	$195–$330	79	3			3	yes	mass.				St. Kitts
Old Manor Hotel	plantation atmopshere	$280–$350	14	2			1						Nevis
★ Ottley's Plantation Inn	ideal Caribbean inn	$298–$758	24	yes		1		hot tub	yes				St. Kitts
Oualie Beach Hotel	dive packages	$245–$325	32	yes					yes			yes	Nevis
Rawlins Plantation Inn	former sugar estate	$470	10	yes		1	1						St. Kitts
Rock Haven B&B	homemade ice cream	$110–$130	2	no			1						St. Kitts
St. Kitts Marriott Resort	huge suites	$263–$390	636	8	1 x 18	5	3	yes	yes	yes	5–12		St. Kitts
Sugar Bay Club	cottages	$320–$420	100	2		1	2			yes	4–12		St. Kitts
★ Timothy Beach Resort	apartments	$125–$205	60	yes			1		mass.	yes			St. Kitts
★ Villa Paradiso	villas	$1,285–$1,785	10	no			10		yes	yes			Nevis
St. Lucia													
Almond Morgan Bay	family all-inclusive	$450–$500	250	4	priv.	4	4	yes	yes	yes	nb–16		Gros Islet
★ Anse Chastanet	good dive program	$495–$865	73	2		1	1		yes	yes		yes	Chastanet
★ Auberge Seraphine	spacious, cheerful	$100–$130	28	yes			1	hot tub					Castries
Bay Gardens Hotel	walk to restaurants	$115–$135	71	yes		2	2		yes				Rodney Bay
★ The Body Holiday	inclusive spa resort	$662–$812	154	3	priv.	2	3	yes	yes	yes		yes	Cap Estate
Club St. Lucia	village-style resort	$270–$400	369	5	priv.	9	5	yes	yes	yes	6 m–17	yes	Cap Estate
★ Coco Palm	boutique hotel	$145–$205	72	yes			1			yes			Rodney Bay
Coconut Bay	AI near airport	$380–$410	254	4		4	3	yes	yes	yes			Vieux Fort
Hummingbird Beach	simple, welcoming	$110–$170	10	yes			1		yes	yes			Soufrière
★ Jalousie Plantation	between the Pitons	$450–$500	112	4	1 x 3	4	1	yes	yes	yes	5–12	yes	Pitons
★ Ladera	villas, no 4th wall	$420–$550	24	yes			1		yes	yes			Soufrière
Rendezvous	cottages	$450–$512	100	2		2	2	yes	mass.	yes		yes	Vigie

priv. = golf privileges
mass. = massage only

HOTEL NAME	Worth Noting	Cost	Rooms	Restaurants	Golf Courses	Tennis Courts	Pools	Health Clubs	Spa	On The Beach	Kids' Programs	Dive Shops	Location
St. Lucia *(cont.)*													
★ Royal St. Lucian	best beach	$500–$670	96	3	priv.	2	1	yes	yes	yes	4–12	yes	Rodney Bay
★ Sandals Grande	swim-up verandahs	$680–$780	282	5	priv.	2	5	yes	yes	yes		yes	Gros Islet
★ Sandals Regency	private plunge pools	$680–$780	328	6	1 x 9	5	3	sauna	yes	yes		yes	Castries
Stonefield Estate	villas	$190–$330	16	yes			1		mass.	yes			Soufrière
★ Ti Kaye Village	isolated, views	$200–$380	33	yes			1		mass.	yes			Castries
Windjammer Landing	family-friendly	$290–$420	219	5		2	4	yes	yes	yes	4–12	yes	Labrelotte
St. Maarten/St. Martin													
Alamanda Resort	right on Orient Beach	$240–$605	42	2		2	1			yes			Orientale
Delfina Hotel	gay-owned	$89–$149	12	no			1	hot tub					Cupecoy
Divi Little Bay	lovely beach	$166–$299	235	3		1	3		yes	yes	3–12	yes	Philipsburg
Esmeralda Resort	upscale, hillside	$240–$715	83	2		2	17		mass.	yes			Orientale
★ Grand Case Beach Club	condos	$130–$385	72	yes		1	1			yes		yes	Grand Case
Green Bay Beach Resort	great location	$110–$340	262	3		1	2	hot tub		yes	4–12		Great Bay
Green Cay Village	villas	$396–$1,020	16	no		1	16			yes			Orientale
★ Hôtel L'Esplanade	excellent service	$220–$370	24	no			2						Grand Case
Holland House	right on Front Street	$98–$225	54	yes						yes			Philipsburg
★ The Horny Toad	apartments on beach	$107–$198	8	no						yes			Simpson Bay
Hotel Beach Plaza	great location	$170–$481	144	yes		1						yes	Marigot
★ Hotel La Plantation	Orient Bay views	$131–$325	51	yes		2	1						Orientale
The Inn at Cupecoy	luxury rooms	$150–$295	5	yes			1						Cupecoy
Le Domaine de Lonvilliers	reno. in 2005	$310–$460	138	yes		1	1	hot tub	mass.	yes			Anse Marcel
Le Flamboyant	kitchenettes	$169–$283	271	yes			2	hot tub		yes			Baie Nettlé
Le Petit Hotel	spacious studios	$240–$500	10	no						yes			Grand Case
★ La Samanna	luxury beach resort	$425–$995	81	2		3	1	yes	yes	yes			Baie Longue

Hotel	Comments	Cost	No. Rooms	Restaurant	Tennis	Pools	Beach	Spa	Fitness	Golf priv.	Location
★ La Vista	friendly service	$180–$260	50	yes		2	yes				Simpson Bay
★ Mary's Boon	beachfront guesthouse	$75–$300	32	yes		1	yes				Simpson Bay
Oyster Bay	condos	$120–$400	178	2		1	yes	hot tub	mass.		Oyster Pond
★ Pasanggrahan Royal Inn	old governor's house	$88–$175	31	yes			yes				Philipsburg
Princess Heights	amazing views	$275–$450	15	no	1		yes	mass.			Oyster Pond
Sonesta Maho Beach	big, sprawling resort	$190–$350	600	3	4	2	yes	yes			Maho Bay
St. Vincent & the Grenadines											
Beachcombers Hotel	shower-only	$90–$130	21	yes		1			yes		St. Vincent
Bequia Beachfront Villas	villas	$311	3	no					yes		Bequia
Bigsand Hotel	suites with kitchenettes	$121–$143	10	yes					yes		Union Island
Casa del Mar	good for groups	$150–$400	5	no							Canouan
Cobblestone Inn	small rooms, in-town	$70	19	yes					yes		St. Vincent
★ Cotton House	elegant grand hotel	$700–$1,150	20	3	2	1	yes	yes	yes	yes	Mustique
Dennis's Hideaway	simple guesthouse	$80	5	yes							Mayreau
Firefly	luxury, small inn	$550–$700	4	yes		2	yes				Mustique
Frangipani Hotel	simple, inexpensive	$55–$175	25	yes	1		yes			yes	Bequia
Friendship Bay	family-friendly	$165–$210	28	2	1		yes				Bequia
★ Gingerbread Hotel	all suites, room for 3	$170–$190	9	yes	1		yes			yes	Bequia
★ Grand View	former plantation	$175–$215	19	2	1	1	yes	yes			St. Vincent
The Lagoon	island's busiest	$120	21	yes	1 x 5	1	yes				St. Vincent
Mariners Hotel	in-town, beach access	$145–$175	20	yes		2	yes		yes		St. Vincent
Mustique Villas	fully-staffed, ultra-luxury	$3K–$40K	58	no		1			yes		Mustique
The New Montrose	suites with kitchenettes	$70–$100	25	yes							St. Vincent
The Old Fort Country Inn	romantic greathouse	$130–$160	5	yes	1	1					Bequia
★ Palm Island Resort	great honeymoon spot	$700–$880	37	yes	1	1	yes	mass.			Palm Island

priv. = golf privileges
mass. = massage only

★ HOTEL NAME	Worth Noting	Cost	Rooms	Restaurants	Golf Courses	Tennis Courts	Pools	Health Clubs	Spa	On The Beach	Kids' Programs	Dive Shops	Location
St. Vincent & the Grenadines (cont.)													
Petit Byahaut	secluded eco-resort	$390	4	yes						yes			St. Vincent
★ Petit St. Vincent Resort	luxurious escape	$585–$910	22	yes					mass.	yes			Pt. St. Vincent
★ Raffles Resort Canouan	exclent golf course	$575–$755	156	4	1 x 18	4	1	yes	yes	yes	4–14		Canouan
Roy's Inn	historic inn	$110–$140	22	yes			1	sauna	mass.	yes			St. Vincent
Saltwhistle Bay Club	cottages with sundecks	$380–$540	10	yes						yes		yes	Mayreau
Spring on Bequia	small, family-owned	$130–$220	9	yes		1	1			yes			Bequia
Sunset Shores	low-rise	$150–$180	32	yes			1			yes			St. Vincent
Tamarind Beach Hotel	resort has a sailboat	$310–$490	45	2						yes		yes	Canouan
Villa Lodge Hotel	homey, personalized	$125	18	2		1	1			yes			St. Vincent
★ Young Island Resort	all luxury cottages	$240–$400	29	yes		1	1		mass.	yes			St. Vincent
Trinidad & Tobago													
Arnos Vale Hotel	private cottages	$230	32	yes		1	1			yes		yes	Tobago
Asa Wright Nature Centre	for bird-watchers	$350	25	no									Trinidad
★ Blue Haven Hotel	restored to perfection	$238–$355	52	yes		1			yes	yes		yes	Tobago
★ Blue Waters Inn	eco-friendly, dive shop	$190	38	yes		1	1			yes		yes	Tobago
Coblentz Inn	charming boutique hotel	$145	16	yes				hot tub	mass.	yes			Trinidad
★ Coco Reef Resort	great spa, perfect beach	$330–$350	181	2		2			yes	yes		yes	Tobago
★ Courtyard by Marriott	for business travelers	$150	119	yes			1		mass.				Trinidad
Crews Inn	close to nightlife	$140	46	yes	priv.		1		mass.				Trinidad
Crowne Plaza Trinidad	in Port-of-Spain	$185	238	2			1						Trinidad
Grafton Beach Resort	all-inclusive	$344	106	3			1			yes			Tobago
★ Le Grande Almandier	remote, on beach	$65	10	yes				sauna					Trinidad
Hilton Tobago	good golf, bad beach	$210–$230	200	2	1 x 18	2	3			yes		yes	Tobago

Hotel		Cost	Rooms	Pool	Golf								Island
★ Hilton Trinidad	best business hotel	$200–$245	407	2		2	1						Trinidad
Kapok Hotel	best Port-of-Spain value	$172–$194	94	2			1						Trinidad
★ Kariwak Village	holistic health	$125	24	yes			1	hot tub	mass.				Tobago
Le Grand Courlan	resort with spa	$384	83	3		2	1	yes	yes	yes		yes	Trinidad
Monique's	some kitchenettes	$65	20	no									Tobago
Mt. Irvine Bay Hotel	slightly shabby gentility	$195–$300	157	3	1 x 18	2	1	sauna		yes		yes	Trinidad
★ Pax Guest House	budget-oriented	$104	18	no		1							Tobago
Plantation Beach Villas	luxury villas	$660	6	no			1			yes			Tobago
Villas at Stonehaven	great villas, no beach	$700	14	yes			1						Tobago
Toucan Inn	cheap, sociable	$90	20	yes			1						Tobago
Turks & Caicos Islands													
The Arches of Grand Turk	villas with kitchens	$200	4	no			1						Gr. Turk
Blue Horizon Resort	remote, self-catering	$165–$180	7	no						yes		yes	Mid. Caicos
★ Beaches Turks & Caicos	family all-inclusive	$820–$1,530	462	9		4	5	yes	yes	yes	nb-12	yes	Provo
Bohio Dive Resort	diving and spa	$158–$250	16	yes			1	yes	yes	yes		yes	Gr. Turk
Caribbean Paradise Inn	small inn off the beach	$135–$199	16	no			1			yes			Provo
Club Med Turkoise	party scene, not quiet	$400–$880	293	2		8	1	yes		yes		yes	Provo
Comfort Suites	good Provo budget choice	$150–$170	100	no			1		mass.				Provo
★ Grace Bay Club	stylish, adults-only	$725–$1,095	21	yes	priv.	2	2	hot tub		yes			Provo
Island House	stay longer, get car	$185–$215	8	no			1						Gr. Turk
Le Vele Resort	all suites, family-friendly	$400–$1,200	18	no			1	hot tub					Provo
★ Meridian Club	private, simple, perfect	$895–$995	19	yes		1	1			yes			Pine Cay
Miramar Resort	free beach shuttle	$120–$150	23	yes		1	1			yes			Provo
Ocean Beach Hotel	condos on the beach	$130–$200	10	yes			1			yes		yes	N. Caicos
★ Ocean Club Resorts	good facilities, condos	$225–$525	348	2	priv.	1	2	yes		yes		yes	Provo

priv. = golf privileges
mass. = massage only

★ HOTEL NAME	Worth Noting	Cost	Rooms	Restaurants	Golf Courses	Tennis Courts	Pools	Health Clubs	Spa	On The Beach	Kids' Programs	Dive Shops	Location
Turks & Caicos Islands (cont.)													
Osprey Beach Hotel	welcoming, many suites	$136–$178	27	yes	priv.		1			yes			Gr. Turk
★ Parrot Cay Resort	celebrity hideaway	$590–$2,025	60	2		2	1	yes	yes	yes			Parrot Cay
Pelican Beach Hotel	friendly, good food	$160–$225	16	yes						yes			N. Caicos
Pirate's Hideaway	fun, quirky	$135–$165	3	no						yes			Salt Cay
Point Grace	celebrity hangout	$505–$980	34	2			1	hot tub		yes			Provo
★ Reef Residences at Grace Bay	romantic, quiet	$270–$985	54	2			3		yes	yes	yes		Provo
★ Royal West Indies	mod. prices, kitchenettes	$225–$626	99	yes			2	hot tub	mass.	yes			Provo
Salt Raker Inn	nice little inn	$100–$115	13	yes									Gr. Turk
The Sands at Grace Bay	good off-season rates	$225–$375	118	yes		1	2	hot tub	yes	yes			Provo
Sibonné	small, on the beach	$125–$225	30	yes			1			yes			Provo
Sunset Reef	basic villas	$143–$171	2	no						yes			Salt Cay
Tradewinds	budget-minded	$143–$170	5	no						yes			Salt Cay
Turks & Caicos Club	quiet, all-suites	$645–$845	21	yes			1			yes			Provo
Turtle Cove Inn	inexpensive, off-beach	$85–$145	30	yes			1						Provo
★ Windmills Plantation	romantic, luxurious	$495–$595	8	yes			1			yes			Salt Cay
United States Virgin Islands													
The Anchorage	beachfront suites	$375	11	yes		2	1			yes			St. Thomas
Best Western	near the airport	$260–$280	90	yes			1			yes			St. Thomas
Bolongo Bay	friendly, family-run	$255–$285	77	2		2	1			yes		yes	St. Thomas
The Buccaneer	family-owned, golf course	$295–$890	138	4	1 x 18	8	2		yes	yes	4–12		St. Croix
Cane Bay Reef Club	simple, near diving	$150–$250	9	yes			1			yes			St. Croix
★ Caneel Bay Resort	understated luxury	$450–$1,350	166	4		11	1	yes		yes	in–12	yes	St. John
★ Caribbean Style	home-like, romantic	$130	4	no			1			yes			St. Thomas

Hotel	Description	Price	No. of Rooms				Hot Tub					Island
Carambola	beautiful beach	$209–$240	151	3	2	1			yes		yes	St. Croix
★ Carringtons Inn	island's best small inn	$125–$150	5	no		1						St. Croix
Chenay Bay	family-friendly	$275–$325	50	yes	2	1	hot tub		yes	4–12		St. Croix
Coconut Coast	condos, walk to town	$269–$369	9	no		1			yes			St. John
Colony Cove	condos	$235	62	no		1			yes			St. Croix
Divi Carina Bay	casino	$279–$388	168	2	2	1	hot tub		yes			St. Croix
Estate Lindholm B&B	sophisticated B&B	$300–$350	10	yes		1			yes			St. John
Estate Zootenvaal	peaceful, out of the way	$275–$550	4	no		1						St. John
Gallows Point Resort	condos, walk to town	$435–$575	60	yes		1			yes			St. John
Garden by the Sea B&B	walk into town	$225–$250	3	no								St. John
★ The Green Iguana	B&B, on-site managers	$129–$159	6	no		1						St. Thomas
Harmony Studios	eco-friendly	$200–$225	12	yes					yes	10 & up		St. John
Hibiscus Beach Hotel	nice beachfront	$200	37	yes		1			yes			St. Croix
Holiday Inn St. Thomas	in-town, beach shuttle	$190–$240	151	yes		1					yes	St. Thomas
Hotel Caravelle	in-town	$139–$169	44	yes		1						St. Croix
Hotel 1829	historic inn	$105–$220	15	no		1						St. Thomas
Hotel on the Cay	on a private island	$125–$190	53	yes		1			yes			St. Croix
★ Inn at Pelican Heights	great breakfast	$125–$160	6	no		1						St. Croix
Island View Guesthouse	homey, family-friendly	$79–$129	30	yes		1	hot tub					St. Thomas
King Christian Hotel	in-town, historic	$100–$135	39	no		1					yes	St. Croix
★ Maho Bay Camps	tent cottages, families	$125–$135	114	yes					yes	10 & up		St. John
Marriott Frenchman's	big resort-boutique hotel	$380–$580	531	4	4	2	yes		yes	4–12		St. Thomas
Pink Fancy Hotel	friendly B&B	$95–$175	12	no								St. Croix
Point Pleasant Resort	small but private beach	$255–$355	128	2	1	3			yes			St. Thomas
★ Ritz-Carlton	island's best luxury	$505–$645	281	4	2	2	yes		yes	4–12		St. Thomas

priv. = golf privileges
mass. = massage only

United States

Virgin Islands *(cont.)*

HOTEL NAME	Worth Noting	Cost	Rooms	Restaurants	Golf Courses	Tennis Courts	Pools	Health Clubs	Spa	On The Beach	Kids' Programs	Dive Shops	Location
Sandcastle on the Beach	gay and lesbian	$130–$379	21	yes			2		mass.	yes			St. Croix
Sapphire Beach Resort	suites, excellent beach	$335–$495	171	2		4	1	yes		yes			St. Thomas
Sapphire Village	high-rise condos	$190–$210	15	yes		2	2			yes			St. Thomas
Secret Harbour	low-rise condos	$275–$485	64	yes		3	1	yes		yes	yes		St. Thomas
Serendip	budget-priced, kitchens	$131–$196	10	no									St. John
Sugar Beach	condos on the beach	$179–$365	46	no		2	1			yes			St. Croix
Tamarind Reef	some kitchenettes	$195–$245	46	yes			1						St. Croix
Villa Greenleaf	upscale B&B	$265–$285	6	no			1						St. Croix
★ Villa Madeleine	2-story villas	$275–$355	43	no		1	43						St. Croix
Villa Margarita	quiet, removed	$125–$190	3	no			1						St. Croix
★ Villa Santana	charming, modern B&B	$125–$195	6	no			1						St. Thomas
Waves at Cane Bay	best for divers	$140–$155	12	yes			1					yes	St. Croix
Westin St. John	big, busy	$609–$819	349	4		6	1	hot tub	mass.	yes	3–12	yes	St. John
★ Wyndham Sugar Bay	all-inclusive	$460–$510	309	2		4	1	yes	yes	yes	4–12	yes	St. Thomas

SMART TRAVEL TIPS

There are planners and there are those who, excuse the pun, fly by the seat of their pants. We happily place ourselves among the planners. Our writers and editors try to anticipate all the issues you may face before and during any journey, and then they do their research. This section is the product of their efforts. Use it to get excited about your trip to the Caribbean, to inform your travel planning, or to guide you on the road should the seat of your pants start to feel threadbare.

ADDRESSES

"Whimsical" might best describe some Caribbean addresses. Street names can change for no apparent reason, and most buildings have no numbers. Addresses throughout this guide may include cross streets, landmarks, and other directionals. But to find your destination you might have to ask a local—and be prepared for directions such as "Go down so, turn at the next gap [road], keep goin' past the church, and you'll see it right down the hill."

AIR TRAVEL

Many carriers fly nonstop routes to the Caribbean from major airports in the United States, including Boston, Dallas, New York (JFK), Newark, Philadelphia, Washington (Dulles), Atlanta, Charlotte, Chicago, Houston, and Miami. If you live somewhere else in the United States, you'll probably have to make a connection to get to your Caribbean destination unless you are taking a charter flight. You may also have to make a connection in the Caribbean in San Juan, Montego Bay, Barbados, or St. Maarten. Regularly scheduled charter flights operate in high season, primarily from Canada and the midwestern United States—but also from the United Kingdom and continental Europe. Although there are some nonstops from the United Kingdom to major Caribbean destinations, such as Barbados and Antigua, you may have to connect in New York or Miami. If you're coming from Australia or New Zealand, you'll probably transfer to a Caribbean-bound flight in Miami.

CARRIERS

Most of the major airlines have some flights to the Caribbean. The biggest airline by far is American, which has a major hub in San Juan; its American Eagle subsidiary operates most of the flights from San Juan. Some major U.S. carriers have codeshare partnerships with airlines that fly to the Caribbean. Delta has a codeshare agreement with Air Jamaica, for example, and United codeshares with BWIA. The codeshare agreement allows an airline to sell a certain number of seats on a flight operated by its partner. Bear in mind, however, that if the flight is canceled because of weather or for any other reason not the fault of the operating airline, you'll be rebooked on the next flight that has available seats specifically designated to the codeshare partner that issued your tickets. This may not be the next flight out.

Some destinations are accessible only by small planes operated by local or regional carriers. International carriers will sometimes book those flights for you as part of your overall travel arrangements, or you can confidently book directly with the local carrier, using a major credit card, sometimes online but more often by phone. Unlike the custom among major carriers, schedule changes on most Caribbean airlines normally don't carry a penalty, and your credit card usually won't be charged until after you've taken the flight.

🛪 From the U.S. & Canada **Air Canada** 🕾 888/712-7786, 866/871-4797 in French ⊕ www.aircanada.ca. **Air Jamaica** 🕾 800/523-5585 ⊕ www.airjamaica.com. **American Airlines** 🕾 800/433-7300 ⊕ www.aa.com. **BWIA** 🕾 800/538-2942 ⊕ www.bwee.com. **Cayman Airways** 🕾 800/422-9626 ⊕ www.caymanairways.com. **Continental Airlines** 🕾 800/523-3273 for U.S. and Mexico reservations, 800/231-0856 for international reservations ⊕ www.continental.com. **Delta Airlines** 🕾 800/221-1212 for U.S. reservations, 800/241-4141 for international reservations ⊕ www.delta.com. **JetBlue** 🕾 800/538-2583 ⊕ www.jetblue.com. **Northwest Airlines** 🕾 800/225-2525 for U.S. reservations, 800/447-4747 for international reservations ⊕ www.nwa.com. **Spirit Airlines** 🕾 800/772-7117 or 586/791-7300 ⊕ www.spiritair.com. **United Airlines** 🕾 800/864-8331 for U.S. reservations, 800/538-2929 for international reser-

vations ⊕ www.united.com. **US Airways** 🕾 800/428-4322 for U.S. and Canada reservations, 800/622-1015 for international reservations ⊕ www.usairways.com.

🛪 Within the Caribbean **Air Caraïbes** 🕾 877/772-1005 ⊕ www.aircaraibes.com. **Air Jamaica Express** 🕾 800/523-5585 ⊕ www.airjamaica.com. **American Eagle** 🕾 800/433-7300 ⊕ www.aa.com. **BonairExpress** 🕾 599/717-0808 in Bonaire ⊕ www.bonairexpress.com. **Caribbean Star** 🕾 866-864-6272, 800/744-7827 within the Caribbean ⊕ www.flycaribbeanstar.com. **Caribbean Sun** 🕾 866/864-6272, 800/744-7827 within the Caribbean ⊕ www.flycsa.com. **LIAT** 🕾 888/844-5428 ⊕ www.liatairline.com. **Seabourne Airlines** 🕾 340/773-6442 or 888/359-8687 ⊕ www.seaborneairlines.com. **SkyKing** 🕾 649/941-3136 ⊕ www.skyking.tc. **SVG Air** 🕾 784/457-5124, 800/744-5777 within the Caribbean ⊕ www.svgair.com. **Tobago Express** 🕾 868/627-5160 ⊕ www.tobagoexpress.com. **Trans Island Airways (TIA)** 🕾 246/418-1650 ⊕ www.tia2000.com.

CHECK-IN & BOARDING

Double-check your flight times, especially if you made your reservations far in advance. Airlines change their schedules, and alerts may not reach you. Always **bring a government-issued photo ID to the airport** (even when it's not required, a passport is best), and **arrive when you need to and not before.** Check in usually at least an hour before domestic flights and two to three hours before international flights. But many airlines have more stringent advance check-in requirements at some busy airports. The TSA estimates the waiting time for security at most major airports and publishes the information on its Web site. Not that if you aren't at the gate at least 10 minutes before your flight is scheduled to take off (sometimes earlier), you won't be allowed to board.

Don't stand in a line if you don't have to. Buy an e-ticket, check in at an electronic kiosk, or—even better—check in on your airline's Web site before you leave home. If you don't need to check luggage, you could bypass all but the security lines. You'll ordinarily be allowed to check in at a kiosk or online if you are traveling only to Puerto Rico since it is considered a domestic destination, but not to the USVI or any other Caribbean destinations, which are considered international destinations. These days, most domestic airline tickets are electronic; international tickets may be either electronic or paper. When you are returning from a Caribbean destination, you may also need to pay departure taxes (which are sometimes *not* included in your airfare in the Caribbean); if you have to pay departure taxes, the payment must be made in cash only.

You usually pay a surcharge (usually at least $25) to get a paper ticket, and its sole advantage is that it may be easier to endorse over to another airline if your flight is cancelled and the airline with which you booked can't accommodate you on another flight. With an e-ticket, the only thing you receive is an e-mailed receipt citing your itinerary and reservation and ticket numbers. Be sure to carry this with you, as you'll need it to get past security. If you lose you receipt, though, you can simply print out another copy or ask the airline to do it for you at check-in.

Particularly during busy travel seasons and around holiday periods, if a flight is oversold, the gate agent will usually ask for volunteers and will offer some sort of compensation if you are willing to take a different flight. On Caribbean routes, this happens most frequently on departures heading north out of San Juan or Miami. **Know your rights.** If you are bumped from a flight *involuntarily,* the airline must give you some kind of compensation if an alternate flight can't be found within one hour. If your flight is delayed because of something within the airline's control (so bad weather doesn't count), then the airline has a responsibility to get you to your destination on the same day, even if it has to book you on another airline and in an upgraded class if necessary. Read your airline's Contract of Carriage; it's usually buried somewhere on the airline's Web site.

Be prepared to adjust your plans quickly by programming a few numbers into your cellphone: your airline, an airport hotel or two, your destination hotel, your car service, and/or your travel agent. Bring snacks, water, and sufficient diversions, and you'll

be covered if you get stuck in the airport, on the Tarmac, or even in the air during turbulence.

CONFIRMING FLIGHTS

Be sure to confirm your flights on interisland carriers and **make sure the carrier has a local contact telephone number for you,** as you may be subject to a small carrier's whims: if no other passengers are booked on your flight, particularly if the carrier operates "scheduled charters," you'll be rescheduled onto another flight or at a different departure time (earlier or later than your original reservation) that is more convenient for the airline. Your plane may also make unscheduled stops to pick up more passengers or cargo, which also can affect actual departure and arrival times. Don't be concerned. It's all part of the adventure of interisland travel.

CUTTING COSTS

It's always good to **comparison shop.** Web sites (aka consolidators) and travel agents can have different arrangements with the airlines and offer different prices for exactly the same flight and day. Certain Web sites have tracking features that will e-mail you immediately when good deals are posted. Other people prefer to stick with one or two frequent-flier programs, racking up free trips and accumulating perks that can make trips easier. On some airlines, perks include a special reservations number, early boarding, access to upgrades, and more roomy economy-class seating.

Check early and often. Start looking for cheap fares up to a year in advance, and keep looking until you see something you can live with; you never know when a good deal may pop up. That said, **jump on the good deals.** Waiting even a few minutes might mean paying more. For most people, saving money is more important than having flexibility, so the more affordable non-refundable tickets work. Just remember that you'll pay dearly (often as much as $100) if you must change your travel plans. Check on prices for departures at different times of the day and to and from alternate airports, and look for departures on Tuesday, Wednesday, and Thursday, typically the cheapest days to travel. Remember to

weigh your options, though. A cheaper flight might have a long layover rather than being nonstop, or landing at a secondary airport might substantially increase your ground transportation costs.

Note that many airline Web sites—and most ads—show prices *without* taxes and surcharges. Don't buy until you know the full price. Government taxes add up quickly. Also **watch those ticketing fees.** Surcharges are usually added when you buy your ticket anywhere but on an airline's own Web site. (By the way, that includes for tickets purchased over the phone–even if you call the airline directly—and for paper tickets regardless of how you book.)

When traveling to the Caribbean, you can often save the most money by booking a package that includes airfare, your hotel or resort room, and sometimes even a rental car. **Investigate island-hopping passes.** Air Jamaica's "Caribbean Hopper" program, for example, allows passengers whose travel starts in the U.S. to visit three or more destinations in its Caribbean and Central American network. American Airlines and American Eagle offer a "Caribbean Explorer" fare to 23 Caribbean destinations out of San Juan. BWIA offers a 30-day "Caribbean Traveller" air pass for travel to 12 Caribbean and South American destinations, provided the international flights into and out of the region are also on BWIA. LIAT has three categories of interisland "Explorer" passes for different durations and flight schemes. For information on all these passes, see ⇨ Carriers.

🔁 On-Line Consolidators **AirlineConsolidator.com** ⊕ www.airlineconsolidator.com; for international tickets. **Best Fares** ☎ 800/880-1234 ⊕ www.bestfares.com; $59.90 annual membership. **Cheap Tickets** ⊕ www.cheaptickets.com. **Expedia** ⊕ www.expedia.com. **Hotwire** ⊕ www.hotwire.com. **last-minute.com** ⊕ www.lastminute.com specializes in last-minute travel; the main site is for the U.K., but it has a link to a U.S. site. **Luxury Link** ⊕ www.luxurylink.com has auctions (surprisingly good deals) as well as offers at the high-end side of travel. **Onetravel.com** ⊕ www.onetravel.com. **Orbitz** ⊕ www.orbitz.com. **Priceline.com** ⊕ www.priceline.com. **Travelocity** ⊕ www.travelocity.com.

ENJOYING THE FLIGHT

Get the seat you want. Avoid those on the aisle directly across from the lavatories. Most frequent fliers say those are even worse than the seats that don't recline (e.g., those in the back row and those in front of a bulkhead). For more legroom, you can request emergency-aisle seats, but do so only if you're capable of moving the 35- to 60-pound airplane exit door—a Federal Aviation Administration requirement of passengers in these seats. Seats behind a bulkhead also offer more legroom, but they don't have under-seat storage. Often you can pick a seat when you buy your ticket on an airline's Web site. But it's not always a guarantee, particularly if the airline changes the plane after you book your ticket; check back before you leave. SeatGuru.com has more information about specific seat configurations, which vary by aircraft.

Fewer airlines are providing free food for passengers in economy class. **Don't go hungry.** If you're scheduled to fly during meal times, verify if your airline offers anything to eat; even when it does, be prepared to pay. If you have dietary concerns, request special meals. These can be vegetarian, low-cholesterol, or kosher, for example. It's a good idea to pack some healthful snacks and a small (plastic) bottle of water in your carry-on bag.

Ask the airline about its children's menus, activities, and fares. On some lines infants and toddlers fly for free if they sit on a parent's lap, and older children fly for half price in their own seats. Also inquire about policies involving car seats; having one may limit where you can sit. While you're at it, ask about seat-belt extenders for car seats. And note that you can't count on a flight attendant to automatically produce an extender; you may have to inquire about it again when you board.

FLYING TIMES

The flight from New York to San Juan, Puerto Rico, takes 3½ hours; from Miami to San Juan, 2½ hours. Flights from New York to Kingston or Montego Bay, Jamaica, take about four hours; from Miami, about an hour. Nonstop flights from New York to Barbados or Grenada take about five hours. Nonstop flights from London to Antigua and Barbados and from Paris to Guadeloupe, Martinique, and St. Maarten are about seven hours. Once you've arrived in the Caribbean, hops between islands range from 10 minutes to 2 hours.

HOW TO COMPLAIN

If your baggage goes astray or your flight goes awry, complain right away. Most carriers require that you **file a claim immediately.** The Aviation Consumer Protection Division of the Department of Transportation publishes *Fly-Rights,* which discusses airlines and consumer issues and is available online. You can also find articles and information on mytravelrights.com, the Web site of the nonprofit Consumer Travel Rights Center.

🔢 Airline Complaints **Federal Aviation Administration Consumer Hotline** ☎ 866/835-5322 ⊕ www.faa.gov **Office of Aviation Enforcement and Proceedings** (Aviation Consumer Protection Division) ☎ 202/366-2220 ⊕ airconsumer.ost.dot.gov

BUSINESS HOURS

Though business hours vary from island to island, shops are generally closed Saturday afternoon and all day Sunday. Some shops close for an hour at lunchtime during the week, as well, although this practice is becoming increasingly rare. Farmers' markets are often open daily (except Sunday), but Saturday morning is always the most colorful and exciting time to go.

CAR RENTAL

Request car seats and extras such as GPS when you book, and make sure that a confirmed reservation guarantees you a car. Agencies sometimes overbook, particularly for busy weekends and holiday periods. Rates are sometimes—but not always—better if you book in advance or reserve through a rental agency's Web site. There are other reasons to book ahead, though: for popular destinations, during busy times of the year, or for certain type of car (vans, SUVs, exotic sports cars).

Your driver's license may not be recognized outside your home country. You may not be able to rent a car without an Inter-

national Driving Permit (IDP), which can be used only in conjunction with a valid driver's license and which translates your license into 10 languages. Check the AAA Web site for more info as well as for IDPs ($10) themselves. Many Caribbean islands require you to purchase a temporary driving permit for a small cost (usually less than $20).

Major firms, such as Avis, Hertz, and Budget, have agencies or affiliates on many Caribbean islands. But don't overlook local firms, whose cars are usually mechanically sound and prices competitive. Cars often have standard transmission, although automatic is usually an option. On most islands, it's not crucial to reserve a rental car prior to your arrival. Many hotels, especially those far from the airport, include airport transfers, and taxis are always an option. Besides, you may want a rental car only for a day or two of on-your-own sightseeing. For exciting treks into remote areas where roads are hilly or unpaved, rent a four-wheel-drive vehicle.

CUTTING COSTS

Really weigh your options. Find out if a credit card you carry or organization or frequent-renter program to which you belong has a discount program. And check that such discounts really are the best deal. You can often do better with special weekend or weekly rates offered by a rental agency. (And even if you want to rent for only five or six days, ask if you can get the weekly rate; it may very well be cheaper than the daily rate for that period of time.)

Price local car-rental companies as well as the majors. Also investigate wholesalers, which don't own fleets but rent in bulk from those that do and often offer better rates (note that you must usually pay for such rentals before leaving home). Consider adding a car rental onto your air/hotel vacation package; the cost will often be cheaper than if you had rented the car separately on your own.

When traveling abroad, **look for guaranteed exchange rates,** which protect you against a falling dollar. With your rate locked in, you won't pay more, even if the price goes up in the local currency (note to self: not the best thing if the dollar is surging rather than plunging).

Beware of hidden charges. Those great rental rates may not be so great when you add in taxes, surcharges, cancellation penalties, taxes, drop-off charges (if you're planning to pick up the car in one city and leave it in another), and surcharges (for being under or over a certain age, for additional drivers, or for driving over state or country borders or out of a specific radius from your point of rental).

⚑ Major Agencies **Alamo** ☎ 800/522-9696 ⊕ www.alamo.com. **Avis** ☎ 800/331-1084 ⊕ www. avis.com. **Budget** ☎ 800/472-3325 ⊕ www.budget. com. **Hertz** ☎ 800/654-3001 ⊕ www.hertz.com. **National Car Rental** ☎ 800/227-7368 ⊕ www. nationalcar.com.

INSURANCE

Everyone who rents a car wonders about whether the insurance that the rental companies offer is worth the expense. No one—not even us—has a simple answer. This is particularly true abroad, where laws are different than at home.

If you own a car, your personal auto insurance may cover a rental to some degree, though not all policies protect you abroad; always read your policy's fine print. If you don't have auto insurance, then seriously consider buying the collision- or loss-damage waiver (CDW or LDW) from the car-rental company, which eliminates your liability for damage to the car. Some credit cards offer CDW coverage, but it's usually supplemental to your own insurance and rarely covers SUVs, minivans, luxury models, and the like. If your coverage is secondary, you may still be liable for loss-of-use costs from the car-rental company. But no credit-card insurance is valid unless you use that card for *all* transactions, from reserving to paying the final bill. All companies exclude car rental in some countries, so be sure to find out about the destination to which you are traveling.

Some countries require you to purchase CDW coverage or require car-rental companies to include it in quoted rates. Ask your rental company about issues like these in your destination. In most cases, it's cheaper to add a supplemental CDW plan to your comprehensive travel insurance policy (⇨ Trip Insurance *under* Things to Consider *in* Getting Started, *above*) than to purchase it from a rental company. That said, you don't want to pay for a supplement if you're required to buy insurance from the rental company.

Note that you can decline the insurance from the rental company and purchase it through a third-party provider such as Travel Guard (www.travelguard.com)— $9 per day for $35,000 of coverage. That's sometimes just under half the price of the CDW offered by some car-rental companies. Also, Diners Club offers primary CDW coverage on all rentals reserved and paid for with the card. This means that Diners Club's company—not your own car insurance—pays in case of an accident. It *doesn't* mean your car-insurance company won't raise your rates once it discovers you had an accident.

CAR TRAVEL

Your valid local driver's license or anInternational Driving Permit (IDP) is recognized in some Caribbean countries. IDPs—available through the American and Canadian automobile associations and, in the United Kingdom, through the Automobile Association and Royal Automobile Club—are universally recognized but valid only in conjunction with your regular driver's license. On Guadeloupe, Martinique, and St. Barths, a valid U.S. or E.U. license is accepted for 20 days; after that, you need an IDP.

Temporary local driving permits are required in several other countries (Anguilla, Antigua, Barbados, the British Virgin Islands, Cayman Islands, Dominica, Grenada, Nevis, St. Kitts, St. Lucia, and St. Vincent & the Grenadines), which you can get at rental agencies or local police offices upon presentation of a valid license and a small fee. St. Lucia and St. Vincent & the Grenadines require a temporary permit only if you don't have an IDP.

Although exploring on your own can give your sightseeing excursions a sense of adventure, tentative drivers should instead consider hiring a taxi for the day. Locals, who are familiar with the roads, often drive fast and take chances. You don't want to get in their way. And you don't want to get lost on dark, winding roads at night.

RULES OF THE ROAD

On many islands (Anguilla, Antigua, Barbados, the British Virgin Islands, Cayman Islands, Dominica, Grenada, Jamaica, Nevis, St. Kitts, St. Lucia, St. Vincent and the Grenadines, Trinidad and Tobago, Turks and Caicos, and the U. S. Virgin Islands), **be prepared to drive on the left.** Speed limits are low, because it's often hard to find a road long and straight enough to *safely* get up much speed. And always wear your seat belt, which is required by law. Drivers are generally courteous; for example, if someone flashes car headlights at you at an intersection, it means "after you." On narrow mountain or country roads, it's a smart idea to tap your horn as you enter a blind curve to let oncoming traffic know you're there.

CRUISE TRAVEL

Cruising is a relaxing and convenient way to tour this beautiful part of the world. You get all of the amenities of a resort hotel and enough activities to guarantee fun, even on the occasional rainy day. All your important decisions are made long before you board. Your itinerary is set, and you know the basic cost of your vacation beforehand. Ships usually call at several ports on a single voyage but are at each port for only one day. Thus, while you don't get much of a feel for any specific island, you get a taste of what several islands are like and can then choose to vacation on your favorite one for a longer time on a future trip.

If you are planning a Caribbean cruise, consider Fodor's *The Complete Guide to Caribbean Cruises* (available in bookstores everywhere).

🚢 Cruise Lines **Carnival Cruise Line** ☎ 305/599–2600 or 800/227–6482 ⊕ www.carnival.com. **Celebrity Cruises** ☎ 305/539–6000 or 800/647–2251 ⊕ www.celebrity.com. **Clipper Cruise Line** ☎ 314/655–6700 or 800/325–0010 ⊕ www. clippercruise.com. **Costa Cruises** ☎ 954/266–5600 or 800/462–6782 ⊕ www.costacruise.com. **Crystal Cruises** ☎ 800/446–6625 or 310/785–9300 ⊕ www. crystalcruises.com. **Cunard Line** ☎ 661/753–1000 or 800/728–6273 ⊕ www.cunard.com. **Disney Cruise Line** ☎ 407/566–3500 or 800/325–2500 ⊕ www. disneycruise.com. **Holland America Line** ☎ 206/ 281–3535 or 877/932–4259 ⊕ www.hollandamerica. com. **MSC Cruises** ☎ 954/662–6262 or 800/666–9333 ⊕ www.msccruises.com. **Norwegian Cruise Line** ☎ 800/327–7030 ⊕ www.ncl.com. **Oceania Cruises** ☎ 305/514–2300 or 800/531–5658 ⊕ www. oceaniacruises.com. **Princess Cruises** ☎ 661/753–0000 or 800/774–6237 ⊕ www.princess.com. **Regent Seven Seas Cruises** ☎ 954/776–6123 or 800/ 477–7500 ⊕ www.rssc.com. **Royal Caribbean International** ☎ 305/539–6000 or 800/327–6700 ⊕ www.royalcaribbean.com. **Seabourn Cruise Line** ☎ 305/463–3000 or 800/929–9391 ⊕ www. seabourn.com. **SeaDream Yacht Club** ☎ 305/856–5622 or 800/707–4911 ⊕ www.seadreamyachtclub. com. **Silversea Cruises** ☎ 954/522–4477 or 800/ 722–9955 ⊕ www.silversea.com. **Star Clippers** ☎ 305/442–0550 or 800/442–0551 ⊕ www. starclippers.com. **Windjammer Barefoot Cruises** ☎ 305/672–6453 or 800/327–2601 ⊕ www. windjammer.com. **Windstar Cruises** ☎ 206/281–3535 or 800/258–7245 ⊕ www.windstarcruises.com. 🏛 Organizations **Cruise Lines International Association (CLIA)** ✉ 80 Broad St., Suite 1800, New York, NY 10004 ☎ 212/921–0066 ⊕ www.cruising.org.

CUSTOMS & DUTIES

You're always allowed to bring goods of a certain value back home without having to pay any duty or import tax. There's also a limit on the amount of tobacco and liquor you can bring back duty-free, and some countries have separate limits for perfumes; for exact figures, check with your customs department. The values of so-called "duty-free" goods are included in these amounts. When you shop abroad, save all your receipts, as customs inspectors may ask to see them as well as the items you purchased. If the total value of your goods is more than the duty-free limit, then you'll have to pay a tax (most often a flat percentage) on the value of everything beyond that limit.

The value of goods you can bring back into the U.S. from most Caribbean countries is $800 (it's $1,600 from the U.S. Virgin Islands). You can bring back 1 liter of alcohol (2 liters if 1 liter was produced in the Caribbean); it's 5 liters from the USVI.

🖪 U.S. Information **U.S. Customs and Border Protection** ⊕ www.cbp.gov.

DIVING

The Caribbean offers some of the best scuba diving in the world. The reef and waters around Bonaire's entire coast, for instance, incorporate a protected marine park, with scores of dive sites accessible from the beach. The Cayman Islands, Turks and Caicos, the British Virgin Islands, St. Lucia, Dominica, and St. Vincent and the Grenadines also offer world-class diving experiences. The water throughout the Caribbean is crystal-clear, often with visibility up to 200 feet, and the quantity and variety of marine life are astounding.

Resorts often offer guests introductory scuba instruction in a pool, followed by a shallow dive; some hotels have on-site dive shops. All shops offer instruction and certification according to the standards set by either the National Association of Underwater Instructors (NAUI) or the Professional Association of Diving Instructors (PADI). Dive operators offer day and night dives to wrecks, reefs, and underwater walls.

DIVERS ALERT

Don't fly within 24 hours after scuba diving.
🖪 **NAUI Worldwide** ☎ 813/628-6284 or 800/553-6284 ⊕ www.naui.org. **PADI** ☎ 800/729-7234 or 949/858-7234 ⊕ www.padi.com ☎ 604/273-0277 or 800/565-8130 in Canada ☎ 0117/300-7234in the U.K. ☎ 2/9451-2300 in Australia.

EATING OUT

The Caribbean islands offer dining experiences that will delight any palate. You'll find French cuisine with exquisite service, lavish buffets featuring local dishes, fresh seafood served by the waterfront, Italian pasta with a modern twist, Chinese cuisine to eat in or take out, and vegetarian dishes of just-picked produce. Fast-food restaurants usually feature fried chicken, not burgers, but pizza is everywhere.

Local cuisine (which is usually cheaper than what you'll find in upscale international restaurants) could be Spanish-style in Puerto Rico and the Dominican Republic, French creole in St. Lucia and Martinique, Indian in Trinidad, Indonesian in Aruba, jerk (spicy barbecue) in Jamaica, and fresh seafood everywhere. Vegetarians can expect a treat, as the fresh fruit, vegetables, herbs, and spices—both usual and unusual—are plentiful.

For information on food-related health issues *see* Health, *below.*

MEALS & MEALTIMES

Resort breakfasts are frequently lavish buffets that offer tropical fruits and fruit juices, cereal, fresh rolls and pastries, hot dishes (such as codfish, corned-beef hash, and potatoes), and prepared-to-order eggs, pancakes, and French toast. Lunch could be a sit-down meal at a beachfront café or a picnic at a secluded cove. But dinner is the highlight, often combining the expertise of internationally trained chefs with local know-how and ingredients.

Expect breakfast to be served from 7:30 AM to 10 AM; lunch from noon to 2 PM or so; and dinner from 7 PM to about 10 PM—perhaps later on Spanish- or French-heritage islands. Some restaurants have specific mealtimes; others serve continuously all day long.

PAYING

Major credit cards (Access, American Express, Barclaycard, Carte Blanche, Diners Club, Discover, EnRoute, Eurocard, MasterCard, Visa) are accepted in most Caribbean restaurants. We note in reviews when credit cards are not accepted. For guidelines on tipping, *see* Tipping *below.*

RESERVATIONS & DRESS

Regardless of where you are, it's a good idea to make a reservation if you can. In some places (St. Barths, for example), it's expected. We mention specifically only when reservations are essential (there's no other way you'll ever get a table) or when they are not accepted. For popular restaurants, book as far ahead as you can (often 30 days), and reconfirm as soon as you arrive. (Large parties should always call ahead to check the reservations policy.) We mention dress only when men are required to wear a jacket or a jacket and tie. Shorts and T-shirts at dinner and beach attire anytime are universally frowned upon in restaurants throughout the Caribbean.

WINE, BEER & SPIRITS

The Caribbean is where "de rum come from," so rum is the base of most cocktails—often fruity, festive ones that really pack a punch. Many islands also have their own breweries, and the local beers (Red Stripe in Jamaica, Piton in St. Lucia, Banks in Barbados, Carib in Grenada and Trinidad, Hairoun in St. Vincent, Kabuli in Dominica, and so on) are light and refreshing—perfect for hot summer afternoons at the beach. Those who prefer a nonalcoholic drink will love the fresh fruit punch, lime squash, or Ting—a carbonated grapefruit drink from Jamaica but also available elsewhere.

Was the service stellar or not up to snuff? Did the food give you shivers of delight or leave you cold? Did the prices and portions make you happy or sad? Rate restaurants and write your own reviews in Travel Ratings or start a discussion about your favorite places in Travel Talk on www.fodors.com. Your comments might even appear in our books. Yes, you, too, can be a correspondent!

ELECTRICITY

On many islands the electric current is 110 to 120 volts alternating current (AC), and wall outlets take the same two-prong plugs found in the United States. Exceptions include Dominica, Grenada, St. Lucia, St. Vincent and the Grenadines (other than Petit St. Vincent), and the French islands of Guadeloupe, Martinique, St. Barths, and St. Martin, all of which deliver electric current at 220 volts. When making reservations on any of the islands utilizing 220 volts, check with your specific hotel about current, as some also have 110-volt current available. Many hotels will have adaptors available at the front desk.

Consider making a small investment in a universal adapter, which has several types of plugs in one lightweight, compact unit. Most laptops and mobile phone chargers are dual voltage (i.e., they operate equally well on 110 and 220 volts) and so require only an adapter. These days the same is true more of small appliances such as hair dryers. Always check labels and manufacturer instructions to be sure, though. Don't use 110-volt outlets marked FOR SHAVERS ONLY for high-wattage appliances such as hair dryers.

🔁 **Steve Kropla's Help for World Traveler's** ⊕ www.kropla.com has information on electrical and telephone plugs around the world. **Walkabout Travel Gear** ⊕ www.walkabouttravelgear.com has a good discussion about electricity under "adapters."

ETIQUETTE & BEHAVIOR

Most Caribbean countries are conservative and religious. Beachwear is appropriate only for the beach and should never be worn outside of your resort. Indiscreet displays of affection, whether between man and woman or between two people of the same sex, are rarely appropriate. As in any country, you should always ask permission before photographing a person.

Throughout the Caribbean, it's hard to understate how important it is that you smile and say "good morning" or "good evening" to start a conversation off right. Say hello when you enter a business, and try not to get down to business too quickly or rush to make your point. Assertiveness is often equated with rudeness on many islands. Much of the pleasure of traveling in the Caribbean is slowing down and working on island time. Islanders take these informal niceties very seriously and will almost always treat you with more friendliness if you respect their ways.

FURTHER READING

Caribbean Style (Crown Publishers) is a coffee-table book with magnificent photographs of the interiors and exteriors of homes and buildings in the Caribbean. Short stories—some dark, some full of laughs—about life in the southern Caribbean made *Easy in the Islands,* by Bob Schacochis, a National Book Award winner. Schacochis has an ear for local patois and an eye for the absurd. In *Coming About: A Family Passage at Sea*, author Susan Tyler Hitchcock details her family's adventures sailing for nine months in the

Bahamas and the Caribbean; it's an intimate look at the islands and a wonderful meditation on marriage and family. Thinking of running away and starting a business on a sun-drenched island? *A Trip to the Beach* by Robert and Melinda Blanchard is the ultimate inspiration. This funny, adventurous tale of how the Blanchards moved to Anguilla, started a restaurant, and learned innumerable lessons (including how to liberate fresh ingredients from the customs warehouse) will have you fantasizing about your own escape. To familiarize yourself with the sights, smells, and sounds of the West Indies, pick up Jamaica Kincaid's *Annie John*, a richly textured coming-of-age novel about a girl growing up in Antigua. The short stories in *At the Bottom of the River*, also by Kincaid, depict island mysteries and manners.

Omeros is Nobel Prize–winning St. Lucian poet Derek Walcott's imaginative Caribbean retelling of the *Odyssey*. Anthony C. Winkler's novels, *The Great Yacht Race, The Lunatic,* and *The Painted Canoe,* provide scathingly witty glimpses into Jamaica's class structure. Meanwhile, if you're heading for Jamaica, be sure to read *The White Witch of Rosehall,* by Herbert G. De Lisser, which relates the fascinating legend of the Rose Hall Plantation—which you can visit. *Wide Sargasso Sea,* by Dominica's Jean Rhys, is a provocative novel set in Jamaica and Dominica that recounts the early life of the first wife of Edward Rochester (pre–*Jane Eyre*). James Michener depicted the islands' diversity in his novel *Caribbean.* To probe island cultures more deeply, read Trinidad's V. S. Naipaul, particularly his *Guerrillas, The Loss of El Dorado, The Enigma of Arrival,* and *A House for Mr. Bizwas*; Eric Williams's *From Columbus to Castro*; and Michael Paiewonsky's *Conquest of Eden. An Embarrassment of Mangoes : A Caribbean Interlude,* by Ann Vanderhoof, is the more contemporary story of her and her husband's two-year journey around the Caribbean in a 42-foot sailboat, which proves to be both enlightening and entertaining.

Though it was written decades ago, Herman Wouk's hilarious *Don't Stop the Carnival* remains as fresh as ever in its depiction of the trials and tribulations of running a small Caribbean hotel. Mystery lovers should pick up a copy of Agatha Christie's *A Caribbean Mystery.* And kids might enjoy reading the Hardy Boys mystery *The Caribbean Cruise Caper.* If you're keen on specific subjects, such as history, cuisine, folklore, bird-watching, or diving, you'll find wonderful books by local authors on each island.

GAY & LESBIAN TRAVEL

Most of the Caribbean isn't particularly gay- and lesbian-friendly, though some Caribbean islands are more welcoming than others. Puerto Rico is perhaps the most gay-friendly island in the Caribbean—and the only one with extensive gay-oriented nightlife, though it is focused almost exclusively in San Juan. The USVI are also a good choice for gay and lesbian travelers; St. Thomas has a few gay bars and discos, and the West End of St. Croix has quietly become gay- and lesbian-friendly. Curaçao now reaches out to gay and lesbian travelers. Aruba, St. Maarten, and Trinidad all have some gay nightlife. In general, the French and Dutch islands are the most tolerant islands; the historically British islands are the least tolerant, with Jamaica leading the pack. It's important to remember that most Caribbean islands are both religious and conservative, so all travelers need to respect social mores. Nearly every island frowns upon same-sex couples strolling hand in hand down a beach or street, and most public displays of affection (either straight or gay) are frowned upon.

Upscale resorts for adults, where privacy and discretion are the norm, are often the most welcoming to gay and lesbian travelers, but individually rented villas, many of which have private pools, are another good option. Some couples-only resorts in the Caribbean now allow same-sex couples—and this includes the Sandals chain of resorts, which recently changed its policy to welcome "all couples in love"— though none of these resorts exactly roll out the red carpet; so you have to ask yourself if you'll be comfortable in such an environment.

HEALTH

The most common types of illnesses among travelers are caused by contaminated food and water. Especially in developing countries, drink only bottled, boiled, or purified water and drinks; don't drink from public fountains or use ice. You should even consider using bottled water to brush your teeth. Make sure food has been thoroughly cooked and is served to you fresh and hot; avoid vegetables and fruits that you haven't washed (in bottled or purified water) or peeled yourself. If you have problems, mild cases of traveler's diarrhea may respond to Imodium (known generically as loperamide) or Pepto-Bismol. Be sure to drink plenty of fluids; if you can't keep fluids down, seek medical help immediately.

Infectious diseases can be airborne or passed via mosquitoes and ticks and through direct or indirect physical contact with animals or people. Some, including Norwalk-like viruses that affect your digestive tract, can be passed along through contaminated food. If you are traveling in an area where malaria is prevalent, use a repellant containing DEET and take malaria-prevention medication before, during, and after your trip as directed by your physician. Condoms can help prevent most sexually transmitted diseases but aren't absolute, and the quality of them varies from country to country. Speak with your physician and/or check the CDC or World Health Organization Web sites for health alerts, particularly if you're pregnant, traveling with children, or have a chronic illness.

The major health risk in the Caribbean is sunburn or sunstroke. Having a long-sleeve shirt, a hat, and long pants or a beach wrap available is essential on a boat, for midday at the beach, and whenever you go out sightseeing. **Use sunscreen** with an SPF of at least 15 and apply it liberally on your nose, ears, and other sensitive and exposed areas.

Watch out for black, spiny sea urchins; stepping on one is guaranteed to be painful for quite some time.

Poisonous snakes are hard to find in the Caribbean, although you should exercise caution while bird-watching in Trinidad. **Beware of the manchineel tree**, which grows near the beach and has fruit that looks like little green apples but is poisonous and bark and leaves that can burn the skin if you touch them; even the droplets of water that might reach your skin if you seek protection under the tree during a shower can burn you.

The worst insect problem may well be the tiny "no-see-ums" (sand flies) that appear after a rain, near swampy ground, and around sunset. Mosquitoes can also be annoying and, more importantly, may be carriers of dengue fever, which has been found (albeit rarely) in several Caribbean locations. **Bring along a good repellent** and use it, particularly at sundown and in the evening, when mosquitoes are most active.

DIVERS' ALERT
Do not fly within 24 hours of scuba diving.

SHOTS & MEDICATIONS

No special shots or vaccinations are required for Caribbean destinations, but health warnings (especially for malaria) are sometimes issued, particularly after hurricanes or other natural disasters. Dengue fever can be found on many islands, but it has not become a major problem.

🚩 Health Warnings **National Centers for Disease Control & Prevention** (CDC) ☎ 877/394–8747 international travelers' health line ⊕ www.cdc.gov/travel. **World Health Organization** (WHO) ⊕ www.who.int.

INSURANCE

What kind of coverage do you honestly need? Do you even need trip insurance at all? Take a deep breath and read on.

We believe that comprehensive trip insurance is especially valuable if you're booking a very expensive or complicated trip (particularly to an isolated region) or if you're booking far in advance. Who knows what could happen six months down the road? But whether or not you get insurance has more to do with how comfortable you are assuming all that risk yourself.

Comprehensive travel policies typically cover trip-cancellation and interruption, letting you cancel or cut your trip short because of a personal emergency, illness, or, in some cases, acts of terrorism in your destination. Such policies also cover evacuation and medical care. Some also cover you for trip delays because of bad weather or mechanical problems as well as for lost or delayed baggage. Another type of coverage to look for is financial default—that is, when your trip is disrupted because a tour operator, airline, or cruise line goes out of business. Generally you must buy this when you book your trip or shortly thereafter, and it's only available to you if your operator isn't on a list of excluded companies.

If you're going abroad, consider buying medical-only coverage at the very least. Neither Medicare nor some private insurers cover medical expenses anywhere outside the U.S. besides Mexico and Canada (including time aboard a cruise ship, even if it leaves from a U.S. port). Medical-only policies typically reimburse you for medical care (excluding that related to preexisting conditions) and hospitalization abroad and provide for evacuation. You still have to pay the bills and await reimbursement from the insurer, though.

Expect comprehensive travel insurance policies to cost about 4% to 7% of the total price of your trip (it's more like 12% if you're over age 70). A medical-only policy may or may not be cheaper than a comprehensive policy. Always read the fine print of your policy to make sure that you are covered for the risks that are of the most concern to you. Compare several policies to make sure you're getting the best price and range of coverage available.

Just as an aside: You know you can save a bundle on trips to warm-weather destinations by traveling in rainy season. But there's also a chance that a severe storm will disrupt your plans. The solution? Look for hotels and resorts that offer storm/hurricane guarantees. Although they rarely allow refunds, most guarantees do let you rebook later if a storm strikes.

🔁 Insurance Comparison Sites **Insure My Trip. com** ⊕ www.insuremytrip.com. **Square Mouth.com** ⊕ www.quotetravelinsurance.com.

🔁 Comprehensive Travel Insurers **Access America** ☎ 800/729-6021 ⊕ www.accessamerica.com. **CSA Travel Protection** ☎ 800/729-6021 ⊕ www. csatravelprotection.com. **HTH Worldwide** ☎ 610/254-8700 or 888/243-2358 ⊕ www.hthworldwide. com. **Travelex Insurance** ☎ 888/457-4602 ⊕ www.travelex-insurance.com. **Travel Guard International** ☎ 715/345-0505 or 800/826-4919 ⊕ www.travelguard.com. **Travel Insured International** ☎ 800/243-3174 ⊕ www.travelinsured.com.

🔁 Medical-Only Insurers **International Medical Group** ☎ 800/628-4664 ⊕ www.imglobal.com. **International SOS** ☎ 215/942-8000 or 713/521-7611 ⊕ www.internationalsos.com. **Wallach & Company** ☎ 800/237-6615 or 504/687-3166 ⊕ www.wallach. com.

LANGUAGE

It becomes obvious that the Caribbean region's history is linked with that of European and African countries when you consider all the languages and dialects that are spoken on the islands. English is the official language of most island nations and widely spoken on most of the others. The main exceptions are much of the Dominican Republic, remote parts of Puerto Rico, and the islands of the French West Indies.

Spanish is the official language in the Dominican Republic, and Puerto Rico is bilingual (Spanish and English). French is spoken almost exclusively on Guadeloupe, Martinique, and St. Barths. St. Maarten/St. Martin is split—geographically, culturally, and linguistically—with French spoken on the St. Martin side and Dutch (as well as English) spoken in St. Maarten. Dutch is also the official language on Aruba, Bonaire, Curaçao, Saba, and St. Eustatius, although everyone also speaks English.

You'll hear strong West Indian lilts throughout the islands, along with locals speaking to each other in Jamaican patois (a mix of English, French, and African words) and, particularly in Dominica and St. Lucia, French Creole (a patois that sounds more like French). On French-speaking St. Barths, some people use the Norman dialect of their ancestors. And on Aruba, Bonaire, and Curaçao you'll encounter Papiamento—perhaps the most worldly language of all—which is a mixture of African languages and Dutch, English, French, Portuguese, *and* Spanish.

LANGUAGES FOR TRAVELERS

A phrase book and language-tape set can help get you started.*Fodor's French for Travelers and Fodor's Spanish for Travelers* (available at bookstores everywhere) are excellent.

LODGING

Most hotels and resorts are on the leeward side of an island, where the calm water is good for snorkeling and swimming. You'll find a few hotels on the windward side, where the surf is rough—good for surfing but treacherous for swimming. Decide whether you want to pay the extra price for a room overlooking the ocean. At less expensive properties, location may mean a difference in price of only $10 to $20 per room. At luxury resorts on pricey islands, however, it could amount to as much as $100 per room. Also **find out how close the property is to a beach.** At some hotels you can walk barefoot from your room onto the sand; others may be across a road, a couple of blocks, or a 10-minute drive away.

If you go to sleep early or are a light sleeper, ask for a room away from the entertainment area or pool. Air-conditioning isn't a necessity on all islands, many of which are cooled by trade winds, but it can be a plus if you enjoy an afternoon snooze or are bothered by humidity—which is most prevalent in September, October, and November. Breezes are best in second-floor rooms, particularly corner rooms. If you like to sleep without air-conditioning, make sure that windows can be opened and have screens. If you're staying away from the water, you'll want a ceiling fan. You'll likely notice a candle and box of matches in your room. In even the most luxurious resorts, there are times when the electricity goes off for a while or things simply *don't* work; it's a fact of Caribbean life. And no matter how

diligent the upkeep, humidity and salt air also take their toll on metal fixtures.

Most hotels and other lodgings require you to give your credit-card details before they will confirm your reservation. If you don't feel comfortable e-mailing this information, ask if you can fax it (some places even prefer faxes). However you book, get confirmation in writing and have a copy of it handy when you check in.

Be sure you understand the hotel's cancellation policy. Some places allow you to cancel without any kind of penalty—even if you prepaid to secure a discounted rate—if you cancel at least 24 hours in advance. Others require you to cancel a week in advance or penalize you for the cost of one night. Small inns and B&Bs are most likely to require you to cancel far in advance. Most hotels allow children under a certain age to stay in their parents' room at no extra charge, but others charge for them as extra adults; find out the cutoff age for discounts.Assume that hotels operate on the European Plan (**EP,** no meals) unless we specify that they use the Breakfast Plan (**BP,** with full breakfast), Continental Plan (**CP,** Continental breakfast), Full American Plan (**FAP,** all meals), Modified American Plan (**MAP,** breakfast and dinner) or are **all-inclusive** (or **AI,** including all meals, drinks, and most activities).

Did the resort look as good in real life as it did in the photos? Did you sleep like a baby, or were the walls paper thin? Did you get your money's worth? Rate hotels and write your own reviews in Travel Ratings or start a discussion about your favorite places in Travel Talk on www. fodors.com. Your comments might even appear in our books. Yes, you, too, can be a Fodor's correspondent!

APARTMENT & HOUSE RENTALS

If you want a home base that's roomy enough for a family and comes with cooking facilities, consider renting a furnished apartment, villa, or house. Rentals can save you money, especially if you're traveling with a group. Home-exchange directories sometimes list rentals as well as exchanges. We list island-specific agents in the individual chapters; the general agencies listed here represent villas and apartments on many islands throughout the Caribbean.

At Home Abroad ☎ 212/421–9165 ⊕ www.athomeabroadinc.com. **Barclay International Group** ☎ 516/364–0064 or 800/845–6636 ⊕ www.barclayweb.com. **Vacation Home Rentals Worldwide** ☎ 201/767–9393 or 800/633–3284 ⊕ www.vhrww.com. **Villanet** ☎ 206/417–3444 or 800/964–1891 ⊕ www.rentavilla.com. **Villas & Apartments Abroad** ☎ 212/213–6435 ⊕ www.vaanyc.com. **Villas of Distinction** ☎ 707/778–1800 or 800/289–0900 ⊕ www.villasofdistinction.com. **Villas International** ☎ 415/499–9490 or 800/221–2260 ⊕ www.villasintl.com. **Wimco** ☎ 800/449–1553 ⊕ www.wimco.com.

HOTELS

Weigh all your options (we can't say this enough). Join "frequent guest" programs. You may get preferential treatment in room choice and/or upgrades in your favorite chains. Check general travel sites and hotel Web sites, as not all chains are represented on all travel sites. Always research or inquire about special packages and corporate rates. If you prefer to book by phone, note you can sometimes get a better price if you call the hotel's local toll-free number (if one is available) rather than the central reservations number.

If your destination's high season is December through April and you're trying to book, say, in late April, you might save considerably by changing your dates by a week or two. Note, though, that many properties charge peak-season rates for your entire stay even if your travel dates straddle peak and nonpeak seasons. High-end chains catering to businesspeople are often busy only on weekdays and often drop rates dramatically on weekends to fill up rooms. **Ask when rates go down.**

Watch out for hidden costs, including resort fees, energy surcharges, and "convenience" fees for such things as unlimited local phone service you won't use and a free newspaper—possibly written in a language you can't read. Always verify whether local hotel taxes are included in the rates you are quoted, so that you'll know the real price of your stay. In some places, taxes can add 20% or more to your bill. If you're traveling to one of the euro-islands, **look for price guarantees,** which protect you against a falling dollar. With your rate locked in, you won't pay more, even if the price goes up in the local currency.

All hotels listed have private bath unless otherwise noted.

MAIL & SHIPPING

Airmail between Caribbean islands and the U.S. or Canada takes 7 to 14 days; surface mail can take four to six weeks. Airmail to the U.K. takes two to three weeks; to Australia and New Zealand, three to four weeks.

SHIPPING PACKAGES

Courier services (such as DHL, FedEx, UPS, and others) operate throughout the Caribbean, although not every company serves each island. "Overnight" service is more likely to take two or more days, because of the limited number of flights on which packages can be shipped.

MONEY MATTERS

Banks rarely have every foreign currency on hand, and it may take as long as a week to order. If you're planning to exchange funds before leaving home, don't wait 'til the last minute.

Prices throughout this guide are given for adults. Substantially reduced fees are almost always available for children, students, and senior citizens. For information on taxes, *see* Taxes.

For island-specific information on banks, currency, service charges, taxes, and tipping in the Caribbean, *see* the A to Z sections *in* individual island chapters.

ATMS & BANKS

Your own bank will probably charge a fee for using ATMs abroad; the foreign bank you use may also charge a fee. Nevertheless, you'll usually get a better rate of exchange via an ATM than you will at a currency-exchange office or even when changing money in a bank. And extracting funds as you need them is a safer option than carrying around a large amount of cash. Note that PINs (personal identification numbers) with more than four digits are not recognized at ATMs in many countries.

Debit cards still aren't widely used in the islands, although you can use bank cards and major credit cards to withdraw cash (in local currency) at automatic teller machines (ATMs). ATMs can be found on most islands at airports, cruise-ship terminals, bank branches, shopping centers, gas stations, and other convenient locations. Although ATM transaction fees may be higher abroad, the exchange rates are excellent because they're based on wholesale rates offered only by major banks.

CREDIT CARDS

Major credit cards are widely accepted at hotels, restaurants, shops, car-rental agencies, other service providers, and ATM machines throughout the Caribbean. The only places that might not accept them are open-air markets or tiny shops in out-of-the-way villages.

Throughout this guide, the following abbreviations are used: **AE**, American Express; **D**, Discover; **DC**, Diners Club; **MC**, MasterCard; and **V**, Visa.

It's a good idea to inform your credit-card company before you travel, especially if you're going abroad and don't travel internationally very often. Otherwise, the credit-card company might put a hold on your card owing to unusual activity—not a good thing halfway through your trip. Record all your credit-card numbers—as well as the phone numbers to call if your cards are lost or stolen—in a safe place so you're prepared should something go wrong. Both MasterCard and Visa have general numbers you can call (collect if you're abroad) if your card is lost, but you're better off calling the number of your issuing bank, since MasterCard and Visa usually just transfer you to your bank; your bank's number is usually printed on your card.

If you plan to use your credit card for cash advances, you'll need to apply for a PIN at least two weeks before your trip. Although it's usually cheaper (and safer) to use a credit card abroad for large purchases (so you can cancel payments or be reimbursed if there's a problem), note that some credit card companies *and* the banks that issue them add substantial percentages to all foreign transactions, whether they're done in a foreign currency or not. Check on these fees before leaving home so that there won't be any surprises when you get the bill.

Reporting Lost Cards American Express ☎ 800/992-3404 in U.S. or 336/393-1111 collect from abroad ⊕ www.americanexpress.com. **Diners Club** ☎ 800/234-6377 in U.S. or 303/799-1504 collect from abroad ⊕ www.dinersclub.com. **Discover** ☎ 800/347-2683 in U.S. or 801/902-3100 collect from abroad ⊕ www.discovercard.com. **MasterCard** ☎ 800/622-7747 in U.S. or 636/722-7111 collect from abroad ⊕ www.mastercard.com. **Visa** ☎ 800/847-2911 in U.S. or 410/581-9994 collect from abroad ⊕ www.visa.com.

CURRENCY & EXCHANGE

The U.S. dollar is the official currency in Puerto Rico, the U.S. Virgin Islands, and the British Virgin Islands. On Grand Cayman you'll usually have a choice of Cayman or U.S. dollars when you take money out of an ATM and may even be able to get change in U.S. dollars. On most other islands, U.S. paper currency (not coins) is usually accepted. When you pay in dollars, however, you'll almost always get change in local currency, so it's best to carry bills in small denominations. The exceptions are at airports—departure-tax payment locations and duty-free shops in the departure lounges—which will generally make every attempt to give you change in U.S. dollars, if you wish. Canadian dollars and British pounds are occasionally accepted, but don't count on this as the norm. The exception to these general rules are the French islands (except for St. Martin), which use the euro; other currency is usually not accepted. If you do need local currency (say, for a trip to one of the French islands), change money at a local bank for the best rate.

With regard to the EC dollar and Barbadian dollar, the exchange rate is fixed, so it makes little difference if you exchange your money in your hotel or at a bank. The exchange rates for the Dominican peso and Jamaican dollar can change.

Exchange Rate Information Oanda.com ⊕ www.oanda.com allows you to print out a handy table with the current day's conversion rates. XE.

com ⊕ www.xe.com. **Yahoo Finance** ⊕ finance. yahoo.com/currency.

TRAVELER'S CHECKS & CARDS

Some consider this the currency of the cave man, and it's true that fewer establishments accept traveler's checks these days. Nevertheless, they're a cheap and secure way to carry extra money, particularly on trips to urban areas. Both Citibank (under the Visa brand) and American Express issue traveler's checks in the U.S., but Amex is better known and more widely accepted; you can also avoid hefty surcharges by cashing Amex checks at Amex offices. Whatever you do, keep track of all the serial numbers in case the checks are lost or stolen.

American Express now offers a stored-value card called a Travelers Cheque Card, which you can use wherever American Express credit cards are accepted, including ATMs. The card can carry a minimum of $300 and a maximum of $2,700, and it's a very safe way to carry your funds. Although you can get replacement funds in 24 hours if your card is lost or stolen, it doesn't really strike us as a very good deal. In addition to a high initial cost ($14.95 to set up the card, plus $5 each time you "reload"), you still have to pay a 2% fee for each purchase in a foreign currency (similar to that of any credit card). Further, each time you use the card in an ATM you pay a transaction fee of $2.50 on top of the 2% transaction fee for the conversion—add it all up and it can be considerably more than you would pay for simply using your own ATM card. Regular traveler's checks are just as secure and cost less.

🖪 **American Express** ☎ 888/412-6945 in U.S., 801/945-9450 collect outside U.S. to add value or speak to customer service ⊕ www.americanexpress.com.

PACKING

Why do some people travel with a convoy of suitcases the size of large-screen TVs and yet never have a thing to wear? How do others pack a toaster-oven-size duffle with a week's worth of outfits *and* supplies for every possible contingency? We realize that packing is a matter of style—a

very personal thing—but there's a lot to be said for traveling light. The tips in this section will help you win the battle of the bulging bag.

Make a list. In a recent Fodor's survey, 29% of respondents said they make lists (and often pack) at least a week before a trip. Lists can be used at least twice—once to pack and once to repack at the end of your trip. You'll also have a record of the contents of your suitcase, just in case it disappears in transit.

Think it through. What's the weather like? Is this a business trip or a cruise or resort vacation? Going abroad? In some places and/or sights, traditions of dress may be more or less conservative than you're used to. As your itinerary comes together, jot activities down and note possible outfits next to each (don't forget those shoes and accessories).

Edit your wardrobe. Plan to wear everything twice (better yet, thrice) and to do laundry along the way. Stick to one basic look—urban chic, sporty casual, etc. Build around one or two neutrals and an accent (e.g., black, white, and olive green). Women can freshen looks by changing scarves or jewelry. For a week's trip, you can look smashing with three bottoms, four or five tops, a sweater, and a jacket you can wear alone or over the sweater.

Be practical. Put comfortable shoes at the top of your list. (Did we need to tell you this?) Pack items that are lightweight, wrinkle resistant, compact, and washable. (Or this?) Try a simple wrinkling test: Intentionally fold a piece of fabric between your fingers for a couple minutes. If it refuses to crease, it will probably come out of your suitcase looking fresh. That said, if you stack and then roll your clothes when packing, they'll wrinkle less.

Check weight and size limitations. In the United States you may be charged extra for checked bags weighing more than 50 pounds. Abroad some airlines don't allow you to check bags weighing more than 60 to 70 pounds, or they charge outrageous fees for every pound your luggage is over. Carry-on size limitations can be stringent, too.

Be prepared to lug it yourself. If there's one thing that can turn a pack rat into a minimalist, it's a vacation spent lugging heavy bags over long distances. Unless you're on a guided tour or a cruise, select luggage that you can readily carry. Porters, like good butlers, are hard to find these days.

Lock it up. Several companies sell locks (about $10) approved by the Transportation Safety Administration that can be unlocked by all U.S. security personnel should they decide to search your bags. Alternatively, you can use simple plastic cable ties, which are sold at hardware stores in bundles.

Tag it. Always put tags on your luggage with some kind of contact information; use your business address if you don't want people to know your home address. Put the same information (and a copy of your itinerary) inside your luggage, too.

Don't check valuables. On U.S. flights, airlines are liable for only about $2,800 per person for bags. On international flights, the liability limit is around $635 per bag. But just try collecting from the airline for items like computers, cameras, and jewelry. It isn't going to happen; they aren't covered. And though comprehensive travel policies may cover luggage, the liability limit is often a pittance. Your homeowners' policy may cover you sufficiently when you travel—or not. You're really better off stashing baubles and gizmos in your carry-on—right near those prescription meds.

Report problems immediately. If your bags—or things in them—are damaged or go astray, file a written claim with your airline *before you leave the airport.* If the airline is at fault, it may give you money for essentials until your luggage arrives. Most lost bags are found within 48 hours, so alert the airline to your whereabouts for two or three days. If your bag was opened for security reasons in the U.S. and something is missing, file a claim with the TSA.

WHAT YOU'LL NEED IN THE CARIBBEAN

Dress on most islands is generally casual. Bring loose-fitting clothing made of natural fabrics to see you through days of heat and humidity, but leave camouflage-pattern clothing at home. It's not permitted for civilians—even small children—in some Caribbean countries and may be confiscated if worn. Pack a beach cover-up and/or long-sleeve shirt to protect yourself from the sun. A sun hat is advisable, but you don't have to pack one—inexpensive straw hats are available everywhere.

For shopping and sightseeing, shorts and T-shirts are appropriate. On all islands, bathing suits and immodest attire off the beach are frowned upon. Evening dress can range from really informal to casually elegant, depending on the establishment. A tie is practically never required for gentlemen, but a jacket may be required in the fancier restaurants or at some resorts, particularly during high season.

Bring sunscreen from home; it's much more expensive in the Caribbean than at your local drugstore. You can get most over-the-counter medications at local drugstores, but they may be expensive. If you are going to the Dominican Republic or Jamaica, you'll likely be in a relatively isolated, all-inclusive resort, where the gift shop will sell everything at a huge premium, so pack wisely.

PASSPORTS & VISAS

At this writing, passport requirements for most Caribbean destinations were expected to change by **January 1, 2007,** when all U.S. citizens traveling to the Caribbean by air or sea will be required to carry a valid passport to reenter the United States. A birth certificate and photo ID will no longer be sufficient, **except for** travel to Puerto Rico and the U.S. Virgin Islands, both of which are still considered part of the U.S. Document requirements for Canadian and British citizens are not expected to change in most Caribbean countries, and in some cases a birth certificate (with a raised seal) and a government-issued photo ID may still be sufficient to prove citizenship—though not if Canadians must make an air connection in the U.S.—but you should always verify requirements shortly before any trip abroad, as laws regarding documentation are changing and becoming more stringent. A valid passport is already required of Americans who visit Barbados, the British Virgin Islands, and the French West Indies (Guadeloupe, Martinique, St. Barthélemy, and St. Martin). We strongly advise all travelers to carry a valid passport to any Caribbean country—*including* the U.S. Virgin Islands and Puerto Rico—so there's no chance you'll be turned away at the airport. All travelers must also have a return or ongoing ticket.

PASSPORTS

We're always surprised at how few Americans have passports—only 25% at this writing, though the number is expected to grow in coming years, when it becomes impossible to reenter the United States from trips to neighboring Canada or Mexico without one. Remember this: A passport verifies both your identity and nationality—a great reason to have one.

U.S. passports are valid for 10 years. Applications are available online and at post offices as well as passport offices. The cost to apply is $97 for adults, $82 for children under 16; renewals are $67. Allow six weeks to process the paperwork for either a new or renewed passport. For an expediting fee of $60, you can reduce the time to about two weeks. If your trip is less than two weeks away, you can get a passport even more rapidly by going to a passport office with the necessary documentation. Private expediters can get things done in as little as 48 hours but charge hefty fees for their services. Children under 14 must appear in person to apply for or renew a passport; both parents must accompany the child (or send a notarized statement with their permission) and provide proof of their relationship to the child.

Before your trip, make two copies of your passport's data page (one for someone at home and another for you to carry separately). Or scan the page and e-mail it to someone at home and/or yourself.

VISAS

Visas are essentially formal permissions to travel to a country. They allow countries to keep track of you and other visitors and to generate revenue (from visa fees). You *always* need a visa to enter a foreign country; however, many countries routinely issue tourist visas on arrival, particularly to U.S. citizens. When your passport is stamped or scanned in the immigration line, you're actually being issued a visa. Sometimes you have to stand in a separate line and pay a small fee to get your stamp before going through immigration, but you can still do this at the airport on arrival. Getting a visa isn't always that easy. Some countries require you to arrange for one in advance of your trip. There's usually—but not always—a fee involved, and said fee may be nominal ($10 or less) or substantial ($100 or more).

If you must apply for a visa in advance, you can usually do it in person or by mail. When you apply by mail, you send your passport to a designated consulate, where your passport will be examined and the visa issued. Expediters—usually the same ones who handle expedited passport applications—can do all the work to obtain your visa for you; however, there's always an additional cost (often more than $50 per visa).

Most visas limit you to a single trip—basically during the actual dates of your planned vacation. Other visas allow you to visit as many times as you wish for a specific period of time. Remember that requirements change, sometimes at the drop of a hat, and the burden is on you to make sure that you have the appropriate visas. Otherwise, you'll be turned away at the airport or, worse, deported after you arrive in the country. No company or travel insurer gives refunds if your travel plans are disrupted because you didn't have the correct visa.

🚹 **U.S. Passport & Visa Expediters A. Briggs Passport & Visa Expeditors** ☎ 800/806-0581 or 202/464-3000 ⊕ www.abriggs.com. **American Passport Express** ☎ 800/455-5166 or 603/559-9888 ⊕ www.americanpassport.com. **Passport Express** ☎ 800/362-8196 or 401/272-4612 ⊕ www.passportexpress.com. **Travel Document Systems** ☎ 800/874-5100 or 202/638-3800 ⊕ www.traveldocs.com. **Travel the World Visas** ☎ 866/886-8472 or 301/495-7700 ⊕ www.world-visa.com.

PHONES

The good news is that you can now make a direct-dial telephone call from virtually any point on earth. The bad news? You can't always do so cheaply. Calling from a hotel is almost always the most expensive option; hotels usually add huge surcharges to all calls, particularly international ones. In some countries, you can phone from call centers or even the post office. Calling cards usually keep costs to a minimum, but only if you purchase them locally. And then there are mobile phones (⇨ *below*), which are sometimes more prevalent—particularly in the developing world—than land lines; as expensive as mobile phone calls can be, they are still usually a much cheaper option than a phone call from your hotel.

Phone and fax service to and from the Caribbean is up-to-date and efficient. Phone cards are used throughout the islands; you can buy them (in various denominations) at many retail shops and convenience stores. Some must be used in special card phones, which are also widely available.

For island area and country codes, *see* the Essentials sections *in* individual island chapters. When you are calling home, the country code is 1 for the U.S. and Canada, 61 for Australia, 64 for New Zealand, and 44 for the U.K.

MOBILE PHONES

If you have a multiband phone (some countries use different frequencies than what's used in the United States) and your service provider uses the world-standard GSM network (as do T-Mobile, Cingular, and Verizon), you can probably use your phone abroad. Roaming fees can be steep, though: 99¢ a minute is considered reasonable. And overseas, you normally pay the toll charges for incoming calls. It's almost always cheaper to send a text message than to make a call, since text messages have a very low set fee (often less than 5¢).

If you just want to make local calls, consider buying a new SIM card (note that your provider may have to unlock your phone for you to use a different SIM card) and a prepaid service plan in the destination. You'll then have a local number and can make local calls at local rates. If your trip is extensive you could also simply buy a new cell phone in your destination, as the initial cost will be offset over time.

If you travel internationally frequently, save one of your old mobile phones or buy a cheap one on the Internet; ask your cell phone company to unlock it for you, and take it with you as a travel phone, buying a new SIM card with pay-as-you-go service in each destination.

U.S. nationwide calling plans for some carriers, such as Cingular, already include Puerto Rico and the U. S. Virgin Islands at no additional charge. On some islands served by Cable & Wireless, for instance, you can use your TDMA digital cell phone for outbound calls only. Digicel, which has competing service on several islands, has roaming agreements with many GSM operations worldwide, allowing customers of those partner carriers to use their compatible phones in the Caribbean.

Access the Caribbean Roamers Guide online to find the various services available listed for each island. Remember, too, that the electrical current on some islands is 220 volts (as opposed to the 110-volt current found in the United States and Canada). You'll need to make sure your cell phone charger is compatible with 220-volt current and bring an appropriate electrical plug adapter if you expect to charge your cell phone battery while you're away.

🛈 **Caribbean Roamers Guide** ⊕ www. roamersguide.com. **Cellular Abroad** ☎ 800/287-3020 or 310/829-6878 ⊕ www.cellularabroad.com rents cell phones and sells country-specific SIM cards as well as mobile phones that work in many countries. **Mobal** ☎ 888/888-9162 ⊕ www. mobalrental.com rents mobiles and sells GSM phones ($49 or $99) that will operate in 140 countries. Per-call rates vary throughout the world. **Planet Fone** ☎ 888/988-4777 ⊕ www.planetfone. com rents cell phones, but the per-minute rates are expensive.

SAFETY

Most Caribbean destinations are safer than major U.S. cities, but street crime is always a possibility where relatively affluent tourists mingle with significantly poorer locals. As at home, petty crime can be a problem in large urban areas, but violent crimes against tourists—even on higher-crime islands like Jamaica and St. Thomas—are rare. You will avoid most problems by using common sense and simply being as cautious as you would at home, which means not walking alone in unfamiliar places (especially at night), not going alone to deserted beaches, locking away valuables, and not flaunting expensive jewelry in public places. Additionally, don't swim alone in unfamiliar waters, and don't swim too far offshore; most beaches have no lifeguards.

If you carry a purse, choose one with a zipper and a thick strap that you can drape across your body; adjust the length so that the purse sits in front of you at or above hip level. If you use a waist pack, attach it so the purse is in the front, not at your back. Carry only enough money in the purse to cover casual spending and utilize your hotel's in-room safe or its front-desk safe deposit box for your remaining valuables.

Distribute your cash, credit cards, IDs, and other valuables between a deep front pocket, an inside jacket or vest pocket, and a hidden money pouch. Don't reach for the money pouch once you're in public.

GOVERNMENT ADVISORIES

As different countries have different world views, look at travel advisories from a range of governments to get more of a sense of what's going on out there. And be sure to parse the language carefully. For example, a warning to "avoid all travel" carries more weight than one urging you to "avoid nonessential travel," and both are much stronger than a plea to "exercise caution." A U.S. government travel warning is more permanent (though not necessarily more serious) than a so-called public announcement, which carries an expiration date.

The U.S. Department of State's Web site has more than just travel warnings and advisories. The consular information sheets issued for every country have general safety tips, entry requirements (though be sure to verify these with the country's embassy), and other useful details.

Consider registering online with the state department (travelregistration.state.gov/ibrs), so the government will know to look for you should a crisis occur in the country you're visiting. If you travel frequently also look into the Registered Traveler program of the Transportation Security Administration (TSA; www.tsa.gov). The program, which is still being tested in five U.S. airports, is designed to cut down on gridlock at security checkpoints by allowing prescreened travelers to pass quickly through kiosks that scan an iris and/or a fingerprint. How sci-fi is that?

General Information & Warnings Australian Department of Foreign Affairs & Trade ⊕ www.smartraveller.gov.au. **Consular Affairs Bureau of Canada** ⊕ www.voyage.gc.ca. **U.K. Foreign & Commonwealth Office** ⊕ www.fco.gov.uk/travel. **U.S. Department of State** ⊕ www.travel.state.gov.

TAXES

Often, departure taxes are now included in your airline ticket, but several Caribbean countries still require travelers to pay departure taxes in cash at the time you check in for your flight home. In most cases, you can pay in either local or U.S. currency, though setting aside the exact change is a wise move. For specific departure taxes, see ⇨ "Taxes" *in* the Essentials section of each chapter.

TIME

The Caribbean islands fall into two time zones. The Cayman Islands, Cuba, Haiti, Jamaica, and the Turks and Caicos Islands are all in the Eastern Standard Time zone, which is five hours earlier than Greenwich Mean Time (GMT). All other Caribbean islands are in the Atlantic Standard Time zone, which is one hour later than Eastern Standard and four hours earlier than GMT. Caribbean islands don't observe Daylight

Saving Time between April and October, so during that period Eastern Standard is one hour behind, and Atlantic Standard is the same time as Eastern Daylight Time.

TOURS & PACKAGES

VACATION PACKAGES

Packages *are not* guided tours. Packages combine airfare, accommodations, and perhaps a rental car or other extras (theater tickets, guided excursions, boat trips, reserved entry to popular museums, transit passes), but they let you do your own thing. During busy periods, packages may be your only option because flights and rooms may be otherwise sold out. Packages will definitely save you time. They can also save you money, particularly in peak seasons, but—and this is a really big "but"—you should price each part of the package separately to be sure. And be aware that prices advertised on Web sites and in newspapers rarely include service charges or taxes, which can up your costs by hundreds of dollars.

Note that local tourism boards can provide information about lesser-known and small-niche operators that sell packages to just a few destinations. And don't always assume that you can get the best deal by booking everything yourself. Some packages and cruises are sold only through travel agents.

Each year consumers are stranded or lose their money when packagers—even large ones with excellent reputations—go out of business. How can you protect yourself? First, always pay with a credit card; if you have a problem, your credit-card company may help you resolve it. Second, buy trip insurance that covers default. Third, choose a company that belongs to the United States Tour Operators Association, whose members must set aside funds ($1 million) to cover defaults. Finally, choose a company that also participates in the Tour Operator Program of the American Society of Travel Agents (ASTA), which will act as mediator in any disputes. You can also check on the tour operator's reputation among travelers by posting an inquiry on one of the Fodors.com forums.

Most major air carriers that fly to the Caribbean offer vacation packages that combine round-trip airfare and lodgings for four, seven, or more nights. More developed islands (St. Thomas, St. Maarten/St. Martin, Aruba, Puerto Rico, Jamaica, and Grand Cayman, for example) tend to be more competitive and creative with their package pricing.

🚩 Organizations **American Society of Travel Agents (ASTA)** ☎ 703/739-2782 or 800/965-2782 24-hr hotline ⊕ www.astanet.com. **United States Tour Operators Association (USTOA)** ☎ 212/599-6599 ⊕ www.ustoa.com.

🚩 Airline Vacation Packages **Air Jamaica Vacations** ☎ 800/568-3247 ⊕ www.airjamaicavacations.com. **American Airlines Vacations** ☎ 800/321-2121 ⊕ www.aavacations.com. **BWIA Vacations** ☎ 877/386-2942 ⊕ www.bwee.com. **Continental Airlines Vacations** ☎ 800/301-3800 ⊕ www.covacations.com. **Delta Vacations** ☎ 800/654-6559 ⊕ www.deltavacations.com. **US Airways Vacations** ☎ 800/422-3861 ⊕ www.usairwaysvacations.com.

🚩 Large Agency Packagers **American Express Vacations** ☎ 800/335-3342 ⊕ www.americanexpressvacations.com. **Apple Vacations** ⊕ www.applevacations.com are mostly sold through travel agents. **Funjet Vacations** ☎ 888/558-6654 ⊕ www.funjet.com. **GoGo Worldwide Vacations** ☎ 800/541-3788 ⊕ www.gogowwv.com are sold through travel agents. **Liberty Travel** ☎ 888/271-1584 ⊕ www.libertytravel.com.

🚩 Online Agency Packagers **Cheap Tickets** ⊕ www.cheaptickets.com. **Expedia** ⊕ www.expedia.com. **Orbitz** ⊕ www.orbitz.com. **Priceline** ⊕ www.priceline.com. **Travelocity** ⊕ www.travelocity.com.

TRAVEL AGENTS

If you use an agent—brick-and-mortar or virtual—you'll pay a fee for the service. And know that the service you get from some online agents isn't comprehensive. For example, Expedia and Travelocity don't search for prices on budget airlines like JetBlue, Southwest, or small foreign carriers. That said, some agents (online or not) *do* have access to fares that are difficult to find otherwise, and the savings can more than make up for any surcharge.

A knowledgeable brick-and-mortar travel agent can be a godsend if you're booking a cruise, a package trip that's not available to you directly, an air pass, or a complicated itinerary including several overseas flights. What's more, travel agents who specialize in a destination may have exclusive access to certain deals and insider information on things such as charter flights. Agents who specialize in types of travelers (senior citizens, gays and lesbians, naturists) or types of trips (cruises, luxury travel, safaris) can also be invaluable.

A top-notch agent planning your trip to Russia will make sure you get the correct visa application and complete it on time; the one booking your cruise may get you a cabin upgrade or arrange to have a bottle of champagne chilling in your cabin when you embark. And complain about the surcharges all you like, but when things don't work out the way you'd hoped, it's nice to have an agent to put things right.

Travel agents can still find you good deals for Caribbean travel—sometimes deals you can't book on our own—and agents who specialize in the Caribbean may know about offers that you won't easily find out about yourself. A few resort companies—Iberostar, for example, which has a big presence in the Dominican Republic—do not allow individuals to book their rooms, so you must book through a travel agent. Some big packagers like Apple Tours and GoGo Tours now allow customers to book directly through their Web sites, but they still sell the majority of their trips through affiliated travel agents. Other companies, including Sandals, offer lowest-price guarantees only when you book rooms through travel agents. If you're traveling to the Caribbean from Europe, where air charters are common in high season, you will almost certainly get a better deal on your travel package if you book through a travel agent.

🚩 Agent Resources **American Society of Travel Agents** ☎ 703/739-2782 ⊕ www.travelsense.org.

🚩 Online Agents **Expedia** ⊕ www.expedia.com. **Onetravel.com** ⊕ www.onetravel.com. **Orbitz** ⊕ www.orbitz.com. **Priceline.com** ⊕ www.priceline.com. **Travelocity** ⊕ www.travelocity.com.

VISITOR INFORMATION

Island tourist-board offices in Canada, the U.K., and the U.S. are good sources of general information, up-to-date calendars of events, and listings of hotels, restaurants, sights, and shops. For a listing of tourist-board offices to contact for information before you go, also *see* Visitor Information *in* the A to Z section of each island chapter. The Caribbean Tourism Organization (CTO) is another resource, especially for information on the islands that have limited representation overseas.

🚩 Caribbean-Wide Tourist Information **Caribbean Tourism Organization (CTO)** ✉ 80 Broad St., New York, NY 10004 ☎ 212/635-9530 🖷 212/635-9511 ⊕ www.doitcaribbean.com ✉ 512 Duplex Ave., Toronto, Ontario M4R 2E3, Canada ☎ 416/485-8724 🖷 416/485-8256 ✉ 42 Westminster Palace Gardens Artillery Row, London SW1P 1RR, UK ☎ 0207/222-4335 🖷 0207/222-4325.

🚩 Caribbean Island Tourist Boards **Anguilla** ☎ 914/287-2400, 800/553-4939 in U.S., 416/944-8105 in Canada, or 0208/871-0012 in U.K. ⊕ www.anguilla-vacation.com. **Antigua & Barbuda** ☎ 212/541-4117 or 888/268-4227 in U.S., 416/961-3085 in Canada, or 0207/486-7073 in U.K. ⊕ www.antigua-barbuda.org. **Aruba** ☎ 800/862-7822 in U.S., 905/264-3434 in Canada, or 0207/928-1700 in U.K. ⊕ www.aruba.com. **Barbados** ☎ 212/986-6516 or 800/221-9831 in U.S., 416/214-9880 or 800/268-9122 in Canada, 20/7636-9447 in U.K., or 2/9221-9988 in Australia ⊕ www.barbados.org. **Bonaire** ☎ 212/956-5913 or 800/266-2473 in U.S. or Canada ⊕ www.infobonaire.com. **British Virgin Islands** ☎ 212/696-0400 or 800/835-8530 in U.S. or Canada, 0207/355-9585 in U.K. ⊕ www.bvitouristboard.com. **Cayman Islands** ☎ 212/889-9009 in U.S., 416-485-1550 or 800/263-5805 in Canada, 0207/491-7771 in U.K. ⊕ www.caymanislands.ky. **Curaçao** ☎ 954/370-5887 or 800/328-7222 in U.S. or Canada, 0207/431-4045 in U.K. ⊕ www.curacao-tourism.com. **Dominica** ☎ 718/261-0702 or 888/645-5637 in U.S., 0207/928-1600 in U.K. ⊕ www.dominica.dm. **Dominican Republic** ☎ 212/575-4966 or 888/374-6361 in U.S.,

514/933-6126 in Canada, 0171/723-1552 in U.K. ⊕ www.dominicana.com.do. **Grenada** 🖷 561/588-8176 or 800/927-9554 in U.S., 416/595-1339 in Canada, 0208/774-4516 in U.K. ⊕ www. grenadagrenadines.com. **Guadeloupe** 🖷 310/276-2835 or 312/337-6339 in U.S., 514/288-4264 in Canada, 0171/499-6911 in U.K. ⊕ www. lesilesdeguadeloupe.com. **Jamaica** 🖷 305/665-0557 or 800/233-4582 in U.S., 416/482-7850 or 800/465-2624 in Canada, 0207/224-0505 in U.K. ⊕ www.visitjamaica.com. **Martinique** 🖷 313/838-7800 in U.S., 514/844-8566 in Canada, 0207/399-3500 in U.K. ⊕ www.martinique.org. **Nevis** 🖷 866/556-3847 in U.S. or Canada, 0142/052-0810 or 0870/200-1413 in U.K. ⊕ www.nevisisland.com. **Puerto Rico** 🖷 800/866-7827 in U.S., 800/667-0394 in Canada ⊕ www.gotopuertorico.com. **Saba** ⊕ www.sabatourism.com. **St. Barthélemy** 🖷 212/838-7800 in U.S. or 514/248-4264 in Canada, 0171/629-9376 in U.K. ⊕ www.st-barths.com. **St. Eustatius** ⊕ www.statiatourism.com. **St. Kitts** 🖷 212/535-1234 or 800/582-6208 in U.S., 416/368-6707 or 888/395-4887 in Canada, 0207/376-0881 in U.K. ⊕ www.stkitts-tourism.com. **St. Lucia** 🖷 212/867-2950 or 800/456-3984 in U.S., 416/362-4242 in Canada, 0870/900-7697 in U.K. ⊕ www.stlucia.org. **St. Maarten** 🖷 212/953-2084 or 800/786-2278 in U.S., 416/622-4300 in Canada ⊕ www.st-maarten.com. **St. Martin** 🖷 212/475-8970 or 877/956-1234 in U.S., 514/288-4264 in Canada ⊕ www.st-martin.org. **St. Vincent & the Grenadines** 🖷 212/687-4981 or 800/729-1726 in U.S., 416/633-3100 in Canada, 0207/937-6570 in U.K. ⊕ www.svgtourism.com. **Trinidad & Tobago** 🖷 868/624-5082 or 868/623-1425 in U.S. or Canada, 0800/804-8787 in U.K. ⊕ www.visitTNT.com. **Turks and Caicos** 🖷 305/891-4117 or 800/241-0824 in U.S., 613/332-6473 or 800/241-0824 in Canada, 0181/350-1000 in U.K. ⊕ www.turksandcaicostourism.com. **U.S. Virgin Islands** 🖷 212/332-2222 or 800/372-8784 in U.S., 416/233-1414 in Canada, 207/978-5222 in U.K. ⊕ www.usvitourism.vi.

WEB SITES

We're really proud of our Web site: Fodors.com is a great place to begin any journey. Scan Travel Wire for suggested itineraries, travel deals, restaurant and hotel openings, and other up-to-the-minute info. Check out Booking to research prices and book plane tickets, hotel rooms, rental cars, and vacation packages. Head to Talk for on-the-ground pointers from travelers who frequent our message boards. You can also link to loads of other travel-related resources.

After your trip, be sure to rate the places you visited and share your experiences and travel tips with us and other Fodorites in Travel Ratings and Talk on www.fodors.com.

For island-specific Web sites, *see* Visitor Information *in* the Essentials section at the end of each chapter.

🔁 Currency Conversion **Google** ⊕ www.google.com does currency conversion. Just type in the amount you want to convert and an explanation of how you want it converted (e.g., "14 Swiss francs in dollars"), and then voilà. **XE.com** ⊕ www.xe.com is another good currency conversion Web site.

🔁 Time Zones **Timeanddate.com** ⊕ www.timeanddate.com/worldclock can help you figure out the correct time anywhere in the world.

🔁 Weather **Accuweather.com** ⊕ www.accuweather.com is an independent weather-forecasting service with especially good coverage of hurricanes. **Weather.com** ⊕ www.weather.com is the Web site for the Weather Channel.

🔁 Other Resources **CIA World Factbook** ⊕ www.odci.gov/cia/publications/factbook/index.html has profiles of every country in the world. It's a good source if you need some quick facts and figures.

INDEX

PHOTO CREDITS

Cover Photo (Windsurfers, Aruba): *Darrell Jones/Stone/Getty Images.* 16, *Peter Phipp/age fotostock.* 17 (left), *Philip Coblentz/Medioimages.* 17 (right), *TIDCO.* 18, *St. Maarten Tourist Bureau.* 19 (left), *Aruba Tourism Authority.* 19 (right), *Philip Coblentz/Medioimages.* 20, *Jamaica Tourist Board.* 21 (left), *Suzi Swygert/Bonaire Tourist Office.* 21 (right), *Aruba Tourism Authority.* 22, *Peter Adams/age fotostock.* 23 (left), *Curaçao Tourism.* 23 (right), *Walter Bibikow/age fotostock.* 25, *St. Maarten Tourist Bureau.* 26, *Barbados Tourism Authority.* 27 (left), *Barbados Tourism Authority.* 27 (right), *Joe Viesti/www. viestiphoto.com.* 28, *Dennis Cox/age fotostock.* 29 (left and center), *Joe Viesti/www.viestiphoto.com.* 29 (right), *Alvaro Leiva/age fotostock.* **Chapter 1: Anguilla:** 31, *J. D. Heaton/Picture Finders/age fotostock.* 32 (top), *Philip Coblentz/Digital Vision.* 32 (bottom), *Joe Viesti/www.viestiphoto.com.* 34, *Philip Coblentz/Digital Vision.* **Chapter 2: Antigua and Barbuda:** 59, *Philip Coblentz/Medioimages.* 60 (top), *Philip Coblentz/Digital Vision.* 60 (bottom), *Philip Coblentz/Digital Vision.* 61, *Philip Coblentz/ Medioimages.* 62, *Philip Coblentz/Medioimages.* **Chapter 3: Aruba:** 95, *Eric Sanford/age fotostock.* 96 (top), *Joe Viesti/www.viestiphoto.com.* 96 (bottom), *Philip Coblentz/Medioimages.* 99, *Philip Coblentz/ Digital Vision.* **Chapter 4: Barbados:** 127, *Doug Pearson/Agency Jon Arnold Images/age fotostock.* 128, *Doug Scott/age fotostock.* 130, *Corbis.* 131, *Barbados Tourism Authority.* **Chapter 5: Bonaire:** 171, *Philip Coblentz/Medioimages.* 172 (top), *Suzi Swygert/Bonaire Tourist Office.* 172 (bottom), *Suzi Swygert for the Bonaire Tourist Office.* 173, *Ken Ross/www.viestiphoto.com.* **Chapter 6: British Virgin Islands:** 199, *Philip Coblentz/Medioimages.* 200 (top), *Philip Coblentz/Digital Vision.* 200 (bottom), *Philip Coblentz/ Digital Vision.* 203 (left), *Philip Coblentz/Digital Vision.* 203 (right), *Philip Coblentz/Digital Vision.* **Chapter 7: Cayman Islands:** 247, *Corbis.* 248 (top), *Cayman Islands Department of Tourism.* 248 (bottom), *Cayman Islands Department of Tourism.* 251, *Cayman Islands Department of Tourism.* **Chapter 8: Curaçao:** 285, *Philip Coblentz/Digital Vision.* 286 (top), *Curaçao Tourism.* 286 (bottom), *Fotoconcept Inc./age fotostock.* 288, *Philip Coblentz/Digital Vision.* 289, *Joe Viesti/www.viestiphoto.com.* **Chapter 9: Dominica:** 321, *Xavier Font/age fotostock.* 322, *Dominica Tourist Office.* 323 (top), *Peter Purchia/www.viestiphoto. com.* 323 (bottom), *Alvaro Leiva/age fotostock.* 324, *Ann Duncan/www.viestiphoto.com.* **Chapter 10: Dominican Republic:** 351, *Doug Scott/age fotostock.* 352 (top), *Guy Thouvenin/age fotostock.* 352 (bottom), *Doug Scott/age fotostock.* 355 (left), *DominicanRepublic.com.* 355 (right), *DominicanRepublic.com.* **Chapter 11: Grenada:** 405, *Doug Scott/age fotostock.* 406 (top), *Grenada Board of Tourism.* 406 (bottom), *Grenada Board of Tourism.* **Chapter 12: Guadeloupe:** 439, *Bruno Morandi/age fotostock.* 440, *Bruno Morandi/age fotostock.* **Chapter 13: Jamaica:** 479, *Ken Ross/www.viestiphoto.com.* 480 (top), *Jamaica Tourist Board.* 480 (bottom), *Philip Coblentz/Digital Vision.* 483, *Corbis.* **Chapter 14: Martinique:** 531, *Gonzalo Azumendi/age fotostock.* 532, *Philip Coblentz/Medioimages.* 533, *Nicole Lejeune/ Maison de la France.* 535 (left), *Nicole Lejeune/Maison de la France.* 535 (right), *Walter Bibikow/age fotostock.* **Chapter 15: Montserrat:** 567, *John Cole.* 568, *John Angerson/Alamy.* 569, *Igor Kravtchenko/ KiMAGIC Photo and Design.* **Chapter 16: Puerto Rico:** 585, *Philip Coblentz/Medioimages.* 586 (top), *Morales/age fotostock,* 586 (bottom), *Atlantide S.N.C./age fotostock.* 588, *Doug Scott/age fotostock.* **Chapter 17: Saba:** 639, *Michael S. Nolan/age fotostock.* 640 (top), *Joe Viesti/www.viestiphoto.com.* 640 (bottom), *Joe Viesti/www.viestiphoto.com.* **Chapter 18: St. Barthélemy:** 657, *Angelo Cavalli/age fotostock.* 658 (top), *Philip Coblentz/Digital Vision.* 658 (bottom), *SuperStock/age fotostock.* **Chapter 19: St. Eustatius:** 685, *SuperStock/age fotostock.* 686, *Helene Rogers/www.viestiphoto.com.* 687, *Bob Turner/www. viestiphoto.com.* **Chapter 20: St. Kitts & Nevis:** 701, *Peter Phipp/age fotostock.* 702, *Doug Scott/age fotostock.* 703, *Peter Phipp/age fotostock.* **Chapter 21: St. Lucia:** 745, *Walter Bibikow/age fotostock.* 746 (top), *Bruno Morandi/age fotostock.* 746 (center), *Philip Coblentz/Medioimages.* 746 (bottom), *Angelo Cavalli/age fotostock.* **Chapter 22: St. Maarten/St. Martin:** 783, *Angelo Cavalli/age fotostock.* 784 (top), *Angelo Cavalli/age fotostock.* 784 (bottom), *St. Maarten Tourist Bureau.* 786, *St. Martin Tourist Office.* 787, *Philip Coblentz/Digital Vision.* **Chapter 23: St. Vincent & the Grenadines:** 817, *Alvaro Leiva/age fotostock.* 818, *St. Vincent Tourism.* 819, *SuperStock/age fotostock.* **Chapter 24: Trinidad & Tobago:** 863, *David Sanger Photography/Alamy.* 864 (top), *Philip Coblentz/Digital Vision (Own).* 864 (bottom), *Angelo Cavalli/age fotostock.* 866, *Philip Coblentz/Medioimages.* **Chapter 25: Turks & Caicos:** 905, *Turks & Caicos Tourism.* 906 (top), *Turks & Caicos Tourism.* 906 (bottom), *Angelo Cavalli/age fotostock.* 907, *Turks & Caicos Tourism.* 908, *Turks & Caicos Tourism.* 909, *Turks & Caicos Tourism.* **Chapter 26: United States Virgin Islands:** 945, *U.S. Virgin Islands Department of Tourism.* 946 (top), *U.S. Virgin Islands Department of Tourism.* 946 (bottom), *Philip Coblentz/Medioimages.*

ABOUT OUR WRITERS

Although there's no substitute for travel advice from a good friend who knows your style, our contributors are the next best thing—the kind of people you would poll for travel advice if you knew them.

St. Thomas–based writer and dietitian Carol M. Bareuther writes about food for the *Virgin Islands Daily News* and serves as the USVI stringer for Reuters. She's the author *Sports Fishing in the Virgin Islands.*

A renowned expert in the field of underwater photography, Cathy Church has been teaching her techniques in Grand Cayman since 1972. Her latest book, *My Underwater Photo Journey,* was published in 2005.

Katherine Dykstra is a senior editor at *The Independent Film & Video Monthly* and an avid freelancer. She's covered travel for the *New York Post,* where she still contributes articles, and *Redbook.* Katherine visits Saba, where her father lives, frequently.

Long-time St. John resident Lynda Lohr lives above Coral Bay and writes for numerous publications as well as travel Web sites. She prefers swimming at Great Maho Bay and hiking the island's numerous trails.

Friends of Elise Meyer often joke that her middle name is "Let's Go." She has contributed articles to myriad newspapers, magazines, and Web sites. She lives in Connecticut with her husband and children.

Londoner Jackie Mulligan escaped to peaceful (and significantly warmer) Grand Turk, where she has worked in communications and as a tourism and development consultant. She edits the national museum's newsletter, *Astrolabe,* and has written for the BBC.

Vernon O'Reilly-Ramesar is a broadcaster and writer who divides his life between Trinidad and Canada. He spends much of his time exploring the miracles of the rain forest.

Husband-wife team Paris Permenter and John Bigley have authored numerous guides to the Caribbean. When they're not in the islands, they edit Lovetripper.com Romantic Travel Magazine and ParisandJohn.com from their home base in Texas.

Elise Rosen is a writer and editor in New York. Her affinity for the Dutch Caribbean islands has prompted her to begin studying Papiamento, the local vernacular. She's also contributed to *Fodor's Israel.*

Eileen Robinson Smith moved from the Caribbean to Charleston, South Carolina. She's lived all over the Virgin Islands and has written about about food and travel for *Sky, Caribbean Travel & Life,* and *Condé Nast Traveler.*

Jordan Simon began his West Indies love affair as a child when his artist mother took him to Haiti. He has since visited and written about nearly every Caribbean island. He writes regularly for national magazines and newspapers and has authored several books, including *Fodor's Colorado* and the *Gousha/USA Today Ski Atlas.*

Chicago native Roberta Sotonoff is a confessed travel junkie who writes to support her habit. Her work has appeared in dozens of domestic and international publications, Web sites, and guidebooks. She writes frequently about the Caribbean.

Mark Sullivan, formerly an editor at Fodor's, is now a freelance writer. In addition to updating our Puerto Rico coverage, he has contributed to several other Fodor's guides and many other publications.

Jane E. Zarem travels frequently to the Caribbean from her Connecticut home. She has contributed to numerous Fodor's guides, among them *New England, USA, Cape Cod, Bahamas, Healthy Escapes,* and *Great American Sports & Adventure Vacations.*